▪ For Students

MyAccountingLab provides students with a personalized interactive learning environment, where they can learn at their own pace and measure their progress.

Interactive Tutorial Exercises

MyAccountingLab's homework and practice questions are correlated to the textbook, and they regenerate algorithmically to give students unlimited opportunity for practice and mastery. Questions include guided solutions, and learning aids for extra help at point-of-use, and they offer helpful feedback when students enter incorrect answers.

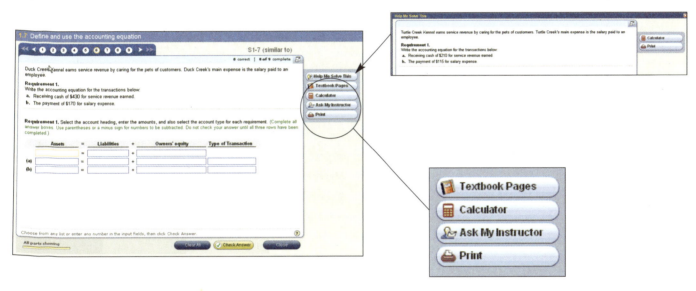

Study Plan for Self-Paced Learning ▶

MyAccountingLab's study plan helps students monitor their own progress, letting them see at a glance exactly which topics they need to practice. MyAccountingLab generates a personalized study plan for each student based on his or her test results, and the study plan links directly to interactive, tutorial exercises for topics the student hasn't yet mastered. Students can regenerate these exercises with new values for unlimited practice, and the exercises include guided solutions and multimedia learning aids to give students the extra help they need.

View a guided tour of MyAccountingLab at http://www.myaccountinglab.com/support/tours.

FIFTEENTH EDITION

Introduction to
MANAGEMENT ACCOUNTING

Charles T. Horngren
Stanford University

Gary L. Sundem
University of Washington – Seattle

William O. Stratton
Dixie State College of Utah

David Burgstahler
University of Washington – Seattle

Jeff Schatzberg
University of Arizona

Prentice Hall

Boston Columbus Indianapolis New York San Francisco Upper Saddle River
Amsterdam Cape Town Dubai London Madrid Milan Munich Paris Montréal Toronto
Delhi Mexico City São Paulo Sydney Hong Kong Seoul Singapore Taipei Tokyo

To Joan, Chelsea, Erik, Marissa
Liz, Garth, Jens, Reed, Grant
Norma, Gina, Adam, Nisha, Tiana
Sheryl, Travis
Jane, Vanessa, Courtney

VP/Editorial Director: Sally Yagan
AVP/Editor-in-Chief: Donna Battista
Acquisitions Editor: Julie Broich
AVP/Director of Digital Learning & Assessment: Richard Keaveny
AVP/Director of Product Development: Lisa Strite
Product Development Manager: Ashley Santora
Editorial Project Manager: Karin Williams
Editorial Assistant: Christina Rumbaugh
VP/Director of Marketing: Patrice Lumumba Jones
Marketing Manager: Elizabeth Averbeck
Marketing Assistant: Ian Gold
Sr. Managing Editor: Cynthia Zonneveld
Sr. Production Project Manager: Rhonda Aversa
Associate Director of Manufacturing: Alexis Heydt
Sr. Operations Specialist: Diane Peirano
Sr. Art Director: Jon Boylan
Art Director, Cover and Interior: Anthony Gemmellaro

Interior Design: 511 Design
Cover Design: Blair Brown
Manager, Visual Research: Beth Brenzel
Photo Researcher: Kathy Ringrose
Manager, Rights and Permissions: Shannon Barbe
Manager, Cover Visual Research & Permissions: Karen Sanatar
Cover Art: Shutterstock/Orla
Image Permissions Coordinator: Nancy Seise
Photo Researcher: Kathy Ringrose
Media Editor: Allison Longley
Media Project Manager, Production: John Cassar
Full-Service Project Management: GEX Publishing Services
Composition: GEX Publishing Services
Printer/Binder: Webcrafters Inc.
Cover Printer: Lehigh-Phoenix Color/Hagerstown
Text Font: 10/12 Times

Credits and acknowledgments borrowed from other sources and reproduced, with permission, in this textbook appear on appropriate page within text (or on page P1).

Library of Congress Cataloging-in-Publication Data

Introduction to management accounting / Charles T. Horngren ... [et al.]. -- 15th ed.
  v. ; cm.
Includes bibliographical references and index.
ISBN 978-0-13-610265-6 (casebound : alk. paper) -- ISBN 978-0-13-610277-9
(casebound : alk. paper) 1. Managerial accounting. I. Horngren, Charles T., 1926-
HF5635.H814 2010
658.15'11--dc22

                              2010000905

Prentice Hall
is an imprint of

www.pearsonhighered.com

10 9 8 7 6 5 4 3 2 1
ISBN 13: 978-0-13-610277-9
ISBN 10: 0-13-610277-8

Charles T. Horngren Series in Accounting
Charles T. Horngren, Consulting Editor

Auditing and Assurance Services: An Integrated Approach, 13/E
Arens/Elder/Beasley

Governmental and Nonprofit Accounting: Theory & Practice, 9/E
Freeman/Shoulders/Allison/ Patton/Smith

Financial Accounting, 8/E
Harrison/Horngren/Thomas

Cost Accounting: A Managerial Emphasis, 13/E
Horngren/Foster/Datar/Rajan/Ittner

Accounting, 8/E
Horngren/Harrison/Oliver

Introduction to Financial Accounting, 10/E
Horngren/Sundem/Elliott/Philbrick

Introduction to Management Accounting, 15/E
Horngren/Sundem/Stratton/Burgstahler/Schatzberg

About the Authors

Charles T. Horngren is the Edmund W. Littlefield Professor of Accounting, emeritus, at Stanford University. A graduate of Marquette University, he received his MBA from Harvard University and his PhD from the University of Chicago. He is also the recipient of honorary doctorates from Marquette University and DePaul University.

A certified public accountant, Horngren served on the Accounting Principles Board for 6 years, the Financial Accounting Standards Board Advisory Council for 5 years, and the Council of the American Institute of Certified Public Accountants for 3 years. For 6 years, he served as a trustee of the Financial Accounting Foundation, which oversees the Financial Accounting Standards Board and the Government Accounting Standards Board.

Horngren is a member of the Accounting Hall of Fame.

A member of the American Accounting Association, Horngren has been its president and its director of research. He received the association's first annual Outstanding Accounting Educator Award. He also received its Lifetime Contribution to Management Accounting Award.

The California Certified Public Accountants Foundation gave Horngren its Faculty Excellence Award and its Distinguished Professor Award. He is the first person to have received both awards.

The American Institute of Certified Public Accountants presented its first Outstanding Educator Award to Horngren.

Horngren was named Accountant of the Year, Education, by the national professional accounting fraternity, Beta Alpha Psi.

Professor Horngren is also a member of the Institute of Management Accountants, where he has received its Distinguished Service Award. He was a member of the Institute's Board of Regents, which administers the Certified Management Accountant examinations.

Horngren is the author of other accounting books published by Prentice Hall: *Cost Accounting: A Managerial Emphasis*, *Introduction to Financial Accounting*, *Accounting*, and *Financial Accounting*.

Horngren is the Consulting Editor for the Charles T. Horngren Series in Accounting.

Gary L. Sundem is professor of accounting emeritus at the University of Washington, Seattle. He received his BA from Carleton College and his MBA and PhD from Stanford University.

Professor Sundem was the 1992–1993 president of the American Accounting Association. He was executive director of the Accounting Education Change Commission, 1989–1991, and served as editor of *The Accounting Review*, 1982–1986. He is currently vice president of education for the International Association for Accounting Education and Research.

Sundem is past president of the Seattle chapter of the Institute of Management Accountants. He has served on IMA's national board of directors and chaired its Academic Relations and Professional Development committees. He chaired the AACSB's Accounting Accreditation Committee, 1997–1999, and currently serves on the Board of Trustees of Rainier Mutual Funds and the Board of Trustees of Carleton College. He received the Carleton College Outstanding Alumni award in 2002.

Professor Sundem has numerous publications in accounting and finance journals including *Issues in Accounting Education*, *The Accounting Review*, *Journal of Accounting Research*, and *Journal of Finance*. He was selected as the Outstanding Accounting Educator by the American Accounting Association in 1998 and by the Washington Society of CPAs in 1987.

William O. Stratton is professor of accounting at the Udvar-Hazy School of Business of Dixie State College of Utah. He received BS degrees from Florida State University and Pennsylvania State University, his MBA from Boston University, and his PhD from the Claremont Graduate University.

A certified management accountant, Stratton has lectured extensively at management accounting conferences in North America, South America, and Europe. He has developed and delivered professional workshops on activity-based management and performance achievement to manufacturing and service organizations throughout the United States and South America. In 1993, Professor Stratton was awarded the Boeing Competition prize for classroom innovation.

Stratton has numerous publications in accounting and international business journals including *Management Accounting Quarterly*, *Strategic Finance*, *Journal of Management Excellence*, *CMA Management*, *Decision Sciences*, *IIE Transactions*, *Cost Management*, *Synergie*, and *Journal of Corporate Accounting & Finance*.

David Burgstahler is Gerhard G. Mueller Endowed Professor in Accounting at the University of Washington, Seattle. He received his BA degree from the University of Minnesota–Duluth, and his PhD from the University of Iowa. He has been associate dean for masters programs and executive education and acting dean at the University of Washington Business School. He has served on more than 40 PhD supervisory committees and has been recognized multiple times as Beta Alpha Psi Professor of the Year and as MBA Professor of the Quarter at the University of Washington.

Professor Burgstahler was 2007–2009 vice president of publications of the American Accounting Association and has served on a number of Association committees.

Professor Burgstahler received the American Accounting Association's American Institute of Certified Public Accountants Notable Contributions to Accounting Literature Award in 2002. He has numerous publications in journals including *The Accounting Review*, *Journal of Management Accounting Research*, *Journal of Accounting Research*, *Journal of Accounting and Economics*, *Contemporary Accounting Research*, *Auditing: A Journal of Practice and Theory*, *Behavioral Research in Accounting*, and *The CPA Journal*.

Jeff Schatzberg is the Humberto Lopez Professor of Accounting in the Eller College of Management at the University of Arizona. Professor Schatzberg received his BA (in Philosophy), MA (in accounting), and PhD (in business administration), all at the University of Iowa. Professor Schatzberg has numerous publications in the most prestigious accounting and business journals, including the *Journal of Accounting Research*, *The Accounting Review*, *Contemporary Accounting Research*, and *Auditing: A Journal of Practice and Theory*. His teaching and research interests are in managerial accounting and auditing. He has given numerous seminars at several U.S. universities and international schools in Canada, England, Wales, Norway, France, Germany, and Switzerland. Jeff has also served on the editorial board of several scholarly accounting journals.

Professor Schatzberg has been teaching undergraduate, master's, and MBA managerial accounting courses at the University of Arizona for the past 23 years. He has extensive experience in executive education worldwide (e.g., United States, Asia, and Mexico), has developed customized managerial accounting programs and performed consulting for numerous companies (e.g., Raytheon, Honeywell, and Intel), and has taught executives in many multi-national firms (e.g., IBM, Motorola, LG, BenQ, Acer, and Mattel). In 1998, 2002, 2005, and 2009, Jeff received the MBA Faculty of the Year Award from the Eller Graduate School of Business at the University of Arizona, and the Arizona Society of CPA's Excellence in Teaching Award in 1997. Jeff is a CPA and worked for several years as an auditor and tax accountant in the Phoenix office of KPMG Peat Marwick. Jeff's work experience includes both manufacturing and service industry firms, as well as not-for-profit institutions.

Brief Contents

Contents

Preface

Now more than ever, managers have to understand how their decisions affect costs.

Management accounting is an essential tool that enhances a manager's ability to make effective economic decisions. Because understanding concepts is more important than memorizing techniques, *Introduction to Management Accounting*, 15th edition, describes both theory and practice so students understand how to produce information that's useful in day-to-day decision making. From the first chapter, we encourage students to think about the advantages and disadvantages of various techniques, not to simply memorize and apply the techniques.

Introduction to Management Accounting, 15th edition, deals with all business sectors—nonprofit, retail, wholesale, service, selling, and administrative situations—as well as manufacturing. The focus is on planning and control decisions, not on product costing for inventory valuation and income determination.

Our Philosophy

Introduce concepts and principles early, then revisit them at more complex levels as students gain understanding, and provide appropriate real-company examples at every stage.

As management accounting builds on financial accounting, the concepts in management accounting build on one another. Students begin their understanding of managerial decisions by asking, "How will my decisions affect the costs and revenues of the organization?" Students then progress to more complex questions: "What is the most appropriate cost-management system for the company?" "What products or services should we emphasize?" "What do our budget variances mean?"

Our goals are to choose relevant subject matter and to present it clearly and accessibly, using many examples drawn from actual companies. Companies such as Starbucks, Boeing, AT&T, McDonald's, Microsoft, and more set the stage for chapter material and are revisited throughout to help students understand management accounting concepts in a real-company context.

Two different text versions fit your course structure.

Introduction to Management Accounting, 15th edition (Chapters 1–14), provides a concise treatment of management accounting topics suitable for a one-term course.

Introduction to Management Accounting, 15th edition (Chapters 1–17), includes 3 financial accounting chapters in addition to the 14 management accounting chapters. This version is especially suited to continuing education or MBA courses where students need to learn financial and management accounting in a one-term course. The financial accounting chapters also provide material for any student who may need a financial accounting review.

Introduction to Financial Accounting, 10th edition, and *Introduction to Management Accounting*, 15th edition, together provide a seamless presentation for any first-year accounting course. Please contact your Prentice Hall representative about cost-saving discounts when adopting both books.

New Edition Enhancements and Updates

The authors have made changes to both update the topic coverage and to add clarity to the discussion of various topics. The most noteworthy changes include the following:

- **New and revised "Business First" boxes** provide insights into operations at well-known organizations, including Microsoft, General Electric, Southwest Airlines, Harley-Davidson, Nortel Networks, and Harvard University.

- **New and revised chapter-opening vignettes** help students understand accounting's role in current business practice. We revisit the chapter-opening company throughout the chapter so that students can see how accounting influences managers in real companies. Students will recognize many of the companies, such as Starbucks, Boeing, US Airways, McDonald's, Nike, and Dell.
- **A problem** in each chapter based on Nike's Form 10-K. These problems illustrate how publicly available information can lead to insights about a company, its costs, and its management decisions.
- **Increased coverage of ethics**, including an ethics problem in each chapter's assignment material.
- **End-of-chapter material** includes many new and significantly revised exercises and problems to provide fresh, new examples.

Chapter-Specific Updates

Chapter 1 continues to emphasize the importance of ethics in business, with an entire section devoted to "Ethical Conduct for Professional Accountants." We shortened the discussion of the distinction between treasurers and controllers and eliminated this as a separate learning objective. We also pared down descriptions of entry-level careers in accounting.

Chapter 2 begins with a simplified introduction to activities, costs, and cost drivers and continues the clarification theme throughout the chapter. We updated many of the examples in the chapter to include current economic events and their impact on various types of organizations. "Business First" boxes have been updated to explain how companies are using their knowledge of cost behavior and cost-volume-profit relationships to weather the global recession and position for the expected recovery.

Chapter 3 provides a clarified section on cost behavior and regression analysis.

Chapter 4 underwent a major rewrite last edition that has been well received. The ABC portion of the chapter is unchanged except for clarifications in several places. The most significant change is using Dell instead of AT&T as the primary example throughout the chapter. We revised the purposes of the cost allocation section and the example of Li Company's cost allocations to make them more clear. The section on costs for external reporting was condensed and clarified. Finally, we improved the description and examples of benchmarking.

In **Chapter 5** we clarified the pricing focus of the chapter, as well as revised the accounting formats that aid in such decision making, namely the absorption versus contribution margin approaches.

Chapter 6 has been revised to further highlight operating decisions and the incremental analysis framework.

Chapter 7 has the conceptual discussion of budget issues in the first half and discussion of preparing the master budget in the second half, so that the broad discussion of budget issues can be scheduled separately from the mechanics of preparing a detailed budget. The Cooking Hut budgeting example has been shortened to cover just 3 months.

Chapter 8 includes a new diagram to clarify the relation between the static budget variance and the flexible-budget and sales-activity variances. Terminology for basic variances is explained in terms of *price* and *quantity* variances to emphasize that the variances follow from the concept that cost is the product of price times quantity; we also emphasize the fact that variance terminology varies widely in practice to try to get students to think about the concepts underlying the variances rather than memorizing labels.

In **Chapter 9**, discussion of the impact of performance evaluation on motivation, goal congruence, and effort has been moved earlier in the chapter. We present examples of nonfinancial performance measures before integrating performance measures using the balanced scorecard. Finally, the latter half of the chapter has been reorganized.

In **Chapter 10**, we reorganized the discussion of agency theory, with corresponding changes to the diagram in Exhibit 10-1. We also revised the comparison of ROI and economic profit performance measures.

We changed the example company used throughout **Chapter 11** to Toyota Motor Corporation. A "Making Managerial Decisions" example was replaced by a new, more realistic one, and we added a new "Summary Problem for Your Review." We improved the descriptions of real options and benchmarking and simplified the treatment of investments in working capital.

Chapter 12 remains largely unchanged from the substantial revisions of the last edition. However, we have clarified and shortened the opening vignette and several other sections. We added current survey results to augment key concepts and demonstrate the use of allocation methods across the value chain. Some minor changes in text organization were made to improve the readability of the text.

Chapter 13 includes clarified discussion of overhead cost allocation and disposition of overhead variances.

Chapter 14 has been revised to clarify the discussion throughout the chapter, especially regarding process costing.

In **Chapter 15** there is an expanded discussion of the International Accounting Standards Board (IASB) and International Financial Reporting Standards (IFRS). Revisions for clarity included a shorter, more-direct discussion of dividends, an updated discussion of balance sheets for nonprofit organizations, and an improved introduction to adjustments.

A new section in **Chapter 16** introduces other comprehensive income. In addition to updating all examples and deleting redundant explanations, we added the IFRS treatment of research and development and replaced a "Making Managerial Decisions" example with a more decision-relevant one.

Chapter 17 now features Berkshire Hathaway rather than General Motors in the introduction and as a recurring example. In additional to general improvements in presentation, the explanations for consolidated statements and efficient markets were simplified. Finally, we have updated all financial statement references throughout.

Supplements for Instructors and Students

INSTRUCTOR'S RESOURCE MANUAL   Substantially revised, this resource manual provides insightful and useful tips on how to best manage course content when using *Introduction to Management Accounting*, 15th edition, in class. Chapter-by-chapter explanations and pedagogical philosophies are clearly delineated and oriented to greatly aid the teaching process.

SOLUTIONS MANUAL   Comprehensive solutions are provided for all end-of-chapter material. The Solutions Manual includes a listing of problems covering each learning objective, sample assignment schedules, a linking of 14th edition problems to those in this edition, comments on choices of problems in each chapter, and key amounts from suggested solutions to selected problems.

TEST ITEM FILE   This is a ready-to-use bank of testing material that contains, for each chapter, a variety of types of questions, including true/false, multiple-choice, and critical thinking problems. For ease of use, each question is linked to chapter objectives and also provides a suggested difficulty level and references to text pages where answers can be found.

TESTGEN   This testing software is designed to aid in creating custom tests in minutes. Features include question randomization, a point-and-drag interface, and extensive customizable settings.

POWERPOINT PRESENTATION   Complete PowerPoint presentations are provided for each chapter. Instructors may download and use each presentation as it is or customize the slides to create tailor-made slide shows. Each presentation allows instructors to offer an interactive presentation using colorful graphics, outlines of chapter material, and graphical explanations of difficult topics. This is available online at http://www.pearsonhighered.com/horngren.

COURSE WEB SITE AT HTTP://WWW.PEARSONHIGHERED.COM/HORNGREN
This complete online resource offers a variety of Internet-based teaching and learning support. It provides a wealth of resources for students and faculty, including the following:

- An online study guide
- Excel spreadsheet templates

STUDENT STUDY GUIDE   The student study guide contains a wealth of resources designed to aid students in text comprehension. Each chapter includes chapter overviews, study tips, self-test questions, demonstration problems, worked-out solutions, and more.

EXCEL SPREADSHEET TEMPLATES   Ready-made templates to accompany selected end-of-chapter problems can be found at **http://www.pearsonhighered.com/horngren**.

Acknowledgments

We have received ideas, assistance, miscellaneous critiques, and assorted assignment material in conversations with and by mail from many students, professors, and business leaders. Each has our gratitude, but the list is too long to enumerate here. We wish to thank the following reviewers whose feedback was helpful in this and previous editions:

Jim Carroll, Georgian Court University
William Creel, Herzing College
Stan Davis, Indiana University – Purdue University Fort Wayne
Chris Gilbert, Glendale Community College
Valerie Goodwin, Olean Business Institute
Lawrence Grasso, Central Connecticut State University
Henry Huang, Butler University
Agatha Jeffers, Montclair State University
Cody King, Georgia Southwestern State University
Roman J. Klusas, University of Indianapolis
Chuo-Hsuan (Jason) Lee, Plattsburgh State University of New York
Lisa Martin, Hampton College
Maureen Mascha, Marquette University
Jerold R. Miller, Chaparral College
David Mona, Champlain College
Julian Mooney, Georgia Southern University
Behnaz Quigley, Marymount University
Bill Rankin, Colorado State University
Patrick Rogan, Cosumnes River College
Walter Smith, Siena College
Ken Snow, Kaplan University & Florida Community College at Jacksonville
John Stancil, Florida Southern College
Vic Stanton, Stanford Graduate School of Business
Holly Sudano, Florida State University
Diane Tanner, University of North Florida
Geoffrey Tickell, Indiana University of Pennsylvania
Michael Tyler, Barry University
Karen Wisniewski, County College of Morris

We also thank Carolyn Streuly for help in proofing the manuscript and checking the solutions manual. Finally, students in our classes have provided invaluable feedback on previous editions, for which we are grateful.

Many people at Prentice Hall also earn our deepest thanks for their thoughtful contributions, including Sally Yagan, Julie Broich, Ashley Santora, Karen Kirincich, Christina Rumbaugh, Jane Avery, Cynthia Zonneveld, Rhonda Aversa, Anthony Gemmellaro, Allison Longley, and Diane Peirano.

Charles T. Horngren
Gary L. Sundem
William O. Stratton
David Burgstahler
Jeff Schatzberg

Introduction to

MANAGEMENT
ACCOUNTING

Managerial Accounting, the Business Organization, and Professional Ethics

LEARNING OBJECTIVES

When you have finished studying this chapter, you should be able to:

1. Describe the major users and uses of accounting information.

2. Describe the cost-benefit and behavioral issues involved in designing an accounting system.

3. Explain the role of budgets and performance reports in planning and control.

4. Discuss the role accountants play in the company's value-chain functions.

5. Explain why accounting is important in a variety of career paths.

6. Identify current trends in management accounting.

7. Explain why ethics and standards of ethical conduct are important to accountants.

▶ STARBUCKS

If you had asked most people a decade or two ago whether consumers around the world would pay a premium price for a "better" cup of coffee, few would have answered yes. Nevertheless, the expansion of **Starbucks** since its founding in 1971 in Seattle's Pike Place Market has been nothing short of phenomenal. In 2008, Starbucks' total revenues—the amount the company received for all the items sold—were $10.4 billion, compared with only $700 million in 1996. Net income—the profit that Starbucks made—was $504 million, up from only $42 million in 1996. Total assets—the recorded value of the items owned by Starbucks—grew from less than $900 million in 1996 to more than $5.6 billion in 2008. These numbers are accounting measures of the cumulative success of numerous managers of Starbucks stores in many countries. Managers use these figures, and more detailed accounting numbers, to make day-to-day decisions and to measure performance.

Starbucks has established a worldwide reputation to match its financial success. It was ranked seventh among *Fortune* magazine's "100 Best Companies to Work For." *Business Ethics* magazine placed it ninth in its list of "100 Best Corporate Citizens." Brandchannel ranked Starbucks among the best 100 global brands for 2008. Finally, in 2008 *Fortune* named Starbucks the sixth most admired company in America.

How did Starbucks accomplish all this? As we embark on our journey into the world of management accounting, we will explore what it takes for a company such as Starbucks to ensure that when Mei-Hwa Zhang walks into a Starbucks in Beijing, she has much the same quality experience as Mohammad Kumar does in a Starbucks in Kuwait or Franz Mueller does in Zurich. All Starbucks' managers, from baristas to store managers to the chief executive officer, use accounting reports to assess how well their unit meets corporate goals and objectives. Accounting provides a common language to help managers around the world communicate and coordinate their actions. By the time you finish reading this book, you will be comfortable with the accounting information managers use to make their decisions. You will better understand how to use information to develop plans, make short-term and long-term decisions, assess performance, and, in general, be a better manager.

Managerial accounting can help managers with all sorts of decisions. For example consider decisions you might face as a manager in the following situations:

- Suppose you are a **Boeing** engineer preparing manufacturing specifications for a component of its new 787 Dreamliner airplane. There are three possible ways to organize the assembly of the component. Which is the most cost-effective approach?
- Suppose you are a product manager at **General Mills** and you are designing a new marketing plan for Cheerios. Market research predicts that distributing free samples in the mail will increase annual sales by 4%. Will the cost of producing and distributing the free samples be more or less than the profits from the added sales?
- **Bank of America** offers free checking to customers with no minimum balance requirement in their MyAccess™ checking account. How much does it cost the bank to provide this free service?
- Kitsap County Special Olympics holds a series of athletic events for disabled youth. As executive director, you must set a goal for the group's annual fund drive based on the estimated cost to support its planned activities.
- Madison Park Cafe currently is open only for dinner, but the owner is considering opening for lunch. The average lunch is priced at about $9, and the café expects to serve about 40 lunches per day. Can the chef produce a luncheon menu that meets the café's quality standards at an average cost that yields a reasonable profit?
- **Amazon.com** offers free 2-day shipping on all orders for subscribers that pay a single $79 annual fee. Does the fee plus the profits from increased sales to subscribers exceed the cost of providing free shipping?

In making decisions such as these, managers turn to management accountants for information. Larry White, former chair of the Institute for Management Accountants, sums up the role of management accounting as follows: "Management accountants are committed to helping their organization achieve its strategic goals by providing decision support, planning, and control for business operations with a high level of ethics and professional competence."

In this chapter, we consider the purposes and roles of management accounting and accountants in different types of organizations, as well as some of the trends and challenges faced by accountants today. Information is useful only if decision makers can rely on it. Therefore we place special emphasis on ethics—unless accountants have high integrity, their information will have little value. ■

Starbuck's coffee shops have strategic locations throughout the world, including this one in Shanghai.

Accounting and Decision Making

The basic purpose of accounting information is to help decision makers—company presidents, production managers, hospital or school administrators, investors, and others. **Decision making**—choice from among a set of alternative courses of action designed to achieve some objective—drives the need for accounting information. Regardless of who is making the decision, understanding accounting information allows for a more informed, and better, decision.

Users of Accounting Information

Both internal parties (managers) and external parties use accounting information, but they often demand different types of information and use it in different ways. **Management accounting** produces information for managers within an organization. It is the process of identifying, measuring, accumulating, analyzing, preparing, interpreting, and communicating information that helps managers fulfill organizational objectives. In contrast, **financial accounting** produces information for external parties, such as stockholders, suppliers, banks, and government regulatory agencies. We list the major differences between management accounting and financial accounting in Exhibit 1-1. In this book we focus on management accounting.

Objective 1
Describe the major users and uses of accounting information.

	Management Accounting	**Financial Accounting**
Primary users	Organization managers at various levels	Outside parties such as investors and government agencies but also organization managers
Freedom of choice of accounting measures	No constraints other than requiring the benefits of improved management decisions to exceed information costs	Constrained by generally accepted accounting principles (GAAP)
Behavioral implications in selecting accounting measures	Choice should consider how measurements and reports will influence managers' daily behavior	Choice based on how to measure and communicate economic phenomena; behavioral considerations are secondary, although executive compensation based on reported results may have behavioral impacts
Time focus of reports	Future orientation: formal use of budgets as well as historical records. Example: 20X2 budget versus 20X2 actual performance	Past orientation: historical evaluation. Example: 20X2 actual performance versus 20X1 actual performance
Time span of reports	Flexible, varying from hourly to 10–15 years	Less flexible; usually one year or one quarter
Types of reports	Detailed reports: includes details about products, departments, territories, etc.	Summary reports: primarily report on the entity as a whole
Influence of other functional areas	Field is less sharply defined; heavier use of economics, decision sciences, and behavioral sciences	Field is more sharply defined. Lighter use of related disciplines

Exhibit 1-1
Distinctions Between Management Accounting and Financial Accounting

What kinds of accounting information do managers need to achieve their goals and objectives? Good accounting information helps answer three types of questions:

1. Scorecard questions: Is the company doing well or poorly? **Scorekeeping** is the classification, accumulation, and reporting of data that help users understand and evaluate organizational performance. Scorekeeping information must be accurate and reliable to be useful. For example, Starbucks produces numerous reports to evaluate results for stores and divisions.
2. Attention-directing questions: Which areas require additional investigation? **Attention directing** usually involves routine reports that compare actual results to before-the-fact expectations. For example, a manager who sees that a Starbucks store has reported profits of $120,000 when budgeted profit was $150,000 will look for explanations as to why the store did not achieve its budget. Attention-directing information helps managers focus on operating problems, imperfections, inefficiencies, and opportunities.
3. Problem-solving questions: Of the alternatives being considered, which is the best? The **problem-solving** aspect of accounting often involves an analysis of the impacts of each alternative to identify the best course to follow. For example, Starbucks experiments with adding various items to its menu. After an analysis of how a new product will affect revenues and costs, management decides which items to add and which to delete.

The scorecard and attention-directing uses of information are closely related. The same information that helps a manager understand and evaluate performance may also serve an attention-directing function for the manager's superior. For example, by pinpointing where actual results differ from plans, performance reports show managers how they are doing and where to take action. Companies produce most scorecard and attention-directing information on a routine basis every day, month, quarter, or year.

Problem solving sometimes relies on routine information used for scorekeeping and attention directing. However, when organizations make long-range plans or nonrecurring decisions, such as whether to make or to buy parts, replace equipment, or add or drop a product, specially-prepared information is often required. For example, Starbucks uses problem-solving information when deciding whether to run ads during the Super Bowl™ broadcast.

Making Managerial Decisions

Managers use accounting information for many different types of decisions. Accountants must make sure that they produce information that is useful for these various decisions. What type of information—scorekeeping, attention-directing, or problem-solving—would managers use for each of the following decisions? Why?

1. Deciding whether to replace a traditional assembly line with a fully automated robotic process
2. Evaluating the performance of a division for the preceding year
3. Identifying which products exceeded their budgeted profitability and which ones fell short of their budgets

Answers

1. Problem solving. This is a one-time decision for which managers need information about the potential impacts of each of the alternatives under consideration.
2. Scorekeeping. This is a routine evaluation of an organizational unit for which managers want systematic data on a regular basis.
3. Attention directing. To identify products that need attention, managers want information that highlights deviations of actual results from pre-specified expectations in the budget.

Influences on Accounting Systems

An **accounting system** is a formal mechanism for gathering, organizing, and communicating information about an organization's activities. In order to reduce costs and complexity, many organizations use a general-purpose accounting system that attempts to meet the needs of both external and internal users. However, as outlined in Exhibit 1-1, there are important differences between management accounting information and financial accounting information.

There are three categories of requirements imposed on accounting systems designed to meet the requirements of external users. First, public companies' financial reports for external users must adhere to a set of standards known as **generally accepted accounting principles (GAAP)**. The Financial Accounting Standards Board (FASB) determines U.S. GAAP. In the European Union and more than 100 countries worldwide, companies must comply with **International Financial Reporting Standards (IFRS)** set by the International Accounting Standards Board (IASB). Second, every company is also subject to various taxes, and therefore subject to various reporting requirements specified by tax rules and regulations. Finally, many companies are subject to other government regulations.

There are many other governmental regulations that influence accounting systems. For example, in 2002 the **Sarbanes-Oxley Act** added several levels of regulation. Driven by corporate bankruptcies blamed in part on accounting lapses (as well as deficiencies in corporate governance, lax securities regulation, and executive greed), the act requires more top-management oversight of a company's accounting policies and procedures. By requiring chief executive officers to sign a statement certifying the accuracy of the company's financial statements, the act makes accounting numbers the concern of all managers, not just the accountants. Sarbanes-Oxley requires external auditors to examine and prepare a separate report on a company's system of **internal controls**—policies to protect and make the most efficient use of an organization's assets. While some managers insist that the extra costs of compliance with Sarbanes-Oxley exceed the benefits, others believe the regulations provide stronger controls and more informative reports whose benefits exceed the costs. Another example of broad regulation is the **Foreign Corrupt Practices Act**, a U.S. law forbidding bribery and other corrupt practices. The word "Foreign" in the title is misleading because the act's provisions apply to all publicly held companies, even if they do not conduct business outside the United States. This law requires that companies maintain their accounting records in reasonable detail and accuracy. **Internal auditors** review and evaluate accounting systems, including companies' internal controls, and conduct **management audits**—reviews to determine whether managers are implementing the policies and procedures specified by top management. A final specific area of regulation is government contracting. Universities, defense contractors, and others contracting with the U.S. government must comply with numerous reporting requirements.

The requirements of external reporting should not constrain the scorekeeping, attention-directing, and problem-solving information that can be generated to meet the needs of internal users. In later chapters, we will see many examples where information needed for a decision is not being generated by the general-purpose accounting system designed to meet external reporting requirements. As a decision-maker, you must recognize when information from the existing accounting system is not sufficient for your decision and be prepared to ask for additional information to be generated. Your requests for more information should be balanced against the cost of obtaining the information. As explained in the following section, you should only acquire additional costly information when the expected benefit of an improved decision exceeds the cost of the information.

Cost-Benefit and Behavioral Considerations

Objective 2

Describe the cost-benefit and behavioral issues involved in designing an accounting system.

Managers should keep two important ideas in mind when designing accounting systems: (1) cost-benefit balances and (2) behavioral implications.

The **cost-benefit balance**—weighing estimated costs against probable benefits—is the primary consideration in choosing among accounting systems and methods. We will refer again and again to cost-benefit considerations throughout this book. Accounting systems are economic goods—like office supplies or labor—available at various costs. Which system does a manager want to buy: a simple file drawer for amassing receipts and canceled checks, an elaborate budgeting system based on computerized models of the organization and its subunits, or something in between?

The answer depends on the buyer's perceptions of the expected benefits in relation to the costs. For example, consider a manager at University Clinic who is considering installing a HorizonMIS®-computerized system from **American Medical Systems of Ohio** for managing a medical practice. Users enter a piece of information only once and the system automatically integrates it with billing, insurance claims, and patient history records. Such a system is efficient and is subject to few errors, but should it be purchased? That depends on whether its expected value to the clinic is greater than its cost of $300,000. While comparison of costs and benefits is conceptually simple, it is often difficult to estimate both costs and benefits, a point that will be illustrated repeatedly in later chapters.

Managers should also consider **behavioral implications**, that is, the system's effect on the behavior, specifically the decisions, of managers. For example, consider a performance report that a manager's superiors use to evaluate the operations for which the manager is responsible. If the report is too complex or difficult to use, the manager may ignore the report in making decisions. If the report unfairly attributes excessive costs to the manager's operations, the manager may lose confidence in the system and not let it influence future decisions. In contrast, a system that managers understand and believe in can greatly influence their decisions and actions.

In a nutshell, think of management accounting as a balance between costs and benefits of accounting information coupled with an awareness of the importance of behavioral effects. Therefore, management accountants must understand related disciplines, such as economics, the decision sciences, and the behavioral sciences, to make intelligent decisions about the best information to supply to managers.

The Management Process and Accounting

Accounting information helps managers plan and control the organization's operations. In practice, planning and control are so intertwined that it seems artificial to separate them. In studying management, however, we find it useful to concentrate on either the planning phase or the control phase to simplify our analysis.

The Nature of Planning and Control

The left side of Exhibit 1-2 demonstrates the planning and control cycle of current operations that could be used by a particular **Starbucks** store. **Planning** (the top box) refers to setting objectives for an organization and outlining how it will attain them. Thus, planning provides the answers to two questions: What objectives does the organization want to achieve? When and how will the organization achieve these objectives? For example, the Starbucks store's management may want to increase profitability and to achieve it by adding new drinks and increasing advertising.

    Control refers to implementing plans and using feedback to evaluate the attainment of objectives. Feedback is crucial to the cycle of planning and control. Planning determines action, action generates feedback, and the control phase uses this feedback to influence further planning and actions. Timely, systematic reports provided by the internal accounting system are the chief source of useful feedback. The control section in Exhibit 1-2 shows the actions that are intended to increase profitability and how Starbucks will evaluate the actions. The Starbucks store will implement its plan to expand the number of drinks on its menu and increase advertising. Management will evaluate these actions based on three performance measures, the increase in drinks sold, increase in advertising expenditures, and the increase in revenue. Performance evaluation results will in turn be used for further planning and implementation.

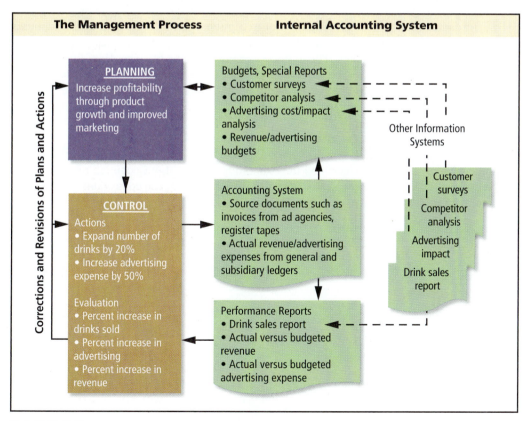

Exhibit 1-2
Starbucks Store—Accounting Framework for Planning and Control

Objective 3

Explain the role of budgets and performance reports in planning and control.

Management by Exception

The right side of Exhibit 1-2 shows that the accounting system formalizes plans by expressing them as budgets. A **budget** is a quantitative expression of a plan of action. Budgets also help to coordinate and implement plans. They are the chief devices for disciplining management planning. Without budgets, planning may not get the front-and-center focus that it deserves. The Starbucks store expresses its plan for product growth and improved marketing through revenue and advertising budgets.

The accounting system records, measures, and classifies actions to produce performance reports (the last box in Exhibit 1-2). **Performance reports** provide feedback by comparing results with plans and by highlighting **variances**, which are deviations from plans. Organizations use performance reports to judge managers' decisions and the productivity of organizational units. Performance reports compare actual results to budgets, thereby motivating managers to achieve the objectives. For example, managers of the Starbucks store evaluate the effectiveness of its advertising plan by comparing the increase in revenue and profits to the increase in advertising costs. Based on their evaluation, managers at Starbucks make corrections and revisions to their plans.

Exhibit 1-3 shows a simple performance report for a hypothetical Starbucks store, the Mayfair Starbucks. The first column of Exhibit 1-3 is the budget for March 20X1. It is based on a predicted level of sales and the estimated costs needed to support that level of sales. After managers and their superiors agree on a budget, it becomes the managers' target for the month. As the store sells its products and incurs costs, Starbucks' accounting system collects the revenue and cost information. At the end of each month (or more often if managers need more frequent feedback), the accounting department prepares a store-level performance report, such as the one in Exhibit 1-3. Managers use the performance report to help evaluate the store's operations.

The Mayfair store report shows that the store met its targeted sales, but the $2,500 unfavorable variance for ingredients shows that these costs were $2,500 over budget. Other variances show that store labor costs were $400 under budget, and other labor was $50 over budget. At the Mayfair store, management would undoubtedly focus attention on ingredients, which had by far the largest unfavorable variance. However, it may also be worthwhile to investigate the $400 favorable labor variance. By investigating favorable variances, managers may find better ways of doing things.

Performance reports spur investigation of exceptions—items for which actual amounts differ significantly from budgeted amounts. Managers then revise operations to conform with the plans or revise the plans. This process is **management by exception**, which means concentrating on areas that deviate from the plan and, in the absence of other evidence, presuming that areas that conform with plans are running smoothly. Thus, the management-by-exception approach frees managers from needless concern with those phases of operations that adhere to plans. However, well-conceived plans incorporate enough discretion or flexibility so that the manager feels free to pursue any unforeseen opportunities.

Notice that although budgets aid planning and performance reports aid control, it is not accountants but operating managers and their subordinates who use accounting reports to plan and control operations. Accounting assists the managerial planning and control functions by providing prompt measurements of actions and by systematically pinpointing trouble spots.

	Budget	Actual	Variance
Sales	$50,000	$50,000	0
Less:			
Ingredients	22,000	$24,500	$2,500 U
Store labor (baristas, etc.)	12,000	11,600	400 F
Other labor (managers, supervisors)	6,000	6,050	50 U
Utilities, maintenance, etc.	4,500	4,500	0
Total expenses	44,500	46,650	2,150 U
Total operating income	$ 5,500	$ 3,350	$2,150 U

U = unfavorable—actual cost greater than budgeted; actual revenue or profit less than budgeted
F = favorable—actual cost less than budgeted; actual revenue or profit greater than budgeted

Exhibit 1-3
Mayfair Starbucks Store—Performance Report for the Month Ended March 31, 20X1

Planning and Control for Product Life Cycles and the Value Chain

Many management decisions relate to a single good or service, or to a group of related products. To effectively plan and control production of goods or services, accountants and other managers must consider the product's life cycle. **Product life cycle** refers to the various stages through which a product passes: conception and product development; introduction into the market; maturation of the market; and, finally, withdrawal from the market. At each stage, managers face differing costs and potential returns. Exhibit 1-4 shows a typical product life cycle.

In the planning process, managers predict revenues and costs over the entire life cycle—however long or short. Then accounting systems track actual costs and revenues throughout the life cycle. Periodic comparisons between planned costs and revenues and actual costs and revenues allow managers to assess the current profitability of a product, determine its current product life-cycle stage, and make any needed changes in strategy.

For example, suppose **Pfizer** is developing a new drug to reduce high blood pressure. There will be substantial development costs and no revenue during the product development stage. Most of the revenues from the product will be received during the introduction and mature market stages when there will also be production costs. During the phase-out of the product, there will be little revenue but Pfizer will need to keep the drug on the market for those who have come to rely on it. Thus, the product pricing strategy must recognize the need for revenues during the introduction and mature market stages to cover both development and phase-out costs as well as the direct costs of producing the drug.

Product life cycles range from a few months (for fashion clothing or faddish toys) to many years (for automobiles or refrigerators). Some products, such as many computer software packages, have long development stages and relatively short market lives. Others, such as **Boeing** 737 airplanes, have a market life many times longer than their development stage. Many companies are working to shorten the product development phase, both to reduce the time during which a product generates no revenue and to bring products to market on a more timely basis.

The Value Chain

In addition to considering a product's life cycle, managers must recognize those activities necessary for a company to create the goods or services that it sells. These activities comprise the **value chain**, the set of business functions or activities that add value to the products or services of an organization. As shown in Exhibit 1-5 these functions include the following:

Objective 4

Discuss the role accountants play in the company's value-chain functions.

- Research and development: the generation of ideas related to new products, services, or processes
- Design of products, services, or processes: the detailed design and engineering of products, services, or processes
- Production: the coordination and assembly of resources to produce a product or deliver a service
- Marketing: the manner by which individuals or groups learn about the value and features of products or services (for example, advertising or selling activities)
- Distribution: the mechanism by which a company delivers products or services to the customer
- Customer service: the support activities provided to the customer

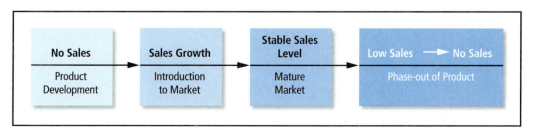

Exhibit 1-4
Typical Product Life Cycle

The Lexus car company case on Angel demonstrate these elements of the value chain.

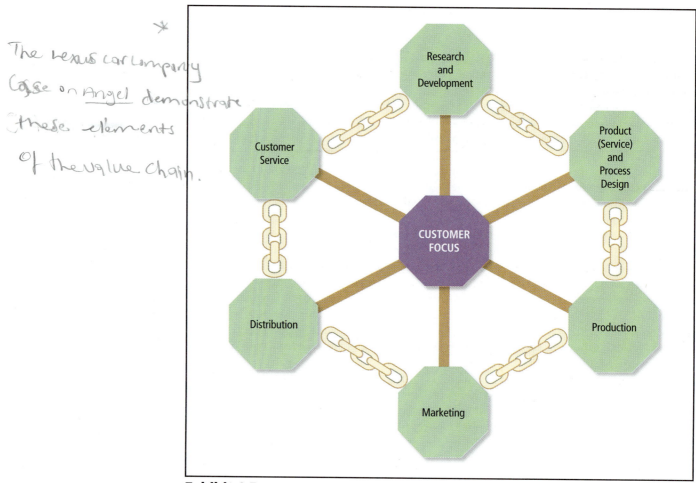

Exhibit 1-5

The Value Chain of Business Functions

Support activities such as management information systems and accounting are not shown. These activities support all other value chain functions.

Not all functions are of equal importance to the success of a company. Senior management must decide which of these functions enables the company to gain and maintain a competitive edge. For example, **Dell Computers** considers the design function a critical success factor. The features designed into Dell's computers create higher quality. In addition, the design of efficient processes used to make and deliver computers lowers costs and speeds up delivery to its customers. Dell also performs the other value-chain functions, but it concentrates on being the best process designer in the computer market.

Accountants play a role in supporting all the value-chain functions. Most obvious is the production stage, where accountants facilitate cost planning and control through the use of budgets and performance reporting and help track the effects of continuous improvement programs. However, accounting can also have a great influence on the two pre-production value-chain functions. For example, accountants provide estimated revenue and cost data during the research and development stage and during the design stage of the value chain. Managers use these data to decide which ideas will move to the production stage and which will be dropped. These data also enable managers and engineers to reduce the life-cycle costs of products or services by changing product and process designs. Accountants can give managers feedback on ideas for cost reductions long before the company must make a commitment to purchase expensive equipment.

Accountants also play a role in post-production value-chain functions. For example, marketing decisions have a significant impact on sales, but the cost of marketing programs is also significant. Accountants analyze the trade-off between increased revenues and costs. In addition, accounting information can influence decisions about distributing products or services to customers. Should a company sell its products directly to a chain of retail stores, or should it sell to a wholesaler? What transportation system should be used—trucks or trains? Accountants provide important information about the costs of each alternative. Finally, accountants provide cost data for customer service activities, such as warranty and repair costs and the costs of goods returned. Managers compare these costs to the benefits generated by better customer service. As you can see, cost management is important throughout the value chain.

Note that customer focus is at the center of Exhibit 1-5. Each value-chain function should focus on activities that create value for the customer. Successful businesses never lose sight of the importance of maintaining a focus on the needs of their customers. For example, one of the main principles in **Starbucks**' mission statement is to "develop enthusiastically satisfied customers all of the time." Customers are also the focus at **Wal-Mart**, as explained by Sam Walton, founder and former chairman:

> *There is only one boss—the customer. Customers can fire everybody in the company from the chairman on down, simply by spending their money somewhere else.*

The value chain and the concepts of adding value and focusing on the customer are essential for success. Therefore, we will return to the value chain and use it as a focus for discussion throughout this book.

Making Managerial Decisions

Measuring costs at various stages of the value chain is important to **Starbucks**. Suppose that you are a Starbucks manager or accountant. For each of the following activities, indicate the value-chain function that is being performed and what accounting information might be helpful to managers in the function:

1. Process engineers investigate methods to reduce the time to roast coffee beans and to better preserve their flavor.
2. A direct-to-your-home mail-order system is established to sell custom-blended coffees.
3. Arabica coffee beans are purchased and transported to company processing plants.
4. Focus groups investigate the feasibility of a new line of Frappuccino drinks.
5. A telephone hotline is established for mail-order customers to call with questions and comments on the quality and speed of delivery.
6. Each company-owned retail store undertakes a campaign to provide information to customers about the processes used to make its coffee products.

Answers

1. Research and development or design. Both the generation of ideas for new processes and the design of new production processes are important parts of the value chain. Managers need the costs of various possible production processes to decide among the alternatives.

2. Distribution. This provides an additional way to deliver products to customers. Managers need information on the costs of a mail-order system to compare to the added profit from mail-order sales.
3. Production. Starbucks purchases only premium beans, but the company is still concerned about the purchase price of beans and transportation. These are part of product costs incurred during production.
4. Research and development or marketing. These costs (mostly wages) are incurred prior to management's final decision to design and produce a new product. Predicted revenues and costs from the Frappuccino market can help managers design a drink that is both marketable and profitable.
5. Customer service. These costs include all expenditures made after Starbucks has delivered the product to the customer; in this case, Starbucks obtains feedback on the quality and speed of delivery. Managers will trade off the cost of the hotline and the value of the information generated from the calls.
6. Marketing. These costs are for activities that enhance the existing or potential customers' awareness and opinion of the product. Like many advertising expenses, it is easy to estimate the costs of such a program but hard to quantify the benefits.

Accounting's Position in the Organization

The role of management accountants in organizations has changed rapidly over the last decade or so. Consider the following four work activities of management accountants:

- Collecting and compiling information
- Preparing standardized reports
- Interpreting and analyzing information
- Being involved in decision making

Trends revealed by recent surveys show that management accountants are spending less time on the first two activities and more time on the last two. In essence, the management accountant is becoming an internal consultant on information-related issues—that is, an advisor for managers about what information would be useful, what information is available, and how to analyze the information and use it in decision making. Decision making is the core of the management process.

Decisions range from the routine (making daily production schedules) to the non-routine (launching a new product line), and accountants are information specialists who aid the decision makers.

Line and Staff Authority

As an organization grows, it must divide responsibilities among a number of managers and executives each with specific responsibilities. **Line managers** are directly involved with making and selling the organization's products or services. Their decisions lead directly to meeting (or not meeting) the organization's objectives. In contrast, **staff managers** are advisory—they support the line managers. They have no authority over line managers, but they help the line managers by providing information and advice. The organization chart in Exhibit 1-6 shows how a traditional manufacturing company divides responsibilities between line and staff managers. The line managers in manufacturing are supported by sales, engineering, personnel, and financial staff support at the corporate level, and by receiving and storeroom, inspection, tool room, purchasing, production control, and maintenance staff at the factory level.

Many modern organizations have abandoned the type of hierarchical structure shown in Exhibit 1-6 in favor of a "flatter" organization. For example, **W. L. Gore & Associates**, maker of GORE-TEX® and other products using fluoropolymer technologies, has gone so far as to eliminate all job titles so everyone shares the same title, "associate." Gore also limits the size of organizational units to 150 associates. In these flatter organizations, specialization by individuals is giving way to decision making by cross-functional teams. In such an organization, management accountants are still the information specialists. However, they are not isolated in one branch of the organization chart and do not sit in their offices and issue reports. Instead, the management accountants are physically located with the line managers, and they work together to determine the optimal information support for the managers. We highlight some other recent changes in the role of accountants in the Business First box on p. 13.

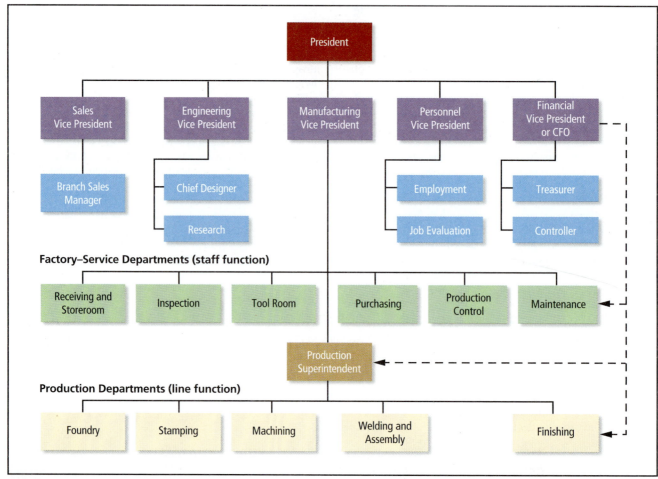

Exhibit 1-6
Partial Organization Chart of a Manufacturing Company

The Accountant's Role at the Marmon Group

The Marmon Group illustrates nearly all the reasons why management accounting is a vital and growing function in today's leading companies. Marmon, a **Berkshire Hathaway** company, is an international association of about 130 manufacturing, distribution, and service companies with annual revenues of about $7 billion. Because operations are spread out in more than 40 different countries with thousands of diverse products and services (such as workers' gloves, water coolers, railroad tank cars, medical products, and credit services for banks), managers at Marmon make extensive use of management accounting information when undertaking important decisions.

What exactly is the role of management accountants at Marmon? According to Jim Smith, Marmon's former director of cost management, "The role of the management accountant is changing dramatically in most of our companies." In the past, Marmon's management accountants were basically clerical workers who spent most of their time analyzing monthly cost variances. Now, however, Marmon's management accountants work closely with operating and sales managers, providing cost information in a format that makes sense to those managers. Says Smith, "In the past few years the management accountant has become much more of a financial and business strategy adviser to senior management.

Operating and sales managers are demanding meaningful cost information, and management accountants are helping them see how their actions affect costs and the bottom line."

Management accountants have become more important to Marmon because recessions and foreign competition have awakened the understanding in most managers that managing costs is an important function. Knowing what a product truly costs or the cost of servicing a particular customer has become essential to Marmon's profitability.

"To help manage costs," says Smith, "accountants and managers are shying away from using one cost, often the cost used for financial reporting purposes, as the only important cost." Instead, they are now using costs calculated for the decision at hand. As Smith said, "Depending on the decision, any of the cost methods described in *Introduction to Management Accounting* are relevant." He believes this is a very positive change, "since it allows and, in fact, requires the management accountant to understand all of the functions in a business and how each one adds value to the product or service."

Source: The Marmon Group Web site (www.marmon.com); discussions with James Smith, former director of cost management, the Marmon Group.

Controller and Treasurer Functions

We have discussed the various roles of management accountants in an organization. The employees carrying out management accounting functions have a variety of titles. The **chief financial officer (CFO)**, a top executive who deals with all finance and accounting issues, oversees the accounting function in most organizations. Both the treasurer and controller generally report to the CFO, as shown in Exhibit 1-6. The **treasurer** is concerned mainly with the company's financial matters such as raising and managing cash, while the **controller** (also called **comptroller** in many government organizations) is concerned with operating matters such as aiding management decision-making. In a small company, one person may perform both treasury and controllership functions. Nevertheless, it is useful to differentiate the two different roles. The **Financial Executives Institute**, an association of corporate treasurers and controllers, distinguishes the two as follows:

Controllership
1. Planning for control
2. Reporting and interpreting
3. Evaluating and consulting
4. Tax administration
5. Government reporting
6. Protection of assets
7. Economic appraisal

Treasurership
1. Provision of capital
2. Investor relations
3. Short-term financing
4. Banking and custody
5. Credit management and cash collections
6. Investments
7. Risk management (insurance)

Management accounting is the primary means of implementing the first three functions of controllership, including advice and help in budgeting, analyzing variances, pricing, and making special decisions.

Management Accounting and Your Career

Objective 5

Explain why accounting is important in a variety of career paths.

A thorough understanding of accounting opens up a broad range of career opportunities. When accounting is mentioned, most people think first of those who devote their careers entirely to accounting such as independent auditors—**certified public accountants (CPAs)** in the United States and **chartered accountants (CAs)** in many other nations—who reassure the public about the reliability of companies' published financial statements. The **International Accounting Education Standards Board (IAESB)**, a part of the International Federation of Accountants, sets educational standards for auditors throughout the world. However, the majority of accountants work in private industry and government. While they produce the organizations' financial statements, they also produce management accounting information for managers.

The **certified management accountant (CMA)** designation is the internal accountant's counterpart to the CPA. The **Institute of Management Accountants (IMA)**, the largest U.S. professional organization focused on internal accounting, oversees the CMA program. CMAs must pass an examination covering (1) Financial planning, performance and control, and (2) Financial decision making.[1] Like the CPA designation, the CMA confers higher status and leads to more responsible positions and higher pay. A recent survey by *Financial Executive* magazine showed that 33% of CEOs in companies with revenues greater than $500 million had risen through the finance/accounting ranks, compared with 26% from operations and 21% from sales and marketing.

Perhaps the most important users of management accounting information are managers who are not accountants. Studying the concepts in this book will help you understand how information can improve decisions in purchasing, manufacturing, wholesaling, retailing, marketing, and many other functional areas. You will develop skills that will help you to be a better manager, regardless of the type of managerial position you hold. By studying accounting, you begin to learn more about the interrelationships among different aspects of an organization, such as production and marketing. In sum, a thorough understanding of management accounting can be an important qualification for the highest-level executive positions in an organization.

Adaptation to Change

Objective 6

Identify current trends in management accounting.

Businesses in the twenty-first century differ from those in the twentieth century. Markets have become more competitive, and access to information has become more important. Many companies today derive their competitive advantage from their information, not their physical facilities. Companies such as **Amazon.com** pride themselves on managing the information obtained from their customers and suppliers. Such companies must continually improve their accounting information. The information that supported traditional companies in the 1980s and 1990s does not adequately support the modern business environment.

Four major business trends are influencing management accounting today:

1. Shift from a manufacturing-based to a service-based economy in the United States
2. Increased global competition
3. Advances in technology
4. Changes in business process management

Service Sector

Accountants in manufacturing organizations developed many of the basic ideas of management accounting. These ideas, however, have evolved so that they apply to all types of organizations, including service and nonprofit organizations. **Service organizations**, for our purposes, are organizations that do not make or sell tangible goods. Public accounting firms, law firms, management consultants, real estate firms, transportation companies,

---

[1]Information can be obtained from the IMA, 10 Paragon Drive, Montvale, NJ 07645, or at www.imanet.org.

banks, insurance companies, and hotels are examples of profit-seeking service organizations. Most nonprofit organizations, such as hospitals, schools, libraries, museums, and government agencies, are also service organizations.

The characteristics of service organizations include the following:

1. *Labor is a major component of costs:* The highest proportions of expenses in service organizations, such as schools and law firms, are typically wages, salaries, and payroll-related costs, not the costs relating to the use of equipment and physical facilities.
2. *Output is usually difficult to measure:* Because service outputs are intangible, they are often hard to measure. For example, the output of a university might be defined as the number of degrees granted, but many critics would maintain that the real output is what is contained in the students' brains.
3. *Service organizations cannot store their major inputs and outputs:* Services cannot usually be stockpiled. For example, an airline cannot save an empty airline seat for a later flight, and a hotel's available labor force and rooms are either used or unused as each day passes.

The service sector now accounts for almost 80% of the employment in the United States. Service industries are extremely competitive, and their managers increasingly rely on accounting information. Many examples in this book are from service companies.

Managers and accountants in service companies, whether profit-seeking or nonprofit organizations, have much in common. They raise and spend money. They prepare budgets and design and implement control systems. They all have an obligation to use resources wisely. Used intelligently, accounting information contributes to efficient operations and helps organizations achieve their objectives.

Simplicity is the watchword for accounting systems in service industries and nonprofit organizations. Why? Because many of the decision-makers using these systems, such as physicians, professors, or government officials, are too busy to try to grapple with a complex system. For them to use the information, it must be in a form that is easy to understand. In fact, simplicity is an important consideration in the design of any accounting system. Complexity generates costs of gathering and interpreting data that may exceed prospective benefits.

Global Competition

Global competition has increased in recent years as many countries have lowered international barriers to trade, such as tariffs and duties. In addition, there has been a worldwide trend toward deregulation. The result has been a shift in the balance of economic power in the world. Nowhere has this been more evident than in the United States. To regain their competitive edge, many U.S. companies redesigned their accounting systems to provide more accurate and timely information about the cost of activities, products, or services. Improved cost information helps managers better understand and predict the effects of their decisions.

Advances in Technology

The dominant influence on management accounting over the past decade has been technological change, affecting both the production and the use of accounting information. The increasing capabilities and decreasing cost of computer processing and storage has changed how accountants gather, store, manipulate, and report data. In many cases, databases allow managers to access data directly and to generate their own reports and analyses. Today managers and accountants work together to assure the availability of the data needed for decisions and to be sure managers know how to assemble and use the data.

One of the most rapidly growing uses of technology is **electronic commerce** or **e-commerce**—conducting business online. While the internet boom that focused on business-to-consumer (**B2C**) transactions ended in 2001, e-commerce focusing on business-to-business (**B2B**) transactions continued to grow at nearly 50% a year. B2B creates real savings to the companies involved. For example, some companies have reduced procurement processing costs by as much as 70% by automating the process.

A major effect of technology on accounting systems has been the growing use of **enterprise resource planning (ERP)** systems—integrated information systems that support all functional areas of a company. Accounting is just one part of such a system. For example, Oracle describes its JD Edwards EnterpriseOne ERP system as one that "helps you integrate all aspects of your business—including customer relationship management, enterprise asset management, enterprise resource planning, supply chain management, and supplier relationship management." Other well-known ERP system providers are **SAP**, **Microsoft Dynamics**, and **The Sage Group**. Accountants must work with managers throughout the organization to ensure that the ERP system provides the financial information that managers need.

Finally, the development and widespread adoption of eXtensible Business Reporting Language (**XBRL**), an XML-based accounting language, helps communicate financial information electronically. This language is greatly influencing both internal and external reporting by making comparisons across companies much simpler.

Changes in Business Process Management

Because management accounting supports business decisions, accounting systems must adapt to changes in management practices. Some companies implement sweeping changes in operations through **business process reengineering**, the fundamental rethinking and radical redesign of business processes to improve performance in areas such as cost, quality, service, and speed. Companies reduce process time by redesigning, simplifying, and automating the production process. They use **computer-aided design (CAD)** to design products that can be manufactured efficiently and **computer-aided manufacturing (CAM)** to direct and control production equipment. **Computer-integrated manufacturing (CIM) systems** use CAD, CAM, robots, and computer-controlled machines. The costs of such a system are quite different from those of a less-automated system. Companies that install a full CIM system use very little labor. Instead, they acquire the robots and computer-controlled machines needed to perform the routine jobs that were previously accomplished by assembly-line workers. Accounting systems of the last century designed primarily around the accounting for labor are not useful in CIM environments.

One management change leading to increased efficiency in business processes has been the adoption of a **just-in-time (JIT) philosophy**. Originally, JIT referred to an inventory system that minimized inventories by arranging for materials and subcomponents to arrive just as they were needed for production and for goods to be made just in time to ship them to customers—no sooner and no later. But JIT has become the cornerstone of a broad management philosophy. It originated in Japanese companies such as **Toyota** and **Kawasaki**. Now many large U.S. companies use JIT, including **Hewlett-Packard**, **Goodyear**, **General Motors**, **Intel**, and **Xerox**, as well as many smaller firms. The essence of the JIT philosophy is to eliminate waste. Managers try to (1) reduce the time that products spend in the production process and (2) eliminate the time that products spend in activities that do not add value (such as inspection and waiting time).

Another management approach focused on efficiency is **lean manufacturing**, which applies continuous process improvements to eliminate waste from the entire enterprise. For example, **Matsushita Electric**'s Saga plant on Japan's Kyushu island decreased the time it takes to produce a finished product from 2½ days to 40 minutes by replacing conveyor belts with clusters of robots. As with JIT, lean ideas are now being extended beyond manufacturing to other business processes.

A focus on quality is also important in today's competitive environment. A decade or more ago, many companies undertook **total quality management (TQM)** initiatives. TQM minimizes costs by maximizing quality. It focuses on continuous improvement in quality and satisfying one's customers. Recently the focus on quality has shifted to **Six Sigma**, a disciplined, *data-driven approach* to eliminating defects in any process. Used by about 35% of major U.S. companies, Six Sigma is essentially a continuous process-improvement effort designed to reduce costs by improving quality. Pioneered in the 1980s by **Motorola**, Six Sigma has also been implemented by companies such as **General Electric** in the United States and **Samsung** in Korea to transform their business. Six Sigma seeks to ensure that internal processes are running as efficiently as possible. Staff functions, such as legal departments, also use Six Sigma today. For example, law departments in both **DuPont** and **Tyco** use Six Sigma to "improve compliance, reduce risk, contain costs, and align the law department more closely with the objectives of the business." Management accountants play a major role in Six Sigma applications as both the experts on the measurements being used and as full members of the cross-functional teams that lead the efforts.

Why do these business process changes affect management accounting? They all directly affect costs, and accountants often measure the actual cost savings, predict anticipated cost savings, and develop costs for products or services for different production environments. For example, one midwestern factory saved production time by redesigning its plant layout to reduce the distance products traveled from one operation to the next during production from 1,384 feet to just 350 feet. Accountants measured the cost the company saved by the reduced production time. A British company reduced the time to manufacture a vacuum pump from 3 weeks to 6 minutes by switching from long assembly lines to manufacturing cells that accomplish all production steps in quick succession. Again, accountants measured the benefits created by the reduced production time. In general, when companies change their production processes to accomplish economic objectives, accountants predict and measure the economic impact.

Making Managerial Decisions

Suppose you are a manager of a DuPont chemical plant. The plant has just undertaken a business process reengineering project and, as a result, has substantially changed its production process. It is much more automated, with newly acquired equipment replacing labor-intensive operations. The plant is also making more use of electronic commerce and moving toward a JIT inventory policy. You have a meeting with your accountant to discuss possible changes in your accounting system. What types of accounting-system changes might be warranted?

Answer

Major changes in production processes generally lead to different information needs. The old accounting system may have focused on accounting for labor, while the new system should focus on the use of the automated equipment. This will direct attention to the most important costs in the process and make sure that they are monitored and controlled. Problem-solving needs will also be different. Initially, the plant's managers will probably want comparative data on the cost of the new process versus the cost of the old. In the future, they will need information about how best to use capacity that the plant owns (the equipment) rather than how much labor to use for the planned level of production.

Implications for the Study of Management Accounting

As you read the remainder of this book, remember that accounting systems change as the world changes. Companies currently apply the techniques described in this book. Tomorrow, however, new techniques will take their place. To adapt to changes, you must understand why companies are using the techniques, not just how they are using them. We urge you to resist the temptation to simply memorize rules and techniques. Instead, develop your understanding of the underlying concepts and principles, because this understanding will continue to be useful no matter what new techniques you encounter.

Ethical Conduct for Professional Accountants

Business processes and accounting systems change. However, the need for accountants to maintain high ethical standards of professional conduct will never change. The Institute of Management Accountants says that **ethics** "deals with human conduct in relation to what is morally good and bad, right and wrong. It is the application of values to decision making. These values include honesty, fairness, responsibility, respect and compassion."

Objective 7

Explain why ethics and standards of ethical conduct are important to accountants.

We like to think of ethics as simply doing what is right. One way to decide whether an action is unethical is to ask yourself whether you would be embarrassed to read about your action in the newspaper the next day. Another warning sign that an action may be unethical is when the justification for the action is "Everybody else is doing it," the phrase Warren Buffett has described as "the five most dangerous words in business." He goes on to say that this excuse should always raise a red flag: "Why would somebody offer such a rationale for an act if there were a good reason available? Clearly the advocate harbors at least a small doubt about the act if he utilizes this verbal crutch."

Why is integrity so important to accountants? Think of it this way: If you buy a car, you can see many of the quality details. Further, if something goes wrong with the car, you will certainly know it. But accounting information is different. You can't see its quality. You might not notice for years that something is wrong—probably not until it's too late to do anything about it. Thus, you rely on the integrity of accountants to assure yourself that the information about a company is correct. If you cannot trust the accountant, then the information is nearly worthless.

In the remainder of this section, we discuss ethical standards and formal codes of conduct that often help resolve ethical issues. We also provide examples of clearly unethical behavior. Finally, we turn to the difficult issue of ethical dilemmas, situations where conflicting values make it unclear which is the ethical action.

Standards of Ethical Conduct

Ethical standards require CPAs and CMAs to adhere to codes of conduct regarding competence, confidentiality, integrity, and credibility. Exhibit 1-7 contains the **IMA Statement of Ethical Professional Practice**. Professional accounting organizations have procedures for reviewing alleged behavior that is not consistent with the standards.

The ethical organization also has policies in place to motivate ethical actions. Integrity and outspoken support for ethical standards by senior managers, in both word and deed, are the greatest motivators of ethical behavior throughout an organization. A **code of conduct**—a document specifying the ethical standards of an organization—is the centerpiece of most ethics programs. (See the Business First box, "Ethics and Corporate Codes of Conduct," on p. 20.) But having a code is not sufficient. Actual policies and practices influence behavior. This means that managers' evaluations must include an assessment of ethical conduct. Organizations cannot tolerate unethical behavior, even if it appears to lead to great financial performance. For example, in the early 2000s Enron, WorldCom, Tyco, Global Crossing, Adelphia, Xerox, and others created accounting entries to make their financial reports look better than their actual performances. In some cases, accountants participated in these fraudulent activities. In other cases, they simply did not step up and challenge what they surely knew (or at least should have known) was misleading information. Fortunately, there are also prominent examples of accountants who stood up and reported wrongdoing to their supervisors despite the personal costs.

In the Spring of 2001, Sherron Watkins began working directly for Enron CFO Andrew Fastow. When she discovered the off-the-books liabilities that have now become famous, she wrote a memo to CEO Kenneth Lay and met with him personally, explaining to him "an elaborate accounting hoax." Later she discovered that, rather than the hoax being investigated, her report had generated a memo from Enron's legal counsel titled "Confidential Employee Matter" that included the following: ". . . how to manage the case with the employee who made the sensitive report. . . . Texas law does not currently protect corporate whistle-blowers. . . ." In addition, her boss confiscated her hard drive, and she was demoted. In the end, Watkins proved to be right. Watkins made the ethical decision to reveal the wrongdoings and did not look back. In June 2002, Cynthia Cooper, vice president of internal audit for WorldCom, told the company's board of directors that fraudulent accounting entries had turned a $662 million loss into a $2.4 billion profit in 2001. This disclosure led to additional discoveries totaling $9 billion in erroneous accounting entries—the largest accounting fraud in history. Cooper was proud of WorldCom and highly committed to its success. Nevertheless, when she and her internal audit team discovered the unethical actions of superiors she admired, she did not hesitate to do the right thing.

Most companies make ethics a top priority. For example, Starbucks includes ethical principles in the first line of its mission statement: "To establish Starbucks as the premier purveyor of the finest coffee in the world while maintaining our uncompromising principles as we grow." Ben & Jerry's, the ice cream company, has a reputation for high ethical standards that focus on its external social obligations, as recognized in its mission statement: "To operate the Company in a way that actively recognizes the central role that business plays in the structure of society by initiating innovative ways to improve the quality of life of a broad community—local, national, and international." There are many more companies with high ethical standards than there are with ethical violations, though the latter receive most of the publicity.

Ethical Dilemmas

The ethical standards of the profession leave much room for individual interpretation and judgment. A first step is to ask two questions: Is this action unethical? Would it be unethical not to take this action? If the answers to these questions are clear, then the ethical action is clear. For example, if WorldCom's accountants had asked whether their recording of expenses as assets was unethical, they would have answered "yes." However, a manager's ethical choice becomes more complex when there are no legal guidelines or clear-cut ethical standards. Ethical dilemmas exist when managers must choose an alternative and there are (1) significant value conflicts among differing interests, (2) several alternatives are justifiable, and (3) there are significant consequences for stakeholders in the situation.

Members of IMA shall behave ethically. A commitment to ethical professional practice includes overarching principles that express our values and standards that guide our conduct.

Principles

IMA's overarching ethical principles include: Honesty, Fairness, Objectivity, and Responsibility. Members shall act in accordance with these principles and shall encourage others within their organizations to adhere to them.

Standards

A member's failure to comply with the following standards may result in disciplinary action.

I. Competence

Each member has a responsibility to
1. Maintain an appropriate level of professional expertise by continually developing knowledge and skills.
2. Perform professional duties in accordance with relevant laws, regulations, and technical standards.
3. Provide decision support information and recommendations that are accurate, clear, concise, and timely.
4. Recognize and communicate professional limitations or other constraints that would preclude responsible judgment or successful performance of an activity.

II. Confidentiality

Each member has a responsibility to
1. Keep information confidential except when disclosure is authorized or legally required.
2. Inform all relevant parties regarding appropriate use of confidential information. Monitor subordinates' activities to ensure compliance.
3. Refrain from using confidential information for unethical or illegal advantage. [insider Trading]

III. Integrity

Each member has a responsibility to
1. Mitigate actual conflicts of interest. Regularly communicate with business associates to avoid apparent conflicts of interest. Advise all parties of any potential conflicts.
2. Refrain from engaging in any conduct that would prejudice carrying out duties ethically.
3. Abstain from engaging in or supporting any activity that might discredit the profession.

IV. Credibility

Each member has a responsibility to
1. Communicate information fairly and objectively.
2. Disclose all relevant information that could reasonably be expected to influence an intended user's understanding of the reports, analyses, or recommendations.
3. Disclose delays or deficiencies in information, timeliness, processing, or internal controls in conformance with organizational policy and/or applicable law.

Resolution of Ethical Conflict

In applying the Standards of Ethical Professional Practice, you may encounter problems identifying unethical behavior or resolving an ethical conflict. When faced with ethical issues, you should follow your organization's established policies on the resolution of such conflict. If these policies do not resolve the ethical conflict, you should consider the following courses of action:
1. Discuss the issue with your immediate supervisor except when it appears that the supervisor is involved. In that case, present the issue to the next level. If you cannot achieve a satisfactory resolution, submit the issue to the next management level. If your immediate superior is the chief executive officer or equivalent, the acceptable reviewing authority may be a group such as the audit committee, executive committee, board of directors, board of trustees, or owners. Contact with levels above the immediate superior should be initiated only with your superior's knowledge, assuming he or she is not involved. Communication of such problems to authorities or individuals not employed or engaged by the organization is not considered appropriate, unless you believe there is a clear violation of the law.
2. Clarify relevant ethical issues by initiating a confidential discussion with an IMA Ethics Counselor or other impartial advisor to obtain a better understanding of possible courses of action.
3. Consult your own attorney as to legal obligations and rights concerning the ethical conflict.

Source: Institute of Management Accountants, Ethical Standards, www.imanet.org/about_ethics_statement.asp.

Exhibit 1-7
IMA Statement of Ethical Professional Practice

Business First

Ethics and Corporate Codes of Conduct

The Sarbanes-Oxley Act of 2002 requires companies "to disclose whether or not, and if not, the reason therefore, such issuer has adopted a code of ethics for senior financial officers, applicable to its principal financial officer and comptroller or principal accounting officer, or persons performing similar functions." This has created increased interest in corporate codes of conduct. However, a code of conduct means different things to different companies. Some of the items included in companies' codes of conduct include maintaining a dress code, avoiding illegal drugs, following instructions of superiors, being reliable and prompt, maintaining confidentiality, not accepting personal gifts from stakeholders as a result of company role, avoiding racial or sexual discrimination, avoiding conflict of interest, complying with laws and regulations, not using an organization's property for personal use, and reporting illegal or questionable activity. Even before the Enron and other corporate scandals, over 80% of U.S. companies had a code of conduct, according to a survey by the Financial Executives Institute (FEI). But the codes differed in type and in level of enforcement.

One company had only one rule: "Don't do anything you would be embarrassed to read about in tomorrow's newspaper." Others have detailed lists of dos and don'ts. Some companies use consulting firms to advise them on their codes. Although the codes and their development differ, the goal is generally the same—to motivate employees to act with integrity.

To encourage development of codes of conduct, the FEI includes examples of codes on its Web site. Two extremes among those presented are those of Wiremold and CSX Corporation. Wiremold has a simple, seven-point code: (1) respect others, (2) tell the truth, (3) be fair, (4) try new ideas, (5) ask why, (6) keep your promises, and (7) do your share. In contrast, CSX has 26 paragraphs detailing expectations of employees under the following headings: Employee Relationships and Conflicts of Interest, Political Contributions and Public Service Involvement, Misrepresentations and False Statements, Employee Discrimination and Harassment, Competition, and Safety and the Environment.

FEI also lists inquiries about corporate codes of conduct among the questions to expect at shareholder annual meetings. As stated on FEI's Web site, "If there's any single issue that overlays the recent corporate and accounting scandals, it is a deficiency in ethical behavior among some company executives. Corporate governance consultants and academics agree that a company needs to have a code of conduct and ethics in place, by which the entire staff and management should conduct themselves in relation to their business activities. . . . In all probability, shareholders will ask questions relating to board committees or subcommittees focused on ethical matters."

While having a code of conduct is important, it is not sufficient. After all, Enron's code of conduct specified that "business is to be conducted in compliance . . . with the highest professional and ethical standards." Top management must set the tone and get out the message. Management must recognize and reward honesty and integrity. As Clarence Otis, CFO of Darden Restaurants, says, "Our senior managers care about honesty and integrity and doing things right, and that influences how they do their job." The corporate culture, more than codes of conduct, is the real influence on the ethical climate of an organization. Codes of conduct can be a part, but only a part, of developing a culture of integrity.

Sources: Sarbanes-Oxley Act of 2002, HR 3763; RedHawk Productions Web site (http://redhawkproductions.com); Financial Executives Institute Web site (www.fei.org); D. Blank, "A Matter of Ethics," *Internal Auditor*, February 2003, pp. 27–31; Enron Corporation, *2000 Corporate Responsibility Report*, p. 3.

Suppose you are an accountant and your boss has asked you to supply the company's banker with a profit forecast for the coming year. A badly needed bank loan rides on the prediction. Your boss is absolutely convinced that profits will be at least $500,000—anything less than that and the loan is not likely to be approved.

Your analysis reveals three possible outcomes: First, if the planned introduction of a new product goes extraordinarily well, profits will exceed $500,000. Second, if there is a modestly successful introduction, there will be a $100,000 profit. You believe this is the most likely outcome. Third, if the product fails, the company stands to lose $600,000. Without the loan, the new product cannot be taken to the market, and there is no way the company can avoid a loss for the year. Bankruptcy is a real possibility.

What forecast would you make? The fundamental issue here is disagreement about the prospects for the new product. If your boss is correct, it would be unethical to make a forecast of less than $500,000, which seems to guarantee financial problems, perhaps even bankruptcy. This would hurt stockholders, management, employees, suppliers, and customers. But if you are correct about the most likely outcome, a forecast of $500,000 may not be fair and objective. It may mislead the bank.

There is no easy answer to this dilemma. It is one of those gray areas where either action includes risks. But remember that a series of gray areas can create a black area. That is, a series of actions that push the boundary of ethical behavior can add up to a clearly unethical situation. Accountants must draw the line someplace, and it is usually better to err on the side of full disclosure than to withhold important information. Enron repeatedly pushed boundaries by reporting only optimistic information. If its managers had done this once or twice, it might not have created a problem. But the pattern of exclusively optimistic projections eventually deteriorated into completely unrealistic, and unethical, projections.

To maintain high ethical standards, accountants and others need to recognize situations that create pressures for unethical behavior. Four such temptations, summarized in *Financial Executive*, are as follows:

1. *Emphasis on short-term results.* This may have been the largest issue in the recent spate of ethical breakdowns. If "making the numbers" is goal number one, accountants may do whatever is necessary to produce the expected profit numbers.
2. *Ignoring the small stuff.* Most ethical compromises start out small. The first step may seem insignificant, but large misdeeds are often the result of many small steps. Toleration of even small lapses can lead to large problems.
3. *Economic cycles.* A down market can reveal what an up market conceals. When Enron was flying high at the turn of the century, no one seemed to question its financial reports. When the economy took a downward turn, managers made ethical compromises to keep pace with expectations of an up market. The result was a huge crisis when scrutiny revealed many questionable practices. Similarly, later in the decade companies such as **AIG**, **Fannie Mae**, and **Freddie Mac** were accused of accounting compromises after the economy started to sour in 2008. Companies need to be especially vigilant to prevent ethical lapses in good times when such lapses are more easily concealed, and thereby avoid revelation of lapses in bad times when their effects are especially damaging.
4. *Accounting rules.* Accounting rules have become more complex and less intuitive, making abuse of the rules harder to identify. Ethical accountants do not just meet the "letter of the law," they seek full and fair disclosure—conveying to users the real economic performance and financial position of the company.

Few organizations are intentionally unethical. Even **Arthur Andersen**, the accounting firm destroyed by failed audits at Enron, **Sunbeam**, **Global Crossing**, and others, had a formal ethical structure, including a partner in charge of ethics. Nevertheless, other pressures, especially the pressure for growing revenues, overrode some of the ethical controls and caused some bad decisions.

Resolution of Ethical Conflicts

Ethical dilemmas also arise when you only observe, rather than commit, unethical behavior. If you discover unethical behavior in an organization, you are obligated to try to halt that behavior. However, you still have confidentiality issues to confront. The section on Resolution of Ethical Conflict in Exhibit 1-7 provides guidance. Most often you can bring the issue to the attention of your supervisor or a special ethics officer (often called an ombudsperson) in the organization. However, if there is not an ethics officer and you suspect your supervisor is involved in unethical activity, your decision becomes more complex. As was the case for Cynthia Cooper at WorldCom described on p. 18, you may need to go all the way to the board of directors. If the case involves legal issues and the board is not responsive, approaching the Securities and Exchange Commission (the body that regulates corporate reporting) or other legal authorities may be necessary.

Summary Problem for Your Review

PROBLEM

Yang Electronics Company (YEC) developed a high-speed, low-cost copying machine marketed primarily for home use. However, as YEC customers learned how easy and inexpensive it was to make copies with it, sales to small businesses soared. Unfortunately, the heavier use by these companies caused breakdowns in a component of the equipment that had been designed only for light use. The copiers were warranted for two years, regardless of the amount of usage. Consequently, YEC began to experience high costs for replacing the damaged component.

As the quarterly meeting of YEC's board of directors approached, the CFO asked Mark Chua, assistant controller, to prepare a report on the situation. It was hard to predict the exact effects but it seemed that many business customers were starting to switch away from the YEC copier to more expensive copiers sold by competitors. It was also clear that the increased warranty costs would significantly affect YEC's profitability. Mark summarized the situation in writing as best he could for the board.

Alice Martinez, YEC's CFO, was concerned about the impact of the report on the board. She did not disagree with the analysis, but she thought it would make management look bad and might even lead the board to discontinue the product. She was convinced from conversations with the head of engineering that the copier could be slightly redesigned to meet the needs of high-volume users, so discontinuing it may pass up a potentially profitable opportunity.

Martinez called Chua into her office and asked him to delete the part of his report dealing with the component failures. She said it was all right to mention this orally to the board, noting that engineering is nearing a solution to the problem. However, Chua felt strongly that such a revision in his report would mislead the board about a potentially significant negative impact on the company's earnings.

Use the IMA Statement of Ethical Professional Practice in Exhibit 1-7 to explain why Martinez's request to Chua is unethical. How should Chua resolve this situation?

SOLUTION

Martinez's request violates requirements for competence, integrity, and credibility. It violates competence because she is asking Chua to prepare a report that is not complete and clear, and omits potentially relevant information. Therefore, the board will not have all the information it should to make a decision about the component failure problem.

The request violates integrity because the revised report may subvert the attainment of the organization's objectives to achieve Martinez's objectives. Management accountants are specifically responsible for communicating unfavorable as well as favorable information.

Finally, the revised report would not be credible. It would not disclose all relevant information that could be expected to influence the board's understanding of operations and, therefore, its decisions.

Chua's responsibility is to discuss this issue with increasingly higher levels of authority within YEC. First, he should let Martinez know about his misgivings. Possibly the issue can be resolved by her withdrawing the request. If not, he should inform her that he intends to take up the matter with the company president, and even the board, if necessary, until the issue is resolved. So that Chua does not violate the standard of confidentiality, he should not discuss the matter with persons outside of YEC.

Highlights to Remember

1. **Describe the major users and uses of accounting information.** Internal managers use accounting information for making short-term planning and control decisions, for making nonroutine decisions, and for formulating overall policies and long-range plans. External users, such as investors and regulators, use published financial statements to make investment decisions, regulatory rulings, and many other decisions. Managers use accounting information to answer scorekeeping, attention-directing, and problem-solving questions.

2. **Describe the cost-benefit and behavioral issues involved in designing an accounting system.** Companies design management accounting information systems for the benefit of managers. These systems should be judged by a cost-benefit criterion—the benefits of better decisions should exceed the cost of the system. Behavioral factors—how the system affects managers and their decisions—greatly influence the benefit of a system.

3. **Explain the role of budgets and performance reports in planning and control.** Budgets and performance reports are essential tools for planning and control. Budgets result from the planning process. Managers use them to translate the organization's goals into action. A performance report compares actual results to the budget. Managers use these reports to monitor, evaluate, and reward performance and, thus, exercise control.

4. **Discuss the role accountants play in the company's value-chain functions.** Accountants play a key role in planning and control. Throughout the company's value chain, accountants gather and report cost and revenue information for decision makers.

5. **Explain why accounting is important in a variety of career paths.** Accounting skills are useful in many functional areas of an organization. Managers with a strong understanding of accounting become prime candidates for promotions to operating and executive positions.

6. **Identify current trends in management accounting.** Many factors have caused changes in accounting systems in recent years. Most significant are a shift to a service-based economy, increased global competition, advances in technology, and changed business processes. Without continuous adaptation and improvement, accounting systems would soon become obsolete.

7. **Explain why ethics and standards of ethical conduct are important to accountants.** Users of accounting information expect accountants to adhere to high standards of ethical conduct. Most users cannot directly assess the quality of that information, and if they cannot rely on accountants to produce unbiased information, the information will have little value to them. That is why professional accounting organizations, as well as most companies, have codes of ethical conduct. Many ethical dilemmas, however, require more than codes and rules. They call for value judgments, not the simple application of standards. ■

Accounting Vocabulary

Vocabulary is an essential and often troublesome phase of the learning process. A fuzzy understanding of terms hampers the learning of concepts and the ability to solve accounting problems. Before proceeding to the assignment material or to the next chapter, be sure you understand the words and terms in the Accounting Vocabulary section of each chapter. Their meaning is explained within the chapter and in the glossary at the end of this book.

accounting system, p. 5
attention directing, p. 4
B2B, p. 15
B2C, p. 16
behavioral implications, p. 6
budget, p. 8
business process
    reengineering, p. 16
certified management
    accountant (CMA), p. 14
certified public accountant
    (CPA), p. 14
chartered accountant (CA), p. 14

chief financial officer
    (CFO), p. 13
code of conduct, p. 18
computer-aided design
    (CAD), p. 16
computer-aided manufacturing
    (CAM) p. 16
computer-integrated
    manufacturing (CIM)
    systems, p. 16
control, p. 7
controller (comptroller), p. 13
cost-benefit balance, p. 6

decision making, p. 3
electronic commerce
    (e-commerce), p. 15
enterprise resource planning
    (ERP) system, p. 15
e-commerce, p. 15
ethics, p. 17
financial accounting, p. 3
Foreign Corrupt Practices
    Act, p. 6
generally accepted
    accounting principles
    (GAAP), p. 5

MyAccountingLab

Fundamental Assignment Material

The assignment material for each chapter is divided into two groups: fundamental and additional. The fundamental assignment material consists of two sets of parallel problems that convey the essential concepts and techniques of the chapter. The additional assignment material covers the chapter in more detail and includes questions, critical thinking exercises, exercises, problems, cases, Excel application exercises, a collaborative learning exercise, and an Internet exercise.

1-A1 Scorekeeping, Attention Directing, and Problem Solving

For each of the following activities, identify the primary function that the accountant is performing—scorekeeping, attention directing, or problem solving—and explain why it best fits that category.

1. Preparing a schedule of depreciation for forklift trucks in the receiving department of a **General Electric** factory in Scotland
2. Analyzing, for a **Sony** production superintendent, the impact on costs of purchasing some new assembly equipment
3. Preparing a scrap report for the finishing department of a **Toyota** parts factory
4. Interpreting why the **Colville Timber Resource Company** did not adhere to its production schedule
5. Explaining the stamping department's performance report
6. Preparing a monthly statement of European sales for the **Ford Motor Company's** vice president of marketing
7. Preparing, for the manager of production control of a **Mittal Steel** plant, a cost comparison of two computerized manufacturing control systems
8. Interpreting variances on the University of Michigan's purchasing department's performance report
9. Analyzing, for an **Airbus** manufacturing manager, the desirability of having some parts for the A380 airplane made in Korea
10. Preparing the budget for the dermatology department of **Providence Hospital**

1-A2 Management by Exception

Beta Alpha Psi (BAP), the accounting honorary fraternity, held a homecoming party. The fraternity expected attendance of 70 persons and prepared the following budget:

Room rental	$ 140
Food	700
Entertainment	600
Decorations	220
Total	$1,660

After BAP paid all the bills for the party, the total cost came to $1,865, or $205 over budget. Details are $140 for room rental; $865 for food; $600 for entertainment; and $260 for decorations. Eighty-five persons attended the party.

1. Prepare a performance report for the party that shows how actual costs differed from the budget. That is, include in your report the budgeted amounts, actual amounts, and variances.
2. Suppose the fraternity uses a management-by-exception rule. Which costs deserve further examination? Why?

1-A3 Professional Ethics

Exhibit 1-7 on page 19 lists four main categories of ethical standards for management account-ants: competence, confidentiality, integrity, and credibility. For each of the following situations, indicate which of these four should influence the manager and what the appropriate action should be:

1. At a dinner party, a guest asked a **General Mills** manager how a major new cereal was doing. The manager had just read a report that said sales lagged much below expectation. What should he say?

2. Felix just graduated from business school with an accounting major and joined the controller's department of Pioneer Enterprises. His boss asked him to evaluate a market analysis for a poten-tial new product prepared by the marketing department. Felix knows very little about the industry, and he never had a class to teach him how to make a market analysis. Should he just do the best he can on the analysis without asking for help?

3. Mary Sue prepared a budget for a division of Southeastern Electronics. Her supervisor, the division manager, was not happy that she included results for an exciting new product that was to be introduced in a month. He asked her to leave the results for the product out of the budget. That way, the financial results for the product would boost actual profits well above the amount budgeted, resulting in favorable reviews for the division and its managers. What should Mary Sue do?

1-B1 Scorekeeping, Attention Directing, and Problem Solving

For each of the following activities, identify the function the accountant is performing—scorekeeping, attention directing, or problem solving. Explain each of your answers.

1. Estimating the operating costs and outputs that could be expected for each of two large metal-stamping machines offered for sale by different manufacturers; only one of these machines is to be acquired by your company
2. Recording daily material purchase vouchers
3. Analyzing the expected costs of acquiring and using each of two alternate types of welding equipment
4. Preparing a report of overtime labor costs by production department
5. Estimating the costs of moving corporate headquarters to another city
6. Interpreting increases in nursing costs per patient-day in a hospital
7. Analyzing deviations from the budget of the factory maintenance department
8. Assisting in a study by the manufacturing vice president to determine whether to buy certain parts needed in large quantities for manufacturing products or to acquire facilities for manufacturing these parts
9. Preparing estimated costs for a new marketing campaign
10. Recording overtime hours of the product finishing department
11. Compiling data for a report showing the ratio of advertising expenses to sales for each branch store
12. Investigating reasons for increased returns and allowances for drugs purchased by a hospital
13. Preparing a schedule of fuel costs by months and government departments
14. Computing and recording end-of-year adjustments for expired fire insurance on the factory warehouse

1-B2 Management by Exception

The Suquamish Indian tribe sells fireworks for the five weeks preceding July 4. The tribe's stand at the corner of Highway 110 and Eagle Drive had budgeted sales of $75,000. Expected expenses were as follows:

Cost of fireworks	$36,000
Labor cost	15,000
Other costs	8,000
Total costs	$59,000

Actual sales were $74,600, almost equal to the budget. The tribe spent $35,500 for fireworks, $18,000 for labor, and $7,910 for other costs.

1. Compute budgeted profit and actual profit.
2. Prepare a performance report to help identify those costs that were significantly different from the budget.
3. Suppose the tribe uses a management-by-exception rule. What costs deserve further explana-tion? Why?

1-B3 Ethical Code of Conduct

According to the **Financial Executives Institute**, "corporate governance consultants and academics agree that a company needs to have a code of conduct" for its employees. Most companies, even many of those who experienced ethical breakdowns, have such a code. Answer the following questions about corporate codes of conduct.

1. What is a corporate code of conduct?
2. What types of issues are covered in a corporate code of conduct? At what level of detail?
3. In some cases codes of conduct were not effective. What, besides simply having a code, is necessary for a code of conduct to be effective?

MyAccountingLab ## Additional Assignment Material

QUESTIONS

1-1 Who uses information from an accounting system?

1-2 "The emphases of financial accounting and management accounting differ." Explain.

1-3 "The field is less sharply defined. There is heavier use of economics, decision sciences, and behavioral sciences." Identify the branch of accounting described in the quotation.

1-4 Distinguish among scorekeeping, attention directing, and problem solving.

1-5 "Generally accepted accounting principles (GAAP) assist the development of management accounting systems." Do you agree? Explain.

1-6 "The Foreign Corrupt Practices Act applies to bribes paid outside the United States." Do you agree? Explain.

1-7 Why is the Sarbanes-Oxley act controversial?

1-8 Why is integrity so important to accountants?

1-9 "Integrity is more important for business professionals than it is for business students." Do you agree? Explain.

1-10 Give three examples of service organizations. What distinguishes service organizations from other types of organizations?

1-11 What two major considerations affect the design of all accounting systems? Explain each.

1-12 "The accounting system is intertwined with operating management. Business operations would be in a hopeless tangle without the recordkeeping that is so often regarded with disdain." Do you agree? Explain, giving examples.

1-13 Distinguish among a budget, a performance report, and a variance.

1-14 "Management by exception means abdicating management responsibility for planning and control." Do you agree? Explain.

1-15 Why are accountants concerned about product life cycles?

1-16 Name the six primary business functions (excluding support functions) that make up the value chain, and briefly describe each.

1-17 "Accountants in every company should measure and report on every function in the company's value chain." Do you agree? Explain.

1-18 Distinguish between the duties of line managers and staff managers.

1-19 The role of management accountants is changing, especially in companies with a "flatter" organizational structure. What are some of the changes?

1-20 Does every company have both a controller and a treasurer? Explain.

1-21 Describe the two parts of the qualifying examination for becoming a CMA.

1-22 "The problem with accounting is that accountants never get to become top managers such as CEOs." Do you agree? Explain.

1-23 How are changes in technology affecting management accounting?

1-24 What is the essence of the JIT philosophy?

1-25 Briefly describe how a change in a plant's layout can make its operation more efficient.

1-26 Standards of ethical conduct for management accountants have been divided into four major responsibilities. Describe each of the four in 20 words or less.

1-27 "Why are there ethical dilemmas? I thought accountants had standards that specified what is ethical behavior." Discuss this quote.

CRITICAL THINKING EXERCISES

1-28 Finance and Management Accounting

Often there is confusion between the roles played by the controller and treasurer in an organization. In many small companies, a single person performs activities related to both functions.

Distinguish between the controller and the treasurer functions by listing typical activities that are associated with each.

1-29 Accounting's Position in the Organization: Controller and Treasurer

For each of the following activities, indicate whether it is more likely to be performed by the controller or by the treasurer. Explain each answer.

1. Prepare divisional financial statements.
2. Help managers prepare budgets.
3. Advise which alternative action is least costly.
4. Meet with financial analysts from Wall Street.
5. Arrange short-term financing.
6. Prepare tax returns.
7. Arrange insurance coverage.
8. Prepare credit checks on customers.

1-30 Marketing and Management Accounting

A cross-functional team of managers, including the management accountant, performs each of the following activities. However, depending on the nature of the decision to be made, one functional area will take the leadership role. Which of these activities is primarily a marketing decision? What would the management accountant contribute to each of the marketing decisions?

1. **Porsche Motor Company** must decide whether to buy a part for one of its cars or to make the part at one of its plants.
2. **Airbus** must decide the price to charge for spare parts it sells over the Internet using its Spare Parts Web site.
3. **St. Luke's Hospital** must decide how to finance the purchase of expensive new medical analysis equipment.
4. **Amazon.com** must forecast the impact on video sales of a new advertising program.
5. **Mission Foods**, a leading producer and distributor of tortillas to retail and food service industries, must decide whether to accept a special order for tortilla chips by a large, national retail chain.
6. **Target Stores** must decide whether to close one of its retail stores that is currently operating at a loss.

1-31 Production and Management Accounting

A cross-functional team of managers, including the management accountant, performed each of the following activities. However, depending on the nature of the decision to be made, one functional area will take the leadership role. Which of these activities is primarily a production decision? What would the management accountant contribute to each of the production decisions?

1. **Saab Automobile AB** must decide whether to buy a part for one of its cars or to make the part at one of its plants.
2. **Boeing Company** must decide the price for spare parts it sells over the Internet using its Spare Parts Web site.
3. **St. Mary's Hospital** must decide how to finance the purchase of expensive new medical analysis equipment.
4. **Amazon.com** must forecast how a new advertising program will affect DVD sales.
5. **Mission Foods**, a leading producer and distributor of tortillas to retail and food service industries, must decide whether to accept a special order for tortilla chips by a large, national retail chain.
6. **Kmart** must evaluate its overall vision and strategic goals in the light of competitive pressures from **Target**, **Sears**, and **Wal-Mart**.
7. **Dell Computers** must decide whether to spend money on training workers to perform setups and changeovers faster. This will free up capacity to be used to make more computers without purchasing more equipment.
8. **Ford Motor Company** must decide whether to keep or replace four-year-old equipment used in one of its Escape plants.

EXERCISES

1-32 Management Accounting and Financial Accounting

Consider the following short descriptions. Indicate whether each of the following descriptions more closely relates to a major feature of financial accounting or management accounting:

1. Field is less sharply defined
2. Provides internal consulting advice to managers
3. Has less flexibility

4. Is characterized by detailed reports
5. Has a future orientation
6. Is constrained by GAAP
7. Behavioral impact is secondary

1-33 Planning and Control, Management by Exception

Study the **Starbucks** store in Exhibit 1-2 on page 7. Suppose that for next year a particular store budgeted revenue of $330,000, a 10% increase over the current revenue of $300,000. The actions listed in Exhibit 1-2 resulted in six new budgeted products and a total advertising budget of $30,000. Actual results were as follows:

New products added	7
Advertising	$ 33,000
Revenues	$326,000

1. Prepare a performance report for revenues and advertising costs using the format of Exhibit 1-3 on page 8.
2. Suppose the remaining cost elements of net income were not available until several months after the store implemented the plan. The net income results were disappointing to management—profits declined even though revenues increased because costs increased by more than revenues. List some factors that might have caused costs to increase so much and that management may not have considered when they formulated the store's plan.

1-34 Line Versus Staff and Value-Chain Responsibility

For each of the following, indicate whether the employee has line or staff responsibility. Also indicate whether the employee primarily provides support for other value chain functions or performs a specific value-chain business function.

1. President
2. District sales manager
3. Market research analyst
4. Cost accountant
5. Head of the legal department
6. Production superintendent

1-35 Microsoft's Value Chain

Microsoft is the world's largest software company. For each of the following value-chain functions, discuss briefly what Microsoft managers would do to achieve that function and how important it is to the overall success of Microsoft.

R&D	Product (service) and process design
Production	Marketing
Distribution	Customer service
Support functions	

1-36 Objectives of Management Accounting

The Institute of Management Accountants (IMA) is composed of nearly 70,000 members. The IMA "Objectives of Management Accounting" states, "The management accountant participates, as part of management, in assuring that the organization operates as a unified whole in its long-run, intermediate, and short-run best interests."

Based on your reading in this chapter, prepare a 100-word description of the principal ways that accountants participate in managing an entity.

1-37 Cost-Benefit of the Ethical Environment

A poor ethical environment results in costs to the company. On the other hand, a good ethical environment creates benefits. List several costs of a poor ethical environment and benefits of a good ethical environment.

1-38 Early Warning Signs of Ethical Conflict

The following statements are early warning signs of ethical conflict:

- "I don't care how you do it, just get it done!"
- "No one will ever know."

List several other statements that are early warning signs of ethical conflict.

PROBLEMS

1-39 Management and Financial Accounting

Lillian Choi, an able mechanical engineer, was informed that she would be promoted to assistant factory manager. Lillian was pleased but uncomfortable. In particular, she knew little about accounting. She had taken one course in financial accounting.

Lillian planned to enroll in a management accounting course as soon as possible. Meanwhile, she asked Walt Greenspan, a cost accountant, to state three or four of the principal distinctions between financial and management accounting.

Prepare Walt's written response to Lillian.

1-40 Use of Accounting Information in Hospitals

Most U.S. hospitals do not derive their revenues directly from patients. Instead, revenues come through third parties, such as insurance companies and government agencies. Until the 1980s, these payments generally reimbursed the hospital's costs of serving patients. Such payments, however, are now generally flat fees for specified services. For example, the hospital might receive $7,000 for an appendectomy or $28,000 for heart surgery—no more, no less.

How might the method of payment change the demand for accounting information in hospitals? Relate your answer to the decisions of top management.

1-41 Costs and Benefits

Marks & Spencer, a huge retailer in the United Kingdom with sales of more than £9 billion, was troubled by its paper bureaucracy. Looked at in isolation, each document seemed reasonable, but overall a researcher reported that there was substantial effort in each department to verify the information. Basically, the effort seemed out of proportion to any value received, and, eventually, the company simplified or eliminated many of the documents.

Describe the rationale that should govern systems design. How should a company such as Marks & Spencer decide what documents it needs and which can be eliminated?

1-42 Importance of Accounting

Some companies are run by engineers and other technical specialists. For example, a manager in a division that is now part of **ArvinMeritor**, an automotive parts supplier, once said that "there'd be sixty or seventy guys talking technical problems, with never a word on profits." Other companies, especially consumer products companies such as **General Mills**, fill top management positions primarily with marketing executives. And still others, like **Berkshire Hathaway** with Warren Buffett as CEO, have top managers with strong finance skills.

How might the role of management accountants differ in these types of companies?

1-43 Changes in Accounting Systems

In the last decade, **Boeing** has made several significant changes to its accounting system. None of these changes were for reporting to external parties. Management believed, however, that the new system gave more accurate costs of the airplanes and other products produced.

1. Boeing had been a very successful company using its old accounting system. What might have motivated it to change the system?
2. When Boeing changed its system, what criteria might its managers have used to decide whether to invest in the new system?
3. Is changing to a system that provides more accurate product costs always a good strategy? Why or why not?

1-44 Value Chain

Nike is an Oregon-based company that focuses on the design, development, and worldwide marketing of high-quality sports footwear, apparel, equipment, and accessory products. Nike is the largest seller of athletic footwear and athletic apparel in the world. The company sells its products to more than 18,000 retail accounts in the United States and through a mix of independent distributors, licensees, and subsidiaries in approximately 180 countries around the world. Nike contracts with more than 700 factories around the world to manufacture virtually all the company's products. Nike produces most footwear and branded apparel products outside the United States.

1. Identify one decision that Nike managers make in each of the six value-chain functions.
2. For each decision in requirement 1, identify one piece of accounting information that would aid the manager's decision.

1-45 Role of Controller

Juanita Veracruz, newly hired controller of Braxton Industries, had been lured away from a competitor to revitalize the controller's department. Her first day on the job proved to be an eye-opener. One of her first interviews was with Adrian Belton, production supervisor in the Cleveland factory. Belton commented, "I really don't want to talk to anyone from the controller's office. The only time we see those accountants is when our costs go over their budget. They wave what they call a 'performance report,' but it's actually just a bunch of numbers they make up. It has nothing to do with what happens on the shop floor. Besides, my men can't afford the time to fill out all the paperwork those accountants want, so I just plug in some numbers and send it back. Now, if you'll let me get back to important matters. . . ." Veracruz left quickly, but she was already planning for her next visit with Belton.

1. Identify some of the problems in the relationship between the controller's department and the production departments (assuming that the Cleveland factory is representative of the production departments).
2. What should Juanita Veracruz do next?

1-46 The Accountant's Role in an Organization

The Business First box on page 13 described the role of accountants in the **Marmon Group**, a collection of operating companies that manufacture such diverse products as copper tubing, water purification products, railroad tank cars, and store fixtures, and provide services such as credit information for banks. Others have described accountants as "internal consultants." Using the information in the box, discuss how accountants at Marmon can act as internal consultants. What kind of background and knowledge would an accountant require to be an effective internal consultant?

1-47 Ethics and Accounting Personnel

McMillan Shipping Company has an equal opportunity employment policy. This policy has the full support of the company's president, Rosemary Creighton, and is included in all advertisements for employee positions.

Hiring in the accounting department is done by the controller, D. W. "Butch" Brigham. The assistant controller, Jack Merton, also interviews candidates, but Brigham makes all decisions. In the last year, the department hired 5 new people from a pool of 175 applicants. Thirteen had been interviewed, including 4 minority candidates. The 5 hired included 3 sons of Brigham's close friends and no minorities. Merton had felt that at least 2 of the minority candidates were very well qualified and that the 3 sons of Brigham's friends were definitely not among the most qualified.

When Merton questioned Brigham concerning his reservations about the hiring practices, he was told that these decisions were Brigham's and not his, so he should not question them.

1. Explain why Brigham's hiring practices were probably unethical.
2. What should Merton do about this situation?

1-48 Ethical Issues

Suppose you are controller of a medium-sized oil exploration company in west Texas. You adhere to the standards of ethical conduct for management accountants. How would those standards affect your behavior in each of the following situations?

1. Late one Friday afternoon you receive a geologist's report on a newly purchased property. It indicates a much higher probability of oil than had previously been expected. You are the only one to read the report that day. At a party on Saturday night, a friend asks about the prospects for the property.
2. An oil industry stock analyst invites you and your spouse to spend a week in Tahiti free of charge. All she wants in return is to be the first to know about any financial information your company is about to announce to the public.
3. It is time to make a forecast of the company's annual earnings. You know that some additional losses will be recognized before the company prepares final statements. The company's president has asked you to ignore these losses in making your prediction because a lower-than-expected earnings forecast could adversely affect the chances of obtaining a loan that is being negotiated and that will be completed before actual earnings are announced.
4. You do not know whether a particular expense is deductible for income tax purposes. You are debating whether to research the tax laws or simply to assume that the item is deductible. After all, if you are not audited, no one will ever know the difference. If you are audited, you can plead ignorance of the law.

1-49 Hundred Best Corporate Citizens

Each year *Corporate Responsibility Officer* magazine publishes its list of the 100 best corporate citizens. The magazine rates companies on performance in 7 stakeholder categories: (1) environment, (2) climate change, (3) human rights, (4) employee relations, (5) philanthropy, (6) financial, and (7) governance. In 2009, the top ten corporate citizens were **Bristol Myers-Squibb**, **General Mills**, **International Business Machines**, **Merck**, **HP**, **Cisco**, **Mattel**, **Abbot Laboratories**, **Kimberly-Clark**, and **Entergy**.

For each of the 7 dimensions on which the magazine reported ratings, give a one-sentence description of what you think would make for good corporate citizenship. Based on your knowledge of these 10 companies, however limited that is, predict the top 2 companies in each of the 7 rated categories.

CASES

1-50 Line and Staff Authority

Fidelity Leasing Company (FLC) leases office equipment to a variety of customers. The company's organization chart is below.

The four positions in blue in the chart are described next.

- J. P. Chen, assistant controller—special projects. Chen works on projects assigned to him by the controller. The most recent project was to design a new accounts payable system.
- Betty Hodge, leasing contracts manager. Hodge coordinates and implements leasing transactions. Her department handles all transactions after the sales department gets a signed contract. This includes requisitioning equipment from the purchasing department, maintaining appropriate insurance, delivering equipment, issuing billing statements, and seeking renewal of leases.
- Larry Paperman, chief accountant. Paperman supervises all the accounting functions. He produces reports for the four supervisors in the functional areas.
- Dawn Shevlin, director of human resources. Shevlin works with all departments of FLC in hiring personnel. Her department advertises all positions and screens candidates, but the individual departments conduct interviews and make hiring decisions. Shevlin also coordinates employee evaluations and administers the company's salary schedule and fringe benefit program.

1. Distinguish between line and staff positions in an organization and discuss why conflicts might arise between line and staff managers.
2. For each of the 4 managers described, identify whether their position is a line or staff position and explain why you classified it that way. Also, indicate any potential conflicts that might arise with other managers in the organization.

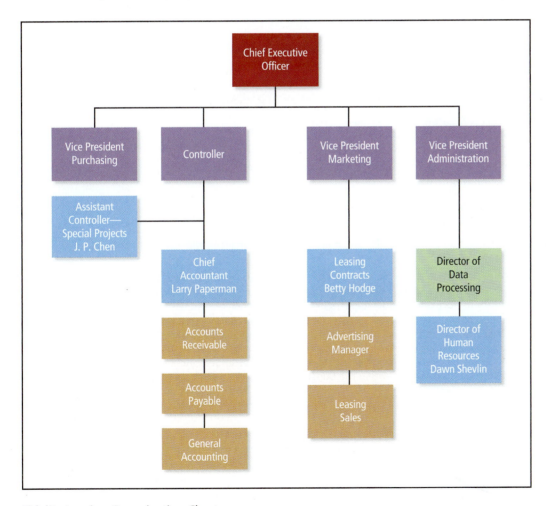

Fidelity Leasing Organization Chart

1-51 Professional Ethics and Toxic Waste

Alberta Mining Company extracts and processes a variety of ores and minerals. One of its operations is a coal-cleaning plant that produces toxic wastes. For many years, the wastes have been properly disposed of through Canadian Disposal, an experienced company. However, disposal of the toxic wastes is becoming an economic hardship because increasing government regulations caused the cost of such disposal to quadruple in the last 6 years.

Rachel O'Casey, director of financial reporting for Alberta Mining, was preparing the company's financial statements for the current year. In researching the material needed for preparing a footnote on environmental contingencies, Rachel found the following note scribbled in pencil at the bottom of a memo to the general manager of the coal-cleaning plant. The body of the memo gave details on the increases in the cost of toxic waste disposals:

> *Ralph—We've got to keep these costs down or we won't meet budget. Can we mix more of these wastes with the shipments of refuse to the Oak Hill landfill? Nobody seems to notice the coal-cleaning fluids when we mix it in well.*

Rachel was bothered by the note. She considered ignoring it, pretending that she had not seen it. But after a couple of hours, her conscience would not let her do it. Therefore, she pondered the following three alternative courses of action:

- Seek the advice of her boss, the vice president of finance for Alberta.
- Anonymously release the information to the local newspaper.
- Give the information to an outside member of Alberta's board of directors, whom she knew because he lived in her neighborhood.

1. Discuss why Rachel has an ethical responsibility to take some action about her suspicion of the illegal dumping of toxic wastes.
2. For each of the three alternative courses of action, explain whether the action is appropriate.
3. Assume that Rachel sought the advice of the vice president of finance and discovered that he both knew about and approved of the dumping of toxic wastes. What steps should she take to resolve the conflict in this situation?

NIKE 10K PROBLEM

1-52 Information in Nike's 10K Report

U.S. companies file 10K reports annually with the SEC. These reports contain the company's annual financial reports and much additional information about the company. Examine **Nike**'s 10K report that is presented in Appendix C. Answer the following questions about Nike:

1. What is Nike's principal business activity?
2. How many retail outlets does Nike have in the United States? How many in other countries?
3. Who is Nike's CFO? What is his accounting background?
4. Where does Nike manufacture most of its footwear? What ethical issues might result from this manufacturing philosophy?

EXCEL APPLICATION EXERCISE

1-53 Budgets and Performance Evaluation

Goal: Create an Excel spreadsheet to prepare a performance report, and use the results to answer questions about your findings.

Scenario: Beta Alpha Psi, the accounting honorary fraternity, has asked you to prepare a performance report about a homecoming party that it recently held. The background data for Beta Alpha Psi's performance report appears in the Fundamental Assignment Material 1-A2.
When you have completed your spreadsheet, answer the following questions:

1. Based on the formatting option used in the exercise, do the negative (red) variances represent amounts that are over or under budget?
2. Which cost/costs changed because the number of attendees increased?
3. Did the fraternity stay within the budgeted amount for food on a per person basis?

Step-by-Step:

1. Open a new Excel spreadsheet.
2. In column A, create a bold-faced heading that contains the following:
   Row 1: Chapter 1 Decision Guideline
   Row 2: Beta Alpha Psi Homecoming Party
   Row 3: Performance Report
   Row 4: Today's Date
3. Merge and center the date across columns A–D.

4. In row 7, create the following bold-faced, right-justified column headings:
   Column B: Budget
   Column C: Actual
   Column D: Variance

5. In column A, create the following row headings:
   Row 8: Room rental
   Row 9: Food
   Row 10: Entertainment
   Row 11: Decorations
   Row 12: Total costs
   Skip a row.
   Row 14: Attendees
   Skip a row.
   Row 16: Food per person

6. Use the data from Fundamental Assignment Material 1-A2 and enter the budget and actual amounts for room, food, entertainment, decorations, and attendees.

7. Use budget minus actual formulas to generate variances for each of the cost categories.

8. Use the SUM function to generate total costs for the budget, actual, and variance columns.

9. Use a formula to generate the "per person" food amount for the budget and actual columns.

10. Format all amounts as follows:

Number tab:	Category:	Currency
	Decimal places:	0
	Symbol:	None
	Negative numbers:	Red with parentheses

11. Change the format of the food per person amounts to display two decimal places and a dollar symbol.

12. Change the format of the room rental and total cost amounts to display a dollar symbol.

13. Change the format of the total costs data (row 12) to display as bold-faced.

14. Change the format of the total costs heading to display as indented:

Alignment tab:	Horizontal:	Left (Indent)
	Indent:	1

15. Save your work to disk, and print a copy for your files.

COLLABORATIVE LEARNING EXERCISE

1-54 The Future Management Accountant

Students should gather in groups of three to six. One-third of each group should read each of the following articles. (Alternatively, you can do this exercise as a whole class, with one-third of the class reading each article.)

- Roth, R. T., "The CFO's Great Balancing Act," *Financial Executive*, July/August 2004, pp. 60–61.
- Johnsson, M, "The Changing Role of the CFO," *Strategic Finance*, June 2002, pp. 54–57, 67.
- Russell, K., G. Siegel, and C. Kulesza, "Counting More, Counting Less: Transformations in the Management Accounting Profession," *Strategic Finance*, September 1999, pp. 39–44.

1. Individually, write down the three most important lessons you learned from the article you read.
2. As a group, list all the lessons identified in requirement 1. Combine those that are essentially the same.
3. Prioritize the list you developed in requirement 2 in terms of their importance to someone considering a career in management accounting.
4. Discuss whether this exercise has changed your impression of management accounting and, if so, how your impression has changed.

INTERNET EXERCISE

1-55 Institute of Management Accountants

The Institute of Management Accountants (IMA) is a major professional organization that is geared toward managerial accounting and finance. The IMA has chapters throughout the United States as well as international chapters. The IMA is very concerned about ethics. Log on to www.imanet.org, the Web site for the IMA.

1. Click on About IMA. What is the IMA dedicated to?
2. Follow the link that shows the mission statement for the IMA. What is the mission of the IMA?
3. One of the stated missions of the IMA is to help its members' professional development through education. Click on the Professional Development link. What options does the IMA provide to help educate the members?
4. Click on the Ethics Center link under About IMA. Follow the link to code of ethics called the Statement of Ethical Professional Practice. Read the code and comment on its importance to management accountants.

Introduction to Cost Behavior and Cost-Volume Relationships

LEARNING OBJECTIVES

When you have finished studying this chapter, you should be able to:

1. Explain how activity cost drivers affect cost behavior.

2. Show how changes in cost driver levels affect variable and fixed costs.

3. Calculate break-even sales volume in total dollars and total units.

4. Create a cost-volume-profit graph and understand the assumptions behind it.

5. Calculate sales volume in total dollars and total units to reach a target profit.

6. Differentiate between contribution margin and gross margin.

7. Explain the effects of sales mix on profits (Appendix 2A).

8. Compute cost-volume-profit relationships on an after-tax basis (Appendix 2B).

▶ BOEING COMPANY

In 1915, William Boeing, a Seattle timberman, assembled his first airplane in a boathouse. In 1954 Boeing introduced its first four-engine 707. The Boeing family of jets has grown to include the 727, 737, 757, 747, 767, and 777. The company expects to deliver its first 787-Dreamliner in 2010. Today, the **Boeing Company** is the world's largest aerospace company, the second largest maker of commercial jets, and the second largest military contractor. Boeing produces 30 to 35 commercial jetliners each month and had annual revenue of $60.9 billion in 2008. The company makes planes with 100 to well over 500 seats and has more than half of the world's market share in airplane sales, and that is growing as Boeing successfully competes for the growing demand for airplanes. How will Boeing maintain its competitive edge and profitability margin? With intense competition from **Airbus**, Boeing knows that it can improve profits more by controlling (reducing) costs than by increasing prices to customers—especially when many of its customers have shrinking profits such as in 2008 and 2009. So, should it build bigger airplanes or more of the existing size but with improvements in features and efficiencies that will lower customers' operating costs? Which alternative has lower costs for Boeing and its customers? To answer these questions, Boeing has to understand its own costs as well as the costs of its customers. This chapter begins your study of costs so that you, too, can assess the costs that are important to Boeing and other companies, big and small, as they make crucial decisions about their products, services, and processes.

Consider a recent decision Boeing faced regarding development and production of a new airplane. Back in 1999, the company started an R&D program for the Sonic Cruiser. The Sonic Cruiser emphasized speed—it was designed to reduce travel time by about 20%. An important part of its research was the assessment of its customers' costs—both of operating their existing fleet of planes and of the costs of the new Sonic Cruisers. In early 2001, discussions with airlines in North America, Asia, and Europe confirmed the design offered exactly what airlines and passengers were looking for: the ability to fly quickly and directly to their destinations while avoiding time-consuming and costly stops at major hubs. In late 2002, after more than three years of research, the company had completed the design of the new airplane and was faced with the final decision to launch. A decision to launch would involve a huge immediate investment in costly plant and equipment resources. To pay for these assets and make a profit, Boeing had to be confident that its customers would be willing to pay more for the airplane than it cost Boeing to design, produce, and sell it.

But production ultimately hinged on whether customers wanted a faster airplane that used the most up-to-date technology both in operating the airplane and producing it. Despite the years of development activities, Boeing decided not to proceed with the Sonic Cruiser. Why? The economic recession and the terrorist attacks of September 11, 2001, had changed the airline industry's needs. According to Alan Mulally, CEO of Boeing Commercial Airplanes at the time, the airlines made it clear that they wanted a cheaper plane rather than a faster plane. Therefore, Boeing management decided to dedicate its resources to developing the 787-Dreamliner—a "super-efficient" version of its existing 777 jetliner. Boeing's managers made their decision after a careful analysis of its own production costs and the airlines' operating costs, comparing them to the predicted demands for airline travel in the next decade.

The design and production of an airplane is a complex process. This is the first assembled Boeing 787 Dreamliner airplane at its production facility at Everett, Washington.

Managers need to understand costs. For example, how much would it cost Boeing to produce each Sonic Cruiser? How much for each 787? How much cost does **Delta Airlines** incur when it adds one more passenger at the last moment to an existing flight, or when it adds one more flight to the schedule? What does it cost **Toyota** to develop a new line of luxury autos, as it did with Lexus? How much does it cost to produce one more Lexus? How will an increase in Arizona's population affect the costs needed to run the state's department of motor vehicles? What does it cost **Nestlé Purina** to meet **Wal-Mart**'s specifications for shipments of pet-care products? What activities contribute most to Nestlé Purina's cost to serve Wal-Mart stores? These questions are really different forms of one general question: What will happen to financial results if a company or organization changes its level of activity?

Although financial results are based on revenues and costs, we will focus primarily on costs in this chapter. As we saw in the case of Boeing, companies usually have more control over their costs than they do over their revenues. One of the main goals of management accounting is helping managers control (and reduce) costs. But managers cannot control costs unless they understand **cost behavior**—how the activities of an organization affect its costs. ■

Identifying Resources, Activities, Costs, and Cost Drivers

Different types of costs behave in different ways. Consider **Boeing**'s costs of making the 737-900ER—Boeing's newest single-aisle airplane. As Boeing produces more airplanes, it buys and uses more resources, such as electrical wire, seats, aluminum, and labor. Therefore, each additional airplane requires Boeing to incur more of these resource costs. In contrast, the cost of other resources such as the factory and salaries of key managers, stay the same, regardless of the number of airplanes made. To predict costs and to manage them on a day-to-day basis, Boeing managers identify

Objective 1
Explain how cost drivers affect cost behavior.

- key activities performed,
- resources used in performing these activities,
- costs of the resources used, and
- **cost drivers**, measures of activities that require the use of resources and thereby cause costs.

Exhibit 2-1 shows how activities link resources and their costs with the output of products or services. For example, an activity that requires resources and therefore causes costs for Boeing is installing seats in the 737-900ER. This activity uses many resources, but let's consider just two: 1) the seats themselves, which Boeing purchases from a subcontractor, and 2) labor for installing the seats. One measure of activity, number of seats installed, is an appropriate cost driver for the cost of the seats. Another measure of activity, labor hours used in installing the seats, is a cost driver for the cost of labor resources.

To control costs, managers usually focus their efforts on managing the activities companies perform to make, sell, and deliver products or services—not necessarily on the products and services themselves. This is why it is important to focus on the activities used to produce outputs, products, or services, and the resources needed to support the activities. For example, a production manager needs to know how routine activities, such as machine maintenance and repairs, affect production costs. Likewise, a sales manager needs to know how activities, such as order processing and post-sales support, affect sales costs. Consider one of the many activities performed as part of the production function at Boeing's plant—receiving parts that production workers install on an airplane. Of course, managers want to know the cost of the parts they purchase, but they also need to know how the receiving activity affects production costs. For example, how does the increase or decrease in receiving activity affect the lease payment for renting the equipment used to move parts from the receiving area to the production floor? How does it affect the cost of fuel for the moving equipment?

An organization has many cost drivers across the various activities of its value chain. For example, one manufacturer of pet foods has a plant in Denver that has more than 50 production activities and a total of 21 cost drivers. Exhibit 2-2 lists examples of resource costs and potential cost drivers for activities in each of the value-chain functions. How well we identify the most appropriate cost drivers determines how well managers understand cost behavior and how well managers can control costs.

In this chapter we focus on a simple situation of one activity and one cost driver for the production of a particular product or service. The activity will include all aspects of the production and sale of the product or service. The cost driver will be the number of units produced and sold, which we assume drives all the resource costs. Therefore, the analysis will examine how decisions about the volume of production and sales affect costs. This simplified analysis is useful to managers who want a rough estimate of the relationship between production volume and costs.

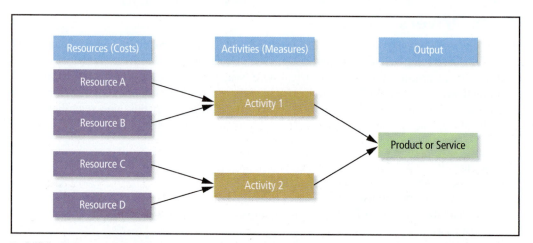

Exhibit 2-1
Linking Resource Costs to Outputs via Activities

Value-Chain Functions and Resource Costs	Example Cost Drivers
Research and development	
• Salaries of sales personnel, costs of market surveys	Number of new product proposals
• Salaries of product and process engineers	Complexity of proposed products
Design of products, services, and processes	
• Salaries of product and process engineers	Number of engineering hours
• Cost of computer-aided design equipment used to develop prototype of product for testing	Number of distinct parts per product
Production	
• Labor wages	Labor hours
• Supervisory salaries	Number of people supervised
• Maintenance wages	Number of mechanic hours
• Depreciation of plant and machinery, supplies	Number of machine hours
• Energy cost	Kilowatt hours
Marketing	
• Cost of advertisements	Number of advertisements
• Salaries of marketing personnel, travel costs, entertainment costs	Sales dollars
Distribution	
• Wages of shipping personnel	Labor hours
• Transportation costs including depreciation of vehicles and fuel	Weight of items delivered
Customer service	
• Salaries of service personnel	Hours spent servicing products
• Costs of supplies, travel	Number of service calls

Exhibit 2-2

Examples of Value-Chain Functions, Resource Costs, and Cost Drivers

Variable- and Fixed-Cost Behavior

To understand cost behavior, it is important to distinguish variable costs from fixed costs. Accountants classify costs as variable or fixed depending on how much they change as the level of a particular cost driver changes. A **variable cost** changes in direct proportion to changes in the cost driver. In contrast, changes in the cost driver do not *immediately* affect a **fixed cost**. Suppose units of production is the cost driver of interest. A 10% increase in the units of production would produce a 10% increase in variable costs. However, the fixed costs would remain unchanged.

Consider some variable costs and assume that the cost driver is the volume of final goods or services produced and sold. Suppose **Watkins Products**, the 140-year-old health food company, pays its sales personnel a 40% straight commission on sales. The total cost of sales commissions to Watkins is 40% of sales dollars—a variable cost with respect to sales revenues. Or suppose Long Lake Bait Shop buys bags of fish bait for $2 each. The total cost of fish bait is $2 times the number of bags purchased—a variable cost with respect to units (number of bags) purchased. Notice that variable costs do not change *per unit*, but that the *total variable costs* change in direct proportion to the cost-driver activity.

Now consider a fixed cost. Suppose **Sony** rents a factory to produce DVD players for $500,000 per year. The number of DVD players produced does not affect the *total fixed cost* of $500,000. The *unit cost* of rent applicable to each DVD player, however, does depend on the total number of DVD players produced. If Sony produces 100,000 DVD players, the unit cost will be $500,000 ÷ 100,000 = $5. If it produces 50,000 DVD players, the unit cost will be $500,000 ÷ 50,000 = $10. Therefore, a fixed cost does not change in total, but the per-unit fixed cost becomes progressively smaller as the volume increases.

Note carefully from these examples that the "variable" or "fixed" characteristic of a cost relates to its total dollar amount and not to its per-unit amount. Exhibit 2-3 summarizes these relationships.

When analyzing costs, you may find these two rules of thumb useful:

1. Think of fixed costs on a total-cost basis. Total fixed costs remain unchanged regardless of changes in the cost-driver.

Objective 2

Show how changes in cost-driver levels affect variable and fixed costs.

If Cost-Driver Level Increases (or Decreases)		
Type of Cost	Total Cost	Cost per Unit*
Fixed costs	No change	Decrease (or increase)
Variable costs	Increase (or decrease)	No change

*Per unit of activity volume, for example, product units, passenger-miles, orders processed, or sales dollars

Exhibit 2-3
Cost Behavior of Fixed and Variable Costs

2. Think of variable costs on a per-unit basis. The per-unit variable cost remains unchanged regardless of changes in the cost-driver. As a result, the total variable cost varies proportionately with the level of the cost-driver.

Now consider again the receiving activity at the **Boeing** plant discussed in the previous section. Exhibit 2-4 shows the relationship between the receiving activity and the costs of the fuel and equipment resources. The receiving activity requires many more resources such as labor and supplies, but we restrict our discussion to just fuel and equipment. The relationships between activities and resources used can be shown using symbols. We introduce some of these symbols here in Chapter 2 and will use these same symbols in later chapters to depict more complex business processes. We denote an activity by the symbol ■. We use the symbol ▬ to represent a variable-cost resource and the symbol ▲ to represent a fixed-cost resource. The total fuel and equipment costs were $24,000 and $45,000, respectively, and the department received 30,000 parts. Notice in Exhibit 2-4 that we apply the two rules of thumb by showing the total fixed lease cost of $45,000 and the per-unit variable fuel cost of $24,000 ÷ 30,000 = $0.80 per part received. Both of these amounts tend to be relatively constant over the wide range of receiving activity. This is an important characteristic because we can use both of these numbers to calculate the activity costs for various levels of the cost driver.

Suppose we want to know what the total fuel and equipment cost would be if only 27,500 parts were received. We can use Exhibits 2-3, 2-4, and our rules of thumb to find the answer. Total fuel cost is variable with respect to parts received, but the fuel cost per part received does not change. Equipment lease cost in total does not change when the number of parts received decreases. So the total cost of receiving 27,500 parts would be (27,500 × $.80) + $45,000 = $67,000. Notice how we used the rules of thumb to answer the question. We used the unit cost of $.80 for variable fuel cost and the total cost of $45,000 for the fixed equipment lease cost. Exhibit 2-5 shows the total cost lines for both resources. These lines can be used to find an estimate of the total costs at any cost-driver level.

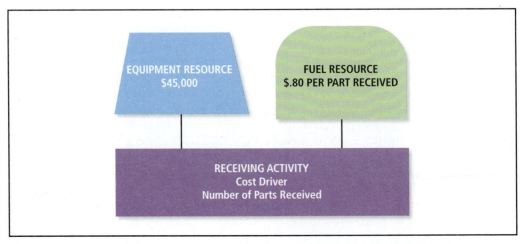

Exhibit 2-4
Receiving Activity and Resources Used

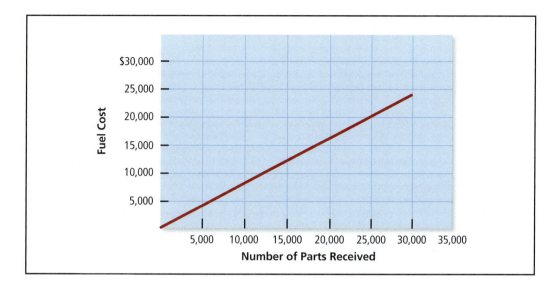

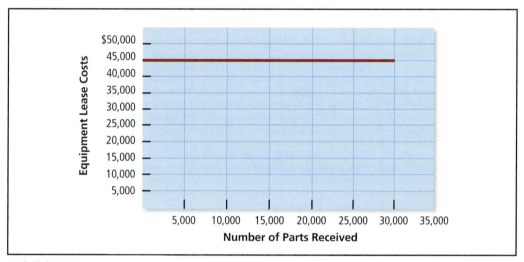

Exhibit 2-5
Total Fuel and Equipment Lease Costs

Summary Problem for Your Review

PROBLEM

Refer to the previous discussion of the receiving activity at the **Boeing** plant and Exhibit 2-4. The plant manager is looking at a monthly report of plant costs and notices that the receiving activity costs vary substantially from month to month. He is interested in knowing more about why the total cost and unit costs of the receiving activity changes when the number of parts received changes. He gives you the data for parts received for the last several months and you note that the range is from 10,000 to 30,000.

1. Prepare a table that shows the cost of each resource, the total cost, and the total cost on a per-part-received basis. Use increments of 5,000 parts beginning with 10,000.
2. Prepare brief explanations of why the total and unit cost patterns change.

SOLUTION

1. The table can be developed by using the two rules of thumb that are based on the relationships shown in Exhibit 2-3. We can also quickly estimate the total costs from the cost lines in Exhibit 2-5.

(1) Parts Received	(2) Equipment Cost	(3) $.80 × (1) Fuel Cost	(4) (2) + (3) Total Cost	(5) (4) ÷ (1) Cost per Part Received
10,000	$45,000	$ 8,000	$53,000	$5.30
15,000	45,000	12,000	57,000	3.80
20,000	45,000	16,000	61,000	3.05
25,000	45,000	20,000	65,000	2.60
30,000	45,000	24,000	69,000	2.30

2. Column (4) shows the total cost of the receiving activity. The total cost increases with increases in the number of parts received due to the increase in variable costs. Whenever we see a pattern of increasing total costs, we may initially assume that it is due to variable-cost resources responding to increasing levels of the cost driver. Column (5) shows the cost per part received. The decreasing cost pattern is due to the fixed equipment cost being spread over increasing levels of the cost driver – number of parts received. For example, when the number of parts received increases from 10,000 to 15,000 parts, the cost per part decreases by $1.50 from $5.30 to $3.80. This is exactly the amount of the decrease in the equipment cost per part, which is $4.50 ($45,000 ÷ 10,000) less $3.00 ($45,000 ÷ 15,000). The variable fuel cost per part stays the same at $0.80.

Making Managerial Decisions

A key factor in helping managers understand cost behavior is distinguishing between variable and fixed costs. Test your understanding by answering the following questions.

1. A producer of premium ice cream uses "gallons of ice cream produced" as a cost driver for the production activity. One of the main resources this activity uses is dairy ingredients. Is the cost of dairy ingredients a variable or a fixed cost?
2. The same company uses "supervisory hours" as a cost driver for the supervision activity. The most costly resource used by this activity is supervisory salaries. Is the supervisory salaries cost variable or fixed?

Answer

The best way to determine whether the cost of a resource is fixed or variable is to ask the question, "If the level of the cost driver changes, what will happen to the cost?" If the company increases (decreases) its production of ice cream, then the cost of dairy ingredients will also increase (decrease). Thus, the cost of dairy ingredients is a variable cost. If the number of supervisory hours increases (decreases), supervisory salaries will not change. Thus, the cost of supervisory salaries is a fixed cost.

Relevant Range

Although we have just described fixed costs as unchanging regardless of changes in the given cost driver, this rule of thumb holds true only within reasonable limits. For example, rent costs, which are generally fixed, will rise if increased production activity requires a larger or additional building—or if the landlord decides to raise the rent. Conversely, rent costs may go down if decreased production activity causes the company to move to a smaller plant. The

relevant range is the limit of cost-driver level within which a specific relationship between costs and the cost driver is valid. Even within the relevant range, though, a fixed cost remains fixed only over a given period of time—usually the budget period. Fixed costs may change from budget year to budget year solely because of changes in insurance and property tax rates, executive salary levels, or rent levels. But these items usually do not change significantly within a given year.

For example, suppose that the relevant range of production activity for a **General Electric** lightbulb plant is between 40,000 and 85,000 cases of lightbulbs per month and that total monthly fixed costs within the relevant range are $100,000. Within the relevant range, fixed costs will remain the same. If production falls below 40,000 cases, changes in production processes would slash fixed costs to $60,000 per month. If operations rise above 85,000 cases, rentals of additional facilities would boost fixed costs to $115,000 per month. Exhibit 2-6 graphs the actual costs in the top figure and the assumed fixed-cost-behavior in the bottom. The two are identical only within the relevant range.

Exhibit 2-6 shows graphically these assumptions—a given period and a given activity range. It is highly unusual, however, for monthly operations to be outside the relevant range. Therefore, the three-level refinement at the top of Exhibit 2-6 is usually not graphed. Instead, a single horizontal line is typically extended through the plotted activity levels, as at the bottom of the exhibit. Often a dashed line is used outside the relevant range.

The basic idea of a relevant range also applies to variable costs. That is, outside a relevant range, some variable costs, such as fuel consumed, may behave differently per unit of cost-driver activity. For example, the variable cost per case for the GE lightbulb plant might increase if production activity exceeds 85,000 cases per month because of the lower efficiency of the new facilities.

Difficulties in Classifying Costs

Is it difficult to classify a cost as exactly variable or exactly fixed? As you may suspect, it often is. Many complications arise, including the possibility of costs behaving in some non-linear way (not producing a straight-line graph). For example, tax preparers often become

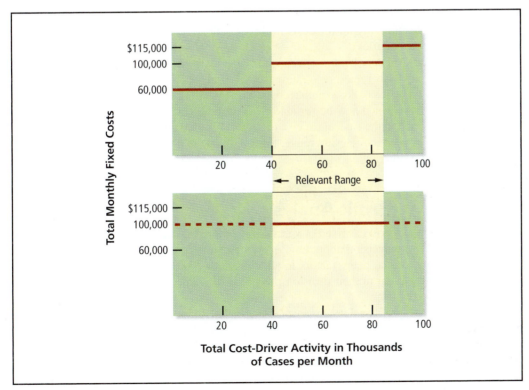

Exhibit 2-6
Fixed Costs and Relevant Range

more efficient as they learn to process the new year's tax forms, thus processing more returns per hour. This means that total variable costs may actually behave as in panel A and not as in panel B.

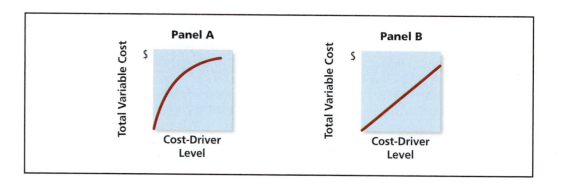

Moreover, more than one cost driver may simultaneously affect costs. For example, both the weight and the number of units handled may affect the costs of shipping labor at an **Amazon.com** warehouse. We will investigate various facets of this problem in succeeding chapters; for now, we assume that we can classify every cost as either totally variable or totally fixed. We assume also that only one cost driver affects a given variable cost and that the variable costs change in direct proportion to the cost driver.

Whether we classify costs as fixed or variable also depends on the situation. More costs are fixed and fewer are variable when decisions for which we use the cost information involve very short time spans and very small changes in activity level. Suppose a **United Airlines** plane with several empty seats will depart from its gate in 2 minutes. A potential passenger is running down a corridor bearing a transferable ticket from a competing airline. Unless the gate attendant holds the airplane for an extra 30 seconds, the passenger will miss the departure and will not switch to United for the planned trip. What are the variable costs to United of delaying the departure and placing one more passenger in an otherwise empty seat? Variable costs (for example, one more meal) are negligible. Virtually all the costs in this situation are fixed (for example, flight crew and maintenance crew salaries).

Now, in contrast, suppose United's decision is whether to add another flight, acquire another gate, add another city to its routes, or acquire another airplane. Many more costs would be variable and fewer would be fixed. For example, in the case of adding a flight, the salaries of the flight and maintenance crews would now be variable. This example underscores the importance of the decision situation itself in the analysis of cost behavior. Whether costs are really "fixed" or "variable" depends heavily on the relevant range, the length of the planning period in question, and the specific decision situation.

Cost-Volume-Profit Analysis

Managers often classify costs as fixed or variable when making decisions that affect the volume of output. Consider the decision about how many units of a product to produce in the coming year. Managers realize that many factors in addition to the volume of output will affect costs. Yet, a useful starting point in their decision process is to predict how the choice of production level will affect costs.

The managers of profit-seeking organizations usually study the effects of output volume on revenue (sales), expenses (costs), and net income (net profit). We call this study **cost-volume-profit (CVP) analysis**. The managers of nonprofit organizations also benefit from the study of CVP relationships. Why? No organization has unlimited resources, and knowledge of how costs fluctuate with changes in volume helps managers to understand how to control costs. For example, administrators of nonprofit hospitals are concerned about the behavior of costs as the volume of patients fluctuates.

To apply CVP analysis, managers usually resort to some simplifying assumptions. The major one is that we can classify costs as either variable or fixed with respect to a single measure of the volume of output activity. This chapter focuses on such a simplified relationship.

CVP Scenario

Amy Winston, the manager of food services for one of Boeing's plants, is trying to decide whether to rent a line of snack vending machines. Although individual snack items have various acquisition costs and selling prices, Winston has decided that an average selling price of $1.50 per unit and an average acquisition cost of $1.20 per unit will suffice for purposes of this analysis. She predicts the following revenue and expense relationships:

	Per Unit	Percentage of Sales
Selling price	$1.50	100%
Variable cost of each item	1.20	80
Selling price less variable cost	$ .30	20%
Monthly fixed expenses		
Rent	$ 3,000	
Wages for replenishing and servicing	13,500	
Other fixed expenses	1,500	
Total fixed expenses per month	$18,000	

We will now use these data in examining several applications of CVP analysis.

Computing the Break-Even Point

[handwritten: Net Income = Zero; Revenues = Expenses]

The most basic CVP analysis computes the monthly **break-even point** in number of units and in dollar sales. The break-even point is the level of sales at which revenue equals expenses and net income is zero. The business press frequently refers to break-even points, especially during times of economic downturn such as in 2001–2002 and in 2008–2009. For example, a news story on hotel occupancy rates in San Francisco stated that "seventy percent [occupancy] is considered a break-even for hoteliers." Another news story stated that Toyota's "operating profit in the first half [of 2008] was ¥582bn, so the group will do little better than break even in the second half." One auto industry analyst summarized the impact of the 2008 downturn on U.S. car manufacturers, saying "the break-even point for Detroit is annual sales of 16.2 million vehicles," while actual sales were about 14.8 million. When a company's sales begin to fall, it may try to lower its break-even point to avoid losing money. The Business First box on p. 44 describes this situation for some high-tech and auto-industry firms.

Some people call the study of cost-volume-profit relationships break-even analysis. However, this term is misleading. Why? Because CVP analysis does much more than compute the break-even point. It is often an important part of a company's planning process. It helps managers to predict how their decisions will affect sales, costs, and net income. Nevertheless, computing a break-even point is one application of CVP analysis.

Objective 3

Calculate break-even sales volume in total dollars and total units.

[handwritten: There is more to CVP than the break-even point!]

Business First

Tech Firms and Auto Makers Lower Break-Even Points During Economic Recession

One might think that break-even is a term that is not often used in business. However when economic conditions result in declining sales, companies are keenly aware of the break-even point.

In 2002–2003, many high-technology companies reported on their attempts to achieve profitability in spite of declining sales. The situation repeated itself for many types of companies in 2008–2009. They often focused on how their efforts to control costs reduced their break-even points. If a company faces rapidly falling sales, it must restructure its costs to be able to break even at a lower volume. Restructuring costs can involve reducing both fixed and variable costs.

Consider Sony's PlayStation 3. It costs Sony about $500 to make a PS3 but the sales price is about $300 and with the recession of 2008–2009 coupled with competitive pressure from Nintendo Wii and Microsoft Xbox 360, raising price was not an option. So how could Sony lower its costs to breakeven? The two actions Sony considered were reducing variable cost and fixed cost. To lower its variable cost, Sony reduced the number of parts and the cost for the console's central processing unit. Reducing the number of parts also lowered Sony's fixed costs,

such as assembly equipment and salaries of purchasing agents responsible for vendor negotiations.

In the severe economic recession beginning in 2008 and continuing into 2009, auto makers worldwide faced dramatic declines in sales, forcing equally dramatic restructuring of their operations to lower their costs in hopes of breaking even. Until the recession, the break-even level of car sales for the "Big Three" U.S. automakers was about 16 million per year. By early in 2009 the annual sales rate was only at a pace of 9 million. Among the actions taken to reduce the break-even sales level by GM, Chrysler, and Ford were massive plant closings, layoffs, and reduction of the number of models produced. Many of the associated costs were fixed and thus not dependent on unit sales. The main idea for automakers is to dramatically reduce fixed cost and variable cost per unit in much greater proportion than sales volume and price, thus lowering breakeven and eventually returning to profitability.

Sources: "Sony PS3 Costs Less To Make, But Still A Money Loser," *Techweb*, December 30, 2008; "Car Sales Not as Horrid In March," *USA Today*, April 2, 2009.

We next illustrate the two basic methods for computing a break-even point: the contribution-margin method and the equation method.

CONTRIBUTION-MARGIN METHOD Consider the following common-sense arithmetic approach. Every unit sold generates a **unit contribution margin** or **marginal income**, which is the unit sales price minus the variable cost per unit. For the vending machine snack items, the unit contribution margin is $.30:

Unit sales price	$1.50
– Unit variable cost	1.20
= Unit contribution margin	$ .30

Fixed Cost = contribution margin

When do we reach the break-even point? When we sell enough units to generate a **total contribution margin** (total number of units sold × unit contribution margin) equal to the total fixed costs. Divide the $18,000 in fixed costs by the $.30 unit contribution margin. The number of units that we must sell to break even is $18,000 ÷ $.30 = 60,000 units. The sales revenue at the break-even point is 60,000 units × $1.50 per unit, or $90,000. (Note that some managers and accountants use the term **contribution margin** to mean either unit contribution margin or total contribution margin, assuming that the context makes clear which they mean.)

Think about the contribution margin of the snack items. Each unit sold generates extra revenue of $1.50 and extra cost of $1.20. Fixed costs are unaffected. If we sell zero units, we incur a loss equal to the fixed cost of $18,000. Each unit sold reduces the loss by $.30 until sales reach the break-even point of 60,000 units. After that point, each unit sold adds (or contributes) $.30 to profit.

The condensed income statement at the break-even point is

	Total	Per Unit	Percentage
Units	60,000		
Sales	$90,000	$1.50	100%
Variable costs	72,000	1.20	80
Contribution margin*	$18,000	$ .30	20%
Fixed costs	18,000		
Net income	$ 0		

*Sales less variable costs

Many companies sell multiple products and, therefore, have no single unit price and unit variable cost. For example, a grocery store sells hundreds of products at many different prices. In such a company, it would not be meaningful to compute a break-even point in overall units sold. Instead, we use total sales and total variable costs to calculate the variable cost percentage and the contribution margin percentage:

Variable-cost percentage = total variable costs ÷ total sales

Contribution-margin percentage = total contribution margin ÷ total sales = 100% − variable cost percentage

Consider our vending machine example:

Sales price	100%
−Variable expenses as a percentage of dollar sales	80
= Contribution-margin percentage	20%

The variable-cost percentage is 80%, and the contribution-margin percentage is 20%. We can also express these percentages as ratios, the **variable-cost ratio** and **contribution-margin ratio**, which are .80 and .20, respectively. Therefore, 20% of each sales dollar is available for the recovery of fixed expenses and the making of net income. Thus, we need $18,000 ÷ .20 = $90,000 of sales to break even. Remember that the contribution-margin percentage is a percentage of dollar sales. Using the contribution-margin percentage, we can compute the break-even volume in dollar sales without determining the break-even point in units.

EQUATION METHOD   The equation method is the most general form of analysis, one you can adapt to any conceivable cost-volume-profit situation. You are familiar with a typical income statement. We can express any income statement in equation form, or as a mathematical model, as follows:

$$\text{sales} - \text{variable expenses} - \text{fixed expenses} = \text{net income} \qquad (1)$$

That is,

$$\left(\begin{matrix} \text{Unit sales} \\ \text{price} \end{matrix} \times \begin{matrix} \text{number} \\ \text{of units} \end{matrix}\right) - \left(\begin{matrix} \text{unit} \\ \text{variable cost} \end{matrix} \times \begin{matrix} \text{number} \\ \text{of units} \end{matrix}\right) - \begin{matrix} \text{fixed} \\ \text{expenses} \end{matrix} = \begin{matrix} \text{net} \\ \text{income} \end{matrix}$$

At the break-even point, net income is zero:

$$\text{sales} - \text{variable expenses} - \text{fixed expenses} = 0$$

Let N = number of units to be sold to break even. Then, for the vending machine example,

$$\$1.50\,N - \$1.20\,N - \$18,000 = 0$$
$$\$.30\,N = \$18,000$$
$$N = \$18,000 \div \$.30$$
$$N = 60,000 \text{ units}$$

Total sales in the equation is a price-times-quantity relationship, which we expressed in our example as $1.50N. To find the dollar sales, multiply 60,000 units by $1.50, which yields the break-even dollar sales of $90,000.

You can also solve the equation for break-even sales dollars without computing the unit break-even point by using the relationship of variable costs and profits as a percentage of sales:

$$\frac{\text{variable-cost}}{\text{ratio or percentage}} = \frac{\text{variable cost per unit}}{\text{sales price per unit}} = \frac{\$1.20}{\$1.50} = .80 \text{ or } 80\%$$

Let S = sales in dollars needed to break even. Then

$$S - .80S - \$18,000 = 0$$
$$.20S = \$18,000$$
$$S = \$18,000 \div .20$$
$$S = \$90,000$$

RELATIONSHIP BETWEEN THE TWO METHODS   You may have noticed that the contribution-margin method is merely a shortcut version of the equation method. Look at the last three lines in the two solutions given for equation 1. They read

Break-Even Volume	
Units	Dollars
$.30N = \$18,000$	$.20S = \$18,000$
$N = \dfrac{\$18,000}{\$.30}$	$S = \dfrac{\$18,000}{.20}$
$N = 60,000$ units	$S = \$90,000$

From these equations, we can derive the following shortcut formulas:

$$\text{break-even volume in units} = \frac{\text{fixed expenses}}{\text{unit contribution margin}} \quad (2)$$

$$\text{break-even volume in dollars} = \frac{\text{fixed expenses}}{\text{contribution-margin ratio}} \quad (3)$$

Which should you use, the equation or the contribution-margin method? Use either. Both yield the same results, so the choice is a matter of personal preference or convenience in a particular case.

Making Managerial Decisions

Managers use CVP analysis to predict effects of changes in sales or costs on the break-even point. Using shortcut formulas (2) and (3), answer the following questions. Remember that the contribution margin per unit equals the sales price per unit minus the variable costs per unit.

1. What would be the effect on the unit and dollar break-even level if fixed costs increase (and there are no other changes)?
2. What would be the effect on the unit and dollar break-even level if variable cost per unit decreases (and there are no other changes)?
3. What would be the effect on the unit and dollar break-even level if sales volume increases (and there are no other changes)?

Answers

1. The break-even level in both units and sales dollars would increase if fixed costs increase.
2. The break-even level in both units and sales dollars would decrease if variable cost per unit decreases.
3. Think before answering this question. The actual (or even planned) volume of sales in units has nothing to do with determining the break-even point. This is why unit sales volume does not appear in either equation (2) or (3).

GRAPHING THE BREAK-EVEN POINT   Exhibit 2-7 is a graph of the cost-volume-profit relationship in our vending machine example. If you fully understand the contribution margin or equation method, you do not need to also learn the graphical method. However, most students find that a careful study of the graphical method leads to a better understanding of CVP analysis. Study the graph as you read the procedure for constructing it.

Objective 4

Create a cost-volume-profit graph and understand the assumptions behind it.

1. Draw the axes. The horizontal axis is the sales volume, and the vertical axis is dollars of cost and revenue.
2. Plot sales volume. Select a convenient sales volume, say, 100,000 units, and plot point A for total sales dollars at that volume: 100,000 × $1.50 = $150,000. Draw the revenue (that is, sales) line from point A to the origin, point 0.
3. Plot fixed expenses. Draw the line showing the $18,000 fixed portion of expenses. It should be a horizontal line intersecting the vertical axis at $18,000, point B.
4. Plot variable expenses. Determine the variable portion of expenses at a convenient level of activity: 100,000 units × $1.20 = $120,000. Add this to the fixed expenses: $120,000 + $18,000 = $138,000. Plot point C for 100,000 units and $138,000. Then draw a line between this point and point B. This is the total expenses line.
5. Locate the break-even point—where the total expenses line crosses the sales line. This is at, 60,000 units or $90,000. On the graph, this is shown where total sales revenues exactly equal total costs, point D.

The break-even point is only one part of this cost-volume-profit graph. The graph also shows the profit or loss at any rate of activity. At any given volume, the vertical distance between the sales line and the total expenses line measures the net income or net loss.

Managers often use break-even graphs because these graphs show potential profits over a wide range of volume more easily than numerical exhibits. Whether you use graphs or other presentations depends largely on your preferences. However, if you need to explain a CVP model to an audience, a graphical approach can be most helpful.

Note that the concept of relevant range applies to the break-even graph. Almost all break-even graphs show revenue and cost lines extending back to the vertical axis as shown in Exhibit 2-7. This approach is misleading because the relationships depicted in such graphs are valid only within a particular relevant range of volume. Nevertheless, for presentation purposes, most managers extend revenue and cost lines beyond the relevant range.

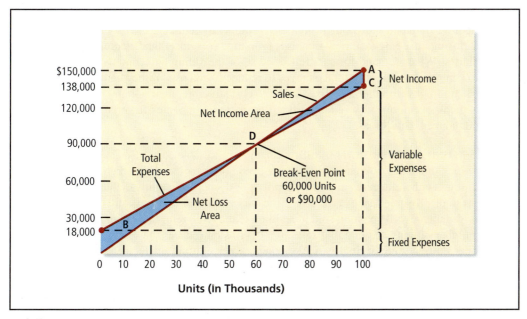

Exhibit 2-7
Cost-Volume-Profit Graph

Regardless of the method used for CVP analysis, it is based on a set of important assumptions. Some of these assumptions follow:

1. We can classify expenses into variable and fixed categories. Total variable expenses vary directly with activity level. Total fixed expenses do not change with activity level.
2. The behavior of revenues and expenses is linear over the relevant range. This means that selling prices per unit and variable costs per unit do not change with changes in sales and production levels.
3. We expect no change in efficiency or productivity.
4. The sales mix remains constant. The **sales mix** is the relative proportions or combinations of quantities of different products that constitute total sales. (See Appendix 2A for more on sales mixes.)
5. The inventory level does not change significantly during the period. That is, the number of units sold equals number of units produced.

CHANGES IN FIXED EXPENSES   Changes in fixed expenses cause changes in the break-even point. For example, if we double the $3,000 monthly rent of the vending machines, what would be the monthly break-even point in number of units and dollar sales?

The fixed expenses would increase from $18,000 to $21,000, so

$$\text{break-even volume in units} = \frac{\text{fixed expenses}}{\text{unit contribution margin}}$$

$$= \frac{\$21,000}{\$.30}$$

$$= 70,000 \text{ units}$$

$$\text{break-even volume in dollars} = \frac{\text{fixed expenses}}{\text{contribution margin ratio}}$$

$$= \frac{\$21,000}{.20}$$

$$= \$105,000$$

Note that a one-sixth increase in fixed expenses altered the break-even point by one-sixth: from 60,000 to 70,000 units and from $90,000 to $105,000. This type of relationship always exists between fixed expenses and the break-even point if everything else remains constant.

Companies frequently lower their break-even points by reducing their total fixed costs. For example, closing or selling factories decreases property taxes, insurance, depreciation, and managers' salaries. When demand for cars fell because of the slumping economy in 2008, the big three auto companies made structural changes to reduce fixed costs. If they had merely produced fewer cars and trucks with the same fixed/variable cost structure, their volume would have fallen below its break-even point. By reducing fixed costs, the companies lowered their break-even points and reduced their losses.

CHANGES IN UNIT CONTRIBUTION MARGIN   Changes in variable costs also cause the break-even point to shift. Companies can reduce their break-even points by increasing their unit contribution margins through either increases in unit sales prices or decreases in unit variable costs, or both.

For example, assume that the fixed rent for the vending machines is still $3,000. (1) If the rental charge includes $.03 per unit sold in addition to the fixed rent, find the monthly break-even point in number of units and in dollar sales. (2) If Winston reduces the selling price from $1.50 to $1.35 per unit and the original variable expenses per unit are unchanged, find the monthly break-even point in number of units and in dollar sales.

Here's what happens to the break-even point:

1. The variable expenses would increase from $1.20 to $1.23 per unit, the unit contribution margin would decline from $.30 to $.27, and the contribution-margin ratio would become

$.27 \div \$1.50 = .18$. The original fixed expenses of $18,000 would stay the same, but the denominators would change from those previously used. Thus,

$$\text{break-even point in units} = \frac{\$18,000}{\$.27} = 66,667 \text{ units}$$

$$\text{break-even point in dollars} = \frac{\$18,000}{.18} = \$100,000$$

2. If Winston reduces the selling price from $1.50 to $1.35 per unit and the original variable expenses are unchanged, the unit contribution margin would fall from $1.50 − $1.20 = $.30 to $1.35 − $1.20 = $.15, and the break-even point would soar to $18,000 ÷ $.15 = 120,000 units. The break-even point in dollars would also change because the selling price per unit and contribution-margin ratio change. The contribution-margin ratio would be $.15 ÷ $1.35 = .11111. The break-even point in dollars would be 120,000 units × $1.35 = $162,000 or, using the formula,

$$\text{break-even volume in dollars} = \frac{\$18,000}{.11111} = \$162,000$$

You can see that small changes in price or variable costs can lead to large changes in the unit contribution margin and, hence, to large changes in the break-even point.

Target Net Profit and an Incremental Approach

Managers also use CVP analysis to determine the total sales, in units and dollars, needed to reach a target profit. For example, in our snack vending example, suppose Winston considers $1,440 per month the minimum acceptable net income. How many units will she have to sell to justify the adoption of the vending machine plan? How does this figure "translate" into dollar sales?

Objective 5
Calculate sales volume in total dollars and total units to reach a target profit.

To compute the target sales volume in units needed to meet the desired or target net income, we adapt the basic break-even formula (equation 1 on p. 45):

$$\text{target sales} - \text{variable expenses} - \text{fixed expenses} = \text{target net income} \qquad (4)$$

or

$$\text{target sales volume in units} = \frac{\text{fixed expenses} + \text{target net income}}{\text{unit contribution margin}}$$

$$= \frac{\$18,000 + \$1,440}{\$.30} = 64,800 \text{ units} \qquad (5)$$

The only real difference from the normal break-even analysis is that here we use a positive target net income instead of a break-even net income of $0.

Another way of getting the same answer is to use your knowledge of the break-even point and adopt an incremental approach. The phrase **incremental effect** refers to the change in total results (such as revenue, expenses, or income) under a new condition in comparison with some given or known condition.

In this case, the given condition is the 60,000-unit break-even point. We would recover all expenses at that volume. Therefore, the change or increment in net income for every unit of sales beyond 60,000 would be equal to the unit contribution margin of $1.50 − $1.20 = $.30. If $1,440 were the target net profit, $1,440 ÷ $.30 would show that the target volume must exceed the break-even volume by 4,800 units; it would therefore be 60,000 + 4,800 = 64,800 units.

To find the answer in terms of dollar sales, multiply 64,800 units by $1.50 or use the formula

$$\text{target sales volume in dollars} = \frac{\text{fixed expenses} + \text{target net income}}{\text{contribution-margin ratio}}$$

$$= \frac{\$18,000 + \$1,440}{.20} = \$97,200 \qquad (6)$$

To solve directly for sales dollars with the incremental approach, we would start at the break-even point in dollar sales of $90,000. Every sales dollar beyond that point contributes $.20 to net profit. Divide $1,440 by $.20. Dollar sales must exceed the break-even volume by $7,200 to produce a net profit of $1,440. Thus, the total dollar sales would be $90,000 + $7,200 = $97,200.

The following table summarizes these computations:

	Break-Even Point	Increment	New Condition
Volume in units	60,000	4,800	64,800
Sales	$90,000	$7,200	$97,200
Variable expenses	72,000	5,760	77,760
Contribution margin	$18,000	$1,440	$19,440
Fixed expenses	18,000	—	18,000
Net income	$ 0	$1,440	$ 1,440

Multiple Changes in Key Factors

So far, we have seen changes in only one CVP factor at a time. In the real world, managers often make decisions about the probable effects of multiple factor changes. For example, Boeing may cut the price of its airplanes to stimulate a larger volume of sales. Mars might decrease the size of its Snickers candy bar, saving variable costs and increasing the unit contribution margin, but also decreasing sales volume. Or Medtronic might automate the production of its insulin infusion pump, replacing variable costs of labor with fixed costs of equipment.

Consider our vending-machine example. Suppose Winston is considering locking the vending machines from 6:00 PM to 6:00 AM, which she estimates will save $2,460 in wages monthly. However, the cutback from 24-hour service would hurt volume substantially because many nighttime employees use the machines. Should the machines remain available 24 hours per day? Assume that monthly sales would decline by 10,000 units from the current sales level. We will perform the analysis for two months representing the lowest and highest predicted sales volume: (1) 62,000 units and (2) 90,000 units.

We will consider two approaches. The first is to construct and solve equations for conditions that prevail under each alternative and select the volume level that yields the highest net income.

Regardless of the current volume level, be it 62,000 or 90,000 units, if we accept the prediction that sales will decline by 10,000 units, closing from 6:00 PM to 6:00 AM will decrease net income by $540:

	Decline from 62,000 to 52,000 Units		Decline from 90,000 to 80,000 Units	
Units	62,000	52,000	90,000	80,000
Sales	$93,000	$78,000	$135,000	$120,000
Variable expenses	74,400	62,400	108,000	96,000
Total contribution margin	$18,600	$15,600	$ 27,000	$ 24,000
Fixed expenses	18,000	15,540	18,000	15,540
Net income	$ 600	$ 60	$ 9,000	$ 8,460
Change in net income	($540)		($540)	

A second approach—an incremental approach—is quicker and simpler. Simplicity is important to managers because it keeps the analysis from being cluttered by irrelevant and potentially confusing data.

What does the insightful manager see in this situation? First, whether the vending machines sell 62,000 or 90,000 units is irrelevant to the decision at hand. The issue is the decline in volume, which is 10,000 units in either case. The essence of this decision is whether the savings in fixed costs exceed the loss in total contribution-margin dollars.

Lost total contribution margin, 10,000 units at $.30	$3,000
Less savings in fixed expenses	−2,460
Prospective decline in net income	$ 540

The incremental analysis also shows that locking the vending machines from 6:00 PM to 6:00 AM would cause a $540 decrease in monthly net income. Whichever way you analyze it, locking the machines is not a sound financial decision.

CVP Analysis and Computer-Based Spreadsheets

The use of spreadsheets simplifies the examination of multiple changes in key factors in a CVP model. Managers in a variety of organizations use a personal computer and a spreadsheet-based CVP modeling program to study combinations of changes in selling prices, unit variable costs, fixed costs, and desired profits. Many nonprofit organizations also use computerized CVP modeling. For example, some private universities have models that help measure how decisions, such as raising tuition, adding programs, and closing dormitories during winter holidays, will affect financial results. The computer quickly calculates the results of changes and can display them both numerically and graphically.

Consider our vending machine example. Exhibit 2-8 is a sample spreadsheet that shows what the sales level would have to be at three different fixed expense levels and three different variable expense levels to reach three different income levels. The computer calculates the 27 different sales levels rapidly and without error. Managers can insert any numbers they want for fixed expenses (column A), variable expense percentage (column B), target net income (row 3 of columns C, D, and E), and the computer will compute the sales level.

In addition to speed and convenience, computers allow a more sophisticated approach to CVP analysis than the one illustrated in this chapter. The assumptions we listed on page 48 are necessary to simplify the analysis enough for most managers to construct a CVP model by hand. Computer analysts, however, can construct a model that does not require all the simplifications. Computer models can include multiple cost drivers, nonlinear relationships between costs and cost drivers, varying sales mixes, and analyses that need not be restricted to a relevant range.

The use of computer models is a cost-benefit issue. The reliability of these models depends on the accuracy of their underlying assumptions about how revenues and costs will actually be affected. More complex models often require fewer assumptions and, thus, are more reliable. However, sometimes the costs of modeling exceed the value of the improved quality of management decisions. In small organizations, simplified CVP models often are accurate enough; more sophisticated (and more expensive) modeling may be unwarranted.

Exhibit 2-8
Spreadsheet Analysis of CVP Relationships

	A	B	C	D	E
1				Sales Required to Earn	
2	Fixed	Variable		Annual Net Income of	
3	Expenses	Expense %	$ 2,000	$ 4,000	$ 6,000
4					
5	$4,000	0.40	$10,000*	$13,333	$16,667
6	$4,000	0.44	$10,714*	$14,286	$17,857
7	$4,000	0.48	$11,538*	$15,385	$19,231
8	$6,000	0.40	$13,333	$16,667	$20,000
9	$6,000	0.44	$14,286	$17,857	$21,429
10	$6,000	0.48	$15,385	$19,231	$23,077
11	$8,000	0.40	$16,667	$20,000	$23,333
12	$8,000	0.44	$17,857	$21,429	$25,000
13	$8,000	0.48	$19,231	$23,077	$26,923

*(A5 + C3)/(1 − B5) = ($4,000 + $2,000)/(1 − $.40) = $10,000
(A6 + C3)/(1 − B6) = ($4,000 + $2,000)/(1 − $.44) = $10,714
(A7 + C3)/(1 − B7) = ($4,000 + $2,000)/(1 − $.48) = $11,538

Business First

Did Blockbuster Violate Disney Contract? Accounting Disagreement or Ethical Issue?

In early 2003, the Walt Disney Company sued Blockbuster, claiming that Blockbuster had violated a 1997 agreement between the two companies. Prior to the agreement, Blockbuster purchased videos from Disney for about $65 each and kept all the rental revenue. Under the pact, Blockbuster agreed to purchase movies from Disney for $7 a copy and then pay the studio a portion of the revenue from each rental.

The contract allowed Blockbuster to buy more copies of each video, which led to the guarantee that customers could rely on Blockbuster to have a copy of any movie they wanted or else the rental was free. With this policy, Blockbuster increased its market share of the video rental market from 28% to 40%. Essentially, Blockbuster turned a fixed cost, $65 per tape, into primarily a variable cost, with a small $7 fixed-cost portion and a larger variable-cost portion that depended on how much revenue Blockbuster generated from its rentals.

The arrangement was similar to that between the owners of shopping malls and many of their retail store tenants. Each store pays a monthly rental fee plus a percentage of its sales. Just as shopping mall owners rely on their tenants to truthfully report their sales, Disney relied on Blockbuster to correctly account for its video rentals.

In addition, Blockbuster and Disney also agreed on when Blockbuster could sell old rental tapes. Since these were so inexpensive for Blockbuster, selling them could be a lucrative business. But Disney did not want these low-cost tapes competing with its own videotape sales. Thus, it placed restrictions on when Blockbuster could sell them.

In the suit, Disney claimed that Blockbuster improperly deducted "promotional" credits from its gross rental fees, failed to account for "hundreds of thousands" of missing videos, and sold videos prematurely. Disney had to rely on Blockbuster to correctly account for its rental revenues and inventory of tapes. Blockbuster claimed that its accounting was in accordance with the original agreement.

This is an example where good ethics and good accounting are both important. The original agreement promised benefits to both companies—more rental income for Disney on hit movies and more cost-structure flexibility for Blockbuster. But such a contract will not work if each party cannot trust the other. It's not clear who is right in this case, but both companies were hurt by the allegations. At a minimum, both will need to include better monitoring provisions in future contracts because other companies will suspect Disney of trying to get more than it deserves and Blockbuster of playing accounting tricks to minimize its payment to Disney.

Source: "Disney Sues Blockbuster Over Contract," *New York Times*, January 4, 2003; "Disney Sues Top Video Chain," *Los Angeles Times*, January 3, 2003.

Additional Uses of Cost-Volume Analysis

Best Cost Structure

Analyzing cost-volume-profit relationships is an important management responsibility. Managers are well advised to gain a thorough understanding of the organization's cost structure—the combination of variable- and fixed-cost resources. For example, purchasing automated machinery may raise fixed costs but reduce labor cost per unit. Conversely, it may be wise to reduce fixed costs to obtain a more favorable combination. Thus, a company may decide to compensate its sales force via sales commissions (variable costs) rather than pay them salaries (a fixed cost). Another example of exchanging a fixed cost for a variable cost is a contract **Blockbuster** signed with **Disney** and other major studios. Instead of buying video tapes for $65 each, a fixed cost for each tape, Blockbuster paid only a $7 fixed cost and an additional variable cost equal to a percentage of the rental revenues. You can see one result of this contract in the Business First box above.

Generally, companies that spend heavily for advertising are willing to do so because they have high contribution-margin percentages (e.g., airlines, cigarette, and cosmetic companies). Conversely, companies with low contribution-margin percentages usually spend less for advertising and promotion (e.g., manufacturers of industrial equipment). As a result, two companies with the same unit sales volumes at the same unit prices could have different attitudes toward risking an advertising outlay. Assume the following:

	Perfume Company	Janitorial Service Company
Unit sales volume	200,000 bottles	200,000 square feet
Dollar sales at $10 per unit	$2,000,000	$2,000,000
Variable costs	200,000	1,700,000
Total contribution margin	$1,800,000	$ 300,000
Contribution-margin percentage	90%	15%

Suppose each company can increase sales volume by 10% with the same expenditure for advertising:

	Perfume Company	Janitorial Service Company
Increase in sales volume, 20,000 × $10	$200,000	$200,000
Increase in total contribution margin, 90%, 15%	180,000	30,000

The perfume company would be inclined to increase advertising considerably to boost the total contribution margin by $180,000. In contrast, the janitorial service company would be foolhardy to spend large amounts to increase the total contribution margin by only $30,000.

Note that when the contribution margin as a percentage of sales is low, great increases in volume are necessary to generate increases in net profits. On the other hand, decreases in profit are also small as volume decreases. High contribution-margin ratios have the opposite effect—large increases in profits as sales grow but also large decreases in profits if sales fall.

Operating Leverage

In addition to weighing the varied effects of changes in fixed and variable costs, managers need to consider their firm's ratio of fixed to variable costs, called **operating leverage**. In highly leveraged companies—those with high fixed costs and low variable costs—small changes in sales volume result in large changes in net income. Changes in sales volume have a smaller effect on companies with less leverage (that is, lower fixed costs and higher variable costs).

Exhibit 2-9 shows cost behavior relationships at two firms, one highly leveraged and one with low leverage. The firm with higher leverage has fixed costs of $14,000 and variable cost per unit of $.10. The firm with lower leverage has fixed costs of only $2,000 but variable costs of $.25 per unit. Expected sales at both companies are 80,000 units at $.30 per unit. At this sales level, both firms would have net incomes of $2,000. If sales fall short of 80,000 units, profits drop most sharply for the highly leveraged business. If sales exceed 80,000 units, however, profits also increase most sharply for the highly leveraged concern.

The highly leveraged alternative is more risky. Why? Because it provides the highest possible net income and the highest possible net losses. In other words, net income is highly variable, depending on the actual level of sales. The low-leverage alternative is less risky because variations in sales lead to only a small variability in net income. At sales of 90,000 units, net income

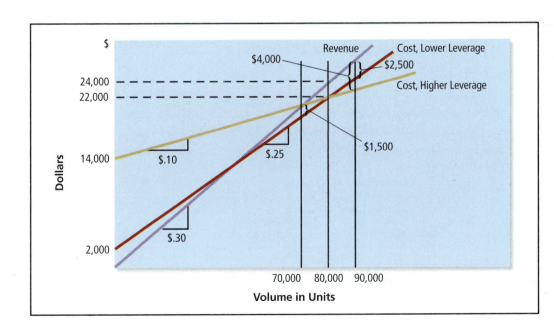

Exhibit 2-9
High Versus Low Operating Leverage

is $4,000 for the higher-leveraged firm but only $2,500 for the lower-leveraged firm. At sales of 70,000 units, however, the higher-leveraged firm has zero profits, compared to $1,500 for the lower-leveraged firm.

Margin of Safety

CVP analysis can also help managers assess risk by providing a measure of the margin of safety. The **margin of safety** shows how far sales can fall below the planned level of sales before losses occur. It compares the level of planned sales with the break-even point:

$$\text{margin of safety} = \text{planned unit sales} - \text{break-even unit sales}$$

The larger the margin of safety, the less likely it is that the company will have an operating loss, that is, operate below the break-even point. A small margin of safety may indicate a more risky situation. If Amy Winston in our vending machine example had predicted a sales volume of 80,000 units, the margin of safety would be 20,000 units:

$$\text{margin of safety} = 80,000 \text{ units} - 60,000 \text{ units} = 20,000 \text{ units}$$

Contribution Margin and Gross Margin

Objective 6

Differentiate between contribution margin and gross margin.

This chapter has focused on the contribution margin. However, accountants also use a similar term, *gross margin*, to mean something quite different. Too often people confuse the terms *contribution margin* and *gross margin*. **Gross margin**, also called **gross profit**, is the excess of sales over the cost of goods sold. **Cost of goods sold** is the cost of the merchandise that a company acquires or produces and then sells. Compare the gross margin with the contribution margin:

$$\text{gross margin} = \text{sales price} - \text{cost of goods sold}$$
$$\text{contribution margin} = \text{sales price} - \text{all variable expenses}$$

Exhibit 2-10 shows costs divided on two different dimensions. As shown at the bottom of the exhibit, the gross margin uses the division on the production or acquisition cost versus selling and administrative cost dimension, and the contribution margin uses the division based on the variable-cost versus fixed-cost dimension.

In our vending-machine illustration, the contribution margin and the gross margin are identical because the cost of goods sold is the only variable cost:

Sales	$1.50
Variable costs: acquisition cost of unit sold	1.20
Contribution margin and gross margin are equal	$ .30

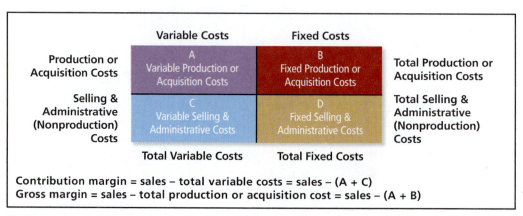

Contribution margin = sales – total variable costs = sales – (A + C)
Gross margin = sales – total production or acquisition cost = sales – (A + B)

Exhibit 2-10
Costs for Gross Margin and Contribution Margin

Now, suppose the firm had to pay a commission of $.12 per unit sold:

		Contribution Margin	Gross Margin
Sales		$1.50	$1.50
Acquisition cost of unit sold	$1.20		1.20
Variable commission	.12		
Total variable expense		1.32	
Contribution margin		$ .18	
Gross margin			$ .30

Nonprofit Application

Consider how cost-volume-profit relationships apply to nonprofit organizations. Suppose a city has a $100,000 lump-sum budget appropriation to conduct a counseling program for drug addicts. The variable costs for counseling are $400 per patient per year. Fixed costs are $60,000 in the relevant range of 50 to 150 patients. If the city spends the entire budget appropriation, how many patients can it serve in a year?

We can use the break-even equation to solve the problem. Let N be the number of patients, substitute the $100,000 lump-sum budget for sales, and note that sales equals variable expenses plus fixed expenses if the city completely spends its budget.

$$\text{sales} = \text{variable expenses} + \text{fixed expenses}$$
$$\$100{,}000 \text{ lump sum} = \$400N + \$60{,}000$$
$$\$400N = \$100{,}000 - \$60{,}000$$
$$N = \$40{,}000 \div \$400$$
$$N = 100 \text{ patients}$$

The city can serve 100 patients. Now, suppose the city cuts the total budget appropriation for the following year by 10%. Fixed costs will be unaffected, but service will decline.

$$\text{sales} = \text{variable expenses} + \text{fixed expenses}$$
$$\$90{,}000 = \$400N + \$60{,}000$$
$$\$400N = \$90{,}000 - \$60{,}000$$
$$N = \$30{,}000 \div \$400$$
$$N = 75 \text{ patients}$$

The percentage reduction in service is $(100 - 75) \div 100 = 25\%$, which is more than the 10% reduction in the budget. Unless the city restructures its operations, the service volume must fall by 25% to stay within budget.

A graphical presentation of this analysis is in Exhibit 2-11. Note that lump-sum revenue is a horizontal line on the graph.

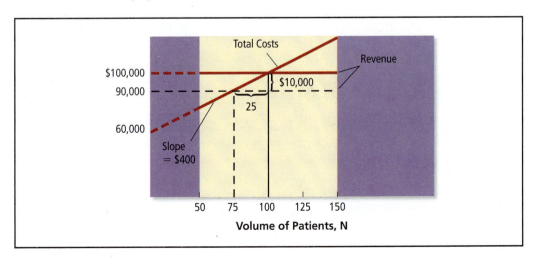

Exhibit 2-11
Graphical Presentation of Nonprofit Application

Summary Problem for Your Review

PROBLEM

A summary of the budgeted income statement of Port Williams Gift Shop follows:

Net revenue	$ 800,000
Less expenses, including $400,000 of fixed expenses	880,000
Net loss	$(80,000)

The manager believes that an additional outlay of $200,000 for advertising will increase sales substantially.

1. At what sales volume in dollars will the shop break even after spending $200,000 on advertising?
2. What sales volume in dollars will result in a net profit of $40,000 after spending the $200,000 on advertising?

SOLUTION

1. Note that all data are in dollars, not units. Most companies have many products, so the overall break-even analysis deals with dollar sales, not units. The variable expenses are $880,000 – $400,000 = $480,000. The variable-cost ratio is $480,000 ÷ $800,000 = .60. (Remember to divide variable costs by sales, not by total costs.) Therefore, the contribution-margin ratio is .40. Let S = break-even sales in dollars. Then

$$S - \text{variable expenses} - \text{fixed expenses} = \text{net profit}$$
$$S - .60S - (\$400,000 + \$200,000) = 0$$
$$.40S = \$600,000$$
$$S = \frac{\$600,000}{.40} = \frac{\text{fixed expenses}}{\text{contribution-margin ratio}}$$
$$S = \$1,500,000$$

2.

$$\text{required sales} = \frac{(\text{fixed expenses} + \text{target net profit})}{\text{contribution-margin ratio}}$$

$$\text{required sales} = \frac{(\$600,000 + \$40,000)}{.40} = \frac{\$640,000}{.40}$$

$$\text{required sales} = \$1,600,000$$

Alternatively, we can use an incremental approach and reason that all dollar sales beyond the $1.5 million break-even point will result in a 40% contribution to net profit. Divide $40,000 by .40. Therefore, sales must be $100,000 beyond the $1.5 million break-even point to produce a net profit of $40,000.

Highlights to Remember

1. **Explain how cost drivers affect cost behavior.** A cost driver is an output measure that causes the use of costly resources. When the level of an activity changes, the level of the cost driver or output measure will also change, causing changes in costs.

2. **Show how changes in cost-driver levels affect variable and fixed costs.** Different types of costs behave in different ways. If the cost of the resource used changes in proportion to changes in the cost-driver level, the resource is a variable-cost resource (its costs are variable). If the cost of the resource used does not change because of cost-driver level changes, the resource is a fixed-cost resource (its costs are fixed).

3. **Calculate break-even sales volume in total dollars and total units.** We can approach CVP analysis (sometimes called break-even analysis) graphically or with equations. To calculate the break-even point in total units, divide the fixed costs by the unit contribution margin. To calculate the break-even point in total dollars (sales dollars), divide the fixed costs by the contribution-margin ratio.

4. **Create a cost-volume-profit graph and understand the assumptions behind it.** We can create a cost-volume-profit graph by drawing revenue and total cost lines as functions of the cost-driver level. Be sure to recognize the limitations of CVP analysis and that it assumes constant efficiency, sales mix, and inventory levels.

5. **Calculate sales volume in total dollars and total units to reach a target profit.** Managers use CVP analysis to compute the sales needed to achieve a target profit or to examine the effects on profit of changes in factors such as fixed costs, variable costs, or cost-driver volume.

6. **Differentiate between contribution margin and gross margin.** The contribution margin—the difference between sales price and variable costs—is an important concept. Do not confuse it with gross margin, the difference between sales price and cost of goods sold. ■

Appendix 2A: Sales-Mix Analysis

Objective 7

Explain the effects of sales mix on profits.

To emphasize fundamental ideas, the cost-volume-profit analysis in this chapter focused on a single product. Nearly all companies, however, sell more than one product. Thus, they must be concerned with sales mix, which you will recall from p. 48 is the relative proportions or combinations of quantities of products that comprise total sales. If the proportions of the mix change, the cost-volume-profit relationships also change.

Suppose Ramos Company has two products, wallets (W) and key cases (K). The income budget follows:

	Wallets (W)	Key Cases (K)	Total
Sales in units	300,000	75,000	375,000
Sales @ $8 and $5	$2,400,000	$375,000	$2,775,000
Variable expenses @ $7 and $3	2,100,000	225,000	2,325,000
Contribution margins @ $1 and $2	$ 300,000	$150,000	$ 450,000
Fixed expenses			180,000
Net income			$ 270,000

What is the break-even point for each product? The typical answer assumes a constant mix of four units of W for every unit of K. Therefore, let K = number of units of product K to break even, and 4K = number of units of product W to break even:

$$sales - variable\ expenses - fixed\ expenses = zero\ net\ income$$
$$[\$8(4K) + \$5(K)] - [\$7(4K) + \$3(K)] - \$180,000 = 0$$
$$\$32K + \$5K - \$28K - \$3K - \$180,000 = 0$$
$$\$6K = \$180,000$$
$$K = 30,000$$
$$4K = 120,000 = W$$

The break-even point is 30,000K + 120,000W = 150,000 units.

This is the only break-even point for a sales mix of four wallets for every key case. Clearly, however, there are other break-even points for other sales mixes. For instance, suppose Ramos Company sells only key cases, and fixed expenses stay at $180,000.

$$break\text{-}even\ point\ in\ units = \frac{fixed\ expenses}{contribution\ margin\ per\ unit}$$
$$= \frac{\$180,000}{\$2}$$
$$= 90,000\ key\ cases$$

If Ramos sells only wallets

$$\text{break-even point} = \frac{\$180,000}{\$1} = 180,000 \text{ wallets}$$

We can see that the break-even point could be 180,000 units (of wallets), 90,000 units (of key cases), or 150,000 units (30,000 key cases and 120,000 wallets).

Managers are not interested in the break-even point for its own sake. Instead, they want to know how changes in a planned sales mix will affect net income. When the sales mix changes, the break-even point and the expected net income at various sales levels change also. For example, suppose overall actual total sales were equal to the budget of 375,000 units. However, Ramos sold only 50,000 key cases.

	Wallets (W)	Key Cases (K)	Total
Sales in units	325,000	50,000	375,000
Sales @ $8 and $5	$2,600,000	$250,000	$2,850,000
Variable expenses @ $7 and $3	2,275,000	150,000	2,425,000
Contribution margins @ $1 and $2	$ 325,000	$100,000	$ 425,000
Fixed expenses			180,000
Net income			$ 245,000

The change in sales mix has resulted in a $245,000 actual net income rather than the $270,000 budgeted net income, an unfavorable difference of $25,000. The budgeted and actual sales in number of units were identical, but the proportion of sales of the product bearing the higher unit contribution margin declined.

Managers usually want to maximize the sales of all their products. Faced with limited resources and time, however, executives prefer to generate the most profitable sales mix achievable. For example, **Neenah Paper, Inc.** included the following in its 2008 annual report: "Net prices increased approximately three and one half percent on average due to . . . a more favorable mix. The mix reflected an increased proportion of sales of higher priced products." **Nissan** had the opposite experience in the first quarter of 2007. Joji Tagawa, Nissan's corporate vice president, explained its fall in profits: "Deterioration in our product mix is the most remarkable in the U.S. market where sales of trucks are decreasing."

Profitability of a given product helps guide executives who must decide to emphasize or deemphasize particular products. For example, given limited production facilities or limited time of sales personnel, should we emphasize wallets or key cases? Other factors beyond the contribution margin can affect these decisions. Chapter 5 explores some of these factors, including the importance of the amount of profit per unit of time rather than per unit of product.

Appendix 2B: Impact of Income Taxes

Objective 8

Compute cost-volume-profit relationships on an after-tax basis.

Thus far we have ignored income taxes. In most nations, however, private enterprises must pay income taxes. Reconsider the vending machine example in this chapter. As part of our CVP analysis, we discussed the sales necessary to achieve a target income before income taxes of $1,440. If Boeing pays income tax at a rate of 40%, the new result would be

Income before income tax	$1,440	100%
Income tax	576	40
Net income	$ 864	60%

Note that

$$\text{net income} = \text{income before income taxes} - .40 \text{ (income before income taxes)}$$
$$\text{net income} = .60 \text{ (income before income taxes)}$$
$$\text{income before income taxes} = \frac{\text{net income}}{.60}$$

or

$$\text{target income before income taxes} = \frac{\text{target after-tax net income}}{1 - \text{tax rate}}$$
$$\text{target income before income taxes} = \frac{\$864}{1 - .40} = \frac{\$864}{.60} = \$1,440$$

Suppose the target net income after taxes was $864. The only change in the general equation approach would be on the right-hand side of the following equation:

$$\text{target sales} - \text{variable expenses} - \text{fixed expenses} = \frac{\text{target after-tax net income}}{1 - \text{tax rate}}$$

Thus, letting N be the number of units to be sold at $1.50 each with a variable cost of $1.20 each and total fixed costs of $18,000,

$$\$1.50N - \$1.20N - \$18,000 = \frac{\$864}{1 - .4}$$
$$\$.30N = \$18,000 + \frac{\$864}{.6}$$
$$\$.18N = \$10,800 + \$864 = 11,664$$
$$N = \$11,664 \div \$.18 = 64,800 \text{ units}$$

Sales of 64,800 units produce an after-tax profit of $864 as shown here and a before-tax profit of $1,440 as shown in the chapter.

Suppose the target net income after taxes was $1,440. The volume needed would rise to 68,000 units, as follows:

$$\$1.50N - \$1.20N - \$18,000 = \frac{\$1,440}{1 - .4}$$
$$\$.30N = \$18,000 + \frac{\$1,440}{.6}$$
$$\$.18N = \$10,800 + \$1,440 = 12,240$$
$$N = \$12,240 \div \$.18 = 68,000 \text{ units}$$

As a shortcut to computing the effects of volume on the change in after-tax income, use the formula

$$\text{change in net income} = \left(\begin{array}{c} \text{change in volume} \\ \text{in units} \end{array} \right) \times \left(\begin{array}{c} \text{contribution margin} \\ \text{per unit} \end{array} \right) \times (1 - \text{tax rate})$$

In our example, suppose operations were at a level of 64,800 units and $864 after-tax net income. The manager is wondering how much after-tax net income would increase if sales become 68,000 units.

$$\text{change in net income} = (68,000 - 64,800) \times \$.30 \times (1 - .4)$$
$$= 3,200 \times \$.30 \times .60 = 3,200 \times \$.18$$
$$= \$576$$

In brief, each unit beyond the break-even point adds to after-tax net profit at the unit contribution margin multiplied by (1 – income tax rate).

Throughout our illustration, the break-even point itself does not change. Why? Because there is no income tax at a level of zero profits.

Accounting Vocabulary

break-even point, p. 43
contribution margin, p. 44
contribution-margin
    percentage, p. 45
contribution-margin ratio, p. 45
cost behavior, p. 35
cost driver, p. 35
cost of goods sold, p. 54

cost-volume-profit (CVP)
    analysis, p. 42
fixed cost, p. 37
gross margin, p. 54
gross profit, p. 54
incremental effect, p. 49
margin of safety, p. 54
marginal income, p. 44
operating leverage, p. 53

relevant range, p. 41
sales mix, p. 48
total contribution margin, p. 44
unit contribution margin, p. 44
variable cost, p. 37
variable-cost percentage, p. 45
variable-cost ratio, p. 45

Fundamental Assignment Material

2-A1 Fixed- and Variable-Cost Behavior

Consider a particular **Boeing** plant. Maintaining a clean working environment is important to Boeing. Cleaning the plant is the responsibility of the maintenance department. Two of the resources needed to clean the plant are labor and cleaning supplies. The cost driver for both resources is square feet cleaned. Plant cleaning laborers are paid the same wages regardless of the number of times the plant is cleaned. Cleaning supplies is a variable cost. The 40,000 square foot plant is thoroughly cleaned from four to eight times a month depending on the level and stage of production. For the most recent month, March, the plant was cleaned four times. The March cost of labor was $24,000 and cleaning supplies used cost $9,600. The production schedule for the next quarter (April through June) indicates that the plant will need to be cleaned five, six, and eight times respectively.

1. Prepare a table that shows how labor cost, cleaning supplies cost, total cost, and total cost per square feet cleaned changes in response to the square feet cleaned. What is the predicted total cost of plant cleaning for the next quarter?
2. Suppose Boeing can hire an outside cleaning company to clean the plant as needed. The charge rate for cleaning is $5,900 per plant cleaning. If the outside cleaning company is hired, Boeing can lay off the workers who are now cleaning the plant and will spend nothing for cleaning supplies. Will Boeing save money with the outside cleaning company over the next quarter? Prepare a schedule that supports your answer.

2-A2 Cost-Volume-Profit and Vending Machines

Enriquez Food Services Company operates and services snack vending machines located in restaurants, gas stations, and factories in four southwestern states. The machines are rented from the manufacturer. In addition, Enriquez must rent the space occupied by its machines. The following expense and revenue relationships pertain to a contemplated expansion program of 40 machines.

Fixed monthly expenses follow:

Machine rental: 40 machines @ $53.50	$2,140
Space rental: 40 locations @ $38.80	1,552
Part-time wages to service the additional 40 machines	2,008
Other fixed costs	300
Total monthly fixed costs	$6,000

Other data follow:

	Per Unit (Snack)	Per $100 of Sales
Selling price	$1.00	100%
Cost of snack	.80	80
Contribution margin	$ .20	20%

These questions relate to the given data unless otherwise noted. Consider each question independently.

1. What is the monthly break-even point in number of units (snacks)? In dollar sales?
2. If 40,000 units were sold, what would be the company's net income?
3. If the space rental cost was doubled, what would be the monthly break-even point in number of units? In dollar sales?
4. Refer to the original data. If, in addition to the fixed space rent, Enriquez Food Services Company paid the vending machine manufacturer $.02 per unit sold, what would be the monthly break-even point in number of units? In dollar sales?
5. Refer to the original data. If, in addition to the fixed rent, Enriquez paid the machine manufacturer $.05 for each unit sold in excess of the break-even point, what would the new net income be if 40,000 units were sold?

2-A3 Exercises in Cost-Volume-Profit Relationships

Barkins Moving Company specializes in hauling heavy goods over long distances. The company's revenues and expenses depend on revenue-miles, a measure that combines both weights and mileage. Summarized budget data for next year are based on predicted total revenue miles of 800,000. At that level of volume, and at any level of volume between 700,000 and 900,000 revenue miles, the company's fixed costs are $120,000. The selling price and variable costs are

Per Revenue-Mile	
Average selling price (revenue)	$1.50
Average variable expenses	1.30

1. Compute the budgeted net income. Ignore income taxes.
2. Management is trying to decide how various possible conditions or decisions might affect net income. Compute the new net income for each of the following changes. Consider each case independently.
    a. A 10% increase in sales price.
    b. A 10% increase in revenue miles.
    c. A 10% increase in variable expenses.
    d. A 10% increase in fixed expenses.
    e. An average decrease in selling price of $.03 per revenue mile and a 5% increase in revenue miles. Refer to the original data.
    f. An average increase in selling price of $.05 and a 10% decrease in revenue miles.
    g. A 10% increase in fixed expenses in the form of more advertising and a 5% increase in revenue miles.

2-B1 Fixed- and Variable-Cost Behavior

Outback Steakhouse has 970 restaurants offering steak, chicken, and seafood served in an Australian-themed atmosphere. Maintaining a clean environment for customers is a key success factor at Outback. Each restaurant is cleaned regularly after closing. In addition to regular cleaning, from 5 to 20 times a month, depending on various factors including the amount of business, a special treatment is given to the floors consisting of breaking down the old wax and rewaxing. So the total number of times a restaurant is cleaned varies from 35 to 50 times a month.

The two most costly resources needed to clean an Outback restaurant are labor and supplies. The cost driver for both resources is square feet cleaned. Cleaning laborers are paid the same wages regardless of the number of times a restaurant is cleaned. Cleaning supplies is a variable cost. The cost of supplies used per square foot for regular and special cleaning is about the same. Suppose one of the local Outback restaurants in Orlando has 5,000 square feet. In October, the restaurant was cleaned 35 times. The cost of cleaning labor was $30,000 for October, and cleaning supplies cost $10,500. The months of November and December are typically much busier, so the restaurant manager expects to clean 45 times and 50 times in November and December, respectively.

1. Prepare a table that shows how labor cost, cleaning supplies cost, total cost, and total cost per square feet cleaned changes in response to square feet cleaned. Use volumes of 35, 40, 45, and 50 times cleaned. What is the predicted total cost of cleaning for November and December?
2. Suppose Outback can hire an outside cleaning company to clean the restaurant as needed. The charge rate for cleaning is $.20 per square foot. If the outside cleaning company is hired, Outback can lay off the workers who are now cleaning and will spend nothing on cleaning supplies. Will Outback save money with the outside cleaning company over the next two months? Prepare a

schedule that supports your answer. What information would you need to make a recommendation about hiring the outside cleaning company on a permanent basis?

2-B2 Cost-Volume-Profit at a Day Care Facility

Beth Durham opened Beth's Corner, a small day care facility, just over 2 years ago. After a rocky start, Beth's Corner has been thriving. Durham is now preparing a budget for November 20X7.

Monthly fixed costs for Beth's Corner are

Rent	$ 800
Salaries	1,400
Other fixed costs	100
Total fixed costs	$ 2,300

The salary is for Ann Page, the only employee, who works with Durham by caring for the children. Durham does not pay herself a salary, but she receives the excess of revenues over costs each month.

The cost driver for variable costs is "child-days." One child-day is one day in day care for one child, and the variable cost is $10 per child-day. The facility is open from 6:00 AM to 6:00 PM weekdays (that is, Monday–Friday), and there are 22 weekdays in November 20X7. An average day has 8 children attending Beth's Corner. State law prohibits Beth's Corner from having more than 14 children, a limit it has never reached. Durham charges $30 per day per child, regardless of how long the child is at the facility.

1. What is the break-even point for November in child-days? In revenue dollars?
2. Suppose attendance for November 20X7 is equal to the average, resulting in 22 × 8 = 176 child-days. What amount will Durham have left after paying all her expenses?
3. Suppose both costs and attendance are difficult to predict. Compute the amount Durham will have left after paying all her expenses for each of the following situations. Consider each case independently.
   a. Average attendance is 9 children per day instead of 8, generating 198 child-days.
   b. Variable costs increase to $12 per child-day.
   c. Rent increases by $220 per month.
   d. Durham spends $300 on advertising (a fixed cost) in November, which increases average daily attendance to 9.5 children.
   e. Durham begins charging $33 per day on November 1, and average daily attendance slips to 7 children.

2-B3 Exercises in Cost-Volume-Profit Relationships

Each problem is unrelated to the others.

1. Given: Selling price per unit, $20; total fixed expenses, $5,000; variable expenses per unit, $16. Find break-even sales in units.
2. Given: Sales, $40,000; variable expenses, $30,000; fixed expenses, $8,000; net income, $2,000. Find break-even sales in dollars.
3. Given: Selling price per unit, $30; total fixed expenses, $33,000; variable expenses per unit, $14. Find total sales in units to achieve a profit of $7,000, assuming no change in selling price.
4. Given: Sales, $50,000; variable expenses, $20,000; fixed expenses, $20,000; net income, $10,000. Assume no change in selling price; find net income if activity volume increases by 10%.
5. Given: Selling price per unit, $40; total fixed expenses, $80,000; variable expenses per unit, $30. Assume that variable expenses are reduced by 20% per unit, and the total fixed expenses are increased by 10%. Find the sales in units to achieve a profit of $20,000, assuming no change in selling price.

MyAccountingLab ## Additional Assignment Material

QUESTIONS

2-1 "Cost behavior is simply identification of cost drivers and their relationships to costs." Comment.

2-2 Give two rules of thumb to use when analyzing cost behavior.

2-3 Give three examples of variable costs and of fixed costs.

2-4 Why is the word *immediately* used in the definition of *fixed cost* and not in the definition of *variable cost*?

2-5 "It is confusing to think of fixed costs on a per-unit basis." Do you agree? Why or why not?

2-6 "All costs are either fixed or variable. The only difficulty in cost analysis is determining which of the two categories each cost belongs to." Do you agree? Explain.

2-7 "The relevant range pertains to fixed costs, not variable costs." Do you agree? Explain.

2-8 Identify the major simplifying assumption that underlies CVP analysis.

2-9 "Classification of costs into variable and fixed categories depends on the decision situation." Explain.

2-10 "Contribution margin is the excess of sales over fixed costs." Do you agree? Explain.

2-11 Why is *break-even analysis* a misnomer?

2-12 "Companies in the same industry generally have about the same break-even point." Do you agree? Explain.

2-13 "It is essential to choose the right CVP method—equation, contribution margin, or graphical. If you pick the wrong one, your analysis will be faulty." Do you agree? Explain.

2-14 Describe three ways of lowering a break-even point.

2-15 "Incremental analysis is quicker, but it has no other advantage over an analysis of all costs and revenues associated with each alternative." Do you agree? Why or why not?

2-16 Define operating leverage and explain why a highly leveraged company may be risky.

2-17 Suppose a company with high operating leverage is also operating at near capacity for all its fixed-cost resources. How could an increase in sales volume result in decreasing economies of scale for this company?

2-18 What is the relationship between the margin of safety and the break-even point?

2-19 "The contribution margin and gross margin are always equal." Do you agree? Explain.

2-20 "CVP relationships are unimportant in nonprofit organizations." Do you agree? Explain.

2-21 Study Appendix 2A. A company sold two products. Total budgeted sales and total actual sales in number of units were identical. Actual unit variable costs and sales prices were the same as budgeted. Actual contribution margin was lower than budgeted. What could be the reason for the lower contribution margin?

2-22 Study Appendix 2B. Given a target after-tax net income, present the CVP formula for computing the income before income taxes.

2-23 Study Appendix 2B. Present the CVP formula for computing the effects of a change in volume on after-tax income.

CRITICAL THINKING EXERCISES

2-24 Marketing Function of Value-Chain and Cost Behavior
Refer to Exhibit 2-2. For the two examples of marketing costs given in Exhibit 2-2, describe their cost behavior in relation to the cost driver listed.

2-25 Production Function of Value-Chain and Cost Behavior
Refer to Exhibit 2-2. For the labor wages and depreciation of plant and machinery examples of production costs given in Exhibit 2-2, describe their cost behavior in relation to the cost driver listed.

2-26 Tenneco Automotive's Value Chain
Tenneco is a leading auto parts company that makes Walker exhaust systems and Monroe ride-control equipment (shocks, struts) for vehicle manufacturers and the replacement market, with annual revenues in excess of $5.9 billion. After reporting weak earnings, the company undertook a strategy to reduce its break-even point by 25% by selling excess capacity, reducing head count, and introducing new high-contribution-margin products. The company's senior vice president listed the key elements of the company's strategy, stating, "We are gaining momentum and transforming our North American aftermarket business with new products, new technology, new positioning strategies, and new pricing." For each of these "new" elements of Tenneco's aftermarket business strategy, list the value-chain function that is most applicable.

EXERCISES

2-27 Identifying Cost Drivers
The following list identifies several potential cost drivers for a manufacturing company that makes eight products. The company uses a JIT production system so it stores finished product for a very limited time. The eight products vary substantially in size from small (plastic casings for pens) to large (plastic casings for truck instrument panels). The company uses order-processing labor to process all orders from customers.
- Number of setups
- Setup time
- Square feet
- Cubic feet

- Cubic feet weeks
- Number of orders
- Number or order line items

For each of the following situations (activity and related resource), identify the best cost driver from the list and briefly justify your choice.

1. To produce a product, production mechanics must set up machinery. It takes about the same time to set up for a production run regardless of the product being produced. What is the best cost driver for the resources used during the setup activity?
2. Instead of the situation described in number 1, what driver should the company use for the setup activity if it takes longer to set up for complex products, such as the instrument panel casings, than for simple products, such as pen casings?
3. What driver should the company use for warehouse occupancy costs (depreciation and insurance)? The company uses the warehouse to store finished products.
4. What driver should the company use for the warehouse occupancy costs if it did not use a JIT system (that is, the company maintains inventories), and upon inspection one of the products had a thick layer of dust on it?
5. What driver should the company use for order processing cost? All orders are similar in terms of types of products ordered and it takes about the same time to process each type of product.
6. What driver should the company use for order processing cost if orders vary substantially in terms of types of products ordered and it takes about the same time to process each type of product?

2-28 Basic Review Exercises

Fill in the blanks for each of the following independent cases (ignore income taxes):

	Sales	Variable Expenses	Contribution Margin	Fixed Expenses	Net Income
1.	$900,000	$500,000	$ —	$330,000	$ —
2.	800,000	—	350,000	—	80,000
3.	—	600,000	360,000	250,000	—

2-29 Variable- and Fixed-Cost Behavior

Refer to Exhibits 2-2 and 2-4 on pages 37 and 38. Part of a company's marketing function is as described in Exhibit 2-2. Two of the many marketing-function activities are advertising and selling. The annual cost behavior of the resources used to perform the advertising activity is depicted in the diagram below using the same symbolic structure as defined in Exhibit 2-4. Which of the two costs is fixed? Which cost is variable? What is the total cost of advertising if the number of advertisements is 50? 100? Does the total cost of advertising double in response to a doubling of the cost driver level? Why or why not?

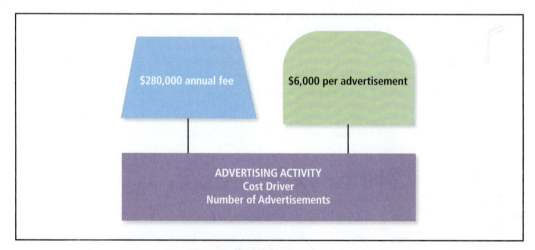

$280,000 annual fee

$6,000 per advertisement

ADVERTISING ACTIVITY
Cost Driver
Number of Advertisements

2-30 Variable- and Fixed-Cost Behavior

Refer to Exhibits 2-2 and 2-4 on pages 37 and 38. Part of a company's marketing function is as described in Exhibit 2-2. Two of the many marketing-function activities are advertising and selling. The annual cost behavior of the resources used to perform the selling activity is depicted in the diagram on page 65 using the same symbolic structure as defined in Exhibit 2-4. Which of the two costs is fixed? Which cost is variable? What is the total cost of the selling activity if sales dollars are $24,000,000? What is the total cost of selling if sales dollars are $12,000,000? Does the total cost of selling decrease by half in response to a 50% decrease in the cost driver level? Why or why not?

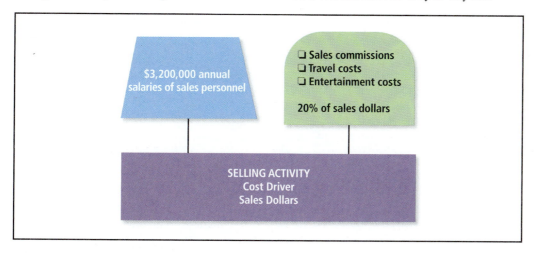

2-31 Basic Review Exercises

Fill in the blanks for each of the following independent cases:

Case	(a) Selling Price per Unit	(b) Variable Cost per Unit	(c) Total Units Sold	(d) Total Contribution Margin	(e) Total Fixed Costs	(f) Net Income
1	$25	$—	120,000	$720,000	$650,000	$ —
2	10	6	100,000	—	320,000	—
3	20	15	—	100,000	—	15,000
4	30	20	60,000	—	—	12,000
5	—	9	80,000	160,000	110,000	—

2-32 Basic Cost-Volume-Profit Graph

Refer to Exercise 2-31. Construct a cost-volume-profit graph for Case 2 that depicts the total revenue, total variable cost, total fixed cost, and total cost lines. Estimate the break-even point in total units sold and the net income for 100,000 units sold.

2-33 Basic Cost-Volume-Profit Graph

Refer to Exercise 2-31. Construct a cost-volume-profit graph for Case 4 that depicts the total revenue, total variable cost, total fixed cost, and total cost lines. Estimate the break-even point in total units sold and the net income (loss) for 50,000 units sold.

2-34 Basic Cost-Volume Graphs

From the following two graphs, construct two graphs that depict the cost behavior on a per-driver-unit basis. Which of the two constructed graphs show fixed-cost behavior? Variable-cost behavior?

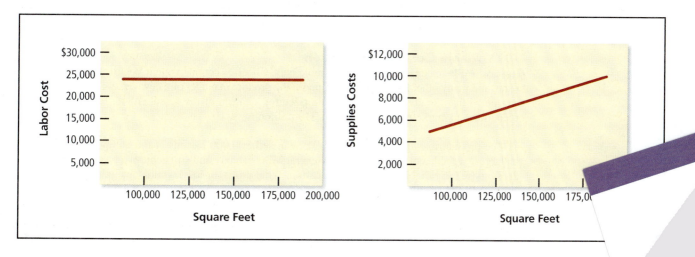

2-35 Basic Cost-Volume Graphs

From the following two graphs, construct two graphs that depict the cost behavior on a total cost basis. Which of the two constructed graphs show fixed-cost behavior? Variable-cost behavior?

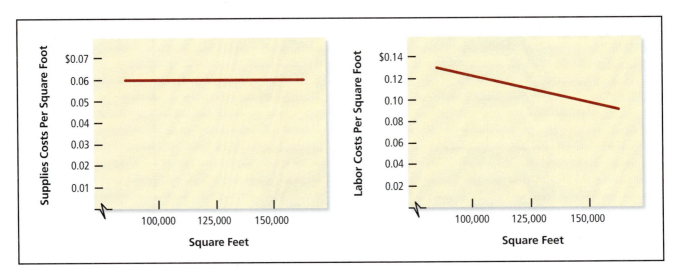

2-36 Hospital Costs and Pricing

St. Martin Hospital has overall variable costs of 20% of total revenue and fixed costs of $40 million per year.

1. Compute the break-even point expressed in total revenue.
2. A patient-day is often used to measure the volume of a hospital. Suppose there are to be 40,000 patient-days next year. Compute the average daily revenue per patient-day necessary to break even.

2-37 Cost-Volume-Profit at a Hospital

Children's Hospital predicts variable costs of 70% of total revenue and fixed costs of $42 million per year for 2011.

1. Compute the break-even point expressed in total revenue.
2. In 2011 Children's Hospital expects total revenue of $150 million from 200,000 patient days. Compute (a) expected profit for 2011 if costs behave as expected, and (b) total profit if variable costs in 2011 are 10% greater than predicted.

2-38 Motel Rentals

Motel 6 pioneered the economy-lodging brand in 1962. It now has 91,000 rooms in 1,000 locations (average is 91 rooms) in the United States and Canada. Suppose a particular Motel 6 has annual fixed costs of $1.2 million for its 100-room motel, average daily room rents of $50, and average variable costs of $10 for each room rented. It operates 365 days per year.

1. How much net income on rooms will Motel 6 generate (a) if the motel is completely full throughout the entire year and (b) if the motel is half full?
2. Compute the break-even point in number of rooms rented. What percentage occupancy for the year is needed to break even?

2-39 Variable Cost to Break Even

General Mills makes Nature Valley granola bars, Cheerios cereal, Yoplait yogurt, Häagen-Dazs ice cream, and many other food products. Suppose the product manager of a new General Mills cereal has determined that the appropriate wholesale price for a carton of the cereal is $48. Fixed costs of the production and marketing of the cereal is $19 million.

1. The product manager estimates that she can sell 800,000 cartons at the $48 price. What is the largest variable cost per carton that General Mills can pay and still achieve a profit of $1 million?
2. Suppose the variable cost is $25 per carton. What profit (or loss) would General Mills expect?

2-40 Sales-Mix Analysis

Study Appendix 2A. Matsunaga Farms produces strawberries and raspberries. Annual fixed costs are $15,600. The cost driver for variable costs is "pints of fruit produced." The variable cost is $.75 per pint of strawberries and $.95 per pint of raspberries. Strawberries sell for $1.10 per pint, raspberries for $1.45 per pint. Two pints of strawberries are produced for every pint of raspberries.

1. Compute the number of pints of strawberries and the number of pints of raspberries produced and sold at the break-even point.
2. Suppose only strawberries are produced and sold. Compute the break-even point in pints.
3. Suppose only raspberries are produced and sold. Compute the break-even point in pints.

2-41 Income Taxes

Review the illustration in Appendix 2B. Suppose the income tax rate were 25% instead of 40%. How many units would the company have to sell to achieve a target after-tax net income of (a) $864 and (b) $1,440? Show your computations.

2-42 Income Taxes and Cost-Volume-Profit Analysis

Study Appendix 2B. Suppose Hernandez Construction Company has a 30% income tax rate, a contribution-margin ratio of 25%, and fixed costs of $440,000. What sales volume is necessary to achieve an after-tax income of $84,000?

PROBLEMS

2-43 Joe's Pub, Cost-Volume-Profit Analysis in a Small Business

Joe Bell recently opened Joe's Pub in the University District. Because of licensing restrictions, the only liquor he can sell is beer. The average price of beer at Joe's Pub is $3.00 per glass, and each glass costs Joe an average of $2.20. Joe has hired a bartender and waiter at $3,000 and $2,000 per month, respectively. His rent, utilities, and other fixed operating costs are $5,000 per month.

Joe is considering selling hamburgers during the lunch hour. He feels that this will increase his daytime business, which is currently quite small. It will also allow him to be more competitive with other local bars that offer a wider variety of food and drinks.

Joe would like to sell the hamburgers for $1.25 each in order to be attractive to customers. Joe will buy buns for $1.20 a dozen and ground beef for $2.80 per pound. Each pound of ground beef will make seven hamburgers. Other ingredients will cost an average of $.20 per hamburger. Joe will also need to hire a part-time cook at $1,200 per month. Other additional fixed costs will run about $360 a month.

1. If Joe sells only beer, how many glasses of beer does he have to sell each month to make a monthly profit of $2,000?
2. If Joe sells only beer, how many glasses of beer does he have to sell each month to make a monthly profit of 5% of sales?
3. Suppose Joe decides to add hamburgers to his menu. How many hamburgers does he need to sell to break even on the hamburgers? Assume that there is no effect on beer sales.
4. The main reason Joe wanted to add hamburgers was to attract more customers. Suppose that 2,000 extra customers per month came for lunch because of the availability of hamburgers and that each bought an average of 1.5 beers. Compute the added profit (or loss) generated by these extra customers.
5. Joe was not sure how many new customers would be attracted by the hamburgers. Give Joe some advice about how many new customers would be needed to just break even on the new business if each new customer bought one hamburger and one beer. Include an assessment of the consequences of volume falling below or above this break-even point.
6. Joe could offer a higher quality hamburger if he spends 50% more on the ingredients. He could then charge $2.00 for them. Explain how Joe could determine whether the higher quality hamburgers would be more profitable than the regular hamburgers.

2-44 Kroger Grocery Chain, Variable and Fixed Costs

Kroger is the nation's number one grocery chain. While Kroger has diversified through acquisitions, adding jewelry and general merchandise to its mix, food stores still account for about 90% of sales. Kroger's 2008 sales were more than $76 billion.

Maintaining a clean shopping environment is a key success factor for Kroger, especially in its food stores. Cleaning a supermarket is the responsibility of the cleaning department. Three of the most costly resources needed to clean a supermarket are labor, equipment, and cleaning supplies. The cost driver for all these resources is "number of times cleaned." Cleaning laborers (called porters) are paid the same wages regardless of the number of times the supermarket is cleaned. Supplies used for regular daily cleaning and special cleaning are about the same. A typical store has 50,000 square feet. The floor is thoroughly cleaned every day from midnight until 7:00 AM. Special cleaning of floors and fixtures is performed in the various departments as needed. Special cleaning varies from 10 to 30 times a month depending on the amount of traffic through the store. Thus, the number of times a store is cleaned varies from 40 to 60 times a month.

3. The managers in the receiving department have a plan that will improve fuel efficiency. What is the predicted total cost of receiving 30,000 parts if the fuel consumption rate is reduced by 20% (assume fuel costs per gallon will not change)? Will the receiving department achieve Boeing's 10% cost-reduction goal? Why or why not?

4. Comment on the benefits of the new cost-driver model compared to the one based solely on one cost driver—"number of parts received."

5. Can you think of other refinements in the cost-driver model based on the data that is given?

2-50 Basic Relationships, Restaurant

Jacqui Giraud owns and operates a restaurant. Her fixed costs are $21,000 per month. She serves luncheons and dinners. The average total bill (excluding tax and tip) is $19 per customer. Giraud's present variable costs average $10.60 per meal.

1. How many meals must she serve to attain a profit before taxes of $8,400 per month?

2. What is the break-even point in number of meals served per month?

3. Giraud's rent and other fixed costs rise to a total of $29,925 per month and variable costs also rise to $12.50 per meal. If Giraud increases her average price to $23, how many meals must she serve to make $8,400 profit per month?

4. Assume the same situation described in requirement 3. Giraud's accountant tells her she may lose 10% of her customers if she increases her prices. If this should happen, what would be Giraud's profit per month? Assume that the restaurant had been serving 3,500 customers per month.

5. Assume the same situation described in requirement 4. To help offset the anticipated 10% loss of customers, Giraud hires a pianist to perform for 4 hours each night for $2,000 per month. Assume that this would increase the total monthly meals from 3,150 to 3,450. Would Giraud's total profit change? By how much?

2-51 Changing Fixed Costs to Variable Costs at Blockbuster Video

According to an article in *Business Week*, when John F. Antioco took charge of **Blockbuster Video** he changed the company's strategy. Traditionally, Blockbuster had bought videotapes from the movie studios for an average cost of about $65 each, planning to rent them out often enough to make a profit. Mr. Antioco replaced this strategy with one that allows Blockbuster to purchase videos for an average of $7 per tape and pay the studio 40% of any rental fee received for the tape. With this arrangement, Blockbuster can afford to stock more copies of each tape and guarantee customers that the tape they want will be in stock—or the rental is free. Suppose that Blockbuster rents videotapes for $2 a day. Assume that operating costs are all fixed.

1. Under the traditional strategy, how many days must each tape be rented before Blockbuster will break even on the tape?

2. Under the new strategy, how many days must each tape be rented before Blockbuster will break even on the tape?

3. Suppose customers rented a particular copy of *Babel* for 50 days. What profit would Blockbuster make on rentals of the tape (considering only the direct costs of the tape, not the costs of operating the rental store) under the traditional strategy? Under the new strategy?

4. Suppose customers rented a particular copy of *The Departed* for only 6 days. What profit would Blockbuster make on rentals of the tape (considering only the direct costs of the tape, not the costs of operating the rental store) under the traditional strategy? Under the new strategy?

5. Comment on how the new arrangement affects the risks Blockbuster accepts when purchasing an additional copy of a particular videotape.

2-52 CVP and Financial Statements for a Mega-Brand Company

Procter & Gamble Company is a Cincinnati-based company that produces household products under brand names such as Gillette, Bounty, Crest, Folgers, and Tide. The company's 2008 income statement showed the following (in millions):

Net sales	$83,503
Costs of products sold	40,695
Selling, general, and administrative expense	25,725
Operating income	$17,083

Suppose that the cost of products sold is the only variable cost; selling, general, and administrative expenses are fixed with respect to sales.

Assume that Procter & Gamble had a 20% decrease in sales in 2009 and that there was no change in costs except for decreases associated with the lower volume of sales. Compute the predicted 2009 operating income for Procter & Gamble and its percentage decrease. Explain why the percentage decrease in income differs from the percentage decrease in sales.

2-53 Bingo and Leverage

Many churches sponsor bingo games, a tradition stemming from the time when only specific nonprofit institutions were allowed to sponsor games of chance. Reverend Justin Olds, the pastor of a new parish in Orange County, is investigating the desirability of conducting weekly bingo nights. The parish has no hall, but a local hotel would be willing to commit its hall for a lump-sum rental of $600 per night. The rent would include cleaning, setting up and taking down the tables and chairs, and so on.

1. A local printer would provide bingo cards in return for free advertising. Local merchants would donate door prizes. The services of clerks, callers, security force, and others would be donated by volunteers. Admission would be $4.00 per person, entitling the player to one card; extra cards would be $1.50 each. Many persons buy extra cards so there would be an average of four cards played per person. What is the maximum in total cash prizes that the church may award and still break even if 200 persons attend each weekly session?
2. Suppose the total cash prizes are $1,100. What will be the church's operating income if 100 persons attend? If 200 persons attend? If 300 persons attend? Briefly explain the effects of the cost behavior on income.
3. After operating for 10 months, Reverend Olds is thinking of negotiating a different rental arrangement but keeping the prize money unchanged at $1,100. Suppose the rent is $200 per night plus $2 per person. Compute the operating income for attendance of 100, 200, and 300 persons, respectively. Explain why the results differ from those in requirement 2.

2-54 Leverage at eBay

In 2008, **eBay** had $8.5 billion in revenue and net income over $1.8 billion. eBay's mission is to "provide a global trading platform where practically anyone can trade practically anything." However, business has not always been as profitable for eBay. The company is one of the survivors of the technology collapse in 2001 and 2002. Consider eBay's situation at that time. In the first quarter of 2001, eBay reported revenue of $154 million and operating expenses of $123 million, for an operating profit of $31 million. In the first quarter of 2002, eBay reported that revenue had increased 59%, to $245 million. eBay's fixed costs were $37 million and variable costs vary with the amount of revenue.

1. Compute eBay's operating income for the first quarter of 2002 and its percentage increase in operating income between 2001 and 2002.
2. Explain how eBay managed to increase its income so much with only a 59% increase in revenue.

2-55 Adding a Product

Mac's Brew Pub, located near State University, serves as a gathering place for the university's more social scholars. Mac sells draft beer and all brands of bottled beer at a contribution margin of $.60 a beer.

Mac is considering also selling hamburgers during selected hours. His reasons are twofold. First, sandwiches would attract daytime customers. A hamburger and a beer are a quick lunch. Second, he has to meet competition from other local bars, some of which provide more extensive menus.

Mac analyzed the costs as follows:

Per Month		Per Hamburger	
Monthly Fixed Expenses		**Variable Expenses**	
Wages of part-time cook	$1,200	Rolls	$.12
Other	360	Meat @ $2.80 per pound	
Total	$1,560	(seven hamburgers per pound)	.40
		Other	.18
		Total	$.70

Mac planned a selling price of $1.20 per hamburger to lure many customers. For all questions, assume a 30-day month.

1. What are the monthly and daily break-even points, in number of hamburgers?
2. What are the monthly and daily break-even points, in dollar sales?
3. At the end of 2 months, Mac finds he has sold 3,600 hamburgers. What is the operating profit per month on hamburgers?

4. Mac thinks that at least 60 extra beers are sold per day because he has these hamburgers available. This means that 60 extra people come to the bar or that 60 buy an extra beer because they are attracted by the hamburgers. How does this affect Mac's monthly operating income?
5. Refer to requirement 3. How many extra beers would have to be sold per day so that the overall effects of the hamburger sales on monthly operating income would be zero?

2-56 Government Organization

A social welfare agency has a government budget appropriation for 20X7 of $900,000. The agency's major mission is to help disabled persons who are unable to hold jobs. On the average, the agency supplements each person's income by $5,000 annually. The agency's fixed costs are $280,000. There are no other costs.

1. How many disabled persons were helped during 20X7?
2. For 20X8, the agency's budget appropriation has been reduced by 15%. If the agency continues the same level of monetary support per person, how many disabled persons will be helped in 20X8? Compute the percentage decline in the number of persons helped.
3. Assume a budget reduction of 15%, as in requirement 2. The manager of the agency has discretion as to how much to supplement each disabled person's income. She does not want to reduce the number of persons served. On the average, what is the amount of the supplement that can be given to each person? Compute the percentage decline in the annual supplement.

2-57 Gross Margin and Contribution Margin

Eastman Kodak Company is a provider of imaging technology products and services to the photographic, graphic communications, and health-care markets. A condensed 2008 income statement follows (in millions):

Sales	$9,416
Cost of goods sold	7,247
Gross margin	2,169
Other operating expenses	2,896
Loss from continuing operations	$ (727)

Assume that $1,400 million of the cost of goods sold is a fixed cost representing depreciation and other production costs that do not change with the volume of production. In addition, $2,000 million of the other operating expenses is fixed.

1. Compute the total contribution margin for 2008 and the contribution margin percentage. Explain why the contribution margin differs from the gross margin.
2. Suppose that sales for Eastman Kodak were predicted to increase by 10% in 2009 and that the cost behavior was expected to continue in 2009 as it did in 2008. Compute the predicted operating income (loss) for 2009.
3. What assumptions were necessary to compute the predicted 2009 operating income in requirement 2?

2-58 Choosing Equipment for Different Volumes

MetroCinemas owns and operates a nationwide chain of movie theaters. The 500 properties in the chain vary from low-volume, small-town, single-screen theaters to high-volume, big-city, multiscreen theaters.

The management is considering installing machines that will make popcorn on the premises. These machines would allow the theaters to sell freshly popped popcorn rather than the prepopped, prebagged corn that it currently sells. This proposed feature would be properly advertised and is intended to increase patronage at the company's theaters.

The machines can be purchased in several different sizes. The annual rental costs and operating costs vary with the size of the machines. The machine capacities and costs are as follows:

	Popper Model		
	Standard	**Deluxe**	**Jumbo**
Annual capacity	50,000 boxes	120,000 boxes	300,000 boxes
Costs			
Annual machine rental	$7,840	$11,200	$20,200
Popcorn cost per box	.14	.14	.14
Cost of each box	.09	.09	.09
Other variable costs per box	.22	.14	.05

1. Calculate the volume level in boxes at which the standard and deluxe poppers would earn the same operating profit (loss).
2. The management can estimate the number of boxes to be sold at each of its theaters. Present a decision rule that would enable MetroCinemas management to select the most profitable machine without having to make a separate cost calculation for each theater. That is, at what anticipated range of unit sales should the theater use the standard model? The deluxe model? The jumbo model?
3. Could the management use the average number of boxes sold per seat for the entire chain and the capacity of each theater to develop this decision rule? Explain your answer.

2-59 Sales Compensation, Variable/Fixed Costs, and Ethics

Most companies compensate their sales forces with a combination of a fixed salary and a commission that is a percentage of sales. Consider two companies competing for the same customers—for example, Kellogg's and Post cereals. Suppose that Kellogg's pays its sales force a large fixed salary and a small commission, while Post pays its sales force a small fixed salary and a large commission. The total pay on average was the same for both companies.

1. Compare the sales cost structure of Kellogg's with that of Post. Which has the larger fixed cost? Which has the larger variable cost? How will this affect each company's risk? (Focus on how the company's profits change with changes in volume.)
2. What incentives does each pay system provide for the sales force?
3. Might either incentive system create potential ethical dilemmas for the sales personnel? Explain.

2-60 Sales-Mix Analysis

Study Appendix 2A. The Rocky Mountain Catering Company specializes in preparing Mexican dinners that it freezes and ships to restaurants in the Denver area. When a diner orders an item, the restaurant heats and serves it. The budget data for 20X5 are

	Product	
	Chicken Tacos	Beef Enchiladas
Selling price to restaurants	$5	$7
Variable expenses	3	4
Contribution margin	$2	$3
Number of units	250,000	125,000

The company prepares the items in the same kitchens, delivers them in the same trucks, and so forth. Therefore, decisions about the individual products do not affect the fixed costs of $735,000.

1. Compute the planned net income for 20X5.
2. Compute the break-even point in units, assuming that the company maintains its planned sales mix.
3. Compute the break-even point in units if the company sells only tacos and if it sells only enchiladas.
4. Suppose the company sells 78,750 units of enchiladas and 236,250 units of tacos, for a total of 315,000 units. Compute the net income. Compute the new break-even point with this new sales mix. What is the major lesson of this problem?

2-61 Hospital Patient Mix

Study Appendix 2A. Hospitals measure their volume in terms of patient-days. We calculate patient-days by multiplying the number of patients by the number of days that the patients are hospitalized. Suppose a large hospital has fixed costs of $54 million per year and variable costs of $600 per patient-day. Daily revenues vary among classes of patients. For simplicity, assume that there are two classes: (1) self-pay patients (S) who pay an average of $1,000 per day and (2) non–self-pay patients (G) who are the responsibility of insurance companies and government agencies and who pay an average of $800 per day. Twenty percent of the patients are self-pay.

1. Compute the break-even point in patient-days, assuming that the hospital maintains its planned mix of patients.
2. Suppose that the hospital achieves 225,000 patient-days but that 25% of the patient-days were self-pay (instead of 20%). Compute the net income. Compute the break-even point.

2-62 Income Taxes on Hotels

Study Appendix 2B. The Four Winds Hotel in downtown Phoenix has annual fixed costs applicable to rooms of $9.2 million for its 600-room hotel, average daily room rates of $105, and average variable costs of $25 daily for each room rented. It operates 365 days per year. The hotel is subject to an income tax rate of 40%.

1. How many rooms must the hotel rent to earn a net income after taxes of $720,000? Of $360,000?
2. Compute the break-even point in number of rooms rented. What percentage occupancy for the year is needed to break even?
3. Assume that the volume level of rooms sold is 150,000. The manager is wondering how much income could be generated by adding sales of 15,000 rooms. Compute the additional net income after taxes.

2-63 Tax Effects, Multiple Choice

Study Appendix 2B. Victor Company is a wholesaler of compact disks. The projected after-tax net income for the current year is $120,000, based on a sales volume of 200,000 CDs. Victor has been selling the CDs at $16 each. The variable costs consist of the $10 unit purchase price and a handling cost of $2 per unit. Victor's annual fixed costs are $600,000, and the company is subject to a 40% income tax rate.

Management is planning for the coming year when it expects that the unit purchase price will increase 30%.

1. Victor Company's break-even point for the current year is (a) 150,000 units, (b) 100,000 units, (c) 50,000 units, (d) 60,000 units, or (e) some amount other than those given.
2. An increase of 10% in projected unit sales volume for the current year would result in an increased after-tax income for the current year of (a) $80,000, (b) $32,000, (c) $12,000, (d) $48,000, or (e) some amount other than those given.
3. The volume of sales in dollars that Victor Company must achieve in the coming year to maintain the same after-tax net income as projected for the current year if unit selling price remains at $16 is (a) $12,800,000, (b) $14,400,000, (c) $11,520,000, (d) $32,000,000, or (e) some amount other than those given.
4. To cover a 30% increase in the unit purchase price for the coming year and still maintain the current contribution-margin ratio, Victor Company must establish a selling price per unit for the coming year of (a) $19.60, (b) $20.00, (c) $20.80, (d) $19.00, or (e) some amount other than those given.

CASES

2-64 Hospital Costs

Gother City Hospital is unionized. In 20X6, nurses received an average annual salary of $45,000. The hospital administrator is considering changes in the contract with nurses for 20X7. In turn, the hospital may also change the way it charges nursing costs to each department.

The hospital holds each department accountable for its financial performance, and it allocates revenues and expenses to departments. Consider the expenses of the obstetrics department in 20X6.

Variable expenses (based on 20X6 patient-days) are

Meals	$ 610,000
Laundry	260,000
Laboratory	900,000
Pharmacy	850,000
Maintenance	150,000
Other	530,000
Total	$3,300,000

Fixed expenses (based on number of beds) are

Rent	$3,000,000
General administrative services	2,200,000
Janitorial	200,000
Maintenance	150,000
Other	350,000
Total	$5,900,000

Management assigns nurses to departments on the basis of annual patient-days as follows:

Volume Level in Patient-Days	Number of Nurses
10,000–12,000	30
12,001–16,000	35

Total patient-days are the number of patients multiplied by the number of days they are hospitalized. The hospital charges each department for the salaries of the nurses assigned to it.

During 20X6, the obstetrics department had a capacity of 60 beds, billed each patient an average of $810 per day, and had revenues of $12.15 million.

1. Compute the 20X6 volume of activity in patient-days.
2. Compute the 20X6 patient-days that would have been necessary for the obstetrics department to recoup all fixed expenses except nursing expenses.
3. Compute the 20X6 patient-days that would have been necessary for the obstetrics department to break even including nurses' salaries as a fixed cost.
4. Suppose obstetrics must pay $200 per patient-day for nursing services. This plan would replace the two-level, fixed-cost system employed in 20X6. Compute what the break-even point in patient-days would have been in 20X6 under this plan.

2-65 CVP in a Modern Manufacturing Environment

A division of Hewlett-Packard Company changed its production operations from one where a large labor force assembled electronic components to an automated production facility dominated by computer-controlled robots. The change was necessary because of fierce competitive pressures. Improvements in quality, reliability, and flexibility of production schedules were necessary just to match the competition. As a result of the change, variable costs fell and fixed costs increased, as shown in the following assumed budgets:

	Old Production Operation	New Production Operation
Unit variable cost		
Material	$ .88	$ .88
Labor	1.22	.22
Total per unit	$ 2.10	$ 1.10
Monthly fixed costs		
Rent and depreciation	$450,000	$ 875,000
Supervisory labor	80,000	175,000
Other	50,000	90,000
Total per month	$580,000	$1,140,000

Expected volume is 600,000 units per month, with each unit selling for $3.10. Capacity is 800,000 units.

1. Compute the budgeted profit at the expected volume of 600,000 units under both the old and the new production environments.
2. Compute the budgeted break-even point under both the old and the new production environments.
3. Discuss the effect on profits if volume falls to 500,000 units under both the old and the new production environments.
4. Discuss the effect on profits if volume increases to 700,000 units under both the old and the new production environments.
5. Comment on the riskiness of the new operation versus the old operation.

2-66 Multiproduct Break Even in a Restaurant

Study Appendix 2A. An article in *Washington Business* included an income statement for **La Brasserie**, a French restaurant in Washington, D.C. A simplified version of the statement follows:

Revenues	$2,098,400
Cost of sales, all variable	1,246,500
Gross profit	851,900
Operating expenses	
Variable	222,380
Fixed	170,940
Administrative expenses, all fixed	451,500
Net income	$ 7,080

The average dinner tab at La Brasserie is $40, and the average lunch tab is $20. Assume that the variable cost of preparing and serving dinner is also twice that of a lunch. The restaurant serves twice as many lunches as dinners. Assume that the restaurant is open 305 days a year.

1. Compute the daily break-even volume in lunches and dinners for La Brasserie. Compare this to the actual volume reflected in the income statement.
2. Suppose that an extra annual advertising expenditure of $15,000 would increase the average daily volume by three dinners and six lunches, and that there is plenty of capacity to accommodate the extra business. Prepare an analysis for the management of La Brasserie, explaining whether this would be desirable.
3. La Brasserie uses only premium food, and the cost of food makes up 25% of the restaurant's total variable costs. Use of average rather than premium ingredients could cut the food cost by 20%. Assume that La Brasserie uses average-quality ingredients and does not change its prices. How much of a drop-off in volume could it endure and still maintain the same net income? What factors in addition to revenue and costs would influence the decision about the quality of food to use?

2-67 Effects of Changes in Costs, Including Tax Effects

Study Appendix 2B. **Pacific Fish Company** is a wholesale distributor of salmon. The company services grocery stores in the Chicago area.

Average selling price per pound		$ 5.00
Average variable costs per pound		
Cost of salmon		$ 2.50
Shipping expenses		.50
Total		$ 3.00
Annual fixed costs		
Selling		$ 210,000
Administrative		356,250
Total		$ 566,250
Expected annual sales volume (390,000 pounds)		$1,950,000
Tax rate		40%

Small but steady growth in sales has been achieved by Pacific Fish over the past few years, while salmon prices have been increasing. The company is formulating its plans for the coming fiscal year. Presented next are the data used to project the current year's after-tax net income of $128,250.

Fishing companies have announced that they will increase prices of their products by an average of 15% in the coming year, owing mainly to increases in labor costs. Pacific Fish Company expects that all other costs will remain at the same rates or levels as in the current year.

1. What is Pacific Fish Company's break-even point in pounds of salmon for the current year?
2. What selling price per pound must Pacific Fish Company charge to cover the 15% increase in the cost of salmon and still maintain the current contribution-margin ratio?

3. What volume of sales in dollars must the Pacific Fish Company achieve in the coming year to maintain the same net income after taxes as projected for the current year if the selling price of salmon remains at $5 per pound and the cost of salmon increases 15%?
4. What strategies might Pacific Fish Company use to maintain the same net income after taxes as projected for the current year?

NIKE 10-K PROBLEM

2-68 Operating Leverage
Examine Nike's 10K report in Appendix C.

1. In the Item 7 of the 10K, review the section titled Operating Segments. Prepare a table that compares the percent change in "Total revenue" to the change in "Pre-tax income" from 2007 to 2008 for the four major regions. Focus on the "Americas" region and the mention of the term *leverage*. How can operating leverage help explain the greater percent increase in income before taxes than the increase in total revenues for this region?
2. While not mentioned, how can operating leverage help explain the lower percent change in income before taxes than total revenues for the United States region?
3. Would you expect Nike's operating leverage to be high or low? Explain. Which assets do you think contribute to Nike's ability to leverage operating overhead?

EXCEL APPLICATION EXERCISE

2-69 CVP and Break Even
Goal: Create an Excel spreadsheet to perform CVP analysis and show the relationship between price, costs, and break-even points in terms of units and dollars. Use the results to answer questions about your findings.

Scenario: Phonetronix is a small manufacturer of telephone and communications devices. Recently, company management decided to investigate the profitability of cellular phone production. They have three different proposals to evaluate. Under all the proposals, the fixed costs for the new phone would be $110,000. Under proposal A, the selling price of the new phone would be $99 and the variable cost per unit would be $55. Under proposal B, the selling price of the phone would be $129 and the variable cost would remain the same. Under proposal C, the selling price would be $99 and the variable cost would be $49.

When you have completed your spreadsheet, answer the following questions:
1. What are the break-even points in units and dollars under proposal A?
2. How did the increased selling price under proposal B impact the break-even points in units and dollars compared to the break-even points calculated under proposal A?
3. Why did the change in variable cost under proposal C not impact the break-even points in units and dollars as significantly as proposal B did?

Step-by-Step:
1. Open a new Excel spreadsheet.
2. In column A, create a bold-faced heading that contains the following:
   Row 1: Chapter 2 Decision Guideline
   Row 2: XPhonetronix
   Row 3: Cost-Volume-Profit (CVP) Analysis
   Row 4: Today's Date
3. Merge and center the four heading rows across columns A–D.
4. In row 7, create the following bold-faced, right-justified column headings:
   Column B: Proposal A
   Column C: Proposal B
   Column D: Proposal C

   Note: Adjust cell widths when necessary as you work.

5. In column A, create the following row headings:
   Row 8: Selling price
   Row 9: Variable cost
   Row 10: Contribution margin
   Row 11: Contribution margin ratio
   Skip a row.
   Row 13: Fixed cost

Skip a row.
Row 15: Break-even in units
Skip a row.
Row 17: Break-even in dollars

6. Use the scenario data to fill in the selling price, variable cost, and fixed cost amounts for the three proposals.

7. Use the appropriate formulas from this chapter to calculate contribution margin, contribution margin ratio, break even in units, and break even in dollars.

8. Format all amounts as follows:

Number tab:	Category:	Currency
	Decimal places:	0
	Symbol:	None
	Negative numbers:	Red with parenthesis

9. Change the format of the selling price, contribution margin, fixed cost, and break even in dollars amounts to display a dollar symbol.

10. Change the format of both contribution margin headings to display as indented:

Alignment tab:	Horizontal:	Left (Indent)
	Indent:	1

11. Change the format of the contribution margin amount cells to display a top border, using the default line style.

Border tab:	Icon:	Top Border

12. Change the format of the contribution margin ratio amounts to display as a percentage with two decimal places.

Number tab:	Category:	Percentage
	Decimal places:	2

13. Change the format of all break-even headings and amounts to display as bold-faced.

14. Activate the ability to use heading names in formulas under Tools → Options:

Calculation tab:	Check the box:	Accept labels in formulas

15. Replace the cell-based formulas with "word-based" equivalents for each formula used in Proposal A.
    Example: Contribution margin for proposal B would be:
    = ('Selling price' 'Proposal B') − ('Variable cost' 'Proposal B')
    Note: The tic marks used in the example help avoid naming errors caused by data having similar titles (i.e., "contribution margin" and "contribution margin ratio"). The parentheses help clarify groupings.
    Help: Ask the Answer Wizard about "Name cells in a workbook."
    Select "Learn about labels and names in formulas" from the right-hand panel.

16. Save your work to a disk, and print a copy for your files.

COLLABORATIVE LEARNING EXERCISE

2-70 CVP for a Small Business

Form into groups of two to six students. Each group should select a very simple business, one with a single product or one with approximately the same contribution margin percentage for all products. Some possibilities are

    A child's lemonade stand
    A retail DVD rental store
    An espresso cart

A retail store selling compact disks

An athletic shoe store

A cookie stand in a mall

However, you are encouraged to use your imagination rather than just select one of these examples.

The following tasks might be split up among the group members:

1. Make a list of all fixed costs associated with running the business you selected. Estimate the amount of each fixed cost per month (or per day or per year, if one of them is more appropriate for your business).

2. Make a list of all variable costs associated with making or obtaining the product or service your company is selling. Estimate the cost per unit for each variable cost.

3. Given the fixed and variable costs you have identified, compute the break-even point for your business in either units or dollar sales.

4. Assess the prospects of your business making a profit.

INTERNET EXERCISE

2-71 Cost Behavior at Southwest Airlines

It is critical that managers understand how costs and revenues behave. One company that is affected by changes in costs and may not have the capability to rapidly change revenues because of competition is **Southwest Airlines**. Let's take a closer look at SWA and its costs and revenues. Log on to SWA's Web site at www.southwest.com. This Web site serves many purposes for the airline, such as providing flight schedules, making reservations and selling tickets, and displaying vacation and airfare specials.

1. Click on the book travel icon. How many cities in the United States does SWA serve? What is the closest city to your current location served by SWA? Click on that city as the departure city and then select any city you like for the arrival city. Now select a date about a month from now for leaving and one for returning. Click to continue to the next screen. What types of fares are available? Why do you think that there are different types of fares offered? Click on one of the fare-type captions to see if Southwest places any restrictions on this fare. If there are any restrictions, what purpose do they serve?

2. Return to the reservations screen and select a departure date that is less than a week away. What types of fare choices are available now? Are the rates the same as those that you found for a trip more than a month away? Why do you think that the choices remaining are for the most part the higher-priced ones? Is there any advantage to the fare(s) still available? Who is the most likely user of a ticket purchased at the last minute?

3. Now that you have looked at the revenue side, let's focus on the expense side. Individuals on the same flight may pay different prices for the ticket. Do you think that the cost of flying a passenger differs due to the price that they pay for the ticket? Why or why not?

4. Return to SWA's home page. Take a look at the costs that SWA actually incurs. Click on the "About Southwest" icon and then click on "Investor Relations." Click on the "Annual Reports" icon and then select the most recent annual report. If not included in the annual report, locate the 10K report submitted to the SEC. Open the annual report (and if separately listed, the 10K report) using Adobe Acrobat Reader. When you have located the annual report and 10K report, notice the summary information that the company has provided in the "Consolidated Highlights" section. Give the most recent year's operating revenues and operating expenses. How much has each changed over the prior year? What does this imply for Southwest's profitability?

5. Now find "Management's Discussion and Analysis of Financial Condition and Results of Operations" that is included in the report. Examine the section that shows "Operating Expenses" and examine operating expenses per ASM. (ASM stands for *available seat miles*, a measure of capacity.) Which of these costs is primarily fixed with respect to ASM? Which is primarily variable? What other cost drivers might be important causes of costs for Southwest?

Measurement of Cost Behavior

LEARNING OBJECTIVES

When you have finished studying this chapter, you should be able to:

1. Explain step- and mixed-cost behavior.

2. Explain management influences on cost behavior.

3. Measure and mathematically express cost functions and use them to predict costs.

4. Describe the importance of activity analysis for measuring cost functions.

5. Measure cost behavior using the engineering analysis, account analysis, high-low, visual-fit, and least-squares regression methods.

▶ AMERICA WEST

US Airways and **America West** came together in 2006 to create the fifth largest domestic airline. US Airways, US Airways Shuttle, and US Airways Express operate approximately 4,000 flights per day and serve more than 225 communities in the United States, Canada, Europe, the Caribbean, and Latin America. Before its merger with US Airways, America West rode the wave of a booming economy to increased revenues in the late 1990s. As a result, management decided to expand by introducing service to new destinations including Acapulco, Miami, and Detroit, and by adding more daily flights to existing markets including Las Vegas, Mexico City, and Boston. To accomplish this, the company had to expand its labor force, add new aircraft, and spend more than $40 million on new technology.

Management did not take lightly the decision to invest large amounts of money in aircraft and equipment. It knew that the decision would have a significant influence on costs, and thus profits, for many years. Management also knew that most of the costs would be fixed but the revenues would fluctuate with the economy. When the economy is bad, revenues may not cover these costs.

How does an airline protect itself against losses when the economy experiences a downturn? According to Richard Goodmanson, former president and chief executive officer of America West, "management has a goal to have from 5% to 10% of the fleet of aircraft leased and thus subject to annual renewal. This enhances the company's ability to decrease capacity (and related costs) in the event of an industry downturn." This example illustrates that understanding how costs behave, as well as how managers' decisions can influence costs, helped the airline improve its cost control.

Chapter 2 demonstrated the importance of understanding the cost structure of an organization and the relationships between an organization's activities and its costs, revenues, and profits. This chapter focuses on **measurement of cost behavior**, which means understanding and quantifying how activities of an organization affect its costs. Recall that activities use resources, and these resources have costs. We measure the relationship between activity and cost using cost drivers. Understanding relationships between costs and their cost drivers allows managers in all types of organizations—profit-seeking, nonprofit, and government—to do the following:

- Evaluate strategic plans and operational improvement programs. (Chapter 4)
- Make proper short-run pricing decisions. (Chapter 5)
- Make short-run operating decisions. (Chapter 6)

- Plan or budget the effects of future activities. (Chapters 7 and 8)
- Design effective management control systems. (Chapters 9 and 10)
- Make proper long-run decisions. (Chapter 11)
- Design accurate and useful product costing systems. (Chapters 12–14)

As you can see, understanding cost behavior is fundamental to management accounting. There are numerous real-world cases in which managers have made very poor decisions to drop product lines, close manufacturing plants, or bid too high or too low on jobs because they had erroneous cost-behavior information. This chapter, therefore, deserves careful study. ■

America West airplanes on the runway at the company's Phoenix hub.

Cost Drivers and Cost Behavior

Accountants and managers often assume that cost behavior is linear over some relevant range of activity levels or cost-driver levels. We can graph **linear-cost behavior** with a straight line because we assume each cost to be either fixed or variable. Recall that the relevant range specifies the limits of cost-driver activity within which a specific relationship between a cost and its cost driver will be valid. Managers usually define the relevant range based on their previous experience operating the organization at different levels of activity.

In this chapter, we focus on those costs for which the volume of a product produced or service provided is the primary cost driver. These costs are easy to identify with, or trace to, products or services. Examples of volume-driven costs include the costs of printing labor, paper, ink, and binding to produce all the copies of this textbook. The number of copies printed affects the total printing labor, paper, ink, and binding costs. We could easily trace the use of these resources to the number of copies of the text printed by using schedules, payroll records, and other documents that show how much of each resource was used to produce the copies of this text.

Activities not directly related to volume also affect costs. Such costs often have multiple cost drivers. For example, the wages and salaries of the editorial staff of the publisher of this textbook are not easy to trace to outputs. These editorial personnel produce many different textbooks, and it would be very difficult to determine exactly what portion of their wages and salaries went into a specific book, such as *Introduction to Management Accounting*.

Understanding and measuring costs that are difficult to trace to outputs can be especially challenging. In practice, many organizations use a linear relationship with a single cost driver to describe each cost, even though many costs have multiple causes. This approach is easier and less expensive than using nonlinear relationships or multiple cost drivers. If we use it carefully, this method often provides cost estimates that are accurate enough for most decisions. It may seem at odds with reality and economic theory, but the added benefit of understanding "true" cost behavior may be less than the cost of determining it, which is consistent with the cost-benefit approach to decision making.

Accountants often describe cost behavior in visual or graphical terms. Exhibit 3-1 shows linear-cost behavior, the relevant range, and an activity or resource cost driver. Note the similarity to the cost-volume-profit (CVP) graphs of Chapter 2.

Step- and Mixed-Cost Behavior Patterns

Chapter 2 described two patterns of cost behavior: variable costs and fixed costs. Recall that, within a relevant range, a purely variable cost changes in proportion to changes in its cost driver's activity, while changes in the cost-driver level do not immediately change a fixed cost. In addition to these pure versions of costs, two additional types of costs combine characteristics of both fixed- and variable-cost behavior. These are step costs and mixed costs.

STEP COSTS **Step costs** change abruptly at different intervals of activity because the resources and their costs are only available in indivisible chunks. If the individual chunks of cost are relatively large and apply to a specific, broad range of activity, we consider the cost a fixed cost over that range of activity. An example is in panel A of Exhibit 3-2, which shows the cost of

Objective 1

Explain step- and mixed-cost behavior.

Exhibit 3-1
Linear-Cost Behavior

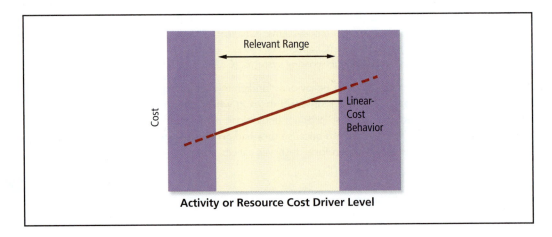

leasing oil and gas drilling equipment. When oil and gas exploration activity reaches a certain level in a given region, the company must lease an entire additional rig. One level of oil and gas rig leasing, however, will support all volumes of exploration activity within a relevant range of drilling. Within each relevant range, this step cost behaves as a fixed cost.

In contrast, accountants often describe step costs as variable when the individual chunks of costs are relatively small and apply to a narrow range of activity. Panel B of Exhibit 3-2 shows the wage cost of cashiers at a supermarket. Suppose one cashier can serve an average of 20 shoppers per hour and that within the relevant range of shopping activity, the number of shoppers can range from 40 per hour to 440 per hour. The corresponding number of cashiers would range between 2 and 22. Because the steps are relatively small, this step cost behaves much like a variable cost, and we could assume it is variable for planning purposes with little loss of accuracy.

MIXED COSTS   **Mixed costs** contain elements of both fixed- and variable-cost behavior. The fixed-cost element is unchanged over a range of cost-driver activity levels. The variable-cost element of the mixed cost varies proportionately with cost-driver activity within the relevant range. You might think of the fixed cost as the cost of having available the capacity necessary to operate at any volume within the relevant range and the variable cost as the additional cost of using that capacity to produce at the specified level of output.

Many costs are mixed costs. For example, consider the monthly facilities maintenance department cost of the Parkview Medical Center (PMC), shown in Exhibit 3-3. Salaries of the maintenance personnel and costs of equipment are fixed at $10,000 per month. In addition, cleaning supplies and repair materials vary at a rate of $5 per patient-day[1] delivered by the hospital.

Exhibit 3-2
Step-Cost Behavior

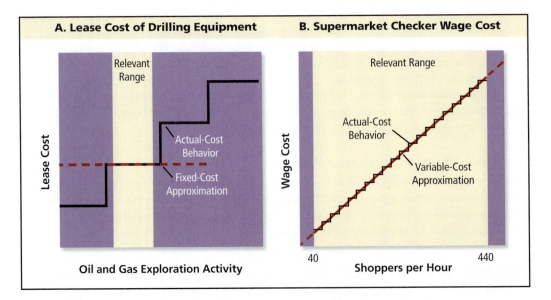

[1]A patient-day is one patient spending 1 day in the hospital. One patient spending 5 days in the hospital is 5 patient-days of service.

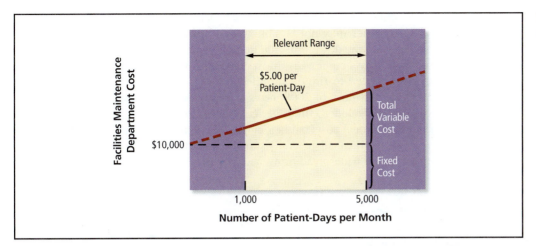

Exhibit 3-3
Mixed-Cost Behavior

The chief administrator at PMC used knowledge of the facilities maintenance department cost behavior to do the following:

1. Plan costs: In May, the hospital expected to service 3,000 patient-days. May's predicted facilities maintenance department costs are $10,000 fixed costs plus the variable cost of $15,000 (3,000 patient-days times $5 per patient-day) for a total of $25,000.
2. Provide feedback to managers: In May, the actual facilities maintenance costs were $34,000 in a month when PMC serviced 3,000 patient-days as planned. The administrator wanted to know why the hospital overspent by $9,000 ($34,000 less the planned $25,000) so that managers could take corrective action.
3. Make decisions about the most efficient use of resources: For example, managers might weigh the long-run trade-offs of increased fixed costs of highly automated floor cleaning equipment against the variable costs of extra hours needed to clean floors manually.

We can see that managers not only passively measure how costs behave, they also actively influence the cost structure of an organization. Let's explore in more detail how managers influence cost behavior.

Management Influence on Cost Behavior

In addition to measuring and evaluating current cost behavior, managers can influence cost behavior through decisions about such factors as product or service attributes, capacity, technology, and policies to create incentives to control costs.

Objective 2
Explain management influences on cost behavior.

Product and Service Decisions and the Value Chain

Throughout the value chain, managers influence cost behavior. This influence occurs through their choices of process and product design, quality levels, product features, distribution channels, and so on. Each of these decisions contributes to the organization's performance, and managers should consider the costs and benefits of each decision. For example, **Hertz**, the car rental company, would add a feature to its services only if the cost of the feature—for example, GPS navigation systems in its vehicles—could be more than recovered in profit from increased business and/or extra fees it could charge for the feature.

Capacity Decisions

Strategic decisions about the scale and scope of an organization's activities generally result in fixed levels of capacity costs. **Capacity costs** are the fixed costs of being able to achieve a desired level of production or to provide a desired level of service while maintaining product or service attributes, such as quality. Most companies make a capacity decision infrequently. They consider capacity decisions as strategic because large amounts of resources are involved. An incorrect capacity decision can have serious consequences for the competitiveness of a company. However, some companies make capacity decisions so frequently that they almost become routine operating decisions, such as opening a new **Starbucks** or **McDonald's**. In this case, the decision to open a new Starbucks is still strategic, but it becomes highly structured.

Companies in industries with long-term variations in demand must be careful when making capacity decisions. Companies may not be able to fully recover fixed capacity costs when demand falls during an economic downturn. Additionally, capacity decisions can entail an ethical commitment to a company's employees. Most companies try to keep a stable employment policy so that they do not need to fire or lay off employees unless there are huge shifts in demand. In the economic downturn of 2008, news stories about companies "downsizing" and initiating extensive layoffs abounded. But other companies managed the decrease in demand without imposing large emotional costs on their employees. Companies that plan their capacity to allow flexibility in meeting demand generally survive economic hard times better, without the emotional upheaval caused by widespread firings and layoffs.

Committed Fixed Costs

Even if a company has chosen to minimize fixed capacity costs, every organization has some costs to which it is committed, perhaps for quite a few years. A company's **committed fixed costs** usually arise from the possession of facilities, equipment, and a basic organizational structure. They include mortgage or lease payments, interest payments on long-term debt, property taxes, insurance, and salaries of key personnel. Only major changes in the philosophy, scale, or scope of operations could change these committed fixed costs in future periods. Recall the example of the facilities maintenance department for the Parkview Medical Center. The capacity of the facilities maintenance department was a management decision, and in this case the decision determined the magnitude of the equipment cost. Suppose PMC were permanently to increase its patient-days per month beyond the relevant range of 5,000 patient-days. Because PMC would need more capacity, the committed equipment cost would rise to a new level per month.

Discretionary Fixed Costs

Some costs are fixed at certain levels only because management decided to incur these levels of cost to meet the organization's goals. These **discretionary fixed costs** have no obvious relationship to levels of capacity or output activity. Companies determine them as part of the periodic planning process. Each planning period, management will determine how much to spend on discretionary items such as advertising and promotion costs, public relations, research and development costs, charitable donations, employee training programs, and purchased management consulting services. These costs then become fixed until the next planning period.

Managers can alter discretionary fixed costs—up or down—even within a budget period, if they decide that different levels of spending are desirable. Conceivably, managers could eliminate such discretionary costs almost entirely for a given year in dire times, whereas they could not reduce committed costs. Discretionary fixed costs may be essential to the long-run achievement of the organization's goals, but managers can vary spending levels broadly in the short run.

Consider Marietta Corporation, which is experiencing financial difficulties. Sales for its major products are down, and Marietta's management is considering cutting back on costs temporarily. Marietta's management must determine which of the following fixed costs it can reduce or eliminate and how much money each would save:

Fixed Costs	Planned Amounts
Advertising and promotion	$ 50,000
Depreciation	400,000
Employee training	100,000
Management salaries	800,000
Mortgage payment	250,000
Property taxes	600,000
Research and development	1,500,000
Total	$3,700,000

Can Marietta reduce or eliminate any of these fixed costs? The answer depends on Marietta's long-run outlook. Marietta could reduce costs but also greatly reduce its ability to compete in the future if it cuts fixed costs carelessly. Rearranging these costs by categories of committed and discretionary costs yields the following analysis:

Fixed Costs	Planned Amounts
Committed	
Depreciation	$ 400,000
Mortgage payment	250,000
Property taxes	600,000
Total committed	$1,250,000
Discretionary (potential savings)	
Advertising and promotion	$ 50,000
Employee training	100,000
Management salaries	800,000
Research and development	1,500,000
Total discretionary	$2,450,000
Total committed and discretionary	$3,700,000

Eliminating all discretionary fixed costs would save Marietta $2,450,000 per year. However, Marietta would be unwise to cut all discretionary costs completely. This would severely impair the company's long-run prospects. Nevertheless, distinguishing committed and discretionary fixed costs would be the company's first step in identifying where costs could be reduced.

Technology Decisions

One of the most critical decisions that managers make is choosing the type of technology the organization will use to produce its products or deliver its services. Choice of technology (for example, labor-intensive versus robotic manufacturing, personal banking services versus automated tellers, or e-commerce versus in-store sales) positions the organization to meet its current goals and to respond to changes in the environment (for example, changes in customer needs or actions by competitors). The use of high-technology methods rather than labor usually means a much greater fixed-cost component to the total cost. This type of cost behavior creates greater risks for companies with wide variations in demand.

Cost-Control Incentives

Finally, the incentives that management creates for employees can affect future costs. Managers use their knowledge of cost behavior to set cost expectations, and employees may receive compensation or other rewards that are tied to meeting these expectations. For example, the administrator of Parkview Medical Center could give the supervisor of the facilities maintenance department a favorable evaluation if the supervisor maintained quality of service and kept department costs below the expected amount for the actual level of patient-days. This feedback motivates the supervisor to watch department costs carefully and to find ways to reduce costs without reducing quality of service.

Cost Functions

As a manager, you will use cost functions often as a planning and control tool. A few of the reasons why cost functions are important are listed here:

1. Planning and controlling the activities of an organization require accurate and useful estimates of future fixed and variable costs.
2. Understanding relationships between costs and their cost drivers allows managers in all types of organizations—profit-seeking, nonprofit, and government—to make better operating, marketing, and production decisions; to plan and evaluate actions; and to determine appropriate costs for short-run and long-run decisions.

The first step in estimating or predicting costs is **cost measurement**—measuring cost behavior as a function of appropriate cost drivers. The second step is to use these cost measures to estimate future costs at expected levels of cost-driver activity. We begin by looking at the form of cost functions and the criteria for choosing the most appropriate cost drivers.

Form of Cost Functions

Objective 3

Measure and mathematically express cost functions and use them to predict costs.

To describe the relationship between a cost and its cost driver(s), managers often use an algebraic equation called a **cost function**. When there is only one cost driver, the cost function is similar to the algebraic CVP relationships discussed in Chapter 2. Consider the mixed cost graphed in Exhibit 3-3 on page 83, the facilities maintenance department cost:

$$\begin{matrix}\text{monthly facilities} \\ \text{maintenance} \\ \text{department costs}\end{matrix} = \begin{matrix}\text{monthly fixed} \\ \text{maintenance cost}\end{matrix} + \begin{matrix}\text{monthly variable} \\ \text{maintenance cost}\end{matrix}$$

$$= \begin{matrix}\text{monthly fixed} \\ \text{maintenance cost}\end{matrix} + \left(\begin{matrix}\text{variable cost per} \\ \text{patient-day}\end{matrix} \times \begin{matrix}\text{number of patient-days} \\ \text{in the month}\end{matrix} \right)$$

Let

Y = monthly facilities maintenance department cost

F = monthly fixed maintenance cost

V = variable cost per patient-day

X = cost-driver activity in number of patient-days per month

We can rewrite the mixed-cost function as

$$Y = F + VX \tag{1}$$

or

$$Y = \$10{,}000 + \$5.00X$$

This mixed-cost function has the familiar form of a straight line—it is called a linear cost function. When we graph a cost function, F is the intercept, the point on the vertical axis where the cost function begins. In Exhibit 3-3, the intercept is the $10,000 fixed cost per month. V, the variable cost per unit of activity, is the slope of the cost function. In Exhibit 3-3, the cost function slopes upward at the rate of $5 for each additional patient-day.

In our example, we use patient-days as the relevant cost driver. How did we choose this cost driver? Why not use number of patients, or number of operations, or facility square footage? In general, how do we develop cost functions?

Developing Cost Functions

Managers should apply two criteria to obtain accurate and useful cost functions: plausibility and reliability.

1. The cost function must be plausible, that is, believable. Personal observation of costs and activities, when it is possible, provides the best evidence of a plausible relationship between a resource cost and its cost driver. Some cost relationships, by nature, are not directly observable, so the cost analyst must be confident that the proposed relationship is valid. Many costs may move together with a number of cost drivers, but no cause-and-effect relationships may exist. A cause-and-effect relationship (that is, the cost driver causes the organization to incur the resource cost) is desirable for cost functions to be accurate and useful. For example, consider three possible cost drivers for the total cost of a **US Airways** round-trip flight from Phoenix to San Diego: miles flown, number of passengers, and passenger-miles (number of passengers times miles flown). Which of these possible cost drivers makes most sense? The answer is passenger-miles—the cost driver used by almost all airlines because both distance AND number of passengers flown impact cost incurrence.

2. In addition to being plausible, a cost function's estimates of costs at actual levels of activity must reliably conform to actually observed costs. We assess reliability in terms of "goodness of fit"—how well the cost function explains past cost behavior. If the fit is good and conditions do not change in the future, the cost function should be a reliable predictor of future costs.

Managers use these criteria together in choosing a cost function. Each is a check on the other. A manager needs to fully understand operations and the way accountants record costs to determine a plausible and reliable cost function that links cause and effect. For example, companies often perform maintenance when output is low because that is when they can take machines out of service. Lower output does not cause increased maintenance costs, however, nor does increased output cause lower maintenance costs. A more plausible explanation is that over a longer period increased output causes higher maintenance costs, but daily or weekly recording of maintenance costs and outputs may make it appear otherwise. Understanding the nature of maintenance costs should lead managers to a reliable, long-run cost function.

Making Managerial Decisions

A cost function is a mathematical expression of how cost drivers affect a particular cost. However, an intuitive understanding of cost functions is just as important as being able to write the mathematical formula. Suppose you have been using a cost function to predict total order-processing activity costs. The cost function is total costs = $25,000 + $89 × (number of orders processed). This formula is based on data that are in the range of 0–700 orders processed. Now, you want to predict the total cost for 680 orders. You have a few fundamental questions to answer before you are comfortable using the cost function in this situation. What does it mean when a cost function is linear? Why do managers want to know whether a cost is linear? What is the importance of the relevant range?

Answer

A linear cost function means that there are two parts to the cost. One part is fixed—that is, it's independent of the cost driver. The other part varies in proportion to the cost driver—that is, if the cost driver increases by X%, this part of the cost also increases by X%. Knowing that a cost is linear allows a manager to separate the cost into fixed and variable components—a simplification that helps you understand how decisions will affect costs. Incidentally, the predicted total cost for 680 orders is $25,000 + ($89 × 680) = $85,520. As long as the operating conditions that existed when the data were collected have not changed significantly, then knowing that the number of orders processed is within the relevant range—0–700, in this case—gives you confidence in the predicted total cost.

Choice of Cost Drivers: Activity Analysis

How do managers construct reliable and plausible cost functions? Well, you cannot have a good cost function without knowing the right cost drivers, so constructing a cost function starts with choosing cost drivers—the X in equation (1) on page 86. Managers use **activity analysis** to identify appropriate cost drivers and their effects on the costs of making a product or providing a service. The final product or service may have several cost drivers because production may involve many separate activities. The greatest benefit of activity analysis is that it directs management accountants to the appropriate cost drivers for each cost.

Consider Northwestern Computers, which makes two products for personal computers: a plug-in music board (Mozart-Plus) and a hard-disk drive (Powerdrive). These two products consist of material costs, labor costs, and support costs. In the past, most of the work on Northwestern's products was done by hand. In such a situation, labor costs were the primary driver of support costs. Support costs were twice as much as labor costs, on average.

Northwestern has just finished upgrading the production process. Now the company uses computer-controlled assembly equipment, which has increased the costs of support activities,

Objective 4

Describe the importance of activity analysis for measuring cost functions.

such as engineering and maintenance, and has reduced labor cost. Its cost function has now changed; specifically, labor cost is now only 5% of the total costs at Northwestern. An activity analysis has shown that the number of components added to products (a measure of product complexity), not labor cost, is the primary cost driver for support costs. Northwestern estimated support costs to be $20 per component. Mozart-Plus has five component parts, and Powerdrive has nine.

Suppose Northwestern wants to predict how much support cost it will incur in producing one Mozart-Plus and how much for one Powerdrive. Using the old cost driver, labor cost, the prediction of support costs would be as follows:

	Mozart-Plus	Powerdrive
Prior labor cost per unit	$ 8.50	$130.00
Predicted support cost		
2 × direct labor cost	$17.00	$260.00

Using the more appropriate cost driver based on the new production process, the number of components added to products, the predicted support costs are as follows:

	Mozart-Plus	Powerdrive
Predicted support cost at $20 per component		
$20 × 5 components	$100.00	
$20 × 9 components		$180.00
Difference in predicted support cost between the old and new cost function	$ 83.00 higher	$ 80.00 lower

By using an appropriate cost driver, Northwestern can predict its support costs much more accurately. Managers will make better decisions with this more accurate information. For example, they can relate prices charged for products more closely to the costs of production. To see how an actual organization uses activity analysis, see the Business First box on page 89.

One major question remains in our discussion of the measurement of cost behavior: How are the estimates of fixed costs and variable cost per cost-driver unit determined? Equation (1) on page 86 denotes these amounts by F = monthly fixed maintenance cost and V = variable cost per patient-day. In practice, organizations use several methods of measuring cost functions and determining values for F and V. Let's look at each of these methods.

Methods of Measuring Cost Functions

Objective 5

Measure cost behavior using the engineering analysis, account analysis, high-low, visual-fit, and least-squares regression methods.

After determining the most plausible drivers behind different costs, managers can choose from a broad selection of methods of approximating cost functions. These methods include (1) engineering analysis, (2) account analysis, (3) high-low analysis, (4) visual-fit analysis, and (5) least-squares regression analysis. These methods are not mutually exclusive; managers frequently use two or more together to avoid major errors in measuring cost behavior. The first two methods rely primarily on logical analysis of the cost environment, whereas the last three involve explicit analysis of prior cost data.

Engineering Analysis

The first method, **engineering analysis**, measures cost behavior according to what costs should be in an on-going process. It entails a systematic review of materials, supplies, labor, support services, and facilities needed for products and services. Analysts can even use engineering analysis successfully for new products and services, as long as the organization has had experience with similar costs. Why? Because they can base measures on information from personnel who are directly involved with the product or service. In addition to actual experience, analysts

Activity Analysis in Health-Care Organizations

Manufacturing companies were the first organizations to use activity analysis. However, its use has spread to many service industries and nonprofit organizations. For example, Hospice and Palliative Care of Central Kentucky (HCK), a health-care organization, has used activity analysis to better understand its costs.

HCK is a Medicare/Medicaid-certified program providing medical care to the terminally ill in 10 counties in central Kentucky. In addition to seeing to the medical needs of its patients, HCK has social workers, home health aides, volunteers, and chaplains. It also provides an 18-month bereavement program for families of patients.

Many of HCK's costs were related directly to patients, and understanding these costs posed no problems. However, support costs were large, and HCK had little information about what caused these costs.

The organization undertook an activity analysis to determine the appropriate cost drivers for support costs. This consisted of two basic tasks: (1) identify the activities being performed and (2) select a cost driver for each activity.

To identify the activities and the costs related to each activity, HCK formed a cross-functional team. The team identified 14 activities. The next step was to select a cost driver for each activity. Some of the activities and their related cost drivers were as follows:

Activity	Cost Driver
Referral	Number of (indexed) referrals
Admission	Number of admissions
Bereavement	Number of deaths
Accounting/finance	Number of (indexed) patient-days
Billing	Number of billings
Volunteer services	Number of volunteers

Using the cost information from the activity analysis, management was able to learn how much each different activity cost and could recognize that patients requiring use of expensive activities were more expensive to treat.

Another organization, a retirement and assisted-living community with 70 living units, took such an activity analysis one step further. Using an activity analysis similar to that of HCK, this organization took the resultant detailed cost information and conducted sensitivity analysis on profitability. Using optimization software called "Solver" from Microsoft Excel the organization was able to construct modified income statements that explicitly displayed how changes in its underlying cost activities would affect its profits. It was subsequently able to maximize its profits by optimizing the levels of these various activities, thus developing a organizational strategy that was best for its cost environment.

Sources: Adapted from Sidney J. Baxendale and Victoria Dornbusch, "Activity-Based Costing for a Hospice," *Strategic Finance*, March 2000, pp. 65–70; Sidney J. Baxendale, Mahesh Gupta, and P. S. Raju, "Profit Enhancement: Using an ABC Model," *Management Accounting Quarterly*, Winter 2005, pp. 11–21; and Hospice and Palliative Care of Central Kentucky's Web site (http://www.hosparus.org).

learn about new costs from experiments with prototypes, accounting and industrial engineering literature, the experience of competitors, and the advice of management consultants. From this information, cost analysts estimate what future costs should be. If the cost analysts are experienced and understand the activities of the organization, then their engineering cost predictions may be quite reliable and useful for decision making. The disadvantages of engineering cost analysis are that the efforts are costly and may not be timely.

Nearly any organization can use this approach to measuring cost behavior. For example, Weyerhaeuser Company, producer of wood products, used engineering analysis to determine the cost functions for its 14 corporate service departments. These cost functions measure the cost of corporate services used by three main business groups. Weyerhaeuser found that its accounts payable costs for each division are a function of three cost drivers: the number of hours spent on each division, number of documents, and number of invoices.

Now consider Parkview Medical Center, introduced earlier in the chapter. An assistant to the hospital administrator interviewed facilities maintenance personnel and observed their activities on several random days for a month. From these data, she confirmed that the most plausible cost driver for facilities maintenance cost is the number of patient-days. She also estimated from current department salaries and equipment charges that monthly fixed costs approximated $10,000 per month. Using interviews and observing supplies usage during the month, she estimated that variable costs are $5 per patient-day. She gave this information to the hospital administrator but cautioned that the cost measures may be wrong because of the following reasons:

1. The month observed may be abnormal.
2. The facilities maintenance personnel may have altered their normal work habits because the assistant was observing them.
3. The facilities maintenance personnel may not have told the complete truth about their activities because of their concerns about the use of the information they revealed.

However, if we assume the observed and estimated information is correct, we could predict facilities maintenance costs in any month by first forecasting that month's expected patient-days and then entering that figure into the following algebraic, mixed-cost function:

$$Y = \$10,000 \text{ per month} + (\$5 \times \text{patient-days})$$

For example, if the administrator expects 3,000 patient-days next month, the prediction of facilities maintenance costs would be as follows:

$$Y = \$10,000 + (\$5 \times 3,000 \text{ patient-days}) = \$25,000$$

Account Analysis

In contrast to engineering analysis, users of **account analysis** look to the accounting system for information about cost behavior. The simplest method of account analysis classifies each account as a variable or fixed cost with respect to a selected cost driver. The cost analyst then looks at each cost account balance and estimates either the variable cost per unit of cost-driver activity or the periodic fixed cost.

To illustrate this approach to account analysis, let's return to the facilities maintenance department at Parkview Medical Center and analyze costs for a recent month. The following table shows costs recorded in a month with 3,700 patient-days:

Monthly Cost	January Amount
Supervisor's salary and benefits	$ 3,800
Hourly workers' wages and benefits	14,674
Equipment depreciation and rentals	5,873
Equipment repairs	5,604
Cleaning supplies	7,472
Total facilities maintenance cost	$37,423

Recall that the most plausible and reliable driver for these costs is the number of patient-days serviced per month. Next, the analyst determines which costs may be fixed and which may be variable. Assume that the analyst has made the following judgments:

Monthly Cost	Amount	Fixed	Variable
Supervisor's salary and benefits	$ 3,800	$3,800	
Hourly workers' wages and benefits	14,674		$14,674
Equipment depreciation and rentals	5,873	5,873	
Equipment repairs	5,604		5,604
Cleaning supplies	7,472		7,472
Total facilities maintenance costs	$37,423	$9,673	$27,750

Measuring total facilities maintenance cost behavior, then, requires only simple arithmetic. First add up all the fixed costs to get the total fixed cost per month. Then divide the total variable costs by the units of cost-driver activity to get the variable cost per unit of cost driver.

$$\text{Fixed cost per month} = \$9,673$$
$$\text{Variable cost per patient-day} = \$27,750 \div 3,700 \text{ patient-days}$$
$$= \$7.50 \text{ per patient-day}$$

The algebraic, mixed-cost function, measured by account analysis, is

$$Y = \$9{,}673 \text{ per month} + (\$7.50 \times \text{patient-days})$$

Account analysis methods are less expensive to conduct than engineering analyses, but they require recording of relevant cost accounts and cost drivers. In addition, like engineering analysis, account analysis is subjective because the analysts decide whether each cost is variable or fixed based on their own judgment.

Summary Problem for Your Review

PROBLEM

The Reliable Insurance Company processes a variety of insurance claims for losses, accidents, thefts, and so on. Account analysis using one cost driver has estimated the variable cost of processing the claims for each automobile accident at 0.5% (.005) of the dollar value of all claims related to a particular accident. This estimate seemed reasonable because high-cost claims often involve more analysis before settlement. To control processing costs better, however, Reliable conducted an activity analysis of claims processing. The analysis suggested that there are three main cost drivers for the costs of processing claims for automobile accidents. The drivers and cost behavior are as follows:

> 0.2% of Reliable Insurance policyholders' property claims
> + 0.6% of other parties' property claims
> + 0.8% of total personal injury claims

Data from two recent automobile accident claims follow:

	Automobile Claim No. 607788	Automobile Claim No. 607991
Policyholder claim	$ 4,500	$23,600
Other party claim	0	3,400
Personal injury claim	12,400	0
Total claim amount	$16,900	$27,000

1. Estimate the cost of processing each claim using data from (a) the single-cost-driver analysis and (b) the three-cost-driver analysis.
2. How would you recommend that Reliable Insurance estimate the cost of processing claims?

SOLUTION

1. Costs are summarized in the table here.

	Automobile Claim No. 607788		Automobile Claim No. 607991	
	Claim Amount	Processing Cost	Claim Amount	Processing Cost
Using single-cost-driver analysis				
Total claim amount	$16,900		$27,000	
Estimated processing cost at 0.5%		$ 84.50		$135.00
Using three-cost-driver analysis				
Policyholder claim	$ 4,500		$23,600	
Estimated processing cost at 0.2%		$ 9.00		$ 47.20
Other party claim	0		3,400	
Estimated processing cost at 0.6%		0		20.40
Personal injury claim	12,400		0	
Estimated processing cost at 0.8%		99.20		0
Total estimated processing cost		$108.20		$ 67.60

2. The three-cost-driver analysis estimates of processing costs are considerably different from those using a single cost driver. If the activity analyses are reliable, then automobile claims that include personal injury losses are more costly to process than property damage claims. If these estimates are relatively inexpensive to keep current and to use, then it seems reasonable to adopt the three-cost-driver approach. Reliable will have more accurate cost estimates and will be better able to plan its claims processing activities. Reliable processes many different types of claims, however. Extending activity analysis to identify multiple cost drivers for all types of claims would result in a complicated system for predicting costs—much more complex (and costly) than simply using the total dollar value of claims. Whether to undertake an activity analysis for all types of policies depends on cost-benefit considerations. Managers can address such considerations by first adopting activity analysis for one type of claim and assessing the usefulness and cost of the more accurate information.

High-Low, Visual-Fit, and Least-Squares Methods

When enough cost data are available, we can use historical data to estimate the cost function mathematically. Three popular methods that use such data are the high-low, visual-fit, and least-squares methods. All three of these methods are more objective than the engineering-analysis and account-analysis methods. Each is based on hard evidence as well as on judgment, and they use more than one period's cost and activity information. Account analysis and engineering analysis will probably remain primary methods of measuring cost behavior because the three mathematical methods require more past cost data. Products, services, technologies, and organizations are changing rapidly in response to increased global competition and technological advances. In some cases, by the time enough historical data are collected to support these analyses, the data are obsolete—the organization has changed, the production process has changed, or the product has changed. The cost analyst must be careful that the historical data are from a past environment that still closely resembles the future environment for which a manager wants to predict costs. Another concern is that historical data may hide past inefficiencies that the company could reduce if it could identify them.

DATA FOR ILLUSTRATION   In discussing the high-low, visual-fit, and least-squares regression methods, we will continue to use the Parkview Medical Center's facilities maintenance department costs. The following table shows monthly data collected on facilities maintenance department costs and on the number of patient-days serviced over the past year:

Facilities Maintenance Department Data

Month	Facilities Maintenance Department Cost (Y)	Number of Patient-Days (X)
January	$37,000	3,700
February	23,000	1,600
March	37,000	4,100
April	47,000	4,900
May	33,000	3,300
June	39,000	4,400
July	32,000	3,500
August	33,000	4,000
September	17,000	1,200
October	18,000	1,300
November	22,000	1,800
December	20,000	1,600

HIGH-LOW METHOD   When sufficient cost data are available, the cost analyst may use historical data to measure the cost function mathematically. The simplest of the three methods to measure a linear-cost function from past cost data is the **high-low method** shown in Exhibit 3-4.

The first step in the high-low method is to plot the historical data points on a graph. This visual display helps the analyst see whether there are obvious errors in the data. Even though many points are plotted, the focus of the high-low method is normally on the highest and lowest activity points. However, if one of these points is an outlier that seems in error or non-representative of normal operations, we should use the next-highest or next-lowest activity point. For example, we should not use a point from a period with abnormally low activity caused by a labor strike or fire. Why? Because that point is not representative of a normal relationship between cost and cost driver.

After selecting the representative high and low points, we can draw a line between them, extending the line to the vertical (Y) axis of the graph. Note that this extension in Exhibit 3-4 is a dashed line, as a reminder that costs may not be linear outside the range of activity for which we have data (the relevant range). Also, managers usually are concerned with how costs behave within the relevant range, not with how they behave either at zero activity or at impossibly high activity levels. Measurements of costs within the relevant range may not be reliable measures or predictors of costs outside the relevant range.

The point at which the line intersects the Y-axis is the intercept, F, or estimate of fixed cost. The slope of the line measures the variable cost, V, per patient-day. The clearest way to measure the intercept and slope with the high-low method is to use algebra:

Month	Facilities Maintenance Department Cost (Y)	Number of Patient-Days (X)
High: April	$47,000	4,900
Low: September	17,000	1,200
Difference	$30,000	3,700

Variable cost per patient-day,

$$V = \frac{\text{change in costs}}{\text{change in activity}} = \frac{\$47,000 - \$17,000}{4,900 - 1,200 \text{ patient-days}}$$

$$V = \frac{\$30,000}{3,700} = \$8.1081 \text{ per patient-day}$$

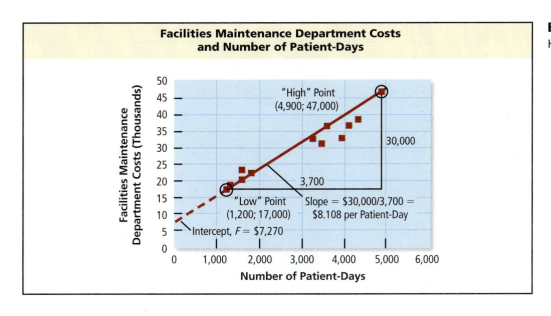

Facilities Maintenance Department Costs and Number of Patient-Days

"High" Point (4,900; 47,000)

30,000

3,700

"Low" Point (1,200; 17,000)

Slope = $30,000/3,700 = $8.108 per Patient-Day

Intercept, F = $7,270

Facilities Maintenance Department Costs (Thousands)

Number of Patient-Days

Exhibit 3-4
High-Low Method

Fixed cost per month, F = total mixed cost less total variable cost

At X (high): F = $47,000 − ($8.1081 × 4,900 patient-days)

= $47,000 − $39,730

= $7,270 per month

At X (low): F = $17,000 − ($8.1081 × 1,200 patient-days)

= $17,000 − $9,730

= $7,270 per month

Therefore, the facilities maintenance department cost function, measured by the high-low method, is

Y = $7,270 per month + ($8.1081 × patient-days)

The high-low method is easy to apply and illustrates mathematically how a change in a cost driver can change total cost. The cost function that resulted in this case is plausible. Before the widespread availability of computers, managers often used the high-low method to measure a cost function quickly. Today, however, the high-low method is not used as often because it makes inefficient use of information, basing the cost function on only two periods' cost experience, regardless of how many relevant data points have been collected.

Summary Problem for Your Review

PROBLEM

The Reetz Company has its own photocopying department. Reetz's photocopying costs include costs of copy machines, operators, paper, toner, utilities, and so on. We have the following cost and activity data:

Month	Total Photocopying Cost	Number of Copies
1	$25,000	320,000
2	29,000	390,000
3	24,000	300,000
4	23,000	310,000
5	28,000	400,000

1. Use the high-low method to measure the cost behavior of the photocopy department in formula form.
2. What are the benefits and disadvantages of using the high-low method for measuring cost behavior?

SOLUTION

1. The lowest and highest activity levels are in months 3 (300,000 copies) and 5 (400,000 copies).

$$\text{Variable cost per copy} = \frac{\text{change in cost}}{\text{change in activity}} = \frac{\$28,000 - \$24,000}{400,000 - 300,000}$$

$$= \frac{\$4,000}{100,000} = \underline{\$0.04} \text{ per copy}$$

Fixed cost per month = total cost less variable cost
at 400,000 copies: $28,000 − ($0.04 × 400,000) = $12,000 per month
at 300,000 copies: $24,000 − ($0.04 × 300,000) = $12,000 per month
Therefore, the photocopy cost function is
Y (total cost) = $12,000 per month + ($0.04 × number of copies)

2. The benefits of using the high-low method are as follows:
- The method is easy to use.
- Not many data points are needed.

The disadvantages of using the high-low method are as follows:
- The choice of the high and low points is subjective.
- The method does not use all available data.
- The method may not be reliable.

VISUAL-FIT METHOD   In the **visual-fit method**, we draw a straight line through a plot of all the available data, using judgment to fit the line as close as possible to all the plotted points. If the cost function for the data is linear, it is possible to draw a straight line through the scattered points that comes reasonably close to most of them and thus captures the general tendency of the data. We can extend that line back until it intersects the vertical axis of the graph.

Exhibit 3-5 shows this method applied to the facilities maintenance department cost data for the past 12 months. By measuring where the line intersects the cost axis, we can estimate the monthly fixed cost—in this case, about $10,000 per month. To find the variable cost per patient-day, select any activity level (for example 1,000 patient-days) and find the total cost at that activity level ($17,000). Then, divide the variable cost (which is total cost less fixed cost) by the units of activity.

$$\text{Variable cost per patient-day} = (\$17,000 - \$10,000) \div 1,000 \text{ patient-days}$$
$$= \$7 \text{ per patient-day}$$

The linear-cost function measured by the visual-fit method is

$$Y = \$10,000 \text{ per month} + (\$7 \times \text{patient-days})$$

Although the visual-fit method uses all the data, the placement of the line and the measurement of the fixed and variable costs are subjective. This subjectivity is the main reason that many

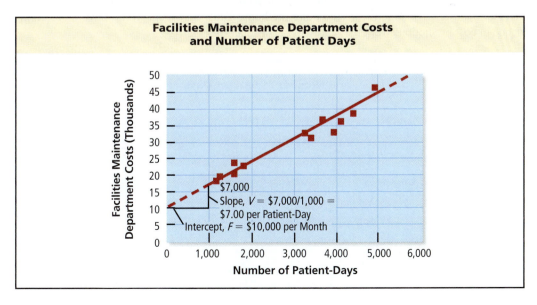

Exhibit 3-5
Visual-Fit Method

companies with sufficient data prefer to use least-squares regression analysis rather than the visual-fit method.

LEAST-SQUARES REGRESSION METHOD   Least-squares regression (or simply **regression analysis**) measures a cost function more objectively and explicitly than does the visual-fit method. Least-squares regression analysis uses statistics rather than human eyesight to fit a cost function to all the historical data. A simple regression uses one cost driver to measure a cost function, while a multiple regression uses two or more cost drivers. We will discuss only simple regression analysis in this chapter. Appendix 3 presents some statistical properties of regression analysis and shows how to use computer regression software.

Regression analysis measures cost behavior more reliably than other cost measurement methods. It also yields important statistical information about the reliability of its cost estimates. These statistics allow analysts to assess their confidence in the cost measures and thereby select the best cost driver. One such measure of reliability, or goodness of fit, is the **coefficient of determination, R^2** (or R-squared), which measures how much of the fluctuation of a cost is explained by changes in the cost driver. Appendix 3 explains R^2 and discusses how to use it to select the best cost driver.

Exhibit 3-6 shows the linear, mixed-cost function for facilities maintenance costs as measured mathematically by regression analysis. The fixed-cost measure is $9,329 per month. The variable-cost measure is $6.951 per patient-day. The linear-cost function is

facilities maintenance department cost = $9,329 per month + ($6.951 × number of patient-days)

or

$$Y = \$9,329 + (\$6.951 \times \text{patient-days})$$

Compare the cost measures produced by each of the five approaches:

Method	Fixed Cost per Month	Variable Cost per Patient-Day
Engineering analysis	$10,000	$5.000
Account analysis	9,673	7.500
High-low	7,270	8.108
Visual-fit	10,000	7.000
Regression	9,329	6.951

Because of their grounding in statistical analysis, the regression-cost measures are more reliable than those obtained from the other methods. Thus, managers would have more confidence in cost predictions from the regression-cost function.

Exhibit 3-6

Least-Squares Regression Method

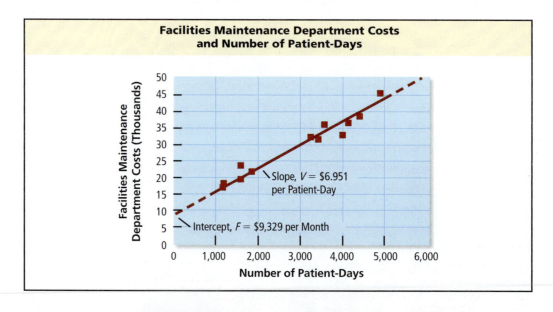

Highlights to Remember

1. **Explain step- and mixed-cost behavior.** Cost behavior refers to how costs change as levels of an organization's activities change. Costs can behave as fixed, variable, step, or mixed costs. Step and mixed costs both combine aspects of variable- and fixed-cost behavior. Step costs form graphs that look like steps. Costs will remain fixed within a given range of activity or cost-driver level, but then will rise or fall abruptly when the cost-driver level is outside this range. Mixed costs involve a fixed element and a variable element of cost behavior. Unlike step costs, mixed costs have a single fixed cost at all levels of activity and in addition have a variable cost element that increases proportionately with activity.

2. **Explain management influences on cost behavior.** Managers can affect the costs and cost behavior patterns of their companies through the decisions they make. Decisions on product and service features, capacity, technology, and cost-control incentives, for example, can all affect cost behavior.

3. **Measure and mathematically express cost functions and use them to predict costs.** The first step in estimating or predicting costs is measuring cost behavior. This is done by finding a cost function. This is an algebraic equation that describes the relationship between a cost and its cost driver(s). To be useful for decision-making purposes, cost functions should be plausible and reliable.

4. **Describe the importance of activity analysis for measuring cost functions.** Activity analysis is the process of identifying the best cost drivers to use for cost estimation and prediction and determining how they affect the costs of making a product or service. This is an essential step in understanding and predicting costs.

5. **Measure cost behavior using the engineering analysis, account analysis, high-low, visual-fit, and least-squares regression methods.** Once analysts have identified cost drivers, they can use one of several methods to determine the cost function. Engineering analysis focuses on what costs should be by systematically reviewing the materials, supplies, labor, support services, and facilities needed for a given level of production. Account analysis involves examining all accounts in terms of an appropriate cost driver and classifying each account as either fixed or variable with respect to the driver. The cost function consists of the variable cost per cost-driver unit multiplied by the amount of the cost driver plus the total fixed cost. The high-low, visual-fit, and regression methods all use historical data to determine cost functions. Of these three methods, regression is the most reliable. ■

Appendix 3: Use and Interpretation of Least-Squares Regression

While we can perform regression analysis of historical cost data by hand, it would be unusual to find cost analysts doing so. Rather, they use computers that are much faster and less prone to error, and also produce explicit statistical analyses of the results. Therefore, we focus on interpretation of the results from a regression performed by a computer.

This appendix is not a substitute for a good statistics class. More properly, think of it as a motivator for studying statistics so that you can better interpret regression cost estimates. Recall that in this textbook we consider only simple regression (one cost driver) analysis. Incorporating more than one cost driver into a cost function via regression (multiple regression) is beyond the scope of this text, and again, you should consult a statistics textbook to learn about such an advanced regression technique.

Assume that there are two potential cost drivers for the costs of the facilities maintenance department in Parkview Medical Center: (1) number of patient-days and (2) total value of hospital room charges. Regression analysis can assist in the determination of which activity is the better (more descriptive) cost driver in explaining and predicting costs. Exhibit 3-7 shows the past 12 months' cost and cost-driver data for the facilities maintenance department.

Regression Analysis Procedures

Most spreadsheet software available for PCs offers basic regression analysis in the Data Analysis or Tools commands. We will use these spreadsheet commands to illustrate regression analysis because many readers will be familiar already with spreadsheet software.

Entering Data

First, create a spreadsheet with the historical cost data in rows and columns. Each row should be data from one period. Each column should be a cost category or a cost driver. For ease of analysis, all the potential cost drivers should be in adjacent columns. Each row and column should be complete (no missing data) and without errors.

Exhibit 3-7

Facilities Maintenance
Department Data

Month	Facilities Maintenance Cost (Y)	Number of Patient-Days (X₁)	Value of Room Charges (X₂)
January	$37,000	3,700	$2,183,000
February	23,000	1,600	2,735,000
March	37,000	4,100	2,966,000
April	47,000	4,900	2,846,000
May	33,000	3,300	2,967,000
June	39,000	4,400	2,980,000
July	32,000	3,500	3,023,000
August	33,000	4,000	2,352,000
September	17,000	1,200	1,825,000
October	18,000	1,300	1,515,000
November	22,000	1,800	1,547,000
December	20,000	1,600	2,117,000

Plotting Data

There are two main reasons why the first step in regression analysis should be to plot the cost against each of the potential cost drivers: (1) Plots may show obvious nonlinear trends in the data; if so, linear regression analysis may not be appropriate for the entire range of the data. (2) Plots help identify outliers—costs that are in error or are otherwise obviously inappropriate.

Plotting with spreadsheets uses Graph commands on the columns of cost and cost-driver data. These Graph commands typically offer many optional graph types (such as bar charts and pie charts), but the most useful plot for regression analysis usually is called the XY graph. This graph is the type shown earlier in this chapter—the X-axis is the cost driver, and the Y-axis is the cost. The XY graph should be displayed without lines drawn between the data points (called data symbols)—an optional command. (Consult your spreadsheet manual for details because each spreadsheet program is different.)

Regression Output

The format of the regression output is different for each software package. However, every package will identify the cost to be explained ("dependent variable") and the cost driver ("independent variable") in the cost function.

Producing regression output with spreadsheets is simple: Just select the Regression command, specify (or highlight) the X-dimension[s] (the cost driver[s]), and specify the Y-dimension or "series" (the cost). Next, specify a blank area on the spreadsheet where the output will be displayed, and select Go. The following is a regression analysis of facilities maintenance department costs using one of the two possible cost drivers, number of patient-days, X_1.

Facilities Maintenance Department Cost Explained by Number of Patient-Days

Regression Output	
Constant	9,329
R^2	0.955
X coefficient(s)	6.951

Interpretation of Regression Output

The fixed-cost measure, labeled "constant" or "intercept" by most programs, is $9,329 per month. The variable cost measure, labeled "X coefficient" (or something similar in other spreadsheets), is $6.951 per patient-day. The linear cost function is

$$Y = \$9,329 \text{ per month} + (\$6.951 \times \text{patient-days})$$

As mentioned in the chapter, it is important to consider plausibility and reliability in evaluating a cost function and its estimates. Plausibility simply refers to whether the estimated cost function makes economic sense. We can assess this by examining the sign of the variable cost estimate. In the preceding cost function, this estimate is +$6.951. The positive sign in this cost function implies that as patient-days increase, facilities maintenance costs also increase (specifically, by $6.951 per patient day). We assess the economic plausibility of this positive relationship by asking ourselves whether it makes economic sense that an increase in patient-days should increase facilities maintenance costs. Based on our economic intuition, it appears that a positive relationship makes sense (that is, we would expect that increasing patient-days would increase the cost of cleaning supplies and repair materials such that total facilities maintenance costs increase). While plausibility appears to be a simple and straightforward item to assess, it is the most important element to assess in a cost function. We would not want to use a cost function to estimate and predict costs if it did not exhibit plausibility (even if it displayed good reliability) because, without plausibility, we do not fundamentally understand the cost function, which makes cost estimation and prediction suspect.

Regarding reliability, the computer output usually gives a number of statistical measures that indicate how well each cost driver explains the cost and how reliable the cost predictions are likely to be. A full explanation of the output is beyond the scope of this text. However, one of the most important statistics, the coefficient of determination, or R^2, is an important measure of reliability—how well the cost function fits the actual cost data. In general, the better a cost driver is at explaining a cost, the closer the data points will lie to the line, and the higher will be the R^2, which varies between 0 and 1. An R^2 of 0 means that the cost driver does not explain variability in the cost data, whereas an R^2 of 1 means that the cost driver explains the variability perfectly. The R^2 of the relationship measured with number of patient-days as the cost driver is 0.955, which is quite high. This value indicates that the number of patient-days explains facilities maintenance department cost extremely well. In fact, the number of patient-days explains 95.5% of the past fluctuations in facilities maintenance department cost. Such a regression is highly reliable.

In contrast, performing a regression analysis on the relationship between facilities maintenance department cost and value of hospital room charges produces the following results:

Facilities Maintenance Department Cost Explained by Value of Hospital Room Charges

Regression Output	
Constant	$ 924
R^2	0.511
X coefficient(s)	0.012

While the positive sign of the variable cost estimate (+.012) appears to satisfy plausibility (that is, as hospital room charges increase we would expect facilities maintenance costs to also increase), the R^2 value, 0.511, indicates that the cost function using value of hospital room charges does not fit facilities maintenance department cost as well as the cost function using number of patient-days.

To use the information generated by regression analysis fully, an analyst must understand the meaning of the statistics and must be able to determine whether the statistical assumptions of regression are satisfied by the cost data. Indeed, one of the major reasons why cost analysts study statistics is to understand the assumptions of regression analysis better. With this understanding, analysts can provide their organizations with the best estimates of cost behavior.

	Sign A	Sign B
Materials cost	$400	$200
Number of power tool operations	3	6
Support cost	?	?

1. Prepare a report showing the support costs of both signs using each cost driver and showing the differences between the two.
2. What advice would you give Evergreen Signs about predicting support costs?

3-A3 Division of Mixed Costs into Variable and Fixed Components

Martina Fernandez, president of Evert Tool, Co., has asked for information about the cost behavior of manufacturing support costs. Specifically, she wants to know how much support cost is fixed and how much is variable. The following data are the only records available:

Month	Machine Hours	Support Costs
May	850	$ 9,000
June	1,300	12,500
July	1,000	7,900
August	1,250	11,400
September	1,750	13,500

1. Find monthly fixed support cost and the variable support cost per machine-hour by the high-low method.
2. Explain how your analysis for requirement 1 would change if new October data were received and machine-hours were 1,700 and support costs were $15,800.
3. A least-squares regression analysis gave the following output:

$$\text{Regression equation: } Y = \$3,355 + \$6.10X$$

What recommendations would you give the president based on these analyses?

3-B1 Identifying Cost Behavior Patterns

At a seminar, a cost accountant spoke on identification of different kinds of cost behavior. Tammy Li, a hospital administrator who heard the lecture, identified several hospital costs of concern to her. After her classification, Li presented you with the following list of costs and asked you to (1) classify their behavior as one of the following: variable, step, mixed, discretionary fixed or committed fixed; and (2) to identify a likely cost driver for each variable or mixed cost.

1. Operating costs of X-ray equipment ($95,000 a year plus $3 per film)
2. Health insurance for all full-time employees
3. Costs incurred by Dr. Rath in cancer research
4. Repairs made on hospital furniture
5. Training costs of an administrative resident
6. Straight-line depreciation of operating room equipment
7. Costs of services of King Hospital Consulting
8. Nursing supervisors' salaries (a supervisor is needed for each 45 nursing personnel)

3-B2 Activity Analysis

Nampa Technology, an Idaho manufacturer of printed circuit boards, has always estimated the support cost of its circuit boards with a 100% "markup" over its material costs. An activity analysis suggests that support costs are driven primarily by the number of manual operations performed on each board, estimated at $4 per manual operation. Compute the estimated support costs of the following two typical circuit boards using the traditional markup and the activity analysis results:

	Board Z15	Board Q52
Material cost	$40.00	$60.00
Manual operations	15	7

Why are the cost estimates different?

3-B3 Division of Mixed Costs into Variable and Fixed Components

The president and the controller of Monterrey Transformer Company (Mexico) have agreed that refinement of the company's cost measurements will aid planning and control decisions. They have asked you to measure the function for mixed-cost behavior of repairs and maintenance from the following sparse data. Currency is the Mexican peso (P).

Monthly Activity in Machine Hours	Monthly Repair and Maintenance Cost
8,000	P200,000,000
12,000	P260,000,000

Additional Assignment Material

MyAccountingLab

QUESTIONS

3-1 What is a cost driver? Give three examples of costs and their possible cost drivers.

3-2 Explain linear-cost behavior.

3-3 "Step costs can be fixed or variable, depending on your perspective." Explain.

3-4 Explain how mixed costs are related to both fixed and variable costs.

3-5 How do management's product and service choices affect cost behavior?

3-6 Why are fixed costs also called capacity costs?

3-7 How do committed fixed costs differ from discretionary fixed costs?

3-8 Why are committed fixed costs the most difficult of the fixed costs to change?

3-9 What are the primary determinants of the level of committed costs? Discretionary costs?

3-10 "Planning is far more important than day-to-day control of discretionary costs." Do you agree? Explain.

3-11 How can a company's choice of technology affect its costs?

3-12 Explain the use of incentives to control cost.

3-13 Why is it important for managers and accountants to measure cost functions?

3-14 Explain plausibility and reliability of cost functions. Which is preferred? Explain.

3-15 What is activity analysis?

3-16 What is engineering analysis? Account analysis?

3-17 Describe the methods for measuring cost functions using past cost data.

3-18 How could account analysis be combined with engineering analysis?

3-19 Explain the strengths and weaknesses of the high-low and visual-fit methods.

3-20 In the high-low method, does the high and low refer to cost-driver levels or to total cost levels? Explain.

3-21 Why is regression analysis usually preferred to the high-low method?

3-22 "You never know how good your fixed- and variable-cost measures are if you use account analysis or if you visually fit a line on a data plot. That's why I like least-squares regression analysis." Explain.

3-23 (Appendix 3) Why should an analyst always plot cost data in addition to applying least-squares regression analysis?

3-24 (Appendix 3) What can we learn from R^2, the coefficient of determination?

3-25 At a conference, a consultant stated, "Before you can control, you must measure." An executive complained, "Why bother to measure when work rules and guaranteed employment provisions in labor contracts prevent discharging workers, using part-time employees, and using overtime?" Evaluate these comments.

CRITICAL THINKING EXERCISES

3-26 Mixed Costs and the Sales Force

Wysocki Company pays its sales force a fixed salary plus a 5% commission on all sales. Explain why sales force costs would be considered a mixed cost.

3-27 Committed and Discretionary Fixed Costs in Manufacturing

Among the fixed costs of Howarth Company are depreciation and research and development (R&D). Using these two costs as examples, explain the difference between committed and discretionary fixed costs.

3-28 Cost Functions and Decision Making

Why is it important that decision makers in a corporation know the cost function for producing the company's products?

3-29 Statistical Analysis and Cost Functions

What advantages does using regression analysis have over the visual-fit method for determining cost functions?

EXERCISES

3-30 Step Costs

Which of the following are step costs? Why?

  a. Rent on a warehouse that is large enough for all anticipated orders
  b. Teachers for a private elementary school; one teacher is needed for every 15 students
  c. Sheet steel for a producer of machine parts; steel is purchased in carload shipments, where each carload contains enough steel for 1,000 parts

3-31 Mixed Costs

The following cost function is a mixed cost. Explain why it is a mixed cost and not a fixed, variable, or step cost.

$$\text{Total cost} = \$8,000 + \$52 \times \text{units produced}$$

3-32 Various Cost-Behavior Patterns

In practice, there is often a tendency to simplify approximations of cost-behavior patterns, even though the "true" underlying behavior is not simple. Choose from the following graphs A–H the one that matches the numbered items. Indicate by letter which graph best fits each of the situations described. Next to each number-letter pair, identify a likely cost driver for that cost.

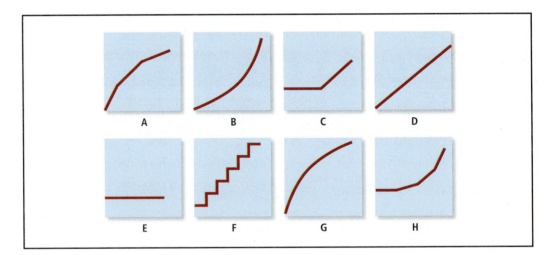

The vertical axes of the graphs represent total dollars of costs incurred, and the horizontal axes represent levels of cost driver activity during a particular time period. The graphs may be used more than once.

  1. Cost of machining labor that tends to decrease as workers gain experience
  2. Price of an increasingly scarce raw material as the quantity used increases
  3. Guaranteed annual wage plan, whereby workers get paid for 40 hours of work per week even at zero or low levels of production that require working only a few hours weekly
  4. Water bill, which entails a flat fee for the first 10,000 gallons used and then an increasing unit cost for every additional 10,000 gallons used
  5. Availability of quantity discounts, where the cost per unit falls as each price break is reached
  6. Depreciation of office equipment
  7. Cost of sheet steel for a manufacturer of farm implements

8. Salaries of supervisors, where one supervisor is added for every 12 phone solicitors
9. Natural gas bill consisting of a fixed component, plus a constant variable cost per thousand cubic feet after a specified number of cubic feet are used

3-33 Plotting Data

The following graph was constructed and data plotted to apply the visual-fit method. Then, the predicted total order-department costs for processing 90 orders was computed. Comment on the accuracy of the analysis. Do your own analysis and explain any differences. Assume the data in parentheses are accurate in thousands of dollars and number of orders.

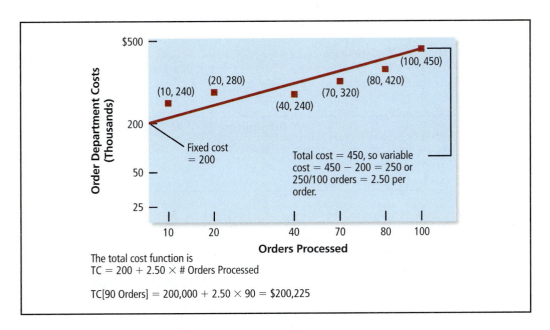

The total cost function is
TC = 200 + 2.50 × # Orders Processed

TC[90 Orders] = 200,000 + 2.50 × 90 = $200,225

3-34 Cost Function for Expedia

Expedia provides travel services on the Internet. 2002 was an important year for Expedia as it reported positive operating income after 3 years of operating losses. In the first quarter of 2001, Expedia reported an operating loss of $19 million on sales revenue of $57 million. In the first quarter of 2002, sales revenue had more than doubled to $116 million, and Expedia had operating income of $18 million. Assume that fixed costs were the same in 2002 as in 2001.

1. Compute the operating expenses for Expedia in the first quarter of 2001 and in the first quarter of 2002.
2. Determine the cost function for Expedia, that is, the total fixed cost and the variable cost as a percentage of sales revenue. Use the same form as equation (1) on page 86.
3. Explain how Expedia's operating income could increase by $37 million with an increase in sales of $59 million, while it had an operating loss of $19 million on its $57 million of sales in the first quarter of 2001.

3-35 Predicting Costs

Given the following four cost behaviors and expected levels of cost-driver activity, predict total costs:

1. Fuel costs of driving vehicles, $0.40 per mile, driven 16,000 miles per month
2. Equipment rental cost, $5,000 per piece of equipment per month for seven pieces for 3 months
3. Ambulance and EMT personnel cost for a soccer tournament, $1,200 for each 200 tournament participants; the tournament is expecting 2,400 participants
4. Purchasing department cost, $7,500 per month plus $5 per material order processed at 4,000 orders in one month

3-36 Identifying Discretionary and Committed Fixed Costs

Identify and compute total discretionary fixed costs and total committed fixed costs from the following list prepared by the accounting supervisor for Huang Building Supply:

Advertising	$22,000
Depreciation	47,000
Health insurance for the company's employees	21,000
Management salaries	85,000
Payment on long-term debt	50,000
Property tax	32,000
Grounds maintenance	9,000
Office remodeling	21,000
Research and development	46,000

3-37 Cost Effects of Technology

Recreational Sports, an outdoor sports retailer, is planning to add a Web site for online sales. The estimated costs of two alternative approaches are as follows:

	Alternative 1	Alternative 2
Annual fixed cost	$200,000	$400,000
Variable cost per order	$ 8	$ 4
Expected number of orders	70,000	70,000

At the expected level of orders, which online approach has the lower cost? What is the indifference level of orders, or the "break-even" level of orders? What is the meaning of this level of orders?

3-38 Mixed Cost, Choosing Cost Drivers, and High-Low and Visual-Fit Methods

Cedar Rapids Implements Company produces farm implements. Cedar Rapids is in the process of measuring its manufacturing costs and is particularly interested in the costs of the manufacturing maintenance activity, since maintenance is a significant mixed cost. Activity analysis indicates that maintenance activity consists primarily of maintenance labor setting up machines using certain supplies. A setup consists of preparing the necessary machines for a particular production run of a product. During setup, machines must still be running, which consumes energy. Thus, the costs associated with maintenance include labor, supplies, and energy. Unfortunately, Cedar Rapids' cost accounting system does not trace these costs to maintenance activity separately. Cedar Rapids employs two full-time maintenance mechanics to perform maintenance. The annual salary of a maintenance mechanic is $25,000 and is considered a fixed cost. Two plausible cost drivers have been suggested: "units produced" and "number of setups."

Data had been collected for the past 12 months and a plot was made for the cost driver—units of production. The maintenance cost figures collected include estimates for labor, supplies, and energy. Cory Fielder, controller at Cedar Rapids, noted that some types of activities are performed each time a batch of goods is processed rather than each time a unit is produced. Based on this concept, he has gathered data on the number of setups performed over the past 12 months. The plots of monthly maintenance costs versus the two potential cost drivers follow:

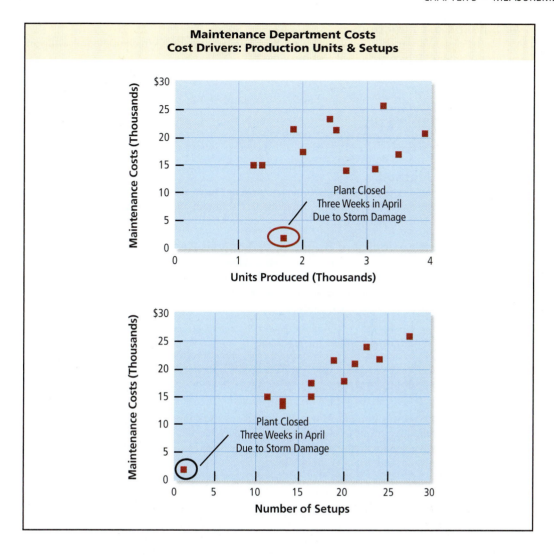

1. Find monthly fixed maintenance cost and the variable maintenance cost per driver unit using the visual-fit method based on each potential cost driver. Explain how you treated the April data.
2. Find monthly fixed maintenance cost and the variable maintenance cost per driver unit using the high-low method based on each potential cost driver.
3. Which cost driver best meets the criteria for choosing cost functions? Explain.

3-39 Account Analysis

Custom Computers is a company started by two engineering students to assemble and market personal computers to faculty and students. The company operates out of the garage of one of the students' homes. From the following costs of a recent month, compute the total cost function and total cost for the month:

Telephone	$ 50, fixed
Utilities	260, fixed: 25% attributable to the garage, 75% to the house
Advertising	75, fixed
Insurance	80, fixed
Materials	7,500, variable, for five computers
Labor	1,800: $1,300 fixed plus $500 for hourly help for assembling five computers

3-40 Linear Cost Functions

Let Y = total costs, X_1 = production volume, and X_2 = number of setups. Which of the following are linear cost functions? Which are mixed cost functions?

a. $Y = \$8X_1$
b. $Y = \$1,500$
c. $Y = \$8,500 + \$1.50X_1$
d. $Y = \$3,000 + \$6X_1 + \$30X_2$
e. $Y = \$9,000 + \$3(X_1 \times X_2)$
f. $Y = \$5,000 + \$4.00X_1$

3-41 High-Low Method

North Manchester Foundry produced 55,000 tons of steel in March at a cost of £1,150,000. In April, the foundry produced 35,000 tons at a cost of £950,000. Using only these two data points, determine the cost function for North Manchester.

3-42 Economic Plausibility of Regression Analysis Results

The head of the Warehousing Division of Lachton, Co., was concerned about some cost behavior information given to him by the new assistant controller, who was hired because of his recent training in cost analysis. His first assignment was to apply regression analysis to various costs in the department. One of the results was presented as follows:

> A regression on monthly data was run to explain building maintenance cost as a function of direct labor hours as the cost driver. The results are

$$Y = \$7,810 - \$.47X$$

> I suggest that we use the building as intensively as possible to keep the maintenance costs down.

The department head was puzzled. How could increased use cause decreased maintenance cost? Explain this counterintuitive result to the department head. What step(s) did the assistant controller probably omit in applying and interpreting the regression analysis?

PROBLEMS

3-43 Controlling Risk, Capacity Decisions, Technology Decisions

Consider the following hypothetical situation in the computer industry. HP had been outsourcing production to Acer and using overtime for as much as 20% of production—HP's plants and assembly lines were running at 100% of capacity and demand was sufficient for an additional 20%. HP had considered increasing its capacity by building new, highly automated assembly lines and plants. However, the investment in high technology and capacity expansion was rejected.

Assume that all material and labor costs are variable with respect to the level of production and that all other costs are fixed. Consider one of HP's plants that makes the Pavillion model. The increase in annual fixed costs to convert the plant to use fully automated assembly lines is $20 million. The resulting labor costs would be significantly reduced and there would be no need for overtime or outsourced production. The annual costs, in millions of dollars, of the build option and the existing costs that include outsourcing and overtime are given in the following tables:

	Build Option		
Percent of current capacity	60	100	120
Material costs	$18	$30	$36
Labor costs	6	10	12
Other costs	40	40	40
Total costs	$64	$80	$88

	HP's Existing Costs Using Outsourcing/Overtime		
Percent of current capacity	60	100	120
Material costs	$18	$30	$ 36
Labor costs	18	30	44
Other costs	20	20	20
Total costs	$56	$80	$100

1. Prepare a line graph showing total costs for the two options: (a) build new assembly lines, and (b) continue to use overtime and outsource production of Pavillions. Give an explanation of the cost behavior of the two options.
2. Which option enables HP's management to control risk better? Explain. Assess the cost-benefit trade-offs associated with each option.
3. A solid understanding of cost behavior is an important prerequisite to effective managerial control of costs. Suppose you are an executive at HP. Currently the production (and sales) level is approaching the 100% level of capacity, and the economy is expected to remain strong for at least one year. While sales and profits are good now, you are aware of the variability inherent in the computer business. Would you recommend committing HP to building automated assembly lines in order to service potential near-term increases in demand, or would you recommend against building, looking to the possible future downturn in business? Discuss your reasoning.

3-44 Step Costs

Algona Beach Jail requires a staff of at least 1 guard for every 4 prisoners. The jail will hold 48 prisoners. Algona Beach attracts numerous tourists and transients in the spring and summer. However, the town is rather sedate in the fall and winter. The jail's fall–winter population is generally between 12 and 16 prisoners. The numbers in the spring and summer can fluctuate from 12 to 48, depending on the weather, among other factors (including phases of the moon, according to some longtime residents).

Algona Beach has 4 permanent guards, hired on a year-round basis at an annual salary of $36,000 each. When additional guards are needed, they are hired on a weekly basis at a rate of $600 per week. (For simplicity, assume that each month has exactly 4 weeks.)

1. Prepare a graph with the weekly planned cost of jail guards on the vertical axis and the number of prisoners on the horizontal axis.
2. What would be the budgeted amount for jail guards for the month of January? Would this be a fixed or a variable cost?
3. Suppose the jail population of each of the 4 weeks in July was 25, 38, 26, and 43, respectively. The actual amount paid for jail guards in July was $19,800. Prepare a report comparing the actual amount paid for jail guards with the amount that would be expected with efficient scheduling and hiring.
4. Suppose Algona Beach treated jail-guard salaries for nonpermanent guards as a variable expense of $150 per week per prisoner. This variable cost was applied to the number of prisoners in excess of 16. Therefore, the weekly cost function was as follows:

$$\text{Weekly jail-guard cost} = \$3{,}000 + \$150 \times (\text{total prisoners} - 16)$$

Explain how this cost function was determined.
5. Prepare a report similar to that in requirement 3 except that the cost function in requirement 4 should be used to calculate the expected amount of jail-guard salaries. Which report, this one or the one in requirement 3, is more accurate? Is accuracy the only concern?

3-45 Government Service Cost Analysis

Auditors for the Internal Revenue Service (IRS) scrutinize income tax returns after they have been prescreened with the help of computer tests for normal ranges of deductions claimed by taxpayers. The IRS uses an expected cost of $7 per tax return, based on measurement studies that allow 20 minutes per return. Each agent has a workweek of 5 days of 8 hours per day. Twenty auditors are employed at a salary of $830 each per week.

The audit supervisor has the following data regarding performance for the most recent 4-week period, when 8,000 returns were processed:

Actual Cost of Auditors	Expected Cost for Processing Returns	Difference or Variance
$66,400	?	?

1. Compute the planned cost and the variance.
2. The supervisor believes that audit work should be conducted more productively and that superfluous personnel should be transferred to field audits. If the foregoing data are representative, how many auditors should be transferred?
3. List some possible reasons for the variance.
4. Describe some alternative cost drivers for processing income tax returns.

3-46 Cost Analysis at US Airways

US Airways is one of the nation's leading commercial air carriers, with hubs in Phoenix and Las Vegas. The following are some of the costs incurred by US Airways. For each cost, select an appropriate cost driver and indicate whether the cost is likely to be fixed, variable, or mixed in relation to your cost driver.

 a. Airplane fuel
 b. Flight attendants' salaries
 c. Baggage handlers' salaries
 d. In-flight meals
 e. Pilots' salaries
 f. Airplane depreciation
 g. Advertising

3-47 Separation of Drug Testing Laboratory Mixed Costs into Variable and Fixed Components

A staff meeting has been called at SportsLab, a drug-testing facility retained by several professional and college sports leagues and associations. The chief of testing, Dr. Hyde, has demanded an across-the-board increase in prices for a particular test because of the increased testing and precision that are now required.

   The administrator of the laboratory has asked you to measure the mixed-cost behavior of this particular testing department and to prepare a short report she can present to Dr. Hyde. Consider the following limited data:

	Average Test Procedures per Month	Average Monthly Cost of Test Procedures
Monthly averages, 20X7	400	$ 60,000
Monthly averages, 20X8	500	80,000
Monthly averages, 20X9	600	140,000

3-48 School Cost Behavior

Lakeview School, a private high school, is preparing a planned income statement for the coming academic year ending August 31, 2010. Tuition revenues for the past two years ending August 31 were as follows: 2009, $820,000; and 2008, $870,000. Total expenses for 2009 were $810,000 and in 2008 were $830,000. No tuition rate changes occurred in 2008 or 2009, nor are any expected to occur in 2010. Tuition revenue is expected to be $810,000 for 2010. What net income should be planned for 2010, assuming that the implied cost behavior remains unchanged?

3-49 Activity Analysis

Des Moines Software develops and markets computer software for the agriculture industry. Because support costs are a large portion of the cost of software development, the director of cost operations of Des Moines, Leslie Paton, is especially concerned with understanding the effects of support cost behavior. Paton has completed a preliminary activity analysis of one of Des Moines's primary software products: FertiMix (software to manage fertilizer mixing). This product is a software template that is customized for specific customers, who are charged for the basic product plus customizing costs. The activity analysis is based on the number of customized lines of FertiMix code. Currently, support cost estimates are based on a fixed rate of 50% of the basic cost. Data are shown for two recent customers:

	Customer	
	West Acres Plants	Beautiful Blooms
Basic cost of FertiMix	$13,000	$13,000
Lines of customized code	490	180
Estimated cost per line of customized code	$22	$22

1. Compute the support cost of customizing FertiMix for each customer using each cost-estimating approach.
2. If the activity analysis is reliable, what are the pros and cons of adopting it for all Des Moines's software products?

3-50 High-Low, Regression Analysis

On November 15, 2009, Sandra Cook, a newly hired cost analyst at Demgren Company, was asked to predict overhead costs for the company's operations in 2010, when 510 units are expected to be produced. She collected the following quarterly data:

Quarter	Production in Units	Overhead Costs
1/06	76	$ 721
2/06	79	715
3/06	71	649
4/06	136	1,131
1/07	125	1,001
2/07	128	1,111
3/07	125	1,119
4/07	133	1,042
1/08	124	997
2/08	129	1,066
3/08	115	996
4/08	84	957
1/09	84	835
2/09	122	1,050
3/09	90	991

1. Using the high-low method to estimate costs, prepare a prediction of overhead costs for 2010.
2. Sandy ran a regression analysis using the data she collected. The result was

$$Y = \$355 + \$5.77 X$$

Using this cost function, predict overhead costs for 2010.
3. Which prediction do you prefer? Why?

3-51 Interpretation of Regression Analysis

Study Appendix 3. The Tent Division of Arizona Outdoor Equipment Company has had difficulty controlling its use of supplies. The company has traditionally regarded supplies as a purely variable cost. Nearly every time production was above average, however, the division spent less than predicted for supplies; when production was below average, the division spent more than predicted. This pattern suggested to Yuki Li, the new controller, that part of the supplies cost was probably not related to production volume, or was fixed.

She decided to use regression analysis to explore this issue. After consulting with production personnel, she considered two cost drivers for supplies cost: (1) number of tents produced, and (2) square feet of material used. She obtained the following results based on monthly data.

	Cost Driver	
	Number of Tents	Square Feet of Material Used
Constant	2,300	1,900
Variable coefficient	0.033	0.072
R^2	0.220	0.686

1. Which is the preferred cost function? Explain.
2. What percentage of the fluctuation of supplies cost depends on square feet of materials? Do fluctuations in supplies cost depend on anything other than square feet of materials? What proportion of the fluctuations is not explained by square feet of materials?

3-52 Regression Analysis

Study Appendix 3. Mr. Liao, CEO of a manufacturer of fine china and stoneware, is troubled by fluctuations in productivity and wants to compute how manufacturing support costs are related to the various sizes of batches of output. The following data show the results of a random sample of 10 batches of one pattern of stoneware:

Sample	Batch Size, X	Support Costs, Y
1	15	$180
2	12	140
3	20	230
4	17	190
5	12	160
6	25	300
7	22	270
8	9	110
9	18	240
10	30	320

1. Plot support costs, Y, versus batch size, X.
2. Using regression analysis, measure the cost function of support costs and batch size.
3. Predict the support costs for a batch size of 25.
4. Using the high-low method, repeat requirements 2 and 3. Should the manager use the high-low or regression method? Explain.

3-53 Choice of Cost Driver

Study Appendix 3. Richard Ellis, the director of cost operations of American Micro Devices, wishes to develop an accurate cost function to explain and predict support costs in the company's printed circuit board assembly operation. Mr. Ellis is concerned that the cost function that he currently uses—based on direct labor costs—is not accurate enough for proper planning and control of support costs. Mr. Ellis directed one of his financial analysts to obtain a random sample of 25 weeks of support costs and three possible cost drivers in the circuit-board assembly department: direct labor hours, number of boards assembled, and average cycle time of boards assembled. (Average cycle time is the average time between start and certified completion—after quality testing—of boards assembled during a week.) Much of the effort in this assembly operation is devoted to testing for quality and reworking defective boards, all of which increase the average cycle time in any period. Therefore, Mr. Ellis believes that average cycle time will be the best support cost driver. Mr. Ellis wants his analyst to use regression analysis to demonstrate which cost driver best explains support costs.

Week	Circuit Board Assembly Support Costs, Y	Direct Labor Hours, X_1	Number of Boards Completed, X_2	Average Cycle Time (Hours), X_3
1	$66,402	7,619	2,983	186.44
2	56,943	7,678	2,830	139.14
3	60,337	7,816	2,413	151.13
4	50,096	7,659	2,221	138.30
5	64,241	7,646	2,701	158.63
6	60,846	7,765	2,656	148.71
7	43,119	7,685	2,495	105.85
8	63,412	7,962	2,128	174.02
9	59,283	7,793	2,127	155.30
10	60,070	7,732	2,127	162.20
11	53,345	7,771	2,338	142.97
12	65,027	7,842	2,685	176.08
13	58,220	7,940	2,602	150.19
14	65,406	7,750	2,029	194.06
15	35,268	7,954	2,136	100.51
16	46,394	7,768	2,046	137.47
17	71,877	7,764	2,786	197.44
18	61,903	7,635	2,822	164.69
19	50,009	7,849	2,178	141.95
20	49,327	7,869	2,244	123.37
21	44,703	7,576	2,195	128.25
22	45,582	7,557	2,370	106.16
23	43,818	7,569	2,016	131.41
24	62,122	7,672	2,515	154.88
25	52,403	7,653	2,942	140.07

1. Plot support costs, Y, versus each of the possible cost drivers, X_1, X_2, and X_3.
2. Use regression analysis to measure cost functions using each of the cost drivers.
3. According to the criteria of plausibility and reliability, which is the best cost driver for support costs in the circuit board assembly department?
4. Interpret the economic meaning of the best cost function.

3-54 Use of Cost Functions for Pricing
Study Appendix 3. Read the previous problem. If you worked that problem, use your measured cost functions. If you did not work the previous problem, assume the following measured cost functions:

$$Y = \$9{,}000/\text{week} + (\$6 \times \text{direct labor hours}); R^2 = .10$$

$$Y = \$20{,}000/\text{week} + (\$14 \times \text{number of boards completed}); R^2 = .40$$

$$Y = \$5{,}000/\text{week} + (\$350 \times \text{average cycle time}); R^2 = .80$$

1. Which of the support cost functions would you expect to be the most reliable for explaining and predicting support costs? Why?
2. Assume that American Micro Devices prices its products by adding a percentage markup to its product costs. Product costs include assembly labor, components, and support costs. Using each of the cost functions, compute the circuit board portion of the support cost of an order that used the following resources:
   a. Effectively used the capacity of the assembly department for 3 weeks
   b. Assembly labor hours: 20,000
   c. Number of boards: 6,000
   d. Average cycle time: 180 hours
3. Which cost driver would you recommend that American Micro Devices use? Why?
4. Assume that the market for this product is extremely cost competitive. What do you think of American Micro Devices's pricing method?

3-55 Review of Chapters 2 and 3
Madison Musical Education Company (MME) provides instrumental music education to children of all ages. Payment for services comes from two sources: (1) a contract with Country Day School to provide private music lessons for up to 150 band students a year (where a year is 9 months of education) for a fixed fee of $150,000, and (2) payment from individuals at a rate of $100 per month for 9 months of education each year. In the 2008–2009 school year, MME made a profit of $5,000 on revenues of $295,000:

Revenues:		
Country Day School contract	$150,000	
Private students	145,000	
Total revenues		$295,000
Expenses:		
Administrative staff	$ 75,000	
Teaching staff	81,000	
Facilities	93,500	
Supplies	40,500	
Total expenses		290,000
Profit		$ 5,000

MME conducted an activity analysis and found that teaching staff wages and supplies costs are variable with respect to student-months. (A student-month is one student educated for one month.) Administrative staff and facilities costs are fixed within the range of 2,000–3,000 student-months. At volumes between 3,000 and 3,500 student-months, an additional facilities charge of $8,000 would be incurred. During the last year, a total of 2,700 student-months of education were provided, 1,450 of which were for private students and 1,250 of which were offered under the contract with Country Day School.

1. Compute the following using cost information from year 2008–2009 operations:
   Fixed cost per year
   Variable cost per student-month

2. Suppose that in 2009–2010 Country Day School decreased its use of MME to 120 students (that is, 1,080 student-months). The fixed contract price of $150,000 was still paid. If everything else stayed as it was in 2008–2009, what profit or loss would be made in 2009–2010?

3. Suppose that at the beginning of 2009–2010 Country Day School decided not to renew its contract with MME, and the management of MME decided to try to maintain business as usual with only private students. How many students (each signing up for 9 months) would MME require to continue to make a profit of $5,000 per year?

CASES

3-56 Government Health Cost Behavior

Dr. Stephanie White, the chief administrator of Uptown Clinic, a community mental health agency, is concerned about the dilemma of coping with reduced budgets in the next year and into the foreseeable future, despite increasing demand for services. In order to plan for reduced budgets, she first must identify where costs can be cut or reduced and still keep the agency functioning. The following are some data from the past year:

Program Area	Costs
Administration	
Salaries	
Administrator	$60,000
Assistant	35,000
Two secretaries	42,000
Supplies	35,000
Advertising and promotion	9,000
Professional meetings, dues, and literature	14,000
Purchased services	
Accounting and billing	15,000
Custodial and maintenance	13,000
Security	12,000
Consulting	10,000
Community mental health services	
Salaries (two social workers)	46,000
Transportation	10,000
Outpatient mental health treatment	
Salaries	
Psychiatrist	86,000
Two social workers	70,000

1. Identify which costs you think are likely to be discretionary or committed costs.
2. One possibility is to eliminate all discretionary costs. How much would be saved? What do you think of this recommendation?
3. How would you advise Dr. White to prepare for reduced budgets?

3-57 Activity Analysis

The costs of the Systems Support (SS) department (and other service departments) of Southeast Pulp and Paper have always been charged to the three business divisions (Forest Management, Lumber Products, and Paper Products) based on the number of employees in each division. This measure is easy to obtain and update, and until recently none of the divisions had complained about the charges. The Paper Products division has recently automated many of its operations and has reduced the number of its employees. At the same time, however, to monitor its new process, Paper Products has increased its requests for various reports provided by the SS department. The other divisions have begun to complain that they are being charged more than their fair share of SS department costs. Based on activity analysis of possible cost drivers, cost analysts have suggested using the number of reports prepared as a means of charging for SS costs and have gathered the following information:

	Forest Management	Lumber Products	Paper Products
2008 number of employees	762	457	502
2008 number of reports	410	445	377
2008 SS costs: $300,000			
2009 number of employees	751	413	131
2009 number of reports	412	432	712
2009 SS costs: $385,000			

1. Discuss the plausibility and probable reliability of each of the cost drivers—number of employees or number of reports.
2. What are the 2008 and 2009 SS costs per unit of cost driver for each division using each cost driver? Do the Forest Management and Lumber Products divisions have legitimate complaints? Explain.
3. What are the incentives that are implied by each cost driver?
4. Which cost driver should Southeast Pulp and Paper use to charge its divisions for SS services? For other services? Why?

3-58 Identifying Relevant Data

eComp.com manufactures personal digital assistants (PDAs). Because these very small computers compete with laptops that have more functions and flexibility, understanding and using cost behavior is very critical to eComp.com's profitability. eComp.com's controller, Kelly Hudson, has kept meticulous files on various cost categories and possible cost drivers for most of the important functions and activities of eComp.com. Because most of the manufacturing at eComp.com is automated, labor cost is relatively fixed. Other support costs comprise most of eComp.com's costs. Partial data that Hudson has collected over the past 25 weeks on one of these support costs, logistics operations (materials purchasing, receiving, warehousing, and shipping), follow:

Week	Logistics Costs, Y	Number of Orders, X
1	$23,907	1,357
2	18,265	1,077
3	24,208	1,383
4	23,578	1,486
5	22,211	1,292
6	22,862	1,425
7	23,303	1,306
8	24,507	1,373
9	17,878	1,031
10	18,306	1,020
11	20,807	1,097
12	19,707	1,069
13	23,020	1,444
14	20,407	733
15	20,370	413
16	20,678	633
17	21,145	711
18	20,775	228
19	20,532	488
20	20,659	655
21	20,430	722
22	20,713	373
23	20,256	391
24	21,196	734
25	20,406	256

1. Plot logistics costs, *Y*, versus number of orders, *X*. What cost behavior is evident? What do you think happened in week 14?
2. What is your recommendation to Kelly Hudson regarding the relevance of the past 25 weeks of logistics costs and number of orders for measuring logistics cost behavior?
3. Hudson remarks that one of the improvements that eComp.com has made in the past several months was to negotiate JIT deliveries from its suppliers. This was made possible by substituting an automated ordering system for the previous manual (labor-intensive) system. Although fixed costs increased, the variable cost of placing an order was expected to drop greatly. Do the data support this expectation? Do you believe that the change to the automated ordering system was justified? Why or why not?

NIKE 10-K PROBLEM

3-59 Step and Mixed Costs and Cost Drivers

Refer to **Nike**'s 10-K in Appendix C and "Item 1. Business." Nike's contract manufacturers make the vast majority of Nike's footwear. Assume these costs are variable to Nike. Nike's largest fixed costs are associated with its distribution system. Consider one of Nike's three distribution and customer service facilities in the United States. List several examples of step-fixed costs and mixed costs at these centers. For each of the following activities at a distribution center, list one plausible cost driver:

1. Receiving activity
2. Unpacking incoming cases of footwear
3. Picking and packing cases of footwear for shipment to retail accounts
4. Processing orders from retail accounts
5. Providing customer service to retail accounts
6. Processing order changes from retail accounts

EXCEL APPLICATION EXERCISE

3-60 Fixed and Variable Cost Data

Goal: Create an Excel spreadsheet to calculate fixed and variable cost data for evaluating alternative approaches. Use the results to answer questions about your findings.

Scenario: Recreational Sports has asked you to evaluate two alternative cost approaches for its new Web site. They would like you to calculate fixed and variable costs at different numbers of orders. The background data for your analysis appear in Exercise 3-37, page 106.

When you have completed your spreadsheet, answer the following questions:

1. At what number of orders are the total costs for the two approaches the same? What does this mean?
2. Which alternative should be selected if the expected number of orders is less than the break-even level of orders? If the expected number of orders is greater than the break-even level of orders?
3. What conclusion regarding cost predictions can be drawn from your analysis?

Step-by-Step:

1. Open a new Excel spreadsheet.
2. In column A, create a bold-faced heading that contains the following:
   Row 1: Chapter 3 Decision Guideline
   Row 2: Recreational Sports
   Row 3: Analysis of Alternative Cost Approaches
   Row 4: Today's Date
3. Merge and center the four heading rows across columns A–K.
4. In row 7, create the following bold-faced, right-justified column headings:
   Column A: Number of Orders
   Column B: Alternative 1
   Column C: Alternative 2

   Note: Adjust column widths as necessary.

5. In column A, rows 8–12, enter order levels from 40,000 to 80,000 in 10,000-unit increments.

6. Use the scenario data to create formulas in columns B and C for calculating the total costs (fixed plus variable costs) for each alternative at the order level in column A.

7. Format all amounts as follows:

Number tab:	Category:	Number
	Decimal places:	0
	Use 1000 Separator (,):	Checked

8. Modify the Page Setup by selecting File, Page Setup.

Page tab:	Orientation:	Landscape
Margins tab:	Top:	.5
	Bottom:	.5

9. Select the data in columns A–C, rows 7–12, and start the Chart Wizard either by inserting a chart (Insert, Chart) or by clicking the Chart Wizard icon on the toolbar.

    Step 1 of 4—Chart Type
    a. **Custom Types tab:**
    b. Chart Type: Smooth Lines
    c. Click "Next >" button

    Note: List is alphabetical.

    Step 2 of 4—Chart Source Data

    d. **Data Range tab:**
    e. Modify Data range to: =*SheetName*!$B$7:$C$12
    f. Series in: Columns
    g. **Series tab:**
    h. Category (X) axis labels: =*SheetName*!$A$8:$A$12
    i. Click "Next >" button

    Step 3 of 4—Chart Options
    j. **Titles tab:**
    k. Chart Title: Analysis of Alternative Cost Approaches
    l. Category (X) axis: Number of Orders
    m. Value (Y) axis: Total Costs
    n. **Gridlines tab:**
    o. Category (X) axis: Major Gridlines (checked)
    p. Value (Y) axis: Major Gridlines (checked)
    q. Click "Next >" button

    Step 4 of 4—Chart Location
    r. As object in SheetName   Checked
    s. Click "Finish" button

10. Move the chart so the upper-left corner is on the left margin, row 14.
    Left-mouse click the upper-left handle and drag it to the designated location.

11. Resize the chart so the lower-right corner fills cell K37.
    Left-mouse click the lower-right handle and drag it to the designated location.

12. Format the Y-axis amounts (Total Costs) to display a dollar symbol by doing the following:
    Double-click any cost amount on the Y-axis to open the "Format Axis" dialog box.

Scale tab:	Minimum:	300,000
Number tab:	Category:	Currency
	Decimal Places:	0
	Symbol:	$

13. Save your work to disk, and print a copy for your files.

    Note: Select cell A8 before printing if you want both the data and the chart to print. If you want only the chart to print, ignore the "Select cell A8" instruction.

    Print your spreadsheet using landscape in order to ensure that all columns appear on one page.

COLLABORATIVE LEARNING EXERCISE

3-61 Cost-Behavior Examples

Select about 10 students to participate in a "cost-behavior bee." The game proceeds like a spelling bee—when a participant is unable to come up with a correct answer, he or she is eliminated from the game. The last one in the game is the winner.

The object of the game is to identify a type of cost that fits a particular cost-behavior pattern. The first player rolls a die.[2] If a 1 or a 6 comes up, the die passes to the next player (and the roller makes it to the next round). If a 2, 3, 4, or 5 comes up, the player has to identify one of the following types of costs:

> If a 2 is rolled, identify a variable cost.
>
> If a 3 is rolled, identify a fixed cost.
>
> If a 4 is rolled, identify a mixed cost.
>
> If a 5 is rolled, identify a step cost.

A scribe should label four columns on the board, one for each type of cost, and list the costs that are mentioned for each category. Once a particular cost has been used, it cannot be used again.

Each player has a time limit of 10 seconds to produce an example. (For a tougher game, make the time limit 5 seconds.) The instructor is the referee, judging if a particular example is acceptable. It is legitimate for the referee to ask a player to explain why he or she thinks the cost mentioned fits the category before making a judgment.

After each player has had a turn, a second round begins with the remaining players taking a turn in the same order as in the first round. The game continues through additional rounds until all but one player has failed to give an acceptable answer within the time limit. The remaining player is the winner.

INTERNET EXERCISE

3-62 Cost Behavior at Southwest Airlines

In this exercise, we will look at some costs and see if we can determine the type of behavior associated with those costs. While firms are concerned about trying to label costs as either variable or fixed to help in planning, very few costs are completely variable or fixed. The information provided by firms to external users also often precludes a user from determining specifics about the cost behaviors—they don't want to give the competitors too much information!

Log on to the **Southwest Airlines** Web site at www.southwest.com. Click on the information icon "About Southwest," and then click on "Investor Relations." This will take you to the site where you can then access the financial information.

1. Click on the "Annual Reports" icon and then select the most recent annual report. Looking at the table of contents, find the page where the 10-year summary starts. Go to this section of the report. What type of information do you find there?
2. When you look at the operating revenue information, what do you see? Look at the information provided concerning operating expenses. Is it categorized in the same manner as the revenues? If the information is not in the same categories, why do you think Southwest did not match it up in the same manner?
3. Now look at the section on consolidated operating statistics. Southwest measures activity in revenue passenger miles (RPMs) and capacity in available seat miles (ASMs). Which of these is larger? How are the RPM and ASM determined? Is it possible for the two numbers to be the same? What information is provided for each of these items in the consolidated operating statistics section?

---

[2]Instead of rolling a die, players could draw one of the four cost categories out of a hat (or similar container) or from a deck of four 3×5 cards. This eliminates the chance element that can let some players proceed to a later round without having to give an example of a particular cost behavior. However, the chance element can add to the enjoyment of the game.

4. Using data from 2002 and 2005 and employing the high-low method, compute the total operating expense per RPM and the variable operating expense per RPM. Compare the total operating expense per RPM and the variable expense per RPM. Is this relationship what you expected? Why or why not?

5. Airlines are often considered to be high-fixed-cost companies. Is this consistent with your findings in requirement 4? Explain why the high-low method over this time might overestimate the amount of variable costs.

you read about in Chapter 2. All of these tools and techniques have one thing in common—the need for accurate information about costs. This chapter focuses on **cost accounting**, the part of a cost management system that measures costs for the purposes of management decision making and financial reporting.

Cost Accounting Systems

Objective 2

Explain the relationship among cost, cost object, cost accumulation, and cost assignment.

We define **cost** as a sacrifice or giving up of resources for a particular purpose. Consider the cost of labor resources. An organization pays (gives up) cash or its equivalent to employees in exchange for their work. We measure the cost of labor resources by the dollars (or other monetary units such as yen or euros) paid to obtain the labor resources. However, managers generally want more from their accountants than simply the cost of the resources used. They often want to know the cost of something in particular, such as a product or a service. Anything for which decision makers desire a separate measurement of costs is a **cost object** (or **cost objective**). Although managers most often want to know the cost of a product or service, there are many other possible cost objects. Examples include customers, departments, territories, and activities such as processing orders or moving materials. For example, one large manufacturer of pet food products recently changed its cost management system to report both the cost of products it makes and the cost to serve the company's major retail customers such as **Wal-Mart** and **PETCO**. It discovered that all its products were profitable, but the cost to sell to and service some customers was greater than the profit margin on the products sold to these customers. Knowing this, the company was able to develop a strategy to improve the profitability of these customers.

The cost data that managers use for decision making come from the **cost accounting system**—the techniques used to determine the cost of a product, service, customer, or other cost object. The cost accounting system is the most fundamental component of a cost management system. It supports all other cost management system tools and techniques.

Cost accounting systems need to provide accurate and timely cost information to help managers make decisions. Without accurate and timely cost information, many decisions can be downright harmful. For example, several years ago a large U.S. grocery chain, **A&P**, ran into profit difficulties and began retrenching by closing many stores. Management's lack of adequate cost information about individual store operations made the closing program a hit-or-miss affair. A news story reported the following:

> *Because of the absence of detailed profit-and-loss statements, and a [cost accounting] system that did not reflect true costs, A&P's strategists could not be sure whether an individual store was really unprofitable. For example, distribution costs were shared equally among all the stores in a marketing area without regard to such factors as a store's distance from the warehouse. Says one close observer of the company: "When they wanted to close a store, they had to wing it. They could not make rational decisions, because they did not have a fact basis."*

All kinds of organizations—manufacturing firms, service companies, and nonprofit organizations—need some form of cost accounting. Consider the following commentaries on the modern role of management accountants and cost accounting systems:

> *We [management accountants] have to understand what the numbers mean, relate the numbers to business activity, and recommend alternative courses of action. Finally, we have to evaluate alternatives and make decisions to maximize business efficiency.*

> —**South Central Bell**

> *Because the [cost accounting] system now mirrors the manufacturing process, the engineers and production staff believe the cost data produced by the cost accounting system. Engineering and production regularly ask accounting to help find the product design combination that will optimize costs. . . . The accountants now participate in product design decisions. They help engineering and production understand how costs behave. . . . The system makes the professional lives of the accountants more rewarding.*

> —**Hewlett-Packard Company**

A cost accounting system typically includes two processes:

1. **Cost accumulation:** Collecting costs by some "natural" classification, such as materials or labor, or by activities performed such as order processing or machine processing.
2. **Cost assignment:** Attaching costs to one or more cost objects, such as activities, processes, departments, customers, or products.

Exhibit 4-1 is a simple illustration of these two basic processes for materials costs. First, the system collects the costs of all materials. Then, it assigns these costs to the departments that use the materials and further to the specific activities performed in these departments. Last, the system assigns the accumulated costs to the products made—cabinets, tables, and desks. The total materials cost of a particular product is the sum of the materials costs assigned to it in the various departments. For example, the cost of a finished desk would include the following materials costs:

- Metal top, sides, and legs produced by the various activities in the machining department
- Bolts, brackets, screws, drawers, handles, and knobs pieced together by finishing department activities

A company's cost accounting system can have a great influence on managers' decisions. Any manager who makes a decision based on financial data relies on the accuracy of the cost accounting system. In today's business environment, characterized by highly-competitive global markets and complex production processes, designing cost accounting systems that provide accurate and useful information is a key success factor for all types of organizations. The financial vice president of a major manufacturing firm recently told one of the authors that the company's main competitive advantage was its financial information system, not its manufacturing or distribution capabilities.

This chapter describes some major types of cost accounting systems. However, before describing the systems, we need to develop an understanding of the various cost terms that managers and accountants commonly use.

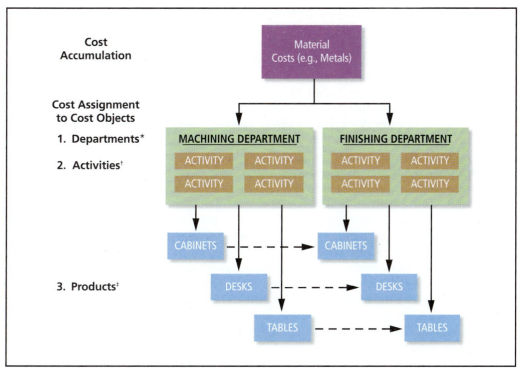

*Purpose: to evaluate performance of manufacturing departments.
†Purpose: to measure and evaluate the efficiency of various activities.
‡Purpose: to obtain costs of various products for valuing inventory, determining income, and judging product profitability.

Exhibit 4-1
Cost Accumulation and Assignment

Cost Terms Used for Strategic Decision Making and Operational Control Purposes

Accountants have their own language laced with jargon. As a manager, you will need to understand the basics of this language. This section focuses on three key terms: direct costs, indirect costs, and cost allocation.

Direct Costs, Indirect Costs, and Cost Allocation

Objective 3

Distinguish between direct and indirect costs.

Costs may be direct or indirect with respect to a particular cost object. Accountants can identify **direct costs** specifically and exclusively with a given cost object in an economically feasible way. Parts and materials included in a product are the most common types of direct cost. For example, to determine the cost of parts assembled into a **Dell** laptop computer, Dell's accountants simply look at the purchase orders for the specific parts used. A key characteristic of direct costs is that accountants can physically identify the amount of the cost that relates exclusively to a particular cost object. We call this **tracing** the direct cost to the cost object. In contrast, accountants cannot specifically and exclusively identify the amount of **indirect costs** related to a given cost object in an economically feasible way. Examples of indirect costs include facilities rental costs, depreciation on equipment, and many staff salaries.

Consider whether the cost of labor is direct or indirect to the products being made. Some employees work specifically on particular products. Their costs are direct to those products because accountants can trace the costs to the products. Others, such as supervisors, general managers, accountants, and legal staff, do not work on individual products. Because accountants cannot trace such labor costs to the products, they are indirect costs. A century ago, a large proportion of labor costs were direct. Why? Because most companies had a labor-intensive production process where a majority of the workers had hands-on involvement with producing their company's products. To produce 10% more units of a particular product, a company typically needed about 10% more workers. Today the situation is different. Automated production processes have eliminated many hands-on jobs, and more employees just oversee automated processes that make many different products. The costs of such labor are indirect. Why? Because it is not economically feasible to trace their costs to the individual products.

Just because a cost is indirect does not mean it is unimportant. Companies cannot continue to make products without facilities, equipment, supervisors, and even accountants. One of the most challenging tasks of a cost accounting system is to assign indirect costs to cost objects. Because indirect costs in many companies today exceed 50% of total costs, accurate assignment of indirect costs is crucial. Decision makers who ignore indirect costs or receive inaccurate measures of indirect costs often make poor decisions.

In addition to knowing that a cost is indirect, managers also want to know whether it is fixed or variable—that is, whether it varies in proportion to production volume—as discussed in Chapter 2. Some indirect costs are variable. Examples are supplies such as tacks and glue in a furniture-making company and the cost of ink in a printing company. Others, such as most depreciation and supervisors' salaries, are fixed. Managers must distinguish between variable and fixed indirect costs to make informed decisions.

To assign indirect costs to cost objects, we use **cost allocation**, which assigns indirect costs to cost objects in proportion to the cost object's use of a particular cost-allocation base. A **cost-allocation base** is some measure of input or output that determines the amount of cost to be allocated to a particular cost object. An ideal cost-allocation base measures how much of the particular cost is *caused by* the cost object. Note the similarity of this definition to that of a cost driver—an output measure that causes costs. Therefore, *most cost-allocation bases are cost drivers*. Consider how much assembly-equipment depreciation, an indirect cost, Dell's accountants should assign to a particular model of laptop. They might allocate this indirect cost to various models based on the allocation base "machine hours," a measure of the amount of assembly equipment time used to make a particular computer. If making a Latitude laptop uses two machine hours while making an Inspiron laptop uses only one, then Dell would allocate twice as much machine depreciation cost to the Latitude. Whenever an accountant uses the term *allocated*, we know the related cost is an indirect cost assigned to a cost object using a cost-allocation base.

Decision makers should be careful in using allocated indirect costs. When the allocation base measures how much cost is *caused by* the cost objects, allocated costs will be relevant for many decisions. When the allocation is not related to the cause of the costs, managers have reason to suspect the accuracy of the resulting costs.

Because cost allocations are so important to cost measurement in today's companies, let's look more deeply into why and how companies allocate their indirect costs.

Purposes of Cost Allocation

What logic should we use for allocating costs? The answer depends on the purpose(s) of the cost allocation. In short, there are no firm rules that we can rely on—there is no universally best cost-allocation system. Instead of cost allocation rules, we focus on general concepts that provide guidance when managers design these systems.

Objective 4

Explain the major reasons for allocating costs.

Recall that cost allocations support a company's CMS—the system providing cost measurements for strategic decision making, operational control, and external reporting. Following are four purposes of cost allocation. The first two support strategic decision making and operational control, the third supports external reporting, and the last one supports elements of all three:

1. *To predict the economic effects of strategic and operational control decisions:* Major strategic decisions include setting the optimal product and customer mix, establishing pricing policy, and setting policy about which value-chain functions to develop as core competencies. Managers also need to predict the economic effects—both benefits and costs—of process improvement efforts. Managers within an organizational unit should be aware of all the consequences of their decisions, even consequences outside of their unit. Examples are the addition of a new course in a university that causes additional work in the registrar's office, the addition of a new flight or an additional passenger on an airline that requires reservation and booking services, and the addition of a new specialty in a medical clinic that produces more work for the medical records department.

2. *To provide desired motivation and to give feedback for performance evaluation:* Companies often hold managers responsible for total costs that include allocated costs. Therefore, cost allocations influence management behavior and can help motivate managers to make decisions that are in the company's best interests. For example, some organizations allocate the costs of legal services or internal management consulting services to spur managers to make sure the benefits of the services exceed the costs. Other organizations do not allocate such costs because top management wants to encourage their use.

3. *To compute income and asset valuations for financial reporting:* Companies allocate costs to products to measure inventory costs for their balance sheets and cost of goods sold for their income statements.

4. *To justify costs or obtain reimbursement:* Sometimes organizations base prices directly on costs. For example, government contracts often specify a price that includes reimbursement for costs plus some profit margin. In these instances, cost allocations directly determine the revenue received from a product or service.

Ideally, a single cost allocation would serve all four purposes simultaneously. But thousands of managers and accountants will testify that most systems fail to achieve this ideal. Instead, cost allocations are often a major source of discontent and confusion to the affected parties. Allocating fixed costs usually causes the greatest problems. Why? Because it is often hard to find a cost-allocation base that accurately measures the amount of a fixed cost resource used by a cost object. When a system cannot meet all purposes simultaneously, managers and accountants need to identify which of the purposes are most important in a particular situation.

Often external reporting rules for measuring inventory and cost of goods sold dominate by default because they are externally imposed. Generally accepted accounting principles (GAAP) require a company to assign all production-related costs and only production-related costs to its products. Often these are not the costs managers want assigned to products for their decision-making purposes. For example, managers may prefer not to allocate all production-related indirect fixed costs. If a particular management decision does not affect such fixed costs, it can be misleading to include them as part of the cost of the product. In addition, managers may want to allocate costs from nonproduction parts of the value chain, such as R&D,

marketing, or administrative expenses. Management decisions might have a major effect on such costs, and allocating them can make managers more aware of this effect. Thus, when managers need individual product or customer costs for decision making and performance evaluation, they often have to adjust the GAAP allocations. Generally, using allocations for planning and control that differ from those used for inventory-costing purposes creates benefits that exceed the added cost.

Methods of Cost Allocation

Now let's turn to the question of how companies allocate costs. Because final products or services are important cost objects to nearly all organizations, we focus on how companies trace direct costs and allocate indirect costs to these cost objects. Examine Exhibit 4-2 to see the difference between assigning direct costs (tracing) and indirect costs (allocation) to final products.

Physically tracing the direct costs is usually straightforward. For example, the cost accounting system can measure the amount and cost of each material added to a product. Workers can record the time spent on each product and the system can value each hour at the worker's appropriate wage rate. Systems to accurately measure direct costs have been available for decades, even centuries.

Allocating indirect costs is more complex, and accountants have more chance to influence the resulting costs by the allocation choices they make. Because of the growth in indirect costs for most companies, allocating indirect costs is especially important. Allocation is a five-step process:

1. Accumulate indirect costs for a period of time, for example one month, into one or more cost pools. A **cost pool** is a group of individual costs that a company allocates to cost objects using a single cost-allocation base. Many simple cost accounting systems place all indirect production costs in a single cost pool.
2. Select an allocation base for each cost pool. If possible, choose a cost driver—a measure that causes the costs in the cost pool. Companies that have a single cost pool for indirect costs often use direct-labor hours or direct-labor cost as the cost-allocation base.
3. Measure the units of the cost-allocation base used for each cost object (for example, the number of direct-labor hours used on a particular product) and compute the total units used for all cost objects.
4. Determine the percentage of total cost-allocation base units used for each cost object.
5. Multiply the percentage in step 4 by the total costs in the cost pool to determine the cost allocated to each cost object.

Consider the depreciation on Dell's assembly equipment mentioned on page 124. How would Dell's accountants allocate July's $400,000 depreciation cost to Inspiron and Latitude laptop computers? Let's apply the five steps:

1. In July accountants measured the depreciation cost, the only cost in this cost pool, at $400,000.
2. The cost-allocation base selected is machine hours.

Exhibit 4-2

Assignment of Direct and Indirect Costs to Products, Services, Customers, or Activities

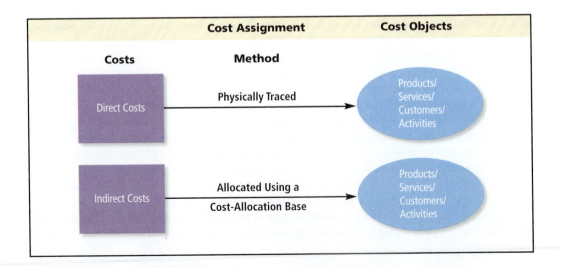

3. Dell used 2,000 machine hours in July to make Inspiron laptops and 3,000 machine hours to make Latitude laptops, for a total of 5,000 machine hours.
4. This means that Dell used 2,000 ÷ 5,000 = 40% of the machine hours for Inspiron and 3,000 ÷ 5,000 = 60% of the machine hours for Latitude.
5. The depreciation cost allocated to Inspiron is 40% × $400,000 = $160,000, and that allocated to Latitude is 60% × 400,000 = $240,000.

Another way of calculating this allocation is to compute the depreciation cost per machine hour or $400,000 ÷ (3,000 + 2,000) = $80. Then the allocation to Inspiron is $80 × 2,000 = $160,000 and the allocation to Latitude is $80 × 3,000 = $240,000. The allocation can be depicted using symbols as follows:

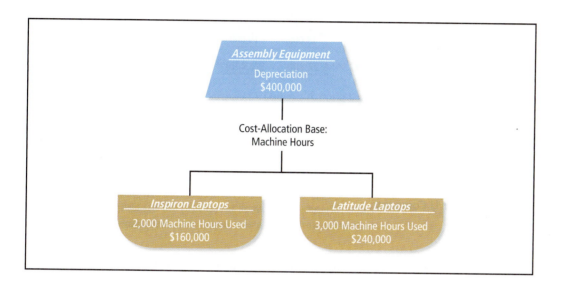

Companies also use cost allocation to assign indirect costs to cost objects other than products or services. Suppose we are allocating costs to departments. A logical cost-allocation base for allocating rent costs to departments is the square feet that each department occupies. Other logical cost-allocation bases include cubic feet for allocating depreciation of heating and air conditioning equipment and total direct cost for allocating general administrative expense.

Also note the varying terminology you will see in practice. Accountants use many different terms to describe cost allocation. You may encounter terms such as *allocate, apply, absorb, attribute, reallocate, assign, distribute, redistribute, load, burden, apportion*, and *reapportion* being used interchangeably to describe the allocation of indirect costs to cost objects.

Unallocated Costs

There are some costs that lack an identifiable relationship to a cost object. Often it is best to leave such costs unallocated. **Unallocated costs** are costs that an accounting system records but does not allocate to any cost object. They might include research and development (R&D), process design, legal expenses, accounting, information services, and executive salaries. Keep in mind, though, that an unallocated cost for one company may be an allocated cost or even a direct cost for another. Why? Because businesses vary considerably in their value chains and operating processes. For example, product design is a critical success factor for some businesses, and therefore, managers in such companies are willing to spend the time and effort to deploy sophisticated accounting systems to allocate or even directly trace product design costs. For other companies, this cost is not important enough to warrant special treatment.

Consider the statement of operating income for Li Company in panel A of Exhibit 4-3. Li Company makes cabinets, tables, and chairs. Each item in panel A represents accumulated totals for all products sold for an entire reporting period. To help make a strategic decision regarding which of the three products to emphasize, it would be useful to "unbundle" these totals to find the profitability of each product. How can we do this?

with the production process that a company cannot trace to products or services in an economically feasible way. Accountants consider many labor costs, such as that of janitors, forklift truck operators, plant guards, and storeroom clerks, to be indirect labor because it is impossible or economically infeasible to trace such activity to specific products. Other examples of factory overhead costs are power, supplies, supervisory salaries, property taxes, rent, insurance, and depreciation.

Regardless of the type of cost accounting system a company uses for internal decision-making purposes, its production costs must appear in its financial statements for external financial reporting purposes. The costs appear both on the income statement, as cost of goods sold, and on the balance sheet, as inventory amounts.

Product Costs and Period Costs

When preparing income statements and balance sheets, accountants frequently distinguish between product costs and period costs. **Product costs** are costs identified with products manufactured or purchased for resale. In a manufacturing company, product costs include direct materials, direct labor, and indirect production costs. These costs first become part of the inventory; thus, we sometimes call them **inventoriable costs**. These inventoriable costs become expenses in the form of cost of goods sold when the company sells the inventory.

In contrast, **period costs** become expenses during the current period without becoming part of inventory. Period costs are associated with nonproduction value-chain functions (research and development, design, marketing, distribution, and customer service). Accounting information systems accumulate these costs by departments, such as R&D, advertising, and sales. Most firms' financial statements report these costs as selling and administrative expenses. In short, these costs do not become a part of the reported inventory cost of the manufactured products for financial reporting purposes.

Exhibit 4-4 illustrates product and period costs. The top half shows a merchandising company, such as a retailer or wholesaler, that acquires goods for resale without changing their basic form. The only product cost is the purchase cost of the merchandise. The company holds unsold goods as merchandise inventory and shows their costs as an asset on a balance sheet. As the company sells the goods, their costs become expenses in the form of "cost of goods sold." A merchandising company also has a variety of selling and administrative expenses. These costs are period costs because the company deducts them from revenue as expenses without ever being regarded as a part of inventory.

The bottom half of Exhibit 4-4 shows product and period costs in a manufacturing company. Note that the company transforms direct materials into salable items with the help of direct-labor and indirect production costs. You can see that the balance sheets of manufacturers and merchandisers differ with respect to inventories. Instead of one inventory account, a manufacturing concern has three inventory accounts that help managers trace all product costs through the production process to the time of sales. These accounts are as follows:

- **Direct-material inventory:** Material on hand and awaiting use in the production process.
- **Work-in-process inventory:** Goods undergoing the production process but not yet fully completed. Costs include appropriate amounts of the three major manufacturing costs: direct material, direct labor, and indirect production costs.
- **Finished-goods inventory:** Goods fully completed but not yet sold.

The only accounting difference between manufacturing and merchandising companies is in the composition of product costs. A merchandising company includes in product cost only the amount paid for the merchandise it sells. In contrast, a manufacturing company includes in product cost such items as insurance, depreciation, and wages that are incurred in the production process in addition to the cost of materials. Although merchandising and manufacturing companies differ in how they account for product costs, they account for period costs the same. Regardless of the type of company, selling and administrative costs never become part of inventory—they are period costs.

Objective 6

Explain how the financial statements of merchandisers and manufacturers differ because of the types of goods they sell.

Balance Sheet and Income Statement Presentation of Costs

How do published financial statements of merchandising and manufacturing companies differ in presenting costs? Let's first examine balance sheets and notice the extra detail provided by a manufacturer:

Current Asset Sections of Balance Sheets

Manufacturer			Retailer or Wholesaler	
Cash		$ 4,000	Cash	$ 4,000
Receivables		25,000	Receivables	25,000
Finished goods	$32,000			
Work in process	22,000			
Direct material	23,000			
Total inventories		77,000	Merchandise inventories	77,000
Other current assets		1,000	Other current assets	1,000
Total current assets		$107,000	Total current assets	$107,000

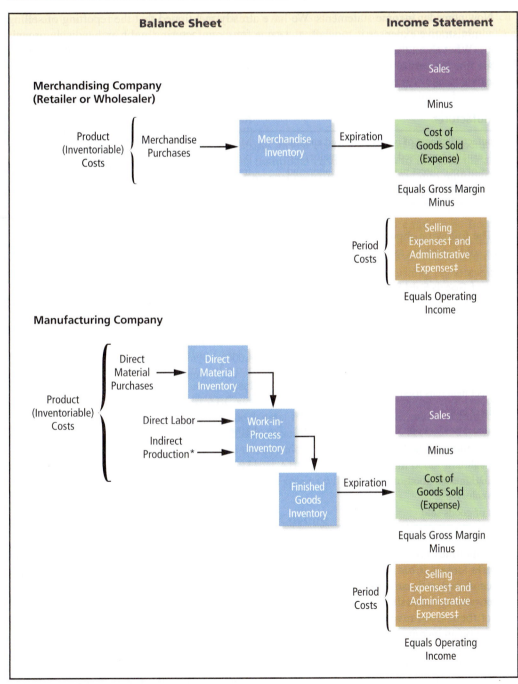

Balance Sheet	Income Statement

Exhibit 4-4

Relationships of Product Costs and Period Costs

*Examples: indirect labor, factory supplies, insurance on inventories, and depreciation on plant.

†Examples: insurance on salespersons' cars, depreciation on salespersons' cars, salespersons' salaries.

‡Examples: insurance on corporate headquarters building, depreciation on office equipment, clerical salaries.

Note particularly that when insurance and depreciation relate to the manufacturing function, they are inventoriable, but when they relate to selling and administration, they are not inventoriable.

"number of customer-generated engineering changes" and "number of distinct parts." The cost-allocation base should be a good measure of the consumption of production-support activity. Let's assume this is "number of distinct parts." Suppose pen casings have only 5 distinct parts compared to 20 for cell phone casings. We would allocate $20 \div (20 + 5) \times \$77,000 = \$61,600$ of the production-support activity costs to cell phone casings and the remaining \$15,400 to pen casings. This allocation better measures the use of engineering services than does the allocation based on the traditional system. Why? Because cell phone casings cause $(20 \div 25) = 80\%$ of the production-support activity costs, but the traditional system allocates only 10% of such costs to cell phone casings. In contrast, the ABC system allocates the appropriate 80% of the production-support activity costs to cell phone casings.

We will continue this example in the Summary Problem for Your Review below, but first let's consider one more advantage of ABC systems. In many companies, managers try to gain cost savings by efficiently managing activities. If Lopez Plastics wants its managers to reduce the cost of producing cell phone casings, the managers will probably focus on possible cost savings in either processing or production support. They may also redesign the product to reduce direct materials costs or reengineer the production process to reduce direct labor costs. But often the largest potential savings are in the indirect costs. By carrying out activities more efficiently, managers reduce the costs of the products that use those activities.

What information do managers need to examine the efficiency of activities? At a minimum, they need to know the cost of each activity. Traditional systems do not generate this cost information, while ABC systems do. Therefore, in addition to providing better costing activity, ABC systems can also promote better operating efficiency.

We now are in a position to complete our ABC analysis and answer our strategic issue regarding our product mix strategy. We do this in the following Summary Problem for Your Review. It is important for you to carefully work this problem to gain a clear understanding of the basic concepts and value of an ABC system.

Summary Problem for Your Review
PROBLEM

Refer to the Lopez Plastics illustration, starting with the financial reports based on the traditional cost accounting system in panel B of Exhibit 4-6, p. 136. Based on these reports, a marketing manager has proposed a plan that emphasizes cell phone casings due to their large gross profit margin (38.75%) compared to that of pen casings (1.25%).

Now, management implements the ABC system shown in Exhibit 4-7, p. 137. The first stage of the two-stage ABC system has been completed, and the results are the activity-cost-pool figures given in Exhibit 4-7—processing activity costs of \$143,000 and production-support activity costs of \$77,000. You need to perform the second-stage allocations to determine the profitability of each product line. The cost-allocation base for processing activity is direct-labor hours and the cost-allocation base for production-support activity is number of distinct parts. Data on the use of these cost-allocation bases for the last quarter are as follows:

	Pen Casings	Cell Phone Casings
Direct labor hours	4,500	500
Distinct parts	5	20

Calculate the gross profit and gross profit margin for each product based on ABC. Do your results differ significantly from those based on the traditional cost accounting system in Exhibit 4-6, p. 136? Explain. Evaluate marketing's plan. Propose a product-mix strategy for the company.

SOLUTION

The table that follows shows the gross profit for each product using ABC costs.

Financial Reports for Lopez Plastics Company Activity-Based Cost Allocation System

	Panel A Statement of Operating Income [External Reporting Purpose]	Panel B Contribution to Corporate Costs and Profit [Internal Strategic Decision-Making and Operational-Control Purposes]	
		Pen Casings	*Cell Phone Casings*
Sales	$440,000	$360,000	$ 80,000
Cost of goods sold:			
Direct material	34,500	22,500	12,000
Direct labor	150,000	135,000	15,000
Processing activity	143,000	128,700*	14,300
Production-support activity	77,000	15,400†	61,600
Cost of goods sold	404,500	301,600	102,900
Gross profit	35,500	$ 58,400	$ (22,900)
Corporate expenses (Unallocated):	100,000		
Operating loss	$ (64,500)		
Gross profit margin	8.07%	16.22%	(28.63%)

* The cost driver is direct-labor hours. The company used 4,500 ÷ (4,500 + 500) = 90% of direct-labor hours to produce pen casings. Thus, the allocation is $143,000 × .90 = $128,700.
† The cost driver is distinct parts. The company used 5 ÷ (20 + 5) = 20% of distinct parts to make pen casings. Thus, the allocation is $77,000 × .20 = $15,400.

The ABC system gives results that are dramatically different from those of the traditional cost allocation system. Pen casings are generating substantial profits for the company, while cell phone casings are losing money. Why is there such a dramatic difference between the two cost accounting systems? It's because the traditional cost-accounting system doesn't recognize differences in the production process for each of the two products. Only the cell phone casings require large amounts of the production-support activity. The ABC system correctly allocates most of this cost to the cell phone casings, while the traditional system allocates most of it to the pen casings. The ABC system first separates the processing-related costs from the production-support costs. Then, it allocates each activity cost to the products based on the proportion of the activity used by each product.

Marketing's plan most likely will result in significantly lower profitability. The company's top management should make the strategic decision to emphasize pen casings because of its large gross profit margin when accurately measured. The cell phone casings are losing money, so that product line needs to be carefully evaluated. Possible actions include raising prices, changing the design by reducing the number of distinct parts, working with suppliers to reduce the cost of direct materials, improving the efficiency of direct labor, or dropping the product line.

Making Managerial Decisions

Suppose you have been asked to attend a meeting of top management of your company. When the meeting begins, you are asked to explain in general terms the main differences and similarities in traditional and ABC systems and why managers might prefer ABC costs for decision-making purposes. You have only Exhibits 4-6 and 4-7 as a guide, so you quickly display these side-by-side on a PowerPoint slide, and, after taking a deep breath, you begin to talk. What similarities and differences would you point out? What advantages do ABC costs have?

Answer

1. Traditional costing systems are much simpler than ABC systems and are usually less costly to maintain.
2. Traditional systems and ABC systems both have all three types of costs: direct, indirect, and unallocated.
3. ABC systems identify multiple cost pools, each representing a particular production activity. Traditional systems use only one cost pool that includes all indirect resource costs. This allows ABC systems to better match costs with the causes of those costs.
4. ABC systems assign indirect resource costs to cost objects in two stages of allocation, where the first stage allocates costs to activities and the second stage allocates activity costs to final cost objects such as products, services, or customers. Traditional systems assign indirect resource costs to final cost objects in just one stage.
5. ABC systems require many more cost-allocation bases than do traditional systems. When these cost-allocation bases are both plausible and reliable cost drivers, the overall accuracy of product, service, or customer cost is improved.
6. ABC systems provide more operational information on the costs of activities, which managers can use to reduce costs by improving operating efficiencies for each activity.

Activity-Based Management: A Cost Management System Tool

Objective 8

Use activity-based management (ABM) to make strategic and operational control decisions.

As we mentioned previously, ABC systems not only develop more accurate costs, they also aid in the control of costs. Recall that managers' day-to-day focus is on managing activities, not costs. Because ABC systems also focus on activities, they are a very useful tool in cost management systems. **Activity-based management (ABM)** is using the output of an activity-based cost accounting system to aid strategic decision making and to improve operational control of an organization. The strategic decision to emphasize pen casings at Lopez Plastics is an example of ABM. In the broadest terms, ABM aims to improve the value received by customers and to improve profits by identifying opportunities for improvements in strategy and operations.

One of the most useful applications of ABM is distinguishing between value-added and non-value-added costs. A **value-added cost** is the cost of an activity that a company cannot eliminate without affecting a product's value to the customer. Value-added costs are necessary (as long as the activity that drives such costs is performed efficiently). In contrast, companies try to minimize **non-value-added costs**, costs that a company can eliminate without affecting a product's value to the customer. Activities such as handling and storing inventories, transporting partly finished products from one part of the plant to another, and changing the setup of production-line operations to produce a different model of the product are all non-value-adding activities. A company can often reduce, if not eliminate, them by careful redesign of the plant layout and the production process.

Another ABC-related technique is **benchmarking**, the continuous process of comparing products, services, and activities to the best industry standards. Benchmarking is a tool to help an organization measure its competitive posture. Benchmarks can come from within the organization, from competing organizations, or from other organizations having similar processes.

Consider the production of laptops at **Dell**. Unit costs for key activities provides the basis for benchmarking the work groups in one production facility with those at others and possibly with industry standards. In addition, Dell can use the cost-allocation bases for key activities—for example, the time to assemble a motherboard—as operational benchmarks. The most efficient work groups and centers can share their ideas for process improvements with other groups and centers.

Companies must exercise caution when benchmarking, especially when using financial benchmarks. Compare a California bank's branches in Chico and San Francisco. The bank's benchmarking system uses the financial benchmark *cost per deposit* to measure deposit-processing efficiency. The San Francisco branch managers pointed out at least two problems that put them at a disadvantage. First, costs, especially labor costs, differ between Chico and San Francisco. Employees in metropolitan areas generally receive higher salaries because of their higher cost of living. Therefore, higher teller salaries in San Francisco increase the cost per deposit. Second, different branches can implement an ABC system in different ways. In this case, Chico's ABC system does not allocate equipment depreciation to the deposit-processing activity; these costs remain unallocated. In contrast, the San Francisco branch allocates this cost to the processing activity. This will also cause the cost per deposit to be higher at the San Francisco branches. As a result, even if the tellers process deposits faster and more accurately at the San Francisco branch, their performance will not appear to be as good as the tellers at the Chico branch. Perhaps a better measure of the deposit process would be the *time to process a deposit*, a strictly nonfinancial benchmark.

Benefits of Activity-Based Costing and Activity-Based Management

Activity-based costing systems are more complex and costly than traditional systems. Thus, companies that have relatively simple operating systems may not realize sufficient benefits to warrant using ABC systems. But more organizations in both manufacturing and nonmanufacturing industries are adopting activity-based costing systems for a variety of reasons:

- Fierce competitive pressure has resulted in shrinking profit margins. Companies may know their overall margin, but they often do not have confidence in the accuracy of the margins for individual products or services. Some are winners and some are losers—but which ones are which? Accurate costs are essential for answering this question. Consider **Taylor Corporation**, one of the largest specialty printers in the United States with annual sales of more than $1.3 billion. One of its operating divisions implemented an ABC system to provide better information on the profitability of more than 3,500 products. Managers used the ABC information to set an optimal product mix and to estimate the profit margins of new products.
- Greater diversity in the types of products and services as well as customer classes results in greater operating complexity. Often in such situations the consumption of a company's shared resources also varies substantially across products and customers—a condition that adds to the value of ABC systems.
- Indirect costs are far more important in today's automated world-class manufacturing environment than they have been in the past. In many industries, automated equipment is replacing direct labor. Indirect costs are sometimes more than 50% of total cost. Because ABC systems focus on indirect costs, they are more common in companies with automated production processes.
- The rapid pace of technological change has shortened product life cycles. Hence, companies do not have time to make price or cost adjustments once they discover costing errors. The accurate costs produced by ABC systems are essential.
- The costs associated with bad decisions that result from inaccurate cost estimates are substantial. Examples include bids lost due to overcosted products, hidden losses from undercosted products, and failure to detect activities that are not cost effective. Companies with accurate ABC product costs have a competitive advantage over those with inaccurate costs.
- Computer technology has reduced the costs of developing and operating ABC systems. Most ERP systems (see p. 15) routinely include ABC modules.

While many companies throughout the world are adopting ABC systems, some German companies, including **Deutsche Telekom** and **DaimlerChrysler**, have gone a step further. They use a cost accounting system called **Grenzplankostenrechnung (GPK)**. Most GPK systems use between 400 and 2,000 cost pools to allocate indirect manufacturing costs. The Business First box on p. 142 summarizes some of the characteristics of GPK.

Business First

GPK and ABC: Support for Short-Term and Long-Term Decisions

Many companies throughout the world have developed sophisticated cost accounting systems. While many U.S. companies have adopted ABC, many northern European companies, especially in France, Norway, Sweden, the Netherlands, and Germany, are increasingly using GPK, a system first developed 50 years ago in Germany. Among the GPK companies are **Porsche**, **STIHL**, **Deutsche Telekom**, and **DaimlerChrysler**.

Advances in computer technology have made widespread use of these cost accounting systems more practical. When companies adopt Enterprise Resource Planning (ERP) systems that include software for ABC and GPK, they can upgrade their cost accounting systems without a huge additional investment. The ERP system of **SAP**, a German software company that helped pioneer such systems, offers the framework for GPK as part of its management accounting module, a main factor in the expanding use of GPK. Because STIHL uses SAP worldwide, it was able to more easily roll out the use of GPK in its U.S. subsidiary.

ABC and GPK embody both similarities and differences. Both allocate costs to products, services, or customers using multiple cost pools with various cost-allocation bases. A main difference is that GPK separates fixed and variable costs and applies only variable costs to products or services. Although the ABC approach could do the same, most ABC systems focus on applying all production-related costs (and, often, some non-production value-chain costs). Thus, GPK systems measure profitability on a contribution-margin basis, while ABC systems generally produce full-cost margins. Another difference between ABC and GPK is how they define cost pools for allocation. ABC companies focus on activities, with only a few major identified activities. In contrast, GPK companies focus on cost centers and may have thousands of them. Deutsche Telekom has about 20,000, although Porsche has only 450, and most companies have between 400 and 2,000. Most cost centers are work units of only a few people, often 10 workers or fewer. In both systems, the cost center or activity is the focus of day-to-day cost control. The GPK systems bring this focus down to a much lower level than do most ABC systems.

Which is best, ABC or GPK? Like many management accounting issues, the answer is "it depends." Because GPK focuses on contribution margins, it provides information that is more relevant for short-term decisions. In contrast, ABC starts with a long-term perspective and produces information more suited to strategic decisions. However, GPK systems can add a full-cost calculation for long-term decision purposes, and many ABC systems can separate fixed and variable costs for short-term decisions. Further, the difference between cost-center and activity-based cost pools may not be especially significant because underlying cost pools and cost drivers can be similar in both systems. Although there remain basic philosophical differences related to allocation of fixed costs and definitions of cost pools, in practice companies that use a combination of GPK and ABC principles may find the best of both worlds. For example, the **Hospital for Sick Children** in Toronto merged GPK with its ABC system to produce financial information that was more useful to management.

Sources: G. Friedl, H. Kupper, and B. Pedell, "Relevance Added: Combining ABC with German Cost Accounting," *Strategic Finance*, June 2005, pp. 56–61; K. Krumwiede, "Rewards and Realities of German Cost Accounting," *Strategic Finance*, April 2005, pp. 27–34; . Carl S. Smith, "Going for GPK," *Strategic Finance*, April 2005, pp. 36–39. Brian Mackie, "Merging GPK and ABC on the Road to RCA," *Strategic Finance*, November 2006, pp. 33–39. P. Sharman and B. Mackie, "Grenzplankostenrechnung (GPK): German Cost Accounting, Flexible Planning and Control," IMA Web site, http://www.imanet.org/pdf/3202.pdf

Highlights to Remember

1. **Describe the purposes of cost management systems.** Cost management systems provide cost information for external financial reporting, for strategic decision making, and for operational cost control.

2. **Explain the relationship among cost, cost object, cost accumulation, and cost assignment.** Cost accounting systems provide cost information about various types of objects— products, customers, activities, and so on. To do this, a system first accumulates resource costs by natural classifications, such as materials, labor, and energy. Then, it assigns these costs to cost objects, either tracing them directly or assigning them indirectly through allocation.

3. **Distinguish between direct and indirect costs.** Accountants can specifically and exclusively identify direct costs with a cost object in an economically feasible way. When this is not possible, accountants may allocate costs to cost objects using a cost driver. Such costs are called indirect costs. The greater the proportion of direct costs, the greater the accuracy of the cost system. When the proportion of indirect costs is significant, accountants must take care to find the most appropriate cost drivers.

4. **Explain the major reasons for allocating costs.** The four main purposes of cost allocation are to predict the economic effects of planning and control decisions, to motivate managers and employees, to measure the costs of inventory and cost of goods sold, and to justify costs for pricing or reimbursement. Some costs are unallocated because the accountants can determine no plausible and reliable relationship between resource costs and cost objects.

5. **Identify the main types of manufacturing costs: direct materials, direct labor, and indirect production costs.** The main types of manufacturing costs are direct materials, direct labor, and indirect production costs. Accountants can trace direct materials and direct labor to most cost objects, and they allocate the indirect production costs using a cost allocation base.

6. **Explain how the financial statements of merchandisers and manufacturers differ because of the types of goods they sell.** The primary difference between the financial statements of a merchandiser and a manufacturer is the reporting of inventories. A merchandiser has only one type of inventory, whereas a manufacturer has three types of inventory—raw materials, work-in-process, and finished goods.

7. **Understand the main differences between traditional and activity-based costing (ABC) systems and why ABC systems provide value to managers.** Traditional systems usually allocate only the indirect costs of the production function. ABC systems often allocate many of the costs of the value-chain functions. Traditional costing accumulates costs using categories such as direct material, direct labor, and production overhead. ABC systems accumulate costs by activities required to produce a product or service. The key value of ABC systems is in their increased costing accuracy and better information provided that can lead to process improvements.

8. **Use activity-based management (ABM) to make strategic and operational control decisions.** Activity-based management is using ABC information to improve operations. A key advantage of an activity-based costing system is its ability to aid managers in decision making. ABC improves the accuracy of cost estimates, including product and customer costs and the costs of value-added versus non-value-added activities. ABC also improves managers' understanding of operations. Managers can focus their attention on making strategic decisions, such as product mix, pricing, and process improvements. ■

Appendix 4: Detailed Illustration of Traditional and Activity-Based Cost Accounting Systems

As we mentioned in the chapter, ABC systems are more complex than traditional systems. In this appendix, we go more in depth than in the Lopez Plastics Company example. You will notice, however, that the main concepts are exactly the same—only the details will change.

Suppose the billing department of one of **AT&T**'s smaller customer care centers requires accurate and useful information about the cost of providing account inquiry and bill printing services for its 120,000 residential and 20,000 commercial customer accounts. A local service bureau has offered to provide all the services currently performed by the billing department at $4.30 per residential account and $8.00 per commercial account. To make informed decisions, AT&T's managers need accurate estimates of the department's own cost per residential account and cost per commercial account. They also need to know the costs of the key activities performed in the department to determine whether they can achieve cost savings through better control of their activities.

Exhibit 4-8 depicts the residential and commercial customer classes (cost objects) and the resources used to support the billing department. All the costs incurred in the billing department are indirect. There are no direct costs or unallocated costs. The billing department currently uses a traditional costing system that allocates all indirect production costs based on the number of account inquiries.

Exhibit 4-8 shows that the resources used in the billing department last month cost $687,500. The traditional cost accounting system simply adds together all indirect costs and then allocates them based on the number of inquiries the department receives from each customer class. The billing department received 25,000 account inquiries during the month, so the cost per inquiry was $687,500 ÷ 25,000 = $27.50. There were 20,000 residential account inquiries, 80% of the total. Thus, we assign 80% of the indirect production cost to residential accounts and 20% to commercial accounts. The resulting cost per account is ($687,500 × .8) ÷ 120,000 = $4.58 and ($687,500 × .2) ÷ 20,000 = $6.88 for residential and commercial accounts, respectively. Does this traditional cost accounting system provide managers with accurate estimates of the cost to serve residential and commercial customers? If the answer is yes, the billing department management would accept the service bureau's proposal to service residential accounts because of the apparent savings of $4.58 – $4.30 = $.28 per account. The billing department would continue to service its commercial accounts because its costs are $8.00 – $6.88 = $1.12 less than the service bureau's bid.

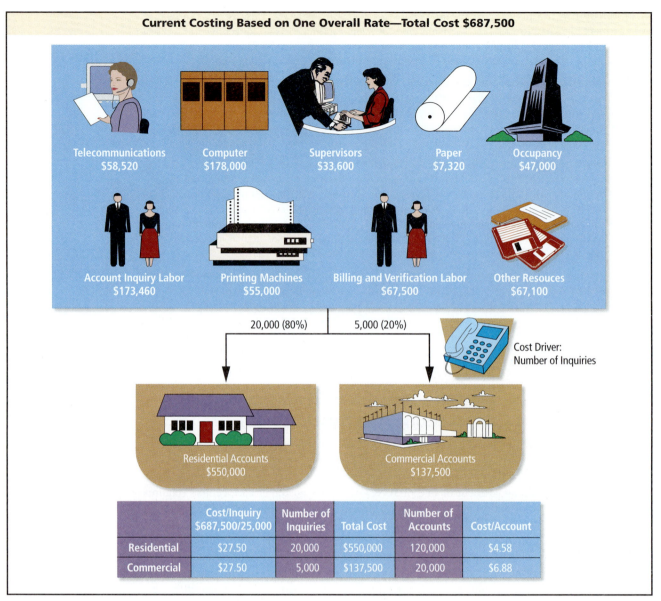

Current Costing Based on One Overall Rate—Total Cost $687,500

Telecommunications $58,520

Computer $178,000

Supervisors $33,600

Paper $7,320

Occupancy $47,000

Account Inquiry Labor $173,460

Printing Machines $55,000

Billing and Verification Labor $67,500

Other Resouces $67,100

20,000 (80%)   5,000 (20%)

Cost Driver: Number of Inquiries

Residential Accounts $550,000

Commercial Accounts $137,500

	Cost/Inquiry $687,500/25,000	Number of Inquiries	Total Cost	Number of Accounts	Cost/Account
Residential	$27.50	20,000	$550,000	120,000	$4.58
Commercial	$27.50	5,000	$137,500	20,000	$6.88

Exhibit 4-8
Traditional Costing System at the Billing Department

Making Managerial Decisions

Suppose **AT&T**'s management retains its traditional cost accounting system but believes that a more plausible and reliable cost driver is "number of printed lines." Each residential bill averages 12 lines and each commercial bill averages 50 lines. What would be the new cost per account for residential and commercial customers based on number of lines per bill? How would this new cost accounting information affect the outsourcing decision?

Answer

The total costs would be the same, but the allocation of the total cost to each customer class would change. Instead of allocating 80% of total costs to residential customers, we would allocate

only $(12 \times 120,000) \div [(12 \times 120,000) + (50 \times 20,000)] =$ 59% of total costs to residential customers and the other 41% to commercial accounts. The cost per account for residential customers would then be $(59\% \times \$687,500) \div 120,000 = \$3.38$, and the cost per commercial account would be $(41\% \times \$687,500) \div 20,000 = \$14.09$. The outsourcing decision would likely change. We would outsource commercial accounts but not residential accounts. A key issue is how much confidence management has in the costs it uses for decision making. Poor cost data can lead to poor decisions.

Now suppose you are the billing department manager and you know that billing employees spend much of their time verifying the accuracy of commercial bills and very little time verifying residential bills. Yet the traditional cost accounting system allocates 80% of the costs of this work to residential customers. Does this make sense to you? Do you have some doubt about the accuracy of the cost-per-account data? You also know that commercial accounts average 50 lines or two pages per bill, compared with only 12 lines or one page for residential accounts. This means that the billing department uses much more paper, computer time, and printing machine time for each commercial account. Again, this does not agree with the percentage of allocations based on number of inquiries. In addition, you believe that the actual consumption of support resources for commercial accounts is much greater than 20% because of their complexity.

As the billing department manager, you are also concerned about activities such as verification of commercial bills, inquiries from customers, and correspondence resulting from customer inquiries. These activities consume costly resources but do not add value to AT&T's services from the customer's perspective. To reduce these costs, management needs a more thorough understanding of the relationships among key activities and resource costs.

In summary, you would probably conclude that AT&T needs to improve the billing department's traditional cost accounting system because it is not providing managers with useful information for strategic decisions or operational control. This is exactly what AT&T's management concluded. So, let's see how we might design an activity-based costing system for the billing department.

Design of an Activity-Based Cost Accounting System

How do managers actually design ABC systems? At the billing department of AT&T's customer-care center, a team of managers from the billing department and AT&T's regional controller used the following four-step procedure to design their new cost accounting system.

Step 1: **Determine the Key Components of the Activity-Based Cost Accounting System**

The key components of an activity-based cost accounting system are cost objects, key activities, resources, and related cost drivers. These components, together with the purpose of the new system, determine the scope of the ABC system. Management at AT&T wanted the system to (1) determine the billing department cost per account for each customer class to better support the strategic decision regarding outsourcing accounts to the local service bureau and (2) enhance the managers' understanding of key billing department activities to support operational cost control. Because the bid from the local service bureau includes performing all the activities of the department, the ABC system must include all department costs. Further, because management wants to understand the key activities and related costs, the team designed an activity-based system.

Objective 9

Describe the steps in designing an activity-based costing system.

Through interviews with the department supervisors, management identified the following activities and related cost drivers to use as cost-allocation bases for the billing department.

Activity	Cost-Allocation Base
Account billing	Number of printed pages
Bill verification	Number of accounts verified
Account inquiry	Number of inquiries
Correspondence	Number of letters
Other activities	Number of printed pages

The four key billing department activities are account billing, bill verification, account inquiry, and correspondence. These activities require the vast majority of the work done in the billing department. There are other activities performed in the billing department, such as routine printer and computer maintenance, training, and preparing monthly reports. Management did not identify these as individual activities. Instead, the team lumped them together and labeled them "other activities." Why? Because the cost of the resources used for each of these individual activities was relatively small, the team could not find plausible and reliable cost drivers for them, or the cost of collecting data was too high. The cost-allocation base selected for the "other activities" cost pool is number of printed pages because most of the other activities, such as maintenance and training, are associated in some way with the printing function. Exhibit 4-8 shows the resources used by the billing department.

Step 2: **Determine the Relationships Among Cost Objects, Activities, and Resources**

An important phase of any activity-based analysis is identifying the relationships among key activities and the resources consumed. The management team does this by interviewing personnel and analyzing various internal data. AT&T interviewed all employees as part of its ABC study. For example, the company asked supervisors how they spend their time. Based on time records, the supervisors estimated that they spend most of their time (40%) supervising account inquiry activity. They also estimated that they spend about 30% of their time supervising billing activity and about 10% of their time reviewing and signing correspondence. They spend the remaining 20% of their time on all other department activities. Exhibit 4-9 shows the results of the interviews.

Implementing an ABC system requires a careful study of operations. As a result, managers often discover that they can trace directly to cost objects some previously indirect or even unallocated costs, thus improving the accuracy of product or service costs. During interviews with the billing department supervisors, the ABC team learned that several of the billing employees work exclusively on verification of commercial bills. Thus, the team could trace their salaries—$11,250—directly to the verification activity. Further, because the billing department performs verification activity for only commercial accounts, they could also trace this cost pool directly to the commercial customer cost object.

Look at the computer resource row in Exhibit 4-9. The supervisor indicated that 45% of this resource supports account inquiry, 5% supports correspondence, and so on. How did the supervisor determine these percentages? Initially, he or she might simply estimate them. Later, the supervisor might gather data to support the estimates. Now consider the occupancy resource row. The percentages used to allocate this resource might be based on the square feet used by the various employees for each activity compared to the total square feet in the department.

Next, the team determined which activities were needed by each cost object. The supervisors indicated that residential customers needed account inquiry, correspondence, and billing activities. Commercial customers needed account inquiry, correspondence, billing, and verification activities. Both also need other activities.

Resource Used to Perform Activity	Account Inquiry Activity	Correspondence Activity	Billing Activity	Verification Activity	All Other Activities	Total
Supervisor	40%	10%	30%		20%	100%
Account inquiry labor	90	10				100%
Billing labor			30	70		100%
Verification labor				100		100%
Paper			100			100%
Computer	45	5	35	10	5	100%
Telecommunications	90				10	100%
Occupancy	65		15		20	100%
Printing machines		5	90		5	100%
All other department resources					100	100%

Exhibit 4-9
Analysis of Interviews with Supervisors from the Billing Department

The process map in Exhibit 4-10 depicts the same information that was gathered from interviews. We allocate the costs of the 10 resources to the 5 activities. For example, account inquiry activity consumes 40% of supervisor resources, 90% of account inquiry labor, 45% of computer resources, 90% of telecommunication resources, and 65% of occupancy costs. Then, we allocate the costs of the five activities to the two customer cost objects—residential and commercial. For example, commercial accounts require account inquiry, correspondence, billing, verification, and other activities. We allocate the activity costs based on a measure of the amount of activity that each customer uses. For example, we allocate the account inquiry activity cost pool based on the number of inquiries received from residential and commercial accounts.

Process maps can be a key tool for managers to gain an understanding of operations. For example, AT&T's managers considered this process map critical because it revealed how AT&T conducted business. Managers were able to see how operating activities consume costly resources. Normally, we do not collect the cost data and the cost driver data shown in Exhibit 4-10 until we have drawn the process map and identified the resources and cost drivers. The ABC team uses the process map as a guide for the next step in designing the ABC system—data collection.

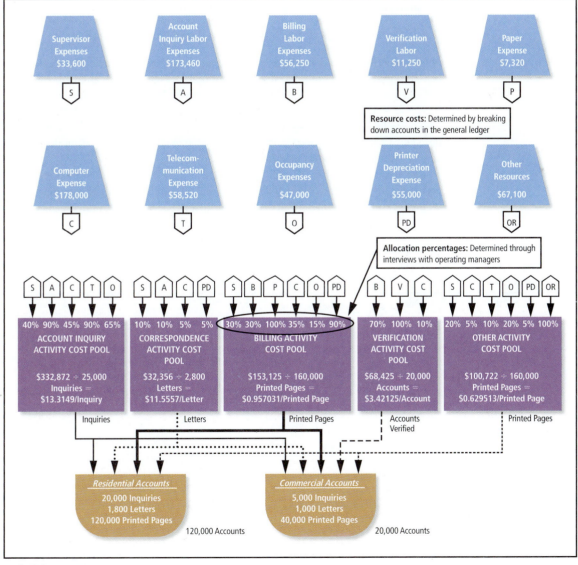

Exhibit 4-10

Two-Stage Cost Allocation for Billing Department Operations

Exhibit 4-11

Number of Cost Driver Units for the Billing Department

		Number of Cost Driver Units		
Activity	Cost Driver Units	Residential	Commercial	Total
Account inquiry	Inquiries	20,000	5,000	25,000
Correspondence	Letters	1,800	1,000	2,800
Billing	Printed pages	120,000	40,000	160,000
Verification	Accounts verified		20,000	20,000
Other activities	Printed pages	120,000	40,000	160,000

Step 3: **Collect Relevant Data Concerning Costs and the Physical Flow of the Cost-Driver Units Among Resources and Activities**

Using the process map as a guide, billing department managers collected the required cost and operational data by further interviews with relevant personnel. Sources of data include the accounting records, special studies, and sometimes "best estimates of managers." The managers collected resource cost information from the general ledger (Exhibit 4-8) and data on the flow of cost drivers from various operational reports (Exhibits 4-9 and 4-11). Exhibit 4-10 shows the data collected.

Management can now use the completed process map to determine costs for the strategic and operational decisions that they must make.

Step 4: **Calculate and Interpret the New Activity-Based Cost Information**

After collecting all required financial and operational data, we can calculate the new activity-based information. Exhibit 4-12 summarizes stage 1 allocations. It shows the total costs for each of the five activity cost pools. Notice that the total costs of $332,872 + $32,356 + $153,125 + $68,425 + $100,722 = $687,500 in Exhibit 4-12 equals the total indirect costs in Exhibit 4-8. Now we can determine the activity-based cost per account for each customer class (stage 2 allocations) from the data in step 3. Exhibit 4-13 shows the computations.

Examine the last two rows in Exhibit 4-13. Notice that traditional costing over-costed the high-volume residential accounts and substantially undercosted the low-volume, complex commercial accounts. The cost per account for residential accounts

		Activity Cost Pool				
Resource	Cost (from Exhibit 4-8)	Account Inquiry	Correspondence	Billing	Verification	Other
Supervisors	$ 33,600	$ 13,440*	$ 3,360**	$ 10,080***		$ 6,720****
Account inquiry labor	173,460	156,114	17,346			
Billing labor	56,250			16,875	$39,375	
Verification labor	11,250				11,250	
Paper	7,320			7,320		
Computer	178,000	80,100	8,900	62,300	17,800	8,900
Telecommunication	58,520	52,668				5,852
Occupancy	47,000	30,550		7,050		9,400
Printers	55,000		2,750	49,500		2,750
Other resources	67,100					67,100
Total cost	$687,500	$332,872	$32,356	$153,125	$68,425	$100,722

* From Exhibits 4-9 and 4-10, account inquiry activity uses 40% of the supervisor resource. So the allocation is 40% × $33,600 = $13,440.

** 10% × $33,600

*** 30% × $33,600

**** 20% × $33,600

Exhibit 4-12

Total Cost of Each Activity in the Billing Department

Driver Costs

Activity (Driver Units)	Total Costs (from Exhibit 4-12) (1)	Total Number of Driver Units (From Exhibit 4-11) (2)	Cost per Driver Unit (1) ÷ (2)
Account inquiry (inquiries)	$332,872	25,000 Inquiries	$13.314880
Correspondence (letters)	$ 32,356	2,800 Letters	$11.555714
Account billing (printed pages)	$153,125	160,000 Printed pages	$ 0.957031
Bill verification (accounts verified)	$ 68,425	20,000 Accounts verified	$ 3.421250
Other activities (printed pages)	$100,722	160,000 Printed pages	$ 0.629513

Cost per Customer Class

		Residential		Commercial	
	Cost per Driver Unit	Number of Driver Units	Cost	Number of Driver Units	Cost
Account inquiry	$13.314880	20,000 Inquiries	$266,298	5,000 Inquiries	$ 66,574
Correspondence	$11.555714	1,800 Letters	20,800	1,000 Letters	11,556
Account billing	$ 0.957031	120,000 Pages	114,844	40,000 Pages	38,281
Bill verification	$ 3.421250			20,000 Accts.	68,425
Other activities	$ 0.629513	120,000 Pages	75,541	40,000 Pages	25,181
Total cost			$477,483		$210,017
Number of accounts			120,000		20,000
Cost per account			$ 3.98		$ 10.50
Cost per account, traditional system from Exhibit 4-8			$ 4.58		$ 6.88

Exhibit 4-13
Key Results of Activity-Based Costing Study

using ABC is $3.98, which is $0.60 (or 13%) less than the $4.58 cost generated by the traditional costing system. The cost per account for commercial accounts is $10.50, which is $3.62 (or 53%) more than the $6.88 cost from the traditional costing system. The analysis confirms management's belief that the traditional system under-costed commercial accounts. AT&T's management now has more accurate cost information for strategic decision-making and cost-control purposes.

Results like these are common when companies perform activity-based costing studies. Traditional systems generally overcost high-volume cost objects with simple processes. Which system makes more sense—the traditional allocation system that "spreads" all support costs to customer classes based solely on the number of inquiries, or the ABC system that identifies key activities and assigns costs based on the consumption of units of cost drivers for each key activity? For AT&T, the probable benefits of the new ABC system appear to outweigh the costs of implementing and maintaining the new cost system.

Strategic Decisions, Operational Cost Control, and ABM

Now let's see how billing department managers can use the ABC system to improve their strategic decisions and operational cost control. Suppose that the billing department needed to find a way to increase its capacity to handle more accounts due to an expected large increase in demand from a new housing development and a business center. Managers proposed a strategic action—outsource certain customer accounts to a local service bureau. Billing department managers were also interested in reducing the operating costs of the department while not impairing the quality of the service it provided to its customers. To address both of these issues, they used the ABC information from Exhibit 4-13 to identify non-value-added activities that had significant costs. Account inquiry and bill verification activities are non-value-added and costly so management asked for ideas for cost reductions. The new information provided by the ABC system generated the following ideas:

- Use the service bureau for commercial accounts because of the significant cost savings. From Exhibit 4-13, the service bureau's bid is $8.00 per account, compared to the billing department's activity-based cost of $10.50, a potential savings of $2.50 per account! In addition, department managers would try to eliminate or reduce bill verification, commercial account inquiry, and commercial account correspondence activities, all non-value-adding activities.

  Suppose AT&T outsourced commercial customers to the service bureau. Would actual costs immediately decrease by $50,000 ($2.50 for each of 20,000 commercial accounts)? No. Only the variable portion of resource costs, such as paper, variable telecommunication charges, variable computer charges, and overtime or part time labor, would decrease immediately. The fixed cost portion of all these resources would not change without some specific management actions. For example, suppose billing labor used for verification is a fixed-cost resource. Then, the time formerly required for verification is idle time, but the company must still pay wages. Management would have to decide whether to lay off billing employees or to keep them in anticipation of the increase in printing activity due to the expected increase in residential customers.

- Exhibit 4-13 indicates that account inquiry activity is very costly, accounting for a significant portion of total billing department costs. A benchmarking analysis showed the cost per inquiry of $13.31 was unusually high compared to similar measures at other customer care centers. By meeting with managers from centers that had significantly lower activity cost rates, the billing department managers developed ideas for process improvements. One idea that resulted from these meetings was to implement a Web-based inquiry system to handle routine questions about bills.

The billing department, like so many companies that have adopted ABC and ABM, improved both strategic and operating decisions.

Summary Problem for Your Review

PROBLEM

Refer to the billing department illustration. Suppose that management at **AT&T**'s Youngstown area customer care center is implementing an ABC system. The center has 98,000 residential customers and 25,000 commercial customers. An ABC team has collected the data shown in Exhibit 4-14. Management has decided not to allocate the other resource costs.

1. Using the same format as Exhibits 4-12 and 4-13, prepare schedules to determine the cost per driver unit for each activity and the activity-based cost per account for each customer type.
2. Consider the verification activity. Suppose the cost per account verified is $0.45. The center verifies 50% of residential and commercial bills. Given that there are, on average, 50 lines on each commercial bill and only 12 lines on each residential bill, criticize the use of accounts verified as a cost driver and suggest a more plausible and reliable cost driver.

SOLUTION

1. Exhibit 4-15 is a schedule showing the total cost of each activity of the billing department. From this we can determine the cost per driver unit and the activity-based cost per account for each customer class, as shown in Exhibit 4-16.
2. The ABC system allocates $49,000 \div (49,000 + 12,500) = 79.7\%$ of verification costs to residential accounts based on the number of accounts verified. However, the work performed to verify a bill is probably closely related to the number of lines on the bill. Using accounts verified assumes that employees expend the same amount of effort verifying residential accounts and commercial accounts, even though there are many fewer lines on residential bills. Thus, the cost driver "lines verified" is more plausible and reliable. The number of lines verified for commercial accounts are 50 lines per

		Percent of Resource Used in Activity				
Resource	Monthly Cost	Billing	Account Inquiry	Correspondence	Verification	Other
Supervisors	$ 30,500	40%	35%	8%		17%
Account inquiry labor	102,000		85	15		
Billing labor	45,000	70			30	
Paper	5,800	100				
Computers	143,000	30	48	7	10	5
Telecommunications	49,620		85			15
Occupancy	56,000	15	70			15
Printers	75,000	80		5		15
Other	59,000					100
Total	$565,920					

		Monthly Number of Cost Driver Units		
Activity	Cost Driver	Residential	Commercial	Total
Billing	Lines	1,176,000	1,250,000	2,426,000
Account inquiry	Inquiries	9,800	7,500	17,300
Correspondence	Letters	1,960	2,500	4,460
Verification	Accounts verified	49,000	12,500	61,500

Exhibit 4-14
First Stage Percentage Allocations and Monthly Number of Cost Driver Units

account × 12,500 accounts = 625,000 lines and for residential accounts are 12 lines per account × 49,000 accounts = 588,000 lines. Thus, we would allocate 588,000 ÷ (588,000 + 625,000) = 48.5% of verification costs to residential accounts based on lines verified. ABC teams should always exercise care when choosing cost drivers to use as allocation bases. The Youngstown team might also want to investigate the plausibility and reliability of the "number of inquiries" cost driver because this assumes that residential and commercial customer inquiries require the same amount of work.

		Activity				
Resource	Cost (from Exhibit 4-14)	Billing	Account Inquiry	Correspondence	Verification	Other
Supervisors	$ 30,500	$ 12,200 *	$ 10,675**	$ 2,440***		$ 5,185****
Account inquiry labor	102,000		86,700	15,300		
Billing labor	45,000	31,500			$13,500	
Paper	5,800	5,800				
Computer	143,000	42,900	68,640	10,010	14,300	7,150
Telecommunication	49,620		42,177			7,443
Occupancy	56,000	8,400	39,200			8,400
Printers	75,000	60,000		3,750		11,250
Other resources	59,000					59,000
Total cost	$565,920	$160,800	$247,392	$31,500	$27,800	$98,428

*40% × $30,500
**35% × $30,500
***8% × $30,500
****17% × $30,500

Exhibit 4-15
Total Cost of Each Activity in the Billing Department

Driver Costs			
Activity (Driver Units)	Total Costs (From Exhibit 4-15) (1)	Total Number of Driver Units (From Exhibit 4-14) (2)	Cost per Driver Unit (1) ÷ (2)
Account inquiry (inquiries)	$247,392	17,300 Inquiries	$14.300116
Correspondence (letters)	$ 31,500	4,460 Letters	$ 7.062780
Account billing (lines)	$160,800	2,426,000 Lines	$ 0.066282
Bill verification (accounts verified)	$ 27,800	61,500 Accounts Verified	$ 0.452033

Cost per Customer Class					
		Residential		Commercial	
	Cost per Driver Unit	Number of Driver Units	Cost	Number of Driver Units	Cost
Account inquiry	$14.300116	9,800 Inquiries	$140,141	7,500 Inquiries	$107,251
Correspondence	$ 7.062780	1,960 Letters	13,843	2,500 Letters	17,657
Account billing	$ 0.066282	1,176,000 Lines	77,947	1,250,000 Lines	82,853
Bill verification	$ 0.452033	49,000 Accounts	22,149	12,500 Accounts	5,650
Total cost			$254,081		$213,411
Number of accounts			98,000		25,000
Cost per account			$ 2.59		$ 8.54

Exhibit 4-16
Cost Per Driver Unit and Activity-Based Cost Per Account

Accounting Vocabulary

activity-based costing (ABC) systems, p. 133
activity-based management (ABM), p. 140
benchmarking, p. 140
cost, p. 122
cost accounting, p. 122
cost accounting systems, p. 122
cost accumulation, p. 123
cost allocation, p. 124
cost assignment, p. 123
cost management system (CMS), p. 121
cost object, p. 122
cost objective, p. 122

cost pool, p. 126
cost-allocation base, p. 124
direct costs, p. 124
direct-labor costs, p. 129
direct-material costs, p. 129
direct-material inventory, p. 130
factory burden, p. 130
factory overhead, p. 130
finished-goods inventory, p. 130
Grenzplankostenrechnung (GPK), p. 141
indirect costs, p. 124
indirect manufacturing costs, p. 130

indirect production costs, p. 130
inventoriable costs, p. 130
manufacturing overhead, p. 130
non-value-added costs, p. 140
period costs, p. 130
process map, p. 133
product costs, p. 130
tracing, p. 124
traditional costing systems, p. 133
two-stage ABC system, p. 136
unallocated costs, p. 127
value-added cost, p. 140
work-in-process inventory, p. 130

 **Fundamental Assignment Material**

4-A1 Direct, Indirect, and Unallocated Costs, Process Map

Lockyear Window Company makes and sells three product lines—custom detailed windows, large standard windows, and small standard windows. The statement of operating income for the most recent period is shown next.

Lockyear Window Company
Statement of Operating Income

		Total
Sales		$155,000
Cost of goods sold		
Direct material	$40,000	
Indirect production costs	41,000	81,000
Gross profit		74,000
Selling and administrative expenses:		
Commissions	15,000	
Distribution to warehouses	10,400	25,400
Income before unallocated expenses		48,600
Unallocated expenses		
Administrative salaries	8,000	
Other administrative expenses	4,000	12,000
Operating income before taxes		
		$ 36,600

Lockyear uses a traditional cost accounting system. A process map developed to describe this system is shown in Exhibit 4-17. To aid in the company's analysis of its product mix strategy, you have been asked to determine operating income (loss) for each product line. Use a format similar to Exhibit 4-3 on page 128 in the text.

4-A2 Financial Statements for Manufacturing and Merchandising Companies
Orinoco, Inc., produces and sells wireless reading devices. A competitor, Nile Electronic Products (NEP) sells similar wireless reading devices that it purchases at wholesale from Sonex for $97 each. Both sell the devices for $170. In 20X9 Orinoco produced 10,000 devices at the following costs:

Direct materials purchased		$570,000
Direct materials used		$530,000
Direct labor		290,000
Indirect production:		
Depreciation	$50,000	
Indirect labor	60,000	
Other	40,000	150,000
Total cost of production		$970,000

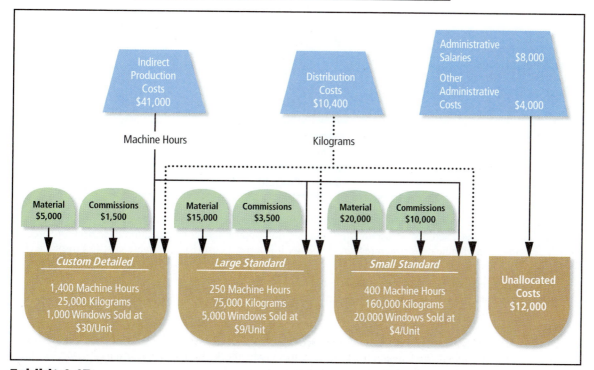

Exhibit 4-17
Process Map for LockYear Window Company's Traditional Cost Allocation System

Assume that Orinoco had no beginning inventory of direct materials. Neither company had any beginning inventory of finished devices, but both had ending inventory of 1,000 finished devices. Ending work-in-process inventory for Orinoco was negligible.

Each company sold 9,000 devices for $1,530,000 in 20X9 and incurred the following selling and administrative costs:

Sales salaries and commissions	$105,000
Depreciation on retail store	40,000
Advertising	25,000
Other	15,000
Total selling and administrative cost	$185,000

1. Prepare the inventories section of the balance sheet for December 31, 20X9, for Nile.
2. Prepare the inventories section of the balance sheet for December 31, 20X9, for Orinoco.
3. Using the cost of goods sold format on page 132 as a model, prepare an income statement for the year 20X9 for Nile.
4. Using the cost of goods sold format on page 132 as a model, prepare an income statement for the year 20X9 for Orinoco.
5. Summarize the differences between the financial statements of Nile, a merchandiser, and Orinoco, a manufacturer.
6. What purpose of a cost management system is being served by reporting the items in requirements 1–4?

4-A3 Activities, Resources, Cost Drivers, and the Banking Industry

Silver Springs Bank is a local bank located in a residential area, and it services mostly individuals and local businesses. Silver Springs' four main services are transaction processing (withdrawals, checks, currency exchange), loans, simple investments (individual clients), and complex investments (portfolios of large businesses).

To support these activities, Silver Springs employs 10 front-office staff, 12 back-office staff dealing with loan applications and investments, and 2 people to consult with customers and manage complex portfolio investments. A team of 3 supervisors manages the overall operations of the bank. As part of Silver Springs' implementation of activity-based costing, it needed to identify activities, resources, and cost drivers. The following table summarizes the cost-allocation bases Silver Springs has chosen for its activities and resources:

Cost-Allocation Base
number of investments
number of applications
number of loans
number of person hours
number of minutes
number of computer transactions
number of square feet
number of loan inquiries
number of transactions
number of schedules
number of securities

For each of the brief descriptions that follows, indicate whether it is an activity (A) or a resource (R). For each activity or resource, choose the most appropriate cost-allocation base from the preceding list and indicate for each resource whether it is a fixed-cost (F) or variable-cost (V) resource. The first item is completed as a guide.

a. Contract maintenance of building (R; number of square feet; F)
b. Staff for front-line customer service
c. External computing services
d. Development of repayment schedules
e. Staff for consulting with customers and arranging the portfolios
f. External service bureau providing customer credit checks for loan applications
g. Preparing investment documents for customers
h. Research to evaluate a loan application

   i. Overtime by back-office staff
   j. Telephones/facsimile
   k. Staff for service and background research
   l. Establish customer collateral for approved loans

4-A4 Activity-Based Costing in an Electronics Company

The wireless phone manufacturing division of a Denver-based consumer electronics company uses activity-based costing. For simplicity, assume that its accountants have identified only the following three activities and related cost drivers for indirect production costs:

Activity	Cost Driver
Materials handling	Direct-materials cost
Engineering	Engineering change notices
Power	Kilowatt hours

Three types of cell phones are produced: Senior, Basic, and Deluxe. Direct costs and cost-driver activity for each product for a recent month are as follows:

	Senior	Basic	Deluxe
Direct-materials cost	$25,000	$ 50,000	$125,000
Direct-labor cost	$ 4,000	$ 1,000	$ 3,000
Kilowatt hours	50,000	200,000	150,000
Engineering change notices	13	5	2

Indirect production costs for the month were as follows:

Materials handling	$12,000
Engineering	20,000
Power	16,000
Total indirect production cost	$48,000

1. Compute the indirect production costs allocated to each product with the ABC system.
2. Suppose all indirect production costs had been allocated to products in proportion to their direct-labor costs. Compute the indirect production costs allocated to each product.
3. In which product costs, those in requirement 1 or those in requirement 2, do you have the most confidence? Why?

4-B1 Direct, Indirect, and Unallocated Costs

Minneapolis Tool Co. is a supplier that assembles purchased parts into components for three distinct markets—scooter parts, lawn mower parts, and hand tool parts. Following is the statement of operating income for the most recent period:

Minneapolis Tool: Statement of Operating Income

		Total
Sales		$990,000
Cost of goods sold		
Direct material	$400,000	
Indirect production (allocated based on machine hours)	94,000	494,000
Gross profit		496,000
Selling and administrative expenses:		
Commissions	55,000	
Distribution to warehouses (allocated based on weight in kilograms)	150,000	205,000
Income before unallocated expenses		291,000
Unallocated expenses		
Corporate salaries	11,000	
Other general expenses	17,000	28,000
Operating income before taxes		$263,000

Minneapolis Tool uses a traditional cost accounting system. Operating data used in the cost accounting system are as follows:

	Scooter Parts	Lawn Mower Parts	Hand Tool Parts
Purchase cost of parts assembled	$175,000	$125,000	$100,000
Machine hours	8,500	1,750	1,500
Weight of parts shipped to distributors (kilograms)	100,000	400,000	250,000
Sales commissions per unit	$ 5.00	$ 0.80	$ 0.20
Units assembled and sold	5,000	25,000	50,000
Sales price per unit	$ 70.00	$ 15.20	$ 5.20

You have been asked to determine operating income (loss) for each product line. Use a format similar to Exhibit 4-3 on p. 128.

4-B2 Allocation, Department Rates, and Direct-Labor Hours Versus Machine Hours

The Garcia Manufacturing Company has two producing departments, machining and assembly. Mr. Garcia recently automated the machining department. The installation of a CAM system, together with robotic workstations, drastically reduced the amount of direct labor required. Meanwhile, the assembly department remained labor intensive. The company had always used one firm-wide rate based on direct-labor hours as the cost-allocation base for applying all costs (except direct materials) to the final products. Mr. Garcia was considering two alternatives: (1) continue using direct-labor hours as the only cost-allocation base, but use different rates in machining and assembly, and (2) using machine hours as the cost-allocation base in the machining department while continuing with direct-labor hours in assembly. Budgeted data for 20X0 are as follows:

	Machining	Assembly	Total
Total cost (except direct materials)	$585,000	$495,000	$1,080,000
Machine hours	97,500	*	105,000
Direct-labor hours	15,000	30,000	45,000

*Not applicable.

1. Suppose Garcia continued to use one firm-wide rate based on direct-labor hours to apply all manufacturing costs (except direct materials) to the final products. Compute the cost-application rate that would be used.
2. Suppose Garcia continued to use direct-labor hours as the only cost-allocation base but used different rates in machining and assembly.
   a. Compute the cost-application rate for machining.
   b. Compute the cost-application rate for assembly.
3. Suppose Garcia changed the cost accounting system to use machine hours as the cost-allocation base in machining and direct-labor hours in assembly.
   a. Compute the cost-application rate for machining.
   b. Compute the cost-application rate for assembly.
4. Three products use the following machine hours and direct-labor hours:

	Machine Hours in Machining	Direct-Labor Hours in Machining	Direct-Labor Hours in Assembly
Product A	12.0	1.0	14.0
Product B	17.0	1.5	3.0
Product C	14.0	1.3	8.0

   a. Compute the manufacturing cost of each product (excluding direct materials) using one firm-wide rate based on direct-labor hours.
   b. Compute the manufacturing cost of each product (excluding direct materials) using direct-labor hours as the cost-allocation base, but with different cost-allocation rates in machining and assembly.

c. Compute the manufacturing cost of each product (excluding direct materials) using a cost-allocation rate based on direct-labor hours in assembly and machine hours in machining.

d. Compare and explain the results in requirements 4a, 4b, and 4c.

4-B3 Traditional Versus ABC Costing Systems

Kiku Yamamoto is the controller of Watanabe, Inc., an electronic controls company located in Osaka. She recently attended a seminar on activity-based costing (ABC) in Tokyo. Watanabe's traditional cost accounting system has three cost categories: direct materials, direct labor, and indirect production costs. The company allocates indirect production costs on the basis of direct labor cost. The following is the 20X0 budget for the automotive controls department (in thousands of Japanese yen):

Direct materials	¥ 60,000
Direct labor	35,000
Indirect production costs	24,500
Total cost	¥119,500

After Ms. Yamamoto attended the seminar, she suggested that Watanabe experiment with an ABC system in the Automotive Controls Department. She identified four main activities that cause indirect production costs in the department and selected a cost driver to use as a cost-allocation base for each activity as follows:

Activity	Cost-Allocation Base	Predicted 20X0 Cost (¥000)
Receiving	Direct materials cost	¥ 4,800
Assembly	Number of control units	13,800
Quality control	QC hours	1,800
Shipping	Number of boxes shipped	4,100
TOTAL		¥24,500

In 20X0 the Automotive Controls Department expects to produce 92,000 control units, use 600 quality control hours, and ship 8,200 boxes.

1. Explain how Watanabe, Inc., allocates its indirect production costs using its traditional cost system. Include a computation of the allocation rate used.

2. Explain how Watanabe, Inc., would allocate indirect production costs under Ms. Yamamoto's proposed ABC system. Include a computation of all the allocation rates used.

3. Suppose Watanabe prices its products at 30% above total production cost. An order came in from **Nissan** for 5,000 control units. Yamamoto estimates that filling the order will require ¥8,000,000 of direct materials cost and ¥2,000,000 of direct labor. It will require 50 hours of QC inspection time and will be shipped in 600 boxes.

   a. Compute the price charged for the 5,000 control units if Watanabe uses its traditional cost accounting system.

   b. Compute the price charged for the 5,000 control units if Watanabe uses the ABC system proposed by Ms. Yamamoto.

4. Explain why costs are different in the two costing systems. Include an indication of which costs you think are most accurate and why.

4-B4 Traditional Costing and ABC, Activity-Based Management

Refer to the text discussion of Lopez Plastics Company on pages 134–138. Assume that the company has the traditional cost accounting system described in Exhibit 4-6. The top management team wants to reverse the pattern of quarterly losses. The company president, Angie Oaks, has emphasized the importance of profit improvement by linking future pay raises of the two product-line managers to their respective gross profit margins. She is concerned about the profitability of the pen casing product line, while pleased with the profitability of the cell phone casing line. She also believes that the unallocated costs of the company are too high compared to competitors. The office of controller, whose costs are included in the unallocated costs, is responsible for vendor relations and purchasing of direct materials. The controller and head of the engineering department present the following idea:

> *We should use more standard parts in cell phone casings, which will dramatically reduce the purchasing department's work required for purchasing. I believe this should cut our office's costs by as much as $20,000 per quarter. Product engineering agrees that this idea is not only feasible but, if implemented, would substantially reduce the design work required for cell phone casings. Quality would also improve.*

The controller, marketing manager, and head of the engineering department provided the following summary of actions and related effects.

Action	Related effects
Reduce prices of cell phone casings 25%.	The vice president of sales estimates that the improved quality of cell phone casings combined with the price reduction will yield a 100% increase in demand for cell phone casings per quarter.
Use standard parts wherever possible in cell phone casings.	The use of fewer suppliers will reduce vendor-relations work by the purchasing department. This will result in unallocated costs decreasing by $20,000.
	One of the two engineers can be let go at an annual cost savings of $80,000.
	Less of the plant and machinery will be used by production support so the allocation percentages will change from 75% and 25% to 80% and 20%. Much less engineer and CAD equipment costs will be needed for production support so these percentages will change from 80% and 20% to 50% and 50%.
	Processing time, measured in direct-labor hours, will increase by 500 hours due to expected 100% increase in sales and production of cell phone casings, but there is adequate capacity of labor and machine time. Direct-labor costs are fixed as are all of the indirect production costs.
	Quality of cell phone casings will improve due to reduced complexity of processing.

1. Evaluate this idea using the traditional cost allocation system shown in Exhibit 4-6 on page 136. What would be the predicted profitability for each product line and the company as a whole? What would be the most likely level of support for the controller's idea by the product managers of the pen casing product line and the cell phone casing product line? What would be the level of support by the president?

2. Assume that you have the ABC system described in Exhibit 4-7 on page 137 with the gross margin percentages as shown in the table on page 139. Often, managers with ABC systems can anticipate more effects of improvement ideas because of their increased understanding of the operating system. In this case, although the total number of parts used would not change, the idea would reduce the number of distinct parts for cell phone casings from 20 to 11. Evaluate the controller's idea using the ABC system described in Exhibit 4-7. What would be the predicted profitability for each product line and the company as a whole? What would be the most likely level of support for the controller's idea by the product managers of the pen casing product line and the cell phone casing product line? What would be the level of support by the president?

3. As vice president, you have expressed concern about the traditional cost-allocation system's product-cost accuracy and its ability to provide relevant information for operational control. Does the new ABC system satisfy your concerns? Explain.

MyAccountingLab ## Additional Assignment Material

QUESTIONS

4-1 Define a cost management system and give its three purposes.

4-2 Cost management systems have three primary purposes. For each of the decisions listed next, indicate the purpose of the CMS being applied.
  a. A production manager wants to know the cost of performing a setup for a production run in order to compare it to a target cost established as part of a process improvement program.
  b. Top management wants to identify the profitability of several product lines to establish the optimum product mix.
  c. Financial managers want to know the manufactured cost of inventory to appear on the balance sheet of the annual report.

4-3 Name four cost objects.

4-4 "Products are the main cost objects. Departments are seldom cost objects." Do you agree? Explain.

4-5 What is the major purpose of detailed cost accounting systems?

4-6 What are the two major processes performed by a cost accounting system? Describe both of them.

4-7 Why are cost accounting systems critically important to managers?

4-8 Distinguish between direct, indirect, and unallocated costs.

4-9 "The same cost can be direct and indirect." Do you agree? Explain.

4-10 How does the idea of economic feasibility relate to the distinction between direct and indirect costs?

4-11 What are four purposes for cost allocation?

4-12 Why do companies assign all production costs and only production costs to products for external reporting purposes?

4-13 "A cost pool is a group of costs that accounting systems physically trace to the appropriate cost objective." Do you agree? Explain.

4-14 List five terms that are sometimes used as substitutes for the word *allocate*.

4-15 "The typical traditional accounting system does not allocate costs associated with value-chain functions other than production to units produced." Do you agree? Explain.

4-16 "It is better not to allocate some costs than to use a cost-allocation base that does not make any sense." Do you agree? Explain.

4-17 Production equipment maintenance, sales commissions, and process design costs are part of a company's costs. Identify which of these costs are most likely direct, indirect, and unallocated with respect to the products manufactured.

4-18 "For a furniture manufacturer, glue or tacks become an integral part of the finished product, so they would be direct material." Do you agree? Explain.

4-19 "Depreciation is a period expense for financial statement purposes." Do you agree? Explain.

4-20 Distinguish between costs and expenses.

4-21 Distinguish between manufacturing and merchandising companies. How do their accounting systems differ?

4-22 Why is there a direct-materials inventory account but no direct-labor inventory account on a manufacturing company's balance sheet?

4-23 "ABC systems are always more accurate than traditional costing systems." Do you agree? Explain.

4-24 Contrast activity-based costing (ABC) with activity-based management (ABM).

4-25 Explain how the layout of a plant's production equipment can reduce non-value-added costs.

4-26 Why do managers want to distinguish between value-added activities and non-value-added activities?

4-27 What is benchmarking? What do companies use it for? How do they determine benchmarks?

4-28 Why should caution be exercised when comparing company performance to benchmarks?

4-29 Why are more organizations adopting ABC systems?

4-30 (Appendix 4) Name four steps in the design and implementation of an ABC system.

CRITICAL THINKING EXERCISES

4-31 Marketing and Capacity Planning

A company has just completed its marketing plan for the coming year. When the company's management accountant entered the projected increases in sales volume into a process map (which relates activities and resources), the accountant discovered that the company will exceed several key resource capacities. What are the three alternative courses of action to solve this dilemma?

4-32 ABC and ABM Compared

During seminars on ABM, participants often ask about the difference between ABC and ABM. Explain briefly. Why is this important to managers?

4-33 ABC for Product Costing and Operational Control

When companies implement an ABC system they often use it first for product costing. Some managers think that is the only use for an ABC system. A typical comment is, "Activity-based allocation is useful for product costing, but not for operational control." Do you agree? Explain.

4-34 ABC and Cost Management Systems

Cost management systems have three primary purposes. Two of these are providing information for strategic and operational purposes. Companies often adopt ABC systems to increase the accuracy of cost information used by managers for strategic and operational decisions. Suppose a company produces only one product. This means that 100% of its costs are direct with respect to the product cost object. The accurate product unit cost is simply all costs incurred divided by the total units produced. Might this company be interested in an ABC system? Why or why not?

4-35 ABC and Benchmarking

Suppose that AT&T used benchmarking to compare the activity-based costs among its various divisions. As part of its benchmarking efforts, AT&T compared the activity cost per driver unit for similar activities and cost per customer for its billing departments in various geographic regions. For example, AT&T compared the costs at the Youngstown area billing department with the similar costs in the Los Angeles area. Are these meaningful comparisons? Why or why not?

EXERCISES

4-36 Classification of Manufacturing Costs

Costs are either direct or indirect depending on whether they can be traced to a cost object and either variable or fixed depending on whether they vary with changes in volume. Classify each of the following as direct (D) or indirect (I) and as variable (V) or fixed (F). For each of the 10 items you will have two answers, D or I and V or F.

1. Factory rent
2. Salary of a factory storeroom clerk
3. Cement for a road builder
4. Supervisor training program
5. Abrasives (e.g., sandpaper)
6. Cutting bits in a machinery department
7. Food for a factory cafeteria
8. Workers' compensation insurance in a factory
9. Steel scrap for a blast furnace
10. Paper towels for a factory washroom

4-37 Confirm Your Understanding of the Classification of Manufacturing Costs

Classify each of the following as direct or indirect with respect to traceability to product and as variable or fixed with respect to whether the costs fluctuate in total as volume of production changes over wide ranges. Explain your classifications.

1. The cost of components that are assembled into a final product
2. The cost of supplies consumed when maintenance is performed on machines
3. The wages of machine operators who work on only one product
4. The cost of training mechanics who service processing machinery

4-38 Variable Costs and Fixed Costs; Manufacturing and Other Costs

For each of the numbered items, choose the appropriate classifications from the lettered items for a manufacturing company. If in doubt about whether the cost behavior is basically variable or fixed, decide on the basis of whether the total cost will fluctuate substantially over a wide range of volume. Most items have two answers among the following possibilities:

a. Manufacturing costs, direct
b. Manufacturing costs, indirect
c. General and administrative cost
d. Selling cost
e. Fixed cost
f. Variable cost
g. Other (specify)

Examples:

Direct material	a, f
President's salary	c, e
Bond interest expense	e, g (financial expense)

Items for your consideration:

1. Welding supplies
2. Salespersons' commissions
3. Salespersons' salaries
4. Supervisory salaries, production control
5. Supervisory salaries, assembly department
6. Supervisory salaries, factory storeroom
7. Factory power for machines
8. Fire loss
9. Sandpaper
10. Company picnic costs
11. Overtime premium, punch press
12. Idle time, assembly
13. Freight out

14. Property taxes
15. Paint for finished products
16. Heat and air conditioning, factory
17. Materials-handling labor, punch press
18. Straight-line depreciation, salespersons' automobiles

4-39 Direct, Indirect, and Unallocated Costs

Refer to the Lopez Plastics Company example on pages 134–138 and to Exhibit 4-7. The following list gives various resources used by Lopez Plastics Company. Use the letters *D*, *I*, and *U* to indicate how the cost of each resource cost would be classified with respect to products manufactured: *D* = direct, *I* = indirect, and *U* = unallocated.

1. Depreciation of the plant
2. Resin used to make pen casings
3. Salary of plant manager
4. Salaries of cost accountants
5. Depreciation on computers used by engineers to design cell phone casings
6. Salaries of engineers
7. Salaries of operating labor processing pen casings
8. Travel costs of purchasing agent while investigating potential new suppliers of resin

4-40 Cost Allocation in ABC

Refer to the Lopez Plastics Company illustration on pages 134–138 and to Exhibit 4-7. Also see the table on page 139. Based on new information, management has adjusted the percentages that apply to the first stage of the ABC system as shown in the following table. Prepare a schedule that shows the gross margins for both products.

| | Indirect Resource | |
Percent of Resource Used in	Plant and Machinery	Engineers and CAD Equipment
Processing activity	90%	30%
Production support activity	10%	70%

4-41 Activity-Based Costing

The Deutsche Toy Company makes a variety of alpine dolls at its operation in Munich.

Its manufacturing process is highly automated. A recently installed ABC system has four activity centers:

Activity Center	Cost Driver	Cost per Driver Unit
Materials receiving and handling	Kilograms of materials	€1.20 per kg
Production setup	Number of setups	€60 per setup
Cutting, sewing, and assembly	Number of units	€.40 per unit
Packing and shipping	Number of orders	€10 per order

Two dolls are called "Hansel" and "Gretel." They require .20 and .40 kg of materials, respectively, at a materials cost of €1.50 for Hansel and €2.20 for Gretel. One computer-controlled assembly line makes all dolls. When a production run of a different doll is started, a setup procedure is required to reprogram the computers and make other changes in the process. Normally, 600 Hansel dolls are produced per setup, but only 240 Gretel dolls. Products are packed and shipped separately so a request from a customer for, say, three different products is considered three different orders.

Suppose the gift shop at the Munich Toy Museum (Spielzeugmuseum) just placed an order for 100 Hansel dolls and 50 Gretel dolls.

1. Compute the cost of the products shipped to the Munich Toy Museum gift shop.
2. Suppose the products made for the Munich Toy Museum gift shop required "Spielzeugmuseum" to be printed on each doll. Because of the automated process, printing the letters takes no extra time or materials, but it requires a special production setup for each product. Compute the cost of the products shipped to the Munich Toy Museum gift shop.
3. Explain how the activity-based-costing system helps Deutsche Toy Company to measure costs of individual products or orders better than a traditional system that allocates all non-materials costs based on direct labor.

4-42 Two-Stage Activity-Based Costing—Stage One

The Marietta branch of Atlanta State Savings Bank (ASSB) is a retail branch in a rapidly growing residential area. It services individuals and local businesses. To support its services, the branch employs 14 tellers, 3 retail sales managers (RSMs), and the branch managing officer. The branch services about 2,900 customers. Each of the 70 branches of ASSB is implementing ABC in order to improve profitability. ASSB's branch managing officers have been given the responsibility to implement activity-based costing. The managing officer at the Marietta branch decided to implement a two-stage ABC system. Exhibit 4-18 depicts its two-stage ABC system.

The Marietta branch has the following cost data for the last year:

Teller wages	$ 350,000
RSM salaries and benefits	210,000
Managing officer salary and benefits	100,000
Other bank costs	430,000
Total	$1,090,000

The "other bank costs" include depreciation on the facility including furniture, building, equipment, insurance, rentals of computers, contracted computer services, telecommunications, and utilities. These costs cannot be directly or indirectly related to routine bank activities, such as processing new accounts or processing deposits or withdrawals, and, thus, are unallocated. There are no costs that can be traced

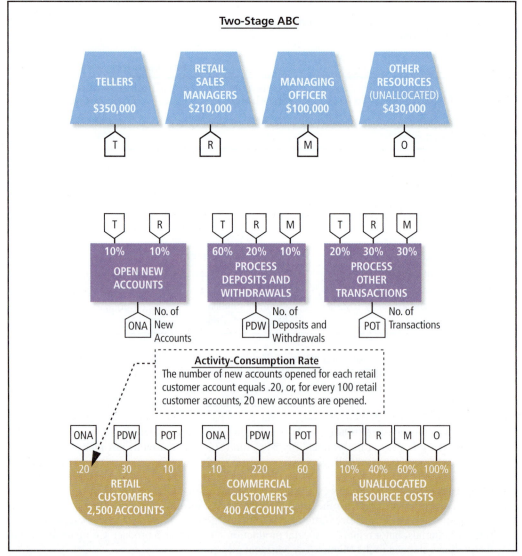

Exhibit 4-18
Two-Stage ABC at the Marietta Branch of ASSB

directly to customers so the Marietta branch has just two types of costs—indirect and unallocated. All employees have been interviewed as part of the ABC study. For example, tellers were asked how they spent their time. Three major activities were identified. They said that they spent most of their time (60%) processing deposits and withdrawals. They also estimated that they spent about 10% of their time processing new accounts and about 20% of their time processing other transactions. The remaining 10% of their time was spent on all other banking activities. The results of the interviews appear next.

Internal Activity Analysis

	Open New Accounts	Process Deposits and Withdrawals	Process Other Transactions	All Other Banking Activities	Total
Teller wages	10%	60%	20%	10%	100%
Retail sales manager salary	10%	20%	30%	40%	100%
Managing officer salary	0%	10%	30%	60%	100%

Determine the total cost of each of the three major activities conducted at the Marietta branch of ASSB. Use Exhibit 4-18 as a guide. (Note that this represents the first stage in the two-stage ABC method.)

4-43 Two-Stage Activity-Based Costing, Banking, Benchmarking
(This exercise is a continuation of Exercise 4-42 and should be assigned only if Exercise 4-42 is also assigned.)

A part of the activity analysis conducted at the Marietta branch of Atlanta State Savings Bank (ASSB) was identifying potential cost drivers for each major activity. The following cost drivers were chosen because they were both plausible and reliable and data were available:

Activity	Cost Driver	Annual Flow of Cost Driver
Process new accounts	Number of new accounts	540
Process deposits and withdrawals	Number of deposits and withdrawals	163,000
Process other transactions	Number of other transactions	49,000

Of the 2,900 customers of the branch, only 400 are local businesses. The business-customer class generated 40 new accounts, 88,000 deposits and withdrawals, and 24,000 other transactions. The implementation of ABC at all branches of ASSB provided sufficient data for internal benchmarking. The following are the lowest activity costs among all branches implementing two-stage ABC systems:

Activity	Lowest Activity Cost per Driver Unit
Open new accounts	$81.67 per new account
Process deposits and withdrawals	$ .75 per deposit or withdrawal
Process other transactions	$ 3.05 per transaction

Customer Class	Lowest Customer Cost per Account
Retail	$ 88
Commercial	$508

1. Determine the allocated (indirect) cost per account for retail and commercial accounts. Use Exhibit 4-18 as a guide.
2. Under what conditions would benchmarking between the Marietta branch of ASSB and the other branches be inappropriate?
3. What do the results of the ABC study suggest?

4-44 Direct, Indirect, and Unallocated Costs
Listed below are several activities and related costs that have been observed at Santana Company, a manufacturing company. The company makes a variety of products and currently uses a traditional costing system that allocates only production overhead based on direct-labor hours. It is implementing an ABC system for the design, production, and distribution functions of its value chain. You have been

asked to complete the following table by indicating for each activity whether the related cost is direct, indirect, or unallocated. For each indirect cost, indicate one appropriate cost-allocation base (more than one cost-allocation base may be appropriate). The first two items have been completed for you.

Activity	Related Cost	Traditional	ABC
Supervising production	Supervisor salaries	Indirect (direct-labor hours)	Indirect (people supervised)
Designing a prototype for new product	Depreciation of computers	Unallocated	Indirect (number of parts)
Setting up for a production run	Mechanic wages		
Purchasing materials and parts to be used in products	Materials and parts cost		
Shipping sold products to customers (distributors)	Fuel used on company's fleet of trucks		
Market research study conducted by marketing staff to assess demand for potential new product	Salaries of market research staff		
Production scheduling	Salaries of production scheduling managers		
Purchasing materials and parts to be used in products	Salaries of purchasing agents		
Order processing of customer orders	Salaries of order processing staff		
Preparing cost analyses	Cost accountant salary		
Designing a new product	Salaries of design engineers that are fully dedicated to this new product		
Managing overall operations	Salary of executive of company		

PROBLEMS

4-45 Cost Accumulation and Allocation

Zhao Manufacturing Company has two departments, machining and finishing. For a given period, the following costs were incurred by the company as a whole: direct material, $200,000; direct labor, $75,000; and indirect production, $80,000. The grand total was $355,000.

The machining department incurred 70% of the direct-material costs, but only 33⅓% of the direct-labor costs. As is commonplace, indirect production costs incurred by each department were allocated to products in proportion to the direct-labor costs of products within the departments. Three products were produced.

Product	Direct Material	Direct Labor
Sigma	40%	30%
Chi	30%	30%
Delta	30%	40%
Total for the machining department	100%	100%
Sigma	33⅓%	40%
Chi	33⅓%	40%
Delta	33⅓%	20%
Total added by finishing department	100%	100%

The indirect production costs incurred by the machining and finishing departments and allocated to all products therein amounted to machining, $38,000 and finishing, $42,000.

1. Compute the total costs incurred by the machining department and added by the finishing department.
2. Compute the total costs of each product that would be shown as finished-goods inventory if all the products were transferred to finished stock on completion. (There were no beginning inventories.)

4-46 Hospital Allocation Base

Emilio Moreno, the administrator of Cook Community Hospital, has become interested in obtaining more accurate cost allocations on the basis of cause and effect. The $210,000 of laundry costs had been allocated on the basis of 600,000 pounds processed for all departments, or $.35 per pound.

Moreno is concerned that government health care officials will require weighted statistics to be used for cost allocation. He asks you, "Please develop a revised base for allocating laundry costs. It should be better than our present base, but not be overly complex either."

You study the situation and find that the laundry processes a large volume of uniforms for student nurses and physicians and for dietary, housekeeping, and other personnel. In particular, the coats or jackets worn by personnel in the radiology department take an unusual amount of handwork.

A special study of laundry for radiology revealed that 7,500 of the 15,000 pounds were jackets and coats that were five times as expensive to process as regular laundry items. Several reasons explained the difference, but it was principally because of handwork involved.

Assume that no special requirements were needed in departments other than radiology. Revise the cost-allocation base and compute the new cost-allocation rate. Compute the total cost charged to radiology using pounds and using the new base.

4-47 Traditional and ABC Cost Accounting, Activity-Based Management

Refer to the text discussion of Lopez Plastics Company on pages 134–138. Assume that the company has the traditional cost accounting system described in Exhibit 4-6. The top management team wants to reverse the pattern of quarterly losses. The company president, Angie Oaks, has emphasized the importance of profit improvement by linking future pay raises of the two product-line managers to their respective gross profit margins. She is concerned about the profitability of the pen casing product line while pleased with the profitability of the cell phone casing line. She also believes that the unallocated costs of the company are too high compared to those of competitors. The office of controller, whose costs are included in the unallocated costs, is responsible for vendor relations and purchasing of direct materials. The controller presents the following idea:

> We should use more standard parts in cell phone casings, which will dramatically reduce the purchasing department's work required for purchasing. I believe this should cut our office's costs by as much as $25,000 per quarter. In addition, using standard parts eliminates the need to purchase several expensive resins. The larger volume of purchases of less costly resin from fewer vendors will cut the cell phone casing direct material cost by 10%. Product engineering agrees that this idea is not only feasible but, if implemented, would improve the overall quality of cell phone casings.

The controller and marketing manager provided the following summary of actions and related effects:

Action	Expected effects
Reduce prices of cell phone casings 25%.	The vice president of sales estimates that the improved quality of cell phone casings combined with the price reduction will yield a 100% increase in demand for cell phone casings per quarter.
Use standard parts wherever possible in cell phone casings.	Total number of parts for each cell phone casing will not change, but the direct material cost per casing will be reduced by 10% due to volume discounts from preferred vendors. The use of fewer suppliers will reduce vendor-relations work by the purchasing department. This will result in unallocated costs decreasing by $25,000.
	Processing time, measured in direct-labor hours, will increase by 500 hours due to expected 100% increase in sales and production of cell phone casings, but there is adequate capacity of labor and machine time. Direct-labor costs are fixed as are all of the indirect manufacturing costs.
	Quality of cell phone casings will improve due to reduced complexity of processing.

1. Evaluate this idea using the traditional cost allocation system shown in Exhibit 4-6 on page 136. What would be the predicted profitability for each product line and the company as a whole? What would be the most likely level of support for the controller's idea by the product managers of the pen casing product line and the cell phone casing product line? What would be the level of support by the president?

2. Assume that you have the ABC system described in Exhibit 4-7 on page 137 with the gross profit margins shown in the table on page 139. Often, managers with ABC systems can anticipate more effects of improvement ideas because of their increased understanding of the operating system. In this case, although the total number of parts would not change, the idea would reduce the number of distinct parts for cell phone casings from 20 to 9. Evaluate the controller's idea using the ABC system described in Exhibit 4-7. What would be the predicted profitability for each product line and the company as a whole? What would be the most likely level of support for the controller's idea by the product managers of the pen casing product line and the cell phone casing product line? What would be the level of support by the president?

3. As vice president, you have expressed concern about the traditional cost-allocation system's product-cost accuracy and its ability to provide relevant information for operational control. Does the new ABC system satisfy your concerns? Explain.

4-48 Activity-Based Costing and Product Line Profitability

Hipercor is a grocery company with stores throughout Spain. Suppose the company is planning an expansion of its store in central Madrid. A preliminary analysis has shown the packaged food department to be the most profitable, so the company plans to increase its space the most.

Assume that the Madrid store has just three departments: produce, packaged food, and meat. The most recent annual report for the store showed sales of €3,283,200, which generated a gross margin of €883,200. Sales and gross margins of the three departments were as follows:

	Produce	Packaged Food	Meat	Total
Revenues	€634,800	€1,680,480	€967,920	€3,283,200
Cost of products sold	480,000	1,200,000	720,000	2,400,000
Gross margin	€154,800	€ 480,480	€247,920	€ 883,200

In addition to cost of products sold, the store has €720,000 of support costs, so operating income is €883,200 – €720,000 = €163,200. Hipercor currently uses an accounting system that uses cost of products sold as a cost-allocation base for allocating support costs.

Ramon Flores, controller of Hipercor, recently attended a seminar on activity-based costing. He suggests that Hipercor management should undertake further analysis before deciding which product gets the largest increase in space in the expansion. He has asked you, his assistant, to lead this analysis.

1. The starting point of your analysis is to determine product profitability under the existing cost accounting system. Compute the operating income and the operating income as a percent of sales for each department using Hipercor's existing system. Use this information to assess the relative profitability per dollar of sales of each of the three departments.

2. Flores asks you next to develop product costs using an activity-based accounting system. You determine that there are five major activities, each with a different cost driver to be used as a cost-allocation base:
   a. Ordering—Placing of orders for purchases
   b. Delivery—Physical delivery and receipt of merchandise
   c. Shelf-stocking—Stocking of merchandise on store shelves, including ongoing restocking
   d. Customer support—Assistance to customers, including check out and bagging
   e. Produce monitoring—Constantly checking on the stacking and freshness of produce

The cost drivers for each activity are as follows:

Ordering	Number of purchase orders
Delivery	Number of deliveries
Shelf-stocking	Hours of stocking time
Customer support	Number of items sold
Produce monitoring	Direct trace to the Produce Department

You have determined the following information about the cost drivers:

	Produce	Packaged Food	Meat	Total
Number of purchase orders	1,440	3,360	1,440	6,240
Number of deliveries	1,200	8,760	2,640	12,600
Hours of shelf-stocking	216	2,160	1,080	3,456
Items sold	50,400	441,600	122,400	614,400

The total cost of each activity was as follows:

Ordering	€124,800
Delivery	201,600
Shelf-stocking	138,240
Customer support	245,760
Product monitoring	9,600
Total	€720,000

Using these data and activity-based costing, calculate the operating income and operating income as a percent of sales for each product. (For example, note that each purchase order costs €124,800 ÷ 6,240 = €20 to process.)

3. Propose a strategy for expansion. Which information, that based on the current costing system or that based on the activity-based costing system, is most useful? Why? What additional information would you like to have before making a more definitive recommendation on an expansion strategy?

4-49 Activity-Based Costing and Activity-Based Management, Automotive Supplier

O'Sullivan Company is an automotive component supplier. O'Sullivan has been approached by Honda of America's Ohio plant to consider expanding its production of part 24Z2 to a total annual quantity of 2,000 units. This part is a low-volume, complex product with a high gross margin that is based on a proposed (quoted) unit sales price of $7.50. O'Sullivan uses a traditional costing system that allocates indirect manufacturing costs based on direct-labor costs. The rate currently used to allocate indirect manufacturing costs is 400% of direct-labor cost. This rate is based on the $3,200,000 annual factory overhead cost divided by $800,000 annual direct-labor cost. To produce 2,000 units of 24Z2 requires $5,000 of direct materials and $1,000 of direct labor. The unit cost and gross margin percentage for part 24Z2 based on the traditional cost system are computed as follows:

	Total	Per Unit (÷2,000)
Direct material	$ 5,000	$2.50
Direct labor	1,000	.50
Indirect production: (400% × direct labor)	4,000	2.00
Total cost	$10,000	$5.00
Sales price quoted		7.50
Gross margin		$2.50
Gross margin percentage		33.3%

The management of O'Sullivan decided to examine the effectiveness of their traditional costing system versus an activity-based costing system. The following data have been collected by a team consisting of accounting and engineering analysts:

Activity Center	Factory Overhead Costs (Annual)
Quality	$ 500,000
Production scheduling	50,000
Setup	700,000
Shipping	300,000
Shipping administration	50,000
Production	1,600,000
Total indirect production cost	$3,200,000

Activity Center: Cost Drivers	Annual Cost-Driver Quantity
Quality: Number of pieces scrapped	10,000
Production scheduling and set up: Number of setups	500
Shipping: Number of containers shipped	60,000
Shipping administration: Number of shipments	1,000
Production: Number of machine hours	10,000

The accounting and engineering team has performed activity analysis and provides the following estimates for the total quantity of cost drivers to be used to produce 2,000 units of part 24Z2:

Cost Driver	Cost-Driver Consumption
Pieces scrapped	120
Setups	4
Containers shipped	10
Shipments	5
Machine hours	15

1. Prepare a schedule calculating the unit cost and gross margin of part 24Z2 using the activity-based costing approach. Use the cost drivers given as cost-allocation bases.
2. Based on the ABC results, which course of action would you recommend regarding the proposal by Honda of America? List the benefits and costs associated with implementing an ABC system at O'Sullivan.

4-50 Library Research in Activity-Based Costing or Activity-Based Management

Select an article from *Strategic Finance, Cost Management*, or *Management Accounting Quarterly* (an online journal) or any other journal that describes a particular company's application of either (a) an activity-based costing system, or (b) activity-based management. Prepare a summary of 300 words or fewer that includes the following:

- Name of the company (if given)
- Industry of the company
- Description of the particular application
- Assessment of the benefits the company received from the application
- Any difficulties encountered in implementation

4-51 Review of Chapters 2, 3, and 4

The Sharma Company provides you with the following miscellaneous data regarding operations in 20X9:

Gross profit	$ 40,000
Net profit	15,000
Sales	120,000
Direct material used	35,000
Direct labor	25,000
Fixed manufacturing overhead	15,000
Fixed selling and administrative expenses	12,000

There are no beginning or ending inventories.

Compute (a) variable selling and administrative expenses, (b) contribution margin in dollars, (c) variable manufacturing overhead, (d) break-even point in sales dollars, and (e) manufacturing cost of goods sold.

4-52 Review of Chapters 2, 3, and 4

Kyu Lee Corporation provides you with the following miscellaneous data regarding operations for 20X0 (in thousands of South Korean won, ₩):

Break-even point in sales	₩ 84,000
Direct material used	29,000
Gross profit	20,000
Contribution margin	25,000
Direct labor	30,000
Sales	100,000
Variable manufacturing overhead	5,000

There are no beginning or ending inventories.

Compute (a) the fixed manufacturing overhead, (b) variable selling and administrative expenses, and (c) fixed selling and administrative expenses.

4-53 Review of Chapters 2, 3, and 4

Beverly High Fashions Company manufactured and sold 1,000 pair of leather handbags during July. Selected data for this month follow:

Sales	$110,000
Direct materials used	31,000
Direct labor	16,000
Variable manufacturing overhead	13,000
Fixed manufacturing overhead	11,000
Variable selling and administrative expenses	?
Fixed selling and administrative expenses	?
Contribution margin	40,000
Operating income	22,000

There were no beginning or ending inventories.

1. What were the variable selling and administrative expenses for July?
2. What were the fixed selling and administrative expenses for July?
3. What was the cost of goods sold during July?
4. Without prejudice to your earlier answers, assume that the fixed selling and administrative expenses for July amounted to $4,000.
   a. What was the break-even point in units for July?
   b. How many units must be sold to earn a target operating income of $14,000?
   c. What would the selling price per unit have to be if the company wanted to earn an operating income of $22,500 on the sale of 900 units?

CASES

4-54 Multiple Allocation Bases

The Liverpool Company produces three types of circuit boards; call them Alpha, Beta, and Gamma. The cost accounting system used by Liverpool until 2009 applied all costs except direct materials to the products using direct-labor hours as the only cost driver. In 2009, the company undertook a cost study. The study determined that there were six main factors that incurred costs. A new system was designed with a separate cost pool for each of the six factors. The factors and the costs associated with each are as follows:

1. Direct-labor hours—direct-labor cost and related fringe benefits and payroll taxes
2. Machine hours—depreciation and repairs and maintenance costs
3. Pounds of materials—materials receiving, handling, and storage costs
4. Number of production setups—labor used to change machinery and computer configurations for a new production batch
5. Number of production orders—costs of production scheduling and order processing
6. Number of orders shipped—all packaging and shipping expenses

The company is now preparing a budget for 2010. The budget includes the following predictions:

	Alpha	Beta	Gamma
Units to be produced	10,000	800	5,000
Direct-materials cost	£70/unit	£88/unit	£45/unit
Direct-labor hours	4/unit	18/unit	9/unit
Machine hours	7/unit	15/unit	7/unit
Pounds of materials	3/unit	4/unit	2/unit
Number of production setups	100	50	50
Number of production orders	300	200	70
Number of orders shipped	1,000	800	2,000

The total budgeted cost for 2010 is £3,866,250, of which £995,400 was direct-materials cost, and the amount in each of the six cost pools defined above is as follow:

Cost Pool*	Cost
1	£1,391,600
2	936,000
3	129,600
4	160,000
5	25,650
6	228,000
Total	£2,870,850

*Identified by the cost driver used.

1. Prepare a budget that shows the total budgeted cost and the unit cost for each circuit board. Use the new system with six cost pools (plus a separate direct application of direct-materials cost).
2. Compute the budgeted total and unit costs of each circuit board if the old direct-labor-hour system had been used.
3. How would you judge whether the new system is better than the old one?

4-55 Traditional Versus ABC Systems

Northwest Desserts, Inc., (NDI) produces a variety of premium cheesecakes and sells them in individual packages directly to retail customers and in packages of 10 cakes to restaurants in Washington, Oregon, Idaho, and Northern California. NDI started as a small retail outlet, where it developed a superb reputation for quality. In the late 1990s it opened a chain of retail outlets. Only recently it started selling cheesecakes to restaurants. Its penetration into the restaurant market has been slower than predicted.

Although NDI produces several types of cheesecakes, all are about the same size and are considered a single product for costing purposes. NDI's existing costing system has a single direct-cost category, ingredients, and a single indirect-cost pool, production overhead costs. The system does not trace labor costs to the products; it considers them part of production overhead. Production overhead costs are allocated on the basis of number of cheesecakes produced. The 2011 budget projected production of 500,000 cheesecakes, 400,000 for the retail market and 100,000 for restaurants. Predicted costs were as follows:

Ingredients	$ 900,000	Direct cost
Production overhead	2,216,000	indirect cost
Total	$3,116,000	

In early 2010 NDI had unsuccessfully bid for a large restaurant contract from the **Applebee's** chain. Its bid had been 30% above that of the successful bidder. This came as a shock because NDI had budgeted only a small profit into the bid. In addition, the NDI plant was one of the newest and most efficient in the industry.

Before completing the budget for 2011, top management of NDI asked Naomi Lester, controller of NDI, to examine the company's cost accounting system. Naomi had attended a short course by the Institute of Management Accountants on activity-based costing (ABC), and she thought some of the principles of ABC might apply to NDI. She felt that accounting for the ingredients was not a problem; the ingredients cost the same whether a cheesecake was produced for retail or restaurant markets. However, when she analyzed production overhead costs, she saw several possible improvements.

Naomi found that production overhead costs could be divided into cost pools for four activities: 1) administration, 2) facilities operations and maintenance, 3) mixing/baking, and 4) decorating/packaging. The activities in administration and facilities operations and maintenance do not involve working directly on cheesecakes, but they support the areas in which the cheese-cakes are produced. Mixing/baking and decorating/packaging are the activities that directly produce the cheesecakes. Naomi described the four activities as follows:

Administrative: Three administrative employees work in a 600 sq. ft. office providing a variety of services to NDI, including accounting, personnel, etc. It is difficult to measure the amount of administrative services provided to each product, but they are roughly proportional to the number of employees. The administrative costs are budgeted at $140,000 for 2011.

Facilities Operations and Maintenance: Two employees, located in an 800 sq. ft. office wing, operate and maintain the facilities. In addition, rent and depreciation charges and the cost of supplies for operating and maintaining the facilities are included in this cost pool. These facilities operations and maintenance costs are closely related to the number of square feet of space used. Budgeted facilities operations and maintenance costs for 2011 are $320,000.

Mixing and Baking: Five employees are located in 4,000 sq. ft. of space with a capacity to produce 600,000 cheesecakes per year. Much of the mixing and baking operation is the same for all cheesecakes produced. However, the cheesecakes sold through NDI's own retail outlets require some special handling to give them a distinctive quality. The production line produces 80 retail cheesecakes per processing-hour and 100 restaurant cheesecakes per processing hour. Costs are driven by the number of processing-hours. Budged costs in mixing and baking for 2011 are $540,000.

Decorating and Packaging: Decorating and packaging require two employees and 1,000 sq. ft. of space. There are two separate decorating/packaging lines. Only 10 retail cheesecakes can be decorated and packaged per hour, while 50 restaurant cheesecakes can be decorated and packaged in the same amount of time. Costs vary with the number of decorating/packaging hours. Budgeted costs for 2011 were $1,216,000. Of this total cost, $376,000 was for packaging materials that could be traced to individual products, $360,000 to retail, and $16,000 to restaurants sales.

1. Use the existing costing system to find the budgeted cost per cheesecake for (a) the retail market and (b) the restaurant market. Comment briefly on the weaknesses of this system.
2. Use the ABC system to find the budgeted cost per cheesecake for (a) the retail market and (b) the restaurant market.
3. Prepare a memo from Naomi Lester to the president of NDI commenting on the differences in the costs between the traditional and ABC systems. Why are they different? What decisions should be made differently now that NDI has the information from the ABC system rather the information from the traditional system? How should managers use the ABC information to make better decisions?

4-56 ABC and Customer Profitability in Financial Services

To increase its share of the checking account market, Columbia City Bank in Seattle took two actions: It established a customer call center to respond to customer inquiries about account balances, checks cleared, fees charged, etc., and it paid year-end bonuses to branch managers who met their branch's target increase in the number of customers. While 80% of the branch managers met the target increase in the number of customers, Columbia City Bank's profits continued to decline. John Diamond, the CEO, didn't understand why profits were declining, even though the bank was serving more customers. The Pierce County branch manager, Rose Perez, noticed that while small retail customers flocked to the bank, the number of business customers was declining.

Columbia City Bank's costing system, developed back in 1988, is straightforward. No costs are traced directly to customers. The bank simply assigns the total indirect costs to customer lines (retail customer line or business customer line) based on the total number of checks processed.

Perez suspected that Columbia City Bank's cost system might be part of the problem. Perez learned about ABC in school, but the applications involved manufacturing firms. She wonders whether Columbia City Bank could develop an ABC system, with the customer-line as the primary cost object.

Rose's boss was skeptical. ("Our profits are going down the tubes and you want me to spend money developing a new accounting system?") However, Rose persuaded her boss to allow a pilot ABC study, using the three Tacoma branches for the pilot test.

The ABC implementation team included Perez, the managers of each of the three Tacoma branches, a bank teller, and a customer service representative from the customer call center. The team began by identifying the following three activities:

- Check payments
- Teller withdrawals and deposits
- Customer service call center

The ABC team then scrutinized the Tacoma branches' total indirect cost of $2,850,000. They classified the components of this total indirect cost into the appropriate activity pool, coming up with the following estimates (in thousands of dollars):

Cost	Activity Cost Pool to Which Cost Is Assigned	Estimated Total Costs for Tacoma Branches
Salaries of check-processing personnel	Check payments	$ 440
Depreciation on check-processing equipment	Check payments	700
Teller salaries	Teller withdrawals and deposits	1,200
Salaries of customer representatives at call center	Customer service call center	450
Toll-free phone lines at customer call center	Customer service call center	60
Total indirect costs		$2,850

The team then identified the following cost drivers for each activity cost pool:

Activity Cost Pool	Activity Cost Driver
Check payments	number of checks processed
Teller withdrawals and deposits	number of teller transactions
Customer service call center	number of calls

The ABC team estimated that for the Tacoma branches, the retail customer line and the business customer line would require the following total resources (in thousands):

Activity Cost Driver	Number of Units of Activity Cost Driver Used by Business Customers	Number of Units of Activity Cost Driver Used by Retail Customers	Total
Checks processed	2,280	9,120	11,400
Teller transactions	320	80	400
Customer calls to call center	95	5	100
Checking accounts	150	50	200

That is, the retail customers have 320,000 teller transactions, make 95,000 calls to the customer service center, and so on.

On average, Columbia City Bank earns revenue from each type of account (from interest earned on checking account balances) as follows:

Average revenue per retail customer account $10
Average revenue per business customer account $40

1. Using the original (old) cost system complete the following:
   a. Compute the indirect cost allocation rate.
   b. Determine the total indirect cost assigned to the retail customer line and the business customer line.
   c. Compute the proportion of the total indirect cost assigned to the retail customer line and the business customer line.
   d. Determine the indirect cost per retail account and the indirect cost per business account.
   e. Assuming that there are no direct costs, compute the average profit per account for retail customers and for business customers.
   f. Assess the likely business strategy that might be adopted by managers using data from this original cost system.
2. What are the signs that Columbia City Bank's original cost system was broken or in need of refinement?
3. Using the new activity-based costing system complete the following:
   a. Compute the indirect cost allocation rates for each of the three activities:

   - Check payments
   - Teller withdrawals and deposits
   - Customer call center

   b. Use the schedule below to compute the total indirect cost allocated to each customer line:

Activity	Total Indirect Cost Assigned to Retail Customer Line	Total Indirect Cost Assigned to Business Customer Line
Check payments		
Teller withdrawals and deposits		
Customer call center		
Total indirect costs		

   c. What proportion of each activity's resources are used by the retail customer line and the business customer line?
   d. Using the ABC data from requirement 3b, compute the indirect cost per retail customer account and the indirect cost per business customer account.
   e. Explain why the results in requirement 1d and requirement 3d differ in the direction they do. Be precise and specific.
   f. Using the new ABC data, compute the average profit per account for both retail and business customers. Assess the likely business strategy that might be adopted by managers using data from this ABC cost system.

4. Be prepared to discuss the following questions:
   a. Was Columbia City Bank's bonus-based incentive plan to increase the number of checking account customers a wise strategy? Would you suggest any change in the strategy based on the ABC analysis?
   b. What benefits can Columbia City Bank reap from the ABC analysis?
   c. Why might Rose Perez have suspected that the benefits of ABC would likely outweigh the costs of implementing ABC at Columbia City Bank?
   d. Why is it important for nonaccounting managers to understand ABC?

4-57 Identifying Activities, Resources, and Cost Drivers in Manufacturing

International Plastics is a multinational, diversified organization. One of its manufacturing divisions, Northeast Plastics, has become less profitable due to increased competition. The division produces three major lines of plastic products within its single plant. Product line A is high-volume, simple pieces produced in large batches. Product line B is medium-volume, more complex pieces. Product line C is low-volume, small-order, highly complex pieces.

Currently, the division allocates indirect production costs based on direct labor cost. The vice president of manufacturing is uncomfortable using the traditional cost figures. He thinks the company is underpricing the more complex products. He decides to conduct an ABC analysis of the business.

Interviews were conducted with the key managers in order to identify activities, resources, cost drivers, and their interrelationships.

INTERVIEWEE: PRODUCTION MANAGER

Q1. *What activities are carried out in your area?*
A1. All products are manufactured using three similar, complex, and expensive molding machines. Each molding machine can be used in the production of the three product lines. Each setup takes about the same time irrespective of the product.
Q2. *Who works in your area?*
A2. Last year, we employed 30 machine operators, 2 maintenance mechanics, and 2 supervisors.
Q3. *How are the operators used in the molding process?*
A3. It requires nine operators to support a machine during the actual production process.
Q4. *What do the maintenance mechanics do?*
A4. Their primary function is to perform machine setups. However, they are also required to provide machine maintenance during the molding process.
Q5. *Where do the supervisors spend their time?*
A5. They provide supervision for the machine operators and the maintenance mechanics. For the most part, the supervisors appear to spend the same amount of time with each of the employees that they supervise.
Q6. *What other resources are used to support manufacturing?*
A6. The molding machines use energy during the molding process and during the setups. We put meters on the molding machines to get a better understanding of their energy consumption. We discovered that for each hour that a machine ran, it used 6.3 kilowatts of energy. The machines also require consumable shop supplies (e.g., lubricants, hoses, and so on). We have found a direct correlation between the amount of supplies used and the actual processing time.
Q7. *How is the building used, and what costs are associated with it?*
A7. We have a 100,000-square-foot building. The total rent and insurance costs for the year were $675,000. These costs are allocated to production, sales, and administration based on square footage.

1. Identify the activities and resources for the division. For each activity, suggest an appropriate cost driver.
2. For each resource identified in requirement 1, indicate its cost behavior with respect to the activities it supports (assume a planning period of 1 month).

NIKE 10-K PROBLEM

4-58 Nike's Cost Accounting System

Examine the inventory account in the balance sheet in Nike's 10-K in Appendix C. Note especially footnote 2, "Inventories." What does the explanation of Nike's inventory imply about the company's manufacturing operations? Is Nike primarily a manufacturer or merchandiser? Can you confirm this elsewhere in the 10-K?

Nike describes its properties in Item 2 of the 10-K. One of the properties is a distribution and customer service facility in Wilsonville, Oregon. Suppose Nike wanted to set up an ABC system for this facility. Based on your understanding of Nike's operations from the descriptions in the 10-K, what major activities might they identify (at least three)? Identify two resources used by each activity and a possible cost-allocation base for assigning each resource cost to the activity.

EXCEL APPLICATION EXERCISE

4-59 Traditional Costing Versus Activity-Based Costing

Goal: Create an Excel spreadsheet to compare traditional costing versus activity-based costing. Use the results to answer questions about your findings.

Scenario: Suppose Sunstar Corporation is one of **Dell**'s circuit board suppliers. Sunstar currently uses traditional costing for making business decisions. At the urging of Dell, however, the company has decided to move to activity-based costing for circuit board production related to products PCB124 and PCB136. As one of the company's accountants, you have been asked to prepare a spreadsheet comparing the two costing methods for the next company board meeting. Your supervisor has given you the following quarterly data:

Total Indirect Costs for the Quarter:			
Assembly	$630,000		
Soldering	$270,000		
Inspection	$160,000		
		PCB124	PCB136
Direct costs (materials, labor)		$162,400	$178,240
Machine hours (assembly)		480	1,080
Number of units produced (soldering)		6,000	4,000
Testing hours (inspection)		6,000	8,000

When you have completed your spreadsheet, answer the following questions:

a. What is the total manufacturing cost per unit using traditional costing for PCB124? For PCB136?
b. What is the total manufacturing cost per unit using activity-based costing for PCB124? For PCB136?
c. What conclusions can be drawn from your spreadsheet results?

Step-by-Step:
1. Open a new Excel spreadsheet.
2. In column A, create a bold-faced heading that contains the following:
   Row 1: Chapter 4 Decision Guideline
   Row 2: Sunstar Corporation
   Row 3: Traditional Versus Activity-Based Costing
   Row 4: Today's Date

   Note: Adjust column widths as follows: Column A (41.57), Columns B, C, and D (21.0). Column D is for check figures only. The column widths have been designed to ensure that Column D will not print on the final version of the spreadsheet if only page 1 is printed.

3. Merge and center the four heading rows across columns A–C.
4. In column A, create the following row headings:
   Row 7: Raw data
   Row 8: Indirect costs for the quarter:
   Row 9: Assembly
   Row 10: Soldering
   Row 11: Inspection
   Row 12: Total indirect costs
   Skip two rows.
   Row 15: Direct costs (Materials, labor)

Row 16: Machine hours (Assembly)
Row 17: Number of units produced (Soldering)
Row 18: Testing hours (Inspection)
Skip two rows.
Row 21: Traditional costing system
Row 22: Indirect cost driver (machine hours)
Row 23: Allocated indirect costs
Skip a row.
Row 25: Cost per product
Row 26: Direct costs
Row 27: Manufacturing overhead
Row 28: Total manufacturing costs per product
Skip a row.
Row 30: Number of units
Row 31: Total manufacturing costs per unit
Skip two rows.
Row 34: Activity-based costing system
Row 35: Assembly cost driver (machine hours)
Row 36: Allocated assembly cost
Row 37: Soldering cost driver (units)
Row 38: Allocated soldering cost
Row 39: Inspection cost driver (testing hours)
Row 40: Allocated inspection cost
Skip a row.
Row 42: Cost per product
Row 43: Direct costs
Row 44: Manufacturing overhead
Row 45: Assembly
Row 46: Soldering
Row 47: Inspection
Row 48: Total manufacturing costs per product
Skip a row.
Row 50: Number of units
Row 51: Total manufacturing costs per unit

5. Change the format of Raw Data (row 7), Traditional costing system (row 21), and Activity-based costing system (row 34) to bold-faced headings.

    Hint: Use the control key for highlighting multiple cells or rows when making changes.

6. Change the format of Cost per product (rows 25 and 42) to underlined headings.
7. In rows 14, 21, 25, 34, and 42 create the following bold-faced, right-justified column headings:
    Column B: PCB124
    Column C: PCB136
8. In rows 21 and 34 create the following bold-faced, right-justified column headings:
    Column D: Total
9. Use the scenario data to fill in the Raw data section.
    Use the SUM function to calculate Total indirect costs (row 12).
10. Traditional costing system:
    Fill in rows 26 and 30 with information from the Raw data section.
    Use appropriate formulas from this chapter to calculate the cost driver and allocated costs.
    Use the SUM function to calculate the Total column for manufacturing overhead costs.
    Complete the remainder of the Cost per product data using formulas and calculations.
    Calculate the Total manufacturing costs per product.
11. Activity-based costing system:
    Fill in rows 43 and 50 with information from the Raw data section.
    Use appropriate formulas from this chapter to calculate the cost drivers and allocated costs.
    Use the SUM function to calculate the Total columns for all allocated costs.
    Complete the remainder of the Cost per product data using formulas and calculations.
    Calculate the Total manufacturing costs per product.

    Hint: If using the SUM function to calculate Total manufacturing costs, verify range.

12. Format all amounts as follows:

Number tab:	Category:	Currency
	Decimal places:	2
	Symbol:	None
	Negative numbers:	Red with parentheses

13. Change the format of hours and units in rows 16–18, 30, and 50 to display no decimal places.
14. Change the format of the amounts in rows 9, 12, 15, 23, 26, 28, 31, 36, 38, 40, 43, 48, and 51 to display a dollar symbol.
15. Change the format of the row headings in rows 9–11, 15–18, 23, 36, 38, 40, and 45–47 to display as indented.

| **Alignment tab:** | Horizontal: | Left (Indent) |
| | Indent: | 1 |

16. Change the format of the amounts in rows 12, 28, and 48 to display a top border, using the default Line Style.

| **Border tab:** | Icon: | Top Border |

17. Change the format of the cost driver calculations in rows 22, 35, 37, and 39 to display as left-justified percentages with two decimal places.

Number tab:	Category:	Percentage
	Decimal places:	2
Alignment tab:	Horizontal:	Left (Indent)
	Indent:	0

18. Accentuate the Cost per product information for each costing method by applying cell shading to columns A, B, and C of rows 25–31 and 42–51.

| **Patterns tab:** | Color: | Lightest grey |

19. Save your work to disk, and print a copy for your files.

Note: The final version of the spreadsheet will be on page 1. You do not need to print page 2 as it should contain only the check figures.

COLLABORATIVE LEARNING EXERCISE

4-60 Internet Research, ABC, and ABM

Form groups of three to five people each. Each member of the group should pick one of the following industries:

- Manufacturing
- Insurance
- Health care
- Government
- Service

Each person should explore the Internet for an example of a company that implemented activity-based costing and activity-based management. Prepare and give a briefing for your group. Do this by completing the following:

1. Describe the company and its business.
2. What was the scope of the ABC/ABM project?
3. What were the goals for the ABC/ABM project?
4. Summarize the results of the project.

After each person has briefed the group on his or her company, discuss within your group the commonalities between the ABC/ABM applications.

INTERNET EXERCISE

4-61 Vermont Teddy Bear Factory

Costs are very important to any manager. Managers focus on trying to keep costs as low as possible. There are many ways to report costs, such as the total amount that is often seen on the income statement or an individual cost for a particular component part.

1. Go to the home page at www.vermontteddybear.com. When you click onto the Web site, what does it suggest that you should do? What is the current headline offering on the site?
2. Click the "What is a Bear-Gram?" icon under "Customer Services" at the bottom of the page. What is a Bear-Gram gift is and what does it contain?
3. Take a tour of the factory. Click on "Online Factory Tour" near the bottom of the home page. Take the online tour. List several activities shown in the tour. What are some resources that are consumed by these activities? For one of the activities you listed, give at least one fixed-cost and one variable-cost resource. Suggest a cost driver for one of the activities you listed.
4. Do you think that the Vermont Teddy Bear factory would be a good candidate for using activity-based costing? Explain.
5. From the description of the Vermont Teddy Bear Company, is it a manufacturer or merchandiser? If you looked at the details of its balance sheet, what would you expect to find under Inventories? Do you expect Vermont Teddy Bear Company to have large work-in-process inventories or finished-goods inventories?

Relevant Information for Decision Making with a Focus on Pricing Decisions

LEARNING OBJECTIVES

When you have finished studying this chapter, you should be able to:

1. Discriminate between relevant and irrelevant information for making decisions.

2. Apply the decision process to make business decisions.

3. Construct absorption and contribution-margin income statements, and identify their relevance for decision making.

4. Decide to accept or reject a special order using the contribution-margin technique.

5. Explain why pricing decisions depend on the characteristics of the market.

6. Identify the factors that influence pricing decisions in practice.

7. Compute a sales price by various approaches, and compare the advantages and disadvantages of these approaches.

8. Use target costing to decide whether to add a new product.

▶ GRAND CANYON RAILWAY

While you are on vacation, the last thing you want to worry about is transportation. For visitors to Grand Canyon National Park, the **Grand Canyon Railway** provides a relaxing alternative to driving to the canyon. Why drive when you can sit back and enjoy the scenery across 65 miles of beautiful Arizona countryside from the comfort of a fully reconditioned steam-powered train? Strolling musicians serenade you, and western characters stage attacks and holdups that offer a glimpse into what train travel might have been like for old-west loggers, miners, and ranchers at the turn of the century. The Grand Canyon Railway offers a ride not only to the canyon itself but into the past as well.

Rides into the past aren't exactly cheap. Tracks for the narrow-gauge train as well as the authentic steam engines and passenger cars required an investment of more than $20 million. Recovering that initial investment while earning a profit is not easy. According to the company CFO, Kevin Call, "Pricing is really the key in running a successful operation."

The railway offers five different classes of service, and setting the pricing on each one determines the company's profit. To set prices, management uses the contribution-margin technique introduced in Chapter 2. Among the influences on pricing discussed in this chapter, costs and customer demands are the most important to the railway. The prices charged must not only ensure a reasonable profit, they also must be attractive to the customer.

Costs are important in the pricing decisions of many types of companies. What price should a **Safeway** store charge for a pound of hamburger? What should **Boeing** charge for a 787 airplane? Should a clothing manufacturer accept a special order from **Wal-Mart**? Managers rely on accounting information to answer these questions and to make important decisions on a daily basis. However, not all accounting information applies to each type of decision. In this chapter, we'll focus on identifying relevant information for decision making and apply what we learn to pricing decisions. The ability to separate relevant from irrelevant information is often the difference between success and failure in modern business. ■[1]

Riding the Grand Canyon Railroad is like going back in time to the grand era of train travel.

The Concept of Relevance

What information is relevant? That depends on the decision being made. Decision making is essentially choosing among several alternative courses of action. Decision makers identify the available alternatives by an often time-consuming search and screening process, perhaps carried out by a company team that includes engineers, accountants, and operating executives. The accountant's role is primarily that of a technical expert on financial analysis who provides information that may be useful to the decision maker. However, the decision maker, who has the best understanding of the decision and the available alternatives, must understand what information is relevant.

What Is Relevance?

Making business decisions requires managers to compare two or more alternative courses of action. Two criteria determine whether information is relevant: (1) Information must be an expected future revenue or cost, and (2) it must have an element of difference among the alternatives. That is, **relevant information** is the predicted future costs and revenues that will differ among the alternatives.

> **Objective 1**
>
> Discriminate between relevant and irrelevant information for making decisions.

Note that relevant information is a prediction of the future, not a summary of the past. Historical (past) information has no direct bearing on a decision. Such information can have an indirect bearing on a decision because it may help in predicting the future. But past figures, in themselves, are irrelevant to the decision itself. Why? Because the decision cannot change the past. Decisions affect the future. Nothing can alter what has already happened.

Of the expected future information, only data that will differ across alternatives are relevant to the decision. Any item that will remain the same regardless of the alternative selected is irrelevant. For instance, if a department manager's salary will be the same regardless of the products produced, the salary is irrelevant to the selection of products. Here are some examples to help you clarify the sharp distinctions between relevant and irrelevant information.

Suppose you always buy gasoline from either of two nearby gasoline stations. Yesterday you noticed that one station was selling gasoline at $2.00 per gallon. The other was selling it at $1.90. Your automobile needs gasoline today, and in making your choice of stations, you assume that these prices have not changed. The relevant costs are $2.00 and $1.90, the expected future costs that will differ between the alternatives. You use your past experience (that is, what you observed yesterday) for predicting today's price. Note that the relevant cost is not what you paid in the past, or what you observed yesterday, but what you expect to pay when you drive in to get gasoline. This cost meets our two criteria: (1) It is the expected future cost, and (2) it differs between the alternatives.

You may also plan to buy a bag of potato chips when you stop for gasoline. Suppose you expect the price of a bag of chips to be the same at either station. This expected future cost is irrelevant to your decision about which station to stop at because it will be the same under either alternative. It does not meet our second criterion.

On a business level, consider the following decision. A food container manufacturer is thinking of using aluminum instead of tin in making a line of large cans. The cost of direct

---

[1]Throughout this and the next chapter, to concentrate on the fundamental ideas, we shall ignore the time value of money and income taxes (discussed in Chapter 11).

material is expected to decrease from $.30 per can if tin is used to $.20 per can if the manufacturer uses aluminum. The direct-labor cost will continue to be $.70 per unit regardless of the material used. Direct-labor cost is irrelevant because our second criterion—an element of difference between the alternatives—is not met.

	Aluminum	Tin	Difference
Direct material	$.20	$.30	$.10
Direct labor	.70	.70	—

In this example, the relevant costs are the costs of direct materials. We can safely exclude direct labor from the comparison of alternatives because it does not differ between the alternatives.

A Decision Model

Objective 2

Apply the decision process to make business decisions.

Exhibit 5-1 illustrates this simple decision process, and it serves to show the appropriate framework for more complex decisions. Box 1(A) represents historical data from the accounting system. Box 1(B) represents other data, such as price indices or industry statistics, gathered from outside the accounting system. Regardless of their source, the data in step 1 help the formulation of predictions in step 2. (Remember that historical data are only relevant as a guide to predicting future costs and revenues. In the large can manufacturing example, the historical costs of tin and aluminum are only relevant as predictors of future prices.)

In step 3, these predictions become inputs to the decision model. A **decision model** is any method used for making a choice. Such models sometimes require elaborate quantitative procedures, such as a petroleum refinery's mathematical method for choosing what products to manufacture for any given day or week. A decision model, however, may also be simple. It may be confined to a single comparison of costs for choosing between two materials, as in the previous example of the tin versus aluminum cans. In this example, our decision model is to compare the predicted unit costs and, assuming that everything else is equal, select the alternative with the lower cost.

The decision process in Exhibit 5-1 applies to all business decisions, no matter how simple or complicated they may be. By using this process, you will be able to focus squarely on the relevant information—the predicted future differences between alternatives—in any decision. In the rest of this chapter, we will use this decision process to apply the concept of relevance to several specific pricing decisions.

Accuracy and Relevance

In the best of all possible worlds, decision-making information would always be both perfectly relevant and precisely accurate. However, in reality, such information is often too difficult or too costly to obtain. Accountants are sometimes forced to choose between more relevance or more accuracy.

Precise but irrelevant information is worthless for decision making. For example, a university president's salary may be $340,000 per year, to the penny, but may have no bearing on the question of whether to buy or rent data-processing equipment. In contrast, imprecise but relevant information can be useful. For example, sales predictions for a new product may be subject to error, but they still are helpful in deciding whether to manufacture the product. Relevant information must be reasonably accurate but not precisely so.

The degree to which information is relevant or precise often depends on the degree to which it is qualitative or quantitative. Qualitative aspects are those for which measurement in dollars and cents is difficult and imprecise; quantitative aspects are those for which measurement is easy and precise. Accountants, statisticians, and mathematicians try to express as many decision factors as feasible in quantitative terms. Why? Because this approach reduces the number of qualitative (subjective) factors they need to consider. Just as we noted that relevance is more crucial than precision in decision making, so qualitative aspects may dominate quantitative (financial) impacts in many decisions. For example, the extreme opposition of a militant labor union to new labor-saving machinery may cause a manager to forgo installation of such machinery even if it would reduce manufacturing costs. In a similar way, a company may pass up the opportunity to

Exhibit 5-1
Decision Process and Role of Information

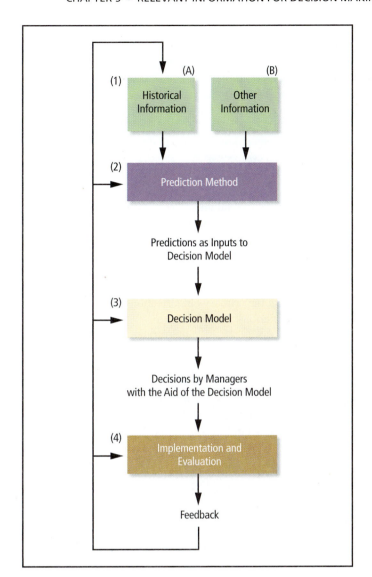

purchase a component from a supplier at a price below the cost of producing it themselves to avoid a long-range dependence on that particular supplier.

Likewise, managers sometimes introduce new technology (for example, advanced computer systems or automated equipment) even though the expected quantitative results seem unattractive. Managers defend such decisions on the grounds that failure to keep abreast of new technology will surely bring unfavorable financial results in the long run.

The Relevance of Alternative Income Statements

In many cases, income statement information is relevant to decision making because it specifies how alternative choices impact income. Additionally, since executives use income statements to evaluate performance, managers need to know how their decisions will affect income as reported on the statements. There are different ways to organize income statement information. Some income statements track fixed and variable costs using the contribution approach, whereas others adopt the absorption approach used in reporting to external parties.

Let's examine the relevance of contribution and absorption income statements. To highlight the different effects of these approaches, consider the Cordell Company. Suppose Cordell produces and sells 1,000,000 units of seat covers for seats on airplanes, buses, and railroad passenger cars. Cordell sells these to companies such as **US Airways** and the **Grand Canyon Railway Company**. The total manufacturing cost of making 1,000,000 seat covers is $30,000,000. The unit manufacturing cost of the product is $30,000,000 ÷ 1,000,000, or $30 per unit. We will assume

Objective 3

Construct absorption and contribution-margin income statements, and identify their relevance for decision making.

that in 20X1 the Cordell Company has direct-materials costs of $14 million and direct-labor costs of $6 million. Assume also that the company incurs the indirect manufacturing costs illustrated in Exhibit 5-2 and the selling and administrative expenses illustrated in Exhibit 5-3. Finally, assume there are no beginning or ending inventories, and total sales are predicted at $40 million.

Note that Exhibits 5-2 and 5-3 subdivide costs as variable or fixed. As explained next, most companies do not make such subdivisions in their absorption income statements for external reporting. However, many companies use these subdivisions in contribution income statements to align with the information managers should use in decision making. Note also that it is sometimes difficult to classify a given cost as variable, fixed, or partially fixed (for example, repairs).

Absorption Approach

Exhibit 5-4 presents Cordell's income statement using the **absorption approach** (or **absorption costing**), the approach used by companies for external financial reporting. Firms that take this approach consider all direct and indirect manufacturing costs (both variable and fixed) to be product (inventoriable) costs that become an expense in the form of manufacturing cost of goods sold only as sales occur.

Note that gross profit or gross margin is the difference between sales and the manufacturing cost of goods sold. Note too that the primary classifications of costs on the income statement are by three major management functions: manufacturing, selling, and administrative.

Contribution Approach

In contrast, Exhibit 5-5 presents Cordell's income statement using the **contribution approach** (also called variable costing or direct costing). United States and international accounting standards do not allow the contribution approach for external financial reporting. However, many companies use the contribution approach for internal decision-making purposes and an absorption format for external purposes. Why? Because they expect the benefits of making better decisions using the contribution approach to exceed the extra costs of using two different reporting systems simultaneously.

For decision purposes, the major difference between the contribution approach and the absorption approach is that the former emphasizes the distinction between variable and fixed costs. Its primary classifications of costs is by variable- and fixed-cost behavior patterns, not by business functions.

The contribution income statement provides a contribution margin—revenue less all variable costs, including variable selling and administrative costs. This approach makes it easier to understand the impact of changes in sales demand on operating income. It also dovetails nicely with the cost-volume-profit (CVP) analysis illustrated in Chapter 2 and the decision analyses in this chapter and Chapter 6.

Another major benefit of the contribution approach is that it stresses the role of fixed costs in operating income. Before a company can earn income, its total contribution margin must exceed the fixed costs it has incurred for manufacturing and other value-chain functions. This highlighting of contribution margin and total fixed costs focuses management attention on cost behavior and control in making both short-run and long-run decisions. Remember that advocates of the contribution

Exhibit 5-2

Cordell Company

Schedules of Predicted Indirect Manufacturing Costs for the Year Ended December 31, 20X1 (thousands of dollars)

Schedule 1: Variable Costs		
Supplies (lubricants, expendable tools, coolants, sandpaper)	$ 600	
Materials-handling labor (forklift operators)	2,800	
Repairs on manufacturing equipment	400	
Power for factory	200	$ 4,000
Schedule 2: Fixed Costs		
Managers' salaries in factory	$ 400	
Factory employee training	180	
Factory picnic and holiday party	20	
Factory supervisory salaries	1,400	
Depreciation, plant, and equipment	3,600	
Property taxes on plant	300	
Insurance on plant	100	6,000
Total indirect manufacturing costs		$10,000

Schedule 3: Selling Expenses		
Variable		
Sales commissions	$1,400	
Shipping expenses for products sold	600	$2,000
Fixed		
Advertising	$1,400	
Sales salaries	2,000	
Other	600	4,000
Total selling expenses		$6,000
Schedule 4: Administrative Expenses		
Variable		
Some clerical wages	$ 160	
Computer time rented	40	$ 200
Fixed		
Office salaries	$ 200	
Other salaries	400	
Depreciation on office facilities	200	
Public-accounting fees	80	
Legal fees	200	
Other	720	1,800
Total administrative expenses		$2,000

Exhibit 5-3
Cordell Company
Schedules of Predicted Selling and Administrative Expenses for the Year Ended December 31, 20X1 (thousands of dollars)

approach do not maintain that fixed costs are unimportant or irrelevant. They do stress, however, that the distinctions between behaviors of variable and fixed costs are crucial for certain decisions. Decisions usually affect fixed costs in a different way than they affect variable costs.

The distinction between the gross margin (from the absorption approach) and the contribution margin (from the contribution approach) is important for manufacturing companies. Why? Because absorption-costing systems regard fixed manufacturing costs as a part of cost of goods sold, and these fixed costs reduce the gross margin accordingly. However, fixed manufacturing costs do not reduce the contribution margin, which is simply the difference between revenues and variable costs. On the other hand, the contribution approach regards variable selling and administrative costs as part of total variable expenses, and these reduce contribution margin accordingly. However, variable selling and administrative costs do not reduce gross margin.

Comparing Contribution and Absorption Approaches

In essence, the contribution approach separates fixed costs from variable costs. It deducts variable costs from sales to compute a contribution margin and then deducts fixed costs to measure profit. In contrast, the absorption approach separates manufacturing costs from nonmanufacturing costs. It deducts manufacturing costs from sales to compute a gross margin and then deducts nonmanufacturing costs to measure profit. Both formats can be relevant for decision making, depending on the type of decision being contemplated. In situations where decisions affect variable costs differently than they affect fixed costs, such as the short-run pricing decisions we will discuss in this chapter, the contribution approach will yield great value. In contrast, the absorption approach is well suited for long-run pricing decisions, where it is important that the prices over a product's life cover all manufacturing costs, including fixed costs.

Sales		$40,000
Less: Manufacturing costs of goods sold		
Direct materials	$14,000	
Direct labor	6,000	
Indirect manufacturing (Schedules 1 plus 2)*	10,000	30,000
Gross margin or gross profit		$10,000
Selling expenses (Schedule 3)	$ 6,000	
Administrative expenses (Schedule 4)	2,000	
Total selling and administrative expenses		8,000
Operating income		$ 2,000
*Schedules 1 and 2 are in Exhibit 5-2. Schedules 3 and 4 are in Exhibit 5-3.		

Exhibit 5-4
Cordell Company
Predicted Absorption Income Statement for the Year Ended December 31, 20X1 (thousands of dollars)

Exhibit 5-5
Cordell Company
Predicted Contribution Income Statement for the Year Ended December 31, 20X1 (thousands of dollars)

Sales		$40,000
Less: Variable expenses		
Direct materials	$14,000	
Direct labor	6,000	
Variable indirect manufacturing costs (Schedule 1)*	4,000	
Total variable manufacturing cost of goods sold	$24,000	
Variable selling expenses (Schedule 3)	2,000	
Variable administrative expenses (Schedule 4)	200	
Total variable expenses		26,200
Contribution margin		$13,800
Less: Fixed expenses		
Manufacturing (Schedule 2)	$ 6,000	
Selling (Schedule 3)	4,000	
Administrative (Schedule 4)	1,800	11,800
Operating income		$ 2,000

*Note: Schedules 1 and 2 are in Exhibit 5-2. Schedules 3 and 4 are in Exhibit 5-3.

Pricing Special Sales Orders

Before considering more general approaches to pricing, it is helpful to examine how a manager might approach a specific pricing decision—whether to accept a proposed price for a special sales order. We will highlight the value of the contribution approach in such a decision.

Illustrative Example

In our illustration, we'll focus again on the Cordell Company. Suppose **Branson Gray Line Tours** offered Cordell $26 per unit for a 100,000-unit special order of seat covers that (1) would not affect Cordell's regular business in any way, (2) would not affect total fixed costs, (3) would not require any additional variable selling and administrative expenses, (4) would use some otherwise idle manufacturing capacity, and (5) would not raise any antitrust issues concerning price discrimination. Should Cordell sell the 100,000 seat covers for the price of $26 each?

Perhaps we should state the question more succinctly: What is the difference in the short-run financial results between not accepting and accepting the order? As usual, the key question is as follows: What are the differences between alternatives? Exhibit 5-5 presents the income statement of the Cordell Company without the special order, using the contribution approach. Let's see how Cordell's operating income would change if it accepts the special order.

Correct Analysis—Focus on Relevant Information and Cost Behavior

Objective 4

Decide to accept or reject a special order using the contribution-margin technique.

The correct analysis focuses on determining relevant information and cost behavior. It employs the contribution-margin technique. As Exhibit 5-6 shows, this particular order affects only variable manufacturing costs, at a rate of $24 per unit. All other variable costs and all fixed costs are unaffected and, thus, irrelevant. Therefore, a manager may safely ignore them in making this special-order decision. Note how the contribution-margin technique's distinction between variable- and fixed-cost behavior patterns aids the necessary cost analysis. Total short-run income will increase by $200,000 if Cordell accepts the order—despite the fact that the unit selling price of $26 is less than the total unit manufacturing cost of $30.

Why did we include fixed costs in Exhibit 5-6? After all, they are irrelevant because they do not differ across the alternatives considered in this decision. We included them because management often focuses on the bottom line—operating income. Both the contribution margin and the operating income increase by $200,000 so we could ignore the fixed costs and come to the same conclusion. However, management may prefer to see the effect of its decisions on operating income, so we include the irrelevant fixed costs in the presentation.

	Without Special Order 1,000,000 Units	Effect of Special Order, 100,000 Units		With Special Order, 1,100,000 Units
		Total	Per Unit	
Sales	$40,000,000	$2,600,000	$26	$42,600,000
Less: Variable expenses				
Manufacturing	$24,000,000	$2,400,000	$24	$26,400,000
Selling and administrative	2,200,000	—	—	2,200,000
Total variable expenses	$26,200,000	$2,400,000	$24	$28,600,000
Contribution margin	$13,800,000	$ 200,000	$ 2	$14,000,000
Less: Fixed expenses				
Manufacturing	$ 6,000,000	—	—	$ 6,000,000
Selling and administrative	5,800,000	—	—	5,800,000
Total fixed expenses	$11,800,000	—	—	$11,800,000
Operating income	$ 2,000,000	$ 200,000	$ 2	$ 2,200,000

Exhibit 5-6

Cordell Company
Comparative Predicted Income Statements, Contribution-Margin Technique for Year Ended December 31, 20X1

Making Managerial Decisions

Suppose you are at a meeting of Cordell Company managers and someone asked the following questions. Some of the answers given by your colleagues follow:

Q: What will be the change in the contribution margin if we accept this order?

A: The contribution margin will increase to $14,000,000.

Q: In your analysis (Exhibit 5-6), you show that fixed costs do not change if we accept the order. Are these costs relevant?

A: No. Fixed costs are not relevant.

Q: OK. But do fixed costs that we incur have an effect on the bottom line of our company?

A: Certainly. That is why we deduct fixed costs from the contribution margin to get operating income.

Q: Well, if fixed costs affect the bottom line, how can you say they are not relevant?

Comment on your colleague's answers, and answer the last question.

Answer

Your colleague's answer to the first question is technically incorrect. The question asks for change, not the new total contribution margin. The correct answer to this question is that contribution margin will increase by $200,000 (and therefore become $14,000,000 in total). Be careful to differentiate between terms that imply totals and terms that imply changes. In this case, $14,000,000 is the answer to "What is the new total contribution margin if we accept the order?"

Your colleague's responses to the second and third questions are correct. The fixed costs of Cordell are not relevant for this particular special order situation. Nevertheless, the bottom line—operating income—includes all costs or total costs and revenues. Do not confuse this with the relevant costs—a term we associated with this specific decision. In a decision situation, relevant costs include only those future costs that will differ if we accept the order. If a manager wants to know the "bottom line" after accepting the order, we would need to include the fixed cost. However, the fixed costs do not affect the difference between the preorder bottom line and the bottom line after accepting the order. The difference is the same $200,000 amount by which the contribution margin increases.

Analysis—Misuse of Unit Cost

Faulty cost analysis sometimes occurs because of misinterpreting unit fixed costs, especially with an absorption approach. For instance, Cordell's managers might erroneously use the $30 per-unit total manufacturing cost under the absorption approach ($30,000,000 ÷ 1,000,000 units per Exhibit 5-4) to make the following prediction for the year:

Incorrect Analysis	Without Special Order 1,000,000 Units	Incorrect Effect of Special Order 100,000 Units	With Special Order 1,100,000 Units
Sales	$40,000,000	$2,600,000	$42,600,000
Less: Manufacturing cost of goods sold at $30	30,000,000	3,000,000	33,000,000
Gross margin	10,000,000	(400,000)	9,600,000
Selling and administrative expenses	8,000,000	—	8,000,000
Operating income	$ 2,000,000	$ (400,000)	$ 1,600,000

The incorrect prediction of a $3 million increase in costs results from multiplying 100,000 units by $30. The fallacy in this approach is that it treats a fixed cost (fixed manufacturing cost) as if it were variable. Avoid the temptation to use total unit costs as a basis for predicting how total costs will behave. Unit costs are useful for predicting variable costs, but unit costs can be misleading when used to predict fixed costs.

Confusion of Variable and Fixed Costs

Consider the relationship between total fixed manufacturing costs and a fixed manufacturing cost per unit of product (per Exhibit 5-5):

$$\frac{\text{fixed manufacturing cost}}{\text{per unit of product}} = \frac{\text{total fixed manufacturing costs}}{\text{some selected volume level as the denominator}}$$

$$= \frac{\$6,000,000}{1,000,000 \text{ units}} = \$6 \text{ per unit}$$

As we noted in Chapter 1, the typical cost accounting system serves two purposes simultaneously: (1) planning and control and (2) product costing. We can graph the total fixed cost for planning and control purposes as a lump sum:

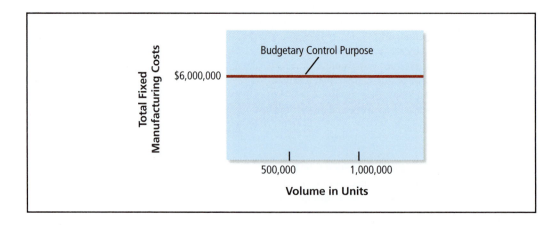

For product-costing purposes, however, using the total unit manufacturing cost implies that these fixed costs behave as if they are variable costs, which is contrary to fixed-cost behavior:

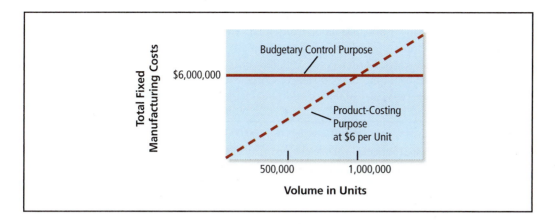

The addition of 100,000 units will not add any fixed costs as long as total output is within the relevant range. The incorrect analysis, however, includes $100,000 \times \$6 = \$600,000$ of additional fixed cost in the predictions of increases in total costs.

In short, we should compute the increase in manufacturing costs by multiplying 1,000,000 units by $24, not by $30. The $30 includes a $6 component that will not affect the total manufacturing costs as volume changes within the relevant range. Alternatively, one could entirely avoid this pitfall of unitizing fixed costs by using the contribution approach as in Exhibit 5-6.

Making Managerial Decisions

We have presented two key lessons so far in this chapter: relevant information and misuse of unit costs. We cannot stress enough how important it is to clearly understand the definition and concept of relevant information. It is also important to understand why the use of unit fixed costs can lead to an incorrect analysis.

Suppose you are a manager in a company that makes small appliances. You are deciding whether to accept or reject a special order for 1,000 units. (Assume there is sufficient excess capacity available for the order.)
1. Which of the following costs are relevant: (a) parts for the order, (b) supervisor's salary, (c) assembly equipment depreciation, (d) power to operate the assembly equipment?
2. Suppose the total unit manufacturing cost for the 1,000 units is $100 per unit. We determined this amount by dividing the total cost by 1,000 units. If the customer decided to double the order to 2,000 units, which costs listed in number 1 would change? Which costs per unit would change? Would the total cost of the order double?

Answers

1. Relevant costs and revenues are predicted future costs and revenues that differ among alternative courses of action. In this case, the cost of parts and power would increase if management accepts the order, and, thus, they are relevant. The other costs are fixed costs that would not change because excess capacity is available.
2. Only the relevant costs, in this case the variable costs, would change: parts and power. Fixed costs would be unaffected. In contrast, the fixed cost per unit will change, whereas the variable cost per unit will stay the same. For example, fixed supervisory salaries will be divided by 2,000 units instead of by only 1,000 units, and hence per-unit supervisory cost will decrease. The parts cost per unit would stay the same, as would the power cost per unit. So, the total unit cost would fall, and the total cost of the order would not double.

Activity-Based Costing, Special Orders, and Relevant Costs

To identify relevant costs affected by a special order (or by other special decisions), more firms are going a step beyond simply identifying fixed and variable costs. As we pointed out in Chapters 3 and 4, a company's operations include many different activities. Businesses that have identified all their significant activities and related cost drivers can produce more detailed relevant information to predict the effects of special orders more accurately.

Suppose the Cordell Company examined its $24 million of variable manufacturing costs very closely and identified two significant activities and related cost drivers: $21 million of processing activity that varies directly with units produced ($14 million in direct materials, $6 million in direct labor, and $1 million of variable manufacturing overhead) at a rate of $21 per unit and $3 million of setup activity (the remainder of variable manufacturing overhead) that varies with the number of production setups. Normally, Cordell produces 2,000 units per setup. Therefore, for processing 1,000,000 units, Cordell has 500 setups at a cost of $6,000 per setup. Additional sales generally require a proportional increase in the number of setups.

Now suppose the special order is for 100,000 units that vary only slightly in production specifications. Instead of the normal 50 setups, Cordell will need only 5 setups. So processing 100,000 units will take only $2,130,000 of additional variable manufacturing cost:

Additional unit-based variable manufacturing cost, 100,000 × $21	$2,100,000
Additional setup-based variable manufacturing cost, 5 × $6,000	30,000
Total additional variable manufacturing cost	$2,130,000

Instead of the original estimate of 100,000 × $24 = $2,400,000 additional variable manufacturing cost, the special order will cost only $2,130,000, or $270,000 less than the original estimate. Therefore, activity-based costing (ABC) allows managers to realize that the special order is $270,000 more profitable than predicted from the simple unit-based assessment of variable manufacturing cost.

A special order may also be more costly than predicted by a simple fixed- and variable-cost analysis. Suppose the 100,000-unit special order called for a variety of models and colors delivered at various times so that it requires 100 setups. The variable cost of the special order would be $2.7 million, $300,000 more than the original estimate of $2.4 million:

Additional unit-based variable manufacturing cost, 100,000 × $21	$2,100,000
Additional setup-based variable manufacturing cost, 100 × $6,000	600,000
Total additional variable manufacturing cost	$2,700,000

ABC systems provide useful operating information for special-order decisions, but the fundamental concepts remain the same—focus your attention on future costs and revenues that differ because of the special order. Also, be careful to recognize and properly use terms such as *impact, change,* and *total.* The summary problem for your review that follows gives you more practice at analyzing a special order.

Summary Problem for Your Review

PROBLEM

1. Suppose Nike produces and sells 500,000 units of the LeBron James "Six Chalk Edition" basketball shirt. The selling price is $35, and there is excess capacity to produce an additional 300,000 shirts. The absorption cost of the shirts is $10,000,000 ÷ 500,000, or $20 per shirt, consisting of variable manufacturing costs of $7,000,000 ($7,000,000 ÷ 500,000 or $14 per shirt) and fixed manufacturing costs of $3,000,000 ($3,000,000 ÷ 500,000 or $6 per shirt). Variable selling and administrative costs are $3 per shirt, and fixed selling and administrative costs are $2,000,000. Assume Nike receives an offer from Sports Authority to buy 100,000 shirts at a price of $18.00 per shirt. If Nike accepts the order it would not incur any additional variable selling and administrative costs, but it would have to pay a flat fee of $80,000 to the manufacturer's agent who had obtained the potential order. Should Nike accept the special order?

2. What if the order was for 250,000 units at a selling price of $13.00 and there was no $80,000 agent's fee? One manager argued for acceptance of such an order as follows: "Of course, we will lose $1.00 each on the variable manufacturing costs ($13 − $14), but we will gain $2.00 per unit by spreading our fixed manufacturing costs over

750,000 shirts instead of 500,000 shirts. Consequently, we should take the offer because it represents an advantage of $1.00 per shirt." The manager's analysis follows:

Old fixed manufacturing cost per unit, $3,000,000 ÷ 500,000	$6.00
New fixed manufacturing cost per unit, $3,000,000 ÷ 750,000	4.00
"Savings" in fixed manufacturing cost per unit	$2.00
Loss on variable manufacturing cost per unit, $13.00 − $14.00	1.00
Net savings per unit in manufacturing cost	$1.00

Explain why this is faulty thinking.

SOLUTION

1. Focus on relevant information—the differences in revenues and costs. In this problem, in addition to the difference in variable costs, there is a difference in fixed costs between the two alternatives.

Additional revenue, 100,000 units at $18.00 per shirt	$1,800,000
Less: Additional costs	
Variable costs, 100,000 units at $14 per unit	1,400,000
Fixed costs, agent's fee	80,000
Increase in operating income from special order	$ 320,000

So, from a strictly financial perspective, Nike should accept the special order.
2. The faulty thinking comes from attributing a "savings" to the decrease in unit fixed costs. Regardless of how we "unitize" the fixed manufacturing costs or "spread" them over the units produced, the special order will not change the total of $3 million. Remember that we have a negative contribution margin of $1.00 per unit on this special order. Thus, there is no way we can cover any amount of fixed costs! Fixed costs are not relevant to this decision.

Basic Principles for Pricing Decisions

One of the major decisions managers face is pricing. Actually, pricing can take many forms. In addition to pricing special orders, managers make the following pricing decisions:

1. Setting the price of a new or refined product
2. Setting the price of products sold under private labels
3. Responding to a new price of a competitor
4. Pricing bids in both sealed and open bidding situations

Pricing decisions are so important that we will spend the rest of the chapter discussing the many aspects of pricing. Let us now take a look at some of the basic concepts behind pricing.

The Concept of Pricing

Pricing decisions depend on the market characteristics in which a firm operates. In **perfect competition** all competing firms sell the same type of product at the same price. Thus, a firm can sell as much of a product as it can produce, all at a single market price. If it charges more, no

Objective 5

Explain why pricing decisions depend on the characteristics of the market.

customer will buy. If it charges less, it sacrifices profits. Therefore, every firm in such a market will charge the market price, and the only decision for managers is how much to produce.

Although costs do not directly influence prices in perfect competition, they do affect the production decision. Consider the marginal cost curve in Exhibit 5-7. The **marginal cost** is the additional cost resulting from producing and selling one additional unit—for the Grand Canyon Railway, it's one additional passenger; for General Motors, it's one additional car. With a fixed set of production facilities, the marginal cost often decreases as production increases up to a point because of efficiencies created by larger volumes. At some point, however, marginal costs begin to rise with increases in production because facilities become overcrowded or overused, resulting in inefficiencies.

Exhibit 5-7 also includes a marginal revenue curve. The **marginal revenue** is the additional revenue resulting from the sale of an additional unit. In perfect competition, the marginal revenue curve is a horizontal line equal to the price per unit at all volumes of sales.

As long as the marginal cost is less than the marginal revenue (price), additional production and sales are profitable. When marginal cost exceeds price, however, the firm loses money on each additional unit. Therefore, the profit-maximizing volume is the quantity at which marginal cost equals price. In Exhibit 5-7, the firm should produce V_0 units. Producing fewer units passes up profitable opportunities, and producing more units reduces profit because each additional unit costs more to produce than it generates in revenue.

In **imperfect competition**, the price a firm charges for a unit influences the quantity of units it sells. At some point, the firm must reduce prices to generate additional sales. Exhibit 5-8 contains a *demand curve* (also called the *average revenue curve*) for imperfect competition that shows the volume of sales at each possible price. To sell additional units, the firm must reduce the price of all units sold. Therefore, the *marginal revenue curve*, also shown in Exhibit 5-8, is below the demand curve. That is, the marginal revenue for selling one additional unit is less than the price at which the company sells it because the price of all other units falls as well. For example, suppose a firm can sell 10 units for $50 per unit. However, the firm must drop the price to $49 per unit to sell 11 units, to $48 to sell 12 units, and to $47 to sell 13 units. The fourth column of Exhibit 5-9 shows the marginal revenue for units 11–13. Notice that the marginal revenue decreases as volume increases.

To estimate marginal revenue, managers must predict the **price elasticity**—the effect of price changes on sales volume. If small price increases cause large volume declines, demand is highly elastic. If prices have little or no effect on volume, demand is highly inelastic.

For the marginal costs shown in the fifth column of Exhibit 5-9, the optimal production and sales level is 12 units. The last column of that exhibit illustrates that the eleventh unit adds $4 to profit, and the twelfth adds $1, but production and sale of the thirteenth unit would decrease profit by $2. In general, firms should produce and sell units until the marginal revenue equals the marginal cost, represented by volume V_0 in Exhibit 5-8. The optimal price charged will be the amount that creates a demand for V_0 units.

Notice that the marginal cost is relevant for pricing decisions. In managerial accounting, marginal cost is essentially the variable cost. What is the major difference between marginal cost and variable cost? Accountants assume that variable cost is constant within a relevant range of

Exhibit 5-7
Marginal Revenue and Cost in Perfect Competition

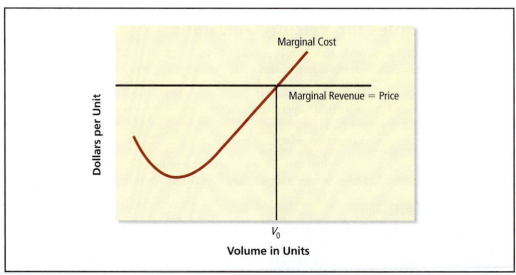

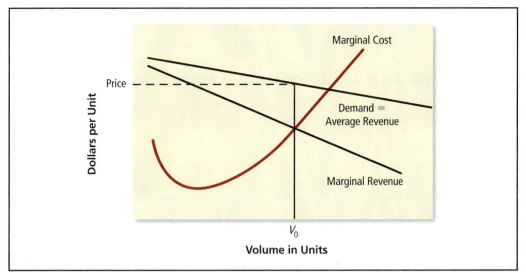

Exhibit 5-8
Marginal Revenue and Cost in Imperfect Competition

volume, whereas marginal cost may change with each unit produced. Within large ranges of production volume, however, changes in marginal cost are often small. Therefore, variable cost can be a reasonable approximation of marginal cost in many situations.

Pricing and Accounting

Accountants seldom compute marginal revenue and marginal cost curves. Instead, they use estimates based on judgment to predict the effects of additional production and sales on profits. In addition, they examine selected volumes, not the whole range of possible volumes. Such simplifications are justified because the cost of a more sophisticated analysis would exceed the benefits.

Consider a division of **General Electric (GE)** that makes microwave ovens. Suppose market researchers estimate that GE can sell 700,000 ovens at $200 per unit and 1,000,000 ovens at $180. The variable cost of production is $130 per unit at production levels of both 700,000 and 1,000,000. Both volumes are also within the relevant range so that changes in volume do not affect fixed costs. Which price should GE charge?

GE's accountant would determine the relevant revenues and costs. The additional revenue and additional costs of the 300,000 additional units of sales at the $180 prices are as follows:

Additional revenue: (1,000,000 × $180) − (700,000 × $200) =	$40,000,000
Additional costs: 300,000 × $130 =	39,000,000
Additional profit	$ 1,000,000

So the $180 price is optimal since it generates $1,000,000 more profit. On the other hand, the accountant could compare the total contribution for each alternative:

Contribution at $180: ($180 − $130) × 1,000,000 =	$50,000,000
Contribution at $200: ($200 − $130) × 700,000 =	49,000,000
Difference	$ 1,000,000

Exhibit 5-9
Profit Maximization in Imperfect Competition

Units Sold	Price per Unit	Total Revenue	Marginal Revenue	Marginal Cost	Profit from Production and Sale of Additional Unit
10	$50	10 × $50 = $500			
11	49	11 × 49 = 539	$539 − $500 = $39	$35	$39 − $35 = $4
12	48	12 × 48 = 576	576 − 539 = 37	36	37 − 36 = 1
13	47	13 × 47 = 611	611 − 576 = 35	37	35 − 37 = (2)

Notice that comparing the total contributions is essentially the same as computing the additional revenues and costs—both use the same relevant information. Further, both approaches correctly ignore fixed costs, which are unaffected by this pricing decision.

General Influences on Pricing in Practice

Several factors interact to shape the market in which managers make pricing decisions. Legal requirements, competitors' actions, and customer demands all influence pricing.

Legal Requirements

Objective 6

Identify the factors that influence pricing decisions in practice.

Managers must consider constraints imposed by United States and international laws when making pricing decisions. These laws often protect consumers, but they also help protect competing companies from predatory and discriminatory pricing.

Predatory pricing means setting prices so low that they drive competitors out of the market. The predatory pricer then has no significant competition and can raise prices dramatically. For example, lawsuits have accused **Wal-Mart** of predatory pricing—selling at low cost to drive out local competitors. However, in a 4-to-3 vote, the Arkansas Supreme Court ruled in favor of Wal-Mart. Courts in the United States have generally ruled that pricing is predatory only if companies set prices below their average variable cost and actually lose money in order to drive their competitors out of business.

Discriminatory pricing is charging different prices to different customers for the same product or service. For example, a large group of retail druggists and big drugstore chains sued several large drug companies. The drugstores alleged that the drug companies' practice of allowing discounts, some as large as 40%, to mail-order drug companies, health maintenance organizations, and other managed-care entities constitutes discriminatory pricing. However, pricing is not discriminatory if it reflects a cost differential incurred in providing the good or service.

Both predatory and discriminatory pricing practices are not only illegal but unethical business practices. Management accountants have an ethical obligation to perform their duties in accordance with relevant laws and to refrain from engaging in or supporting any activity or practice that would discredit the profession.

Competitors' Actions

Competitors usually react to the price changes of their rivals. Many companies gather information regarding a rival's capacity, technology, and operating policies. In this way, managers make more informed predictions of competitors' reactions to a company's prices. The study of game theory focuses on predicting and reacting to competitors' actions.

A manager's expectations of competitors' reactions and of the overall effects of price changes on the total industry demand for the good or service in question heavily influence pricing policies. For example, an airline might cut prices even if it expects matching price cuts from its rivals, hoping that total customer demand for the tickets of all airlines will increase sufficiently to offset the reduction in the price per ticket.

Competition is becoming increasingly global in its scope. Overcapacity in some countries often causes aggressive pricing policies for a company's exported goods. For example, companies might "dump" products by selling them at a low price in a foreign market that is isolated from its other markets. As you can imagine, when companies' markets expand globally, their pricing policies become more complex.

Customer Demands

More than ever before, managers are recognizing the needs of customers. Pricing is no exception. If customers believe a price is too high, they may turn to other sources for the product or service, substitute a different product, or decide to produce the item themselves. As the controller for the **Grand Canyon Railway** states, ". . . prices charged must be attractive to the customer." If not, customers can simply drive their own cars to the Grand Canyon or choose to ride a bus.

Cost-Plus Pricing

Accounting influences pricing by providing costs. The exact role costs play in pricing decisions depends on both the market conditions and the company's approach to pricing. This section discusses cost-plus pricing, the most common use of costs in pricing decisions.

What Is Cost-Plus Pricing?

Many managers set prices by "cost-plus" pricing. For example, Grand Canyon Railway sets its prices by computing an average cost and then adding a desired **markup**—the amount by which price exceeds cost—that will generate a desired level of income. The key, however, is the "plus" in cost plus. Instead of being a fixed markup, the "plus" will usually depend on both costs and the demands of customers. For example, the railway has a standard (rack rate) price that does not change during the year, but it often offers discounts during the slow winter season.

Prices are most directly related to costs in industries where revenue is based on cost reimbursement. Cost-reimbursement contracts generally specify how to measure costs and what costs are allowable. For example, the government reimburses only coach-class (not first-class) airfares for business travel on defense contracts.

Ultimately, though, the market sets prices. Why? Because companies inevitably adjust the price as set by a cost-plus formula "in light of market conditions." The maximum price a company can charge is the one that does not drive the customer away. The minimum price might be considered to be zero (for example, companies may give out free samples to gain entry into a market).

A more practical guide is that, in the short run, the minimum price sales personnel should quote on an order is the marginal cost that the company incurs if it gets the order (in effect its relevant costs of filling the order)—often all variable costs of producing, selling, and distributing the good or service. However, in the long run, the price must be high enough to cover all costs, including fixed costs. Therefore, many companies add allocated fixed unit costs to the variable costs to get a minimum price they want to achieve in the long run. They acknowledge that market conditions sometimes dictate sales at a price lower than this long-run minimum price. Yet, to continue to produce and sell such a product, there must be a prospect of eventually achieving a price at or above the long-run minimum.

Cost Bases for Cost-Plus Pricing

To set a desired price for products or services, managers often add a markup to some measure of costs—thus, the term *cost plus*. The size of the "plus" depends on the definition of cost and the desired operating income. Prices can be based on a host of different markups that are in turn based on a host of different definitions of cost. Thus, there are many ways to arrive at the same price.

Exhibit 5-10 displays the relationships of costs to selling prices, assuming a desired operating income of $1 million on a volume of 1 million units. The exhibited percentages represent four popular markup formulas for pricing: (1) as a percentage of variable manufacturing costs, (2) as a percentage of total variable costs, (3) as a percentage of total manufacturing cost, and (4) as a percentage of full costs. Notice that the first two formulas are consistent with the contribution approach and the latter two are based on absorption costing numbers. Note also that **full cost** means the total of all manufacturing costs plus the total of all selling and administrative costs. As noted in earlier chapters, we use "selling and administrative" to include all value-chain functions other than production.

Objective 7

Compute a sales price by various approaches, and compare the advantages and disadvantages of these approaches.

			Alternative Markup Percentages to Achieve Same Sales Price
	Sales price	$20.00	
	Variable cost:		
(1)	Manufacturing	$12.00	($20.00 − $12.00) ÷ $12.00 = 66.67%
	Selling and administrative*	1.10	
(2)	Unit variable costs	$13.10	($20.00 − $13.10) ÷ $13.10 = 52.67%
	Fixed costs:		
	Manufacturing[†]	$ 3.00	
	Selling and administrative	2.90	
	Unit fixed costs	$ 5.90	
(3)	Full costs	$19.00	($20.00 − $19.00) ÷ $19.00 = 5.26%
	Desired operating income	$ 1.00	

*Selling and administrative costs include costs of all value chain functions other than production.
[†](4) A frequently used formula is based on total manufacturing costs: [$20.00 − ($12.00 + $3.00)] ÷ $15.00 = 33.33%.

Exhibit 5-10

Relationships of Costs to Same Target Selling Price

To achieve the same prices, the percentages in Exhibit 5-10 differ for each definition of cost. For instance, the markup on variable manufacturing costs is 66.67%, and on full costs it is only 5.26%. Regardless of the formula used, the pricing decision maker will be led toward the same $20 price. If the decision maker is unable to obtain such a price consistently, the company will not achieve its $1 million operating income objective.

We have seen that managers can base prices on various types of cost information, from variable manufacturing costs to full costs. Each of these costs can be relevant to the pricing decision. Each approach has advantages and disadvantages.

Advantages of the Contribution Approach in Cost-Plus Pricing

Prices based on variable costs represent a contribution approach to pricing. When used intelligently, the contribution approach has some advantages over the total-manufacturing-cost and full-cost approaches because the latter two often fail to highlight different cost behavior patterns.

The contribution approach offers more detailed information because it displays variable- and fixed-cost behavior patterns separately. Because the contribution approach is sensitive to cost-volume-profit relationships, it is a helpful basis for developing pricing formulas. As a result, this approach allows managers to prepare price schedules at different volume levels.

The correct analysis in Exhibit 5-11 shows how changes in volume affect operating income. The contribution approach helps managers with pricing decisions by readily displaying the inter-relationships among variable costs, fixed costs, and potential changes in selling prices.

In contrast, pricing with full costing presumes a given volume level. When the volume changes, the unit cost used at the original planned volume may mislead managers. Managers sometimes erroneously assume that they can compute the change in total costs by multiplying any change in volume by the full unit cost.

The incorrect analysis in Exhibit 5-11 shows how using the $19 full cost per unit (based on a volume of 1,000,000 units from Exhibit 5-10) to predict effects of volume changes on operating income can mislead managers. Suppose a manager uses the $19 figure to predict an operating income of $900,000 if the company sells 900,000 instead of 1,000,000 units. If actual operating income is $310,000 instead, as the correct analysis predicts, that manager may be stunned—and possibly looking for a new job. Notice the only volume where the incorrect analysis is actually correct is at the 1 million unit volume level, which is also the only volume where the $19 full cost per unit is valid.

The contribution approach also offers insight into the short-run versus long-run effects of cutting prices on special orders. For example, recall the 100,000 unit special order at a lower than normal selling price ($26 versus $40) for Cordell Company displayed in Exhibit 5-6 (page 185). As you saw earlier, the contribution approach generated the most relevant information, showing that accepting this special order yielded a short-run advantage of $200,000.

However, the manager should also consider long-run effects. Will acceptance of the offer undermine the long-run price structure? In other words, is the short-run advantage of $200,000 more than

	Correct Analysis			Incorrect Analysis		
Volume in units	900,000	1,000,000	1,100,000	900,000	1,000,000	1,100,000
Sales at $20.00	$18,000,000	$20,000,000	$22,000,000	$18,000,000	$20,000,000	$22,000,000
Unit variable costs at $13.10*	11,790,000	13,100,000	14,410,000			
Contribution margin	6,210,000	6,900,000	7,590,000			
Fixed costs†	5,900,000	5,900,000	5,900,000			
Full costs at $19.00*				17,100,000	19,000,000	20,900,000
Operating income	$ 310,000	$ 1,000,000	$ 1,690,000	$ 900,000	$ 1,000,000	$ 1,100,000

*From Exhibit 5-10.

†Fixed manufacturing costs	$3,000,000
Fixed selling and administrative costs	2,900,000
Total fixed costs	$5,900,000

Exhibit 5-11
Analyses of Effects of Changes in Volume on Operating Income

offset by highly probable long-run financial disadvantages? The manager may think so and, thus, reject the offer. But—and this is important—by doing so the manager is, in effect, forgoing $200,000 now to protect certain long-run market advantages. Generally, the manager can assess problems of this sort by asking whether the probability of long-run benefits is worth an "investment" equal to the forgone contribution margin ($200,000, in this case). Under full-cost approaches, the manager must ordinarily conduct a special study to find the immediate effects. Under the contribution approach, the manager has a system that will routinely provide such information.

Advantages of Absorption-Cost Approaches in Cost-Plus Pricing

Frequently, companies do not employ a contribution approach because they fear that managers will indiscriminately substitute variable costs for full costs and will, therefore, lead to suicidal price cutting. This problem should not arise if managers use the data wisely. However, if top managers perceive a pronounced danger of underpricing when they reveal variable-cost data, they may justifiably prefer an absorption-cost approach (either total manufacturing costs or full costs) for guiding pricing decisions.

Actually, absorption costs are far more widely used in practice than is the contribution approach. Why? In addition to the reasons we have already mentioned, managers have cited the following:

1. In the long run, a firm must recover all costs to stay in business. Sooner or later, fixed costs do indeed fluctuate as volume changes. Therefore, it is prudent to assume that all costs are variable (even if some are fixed in the short run).
2. Computing prices based on absorption cost may indicate what competitors might charge, especially if they have approximately the same level of efficiency as you and also aim to recover all costs in the long run.
3. Absorption-cost formula pricing meets the cost-benefit test. It is too expensive to conduct individual cost-volume tests for the many products (sometimes thousands) that a company offers.
4. There is much uncertainty about the shape of the demand curves and the correct price-output decisions. Absorption-cost pricing copes with this uncertainty by not encouraging managers to take too much marginal business.
5. Absorption-cost pricing tends to promote price stability. Managers prefer price stability, primarily because it makes planning more dependable.
6. Absorption-cost pricing provides the most defensible basis for justifying prices to all interested parties, including government antitrust investigators.
7. Absorption-cost pricing provides convenient reference points to simplify hundreds or thousands of pricing decisions.

Using Multiple Approaches

To say that either a contribution approach or an absorption-cost approach provides the "best" guide to pricing decisions is a dangerous oversimplification of one of the most perplexing issues in business. Lack of understanding and judgment can lead to unprofitable pricing regardless of the kind of cost data available or cost accounting system used.

Basically, no single method of pricing is always best. Many companies use both full-cost and variable-cost information in pricing decisions. Modern accounting systems, such as ERP systems, often identify variable and fixed costs, producing both full-cost and variable-cost information. This allows assessment of both short-run and long-run effects. In contrast, most older systems focus on absorption-cost and do not organize their data collection to distinguish between variable and fixed costs. When using such older systems, managers must use special studies or educated guesses to designate costs as variable or fixed.

Managers are especially reluctant to focus on variable costs and ignore allocated fixed costs when their performance evaluations, and possibly their bonuses, are based on income shown in published financial statements. Why? Because companies base such statements on full costing, and thus allocations of fixed costs affect reported income.

Formats for Pricing

Exhibit 5-10 showed how to compute alternative general markup percentages that would produce the same selling prices if used day after day. In practice, the format and arithmetic of quote sheets, job proposals, or similar records vary considerably.

Exhibit 5-12 is from an actual quote sheet used by the manager of a small job shop that bids on welding machinery orders in a highly competitive industry. The approach in Exhibit 5-12 is a tool for informed pricing decisions. Notice that the maximum price is not a matter of cost at all. It is what you think you can obtain. The minimum price is the total variable cost.

The manager will rarely bid the minimum price. Businesses do need to make a profit. Still, the manager wants to know the effect of a job on the company's total variable costs. Occasionally, a company will bid near or even below that minimum price to establish a presence in new markets or with a new customer, especially when cost reductions can be achieved in the future or when the new product is tied to other products that generate profits for the firm, as in the Business First box on page 197 regarding **Microsoft**'s Xbox.

Note that Exhibit 5-12 classifies costs specifically for the pricing task. More than one person may make pricing decisions in a particular company. The accountant's responsibility is to prepare an understandable format that requires a minimum of computations. Exhibit 5-12 combines direct labor and variable manufacturing overhead. It lumps together all fixed costs, whether manufacturing, selling, or administrative, and applies them to the job using a single fixed-overhead rate per direct labor hour. If the company wants more accuracy, it could formulate many more detailed cost items and overhead rates. To obtain the desired accuracy, many companies are turning to activity-based costing.

Some managers, particularly in construction and in service industries (such as auto repair), compile separate categories of costs of (1) direct materials, parts, and supplies and (2) direct labor. These managers then use different markup rates for each category. They use these rates to provide enough revenue to cover both indirect and unallocated costs and operating profit. For example, an automobile repair shop might have the following format for each job:

	Billed to Customers
Auto parts ($200 cost plus 40% markup)	$280
Direct labor (Cost is $20 per hour. Bill at 300% to recover indirect and unallocated costs and provide for operating profit. Billing rate is $20 × 300% = $60 per hour. Total billed for 10 hours is $60 × 10 = $600.)	600
Total billed to customer	$880

Another example is an Italian printing company in Milan that wants to price its jobs so that each one generates a margin of 28% of revenues—14% to cover selling and administrative expenses and 14% for profit. To achieve this margin, the manager uses a pricing formula of 140% times predicted materials cost plus €25 per hour of production time. The latter covers labor and overhead costs of €18 per hour. For a product with €400 of materials cost and 30 hours of production time, the price would be €1,310:

	Cost	Price	Margin
Materials	€400	€ 560	€160
Labor and overhead	540	750	210
Total	€940	€1,310	€370

The profit of €370 is approximately 40% of the cost of €940 and 28% of the price of €1,310.

Exhibit 5-12
Quote Sheet for Pricing

Direct materials, at cost	$25,000
Direct labor and variable manufacturing overhead, 600 direct labor hours × $30 per hour	18,000
Sales commission (varies with job)	2,000
Total variable costs—minimum price*	45,000
Add fixed costs allocated to job, 600 direct labor hours × $20 per hour	12,000
Total costs	57,000
Add desired markup	30,000
Selling price—maximum price that you think you can obtain*	$87,000

*This sheet shows two prices, maximum and minimum. Any amount you can get above the minimum price provides contribution margin.

Business First

Xbox Pricing

Despite all the hype surrounding the Xbox 360 video game console in May of 2005, **Microsoft** didn't initially make any money on the machine itself. A tear-down analysis by market researcher **iSuppli** of the high-end Xbox 360 found that the materials (e.g., hard drive, computer chip, cables, etc.) cost Microsoft $525 before assembly. The console initially sold at retail for $399, for a loss of $126 per unit. iSuppli analyst Chris Crotty said efficiency gains would shave $50 off chip costs, which, with other reductions over time, would get Microsoft closer to breakeven. Microsoft expected that, including sales of its own game software, the Xbox line would start out "gross margin neutral"—breakeven—and would eventually turn a profit.

Microsoft continued this low-price strategy by reducing the price of its Xbox 360 Arcade system to less than $200 in 2008. As a result, Asian shipments of the Xbox in October 2008 grew by 53% compared to the prior month. Microsoft officials claim "...what is really driving our growth momentum right now is how we are broadening our consumer base to include not only hardcore gamers but also individuals who would have previously not thought about buying a game console." Microsoft also commented that "... current shipment volumes had reached such high levels that the company could afford to depend on volume to rake in a profit despite the lower prices." This pricing strategy is also sure to boost company profits from related software-game sales for the Xbox, which is consistent with its fundamental claim that "Microsoft is a software company by heart, and we will continue to work with our partners and by ourselves to develop new software for the market."

Sources: Arik Kesseldahl, "For Every Xbox, A Big Fat Loss," *Business Week*, December 5, 2005; Reuters, "Microsoft Eyes '09 Market-Beating Xbox Sales," December 17, 2008.

You can see there are numerous ways to compute selling prices. However, some general words of caution are appropriate here. Managers are better able to understand their options and the effects of their decisions on profits if they know their costs. That is, it is more informative to pinpoint costs first, before adding markups, than to have a variety of markups already embedded in the "costs" used as guides for setting selling prices. For example, if materials cost $1,000, a price quotation guide should show them at $1,000, not at, for example, a marked-up $1,400 because that is what the seller hopes to get.

Summary Problem for Your Review

PROBLEM

Custom Graphics is a Chicago printing company that bids on a wide variety of design and printing jobs. The owner of the company, Janet Solomon, prepares the bids for most jobs. Her cost budget for 20X1 follows:

Materials		$ 350,000
Labor		250,000
Overhead		
Variable	$300,000	
Fixed	150,000	450,000
Total production cost of jobs		1,050,000
Selling and administrative expenses[*]		
Variable	$ 75,000	
Fixed	125,000	200,000
Total costs		$1,250,000

[*]These expenses include costs of all value chain functions other than production.

Solomon has a target profit of $250,000 for 20X1.

Compute the average target markup percentage for setting prices as a percentage of the following:

1. Materials plus labor
2. Variable production cost of jobs (assume labor is a variable-cost resource)
3. Total production cost of jobs
4. All variable costs
5. All costs

SOLUTION

The purpose of this problem is to emphasize that many different approaches to pricing might be used that would achieve the same selling price. To achieve $250,000 of profit, the desired revenue for 20X1 is $1,250,000 + $250,000 = $1,500,000. The required markup percentages are as follow:

1. Percent of materials and labor $= \dfrac{(\$1,500,000 - \$600,000)}{\$600,000} = 150\%$

2. Percent of variable production cost of jobs $= \dfrac{(\$1,500,000 - \$900,000)}{\$900,000} = 66.7\%$

3. Percent of total production cost of jobs $= \dfrac{(\$1,500,000 - \$1,050,000)}{\$1,050,000} = 42.9\%$

4. Percent of all variable costs $= \dfrac{(\$1,500,000 - \$975,000)}{\$975,000} = 53.8\%$

5. Percent of all costs $= \dfrac{(\$1,500,000 - \$1,250,000)}{\$1,250,000} = 20\%$

Target Costing

Objective 8

Use target costing to decide whether to add a new product.

The pricing approaches so far have all developed a price based on measures of costs. Another approach to the relationship between costs and prices is to take a product's market price as given and determine the maximum cost the company can spend to make the product and still achieve the desired profitability. We call this **target costing**.

Consider a company that is deciding whether to develop and market a new product. In evaluating the feasibility of the new product, management must predict both the cost to produce the product and the price at which it will sell. The degree to which management actions can affect price and cost determines the most effective approach to use for pricing and cost management purposes. Companies use cost-plus pricing for products where management actions (for example, advertising) can influence the market price. Although cost management is important in this case, there is a strong focus on marketing and the revenue side of the profit equation.

But what if the market conditions are such that management cannot influence prices? If a company is to achieve management's desired profit, it must focus on the product's cost. What management needs is an effective tool to reduce costs without reducing value to the customer. A growing number of companies faced with this situation are adopting target costing. Based on the product's predicted price and the company's desired profit, managers set a desired, or target, cost before creating or even designing the product. Managers must then design the product and manufacturing process so that the product's cost does not exceed its target cost. Why focus on the product design phase? Because the design affects a vast majority of costs. For example, the design of the product and the associated production process largely determines the costs of resources, such as new machinery, materials, parts, and even future refinements. It is not easy to reduce these costs once production begins. So, the emphasis of target costing is on proactive, up-front planning throughout every activity of the new-product development process.

Target Costing and New Product Development

Exhibit 5-13 shows a real company's target costing process for a new product. Based on the existing technology and related cost structure, the new product has three parts, requires direct labor, and has four types of indirect costs. The first step in the target-costing process is to determine the market price. The market sets this price. So why does management have to determine it? Remember that the product is new and has not actually been on the market. So, management has to estimate what the market will pay for the product. There are several tools, such as market focus group studies and surveys, that a firm can use to determine this price. Management also sets a desired gross margin for the new product. The market price less the gross margin is the target cost for the new product. The company determines the existing cost structure for the product by building up costs on an individual component level. This product has two components. Component 1 consists of parts A and B. Component 2 is part C. Both components and the final assembly use direct labor. Finally, the activities necessary to plan and process the product create indirect costs.

Marketing plays a large role in target costing. Market research in the early planning stages guides the whole product development process by supplying information about customer demands and requirements. One of the key characteristics of successful target costing is a strong emphasis on understanding customer demands. Many companies actively seek customer input on the design of product features. Then, they compare the cost of each feature to its value to determine whether to add it to the product. For example, one of Boeing's customers wanted heated floors in its airplanes. However, the cost of the heated floors was too high, and the customer reconsidered.

In the example in Exhibit 5-13, the existing cost is too large to generate the desired profit. Does this mean that the new product is not feasible? Not necessarily. A cross-functional team consisting of engineers, sales personnel, key suppliers, and accountants now must determine if the company can implement cost reductions large enough to meet the target cost. In the example in Exhibit 5-13, the company reduced the cost of parts by changing the design of the product so that it could use part C in place of part B. The company also asked suppliers of parts A and C to

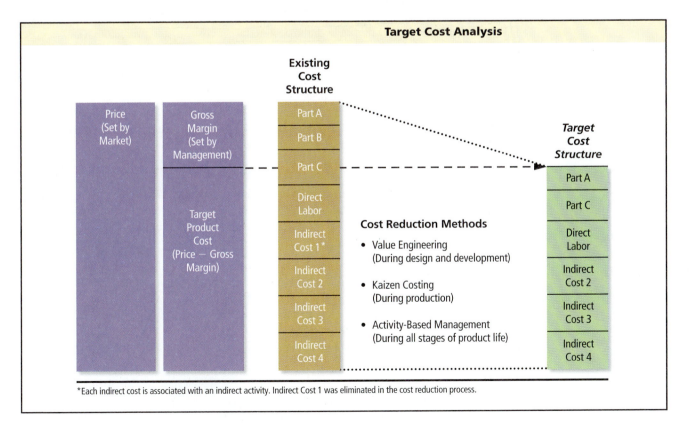

Target Cost Analysis

Existing Cost Structure

Price (Set by Market)

Gross Margin (Set by Management)

Target Product Cost (Price − Gross Margin)

Part A
Part B
Part C
Direct Labor
Indirect Cost 1*
Indirect Cost 2
Indirect Cost 3
Indirect Cost 4

Cost Reduction Methods

- Value Engineering (During design and development)
- Kaizen Costing (During production)
- Activity-Based Management (During all stages of product life)

Target Cost Structure

Part A
Part C
Direct Labor
Indirect Cost 2
Indirect Cost 3
Indirect Cost 4

*Each indirect cost is associated with an indirect activity. Indirect Cost 1 was eliminated in the cost reduction process.

Exhibit 5-13
The Target Costing Process

reduce their costs. Design and process engineers were also able to eliminate the activity that generated the first type of indirect cost. These cost reductions resulted from **value engineering**—a cost-reduction technique, used primarily during the design stage, that uses information about all value-chain functions to satisfy customer needs while reducing costs. In total, the planned cost reductions were adequate to reduce costs to the target.

Not all the reductions in cost have to take place before production begins. For example, **kaizen costing** is the Japanese term for continuous improvement during manufacturing. How do companies apply kaizen costing? They establish kaizen goals each year as part of the planning process. Examples include the continual reduction in setup and processing times due to increased employee familiarity with the procedure. In total, target costing during design and kaizen costing during manufacturing may allow the firm to achieve the target cost over the product's life, even if initial cost predictions look too high.

Might not achieve target cost right away

Underlying these cost-reduction methods is the need for accurate cost information. Activity-based costing often provides this information. Companies can then use activity-based management (ABM) to identify and eliminate non-value-added activities, waste, and their related costs. ABM is applied throughout both the design and manufacturing stages of the product's life. For examples of how accountants are using ABC and ABM in target costing, see the Business First box on page 201.

Illustration of Target Costing

Consider the target-costing system used by **ITT Automotive**—one of the world's largest automotive suppliers. The company designs, develops, and manufactures a broad range of products including brake systems, electric motors, and lamps. Also, the company is the worldwide market leader in antilock braking systems (ABS), producing 20,000 such systems per day.

What pricing approach does ITT Automotive use for the ABS? The pricing process starts when one of ITT's customers, for example **Mercedes-Benz**, sends an invitation to bid. The market for brake systems is so competitive that very little variance exists in the prices companies can ask (bid). ITT then forms a target-costing group and charges it with determining whether the price and costs allow for enough of a profit margin. This group includes engineers, management accountants, and sales personnel. Factors the group considers in determining the feasibility of earning the desired target profit margin include competitor pricing, inflation rates, interest rates, and potential cost reductions during both the design (target costing) and production (kaizen costing) stages of the ABS product life. ITT purchases many of the component parts that make up the ABS. Thus, the target-costing group works closely with suppliers. After making product and process design improvements and receiving commitments from suppliers, the company has the cost information needed to decide the price to bid.

The target-costing system has worked well at ITT Automotive. The company's bid for the ABS resulted in Mercedes-Benz U.S. International selecting ITT Automotive as the developer and supplier of ABS for the automaker's M-Class All-Activity Vehicle.

Target Costing and Cost-Plus Pricing Compared

Successful companies understand the market in which they operate and use the most appropriate pricing approach. To see how target costing and cost-plus pricing can lead to different decisions, suppose that ITT Automotive receives an invitation from Ford to bid on the ABS to be used in a new model car.

Assume the following data apply:

- The specifications contained in Ford's invitation lead to an estimated current manufacturing cost (component parts, direct labor, and manufacturing overhead) of $154.
- ITT Automotive had a desired gross margin rate of 30% on sales, which means that actual cost should make up 70% of the price.
- Highly competitive market conditions exist and have established a sales price of $200 per unit.

If ITT had used cost-plus pricing to bid on the ABS, the bid price would be $154 ÷ .7 = $220. Ford would most likely reject this bid because others are likely to bid $200. ITT Automotive's pricing approach would lead to a lost opportunity.

Suppose that managers at ITT Automotive recognize that market conditions dictate a set price of $200. If ITT used a target-costing system, what would be its pricing decision? The target cost is $140 (that is, $200 × .7) so a required cost reduction of $14 per unit is necessary. The target-costing

Business First

Target Costing, ABC, and the Role of Management Accounting

Many companies use target costing together with an ABC system. Target costing requires a company to first determine what a customer will pay for a product and then work backward to design the product and production process that will generate a desired level of profit. ABC provides data on the costs of the various activities needed to produce the product. Knowing the costs of activities allows product and production process designers to predict the effects of their designs on the product's cost. Target costing essentially takes activity-based costs and uses them for strategic product decisions.

For example, Culp, a North Carolina manufacturer of furniture upholstery fabrics and mattress fabrics, uses target costing and ABC to elevate cost management into one of the most strategically important areas of the firm. Culp found that 80% of its product costs are predetermined at the design stage, but earlier cost control efforts had focused only on the other 20%. By shifting cost management efforts to the design stage and getting accurate costs of the various activities involved in production, cost management at Culp evolved into a process of cutting costs when engineers design a product, not identifying costs that are out of line after the production is complete.

A basic goal of target costing is to reduce costs before they occur. After all, once a company has incurred costs, it cannot change them. Such a strategy is especially important when product life cycles are short. Because most product life cycles are shrinking, use of target costing is expanding. Target costing focuses on reducing costs in the product design and development stages—when costs can really be affected. For example,

target costing heavily influenced Boeing's pricing of specialized design features in its planes, and Procter & Gamble's CEO credits target costing for helping eliminate costs that could cause managers to price products too high for the market to bear. According to Ron Gallaway, CFO of Micrus Semiconductors (now part of Phillips Semiconductors), "The design process is where you can truly leverage [reduce] your costs."

What role does management accounting play in target costing? At Micrus, management accountants are responsible for setting final target costs for all components and processes. One survey reports that 86% of companies using target costing take data directly from their cost systems to estimate product costs during product design. At Eastman Kodak, management accountants are a vital part of the cross-functional team that implements target costing. This team includes design and manufacturing engineers, procurement, and marketing, as well as management accounting. Peter Zampino, director of research at the Consortium for Advanced Manufacturing—International, agrees: "It's like anything else; if finance doesn't bless the numbers, they won't have the credibility throughout the organization."

Sources: Adapted from R. Banham, "Off Target," *CFO*, May 2000; D. Swensen, S. Anasri, J. Bell, and I. Kim, "Best Practices in Target Costing," *Management Accounting Quarterly*, Winter, 2003, pp. 12–17; G. Boer and J. Ettlie, "Target Costing Can Boost Your Bottom Line," *Strategic Finance*, July 1999, pp. 49–52; J. Brausch, "Target Costing for Profit Enhancement," *Management Accounting*, November 1994, pp. 45–49; G. Hoffman, "Future Vision," *Grocery Marketing*, March 1994, p. 6.

group would work with product and process engineers and suppliers to determine if they could reduce the average unit cost by $14 over the product's life. Note that it is not necessary to get costs down to the $140 target cost before production begins. The initial unit cost will likely be higher, for example, $145. Continuous improvement over the product's life will result in the final $5 of cost reductions. If the managers receive commitments for cost reductions, they will decide to bid $200 per unit. Note that if ITT Automotive wins the bid, it must carry through with its focus on cost management throughout the life of the product.

Target costing originated in Japan and is a common practice there. However, a growing number of companies now use it worldwide, including Boeing, Eastman Kodak, Honda of America, Mercedes-Benz, Procter & Gamble, and Caterpillar, as well as ITT Automotive. Even some hospitals use target costing.

Why the increasing popularity of target costing? With increased global competition in many industries, companies are increasingly limited in influencing market prices. Cost management then becomes the key to profitability. Target costing forces managers to focus on costs to achieve the desired profits.

Highlights to Remember

1. **Discriminate between relevant and irrelevant information for making decisions.** To be relevant to a particular decision, a cost (or revenue) must meet two criteria: (1) It must be an expected future cost (or revenue), and (2) it must have an element of difference among the alternative courses of action.

2. **Apply the decision process to make business decisions.** All managers make business decisions based on some decision process. The best processes help decision making by focusing the manager's attention on relevant information.

3. **Construct absorption and contribution-margin income statements, and identify their relevance for decision making.** The major difference between the absorption and contribution approaches for the income statement is that the contribution approach focuses on cost behavior (fixed and variable), whereas the absorption approach reports costs by business functions (manufacturing versus nonmanufacturing). The contribution approach makes it easier for managers to evaluate the effects of changes in volume on income and thus is well suited for shorter-run decision making.

4. **Decide to accept or reject a special order using the contribution-margin technique.** Decisions to accept or reject a special sales order should use the contribution-margin technique and focus on the additional revenues and additional costs of the order.

5. **Explain why pricing decisions depend on the characteristics of the market.** Market demand and supply, the degree of competition, and marginal revenue and marginal cost concepts impact market price and must be incorporated into any pricing decision.

6. **Identify the factors that influence pricing decisions in practice.** Market conditions, the law, customers, competitors, and costs influence pricing decisions. The degree that management actions can affect price and cost determines the most effective approach to use for pricing and cost-management purposes.

7. **Compute a sales price by various approaches, and compare the advantages and disadvantages of these approaches.** Companies use cost-plus pricing for products when management actions can influence the market price. They can add profit markups to a variety of cost bases including variable manufacturing costs, all variable costs, full manufacturing costs, or all costs. The contribution approach to pricing has the advantage of providing detailed cost behavior information that is consistent with cost-volume-profit analysis.

8. **Use target costing to decide whether to add a new product.** When market conditions are such that management cannot significantly influence prices, companies must focus on cost control and reduction. They use target costing primarily for new products, especially during the design phase of the value chain. They deduct a desired target margin from the market-established price to determine the target cost. Cost management then focuses on controlling and reducing costs over the product's life cycle to achieve that target cost. ■

Accounting Vocabulary

absorption approach, p. 182	imperfect competition, p. 190	predatory pricing, p. 192
absorption costing, p. 182	kaizen costing, p. 200	price elasticity, p. 190
contribution approach, p. 182	marginal cost, p. 190	relevant information, p. 179
decision model, p. 180	marginal revenue, p. 190	target costing, p. 198
discriminatory pricing, p. 192	markup, p. 193	value engineering, p. 200
full cost, p. 193	perfect competition, p. 189	

Fundamental Assignment Material

5-A1 Straightforward Income Statements
The Independence Company had the following manufacturing data for the year 2009 (in thousands of dollars):

Beginning and ending inventories	None
Direct material used	$400
Direct labor	330
Supplies	20
Utilities—variable portion	40
Utilities—fixed portion	15
Indirect labor—variable portion	90
Indirect labor—fixed portion	50
Depreciation	200
Property taxes	20
Supervisory salaries	60

Selling expenses were $300,000 (including $80,000 that were variable) and general administrative expenses were $144,000 (including $25,000 that were variable). Sales were $2.2 million.

Direct labor and supplies are regarded as variable costs.

1. Prepare two income statements, one using the contribution approach and one using the absorption approach.
2. Suppose that all variable costs fluctuate directly in proportion to sales and that fixed costs are unaffected over a very wide range of sales. What would operating income have been if sales had been $2.0 million instead of $2.2 million? Which income statement did you use to help obtain your answer? Why?

5-A2 Special Order

Consider the following details of the income statement of the Manteray Pen Company (MPC) for the year ended December 31, 20X0:

Sales	$11,000,000
Less cost of goods sold	6,500,000
Gross margin or gross profit	$ 4,500,000
Less selling and administrative expenses	3,000,000
Operating income	$ 1,500,000

MPC's fixed manufacturing costs were $3.0 million and its fixed selling and administrative costs were $2.2 million. Sales commissions of 3% of sales are included in selling and administrative expenses.

The division had produced and sold 2 million pens. Near the end of the year, **Pizza Hut** offered to buy 150,000 pens on a special order. To fill the order, a special Pizza Hut logo would have to be added to each pen. Pizza Hut intended to use the pens for special promotions in an eastern city during early 20X1.

Even though MPC had some idle plant capacity, the president rejected the Pizza Hut offer of $660,000 for the 150,000 pens. He said,

> The Pizza Hut offer is too low. We'd avoid paying sales commissions, but we'd have to incur an extra cost of $.40 per pen to add the logo. If MPC sells below its regular selling prices, it will begin a chain reaction of competitors' price cutting and of customers wanting special deals. I believe in pricing at no lower than 8% above our full costs of $9,500,000 ÷ 2,000,000 units = $4.75 per unit plus the extra $.40 per pen less the savings in commissions.

1. Using the contribution-margin technique, prepare an analysis similar to that in Exhibit 5-6 on page 185. Use four columns: without the special order, the effect of the special order (one column total and one column per unit), and totals with the special order.
2. By what percentage would operating income increase or decrease if the order had been accepted? Do you agree with the president's decision? Why?

5-A3 Formulas for Pricing

Randy Azarski, a building contractor, builds houses in tracts, often building as many as 20 homes simultaneously. Azarski has budgeted costs for an expected number of houses in 20X0 as follows:

Direct materials	$3,500,000
Direct labor	1,000,000
Job construction overhead	1,500,000
Cost of jobs	$6,000,000
Selling and administrative costs	1,500,000
Total costs	$7,500,000

The job construction overhead includes approximately $800,000 of fixed costs, such as the salaries of supervisors and depreciation on equipment. The selling and administrative costs include $500,000 of variable costs, such as sales commissions and bonuses that depend fundamentally on overall profitability.

Azarski wants an operating income of $1.5 million for 20X0.

Compute the average target markup percentage for setting prices as a percentage of the following:

1. Direct materials plus direct labor
2. The full "cost of jobs"

3. The variable "cost of jobs"
4. The full "cost of jobs" plus selling and administrative costs
5. The variable "cost of jobs" plus variable selling and administrative costs

5-A4 Target Costing

Lowest Cost Corporation uses target costing to aid in the final decision to release new products to production. A new product is being evaluated. Market research has surveyed the potential market for this product and believes that its unique features will generate a total demand over the product's life of 70,000 units at an average price of $360. The target costing team has members from market research, design, accounting, and production engineering departments. The team has worked closely with key customers and suppliers. A value analysis of the product has determined that the total cost for the various value-chain functions using the existing process technology are as follows:

Value-Chain Function	Total Cost over Product Life
Research and development	$ 2,300,000
Design	750,000
Manufacturing (70% outsourced to suppliers)	8,000,000
Marketing	1,800,000
Distribution	2,200,000
Customer service	950,000
Total cost over product life	$16,000,000

Management has a target contribution to profit percentage of 40% of sales. This contribution provides sufficient funds to cover corporate support costs, taxes, and a reasonable profit.

1. Should the new product be released to production? Explain.
2. Approximately 70% of manufacturing costs for this product consists of materials and parts that are purchased from suppliers. Key suppliers on the target-costing team have suggested process improvements that will reduce supplier cost by 20%. Should the new product be released to production? Explain.
3. New process technology can be purchased at a cost of $220,000 that will reduce non-outsourced manufacturing costs by 25%. Assuming the supplier's process improvements and new process technology are implemented, should the new product be released to production? Explain.

5-B1 Contribution and Absorption Income Statements

The following information is taken from the records of the Kingland Manufacturing Company for the year ending December 31, 2009. There were no beginning or ending inventories.

Sales	$13,000,000	Long-term rent, factory	$ 100,000
Sales commissions	500,000		
Advertising	400,000	Factory superintendent's salary	30,000
Shipping expenses	300,000	Factory supervisors' salaries	100,000
		Direct materials used	4,000,000
Administrative executive salaries	100,000	Direct labor	2,000,000
		Cutting bits used	60,000
Administrative clerical salaries (variable)	400,000	Factory methods research	40,000
		Abrasives for machining	100,000
Fire insurance on factory equipment	2,000	Indirect labor	800,000
Property taxes on factory equipment	30,000	Depreciation on factory equipment	400,000

1. Prepare a contribution income statement and an absorption income statement. If you are in doubt about any cost behavior pattern, decide on the basis of whether the total cost in question will fluctuate substantially over a wide range of volume. Prepare a separate supporting schedule of indirect manufacturing costs subdivided between variable and fixed costs.
2. Suppose that all variable costs fluctuate directly in proportion to sales, and that fixed costs are unaffected over a wide range of sales. What would operating income have been if sales had been $12 million instead of $13 million? Which income statement did you use to help get your answer? Why?

5-B2 Special Order, Terminology, and Unit Costs

Following is the income statement of Danube Company, a manufacturer of men's blue jeans:

Danube Company Income Statement for the Year Ended December 31, 20X0	Total	Per Unit
Sales	$40,000,000	$20.00
Less: Cost of goods sold	22,000,000	11.00
Gross margin	$18,000,000	$ 9.00
Less selling and administrative expenses	15,000,000	7.50
Operating income	$ 3,000,000	$ 1.50

Danube had manufactured 2 million pairs of jeans, which had been sold to various clothing wholesalers and department stores. At the start of 20X0, the president, Rosie Valenzuela, died unexpectedly. Her son, Ricardo, became the new president. Ricardo had worked for 15 years in the marketing phases of the business. He knew very little about accounting and manufacturing, which were his mother's strengths. Ricardo has several questions, including inquiries regarding the pricing of special orders.

1. To prepare better answers, you decide to recast the income statement in contribution form. Variable manufacturing cost was $18 million. Variable selling and administrative expenses, which were mostly sales commissions, shipping expenses, and advertising allowances paid to customers based on units sold, were $9 million. Prepare the revised income statement.
2. Ricardo asks, "I can't understand financial statements until I know the meaning of various terms. In scanning my mother's assorted notes, I found the following pertaining to both total and unit costs: full manufacturing cost, variable cost, full cost, fully allocated cost, gross margin, and contribution margin. Using our data for 20X0, please give me a list of these costs, their total amounts, and their per-unit amounts."
3. He also says, "Near the end of 20X0, I brought in a special order from **Costco** for 100,000 jeans at $16 each. I said I'd accept a flat $20,000 sales commission instead of the usual 6% of selling price, but my mother refused the order. She usually upheld a relatively rigid pricing policy, saying that it was bad business to accept orders that did not at least generate full manufacturing cost plus 80% of full manufacturing cost.

    That policy bothered me. We had idle capacity. The way I figured, our manufacturing costs would go up by 100,000 × $11 = $1,100,000, but our selling and administrative expenses would go up by only $20,000. That would mean additional operating income of 100,000 × ($16 − $11) minus $20,000, or $500,000 minus $20,000, or $480,000. That's too much money to give up just to maintain a general pricing policy. Was my analysis of the impact on operating income correct? If not, please show me the correct additional operating income."
4. After receiving the explanations offered in number 2 and 3, Ricardo said, "Forget that I had the Costco order. I had an even bigger order from **Lands' End**. It was for 500,000 units and would have filled the plant completely. I told my mother I'd settle for no commission. There would have been no selling and administrative costs whatsoever because Lands' End would pay for the shipping and would not get any advertising allowances.

    Lands' End offered $8.70 per unit. Our fixed manufacturing costs would have been spread over 2.5 million instead of 2 million units. Wouldn't it have been advantageous to accept the offer? Our old fixed manufacturing costs were $2.00 per unit. The added volume would reduce that cost more than our loss on our variable costs per unit.

    Am I correct? What would have been the impact on total operating income if we had accepted the order?"

5-B3 Cost-Plus Pricing and Target Costing

A Fortune 100 company, **Caterpillar** is the world's leading manufacturer of construction and mining equipment, diesel and natural gas engines, and industrial gas turbines. Caterpillar also manufactures custom piston pins for other manufacturers in the same facility used to make pins for its own heavy-duty engines. Piston pins are made with cost effective CNC bar feeders and multispindle barstock machines. This process is a high-output, high-efficiency operation that eliminates the added costs of purchasing special cut-to-length barstock or cutting barstock to specific lengths.

The market research department has indicated that a proposed new piston pin for a manufacturer of truck engines would likely sell for $46. A similar piston pin currently being produced has the following manufacturing costs:

Direct materials	$24.00
Direct labor	10.00
Overhead	16.00
Total	$50.00

Assume that Caterpillar desires a gross margin of 30% of the manufacturing cost.

1. Suppose Caterpillar used cost-plus pricing, setting the price 30% above the manufacturing cost. What price would be charged for the piston pin? Would you produce such a piston pin if you were a manager at Caterpillar? Explain.
2. Caterpillar uses target costing. What price would the company charge for a piston pin? What is the highest acceptable manufacturing cost for which Caterpillar would be willing to produce the piston pin?
3. As a user of target costing, what steps would Caterpillar managers take to try to make production of this product feasible?

Additional Assignment Material

QUESTIONS

5-1 "The distinction between precision and relevance should be kept in mind." Explain.

5-2 Distinguish between the quantitative and qualitative aspects of decisions.

5-3 Describe the accountant's role in decision making.

5-4 "Any future cost is relevant." Do you agree? Explain.

5-5 Why are historical or past data irrelevant to special decisions?

5-6 Describe the role of past or historical costs in the decision process. That is, how do these costs relate to the prediction method and the decision model?

5-7 What is the advantage of the contribution approach as compared with the absorption approach?

5-8 "The primary classifications of costs are by variable and fixed-cost behavior patterns, not by business functions." Name three commonly used terms that describe this type of income statement.

5-9 "There is a commonality of approach to various special decisions." Explain.

5-10 "Fixed costs are not relevant costs." Do you agree? Explain.

5-11 Why are customers one of the factors influencing pricing decisions?

5-12 What is target cost per unit?

5-13 What is value engineering?

5-14 What is kaizen costing?

5-15 "In target costing, prices determine costs rather than vice versa." Explain.

5-16 Many companies that use target costing involve both customers and suppliers in product and process design. Explain why.

5-17 If a target-costing system is used and the existing cost cannot be reduced to the target cost through cost reductions, management should discontinue producing and selling the product. Do you agree? Explain.

5-18 "Basing pricing on only the variable costs of a job results in suicidal underpricing." Do you agree? Why?

5-19 Provide three examples of pricing decisions other than the special order.

5-20 List three popular markup formulas for pricing.

5-21 Describe two long-run effects that may lead to managers' rejecting opportunities to cut prices and obtain increases in short-run profits.

5-22 Give two reasons why full costs are more widely used than variable costs for guiding pricing.

CRITICAL THINKING EXERCISES

5-23 Fixed Costs and the Sales Function
Many sales managers have a good intuitive understanding of costs, but they often are imprecise in how they describe the costs. For example, one manager said the following: "Increasing sales will decrease fixed costs because it spreads them over more units." Do you agree? Explain.

5-24 Income Statements and Sales Managers
Suppose Chee Wong is in charge of selling Nantucket Nectars' Juice Cocktails. What type of income statement, absorption or contribution, would Wong find most useful for his decisions? Why?

5-25 The Economics of the Pricing Decision

Economic theory states that managers should set price equal to marginal cost in perfect competition. Accountants use variable cost to approximate marginal costs. Compare and contrast marginal cost and variable cost, and explain whether using variable costs as an approximation for marginal cost is appropriate for making pricing decisions.

5-26 Pricing Decisions, Ethics, and the Law

Managers should base pricing decisions on both cost and market factors. In addition, they must also consider ethical and legal issues. Describe the influence that ethics and the law have on pricing decisions.

5-27 Target Costing and the Value Chain

According to Keith Hallin, program affordability manager (target costing) for **Boeing**'s MMA Program in Integrated Defense Systems, reaching target costs is a challenge for the company's entire value chain. Explain how managers of the various value-chain functions at Boeing might be involved in the target costing process.

EXERCISES

5-28 Pinpointing Relevant Costs

Today you are planning to see a motion picture, and you can attend either of two theaters. You have only a small budget for entertainment so prices are important. You have attended both theaters recently. One charged $5 for admission; the other charged $7. You habitually buy popcorn in the theater—each theater charges $3. The motion pictures now being shown are equally attractive to you, but you are virtually certain that you will never see the picture that you reject today.

Identify the relevant costs. Explain your answer.

5-29 Information and Decisions

Suppose the historical costs for the manufacture of a calculator by **Radio Shack** were as follows: direct materials, $5.00 per unit; and direct labor, $6.00 per unit. Management is trying to decide whether to replace some materials with different materials. The replacement should cut material costs by 10% per unit. However, direct-labor time will increase by 5% per unit. Moreover, direct-labor rates will be affected by a recent 10% wage increase.

Prepare an exhibit like Exhibit 5-1 (p. 181), showing where and how the data about direct material and direct labor fit in the decision process.

5-30 Identification of Relevant Costs

Paul and Paula Petroceli were trying to decide whether to go to the symphony or to the baseball game. They already have two nonrefundable tickets to "Pops Night at the Symphony" that cost $40 each. This is the only concert of the season they considered attending because it is the only one with the type of music they enjoy. The baseball game is the last one of the season, and it will decide the league championship. They can purchase tickets to the game for $20 each.

The Petrocelis will drive 50 miles round-trip to either event. Variable costs for operating their automobile are $.18 per mile, and fixed costs average $.13 per mile for the 15,000 miles they drive annually. Parking at the symphony is free, but it costs $6 at the baseball game.

To attend either event, Paul and Paula will hire a babysitter at $7 per hour. They expect to be gone 5 hours to attend the baseball game but only 4 hours to attend the symphony.

Compare the cost of attending the baseball game with the cost of attending the symphony. Focus on relevant costs. Compute the difference in cost, and indicate which alternative is more costly to the Petrocelis.

5-31 Straightforward Absorption Statement

The Pierce Company had the following data (in thousands) for a given period:

Sales	$800
Direct materials	200
Direct labor	200
Indirect manufacturing costs	170
Selling and administrative expenses	150

There were no beginning or ending inventories. Compute the (1) manufacturing cost of goods sold, (2) gross profit, (3) operating income, and (4) conversion cost (total manufacturing cost less materials cost).

5-32 Straightforward Contribution Income Statement

Yoko, Ltd., had the following data (in millions of yen) for a given period:

Sales	¥950
Direct materials	290
Direct labor	160
Variable factory overhead	60
Variable selling and administrative expenses	100
Fixed factory overhead	120
Fixed selling and administrative expenses	45

There were no beginning or ending inventories. Compute the (a) variable manufacturing cost of goods sold, (b) contribution margin, and (c) operating income.

5-33 Straightforward Absorption and Contribution Statement

Anzola Company had the following data (in millions) for a recent period. Fill in the blanks. There were no beginning or ending inventories.

a.	Sales	$920
b.	Direct materials used	350
c.	Direct labor	210
	Indirect manufacturing costs:	
d.	Variable	100
e.	Fixed	50
f.	Variable manufacturing cost of goods sold	—
g.	Manufacturing cost of goods sold	—
	Selling and administrative expenses:	
h.	Variable	90
i.	Fixed	80
j.	Gross profit	—
k.	Contribution margin	—

5-34 Absorption Statement

Stein Jewelry had the following data (in thousands of South African rands, ZAR) for a given period. Assume there are no inventories. Fill in the blanks.

Sales	ZAR ____
Direct materials	370
Direct labor	____
Indirect manufacturing	____
Manufacturing cost of goods sold	780
Gross margin	120
Selling and administrative expenses	____
Operating income	20
Prime cost (direct materials + direct labor)	600

5-35 Contribution Income Statement

Jackson Company had the following data (in thousands) for a given period. Assume there are no inventories.

Direct labor	$170
Direct materials	150
Variable indirect manufacturing	110
Contribution margin	200
Fixed selling and administrative expenses	100
Operating income	10
Sales	890

Compute the (a) variable manufacturing cost of goods sold, (b) variable selling and administrative expenses, and (c) fixed indirect manufacturing costs.

5-36 Special-Order Decision

Belltown Athletic Supply (BAS) makes game jerseys for athletic teams. The F. C. Kitsap soccer club has offered to buy 100 jerseys for the teams in its league for $15 per jersey. The team price for such jerseys normally is $18, an 80% markup over BAS's purchase price of $10 per jersey. BAS adds a name and number to each jersey at a variable cost of $2 per jersey. The annual fixed cost of equipment used in the printing process is $6,000, and other fixed costs allocated to jerseys are $2,000. BAS makes about 2,000 jerseys per year, so the fixed cost is $4 per jersey. The equipment is used only for printing jerseys and stands idle 75% of the usable time.

The manager of BAS turned down the offer, saying, "If we sell at $15 and our cost is $16, we lose money on each jersey we sell. We would like to help your league, but we can't afford to lose money on the sale."

1. Compute the amount by which the operating income of BAS would change if it accepted F. C. Kitsap's offer.
2. Suppose you were the manager of BAS. Would you accept the offer? In addition to considering the quantitative impact computed in requirement 1, list two qualitative considerations that would influence your decision—one qualitative factor supporting acceptance of the offer and one supporting rejection.

5-37 Unit Costs and Total Costs

You are a CPA who belongs to a downtown business club. Annual dues are $150. You use the club solely for lunches, which cost $9 each. You have not used the club much in recent years, and you are wondering whether to continue your membership.

1. You are confronted with a variable-cost plus a fixed-cost behavior pattern. Plot each on a graph, where the vertical axis is total cost and the horizontal axis is annual volume in number of lunches. Also plot a third graph that combines the previous two graphs.
2. What is the cost per lunch if you pay for your own lunch once a year? Twelve times a year? Two hundred times a year?
3. Suppose the average price of lunches elsewhere is $10. (a) How many lunches must you have at the luncheon club so that the total costs of the lunches would be the same, regardless of where you ate for that number of lunches? (b) Suppose you ate 200 lunches a year at the club. How much would you save in relation to the total costs of eating elsewhere?

5-38 Advertising Expenditures and Nonprofit Organizations

Many colleges and universities have been extensively advertising their services. For example, a university in Philadelphia used a biplane to pull a sign promoting its evening program, and one in Mississippi designed bumper stickers and slogans as well as innovative programs.

Suppose Wilton College charges a comprehensive annual fee of $14,500 for tuition, room, and board, and it has capacity for 2,500 students. The admissions department predicts enrollment of 2,000 students for 20X1. Costs per student for the 20X1 academic year are as follows:

	Variable	Fixed	Total
Educational programs	$4,000	$4,200	$ 8,200
Room	1,300	2,200	3,500
Board	2,600	600	3,200
	$7,900	$7,000*	$14,900

*Based on 2,000–2,500 students for the year.

The assistant director of admissions has proposed a 2-month advertising campaign using radio and television advertisements, together with an extensive direct mailing of brochures.

1. Suppose the advertising campaign will cost $1.65 million. What is the minimum number of additional students the campaign must attract to make the campaign break even?
2. Suppose the admissions department predicts that the campaign will attract 350 additional students. What is the most Wilton should pay for the campaign and still break even?
3. Suppose a 3-month (instead of 2-month) campaign will attract 450 instead of 350 additional students. What is the most Wilton should pay for the 1-month extension of the campaign and still break even?

5-39 Variety of Cost Terms

Consider the following data:

Variable selling and administrative costs per unit	$ 4.00
Total fixed selling and administrative costs	$2,900,000
Total fixed manufacturing costs	$3,000,000
Variable manufacturing costs per unit	$ 10.00
Units produced and sold	500,000

1. Compute the following per unit of product: (a) total variable costs, (b) full manufacturing cost, (c) full cost.

5-40 Acceptance of Low Bid

The Velasquez Company, a maker of a variety of metal and plastic products, is in the midst of a business downturn and is saddled with many idle facilities. Columbia Health Care has approached Velasquez to produce 300,000 nonslide serving trays. Columbia will pay $1.50 each.

Velasquez predicts that its variable costs will be $1.60 each. Its fixed costs, which had been averaging $1 per unit on a variety of other products, will now be spread over twice as much volume. The president commented, "Sure we'll lose $.10 each on the variable costs, but we'll gain $.50 per unit by spreading our fixed costs. Therefore, we should take the offer because it represents an advantage of $.40 per unit."

Suppose the regular business had a current volume of 300,000 units, sales of $600,000, variable costs of $480,000, and fixed costs of $300,000. Do you agree with the president? Why?

5-41 Pricing by Auto Dealer

Many automobile dealers have an operating pattern similar to that of Austin Motors, a dealer in Texas. Each month, Austin initially aims at a unit volume quota that approximates a break-even point. Until the break-even point is reached, Austin has a policy of relatively lofty pricing, whereby the "minimum deal" must contain a sufficiently high markup to ensure a contribution to profit of no less than $400. After the break-even point is attained, Austin tends to quote lower prices for the remainder of the month.

What is your opinion of this policy? As a prospective customer, how would you react to this policy?

5-42 Pricing to Maximize Contribution

Reynolds Company produces and sells picture frames. One particular frame for 8 × 10 photos was an instant success in the market, but recently competitors have come out with comparable frames. Reynolds has been charging $12.50 wholesale for the frames, and sales have fallen from 10,000 units last year to 7,000 units this year. The product manager in charge of this frame is considering lowering the price to $10 per frame. He believes sales will rebound to 10,000 units at the lower price, but they will fall to 6,000 units at the $12.50 price. The unit variable cost of producing and selling the frames is $6, and $60,000 of fixed cost is assigned to the frames.

1. Assuming that the only prices under consideration are $10 and $12.50 per frame, which price will lead to the largest profit for Reynolds? Explain why.
2. What subjective considerations might affect your pricing decision?

5-43 Target Selling Prices

Consider the following data from Blackmar Company's budgeted income statement (in thousands of dollars):

Target sales	$90,000
Variable costs	
Manufacturing	30,000
Selling and administrative	6,000
Total variable costs	36,000
Fixed costs	
Manufacturing	8,000
Selling and administrative	6,000
Total fixed costs	14,000
Total of all costs	50,000
Operating income	$40,000

Compute the following markup percentages that would be used for obtaining the same target sales as a percentage of (1) total variable costs, (2) full costs, and (3) variable manufacturing costs.

5-44 Competitive Bids

Griffy, Rodriguez, and Martinez, a CPA firm, is preparing to bid for a consulting job. Although Alicia Martinez will use her judgment about the market in finalizing the bid, she has asked you to prepare a cost analysis to help in the bidding. You have estimated the costs for the consulting job to be as follows:

Materials and supplies, at cost	$ 30,000
Hourly pay for consultants, 2,000 hours at $35 per hour	70,000
Fringe benefits for consultants, 2,000 hours at $12 per hour	24,000
Total variable costs	124,000
Fixed costs allocated to the job	
Based on labor, 2,000 hours at $10 per hour	20,000
Based on materials and supplies, 80% of 30,000	24,000
Total cost	$168,000

Of the $44,000 allocated fixed costs, $35,000 will be incurred even if the job is not undertaken.

Alicia normally bids jobs at the sum of (1) 150% of the estimated materials and supplies cost and (2) $75 per estimated labor hour.

1. Prepare a bid using the normal formula.
2. Prepare a minimum bid equal to the additional costs expected to be incurred to complete the job.
3. Prepare a bid that will cover full costs plus a markup for profit equal to 20% of full cost.

5-45 Target Costing

Quality Corporation believes that there is a market for a portable electronic toothbrush that can be easily carried by business travelers. Quality's market research department has surveyed the features and prices of electronic brushes currently on the market. Based on this research, Quality believes that $70 would be about the right price. At this price, marketing believes that about 80,000 new portable brushes can be sold over the product's life cycle. It will cost about $1,000,000 to design and develop the portable brush. Quality has a target profit of 20% of sales.

Determine the total and unit target cost to manufacture, sell, distribute, and service the portable brushes.

5-46 Target Costing

Best Cost Corporation has an aggressive research and development (R&D) program and uses target costing to aid in the final decision to release new products to production. A new product is being evaluated. Market research has surveyed the potential market for this product and believes that its unique features will generate a total demand of 50,000 units at an average price of $230. Design and production engineering departments have performed a value analysis of the product and have determined that the total cost for the various value-chain functions using the existing process technology are as follows:

Value-Chain Function	Total Cost over Product Life
Research and Development	$ 1,500,000
Design	750,000
Manufacturing	5,000,000
Marketing	800,000
Distribution	1,200,000
Customer Service	750,000
Total Cost over Product Life	$10,000,000

Management has a target profit percentage of 20% of sales. Production engineering indicates that a new process technology can reduce the manufacturing cost by 40%, but it will cost $1,100,000.

1. Assuming the existing process technology is used, should the new product be released to production? Explain.
2. Assuming the new process technology is purchased, should the new product be released to production? Explain.

PROBLEMS

5-47 Pricing, Ethics, and the Law

Great Lakes Pharmaceuticals, Inc. (GLPI), produces both prescription and over-the-counter medications. In January, GLPI introduced a new prescription drug, Capestan, to relieve the pain of arthritis. The company spent more than $50 million over the last 5 years developing the drug, and advertising alone during the first year of introduction will exceed $10 million. Production cost for a bottle of 100 tablets is approximately $12. Sales in the first 3 years are predicted to be 500,000, 750,000, and 1,000,000 bottles, respectively. To achieve these sales, GLPI plans to distribute the medicine through three sources: directly to physicians, through hospital pharmacies, and through retail pharmacies. Initially, the bottles will be given free to physicians to give to patients, hospital pharmacies will pay $25 per bottle, and retail pharmacies will pay $40 per bottle. In the second and third year, the company plans to phase out the free distributions to physicians and move all other customers toward a $50-per-bottle sales price.

Comment on the pricing and promotion policies of GLPI. Pay particular attention to the legal and ethical issues involved.

5-48 Analysis with Contribution Income Statement

The following data have been condensed from LaGrande Corporation's report of 2009 operations (in millions of euros):

	Variable	Fixed	Total
Manufacturing cost of goods sold	€300	€280	€580
Selling and administrative expenses	140	60	200
Sales			900

1. Prepare the 2009 income statement in contribution form, ignoring income taxes.
2. LaGrande's operations have been fairly stable from year to year. In planning for the future, top management is considering several options for changing the annual pattern of operations. You are asked to perform an analysis of their estimated effects. Use your contribution income statement as a framework to compute the estimated operating income (in millions) under each of the following separate and unrelated assumptions:
   a. Assume that a 10% reduction in selling prices would cause a 30% increase in the physical volume of goods manufactured and sold.
   b. Assume that an annual expenditure of €30 million for a special sales promotion campaign would enable the company to increase its physical volume by 10% with no change in selling prices.
   c. Assume that a basic redesign of manufacturing operations would increase annual fixed manufacturing costs by €80 million and decrease variable manufacturing costs by 15% per product unit, but with no effect on physical volume or selling prices.
   d. Assume that a basic redesign of selling and administrative operations would double the annual fixed expenses for selling and administration and increase the variable expenses for selling and administration by 25% per product unit; it would also increase physical volume by 20%. Selling prices would be increased by 5%.
   e. Would you prefer to use the absorption form of income statement for the preceding analyses? Explain.
3. Discuss the desirability of alternatives a–d in number 2. If only one alternative could be selected, which would you choose? Explain.

5-49 Pricing and Contribution-Margin Technique

The Transnational Trucking Company has the following operating results to date for 20X1:

Operating revenues	$50,000,000
Operating costs	40,000,000
Operating income	$10,000,000

A large Boston manufacturer has inquired about whether Transnational would be interested in trucking a large order of its parts to Chicago. Steve Goldmark, operations manager, investigated the situation and estimated that the "fully allocated" costs of servicing the order would be $45,000. Using his general pricing formula, he quoted a price of $50,000. The manufacturer replied, "We'll give you $39,000, take it or leave it. If you do not want our business, we'll truck it ourselves or go elsewhere."

A cost analyst had recently been conducting studies of how Transnational's operating costs tended to behave. She found that $30 million of the $40 million could be characterized as variable costs. Goldmark discussed the matter with her and decided that this order would probably generate cost behavior about the same as Transnational's general operations.

1. Using a contribution-margin technique, prepare an analysis for Transnational.
2. Should Transnational accept the order? Explain.

5-50 Cost Analysis and Pricing

The budget for the Oxford University Printing Company for 20X1 follows:

Sales		£1,100,000
Direct material	£280,000	
Direct labor	320,000	
Overhead	400,000	1,000,000
Net income		£ 100,000

The company typically uses a so-called cost-plus pricing system. Direct-material and direct-labor costs are computed, overhead is added at a rate of 125% of direct labor costs, and 10% of the total cost is added to obtain the selling price.

Edith Smythe, the sales manager, has placed a £22,000 bid on a particularly large order with a cost of £5,600 direct material and £6,400 direct labor. The customer informs her that she can have the business for £18,000, take it or leave it. If Smythe accepts the order, total sales for 20X1 will be £1,118,000.

Smythe refuses the order, saying, "I sell on a cost-plus basis. It is bad policy to accept orders at below cost. I would lose £2,000 on the job."

The company's annual fixed overhead is £160,000.

1. What would operating income have been with the order? Without the order? Show your computations.
2. Give a short description of a contribution-margin technique to pricing that Smythe might follow to achieve a price of £22,000 on the order.

5-51 Pricing of Education

You are the director of continuing education programs for a state university. Courses for executives are especially popular, and you have developed an extensive menu of one-day and two-day courses that are presented in various locations throughout the state. The performance of these courses for the current fiscal year, excluding the final course, which is scheduled for the next Saturday, is as follows:

Tuition revenue	$2,000,000
Costs of courses	800,000
Contribution margin	1,200,000
General administrative expenses	400,000
Operating income	$ 800,000

The costs of the courses include fees for instructors, rentals of classrooms, advertising, and any other items, such as travel, that can be easily and exclusively identified as being caused by a particular course.

The general administrative expenses include your salary, your secretary's compensation, and related expenses, such as a lump-sum payment to the university's central offices as a share of university overhead.

The enrollment for your final course of the year is 30 students, who have paid $200 each. Two days before the course is to begin, a city manager telephones your office. "Do you offer discounts to nonprofit institutions?" he asks. "If so, we'll send 10 managers. But our budget will not justify our spending more than $100 per person." The extra cost of including these 10 managers would entail lunches at $20 each and course materials at $30 each.

1. Prepare a tabulation of the performance for the full year including the final course. Assume that the costs of the final course for the 30 enrollees' instruction, travel, advertising, rental of hotel classroom, lunches, and course materials would be $3,000. Show a tabulation in four columns: before final course, final course with 30 registrants, effect of 10 more registrants, and grand totals.
2. What major considerations would probably influence the pricing policies for these courses? For setting regular university tuition in private universities?

5-52 DVD Sales and Rental Markets

Is it more profitable to sell your product for $50 or $15? This is a difficult question for many movie studio executives. Consider a movie that cost $60 million to produce and required another $40 million to promote. After its theater release, the studio must determine whether to sell DVDs directly to the public at a wholesale price of about $15 per DVD or to sell to video rental store distributors for about $50 per DVD. The distributors will then sell to about 14,000 video rental stores in the United States.

Assume that the variable cost to produce and ship 1 DVD is $3.00.

1. Suppose each video rental store would purchase 10 DVDs of this movie. How many DVDs would need to be sold directly to customers to make direct sales a more profitable option than sales to video store distributors?
2. How does the cost of producing and promoting the movie affect this decision?
3. **Walt Disney Co.** elected to sell *The Lion King* directly to consumers, and it sold 30 million copies at an average price of $15.40 per DVD. How many DVDs would each video rental store have to purchase to provide Disney as much profit as the company received from direct sales? Assume that Disney would receive $50 per DVD from the distributors.

5-53 Use of Passenger Jets

In a recent year **Continental Airlines** filled about 50% of the available seats on its flights, a record about 15% below the national average.

Continental could have eliminated about 4% of its runs and raised its average load considerably. The improved load factor would have reduced profits, however. Give reasons for or against this elimination. What factors should influence an airline's scheduling policies?

When you answer this question, suppose that Continental had a basic package of 3,000 flights per month, with an average of 100 seats available per flight. Also suppose that 52% of the seats were filled at an average ticket price of $200 per flight. Variable costs are about 70% of revenue.

Continental also had a marginal package of 120 flights per month, with an average of 100 seats available per flight. Suppose that only 20% of the seats were filled at an average ticket price of $100 per flight. Variable costs are about 50% of this revenue. Prepare a tabulation of the basic package, marginal package, and total package, showing percentage of seats filled, revenue, variable expenses, and contribution margin.

5-54 Effects of Volume on Operating Income

The Wittred Division of Melbourne Sports Company manufactures boomerangs, which are sold to wholesalers and retailers. The division manager has set a target of 250,000 boomerangs for next month's production and sales has developed an accurate budget for that level of sales. The manager has also prepared an analysis of the effects on operating income of deviations from the target:

Volume in units	200,000	250,000	300,000
Sales at $3.00	$600,000	$750,000	$900,000
Full costs at $2.00	400,000	500,000	600,000
Operating income	$200,000	$250,000	$300,000

The costs have the following characteristics: Variable manufacturing costs are $.80 per boomerang; variable selling costs are $.60 per boomerang; fixed manufacturing costs per month are $125,000; and fixed selling and administrative costs per month are $25,000.

1. Prepare a correct analysis of the changes in volume on operating income. Prepare a tabulated set of income statements at levels of 200,000, 250,000, and 300,000 boomerangs. Also show percentages of operating income in relation to sales.
2. Compare your tabulation with the manager's tabulation. Why is the manager's tabulation incorrect?

5-55 Pricing at the Grand Canyon Railway

Suppose a tour agent approached the general manager of the **Grand Canyon Railway** with a proposal to offer a special guided tour to the agent's clients. The tour would occur 20 times each summer and be part of a larger itinerary that the agent is putting together. The agent presented two options: (a) a special 65-mile tour with the agent's 30 clients as the only passengers on the train, or (b) adding a car to an existing train to accommodate the 30 clients on an already scheduled 65-mile tour.

Under either option, Grand Canyon would hire a tour guide for $200 for the trip. Grand Canyon has extra cars in its switching yard, and it would cost $40 to move a car to the main track and hook it up. The extra fuel cost to pull one extra car is $.20 per mile. To run an engine and a passenger car on the trip would cost $2.20 per mile, and an engineer would be paid $400 for the trip.

Depreciation on passenger cars is $5,000 per year, and depreciation on engines is $20,000 per year. Each passenger car and each engine travels about 50,000 miles a year. They are replaced every 8 years.

The agent offered to pay $32 per passenger for the special tour and $15 per passenger for simply adding an extra car.

1. Which of the two options is more profitable to Grand Canyon? Comment on which costs are irrelevant to this decision.
2. Should Grand Canyon accept the proposal for the option you found best in number 1? Comment on what costs are relevant for this decision but not for the decision in number 1.

5-56 Pricing of Special Order

The Drosselmeier Corporation, located in Munich, makes Christmas nutcrackers and has an annual plant capacity of 2,400 product units. Suppose its predicted operating results (in euros) for the year are as follows:

Production and sales of 2,000 units, total sales	€180,000
Manufacturing costs	
Fixed (total)	70,000
Variable (per unit)	25
Selling and administrative expenses	
Fixed (total)	30,000
Variable (per unit)	10

Compute the following, ignoring income taxes:

1. If the company accepts a special order for 300 units at a selling price of €40 each, how would the total predicted net income for the year be affected, assuming no effect on regular sales at regular prices?
2. Without decreasing its total net income, what is the lowest unit price for which the Drosselmeier Corporation could sell an additional 100 units not subject to any variable selling and administrative expenses, assuming no effect on regular sales at regular prices?
3. List the numbers given in the problem that are irrelevant (not relevant) in solving number 2.
4. Compute the expected annual net income (with no special orders) if plant capacity can be doubled by adding additional facilities at a cost of €500,000. Assume that these facilities have an estimated life of 4 years with no residual scrap value, and that the current unit selling price can be maintained for all sales. Total sales are expected to equal the new total plant capacity each year. No changes are expected in variable costs per unit or in total fixed costs except for depreciation.

5-57 Pricing and Confusing Variable and Fixed Costs

Goldwyn Electronics had a fixed factory overhead budget for 20X0 of $10 million. The company planned to make and sell 2 million units of a particular communications device. All variable manufacturing costs per unit were $10. The budgeted income statement contained the following:

Sales	$40,000,000
Manufacturing cost of goods sold	30,000,000
Gross margin	10,000,000
Deduct selling and administrative expenses	4,000,000
Operating income	$ 6,000,000

For simplicity, assume that the actual variable costs per unit and the total fixed costs were exactly as budgeted.

1. Compute Goldwyn's budgeted fixed factory overhead per unit.
2. Near the end of 20X0, a large computer manufacturer offered to buy 100,000 units for $1.3 million on a one-time special order. The president of Goldwyn stated, "The offer is a bad deal. It's foolish to sell below full manufacturing costs per unit. I realize that this order will have only a modest effect on selling and administrative costs. They will increase by a $20,000 fee paid to our sales agent." Compute the effect on operating income if the offer is accepted.
3. What factors should the president of Goldwyn consider before finally deciding whether to accept the offer?
4. Suppose the original budget for fixed manufacturing costs was $10 million, but budgeted units of product were 1 million. How would your answers to numbers 1 and 2 change? Be specific.

5-58 Demand Analysis

Zimmerman Manufacturing Limited produces and sells one product, a three-foot Canadian flag. During 20X0, the company manufactured and sold 50,000 flags at $26 each. Existing production capacity is 60,000 flags per year.

In formulating the 20X1 budget, management is faced with several decisions concerning product pricing and output. The following information is available:

1. A market survey shows that the sales volume depends on the selling price. For each $1 drop in selling price, sales volume would increase by 10,000 flags.
2. The company's expected cost structure for 20X1 is as follows:
   a. Fixed cost (regardless of production or sales activities), $360,000
   b. Variable costs per flag (including production, selling, and administrative expenses), $15
3. To increase annual capacity from the present 60,000 flags to 90,000 flags, additional investment for plant, building, equipment, and the like of $500,000 would be necessary. The estimated average life of the additional investment would be 10 years, so the fixed costs would increase by an average of $50,000 per year. (Expansion of less than 30,000 additional units of capacity would cost only slightly less than $500,000.)

Indicate, with reasons, what the level of production and the selling price should be for the coming year. Also indicate whether the company should approve the plant expansion. Show your calculations. Ignore income tax considerations and the time value of money.

5-59 Target Costing

Memphis Electrical makes small electric motors for a variety of home appliances. Memphis sells the motors to appliance makers, who assemble and sell the appliances to retail outlets. Although Memphis makes dozens of different motors, it does not currently make one to be used in garage-door openers. The company's market research department has discovered a market for such a motor.

The market research department has indicated that a motor for garage-door openers would likely sell for $26. A similar motor currently being produced has the following manufacturing costs:

Direct materials	$13.00
Direct labor	6.00
Overhead	8.00
Total	$27.00

Memphis desires a gross margin of 20% of the manufacturing cost.

1. Suppose Memphis used cost-plus pricing, setting the price 20% above the manufacturing cost. What price would be charged for the motor? Would you produce such a motor if you were a manager at Memphis? Explain.
2. Suppose Memphis uses target costing. What price would the company charge for a garage-door-opener motor? What is the highest acceptable manufacturing cost for which Memphis would be willing to produce the motor?
3. As a user of target costing, what steps would Memphis managers take to try to make production of this product feasible?

5-60 Target Costing and ABM

Cleveland Plastics makes plastic parts for other manufacturing companies. Cleveland has an ABC system for its production, marketing, and customer service functions. The company uses target costing as a strategic decision-making tool. One of Cleveland's product lines—consumer products—has over 100 individual products with life cycles of less than 3 years. This means that about 30–40 products are discontinued and replaced with new products each year. Cleveland's top management has established the following tool to be used by the target-cost team for evaluating proposed new products:

Required Cost Reduction (RCR) as a Percent of Market Price	Action
RCR ≤ 0%	Release to production
0 < RCR ≤ 5%	Release to production and set kaizen improvement plan
5% < RCR ≤ 25%	Product and process redesign
RCR > 25%	Abandon subject to top management review and approval

The following operational and ABC data are for four proposed new products:

Value-Chain Function	Cost per Driver Unit	Estimated Number of Driver Units over Product Life Cycle			
		C-200472	C-200473	C-200474	C-200475
Production					
Direct material	$1.60 per pound	2,000	1,000	4,000	800
Setup/Maintenance	$1,015 per setup	10	4	12	5
Processing hour	$370 per machine	20	12	32	12
Marketing	$860 per order	30	10	50	16
Customer service	$162 per sales call	55	35	20	28
Estimated life-cycle demand		2,000 Units	1,400	4,000	600
Estimated market price per unit		$39	28	35	50

Top management has set a desired contribution to cover unallocated value-chain costs, taxes, and profit of 40% of the estimated market price.

Prepare a schedule that shows for each proposed new product, the target cost, estimated cost using existing technology, and any required cost reduction as a percent of the estimated market price. Use the evaluation tool to make a decision regarding the four proposed new products.

5-61 Target Costing Over Product Life Cycle

Southeast Equipment makes a variety of motor-driven products for homes and small businesses. The market research department recently identified power lawn mowers as a potentially lucrative market. As a first entry into this market, Southeast is considering a riding lawn mower that is smaller and less expensive than those of most of the competition. Market research indicates that such a lawn mower would sell for about $995 at retail and $800 wholesale. At that price, Southeast expects life-cycle sales as follows:

Year	Sales
20X1	1,000
20X2	5,000
20X3	10,000
20X4	10,000
20X5	8,000
20X6	6,000
20X7	4,000

The production department has estimated that the variable cost of production will be $475 per lawn mower, and annual fixed costs will be $900,000 per year for each of the 7 years. Variable selling costs will be $25 per lawn mower and fixed selling costs will be $50,000 per year. In addition, the product development department estimates that $5 million of development costs will be necessary to design the lawn mower and the production process for it.

1. Compute the expected profit over the entire product life cycle of the proposed riding lawn mower.
2. Suppose Southeast expects pretax profits equal to 10% of sales on new products. Would the company undertake production and selling of the riding lawn mower?
3. Southeast Equipment uses a target costing approach to new products. What steps would management take to try to make a profitable product of the riding lawn mower?

CASES

5-62 Use of Capacity

St. Tropez S.A. manufactures several different styles of jewelry cases in southern France. Management estimates that during the second quarter of 20X1 the company will be operating at 80% of normal capacity. Because the company desires a higher utilization of plant capacity, it will consider a special order.

St. Tropez has received special-order inquiries from two companies. The first is from Lyon, which would like to market a jewelry case similar to one of St. Tropez's cases. The Lyon jewelry case would be marketed under Lyon's own label. Lyon has offered St. Tropez €67.5 per jewelry case for

20,000 cases to be shipped by July 1, 20X1. The cost data for the St. Tropez jewelry case, which would be similar to the specifications of the Lyon special order, are as follows:

Regular selling price per unit	€100
Costs per unit:	
Raw materials	€ 35
Direct labor, .5 hour at €60	30
Overhead, .25 machine hour at €40	10
Total cost per unit	€ 75

According to the specifications provided by Lyon, the special-order case requires less expensive raw materials, which will cost only €32.5 per case. Management has estimated that the remaining costs, labor time, and machine time will be the same as those for the St. Tropez jewelry case.

The second special order was submitted by the Avignon Co., for 7,500 jewelry cases at €85 per case. These cases would be marketed under the Avignon label and would have to be shipped by July 1, 20X1. The Avignon jewelry case is different from any jewelry case in the St. Tropez line. Its estimated per-unit costs are as follows:

Raw materials	€43
Direct labor, .5 hour at €60	30
Overhead, .5 machine hour at €40	20
Total costs	€93

In addition, St. Tropez will incur €15,000 in additional setup costs and will have to purchase a €20,000 special device to manufacture these cases; this device will be discarded once the special order is completed.

The St. Tropez manufacturing capabilities are limited by the total machine hours available. The plant capacity under normal operations is 90,000 machine hours per year, or 7,500 machine hours per month. The budgeted fixed overhead for 20X1 amounts to €2.16 million, or €24 per hour. All manufacturing overhead costs are applied to production on the basis of machine hours at €40 per hour.

St. Tropez will have the entire second quarter to work on the special orders. Management does not expect any repeat sales to be generated from either special order. Company practice precludes St. Tropez from subcontracting any portion of an order when special orders are not expected to generate repeat sales.

Should St. Tropez accept either special order? Justify your answer and show your calculations. (Hint: Distinguish between variable and fixed overhead.)

NIKE 10-K PROBLEM

5-63 Special Order

As discussed in Item 1 of **Nike**'s 10-K, one of the companies it owns is **Cole Haan**. Cole Haan makes a variety of fashion footwear, such as dress shoes. One of these products is a men's loafer. This shoe is in strong demand. Suppose sales on this loafer during the present year, 20X0, are expected to hit the 1,000,000 mark. Full plant capacity is 1,150,000 units, but the 1,000,000 unit mark is considered normal capacity. The following unit price and cost breakdown is applicable in 20X0:

		Per unit
Sales price		$145.00
Less: Manufacturing costs		
Materials		$ 49.00
Direct labor		22.00
Overhead:	Variable	14.00
	Fixed	16.00
Total manufacturing costs		$101.00
Gross margin		$ 44.00
Less selling and administrative expenses		
Selling:	Variable	$ 5.50
	Fixed	9.00
Administrative, fixed		12.00
Packaging, variable*		3.50
Total selling and administrative expenses		$ 30.00
Net profit before taxes		$ 14.00

*Two types of packaging are available: deluxe, $3.50 per unit; and standard, $2.00 per unit.

During March, the company received two special-order requests from **Nordstrom** and **Macy's**. These orders are not part of the budgeted 1,000,000 unit sales for 20X0, but there is sufficient capacity for possibly one order to be accepted. Orders received and their terms are as follows:

Order from Nordstrom: 75,000 loafers at $136.00 per unit, deluxe packaging

Order from Macy's: 90,000 loafers at $130.00 per unit, standard packaging
    Since these orders were made directly to Cole Haan, no variable selling costs will be incurred.

1. Analyze the profitability of each of these two special orders. Which special order should be accepted?
2. What other aspects need to be considered in addition to profitability?

EXCEL APPLICATION EXERCISE

5-64 Determining Whether to Accept a Special Order

Goal: Create an Excel spreadsheet to determine which special order to accept. Use the results to answer questions about your findings.

Scenario: The Ibunez Tool Company has been offered two different special orders: (1) the production of 40,000 plain circular saws or (2) the production of 20,000 professional circular saws. The company has enough excess capacity to accept either offer, but not both. The plain saw sells for $65 and has a variable cost of $50. The professional saw sells for $100 and has a variable cost of $75.

When you have completed your spreadsheet, answer the following questions:
1. What is the contribution margin and contribution-margin ratio per unit for the plain circular saw? For the professional circular saw?
2. What is the total contribution margin for the plain circular saw if the company fills this special order? For the professional circular saw special order?
3. What general conclusion can you draw from the data illustrated by the Excel problem?

Step-by-Step:
1. Open a new Excel spreadsheet.
2. In column A, create a bold-faced heading that contains the following:
    Row 1: Chapter 5 Decision Guideline
    Row 2: Ibunez Tool Company
    Row 3: Special Order Analysis
    Row 4: Today's Date
3. Merge and center the four heading rows across columns A–E.

4. Adjust column widths as follows:
   Column A: 17
   Column B: 15
   Column C: 10
   Column D: 15
   Column E: 10
5. In row 7, create the following bold-faced column heading:
   Column B: Products
6. Merge and center the Products heading across columns B–E.
7. In row 8, create the following bold-faced column headings:
   Column B: Plain Circular Saw
   Column D: Professional Circular Saw
8. Merge and center the Plain Circular Saw heading across columns B–C.
9. Merge and center the Professional Circular Saw heading across columns D–E.
10. In column A, create the following row headings:
    Row 9: Selling price
    Row 10: Variable cost
    Row 11: Contribution margin
    Skip four rows.
    Row 16: Special order units:
    Skip one row.
    Row 18: Total contribution margin:
11. Merge the headings in rows 16–18 across columns A and B, then right-justify.
    Alignment tab: Horizontal: Right
12. Enter the selling price and variable cost for plain and professional saws in columns B and D, respectively.
13. In row 11, create formulas to calculate the contribution margin for each type of saw in columns B and D, respectively.
14. In row 11, create formulas to calculate the contribution-margin percent for each type of saw in columns C and E, respectively.
15. In row 16, enter the number of units requested in the special order for each type of saw in columns C and E, respectively.
16. In row 18, create formulas to calculate the total contribution margin for each type of saw in columns C and E, respectively.
17. Format all amounts in columns B and D as follows:

Number tab:	Category:	Accounting ($ sign is left-justified)
	Decimal places:	2
	Symbol:	$

18. Modify the format of the variable cost amounts to exclude the dollar ($) sign:

Number tab:	Symbol:	None

19. Modify the format of the contribution-margin amounts to display a top border, using the default Line Style:

Border tab:	Icon:	Top Border

20. Format the contribution-margin percent in columns C and E as follows:

Number tab:	Category:	Percentage
	Decimal places:	0
Alignment tab:	Horizontal:	Center

21. Format the amount in row 16 as follows:

Number tab:	Category:	Number
	Decimal places:	0
	Use 1000 Separator (,):	Checked
Alignment tab:	Horizontal:	Center

22. Format total contribution-margin amounts as follows:

Number tab:	Category:	Accounting
	Decimal places:	0
	Symbol:	$

23. Save your work to disk, and print a copy for your files.

COLLABORATIVE LEARNING EXERCISE

5-65 Understanding Pricing Decisions

Form teams of three to six students. Each team should contact and meet with a manager responsible for pricing in a company in your area. This might be a product manager or brand manager for a large company or a vice president of marketing or sales for a smaller company.

Explore with the manager how his or her company sets prices. Among the questions you might ask are the following:

- How do costs influence your prices? Do you set prices by adding a markup to costs? If so, what measure of costs do you use? How do you determine the appropriate markup?
- How do you adjust prices to meet market competition? How do you measure the effects of price on sales level?
- Do you use target costing? That is, do you find out what a product will sell for and then try to design the product and production process to make a desired profit on the product?
- What is your goal in setting prices? Do you try to maximize revenue, market penetration, contribution margin, gross margin, or some combination of these, or do you have other goals when setting prices?

After each team has conducted its interview, it would be desirable, if time permits, to get together as a class and share your findings. How many different pricing policies did the groups find? Can you explain why policies differ across companies? Are there characteristics of different industries or different management philosophies that explain the different pricing policies?

INTERNET EXERCISE

5-66 Marketing Decisions at Colgate-Palmolive

Managers need information of all types in order to make decisions. Many marketing decisions are strategic, such as setting pricing policies. Managers rely on multiple sources to help locate relevant information to support these decisions. Managers must know how to use the information that is available and what weight to assign to the information that is deemed to be useful.

A firm is not going to give us detailed information about its marketing strategy on its Web site. However, we can view a firm's Web site to look at some of the relevant information that managers might use to help make marketing decisions. Let's look at the **Colgate-Palmolive Company** to see what information on its site would be relevant for some marketing decisions.

1. Go to Colgate-Palmolive's home page at www.colgate.com. Move your cursor to the heading "For Investors" at the top of the page. Click on "For Investors," then on "Financial Info," then "Annual Reports," and then on the "Dear Colgate Shareholder" in the 2008 annual report. In this section, Colgate shares its worldwide strategy. What types of pricing decisions that are discussed in this chapter are part of Colgate's strategy? What does this strategy reveal about the need for relevant information?
2. Many companies place a high priority on ethics. Examine the section "Living Our Values" under the "Our Company" heading. Give two examples that show Colgate's commitment to ethical behavior.
3. One area that many companies identify as a key component to strategy is new product development. Locate where Colgate highlights its newest products (you may want to use the search option on the Web site). Based on the information, what was the last new product to be released? Is this a "new" product or is it simply a variation of an existing product?
4. Now, look at the products that the firm manufactures. What format is offered for learning about these products? Look at the fabric conditioner products. How many fabric conditioners does the firm offer? From looking at the information provided, can you tell what differentiates the products? Does the Web site provide any information on how or when to use the products? Would you want to make a decision about the "best" fabric conditioner for a specific type of laundry based on the information found on the Web site? Why or why not?
5. Let's look at the most recent annual report again. Is there evidence in the financial statements that Colgate is achieving its worldwide strategy? Is the company improving profitability?

6

Relevant Information for Decision Making with a Focus on Operational Decisions

LEARNING OBJECTIVES

When you have finished studying this chapter, you should be able to:

1. Use a differential analysis to examine income effects across alternatives and show that an opportunity-cost analysis yields identical results.

2. Decide whether to make or to buy certain parts or products.

3. Choose whether to add or delete a product line using relevant information.

4. Compute the optimal product mix when production is constrained by a scarce resource.

5. Decide whether to process a joint product beyond the split-off point.

6. Decide whether to keep or replace equipment.

7. Identify irrelevant and misspecified costs.

8. Discuss how performance measures can affect decision making.

▶ NANTUCKET NECTARS

Starting a beverage business can be a complex maze of decisions. Tom First and Tom Scott should know. After graduating from college, they operated a two-person boat service business off Nantucket Island, provisioning and cleaning yachts during the summer. In 1989, they received the inspiration for a juice drink made with fresh peaches. After a bit of experimentation, the self-proclaimed "juice guys" began bottling and selling their nectar drink from their boat. That first summer, they sold 2,000 bottles at $1.00 each. Today, Nantucket Nectars, bought by Cadbury-Schweppes in 2002 and now owned by Dr Pepper Snapple Group, sells millions of cases each year. Product lines include Nantucket Nectars' Organic, 100% fruit juices, juice cocktails, carbonated juice drinks, and not-from-concentrate teas and lemonades.

Getting to this point, however, has been anything but smooth sailing. First and Scott's early attempts to sell juice to retailers failed; profits were nonexistent. They sold half the business to an equity partner for $500,000 to venture into distribution, but ended up losing $1 million the first year. Employees stole caseloads of merchandise from the warehouse, and there were product disappointments, such as Bayberry Tea. But the juice guys were quick learners. They got out of distribution, changed their marketing approach, and stopped the flow of red ink.

As the company grew, it tackled important operational decisions. For example, should it build and operate its own bottling facilities? What criteria should be used for developing new products? What's the best approach for tracking and analyzing the growing volume of production, distribution, and sales data?

After examining the cost of building and operating bottling plants, Nantucket Nectars chose to contract with existing beverage co-packers in Rhode Island, Nevada, Florida, Pennsylvania, and Maryland. This approach gave the company broader distribution options without the capital expenditure and overhead of multiple plants. Its managers scrutinized unit costs associated with new product ideas emerging from the test kitchen to be sure margins were on target, and they meticulously tracked every detail—from operational costs to pricing promotions—through an enterprise resource planning (ERP) information system from **Oracle**.

As with Nantucket Nectars, managers in other companies must make similar operational decisions. Should **Toyota** make the tires it mounts on its cars, or should it buy them from suppliers? Should **General Mills** sell the flour it mills, or should it use the flour to make more breakfast cereal? Should **Air France** add routes to use idle airplanes, or should it sell the planes? These decisions all require a good deal of accounting information. But what information will be relevant to each decision? In Chapter 5, we identified relevant information for pricing decisions. We now need to determine relevance in the operational area. The basic framework for identifying relevant information remains the same for operations as it was for pricing. We are still looking only for future costs that differ among alternatives. However, we now expand our analysis by introducing the concepts of opportunity costs and differential costs. ■

Analyzing Relevant Information: Focusing on the Future and Differential Attributes

Opportunity, Outlay, and Differential Costs and Analysis

Management decision making is a matter of comparing two or more alternative courses of action. Suppose a manager has only two alternatives to compare. The key to determining the financial difference between the alternatives is to identify the differential costs and revenues. **Differential cost** (**differential revenue**) is the difference in total cost (revenue) between two alternatives. For example, consider the decision about which of two machines to purchase. Both machines perform the same function. The differential cost is the difference in the price paid for the machines plus the difference in the costs of operating the machines. We call a decision process that compares the differential revenues and costs of alternatives a **differential analysis**.

When managers analyze the differential costs between the existing situation and a proposed alternative, they often refer to this as **incremental analysis**. They examine the incremental (additional) costs and benefits of the proposed alternative compared with the current situation. The **incremental costs** are additional costs or reduced revenues generated by the proposed alternative. **Incremental benefits** are the additional revenues or reduced costs generated by the proposed alternative. For instance, suppose **Nantucket Nectars** proposes to increase production of its NectarFizz juice drink from 1,000 bottles to 1,200 bottles per week. The incremental costs of the proposed alternative are the costs of producing the additional 200 bottles each week. The incremental benefits are the additional revenues generated by selling the extra 200 bottles.

When there are multiple alternative courses of action, managers often compare one particular action against the entire set of alternatives. For example, Nantucket Nectars might consider introducing a new 100% juice drink, Papaya Mango. There are many alternatives to introducing Papaya Mango, including introducing other new 100% juice drinks, expanding production of existing drinks such as juice cocktails or blended nectars, or producing non-juice products. Computing the differential costs and revenues between producing Papaya Mango and every alternative could be cumbersome. Thus, Nantucket Nectars managers might use another approach.

Introducing Papaya Mango would entail two types of costs, outlay costs and opportunity costs. An **outlay cost** requires a future cash disbursement. Outlay costs include costs for items such as materials and labor. **Opportunity cost** applies to a resource that a company already owns or that it has already committed to purchase. It is the maximum available benefit forgone (or passed up) by using such a resource for a particular purpose instead of the best alternative use. Suppose Nantucket Nectars has a machine for which it paid $100,000 several years ago and it is sitting idle. It can use the machine to produce Papaya Mango or to increase the production of the Original Peach 100% Juice. The contribution margin from the additional sales of the Original Peach would be $60,000. A third alternative is selling the machine for $50,000 cash. What is the opportunity cost of the machine when we analyze the Papaya Mango alternative? It is $60,000, the larger of the $50,000 or $60,000, the two possible gains that the company could achieve using the machine in its alternative uses. The $100,000 paid for the machine is not relevant because, as we learned from our discussion of relevant costs in Chapter 5, it is not a future cost.

Objective 1

Use a differential analysis to examine income effects across alternatives and show that an opportunity-cost analysis yields identical results.

Now suppose that Nantucket Nectars will have total sales over the life cycle of Papaya Mango 100% Juice of $500,000. The production and marketing costs (outlay costs), excluding the cost of the machine, are $400,000. The net financial benefit from the Papaya Mango is $40,000:

Revenues	$500,000
Costs:	
Outlay costs	400,000
Financial benefit before opportunity costs	$100,000
Opportunity cost of machine	60,000
Net financial benefit	$ 40,000

Nantucket Nectars will gain $40,000 more financial benefit using the machine to make Papaya Mango than it would make using it for the next most profitable alternative.

An alternative to the opportunity-cost analysis is to conduct an incremental analysis. In an incremental analysis, we compare the revenues and outlay costs of the proposed alternative to those of the next best alternative use of the machine. In this case, the revenue less outlay costs for Papaya Mango of $100,000 is $40,000 higher than the predicted contribution margin on the Original Peach. The result of the incremental analysis is equivalent to that of the opportunity-cost approach.

To further illustrate this equivalence, consider Maria Morales, a certified public accountant employed by a large accounting firm for a salary of $60,000 per year. She is considering an alternative use of her time, her most valuable resource. The alternative is to start an independent accounting practice. Maria's practice would have revenues of $200,000. This is $140,000 more than she would make as an employee of the large firm. However, she would also have to pay $120,000 to rent office space, lease equipment, buy advertising, and cover other out-of-pocket expenses.

An incremental analysis follows:

Assume Maria Opens Her Own Independent Practice

Incremental benefits, $200,000 – $60,000 of increased revenues	$140,000
Incremental costs, $120,000 – $0 of additional costs	120,000
Incremental income effects per year	$ 20,000

If Maria opens her own practice, her income will be $20,000 higher than it is as an employee of the large firm.

Now let's take an opportunity-cost approach. We will look at the alternative of operating an independent practice, essentially comparing it to the alternative uses of Maria's time (which in this case is simply the alternative of working for the large firm). To do this we must consider another cost. Had Maria remained an employee, she would have made $60,000. By starting her own company, Maria will forgo this profit. Thus, the $60,000 is an opportunity cost of starting her own business:

		Alternative Chosen: Independent Practice
Revenue		$200,000
Expenses		
Outlay costs (operating expenses)	$120,000	
Opportunity cost of employee salary	60,000	180,000
Income effects per year		$ 20,000

Consider the two preceding tabulations. Each produces the correct key difference between alternatives, $20,000. The first tabulation does not mention opportunity cost because we measured the differential economic impacts—differential revenues and differential costs—compared to the alternative. The second tabulation mentions opportunity cost because we included the $60,000 annual net economic impact of the excluded alternative as a cost of the chosen alternative. If we had failed to recognize opportunity cost in the second tabulation, we would have misstated the difference between the alternatives.

Why do we use opportunity costs when an incremental analysis produces the same result? When there is only one resource and one alternative opportunity to use that resource, the incremental analysis is more straightforward. However, suppose you were analyzing a project that uses five existing machines each with 10 alternative uses. An incremental analysis would require comparing the project with $10^5 = 100,000$ alternatives—every combination of alternative uses of the five machines. Using opportunity costs allows you to simplify the analysis. You just assess the 10 alternatives for each machine, pick the best one to use in determining each machine's opportunity cost, and add the five opportunity costs to the outlay costs of the project. The opportunity-cost approach is simpler than the incremental approach in such a situation.

This does not mean that estimating opportunity costs is easy. They depend on estimated revenues and costs for hypothetical alternatives—alternatives not taken. Furthermore, they depend on the alternatives that are available at a particular point in time. The same alternatives may not be available at a different time. For example, excess capacity in September does not mean that there will also be excess capacity in October. Finally, there is little historical information—sale or purchase prices—to help predict benefits for hypothetical alternatives.

We will next use the concepts in this section to analyze a variety of operational decisions. Just as we focused on relevant costs for pricing decisions in Chapter 5, we will focus on relevant costs for operational decisions in this chapter.

Making Managerial Decisions

Suppose you are a warehouse manager at **Mattel**, the toy company. **Ace Hardware** approaches you asking to rent warehouse space for January–April for storage of garden tools for the spring sales season. What is the likely opportunity cost to Mattel of the warehouse space? What if the request were for September–November?

Answer

At a toy company, excess warehouse space is a seasonal phenomenon. There is unlikely to be excess space late in the year as the holiday season approaches, but in January–April Mattel may have little use for the space. You might look for other temporary alternatives, ones that use the space for only a few months. If there are no such alternatives, the opportunity cost would be close to zero. If other alternatives exist, the opportunity cost would be the benefit received from the next best alternative use. If the request came in September, the opportunity cost would likely be high because Mattel needs the space to accommodate its own toy inventory for holiday sales.

Make-or-Buy Decisions

Managers often must decide whether to produce a product or service within the firm or purchase it from an outside supplier. If they purchase products or services from an outside supplier, we often call it **outsourcing**. They apply relevant cost analysis to a variety of outsourcing decisions such as the following:

Objective 2

Decide whether to make or to buy certain parts or products.

- **Boeing** must decide whether to buy or make many of the tools used in assembling 787 airplanes.
- **Apple** must decide whether to develop its own Internet search software for a new computer or to buy it from a software vendor.

The Business First box on page 226 describes outsourcing and its growing popularity.

Business First

An Example of Make or Buy: Outsourcing

Make-or-buy decisions (or outsourcing decisions) apply to services as well as to products. Companies are increasingly deciding to hire service firms to handle some of their internal operations. According to the Outsourcing Institute, outsourcing is "the strategic use of outside resources to perform activities traditionally handled by internal staff and resources."

Companies use outsourcing for many business processes within various value-chain functions. The most common business functions outsourced fall within the value-chain functions of corporate support (e.g., administration, human resources, finance, and IT) and marketing (e.g., sales and call centers). Additionally, some companies outsource production processes and even research and development activities. For example, Eli Lilly has moved some of its chemistry lab work to China and is conducting more clinical trial activities overseas, primarily to reduce costs.

Although companies can outsource many processes, the Internet has driven much of the recent growth in outsourcing of computer applications. By the beginning of the twenty-first century, many companies realized that the huge investments necessitated by ERP systems may be unnecessary. They could purchase the required services over the Internet without investing in the systems' purchase and development costs. The formerly expensive process of communication using service providers had become essentially free via the Internet. A new group of computing service providers—called application service providers (ASPs)—arose to provide outsourcing opportunities for a variety of computing applications.

What are the key reasons for outsourcing? Over half of the companies in Outsourcing Institute's annual survey said they wanted to improve the company's focus and reduce operating costs. According to Todd Kertley, who manages IBM's outsourcing services, "Corporations increasingly want to focus on their core businesses, not technology." As the complexity of data processing and especially networking has grown, companies have found it harder and harder to keep current with the technology. Instead of investing huge sums in personnel and equipment and diverting attention from the value-added activities of their own businesses, many firms have found outsourcing financially attractive. Additionally, many companies are discovering that outsourcing aids corporate growth, making better use of skilled labor, and even job creation. Such "transformational outsourcing" exploits the enormous gains in efficiency, productivity, and revenues that accrue to firms from leveraging offshore talent.

The big stumbling block to outsourcing has been subjective factors, such as control. To make outsourcing attractive, the services must be reliable, be available when needed, and be flexible enough to adapt to changing conditions. Companies that have successful outsourcing arrangements have been careful to include the subjective factors in their decisions.

Outsourcing has become so profitable that more than 75% of *Fortune* 500 companies outsource some aspect of their business support services. The McKinsey Global Institute estimates that companies have shifted abroad more than $18 billion in global IT work and over $11 billion in business process services.

Sources: Adapted from T. Kearney, "Why Outsourcing Is In," *Strategic Finance*, January 2000, pp. 34–38; J. Hechinger, "IBM to Take Over Operations of Auto-Parts Maker Visteon," *Wall Street Journal*, February 12, 2003; P. Engardio, M. Arndt, and D. Foust, "The Future of Outsourcing," *Business Week*, January 30, 2006; and the Outsourcing Institute (www.outsourcing.com).

Basic Make-or-Buy Decisions and Idle Facilities

A basic make-or-buy question is whether a company should make its own parts that it will use in its final products or buy the parts from vendors. Sometimes the answer to this question is based on qualitative factors. For example, some manufacturers always make parts because they want to control quality. Alternatively, some companies always purchase parts to protect long-run relationships with their suppliers. These companies may deliberately buy from vendors even during slack times to avoid difficulties in obtaining needed parts during boom times, when there may well be shortages of materials and workers, but no shortage of sales orders.

What quantitative factors are relevant to the decision of whether to make or buy? The answer, again, depends on the situation. A key factor is whether there are idle facilities. Many companies make parts only when they cannot use their facilities to better advantage.

Assume that Nantucket Nectars reports the following costs:

Nantucket Nectars Company
Cost of Making 12-Ounce Glass Bottles

	Total Cost for 1,000,000 Bottles	Cost per Bottle
Direct materials	$ 60,000	$.06
Direct labor	20,000	.02
Variable factory overhead	40,000	.04
Fixed factory overhead	80,000	.08
Total costs	$200,000	$.20

Another manufacturer offers to sell Nantucket Nectars the bottles for $.18. Should Nantucket Nectars make or buy the bottles?

Although the $.20 unit cost seemingly indicates that the company should buy, the answer is rarely so obvious. The essential question is "What is the difference in expected future costs between the alternatives?" If the $.08 fixed overhead per bottle consists of costs that will continue regardless of the decision, the entire $.08 becomes irrelevant. Examples of such fixed factory costs include depreciation, property taxes, insurance, and foreman salaries for the plant.

Are only the variable costs relevant? No. Perhaps Nantucket Nectars will eliminate $50,000 of the fixed costs if the company buys the bottles instead of making them. For example, the company may be able to release a supervisor with a $50,000 salary. In that case, the fixed costs that the company will be able to avoid in the future are relevant.

For the moment, suppose the capacity now used to make bottles will become idle if the company purchases the bottles. Further, the $50,000 supervisor's salary is the only fixed cost that the company would eliminate. The relevant computations follow:

	Make		Buy	
	Total	Per Bottle	Total	Per Bottle
Purchase cost			$180,000	$.18
Direct materials	$ 60,000	$.06		
Direct labor	20,000	.02		
Variable factory overhead	40,000	.04		
Fixed factory overhead that can be avoided by not making (supervisor's salary)	50,000*	.05*		
Total relevant costs	$170,000	$.17	$180,000	$.18
Difference in favor of making	$ 10,000	$.01		

*Note that unavoidable fixed costs of $80,000 – $50,000 = $30,000 are irrelevant. Thus, the irrelevant costs per unit are $.08 – $.05 = $.03.

The key to wise make-or-buy decisions is identifying and accurately measuring the additional costs for making (or the costs avoided by buying) a part or component. Companies with accurate cost accounting systems, such as ABC systems discussed in Chapter 4, are in a better position to perform make-or-buy analysis.

Make or Buy and the Use of Facilities

Make-or-buy decisions are rarely as simple as the one in our Nantucket Nectars example. As we said earlier, the use of facilities is a key to the make-or-buy decision. For simplicity, we assumed that the Nantucket Nectars facilities would remain idle if the company chose to buy the bottles. This means that the opportunity cost of the facilities is zero. In most cases, companies will not leave their facilities idle. Instead, they will often put idle facilities to some other use, and we must consider the financial outcomes of these uses when choosing to make or buy. The value received from the best of these alternative uses is an opportunity cost for the internal production of the parts or components.

Suppose Nantucket Nectars can use the released facilities in our example in some other manufacturing activity to produce a contribution to profits of $55,000 or can rent them out for $25,000. We now have four alternatives to consider. The following table is an incremental analysis that summarizes all the costs and revenues that differ among the four alternatives (amounts are in thousands):

	Make	Buy and Leave Facilities Idle	Buy and Rent Out Facilities	Buy and Use Facilities for Other Products
Rent revenue	$ —	$ —	$ 25	$ —
Contribution from other products	—	—	—	55
Relevant cost of bottles	(170)	(180)	(180)	(180)
Net relevant costs	$(170)	$(180)	$(155)	$(125)

The final column indicates that buying the bottles and using the vacated facilities for the production of other products would yield the lowest net costs in this case, $170,000 – $125,000 = $45,000 less than the cost of making the bottles.

We can also analyze this choice using opportunity costs. The opportunity cost of the facilities is $55,000 because that is the maximum benefit Nantucket Nectars could get if it did not use the facilities to make bottles. Add that to the outlay cost, and the total cost of making the bottles is $225,000. This is $45,000 higher than the $180,000 cost of purchasing them.

Making Managerial Decisions

Suppose a company uses its facilities, on average, 80% of the time. However, because of seasonal changes in the demand for its product, the actual demand for the facilities varies from 60% in the off season to over 100% in the peak season when it must outsource production of some parts. Under what circumstances would the company choose to take on work for other companies during the off season? Why might it continue to outsource production of parts during the peak season—that is, why would the company choose not to expand its capacity?

Answer

During the off season, the company would decide to take on work for other manufacturers (on a subcontract) if it is profitable. Such work may not be profitable enough to cover the cost of expanding the capacity of the facilities. The company will use facilities for these orders only when the opportunity cost of using the facilities is close to zero, that is, when there are no other more profitable uses for them. In contrast, during the peak season, the company meets the high volume by outsourcing the production of some parts. Again, the cost of purchased parts may be higher than the cost to make them in the company's own facilities if there were idle capacity, but purchasing the parts is less costly than expanding the facilities to produce them. Additionally, a company may increase production above demand (but below capacity) in the off-season in order to build inventory for the busy season.

Summary Problem for Your Review

PROBLEM

Exhibit 6-1 contains data for the Block Company for the year just ended. The company makes industrial power drills. Exhibit 6-1 shows the costs of the plastic housing separately from the costs of the electrical and mechanical components. Answer each of the following questions independently. (Requirement 1 reviews Chapter 5.)

	A	B	A + B
	Electrical and Mechanical Components*	Plastic Housing	Industrial Drills
Sales: 100,000 units, at $100			$10,000,000
Variable costs			
Direct materials	$4,400,000	$ 500,000	$ 4,900,000
Direct labor	400,000	300,000	700,000
Variable factory overhead	100,000	200,000	300,000
Other variable costs	100,000	—	100,000
Sales commissions, at 10% of sales	1,000,000	—	1,000,000
Total variable costs	$6,000,000	$1,000,000	$ 7,000,000
Contribution margin			$ 3,000,000
Total fixed costs	$2,220,000	$ 480,000	2,700,000
Operating income			$ 300,000

*Not including the costs of plastic housing (column B).

Exhibit 6-1
Block Company Cost of Industrial Drills

1. During the year, a prospective customer in an unrelated market offered $82,000 for 1,000 drills. The drills would be manufactured in addition to the 100,000 units sold. Block Company would pay the regular sales commission rate on the 1,000 drills. The president rejected the order because "it was below our costs of $97 per unit." What would operating income have been if Block Company had accepted the order?

2. A supplier offered to manufacture the year's supply of 100,000 plastic housings for $12.00 each. What would be the effect on operating income if the Block Company purchased rather than made the housings? Assume that Block Company would avoid $350,000 of the fixed costs assigned to housings if it purchases the housings.

3. Suppose that Block Company could purchase the housings for $13.00 each and use the vacated space for the manufacture of a deluxe version of its drill. Assume that it could make 20,000 deluxe units (and sell them for $130 each in addition to the sales of the 100,000 regular units) at a unit variable cost of $90, exclusive of housings and exclusive of the 10% sales commission. The company could also purchase the 20,000 extra plastic housings for $13.00 each. All the fixed costs pertaining to the plastic housings would continue because these costs relate primarily to the manufacturing facilities used. What would operating income have been if Block had bought the housings and made and sold the deluxe units?

SOLUTION

1. The costs of filling the special order follow:

Direct materials	$49,000
Direct labor	7,000
Variable factory overhead	3,000
Other variable costs	1,000
Sales commission at 10% of $82,000	8,200
Total variable costs	$68,200
Selling price	82,000
Contribution margin	$13,800

Operating income would have been $300,000 + $13,800 = $313,800 if Block Company had accepted the order. In a sense, the decision to reject the offer implies that the Block Company is willing to forego $13,800 in immediate gains (an opportunity cost) in order to preserve the long-run selling price structure.

2. Assuming that Block Company could have avoided $350,000 of the fixed costs by not making the housings and that the other fixed costs would have continued, we can summarize the incremental costs and benefits of buying the housings compared with making them as follows:

Incremental cost (Purchase cost of 100,000 × $12)	$1,200,000
Incremental benefits:	
Variable costs	$1,000,000
Avoidable fixed costs	350,000
Net incremental benefit	$ 150,000

If the facilities used for plastic housings became idle, the Block Company would prefer to buy the housings. Operating income would increase by $150,000.

3. The effect of purchasing the plastic housings and using the vacated facilities for the manufacture of a deluxe version of its drill follows:

Incremental Benefit:			
Sales increase, 20,000 units, at $130			$2,600,000
Variable costs exclusive of housings increase, 20,000 units, at $90		$1,800,000	
Plus: sales commission, 10% of $2,600,000		260,000	$2,060,000
Contribution margin on 20,000 units			$ 540,000
Incremental Cost:			
Housings: 120,000 rather than 100,000 would be needed; Buy 120,000 at $13		$1,560,000	
Versus make 100,000 at $10 (only the variable costs are relevant)		1,000,000	
Incremental cost of outside purchase			560,000
Fixed costs, unchanged			—
Net incremental cost to buying			$ 20,000

Operating income would decline to $300,000 − $20,000 = $280,000. The deluxe units bring in a contribution margin of $540,000, but the additional costs of buying rather than making housings is $560,000, leading to a net disadvantage of $20,000.

Deletion or Addition of Products, Services, or Departments

Objective 3

Choose whether to add or delete a product line using relevant information.

Relevant information also plays an important role in decisions about adding or deleting products, services, or departments.

Avoidable and Unavoidable Costs

Often, existing businesses will want to expand or contract their operations to improve profitability. Decisions about whether to add or to drop products or whether to add or to drop departments will use the same analysis: examining all the relevant costs and revenues. For example, consider a store that has three major departments: groceries, general merchandise, and drugs. Management is considering dropping the grocery department, which has consistently shown an operating loss. The following table reports the store's present annual operating income (in thousands of dollars):

		Departments		
	Total	Groceries	General Merchandise	Drugs
Sales	$1,900	$1,000	$800	$100
Variable cost of goods sold and expenses*	1,420	800	560	60
Contribution margin	$ 480 (25%)	$ 200 (20%)	$240 (30%)	$ 40 (40%)
Fixed expenses (salaries, depreciation, insurance, property taxes, and so on):				
Avoidable	$ 265	$ 150	$100	$ 15
Unavoidable	180	60	100	20
Total fixed expenses	$ 445	$ 210	$200	$ 35
Operating income (loss)	$ 35	$ (10)	$ 40	$ 5

*Examples of variable expenses include product, paper shopping bags, and sales commissions.

Notice that we have divided the fixed expenses into two categories, avoidable and unavoidable. **Avoidable costs**—costs that will not continue if an ongoing operation is changed or deleted—are relevant. In our example, avoidable costs include department salaries and other costs that the store could eliminate by not operating the specific department. **Unavoidable costs**—costs that continue even if a company discontinues an operation—are not relevant in our example because a decision to delete the department does not affect them. Unavoidable costs include many **common costs**, which are those costs of facilities and services that are shared by users. For example, store depreciation, heating, air conditioning, and general management expenses are costs of shared resources used by all departments. For our example, assume first that we will consider only two alternatives, dropping or continuing the grocery department, which shows a loss of $10,000. Assume further that the decision will not affect the total assets invested in the store. The vacated space would be idle, and the unavoidable costs would continue. Which alternative would you recommend? An analysis (in thousands of dollars) follows:

	Store as a Whole		
Income Statements	Total Before Change (a)	Effect of Dropping Groceries (b)	Total After Change (a) – (b)
Sales	$1,900	$1,000	$900
Variable expenses	1,420	800	620
Contribution margin	$ 480	$ 200	$280
Avoidable fixed expenses	265	150	115
Profit contribution to common space and other unavoidable costs	$ 215	$ 50	$165
Common space and other unavoidable costs	180	—	180
Operating income (loss)	$ 35	$ 50	$ (15)

The preceding analysis shows that matters would be worse, rather than better, if the store drops the groceries department and leaves the vacated facilities idle. In short, as the income statement shows, groceries bring in a contribution margin of $200,000, which is $50,000 more than the $150,000 fixed expenses the store would save by closing the grocery department. The grocery department showed a loss in the first income statement because of the unavoidable fixed costs charged (allocated) to it.

Most companies do not like having space left idle, so perhaps the preceding example was a bit too basic. Assume now that the store could use the space made available by the dropping of groceries to expand the general merchandise department. The space would be occupied by merchandise that would increase sales by $500,000, generate a 30% contribution-margin percentage, and have additional (avoidable) fixed costs of $70,000. The $80,000 increase in operating income of general merchandise more than offsets the $50,000 decline from eliminating groceries, providing an overall increase in operating income of $65,000 – $35,000 = $30,000. The analysis is as follows:

	Effects of Changes			
	Total Before Change (a)	Drop Groceries (b)	Expand General Merchandise (c)	Total After Changes (a) – (b) + (c)
(in thousands of dollars)				
Sales	$1,900	$1,000	$500	$1,400
Variable expenses	1,420	800	350	970
Contribution margin	$ 480	$ 200	$150	$ 430
Avoidable fixed expenses	265	150	70	185
Contribution to common space and other unavoidable costs	$ 215	$ 50	$ 80	$ 245
Common space and other unavoidable costs*	180	—	—	180
Operating income	$ 35	$ 50	$ 80	$ 65

*Includes the $60,000 of former grocery fixed costs, which were allocations of unavoidable common costs that will continue regardless of how the space is occupied.

This example illustrates that relevant costs are not always variable. The key to decision making is not relying on a hard and fast rule about what to include and what to ignore. Rather, you need to analyze all pertinent costs and revenues to determine what is and what is not relevant. In this case, the relevant costs included the avoidable fixed costs.

It is also important to remember that nonfinancial information can influence decisions to add or delete products or departments. For example, when deciding to delete a product or to close a plant, there are ethical considerations. What happens to the employees in the area being discontinued? What about customers who might be relying on customer support in the future? What about the community in which a discontinued operation is located? While the nonfinancial impacts of such considerations are hard to determine, they are still factors a company should consider. In addition, a stable, committed workforce and a supportive community can be important assets to a company. This may be a situation where good ethics is good business. Any negative impacts on employees, customers, or communities could create future financial problems for the company that are much larger than short-term cost savings from discontinuing a product or plant.

Making Managerial Decisions

When managers face a decision about whether to add or delete a product, service, or department, it is useful to classify the associated fixed costs as avoidable or unavoidable. Indicate whether the following fixed costs are typically avoidable or unavoidable if a company deletes a product. Assume that the company produces many products in a single plant.

1. Advertising costs for the product. The company places specific ads just for this product.
2. Salary of the plant manager.
3. Rent for the plant building.

4. Insurance costs on equipment used to produce the product. The company will sell the equipment if it discontinues the product.

Answer

Numbers 1 and 4 are avoidable fixed costs. The company is unlikely to change the salary of the plant manager if it discontinues only one product. Thus, it is unavoidable. The same is true for the plant rent. Hence, it is also an unavoidable cost.

Optimal Use of Limited Resources: Product-Mix Decisions

Objective 4

Compute the optimal product mix when production is constrained by a scarce resource.

Suppose a plant makes more than one product and is operating at capacity. If demand for its products exceeds the amount the company can produce, managers must decide which product mix to produce. The product-mix decision requires a focus on each product's contribution margin and its use of capacity. Managers should emphasize the product that makes the largest contribution per unit of the limiting factor. A **limiting factor** or **scarce resource** restricts or constrains the production or sale of a product or service. Limiting factors include labor hours and machine hours that limit production (and hence sales) in manufacturing firms, and square feet of floor space or cubic meters of display space that limit sales in department stores.

Managers must use the contribution margin technique wisely. They sometimes mistakenly favor those products with the biggest contribution margin or gross margin per unit or per sales dollar, without regard to scarce resources. This could lead to incorrect decisions.

Consider two different athletic shoes produced by **Nike**, the Air Court tennis shoe and the Air Max running shoe. Assume that one factory is the only facility that produces these shoes, and Nike managers must decide how many shoes of each type to produce. Suppose machine time is the measure of capacity in this factory, and there is a maximum of 10,000 hours of machine time. The factory can produce 10 pairs of Air Court shoes or 5 pairs of Air Max shoes in 1 hour of machine time. Unit data follow:

	Air Court	Air Max
Selling price per pair	$80	$120
Variable costs per pair	60	84
Contribution margin per pair	$20	$ 36
Contribution margin ratio	25%	30%

Which is more profitable, the Air Court or Air Max? On which should Nike spend its resources? The correct answer is "It depends." Suppose the factory has excess capacity of 1,000 hours of machine time. Now a sports retailer approaches Nike and wants it to fill a special order for 1,000 pairs of shoes of either type. Which shoe would be most profitable to fill this order, the Air Court or the Air Max? It would be better to produce and sell an Air Max pair contributing $36 than an Air Court pair contributing $20. In this case, Air Max shoes generate more profit per pair. Thus, if the limiting factor is demand, that is, pairs of shoes, the more profitable product is the one with the higher contribution per unit.

Now suppose the demand for either shoe would exceed the factory's capacity. Capacity is now the limiting factor because there is only one factory in which to make either the Air Max or the Air Court. In this case, the Air Court shoe is more profitable. Why? Because it generates $2,000,000 of contribution margin from the capacity that is available compared to $1,800,000 for Air Max:

	Air Court	Air Max
1. Pairs of shoes from 10,000 hours	100,000	50,000
2. Contribution margin per pair	$ 20	$ 36
3. Contribution margin from 10,000 hours of capacity, (1) × (2)	$2,000,000	$1,800,000
Contribution margin per machine-hour, (3) ÷ 10,000	$ 200	$ 180

Each machine-hour used to produce Air Court shoes generates $200 of contribution, while an hour used to produce Air Max shoes generates only $180.

Now suppose that neither shoe alone has enough demand to fill the entire capacity, but the combined demand will more than fill the capacity. What our analysis tells us is the Air Court shoe is a better use of the production capacity than the Air Max shoe. Nike would want to make sure there are as many pairs of Air Court shoes available as customers demand, and only after satisfying this demand is it worth producing Air Max shoes.

This analysis depends on the relative use of capacity by the two products. Suppose the factory can produce seven instead of five Air Max shoes per hour of machine time. Then, the Air Max would be the most profitable use of the capacity. It would have a $252 contribution for each machine-hour compared with Air Court's $200.

	Air Court	Air Max
Contribution from 10,000 machine-hours	10,000 × 10 × $20 = $2,000,000	10,000 × 7 × $36 = $2,520,000
Contribution per machine-hour	$2,000,000 ÷ 10,000 = $200	$2,520,000 ÷ 10,000 = $252

Any way we express it, Air Max shoes will have more contribution per unit of capacity—per hour or per 10,000 hours. Note that each of these financial measures shows that Air Max shoes are 26% more profitable than the Air Court. That is, ($252 − $200) ÷ $200 = 26%, and ($2,520,000 − $2,000,000) ÷ $2,000,000 = 26%.

This issue of optimizing the use of scarce resources is important in non-manufacturing companies as well. In retail stores, the limiting resource is often floor space. Thus, they often focus either on products taking up less space or on using the space for shorter periods of time—greater **inventory turnover** (number of times the average inventory is sold per year). However, the product that is most profitable when one particular factor limits sales may be the least profitable if a different factor restricts sales. Consider an example of two department stores. The conventional gross profit percentage (gross profit ÷ selling price) is an insufficient clue to profitability because, as we said, profits depend on the space occupied and the inventory turnover. Discount department stores, such as **Wal-Mart**, **Target**, and **Kmart**, have succeeded in using lower markups than traditional department stores because they have been able to increase turnover and, thus, increase the contribution to profit per unit of space. Exhibit 6-2 illustrates the same product, taking up the same amount of space, in each of two stores. The contribution margins per unit and per sales dollar are less in the discount store, but faster turnover makes the same product a more profitable use of space in the discount store. In general, retail companies seek faster inventory

	Regular Department Store	Discount Department Store
Retail price	$ 4.00	$ 3.50
Cost of merchandise and other variable costs	3.00	3.00
Contribution to profit per unit	$ 1.00 (25%)	$ .50 (14%)
Units sold per year	10,000	22,000
Total contribution to profit, assuming the same space allotment in both stores	$10,000	$11,000

Exhibit 6-2

Effect of Inventory Turnover on Profit

turnover. A survey of retail shoe stores showed that those with above-average financial performance had an inventory turnover of 2.6 times per year compared to an industry average of 2.0.

Joint Product Costs: Sell or Process Further Decisions

Objective 5

Decide whether to process a joint product beyond the split-off point.

We now examine another operating decision for which relevant costs are important—decisions about whether to sell a product as it is or to further process it. In this section, we will examine how joint product costs affect such decisions.

Consider **ConAgra**, which produces meat products with brand names such as Swift, Armour, and Butterball. ConAgra cannot kill a sirloin steak; it has to purchase and slaughter a steer, which supplies various cuts of dressed meat, hides, and trimmings. So how does ConAgra determine the proper allocation of the purchase cost paid for the steer to the various manufactured meat products? When two or more manufactured products (1) have relatively significant sales values and (2) are not separately identifiable as individual products until their split-off point, we call them **joint products**. The **split-off point** is that juncture of manufacturing where the joint products become individually identifiable. Any costs beyond that stage are **separable costs** because they are not part of the joint process and the accounting system can exclusively identify them with individual products. We call the costs of manufacturing joint products prior to the split-off point **joint costs**. Further examples of joint products include chemicals, lumber, flour, and the products of petroleum refining.

To illustrate joint costs, suppose **Dow Chemical Company** produces two chemical products, X and Y, as a result of a particular joint process. The joint processing cost is $100,000. This includes raw material costs and the cost of processing before the joint products X and Y reach the split-off point. At the split-off point, Dow either sells X and Y or processes them further before selling them to the petroleum industry, which uses them as ingredients of gasoline. The relationships follow:

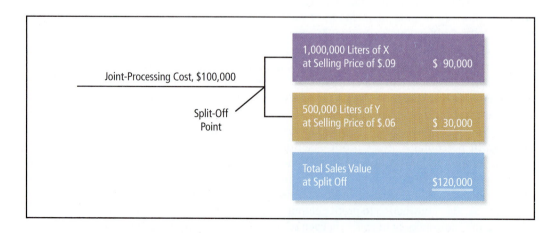

Let's see how Dow's managers develop relevant information to help them decide whether to sell joint products X and Y at the split-off point or to further process one or both of them.

Sell or Process Further

Suppose Dow can further process the 500,000 liters of Y and sell it to the plastics industry as product YA, an ingredient for plastic sheeting. The additional processing cost would be $.08 per liter for manufacturing and distribution, a total of $40,000 for 500,000 liters. The net sales price of YA would be $.16 per liter, a total of $80,000.

Dow cannot process product X further and will sell it at the split-off point, but management is undecided about product Y. Should the company sell Y at the split-off point, or should it process Y into YA? To answer this question, we need to find the relevant costs involved. Consider first the joint costs—those before the split-off point. They cannot affect anything beyond the split-off point. They violate both attributes of relevancy; they are neither future costs nor differential across alternatives. Therefore they are irrelevant to the question of whether to sell or process further. The only approach that will yield valid results is to concentrate on the separable costs and revenues beyond split-off, as shown in Exhibit 6-3.

This analysis shows that it would be $10,000 more profitable to process Y beyond split-off than to sell Y at split-off. The rule is to extend processing on a joint product if the additional revenue exceeds the additional expenses.

Exhibit 6-4 illustrates another way to compare the alternatives of (1) selling Y at the split-off point and (2) processing Y beyond split-off. It includes the joint costs, which are the same for each alternative and, therefore, do not affect the difference.

Because joint costs would not affect the decision (as Exhibit 6-4 demonstrates), we have not allocated the joint costs to products. However, no matter how we might allocate them, the total income effects for the firm would not change. We provide additional coverage of the allocation of joint costs and inventory valuation in Chapter 12.

	Sell at Split-Off as Y	Process Further and Sell as YA	Difference
Revenues	$30,000	$80,000	$50,000
Separable costs beyond split-off at $.08	—	40,000	40,000
Income effects	$30,000	$40,000	$10,000

Exhibit 6-3
Illustration of Sell or Process Further

	(1) Alternative One			(2) Alternative Two			(3)
	X	Y	Total	X	YA	Total	Differential Effects
Revenues	$90,000	$30,000	$120,000	$90,000	$80,000	$170,000	$50,000
Joint costs			$100,000			$100,000	—
Separable costs			—		40,000	40,000	40,000
Total costs			$100,000			$140,000	$40,000
Income effects			$ 20,000			$ 30,000	$10,000

Exhibit 6-4
Sell or Process Further Analysis—Firm as a Whole

Keeping or Replacing Equipment

We next examine a common decision in business, the replacement of old equipment. One important aspect of such a situation is that the book value of the old equipment is not a relevant consideration in deciding whether to purchase a replacement. Why? Because it is a past cost, not a future cost. When a company purchases equipment, it spreads the cost via a **depreciation** expense over the future periods in which it will use the equipment. The equipment's **book value**, or **net book value**, is the original cost less accumulated depreciation. **Accumulated depreciation** is the sum of all depreciation charged to past periods. For example, suppose a $10,000 machine with a 10-year life span has depreciation of $1,000 per year. At the end of 6 years, accumulated depreciation is 6 × $1,000 = $6,000, and the book value is $10,000 – $6,000 = $4,000.

Consider the following data for a decision about whether to replace an old machine:

	Old Machine	Replacement Machine
Original cost	$10,000	$8,000
Useful life in years	10	4
Current age in years	6	0
Useful life remaining in years	4	4
Accumulated depreciation	$ 6,000	0
Book value	$ 4,000	Not acquired yet
Disposal value (in cash) now	$ 2,500	Not acquired yet
Disposal value in 4 years	0	0
Annual cash operating costs (maintenance, power, repairs, coolants, and so on)	$ 5,000	$3,000

Let's prepare a comparative analysis of the two alternatives. Before proceeding, consider some important concepts. The most widely misunderstood facet of replacement decision making is the role of the book value of the old equipment in the decision. We often call the book value a **sunk cost**, which is really just another term for historical or past cost, a cost that the company has already incurred and, therefore, is irrelevant to the decision-making process. Nothing can change what has already happened. The Business First box on page 237 illustrates this concept.

The irrelevance of past costs for decisions does not mean that knowledge of past costs is useless. Often managers use past costs to help predict future costs. In addition, past costs affect future payments for income taxes (as explained in Chapter 11). However, the past cost itself is not relevant. The only relevant cost is the predicted future cost.

In deciding whether to replace or keep existing equipment, we must consider the relevance of four commonly encountered items:

1. Book value of old equipment: irrelevant because it is a past (historical) cost. Therefore, depreciation on old equipment is also irrelevant.
2. Disposal value of old equipment: relevant because it is an expected future inflow that usually differs across alternatives.
3. Gain or loss on disposal: This is the difference between book value and disposal value. It is therefore a meaningless combination of irrelevant and relevant items. The combination form, loss (or gain) on disposal, blurs the distinction between the irrelevant book value and the relevant disposal value. Consequently, it is best to think of each separately.
4. Cost of new equipment: relevant because it is an expected future outflow that will differ across alternatives. Therefore, the initial cost of new equipment (or its allocation in subsequent depreciation charges) is relevant.

Business First

Sunk Costs and Government Contracts

It is easy to agree that—in theory—managers should ignore sunk costs when making decisions. But in practice, sunk costs often influence important decisions, especially when a decision maker doesn't want to admit that a previous decision to invest funds was a bad decision.

Consider the governmental claims made during the famous Congressional debates regarding the termination of funding for the military's B-2 aircraft. As documented in the *St. Louis Post Dispatch*, Larry O. Welch, the air force chief of staff, claimed "the B-2 already is into production; cancel it and the $17 billion front end investment is lost," and Les Aspin, chairman of the House Armed Services Committee, stated "with $17 billion already invested in it, the B-2 is too costly to cancel."

The $17 billion already invested in the B-2 is a sunk cost. What matters are the future incremental costs and benefits, the costs necessary to complete production compared to the value of the completed B-2s. We want to avoid throwing good money after bad—that is, if the value of the B-2 is not at least

equal to the future investment in it, Congress should cancel funding regardless of the amount previously spent.

Failure to ignore sunk costs is not unique to the U.S. government. More than a decade ago, Motorola made critical decisions to ignore digital technology, and insisted that analog communications, in which it was heavily invested, was the wave of the future. Despite intense demands from wireless providers for digital cell phones, Motorola refused to even consider switching from analog to digital technology. It refused to acknowledge that its analog investments were a sunk cost. Motorola completely lost its dominance in the cell phone market, with its U.S. market share falling from 60% to 13% within three years.

Sources: Adapted from J. Berg, J. Dickhaut, and C. Kanodia, "The Role of Private Information in the Sunk Cost Phenomenon," unpublished paper, November 12, 1991; and W. Y. Davis, "Return the 'Sunk Costs are Sunk' Concept to Principles of Economics Textbooks," *Journal of Business and Economic Research*, Volume 3, Number 6, 2005.

Exhibit 6-5 shows the relevance of these items in our example. Book value of old equipment is irrelevant regardless of the decision-making technique we use. The "difference" column in Exhibit 6-5 shows that the $4,000 book value of the old equipment does not differ between alternatives. We should completely ignore it for decision-making purposes. The difference is merely one of timing. The amount written off is still $4,000, regardless of any available alternative. The $4,000 appears on the income statement either as a $4,000 deduction from the $2,500 cash proceeds received to obtain a $1,500 loss on disposal in the first year or as $1,000 of depreciation in each of 4 years. But how it appears is irrelevant to the replacement decision. In contrast, the $2,000 annual depreciation on the new equipment is relevant because the total $8,000 depreciation is a future cost that we can avoid by not replacing. The three relevant items—operating costs, disposal value, and acquisition cost—give replacement a net advantage of $2,500.

	Four Years Together		
	Keep	Replace	Difference
Cash operating costs	$20,000	$12,000	$8,000
Old equipment (book value)			
Periodic write-off as depreciation	4,000	—	—
or			
Lump-sum write-off		4,000*	
Disposal value	—	−2,500*	2,500
New machine			
Acquisition cost	—	8,000†	−8,000
Total costs	$24,000	$21,500	$2,500

The advantage of replacement is $2,500 for the 4 years together.

*In a formal income statement, these two items would be combined as "loss on disposal" of $4,000 − $2,500 = $1,500.

† In a formal income statement, written off as straight-line depreciation of $8,000 ÷ 4 = $2,000 for each of 4 years.

Exhibit 6-5

Cost Comparison—Replacement of Equipment Including Relevant and Irrelevant Items

Making Managerial Decisions

It is sometimes difficult to accept the proposition that past or sunk costs are irrelevant to decisions. Consider the ticket you have to a major football game in December. After getting the ticket, you learn that the game will be on TV, and you really prefer to watch the game in the comfort of your warm home. Does your decision about attending the game or watching it on TV depend on whether you were given the ticket for free or you paid $80 for it? What does this tell you about a manager's decision to replace a piece of equipment?

Answer

The amount paid, whether it be $0, $80, or $1,000, should make no difference to the decision. You have the ticket, and you have paid for it. That cannot be changed. If you really prefer to

watch the game on TV, it may have been a bad decision to pay $80 for a ticket. But you cannot erase that bad decision. All you can do is choose the future action that has the most value to you. You should not suffer through a less pleasant experience just because you paid $80 for the ticket.

A manager must make the same analysis regarding the replacement of a piece of equipment. What the company spent for the old equipment is irrelevant. Keeping equipment that is no longer economical is just like using a ticket for an event that you would rather not attend. Additionally, keeping the equipment creates an opportunity cost because the company forgoes the disposal value of the old equipment, in the same way that keeping the ticket prevents you from reselling it to another fan (which is a relevant item in this scenario).

Summary Problem for Your Review

PROBLEM

Exhibit 6-5 looks beyond 1 year. Examining the alternatives over the equipment's entire life ensures that peculiar nonrecurring items, such as loss on disposal, will not obstruct the long-run view vital to many managerial decisions. However, Exhibit 6-5 presents both relevant and irrelevant items. Prepare an analysis that concentrates on relevant items only.

SOLUTION

Exhibit 6-6 presents the analysis with relevant items only—the cash operating costs, the disposal value of the old equipment, and the acquisition cost of the new equipment. To demonstrate that the amount of the old equipment's book value will not affect the answer, suppose the book value of the old equipment is $500,000 rather than $4,000. Your final answer will not change. The cumulative advantage of replacement is still $2,500. (If you are in doubt, rework this example, using $500,000 as the book value.)

	Four Years Together		
	Keep	**Replace**	**Difference**
Cash operating costs	$20,000	$12,000	$8,000
Disposal value of old machine	—	−2,500	2,500
New machine, acquisition cost	—	8,000	−8,000
Total relevant costs	$20,000	$17,500	$2,500

Exhibit 6-6

Cost Comparison—Replacement of Equipment, Relevant Items Only

Identify Irrelevant or Misspecified Costs

Objective 7

Identify irrelevant and misspecified costs.

The ability to recognize irrelevant or misspecified costs is sometimes just as important to decision makers as identifying relevant costs. How do we know that past costs, although sometimes good predictors of future costs, are irrelevant in decision making? Let's consider such past costs as obsolete inventory and see why they are irrelevant to decisions.

Suppose **General Dynamics** has 100 obsolete aircraft parts in its inventory. The original manufacturing cost of these parts was $100,000. General Dynamics can (1) re-machine the parts for $30,000 and then sell them for $50,000 or (2) sell them as scrap for $5,000. Which should it do? This is an unfortunate situation, yet the $100,000 past cost is irrelevant to the decision to re-machine or scrap. The only relevant factors are the expected future revenues and costs:

	Remachine	Scrap	Difference
Expected future revenue	$ 50,000	$ 5,000	$45,000
Expected future costs	30,000	—	30,000
Relevant excess of revenue over costs	$ 20,000	$ 5,000	$15,000
Accumulated historical inventory cost*	100,000	100,000	—
Net overall loss on project	$ (80,000)	$ (95,000)	$15,000

*Irrelevant because it is unaffected by the decision.

As you can see from the fourth line of the preceding table, we can completely ignore the $100,000 historical cost and still arrive at the $15,000 difference, the key figure in the analysis that yields re-machining as the optimal decision.

In addition to past costs, some future costs may be irrelevant because they will be the same under all feasible alternatives. These, too, we may safely ignore for a particular decision. Top management salaries are examples of expected future costs that may be unaffected by the decision at hand.

Other irrelevant future costs include fixed costs that will be the same whether a company selects machine X or machine Y. However, it is not merely a case of saying that fixed costs are irrelevant and variable costs are relevant. Variable costs can be irrelevant, and fixed costs can be relevant. For instance, sales commissions are a variable cost that is irrelevant to a decision on whether to produce a product in plant G or plant H. The rental cost of a warehouse is a fixed cost that is relevant if one alternative requires the warehouse while the other does not. In sum, future costs (both variable and fixed) are irrelevant whenever they do not differ among the alternatives at hand and are relevant whenever they do differ between the alternatives.

Finally, it is also critical in decision making to identify misspecified costs. The pricing illustration in Chapter 5 showed that managers should analyze unit costs with care in decision making. There are two major ways to go wrong: (1) including irrelevant costs, such as the $.03 allocation of unavoidable fixed costs in the **Nantucket Nectars** make-or-buy example (pp. 226–227) that would result in a unit cost of $.20 instead of the relevant unit cost of $.17 and (2) comparing unit costs not computed on the same volume basis, as the following example demonstrates. Machinery sales personnel often brag about the low unit costs of using the new machines. Sometimes they neglect to point out that the unit costs are based on outputs far in excess of the volume of activity of their prospective customer. Assume that a new $100,000 machine with a 5-year life span can produce 100,000 units a year at a variable cost of $1 per unit, as opposed to a variable cost per unit of $1.50 with an old machine. A sales representative claims that the new machine will reduce total cost by $.30 per unit after allowing $.20 per unit for depreciation on the new machine. Is the new machine a worthwhile acquisition?

The new machine is attractive at first glance. If the customer's expected volume is 100,000 units, unit-cost comparisons are valid, provided that new depreciation is also considered. Assume that the disposal value of the old equipment is zero. Because depreciation is an allocation of historical cost, the depreciation on the old machine is irrelevant. In contrast, the depreciation on the new machine is relevant because the new machine entails a future cost that the customer can avoid by not acquiring it.

	Old Machine	New Machine
Units	100,000	100,000
Variable costs	$150,000	$100,000
Straight-line depreciation	—	20,000
Total relevant costs	$150,000	$120,000
Unit relevant costs	$ 1.50	$ 1.20

Apparently, the sales representative is correct. However, if the customer's expected volume is only 30,000 units per year, the unit costs change in favor of the old machine.

	Old Machine	New Machine
Units	30,000	30,000
Variable costs	$45,000	$30,000
Straight-line depreciation	—	20,000
Total relevant costs	$45,000	$50,000
Unit relevant costs	$ 1.50	$1.6667

Generally, be wary of unit fixed costs. When feasible, use total fixed cost in your analysis, not fixed cost per unit. Why? Because you need to calculate a new fixed cost per unit for every different volume of production—often a cumbersome task—and if you don't recalculate it, your costs will be misspecified.

Conflicts Between Decision Making and Performance Evaluation

Objective 8

Discuss how performance measures can affect decision making.

You should now know how to make good decisions based on relevant data. However, knowing how to make these decisions and actually making them are two different things. Managers might be tempted to make decisions they know are poor—not in the best interests of the company—if the performance measures in place will reward them for those decisions. To motivate managers to make optimal decisions, methods of evaluating managers' performance should be consistent with their appropriate decision model.

Let's look at an example of a conflict between the analysis for decision making and the method used to evaluate performance. Consider the replacement decision shown in Exhibit 6-6 on page 238, where replacing the machine had a $2,500 advantage over keeping it. To motivate managers to make the right choice, the method used to evaluate performance should be consistent with the decision model—that is, it should show better performance when managers replace the machine than when they keep it. Assume that top management uses accounting income to measure a manager's performance. The effect on accounting income in the first year after replacement compared with that in years 2, 3, and 4 follows:

	Year 1		Years 2, 3, and 4	
	Keep	Replace	Keep	Replace
Cash operating costs	$5,000	$3,000	$5,000	$3,000
Depreciation	1,000	2,000	1,000	2,000
Loss on disposal ($4,000 – $2,500)	—	1,500	—	—
Total cost	$6,000	$6,500	$6,000	$5,000

First-year costs will be $6,500 – $6,000 = $500 lower, making first-year income $500 higher, if the manager keeps the machine rather than replacing it. Because managers naturally want to make decisions that maximize the measure of their performance, the manager may be inclined to keep the machine.

The conflict is especially severe if a company often transfers managers from one position to another. Why? Because the $500 first-year increase in income for keeping the machine will be offset by a $1,000 annual decrease in income in years 2 to 4. (Note that the net difference of $2,500 in favor of replacement over the 4 years together is the same as in Exhibit 6-6.) A manager who moves to a new position after the first year, however, bears the entire loss on disposal without reaping the benefits of lower operating costs in years 2 to 4.

The decision to replace a machine earlier than planned also reveals a possible error in the original decision to purchase the machine. The company bought the old machine 6 years ago for $10,000. Its expected life span was 10 years. However, if a better machine is now available, then the useful life of the old machine was really 6 years, not 10. This feedback on the actual life of the old machine has two possible effects, the first good and the second bad. First, managers might learn from the earlier mistake. If the manager overestimated the useful life of the old machine, how believable is the prediction that the new machine will have a 4-year life span? Feedback can help avoid repeating past mistakes. Second, another mistake might be made to cover up the earlier one. A "loss on disposal" could alert superiors to the incorrect economic-life prediction used in the earlier decision. By avoiding replacement, the manager can spread the $4,000 remaining book value over the future as "depreciation," a more appealing term than "loss on disposal." The superiors may never find out about the incorrect prediction of economic life. Using accounting income for performance evaluation mixes the financial effects of various decisions, hiding both the earlier misestimation of useful life and the current failure to replace.

The conflict between decision making and performance evaluation is a widespread problem in practice. Unfortunately, there are no easy solutions. In theory, accountants could evaluate performance in a manner consistent with decision making. In our equipment example, this would mean predicting year-by-year income effects over the planning horizon of 4 years, noting that the first year would be poor, and evaluating actual performance against the predictions.

The trouble is that evaluating performance decision by decision is a costly procedure. Therefore, we generally use aggregate measures. For example, an income statement shows the results of many decisions, not just the single decision of buying a machine. Consequently, in many cases like our equipment example, the first-year effects on the income statement may be the major influence on managers' decisions. Thus, managers refrain from taking the longer view that would benefit the company.

Chapters 5 and 6 introduced the important topics of relevant information and decision making. Our major focus was on how to determine and use relevant information when faced with various managerial decisions such as pricing, special orders, make or buy, adding or deleting a product line, and equipment replacement. We have emphasized the importance of understanding cost behavior in each of these decision situations. Now, we shift our emphasis from decision-making techniques to planning and control techniques. One of the most important planning techniques you will use as a manager is budgeting—the major topic in Chapters 7 and 8.

Highlights to Remember

1. **Use a differential analysis to examine income effects across alternatives, and show that an opportunity-cost analysis yields identical results.** A differential analysis is a valuable tool for analyzing decisions; it focuses on the relevant items in the situation—differential revenues and differential costs. One should always consider opportunity costs when deciding on the use of limited resources. The opportunity cost of a course of action is the maximum profit forgone from other alternative actions. Decision makers may fail to consider opportunity costs because accountants do not report them in the financial accounting system.

2. **Decide whether to make or to buy certain parts or products.** One of the most important production decisions is the make-or-buy decision. Should a company make its own parts or products or should it buy them from outside sources? Both qualitative and quantitative factors affect this decision. In applying relevant cost analysis to a make-or-buy situation, a key factor to consider is often the opportunity cost of facilities.

3. **Choose whether to add or delete a product line using relevant information.** Relevant information also plays an important role in decisions about adding or deleting products, services, or departments. Decisions on whether to delete a department or product line require analysis of the revenues forgone and the costs saved from the deletion.

4. **Compute the optimal product mix when production is constrained by a scarce resource.** When production is constrained by a limiting resource, the key to obtaining the maximum profit from a given capacity is to obtain the greatest possible contribution to profit per unit of the limiting or scarce resource.

5. **Decide whether to process a joint product beyond the split-off point.** Another typical production situation is deciding whether to process further a joint product or sell it at the split-off point. The relevant information for this decision includes the costs that differ beyond the split-off point. Joint costs that occur before split-off are irrelevant.

6. **Decide whether to keep or replace equipment.** In the decision to keep or replace equipment, the book value of old equipment is irrelevant. This sunk cost is a past or historical cost that a company has already incurred. Relevant costs normally include the disposal value of old equipment, the cost of new equipment, and the difference in the annual operating costs.

7. **Identify irrelevant and misspecified costs.** In certain production decisions, it is important to recognize and identify irrelevant costs. In the decision to dispose of obsolete inventory, the original cost of the inventory is irrelevant. Unit fixed costs can be misleading because of the differences in the assumed level of volume on which they are based. The more units a company makes, the lower the unit fixed cost will be. You can avoid being misled by unit costs by always using total fixed costs.

8. **Discuss how performance measures can affect decision making.** If companies evaluate managers using performance measures that are not in line with relevant decision criteria, there could be a conflict of interest. Managers often make decisions based on how the decision affects their performance measures. Thus, performance measures work best when they are consistent with the long-term good of the company. ∎

Accounting Vocabulary

accumulated depreciation, p. 236	incremental analysis, p. 223	opportunity cost, p. 223
avoidable costs, p. 231	incremental benefits, p. 223	outlay cost, p. 223
book value, p. 236	incremental costs, p. 223	outsourcing, p. 225
common costs, p. 231	inventory turnover, p. 233	scarce resource, p. 232
depreciation, p. 236	joint costs, p. 234	separable costs, p. 234
differential analysis, p. 223	joint products, p. 234	split-off point, p. 234
differential cost, p. 223	limiting factor, p. 232	sunk cost, p. 236
differential revenue, p. 223	net book value, p. 236	unavoidable costs, p. 231

 # Fundamental Assignment Material

6-A1 Make or Buy
Sunshine State Fruit Company sells premium-quality oranges and other citrus fruits by mail order. Protecting the fruit during shipping is important so the company has designed and produces shipping boxes. The annual cost to make 80,000 boxes is

Materials	$112,000
Labor	20,000
Indirect manufacturing costs	
Variable	16,000
Fixed	60,000
Total	$208,000

Therefore, the cost per box averages $2.60.

Suppose **Weyerhaeuser** submits a bid to supply Sunshine State with boxes for $2.10 per box. Sunshine State must give Weyerhaeuser the box design specifications, and the boxes will be made according to those specs.

1. How much, if any, would Sunshine State save by buying the boxes from Weyerhaeuser?
2. What subjective factors should affect Sunshine State's decision about whether to make or buy the boxes?
3. Suppose all the fixed costs represent depreciation on equipment that was purchased for $600,000 and is just about at the end of its 10-year life. New replacement equipment will cost $800,000 and is also expected to last 10 years. In this case, how much, if any, would Sunshine State save by buying the boxes from Weyerhaeuser?

6-A2 Choice of Products

The Ibunez Tool Company has two products: a plain circular saw and a professional circular saw. The plain saw sells for $70 and has a variable cost of $55. The professional saw sells for $100 and has a variable cost of $75.

1. Compute contribution margins and contribution-margin ratios for plain and professional saws.
2. The demand is for more units than the company can produce. There are only 20,000 machine-hours of manufacturing capacity available. Two plain saws can be produced in the same average time (1 hour) needed to produce one professional saw. Compute the total contribution margin for 20,000 hours for plain saws only and for professional saws only. Which product is the best use of machine hours?
3. Use two or three sentences to state the major lesson of this problem.

6-A3 Joint Products: Sell or Process Further

The Mussina Chemical Company produced three joint products at a joint cost of $117,000. These products were processed further and sold as follows:

Chemical Product	Sales	Additional Processing Costs
A	$230,000	$190,000
B	330,000	300,000
C	175,000	100,000

The company has had an opportunity to sell at split-off directly to other processors. If that alternative had been selected, sales would have been A, $54,000; B, $32,000; and C, $54,000.

The company expects to operate at the same level of production and sales in the forthcoming year. Consider all the available information, and assume that all costs incurred after split-off are variable.

1. Could the company increase operating income by altering its processing decisions? If so, what would be the expected overall operating income?
2. Which products should be processed further and which should be sold at split-off?

6-A4 Role of Old Equipment Replacement

On January 2, 2010, the S. H. Park Company installed a brand new $90,000 special molding machine for producing a new product. The product and the machine have an expected life of 3 years. The machine's expected disposal value at the end of 3 years is zero.

On January 3, 2010, Kimiyo Lee, a star salesperson for a machine tool manufacturer, tells Mr. Park, "I wish I had known earlier of your purchase plans. I can supply you with a technically superior machine for $99,000. The machine you just purchased can be sold for $15,000. I guarantee that our machine will save $38,000 per year in cash operating costs, although it too will have no disposal value at the end of 3 years."

Park examines some technical data. Although he has confidence in Lee's claims, Park contends, "I'm locked in now. My alternatives are clear: (a) Disposal will result in a loss, (b) keeping and using the 'old' equipment avoids such a loss. I have brains enough to avoid a loss when my other alternative is recognizing a loss. We've got to use that equipment until we get our money out of it."

The annual operating costs of the old machine are expected to be $60,000, exclusive of depreciation. Sales, all in cash, will be $910,000 per year. Other annual cash expenses will be $810,000 regardless of this decision. Assume that the equipment in question is the company's only fixed asset.

Ignore income taxes and the time value of money.

1. Prepare statements of cash receipts and disbursements as they would appear in each of the next 3 years under both alternatives. What is the total cumulative increase or decrease in cash for the 3 years?
2. Prepare income statements as they would appear in each of the next 3 years under both alternatives. Assume straight-line depreciation. What is the cumulative increase or decrease in net income for the 3 years?
3. Assume that the cost of the "old" equipment was $1 million rather than $90,000. Would the net difference computed in numbers 1 and 2 change? Explain.
4. As Kimiyo Lee, reply to Mr. Park's contentions.
5. What are the irrelevant items in each of your presentations for numbers 1 and 2? Why are they irrelevant?

6-B1 Make or Buy

Suppose a **BMW** executive in Germany is trying to decide whether the company should continue to manufacture an engine component or purchase it from Frankfurt Corporation for €50 each. Demand for the coming year is expected to be the same as for the current year, 200,000 units. Data for the current year follow:

Direct material	€ 5,000,000
Direct labor	1,900,000
Factory overhead, variable	1,100,000
Factory overhead, fixed	3,000,000
Total costs	€11,000,000

If BMW makes the components, the unit costs of direct material will increase by 10%.

If BMW buys the components, 30% of the fixed costs will be avoided. The other 70% will continue regardless of whether the components are manufactured or purchased. Assume that variable overhead varies with output volume.

1. Prepare a schedule that compares the make-or-buy alternatives. Show totals and amounts per unit. Compute the numerical difference between making and buying. Assume that the capacity now used to make the components will become idle if the components are purchased.
2. Assume also that the BMW capacity in question can be rented to a local electronics firm for €1,150,000 for the coming year. Prepare a schedule that compares the net relevant costs of the three alternatives: make, buy and leave capacity idle, buy and rent. Which is the most favorable alternative? By how much in total?

6-B2 Unit Costs and Capacity

Fargo Manufacturing Company produces two industrial solvents for which the following data have been tabulated. Fixed manufacturing cost is applied to products at a rate of $1.00 per machine-hour.

Per Unit	XY-7	BD-4
Selling price	$6.00	$4.00
Variable manufacturing costs	3.00	1.50
Fixed manufacturing cost	.75	.25
Variable selling cost	2.00	2.00

The sales manager has had a $150,000 increase in her budget allotment for advertising and wants to apply the money on the most profitable product. The solvents are not substitutes for one another in the eyes of the company's customers.

1. How many machine-hours does it take to produce one XY-7? To produce one BD-4? (Hint: Focus on applied fixed manufacturing cost.)
2. Suppose Fargo has only 100,000 machine-hours that can be made available to produce XY-7 and BD-4. If the potential increase in sales units for either product resulting from advertising is far in excess of these production capabilities, which product should be produced and advertised, and what is the estimated increase in contribution margin earned?

6-B3 Dropping a Product Line

Hamleys Toy Store is on Regent Street in London. It has a magic department near the main door. Suppose that management is considering dropping the magic department, which has consistently shown an operating loss. The predicted income statements, in thousands of pounds (£), are at the top of page 245 (for ease of analysis, only three product lines are shown).

The £300,000 of magic department fixed expenses include the compensation of employees of £120,000. These employees will be released if the magic department is abandoned. All of the magic department's equipment is fully depreciated, so none of the £300,000 pertains to such items. Furthermore, disposal values of equipment will be exactly offset by the costs of removal and remodeling.

If the magic department is dropped, the manager will use the vacated space for either more general merchandise or more electronic products. The expansion of general merchandise would not entail

	Total	General Merchandise	Electronic Products	Magic Department
Sales	£6,000	£5,000	£400	£ 600
Variable expenses	4,090	3,500	200	390
Contribution margin	£1,910 (32%)	£1,500 (30%)	£200 (50%)	£ 210 (35%)
Fixed expenses (compensation, depreciation, property taxes, insurance, etc.)	1,100	750	50	300
Operating income (loss)	£ 810	£ 750	£150	£(90)

hiring any additional salaried help, but more electronic products would require an additional person at an annual cost of £30,000. The manager thinks that sales of general merchandise would increase by £250,000; electronic products, by £200,000. The manager's modest predictions are partially based on the fact that she thinks the magic department has helped lure customers to the store and, thus, improved overall sales. If the magic department is closed, that lure would be gone.

Should the magic department be closed? Explain, showing computations.

6-B4 Sell or Process Further

ConAgra produces meat products with brand names such as Healthy Choice, Armour, and Butterball. Suppose one of the company's plants processes beef cattle into various products. For simplicity, assume that there are only three products: steak, hamburger, and hides, and that the average steer costs $700. The three products emerge from a process that costs $100 per steer to run, and output from one steer can be sold for the following net amounts:

Steak (100 pounds)	$ 400
Hamburger (500 pounds)	600
Hide (120 pounds)	100
Total	$1,100

Assume that each of these three products can be sold immediately or processed further in another ConAgra plant. The steak can be the main course in frozen dinners sold under the Healthy Choice label. The vegetables and desserts in the 400 dinners produced from the 100 pounds of steak would cost $110, and production, sales, and other costs for the 400 meals would total $330. Each meal would be sold wholesale for $2.10.

The hamburger could be made into frozen Salisbury steak patties sold under the Armour label. The only additional cost would be a $200 processing cost for the 500 pounds of hamburger. Frozen Salisbury steaks sell wholesale for $1.70 per pound.

The hide can be sold before or after tanning. The cost of tanning one hide is $80, and a tanned hide can be sold for $170.

1. Compute the total profit if all three products are sold at the split-off point.
2. Compute the total profit if all three products are processed further before being sold.
3. Which products should be sold at the split-off point? Which should be processed further?
4. Compute the total profit if your plan in number 3 is followed.

6-B5 Replacing Old Equipment

Consider the data regarding Douglas County's photocopying requirements at the top of page 246.

The county administrator is trying to decide whether to replace the old equipment. Because of rapid changes in technology, she expects the replacement equipment to have only a 3-year useful life. Ignore the effects of taxes.

1. Prepare a schedule that compares both relevant and irrelevant items for the next 3 years. (Hint: See Exhibit 6-5, page 237.)
2. Prepare a schedule that compares all relevant items for the next 3 years. Which tabulation is clearer, this one or the one in requirement 1? (Hint: See Exhibit 6-6, page 238.)
3. Prepare a simple "shortcut" or direct analysis to support your choice of alternatives.

	Old Equipment	Proposed Replacement Equipment
Useful life, in years	5	3
Current age, in years	2	0
Useful life remaining, in years	3	3
Original cost	$25,000	$15,000
Accumulated depreciation	10,000	0
Book value	15,000	Not acquired yet
Disposal value (in cash) now	6,000	Not acquired yet
Disposal value in 3 years	0	0
Annual cash operating costs for power, maintenance, toner, and supplies	14,000	9,000

6-B6 Decision and Performance Models
Refer to the preceding problem.

1. Suppose the "decision model" favored by top management consisted of a comparison of a 3-year accumulation of cash under each alternative. As the manager of office operations, which alternative would you choose? Why?
2. Suppose the "performance evaluation model" emphasized the minimization of overall costs of photocopying operations for the first year. Which alternative would you choose?

 **Additional Assignment Material**

QUESTIONS

6-1 Distinguish between an opportunity cost and an outlay cost.

6-2 "I had a chance to rent my summer home for 2 weeks for $800. But I chose to have it idle. I didn't want strangers living in my summer house." What term in this chapter describes the $800? Why?

6-3 "Accountants do not ordinarily record opportunity costs in the formal accounting records." Why?

6-4 Distinguish between an incremental cost and a differential cost.

6-5 "Incremental cost is the addition to costs from the manufacture of one unit." Do you agree? Explain.

6-6 "The differential costs or incremental costs of increasing production from 1,000 automobiles to 1,200 automobiles per week would be the additional costs of producing the additional 200 automobiles." If production were reduced from 1,200 to 1,000 automobiles per week, what would the decline in costs be called?

6-7 "Qualitative factors generally favor making over buying a component." Do you agree? Explain.

6-8 "Choices are often mislabeled as simply make or buy." Do you agree? Explain.

6-9 "The key to decisions to delete a product or department is identifying avoidable costs." Do you agree? Explain.

6-10 Give four examples of limiting or scarce factors.

6-11 What are joint products? Name several examples of joint products.

6-12 What is the split-off point, and why is it important in analyzing joint costs?

6-13 "No technique used to assign the joint cost to individual products should be used for management decisions regarding whether a product should be sold at the split-off point or processed further." Do you agree? Explain.

6-14 "Inventory that was purchased for $5,000 should not be sold for less than $5,000 because such a sale would result in a loss." Do you agree? Explain.

6-15 "Recovering sunk costs is a major objective when replacing equipment." Do you agree? Explain.

6-16 "Past costs are indeed relevant in most instances because they provide the point of departure for the entire decision process." Do you agree? Why?

6-17 Which of the following items are relevant to replacement decisions? Explain.
  a. Book value of old equipment
  b. Disposal value of old equipment
  c. Cost of new equipment

6-18 "Some expected future costs may be irrelevant." Do you agree? Explain.

6-19 "Variable costs are irrelevant whenever they do not differ among the alternatives at hand." Do you agree? Explain.

6-20 There are two major reasons why unit costs should be analyzed with care in decision making. What are they?

6-21 "Machinery sales personnel sometimes erroneously brag about the low unit costs of using their machines." Identify one source of an error concerning the estimation of unit costs.

6-22 Give an example of a situation in which the performance evaluation model is not consistent with the decision model.

6-23 "Evaluating performance, decision by decision, is costly. Aggregate measures, such as the income statement, are frequently used." How might the wide use of income statements affect managers' decisions about buying equipment?

CRITICAL THINKING EXERCISES

6-24 Measurement of Opportunity Cost
"Accountants cannot measure opportunity cost. Only managers have the knowledge to measure it." Do you agree with this statement? Why or why not?

6-25 Outsourcing Decisions
Decisions on whether to outsource services such as payroll accounting and systems development are much like make-or-buy decisions. What cost factors should influence the decision on whether to outsource payroll functions?

6-26 Unitized Costs
Suppose you are a manager in a manufacturing company. Your accountant has just presented you with a very detailed cost analysis for a decision about whether to outsource or make a component of a product. You have to use this analysis in a meeting with other managers. Since the analysis is shown in totals and your colleagues prefer simple reports and unit costs, you divide the bottom-line amounts by the total units to be made or bought (outsourced) and present just these in a simple report. Your colleagues are pleased that your report is so easy to understand and simple to use. Then they begin to predict the total cost differences for several other possible numbers of units to be made or outsourced by simply multiplying the unit costs by the volume to be outsourced. Why should you feel uncomfortable?

6-27 Historical Costs and Inventory Decisions
Explain why it is sometimes best to sell inventory for less than the amount paid for it.

EXERCISES

6-28 Opportunity Costs
Martina Bridgeman is an attorney employed by a large law firm at a salary of $110,000 per year. She is considering whether to become a sole practitioner, which would probably generate annually $350,000 in operating revenues and $220,000 in operating expenses.

1. Present two tabulations of the annual income effects of these alternatives. The second tabulation should include the opportunity cost of Bridgeman's compensation as an employee.
2. Suppose Bridgeman prefers less risk and chooses to stay an employee. Show a tabulation of the income effects of rejecting the opportunity of independent practice.

6-29 Opportunity Cost of Home Ownership
Oliver Kamp has just made the final payment on his mortgage. He could continue to live in the home; cash expenses for repairs and maintenance (after any tax effects) would be $500 monthly. Alternatively, he could sell the home for $200,000 (net of taxes), invest the proceeds in 5% municipal tax-free bonds, and rent an apartment for $12,000 annually. The landlord would then pay for repairs and maintenance.

Prepare two analyses of Kamp's alternatives, one showing no explicit opportunity cost and the second showing the explicit opportunity cost of the decision to hold the present home.

6-30 Opportunity Cost at Nantucket Nectars
Suppose Nantucket Nectars has a machine for which it paid $160,000 several years ago and is currently not being used. It can use the machine to produce 12 oz. bottles of its Juice Cocktails or 12 oz. bottles of its 100% Juices. The contribution margin from the additional sales of 100% Juices would be $90,000. A third alternative is selling the machine for cash of $75,000. What is the opportunity cost of the machine when we analyze the alternative to produce 12 oz. bottles of Juice Cocktails?

6-31 Hospital Opportunity Cost

An administrator at **Saint Jude Hospital** is considering how to use some space made available when the outpatient clinic moved to a new building. She has narrowed her choices, as follows:

   a. Use the space to expand laboratory testing. Expected future annual revenue would be $330,000; future costs, $290,000.
   b. Use the space to expand the eye clinic. Expected future annual revenue would be $500,000; future costs, $480,000.
   c. The gift shop is rented by an independent retailer who wants to expand into the vacated space. The retailer has offered $11,000 for the yearly rental of the space. All operating expenses will be borne by the retailer.

The administrator's planning horizon is unsettled. However, she has decided that the yearly data given will suffice for guiding her decision.

Tabulate the total relevant data regarding the decision alternatives. Omit the concept of opportunity cost in one tabulation, but use the concept in a second tabulation. As the administrator, which tabulation would you prefer if you could receive only one?

6-32 Make or Buy

Assume that a division of **Bose** makes an electronic component for its speakers. Its manufacturing process for the component is a highly automated part of a just-in-time production system. All labor is considered to be an overhead cost, and all overhead is regarded as fixed with respect to output volume. Production costs for 100,000 units of the component are as follows:

Direct materials		$400,000
Factory overhead		
Indirect labor	$80,000	
Supplies	30,000	
Allocated occupancy cost	40,000	150,000
Total cost		$550,000

A small, local company has offered to supply the components at a price of $4.20 each. If the division discontinued its production of the component, it would save two-thirds of the supplies cost and $30,000 of indirect-labor cost. All other overhead costs would continue.

The division manager recently attended a seminar on cost behavior and learned about fixed and variable costs. He wants to continue to make the component because the variable cost of $4.00 is below the $4.20 bid.

   1. Compute the relevant cost of (a) making and (b) purchasing the component. Which alternative is less costly and by how much?
   2. What qualitative factors might influence the decision about whether to make or to buy the component?

6-33 Make or Buy at Nantucket Nectars

Assume that Nantucket Nectars reports the following costs to make 17.5 oz. bottles for its Juice Cocktails:

Nantucket Nectars Company
Cost of Making 17.5-Ounce Bottles

	Total Cost for 1,000,000 Bottles	Cost per Bottle
Direct materials	$ 80,000	$.080
Direct labor	30,000	.030
Variable factory overhead	60,000	.060
Fixed factory overhead	85,000	.085
Total costs	$255,000	$.255

Another manufacturer offers to sell Nantucket Nectars the bottles for $.25. The capacity now used to make bottles will become idle if the company purchases the bottles. Further, one supervisor with a salary of $60,000, a fixed cost, would be eliminated if the bottles were purchased. Prepare a schedule that compares the costs to make and buy the 17.5 oz. bottles. Should Nantucket Nectars make or buy the bottles?

6-34 Make or Buy and the Use of Idle Facilities at Nantucket Nectars

Refer to the preceding exercise. Suppose Nantucket Nectars can use the released facilities in another manufacturing activity that makes a contribution to profits of $75,000 or can rent them out for $55,000. Prepare a schedule that compares the four alternative courses of action. Which alternative would yield the lowest net cost?

6-35 Profit per Unit of Space

1. Several successful chains of warehouse stores such as Costco and Sam's Club have merchandising policies that differ considerably from those of traditional department stores. Name some characteristics of these warehouse stores that have contributed to their success.
2. Food chains such as Safeway have typically regarded approximately 20% of selling price as an average target gross profit on canned goods and similar grocery items. What are the limitations of such an approach? Be specific.

6-36 Deletion of Product Line

Zurich American School is an international private elementary school. In addition to regular classes, after-school care is provided between 3:00 PM and 6:00 PM at CHF 12 per child per hour. Financial results for the after-school care for a representative month are

Revenue, 600 hours at CHF 12 per hour		CHF 7,200
Less		
Teacher salaries	CHF 6,000	
Supplies	800	
Depreciation	1,300	
Sanitary engineering	100	
Other fixed costs	200	8,400
Operating income (loss)		CHF (1,200)

The director of Zurich American School is considering discontinuing the after-school care services because it is not fair to the other students to subsidize the after-school care program. He thinks that eliminating the program will free up CHF 1,200 a month to support regular classes.

1. Compute the financial impact on Zurich American School from discontinuing the after-school care program.
2. List three qualitative factors that would influence your decision.

6-37 Sell or Process Further

An Exxon petrochemical factory produces two products, L and M, as a result of a particular joint process. Both products are sold to manufacturers as ingredients for assorted chemical products.
   Product L sells at split off for $.25 per gallon; M, for $.30 per gallon. Data for April follow:

Joint processing cost	$1,600,000
Gallons produced and sold	
L	4,000,000
M	2,500,000

Suppose that in April the 2,500,000 gallons of M could have been processed further into Super M at an additional cost of $165,000. The Super M output would be sold for $.36 per gallon. Product L would be sold at split off in any event.
   Should M have been processed further in April and sold as Super M? Show your computations.

6-38 Joint Products, Multiple Choice

From a particular joint process, Edgerton company produces three products, A, B, and C. Each product may be sold at the point of split-off or processed further. Additional processing requires no special facilities, and production costs of further processing are entirely variable and traceable to the products involved. In 2009, all three products were processed beyond split-off. Joint production costs for the year were $72,000. Sales values and costs needed to evaluate Edgerton's 2009 production policy follow:

Product	Units Produced	Net Realizable Values (Sales Values) at Split Off	Additional Costs and Sales Values if Processed Further	
			Sales Values	Added Costs
A	6,000	$25,000	$42,000	$ 9,000
B	4,000	41,000	45,000	7,000
C	2,000	24,000	32,000	10,000

Answer the following multiple-choice questions:

1. For units of C, the unit production cost most relevant to a sell-or-process-further decision is (a) $5, (b) $12, (c) $4, (d) $9.
2. To maximize profits, Edgerton should subject the following products to additional processing: (a) A only, (b) A, B, and C, (c) B and C only, (d) C only.

6-39 Obsolete Inventory

The Ohio State bookstore bought more "Buckeye Champs" calendars than it could sell. It was nearly June and 200 calendars remained in stock. The store paid $4.50 each for the calendars and normally sold them for $8.95. Since February, they had been on sale for $6.00, and 2 weeks ago the price was dropped to $5.00. Still, few calendars were being sold. The bookstore manager thought it was no longer worthwhile using shelf space for the calendars.

The proprietor of Hurricane Collectibles offered to buy all 200 calendars for $100. He intended to store them until the 2009 football season was over and then sell them as novelty items.

The bookstore manager was not sure she wanted to sell for $.50 calendars that cost $4.50. The only alternative, however, was to scrap them because the publisher would not take them back.

1. Compute the difference in profit between accepting the $100 offer and scrapping the calendars.
2. Describe how the $4.50 × 200 = $900 paid for the calendars affects your decision.

6-40 Replacement of Old Equipment

Three years ago, the Oak Street **TCBY** bought a frozen yogurt machine for $8,000. A salesman has just suggested to the TCBY manager that she replace the machine with a new, $12,500 machine. The manager has gathered the following data:

	Old Machine	New Machine
Original cost	$8,000	$12,500
Useful life in years	8	5
Current age in years	3	0
Useful life remaining in years	5	5
Accumulated depreciation	$3,000	Not acquired yet
Book value	$5,000	Not acquired yet
Disposal value (in cash) now	$2,000	Not acquired yet
Disposal value in 5 years	0	0
Annual cash operating cost	$4,500	$ 3,000

1. Compute the difference in total costs over the next 5 years under both alternatives, that is, keeping the original machine or replacing it with the new machine. Ignore taxes.
2. Suppose the Oak Street TCBY manager replaces the original machine. Compute the "loss on disposal" of the original machine. How does this amount affect your computation in number 1? Explain.

6-41 Unit Costs

Brandon Company produces and sells a product that has variable costs of $8 per unit and fixed costs of $250,000 per year.

1. Compute the unit cost at a production and sales level of 10,000 units per year.

2. Compute the unit cost at a production and sales level of 20,000 units per year.
3. Which of these unit costs is most accurate? Explain.

6-42 Relevant Investment

Roberta Thomas had obtained a new truck with a list price, including options, of $21,000. The dealer had given her a "generous trade-in allowance" of $5,000 on her old truck that had a wholesale price of $3,000. Sales tax was $1,260.

The annual cash operating costs of the old truck were $4,200. The new truck was expected to reduce these costs by one-third, to $2,800 per year.

Compute the amount of the original investment in the new truck. Explain your reasoning.

6-43 Weak Division

Lake Forest Electronics Company paid $7 million in cash 4 years ago to acquire a company that manufactures CD-ROM drives. This company has been operated as a division of Lake Forest and has lost $500,000 each year since its acquisition.

The minimum desired return for this division is that, when a new product is fully developed, it should return a net profit of $500,000 per year for the foreseeable future.

Recently, the **IBM Corporation** offered to purchase the division from Lake Forest for $5 million. The president of Lake Forest commented, "I've got an investment of $9 million to recoup ($7 million plus losses of $500,000 for each of 4 years). I have finally got this situation turned around, so I oppose selling the division now."

Prepare a response to the president's remarks. Indicate how to make this decision. Be as specific as possible.

6-44 Opportunity Cost

Renee Behr, MD, is a psychiatrist who is in heavy demand. Even though she has raised her fees considerably during the past 5 years, Dr. Behr still cannot accommodate all the patients who wish to see her.

Behr has conducted 6 hours of appointments a day, 6 days a week, for 48 weeks a year. Her fee averages $150 per hour.

Her variable costs are negligible and may be ignored for decision purposes. Ignore income taxes.

1. Behr is weary of working a 6-day week. She is considering taking every other Saturday off. What would be her annual income (a) if she worked every Saturday and (b) if she worked every other Saturday?
2. What would be her opportunity cost for the year of not working every other Saturday?
3. Assume that Dr. Behr has definitely decided to take every other Saturday off. She loves to repair her sports car by doing the work herself. If she works on her car during half a Saturday when she otherwise would not see patients, what is her opportunity cost?

PROBLEMS

6-45 Hotel Rooms and Opportunity Costs

The **Marriott Corporation** operates many hotels throughout the world. Suppose one of its Chicago hotels is facing difficult times because of the opening of several new competing hotels.

To accommodate its flight personnel, **American Airlines** has offered Marriott a contract for the coming year that provides a rate of $70 per night per room for a minimum of 50 rooms for 365 nights. This contract would assure Marriott of selling 50 rooms of space nightly, even if some of the rooms are vacant on some nights. Assume zero variable costs.

The Marriott manager has mixed feelings about the contract. On several peak nights during the year, the hotel could sell the same space for $150 per room.

1. Suppose the Marriott manager signs the contract. What is the opportunity cost of the 50 rooms on October 20, the night of a big convention of retailers when every nearby hotel room is occupied? What is the opportunity cost on December 28, when only 10 of these rooms would be expected to be rented at an average rate of $100?
2. If the year-round rate per room averaged $110, what percentage of occupancy of the 50 rooms in question would have to be rented to make Marriott indifferent about accepting the offer?

6-46 Extension of Preceding Problem

Assume the same facts as in the preceding problem. However, also assume that the variable costs per room, per day are $10.

1. Suppose the best estimate is a 62% general occupancy rate for the 50 rooms at an average $110 room rate for the next year. Should Marriott accept the contract?

2. What percentage of occupancy of the 50 rooms in question would make Marriott indifferent about accepting the offer?

6-47 Make or Buy

Dana Corporation, based in Toledo, Ohio, is a global manufacturer of highly engineered products that serve industrial, vehicle, construction, commercial, aerospace, and semiconductor markets. Dana's 2009 sales were $10.3 billion. It frequently subcontracts work to other manufacturers, depending on whether Dana's facilities are fully occupied. Suppose Dana is about to make some final decisions regarding the use of its manufacturing facilities for the coming year.

The following are the costs of making part EC113, a key component of an emissions control system:

	Total Cost for 50,000 Units	Cost per Unit
Direct materials	$ 400,000	$ 8
Direct labor	250,000	5
Variable factory overhead	150,000	3
Fixed factory overhead	300,000	6
Total manufacturing costs	$1,100,000	$22

Another manufacturer has offered to sell the same part to Dana for $20 each. The fixed overhead consists of depreciation, property taxes, insurance, and supervisory salaries. All the fixed overhead would continue if Dana bought the component except that the cost of $150,000 pertaining to some supervisory and custodial personnel could be avoided.

1. Assume that the capacity now used to make parts will become idle if the parts are purchased. Should Dana buy or make the parts? Show computations.
2. Assume that the capacity now used to make parts will either (a) be rented to a nearby manufacturer for $75,000 for the year or (b) be used to make oil filters that will yield a profit contribution of $100,000. Should Dana buy or make part EC113? Show your computations.

6-48 Relevant-Cost Analysis

Following are the unit costs of making and selling a single product at a normal level of 5,000 units per month and a current unit selling price of $90:

Manufacturing costs	
Direct materials	$35
Direct labor	12
Variable overhead	8
Fixed overhead (total for the year, $300,000)	5
Selling and administrative expenses	
Variable	15
Fixed (total for the year, $480,000)	8

Consider each requirement separately. Label all computations, and present your solutions in a form that will be comprehensible to the company president.

1. This product is usually sold at a rate of 60,000 units per year. It is predicted that a rise in price to $98 will decrease volume by 10%. How much may advertising be increased under this plan without having annual operating income fall below the current level?
2. The company has received a proposal from an outside supplier to make and ship this item directly to the company's customers as sales orders are forwarded. Variable selling and administrative costs would fall 40%. If the supplier's proposal is accepted, the company will use its own plant to produce a new product. The new product would be sold through manufacturer's agents at a 10% commission based on a selling price of $40 each. The cost characteristics of this product, based on predicted yearly normal volume, are at the top of page 253.
   What is the maximum price per unit that the company can afford to pay to the supplier for subcontracting production of the entire old product? Assume the following:
   • Total fixed factory overhead and total fixed selling expenses will not change if the new product line is added.

	Per Unit
Direct materials	$ 6
Direct labor	12
Variable overhead	8
Fixed overhead	6
Manufacturing costs	$32
Selling and administrative expenses	
Variable (commission)	10% of selling price
Fixed	$ 2

- The supplier's proposal will not be considered unless the present annual net income can be maintained.
- Selling price of the old product will remain unchanged.
- All $300,000 of fixed manufacturing overhead will be assigned to the new product.

6-49 Hotel Pricing and Use of Capacity

A growing corporation in a large city has offered a 200-room **Holiday Inn** a 1-year contract to rent 40 rooms at reduced rates of $50 per room instead of the regular rate of $86 per room. The corporation will sign the contract for 365-day occupancy because its visiting manufacturing and marketing personnel are virtually certain to use all the space each night.

Each room occupied has a variable cost of $12 per night (for cleaning, laundry, lost linens, and extra electricity).

The hotel manager expects an 85% occupancy rate for the year so she is reluctant to sign the contract. If the contract is signed, the occupancy rate on the remaining 160 rooms will be 95%.

1. Compute the total contribution margin for the year with and without the contract. Is the contract profitable to Holiday Inn?
2. Compute the lowest room rate that the hotel should accept on the contract so that the total contribution margin would be the same with or without the contract.

6-50 Special Air Fares

Denver-based **Frontier Airlines** provides service to 39 cities in the United States and Mexico. Frontier operates a fleet of 37 aircraft including sixteen 134-passenger **Boeing** 737-300 jets. The manager of operations of Frontier Airlines is trying to decide whether to adopt a new discount fare. Focus on one 134-seat 737 airplane now operating at a 56% load factor. That is, on average the airplane has .56 × 134 = 75 passengers. The regular fares produce an average revenue of $.12 per passenger mile.

Suppose an average 40% fare discount (which is subject to restrictions regarding time of departure and length of stay) will produce three new additional passengers. Also suppose that three of the previously committed passengers accept the restrictions and switch to the discount fare from the regular fare.

1. Compute the total revenue per airplane-mile with and without the discount fares.
2. Suppose the maximum allowed allocation to new discount fares is 50 seats. These will be filled. As before, some previously committed passengers will accept the restrictions and switch to the discount fare from the regular fare. How many will have to switch so that the total revenue per mile will be the same either with or without the discount plan?

6-51 Choice of Products

Gulf Coast Fashions sells both designer and moderately priced women's wear in Tampa. Profits have been volatile. Top management is trying to decide which product line to drop. Accountants have reported the following data:

	Per Item	
	Designer	**Moderately Priced**
Average selling price	$240	$150
Average variable expenses	120	85
Average contribution margin	$120	$ 65
Average contribution-margin percentage	50%	43%

The store has 8,000 square feet of floor space. If moderately priced goods are sold exclusively, 400 items can be displayed. If designer goods are sold exclusively, only 300 items can be displayed.

Moreover, the rate of sale (turnover) of the designer items will be two-thirds the rate of moderately priced goods.

1. Prepare an analysis to show which product to drop.
2. What other considerations might affect your decision in number 1?

6-52 Analysis of Unit Costs

Home Appliances Company manufactures small appliances, such as electric can openers, toasters, food mixers, and irons. The peak manufacturing season is at hand, and the president is trying to decide whether to produce more of the company's standard line of can openers or its premium line that includes a built-in knife sharpener, a better finish, and a higher-quality motor. The unit data follow:

	Product	
	Standard	**Premium**
Selling price	$29	$39
Direct material	$ 8	$13
Direct labor	2	1
Variable factory overhead	4	6
Fixed factory overhead	6	9
Total cost of goods sold	$20	$29
Gross profit per unit	$ 9	$10

The sales outlook is very encouraging. The plant could operate at full capacity by producing either product or both products. Both the standard and the premium products are processed through the same departments. Selling and administrative costs will not be affected by this decision so they may be ignored.

Many of the parts are produced on automatic machinery. The factory overhead is allocated to products by developing separate rates per machine-hour for variable and fixed overhead. For example, the total fixed overhead is divided by the total machine-hours to get a rate per hour. Thus, the amount of overhead allocated to products is dependent on the number of machine-hours used by the product. It takes 1 hour of machine time to produce one unit of the standard product.

Direct labor may not be proportionate with overhead because many workers operate two or more machines simultaneously.

Which product should be produced? If more than one should be produced, indicate the proportions of each. Show computations. Explain your answers briefly.

6-53 Use of Available Facilities

The Oahu Audio Company manufactures electronic subcomponents that can be sold as is or can be processed further into "plug-in" assemblies for a variety of intricate electronic equipment. The entire output of subcomponents can be sold at a market price of $2.20 per unit. The plug-in assemblies have been generating a sales price of $5.70 for 3 years, but the price has recently fallen to $5.30 on assorted orders.

Janet Oh, the vice president of marketing, has analyzed the markets and the costs. She thinks that production of plug-in assemblies should be dropped whenever the price falls below $4.70 per unit. However, at the current price of $5.30, the total available capacity should currently be devoted to producing plug-in assemblies. She has cited the data in Exhibit 6-7.

Direct-materials and direct-labor costs are variable. The total overhead is fixed; it is allocated to units produced by predicting the total overhead for the coming year and dividing this total by the total hours of capacity available.

The total hours of capacity available are 600,000. It takes 1 hour to make 60 subcomponents and 2 hours of additional processing and testing to make 60 plug-in assemblies.

1. If the price of plug-in assemblies for the coming year is to be $5.30, should sales of subcomponents be dropped and all facilities devoted to the production of plug-in assemblies? Show your computations.
2. Prepare a report for the vice president of marketing to show the lowest possible price for plug-in assemblies that would be acceptable.
3. Suppose 40% of the manufacturing overhead is variable with respect to processing and testing time. Repeat numbers 1 and 2. Do your answers change? If so, how?

6-54 Joint Costs and Incremental Analysis

Jacque de Paris, a high-fashion women's dress manufacturer, is planning to market a new cocktail dress for the coming season. Jacque de Paris supplies retailers in Europe and the United States.

	Subcomponents	
Selling price, after deducting relevant selling costs		$2.20
Direct materials	$1.10	
Direct labor	.30	
Manufacturing overhead	.60	
Cost per unit		2.00
Operating profit		$ .20
	Plug-In Assemblies	
Selling price, after deducting relevant selling costs		$5.30
Transferred-in variable cost for subcomponents	$1.40	
Additional direct materials	1.45	
Direct labor	.45	
Manufacturing overhead	1.20*	
Cost per unit		4.50
Operating profit		$ .80

Exhibit 6-7
Oahu Audio Company
Product Profitability Data

*For additional processing to make and test plug-in assemblies.

Four yards of material are required to lay out the dress pattern. Some material remains after cutting, which can be sold as remnants. The leftover material could also be used to manufacture a matching cape and handbag. However, if the leftover material is to be used for the cape and handbag, more care will be required in the cutting, which will increase the cutting costs.

The company expects to sell 1,250 dresses if no matching cape or handbag is available. Market research reveals that dress sales will be 20% higher if a matching cape and handbag are available. The market research indicates that the cape and handbag will not be sold individually, but only as accessories with the dress. The various combinations of dresses, capes, and handbags that are expected to be sold by retailers are as follows:

Percent of Total	
Complete sets of dress, cape, and handbag	70%
Dress and cape	6%
Dress and handbag	15%
Dress only	9%
Total	100%

The material used in the dress costs €80 a yard, or €320 for each dress. The cost of cutting the dress if the cape and handbag are not manufactured is estimated at €100 a dress, and the resulting remnants can be sold for €28 for each dress cut out. If the cape and handbag are to be manufactured, the cutting costs will be increased by €30 per dress. There will be no salable remnants if the capes and handbags are manufactured in the quantities estimated. The selling prices and the costs to complete the three items once they are cut are as follows:

	Selling Price per Unit	Unit Cost to Complete (Excludes Cost of Material and Cutting Operation)
Dress	€1,050	€400
Cape	140	100
Handbag	50	30

1. Calculate the incremental profit or loss to Jacque de Paris from manufacturing the capes and handbags in conjunction with the dresses.
2. Identify any non-quantitative factors that could influence the company's management in its decision to manufacture the capes and handbags that match the dress.

6-55 Joint Products: Sell or Process Further

Western, Corp., produces two products, cigars and chewing tobacco, from a joint process involving the processing of tobacco leaves. Joint costs are $60,000 for this process, and yield 2,000 pounds of cigars and 4,000 pounds of chewing tobacco. Cigars sell for $80 per pound, and chewing tobacco sells for $20 per pound. Cigars require $80,000 in separable costs, while chewing tobacco requires $50,000 in separable costs. Chewing tobacco can be processed further (for $30,000 in additional separable costs) into a mint-flavored premium chewing tobacco that would sell for $30 per pound.

1. Should Western process chewing tobacco into premium chewing tobacco?
2. What is the maximum amount that joint costs can increase before (a) it would not be better to process chewing tobacco further into premium chewing tobacco, and (b) it would be better to cease processing tobacco leaves to produce cigars and premium chewing tobacco?

6-56 Relevant Cost

Debraceny Company's unit costs of manufacturing and selling a given item at the planned activity level of 10,000 units per month are

Manufacturing costs	
Direct materials	$4.20
Direct labor	.60
Variable overhead	.90
Fixed overhead	.80
Selling expenses	
Variable	3.20
Fixed	1.15

Ignore income taxes in all requirements. These four parts have no connection with each other.

1. Compute the planned annual operating income at a selling price of $13 per unit.
2. Compute the expected annual operating income if the volume can be increased by 20% when the selling price is reduced to $12. Assume that the implied cost behavior patterns are correct.
3. The company desires to seek an order for 5,000 units from a foreign customer. The variable selling expenses for the order will be 40% less than usual, but the fixed costs for obtaining the order will be $6,000. Domestic sales will not be affected. Compute the minimum break-even price per unit to be considered.
4. The company has an inventory of 3,000 units of this item left over from last year's model. These must be sold through regular channels at reduced prices. The inventory will be valueless unless sold this way. What unit cost is relevant for establishing the minimum selling price of these 3,000 units?

6-57 New Machine

A new $300,000 machine is expected to have a 5-year life and a terminal value of zero. It can produce 40,000 units a year at a variable cost of $4 per unit. The variable cost is $6.50 per unit with an old machine, which has a book value of $100,000. It is being depreciated on a straight-line basis at $20,000 per year. It too is expected to have a terminal value of zero. Its current disposal value is also zero because it is highly specialized equipment.

The salesperson of the new machine prepared the following comparison:

	New Machine	Old Machine
Units	40,000	40,000
Variable costs	$160,000	$260,000
Straight-line depreciation	60,000	20,000
Total cost	$220,000	$280,000
Unit cost	$ 5.50	$ 7.00

He said, "The new machine is obviously a worthwhile acquisition. You will save $1.50 for every unit you produce."

1. Do you agree with the salesperson's analysis? If not, how would you change it? Be specific. Ignore taxes.
2. Prepare an analysis of total and unit differential costs if the annual volume is 20,000 units.
3. At what annual volume would both the old and new machines have the same total relevant costs?

6-58 Conceptual Approach

A large automobile-parts plant was constructed 4 years ago in a Pennsylvania city served by two railroads. The PC Railroad purchased 40 specialized 60-foot freight cars as a direct result of the additional traffic generated by the new plant. The investment was based on an estimated useful life of 20 years.

Now the competing railroad has offered to service the plant with new 86-foot freight cars that would enable more efficient shipping operations at the plant. The automobile-parts company has threatened to switch carriers unless PC Railroad buys 10 new 86-foot freight cars.

The PC marketing management wants to buy the new cars, but PC operating management says, "The new investment is undesirable. It really consists of the new outlay plus the loss on the old freight cars. The old cars must be written down to a low salvage value if they cannot be used as originally intended."

Evaluate the comments. What is the correct conceptual approach to the quantitative analysis in this decision?

6-59 Book Value of Old Equipment

Consider the following data:

	Old Equipment	Proposed New Equipment
Original cost	$24,000	$12,000
Useful life in years	8	3
Current age in years	5	0
Useful life remaining in years	3	3
Accumulated depreciation	$15,000	0
Book value	9,000	*
Disposal value (in cash) now	3,000	*
Annual cash operating costs (maintenance, power, repairs, lubricants, etc.)	$11,000	$ 6,000

*Not acquired yet.

1. Prepare a cost comparison of all relevant items for the next 3 years together. Ignore taxes.
2. Prepare a cost comparison that includes both relevant and irrelevant items. (See Exhibit 6-5, p. 237.)
3. Prepare a comparative statement of the total charges against revenue for the first year. Would the manager be inclined to buy the new equipment? Explain.

6-60 Decision and Performance Models

Refer to problem 6-A4.

1. Suppose the "decision model" favored by top management consisted of a comparison of a 3-year accumulation of wealth under each alternative. Which alternative would you choose? Why? (Accumulation of wealth means cumulative increase in cash.)
2. Suppose the "performance evaluation model" emphasized the net income of a subunit, such as a division, each year rather than considering each project, one by one. Which alternative would you expect a manager to choose? Why?
3. Suppose the same quantitative data existed, but the "enterprise" was a city and the "machine" was a computer in the treasurer's department. Would your answers to the first two parts change? Why?

6-61 Review of Relevant Costs

Since the early 1960s, Neil Simon has been one of Broadway's most successful playwrights. The *New York Times* reported that Neil Simon planned to open his play, *London Suite*, off Broadway. Why? For financial reasons. Producer Emanuel Azenberg predicted the following costs before the play even opened:

	On Broadway	Off Broadway
Sets, costumes, lights	$ 357,000	$ 87,000
Loading in (building set, etc.)	175,000	8,000
Rehearsal salaries	102,000	63,000
Director and designer fees	126,000	61,000
Advertising	300,000	121,000
Administration	235,000	100,000
Total	$1,295,000	$440,000

Broadway ticket prices average $60, and theaters can seat about 1,000 persons per show. Off-Broadway prices average only $40, and the theaters seat only 500. Normally, plays run eight times a week, both on and off Broadway. Weekly operating expenses off Broadway average $102,000; they average an extra $150,000 on Broadway for a weekly total of $252,000.

1. Suppose 400 persons attended each show, whether on or off Broadway. Compare the weekly financial results from a Broadway production to one produced off Broadway.
2. Suppose attendance averaged 75% of capacity, whether on or off Broadway. Compare the weekly financial results from a Broadway production to one produced off Broadway.
3. Compute the attendance per show required just to cover weekly expenses (a) on Broadway and (b) off Broadway.
4. Suppose average attendance on Broadway was 600 per show and off Broadway was 400. Compute the total net profit for a 26-week run (a) on Broadway and (b) off Broadway. Be sure to include the pre-opening costs.
5. Repeat requirement 4 for a 100-week run.
6. Using attendance figures from numbers 4 and 5, compute (a) the number of weeks a Broadway production must run before it breaks even, and (b) the number of weeks an off-Broadway production must run before it breaks even.
7. Using attendance figures from numbers 4 and 5, determine how long a play must run before the profit from a Broadway production exceeds that from an off-Broadway production.
8. If you were Neil Simon, would you prefer *London Suite* to play on Broadway or off Broadway? Explain.

6-62 Make or Buy

Tempor, Corp., estimates it will produce 30,000 units of a part that goes into its final product. It currently produces this part internally, but is considering outsourcing this activity. Current internal capacity permits for a maximum of 60,000 units of the part. The production manager has prepared the following information concerning the internal manufacture of 60,000 units of the part:

	Per unit
Direct materials	$ 3.00
Direct labor	4.00
Variable overhead	5.00
Fixed overhead	6.00
Total cost	$18.00

The fixed overhead of $6 per unit includes a $1.50 per unit allocation for salary paid to a supervisor to oversee production of the part. The fixed costs would not be reduced by outsourcing, except the supervisor would be terminated. Assume that if Tempor outsources, its purchase price from the outsourcer is $12 per unit.

1. Should Tempor outsource?
2. Assume Tempor has received a special order for 10,000 units of the part from Adigen, Co. Adigen will pay Tempor $23 per part, but will take the parts only if they have been manufactured by Tempor. Thus, Adigen will engage in the special order only if Tempor does not outsource any of its production. Should Tempor accept the special order?

6-63 Make or Buy, Opportunity Costs, and Ethics

Agribiz Food Products produces a wide variety of food and related products. The company's tomato-canning operation relies partly on tomatoes grown on Agribiz's own farms and partly on tomatoes bought from other growers.

Agribiz's tomato farm is on the edge of Sharpestown, a fast-growing, medium-sized city. It produces 8 million pounds of tomatoes a year and employs 55 persons. The annual costs of tomatoes grown on this farm are

Variable production costs	$ 550,000
Fixed production costs	1,200,000
Shipping costs (all variable)	200,000
Total costs	$1,950,000

Fixed production costs include depreciation on machinery and equipment, but not on land because land should not be depreciated. Agribiz owns the land, which was purchased for $600,000 many years ago. A recent appraisal placed the value of the land at $18 million because it is a prime site for an industrial park and shopping center.

Agribiz could purchase all the tomatoes it needs on the market for $.25 per pound delivered to its factory. If it did this, it would sell the farmland and shut down the operations in Sharpestown. If the farm were sold, $300,000 of the annual fixed costs would be saved. Agribiz can invest excess cash and earn an annual rate of 10%.

1. How much does it cost Agribiz annually for the land used by the tomato farm?
2. How much would Agribiz save annually if it closed the tomato farm? Is this more or less than would be paid to purchase the tomatoes on the market?
3. What ethical issues are involved with the decision to shut down the tomato farm?

6-64 Irrelevance of Past Costs at Starbucks

Starbucks purchases and roasts high-quality, whole-bean coffees, its hallmark, and sells them along with other coffee-related products primarily through its company-operated retail stores.

Suppose that the quality-control manager at Starbucks discovered a 1,000-pound batch of roasted beans that did not meet the company's quality standards. Company policy would not allow such beans to be sold with the Starbucks name on them. However, they could be reprocessed, at which time they could be sold by Starbucks' retail stores, or they could be sold as is on the wholesale coffee bean market.

Assume that the beans were initially purchased for $3,000, and the total cost of roasting the batch was $2,500, including $500 of variable costs and $2,000 of fixed costs (primarily depreciation on the equipment).

The wholesale price at which Starbucks could sell the beans was $3.65 per pound. Purchasers would pay the shipping costs from the Starbucks plant to their individual warehouses.

If the beans were reprocessed, the processing cost would be $800 because the beans would not require as much processing as new beans. All $800 would be additional costs, that is, costs that would not be incurred without the reprocessing. The beans would be sold to the retail stores for $5.00 per pound, and Starbucks would have to pay an average of $.20 per pound to ship the beans to the stores.

1. Should Starbucks sell the beans on the market as is for $3.65 per pound, or should the company reprocess the beans and sell them through its own retail stores? Why?
2. Compute the amount of extra profit Starbucks earns from the alternative you selected in number 1 compared to what it would earn from the other alternative.
3. What cost numbers in the problem were irrelevant to your analysis? Explain why they were irrelevant.

CASES

6-65 Make or Buy

The Minnetonka Corporation, which produces and sells to wholesalers a highly successful line of water skis, has decided to diversify to stabilize sales throughout the year. The company is considering the production of cross-country skis.

After considerable research, a cross-country ski line has been developed. Because of the conservative nature of the company management, however, Minnetonka's president has decided to introduce only one type of the new skis for this coming winter. If the product is a success, further expansion in future years will be initiated.

The ski selected is a mass-market ski with a special binding. It will be sold to wholesalers for $80 per pair. Because of available capacity, no additional fixed charges will be incurred to produce the skis. A $125,000 fixed charge will be absorbed by the skis, however, to allocate a fair share of the company's present fixed costs to the new product.

Using the estimated sales and production of 10,000 pair of skis as the expected volume, the accounting department has developed the following costs per pair of skis and bindings:

Direct labor	$35
Direct materials	30
Total overhead	15
Total cost	$80

Minnetonka has approached a subcontractor to discuss the possibility of purchasing the bindings. The purchase price of the bindings from the subcontractor would be $5.25 per binding, or $10.50 per pair. If the Minnetonka Corporation accepts the purchase proposal, it is predicted that direct-labor and variable-overhead costs would be reduced by 10% and direct-materials costs would be reduced by 20%.

1. Should the Minnetonka Corporation make or buy the bindings? Show calculations to support your answer.

2. What would be the maximum purchase price acceptable to the Minnetonka Corporation for the bindings? Support your answer with an appropriate explanation.

3. Instead of sales of 10,000 pairs of skis, revised estimates show sales volume at 12,500 pairs. At this new volume, additional equipment, at an annual rental of $10,000, must be acquired to manufacture the bindings. This incremental cost would be the only additional fixed cost required, even if sales increased to 30,000 pairs. (The 30,000 level is the goal for the third year of production.) Under these circumstances, should the Minnetonka Corporation make or buy the bindings? Show calculations to support your answer.

4. The company has the option of making and buying at the same time. What would be your answer to number 3 if this alternative were considered? Show calculations to support your answer.

5. What nonquantifiable factors should the Minnetonka Corporation consider in determining whether they should make or buy the bindings?

6-66 Make or Buy

The Rohr Company's old equipment for making subassemblies is worn out. The company is considering two courses of action: (a) completely replacing the old equipment with new equipment or (b) buying subassemblies from a reliable outside supplier, who has quoted a unit price of $1 on a 7-year contract for a minimum of 50,000 units per year.

Production was 60,000 units in each of the past 2 years. Future needs for the next 7 years are not expected to fluctuate beyond 50,000 to 70,000 units per year. Cost records for the past 2 years reveal the following unit costs of manufacturing the subassembly:

Direct materials	$ .30
Direct labor	.35
Variable overhead	.10
Fixed overhead (including $.10 depreciation and	
$.10 for direct departmental fixed overhead)	.25
	$1.00

The new equipment will cost $188,000 cash, will last 7 years, and will have a disposal value of $20,000. The current disposal value of the old equipment is $10,000.

The sales representative for the new equipment has summarized her position as follows: The increase in machine speeds will reduce direct labor and variable overhead by $.35 per unit. Consider last year's experience of one of your major competitors with identical equipment. It produced 100,000 units under operating conditions very comparable to yours and showed the following unit costs.

Direct materials	$.30
Direct labor	.05
Variable overhead	.05
Fixed overhead, including depreciation of $.24	.40
Total	$.80

For purposes of this case, assume that any idle facilities cannot be put to alternative use. Also assume that $.05 of the old Rohr unit cost is allocated fixed overhead that will be unaffected by the decision.

1. The president asks you to compare the alternatives on a total-annual-cost basis and on a per-unit basis for annual needs of 60,000 units. Which alternative seems more attractive?

2. Would your answer to number 1 change if the needs were 50,000 units? 70,000 units? At what volume level would Rohr be indifferent between making and buying subassemblies? Show your computations.

3. What factors, other than the preceding ones, should the accountant bring to the attention of management to assist them in making their decision? Include the considerations that might be applied to the outside supplier.

6-67 Make or Buy

Levoy, Corp., estimates it will produce 25,000 units of an electronic sensor part that goes into one of its final products, called a Fluctotron. It currently produces this sensor internally but is considering outsourcing this activity. Current internal capacity permits the production of a maximum of 40,000 sensors. The production manager has prepared the following information concerning the internal manufacture of 40,000 sensors:

	Per sensor
Direct materials	$15.00
Direct labor	8.00
Variable overhead	10.00
Fixed overhead	11.00
Total cost	$44.00

The fixed overhead of $11 per unit includes a $2 per unit allocation for salary paid to a supervisor to oversee production of sensors. The fixed costs would not be reduced by outsourcing, except the supervisor would be fired (the company would terminate his contract). Assume that if Levoy outsources, its purchase price from the outsourcer is $38 per unit.

1. Should Levoy outsource? Why or why not?
2. Assume that if Levoy outsourced, it would create sufficient excess capacity such that it would retain the supervisor and have him oversee production of a new optical reading product, called a Scanmeister. If each Scanmeister generates a contribution margin of $15 and the company produces 10,000 Scanmeisters, what is the maximum price Levoy would accept for outsourcing the sensors?

NIKE 10-K PROBLEM

6-68 Make or Buy

As described in Item 1 of **Nike**'s 10-K, virtually all of its products are produced by independent contractors. Suppose that in one of those contracted production facilities where Nike Golf clubs are produced, Nike estimates the need for 20,000 specialized head casings per year over the next 5 years for a custom driver club it manufactures. It can either make the casings internally or purchase them from an outside supplier for $29.75 per unit. If it makes the casings, it will have to purchase equipment costing $300,000 that has a 5-year life and no salvage value (assume straight line depreciation). The machine can produce up to 40,000 casings per year. The production manager thinks the company should purchase the casings based on the following information he has prepared concerning the internal manufacture of 20,000 casings per year:

	Per unit
Direct materials	$12.00
Direct labor	8.00
Variable overhead	4.50
Depreciation	3.00
Supervision	1.50
Rent	3.00
Total cost	$32.00

A supervisor would have to be hired and paid a salary of $30,000 to oversee production of the casings. The rent charge is based on the space utilized in the plant, but there is excess plant space available to manufacture the casings. Total rent on the plant is $250,000 per period.

1. If the casings are made internally, will the company be better off or worse off, and by how much?
2. If it is estimated that only 15,000 casings per year were required, should Nike make or buy them?

EXCEL APPLICATION EXERCISE

6-69 Identifying Relevant Revenue, Costs, and Income Effects

Goal: Create an Excel spreadsheet to assist with sell-or-process-further decisions by identifying the relevant revenue, costs, and income effects. Use the results to answer questions about your findings.

Scenario: Mussina Chemical Company has asked you to prepare an analysis to help it make decisions about whether to sell joint products at the split-off point or process them further. The background data for the analysis appears in the Fundamental Assignment Material 6-A3. Prepare the analysis report using a format similar to Exhibit 6-3 on page 235.

When you have completed your spreadsheet, answer the following questions:

1. How should the $117,000 be allocated to the three products?

2. Is the company currently making the right processing decisions? Explain.
3. If the company alters its processing decisions, what would be the expected combined operating income from the three products?

Step-by-Step:

1. Open a new Excel spreadsheet.
2. In column A, create a bold-faced heading that contains the following:
   Row 1: Chapter 6 Decision Guideline
   Row 2: Mussina Chemical Company
   Row 3: Sell-or-Process-Further Analysis
   Row 4: Today's Date
3. Merge and center the four heading rows across columns A–J.
4. In row 7, create the following bold-faced column headings:
   Column B: Chemical Product A
   Skip two columns
   Column E: Chemical Product B
   Skip two columns
   Column H: Chemical Product C
5. Merge and center the heading in row 7, column B across columns B–D.
   Merge and center the heading in row 7, column E across columns E–G.
   Merge and center the heading in row 7, column H across columns H–J.
6. In row 8, create the following center-justified column headings:
   Column B: Sell at Split-Off
   Column C: Process Further
   Column D: Difference
   Column E: Sell at Split-Off
   Column F: Process Further
   Column G: Difference
   Column H: Sell at Split-Off
   Column I: Process Further
   Column J: Difference
7. Change the format of the column headings in row 8 to permit the titles to be displayed on multiple lines within a single cell.

Alignment tab:	Wrap Text:	Checked

8. In column A, create the following bold-faced row headings:
   Row 9: Revenues
   Row 10: Costs Beyond Split-Off
   Skip a row
   Row 11: Income Effects

   Note: Adjust the width of column A to accommodate row headings.

9. Use the scenario data to fill in revenues and costs beyond split-off amounts for each of the products.
10. Use appropriate formulas to calculate the difference and income effects columns for each product as absolute values.
    5ABS(formula)
11. Format all amounts as

Number:	Category:	Accounting
	Decimal places:	0
	Symbol:	$

12. Change the format of the costs beyond split-off amounts to not display a dollar symbol.
13. Change the format of the income effects amounts to display as bold.
14. Change the format of the revenues amounts to display a top border, using the default line style.

Border tab:	Icon:	Top Border

15. Change the format of the costs beyond split-off amounts to display a bottom border, using the default line style.

Border tab:	Icon:	Bottom Border

16. Change the format of row 7, column B to display an outline border, using the default line style.

Border tab:	Presets:	Outline

Repeat this step for column E.
Repeat this step for column H.

17. Save your work to disk, and print a copy for your files.

Note: Print your spreadsheet using landscape in order to ensure that all columns appear on one page.

COLLABORATIVE LEARNING EXERCISE

6-70 Outsourcing

A popular term for make-or-buy decisions is *outsourcing decisions*. There are many examples of outsourcing, from **Nike**'s outsourcing of nearly all its production activities to small firms' outsourcing of their payroll activities. Especially popular outsourcing activities are warehousing and computer systems.

The purpose of this exercise is to share information on different types of outsourcing decisions. It can be done in small groups or as an entire class. Each student should pick an article from the literature that tells about a particular company's outsourcing decision. There are many such articles: A recent electronic search of the business literature turned up more than 4,000 articles. An easy way to find such an article is to search an electronic database of business literature. Magazines that have published outsourcing articles include *Fortune*, *Forbes*, *Business Week*, and *Strategic Finance*. Many business sections of newspapers also include such articles. The *Wall Street Journal* usually has a couple of articles on outsourcing each month.

1. List as many details about the outsourcing decision as you can. Include the type of activity that is being outsourced, the size of the outsourcing, and the type of company providing the outsourcing service.
2. Explain why the company decided to outsource the activity. If reasons are not given in the article, prepare a list of reasons that you think influenced the decision.
3. What disadvantages are there to outsourcing the activity?
4. Be prepared to make a 3- to 5-minute presentation to the rest of the group or to the class, covering your answers to numbers 1, 2, and 3.

INTERNET EXERCISE

6-71 Green Mountain Coffee Company

How do firms determine what type of information is useful for a given decision? Is it possible for firms to have too much information? While a look at a firm's Web site provides us with lots of information, not all of it is necessarily useful for a particular decision. Let's look at the **Green Mountain Coffee Company** and see what information on the site would be useful for some specific decisions.

1. Go to the home page of Green Mountain Coffee at www.greenmountaincoffee.com. What are the major topics on which a user can click to be taken to a page with more detailed information? Would you likely find the same type of information if you clicked on the links to any one of these? Why do you suppose Green Mountain Coffee chose those particular subtopics for its home page?
2. Where would you look on the site if you wanted to know more about Green Mountain Coffee's financial information? Locate the most recent annual report posted on this section of the Web site, and answer the following questions. Did the company make a profit for the year? What was the major expense that the firm encountered? Did the firm pay any dividends? If you were interested in an income-producing stock, would you want to invest in Green Mountain Coffee Roasters?
3. Which link would you want to use if you wanted to gain knowledge concerning the story of coffee and its history? Click on this link now. This page has additional links about coffee. Which one(s) are likely to provide information to help you learn about the different coffees? Click on one of the links you just identified. What type of information about coffee differences does it provide? Did your link provide any information concerning prices as being a difference? Do you think that this would be a difference between coffees?
4. The site provides extensive information about social and environmental initiatives. What areas in particular does the firm highlight? Is this information useful in helping determine if the company's coffee products taste good? What about the quality of the product? Would this information be useful to a potential investor in Green Mountain Coffee's common stock?

CHAPTER

7

Introduction to Budgets and Preparing the Master Budget

LEARNING OBJECTIVES

When you have finished studying this chapter, you should be able to:

1. Explain how budgets facilitate planning and coordination.

2. Anticipate possible human relations problems caused by budgets.

3. Explain potentially dysfunctional incentives in the budget process.

4. Explain the difficulties of sales forecasting.

5. Explain the major features and advantages of a master budget.

6. Follow the principal steps in preparing a master budget.

7. Prepare the operating budget and the supporting schedules.

8. Prepare the financial budget.

9. Use a spreadsheet to develop a budget (Appendix 7).

▶ RITZ-CARLTON

If you have ever traveled, you know that there is a big difference between staying in a cheap motel and staying in a five-star, world-class hotel. The cheap motel takes care of your basic needs, but the five-star hotel surrounds you in comfort and luxury, catering to your every whim. No one understands the difference better than the managers of the **Ritz-Carlton** chain of hotels. After all, the word *ritzy*, which means glamorous and luxurious, is actually derived from the name of the Ritz Hotel. Thanks to fierce competition in the industry, though, Ritz-Carlton managers have their share of challenges in maintaining standards that keep their hotels successful.

What does it take to run a world-class hotel successfully? Good location, exquisite food, luxury, personalized service, and quality are all essential ingredients. But you might be surprised to learn that the budgeting process is also a key to success. According to Ralph Vick, former general manager of the Phoenix Ritz-Carlton, "Budgets are crucial to the ultimate financial success of our hotels." Why are budgets so important? Mainly because they serve as a road map toward achieving goals. Budgets are a manager's tool to understand, plan, and control operations, and Ritz-Carlton wants to give its managers the best tools possible. As a result, the company takes the budgeting process very seriously.

At the Ritz-Carlton hotels, all employees, from the hotel manager, to the controller, to the newest housekeeper, are involved in the budgeting process. Working in teams, managers set budget targets for the expenses they can control. These target figures help not only in planning, but also in controlling and evaluating employee performance. Managers compare actual results with previously budgeted target figures, and they evaluate performance based on the differences. In addition to financial reports, Ritz-Carlton managers also use nonfinancial measures, such as quality and customer satisfaction, to evaluate and reward employees.

Planning is the key to good management. This statement is certainly true for Ritz-Carlton, and it is also true for other types of organizations—small, family-owned companies, large corporations, government agencies, and nonprofit organizations. All organizations need budgets to make the best and most profitable use of their resources. Budgeting can cover such diverse issues as how much time to spend inspecting a product and how much money the company will allot to research and development in the coming year. In this chapter, we look at the benefits (and costs) of budgets and illustrate the construction of a comprehensive, detailed budget. ■

A Ritz-Carlton hotel projects an image of quality. High quality is expensive so during the master budgeting process Ritz-Carlton managers must assess the planned expenditures for quality-enhancing features versus the added revenues these features will bring.

Budgets and the Organization

Many people associate the word *budget* primarily with limitations on spending. For example, management often gives individual units within an organization a spending budget and then expects them to maintain expenditures within the limits prescribed by the budget. However, well-managed organizations use budgets for more than simple limits on spending. Budgets formalize the planning process, allowing managers to take steps to avoid problems or take advantage of opportunities. Budgets provide a comprehensive financial overview that helps coordinate financial and operational activities. Budgets provide an important two-way communication channel. They convey information about strategies and expectations downward from the upper-levels of the organization and communicate information about capabilities and opportunities upward from the lower-levels of the organization. Managers also use budgets for performance evaluation. Budgets act as a benchmark—a measure of expected or desired performance—against which they compare actual performance.

Budgeting moves planning to the forefront of the manager's mind. There are numerous examples of seemingly healthy businesses that failed because managers did not bother to construct budgets that would have identified problems in advance or they failed to monitor and adjust budgets to changing conditions. While there will always be debate about the costs and benefits of budgeting, as indicated in the Business First box on page 266, the vast majority of managers continue to use budgeting as an effective cost-management tool. One study of more than 150 organizations in North America listed budgeting as the most frequently used cost-management tool.

Advantages of Budgets

In Chapter 1, we defined a budget as a quantitative expression of a plan of action. Sometimes plans are informal, perhaps even unwritten, and informal plans sometimes work in a small organization. However, as an organization grows, seat-of-the-pants planning is not enough. Budgets impose the formal structure—a budgetary system—that is needed for all but the smallest organizations.

Budgeting is the process of formulating an organization's plans. Four major benefits of effective budgeting are as follows:

1. Budgeting compels managers to think ahead by formalizing their responsibilities for planning.
2. Budgeting provides an opportunity for managers to reevaluate existing activities and evaluate possible new activities.
3. Budgeting aids managers in communicating objectives and coordinating actions across the organization.
4. Budgeting provides benchmarks to evaluate subsequent performance.

Let's look more closely at each of these benefits.

FORMALIZATION OF PLANNING Budgeting forces managers to devote time to planning. On a day-to-day basis, managers often move from extinguishing one business brush fire to another, leaving no time for thinking beyond the next day's problems. Planning takes a backseat to, or is actually obliterated by, daily pressures.

Objective 1

Explain how budgets facilitate planning and coordination.

Business First

Budgeting: Value Driver or Value Buster?

There is an ongoing debate about the costs and benefits of budgeting, focusing on four issues: (1) The budgeting process is time-consuming and expensive; (2) budgets are not accurate because marketplace change is frequent and unpredictable; (3) evaluating performance against a budget causes managers to bias their budgets, resulting in inaccurate planning; and (4) budget targets create incentives for individuals to take actions to meet targets even when the actions make the firm as a whole worse off.

Some studies suggest that the annual budgeting process can take up to 30% of management's time. For example, estimates place Ford Motor Company's cost of budgeting at $1.2 billion a year. Companies can justify such large budgeting costs only when there are corresponding large benefits. Companies that fail to incorporate budgeting in their planning activities and those that react to changing economic conditions by ignoring the budget rather than learning and then adapting the budget will find it hard to justify large budgeting costs.

Skeptical managers sometimes claim, "I face too many uncertainties and complications to make budgeting worthwhile for me." While it is true that budgeting is more difficult in uncertain or complicated environments, it is also true that the potential benefits are largest in these environments. When conditions are changing rapidly, a budget provides a framework for systematic response rather than chaotic reaction.

When managers anticipate that budget information will be used to set targets used in their subsequent performance evaluations, they may provide budget information that is biased to make it easier to meet the targets. Biases severely limit the usefulness of budget information for planning and coordination. Moreover, widespread understanding and acceptance of built-in biases can create a pernicious "culture of lying" within the organization.

When managers realize that meeting budget targets affects their rewards, either explicitly through bonus plans or implicitly through promotion and recognition, they have incentives to take actions to meet the targets. This can be a positive motivation, but it can also lead to unethical behavior, such as "cooking the books" or putting pressure on employees to meet targets using whatever means possible. For example, the director of the Office of Federal Housing Enterprise Oversight (OFHEO) denounced "an arrogant and unethical culture" at Fannie Mae, the giant mortgage finance company. An OFHEO report cited a corporate culture that allowed managers to disregard accounting standards when they got in the way of achieving earnings targets that were tied to bonuses. In other cases, managers have taken actions to ship faulty or incomplete products to meet budgeted sales targets, despite clear adverse effects on customer relations and the reputation of the firm.

Most companies that have experienced problems with their budgeting process are not abandoning traditional budgeting but instead are modifying their approach to budgeting. For example, some companies now separate planning budgets from control budgets, comparing actual performance to benchmarks based on actual performance of peers and best-in-class operations rather than to budgets. Further, most managers still agree that budgeting, when correctly used, has significant value to management. More than 92% of the companies in a recent survey use budgets, and they rank budgeting among their top three cost-management tools.

Companies such as Allstate, Owens Corning, Sprint, Battelle, and Texaco are modifying their approach to budgeting by implementing new technologies. For example, Battelle's Pacific Northwest National Laboratory uses an intranet to reduce the time and expense of developing the annual budget. The new system enables support staff and managers to input their budget data and plans directly on this corporate intranet. In addition to decreasing the cost of budgeting, managers at Battelle report that the new system "results in higher quality and more accurate budgeting, reporting, and analysis." Many companies are tying their budgeting process more closely to their overall strategy and have expanded their performance measures beyond traditional financial measures to also consider nonfinancial measures, such as time to market for new products or services.

Sources: Adapted from R. Banham, "Better Budgets," *Journal of Accountancy*, February 2000, pp. 37–40; J. Hope and R. Fraser, "Who Needs Budgets?" *Harvard Business Review*, February 2003, pp. 108–115; P. Smith, C. Goranson, and M. Astley, "Intranet Budgeting," *Strategic Finance*, May 2003, pp. 30–33; T. Hatch and W. Stratton, "Scorecarding in North America: Who is Doing What?" Paper presented at the CAM-I/CMS 3rd quarter meeting, Portland, Oregon, September 10, 2002; M. Jensen, "Corporate Budgeting Is Broken, Let's Fix It," *Harvard Business Review*, November 2001, pp. 94–101; M. Jensen, "Paying People to Lie: the Truth About the Budgeting Process," *European Financial Management*, Vol. 9 No. 3, (2003), pp. 379–406; and "Fannie Mae Ex-Officials May Face Legal Action over Accounting," The *Wall Street Journal*, May 24, 2006, p. A1.

To prepare a budget, a manager should set goals and objectives and establish policies to aid their achievement. The objectives are the destination points, and budgets are the road maps guiding us to those destinations. In the absence of goals and objectives, results are difficult to interpret, managers do not foresee problems, and company operations lack direction. The budgeting process formalizes the need to anticipate and prepare for changing conditions.

EVALUATION OF ACTIVITIES Budgeting typically uses the current activities of the organization as a starting point for planning, but how managers use this starting point varies widely. At one extreme, in some organizations the budget process automatically assumes that activities for the new budget period will be the same as the activities for the previous period. At the other extreme, some organizations use a form of **zero-base budget**, which starts with the assumption that current activities will not automatically be continued. The term zero-base comes from the fundamental assumption that the budget for every activity starts at zero, and managers must justify all activities (including continuation of existing activities) in each new budget.

In practice, budgeting for most organizations falls somewhere between these two extremes. An effective budget process will encourage managers to think carefully about whether to continue current activities and methods, whether there are opportunities to modify activities, and whether to add new activities to help the organization better achieve its goals in response to changing conditions. Used in this way, budgeting encourages managers to review whether a particular plan allocates resources optimally among the firm's various activities.

COMMUNICATION AND COORDINATION   The most effective budget processes facilitate communication both from the top down and from the bottom up. Top management communicates the broad goals and objectives of the organization in its budgetary directives. Lower-level managers and employees contribute their own ideas and provide feedback on the goals and objectives. The result is two-way communication about opportunities and challenges that lie ahead.

Budgets also help managers coordinate activities across the organization. For example, a budget allows purchasing personnel to integrate their plans with production requirements, while production managers use the sales budget and delivery schedule to help them anticipate and plan for the employees and physical facilities they will need. Similarly, financial officers use the sales budget, purchasing requirements, and other planned expenditures to anticipate the company's need for cash. Thus, budgeting forces managers to visualize and quantify the relationship of their department's activities to those of other departments and the company as a whole.

PERFORMANCE EVALUATION   Budgeted performance goals generally provide a better basis for evaluating actual results than would a simple comparison with past performance. The news that a company had sales of $100 million this year, as compared with $80 million the previous year, may or may not indicate that company objectives have been met—perhaps the sales goal for this year was $110 million. The major drawback of relying only on historical results for judging current performance is that inefficiencies may be concealed in past performance. Changes in economic conditions, technology, personnel, competition, and other factors also limit the usefulness of comparisons with the past. And for start-up companies and firms with new products or services, there is no prior performance to compare against current results.

Making Managerial Decisions

Level 3 Communications is "a facilities based provider of a broad range of integrated communications services." The company has had losses for a number of years, which it attributes to a difficult competitive environment. The 2008 annual report states "We believe that ... these factors created an unsustainable level of competition in the market. We believe that this was evidenced by both the number of competitors vying for similar business and by the amount of inventory or capacity each brought to the market for many services. The result of these actions was an oversupply of capacity and an intensely competitive environment." The net loss has steadily increased from $458 million in 2004 to $638 million in 2005 to $744 million in 2006 to $1,114 million in 2007.

Level 3 Communication's actual loss for 2008 was $290 million. Suppose the company budgeted to break even for 2008. Evaluate operating performance for 2008.

Answer

Level 3's performance in 2008 is substantially better than would be projected by looking at past results and the trend of steadily increasing losses over the past 4 years. However, if the company budgeted for break even in 2008, then performance is much worse than budgeted. This situation illustrates that comparisons to past results can provide a very different conclusion than comparisons to the budget.

Potential Problems in Implementing Budgets

In this section, we discuss three problems that can limit, in some cases severely, the advantages of budgeting:

1. Low levels of participation in the budget process and lack of acceptance of responsibility for the final budget
2. Incentives to lie and cheat in the budget process
3. Difficulties in obtaining accurate sales forecasts

BUDGET PARTICIPATION AND ACCEPTANCE OF THE BUDGET The advantages of budgeting are fully realized only when employees throughout the organization fully accept and take responsibility for the final budget. The main factors affecting budget acceptance are the perceived attitude of top management, the level of participation in the budget process, and the degree of alignment between the budget and other performance goals.

The attitude of top management will heavily influence lower-level managers' and employees' attitudes toward budgets. If top management does not use budgets effectively in controlling operations and adapting to change, others in the organization may come to view budgeting as irrelevant. Even with the support of top management, however, budgets—and the managers who implement them—can run into opposition.

Lower-level managers sometimes have negative attitudes toward budgets because they believe the primary purpose of the budget is to limit spending. These negative attitudes are reinforced when companies evaluate managerial performance by comparing actual expenditures against amounts budgeted without substantive input from the managers. Ensuring that managers at all levels participate in setting budgets is one way to reduce negative attitudes and improve the quality of planning decisions. Budgets created with the active participation of all affected employees—called **participative budgeting**—are generally more effective than budgets imposed on subordinates. For example, Ritz-Carlton's budgeting system involves all hotel employees and is thus a participative system. Employee "buy-in" to the budget is so important at Ritz-Carlton that self-directed employee teams at all levels of the company have the authority to change operations based on budgets as they see fit.

Misalignment between the performance goals stressed in budgets versus the performance measures the company uses to reward employees and managers can also limit the advantages of budgeting. For example, suppose a company rewards managers based on actual profit compared to budgeted profit and also on quality (defect rate) and timely delivery to customers (percent on time). Increased quality and more timely deliveries typically require higher costs so the message conveyed by the budget system (minimize cost) may be misaligned with the incentives provided by the compensation system (maximize quality and timely delivery). Companies can manage the apparent misalignment by clearly specifying and communicating the tradeoff between costs and quality measures. This is particularly important for performance goals where the short-term impact on current performance relative to budget is negative but the long-term impact due to improved customer satisfaction is positive. We explore these issues in more detail in Chapter 9.

There is often too much concern with the mechanics of budgets and too little attention paid to the fact that the effectiveness of any budgeting system depends directly on whether the affected managers and employees understand and accept the budget. Management should seek to create an environment where there is a true two-way flow of information in the budget process where lower level managers and employees perceive that their input has a real effect on budget outcomes. Top management must emphasize the importance of budgets in planning and communication and demonstrate how budgets can help each manager and employee achieve better results. Only then will the budgets become a positive aid in motivating employees at all levels to work toward goals, set objectives, measure results accurately, and direct attention to the areas that need investigation.

INCENTIVES TO LIE AND CHEAT Effective budgets provide targets for managers and motivate them to achieve the organization's objectives. However, misuse of budgets can lead to undesirable incentives—what Professor Michael Jensen calls incentives to lie and cheat. Not only do such incentives lead managers to make poor decisions, they undercut attempts to maintain high ethical standards in the organization.

Let's first consider lying. Lying can arise if the budget process creates incentives for managers to bias the information that goes into their budgets. What might cause managers to create biased budgets—essentially to lie about their plans? Managers may want to increase the resources allocated to their department—resources such as space, equipment, and personnel—and larger budgets may justify such allocations. Why do managers want more resources? Day-to-day managing is easier when the department has more resources to achieve its output targets. Further, it is common for managers of larger units with more resources to receive higher pay, higher status, and greater prospects for promotion. Recognizing the incentives for bias allows organizations to implement budgets in a way that minimizes bias. For example, when employees understand, accept, and participate in the budget process, they are less likely to introduce biased information. Also, decision makers can be aware of expected bias when they make decisions based on budget information.

Additional lying incentives arise when organizations use budgets as a target for performance evaluations. This may prompt managers to create **budgetary slack** or **budget padding**—that is, managers may overstate their budgeted costs or understate their budgeted revenues to create a budget target that is easier to achieve. Budgetary slack also helps buffer managers from budget cuts imposed by higher-level management and provides protection against cost increases or revenue shortfalls due to unforeseen events. But these incentives can lead to the following deleterious cycle: Lower-level managers bias budgets to create budgetary slack, so upper-level managers attempt to correct for this bias in their inputs to the budget process. Lower-level managers, recognizing that upper-level managers are making this correction, then incorporate additional bias to compensate. Upper-level managers then introduce larger corrections to compensate for the increased bias, and the cycle of increasing distortion continues. This cycle of increasing bias and increasing bias corrections can cause the budget process to spiral out of control as inputs from both upper-level and lower-level managers become increasingly meaningless.

Now let's add one more complication—managerial bonuses based on making budget. Suppose a manager with a $100,000 annual salary will receive a bonus ranging from 80% to 120% of a target bonus of $50,000 if her division achieves between 80% and 120% of its budgeted profit target, as shown in Exhibit 7-1. In this example, representative of bonus plans commonly encountered in practice, there is a minimum level of division profit below which no bonus is paid (the bonus drops from a $40,000 bonus at 80% of budgeted profit to zero bonus at any profit level below 80% of budgeted profit) and a maximum level of division profit above which the maximum bonus is capped (above 120% of budgeted profit, the bonus is capped at $60,000).

We should first recognize that within the relevant range of 80%–120% of profits this system creates appropriate incentives to work harder, more efficiently, and more effectively to achieve desired results. But suppose, despite a manager's best efforts, it appears that reported profit will fall below 80% of the target profit in Exhibit 7-1. What inappropriate incentives does this bonus system provide for the manager? There are incentives to "cheat," to make results appear better or worse than they actually are. The incentive to cheat is particularly strong when the division is in danger of falling just short of 80% of the profit target, so that a small increase in reported profit would lead to a large jump in the amount of the bonus.

An extreme form of cheating is to "cook the books," that is, report false profit numbers. The division manager may accomplish this by recording fictitious sales or omitting costs. For example, a few years ago Enron and other energy companies recorded questionable sales of energy contracts, and WorldCom increased reported income by treating expenses as capital investments. Such actions have serious ethical and legal consequences, but sometimes the pressure to meet profit targets has been great enough to motivate managers to go to such extremes.

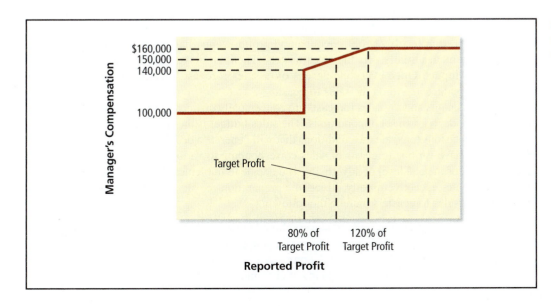

Exhibit 7-1
Bonus Payments Tied to Profit Levels

Managers may instead choose less extreme actions to increase reported profits. They may increase current sales by offering customers discounts that cause them to accelerate purchases from future periods to the current period, or offer better credit terms that are costly to the company through increased financing costs or increased credit risk. Managers may cut discretionary expenditures, such as research and development (R&D) and advertising, trading future sales for current profits. These short-term actions allow managers to achieve their current bonus, but cheat the company and its shareholders whenever the actions are not in the company's best long-run interests.

There are also incentives to *decrease* profits when the manager sees actual profits exceeding 120% of the profit target in Exhibit 7-1 or when profits fall so far short of the 80% profit target that there is no hope of achieving a bonus. Why would managers take actions to decrease current reported profit? First, moving this year's sales into next year or moving next year's expenses into this year increases next year's income, ensuring a higher level of reported profit (and probably a higher bonus) next year. Second, by decreasing this year's income, the manager may avoid increasing performance expectations for the next year—and thus may avoid a higher budgeted profit target for next year. Managers may move current sales into the next year by encouraging customers to defer purchases until the next year, thus effectively transferring current income to the future. They might also speed up actual expenditures (for example, moving maintenance planned for future years into the current year) or accelerate recognition of expenses (for example, writing off costs of equipment that remains in use), taking as current period expenses some costs that rightly belong to future periods.

Perhaps the most serious concern raised by these inappropriate incentives for lying and cheating is that they foster cynicism about the budget process and create a culture of unethical behavior in the organization. When managers know that the budget and evaluation processes encourage employees to provide biased information and make questionable decisions, not only does information quality suffer, but a lack of trust begins to pervade the organization.

How can organizations avoid unwanted incentives in budgetary systems? The main way to avoid lying in preparing the budget is to reward good budget forecasts as well as good performance against the budget. If managers take personal responsibility for their budgets and their superiors take the budgeting process seriously so that good planning is just as important as good performance for managers, accurate budgets will generally result. To minimize the incentives to cheat, performance-linked payment plans should avoid "discontinuities" in payments. Note that in Exhibit 7-1 the manager's payment jumps up—that is, it is discontinuous—at 80% of the target profit level and the payment levels off—is discontinuous—at the maximum bonus level. To minimize incentives to transfer income between periods, we can make bonuses and total payments increase continuously over the entire range of possible performance so that there is no point at which a small change in profit has a large effect on pay.

Objective 4

Explain the difficulties of sales forecasting.

DIFFICULTIES OF OBTAINING ACCURATE SALES FORECASTS   The third problem that limits the advantages of budgets is the difficulty of obtaining accurate sales forecasts. The sales budget is the foundation of budgeting. Why? Because the accuracy of all components of the budget depends on the accuracy of budgeted sales, as illustrated later in the chapter in the discussion of the master budget. At the **Ritz-Carlton** hotels, the process of developing the sales budget involves forecasting levels of room occupancy, group events, banquets, and other activities. Upper management initially sets the sales targets. Then, employee teams in each department provide their inputs. Once everyone agrees on a sales forecast, managers prepare monthly departmental budgets based on the sales forecast.

The sales budget and the sales forecasts are conceptually distinct. A **sales forecast** is a prediction of sales under a given set of conditions. The **sales budget** is the specific sales forecast that is the result of decisions to create the conditions that will generate a desired level of sales. For example, you may have various forecasts of sales corresponding to various levels of advertising. The sales forecast for the one level of advertising you decide to implement becomes the sales budget.

The top sales executive usually directs the preparation of sales forecasts. Important factors considered by sales forecasters include the following:

1. Past patterns of sales: Past experience combined with detailed past sales by product line, geographic region, and type of customer can help predict future sales.
2. Estimates made by the sales force: A company's sales force is often the best source of information about the desires and plans of customers.

3. General economic conditions: The financial press regularly publishes predictions for many economic indicators, such as gross domestic product and industrial production indexes (local and foreign). Knowledge of how sales relate to these indicators can aid sales forecasting.

4. Competitors' actions: Sales depend on the strength and actions of competitors. To forecast sales, a company should consider the likely strategies and reactions of competitors, such as changes in their prices, product quality, or services.

5. Changes in the firm's prices: A company should consider the effects of planned price changes on customer demand (see Chapter 5). Normally, lower prices increase unit sales while higher prices decrease unit sales.

6. Changes in product mix: Changing the mix of products often can affect not only sales levels but also overall contribution margin. Identifying the most profitable products and devising methods to increase their sales is a key part of successful management.

7. Market research studies: Some companies hire marketing experts to gather information about market conditions and customer preferences. Such information is useful to managers making sales forecasts and product-mix decisions.

8. Advertising and sales promotion plans: Advertising and other promotional costs affect sales levels. A sales forecast should be based on anticipated effects of promotional activities.

Sales forecasting usually combines various techniques. In addition to the opinions of the sales staff, statistical analysis of correlations between sales and economic indicators (prepared by economists and members of the market research staff) provide valuable help. The opinions of line management also heavily influence the final sales forecasts. No matter how many technical experts a company uses in forecasting, the sales budget should ultimately be the responsibility of line management. Line managers who participate fully in setting the sales budget will be more committed to achieving the budget goals.

Governments and other nonprofit organizations face a similar problem in forecasting revenues from taxes, contributions, or other sources. For example, city revenues may depend on a variety of factors, such as property taxes, traffic fines, parking fees, license fees, and city income taxes. In turn, property taxes depend on the extent of new construction and general increases in real estate values. Thus, forecasting revenues for a government or nonprofit organization may require just as much sophistication as sales forecasts of a for-profit firm.

Types of Budgets

Businesses use several different types of budgets. The most forward-looking and least detailed budget is the **strategic plan**, which sets the overall goals and objectives of the organization. While the strategic plan does not deal with a specific time frame and does not produce forecasted financial statements, it provides the overall framework for the **long-range plan**. Long-range plans typically produce forecasted financial statements for 5- to 10-year periods. Decisions made during long-range planning include addition or deletion of product lines, design and location of new plants, acquisitions of buildings and equipment, and other long-term commitments. Companies coordinate their long-range plans with **capital budgets**, which detail the planned expenditures for facilities, equipment, new products, and other long-term investments. Short-term plans and budgets guide day-to-day operations.

Managers who pay attention only to short-term budgets will quickly lose sight of long-term goals. Similarly, managers who pay attention only to the long-term budget could wind up mismanaging day-to-day operations. Effective managers balance detailed attention to their short-term budgets with a broad awareness of long-term plans.

The **master budget** is a detailed and comprehensive analysis of the first year of the long-range plan. It quantifies targets for sales, purchases, production, distribution, and financing in the form of forecasted financial statements and supporting operating schedules. These schedules provide detailed information beyond what appears in the forecasted financial statements. Thus, the master budget includes forecasts of sales, expenses, balance sheets, and cash receipts and disbursements.

Many companies break their annual budgets into 4 quarterly or even 12 monthly budgets. **Continuous budgets** or **rolling budgets** are master budgets that simply add a month (or quarter) in the future as they drop the month (or quarter) just ended. In this way, budgeting becomes an ongoing process instead of an annual exercise. Continuous budgets force managers to always think about the next full year, not just the remainder of the current fiscal year.

Objective 5

Explain the major features and advantages of a master budget.

Components of the Master Budget

The two major parts of a master budget are the operating budget and the financial budget. The **operating budget**—sometimes called the **profit plan**—focuses on the income statement and its supporting schedules or, in an organization with no sales revenues, on budgeted expenses and supporting schedules. In contrast, the **financial budget** focuses on the effects that the operating budget and other plans (such as capital budgets and repayments of debt) will have on cash balances. The distinction between the operating budget and the financial budget is important because of the distinction between profitability and financial position. There are many examples of firms with strong profits where a weak cash position placed them in bankruptcy. There are also many examples of firms whose strong financial position allowed them to survive periods of temporary unprofitability.

The terms used to describe specific budget schedules vary from organization to organization. However, most master budgets share common elements. The usual master budget for a merchandising company has the following components as shown in Exhibit 7-2:

A. Operating budget
   1. Sales budget
   2. Purchases and cost-of-goods-sold budget
   3. Operating expense budget
   4. Budgeted statement of income
B. Financial budget
   1. Capital budget
   2. Cash budget
   3. Budgeted balance sheet

Other companies add to or adapt these categories depending on the nature of their operations. For example, manufacturing companies add budgets for raw material, work-in-process,

Exhibit 7-2
Preparation of the Master Budget for a Merchandising Company

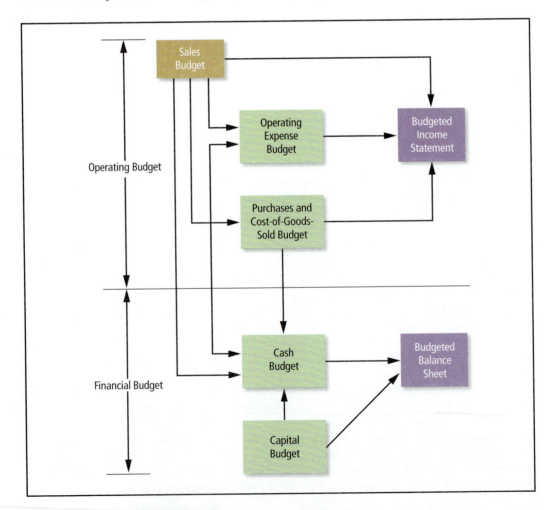

and finished good inventories, and budgets for each type of resource activity, such as labor, materials, and factory overhead. Similarly, a consulting company might adapt the operating expense budget to focus on its major cost, consultant salaries. In addition to the master budget, there are countless forms of special budgets and related reports. For example, a report might detail goals and objectives for improvements in quality or customer satisfaction during the budget period.

Preparing the Master Budget

Let's return to Exhibit 7-2 and trace the preparation of the master budget components. Although the process involves a large number of detailed calculations, always keep the big picture in mind. Remember that the master budgeting process provides an overview of company operations and an opportunity to review key decisions regarding all aspects of the company's value chain. Early drafts of the budget often lead to decisions that, in turn, lead to revisions in subsequent budget drafts. This cycle may be repeated several times before the budget is finalized.

The Cooking Hut

We illustrate the budgeting process using the Cooking Hut Company (CHC), a Denver retailer of a wide variety of kitchen and dining room items, such as coffeemakers, silverware, and table linens. Although master budgets normally cover a full year, for the sake of brevity this illustration shows only the first 3 months of CHC's fiscal year, April–June. Exhibit 7-3 is the closing balance sheet for the previous fiscal year ending March 31, 20X1.

SALES BUDGET   Preparation of the master budget for the first 3 months of the new fiscal year requires a sales budget for 1 month beyond the 3 months because CHC bases its budgeted inventory purchases on the following month's sales. The sales budget for the next 4 months is as follows:

April	$50,000
May	$80,000
June	$60,000
July	$50,000

The master budget also requires information about actual sales in the previous month because CHC collects cash for the credit sales in the month following the sale. On average, 60% of sales are cash sales and the remaining 40% are credit sales. Sales in March were $40,000 and the $16,000 of accounts receivable on March 31 represents credit sales made in March (40% of $40,000). Uncollectible accounts are negligible and thus ignored. For simplicity's sake, we also ignore all local, state, and federal taxes for this illustration.

Assets		
Current assets		
Cash	$10,000	
Accounts receivable, net (.4 × March sales of $40,000)	16,000	
Merchandise inventory, $20,000 + .7 (.8 × April sales of $50,000)	48,000	
Unexpired insurance (for April–December 20X1)	1,800	$ 75,800
Plant assets		
Equipment, fixtures, and other	$37,000	
Accumulated depreciation	12,800	24,200
Total assets		$100,000
Liabilities and Owners' Equity		
Current liabilities		
Accounts payable (.5 × March purchases of $33,600)	$16,800	
Accrued wages and commissions payable ($1,250 + $3,000)	4,250	$ 21,050
Owners' equity		78,950
Total liabilities and owners' equity		$100,000

Exhibit 7-3
The Cooking Hut Company
Balance Sheet March 31, 20X1

PLANNED INVENTORY LEVELS   Because deliveries from suppliers and customer demands are uncertain, at the end of each month CHC wants to have on hand a base inventory of $20,000 plus additional inventory equal to 80% of the expected cost of goods sold for the following month. The cost of goods sold averages 70% of sales. Therefore, the inventory on March 31 is $20,000 + .7(.8 × April sales of $50,000) = $20,000 + $28,000 = $48,000. The purchase terms available to CHC are net, 30 days. CHC pays for each month's purchases as follows: 50% during the month of purchase and 50% during the next month. Therefore, the accounts payable balance on March 31 is 50% of March purchases, or $33,600 × .5 = $16,800.

WAGES AND COMMISSIONS   CHC pays wages and commissions twice each month, with payments lagged half a month after they are earned. Each payment consists of two components: (i) one-half of monthly fixed wages of $2,500, and (ii) commissions, equal to 15% of sales, which we assume are uniform throughout each month. To illustrate the wage and commission payments, the March 31 balance of accrued wages and commissions payable is (.5 × $2,500) + .5(.15 × $40,000) = $1,250 + $3,000 = $4,250. Because of the half-month lag, CHC will pay this $4,250 balance on April 15.

CAPITAL EXPENDITURES AND OPERATING EXPENDITURES   CHC's only planned capital expenditure is the purchase of new fixtures for $3,000 cash in April. CHC has monthly operating expenses as follows:

Miscellaneous expenses	5% of sales, paid as incurred
Rent	$2,000, paid as incurred
Insurance	$200 expiration per month
Depreciation, including new fixtures	$500 per month

CASH BALANCES   Because collections lag credit sales, CHC often struggles to come up with the cash to pay for purchases, employee wages, and other outlays. To meet cash needs, CHC uses short-term loans from local banks, paying them back when excess cash is available. CHC maintains a minimum $10,000 cash balance at the end of each month for operating purposes and can borrow or repay loans only in multiples of $1,000. Assume that borrowing occurs at the beginning and repayments occur at the end of the month. Also assume that interest of 1% per month is paid in cash at the end of each month.

Steps in Preparing the Master Budget

The principal steps in preparing the master budget are as follows:

Supporting Budgets and Schedules

1. Using the data given, prepare the following budgets and schedules for each of the months of the planning horizon:
   Schedule a. Sales budget
   Schedule b. Cash collections from customers
   Schedule c. Purchases and cost-of-goods-sold budget
   Schedule d. Cash disbursements for purchases
   Schedule e. Operating expense budget
   Schedule f. Cash disbursements for operating expenses

Operating Budget

2. Using the supporting budgets and schedules, prepare a budgeted income statement for the 3 months ending June 30, 20X1 (Exhibit 7-4).

Financial Budget

3. Prepare the following budgets and forecasted financial statements:
   a. Capital budget
   b. Cash budget, including details of borrowings, repayments, and interest for each month of the planning horizon (Exhibit 7-5)
   c. Budgeted balance sheet as of June 30, 20X1 (Exhibit 7-6)

Objective 6

Follow the principal steps in preparing a master budget.

Organizations with effective budget systems have specific guidelines for the steps and timing of budget preparation. Although the details differ, the guidelines invariably include the preceding steps. As we follow these steps to prepare CHC's master budget, be sure that you understand the source of each figure in each schedule and budget.

Step 1: Preparing Basic Data

STEP 1A: SALES BUDGET   The sales budget is the starting point for budgeting because planned inventory levels, purchases, and operating expenses all depend on the expected level of sales. Schedule a includes information about actual March sales because March credit sales affect cash collections in April.

Objective 7
Prepare the operating budget and the supporting schedules.

Schedule a: Sales Budget

	March	April	May	June	April–June Total
Total sales	$40,000	$50,000	$80,000	$60,000	$190,000

STEP 1B: CASH COLLECTIONS FROM CUSTOMERS   Schedule b uses the sales budget to plan when CHC will collect cash. In turn, we will use Schedule b to prepare the cash budget in Step 3. Cash collections from customers include the current month's cash sales plus collection of the previous month's credit sales.

Schedule b: Cash Collections from Customers

	April	May	June
Cash sales (60% of current month sales)	$30,000	$48,000	$36,000
Collection of last month's credit sales (40% of previous month sales)	16,000	20,000	32,000
Total collections	$46,000	$68,000	$68,000

STEP 1C: PURCHASES BUDGET   The elements of the purchases budget are tied together by a simple intuitive identity that ignores minor complications such as returns and defects but relates the fundamental uses of inventory to the sources: Inventory is either sold or else carried over to the next period as ending inventory. Inventory comes from either beginning inventory or purchases. Therefore, cost of goods sold plus ending inventory equals beginning inventory plus purchases.

We budget cost of goods sold by multiplying the cost of merchandise sold percentage (70%) by budgeted sales. The total merchandise needed is the sum of budgeted cost of goods sold plus the desired ending inventory. Finally, we compute required purchases by subtracting beginning inventory from the total merchandise needed:

Schedule c: Purchases Budget

	March	April	May	June	April–June Total
Budgeted cost of goods sold†		$35,000	$ 56,000	$42,000	$133,000
Plus: Desired ending inventory		64,800	53,600	48,000	
Total merchandise needed		$99,800	$109,600	$90,000	
Less: Beginning inventory		48,000‡	64,800	53,600	
Purchases	$33,600*	$51,800	$ 44,800	$36,400	

*Purchases for March were ending inventory ($48,000 as shown in Exhibit 7-3) plus cost of goods sold (.7 × March sales of $40,000) less beginning inventory ($42,400 = $20,000 + [.8 × March cost of goods sold of $28,000]).

†.7 × April sales of $50,000 = $35,000; .7 × May sales of $80,000 = $56,000; .7 × June sales of $60,000 = $42,000
‡Ending inventory from March was $48,000 as shown in Exhibit 7-3.

STEP 1D: DISBURSEMENTS FOR PURCHASES   We use the purchases budget to develop Schedule d. In our example, disbursements are 50% of the current month's purchases and 50% of the previous month's purchases.

Schedule d: Cash Disbursements for Purchases

	April	May	June
50% of last month's purchases	$16,800	$25,900	$22,400
Plus 50% of this month's purchases	25,900	22,400	18,200
Disbursements for purchases	$42,700	$48,300	$40,600

STEP 1E: OPERATING EXPENSE BUDGET   Month-to-month changes in sales volume and other cost-driver activities directly influence many operating expenses. Examples of expenses driven by sales volume include sales commissions and delivery expenses—these are included in miscellaneous expenses for CHC. Other expenses, such as rent, insurance, depreciation, and wages, are not influenced by sales (within appropriate relevant ranges), and we regard them as fixed. Schedule e summarizes operating expenses for CHC.

Schedule e: Operating Expense Budget

	March	April	May	June	April–June Total
Wages (fixed)	$2,500	$ 2,500	$ 2,500	$ 2,500	
Commissions (15% of current month's sales)	6,000	7,500	12,000	9,000	
Total wages and commissions	$8,500	$10,000	$14,500	$11,500	$36,000
Miscellaneous expenses (5% of current sales)		2,500	4,000	3,000	9,500
Rent (fixed)		2,000	2,000	2,000	6,000
Insurance (fixed)		200	200	200	600
Depreciation (fixed)		500	500	500	1,500
Total operating expenses		$15,200	$21,200	$17,200	$53,600

STEP 1F: DISBURSEMENTS FOR OPERATING EXPENSES   Disbursements for operating expenses are based on the operating expense budget. Disbursements include 50% of last month's wages and commissions, 50% of this month's wages and commissions, and miscellaneous and rent expenses. There is no monthly cash disbursement for Insurance (which is paid annually at the beginning of the year) nor for depreciation (which does not involve any periodic cash disbursement). We use the total of these disbursements for each month in preparing the cash budget, Exhibit 7-5.

Schedule f: Disbursements for Operating Expenses

	April	May	June
Wages and commissions			
50% of last month's expenses	$ 4,250	$ 5,000	$ 7,250
50% of this month's expenses	5,000	7,250	5,750
Total wages and commissions	$ 9,250	$12,250	$13,000
Miscellaneous expenses	2,500	4,000	3,000
Rent	2,000	2,000	2,000
Total disbursements	$13,750	$18,250	$18,000

Step 2: Preparing the Operating Budget

Steps 1a, 1c, and 1e, along with interest expense from Exhibit 7-5, provide information to construct the budgeted income statement in Exhibit 7-4. Budgeted income from operations is often a benchmark for judging management performance.

Step 3: Preparation of Financial Budget

Objective 8

Prepare the financial budget.

The second major part of the master budget is the financial budget, which consists of the capital budget, cash budget, and ending balance sheet.

STEP 3A: CAPITAL BUDGET   In our illustration, the $3,000 planned purchase of new fixtures in April is the only item in the capital budget. More complex capital budgets are illustrated in Chapter 11.

		Data	Source of Data
Sales		$190,000	Schedule a
Cost of goods sold		133,000	Schedule c
Gross margin		$ 57,000	
Operating expenses:			
Wages and commissions	$36,000		Schedule e
Rent	6,000		Schedule e
Miscellaneous	9,500		Schedule e
Insurance	600		Schedule e
Depreciation	1,500	53,600	Schedule e
Income from operations		$ 3,400	
Interest expense		410	
Net income		$ 2,990	

Exhibit 7-4

The Cooking Hut Company
Budgeted Income Statement for Three Months Ending June 30, 20X1

STEP 3B: CASH BUDGET The **cash budget** is a statement of planned cash receipts and disbursements. Cash budgets help management avoid having unnecessary idle cash, on the one hand, or unnecessary cash deficiencies, on the other. The cash budget is heavily affected by the level of operations summarized in the budgeted income statement.

The cash budget has the following major sections, where the letters x, y, and z refer to the lines in Exhibit 7-5 that summarize the effects of that section:

- The available cash balance (x) is the amount by which the beginning cash balance exceeds CHC's $10,000 minimum cash balance. Companies maintain a minimum cash balance to allow for fluctuations in the level of cash during the month—daily balances during the month typically fluctuate relative to the beginning and ending cash balances—and also to provide for unexpected cash needs.

	April	May	June
Beginning cash balance	$ 10,000	$10,410	$ 10,720
Minimum cash balance desired	10,000	10,000	10,000
Available cash balance (x)	$ 0	$ 410	$ 720
Cash receipts and disbursements			
Collections from customers (Schedule b*)	$ 46,000	$68,000	$ 68,000
Payments for merchandise (Schedule d)	(42,700)	(48,300)	(40,600)
Payments for operating expenses (Schedule f)	(13,750)	(18,250)	(18,000)
Purchase of new fixtures (Step 3a)	(3,000)		
Net cash receipts and disbursements (y)	$ (13,450)	$ 1,450	$ 9,400
Excess (deficiency) of cash before financing $(x + y)$	(13,450)	$ 1,860	$ 10,120
Borrowing (at beginning of month)	$ 14,000†		
Repayments (at end of month)		$ (1,000)	$ (9,000)
Interest payments (1% per month, end of month‡)	(140)	(140)	(130)
Total cash increase (decrease) from financing (z)	$ 13,860	$ (1,140)	$ (9,130)
Ending cash balance (beginning + y + z)	$ 10,410	$10,720	$ 10,990

*Letters x, y, and z are keyed to the explanation in the text.
†Borrowing and repayment of principal are made in multiples of $1,000, at an interest rate of 1% per month.
‡Interest computations: $14,000 × .01 = $140; $14,000 × .01 = $140; $13,000 × .01 = $130.

Exhibit 7-5

The Cooking Hut Company
Cash Budget for Three Months Ending June 30, 20X1

- Net cash receipts and disbursements (y):
  1. Cash receipts depend on collections from customers' accounts receivable, cash sales, and on other operating cash income sources, such as interest received on notes receivable. Trace total collections from Schedule b to Exhibit 7-5.
  2. Disbursements for purchases depend on the credit terms extended by suppliers and the bill-paying habits of the buyer. Trace disbursements for merchandise from Schedule d to Exhibit 7-5.
  3. Payroll depends on wages and commission terms and on payroll dates. Some costs and expenses depend on contractual terms for installment payments, mortgage payments, rents, leases, and miscellaneous items. Trace disbursements for operating expenses from Schedule f to Exhibit 7-5.
  4. Other disbursements include outlays for fixed assets, long-term investments, dividends, and the like. An example is the $3,000 expenditure for new fixtures.
- The total cash increase (decrease) from financing (z) depends on the total available cash balance (x) and the net cash receipts and disbursements (y). If cash available plus net cash receipts less disbursements is negative, borrowing is necessary—Exhibit 7-5 shows that CHC will borrow $14,000 in April to cover the planned deficiency. If cash available plus net cash receipts less disbursements is sufficiently positive, CHC can repay loans—it repays $1,000 and $9,000 in May and June, respectively. This section of the cash budget also generally contains the outlays for interest expense. Trace the calculated interest expense, which in our example is the same as the cash interest payments for the 3 months, to Exhibit 7-4, which then will be complete.
- The ending cash balance is the beginning cash balance $+ y + z$. Financing, z, has either a positive (borrowing) or a negative (repayment) effect on the cash balance. The illustrative cash budget shows the pattern of short-term, "self-liquidating" financing. Seasonal peaks often result in heavy drains on cash—for merchandise purchases and operating expenses—before the company makes sales and collects cash from customers. The resulting loan is "self-liquidating"—that is, the company uses borrowed money to acquire merchandise for sale, and uses the proceeds from sales to repay the loan. This "working capital cycle" moves from cash to inventory to receivables and back to cash.

Exhibit 7-6

The Cooking Hut Company
Budgeted Balance Sheet
June 30, 20X1

Assets

Current Assets		
Cash (Exhibit 7-5)	$10,990	
Accounts receivable, net (.4 × June Sales of $60,000)	24,000	
Inventory (Schedule c)	48,000	
Unexpired insurance (for July–December)	1,200	$ 84,190
Plant Assets		
Equipment, fixtures, and other ($37,000 + $3,000)	$40,000	
Accumulated Depreciation ($12,800 + $1,500)	(14,300)	25,700
Total assets		$109,890

Liabilities and Owners' Equity

Current liabilities		
Accounts payable (.5 × June purchases of $36,400)	$18,200	
Short-term bank loan	4,000	
Accrued wages and commissions payable (.5 × 11,500)	5,750	$ 27,950
Owners' equity (78,950 + 2,990 net income)		81,940
Total liabilities and owners' equity		$109,890

Note: March 31, 20X1 beginning balances are used for computations of unexpired insurance, plant assets, and owners' equity.

Business Plans and Budgets

Start-up companies in a variety of industries have mushroomed into multibillion-dollar companies. How do these companies get started? An essential component in securing initial funding for a start-up is the development of a business plan. The federal government's Small Business Administration recommends a business plan with three sections:

1. The Business—includes a description of the business, a marketing plan, an assessment of the competition, a list of operating procedures, and a roster of personnel
2. Financial Data—includes the following items:
    Loan applications
    Capital equipment and supply list
    Pro forma balance sheet
    Break-even analysis
    Pro forma income projections (income statements):
        Three-year summary
        Detail by month, first year
        Detail by quarters, second and third years
        Assumptions upon which projections were based
    Pro forma cash flow statements
3. Supporting Documents—includes a variety of legal documents and information about the principals involved, suppliers, customers, etc.

Financial data are an important part of a business plan, the centerpiece of which is the master budget. The budgeted income statement and budgeted cash flow statement are essential to predicting the future prospects of any business. They are especially critical to assessing the prospects of a new company that has little history to analyze.

The importance of a budget to a start-up company was emphasized by Jim Rowan, former senior vice president of **SunAmerica**, who left to form a new company, **EncrypTix**. He raised $36 million in investment funding to spin EncrypTix off from **Stamps.com**. The company focuses on Internet delivery and storage of tickets, coupons, and vouchers. Rowan stated, "The key thing for a start-up is to develop a budget and put it like a stake in the ground, so you can measure against it. It's not a ceiling, it's not carved in stone, but you have to have something that's a benchmark."

Budgeting is often not the most exciting task for entrepreneurs. However, lack of a credible budget is one of the main reasons venture capitalists cite when they refuse funding for a start-up. Further, a cash shortage is one of the main causes of failure among start-up companies. Anyone wanting to be an entrepreneur would be well-advised to study budgeting and learn how it can be a powerful tool both for managing the company and for promoting the company to potential investors.

Sources: Adapted from Small Business Administration, *The Business Plan: Roadmap to Success* (www.sba.gov/starting/indexbusplans.html); and K. Klein, "Budgeting Helps Secure Longevity," *Los Angeles Times*, August 2, 2000, p. C6.

STEP 3C: BUDGETED BALANCE SHEET   The final step in preparing the master budget is to construct the budgeted balance sheet (Exhibit 7-6) that projects each balance sheet item in accordance with the business plan as expressed in the previous schedules. Specifically, the beginning balances at March 31 would be increased or decreased in light of the expected cash receipts and cash disbursements in Exhibit 7-5 and in light of the effects of noncash items appearing on the income statement in Exhibit 7-4. For example, unexpired insurance is a noncash item that would decrease from its balance of $1,800 on March 31 to $1,200 on June 30.

The master budget is an important management tool for evaluating and revising strategy. For example, the initial formulation of the financial statements may prompt management to consider new sales strategies to generate more demand. Alternatively, management may explore the effects of various adjustments in the timing of cash receipts and disbursements. The large cash deficiency in April, for example, may lead to an emphasis on cash sales or an attempt to speed up collection of accounts receivable. In any event, the first draft of the master budget is rarely the final draft. As managers revise strategy, the budgeting process becomes an integral part of the management process itself—budgeting is planning and communicating. The Business First box above describes the important role of budgets in start-up companies.

Making Managerial Decisions

Some managers focus on the operating budget, while others are more concerned with the financial budget. How does the operating budget differ from the financial budget?

Answer

The operating budget focuses on the income statement, which uses accrual accounting. It measures revenues and expenses. Line operating managers usually prepare and use the operating budget. In contrast, the financial budget focuses primarily on cash flow. It measures the receipts and disbursements of cash. Financial managers, such as controllers and treasurers, focus on the financial budget. The operating budget is a better measure of long-run performance, but the financial budget is essential to plan for short-term cash needs and manage cash balances. A shortage of cash can get a company into financial trouble even when operating performance appears to be okay. Thus, both operating and financial budgets are important to an organization.

Summary Problem for Your Review

Be sure you understand every step of the CHC example before you tackle this review problem.

PROBLEM

The Country Store is a retail outlet for a variety of hardware and housewares. The owner is eager to prepare a budget and is especially concerned with her cash position. The company will have to borrow in order to finance purchases made in preparation for high expected sales during the busy last quarter of the year. When the company needs cash, borrowing occurs at the end of a month. When cash is available for repayments, the repayment occurs at the end of a month. The company pays interest in cash at the end of every month at a monthly rate of 1% on the amount outstanding during that month.

Review the structure of the example in the chapter and then prepare the Country Store's master budget for the months of October, November, and December. The owner has gathered the data shown in Exhibit 7-7 to prepare the simplified budget. In addition, she will purchase equipment in October for $19,750 cash and pay dividends of $4,000 in December.

Balance Sheet as of September 30, 20X1

Assets	
Cash	$ 9,000
Accounts receivable	48,000
Inventory	12,600
Plant and equipment (net)	200,000
Total assets	$269,600

Liabilities and stockholders' equity	
Interest payable	0
Note payable	0
Accounts payable	18,300
Capital stock	180,000
Retained earnings	71,300
Total liabilities and stockholders' equity	$269,600

Budgeted expenses (per month):

Wages and salaries	$ 7,500
Freight out as a percent of sales	6%
Advertising	$ 6,000
Depreciation	$ 2,000
Other expense as a percent of sales	4%
Minimum inventory policy as a percent of next month's cost of goods sold	30%

Budgeted sales:

September (actual)	$60,000
October	70,000
November	85,000
December	90,000
January 20X2	50,000

Other data:

Required minimum cash balance	$ 8,000
Sales mix, cash/credit	
Cash sales	20%
Credit sales (collected the following month)	80%
Gross profit rate	40%
Loan interest rate (interest paid in cash monthly)	12%
Inventory paid for in	
Month purchased	50%
Month after purchase	50%
Wages and salaries, freight-out advertising, and other expenses are paid in cash in the month incurred.	

Exhibit 7-7
The Country Store
Budget Data

SOLUTION

Schedule a: Sales budget

	October	November	December	Total
Credit sales, 80%	$56,000	$68,000	$72,000	$196,000
Cash sales, 20%	14,000	17,000	18,000	49,000
Total sales	$70,000	$85,000	$90,000	$245,000

Schedule b: Cash collections from customers

	October	November	December	Total
Cash sales	$14,000	$17,000	$18,000	$ 49,000
Collections from prior month	48,000	56,000	68,000	172,000
Total collections	$62,000	$73,000	$86,000	$221,000

Schedule c: Purchases budget

	October	November	December	Total
Desired ending inventory	$15,300	$16,200	$ 9,000	$ 40,500
Plus cost of goods sold	42,000	51,000	54,000	147,000
Total needed	$57,300	$67,200	$63,000	$187,500
Less: Beginning inventory	12,600	15,300	16,200	44,100
Total purchases	$44,700	$51,900	$46,800	$143,400

Schedule d: Cash disbursements for purchases

	October	November	December	Total
For September*	$18,300			$ 18,300
For October	22,350	$22,350		44,700
For November		25,950	$25,950	51,900
For December			23,400	23,400
Total disbursements	$40,650	$48,300	$49,350	$138,300

*The amount payable on the September 30, 20X1, balance sheet.

Schedules e and f: Operating expenses and disbursements for expenses (except interest)

	October	November	December	Total
Cash expenses:				
Salaries and wages	$ 7,500	$ 7,500	$ 7,500	$22,500
Freight-out	4,200	5,100	5,400	14,700
Advertising	6,000	6,000	6,000	18,000
Other expenses	2,800	3,400	3,600	9,800
Total disbursements for expenses	$20,500	$22,000	$22,500	$65,000
Noncash expenses:				
Depreciation	2,000	2,000	2,000	6,000
Total expenses	$22,500	$24,000	$24,500	$71,000

The Country Store
Cash Budget for the months of October–December, 20X1

	October	November	December
Beginning cash balance	$ 9,000	$ 8,000	$ 8,000
Minimum cash balance desired	8,000	8,000	8,000
Available cash balance	1,000	0	0
Cash receipts and disbursements:			
Collections from customers	62,000	73,000	86,000
Payments for merchandise	(40,650)	(48,300)	(49,350)
Operating expenses	(20,500)	(22,000)	(22,500)
Equipment purchases	(19,750)	0	0
Dividends	0	0	(4,000)
Interest*	0	(179)	(154)
Net cash receipts and disbursements	(18,900)	2,521	9,996
Excess (deficiency) of cash before financing	$(17,900)	$ 2,521	$ 9,996
Financing:			
Borrowing†	$17,900	$ 0	$ 0
Repayments	0	(2,521)	(9,996)
Total cash from financing	17,900	(2,521)	(9,996)
Ending cash balance	$ 8,000	$ 8,000	$ 8,000

*Interest is paid on the loan amounts outstanding during the month. November: $(.01) \times (\$17,900) = \$179$; December: $(.01) \times (\$17,900 - \$2,521) = \$154$.

†Borrowings are at the end of the month in the amounts needed. Repayments also are made at the end of the month in the amount that excess cash permits.

The Country Store
Budgeted Income Statement for October–December, 20X1

	October	November	December	October–December Total
Sales	$70,000	$85,000	$90,000	$245,000
Cost of goods sold	42,000	51,000	54,000	147,000
Gross margin	28,000	34,000	36,000	98,000
Operating expenses				
Salaries and wages	7,500	7,500	7,500	22,500
Freight-out	4,200	5,100	5,400	14,700
Advertising	6,000	6,000	6,000	18,000
Other	2,800	3,400	3,600	9,800
Interest*	—	179	154	333
Depreciation	2,000	2,000	2,000	6,000
Total operating expense	$22,500	$24,179	$24,654	$ 71,333
Net operating income	$ 5,500	$ 9,821	$11,346	$ 26,667

*Interest expense is the monthly interest rate times the borrowed amount held for the month. November: $(.01) \times \$17,900 = \$179$; December: $(.01) \times \$15,379 = \$154$.

The Country Store
Budgeted Balance Sheets as of the Ends of October–December, 20X1

Assets	October	November	December*
Current assets			
Cash	$ 8,000	$ 8,000	$ 8,000
Accounts receivable	56,000	68,000	72,000
Inventory	15,300	16,200	9,000
Total current assets	79,300	92,200	89,000
Plant, less accumulated depreciation[†]	217,750	215,750	213,750
Total assets	$297,050	$307,950	$302,750
Liabilities and Equities			
Liabilities			
Accounts payable	$ 22,350	$ 25,950	$ 23,400
Notes payable	17,900	15,379	5,383
Total liabilities	40,250	41,329	28,783
Stockholders' equity			
Capital stock	180,000	180,000	180,000
Retained earnings	76,800	86,621	93,967
Total equities	256,800	266,621	273,967
Total liabilities and equities	$297,050	$307,950	$302,750

*The December 30, 20X1, balance sheet is the ending balance sheet for the quarter.

[†]October ending balance in Plant = beginning balance + equipment purchases − depreciation = $200,000 + $19,750 − $2,000 = $217,750.

Activity-Based Master Budgets

The budget process we have described thus far in this chapter can be called **functional budgeting** because the focus is on preparing budgets by function, such as production, selling, and administrative support. Organizations that have implemented activity-based cost accounting systems often use these systems as a vehicle to prepare **activity-based budgets (ABB)**—budgets that focus on the budgeted cost of activities required to produce and sell products and services.

An activity-based budgetary system emphasizes the planning and control purpose of cost management. Our discussion of activity-based costing (ABC) in Chapter 4 focused on designing cost accounting and cost allocation systems that provided more accurate product and service costs. However, once a company has designed and implemented an ABC system, it can use the same framework for its budgetary system. Exhibit 7-8 highlights the main concepts and differences between ABC allocation of resource costs to activities and products, and ABB.

Just as in functional budgeting (see Exhibit 7-2), ABB begins with the forecasted demand for products or services—the sales budget. In functional budgeting, the next step is to determine the ending-inventory budget, then the material purchases, and the cost-of-goods-sold budget. In ABB, the focus is on estimating the demand for each activity's output as measured by its cost driver. Then, we use the rate at which activities consume resources to estimate or budget the resources needed. As we can see from comparing Exhibits 7-2 and 7-8, functional budgeting determines the resources needed directly from the predicted sales of products or services, while ABB uses the sales predictions to estimate the required activities, which in turn determines the resources needed. Because of the emphasis on activities and their consumption of resources, some managers believe that ABB is more useful for controlling waste and improving efficiency—a primary objective of budgeting.

Exhibit 7-8

ABC and ABB Compared

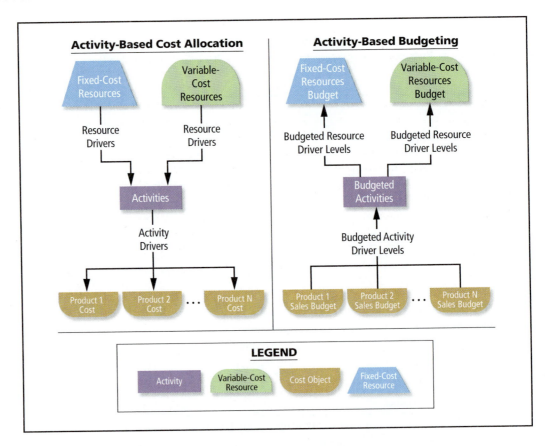

Most companies do not realize the full benefits of ABC until they also integrate it into their budgeting system. Often accountants "own" the costing system of a company, but the budgeting system "belongs" to managers. ABB requires managers to focus on managing activities as they prepare their budgets using the same framework used by the ABC system. For example, when Dow Chemical integrated its new ABC system with its budgeting process, it undertook a massive training effort for "controllers, accountants, work process subject matter experts, cost center owners, business manufacturing leaders, and site general managers." By creating budgets consistent with cost reports, Dow gained much greater benefit from its ABB system.

Government organizations such as the U.S. Small Business Administration (SBA) also use ABB. The SBA is one of the five largest federal credit agencies with over $50 billion in loans. An article published by the SBA touted its use of ABB:

Our goal is to clearly identify the activities that must be performed to produce critical outputs and then determine the level of resources that must be committed to successfully complete the activity. Once this is done, we can determine how various funding levels affect the outputs produced by the SBA. The ABB process provides SBA management the quality information necessary for sound decision making.

Budgets as Financial Planning Models

A well-made master budget that considers all aspects of the company (the entire value chain) provides the basis for an effective **financial planning model**, a mathematical model that can incorporate the effects of alternative assumptions about sales, costs, or product mix. Today, many large companies have developed large-scale financial planning models based on the master budget to predict how various decisions might affect the company. For example, a manager might want to predict the consequences of changing the mix of products offered for sale to emphasize several products with the highest prospects for growth. A financial planning model would provide operational and financial budgets under alternative assumptions about the product mix, sales levels, production constraints, quality levels, scheduling, and so on. Most importantly, managers can get answers to what-if questions, such as "What if sales are 10% below forecasts?

What if material prices increase 8% instead of 4% as expected? What if the new union contract grants a 6% raise in consideration for productivity improvements?"

Using the master budget in this way is a step-by-step process in which managers revise their tentative plans as they exchange views on various aspects of expected activities. For instance, Dow Chemical's model uses 140 separate, constantly revised cost inputs that are based on several different cost drivers. By mathematically describing the relationships among all the operating and financial activities and among the other major internal and external factors that affect the results of management decisions, financial planning models allow managers to assess the predicted impacts of various alternatives before they make final decisions.

Financial planning models have shortened managers' reaction times dramatically. We can prepare in minutes (or even seconds) a revised plan for a large company that once took many accountants many days to prepare by hand. For example, Public Service Enterprise Group, a New Jersey utility company, can run its total master budget several times a day, if necessary.

The use of spreadsheet software has put financial planning models within reach of even the smallest organizations. Appendix 7 illustrates how to use a spreadsheet model for planning. Ready access to powerful modeling, however, does not guarantee plausible or reliable results. Financial planning models are only as good as the assumptions and the inputs used to build and manipulate them—what computer specialists call GIGO (garbage in, garbage out). Nearly every CFO has a horror story to tell about following the bad advice generated from a financial planning model with accurate calculations but faulty assumptions or inputs.

Highlights to Remember

1. **Explain how budgets facilitate planning and coordination.** A budget expresses, in quantitative terms, an organization's objectives and possible steps for achieving them. Thus, a budget is a tool that helps managers in both their planning and control functions. Budgets provide a mechanism for communication between units and across levels of the organization. In an environment that encourages open communication of the opportunities and challenges facing the organization, the budget process allows managers to coordinate ongoing activities and plan for the future.

2. **Anticipate possible human relations problems caused by budgets.** The success of a budget depends heavily on employee reaction to it. Negative attitudes toward budgets often prevent realization of many of the potential benefits. Such attitudes are usually caused by managers who use budgets only to limit spending or to punish employees. Budgets generally are more useful when all affected parties participate in their preparation.

3. **Explain potentially dysfunctional incentives in the budget process.** When managers want to increase the resources allocated to their unit or when managers are evaluated based on performance relative to budgeted amounts, there are incentives to bias the information that goes into their budgets. When managers are compensated using typical bonus schemes, there may be pressure to report inflated results and incentives to make short-run decisions that are not in the best long-run interests of the organization. Not only do such incentives lead managers to make poor decisions, they undercut efforts to maintain high ethical standards in the organization.

4. **Explain the difficulties of sales forecasting.** Sales forecasting combines various techniques as well as opinions of sales staff and management. Sales forecasters must consider many factors, such as past patterns of sales, economic conditions, and competitors' actions. Sales forecasting is difficult because of its complexity and the rapid changes in the business environment in which most companies operate.

5. **Explain the major features and advantages of a master budget.** The two major parts of a master budget are the operating budget and the financial budget. Advantages of budgets include formalization of planning, providing a framework for judging performance, and aiding managers in communicating and coordinating their efforts.

6. **Follow the principal steps in preparing a master budget.** Master budgets typically cover relatively short periods—usually 1 month to 1 year. The steps involved in preparing the master budget vary across organizations but follow the general outline given on pages 274–279. Invariably, the first step is to forecast sales or service levels. The next step should be to forecast cost-driver activity levels, given expected sales and service. Using these forecasts and knowledge of cost behavior, collection patterns, and so on, managers can prepare the operating and financing budgets.

7. **Prepare the operating budget and the supporting schedules.** The operating budget includes the income statement for the budget period. Managers prepare it using the following supporting schedules: sales budget, purchases budget, and operating expense budget.

8. **Prepare the financial budget.** The second major part of the master budget is the financial budget. The financial budget consists of a cash budget, capital budget, and a budgeted balance sheet. Managers prepare the cash budget from the following supporting schedules: cash collections, disbursements for purchases, disbursements for operating expenses, and other disbursements. ■

Appendix 7: Use of Spreadsheet Models for Sensitivity Analysis

Objective 9

Use a spreadsheet to develop a budget.

Spreadsheet software is an extremely powerful and flexible tool for budgeting. An obvious advantage of a spreadsheet is that arithmetic errors are virtually nonexistent. The real value of spreadsheets, however, is that they can be used to make a mathematical model (a financial planning model) of the organization. At very low cost, this model can be applied with a variety of assumptions that reflect possible changes in expected sales, cost drivers, cost functions, and so on. The objective of this appendix is to illustrate how to use a spreadsheet model for sensitivity analysis.

Recall the chapter's Cooking Hut Company (CHC) example. Suppose CHC has prepared its master budget using spreadsheet software. To simplify making changes to the budget, we have placed the relevant forecasts and other budgeting details in Exhibit 7-9. Note that for simplification, we have included only the data necessary for the purchases budget. The full master budget would require a larger table with all the data given in the chapter.

Each cell of the spreadsheet is referenced by its column (a letter) and its row (a number). For example, the beginning inventory for the budget period is in "D4," which is shown as $48,000. By referencing the budget data's cell addresses, you can generate the purchases budget (Exhibit 7-11) within the same spreadsheet by entering formulas instead of numbers into the schedule. Consider Exhibit 7-10. Instead of typing $48,000 as April's beginning inventory in the purchases budget at cell D17, type a formula with the cell address for the beginning inventory from the preceding table, =D4 (the cell address preceded by an "=" sign—the common spreadsheet indicator for a formula). Likewise, all the cells of the purchases budget will contain formulas that include cell addresses instead of numbers. The total inventory needed in April (cell D16) is =D13 + D14, and budgeted purchases in April (cell D19) are =D16 − D17. We can compute the figures for May and June similarly within the respective columns. This approach gives the spreadsheet the most flexibility because you can change any number in the budget data in Exhibit 7-9 (for example, a sales forecast), and the software automatically recalculates the numbers in the entire purchases budget. Exhibit 7-10 shows the formulas used for the purchases budget. Exhibit 7-11 is the purchases budget displaying the numbers generated by the formulas in Exhibit 7-10 using the input data in Exhibit 7-9.

	A	B	C	D	E	F
1	Budgeted data					
2	Sales forecasts		Other information			
3						
4	March (actual)	$40,000	Beginning inventory	$48,000		
5	April	50,000	Desired ending inventory:			
			Base amount	$20,000		
6	May	80,000	Plus percent of next			
7	June	60,000	month's cost of			
8	July	50,000	goods sold	80%		
9			Cost of goods sold			
10			as percent of sales	70%		

Exhibit 7-9
The Cooking Hut Company
Budget Data (Column and row labels are given by the spreadsheet.)

	A	B	C	D	E	F
11	Schedule c					
12	Purchases budget			April	May	June
13	Desired ending inventory			= D5 + D8* (D10*B6)	= D5 + D8* (D10*B7)	= D5 + D8* (D10*B8)
14	Plus cost of goods sold			= D10*B5	= D10*B6	= D10*B7
15						
16	Total needed			= D13 + D14	= E13 + E14	= F13 + F14
17	Less beginning inventory			= D4	= D13	= E13
18						
19	Purchases			= D16 − D17	= E16 − E17	= F16 − F17

Exhibit 7-10

The Cooking Hut Company
Purchases Budget Formulas

Now, what if you want to know the effect on budgeted purchases if the sales forecast is revised upward by 10%? By changing the sales forecasts in spreadsheet Exhibit 7-9, you obtain a nearly instantaneous revision of the purchases budget. Exhibit 7-12 shows the revised budget based on these alternative sales forecasts. The revised sales forecasts are shown in red type and the revised purchases budget is shown in blue type. We could alter any piece of budget data in the table, and easily view or print out the effects on purchases. This sort of analysis, assessing the effects of varying one of the budget inputs, up or down, is sensitivity analysis. **Sensitivity analysis** for budgeting is the systematic varying of budget data input to determine the effects of each variation on the budget. This type of what-if analysis is one of the most powerful uses of spreadsheets for financial planning models. Note that while you can vary more than one type of budget input at a time, it becomes more difficult to isolate the effects of each change.

We can prepare every schedule, operating budget, and financial budget of the master budget on a spreadsheet. We link each schedule by the appropriate cell addresses just as we linked the budget input data (Exhibit 7-9) to the purchases budget (Exhibits 7-10 and 7-11). As in the purchases budget, ideally all cells in the master budget are formulas, not numbers. That way, every budget input can be the subject of sensitivity analysis by simply changing the budget data in Exhibit 7-9.

Preparing the master budget on a spreadsheet is time-consuming the first time. Once the spreadsheet is prepared, the time savings in subsequent periods and the benefits from increased planning and sensitivity analysis capabilities are enormous. In order to obtain these benefits, it is essential for the master budget model to be well documented. Any assumptions that are made should be described either within the spreadsheet or in a separate budget preparation document that is readily available to subsequent users.

	A	B	C	D	E	F
11	Schedule c					
12	Purchases budget			April	May	June
13	Desired ending inventory			$64,800	$53,600	$48,000
14	Plus cost of goods sold			35,000	56,000	42,000
15						
16	Total needed			99,800	109,600	90,000
17	Less beginning inventory			48,000	64,800	53,600
18						
19	Purchases			$51,800	$44,800	$36,400

Exhibit 7-11

The Cooking Hut Company
Purchases Budget

	A	B	C	D	E	F
1	Budgeted data					
2	Sales forecasts		Other information			
3						
4	March (actual)	$40,000	Beginning inventory	$48,000		
5	April	55,000	Desired ending inventory:			
			Base amount	$20,000		
6	May	88,000	Plus percent of next			
7	June	66,000	month's cost of			
8	July	55,000	goods sold	80%		
9			Cost of goods sold			
10			as percent of sales	70%		
11	Schedule c					
12	Purchases budget			April	May	June
13	Desired ending inventory			$ 69,280	$ 56,960	$50,800
14	Plus cost of goods sold			38,500	61,600	46,200
15						
16	Total needed			107,780	118,560	97,000
17	Less beginning inventory			48,000	69,280	56,960
18						
19	Purchases			$ 59,780	$ 49,280	$40,040

Exhibit 7-12
The Cooking Hut Company
Purchases Budget

Accounting Vocabulary

activity-based budgets (ABB), p. 283
budgetary slack, p. 269
budget padding, p. 269
capital budget, p. 271
cash budget, p. 277
continuous budget, p. 271
financial budget, p. 272

financial planning model, p. 284
functional budgeting, p. 283
long-range plan, p. 271
master budget, p. 271
operating budget, p. 272
participative budgeting, p. 268
profit plan, p. 272

rolling budget, p. 271
sales budget, p. 270
sales forecast, p. 270
sensitivity analysis, p. 287
strategic plan, p. 271
zero-base budget, p. 266

MyAccountingLab

Fundamental Assignment Material

Special note: Problems 7-A1 and 7-B1 provide single-problem reviews of most of the chapter topics. Those readers who prefer to concentrate on the fundamentals in smaller chunks should consider any of the other problems.

7-A1 Prepare Master Budget

You are the new manager of the Rapidbuy Electronics store in the Mall of America. Top management of Rapidbuy Electronics is convinced that management training should include the active participation of store managers in the budgeting process. You have been asked to prepare a complete master budget for your store for June, July, and August. All accounting is done centrally so you have no expert help on the premises. In addition, tomorrow the branch manager and the assistant controller will be here to examine your work; at that time, they will assist you in formulating the final budget document. The idea is to have you prepare the initial budget on your own so that you gain more confidence about accounting matters. You want to make a favorable impression on your superiors, so you gather the data at the top of page 289 as of May 31, 20X8:

Credit sales are 90% of total sales. Eighty percent of each credit account is collected in the month following the sale and 20% is collected in the subsequent month. Assume that bad debts are negligible and can be ignored. The accounts receivable on May 31 are the result of the credit sales for April and May:

$$(.20 \times .90 \times \$60,000) + (1.0 \times .90 \times \$70,000) = \$73,800.$$

		Recent and Projected Sales	
Cash	$ 5,800		
Inventory	86,800	April	$ 60,000
Accounts receivable	73,800	May	70,000
Net furniture and fixtures	33,600	June	140,000
Total assets	$200,000	July	80,000
Accounts payable	$ 97,800	August	80,000
Owners' equity	102,200	September	60,000
Total liabilities and owners' equities	$200,000		

The average gross profit on sales is 38%.

The policy is to acquire enough inventory each month to equal the following month's projected cost of goods sold. All purchases are paid for in the month following purchase.

Salaries, wages, and commissions average 20% of sales; all other variable expenses are 4% of sales. Fixed expenses for rent, property taxes, and miscellaneous payroll and other items are $11,000 monthly. Assume that these variable and fixed expenses require cash disbursements each month. Depreciation is $500 monthly.

In June, $11,000 is going to be disbursed for fixtures acquired and recorded in furniture and fixtures in May. The May 31 balance of accounts payable includes this amount.

Assume that a minimum cash balance of $5,000 is to be maintained. Also assume that all borrowings are effective at the beginning of the month and all repayments are made at the end of the month of repayment. Interest is compounded and added to the outstanding balance each month, but interest is paid only at the ends of months when principal is repaid. The interest rate is 10% per year; round interest computations and interest payments to the nearest dollar. Interest payments may be any dollar amount, but all borrowing and repayments of principal are made in multiples of $1,000.

1. Prepare a budgeted income statement for the coming June–August quarter, a cash budget (for each of the next 3 months), and a budgeted balance sheet for August 31, 20X8. All operations are evaluated on a before-income-tax basis, so income taxes may be ignored here.
2. Explain why there is a need for a bank loan and what operating sources supply cash for repaying the bank loan.

7-B1 Prepare Master Budget

Wallaby Kite Company, a small Melbourne firm that sells kites on the Web, wants a master budget for the 3 months beginning January 1, 20X2. It desires an ending minimum cash balance of $20,000 each month. Sales are forecasted at an average wholesale selling price of $8 per kite. Merchandise costs average $4 per kite. All sales are on credit, payable within 30 days, but experience has shown that 60% of current sales are collected in the current month, 30% in the next month, and 10% in the month thereafter. Bad debts are negligible.

In January, Wallaby Kite is beginning just-in-time (JIT) deliveries from suppliers, which means that purchases will equal expected sales. On January 1, purchases will cease until inventory decreases to $24,000, after which time purchases will equal sales. Purchases during any given month are paid in full during the following month.

Monthly operating expenses are as follows:

Wages and salaries	$60,000
Insurance expired	500
Depreciation	1,000
Miscellaneous	10,000
Rent	$1,000/month + 10% of quarterly sales over $40,000

Cash dividends of $6,000 are to be paid quarterly, beginning January 15, and are declared on the fifteenth of the previous month. All operating expenses are paid as incurred, except insurance, depreciation, and rent. Rent of $1,000 is paid at the beginning of each month, and the additional 10% of sales is settled quarterly on the tenth of the month following the end of the quarter. The next rent settlement date is January 10.

The company plans to buy some new fixtures for $12,000 cash in March.

Money can be borrowed and repaid in multiples of $2,000. Management wants to minimize borrowing and repay rapidly. Simple interest of 10% per annum is computed monthly but paid when the principal is repaid. Assume that borrowing occurs at the beginning, and repayments at the end, of the months in question. Compute interest to the nearest dollar.

Assets as of December 31, 20X1		Liabilities and Equities as of December 31, 20X1	
Cash	$ 20,000	Accounts payable	$142,200
Accounts receivable	50,000	(merchandise)	
Inventory*	156,200	Dividends payable	6,000
Unexpired insurance	6,000	Rent payable	31,200
Fixed assets, net	50,000	Owners' Equity	102,800
	$282,200		$282,200

*November 30 inventory balance = $64,000.

Recent and forecasted sales:

October	$152,000	December	$100,000	February	$280,000	April	$180,000
November	100,000	January	248,000	March	152,000		

1. Prepare a master budget including a budgeted income statement, balance sheet, cash budget, and supporting schedules for the months January–March 20X2.
2. Explain why there is a need for a bank loan and what operating sources provide the cash for the repayment of the bank loan.

 **Additional Assignment Material**

QUESTIONS

7-1 What are the major benefits of budgeting?

7-2 Is budgeting used primarily for scorekeeping, attention directing, or problem solving?

7-3 How do strategic planning, long-range planning, and budgeting differ?

7-4 "I oppose continuous budgets because they provide a moving target. Managers never know at what to aim." Discuss.

7-5 Why is it important to align performance goals of the company and the system used to evaluate and reward employees?

7-6 Explain the cycle of bias by lower-level managers and bias-adjustment by upper-level managers that can spiral out of control and result in meaningless budgets.

7-7 What are the incentives for inappropriate behaviors to *increase* reported profit when it appears that profits are likely to fall just short of a manager's bonus target?

7-8 Why is there an incentive for a manager to inappropriately *reduce* reported profit when it appears that profits are likely to be above the upper limit of a manager's bonus range?

7-9 Why is budgeted performance better than past performance as a basis for judging actual results?

7-10 "Budgets are okay in relatively certain environments. But everything changes so quickly in the electronics industry that budgeting is a waste of time." Comment on this statement.

7-11 "Budgeting is an unnecessary burden on many managers. It takes time away from important day-to-day problems." Do you agree? Explain.

7-12 Why is the sales forecast the starting point for budgeting?

7-13 What factors influence the sales forecast?

7-14 Differentiate between an operating budget and a financial budget.

7-15 Distinguish between operating expenses and disbursements for operating expenses.

7-16 What is the principal objective of a cash budget?

7-17 "Education and salesmanship are key features of budgeting." Explain.

7-18 What are the main differences between functional and activity-based budgets?

7-19 "Financial planning models guide managers through the budget process so that managers do not really need to understand budgeting." Do you agree? Explain.

7-20 Study Appendix 7. "I cannot be bothered with setting up my monthly budget on a spreadsheet. It just takes too long to be worth the effort." Comment.

7-21 Study Appendix 7. How do spreadsheets aid the application of sensitivity analysis?

CRITICAL THINKING EXERCISES

7-22 Budgets as Limitations on Spending
Many nonprofit organizations use budgets primarily to limit spending. Why does this limit the effectiveness of budgets?

7-23 Sales Personnel and Budgeting
The sales budget is the foundation of the entire master budget. How do sales personnel help formulate the budget? Compare the role of sales personnel to that of a central staff function, such as market research.

7-24 Master Budgets for Research and Development
The text focuses on budgets for organizations that have revenues and expenses. Suppose you were the manager of a research and development division of a biotech company that has no revenue. How would budgets be helpful to you?

7-25 Production Budgets and Performance Evaluation
The Akron plant of American Tire Company prepares an annual master budget each November for the following year. At the end of each year, it compares the actual costs incurred to the budgeted costs. How can American Tire get employees to accept the budget and strive to meet or beat the budgeted costs?

EXERCISES

7-26 Fill In the Blanks
Enter the word or phrase that best completes each sentence.

1. The financial budget process includes the following budgets:
   a. _____
   b. _____
   c. _____
2. The master budget process usually begins with the _____ budget.
3. A _____ budget is a plan that is revised monthly or quarterly, dropping one period and adding another.
4. Strategic planning sets the _____.

7-27 Cash Budgeting
Blake Henderson and Anna Kraft are preparing a plan to submit to venture capitalists to fund their business, Music Masters. The company plans to spend $380,000 on equipment in the first quarter of 2008. Salaries and other operating expenses (paid as incurred) will be $35,000 per month beginning in January 2008 and will continue at that level thereafter. The company will receive its first revenues in January 2009, with cash collections averaging $30,000 per month for all of 2009. In January 2010, cash collections are expected to increase to $100,000 per month and continue at that level thereafter.

Assume that the company needs enough funding to cover all its cash needs until cash receipts start exceeding cash disbursements. How much venture capital funding should Blake and Anna seek?

7-28 Purchases and Cost of Goods Sold
Ronco Products, a wholesaler of fishing equipment, budgeted the following sales for the indicated months:

	June 20X8	July 20X8	August 20X8
Sales on account	$1,820,000	$1,960,000	$2,100,000
Cash sales	280,000	240,000	260,000
Total sales	$2,100,000	$2,200,000	$2,360,000

All merchandise is marked up to sell at its invoice cost plus 25%. Target merchandise inventories at the beginning of each month are 30% of that month's projected cost of goods sold.

1. Compute the budgeted cost of goods sold for the month of June 20X8.
2. Compute the budgeted merchandise purchases for July 20X8.

7-29 Purchases and Sales Budgets
All sales of Jenny's Jeans and Uniforms (JJU) are made on credit. Sales are billed twice monthly, on the fifth of the month for the last half of the prior month's sales and on the twentieth of the month for the first half of the current month's sales. For accounts paid within the first 10 days after the billing date, JJU gives

customers a 3% discount; otherwise the full amount is due within 30 days of the billing date, and customers that do not pay within the 10-day discount period generally wait the full 30 days before making payment. Based on past experience, the collection experience of accounts receivable is as follows:

Within the 10-day discount period	80%
At 30 days after billing	18%
Uncollectible	2%

Sales for May 20X8 were $700,000. The forecast sales for the next 4 months are as follows:

June	$800,000
July	950,000
August	900,000
September	600,000

JJU's average markup on its products is 40% of the sales price.

JJU purchases merchandise for resale to meet the current month's sales demand and to maintain a desired monthly ending inventory of 25% of the next month's cost of goods sold. All purchases are on credit. JJU pays for one-half of a month's purchases in the month of purchase and the other half in the month following the purchase.

All sales and purchases occur uniformly throughout the month.

1. How much cash can JJU plan to collect from accounts receivable collections during July 20X8?
2. Compute the budgeted dollar value of JJU inventory on May 31, 20X8.
3. How much merchandise should JJU plan to purchase during June 20X8?
4. How much should JJU budget in August 20X8 for cash payments for merchandise purchased?

7-30 Sales Budget

Suppose a lumber yard has the following data:
- Accounts receivable, May 31: (.3 × May sales of $350,000) = $105,000
- Monthly forecasted sales: June, $430,000; July, $440,000; August, $500,000; September, $530,000

Sales consist of 70% cash and 30% credit. All credit accounts are collected in the month following the sales. Uncollectible accounts are negligible and may be ignored.

Prepare a sales budget schedule and a cash collections budget schedule for June, July, and August.

7-31 Sales Budget

A Kyoto clothing wholesaler was preparing its sales budget for the first quarter of 20X8. Forecast sales are as follows (in thousands of yen):

January	¥200,000
February	¥220,000
March	¥240,000

Sales are 20% cash and 80% on credit. Fifty percent of the credit accounts are collected in the month of sale, 40% in the month following the sale, and 10% in the following month. No uncollectible accounts are anticipated. Accounts receivable at the beginning of 20X8 are ¥96 million (10% of November credit sales of ¥180 million and 50% of December credit sales of ¥156 million).

Prepare a schedule showing sales and cash collections for January, February, and March, 20X8.

7-32 Cash Collection Budget

Northwest Equipment offers a 2% discount to customers who pay cash at the time of sale and a 1% discount to customers who pay within the first 10 days of the month after sale. Past experience shows that cash collections from customers tend to occur in the following pattern:

Cash collected at time of sale	50%
Collected within cash discount period in first 10 days of month after sale	10
Collected after cash discount period in first month after month of sale	25
Collected after cash discount period in second month after month of sale	12
Never collected	3

Compute the total cash budgeted to be collected in March if sales forecasts are $360,000 for January, $400,000 for February, and $450,000 for March.

7-33 Purchases Budget

Renovation Lighting Supply plans inventory levels (at cost) at the end of each month as follows: May, $275,000; June, $220,000; July, $200,000; and August, $240,000.

Sales are expected to be June, $440,000; July, $350,000; and August, $300,000. Cost of goods sold is 60% of sales.

Purchases in April were $250,000 and in May they were $180,000. Payments for each month's purchases are made as follows: 10% during that month, 80% the next month, and the final 10% the next month.

Prepare budget schedules for June, July, and August for purchases and for disbursements for purchases.

7-34 Purchases Budget

Linkenheim GmbH has adopted the following policies regarding merchandise purchases and inventory. At the end of any month, the inventory should be €15,000 plus 90% of the cost of goods to be sold during the following month. The cost of merchandise sold averages 60% of sales. Purchase terms are generally net, 30 days. A given month's purchases are paid as follows: 20% during that month and 80% during the following month.

Purchases in May had been £150,000 and the inventory on May 31 was higher than planned at £210,000. The manager was upset because the inventory was too high. Sales are expected to be June, £300,000; July, £290,000; August, £340,000; and September, £400,000.

1. Compute the amount by which the inventory on May 31 exceeded the company's policies.
2. Prepare budget schedules for June, July, and August for purchases and for disbursements for purchases.

7-35 Cash Budget

Consider the budgeted income statement for Carlson Company for June 20X4 in Exhibit 7-13.

The cash balance, May 31, 20X4, is $15,000.

Sales proceeds are collected as follows: 80% the month of sale, 10% the second month, and 10% the third month.

Accounts receivable are $44,000 on May 31, 20X4, consisting of $20,000 from April sales and $24,000 from May sales.

Accounts payable on May 31, 20X4, are $145,000.

Carlson Company pays 25% of purchases during the month of purchase and the remainder during the following month.

All operating expenses requiring cash are paid during the month of recognition, except that insurance and property taxes are paid annually in December for the forthcoming year.

Prepare a cash budget for June. Confine your analysis to the given data. Ignore income taxes.

Sales		$290
Inventory, May 31	$ 50	
Purchases	192	
Available for sale	242	
Inventory, June 30	40	
Cost of goods sold		202
Gross margin		$ 88
Operating expenses		
Wages	$ 36	
Utilities	5	
Advertising	10	
Depreciation	1	
Office expenses	4	
Insurance and property taxes	3	59
Operating income		$ 29

Exhibit 7-13

Carlson Company
Budgeted Income Statement for the Month Ended June 30, 20X4 (in thousands)

PROBLEMS

7-36 Cash Budget

Daniel Merrill is the manager of an airport gift shop, Merrill News and Gifts. From the following data, Mr. Merrill wants a cash budget showing expected cash receipts and disbursements for the month of April, and the cash balance expected as of April 30, 20X7.

- Planned cash balance, March 31, 20X7: $100,000
- Customer receivables as of March 31: $530,000 total, $80,000 from February sales, $450,000 from March sales
- Accounts payable, March 31: $460,000 ✓
- Merchandise purchases for April: $450,000, 40% paid in month of purchase, 60% paid in next month
- Payrolls due in April: $90,000
- Other expenses for April, payable in April: $45,000
- Accrued taxes for April, payable in June: $7,500
- Bank note due April 10: $90,000 plus $7,200 interest
- Depreciation for April: $2,100
- Two-year insurance policy due April 14 for renewal: $1,500, to be paid in cash
- Sales for April: $1,000,000, half collected in month of sale, 40% in next month, 10% in third month

Prepare the cash budget for the month ending April 30, 20X7.

7-37 Cash Budget

Prepare a statement of estimated cash receipts and disbursements for October 20X7 for the Botanica Company, which sells one product, herbal soap, by the case. On October 1, 20X7, part of the trial balance showed the following:

	DR	CR
Cash	$ 4,800	
Accounts receivable	15,600	
Allowance for bad debts		$1,900
Merchandise inventory	9,000	
Accounts payable, merchandise		6,600

The company pays for its purchases within 10 days of purchase so assume that one-third of the purchases of any month are due and paid for in the following month.

The cost of the merchandise purchased is $12 per case. At the end of each month, it is desired to have an inventory equal in units to 50% of the following month's sales in units.

Sales terms include a 1% discount if payment is made by the end of the calendar month. Past experience indicates that 60% of sales will be collected during the month of the sale, 30% in the following calendar month, 6% in the next following calendar month, and the remaining 4% will be uncollectible. The company's fiscal year begins August 1.

Unit selling price	$ 20
August actual sales	$ 12,000
September actual sales	36,000
October estimated sales	30,000
November estimated sales	22,000
Total sales expected in the fiscal year	$360,000

Exclusive of bad debts, total budgeted selling and general administrative expenses for the fiscal year are estimated at $61,500, of which $24,000 is fixed expense (which includes a $13,200 annual depreciation charge). The Botanica Company incurs these fixed expenses uniformly throughout the year. The balance of the selling and general administrative expenses varies with sales. Expenses are paid as incurred.

7-38 Budgeting at Ritz-Carlton

The Ritz-Carlton has four hotels and resorts in the Caribbean and Mexico. For one of these hotels, management expects occupancy rates to be 95% in December, January, and February; 85% in November, March, and April; and 70% the rest of the year. This hotel has 300 rooms and the average room rental is $290 per night. Of this, on average 10% is received as a deposit the month before the stay, 60% is received in the month of the stay, and 28% is collected the month after. The remaining 2% is never collected.

Most of the costs of running the hotel are fixed. The variable costs are only $30 per occupied room per night. Fixed salaries (including benefits) run $400,000 per month, depreciation is $350,000 a month, other fixed operating costs are $120,000 per month, and interest expense is $600,000 per month. Variable costs and salaries are paid in the month they are incurred, depreciation is recorded at the end of each quarter, other fixed operating costs are paid as incurred, and interest is paid semi-annually each June and December.

1. Prepare a monthly cash budget for this Ritz-Carlton hotel for the entire year. For simplicity, assume that there are 30 days in each month.
2. How much would the hotel's annual profit increase if occupancy rates increased by 5% each month in the off-season (that is, from 70% to 75% in May–October)?

7-39 Activity-Based Budgeting

A recent directive from Sandy Jensen, CEO of Duluth Manufacturing, had instructed each department to cut its costs by 10%. The traditional functional budget for the shipping and receiving department was as follows:

Salaries, four employees at $42,000	$168,000
Benefits at 20%	33,600
Depreciation, straight-line basis	76,000
Supplies	43,400
Overhead at 35% of direct costs	112,350
Total	$433,350

Therefore, the shipping and receiving department needed to find $43,335 to cut.

June Steele, a recent MBA graduate, was asked to pare $43,335 from the shipping and receiving department's budget. As a first step, she recast the traditional budget into an activity-based budget.

Receiving, 620,000 pounds	$ 93,000
Shipping, 404,000 boxes	202,000
Handling, 11,200 moves	112,000
Record keeping, 65,000 transactions	26,350
Total	$433,350

1. What actions might Steele suggest to attain a $43,335 budget cut? Why would these be the best actions to pursue?
2. Which budget helped you most in answering number 1? Explain.

7-40 Budgeting, Behavior, and Ethics

Mathew Philp, president of North Idaho Mining, Ltd., has made budgets a major focus for managers. Making budget was such an important goal that the only two managers who had missed their budgets in 20X7 (by 2% and 4%, respectively) had been summarily fired. This caused all managers to be wary when setting their 20X8 budgets.

The Red Mountain Copper Division of North Idaho Mining had the following results for 20X7:

Sales, 1.6 million pounds at $.95/pound	$1,520,000
Variable costs	880,000
Fixed costs, primarily depreciation	450,000
Pretax profit	$ 190,000

Molly Stark, general manager of Red Mountain Copper, received a memo from Philp that contained the following:

> We expect your profit for 20X8 to be at least $209,000. Prepare a budget
> showing how you plan to accomplish this.

Stark was concerned because the market for copper had recently softened. Her market research staff forecast that sales would be at or below the 20X7 level, and prices would likely be between

$.92 and $.94 per pound. Her manufacturing manager reported that most of the fixed costs were committed and there were few efficiencies to be gained in the variable costs. He indicated that perhaps a 2% savings in variable costs might be achievable but certainly no more.

1. Prepare a budget for Stark to submit to headquarters. What dilemmas does Stark face in preparing this budget?
2. What problems do you see in the budgeting process at North Idaho Mining?
3. Suppose Stark submitted a budget showing a $209,000 profit. It is now late in 20X8, and she has had a good year. Despite an industry-wide decline in sales, Red Mountain Copper's sales matched last year's 1.6 million pounds, and the average price per pound was $.945, nearly at last year's level and well above that forecast. Variable costs were cut by 2% through extensive efforts. Still, profit projections were more than $9,000 below budget. Stark was concerned for her job so she approached the controller and requested that depreciation schedules be changed. By extending the lives of some equipment for 2 years, depreciation in 20X8 would be reduced by $15,000. Estimating the economic lives of equipment is difficult, and it would be hard to prove that the old lives were better than the new proposed lives. What should the controller do? What ethical issues does this proposal raise?

7-41 Spreadsheets and Sensitivity Analysis of Income Statement

Study Appendix 7. A Speedy-Mart Store in Northcenter Mall has the following budgeted sales, which are uniform throughout the month:

May	$450,000
June	375,000
July	330,000
August	420,000

Cost of goods sold averages 70% of sales, and merchandise is purchased and paid for essentially as needed. Employees earn fixed salaries of $22,000 monthly and commissions of 10% of the current month's sales, paid as earned. Other expenses are rent, $6,000, paid on the first of each month for that month's occupancy; miscellaneous expenses, 6% of sales, paid as incurred; insurance, $450 per month, from a 1-year policy that was paid for on January 2; and depreciation, $2,850 per month.

1. Using spreadsheet software, prepare a table of budget data for the Speedy-Mart Store.
2. Continue the spreadsheet in number 1 to prepare budget schedules for (a) disbursements for operating expenses and (b) operating income for June, July, and August.
3. Adjust the budget data appropriately for each of the following scenarios independently and recompute operating income using the spreadsheet:
   a. A sales promotion that will cost $30,000 in May could increase sales in each of the following 3 months by 5%.
   b. Eliminating the sales commissions and increasing employees' salaries to $52,500 per month could decrease sales thereafter by a net of 2%.

7-42 Spreadsheets and Sensitivity Analysis of Operating Expenses

Study Appendix 7. The High Definition LCD Division (HDLD) of Fisher Displays produces displays for HD LCD TVs. The displays are assembled from purchased components. The costs (value) added by HDLD are indirect costs, which include assembly labor, packaging, and shipping. HDLD produces two sizes of displays: 42″ and 50″. Cost behavior of HDLD is as follows:

	Fixed Cost/Month	Variable Cost
Purchased components		
50″ Displays		$80 per component
42″ Displays		55 per component
Assembly labor	$40,000	16 per component
Packaging	8,000	4 per display
Shipping	8,000	2 per display

Both displays require five components per display. Therefore, the total cost of components for 50″ displays is $400 and for 42″ displays is $275. HDLD uses a 6-month continuous budget that is revised monthly. Sales forecasts for the next 8 months are as follows:

	50" Displays	42" Displays
October	3,200 units	4,000 units
November	2,400	3,000
December	5,600	7,000
January	3,200	4,000
February	3,200	4,000
March	2,400	3,000
April	2,400	3,000
May	2,800	3,500

Treat each event in succession.

1. Use spreadsheet software to prepare a table of budgeting information and an operating expense budget for HDLD for October–March. Incorporate the expectation that sales of 42" displays will be 125% of 50" displays. Prepare a spreadsheet that can be revised easily for succeeding months in parts 2 and 3.
2. October's actual sales were 2,800 50" displays and 3,600 42" displays. This outcome has caused HDLD to revise its sales forecasts downward by 10%. Revise the operating expense budget for November–April.
3. At the end of November, HDLD decides that the proportion of 50" to 42" displays is changing. Sales of 42" displays are expected to be 150% of 50" displays sales. Expected sales of 50" displays are unchanged from number 2. Revise the operating expense budget for December–May.

CASES

7-43 Comprehensive Cash Budgeting

Christine Morrison, treasurer of Salt Lake Light Opera (SLLO), was preparing a loan request to the South Utah National Bank in December 20X4. The loan was necessary to meet the cash needs of the SLLO for year 20X5. In a few short years, the SLLO had established itself as a premier opera company. In addition to its regular subscription series, it started a series for new composers and offered a very popular holiday production. The holiday production was the most financially successful of the SLLO's activities, providing a base to support innovative productions that were artistically important to the SLLO but did not usually succeed financially.

In total, the SLLO had done well financially, as shown in Exhibits 7-14 and 7-15. Its profitable operations had enabled it to build its own building and generally acquire a large number of assets. It had at least broken even every year since its incorporation, and management anticipates continued

Exhibit 7-14

Salt Lake Light Opera

Balance Sheets as of December 31 (in thousands of dollars)

	20X2	20X3	20X4
Assets			
Cash	$2,688	$ 229	$ 208
Accounts receivable	2,942	3,372	4,440
Supplies inventory	700	700	500
Total current assets	$6,330	$4,301	$ 5,148
Plant and equipment	2,643	4,838	5,809
Total assets	$8,973	$9,139	$10,957
Liabilities and Equities			
Bank loan	$ 0	$ 0	$ 1,620*
Accounts payable	420	720	780
Accrued payroll expenses	472	583	646
Mortgage, current	250	250	250
Total current liabilities	$1,142	$1,553	$ 3,296
Other payables	270		
Mortgage payable, long-term	3,750	3,500	3,250
Net assets†	3,811	4,086	4,411
Total liabilities and equities	$8,973	$9,139	$10,957

*Includes $32,000 of accrued interest.

†The "Net assets" account for a nonprofit organization is similar to "Stockholders' equity" for a corporation.

	20X2	20X3	20X4
Ticket sales	$3,303	$4,060	$5,263
Contributions	1,041	1,412	1,702
Grants and other revenues	1,202	1,361	1,874
Total revenues	$5,546	$6,833	$8,839
Expenses*			
Production	$4,071	$4,805	$6,307
Operations	271	332	473
Public relations and			
community development	1,082	1,421	1,734
Total expenses	$5,424	$6,558	$8,514
Excess of revenues over expenses	$ 122	$ 275	$ 325

*Expenses include depreciation of $355, $370, and $470 and general and administrative expenses of $1,549, $1,688, and $2,142 in the years 20X2, 20X3, and 20X4, respectively.

Exhibit 7-15
Salt Lake Light Opera
Income Statements for the Year Ended December 31 (in thousands of dollars)

profitable operations. The Corporate Community for the Arts in Salt Lake and several private foundations had made many grants to the SLLO, and such grants are expected to continue. Most recently, the largest bank in town had agreed to sponsor the production of a new opera by a local composer. The SLLO's director of development, Harlan Wayne, expected such corporate sponsorships to increase in the future.

To provide facilities for the Opera's anticipated growth, SLLO began work on an addition to its building 2 years ago. The new facilities are intended primarily to support the experimental offerings that were becoming more numerous. The capital expansion was to be completed in 20X5; all that remained was acquisition and installation of lighting, sound equipment, and other new equipment to be purchased in 20X5.

SLLO had borrowed working capital from South Utah National Bank for the past several years. To qualify for the loans, the SLLO had to agree to the following:

1. Completely pay off the loan for 1 month during the course of the year.
2. Maintain cash and accounts receivable balances equal to (or greater than) 120% of the loan.
3. Maintain a compensating cash balance of $200,000 at all times.

In the past, the SLLO has had no problem meeting these requirements. However, in 20X4 the SLLO had been unable to reduce the loan to zero for an entire month. Although South Utah continued to extend the needed credit, the loan manager expressed concern over the situation. She asked for a quarterly cash budget to justify the financing needed for 20X5. Ms. Morrison began to assemble the data needed to prepare such a budget.

SLLO received revenue from three main sources: ticket sales, contributions, and grants. Ms. Morrison formed Exhibit 7-16 to calculate the accounts receivable balance for each of these sources for 20X5. She assumed that SLLO would continue its normal practices for collecting pledges and grant revenues.

	Ticket Sales		Contributions		Grants	
	Revenues	End of Quarter Receivables	Revenues	End of Quarter Receivables	Revenues	End of Quarter Receivables
First Quarter	$ 852	$2,795	$ 75	$ 794	$ 132	$1,027
Second Quarter	1,584	3,100	363	888	448	1,130
Third Quarter	2,617	3,407	1,203	1,083	1,296	1,240
Fourth Quarter	1,519	3,683	442	1,170	528	1,342

Exhibit 7-16
Salt Lake Light Opera
Estimated Quarterly Revenues and End of Quarter Receivables for the Year Ended December 31, 20X5 (in thousands of dollars)

Most expenses were constant from month to month. An exception was supplies, which were purchased twice a year in December and June. In 20X5, SLLO expects to purchase $200,000 of supplies in June and $700,000 in December on terms of net, 30 days. The supplies inventory at the end of December was expected to be $600,000. Depreciation expense of $500,000 was planned for 20X5, and other expenses were expected to run at a steady rate of $710,000 a month throughout the year, of which $700,000 was payroll costs. Salaries and wages were paid on the Monday of the first week following the end of the month. The remaining $10,000 of other expenses were paid as incurred.

The major portion of the new equipment to be installed in 20X5 was to be delivered in September; payments totaling $400,000 would be made in four equal monthly installments beginning in September. In addition, small equipment purchases are expected to run $20,000 per month throughout the year. They will be paid for on delivery.

In late 20X2, SLLO had borrowed $4 million (classified as a mortgage payable) from Farmers' Life Insurance Company. The SLLO is repaying the loan over 16 years, in equal principal payments in June and December of each year. Interest at 8% annually is also paid on the unpaid balance on each of these dates. Total interest payments for 20X5, according to Ms. Morrison's calculations, would be $275,000.

Interest on the working capital loan from South Utah National Bank was at an annual rate of 10%. Interest is accrued quarterly but paid annually; payment for 20X4's interest would be made on January 10, 20X5, and that for 20X5's interest would be made on January 10, 20X6. Working capital loans are taken out on the first day of the quarter that funds are needed, and they are repaid on the last day of the quarter when extra funds are generated. SLLO has tried to keep a minimum cash balance of $200,000 at all times, even if loan requirements do not require it.

1. Compute the cash inflows and outflows for each quarter of 20X5. What are SLLO's loan requirements each quarter?
2. Prepare a projected income statement and balance sheet for SLLO for 20X5.
3. Prepare the projected statement of cash flows for 20X5.
4. What financing strategy would you recommend for SLLO?

7-44 Cash Budgeting for a Hospital

Evergreen Hospital provides a wide range of health services in its community. Evergreen's board of directors has authorized the following capital expenditures:

Intra-aortic balloon pump	$1,400,000
Computed tomographic scanner	850,000
X-ray equipment	550,000
Laboratory equipment	1,200,000
Total	$4,000,000

The expenditures are planned for October 1, 20X7, and the board wishes to know the amount of borrowing, if any, necessary on that date. Rebecca Singer, hospital controller, has gathered the following information to be used in preparing an analysis of future cash flows.

Billings, made in the month of service, for 20X7 are shown next, with actual amounts for January–June and estimated amounts for July–December:

Month	Amount Billed
January	$5,300,000
February	5,300,000
March	5,400,000
April	5,400,000
May	6,000,000
June	6,000,000
July (estimated)	5,800,000
August (estimated)	6,200,000
September (estimated)	6,600,000
October (estimated)	6,800,000
November (estimated)	7,000,000
December (estimated)	6,600,000

Ninety percent of Evergreen billings are made to third parties, such as BlueCross, federal or state governments, and private insurance companies. The remaining 10% of the billings are made directly to patients. Historical patterns of billing collections are as follows:

	Third-Party Billings	Direct-Patient Billings
Month of service	20%	10%
Month following service	50	40
Second month following service	20	40
Uncollectible	10	10

Singer expects the same billing and collection patterns that have been experienced during the first 6 months of 20X7 to continue during the last 6 months of the year. The following schedule presents the purchases that have been made during the past 3 months and the planned purchases for the last 6 months of 20X7.

Month	Amount
April	$1,300,000
May	1,450,000
June	1,450,000
July	1,500,000
August	1,800,000
September	2,200,000
October	2,350,000
November	2,700,000
December	2,100,000

All purchases are made on account, and accounts payable are remitted in the month following the purchase.
- Salaries for each month during the remainder of 20X7 are expected to be $1,800,000 per month plus 20% of that month's billings. Salaries are paid in the month of service.
- Evergreen's monthly depreciation charges are $150,000.
- Evergreen incurs interest expenses of $180,000 per month and makes interest payments of $540,000 on the last day of each calendar quarter.
- Endowment fund income is expected to continue to total $210,000 per month.
- Evergreen has a cash balance of $350,000 on July 1, 20X7, and has a policy of maintaining a minimum end-of-month cash balance of 10% of the current month's purchases.
- Evergreen Hospital employs a calendar-year reporting period.

1. Prepare a schedule of budgeted cash receipts by month for the third quarter of 20X7.
2. Prepare a schedule of budgeted cash disbursements by month for the third quarter of 20X7.
3. Determine the amount of borrowing, if any, necessary on October 1, 20X7, to acquire the capital items totaling $4,000,000.

7-45 Comprehensive Budgeting for a University

Suppose you are the controller of Minnesota State University. The university president, Lisa Larsson, is preparing for her annual fund-raising campaign for 20X7–20X8. To set an appropriate target, she has asked you to prepare a budget for the academic year. You have collected the following data for the current year (20X6–20X7):

	Undergraduate Division	Graduate Division
Average salary of faculty member	$58,000	$58,000
Average faculty teaching load in semester credit-hours per year (eight undergraduate or six graduate courses)	24	18
Average number of students per class	30	20
Total enrollment (full-time and part-time students)	3,600	1,800
Average number of semester credit-hours carried each year per student	25	20
Full-time load, semester hours per year	30	24

For 20X7–20X8, all faculty and staff will receive a 6% salary increase. Undergraduate enrollment is expected to decline by 2%, but graduate enrollment is expected to increase by 5%.

- The 20X6–20X7 budget for operation and maintenance of facilities was $500,000, which includes $240,000 for salaries and wages. Experience so far this year indicates that the budget is accurate. Salaries and wages will increase by 6% and other operating costs will increase by $12,000 in 20X7–20X8.
- The 20X6–20X7 and 20X7–20X8 budgets for the remaining expenditures are as follows:

	20X6–20X7	20X7–20X8
General administrative	$500,000	$525,000
Library		
Acquisitions	150,000	155,000
Operations	190,000	200,000
Health services	48,000	50,000
Intramural athletics	56,000	60,000
Intercollegiate athletics	240,000	245,000
Insurance and retirement	520,000	560,000
Interest	75,000	75,000

- Tuition is $92 per credit hour. In addition, the state legislature provides $780 per full-time-equivalent student. (A full-time equivalent is 30 undergraduate hours or 24 graduate hours.) Full-tuition scholarships are given to 30 full-time undergraduates and 50 full-time graduate students.
- Revenues other than tuition and the legislative apportionment are as follows:

	20X6–20X7	20X7–20X8
Endowment income	$200,000	$210,000
Net income from auxiliary services	325,000	335,000
Intercollegiate athletic receipts	290,000	300,000

- The chemistry/physics classroom building needs remodeling during the 20X7–20X8 period. Projected cost is $575,000.

1. Prepare a schedule for 20X7–20X8 that shows, by division, (a) expected enrollment, (b) total credit hours, (c) full-time-equivalent enrollment, and (d) number of faculty members needed.
2. Calculate the budget for faculty salaries for 20X7–20X8 by division.
3. Calculate the budget for tuition revenue and legislative apportionment for 20X7–20X8 by division.
4. Prepare a schedule for President Larsson showing the amount that must be raised by the annual fund-raising campaign.

NIKE 10-K PROBLEM

7-46 Budgeting Assumptions at Nike

Examine Nike's 2008 10-K presented in Appendix C. Find the section of the 10-K titled "Results of Operations" showing a condensed income statement for fiscal years 2006, 2007, and 2008. Use the condensed income statement to calculate budgeted net income for fiscal 2009 under the following alternative sets of assumptions:

1. Note that Nike's revenues have increased by about 10% per year for each of the last 2 years. Assume cost of sales is 55% of revenue, selling and administrative expense is 32% of revenue and income tax expense is 25% of income before income taxes. Assume that all costs are variable.
   a. Calculate budgeted net income if revenue increases by 10%.
   b. Calculate budgeted net income if revenue decreases by 10%.
2. Assume cost of sales is a variable cost and is 55% of revenue, selling and administrative expense is fixed, and income tax expense is variable and is 25% of income before income taxes.
   a. Calculate budgeted net income if revenue increases by 10%.
   b. Calculate budgeted net income if revenue decreases by 10%.

3. Note that Nike's gross margin was 45% in fiscal 2008 but was slightly lower in 2006 and 2007, at 44% and 43.9%, respectively. Assume revenue for 2009 will be the same as in 2008, selling and administrative expense is a fixed cost of $5,954 million, and income tax expense is 25% of income before income taxes.
   a. Calculate budgeted net income if the gross margin increases to 46%.
   b. Calculate budgeted net income if the gross margin decreases to 44%.

EXCEL APPLICATION EXERCISE

7-47 Preparing a Cash Budget to Assist Long-Range Planning

Goal: Create an Excel spreadsheet to prepare a cash budget to assist with long-range planning. Use the results to answer questions about your findings.

Scenario: Music Masters has asked you to prepare an analysis of its cash requirements until such time as its forecasted cash receipts begin to exceed its forecasted cash disbursements. The company will use your analysis to determine venture capital funding requests. Additional background information for your spreadsheet appears in Exercise 7-27 on page 291.
When you have completed your spreadsheet, answer the following questions:

1. Based on its stated objective of stopping venture capital funding when cash receipts begin to exceed cash disbursements, in what month/year should Music Masters no longer require venture capital funding? Why?
2. What is the total amount of expenditures Music Masters will incur before its cash receipts begin to exceed its cash disbursements? What is the total amount of venture capital funding that Music Masters should request?
3. Is the amount of venture capital funding that Music Masters should request equal to its total expenditures? If not, why are the amounts different?

Step-by-Step:

1. Open a new Excel spreadsheet.
2. In column A, create a bold-faced heading that contains the following:
   Row 1: Chapter 7 Decision Guideline
   Row 2: Music Masters
   Row 3: Cash Budget for Venture Capital Requirements
   Row 4: Today's Date
3. Merge and center the four heading rows across columns A–F.
4. In row 7, create the following bold-faced, center-justified column headings with a column width of 10.57:
   Column B: 2008
   Column C: 2009
   Column D: 2010
   Column E: 2011
   Column F: Total
5. In column A, create the following row headings:
   Row 8: Equipment Purchase
   Row 9: Salaries and Other Operating Expenses
   Row 10: Revenues
   Row 11: Net Cash Requirements

   Note: Adjust column width as necessary.

6. Use data from Exercise 7-27 to enter the amounts for the yearly cash requirements for the three income/expense categories. Use formulas to calculate the appropriate yearly amounts within each category when necessary.

   Hint: Use different signs for the cash receipt (revenue) and cash disbursement (expense) amounts.

7. Use the SUM function to calculate totals for each column in row 11 and for each row in column F.
8. Format amounts in rows 8 and 11 as follows:

Number tab:	Category:
	Decimal: 0
	Symbol: $

9. Format amounts in Rows 9 and 10 as follows:

Number tab:	Category:
	Decimal: 0
	Symbol: None

10. Apply top and bottom borders to the amounts in row 11 by clicking the drop-down indicator on the Borders icon from the toolbar. Select the "Top and Double Bottom Border."
11. Save your work to disk, and print a copy for your files.

COLLABORATIVE LEARNING EXERCISE

7-48 Personal Budgeting

Budgeting is useful to many different types of entities, including the individual. Consider an entity that you know well, the college or university student. Form a group of two to six students, and pool the information that you have about what it costs to spend a year as a full-time student.

Prepare a revenue and expense budget for an average prospective full-time student at your college or university. Identify possible sources of revenue and the amount to be received from each. Identify the costs a student is likely to incur during the year. You can assume that cash disbursements are made immediately for all expenses so the budgeted income statement and cash budget are identical.

When all groups have completed their budgets, compare those budgets. What are the differences? What assumptions led to the differences?

INTERNET EXERCISES

7-49 Carnival Corporation

The budgeting process helps firms to identify sources of revenues and expenses as well as the timing of cash flows. While many parts of the budgeting process are confidential, there are some things that may be identifiable by someone outside the firm who would like to make some potential budget projections for the following year. Consider **Carnival Corporation**, the cruise ship firm. Go to the Carnival Web site at www.carnivalcorp.com.

1. Look at the list of Carnival Corporation's global brands. How many different brand lines operate under the corporation shell? What are they? Visit a couple of the links. Do the brands each offer exactly the same services? Why might the firm have different names for the cruise lines serving different areas?
2. The sales figure is one of the most important pieces of information the firm uses in beginning the planning process. Carnival's sales figure is made up primarily of two parts—the number of passenger cruise days and the price charged for each passenger cruise day. Go to "Investor Relations" and then "Financial Reports" to open Carnival's annual report (10-K) for the most recent year. Notice the total revenues for the year and then turn to the section, Passengers, Capacity, and Occupancy. Notice the information about passenger capacity and find the occupancy percentage.
3. Find the information provided by management with respect to ships under contract for construction. Does the company expect an increase in passenger capacity during the coming years? Assuming revenue increases in proportion to passenger capacity, what would be the expected revenue when these ships are completed? Should the firm expect an increase in costs associated with the increase in capacity? When budgeting for these costs, would the costs be proportional to the increase in revenues? Why or why not?
4. The other component in revenue is how much the passenger pays for the cruise. Select one of the cruise line links from the main page. Find the subsequent link that takes you to information about cruise prices. Are prices for the same length cruise always the same? Look at the fine print with respect to the cruise pricing. What does it tell about how the price is determined? Why might the capacity level of the cruise determine the price that is charged for the cruise?

Flexible Budgets and Variance Analysis

▶ **MCDONALD'S**

McDonald's is consistently ranked among the world's best-known brands in *BusinessWeek's* annual ranking of global brands. You can eat a Big Mac under the Golden Arches in more than 110 countries.

With sales of more than $45 billion, the challenge is to ensure that the taste of each Big Mac is the same at each of the more than 30,000 company-owned, franchised, or affiliated restaurants. How does McDonald's maintain cost and quality control? How does it ensure that each of the 47 million customers it serves daily receives the same value? It uses standards, budgets, and variance analysis. For example, the standards for material are the same for hamburgers wherever they are sold—1 bun, 1 hamburger patty, 1 pickle slice, 1/8 tablespoon of dehydrated onion, 1/4 tablespoon mustard, and 1/2 ounce of ketchup. For each of these ingredients management determines variances—differences between the amount actually used and what should have been used given the number and types of sandwiches sold.

McDonald's managers budget sales for each hour during the day. Based on the sales budgeted, they construct a budget for each of the materials that make up their menu. They use the budget for planning (to make sure materials will be available when needed) and control (to evaluate the use of materials). McDonald's applies these planning and control concepts not just to material costs, but also to labor and overhead costs. Further, McDonald's uses budgets for planning and control of revenues, as well as costs. Understanding what went wrong and what went right helps managers plan and manage more effectively in future periods.

McDonald's also uses nonfinancial standards to meet its quality and service goals. Here are three examples: (1) The standard time for a drive-through customer is 310 seconds, from pulling up to the menu board to driving away; (2) employees must destroy cooked meat that is not used in a sandwich within 30 minutes; and (3) once employees make a sandwich and place it in the transfer bin, they must sell it within 10 minutes or throw it away.

This chapter focuses on flexible budgets and variances. Flexible budgets extend the budget developed in Chapter 7 for a single level of activity to multiple levels of activity. Variances are deviations of actual results from expected (or planned) results. Each variance should cause a manager to ask, "Why did results differ from plan?" Variances are an important evaluation tool that directs management to areas that deserve attention and helps managers identify ways to improve future decisions and results. (For more background on how managers use variances, you might want to review the discussion of management by exception in Chapter 1, page 8.) ■

Using Budgets and Variances to Evaluate Results

To illustrate how companies use budgets and variances, consider the Dominion Company, a firm in Toronto that manufactures a wheeled, collapsible suitcase carrier popular with airline flight crews. Assume for simplicity that the company produces a single product. To further simplify the example, assume that sales are equal to production and inventory levels are zero. The results for the actual sales volume of 7,000 units in June 20X1 appear in column 1 of Exhibit 8-1.

Using flexible budgets to analyze performance is important to individual McDonald's restaurants, such as this one in Asia, as well as to the company as a whole.

Favorable and Unfavorable Variances

Recall from Chapter 1 that variances are deviations from plans. While we can compute variances for any type of deviation from plans, in this chapter we focus on deviations of profits, revenues, and costs from budgeted amounts. We label profit, revenue, and cost variances as favorable or unfavorable depending on the direction of the effect on profitability. **Favorable profit variances**

	Actual (1)	Static Budget (2)	Static Budget Variances (3)
Units	7,000	9,000	2,000 U
Sales	$217,000	$279,000	$62,000 U
Variable costs			
Variable manufacturing costs	$151,270	$189,000	$37,730 F
Shipping costs (selling)	5,000	5,400	400 F
Administrative costs	2,000	1,800	200 U
Total variable costs	$158,270	$196,200	$37,930 F
Contribution margin	$ 58,730	$ 82,800	$24,070 U
Fixed expenses			
Fixed manufacturing costs	$ 37,300	$ 37,000	$ 300 U
Fixed selling and administrative costs	33,000	33,000	—
Total fixed costs	$ 70,300	$ 70,000	$ 300 U
Operating income (loss)	$(11,570)	$ 12,800	$24,370 U

U = Unfavorable cost variances occur when actual costs are more than budgeted costs. Unfavorable revenue (or profit) variances occur when actual revenues (or profits) are less than budgeted.

F = Favorable cost variances occur when actual costs are less than budgeted costs. Favorable revenue (or profit) variances occur when actual revenues (or profits) are more than budgeted.

Exhibit 8-1
Dominion Company
Performance Report Using a Static Budget for the Month Ended June 30, 20X1

arise when actual profits exceed budgeted profits. **Unfavorable profit variances** arise when actual profits fall below budgeted profits. Because increases in revenues increase profits, revenue variances work in exactly the same way: When actual revenues exceed budgeted revenues we have **favorable revenue variances**, and actual revenues below budgeted revenues result in **unfavorable revenue variances**. However, cost variances work in the opposite way because increases in costs decrease profitability: When actual costs exceed budgeted costs we have **unfavorable cost variances**, and actual costs less than budgeted costs result in **favorable cost variances**. The following chart summarizes these relationships using the abbreviations that we will use for favorable (F) and unfavorable (U) variances.

Favorable (F) Versus Unfavorable (U) Variances

	Profits	Revenues	Costs
Actual > Expected	F	F	U
Actual < Expected	U	U	F

Static Budgets Versus Flexible Budgets

Objective 1

Distinguish between flexible budgets and static budgets.

Let's consider two ways to prepare a budget. A budget prepared for only one expected level of activity is a **static budget**. A budget that adjusts to different levels of activity is a **flexible budget** (sometimes called a **variable budget**). To illustrate these concepts, suppose Dominion Company expects to sell 9,000 units in 20X1. Its static budget consists of the revenues, costs, and profits expected at a volume of 9,000 units. If Dominion Company realizes that there is uncertainty about the expected sales volume, it might prepare a flexible budget that predicts revenues, costs, and profits at, say, any volume between 7,000 and 9,000 units.

How does the master budget introduced in Chapter 7 relate to static and flexible budgets? The modifier "master" refers to the scope of the budget, not to whether it is static or flexible. The master budgets used in Chapter 7 were static master budgets. They presumed one fixed level of volume, the most common way to prepare master budgets. However, there is no reason that a company could not prepare a flexible master budget.

Static-Budget Variances Versus Flexible-Budget Variances

How should we evaluate the performance of Dominion Company for June 20X1? The basic approach is to compare actual amounts with budgeted amounts. However, we now have two candidates for "the" budgeted amount: The static budget for the original expected level of output or the flexible budget for the achieved level of output.

STATIC-BUDGET VARIANCE Let's begin by comparing Dominion Company's actual results with the static budget for a projected sales volume of 9,000 units. Differences between actual results and the static budget for the original planned level of output are **static-budget variances**. Column 2 of Exhibit 8-1 shows the static budget for projected sales of 9,000 units. Column 3 shows the static-budget variances.

Exhibit 8-1 shows the $24,370 U static-budget operating income variance that results from an actual operating loss of $11,570 when budgeted operating income was $12,800. Exhibit 8-1 also shows static-budget variances for the revenue and cost components of the $24,370 U static-budget income variance. First, the $62,000 unfavorable revenue variance shows that sales were $62,000 below the amount budgeted for sales of 9,000 units. The unfavorable revenue variance helps us understand part of the reason why actual results were worse than expected: Lower sales normally lead to lower profit. Second, the $37,930 favorable total variable cost variance shows that total variable costs were less than projected in the static budget. Finally, the $300 unfavorable variance for fixed costs shows that we spent $300 more than the budget.

The static-budget variances show the differences between actual results and the original budgeted amounts for sales of 9,000 units, but they do not take into account that the actual level of sales was only 7,000 units. This is particularly a concern for variable cost variances. Considering the lower-than-projected level of sales activity, was cost control really satisfactory? When you produce only 7,000 units wouldn't you expect variable costs to be lower than the $196,200 amount shown in the static budget for production of 9,000 units? Of course! Therefore, the favorable static-budget variances for the variable costs provide an incomplete picture of how well Dominion Company controlled variable costs.

FLEXIBLE-BUDGET VARIANCE   Differences between actual results and the flexible budget for the actual level of output achieved are **flexible-budget variances**. Flexible budget variances are more useful for evaluating variable costs because deviations from the flexible budget better reflect how costs deviate from what was expected given the actual level of activity. The flexible-budget approach says, "Give me any activity level you choose, and I'll provide a budget tailored to that particular level." For example, when Dominion's sales turn out to be 7,000 units instead of 9,000, the flexible budget shows what the total variable costs should be based on the achieved sales level of 7,000 units. Many companies routinely "flex" their budgets to provide a better benchmark for evaluating performance.

Consider a **McDonald's** restaurant that expects to sell 1 million Big Macs and budgets $100,000 for buns at $.10 per bun. Suppose the restaurant sells only 900,000 Big Macs and pays $94,000 for buns. The static-budget variance is a $100,000 − $94,000 = $6,000 favorable variance. However, the static-budget variance doesn't adjust for the expected decrease in costs due to the decrease in volume relative to the static-budget sales level of 1 million Big Macs. In contrast, the flexible budget yields an expected cost of $90,000 for the actual sales of 900,000 Big Macs, so the flexible-budget variance is $94,000 − $90,000 = $4,000 unfavorable variance. The flexible-budget variance shows that the restaurant spent $4,000 more for buns than it should have given the lower actual sales level of 900,000 Big Macs.

Flexible-Budget Formulas

To develop a flexible budget, managers use flexible-budget formulas that describe revenue and cost behavior with respect to appropriate cost drivers. The cost functions that we introduced in Chapter 2 and estimated in Chapter 3 are examples of flexible-budget formulas. The flexible budget incorporates effects of changes in activity on each revenue and cost.

Exhibit 8-2 shows Dominion Company's flexible budget that uses flexible-budget formulas based on a single cost driver, units of output. The three columns of Exhibit 8-2 are flexible budgets for output levels of 7,000, 8,000, and 9,000 units, respectively. Exhibit 8-3 shows a graphical version of the flexible-budget formula. The solid line between 7,000 and 9,000 units indicates that the relevant range for these flexible-budget formulas is 7,000 to 9,000 units. Within this range, we expect fixed costs to be constant at $70,000 per month, the point where the line meets the vertical axis, and variable costs to be $21.80 per unit, the slope of the line. The dashed line below 7,000 units indicates that this portion of the flexible-budget line is outside the relevant range.

Note that the static budget is just the flexible budget for the original planned level of activity. Thus, the amounts shown in the static budget column in Exhibit 8-1 for sales of 9,000 units

Objective 2

Use flexible-budget formulas to construct a flexible budget based on the volume of sales.

	Flexible-Budget Formula	Flexible Budgets for Various Levels of Sales/Production Activity		
Units		7,000	8,000	9,000
Sales	$ 31.00	$217,000	$248,000	$279,000
Variable costs				
Variable manufacturing costs	$ 21.00	$147,000	$168,000	$189,000
Shipping costs (selling)	.60	4,200	4,800	5,400
Administrative costs	.20	1,400	1,600	1,800
Total variable costs	$ 21.80	$152,600	$174,400	$196,200
Contribution margin	$ 9.20	$ 64,400	$ 73,600	$ 82,800
Fixed costs per month				
Fixed manufacturing costs	$37,000	$ 37,000	$ 37,000	$ 37,000
Fixed selling and administrative costs	33,000	33,000	33,000	33,000
Total fixed costs	$70,000	$ 70,000	$ 70,000	$ 70,000
Operating income (loss)		$ (5,600)	$ 3,600	$ 12,800

Exhibit 8-2

Dominion Company
Flexible Budgets

Exhibit 8-3
Dominion Company
Graph of Flexible Budget of Costs

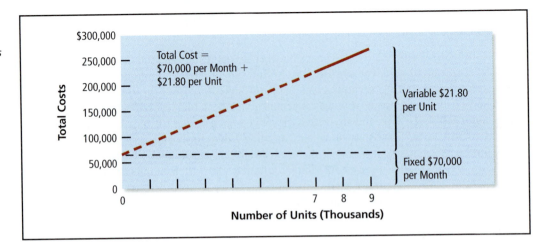

Activity-Based Flexible Budgets

Objective 3

Prepare an activity-based flexible budget.

are exactly the same as the amounts in the far right column of Exhibit 8-2, the flexible budget for sales of 9,000 units.

Dominion Company's flexible budget in Exhibit 8-2 is based on a single cost driver—units of output. This is an appropriate approach to flexible budgeting when "units of output" is a plausible and reliable cost driver for all of a company's costs. But what if some of a company's costs are driven by activities such as order processing or setting up for production? A company that has an activity-based costing system with multiple cost drivers, such as the systems described in Chapter 4, will prepare an **activity-based flexible budget** by budgeting costs for each activity using the related cost driver.

Exhibit 8-4 shows an activity-based flexible budget for the Dominion Company. There are four activities: processing, setup, marketing, and administration. For each activity, costs depend on a different cost driver. For example, in Exhibit 8-4 we assume that setup costs are variable with respect to the "number of setups," whereas in Exhibit 8-2 we assumed that the $12,000 of setup costs included in the manufacturing costs of $37,000 are fixed with respect to "units of output." To see why setup costs might be expected to vary with respect to the number of setups but not with respect to the number of units, consider the example of setup supplies. Each time employees set up a production run, they use a batch of setup supplies. However, once the run is set up, production of additional units uses no additional setup supplies. Thus, the cost of supplies varies directly with the number of setups (at a cost of $500 per setup) but does not vary directly with the number of units produced.

Compare the traditional flexible budget (Exhibit 8-2) and the activity-based flexible budget (Exhibit 8-4). Note that assumptions about fixed and variable costs differ in the two exhibits. Because of differing assumptions about cost behavior, the calculated cost using a single cost driver differs from the calculated cost using multiple activity-based cost drivers.

When should a company use a more sophisticated activity-based flexible budget with multiple cost drivers rather than a simple flexible budget with a single cost driver, such as units of output? When a significant portion of its costs vary with cost drivers other than units of output. For the remainder of this chapter, we return to using a flexible budget based on the assumption of a single cost driver, units of output.

Evaluation of Financial Performance Using Flexible Budgets

Objective 4

Explain the performance evaluation relationship between static budgets, flexible budgets, and actual results.

We saw earlier that two quite different factors combine to cause static-budget variances. Actual results might differ from the static budget because (1) actual output levels were not the same as in the static budget, or (2) actual revenues and costs differed from those in the flexible budget for the actual level of output achieved. The flexible budget allows us to separate these two effects by calculating one set of variances based on differences between the static budget and the flexible budget and a second set of variances based on differences between the flexible budget and actual results. The differences between the static budget amounts and the flexible budget amounts are **activity-level variances**. Differences between the flexible budget amounts and actual results are flexible-budget variances. Thus, the static-budget variance, the difference between actual results

Exhibit 8-4
Dominion Company
*Activity-Based Flexible Budget for
the Month Ended June 30, 20X1*

	Budget Formula	Units		
Sales in units		7,000	8,000	9,000
Sales in dollars	$31.00/unit	$217,000	$248,000	$279,000
ACTIVITY				
Processing		Cost Driver: Number of Machine Hours (MH)		
Cost-driver level		14,000	16,000	18,000
Variable costs	$10.50/MH	$147,000	$168,000	$189,000
Fixed costs	$13,000	$ 13,000	$ 13,000	$ 13,000
Total costs of processing activity		$160,000	$181,000	$202,000
Setup		Cost Driver: Number of Setups		
Cost-driver level		20	22	24
Variable costs	$500/setup	$ 10,000	$ 11,000	$ 12,000
Fixed costs	$12,000	$ 12,000	$ 12,000	$ 12,000
Total costs of setup activity		$ 22,000	$ 23,000	$ 24,000
Marketing		Cost Driver: Number of Orders		
Cost-driver level		350	400	450
Variable costs	$12.00/order	$ 4,200	$ 4,800	$ 5,400
Fixed costs	$15,000	$ 15,000	$ 15,000	$ 15,000
Total costs of marketing activity		$ 19,200	$ 19,800	$ 20,400
Administration		Cost Driver: Number of Units		
Cost-driver level		7,000	8,000	9,000
Variable costs	$.20/unit	$ 1,400	$ 1,600	$ 1,800
Fixed costs	$18,000	$ 18,000	$ 18,000	$ 18,000
Total costs of administration activity		$ 19,400	$ 19,600	$ 19,800
Total costs		$220,600	$243,400	$266,200
Operating income (loss)		$ (3,600)	$ 4,600	$ 12,800

and the static budget, can be divided into two components, 1) the activity-level variance and 2) the flexible-budget variance:

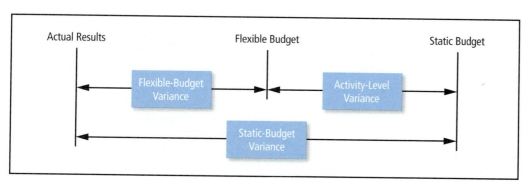

Accountants use flexible-budget variances to draw attention to unexpected results that managers can correct (if the effects are detrimental) or enhance (if the effects are beneficial). Because the flexible budget adjusts planned revenues and planned costs to reflect the actual level of output, only departures of actual costs or revenues from flexible-budget formula amounts cause any variances between the flexible budget and actual results. In contrast, changes in output (activity) levels, not cost control, cause the differences between the static budget and the flexible budget.

The division of static-budget variances into flexible-budget variances and activity-level variances is illustrated for Dominion Company in Exhibit 8-5. The flexible budget (column 3) for sales of 7,000 units taken from Exhibit 8-2 (and simplified) provides an explanatory bridge between the static budget (column 5) for sales of 9,000 units and the actual results (column 1). The bottom lines of Exhibit 8-5 summarize the variances for income. Note that the sum of the activity-level variances (here **sales-activity variances** because sales is used as the cost driver) and the flexible-budget variances equals the total of the static-budget variances: $18,400 U + $5,970 U = $24,370 U.

Isolating the Causes of Variances

When evaluating performance, managers try to distinguish between **effectiveness**—the degree to which an organization meets an objective—and **efficiency**—the degree to which an organization minimizes the resources used to achieve an objective. Performance may be effective, efficient, both, or neither.

For example, Dominion Company set a static-budget objective of manufacturing and selling 9,000 units. It actually made and sold only 7,000 units. Was Dominion's performance effective? No. Dominion failed to meet its sales objective, and, therefore, performance (as measured by sales-activity variances) was ineffective. Was Dominion's performance efficient? Managers judge the degree of efficiency by comparing actual inputs used (such as the costs of direct materials and direct labor) to budgeted inputs for the level of output achieved (7,000 units). The less input used to produce a given output, the more efficient the operation. The unfavorable flexible-budget variances indicate that Dominion was inefficient because the actual cost of its inputs exceeded the cost expected for the actual level of output.

A **McDonald's** restaurant could use this same analysis. Effectiveness—the difference between the static budget and the flexible budget—depends on the degree to which the restaurant meets its sales objectives. Efficiency—the difference between the actual results and the flexible budget—is the difference between actual profit and the profit expected for the level of sales actually attained.

	Actual Results at Actual Activity Level* (1)	Flexible-Budget Variances † (2) = (1) − (3)	Flexible Budget For Actual Sales Activity ‡ (3)	Sales-Activity Variances (4) = (3) − (5)	Static Budget* (5)
Units	7,000	—	7,000	2,000 U	9,000
Sales	$ 217,000	—	$217,000	$62,000 U	$279,000
Variable costs	158,270	5,670 U	152,600	43,600 F	196,200
Contribution margin	$ 58,730	$5,670 U	$ 64,400	$18,400 U	$ 82,800
Fixed costs	70,300	300 U	70,000	—	70,000
Operating income	$ (11,570)	$5,970 U	$ (5,600)	$18,400 U	$ 12,800

Total flexible-budget variances
$5,970 U

Total sales-activity variances
$18,400 U

Total static budget variances, $24,370 U

U = Unfavorable. F = Favorable.
*Figures are from Exhibit 8-1.
†Figures are shown in more detail in Exhibit 8-6.
‡Figures are from the 7,000-unit column in Exhibit 8-2.

Exhibit 8-5
Dominion Company
Summary of Performance for the Month Ended June 30, 20X1

Making Managerial Decisions

Consider a company that plans to sell 1,000 units for $3 per unit. Budgeted variable costs are $2 per unit, budgeted fixed costs are $700, and the static-budget profit is $300. Suppose the company actually sells 800 units and income is $110. Compute and interpret the static-budget profit variance, the sales-activity profit variance, and the flexible-budget profit variance.

Answer

There is a $190 unfavorable static-budget profit variance, the difference between static budgeted profit of $300 and the actual profit of $110. The static budget variance is the sum of two components: the sales-activity variance and the flexible-budget variance. The sales-activity profit variance is the difference between the static-budgeted profit of $300 for planned production of 1,000 units versus the flexible-budgeted profit of $100 for production of 800 units, a $200 unfavorable variance. The flexible-budget profit variance is the difference between the flexible-budgeted profit of $100 versus the actual profit of $110, a favorable variance of $10. The $10 favorable flexible-budget variance indicates that the operation was efficient while the $200 unfavorable sales-activity variance indicates the company was not effective.

Flexible-Budget Variances

Recall that flexible-budget variances measure the efficiency of operations at the actual level of activity. The first three columns of Exhibit 8-5 provide comparisons of actual results with the flexible-budget amounts. The flexible-budget variances are the differences between columns 1 and 3. For income, the flexible-budget variance is $5,970 unfavorable:

Objective 5

Compute activity-level variances and flexible-budget variances.

$$\text{flexible-budget income variance} = \text{actual income} - \text{flexible-budget income (at actual sales level)}$$

$$= (-\$11,570) - (-\$5,600)$$

$$= \$5,970 \text{ unfavorable}$$

Just as we can divide income into its component revenues minus costs, we can divide the flexible-budget income variance into revenue and cost variances. In the Dominion Company example, the flexible-budget revenue variance is zero because there is no difference between the actual sales price and the flexible-budgeted sales price. Therefore, for this example we focus on cost variances for variable and fixed costs, the differences between actual costs and flexible-budget costs.

Exhibit 8-6 gives a line-by-line computation of flexible-budget variances for all cost items at Dominion and provides new details about variable and fixed manufacturing costs. Note that most of the costs with favorable static-budget variances (see Exhibit 8-1) have unfavorable flexible-budget variances. Why is this so? Sales fell far short of the target, and, therefore, budgeted costs in the flexible budget based on actual sales of 7,000 units were much lower than budgeted costs in the static budget based on target sales of 9,000 units, yielding favorable static-budget variances. However, in most instances where actual costs were lower than the static budget, the actual costs were higher than the flexible budget, yielding unfavorable flexible-budget variances.

It is tempting to assume that favorable flexible-budget variances are always good and unfavorable flexible-budget variances are always bad, but beware of this assumption. Favorable flexible-budget variances might at first seem to indicate that costs are well-managed. However, favorable variances, where actual costs are less than the flexible budget, might instead indicate that the company is spending too little. For example, actual maintenance costs that are less than budgeted may indicate that the company is not keeping up with required maintenance. Similarly, shipping costs that are below budget because slow ground shipments are being used instead of air shipments may mean that customers will be alienated by the slower deliveries. On the other hand, significantly unfavorable variances, where costs exceed the flexible budget, may not mean that costs are out of control. For example, higher than budgeted direct-labor costs may be explained by a budget that did not reflect an increase in pay rates. Similarly, higher than budgeted material costs may be explained by a decision to switch to higher-quality, higher-cost materials that are expected to result in labor-cost savings that will more than offset the increase in material costs. In sum, do not assume that the "favorable" and "unfavorable" labels tell you everything you need to know.

	Actual Costs Incurred	Flexible Budget*	Flexible-Budget Variances†	Possible Explanation
Units	7,000	7,000	—	
Variable costs				
Direct materials	$ 69,920	$ 70,000	$ 80 F	Lower prices but higher usage
Direct labor	61,500	56,000	5,500 U	Higher wage rates and higher usage
Indirect labor	9,100	11,900	2,800 F	Decreased setup time
Idle time	3,550	2,800	750 U	Excessive machine breakdowns
Cleanup time	2,500	2,100	400 U	Cleanup of spilled solvent
Supplies	4,700	4,200	500 U	Higher prices and higher usage
Variable manufacturing costs	$151,270	$147,000	$4,270 U	
Shipping	5,000	4,200	800 U	Use of air freight to meet delivery
Administration	2,000	1,400	600 U	Excessive copying and long-distance calls
Total variable costs	$158,270	$152,600	$5,670 U	
Fixed costs				
Factory supervision	$ 14,700	$ 14,400	$ 300 U	Salary increase
Factory rent	5,000	5,000	—	
Equipment depreciation	15,000	15,000	—	
Other fixed factory costs	2,600	2,600	—	
Fixed manufacturing costs	$ 37,300	$ 37,000	$ 300 U	
Fixed selling and administrative costs	33,000	33,000	—	
Total fixed costs	$ 70,300	$ 70,000	$ 300 U	
Total variable and fixed costs	$228,570	$222,600	$5,970 U	

*From 7,000-unit column of Exhibit 8-2.
†This is a line-by-line breakout of the variances in column 2 of Exhibit 8-5.

Exhibit 8-6
Dominion Company
Cost-Control Performance Report for the Month Ended June 30, 20X1

Instead, always look for underlying explanations for any significant deviation of actual cost from the flexible budget. The last column of Exhibit 8-6 provides examples of some possible explanations for Dominion Company's variances.

Sales-Activity Variances

For Dominion Company, we assume that the driver for variable costs in the flexible budget is unit sales volume, so the activity-level variances are sales-activity variances. Dominion Company's sales activity fell 2,000 units short of the planned level. The sales-activity variances (totaling $18,400 U) in the final three columns of Exhibit 8-5 measure the budgeted effect of falling short of the original sales objective. Note that changes in unit prices or unit variable costs do not affect activity-level variances. Why? Only the unit sales volume affects the sales-activity variances because the flexible budget and the static budget differ only due to different assumed levels of activity, but use the same budgeted unit prices, unit variable costs, and total fixed costs. Also note that there can never be a sales-activity variance for fixed costs. Why? Because the total budgeted fixed-costs are the same in the flexible budget and the static budget.

The sales-activity income variance informs the manager that falling short of the sales target by 2,000 units explains $18,400 of the shortfall of income relative to the amount initially budgeted (a $5,600 flexible-budget loss instead of a $12,800 static-budget profit). We can also express this $18,400 variance as the shortfall of 2,000 units multiplied by the budgeted contribution margin of $9.20 per unit (from the first column of Exhibit 8-2):

Sales-activity income variance = (actual units − static budget units) × budgeted contribution per unit

$$= (9,000 - 7,000) \times \$9.20$$

$$= \$18,400 \text{ unfavorable}$$

Who has responsibility for the sales-activity income variance? Marketing managers usually have the primary responsibility for reaching the sales level specified in the static budget. Many factors can cause variations in sales, including poor production quality and missed delivery schedules. Nevertheless, marketing managers are typically in the best position to explain why actual sales levels differed from plans.

Think about the situation for many companies at the end of 2008 as the effects of the economic crisis caused actual sales to fall far short of the original budgeted level of sales. Even if their operations were efficient (that is, no unfavorable flexible-budget variances), large unfavorable sales-activity variances explain why income often fell far below predicted (static-budget) income levels.

Setting Standards

To establish flexible budgets, managers must determine standard costs. A **standard cost** is a carefully developed cost per unit. Standards are popular, used by more than 85% of U.S. companies. But standards mean different things to different companies. Many companies set standard cost equal to **expected cost**, the cost that is most likely to be attained. However, it is also common to intentionally set standards above or below expected costs to create desired incentives. What standard of performance should a company use in its flexible budgets? Should a standard be so strict that the company rarely, if ever, meets it? Should the company attain the standard about 50% of the time? 90%? 20%? Individuals who have worked a lifetime setting and evaluating standards for performance disagree on this question, so there are no universal answers. As described in the Business First box on page 314, more companies are adapting standards to fit their particular needs.

Perfection standards (also called **ideal standards**) are expressions of the most efficient performance possible under the best conceivable conditions, using existing specifications and equipment. Perfection standards make no provision for waste, spoilage, machine breakdowns, and the like. Those who favor using perfection standards maintain that the resulting unfavorable variances will constantly remind personnel of the need for continuous improvement in all phases of operations. Though concern for continuous improvement is widespread, perfection standards are not widely used because they often have an adverse effect on employee motivation. Employees tend to ignore goals that they know cannot be reached.

Currently attainable standards are levels of performance that managers can achieve by realistic levels of effort. They make allowances for normal defectives, spoilage, waste, and nonproductive time. There are at least two popular approaches to setting currently attainable standards.

The first approach sets standards so that employees regard their attainment as highly probable if normal effort and diligence are exercised. Hence, the standards are predictions of what will likely occur, anticipating some normal level of inefficiencies. Under normal conditions this approach yields variances that are random and negligible. Managers accept the standards as being reasonable goals. The major advantages of this approach to setting currently attainable standards are as follows:

1. The resulting standards serve multiple purposes. Because the standards represent what is expected under normal conditions, companies can use the same standard costs for financial budgeting and inventory valuation. In contrast, they cannot use perfection standards for inventory valuation or financial budgeting because they know that the resulting standard costs are unrealistically low.
2. Reasonable standards have a desirable motivational impact on employees, especially when combined with incentives for continuous improvement. The standard represents reasonable future performance, not unrealistic goals. Therefore, unfavorable variances direct attention to performance that is not meeting reasonable expectations.

A second approach to setting currently attainable standards falls somewhere between perfection standards and the first approach to setting currently attainable standards. This approach sets standards so that employees regard them as "stretch goals," where meeting the standard is difficult but possible. Managers can achieve such standards only by very efficient operations. Variances tend to be unfavorable; nevertheless, employees accept the standards as being tough but not unreasonable goals.

Business First

The Need to Adapt Standard Cost Approaches

Critics of standard costs and variance analysis maintain that predetermined standards do not work well in today's dynamic, fast-paced, just-in-time environment. Nonetheless, companies continue to use standards and to measure performance against them. Surveys in nine different countries have shown that between 56% and 92% of manufacturing companies use standard costs. Companies have apparently adapted the approach to fit their modern environments.

To apply standards in a dynamic environment, how should managers measure and report variances? First, they should continually evaluate their standards. If a company is in a state of continuous improvement, it must continually revise its standards. Second, standards and variances should measure key strategic variables. The concept of setting a benchmark, comparing actual results to the benchmark, and identifying causes for any differences is universal. We can apply it to many types of measures, such as production quantity or quality, as well as to costs. Finally, variances should not lead to affixing blame. Standards are plans, and things do not always go according to plan—often with no one being at fault.

One company that has adapted standard costs to meet its particular needs is the Brass Products Division (BPD) at **Parker Hannifin Corporation**, a $10 billion company that produces motion and control technologies and systems. BPD uses standard costs and variances to pinpoint problem areas

that need attention if the division is to meet its goal of continuous improvement. Among the changes that have increased the value of the standard cost information are more timely product cost information, variances computed at more detailed levels, and regular meetings to help employees understand their impact on the variances.

Managers and accountants adapt the standard cost concept to fit the particular needs of a company. For example, BPD created three new variances: (1) The standard run quantity variance examines the effect of actual compared to optimal batch size for production runs; (2) the material substitution variance compares material costs to the costs of alternative materials; and (3) the method variance measures costs using actual machines compared to costs using alternative machines. All three variances use the concept of setting a standard and comparing actual results to the standard, but they do not apply the traditional standard cost-variance formulas.

Sources: Adapted from D. Johnsen and P. Sopariwala, "Standard Costing Is Alive and Well at Parker Brass," *Management Accounting Quarterly*, Winter 2000, pp. 12–20; C. B. Cheatham and L. R. Cheatham, "Redesigning Cost Systems: Is Standard Costing Obsolete?" *Accounting Horizons*, December 1996, pp. 23–31; C. Horngren, G. Foster, and S. Datar, *Cost Accounting: A Managerial Emphasis*, 12th ed. (Upper Saddle River, NJ: Prentice Hall, 2006), p. 229; and Parker Hannifin Corp., *Parker Hannifin 2008 Annual Report*.

Is it possible to achieve continuous improvement using currently attainable standards? Yes, but managers must continually update such standards to recognize improved productivity, and management must also use incentive systems that reward continuous improvement.

Trade-Offs Among Variances

Because the various activities of an organization are interrelated, the level of performance in one area will often affect performance in other areas. Often there are trade-offs among costs. For example, **McDonald's** may generate favorable labor variances by hiring less-skilled and lower-paid employees, but this might also lead to more waste because substandard products need to be scrapped, resulting in unfavorable materials variances. As another example, **Ford** may experience unfavorable materials variances by purchasing higher-quality materials at a higher than planned price, but this may be more than offset by other favorable variances due to lower waste, fewer inspections, and higher-quality products.

Because of the many interdependencies among activities, an "unfavorable" or "favorable" label should not lead a manager to jump to conclusions. By themselves, variances merely raise questions and provide clues to the causes of performance. Variances are attention directors, not problem solvers. Furthermore, the cause of unfavorable variances might be unrealistically high standards rather than poor execution by managers. One of the first questions a manager should consider when investigating a large variance is whether expectations were valid.

When to Investigate Variances

When should management investigate a variance? For some critical items, any deviation may prompt a follow-up. However, for most items, managers recognize that, even if everything operates normally, variances are unlikely to be exactly zero. For these items, managers specify a range of "acceptable" variances based on economic analysis of how big a variance must be before investigation would be worth the effort. While the acceptable range is sometimes stated in percentage terms, it is important to also consider the dollar deviation from budget. For example, a 4% variance in a $1 million material cost may deserve more attention than a 20% variance in a $1,000 repair cost. Because knowing exactly when to investigate is difficult, many organizations have developed rules of thumb that incorporate both absolute and relative size measures such as "Investigate all variances exceeding either $5,000 or 15% of expected cost."

Comparisons with Prior Period's Results

Some organizations compare actual results with last year's results for the same period rather than using flexible-budget benchmarks. For example, an organization might compare June 2010's actual results to June 2009's actual results. However, simplistic comparisons with prior period results should be used cautiously. In general, a carefully developed flexible budget provides a better benchmark than prior period results for evaluating performance. Why? First, using actual results from the prior year as a benchmark assumes that prior year values are what we aspire to achieve and don't contain any inefficiencies or substandard results. Second, many changes occur in the environment and in the organization, and these changes can make a comparison to the prior year invalid. Few organizations and environments are so stable that the only difference between now and a year ago is merely the passage of time. For example, the turmoil in the stock market in 2008 led many financial institutions to make sweeping changes in operations. Comparisons of operating results in 2008 to 2007 would not have been meaningful because the economic climate was so different in 2008. Further changes in the economic climate during 2009 implied that simple comparisons of operating results in 2009 to 2008 were also not meaningful. Even comparisons with the prior month's actual results may not be as useful as comparisons with an up-to-date flexible budget. Comparisons with previous years may be useful for analyzing trends in such key variables as sales volume, market share, and product mix, but they do not help answer questions such as Dominion Company's "Why did we have a loss of $11,570 in June, when we expected a profit of $12,800?"

Summary Problem for Your Review

PROBLEM

Refer to the data in Exhibits 8-1 and 8-2. Suppose actual production and sales were 8,500 units instead of 7,000 units; actual variable costs were $188,800; and actual fixed costs were $71,200. The selling price remained at $31 per unit.

1. Compute the static-budget variance for income. What does this tell you about the efficiency of operations? The effectiveness of operations?
2. Compute the sales-activity variance for income. Is the performance of the marketing function the sole explanation for this variance? Why?
3. Using a flexible budget at the actual activity level, compute the budgeted contribution margin, budgeted income, and flexible-budget variance for income. What do you learn from this variance?

SOLUTION

1.   actual operating income = $(8,500 \times \$31) - \$188,800 - \$71,200 = \$3,500$

static-budget operating income = $12,800$ (from Exhibit 8-1)

static budget variance = $\$12,800 - \$3,500 = \$9,300$ U

Three factors affect the static-budget variance: sales activity, efficiency, and price changes. There is no way to tell from the static-budget variance alone how much of the $9,300 U was caused by each of these factors.

2. sales-activity variance = budgeted unit contribution margin × difference between the
static budget unit sales and the actual unit sales

$$= \$9.20 \text{ per unit CM} \times (8,500 - 9,000)$$

$$= \$4,600 \text{ U}$$

The sales-activity variance for income quantifies the impact of the deviation from an original sales target while holding price and efficiency factors constant. This is a measure of the effectiveness of Dominion in meeting its sales objective. Management might attribute the failure to reach target sales to ineffectiveness of marketing personnel or to causes beyond the control of marketing personnel, such as material shortages, factory breakdowns, delivery problems, and so on.

3. The budget formulas in Exhibit 8-2 are the basis for the following answers:

flexible-budget contribution margin = $\$9.20 \times 8,500 = \$78,200$

flexible-budget operating income = $\$78,200 - \$70,000$ fixed costs = $\$8,200$

actual operating income = $\$3,500$ (from number 1)

flexible budget variance = $\$8,200 - \$3,500 = \$4,700$ U

The flexible-budget variance shows that the company spent $4,700 more to produce and sell the 8,500 units than it should have spent if operations had been efficient and costs had not changed. Note that this $4,700 U flexible-budget variance plus the $4,600 U sales-activity variance total to the $9,300 U static-budget variance.

Flexible-Budget Variances in Detail

The remainder of this chapter explains how to further analyze flexible-budget variances by dividing them into component variances. We begin with direct labor and direct material variances and then briefly discuss overhead variances.

Variances for Direct Material and Direct Labor

We can express the actual cost and flexible-budget cost for labor or materials as quantity multiplied by price. Actual cost is the actual quantity used multiplied by the actual price per unit. Flexible-budget cost is the standard quantity allowed for the actual level of activity multiplied by the standard price per unit. Therefore, the flexible-budget variance (the difference between actual cost incurred and the flexible-budget cost) can be divided into 1) a quantity variance, attributable to the difference between actual quantity used and standard quantity allowed, and 2) a price variance, attributable to the difference between actual price per unit and standard price per unit.

Let's consider the components of the direct-material and direct-labor flexible-budget variances for the Dominion Company. As shown in Exhibit 8-6, the flexible-budget variances for direct material and direct labor are $80 F and $5,500 U, respectively:

	(1) Actual Costs	(2) Flexible Budget	(3) Flexible-Budget Variance
Direct materials	$69,920	$70,000	$ 80 F
Direct labor	61,500	56,000	5,500 U

To divide the flexible-budget variances into quantity and price variances, we need further information about the underlying actual and budgeted quantities and prices of direct labor and materials.

We turn first to the flexible budget quantities and prices. Dominion Company's flexible budget shows the amounts that Dominion expected to spend based on standard quantities and standard costs for direct materials and direct labor to produce the output achieved, computed as follows:

$$\frac{\text{flexible}}{\text{budget}} = \frac{\text{units of actual}}{\text{output achieved}} \times \frac{\text{input allowed}}{\text{per unit of output}} \times \frac{\text{standard unit}}{\text{price of input}}$$

Note that the flexible budget is constructed for the level of actual output achieved. We will refer to the flexible budget for the actual output achieved as "standard cost allowed."

Exhibit 8-6 presented flexible-budget amounts based on $10 per unit of output for direct materials and $8 per unit of output for direct labor. Let's assume the company derived these flexible budget amounts as the product of two components, a standard quantity of an input and a standard price for the input, as shown in the following table:

	Standards		
	Standard Quantity of Input Allowed per Unit of Output	Standard Price per Unit of Input	Flexible Budget Formula per Unit of Output
Direct materials	5 pounds	$2/pound	$10
Direct labor	$\frac{1}{2}$ hour	$16/hour	8

For the 7,000 units of output achieved by Dominion, these flexible-budget amounts for direct material and direct labor translate into the following standard costs allowed:

$$\text{direct-materials cost allowed} = 7{,}000 \text{ units} \times 5 \text{ pounds} \times \$2.00 \text{ per pound} = \$70{,}000$$

$$\text{direct-labor cost allowed} = 7{,}000 \text{ units} \times \tfrac{1}{2} \text{ hour} \times \$16.00 \text{ per hour} = \$56{,}000$$

We next turn to additional information about actual costs. Let's assume the following actual prices and quantities explain the actual direct material and direct labor costs for Dominion:

- Direct materials: Dominion purchased and used 36,800 pounds of material at an actual unit price of $1.90 for a total actual cost of 36,800 × $1.90 = $69,920.
- Direct labor: Dominion used 3,750 hours of labor at an actual hourly price (rate) of $16.40, for a total cost of 3,750 × $16.40 = $61,500.

Computing Price and Quantity Variances

The **price variance** indicates whether management paid more or less than the standard price for each input used:

$$\text{price variance} = (\text{actual price} - \text{standard price}) \times \text{actual quantity used}$$

The **quantity variance** indicates whether management used more or less than the standard quantity of input for the output achieved:

$$\text{quantity variance} = (\text{actual quantity used} - \text{standard quantity allowed for actual output}) \times \text{standard price}$$

Objective 6

Compute and interpret price and quantity variances for materials and labor.

Let's examine the computation of price and quantity variances in more detail, as shown in Exhibit 8-7. Panel A shows the case where the actual price is equal to the standard price so there is solely a quantity variance, Panel B shows the case where the actual quantity is equal to the standard quantity so there is solely a price variance, and Panel C shows the more common case with both quantity and price variances. In all three panels, the flexible budget is the standard quantity multiplied by the standard price—the rectangle shaded blue. However, the variances differ across the panels, depending on the difference between standard and actual price and the difference between standard and actual quantity.

In Panel A where there is solely a quantity variance, the variance is the quantity used in excess of the standard quantity times the standard price—the rectangle shaded green. In Panel B where there is solely a price variance, the variance is the price paid in excess of the standard price times the standard quantity—the rectangle shaded purple.

Panel C illustrates the situation where both quantity and price variances exist. There is a joint effect of the two variances, represented by the cross-hatched purple region. In concept, this joint effect could be defined to be a separate, third variance. In practice, most companies include this joint effect as part of the price variance, and this is the way the price variance was defined previously. This means we calculate the price variance by multiplying the difference between actual and standard price by the total actual quantity used. This definition includes the joint effect represented by the purple cross-hatched area as part of the price variance. The quantity variance is then the difference between actual and standard quantity multiplied by the standard price.

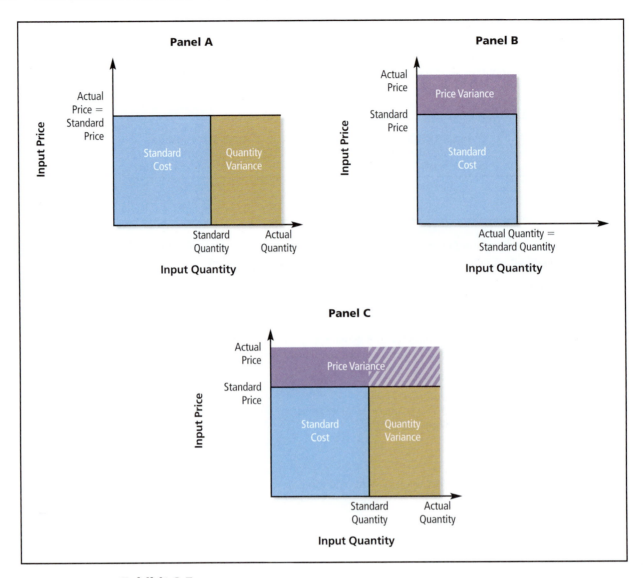

Exhibit 8-7

Graphical Representation of Quantity and Price Variances

We use this approach to divide the Dominion Company's flexible-budget variances (column (3) in the table near the bottom of page 316) into price and quantity variances for material and labor. The price variances are as follows:

$$\text{Direct-materials price variance} = (\text{actual price} - \text{standard price}) \times \text{actual quantity}$$

$$= (\$1.90 - \$2.00) \text{ per pound} \times 36{,}800 \text{ pounds}$$

$$= \$3{,}680 \text{ favorable}$$

$$\text{Direct-labor price (rate) variance} = (\text{actual price} - \text{standard price}) \times \text{actual quantity}$$

$$= (\$16.40 - \$16.00) \text{ per hour} \times 3{,}750 \text{ hours}$$

$$= \$1{,}500 \text{ unfavorable}$$

The quantity (or usage) variances are as follows:

$$\text{Direct-materials quantity variance} = (\text{actual quantity} - \text{standard quantity}) \times \text{standard price}$$

$$= [36{,}800 - (7{,}000 \times 5)] \text{ pounds} \times \$2.00 \text{ per pound}$$

$$= [36{,}800 - 35{,}000] \text{ pounds} \times \$2.00 \text{ per pounds}$$

$$= \$3{,}600 \text{ unfavorable}$$

$$\begin{aligned}
\text{Direct-labor quantity variance} &= (\text{actual quantity} - \text{standard quantity}) \times \text{standard price} \\
&= [3{,}750 - (7{,}000 \times 1/2)] \text{ hours} \times \$16.00 \text{ per hour} \\
&= [3{,}750 - 3{,}500] \text{ hours} \times \$16.00 \text{ per hour} \\
&= \$4{,}000 \text{ unfavorable}
\end{aligned}$$

By definition, the sum of the direct-labor price and quantity variances equals the direct-labor flexible-budget variance. Similarly, the sum of the direct-materials price and quantity variances equals the total direct-materials flexible-budget variance.

$$\begin{aligned}
\text{Direct-materials flexible-budget variance} &= \$3{,}680 \text{ favorable} + \$3{,}600 \text{ unfavorable} \\
&= \$80 \text{ favorable} \\
\text{Direct-labor flexible-budget variance} &= \$1{,}500 \text{ unfavorable} + \$4{,}000 \text{ unfavorable} \\
&= \$5{,}500 \text{ unfavorable}
\end{aligned}$$

You are likely to encounter a variety of terminology for price and quantity variances in practice. For example, many companies call a price variance applied to labor a **rate variance**, and many refer to quantity variances as **usage** or **efficiency variances**. Moreover, you may encounter new variance definitions such as those created by the Brass Products Division in the Business First box on page 314 or in the Making Managerial Decisions section on page 321. Because there is so much variation in definitions and terminology, you should always ask whatever questions are necessary to be sure that you understand the exact definition of any variance that you encounter.

Framework for Calculating Materials and Labor Variances

Exhibit 8-8 summarizes the framework used to divide direct-materials and direct-labor flexible-budget variances into price and quantity variances. Though the exhibit may seem complex at first, studying it will solidify your understanding of variance analysis.

Column A of Exhibit 8-8 contains the actual costs incurred based on the actual quantities used at actual prices. Column C is the flexible-budget amount based on standard input quantities allowed for the outputs achieved multiplied by standard prices. We insert column B, the actual input quantities used multiplied by standard prices, between A and C to separate price and quantity effects. The difference between columns A and B is due to different actual versus standard prices because we hold actual quantity constant across columns A and B. The difference between columns B and C is due to different actual versus standard quantities used because we hold price constant across columns B and C.

We measure activity in a flexible budget in terms of standard inputs allowed for actual outputs achieved (column C in Exhibit 8-8). For Dominion Company, a single-product firm, standard inputs allowed is simply units of output multiplied by the standard quantity of input per unit. For companies that manufacture a variety of products, standard inputs allowed will be aggregated across multiple products, with different standard inputs for the output achieved for each product. For example, consider a furniture manufacturer that produced 12,000 chairs and 3,000 sofas. If each chair requires 1 standard labor hour and each sofa requires 2 standard labor hours, the manufacturer may express standard hours allowed for outputs achieved as $(12{,}000 \times 1) + (3{,}000 \times 2) = 18{,}000$. Standard hours allowed for output achieved is the result of translating disparate output units (chairs and sofas) into a common standard measure of activity (standard labor hours allowed for output achieved).

Interpreting Price and Quantity Variances

By dividing flexible-budget variances into price and quantity variances, we can better evaluate managers on variances that they can control. Consider an operating manager who has control over the quantity of materials used in the production process but little control over the price. In that case, the quantity variance will be more relevant than the price variance in evaluating the operating manager. Who has control over the price variance? The manager in charge of purchasing materials likely has some control over the price, and therefore is responsible for the price variance. However, even the purchasing manager may not have much control over price. Why? Because external market forces often are the primary influence on prices. Irrespective of whether any manager has control of price, it is useful to separate price and quantity variances whenever

Exhibit 8-8

General Approach to Analysis of Direct-Labor and Direct-Materials Variances

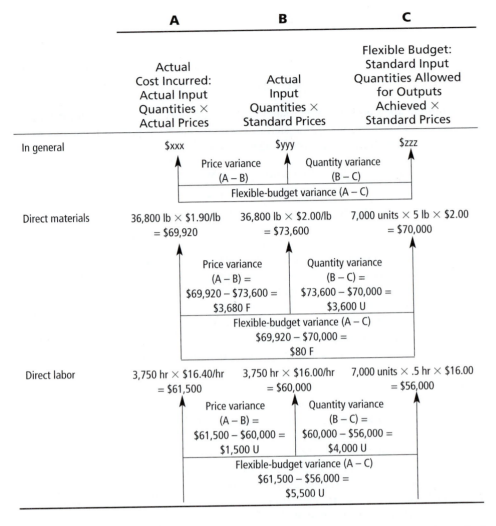

the quantity variance is important for evaluation. For example, the commodity prices of wheat, oats, corn, and rice may be outside the control of **General Mills** managers. By separating price variances from quantity variances, the breakfast cereal maker can focus on the quantity variance to assess whether managers used grain efficiently.

It is important to carefully consider the incentives created by price and quantity variances. Exclusive focus on material price variances can provide incentives that work against an organization's JIT and total quality management goals. For example, a purchasing manager focused only on creating a favorable material price variance may achieve a lower price by buying in large quantities or buying lower-quality material. However, the result could be excessive inventory-handling and opportunity costs caused by large purchase quantities or increased manufacturing defects caused by faulty material. As another example, exclusive focus on labor price variances could motivate managers to use lower-cost (and lower-skilled) workers or to rush workers through critical tasks. In either case, the result could impair quality of products and services.

Companies that use variances primarily to fix blame often find that managers resort to cheating and subversion to beat the system. Lower-level operations managers usually have more information about their operations than higher-level managers. If supervisors use that information against them, lower-level managers might withhold or misstate valuable information for their own protection. For example, one manufacturing firm actually followed a policy of reducing the next period's departmental budget by the amount of the department's unfavorable variances in the current period. If a division had a $50,000 expense budget for labor and $52,000 of actual labor costs resulting in a $2,000 unfavorable labor variance, the following period's budget would be set at $48,000. This system led managers to cheat and to falsify reports to avoid unfavorable variances and avoid reductions in their budgets. We can criticize departmental managers' ethics in this situation, but the system design was also at fault.

Variances by themselves cannot provide the complete picture of why the company achieved or failed to achieve the budgeted income. For instance, one possible explanation for Dominion's set of variances is that a manager made a trade-off. Perhaps the manager purchased substandard-quality materials at a favorable price, saving $3,680 (the favorable materials price variance) knowing that the substandard material would lead to extra waste of materials (the $3,600 unfavorable material quantity variance). In this case, the material price variance more than offset the material quantity variance, as indicated by the net materials flexible-budget variance of $80 favorable.

Of course, to fully understand the effect of the decision to purchase substandard materials, still more investigation and analysis might be required. For example, the material waste due to substandard materials might also have caused at least part of the excess use of direct labor. Why? Perhaps Dominion used direct labor time working on units that ended up being defective, thus wasting that time. Suppose the labor wasted on the defective units was more than the $80 favorable materials flexible budget variance described in the previous paragraph. Then, the decision to purchase substandard material was not successful because the labor cost inefficiencies caused by using substandard materials exceeded the materials cost savings from the favorable price. The important point here is that variances are useful tools that provide clues and direct attention to problems, but variances are only the starting point of the search for answers to the complex question of why actual results differ from expectations.

Making Managerial Decisions

Managers can apply the concepts of variance analysis to construct new variance definitions to fit new situations. For example, consider a production plant that plans to produce 50 units per hour and work 8 hours per day for a total planned production of 400 units each day. On March 23, the plant produced just 276 units for a total unfavorable production variance of 124 units. Because of machine breakdowns, the plant operated for only 6 hours that day. Using a three-column framework like that used in Exhibit 8-8, define variances that separate how much of the 124 unit shortfall in production was caused by operating only 6 hours versus how much was caused by low production efficiency during the 6 hours of actual operation.

Answer

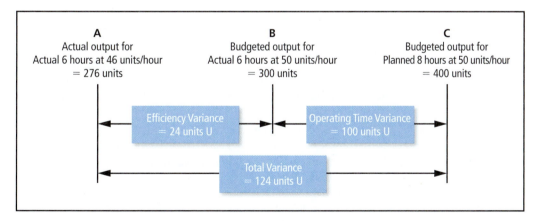

Column A shows actual production of 276 units over 6 actual operating hours equates to 46 units per hour. Column C shows standard production of 8 hours per day × 50 units per hour = 400 units per day. Column B shows standard production rates for actual operating hours, 6 hours of production × 50 units per hour = 300 units. The difference between columns B and C is the production shortfall caused by loss of 2 hours of operating time due to the machine breakdowns, 2 hours × 50 units per hour = 100 unit unfavorable variance. The difference between columns A and B is the shortfall caused by an actual rate of production (276 ÷ 6 × 46 units per hour) lower than the standard rate of 50 units per hour. This difference is the rate shortfall (4 units per hour) multiplied by the actual hours worked for the day (6 hours) = 24 unit unfavorable variance. The total variance, 100 units + 24 units = 124 units, is the difference between columns A and C.

Overhead Variances

Objective 7
Compute variable overhead
spending and efficiency variances.

The evaluation of overhead variances is different from the evaluation of direct materials and direct labor because overhead costs are generally indirect costs that companies allocate rather than trace to output. In this section, we outline the framework used to construct variable overhead variances, and then briefly discuss variances for fixed overhead.

Variable Overhead Variances

Companies allocate variable overhead to output based on some cost driver. For example, the variable-overhead cost driver for Dominion Company is direct-labor hours. The variable-overhead flexible-budget variance can be divided into two variances. When actual cost-driver activity differs from the standard amount allowed for the actual output achieved, we have a **variable-overhead efficiency variance**, calculated as follows:

$$\begin{matrix}\text{variable-overhead} \\ \text{efficiency variance}\end{matrix} = \left(\begin{matrix}\text{actual cost-} \\ \text{driver activity}\end{matrix} - \begin{matrix}\text{standard cost-driver} \\ \text{activity allowed}\end{matrix} \right) \times \begin{matrix}\text{standard} \\ \text{variable-overhead} \\ \text{rate per cost-driver unit}\end{matrix}$$

The variable-overhead efficiency variance depends entirely on whether the quantity of the cost driver used is more or less than the quantity allowed for the actual output achieved. It measures how control of the cost driver activity affected variable overhead costs.

The **variable-overhead spending variance**, arises when actual variable overhead costs differ from the amount predicted for the actual cost-driver activity:

$$\begin{matrix}\text{variable-overhead spending} \\ \text{variance}\end{matrix} = \begin{matrix}\text{actual variable} \\ \text{overhead}\end{matrix} - \left(\begin{matrix}\text{standard variable} \\ \text{overhead rate per} \\ \text{unit of cost-driver}\end{matrix} \times \begin{matrix}\text{actual cost-driver} \\ \text{activity used}\end{matrix} \right)$$

This variance combines price and quantity effects and tells us how the actual variable overhead cost compares to the predicted amount for the actual level of cost-driver activity.

Exhibit 8-9 illustrates the calculation of variable and fixed overhead variances for Dominion Company. The exhibit breaks the $500 unfavorable flexible-budget variable overhead variance for supplies into spending and efficiency variances. We compute the efficiency variance by multiplying

Exhibit 8-9
General Approach to Analysis
of Overhead Variances

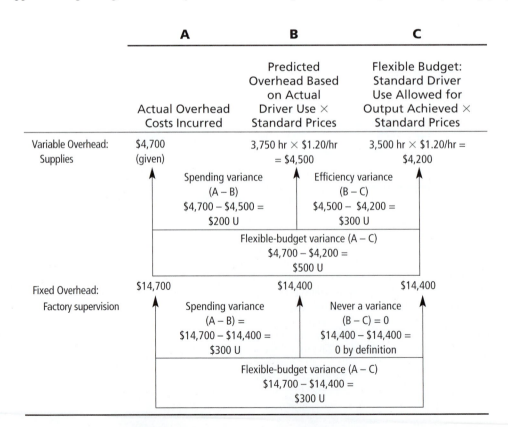

	A	**B**	**C**
	Actual Overhead Costs Incurred	Predicted Overhead Based on Actual Driver Use × Standard Prices	Flexible Budget: Standard Driver Use Allowed for Output Achieved × Standard Prices
Variable Overhead: Supplies	$4,700 (given)	3,750 hr × $1.20/hr = $4,500	3,500 hr × $1.20/hr = $4,200

Spending variance (A – B)
$4,700 – $4,500 = $200 U

Efficiency variance (B – C)
$4,500 – $4,200 = $300 U

Flexible-budget variance (A – C)
$4,700 – $4,200 = $500 U

Fixed Overhead: Factory supervision	$14,700	$14,400	$14,400

Spending variance (A – B) =
$14,700 – $14,400 = $300 U

Never a variance (B – C) = 0
$14,400 – $14,400 = 0 by definition

Flexible-budget variance (A – C)
$14,700 – $14,400 = $300 U

the standard variable overhead rate times the difference between the quantity of the cost driver used and the quantity of the cost driver allowed for the output achieved. For Dominion Company, standards allow 1/2 hour of the cost driver direct labor for each unit of output, or 3,500 hours allowed for the 7,000 units of output achieved. Therefore, the flexible budget amount of $4,200 for supplies in Exhibit 8-6 translates to $4,200 ÷ 3,500 hours = $1.20 per direct-labor hour allowed for output achieved. Because Dominion Company used 3,750 labor hours when the standard for production of 7,000 units is 1/2 hour/unit × 7,000 units = 3,500 standard hours allowed, it used an excess of 250 labor hours. Each labor hour drives $1.20 of variable overhead, so the excess labor hours drive 250 units × $1.20/unit = $300 of extra variable overhead costs.

$$\begin{array}{l}\text{variable-overhead}\\ \text{efficiency variance} \\ \text{for supplies}\end{array} = \left(\begin{array}{c}\text{actual direct-}\\ \text{labor hours}\end{array} - \begin{array}{c}\text{standard direct-labor}\\ \text{hours allowed}\end{array}\right) \times \begin{array}{c}\text{standard}\\ \text{variable-overhead}\\ \text{rate per hour}\end{array}$$

$$= \left(\begin{array}{c}3,750\text{ actual}\\ \text{hours}\end{array} - \begin{array}{c}3,500\text{ standard}\\ \text{hours allowed}\end{array}\right) \times \$1.20\text{ per hour}$$

$$= (250\text{ excess hours}) \times \$1.20\text{ per hour}$$

$$= \$300\text{ unfavorable}$$

This example illustrates a general principle: When actual cost-driver activity exceeds the activity allowed for the actual output achieved, variable-overhead efficiency variances are unfavorable and vice versa. In essence, the variable-overhead efficiency variance tells management how much variable overhead cost it wastes if the variance is unfavorable (or saves, if the variance is favorable) due to cost-driver activity.

The other component of the flexible-budget variance measures control of overhead spending given actual cost-driver activity. The variable-overhead spending variance is the difference between the actual variable overhead and the amount of variable overhead predicted when using 3,750 actual direct-labor hours:

$$\begin{array}{l}\text{variable-overhead spending}\\ \text{variance for supplies}\end{array} = \begin{array}{c}\text{actual variable}\\ \text{overhead}\end{array} - \left(\begin{array}{c}\text{standard variable}\\ \text{overhead rate}\end{array} \times \begin{array}{c}\text{actual direct-}\\ \text{labor hours used}\end{array}\right)$$

$$= \$4,700 - (\$1.20 \times 3,750)$$

$$= \$4,700 - \$4,500$$

$$= \$200\text{ unfavorable}$$

Like other variances, a variable-overhead variance does not by itself identify the causes of results that differ from the static and flexible budgets. The distinction between efficiency and spending variances for variable overhead provides a springboard for more investigation, but the only way for management to discover why overhead performance did not agree with the budget is to investigate possible causes.

Fixed Overhead Variances

The framework for analysis of fixed overhead variances differs from the framework for variable cost variances. Consider factory supervision, a fixed cost, shown at the bottom of Exhibit 8-9. The flexible budget in column B based on actual use of the cost driver and the flexible budget in column C based on standard use of the cost driver are always the same. Why? Because fixed overhead does not vary with the level of use of the cost driver. Because there is no difference between columns B and C, the entire fixed overhead flexible-budget variance in Exhibit 8-9 is due to the difference between columns A and B. This difference between the actual fixed-overhead cost in column A and the budgeted cost in columns B and C is the **fixed-overhead spending variance**. For example, Dominion Company's factory supervision fixed-overhead spending variance is the flexible-budget variance of $14,700 − $14,400 = $300 unfavorable, the difference between the actual cost of factory supervision and the budgeted fixed amount.

In Chapter 13, you will encounter a second type of fixed-overhead variance, the production-volume variance. Because this second type of variance does not involve the control of costs, we consider only the fixed-overhead spending variance in this chapter.

Objective 8
Compute the fixed-overhead spending variance.

Summary Problem for Your Review

PROBLEM

The following questions are based on the data contained in the Dominion Company illustration used in this chapter.

- Direct materials: standard, 5 pounds per unit at $2 per pound
- Direct labor: standard, 1/2 hour at $16 per hour

Suppose the following were the actual results for production of 8,500 units:

- Direct materials: Dominion purchased and used 46,000 pounds at an actual unit price of $1.85 per pound, for an actual total cost of $85,100.
- Direct labor: Dominion used 4,125 hours of labor at an actual hourly rate of $16.80, for a total actual cost of $69,300.

1. Compute the flexible-budget variance and the price and quantity variances for direct labor and direct material.

2. In requirement 1, you should have computed a direct-materials price variance of $6,900 favorable. Is this a good outcome? Explain.

SOLUTION

1. The variances are as follows:

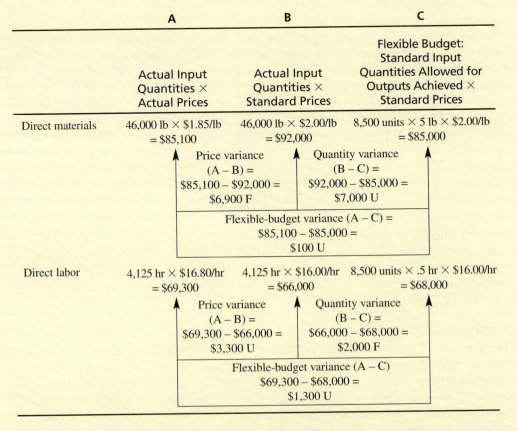

2. The favorable price variance may not be a good outcome. When prices are low, it may motivate Dominion Company managers to buy extra inventory in excess of its immediate needs, causing extra storage and handling costs. The favorable price variance may also mean that lower quality material has been purchased. The favorable materials price variance is a good outcome only if it exceeds any unfavorable material, labor, and overhead variances caused by the volume and quality of materials purchased.

Highlights to Remember

1. **Distinguish between flexible budgets and static budgets.** Flexible budgets are geared to changing levels of cost-driver activity rather than to the single level of the static budget. Organizations tailor flexible budgets to particular levels of sales or cost-driver activity—before or after the fact. Flexible budgets tell how much revenue and cost to expect for any level of activity.

2. **Use flexible-budget formulas to construct a flexible budget based on the volume of sales.** Cost functions, or flexible-budget formulas, reflect fixed- and variable-cost behavior and allow managers to compute budgets for any volume of output achieved. We compute the flexible-budget amounts for variable costs by multiplying the variable cost per unit of output times the level of output. The flexible-budgeted fixed cost is a lump sum, independent of the level of output (within the relevant range).

3. **Prepare an activity-based flexible budget.** When a significant portion of operating costs varies with cost drivers other than volume of production, a company benefits from using activity-based flexible budgets. These budgets are based on budgeted costs for each activity and related cost driver.

4. **Explain the performance evaluation relationship between static budgets, flexible budgets, and actual results.** The differences or variances between the static budget and the flexible budget are due to activity levels, not cost control. The variances between the flexible budget and actual costs reflect cost control given the achieved level of activity.

5. **Compute activity-level variances and flexible-budget variances.** The flexible-budget variance is the difference between the actual result and the corresponding flexible-budget amount. The activity-level variance is the difference between the static budget and the corresponding flexible budget amount.

6. **Compute and interpret price and quantity variances for materials and labor.** Managers often find it useful to subdivide flexible-budget variances for variable inputs into price (or rate or spending) and quantity (or usage or efficiency) variances. Price variances reflect the effects of changing input prices, holding inputs constant at actual input use. Quantity variances reflect the effects of different levels of input usage, holding prices constant at standard prices.

7. **Compute variable-overhead spending and efficiency variances.** The variable-overhead spending variance is the difference between the actual variable overhead and the amount of variable overhead budgeted for the actual level of cost-driver activity. The variable-overhead efficiency variance is the difference between the actual cost-driver activity and the amount of cost-driver activity allowed for the actual output achieved, costed at the standard variable-overhead rate.

8. **Compute the fixed-overhead spending variance.** The fixed-overhead spending variance is the difference between the actual fixed overhead expenditures and the budgeted amount of fixed overhead. ■

Accounting Vocabulary

activity-based flexible
   budget, p. 308
activity-level variances, p. 308
currently attainable
   standards, p. 313
effectiveness, p. 310
efficiency, p. 310
efficiency variance, p. 319
expected cost, p. 313
favorable cost variance, p. 306
favorable profit variance, p. 305
favorable revenue
   variance, p. 306

fixed-overhead spending
   variance, p. 323
flexible budget, p. 306
flexible-budget
   variances, p. 307
ideal standards, p. 313
perfection standards, p. 313
price variance, p. 317
quantity variance, p. 317
rate variance, p. 319
sales-activity variances, p. 310
standard cost, p. 313
static budget, p. 306

static-budget variance, p. 306
unfavorable cost
   variance, p. 306
unfavorable profit
   variance, p. 306
unfavorable revenue
   variance, p. 306
usage variance, p. 319
variable budget, p. 306
variable-overhead spending
   variance, p. 322
variable-overhead efficiency
   variance, p. 322

Fundamental Assignment Material

8-A1 Flexible and Static Budgets

Burton Transportation Company's general manager reports quarterly to the company president on the firm's operating performance. The company uses a budget based on detailed expectations for the forthcoming quarter. The general manager has just received the condensed quarterly performance report shown in Exhibit 8-10.

Although the general manager was upset about not obtaining enough revenue, she was happy that her cost performance was favorable; otherwise, her net income would be even worse.

The president was not satisfied with the performance report and remarked, "I can see some merit in comparing actual performance with budgeted performance because we can see whether actual revenue coincided with our best guess for budget purposes. But I can't see how this performance report helps me evaluate cost-control performance."

1. Prepare a columnar flexible budget for Burton Transportation at revenue levels of $7,200,000, $8,000,000, and $8,800,000. Use the format of the last three columns of Exhibit 8-2, page 307. Assume that the prices and mix of products sold are equal to the budgeted prices and mix.
2. Write out the flexible budget formula for costs as a function of revenue.
3. Prepare a condensed table showing the static budget variance, the sales-activity variance, and the flexible-budget variance. Use the format of Exhibit 8-5, page 310.

8-A2 Activity Level Variances

The systems consulting department of Bennett Baseball Products designs systems for data collection, encoding, and reporting to fit the needs of other departments within the company. An overall cost driver is the number of requests made to the systems consulting department. The expected variable cost of handling a request was $500, and the number of requests expected for June 20X1 was 75. Bennett budgeted its monthly fixed costs for the department (salaries, equipment depreciation, space costs) at $65,000.

The actual number of requests serviced by systems consulting in June 20X1 was 90, and the total costs incurred by the department was $120,000. Of that amount, $76,000 was for fixed costs.

Compute the static budget variances and the flexible-budget variances for variable and fixed costs for the systems consulting department for June 20X1.

	Budget	Actual	Variance
Net revenue	$8,000,000	$7,600,000	$400,000 U
Variable Costs			
Fuel	$ 160,000	$ 157,000	$ 3,000 F
Repairs and maintenance	80,000	85,000	5,000 U
Supplies and miscellaneous	800,000	788,000	12,000 F
Variable payroll	5,360,000	5,200,000	160,000 F
Total variable costs*	$6,400,000	$6,230,000	$ 170,000 F
Fixed Costs			
Supervision	$ 180,000	$ 183,000	$ 3,000 U
Rent	160,000	160,000	—
Depreciation	480,000	480,000	—
Other fixed costs	160,000	158,000	2,000 F
Total fixed costs	980,000	981,000	$ 1,000 U
Total fixed and variable costs	$7,380,000	$7,211,000	$ 169,000 F
Operating income	$ 620,000	$ 389,000	$231,000 U

U = Unfavorable. F = Favorable.

*For purposes of this analysis, assume that all of these costs are totally variable with respect to sales revenue. In practice, many are mixed and would have to be subdivided into variable and fixed components before a meaningful analysis could be made. Also, assume that the prices and mix of services sold remain unchanged.

Exhibit 8-10
Burton Transportation Operating Performance Report
Second Quarter, 20X1

8-A3 Direct-Material and Direct-Labor Variances

Barber Brass manufactures trumpets, trombones, tubas, and other brass instruments. The following standards were developed for a line of trumpets:

	Standard Inputs Expected for Each Unit of Output Achieved	Standard Price per Unit of Input
Direct materials	5 pounds	$10 per pound
Direct labor	10 hours	$25 per hour

During April, Barber scheduled 550 trumpets for production. However, the company produced only 525.

Barber purchased and used 3,100 pounds of direct materials at a unit price of $8.50 per pound. It used 5,500 hours of direct labor at an actual rate of $26.00 per hour.

1. Compute the standard cost per trumpet for direct materials and direct labor.
2. Compute the price variances and quantity variances for direct materials and direct labor.
3. Based on these sketchy data, what clues for investigation are provided by the variances?

8-B1 Summary Performance Reports

Consider the following data for David Skold Tax Services, a firm much like **H&R Block**:
- Static budget data: sales, 2,500 clients at $350 each; variable costs, $250 per client; fixed costs, $150,000
- Actual results at actual prices: sales, 3,000 clients at $360 per client; variable costs, $800,000; fixed costs, $159,500
1. Prepare a summary performance report similar to Exhibit 8-5, page 310.
2. Fill in the blanks:

Static-budget income		$ —
Variances		
Sales-activity variances	$ —	
Flexible-budget variances	—	—
Actual income		$ —

8-B2 Material and Labor Variances

Consider the following data for a manufacturing company:

	Direct Materials	Direct Labor
Actual price per unit of input (lb and hr)	$ 7.80	$12.00
Standard price per unit of input	$ 7.00	$12.75
Standard inputs allowed per unit of output	10	2
Actual units of input	116,000	29,000
Actual units of output (product)	14,400	14,400

1. Compute the price, quantity, and flexible-budget variances for direct materials and direct labor. Use U or F to indicate whether the variances are unfavorable or favorable.
2. Prepare a plausible explanation for the performance.

8-B3 Variable-Overhead Variances

You have been asked to prepare an analysis of the overhead costs in the order processing department of a mail-order company like **Harriet Carter Corporation**. As an initial step, you prepare a summary of some events that bear on overhead for the most recent period. Variable overhead is applied based on hours of processing-clerk labor. The standard variable-overhead rate per order was $.06. The rate of 10 orders per hour is regarded as standard productivity per clerk. The total overhead incurred was $203,600, of which $135,900 was fixed. The fixed-overhead spending variance was $400 unfavorable.

The variable-overhead flexible-budget variance was $5,600 unfavorable. The variable-overhead spending variance was $3,000 favorable.

Find the following:

1. Variable-overhead efficiency variance
2. Actual hours of input
3. Standard hours of input allowed for output achieved
4. Budgeted-fixed overhead

MyAccountingLab ## Additional Assignment Material

QUESTIONS

8-1 Distinguish between favorable and unfavorable cost (and revenue) variances.

8-2 "The flex in the flexible budget relates solely to variable costs." Do you agree? Explain.

8-3 "We want a flexible budget because costs are difficult to predict. We need the flexibility to change budgeted costs as input prices change." Does a flexible budget serve this purpose? Explain.

8-4 Explain the role of understanding cost behavior and cost-driver activities for flexible budgeting.

8-5 "An activity-based flexible budget has a 'flex' for every activity." Do you agree? Explain.

8-6 "Effectiveness and efficiency go hand in hand. You can't have one without the other." Do you agree? Explain.

8-7 Differentiate between a static-budget variance and a flexible-budget variance.

8-8 "Managers should be rewarded for favorable variances and punished for unfavorable variances." Do you agree? Explain.

8-9 "A good control system places the blame for every unfavorable variance on someone in the organization. Without affixing blame, no one will take responsibility for cost control." Do you agree? Explain.

8-10 Who is usually responsible for sales-activity variances? Why?

8-11 Differentiate between perfection standards and currently attainable standards.

8-12 What are two possible approaches to setting "currently attainable standards"?

8-13 "A standard is one point in a band or range of acceptable outcomes." Evaluate this statement.

8-14 "Price variances should be computed even if prices are regarded as being outside of company control." Do you agree? Explain.

8-15 What are some common causes of unfavorable quantity variances?

8-16 "Failure to meet price standards is the responsibility of the purchasing officer." Do you agree? Explain.

8-17 "The variable-overhead efficiency variance is not really an overhead variance." Evaluate this statement.

8-18 Why do the techniques for controlling overhead differ from those for controlling direct materials?

CRITICAL THINKING EXERCISES

8-19 Interpretation of Favorable and Unfavorable Variances

A division budgeted an operating profit of $3,000 on sales of $8,000 and relevant costs of $5,000. However, at the beginning of the period one of the division's machines broke down and could not be fixed until the end of the period. When the machine broke, the division manager determined that there were two feasible alternatives: First, production and sales could be cut back by 25%, reducing sales to $6,000 and relevant costs to $4,000. (Note that costs are not reduced by 25% because some of the costs are fixed.) Second, a replacement machine could be obtained and installed, allowing sales to be maintained at $8,000 but increasing relevant costs to $6,500. The division manager analyzed the alternatives and concluded that revenues less costs would be greater if sales were reduced ($6,000 less $4,000 = $2,000 operating profit) than if the replacement machine was obtained ($8,000 less $6,500 = $1,500 operating profit). The manager, therefore, chose not to replace the machine. However, because revenue was lower than planned by $2,000, there is an unfavorable revenue variance of $2,000. Comment on how the unfavorable revenue variance should be interpreted in evaluating the performance of the manager.

8-20 Marketing Responsibility for Sales-Activity Variances

Suppose a company budgeted an operating profit of $100 on sales of $1,000. Actual sales were $900. The marketing department claimed that because sales were down 10%, it was responsible for only 10% of $100 or $10 of any drop in profit. Any further shortfall must be someone else's responsibility. Comment on this claim.

8-21 Production Responsibility for Flexible-Budget Variances

Suppose a plant manager planned to produce 100 units of product at a total cost of $1,000. Instead, actual production was 10% higher at 110 units. When costs came in at less than a 10% increase in costs or $1,100, the plant manager claimed that she should get credit for a favorable variance equal to the amount by which the actual costs fell short of $1,100. Comment on this claim.

8-22 Responsibility of Purchasing Manager

A company's purchasing manager bought 5,000 pounds of material for $5.50 per pound instead of the budgeted $6.00 per pound, resulting in a favorable variance of $2,500. The company has a policy of rewarding employees with 20% of any cost savings they generate. Before awarding a $500 bonus to the purchasing manager, what other variances would you look at to determine the total effect of the purchasing decision? Explain.

8-23 Variable-Overhead Efficiency Variance

Birmingham Company had a $1,000 U variable-overhead efficiency variance. Neither the plant manager, who was responsible primarily for labor scheduling, nor the administrative manager, who was responsible for most support services, felt responsible for the variance. Who should be held responsible? Why?

EXERCISES

8-24 Flexible Budget

Stang Sports Equipment Company made 40,000 basketballs in a given year. Its manufacturing costs were $256,000 variable and $95,000 fixed. Assume that no price changes will occur in the following year and that no changes in production methods are applicable. Compute the budgeted cost for producing 44,000 basketballs in the following year.

8-25 Basic Flexible Budget

The superintendent of police of the city of Rollag is attempting to predict the costs of operating a fleet of police cars. Among the items of concern are fuel, $.24 per mile, and depreciation, $6,000 per car per year.

The manager is preparing a flexible budget for the coming year. Prepare the flexible-budget amounts for fuel and depreciation for each car at a level of 30,000, 40,000, and 50,000 miles.

8-26 Flexible Budget

Scottish Designs has a department that makes high-quality leather cases for iPods. Consider the following data for a recent month:

	Budget Formula per Unit	Various Levels of Output		
Units		6,000	7,000	8,000
Sales	$15	$?	$?	$?
Variable costs				
Direct materials	?	39,000	?	?
Hand labor	4	?	?	?
Fixed costs				
Depreciation		?	19,000	?
Salaries		?	?	34,000

Fill in the unknowns.

8-27 Basic Flexible Budget

The budgeted prices for materials and direct labor per unit of finished product are $11 and $5, respectively. The production manager is delighted about the following data:

	Static Budget	Actual Costs	Variance
Direct materials	$77,000	$72,000	$5,000 F
Direct labor	35,000	31,000	4,000 F

Is the manager's happiness justified? Prepare a report that might provide a more detailed explanation of why the static budget was not achieved. Good output was 5,800 units.

8-28 Activity-Level Variances

Materials-support costs for the Pittsburgh Steel Company (PSC) are variable costs that depend on the weight of material (plate steel, castings, etc.) moved. For the current budget period and based on scheduled production, PSC expected to move 750,000 pounds of material at a cost of $.25 per pound. Several orders were canceled by customers, and PSC moved only 650,000 pounds of material. Total materials support costs for the period were $177,000.

Compare actual support costs to the static-budget support costs by computing static budget, activity-level, and flexible-budget variances for materials-support costs.

8-29 Direct-Material Variances

Bangkok Custom Shirt Company uses a special fabric in the production of dress shirts. During August, Bangkok Custom Shirt purchased and used 7,900 square yards in the production of 3,800 shirts at a total cost of B5,490,500. (B stands for the Thai baht. There are roughly 35 bahts to a U.S. dollar.) The standard allows two yards at B700 per yard for each shirt.

Calculate the material price variance and the material quantity variance.

8-30 Labor Variances

Elizabeth Chuk, the manager of the city of Reno road maintenance shop uses standards to judge performance. Because a clerk mistakenly discarded some labor records, however, Liz has only partial data for April. She knows that the total direct-labor flexible-budget variance was $1,855 favorable. Moreover, a recent pay raise produced an unfavorable labor price variance for April of $1,085. The actual hours of input were 1,750 and the standard labor price was $14 per hour.

1. Find the actual labor rate per hour.
2. Determine the standard hours allowed for the output achieved.

8-31 Quantity Variances

Tanzania Toy Company produced 10,000 stuffed bears. The standard direct-material allowance is 1.75 kilograms per bear, at a cost per kilo of $3. Actually, 16,500 kilos of materials (input) were used to produce the 10,000 bears (output).

Similarly, the standard allowance for direct labor is 4.6 hours to produce one bear, and the standard hourly labor cost is $6. But 48,000 hours (input) were used to produce the 10,000 bears.

Compute the quantity variances for direct materials and direct labor.

8-32 Labor and Material Variances

Standard direct-labor rate	$14.00
Actual direct-labor rate	$12.20
Standard direct-labor hours	12,000
Direct-labor quantity variance—unfavorable	$9,800
Standard unit price of materials	$ 4.50
Actual quantity purchased and used	1,800
Standard quantity allowed for actual production	1,650
Materials purchase price variance—favorable	$ 198

1. Compute the actual hours worked, rounded to the nearest hour.
2. Compute the actual purchase price per unit of materials, rounded to the nearest penny.

8-33 Material and Labor Variances

Consider the following data:

	Direct Materials	Direct Labor
Costs incurred: actual inputs × actual prices incurred	$154,000	$77,800
Actual inputs × expected prices	170,000	74,000
Standard inputs allowed for actual outputs achieved × expected prices	172,500	71,300

Compute the price, quantity, and flexible-budget variances for direct materials and direct labor. Use U or F to indicate whether the variances are unfavorable or favorable.

PROBLEMS

8-34 National Park Service

The National Park Service prepared the following budget for one of its national parks for 20X1:

Revenue from fees	$5,000,000
Variable costs (miscellaneous)	500,000
Contribution margin	$4,500,000
Fixed costs (miscellaneous)	4,500,000
Income	$ 0

The fees were based on an average of 25,000 vehicle-admission days (vehicles multiplied by number of days in parks) per week for the 20-week season, multiplied by average entry and other fees of $10 per vehicle-admission day.

The season was booming for the first 4 weeks. During the fifth week, however, there were major forest fires. A large percentage of the park was scarred by the fires. As a result, the number of visitors to the park dropped sharply during the remainder of the season.

Total revenues fell $1.2 million short of the original budget. Variable costs fell as expected, and fixed costs were unaffected except for hiring extra firefighters at a cost of $300,000.

Prepare a columnar summary of performance, showing the original (static) budget, sales-activity variances, flexible budget, flexible-budget variances, and actual results.

8-35 Flexible and Static Budgets

Beta Gamma Sigma, the business honor society, recently held a dinner dance. The original (static) budget and actual results were as follows:

	Static Budget	Actual	Variance
Attendees	75	90	
Revenue	$2,625	$3,255	$630 F
Chicken dinners at $19.00	1,425	1,767	342 U
Beverages, $6 per person	450	466	16 U
Club rental, $75 plus 8% tax	81	81	0
Music, 3 hours at $250 per hour	750	875	125 U
Profit	$ (81)	$ 66	$147 F

1. Subdivide each variance into a sales-activity variance portion and a flexible-budget variance portion. Use the format of Exhibit 8-5, page 310.
2. Provide possible explanations for the variances.

8-36 Summary Explanation

Higgins Company produced 80,000 units, 8,000 more than budgeted. Production data are as follows. Except for physical units, all quantities are in dollars.

	Actual Results at Actual Prices	Flexible-Budget Variances	Flexible Budget	Sales-Activity Variances	Static Budget
Physical units	80,000	—	?	?	72,000
Sales	?	6,400 F	?	?	720,000
Variable costs	492,000	?	480,000	?	?
Contribution margin	?	?	?	?	?
Fixed costs	?	30,000 U	?	?	150,000
Income	?	?	?	?	?

1. Fill in the unknowns.
2. Give a brief summary explanation of why the original target income was not attained.

8-37 Explanation of Variance in Income

Damerow Credit Services produces reports for consumers about their credit ratings. The company's standard contribution margins average 70% of dollar sales, and average selling prices are $50 per report. Average productivity is four reports per hour. Some employees work for sales commissions and others for an hourly rate. The static budget for 20X1 had predicted processing 800,000 reports, but Damerow processed only 700,000 reports.

Fixed costs of rent, supervision, advertising, and other items were budgeted at $22 million, but the budget was exceeded by $600,000 because of extra advertising in an attempt to boost revenue. There were no variances from the average selling prices, but the actual commissions paid to preparers and the actual productivity per hour resulted in flexible-budget variances (i.e., total price and quantity variances) for variable costs of $900,000 unfavorable.

The president of Damerow was unhappy because the budgeted income of $6 million was not achieved. He said, "Sure, we had unfavorable variable-cost variances, but our income was down far more than that. Please explain why."

Explain why the budgeted income was not attained. Use a presentation similar to Exhibit 8-5, page 000. Enough data have been given to permit you to construct the complete exhibit by filling in the known items and then computing the unknowns. Complete your explanation by summarizing what happened, using no more than three sentences.

8-38 Activity and Flexible-Budget Variances at KFC

Suppose a chain of **KFC** franchises in Beijing had budgeted sales for 2009 of RMB 7.3 million (where RMB stands for the Chinese unit of currency, officially the renminbi, also called the yuan). Cost of goods sold and other variable costs were expected to be 60% of sales. Budgeted annual fixed costs were RMB 1.8 million. A strong Chinese economy caused actual 2009 sales to rise to RMB 9.2 million and actual profits to increase to RMB 1,570,000. Fixed costs in 2009 were as budgeted. The franchisee was pleased with the increase in profit.

1. Compute the sales-activity variance and the flexible-budget variance for income for 2009. What can the franchisee learn from these variances?
2. Suppose that in 2010 the Chinese economy weakened, and the franchise's sales fell back to the RMB 7.3 million level. Given what happened in 2009, what do you expect to happen to profits in 2010?

8-39 Summary of Airline Performance

The performance (in thousands of dollars) of Kenmore Airlines for the most recent year is shown in the following table:

	Actual Results at Actual Prices	Static Budget	Variance
Revenue	$?	$300,000	$?
Variable expenses	200,000	195,000*	5,000 U
Contribution margin	?	105,000	?
Fixed expenses	87,000	80,000	7,000 U
Income	$?	$ 25,000	$?

*Includes jet fuel of $90,000.

The static budget had been based on a budget of $.20 revenue per passenger mile. A passenger mile is one paying passenger flown one mile. An average airfare decrease of 8% had helped generate an increase in passenger miles flown that was 10% in excess of the static budget for the year.

The price per gallon of jet fuel rose above the price used to formulate the static budget. The average jet fuel price increase for the year was 10%.

1. Prepare a summary report similar to Exhibit 8-5, page 310, to help the president understand performance for the most recent year.
2. Assume that jet fuel costs are purely variable, and the quantity of fuel used was at the same level of efficiency as predicted in the static budget. What part of the flexible-budget variance for variable expenses is attributable to jet fuel expenses? Explain.

8-40 Hospital Costs and Explanation of Variances

The emergency room at Rochester General Hospital uses a flexible budget based on patients seen as the measure of activity. The hospital must maintain an adequate staff of attending and on-call physicians at all times so patient activity does not affect physician scheduling. Nurse scheduling varies as volume changes, however. A standard of .5 nurse-hours per patient visit was set. Hourly pay for nurses ranges from $9 to $18 per hour, and the average pay rate is $15 per hour. The hospital considers all materials to be supplies, a part of overhead; there are no direct materials. A statistical study showed that the cost of supplies and other variable overhead is more closely associated with nurse-hours than with patient visits. The standard for supplies and other variable overhead is $10 per nurse-hour.

The head physician of the emergency room unit, Brad Narr, is responsible for control of costs. During October the emergency room unit treated 4,000 patients. The budget and actual costs were as follows:

	Budget	Actual	Variance
Patient visits	3,800	4,000	200
Nurse-hours	1,900	2,080	180
Nursing cost	$ 28,500	$ 33,180	$4,680
Supplies and other variable overhead	19,000	20,340	1,340
Fixed costs	92,600	92,600	0
Total cost	$140,100	$146,120	$6,020

1. Calculate price and quantity variances for nursing costs.
2. Calculate spending and efficiency variances for supplies and other variable overhead.
3. The hospital's chief administrator has asked Dr. Narr to explain the variances. Provide possible explanations.

8-41 Flexible Budgeting

For the convenience of its reporters and staff based in London, **CNN** operates a motor pool. The motor pool operated with 25 vehicles until February of this year, when it acquired an additional automobile. The motor pool furnishes petrol (gasoline), oil, and other supplies for the cars and hires one mechanic who does routine maintenance and minor repairs. Major repairs are done at a nearby commercial garage. A supervisor manages the operations.

Each year the supervisor prepares an operating budget, informing CNN management of the funds needed to operate the pool. Depreciation on the automobiles is recorded in the budget in order to determine the cost per mile.

The following schedule presents the annual budget approved by the news division. The actual costs for March are compared with one-twelfth of the annual budget.

CNN London Motor Pool				
Budget Report for March 20X1				
	Annual Budget	One-Month Budget	March Actual	Over (Under)
Petrol (gasoline)	£ 82,500	£ 6,875	£ 8,200	£1,325
Oil, minor repairs, parts, and supplies	30,000	2,500	2,540	40
Outside repairs	2,700	225	50	(175)
Insurance	4,800	400	416	16
Salaries and benefits	21,600	1,800	1,800	—
Depreciation	22,800	1,900	1,976	76
Total costs	£164,400	£13,700	£14,982	£1,282
Total kilometers	1,500,000	125,000	140,000	
Cost per kilometer	£ .1096	£ .1096	£ .1070	
Number of automobiles	25	25	26	

The annual budget was constructed based on the following assumptions:

1. 25 automobiles in the pool
2. 60,000 kilometers per year per automobile
3. 8 kilometers per liter of petrol for each automobile
4. £.44 per liter of petrol
5. £.02 per kilometer for oil, minor repairs, parts, and supplies
6. £108 per automobile in outside repairs

The supervisor is unhappy with the monthly report comparing budget and actual costs for March; she claims it presents her performance unfairly. Her previous employer used flexible budgeting to compare actual costs with budgeted amounts.

1. Employing flexible-budgeting techniques, prepare a report that shows budgeted amounts, actual costs, and monthly variation for March.
2. Explain briefly the basis of your budget figure for outside repairs.

8-42 Activity-Based Flexible Budget

Cost behavior analysis for the four activity centers in the billing department of Fargo Power Company is given next.

Traceable Costs

Activity Center	Variable	Fixed	Cost-Driver Activity
Account inquiry	$ 79,910	$156,380	3,300 labor hours
Correspondence	9,800	25,584	2,800 letters
Account billing	154,377	81,400	2,440,000 lines
Bill verification	10,797	78,050	20,000 accounts

The billing department constructs a flexible budget for each activity center based on the following ranges of cost-driver activity.

Activity Center	Cost Driver	Relevant Range	
Account inquiry	Labor hours	3,000	5,000
Correspondence	Letters	2,500	3,500
Account billing	Lines	2,000,000	3,000,000
Bill verification	Accounts	15,000	25,000

1. Develop flexible-budget formulas for each of the four activity centers.
2. Compute the budgeted total cost in each activity center for each of these levels of cost-driver activity: (a) the smallest activity in the relevant range, (b) the midpoint of the relevant range, and (c) the highest activity in the relevant range.
3. Determine the total cost function for the billing department.
4. The following table gives the actual results for the billing department. Prepare a cost-control performance report comparing the flexible budget to actual results for each activity center. Compute flexible-budget variances.

Activity Center	Actual Cost-Driver Level	Actual Cost
Account inquiry	4,300 labor hours	$235,400
Correspondence	3,200 letters	38,020
Account billing	2,950,000 lines	285,000
Bill verification	23,000 accounts	105,320

8-43 Straightforward Variance Analysis

Crescent Tool Works uses a standard cost system. The month's data regarding its iron castings follow:

- Materials purchased and used, 3,300 pounds
- Direct-labor costs incurred, 5,500 hours, $42,350

- Variable-overhead costs incurred, $4,620
- Finished units produced, 1,000
- Actual materials cost, $.97 per pound
- Standard variable-overhead rate, $.80 per direct-labor hour
- Standard direct-labor cost, $8 per hour
- Standard materials cost, $1 per pound
- Standard pounds of material in a finished unit, 3
- Standard direct-labor hours per finished unit, 5

Prepare schedules of all variances, using the formats of Exhibits 8-8 and 8-9 on pages 320 and 322.

8-44 Variance Analysis

The Zurich Chocolate Company uses standard costs and a flexible budget to control its manufacture of fine chocolates. The purchasing agent is responsible for material price variances, and the production manager is responsible for all other variances. Operating data for the past week are summarized as follows:

1. Finished units produced: 4,000 boxes of chocolates.
2. Direct materials: Purchased and used, 4,300 pounds of chocolate at 15.5 Swiss francs (CHF) per pound; standard price is CHF 16 per pound. Standard allowed per box produced is 1 pound.
3. Direct labor: Actual costs, 6,400 hours at CHF 30.5, or CHF 195,200. Standard allowed per box produced is 1.5 hours. Standard price per direct-labor hour is CHF 30.
4. Variable manufacturing overhead: Actual costs, CHF 69,500. Budget formula is CHF 10 per standard direct-labor hour.

Compute the following:
- 1. a. Materials purchase-price variance
  - b. Materials quantity variance
  - c. Direct-labor price variance
  - d. Direct-labor quantity variance
  - e. Variable manufacturing-overhead spending variance
  - f. Variable manufacturing-overhead efficiency variance
  (Hint: For format, see the solution to the Summary Problem for Your Review, page 324.)
- 2. a. What is the budget allowance for direct labor?
  - b. Would it be any different if production were 5,000 boxes?

8-45 Similarity of Direct-Labor and Variable-Overhead Variances

The Kevin Koh Company has had great difficulty controlling costs in Singapore during the past 3 years. Last month, the company installed a standard-cost and flexible-budget system. A condensation of results for a department follows:

	Expected Cost per Standard Direct-Labor Hour	Flexible-Budget Variance
Lubricants	$ .60	$ 330 F
Other supplies	.30	225 U
Rework	.60	450 U
Other indirect labor	1.50	450 U
Total variable overhead	$3.00	$795 U

F = Favorable. U = Unfavorable.

The department had initially planned to manufacture 9,000 audio speaker assemblies in 6,000 standard direct-labor hours allowed. Material shortages and a heat wave resulted in the production of 8,100 units in 5,800 actual direct-labor hours. The standard wage rate is $5.25 per hour, which was $.15 higher than the actual average hourly rate.

1. Prepare a detailed performance report with two major sections: direct labor and variable overhead.
2. Prepare a summary analysis of price and quantity variances for direct labor and spending and efficiency variances for variable overhead.
3. Explain the similarities and differences between the direct-labor and variable-overhead variances. What are some of the likely causes of the overhead variances?

8-46 Material, Labor, and Overhead Variances

Poulsbo Kayak Company makes molded plastic kayaks. Standard costs for an entry-level whitewater kayak are as follows:

Direct materials, 60 lb at $5.50/lb	$330
Direct labor, 1.5 hr at $16/hr	24
Overhead, at $12 per kayak	12
Total	$366

The overhead rate assumes production of 450 kayaks per month. The overhead cost function is $2,808 + ($5.76 × number of kayaks).

During March, Poulsbo produced 430 kayaks and had the following actual results:

Direct materials purchased and used	27,000 pounds at $5.30/lb
Direct labor	670 hours at $15.90/hr
Actual overhead	$5,335

1. Compute material, labor, and overhead variances.
2. Interpret the variances.
3. Suppose the cost function for variable overhead was $3.84 per labor hour instead of $5.76 per kayak. Compute the variable-overhead efficiency variance and the total overhead spending variance. Would these variances lead you to a different interpretation of the overhead variances from the interpretation in requirement 2? Explain.

8-47 Automation and Direct Labor as Overhead

Kilgore Precision Machining (KPM) has a highly automated manufacturing process for producing a variety of auto parts. Through the use of computer-aided manufacturing and robotics, the company has reduced its labor costs to only 5% of total manufacturing costs. Consequently, the company does not account for labor as a separate item but instead accounts for labor as part of overhead.

Consider a part used in antilock braking systems. The static budget for producing 750 units in March 20X1 is as follows

Direct materials	$18,000*
Overhead	
Supplies	1,875
Power	1,310
Rent and other building services	2,815
Factory labor	1,500
Depreciation	4,500
Total manufacturing costs	$30,000

*3 lb/unit × $8/lb × 750 units.

Supplies and power are variable, and the other overhead items are fixed costs.
Actual costs in March 20X1 for producing 900 units of the brake part were as follows:

Direct materials	$21,840*
Overhead	
Supplies	2,132
Power	1,612
Rent and other building services	2,775
Factory labor	1,618
Depreciation	4,500
Total manufacturing costs	$34,477

*KPM purchased and used 2,800 pounds of materials at $7.80 per pound.

1. Compute (a) the direct-materials price and quantity variances and (b) the flexible-budget variance for each overhead item.
2. Comment on the way KPM accounts for and controls factory labor.

8-48 Standard Material Allowances

Chesapeake Chemical Company supplies primarily industrial users. Your superior has asked you to develop a standard product cost for a new solution the company plans to introduce.

The new chemical solution is made by combining altium and bollium, boiling the mixture, adding credix, and bottling the resulting solution in 20-liter containers. The initial mix, which is 20 liters in volume, consists of 24 kilograms of altium and 19.2 liters of bollium. A 20% reduction in volume occurs during the boiling process. The solution is then cooled slightly before adding 10 kilograms of credix to each 20-liter container; the addition of credix does not affect the total liquid volume.

The purchase prices of the raw materials used in the manufacture of this new chemical solution are as follows:

Altium	$2.20 per kilogram
Bollium	$4.60 per liter
Credix	$3.20 per kilogram

Determine the standard quantity for each of the raw materials needed to produce 20 liters of Chesapeake Chemical Company's new chemical solution and the total standard materials cost of 20 liters of the new product.

8-49 Role of Defective Units and Nonproductive Time in Setting Standards

Haig McNamee owns and operates McNamee Machining, a subcontractor to several aerospace industry contractors. When Mr. McNamee wins a bid to produce a piece of equipment, he sets standard costs for the production of the item. He then compares actual manufacturing costs with the standards to judge the efficiency of production.

In April 20X1, McNamee won a bid to produce 15,000 units of a shielded component used in a navigation device. Specifications for the component were very tight, and Mr. McNamee expected that on average 1 out of every 6 finished components would fail his final inspection, even if employees exercise every care in production. There was no way to identify defective items before production was complete. Therefore, the company had to produce 18,000 units to get 15,000 good components. The company set standards to include an allowance for the expected number of defective items.

Each final component contained 3.2 pounds of direct materials, and the company expected normal scrap from production to average an additional .4 pounds per unit. It expected the direct material to cost $11.40 per pound plus $.80 per pound for shipping and handling.

Machining of the components required close attention by skilled machinists. Each component required 4 hours of machining time. McNamee paid the machinists $20 per hour, and they worked 40-hour weeks. Of the 40 hours, employees spent an average of 32 hours directly on production. The other 8 hours consisted of time for breaks and waiting time when machines were broken down or there was no work to be done. Nevertheless, the company considered all payments to machinists to be direct labor, whether or not they represented time spent directly on production. In addition to the basic wage rate, McNamee paid fringe benefits averaging $6 per hour and payroll taxes of 10% of the basic wages.

Determine the standard cost of direct materials and direct labor for each good unit of output.

8-50 Review of Major Points in This Chapter

The following questions are based on the Dominion Company data contained in Exhibit 8-1 (page 305) and in the table near the top of page 317.

1. Suppose actual production and sales were 8,000 units instead of 7,000 units. (a) Compute the sales-activity variance. Is the performance of the marketing function the sole explanation for this variance? Why? (b) Using a flexible budget, compute the budgeted contribution margin, the budgeted income, budgeted direct material, and budgeted direct labor.
2. Suppose the following were the actual results for the production of 8,000 units.
   Direct materials: 42,000 pounds were used at an actual unit price of $1.86, for a total actual cost of $78,120.
   Direct labor: 4,140 hours were used at an actual hourly rate of $16.40, for a total actual cost of $67,896.
   Compute the flexible-budget variance and the price and quantity variances for direct materials and direct labor. Present your answers in the form shown in Exhibit 8-8, page 320.
3. Evaluate Dominion Company's performance based on the variances you calculated in numbers 1 and 2.

8-51 Review Problem on Standards and Flexible Budgets; Answers Are Provided

The Des Moines Leather Company makes a variety of leather goods. It uses standard costs and a flexible budget to aid planning and control. Budgeted variable overhead at a 45,000-direct-labor-hour level is $81,000.

During April, the company had a favorable variable-overhead efficiency variance of $2,970. Material purchases were $241,900. Actual direct-labor costs incurred were $422,100. The direct-labor quantity variance was $15,300 unfavorable. The actual average wage rate was $.60 lower than the standard average wage rate.

The company uses a variable-overhead rate of 20% of standard direct-labor cost for flexible-budgeting purposes. Actual variable overhead for the month was $92,250.

Compute the following amounts; use U or F to indicate whether variances are unfavorable or favorable.

1. Standard direct-labor cost per hour
2. Actual direct-labor hours worked
3. Total direct-labor price variance
4. Total flexible budget for direct-labor costs
5. Total direct-labor flexible-budget variance
6. Variable-overhead spending variance in total

8-51 Answers to Problem 8-51

1. $9. The variable-overhead rate is $1.80, obtained by dividing $81,000 by 45,000 hours. Therefore, the direct-labor rate must be $1.80 ÷ .20 = $9.
2. 50,250 hours. Actual costs, $422,100 ÷ ($9 − $.60) = 50,250 hours.
3. $30,150 F. 50,250 actual hours × $.60 = $30,150.
4. $436,950. Quantity variance was $15,300 U. Therefore, excess hours must have been $15,300 ÷ $9 = 1,700. Consequently, standard hours allowed must be 50,250 − 1,700 = 48,550. Flexible budget = 48,550 × $9 = $436,950.
5. $14,850 F. $436,950 − $422,100 = $14,850 F; or $30,150 F − $15,300 U = $14,850 F.
6. $7,830 U. Flexible budget = 48,550 × 1.80 = $87,390. Total variance = $92,250 − $87,390 = $4,860 U. Spending variance = Total variance − Efficiency variance = $4,860 + $2,970 = $7,830 U. Check: $92,250 − .20 × $422,100 = $7,830.

CASES

8-52 Activity and Flexible-Budget Variances

In 2003, Methodist Hospital initiated its substance abuse program, which focused on counseling current and potential substance abusers. The program was funded by a grant from the state department of health that paid $76 per visit for counseling. Pat Leizinger, CFO of Methodist Hospital, was concerned about the substance abuse program. It had never broken even and, thus, was subsidized by the other patients in the hospital. Mr. Leizinger was preparing the hospital's budget for 2010, and he did not like the substance abuse program's financial situation. The results for 2009 are shown in Exhibit 8-11:

Revenues ($76 per visit; 17,000 visits)	$1,292,000
Cost of services:	
Supplies	$ 114,750
Physician salaries	204,000
Nurse salaries	153,000
Overhead	676,200
Total direct cost of services	1,147,950
General and administrative expenses	194,250
Total expenses	1,342,200
Net loss	$ (50,200)

Exhibit 8-11
Substance Abuse Program
2009 Results

A recent cost analysis had determined the following facts about the behavior of costs in the substance abuse program:

a. Supplies and physician and nurse salaries were totally variable with respect to number of visits within the range of 15,000–30,000.

b. Variable overhead was equal to 20% of labor costs in 2009; the remainder of the overhead was fixed.

c. $181,500 of the general and administrative cost was fixed; the remainder varied with number of visits.

d. Costs in 2010 are expected to behave the same as those in 2009, except that variable-overhead costs will be 21% of labor costs in 2010 compared to only 20% of labor costs in 2009. (Fixed overhead costs will remain the same in 2010 as in 2009.)

Leizinger had been pressuring the director of the substance abuse program, Jody Lee, for the last couple of years to try to get her costs under control. Ms. Lee responded that it was a very important program for the community. Besides, the program was so close to breaking even that all it needed was a little more time and the results would be better. She predicted 18,000 visits in 2010, an increase of nearly 6%, which would certainly make the financial picture brighter.

Leizinger agreed on the importance of the program, but he also said that pressures were building from others in Methodist Hospital to eliminate programs that were a drain on the hospital's resources. Thus, he believed that if the substance abuse program was not at least at a break-even point in 2010, the program would be in jeopardy. He doesn't believe that even the increase of 1,000 visits would be enough to break even.

1. Compute the cost function for the substance abuse program for use in budgeting for 2010. That is, compute the variable cost per visit and the total annual fixed cost based on the cost analysis that Leizinger conducted.

2. Compute the budgeted profit (loss) for 2010, assuming that there will be 18,000 visits at $76 each and the costs behave as expected.

3. Suppose that Methodist Hospital accepted the budget for the substance abuse program that you computed in number 2. At the end of 2010, the actual loss for the program was $15,500 and the actual number of visits was 18,400. Explain the difference between the amount of loss you budgeted in number 2 and the actual loss of $15,500 in as much detail as you can, given the information you have. Based on this, give a one-sentence answer to each of the following questions:

a. What was the financial impact of the extra 400 visits?

b. How well did the substance abuse program control its costs in 2010?

8-53 Activity-Based Costing and Flexible Budgeting

A new printing department provides printing services to the other departments of Farmers & Mechanics Insurance Company (FMIC). Before the establishment of the in-house printing department, the departments contracted with external printers for their printing work. FMIC's printing policy is to charge departments for the variable printing costs on the basis of number of pages printed. The company recovers fixed costs in pricing of external jobs.

The first year's budget for the printing department was based on the department's expected total costs divided by the planned number of pages to be printed.

The projected annual number of pages to be printed was 420,000, and budgeted total variable costs were $420,000. Most government accounts and all internal jobs were expected to use only single-color printing. Commercial accounts use primarily four-color printing. FMIC estimated its variable costs based on the typical mix of single-color versus four-color printing and the average variable cost of printing a four-color page that is one-fourth graphics and three-fourths text. The expected annual costs for each division were as follows:

Department	Planned Pages Printed	Variable Cost per Page	Budgeted Charges
Government accounts	120,000	$1	$ 90,000
Commercial accounts	250,000	1	300,000
Central administration	50,000	1	30,000
Total	420,000		$420,000

After the first month of using the internal printing department, the printing department announced that its variable cost estimate of $1 per page was too low. The first month's actual costs were $51,000 to print 40,000 pages.

Government accounts	9,000 pages
Commercial accounts	27,500
Central administration	3,500

Three reasons were cited for higher-than-expected costs: All departments were using more printing services than planned, and government and internal jobs were using more four-color printing and more graphics than anticipated in the original variable cost projections. The printing department also argued that it would have to purchase additional four-color printing equipment if demand for four-color printing continued to grow.

1. Compare the printing department actual results, static budget, and flexible budget for the month just completed.
2. Discuss possible reasons why the printing department static budget was inaccurate.
3. An ABC study completed by a consultant indicated that printing costs are driven by number of pages (at $.35 per page), and use of colors (at $1 extra per page for color).
   a. Discuss the likely effects of using the ABC results for budgeting and control of printing department use.
   b. Discuss the assumptions regarding cost behavior implied in the ABC study results.
   c. All commercial accounts during the first month (27,500 pages) used four colors per page. Compare the cost of commercial accounts under the old and the proposed ABC system.

8-54 Analyzing Performance

Hopkins Community Hospital operates an outpatient clinic in a town several miles from the main hospital. For several years the clinic has struggled just to break even. The clinic's financial budget for 20X7 is shown in Exhibit 8-12.

On the average, billings for each patient-visit are expected to be $180. Costs in 20X7 are expected to average $183 per patient-visit, as follows:

Physician time	$ 60
Nurse and technician time	45
Supplies	15
Overhead	63
Total	$183

The clinic is generally staffed by one physician who must be present whether or not there is a patient to see. Currently, about 10% of the physician's time is idle. The clinic employs nurses and technicians to meet the actual workload necessitated by patient appointments. Their cost averages $30 per hour, and usage varies proportionately with the number of patient-visits. Supplies cost is also variable with respect to patient-visits. Fixed overhead in 20X7 was expected to be $180,000; the remaining $72,000 of overhead varies with respect to patient visits. Included in the fixed overhead was $30,000 of hospital-wide administrative costs that the hospital allocates to the clinic and $37,500 of depreciation on the clinic's property and equipment.

Cindy Ryden, controller of Hopkins Community Hospital, reported the actual loss of $20,200 in 20X7 shown next. This represented the fifth straight year of losses. She does not feel it is right for patients in the main hospital to subsidize those using the clinic. Therefore, she suggested that unless the situation could be changed, the clinic should be closed. Brett Johnson, administrative vice president of the hospital, charged with oversight of the clinic, disagreed: "We provide a valuable service to the community with the clinic. Even if we are losing money, it is worthwhile to keep it open."

		Total		Per Patient
Revenues (4,000 patients at $180 each)			$720,000	$180
Cost of services				
Physicians	$240,000			
Nurses and technicians	180,000			
Supplies	60,000			
Overhead	252,000		732,000	183
Net loss			$ (12,000)	$ (3)

Exhibit 8-12
Outpatient Clinic
20X7 Budget

At the end of 20X7, the clinic's actual results for the year were as follows:

		Total
Revenues (3,800 patients at $180)		$684,000
Cost of services		
Physicians	$231,000	
Nurses and technicians (5,800 hours)	182,700	
Supplies	58,500	
Overhead	232,000	704,200
Net loss		$ (20,200)

1. Would Hopkins Community Hospital have saved money in 20X7 if the outpatient clinic was closed? Explain.
2. Explain the difference between the budgeted loss of $12,000 and the actual loss of $20,200 (that is, the static-budget variance of $8,200) in as much detail as possible. From the analysis of the 20X7 results, what actions would you suggest to avoid a loss in 20X8?

8-55 Complete Variance Analysis

Gates Video Games manufactures video game machines. Market saturation and technological innovations have caused pricing pressures that have resulted in declining profits. To stem the slide in profits until the company can introduce new products, top management has turned its attention to both manufacturing economies and increased production. To realize these objectives, management developed an incentive program to reward production managers who contribute to an increase in the number of units produced and achieve cost reductions. In addition, the company instituted a JIT purchasing program so that it purchases raw materials on an as-needed basis.

The production managers have responded to the pressure to improve manufacturing performance in several ways that have resulted in an increase in the number of completed units over normal production levels. The video game machines put together by the assembly group require parts from both the printed circuit boards (PCB) and the reading heads (RH) departments. To attain increased production levels, the PCB and RH departments started rejecting parts from suppliers that previously would have been tested and modified to meet manufacturing standards. Preventive maintenance on machines used in the production of these parts has been postponed with only emergency repair work being performed to keep production lines moving. The maintenance staff is concerned that there will be serious breakdowns and unsafe operating conditions.

The more aggressive assembly group production supervisors have pressured maintenance personnel to attend to their machines at the expense of other groups. This has resulted in machine downtime in the PCB and RH departments which, when coupled with demands for accelerated parts delivery by the assembly department, has led to more frequent parts rejections and increased friction among departments. Gates Video Games operates under a standard-costing system. The standard costs at a production level of 24,000 units per year are in part A of Exhibit 8-13.

Gates Video Games prepares monthly income statements based on actual expenses. Part B of Exhibit 8-13 shows the statement for May, when production and sales both reached 2,200 units. The budgeted sales price was $200 per unit, and budgeted (normal) production and sales were 24,000 units per year. Top management was surprised by the low profit in spite of increased sales for May. The original budget had called for income before taxes of $62,000, and with the added sales, the president had expected at least $68,200 of income ($6,200 more income; 200 extra units × $31 per unit). The president called on Michelle Barber, director of cost management, to report on the reasons for the shortfall in income. After a thorough review of the data, Barber prepared the report in part C of Exhibit 8-13.

1. Prepare a budgeted income statement in contribution margin format for Gates Video Games showing why the company expected income before taxes to be $62,000.
2. Assume that you have been given Michelle Barber's task. Prepare a complete analysis explaining the reason for the difference between the original projected income before taxes of $62,000 and the actual of $47,740. Compute all the variances that are helpful in explaining this difference, and explain what you learn from the variances.

	Standard Cost per Unit		
	Quantity	Cost	Total
A. Standard Cost Report			
Direct materials:			
Housing unit	1 unit	$ 20	$ 20
Printed circuit boards (PCB)	2 boards	15	30
Reading heads (RH)	4 heads	10	40
Direct labor:			
Assembly department	2.0 hours	8	$ 16
PCB department	1.0 hour	9	9
RH department	1.5 hours	10	15
Overhead:			
Variable	4.5 hours	$ 2	$ 9
Fixed	4.5 hours	4	18
Total manufacturing cost per unit			$157
Selling and administrative:			
Fixed		$ 12	$ 12
Total standard cost per unit			$169
B. Income Statement for May			
Revenues (2,200 units)		$440,000	
Variable costs:			
Direct materials	220,400		
Direct labor	93,460		
Variable overhead	18,800		
Fixed costs:			
Overhead	37,600		
Selling and administrative	22,000		
Total costs		392,260	
Income before taxes		$ 47,740	

C. Usage Report for May		
Cost Item	Actual Quantity	Actual Cost
Direct materials:		
Housing units	2,200 units	$ 44,000
Printed circuit boards	4,700 boards	75,200
Reading heads	9,200 heads	101,200
Direct labor:		
Assembly department	3,900 hours	31,200
PCB department	2,400 hours	23,760
RH department	3,500 hours	38,500
Overhead:		
Variable		18,800
Fixed		37,600
Total manufacturing costs		$370,260

Exhibit 8-13
Gates Video Games

NIKE 10-K PROBLEM

8-56 Performance Standards

Examine Nike's income statement shown in condensed form as "Results of Operations" for fiscal years 2006, 2007, and 2008 in Appendix C. Suppose that Nike used results for 2007 to set standards for 2008. Also assume that cost of sales is a variable cost and that selling and administrative costs are fixed costs. Prepare a statement showing budgeted income before interest, other income, and income taxes for 2008 based on the assumption that sales (and variable costs) will grow by 10%. Using the actual results for 2008, determine the static-budget variance, the sales-activity variance, and the flexible-budget variance.

EXCEL APPLICATION EXERCISE

8-57 Flexible-Budget and Sales-Activity Variances

Goal: Create an Excel spreadsheet to prepare a summary performance report that identifies flexible-budget and sales-activity variances. Use the results to answer questions about your findings.

Scenario: David Skold Tax Services has asked you to prepare a summary performance report identifying its flexible-budget and sales-activity variances. The background data for the summary performance report appears in the Fundamental Assignment Material 8-B1. Prepare the summary performance report using a format similar to Exhibit 8-5.

When you have completed your spreadsheet, answer the following questions:

1. What caused the flexible-budget variance for sales?
2. What was the change in actual income compared to the income calculated in the static budget?
3. Can the amount in question 2 be explained by the flexible-budget and sales-activity variances? Explain.

Step-by-Step:

1. Open a new Excel spreadsheet.
2. In column A, create a bold-faced heading that contains the following:
   Row 1: Chapter 8 Decision Guideline
   Row 2: Skold Tax Services
   Row 3: Summary Performance Report
   Row 4: Today's Date
3. Merge and center the four heading rows across columns A–H.
4. In column A, create the following row headings:
   Row 8: Clients
   Skip a row.
   Row 10: Sales
   Row 11: Variable Costs
   Row 12: Contribution Margin
   Row 13: Fixed Costs
   Skip a row.
   Row 15: Operating Income
5. Change the format of Contribution margin (row 12) and Operating income (row 15) to boldfaced headings.

   Note: Adjust width of column A to accommodate row headings.

6. In row 7, create the following bold-faced, center-justified column headings:
   Column B: Actual Results at Actual Activity
   Column C: Flexible-Budget Variances
   Skip a column.
   Column E: Flexible Budget at Actual Activity
   Column F: Sales-Activity Variances
   Skip a column.
   Column H: Static Budget
7. Change the format of the column headings in row 7 to permit the titles to be displayed on multiple lines within a single cell.

   Alignment tab: Wrap Text: Checked

   Note: Adjust column widths so that headings use only two lines. Adjust row height to ensure that row is same height as adjusted headings.

8. Change format of the column width of columns D and G to a size of 2.
9. Use the scenario data to fill in client and fixed cost amounts for actual, flexible-budget, and static-budget columns as well as variable costs for the actual column.
10. Calculate variable costs for flexible-budget and static budget columns. Use appropriate formulas to calculate sales, contribution margin, and operating income amounts for actual, flexible-budget, and static-budget columns.
11. Use appropriate formulas to calculate flexible-budget and sales-activity variances and display as absolute values.
    =ABS(*variance formula*)
12. Use one of the following formula templates to indicate whether variances are favorable (F) or unfavorable (U):
    =IF(*variance formula*>0,"F",IF(*variance formula*<0,"U","–"))

For sales, margin and income variances only.
=IF(*variance formula*<0,"F",IF(*variance formula*>0,"U","–"))
For client, variable and fixed cost variances only.

Hint: Go to the "Help" text and type "copy formulas" in the search area to obtain instructions for copying formulas from one cell to another. If done correctly, you should have to type in each of the formula templates only once.

13. Format all amounts as follows:

Number:	Category:	
	Decimal places:	0
	Symbol:	None
	Negative numbers:	Red with parenthesis

14. Change the format of the amounts for sales, contribution margin, and operating income to display a dollar symbol.
15. Change the format of the operating income amounts for actual, flexible budget, and static budget to display as bold.
16. Change the format of the row headings for contribution margin and operating income to display as indented.

Alignment tab:	Horizontal:	Left (Indent)
	Indent:	I

Note: Adjust width of column A to accommodate row headings.

17. Save your work to disk, and print a copy for your files.

Note: Print your spreadsheet using landscape format in order to ensure that all columns appear on one page.

COLLABORATIVE LEARNING EXERCISE

8-58 Setting Standards

Form groups of two to six persons each. The groups should each select a simple product or service. Be creative, but do not pick a product or service that is too complex. For those having difficulty choosing a product or service, some possibilities are as follows:

- One dozen chocolate-chip cookies
- A 10-mile taxi ride
- One copy of a 100-page course syllabus
- A machine-knit wool sweater
- A hand-knit wool sweater
- One hour of lawn mowing and fertilizing
- A hammer

1. Each student should individually estimate the direct materials and direct labor inputs needed to produce the product or service. For each type of direct material and direct labor, determine the standard quantity and standard price. Also, identify the overhead support needed, and determine the standard overhead cost of the product or service. The result should be a total standard cost for the product or service.
2. Each group should compare the estimates of its members. Where estimates differ, determine why there were differences. Did assumptions differ? Did some members have more knowledge about the product or service than others? Form a group estimate of the standard cost of the product or service.
3. After the group has agreed on a standard cost, discuss the process used to arrive at the cost. What assumptions did the group make? Is the standard cost an "ideal" standard or a "currently attainable" standard? Note how widely standard costs can vary depending on assumptions and knowledge of the production process.

INTERNET EXERCISE

8-59 Flexible Budgets at Hershey Food Corporation

This chapter focused on flexible budgets and variance analysis. While the information used to determine both of these is generally for internal purposes only and not available to an outsider, it is possible to look at what information a firm reports and, based on that information, to make some judgments about what occurred.

1. Look at the **Hershey Company** home page at www.hersheys.com. Who is Hershey's home page directed to? What products does Hershey list at the bottom of the page?

2. Click on "Corporate Information" and then on "About The Hershey Company," and read the profile of the company. Hershey has a variety of products. What are total revenues and number of employees for Hershey worldwide? With the large number of products offered, would a static or flexible budget be more useful for planning purposes? Why?

3. Follow the link to "Investor Relations," and examine Hershey's income statement from its most recent 10-K in "SEC Filings." Suppose that in the following year net sales were expected to increase by 5%, but there was no expected increase in selling prices. Also, assume that cost of sales is the only variable cost and that selling, marketing, and administrative costs are fixed costs. (Also assume that realignment and impairment charges, gains on sales of businesses, and any other such one-time charges are not recurring costs.) Prepare a static-budget operating income statement for the following year. Now, suppose that selling prices were exactly as budgeted, but sales actually increased by 8% and operating income increased by 10%. Determine the static-budget variance, the sales-activity variance, and the flexible-budget variance for operating income.

Management Control Systems and Responsibility Accounting

▶ HEALTH NET

It's 2:30 AM. You don't feel well. Should you call your doctor? Go to the emergency room? Is what you're feeling really something to worry about? What you need is good quality health care and you need it now, not tomorrow morning, and you do not want to worry about its cost. Sound familiar? This is a dilemma that we have all faced at some time. One health-care organization that has a solution is **Health Net**, one of the largest managed health-care organizations in the United States. With approximately 10,000 employees and 2008 revenues of more than $15 billion, it provides coverage to 6.7 million health plan members.

Health-care organizations must compete just as any other business, offering high-quality health care at an affordable cost. To maintain its competitive advantage, Health Net undertook a major information systems development program called "fourth generation medical management." According to Dr. Malik Hasan, former chairman and CEO, Health Net created this new management control system "because the greatest opportunity for increasing overall quality and decreasing the cost of health care lies in managing patient care by seamlessly linking the entire health care delivery system electronically." The system "gives physicians and health care providers instant, user-friendly electronic access to comprehensive information about a patient's medical history and the best clinical treatments recommended."

The result? A fast and preapproved referral to the best clinical resource, whether it be a specialist, the emergency room or urgent care center, your regular physician, or safe self-care. In other words, a satisfied customer! And as a bonus, costs are reduced. As Medical Director John Danaher,

MD, explains, "Paper charting and duplicative lab and radiology tests are eliminated."

This chapter builds on concepts developed in previous chapters to explore how managers blend the individual tools of management accounting to help achieve organizational goals. Tools such as activity-based costing, relevant costing, budgeting, and variance analysis are each useful by themselves. They are most useful, however, when they are parts of an integrated system—a comprehensive plan to coordinate and evaluate all the activities of the organization's value chain. Just as in the case of Health Net, managers of most organizations today realize that long-run success requires a focus on cost, quality, and service—the three components of the competitive edge. This chapter considers how the management control system helps managers achieve such a focus. As you will see, no single management control system is inherently superior to another. The "best" system for any organization is the one that most consistently leads to actions that meet the organization's goals and objectives. ■

Doctors and managers at Health Net use a state-of-the-art medical management system and management control system to offer high quality health care at an affordable price.

Management Control Systems

A **management control system** is a logical integration of techniques for gathering and using information to make planning and control decisions, for motivating employee behavior, and for evaluating performance. A well-designed management control system supports and coordinates the decision-making process and motivates individuals throughout the organization to act in concert. It also facilitates forecasting and budgeting. An effective management control system should

- clearly define and communicate the organization's goals;
- ensure that managers and employees understand the specific actions required to achieve organizational goals;
- communicate results of actions across the organization; and
- motivate managers and employees to achieve the organization's goals.

Based on the preceding criteria, Exhibit 9-1 describes elements of the planning and control processes and emphasizes their interrelationships. As we pointed out in Chapter 1, planning and control are so strongly interrelated that it is somewhat artificial to separate them in practice. To the extent we can separate them, planning includes defining goals (A) and establishing and carrying out plans to achieve the goals (B). Control includes measuring and reporting results (C) and performance evaluation (D). The clockwise ordering of the elements represents the order that managers would naturally follow when designing and evaluating the management control system. However, once an organization has implemented the control system, it continuously adapts all the interrelated elements and revises them through feedback and learning. For example, the organization may revise the measures used to monitor and report in C to fit better with the goals in A. Similarly, it might realign the performance evaluation system in D to better fit with the specific plans and objectives in B. We will refer to Exhibit 9-1 often as we consider the design and operation of management control systems.

Management Control Systems and Organizational Goals

The first and most basic component in a management control system is the organization's goals. Exhibit 9-2 illustrates how managers at all levels of the organization set goals and objectives and develop related performance measures for their section of the organization. Top managers set organization-wide goals, performance measures, and targets, which they generally review annually. These goals provide a long-term framework around which an organization will form its comprehensive plan for positioning itself in the market. Goals address the question in Exhibit 9-1, "What do we want to achieve?" However, goals without performance measures do not motivate managers.

A basic adage of management control is that "you get what you measure." Because measures of performance set direction and motivate managers' decisions, every performance measure

Objective 1

Describe the relationship of management control systems to organizational goals.

Exhibit 9-1
The Management
Control System

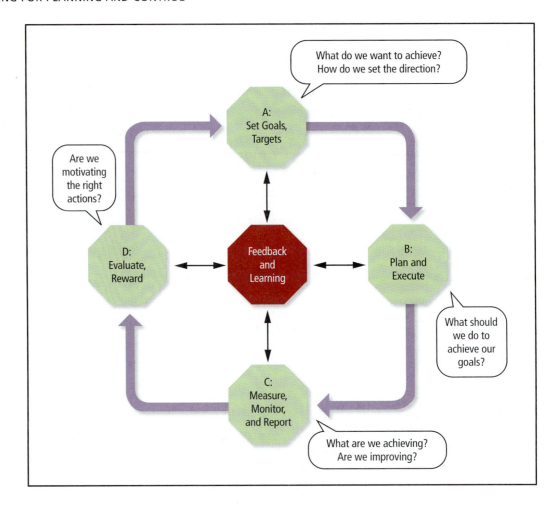

should be consistent with organizational goals. Otherwise, managers who achieve high perform-ance measures may not create value for the company and its owners. An ideal management con-trol system should include at least one performance measure related to every goal. The book *Cracking the Value Code* states this succinctly when it says that we tend to "value what we meas-ure but we do not always measure what we value."

Exhibit 9-2
Translating Goals and
Objectives into Performance
Measures

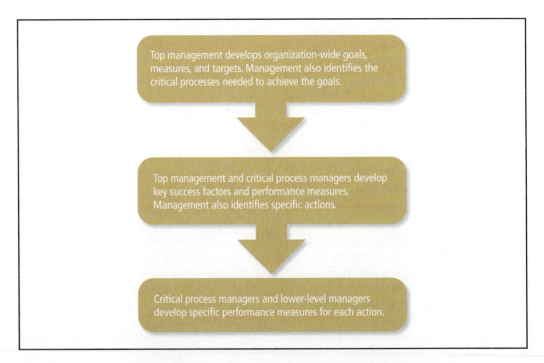

To illustrate the correspondence between organizational goals and performance measures, suppose a major Arizona-based luxury hotel chain, Scottsdale Luxury Suites, has the following goals and related measures:

Organizational Goals	Performance Measures
Exceed guest expectations	• Customer satisfaction index • Number of repeat stays
Maximize revenue yield	• Occupancy rate • Average room rate • Income before fixed costs
Focus on innovation	• New products/services implemented per year • Number of employee suggestions

The company sets quantifiable targets for each of the measures. For example, a target for the performance measure occupancy rate might be "at least 70%." Note that every goal has at least one performance measure, and every measure is related to at least one goal.

As shown in Exhibit 9-2, performance measures become more specific as we move to lower levels of the organization. For example, higher-level managers work with subordinates within each business unit to select specific tangible short-term actions (or activities) that managers can carry out, along with observable performance measures. One approach to selecting these actions and measures is for top managers to identify **key success factors**—characteristics or attributes that managers must achieve in order to drive the organization toward its goals. For Scottsdale Luxury Suites a key success factor for the goal to exceed guest expectations is timeliness. This key success factor suggests that Scottsdale Luxury Suites should consider specific actions, such as implementing an express check-in system. In addition, it should measure timeliness by using performance measures, such as time to check in, time to check out, and response time to guest requests (for example, number of rings before someone at the front desk answers the telephone).

Balancing various goals is an important part of designing a management control system. Managers often face trade-offs. For example, a manager may meet a goal of increased customer satisfaction by establishing a more generous policy for accepting returned merchandise. However, this policy will also impose additional costs that decrease short-term profitability. Choosing the best trade-off between short-term profitability and long-term customer satisfaction is often difficult, especially when the long-term benefits of increased customer satisfaction are hard to predict.

Designing Management Control Systems

To design a management control system that meets the organization's needs, managers must identify what motivates employees, develop performance measures based on these motivations, and establish a monitoring and reporting structure for these measures. Let's look at each of these.

Motivating Employees

An important goal of the management control system is to motivate employees to work in the best interests of the organization. A good management control system fosters both goal congruence and managerial effort. An organization achieves **goal congruence** when employees, working in their own perceived best interests, make decisions that help meet the overall goals of the organization. **Managerial effort**—exertion toward a goal or objective—must accompany goal congruence. Effort here includes not only working harder or faster but also working better. It includes all conscious actions (such as supervising, planning, and thinking) that result in more efficiency and effectiveness.

As we saw in Exhibit 9-1, the challenge of management control system design is to induce (or at least not discourage) employee decisions that would achieve organizational goals. For example, an organization may identify continuous improvement in employee efficiency and effectiveness as one of its goals. Employees, however, might perceive that continuous improvements will result in tighter standards, faster pace of work, and loss of jobs. Even though they may agree with management that continuous improvements are competitively

Objective 2

Explain the importance of evaluating performance and describe how it impacts motivation, goal congruence, and employee effort.

necessary, management should not expect them to exert effort for continuous improvements unless rewards are in place to make this effort in their own best interests.

As another example, students may enroll in a college course because their goal is to learn about management accounting. The faculty and the students share the same goal, but goal congruence is not enough. Faculty also introduce a grading system to reward student effort. Grading is a form of performance evaluation, similar to organizations using management control reports for raises, promotions, and other forms of rewards. Performance evaluation improves effort because most individuals tend to perform better when performance reports lead directly to personal rewards. Thus, manufacturers that set quality improvements as critical organizational goals, such as **Allen-Bradley** and **Corning**, put quality targets into the bonus plans of top managers and factory workers.

Motivation—the drive toward some selected goal that creates effort and action toward that goal—is key to management control. Yet employees differ widely in their motivations. This makes the system designer's task complex and ill-structured. Each system must fit the specific organizational environment and behavioral characteristics of the employees. The system designer must align individuals' self-interest with the goals of the organization. Thus, the designer must predict the motivational impact of a particular system—how it will cause people to respond—and compare it to the motivational impact of other potential systems. Designing performance measures is not a back-office accounting task. It requires direction from top management and the direct involvement of those affected. Stephen Kaufman, former chairman of the board of **Arrow Electronics** put it this way: "It's very difficult to define the right metric and anticipate exactly how your people will react to it. Your best chance of knowing whether it will have the intended effect is to talk to the people directly involved."

Budgets, variances, and the entire inventory of management control tools should constructively influence behavior. These tools are most effective when managers use them positively to encourage employees to improve performance, rather than negatively to punish, place blame, or find fault. Used negatively, these tools pose a threat to employees, who will resist and undermine the use of such techniques. Critics have pointed to **Enron**'s management control system as a major cause of the company's problems. Employees were heavily rewarded for good performance. More importantly, the employees who were ranked lowest at each evaluation were fired. This created intense competition, which at first seemed to create exceptional performance levels for the company. Later, it became clear that the pressure for good performance caused some employees to use unethical methods to increase their performance measures, which eventually led to the demise of the company.

Developing Performance Measures

Objective 3

Develop performance measures and use them to monitor the achievements of an organization.

For most organizations, effective performance measurement requires multiple performance measures, including both financial and nonfinancial measures. Effective performance measures have the following characteristics:

1. Reflect key actions and activities that relate to the goals of the organization
2. Affected by actions of managers and employees
3. Readily understood by employees
4. Reasonably objective and easily measured
5. Used consistently and regularly in evaluating and rewarding managers and employees
6. Balance long-term and short-term concerns

Sometimes accountants and managers focus too much on financial measures, such as operating budgets, profit targets, or required return on investment, because the accounting system readily produces such measures. Further, it is often difficult to construct performance measures for nonfinancial goals such as customer satisfaction, improvements in quality, environmental stewardship, social responsibility, and organizational learning, which many companies list as key goals. However, well-designed management control systems develop and report both financial and nonfinancial measures of performance because "You can't manage something you can't measure."

Nonfinancial measures often motivate employees toward achieving important performance goals. For example, **AT&T Universal Card Services**, which received the prestigious Baldrige National Quality Award (presented by the U.S. Department of Commerce), used 18 performance measures for its customer inquiries process. These measures include average speed of

Business First

Performance Measures in Practice

An organization's performance measures depend on its goals and objectives. For example, a software company and an auto manufacturer have different goals and objectives and therefore have vastly different performance measures. The measures also must span a variety of key success factors for the organization. Performance measures too focused on one aspect of performance may foster neglect of other important factors.

Let's look at a classic management control system, the one developed by **General Electric** in the 1950s. The system focused on eight "key result areas," as GE called them:

Financial Key Result Areas
1. Profitability
2. Productivity
3. Market position

Nonfinancial Key Result Areas
4. Product leadership
5. Personnel development
6. Employee attitudes
7. Public responsibility
8. Balance between short-run and long-range goals

Measures in each of these eight areas are just as relevant today as in the 1950s. These are clearly long-run strategic goals. Measures might change as an organization adapts the means of achieving the goals, but the basic framework of a management control system does not need to change as management fads come and go.

A more recent example is **Southwest Airlines**. The mission of Southwest Airlines is "dedication to the highest quality of customer service delivered with a sense of warmth, friendliness, individual pride, and company spirit." Yet, until recently, the company focused mainly on financial measures in evaluating managers. Recently, Southwest introduced nonfinancial measures into the mix, including the following:

- Load factor (percentage of seats occupied)
- Utilization factors on aircraft and personnel
- On-time performance
- Available seat miles
- Denied boarding rate
- Lost bag reports per 10,000 passengers
- Flight cancellation rate
- Employee head count
- Customer complaints per 10,000 passengers

By including nonfinancial measures, Southwest could focus managers' attention on the key success factors that related most closely to Southwest's mission and goals.

Sources: David Solomons, *Divisional Performance: Measurement and Control* (Homewood, IL: Irwin, 1965); and Southwest Airlines Web site (www.southwest.com).

---

answer, abandon rate, and application processing time (3 days compared to the industry average of 34 days).

Financial measures often are lagging indicators that arrive too late to help prevent problems and ensure the organization's health. The effects of poor nonfinancial performance (for example, lack of organizational learning and low customer satisfaction) may not show up in the financial measures until the company has lost considerable ground. Many companies now stress management of the activities that drive revenues and costs, rather than waiting to explain the revenues or costs themselves. Superior financial performance usually follows from superior nonfinancial performance. Examples of both financial and nonfinancial measures are in the Business First box above.

Monitoring and Reporting Results

Notice that Exhibit 9-1 has feedback and learning at the center of the management control system. Organization-wide learning is a foundation for gaining and maintaining financial strength. Some management experts have said that the only sustainable competitive advantage is the rate at which a company's managers learn. **Harley-Davidson**, a company with 2008 sales of about $5.6 billion, emphasizes learning for operational excellence—getting out waste, improving quality, and helping drive customer satisfaction.

Once a company has superior intellectual capital, how can it best maintain its leadership? Exhibit 9-3 shows how organizational learning leads to financial strength. Measures such as training time, employee turnover, and staff satisfaction scores on employee surveys monitor organizational learning. The result of learning is continuous process improvement. Measures such as cycle time, number of defects (quality), and activity costs can assess improvement. Customers will value improved response time (lower cycle time), higher quality, and lower prices and will increase their demand for products and services. Increased demand, combined with lower costs to make and deliver products and services, results in improved product profitability and earnings. Successful organizations do not stop with one cycle of learning → process improvement → increased customer

Exhibit 9-3

The Components of a
Successful Organization and
Measures of Achievement

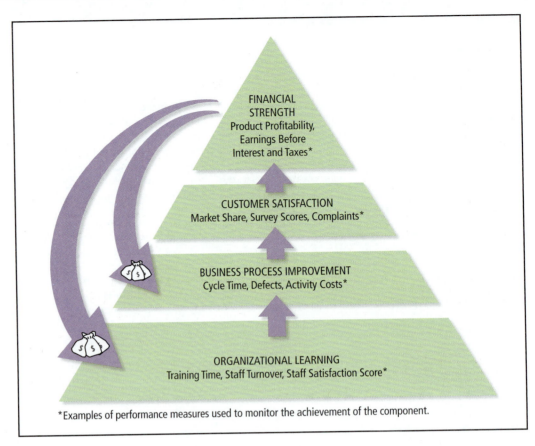

*Examples of performance measures used to monitor the achievement of the component.

satisfaction → improved financial strength. Instead, they continue to reinvest financial resources to further support both continuous learning and continuous process improvement.

There are no guarantees that each of the components automatically follows from success at the previous component. If efforts are not coordinated throughout the value chain, the cause-effect links can be broken. For example, new and improved products or services may fail if marketing and distribution techniques do not place them at the location desired by the customer. As another example, development of a great e-commerce Web site does no good if customers never visit the Web site. The point is that improvement in business processes must be coordinated across all parts of the value chain.

Another message from Exhibit 9-3 is that a key driver of enterprise performance is the culture within the company that fosters continual learning and growth at all levels of management. It is not sufficient to use money to train managers without making sure that the resulting learning translates into improved processes, products, and services. This requires a culture of learning that motivates managers to translate learning into growth.

General Electric provides a good example of the application of the enterprise learning culture. With sales of about $180 billion, GE has demonstrated a remarkable ability to generate formidable profits with products ranging from aircraft engines, power generation, water processing, and security technology to medical imaging, business and consumer financing, and industrial products. GE employs more than 300,000 people worldwide. In 2009, GE was ninth on *Fortune* magazine's "Most Admired Company in America," and has consistently been at or near the top of the list throughout the last decade. Although problems, primarily in the consumer financing part of GE, caused a large drop in its share price in 2008 and 2009, many parts of the company continued to dominate their markets.

In a GE annual report just before he retired, former CEO John Welch attributed GE's success to

. . . . a General Electric culture that values the contributions of every individual, thrives on learning, thirsts for the better idea, and has the flexibility and speed to put the better idea into action every day. We are a learning company, a company that studies its own successes and failures and those of others—a company that has the self-confidence and the resources to take big swings and pursue numerous opportunities based on winning ideas

and insights, regardless of their source. That appetite for learning, and the ability to act quickly on that learning, will provide GE with what we believe is an insurmountable and sustainable competitive advantage.

Exactly what did John Welch mean by the "ability to act quickly on that learning"? According to Welch, GE "opened [its] culture up to ideas from everyone, everywhere, killed NIH (Not Invented Here) thinking, decimated the bureaucracy, and made boundaryless behavior a reflexive and natural part of our culture, thereby creating the learning culture." His successor, Jeff Immelt, points out another important part of the GE learning culture—openness to dropping old management approaches in favor of new and better techniques: "Most people inside GE learn from the past but have a healthy disrespect for history. They have an ability to live in the moment and not be burdened by the past, which is extremely important."

As shown in Exhibit 9-1, monitoring and reporting the results of business activities are key components of a management control system. Exhibit 9-2 indicates that managers identify actions and related performance measures that are linked to the achievement of goals and objectives. The performance-reporting system provides periodic information on the achievement of desired outcomes. Effective performance reports align results with managers' goals and objectives, provide guidance to managers, communicate goals and their level of attainment throughout the organization, and enable organizations to anticipate and respond to change in a timely manner.

Weighing Costs and Benefits

The designer of a management control system must always weigh the costs and benefits of various alternatives. Benefits and costs of management control systems are often difficult to measure, and both may become apparent only after experimentation or use. For example, the director of accounting policy of **Citicorp** stated that, after using a very detailed management control system for several years, the system proved to be too costly to administer relative to the perceived benefits. Accordingly, Citicorp returned to a simpler, less costly—though less detailed—management control system. In contrast, **Home Depot** added detail in the form of additional metrics to its management control system. When employees asked then-CEO Bob Nardelli why they should use the new metrics, he compared the metrics to gauges in a car: "Why do you need a gas gauge? Why do you need a speedometer?" He believed that the metrics were worth the cost because they helped headquarters know what is going on throughout the company.

Summary Problem for Your Review
PROBLEM

The Luxury Suites hotel chain is developing performance measures for each of its major goals. Top management established "exceed guest expectations" as one organization-wide goal. Among the key success factors are timeliness of customer service and quality of personalized service. Patty Bowen, vice president of sales, is the manager responsible for the actions required to meet the goal of exceeding guest expectations. She has already identified one action (objective) for the coming year—upgrade customer service department capabilities.

1. Identify several possible performance measures for the quality-of-personalized-service key success factor.
2. Recommend several specific actions or activities associated with upgrading customer service department capabilities that would drive Luxury Suites toward its goal of exceeding customer expectations.

SOLUTION

1. Performance measures for the quality of personalized service might include the number of changes to registration, rating on the "friendly, knowledgeable staff" question on the guest survey, number of complaints, percentage of return guests, and percentage of customers with completed customer profile (profiles special needs of customers).
2. Specific actions or activities might include training employees, implementing a call checklist (list of services and options available to the guest) and monitoring compliance with the list, developing a customer satisfaction survey, and reengineering the guest registration and reservation processes.

Controllability and Measurement of Financial Performance

Management control systems often distinguish between controllable and uncontrollable events and between controllable and uncontrollable costs. These terms refer to relative rather than absolute controllability—no cost is completely under the control of a manager—and a controllable cost is one that a manager's decisions "affect to a reasonable extent." An **uncontrollable cost** is any cost that management cannot reasonably affect within a given time span. For example, the manager of a **Dow Chemical** factory may not be able to control the market price of the crude oil used to make various chemicals. In contrast, **controllable costs** include those costs that a manager's decisions and actions can influence to a reasonable extent. For example, Dow Chemical is likely to consider labor costs as controllable by the factory manager, even though the manager does not totally control labor costs because union contracts place constraints on both pay rates and labor usage. Similarly, the manager may be able to affect, though not completely control, the amount of crude oil used and most overhead costs in the factory. The distinction between controllable and uncontrollable costs is used in evaluating the performance of a manager. Costs that are completely uncontrollable tell nothing about a manager's decisions and actions because, by definition, nothing the manager does will affect the costs. In contrast, measuring and reporting controllable costs provides evidence about a manager's performance.

Identifying Responsibility Centers

Objective 4

Use responsibility accounting to define an organizational subunit as a cost center, a profit center, or an investment center.

Designers of management control systems identify the responsibilities of each manager in an organization by establishing responsibility centers based on what a manager can control. A **responsibility center** is a set of activities and resources assigned to a manager, a group of managers, or other employees. A set of machines and machining activities, for example, may be a responsibility center for a production supervisor. The full production department may be a responsibility center for the department head. Finally, the entire organization may be a responsibility center for the president. In some organizations, groups of employees share management responsibility to create wide "ownership" of management decisions, to allow creative decision making, and to prevent one person's concern (or lack of concern) for risks of failure to dominate decisions.

An effective management control system gives each manager responsibility for a group of activities and actions and then, as Exhibit 9-1 shows, monitors and reports on (1) the results of the activities and (2) the manager's influence on those results. Such a system has intrinsic appeal for most top managers (because it helps them delegate decision making and frees them to focus on more strategic issues) and lower-level managers (who value the decision-making autonomy they inherit). Thus, system designers apply **responsibility accounting** to identify what parts of the organization have primary responsibility for each action, develop performance measures and targets, and design reports of these measures by responsibility center. Responsibility centers usually have multiple goals and actions that the management control system monitors. We classify responsibility centers as cost centers, profit centers, or investment centers based on their managers' primary financial responsibilities.

COST, PROFIT, AND INVESTMENT CENTERS   In a **cost center**, managers are responsible for costs only. A cost center may encompass an entire department, or a department may contain several cost centers. For example, although one manager may supervise an assembly department, the department may contain several assembly lines and each assembly line may be considered a separate cost center. Likewise, within each line, each separate machine may be its own cost center. The determination of the number of cost centers depends on cost-benefit considerations—do the benefits (for planning, control, and evaluation) of smaller, more numerous cost centers exceed the higher costs of reporting?

Unlike cost-center managers, profit-center managers are responsible for controlling revenues as well as costs—that is, profitability. Despite the name, a **profit center** can exist in non-profit organizations (though it might not be referred to as such) when a responsibility center receives revenues for its services. For example, the **Western Area Power Authority (WAPA)** is charged with recovering its costs of operations through sales of power to electric utilities in the western United States. WAPA is a profit center responsible for both revenues and costs, though its objective is not to maximize profits but rather to break even.

An **investment center** adds responsibility for investment to profit-center responsibilities. Investment-center success depends on both income and invested capital, measured by relating income generated to the value of the capital employed.

Systems designers must understand operating processes and cost behavior to help identify responsibility for controllable costs. For example, by isolating activities and related cost drivers, activity-based costing (see Chapter 4) can help to point out controllable costs. **Procter & Gamble** credited its activity-based management control system with identifying controllable costs in one of its detergent divisions, which led to major strategic changes.

Responsibility center managers are often able to explain their center's uncontrollable costs, even in situations where they are not held responsible for these uncontrollable costs. For example, an importer of grapes from Chile to the United States suffered a sudden loss of sales several years ago after a few grapes were found to contain poisonous cyanide. The tampering was beyond the import manager's control. The company held the manager responsible for efficiency (the flexible-budget variance [see Chapter 8]) but not the effects of activity volume (the sales-activity variance). Even though he was not held responsible for the sales-activity variance, the manager was in the best position to provide an explanation for the variance because he had the best information about the reasons for the decline in sales.

Contribution Margin

Many organizations combine the contribution approach to measuring income with responsibility accounting—that is, they report by cost behavior as well as by degrees of controllability. Exhibit 9-4 is an organization chart showing selected units of a retail grocery company like **Safeway**, **Kroger**, or **SuperValu**. Exhibit 9-5 illustrates the contribution approach to measuring financial performance of the various units shown on the organization chart. **Segments** are responsibility centers for which a company develops separate measures of revenues and costs. Exhibit 9-5 provides perspective on how a management-control system report can stress cost behavior, controllability, manager performance, and responsibility center performance simultaneously.

Line (a) in Exhibit 9-5 shows the contribution margin, sales revenues less variable expenses. The contribution margin ratio, defined as the ratio of contribution margin to sales, is especially helpful for predicting the impact on income of short-run changes in sales volume. Managers may quickly calculate expected changes in income by multiplying the contribution margin ratio by the expected change in dollar sales. For example, the contribution margin ratio for meats in the West Division is $180 ÷ $900 = .20. A $1,000 increase in sales of meats in the West Division should produce a $200 increase in contribution margin and income (.20 × $1,000 = $200) if there are no changes in selling prices, variable operating expenses per unit, fixed costs, or mix of sales.

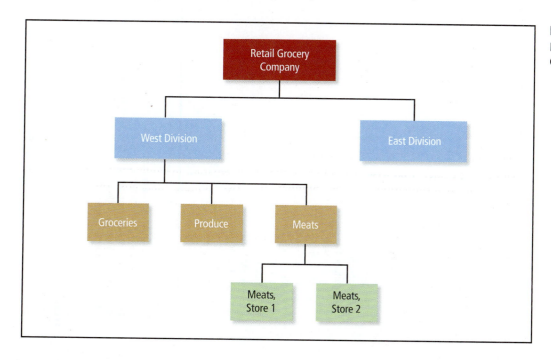

Exhibit 9-4
Retail Grocery Company Organization Chart

	Company as a Whole	Company Breakdown into Two Divisions		Breakdown of West Division Only				Breakdown of West Division, Meats Only		
		East Division	West Division	Not Allocated†	Groceries	Produce	Meats	Not Allocated†	Store 1	Store 2
Net sales	$4,000	$1,500	$2,500	—	$1,300	$300	$900	—	$600	$300
Variable costs										
Cost of merchandise sold	$3,000	$1,100	$1,900	—	$1,000	$230	$670	—	$450	$220
Variable operating costs‡	260	100	160	—	100	10	50	—	35	15
Total variable costs	$3,260	$1,200	$2,060	—	$1,100	$240	$720	—	$485	$235
(a) Contribution margin	$ 740	$ 300	$ 440	—	$ 200	$ 60	$180	—	$115	$ 65
Less: Fixed costs controllable by segment managers§	260	100	160	$ 20	40	10	90	$ 30	35	25
(b) Contribution controllable by segment managers	$ 480	$ 200	$ 280	$(20)	$ 160	$ 50	$ 90	$(30)	$ 80	$ 40
Less: Fixed costs controllable by others¶	200	90	110	20	40	10	40	10	22	8
(c) Contribution by segments	$ 280	$ 110	$ 170	$(40)	$ 120	$ 40	$ 50	$(40)	$ 58	$ 32
Less: Unallocated costs‖	100									
(d) Income before income taxes	$ 180									

*Three different types of segments are illustrated here: divisions, product lines, and stores. As you read across, note that the focus becomes narrower; from East and West divisions to West Division only, to meats in West Division only.

†Only those costs clearly identifiable to a product line or store should be allocated.

‡Principally wages and payroll-related costs.

§Examples are certain advertising, sales promotions, salespersons' salaries, management consulting, training, and supervision costs.

¶Examples are depreciation, property taxes, insurance, and perhaps the segment manager's salary.

‖These costs are not clearly or practically allocable to any segment except by some highly questionable allocation base.

Exhibit 9-5

Retail Grocery Store

Contribution Approach: Model Income Statement by Segments (thousands of dollars)

Contribution Controllable by Segment Managers

Lines (b) and (c) in Exhibit 9-5 separate the contribution that segment managers control (b) from the overall segment contribution (c). Designers of management control systems distinguish between the segment as an economic investment and the manager as a decision maker. For instance, an extended period of drought coupled with an aging population may adversely affect the desirability of continued economic investment in a ski resort, but the resort manager may nonetheless be doing an excellent job under the circumstances.

Exhibit 9-5 separates costs by controllability. The manager of meats at Store 1 may have influence over some local advertising but not other advertising, some fixed salaries but not other salaries, and so forth. Moreover, the meat manager at both the division and store levels may have zero influence over store depreciation or the president's salary. Managers on all levels help explain the total segment contribution, but they are responsible only for the controllable contribution. Note that we deduct the fixed costs controllable by the segment managers from the contribution margin to obtain the contribution controllable by segment managers. These controllable costs are usually discretionary fixed costs such as local advertising and some salaries, but not the manager's own salary.

As we move to the right in Exhibit 9-5, we see allocations of only part of the fixed costs to lower levels in the organization. For example, consider the line with fixed costs controllable by segment managers. Of the $160,000 fixed costs that the West Division manager controls, groceries, produce, and meat departments control only $140,000. We do not allocate the remaining $20,000 of West Division fixed costs because they are not controllable this far down in the organization. That is, the West Division manager controls all $160,000 of fixed costs, but subordinates (grocery, produce, and meat managers) control only $140,000. Similarly, the Meats manager controls $90,000 of fixed costs, but subordinates at Stores 1 and 2 control only $35,000 and $25,000, respectively.

Contribution by Segments

The contribution by segments, line (c) in Exhibit 9-5, is an attempt to approximate the financial performance of the segment, as distinguished from the financial performance of its manager, which we measure in line (b). The "fixed costs controllable by others" typically include committed costs (such as depreciation and property taxes) and discretionary costs (such as the segment manager's salary). Although the segment manager does not control these costs, they are necessary for the operation of the segment.

Unallocated Costs

Exhibit 9-5 shows "unallocated costs" immediately before line (d). These costs might include central corporate costs, such as the costs of top management and some corporate-level services (for example, legal and taxation). When an organization cannot find a persuasive cause-and-effect or activity-based justification for allocating such costs, it generally does not allocate them to segments.

Summary

The correct classification of costs as illustrated in Exhibit 9-5 is sometimes ambiguous. Determining controllability is a problem when a company allocates service department costs to other departments. Should a store manager bear a part of the division headquarters' costs? If so, how much and on what basis? How much, if any, store depreciation or lease expenses should we deduct in computing the controllable contribution? There are no universally correct answers to these questions. Each organization makes choices that balance costs and benefits. (This differs from the situation in external accounting systems, where tax or financial reporting regulations usually specify the required classification of costs.)

Because of the subjectivity involved in classification of costs, measures of financial performance like those illustrated in Exhibit 9-5 are subjective, especially at lower-level units. The calculation of the contribution margin near the top of the report tends to be the most objective, because managers can usually objectively identify and assign variable costs. As you read downward in the report, the allocations become increasingly subjective, and the resulting measures of contributions become more subject to dispute. Nonetheless, many organizations find that allocation of costs to units makes managers more aware of the costs of the entire organization and leads to better organizational cost control.

Objective 5

Prepare segment income statements for evaluating profit and investment centers using the contribution margin and controllable-cost concepts.

Making Managerial Decisions

Managers should try to distinguish between controllable and uncontrollable costs when designing segment financial reports. For each of the following costs of a suburban **Wal-Mart** store, indicate whether it is a variable cost, fixed cost controllable by segment managers, fixed cost controllable by someone other than the segment manager, or a cost that a company normally does not allocate:

Property taxes
Supervision of local sales staff
Depreciation of store
Cost of goods sold
Local store advertising
Corporate-level advertising
Corporate-level public relations
Temporary sales labor

Answer

Variable costs are generally controllable by the store manager. Cost of goods sold and temporary sales labor are examples.

Fixed costs controllable by the segment (store) manager include local store advertising and supervision of the local sales staff. The store manager usually decides the appropriate level for these costs.

Fixed costs controllable by those other than the store manager include property taxes and depreciation of the store. These costs relate directly to the store, but the store manager cannot change them.

Unallocated costs include corporate-level advertising and public relations. These costs have a tenuous link to the store.

Summary Problem for Your Review

PROBLEM

The Book & Game Company has two bookstores: Auntie's and Merlin's. Each store has managers who have a great deal of decision authority over their store. Advertising, market research, acquisition of books, legal services, and other staff functions, however, are handled by a central office. The Book & Game Company's current accounting system allocates all costs to the stores. Results for 20X1 were as follows:

Item	Total Company	Auntie's	Merlin's
Sales revenue	$700,000	$350,000	$350,000
Cost of merchandise sold	450,000	225,000	225,000
Gross margin	250,000	125,000	125,000
Operating expenses			
Salaries and wages	63,000	30,000	33,000
Supplies	45,000	22,500	22,500
Rent and utilities	60,000	40,000	20,000
Depreciation	15,000	7,000	8,000
Allocated staff costs	60,000	30,000	30,000
Total operating expenses	243,000	129,500	113,500
Operating income (loss)	$ 7,000	$ (4,500)	$ 11,500

Each bookstore manager makes decisions that affect salaries and wages, supplies, and depreciation. In contrast, rent and utilities are beyond the managers' control because the managers did not choose the location or the size of the store.

Supplies are variable costs. Variable salaries and wages are equal to 8% of the cost of merchandise sold; the remainder of salaries and wages is a fixed cost. Rent, utilities, and depreciation also are fixed costs. Staff costs represent the cost of activities performed by the central office. Events at the individual bookstores do not affect staff costs; nevertheless, Book & Game Company allocates them as a proportion of sales revenue.

1. Using the contribution approach, prepare a performance report that distinguishes the performance of each bookstore from that of the bookstore manager.
2. Evaluate the financial performance of each bookstore.
3. Evaluate the financial performance of each manager.

SOLUTION

1. See Exhibit 9-6.
2. We can evaluate the financial performances of the bookstores (that is, segments of the company) using the line "contribution by bookstore." Merlin's has a substantially higher contribution, despite equal levels of sales revenues in the two stores. The major reason for this advantage is that Merlin's pays less for rent and utilities.
3. We can evaluate the financial performance of the managers using the line "contribution controllable by managers." By this measure, the performance of Auntie's manager is better than that of Merlin's. The contribution margin is the same for each store, but Merlin's manager paid $4,000 more in controllable fixed costs than did Auntie's manager. Note that the additional fixed costs could be beneficial in the long run. What is missing from each of these segment reports is the year's master budget and a flexible budget, which would be the best benchmark for evaluating both bookstores and bookstore managers.

Item	Total Company	Auntie's	Merlin's
Sales revenue	$700,000	$350,000	$350,000
Variable costs			
Cost of merchandise sold	450,000	225,000	225,000
Salaries and wages—variable portion	36,000	18,000	18,000
Supplies	45,000	22,500	22,500
Total variable costs	531,000	265,500	265,500
Contribution margin by bookstore	169,000	84,500	84,500
Less: Fixed costs controllable by bookstore managers			
Salaries and wages—fixed portion	27,000	12,000	15,000
Depreciation	15,000	7,000	8,000
Total controllable fixed costs	42,000	19,000	23,000
Contribution controllable by managers	127,000	65,500	61,500
Less: Fixed costs controllable by others			
Rent and utilities	60,000	40,000	20,000
Contribution by bookstore	67,000	$ 25,500	$ 41,500
Unallocated costs	60,000		
Operating income	$ 7,000		

Exhibit 9-6
The Book & Game Company
Performance Report

Measurement of Nonfinancial Performance

For many years, organizations have monitored their nonfinancial performance. For example, sales organizations have followed up on customers to ensure their satisfaction, and manufacturers have tracked manufacturing defects and product performance. In recent years, many organizations have developed a new awareness of the importance of controlling nonfinancial performance areas. We first examine important examples of nonfinancial performance measures such as quality, cycle time, and productivity. Then, we discuss the balanced scorecard, a popular approach to performance measurement that integrates financial and nonfinancial measures tied to the organization's fundamental strategy.

Objective 6

Measure performance against nonfinancial performance measures such as quality, cycle time, and productivity.

Control of Quality

Most companies use performance metrics that measure the quality of their products or services. **Quality control** is the effort to ensure that products and services perform to customer requirements. In essence, customers or clients define quality by comparing their needs to the attributes of the product or service. For example, buyers judge the quality of an automobile based on reliability, performance, styling, safety, and image relative to their needs, budget, and the alternatives. Defining quality in terms of customer requirements is only half the battle. There remains the problem of reaching and maintaining the desired level of quality. There are many approaches to controlling quality.

The traditional approach in the United States was to inspect products after completing them and reject or rework those that failed the inspections. Because testing is expensive, companies often inspected only a sample of products. They judged the process to be in control as long as the number of defective products did not exceed an acceptable quality level. This meant that some defective products could still make their way to customers.

Many companies have moved away from the traditional approach to quality control. They have found that it is more cost effective to prevent defects than to detect and correct them. The resources consumed to detect defective products do not add value. If the company must scrap the defective product, it wastes the resources that were consumed to produce it. Even when the company can correct the product defects, it wastes the resources required for rework. When a company does not discover defects until the product reaches the customer, it is costly to repair products already in use by a customer or to win back a dissatisfied customer. IBM's former CEO John Akers was quoted in the *Wall Street Journal* as saying, "I am sick and tired of visiting plants to hear nothing but great things about quality and cycle time—and then to visit customers who tell me of problems."

The high costs of achieving quality by the traditional approach of "inspecting it in" are evident in a **cost of quality report**, which displays the financial impact of quality. The quality cost report shown in Exhibit 9-7 measures four categories of quality costs:

1. Prevention—costs incurred to prevent the production of defective products or delivery of substandard services including engineering analyses to improve product design for better manufacturing, improvements in production processes, increased quality of material inputs, and programs to train personnel
2. Appraisal—costs incurred to identify defective products or services including inspection and testing
3. Internal failure—costs of defective components and final products or services that are scrapped or reworked; also costs of delays caused by defective products or services
4. External failure—costs caused by delivery of defective products or services to customers, such as field repairs, returns, and warranty expenses

Exhibit 9-7 shows that internal or external failures caused most of the costs incurred by Eastside Manufacturing Company. These costs almost certainly are understated, however, because they omit opportunity costs of internal delays and lost sales. For example, quality problems in American-built automobiles in the 1980s caused sales to drop for many years. The opportunity cost of these lost future sales were much more significant than the immediate tangible costs measured in any quality cost report.

In recent years, more U.S. companies have been rethinking this approach to quality control. They have adopted an approach first espoused by an American, W. Edwards Deming, and embraced by Japanese companies decades ago: **total quality management (TQM)**. Following the old adage "an ounce of prevention is worth a pound of cure," it focuses on prevention of defects and on achievement of customer satisfaction. The TQM approach builds on the assumption that an organization minimizes the cost of quality when it achieves high quality levels. TQM is the application of quality principles to all of the organization's endeavors to satisfy customers. TQM has significant implications for organization goals, structure, and management control systems. For TQM to work, though, employees must be well trained in the process, the product or service, and the use of quality-control information.

To implement TQM, an organization trains employees to prepare, interpret, and act on quality-control charts, such as that shown in Exhibit 9-8. The **quality-control chart** is a statistical plot of measures of various product quality dimensions or attributes. This plot helps detect

Month			Quality Cost Area	Year to Date		
Actual	Plan	Variance		Actual	Plan	Variance
			1. Prevention Cost			
3	2	1	A. Quality—administration	5	4	1
16	18	(2)	B. Quality—engineering	37	38	(1)
7	6	1	C. Quality—planning by others	14	12	2
5	7	(2)	D. Supplier assurance	13	14	(1)
31	33	(2)	Total prevention cost	69	68	1
5.5%	6.1%		Percentage of total quality cost	6.2%	6.3%	
			2. Appraisal cost			
31	26	5	A. Inspection	55	52	3
12	14	(2)	B. Test	24	28	(4)
7	6	1	C. Inspection & test of purchased materials	15	12	3
11	11	0	D. Product quality audits	23	22	1
3	2	1	E. Maintenance of inspection & test equipment	4	4	0
2	2	0	F. Materials consumed in inspection & testing	5	4	1
66	61	5	Total appraisal cost	126	122	4
11.8%	11.3%		Percentage of total quality cost	11.4%	11.3%	
			3. Internal failure cost			
144	140	4	A. Scrap & rework—manufacturing	295	280	15
55	53	2	B. Scrap & rework—engineering	103	106	(3)
28	30	(2)	C. Scrap & rework—supplier	55	60	(5)
21	22	(1)	D. Failure investigation	44	44	0
248	245	3	Total internal failure cost	497	490	7
44.3%	45.4%		Percentage of total quality cost	44.9%	45.3%	
345	339	6	Total internal quality cost (1 + 2 + 3)	692	680	12
61.6%	62.8%		Percentage of total quality cost	62.6%	62.8%	
			4. External failure quality cost			
75	66	9	A. Warranty expense—manufacturing	141	132	9
41	40	1	B. Warranty expense—engineering	84	80	4
35	35	0	C. Warranty expense—sales	69	70	(1)
46	40	6	D. Field warranty cost	83	80	3
18	20	(2)	E. Failure investigation	37	40	(3)
215	201	14	Total external failure cost	414	402	12
38.4%	37.2%		Percentage of total quality cost	37.4%	37.2%	
560	540	20	Total quality cost	1,106	1,082	24
9,872	9,800		Total product cost	20,170	19,600	
5.7%	5.5%		Total quality cost as percentage of total production cost	5.5%	5.5%	

*Adapted from Allen H. Seed III, *Adapting Management Accounting Practice to an Advanced Manufacturing Environment* (Montvale, NJ: National Association of Accountants, 1988), Table 5-2, p. 76.

Exhibit 9-7
Eastside Manufacturing Company
Quality Cost Report (thousands of dollars)*

process deviations and identify excessive variation in product dimensions or attributes that process or design engineers should address. The chart in Exhibit 9-8 shows that, except for a brief period near the end of April, the Eastside Manufacturing Company generally is not meeting its defects objective of .6% defects. Managers looking at this chart would know that they should take corrective action.

The most recent trend in quality control is Six Sigma, defined in Chapter 1 as a continuous process improvement effort designed to reduce costs by improving quality. The name Six Sigma comes from the idea of an extremely low defect rate of fewer than 3.4 defects per million (far lower than the rate of 6 defects per thousand in the previous Eastside Manufacturing example). However, the Six Sigma approach has broadened into a general approach to defining, measuring, analyzing, and improving a production process to minimize errors. The focus is on measuring how many defects a company has in its process because, once a company measures the defects, it can take steps to eliminate them. Developed by Motorola, Six Sigma is making large impacts at companies such as General Electric, Dow Chemical, and 3M. At Dow, each Six Sigma project has created an average of $500,000 in savings.

Exhibit 9-8
Eastside Manufacturing Company
Quality-Control Chart

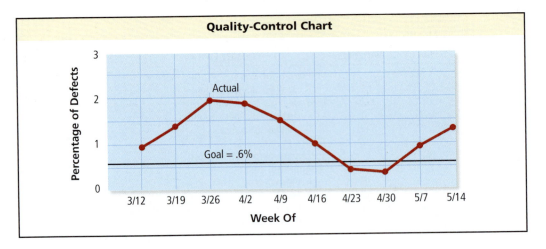

Control of Cycle Time

Reducing cycle time is a key to improving quality. **Cycle time**, or **throughput time**, is the time taken to complete a product or service. It is a summary measure of efficiency and effectiveness and is also an important cost driver. You may find it surprising that lower cycle times often lead to higher quality and lower defect rates. A lower cycle time requires smooth-running processes and high quality. It also creates increased flexibility and quicker reactions to customer needs. As a company decreases cycle time, quality problems become more apparent throughout the process. Decreasing cycle time also results in bringing products or services more quickly to customers, which makes for happy customers.

An effective means of measuring cycle time is to attach an identifier such as a bar code (similar to symbols on most grocery products) to each component or product and use a scanner to read the code at the end of each stage of completion. Cycle time for each stage is the time between readings of bar codes. Bar coding also permits effective tracking of materials and products for inventories, scheduling, and delivery.

Exhibit 9-9 is a sample cycle-time report showing that Eastside Manufacturing Company is meeting its cycle-time objectives at two of its five production process stages. This report is similar to the flexible budget reports of Chapter 8. Explanations of the variances indicate that poor-quality materials and poor design led to extensive rework and retesting.

Control of Productivity

More than half the companies in the United States measure and manage productivity as part of the effort to improve their competitiveness. **Productivity** is a measure of outputs divided by inputs. The fewer inputs needed to produce a given output, the more productive the organization. This simple definition, however, raises difficult measurement questions. How should the company measure outputs and inputs? Specific management control issues usually determine the most appropriate measures. Labor-intensive organizations, especially service organizations,

Exhibit 9-9
Eastside Manufacturing Company
Cycle Time Report for the Second Week of May

Process Stage	Actual Cycle Time*	Standard Cycle Time	Variance	Explanation
Materials processing	2.1	2.5	0.4 F	
Circuit board assembly	44.7	28.8	15.9 U	Poor-quality materials caused rework
Power unit assembly	59.6	36.2	23.4 U	Engineering change required rebuilding all power units
Product assembly	14.6	14.7	0.1 F	
Functional and environmental test	53.3	32.0	21.3 U	Software failure in test procedures required retesting

F = Favorable. U = Unfavorable.
*Average time per stage over the week.

Productivity Performance Is Key in Auto Industry

Productivity is an important component of profitability for auto manufacturers. Each year, *The Harbour Report*™ ranks the most productive auto-assembly companies in North America based on the number of hours of assembly time per vehicle (HPV). In the 2008 report, CAMI Automotive, which produces the Chevrolet Equinox, Pontiac Torrent, and Suzuki XL-7 in Ontario, averaged 17.59 hours to produce each vehicle to lead all companies in North America. A Chrysler plant (Toledo South) took the top place among individual assembly plants with 13.57 HPV. Chrysler had four of the top ten individual assembly plants in terms of HPV, followed by General Motors (GM) with three of the top ten.

Other productivity measures indicate performance in specific parts of the manufacturing process. For example, *Harbour* measures hours per engine (HPE) in the production of engines. Toyota had the best overall engine productivity at 3.13 HPE, while Chrysler finished second at 3.35 HPE, followed by GM at 3.44 HPE. The Chrysler Dundee plant led performance by plant with an HPE of 1.84, while GM's Spring Hill plant had an HPE of 2.53. *Harbour* also evaluates the stamping process, where it measures hits per hour (HPH) and pieces per hour (PPH), among other metrics.

Industry analysts look closely at these productivity numbers and their trends. They are a precursor of future profitability. Further, other companies want to find out how the various plants achieve their productivity levels so that they may copy successful methods and avoid others.

How are companies improving productivity? According to Michelle Hill, director of *The Harbour Report* North America, "There is no doubt, based on our visits to more than 20 plants over the last year, that continuous improvements in manufacturing processes are taking hold in just about every company. Everyone is focused on reducing waste and building quality into their processes more than ever." The factors that determine productivity include the following:

- Quality equals productivity
- Vehicles designed for easy assembly and high first-time quality
- Ability to produce more profitable small and midsize cars
- Balance of people and automation

Source: Oliver Wyman's *The Harbour Report*, June 5, 2008 (www.oliverwyman.com).

focus on increasing the productivity of labor, so labor-based measures are appropriate. Highly automated companies focus on machine use and productivity of capital investments, so capacity-based measures, such as the percentage of time machines are available, may be most important to them. Manufacturing companies, in general, monitor the efficient use of materials. For them, measures of material yield (a ratio of material outputs over material inputs) may be useful indicators of productivity.

Exhibit 9-10 shows 12 examples of productivity measures. As you can see, they vary widely according to the type of resource that management wishes to use efficiently. In all cases, a measure of the resource that management wishes to control is in the denominator (the input) and a measure of the objective of using the resource is in the numerator (the output). The Business First box above shows how managers and analysts measure productivity in the auto industry.

Exhibit 9-10
Measures of Productivity

Resource	Possible Outputs (Numerator)		Possible Inputs (Denominator)
Labor	Standard direct-labor hours allowed for good output	÷	Actual direct-labor hours used
	Sales revenue	÷	Number of employees
	Sales revenue	÷	Direct-labor costs
	Bank deposit/loan activity (by a bank)	÷	Number of employees
	Service calls	÷	Number of employees
	Customer orders	÷	Number of employees
Materials	Weight of output	÷	Weight of input
	Number of good units	÷	Total number of units
Equipment, capital, physical capacity	Time (e.g., hours) used	÷	Time available for use
	Time available for use	÷	Time (e.g., 24 hours per day)
	Expected machine hours for good output	÷	Actual machine hours
	Sales revenue	÷	Direct-labor cost

Choice of Productivity Measures

Which productivity measures should a company choose to manage? The choice depends on the behaviors desired. For example, if top management evaluates subordinates' performance based on direct-labor productivity, lower-level managers will focus on improving that specific measure.

The challenge in choosing productivity measures is to avoid motivating decisions that improve one measure of performance but hurt performance elsewhere in the organization. For example, long production runs may improve productivity per machine but result in excessive inventory handling and holding costs. As another example, improved labor productivity achieved by motivating workers to spend less time on each unit produced may cause a high rate of product defects.

Use of a single measure of productivity is unlikely to result in overall improvements in performance. The choice of management controls requires anticipating the trade-offs that employees will make between performance measures. Many organizations focus management control on all of the most important activities, including nonfinancial measures such as control of quality and service, and use multiple measures to monitor the actual benefits of improvements in these activities.

Productivity Measures Over Time

Be careful when comparing productivity measures over time. Changes in the process or in the rate of inflation can make results misleading. For example, consider labor productivity at **Adobe Systems**. One measure of productivity is sales revenue per employee.

	2001	2008	Percent Change
Total revenue (millions)	$ 1,230	$ 3,579	191%
Employees	÷ 3,043	÷ 7,544	148%
Revenue per employee (unadjusted for inflation)	$404,206	$474,416	17%

By this measure, Adobe appears to have achieved a 17% increase in the productivity of labor because the number of employees grew more slowly than the total revenue. However, total revenue has not been adjusted for the effects of inflation. Because of inflation, each 2001 dollar was equivalent to 1.19 dollars in 2008. Therefore, Adobe's 2001 sales revenue, expressed in 2008 dollars (so we can compare it with 2008 sales revenue), is $1,230 × 1.19 = $1,464. The adjusted 2001 sales revenue per employee is as follows:

	2001 (adjusted)	2008	Percent Change
Total revenue (millions)	$ 1,464	$ 3,579	144%
Employees	÷ 3,043	÷ 7,544	148%
Revenue per employee (adjusted for inflation)	$481,104	$474,416	–1%

Adjusting for the effects of inflation reveals that Adobe's labor productivity has actually decreased by 1% rather than increased by 17%.

The Balanced Scorecard

Objective 7

Use a balanced scorecard to integrate financial and nonfinancial measures of performance.

The best management control systems include both financial and nonfinancial measures. A **balanced scorecard** (BSC) is a system that strikes a balance between financial and nonfinancial measures in the performance measurement process, links performance to rewards, and gives explicit recognition to the link between performance measurement and organizational goals and objectives. The balanced scorecard focuses management attention on measures that drive an organization to achieve its goals. About 50% of the 1,000 largest U.S. firms use some version of the balanced scorecard, including **Microsoft, American Express, ExxonMobil, Allstate, Apple Computer**, and government and nonprofit agencies, such as the U.S. Department of Transportation and the United Way of America. We describe some of the more successful in the Business First box on page 365.

Business First

Balanced Scorecard Hall of Fame

Robert Kaplan and David Norton created the BSC in 1992. In 2000, their company, **Balanced Scorecard Collaborative**, created a Balanced Scorecard Hall of Fame. To be selected for the Hall of Fame, a company must apply one or more of the following five principles to create a strategy-focused organization: "mobilize change through executive leadership; translate the strategy into operational terms; align the organization around its strategy; make strategy everyone's job; and make strategy a continual process." By the end of 2008, the Balanced Scorecard Collaborative had recognized a total of 120 Hall of Fame organizations. The inductees include the following: **Army and Air Force Exchange Service (AAFES)**, **St. Mary's/Duluth Clinic Health System (SMDC)**, the City of Corpus Christi, **BMW Financial Services**, and **Wendy's International**.

AAFES is a $9 billion global retailer with 50,000 employees serving 8.7 million customers in 3,100 stores in 30 countries. AAFES adopted the Balanced Scorecard to prepare the organization to meet growing and diverse demands of its increasingly mobile customers. The BSC helps create alignment, drive accountability, optimize resource allocation, and link strategy to operations. In 4 years revenue has increased by 11%, dividends 19%, employee satisfaction 16%, and customer satisfaction 17%. Inventory has been reduced by about $108 million. Michael Howard, AAFES chief operating officer, observes the following: "The BSC has given us the ability to look beyond traditional financial measures to drive long-term sustainability that focuses on employee optimization. The BSC aligns corporate resources and energies to drive performance that ensure AAFES continues to provide a valued benefit to the military market."

SMDC operates 20 clinics, hospitals, and specialty care facilities in northern Minnesota. It has gross revenue of about $700 million. CEO Peter Person comments "our monthly scorecard review sessions are incredibly valuable to me as CEO. The scorecard enables us to easily scan and digest overall organizational performance, and to identify any necessary course corrections." SMDC has used the BSC to align its operations, link its budget to strategy, and to spread strategic awareness to every employee.

The City of Corpus Christi is Texas's largest coastal city and the nation's sixth largest port. The city employs 3,300 serving a population of 295,000. The city adopted the BSC to clarify and communicate its strategy; align departments, divisions, and employees; and make more timely and better informed decisions that impact citizens' lives. Constituent satisfaction has increased 16%, workforce retention is up, and citizen/customer wait time is down. The city's bond rating improved, fueled in part by the BSC management system. Angel R. Escobar, Interim City Manager says: "Now, with the BSC, we know what we are great at and what we need to improve upon ... our monthly BSC meetings unify departmental directors to collectively focus on and discuss solutions to real issues."

BMW Financial Services was established in 1993 to support the sales and marketing efforts of BMW North America. The company has more than $15 billion in managed assets. It finances over half the new BMW vehicles sold in the United States. BMW Financial Services adopted the BSC in 1998 and has seen remarkable growth in annual sales and number of customer accounts. The company uses the scorecard to link objectives, initiatives, and metrics to its strategy and communicate these links throughout the company.

Wendy's International is one of the world's largest restaurant operating and franchising companies, with more than 6,600 restaurants and 2008 revenue of $1.8 billion. The company implemented the BSC to get a better handle on intangible assets, such as intellectual capital, and customer focus. CEO Jack Schuessler lauded the BSC's success in "establishing targets and measuring our progress in key dimensions ranging from employee retention at the restaurant level, to restaurant evaluation scores, to business processes, to total revenue growth. They are all vitally important, not just the financial measures." The BSC provides a framework for balancing financial and nonfinancial measures.

The BSC has helped these and other award-winning organizations in many different ways. It has gained wide acceptance and successful implementation in many companies since its introduction more than 15 years ago.

Sources: Balanced Scorecard Collaborative Web site (www.bscol.com); St. Mary's/Duluth Clinic Health System Web site (www.smdc.org); BMW Financial Services Web site (www.fs.bmwusa.com); and Wendy's International, Inc., *Wendy's International 2008 Annual Report;* Palladium Group Web site November 6, 2008 press release(www.thepalladiumgroup.com).

The balanced scorecard helps line managers understand the relationship between nonfinancial measures and organizational goals. The balanced scorecard identifies performance measures from each of the four components of the successful organization shown in Exhibit 9-3 on page 352. Links between the measures and organizational objectives help managers throughout the organization understand how their actions support the organization's goals.

What does a balanced scorecard look like? The classic balanced scorecard developed by Robert Kaplan and David Norton includes **key performance indicators**—measures that drive the organization to meet its goals—grouped into four categories: (1) financial, (2) customers, (3) internal business processes, and (4) innovation and learning. Some companies use other terminology and some include additional categories—the most common additional categories are for employees or other stakeholders. However, all develop performance measures for each objective within each category. For example, **Philips Electronics** uses the categories and performance indicators in Exhibit 9-11. Most companies that use a balanced scorecard specify the categories

Exhibit 9-11

Performance Indicators for Philips Electronics' Balanced Scorecard

Financial	Processes
Economic profit realized	Percentage reduction in process cycle time
Income from operations	Number of engineering changes
Working capital	Capacity utilization
Operational cash flow	Order response time
Inventory turns	Process capability
Customers	**Competence**
Rank in customer survey	Leadership competence
Market share	Percentage of patent-protected turnover
Repeat order rate	Training days per employee
Complaints	Quality improvement team participation
Brand index	

that each business segment will use, but they allow the units to choose the relevant performance measures for each category. For example, every Microsoft division has measures for financial, customer, internal processes, and learning perspectives, but the Latin American division has different measures in each category than does the Seattle headquarters. The balanced scorecard should not be a straightjacket; rather it is a flexible framework for motivating and measuring performance.

Making Managerial Decisions

The balanced scorecard emphasizes the connections between performance measures and financial and nonfinancial goals. Indicate where each of the following goals of **Whirlpool** fits with the four components of a successful organization shown in Exhibit 9-3 on page 352, and explain how these components relate to one another:

> People commitment
> Total quality
> Customer satisfaction
> Financial performance
> Growth and innovation

Answer

The components listed in Exhibit 9-3 depict the causal links from organizational learning to business process improvement, to customer satisfaction, and finally to financial strength. The

five goals set by top managers at Whirlpool suggest the following links among the goals:

If Whirlpool makes a solid commitment to its people and invests in growth and innovation, the company will make progress in organizational learning. This will lead to business process improvements that decrease costs, increase efficiency, and increase the total quality of its products, which will then lead to increased customer satisfaction. The ultimate result of satisfied customers is improved financial performance. Sustainable financial strength should allow Whirlpool to repeat the cycle and continue to invest in both organizational learning and internal business processes.

Management Control Systems in Service, Government, and Nonprofit Organizations

Objective 8

Describe the difficulties of management control in service and nonprofit organizations.

Most service, government, and nonprofit organizations face substantial difficulty implementing management control systems. Why? The main problem is that the outputs of service and nonprofit organizations are difficult to measure. For example, what is a good measure of output for a bank's call center (where service representatives answer customers' questions)? Number of calls or total time spent on calls? The measure "number of calls" might motivate many short calls that do not provide thorough answers to customers. The measure "total time spent on calls" might motivate long, time-wasting calls. It may be difficult to know the quality or sometimes even the quantity of the service provided until long after the organization delivers the service. When quality and quantity of output are hard to measure, developing timely measures of input/output relationships is nearly impossible.

The keys to successful management control in any organization are proper training and motivation of employees to achieve the organization's strategic objectives, accompanied by consistent monitoring of measures chosen to fit with these objectives. These keys are equally important in service-oriented organizations. **MBNA America**, a large issuer of bank credit cards, works hard to measure the amount and quality of its service. It identifies customer retention as its primary key success factor. MBNA trains its customer representatives carefully. Each day it measures and reports performance on 14 objectives consistent with customer retention, and it rewards every employee based on those 14 objectives. Measures include answering every call by the second ring, keeping the computer up 100% of the time, and processing credit-line requests within 1 hour. Employees have earned bonuses as high as 20% of their annual salaries by meeting those objectives.

Nonprofit and government organizations have problems designing and implementing an objective that is similar to the financial "bottom line" that often serves as the unifying goal in private industry. Furthermore, in nonprofit organizations, many people seek primarily nonmonetary rewards. For example, volunteers in the **Peace Corps** receive little pay but derive much satisfaction from helping to improve conditions in underdeveloped countries. **AmeriCorps** volunteers have similar objectives domestically. Thus, monetary incentives are generally less effective in nonprofit organizations. Management control systems in nonprofit organizations probably will never be as highly developed as are those in profit-seeking firms because of the following:

1. Organizational goals and objectives are less clear. Moreover, there are often multiple goals and objectives, requiring difficult trade-offs.
2. Professionals (for example, teachers, attorneys, physicians, scientists, economists) tend to dominate nonprofit organizations. Because of their perceived professional status, they are often less receptive to the installation of formal control systems.
3. Measurements are more difficult because
   a. there is no profit measure; and
   b. there are heavy amounts of discretionary fixed costs, which make the relationships of inputs to outputs difficult to specify and measure.
4. There is less competitive pressure from other organizations or "owners" to improve management control systems. As a result, for example, many cities in the United States are "privatizing" some essential services, such as sanitation, by contracting with private firms.
5. The role of budgeting, instead of being a rigorous planning process, is often more a matter of playing bargaining games with sources of funding to get the largest possible authorization.
6. Motivations and incentives of employees may differ from those in for-profit organizations.

Making Managerial Decisions

Study Exhibit 9-3 again. Use the same four general components, but rearrange them a bit to reflect a framework that might help managers of a successful governmental or nonprofit organization.

Answer

For governmental and nonprofit organizations, the ultimate objective is not to focus on financial results but to deliver the maximum benefits to customers (or citizens) based on an available pool of financial resources. Thus, the causal relationships might be as follows:

Organizational learning → process improvements in delivering programs → fiscal or financial strength → greater program benefits for citizens or clients

Future of Management Control Systems

As organizations mature and as environments change, managers expand and refine their management control tools. The management control techniques that were satisfactory 10 or 20 years ago may not be adequate for many organizations today.

A changing environment often means that organizations adjust their goals or key success factors. New goals require different benchmarks for evaluating performance. The management control system must evolve, too, or the organization may not manage its resources effectively or efficiently. A summary of management control principles that will always be important and that can guide the redesign of systems follows:

1. Always expect that individuals will be pulled in the direction of their own self-interest. You may be pleasantly surprised that some individuals will act selflessly, but management control systems should be designed to take advantage of more typical human behavior. Be aware that managers in different cultures may perceive self-interest differently.

2. Design incentives so that individuals who pursue their own self-interest also achieve the organization's objectives. Because there are usually multiple objectives, multiple incentives are appropriate. Do not underestimate the difficulty of balancing these incentives—some experimentation may be necessary to achieve multiple objectives.

3. Evaluate actual performance based on expected or planned performance. Where appropriate, revise planned performance to reflect actual output achieved. You can apply the concept of flexible budgeting to many goals and actions, both financial and nonfinancial.

4. Consider nonfinancial performance to be an important determinant of long-term success. In the short run, a manager may be able to generate good financial performance while neglecting nonfinancial performance, but it is not likely over a longer haul.

5. Array performance measures across the entire value chain of the company. This ensures that the management control system incorporates all activities that are critical to the long-run success of the company.

6. Periodically review the success of the management control system. Is the organization achieving its overall goals? Do the actions motivated by the management control system lead to goal achievement? Do individuals understand the management control system and effectively use the information it provides?

7. Learn from the management control successes (and failures) of competitors around the world. Despite cultural differences, human behavior is remarkably similar. Managers can learn from successful applications of new technology and management controls by reading books or attending courses that describe management control systems at other companies.

Highlights to Remember

1. **Describe the relationship of management control systems to organizational goals.** The starting point for designing and evaluating a management control system is the identification of organizational goals as specified by top management.

2. **Explain the importance of evaluating performance and describe how it impacts motivation, goal congruence, and employee effort.** The way an organization measures and evaluates performance affects individuals' behavior. The more that it ties rewards to performance measures, the more incentive there is to improve the measures. Poorly designed measures may actually work against the organization's goals.

3. **Develop performance measures and use them to monitor the achievements of an organization.** A well-designed management control system measures both financial and nonfinancial performance. Superior nonfinancial performance usually leads to superior financial performance in time. The performance measures should tell managers how well they are meeting the organization's goals.

4. **Use responsibility accounting to define an organizational subunit as a cost center, a profit center, or an investment center.** Responsibility accounting assigns revenue and cost objectives to the management of the subunit that has the greatest influence over them. Cost centers focus on costs only, profit centers on both revenues and costs, and investment centers on profits relative to the amount invested.

5. **Prepare segment income statements for evaluating profit and investment centers using the contribution margin and controllable-cost concepts.** The contribution approach to measuring a segment's income aids performance evaluation by separating a segment's costs into those controllable by the segment management and those beyond management's control. It allows separate evaluation of a segment as an economic investment and the performance of the segment's manager.

6. **Measure performance against nonfinancial objectives such as quality, cycle time, and productivity.** Measuring performance in areas such as quality, cycle time, and productivity causes employees to direct attention to those areas. Achieving goals in these nonfinancial measures can help meet long-run financial objectives.

7. **Use a balanced scorecard to integrate financial and nonfinancial measures of performance.** The balanced scorecard helps managers monitor actions that are designed to meet the various goals of the organization. It integrates key performance indicators that measure how well the organization is meeting its goals.

8. **Describe the difficulties of management control in service and nonprofit organizations.** Management control in service and nonprofit organizations is difficult because of a number of factors, chief of which is a relative lack of clearly observable outcomes. ■

Accounting Vocabulary

balanced scorecard (BSC), p. 364
controllable cost, p. 354
cost center, p. 354
cost of quality report, p. 360
cycle time, p. 362
goal congruence, p. 349
investment center, p. 355

key performance indicators, p. 365
key success factor, p. 349
management control system, p. 347
managerial effort, p. 349
motivation, p. 350
productivity, p. 362
profit center, p. 354
quality control, p. 360

quality-control chart, p. 360
responsibility accounting, p. 354
responsibility center, p. 354
segments, p. 355
throughput time, p. 362
total quality management (TQM), p. 360
uncontrollable cost, p. 354

Fundamental Assignment Material

9-A1 Responsibility of Purchasing Agent

Excel Electronics Company, a privately held enterprise, has a subcontract from a large aerospace company in Chicago. Although Excel was a low bidder, the aerospace company was reluctant to award the business to the company because it was a newcomer to this kind of activity. Consequently, Excel assured the aerospace company of its financial strength by submitting its audited financial statements. Moreover, Excel agreed to a pay a penalty of $5,000 per day for each day of late delivery for whatever cause.

Margie McMahon, the Excel purchasing agent, is responsible for acquiring materials and parts in time to meet production schedules. She placed an order with an Excel supplier for a critical manufactured component. The supplier, who had a reliable record for meeting schedules, gave McMahon an acceptable delivery date. McMahon checked up several times and was assured that the component would arrive at Excel on schedule.

On the date specified by the supplier for shipment to Excel, McMahon was informed that the component had been damaged during final inspection. It was delivered 10 days late. McMahon had allowed 4 extra days for possible delays, but Excel was 6 days late in delivering to the aerospace company and so had to pay a penalty of $30,000.

What department should bear the penalty? Why?

9-A2 Contribution Approach to Responsibility Accounting

Dave Skold owns and operates a small chain of convenience stores in Waterloo and Cedar Rapids. The company has five stores including a downtown store and a Big Rock store in the Waterloo division; and a downtown store, a Solon store, and an airport store in the Cedar Rapids Division. There is also a separate administrative staff that provides market research, personnel, and accounting and finance services.

The company had the following financial results for 20X1 (in thousands):

Sales revenue	$8,000
Cost of merchandise sold	3,500
Gross margin	4,500
Operating expenses	2,200
Income before income taxes	$2,300

The following data about 20X1 operations were also available:

1. All five stores used the same pricing formula; therefore, all had the same gross margin percentage.
2. Sales were largest in the two downtown stores, with 30% of the total sales volume in each. The Solon and airport stores each provided 15% of total sales volume, and the Big Rock store provided 10%.
3. Variable operating costs at the stores were 10% of revenue for the downtown stores. The other stores had lower variable and higher fixed costs. Their variable operating costs were only 5% of sales revenue.
4. The fixed costs over which the store managers had control were $125,000 in each of the downtown stores, $160,000 at Solon and airport, and $80,000 at Big Rock.
5. The remaining $910,000 of operating costs consisted of
   a. $210,000 controllable by the Cedar Rapids division manager but not by individual stores,
   b. $100,000 controllable by the Waterloo division manager but not by individual stores, and
   c. $600,000 controllable by the administrative staff.
6. Of the $600,000 spent by the administrative staff, $350,000 directly supported the Cedar Rapids division, with 20% for the downtown store, 30% for each of the Solon and airport stores, and 20% for Cedar Rapids operations in general. Another $140,000 supported the Waterloo division, 50% for the downtown store, 25% for the Big Rock store, and 25% supporting Waterloo operations in general. The other $110,000 was for general corporate expenses.

Prepare an income statement by segments using the contribution approach to responsibility accounting. Use the format of Exhibit 9-4, page 355. Column headings should be as follows:

Company as a whole	Breakdown into Two Divisions		Breakdown of Waterloo Division			Breakdown of Cedar Rapids Division			
	Waterloo	Cedar Rapids	Not allocated	Downtown	Big Rock	Not allocated	Downtown	Solon	Airport

9-A3 Comparison of Productivity

Wells and Severson are manufacturing companies. Comparative data for 20X1 and 20X7 are as follows:

		Wells	Severson
Sales revenue	20X1	$5,660,000,000	$7,658,000,000
	20X7	$6,000,000,000	$9,667,000,000
Number of employees	20X1	56,600	75,900
	20X7	54,800	76,200

Assume that inflation has totaled 15% during these 6 years so that each 20X1 dollar is equivalent to 1.15 dollars in 20X7, due to inflation.

1. Compute 20X1 and 20X7 productivity measures in terms of revenue per employee for Wells and Severson.
2. Compare the change in productivity between 20X1 and 20X7 for Wells with that for Severson.

9-B1 Responsibility Accounting

The Kephart Company produces precision machine parts. Kephart uses a standard cost system, calculates standard cost variances for each department, and reports them to department managers. Managers use the information to improve their operations. Superiors use the same information to evaluate managers' performance.

Liz Elder was recently appointed manager of the assembly department of the company. She has complained that the system as designed is disadvantageous to her department. Included among the variances charged to the departments is one for rejected units. The inspection occurs at the end of the assembly department. The inspectors attempt to identify the cause of the rejection so that the department where the error occurred can be charged with it. Not all errors can be easily identified with a department, however. The nonidentified units are totaled and apportioned to the departments according to the number of identified errors. The variance for rejected units in each department is a combination of the errors caused by the department plus a portion of the unidentified causes of rejects.

1. Is Elder's complaint valid? Explain the reason(s) for your answer.
2. What would you recommend that the company do to solve its problem with Elder and her complaint?

9-B2 Divisional Contribution, Performance, and Segment Margins

The president of North Shore Railroad wants to obtain an overview of the company's operations, particularly with respect to comparing freight and passenger business. He has heard about "contribution" approaches to cost allocations that emphasize cost behavior patterns and contribution margins, contributions controllable by segment managers, and contributions by segments. The president has hired you as a consultant to help him. He has given you the following information.

Total revenue in 20X3 was $80 million, of which $72 million was freight traffic and $8 million was passenger traffic. Fifty percent of the passenger revenue was generated by division 1, 40% by division 2, and 10% by division 3.

Total variable costs were $40 million, of which $36 million was caused by freight traffic. Of the $4 million allocable to passenger traffic, $2.1, $1.6, and $.3 million could be allocated to divisions 1, 2, and 3, respectively.

Total separable discretionary fixed costs were $8 million, of which $7.6 million applied to freight traffic. For the remaining $400,000 applicable to passenger traffic, $80,000 could not be allocated to specific divisions, while $200,000, $100,000, and $20,000, were allocable to divisions 1, 2, and 3, respectively.

Total separable committed costs, which were not regarded as being controllable by segment managers, were $25 million, of which 80% was allocable to freight traffic. Of the 20% traceable to passenger traffic, divisions 1, 2, and 3 should be allocated $3 million, $700,000, and $300,000, respectively; the balance was unallocable to a specific division.

The common fixed costs not clearly allocable to any part of the company amounted to $800,000.

1. The president asks you to prepare statements, dividing the data for the company as a whole between the freight and passenger traffic and then subdividing the passenger traffic into three divisions.
2. Some competing railroads actively promote a series of one-day sightseeing tours on summer weekends. Most often, these tours are timed so that the cars with the tourists are hitched on with regularly scheduled passenger trains. What costs are relevant for making decisions to run such tours? Other railroads, facing the same general cost structure, refuse to conduct such sightseeing tours. Why?
3. Suppose that the railroad has petitioned government authorities for permission to drop division 1. What would be the effect on overall company net income for 20X4, assuming that the figures are accurate and that 20X4 operations are expected to be in all respects a duplication of 20X3 operations?

9-B3 Balanced Scorecard for a Law Firm

Young, Martinez, and Cheung (YMC) is a law firm in Chicago. The firm has had a very loose and relaxed management style that has served it well in the past. However, more aggressive law firms have been winning new clients faster than YMC has. Thus, the managing partner, Jerry Martinez, recently attended an ABA seminar on performance measurement in law firms, where he learned about the balanced scorecard. He thought it might be a good tool for YMC, one that would allow the firm to keep its culture yet still more aggressively seek new clients.

Martinez identified the following strategic objectives that fit with the firm's core values and provide a framework for assessing progress toward the firm's goals:

Financial
  a. Steadily increase the firm's revenues and profits.

Customer
  a. Understand the firm's customers and their needs.
  b. Value customer service over self-interest.

Internal Business Process
  a. Encourage knowledge sharing among the legal staff.
  b. Communicate with each other openly, honestly, and often.
  c. Empower staff to make decisions that benefit clients.

Organizational Learning
  a. Maintain an open and collaborative environment that attracts and retains the best legal staff.
  b. Seek staff diversity.

1. Develop at least one measure for each of the strategic objectives listed.
2. Explain how YMC can use this balanced scorecard to evaluate staff performance.
3. Should staff compensation be tied to the scorecard performance measures? Why or why not?

Additional Assignment Material

QUESTIONS

9-1 What is a management control system?

9-2 What are the purposes of a management control system?

9-3 What are the major components of a management control system?

9-4 What is a key success factor?

9-5 "Goals are useless without performance measures." Do you agree? Explain.

9-6 "There are corporate goals other than to improve profit." Name three.

9-7 How does management determine its key success factors?

9-8 Give three examples of how managers may improve short-run performance to the detriment of long-run results.

9-9 Name three kinds of responsibility centers.

9-10 How do profit centers and investment centers differ?

9-11 List five characteristics of a good performance measure.

9-12 List four nonfinancial measures of performance that managers find useful.

9-13 "Performance evaluation seeks to achieve goal congruence and managerial effort." Explain what is meant by this statement.

9-14 "Managers of profit centers should be held responsible for the center's entire profit. They are responsible for profit even if they cannot control all factors affecting it." Discuss.

9-15 "Variable costs are controllable and fixed costs are uncontrollable." Do you agree? Explain.

9-16 "The contribution margin is the best measure of short-run performance." Do you agree? Explain.

9-17 Give four examples of segments.

9-18 "Always try to distinguish between the performance of a segment and its manager." Why?

9-19 "The contribution margin approach to performance evaluation is flawed because focusing on only the contribution margin ignores important aspects of performance." Do you agree? Explain.

9-20 What is a balanced scorecard and why are more companies using one?

9-21 What are key performance indicators?

9-22 There are four categories of cost in the quality cost report; explain them.

9-23 Why are companies increasing their quality control emphasis on the prevention of defects?

9-24 "Nonfinancial measures of performance can be controlled just like financial measures." Do you agree? Explain.

9-25 Identify three measures of labor productivity, one using all physical measures, one using all financial measures, and one that mixes physical and financial measures.

9-26 Discuss the difficulties of comparing productivity measures over time.

9-27 "Control systems in nonprofit organizations will never be as highly developed as in profit-seeking organizations." Do you agree? Explain.

CRITICAL THINKING EXERCISES

9-28 Management Control Systems and Innovation

The president of a fast-growing, high-technology firm remarked, "Developing budgets and comparing performance with the budgets may be fine for some firms. But we want to encourage innovation and entrepreneurship. Budgets go with bureaucracy, not innovation." Do you agree? How can a management control system encourage innovation and entrepreneurship?

9-29 Municipal Responsibility Accounting

After barely avoiding bankruptcy, New York City established one of the most sophisticated budgeting and reporting systems of any municipality. The Integrated Financial Management System (IFMS) "clearly identifies managers in line agencies and correlates allocations and expenditures with organizational structure. . . . In addition, managers have more time to take corrective measures when variances between budgeted and actual expenditures start to develop." (*FE—The Magazine for Financial Executives*, 1, no. 8, p. 26.)

Discuss how a responsibility accounting system such as IFMS can help manage a municipality such as New York City.

9-30 Control Systems and Customer Service Function of the Value Chain

Companies increasingly use nonfinancial measures to supplement financial measures of performance. One of the most important areas of nonfinancial performance is customer service. The last decade has brought an increased focus on the customer, and this focus is reflected in many companies' management control systems, where companies use "customer-value metrics." That is, they develop measures that monitor how well the company is meeting its customers' interests. What customer-value metrics might a company such as **Volvo**, the Swedish automobile company, use in its management control system?

9-31 Control Systems and the Production Function of the Value Chain

In recent years, many organizations have focused on the value of controlling nonfinancial performance as a key to improved productivity. In particular, to gain and maintain a competitive edge, companies focus on quality and cycle time. Discuss how quality, cycle time, and productivity are related.

9-32 Key Performance Indicators

Research on performance management suggests that organizations can compete most effectively by identifying and monitoring those elements that are most closely linked to organizational success. A key performance indicator can be thought of as a measure that drives organizational success. For each of the following companies or organizations, identify two possible key performance indicators.

1. **Delta Airlines**
2. **Wal-Mart**
3. **Hewlett Packard**
4. **New York Department of Motor Vehicles**

EXERCISES

9-33 Responsibility for Stable Employment Policy

The Mid-Atlantic Metal Fabricating Company has been manufacturing machine tools for a number of years and has had an industry-wide reputation for doing high-quality work. The company has been faced with fluctuations in demand over the years. It has been company policy to lay off welders as soon as there was insufficient work to keep them busy and to rehire them when demand warranted. Because of this lay-off policy, the company now has poor labor relations and finds it difficult to hire good welders. Consequently, the quality of the products has been declining steadily.

The plant manager has proposed that welders who earn $20 per hour be retained during slow periods to do menial plant maintenance work that is normally performed by workers earning $14 per hour in the plant maintenance department.

You, as controller, must decide the most appropriate accounting procedure to handle the wages of the welders doing plant maintenance work. What department(s) should be charged with this work, and at what rate? Discuss the implications of your plan.

9-34 Salesclerk's Compensation Plan

You are the manager of a department store in Tokyo. Sales are subject to month-to-month variations, depending on the individual salesclerk's efforts and other factors. A new salary-plus-bonus plan has been in effect for 4 months, and you are reviewing a sales performance report. The plan provides for a base salary of ¥50,000 per month, a ¥68,000 bonus each month if the salesclerk meets the monthly sales quota, and an additional commission of 5% of all sales over the monthly quota. Each month, the quota is reset at approximately 3% above the previous month's sales to motivate clerks to continually increase sales. The monthly quotas and actual amounts for the first 4 months of the plan are shown in the sales report below (in thousands).

		Salesclerk A	Salesclerk B	Salesclerk C
January	Quota	¥4,500	¥1,500	¥7,500
	Actual	1,500	1,500	9,000
February	Quota	¥1,545	¥1,545	¥9,270
	Actual	3,000	1,545	3,000
March	Quota	¥3,090	¥1,590	¥3,090
	Actual	5,250	750	9,000
April	Quota	¥5,400	¥ 775	¥9,270
	Actual	1,500	780	4,050

1. Compute the compensation for each salesclerk for each month.
2. Evaluate the compensation plan. Be specific. What changes would you recommend?

9-35 Common Measures on a Balanced Scorecard

Listed next are common performance measures appearing on balanced scorecards. Indicate whether the listed measure is primarily associated with the financial, customer, internal process, or learning and growth perspective. (Note that some measures might reasonably be associated with more than one perspective.)

- Return on sales
- Retention of target customers
- Net cash flow
- Training hours
- Employee turnover rate
- Materials handling cost per unit
- Market share
- Product-development cycle time
- Revenue growth in segments
- Occupational injuries and illness
- Days sales in inventory
- Average cost per invoice

9-36 Goals and Objectives at Health Net

Health Net provides health care to more than 6.7 million members. As a managed health-care organization, the company strives to provide high-quality health care at a reasonable cost. Many stakeholders have an interest in Health Net's operations, including doctors and other medical personnel, patients, insurance companies, government regulators, and the general public.

Prepare a goal and one measure for assessing achievement of that goal for each of the following key areas:

Customer satisfaction
Efficient use of lab tests
Usage of physician time
Maintain state-of-the-art facilities
Overall financial performance

9-37 Performance Evaluation

Daniel Merrill & Co. is a stock brokerage firm that evaluates its employees on sales activity generated. Recently, the firm also began evaluating its stockbrokers on the number of new accounts generated.

Discuss how these two performance measures are consistent and how they may conflict. Do you believe that these measures are appropriate for the long-term goal of profitability?

9-38 Simple Controllable Costs

Chuk's Sweets Chalet is a gourmet dessert restaurant in downtown San Francisco. Elizabeth Chuk, the sole proprietor, expanded to a second location in Burlingame, California, 3 years ago. Recently, Chuk decided to enroll in a PhD program and retire from active management of the individual restaurants but continues to oversee the entire company. She hired a manager for each restaurant. In 20X3, each had sales of $850,000. The Burlingame restaurant is still pricing lower than the San Francisco restaurant to establish a customer base. Variable expenses run 60% of sales for the San Francisco restaurant and 70% of sales for the Burlingame restaurant.

Each manager is responsible for the rent and some other fixed costs for his or her restaurant. These costs amounted to $125,000 for the San Francisco restaurant and $50,000 for the one in Burlingame. The difference is primarily due to lower rent in Burlingame. In addition, several costs, such as advertising, legal services, accounting, and personnel services, were centralized. The managers had no control of these expenses, but some of them directly benefited the individual restaurants. Of the $360,000 cost in this category, $110,000 related to San Francisco and $180,000 to Burlingame, where most of the additional cost in Burlingame is due to the cost of extra advertising to build up its customer base. The remaining $70,000 was general corporate overhead.

1. Prepare income statements for each restaurant and for the company as a whole. Use a format that allows easy assessment of each manager's performance and each restaurant's economic performance.
2. Using only the information given in this exercise do the following:
   a. Evaluate each restaurant as an economic investment.
   b. Evaluate each manager.

9-39 Quality Theories Compared

Examine the two graphs below. Compare the total quality management approach to the traditional theory of quality. Which theory do you believe represents the current realities of today's global competitive environment? Explain.

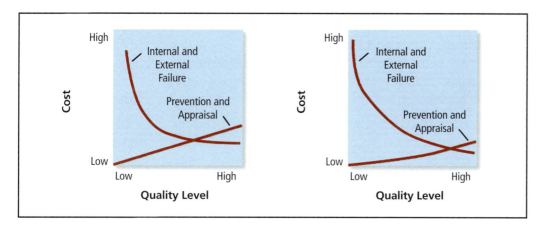

9-40 Quality-Control Chart

San Angelo Manufacturing Company was concerned about a growing number of defective units being produced. At one time, the company had the percentage of defective units down to less than 5 per thousand, but recently rates of defects have been near, or even above, 1%. The company decided to graph its defects for the last 8 weeks (40 working days), beginning Monday, September 1 through Friday, October 24. The graph is shown in Exhibit 9-12 below.

1. Identify two important trends evident in the quality-control chart.
2. What might management of San Angelo do to deal with each trend?

9-41 Cycle-Time Reporting

The Pierre plant of Global Electronics produces computers. The plant monitors its cycle time closely to prevent schedule delays and excessive costs. The standard cycle time for the manufacture of printed circuit boards for one of its computers is 26 hours. Consider the following cycle-time data from the past 6 weeks of circuit board production:

Week	Units Completed	Total Cycle Time
1	564	14,108 hours
2	544	14,592
3	553	15,152
4	571	16,598
5	547	17,104
6	552	16,673

Analyze circuit board cycle time performance in light of the 26-hour objective.

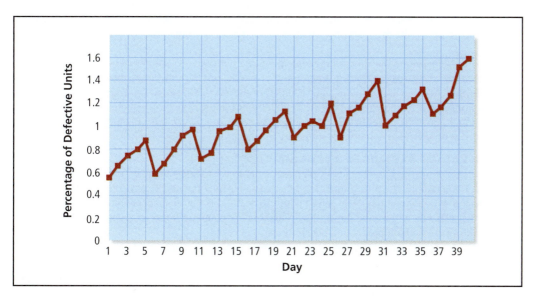

Exhibit 9-12

San Angelo Manufacturing Company

Quality-Control Chart for September 1 Through October 24

PROBLEMS

9-42 Multiple Goals and Profitability

The following multiple goals were identified by General Electric:

Profitability
Market position
Productivity
Product leadership
Personnel development
Employee attitudes
Public responsibility
Balance between short-range and long-range goals

General Electric is a huge, highly decentralized corporation. At the time it developed these goals, GE had approximately 170 responsibility centers called departments, but that is a deceptive term. In most other companies, these departments would be called divisions. For example, some GE departments had sales of more than $500 million.

Each department manager's performance was evaluated annually in relation to the specified multiple goals. A special measurements group was set up to devise ways of quantifying accomplishments in each of the areas. In this way, the evaluation of performance would become more objective as the various measures were developed and improved.

1. How would you measure performance in each of these areas? Be specific.
2. Can the other goals be encompassed as ingredients of a formal measure of profitability? In other words, can profitability per se be defined to include the other goals?

9-43 Responsibility Accounting, Profit Centers, and Contribution Approach

Bloomington Honda had the following data for the year's operations:

Sales of vehicles	$2,400,000
Sales of parts and service	600,000
Cost of vehicle sales	1,920,000
Parts and service materials	180,000
Parts and service labor	240,000
Parts and service overhead	60,000
General dealership overhead	200,000
Advertising of vehicles	120,000
Sales commissions, vehicles	48,000
Sales salaries, vehicles	60,000

The president of the dealership has long regarded the markup on material and labor for the parts and service activity as the amount that is supposed to cover all parts and service overhead plus some general overhead of the dealership. In other words, the parts and service department is viewed as a cost-recovery operation, while the sales of vehicles is viewed as the income-producing activity.

1. Prepare a departmentalized operating statement that harmonizes with the views of the president.
2. Prepare an alternative operating statement that would reflect a different view of the dealership operations. Assume that $24,000 and $120,000 of the $200,000 general overhead can be allocated with confidence to the parts and service department and to sales of vehicles, respectively. The remaining $56,000 cannot be allocated except in some highly arbitrary manner.
3. Comment on the relative merits of numbers 1 and 2.

9-44 Incentives in Planned Economies

Often government-owned companies in planned economies reward managers based on nonfinancial measures. For example, the government might give managers a bonus for exceeding a 5-year-planned target for production quantities. A problem with this method is that managers tend to predict low volumes so that officials will set the targets low. This hinders planning because managers do not provide accurate information about production possibilities.

The former Soviet Union developed an alternative performance measurement and reward system. Suppose F is the forecast of production, A is actual production, and X, Y, and Z are positive constants set by top officials, with X, Y, $Z > 0$. The following performance measure was designed to motivate both high production and accurate forecasts.

$$\text{performance measure} = (Y \times F) + [X \times (A - F)] \text{ if } F \leq A$$
$$(Y \times F) - [Z \times (F - A)] \text{ if } F > A$$

Assume that Cuba adopted this measure at a time when Soviet influence was great. Consider the Havana Television Manufacturing Company (HTMC). During 19X3, the factory manager, Che Chavez, had to predict the number of TVs that HTMC could produce during the next year. He was confident that at least 700,000 TVs could be produced in 19X4, and most likely they could produce 800,000 TVs. With good luck, they might even produce 900,000. Government officials told him that the new performance evaluation measure would be used, and that $X = .50$, $Y = .80$, and $Z = 1.00$ for 19X4 and 19X5.

1. Suppose Chavez predicted production of 800,000 TVs and HTMC actually produced 800,000. Calculate the performance measure.
2. Suppose again that HTMC produced 800,000 TVs. Calculate the performance measure if Chavez had been conservative and predicted only 700,000 TVs. Also calculate the performance measure if he had predicted 900,000 TVs.
3. Now suppose it is November 19X4, and it is clear that HTMC cannot achieve the 800,000 target. Does the performance measure motivate continued efforts to increase production? Suppose it is clear that HTMC will easily meet the 800,000 target. Will the system motivate continued efforts to increase production?

9-45 Balanced Scorecard

Indianapolis Pharmaceuticals Company (IPC) recently revised its performance evaluation system. The company identified four major goals and several objectives required to meet each goal. Kris Nordmark, controller of IPC, suggested that a balanced scorecard be used to report on progress toward meeting the objectives. At a recent meeting, she told the managers of IPC that listing the objectives was only the first step in installing a new performance measurement system. Each objective has to be accompanied by one or more measures to monitor progress toward achieving the objectives. She asked the help of the managers in identifying appropriate measures.

The goals and objectives determined by the top management of IPC are as follows:

1. Maintain strong financial health.
   a. Keep sufficient cash balances to assure financial survival.
   b. Achieve consistent growth in sales and income.
   c. Provide excellent returns to shareholders.
2. Provide excellent service to customers.
   a. Provide products that meet the needs of customers.
   b. Meet customer needs on a timely basis.
   c. Meet customer quality requirements.
   d. Be the preferred supplier to customers.
3. Be among the industry leaders in product and process innovations.
   a. Bring new products to market before competition.
   b. Lead competition in production process innovation.
4. Develop and maintain efficient, state-of-the-art production processes.
   a. Excel in manufacturing efficiency.
   b. Meet or beat product introduction schedules.

Propose at least one measure of performance for each of the objectives of IPC.

9-46 Quality Cost Report

The manufacturing division of Red Lake Enterprises makes a variety of home furnishings. The company prepares monthly reports on quality costs. In early 20X7, Red Lake's president asked you, the controller, to compare quality costs in 20X6 to those in 20X4. He wanted to see only total annual numbers for 20X6 compared with 20X4. You have prepared the report shown in Exhibit 9-13 on page 378.

1. For each of the four quality cost areas, explain what types of costs are included and how those costs have changed between 20X4 and 20X6.
2. Assess overall quality performance in 20X6 compared with 20X4. What do you suppose has caused the changes observed in quality costs?

9-47 Six Sigma, Mean, and Variance

A major objective of Six Sigma quality-control programs is to better meet customers' needs. One place companies have applied Six Sigma is to order delivery times. They have directed efforts at reducing both the mean (average) time to delivery and the variance or standard deviation (dispersion)

Quality Cost Area	20X4 Cost	20X6 Cost
1. Prevention cost	45	107
Percentage of total quality cost	3.3%	12.4%
2. Appraisal cost	124	132
Percentage of total quality cost	9.1%	15.2%
3. Internal failure cost	503	368
Percentage of total quality cost	36.9%	42.5%
Total internal quality cost (1 + 2 + 3)	672	607
Percentage of total quality cost	49.3%	70.1%
4. External failure cost	691	259
Percentage of total quality cost	50.7%	29.9%
Total quality cost	1,363	866
Total product cost	22,168	23,462

Exhibit 9-13

Red Lake Enterprises

Quality Cost Report (thousands of dollars)

of the delivery times. Customers want to get their products sooner, as reflected in the mean. But they also want assurance that the product will arrive when promised. This requires delivery schedules to have little random variance.

Consider the following experience with the implementation of Six Sigma at a major manufacturing company:

Order Delivery Times (Days)	
Before Six Sigma	After Six Sigma
30	22
12	20
11	5
13	8
26	19
14	8
16	7
20	12
24	18
14	21

Compute the mean and standard deviation of order-delivery time before and after implementation of Six Sigma. From a customer's perspective, how would you view the results of this application of Six Sigma?

9-48 Productivity

In early 20X1, United Communications, a U.S.-based international telephone communications company, purchased the controlling interest in Bucharest Telecom, Ltd. (BTL) in Romania. A key productivity measure monitored by United is the number of customer telephone lines per employee. Consider the following data for United:

	20X1 without BTL	20X1 with BTL	20X0
Customer lines	15,054,000	19,994,000	14,615,000
Employees	74,520	114,590	72,350
Lines per employee	202	174	202

1. What are United's 20X0 productivity and 20X1 productivity without BTL?
2. What are BTL's 20X1 productivity and United's 20X1 productivity with BTL?
3. What difficulties do you foresee if United brings BTL's productivity in line?

9-49 Productivity Measurement

Larson's Laundry had the following results in 20X1 and 20X3:

	20X1	**20X3**
Pounds of laundry processed	1,360,000 pounds	1,525,000 pounds
Sales revenue	$720,000	$1,014,000
Direct-labor hours worked	45,100 hours	46,650 hours
Direct-labor cost	$316,000	$408,000

The laundry used the same facilities in 20X3 as in 20X1. During the past 3 years, however, the company put more effort into training its employees. The manager of Larson's was curious about whether the training had increased labor productivity.

1. Compute a measure of labor productivity for 20X3 based entirely on physical measures. Do the same for 20X1. That is, from the data given, choose measures of physical output and physical input, and use them to compare the physical productivity of labor in 20X3 with that in 20X1.
2. Compute a measure of labor productivity for 20X3 based entirely on financial measures. Do the same for 20X1. That is, from the data given, choose measures of financial output and financial input, and use them to compare the financial productivity of labor in 20X3 with that in 20X1.
3. Suppose the following productivity measure was used:

$$\text{Productivity} = \frac{\text{sales revenue}}{\text{direct-labor hours worked}}$$

Because of inflation, each 20X1 dollar is equivalent to 1.12 dollars in 20X3. Compute appropriate productivity numbers for comparing 20X3 productivity with 20X1 productivity.

CASES

9-50 Trade-Offs Among Objectives

Computer Data Services (CDS) performs routine and custom information systems services for many companies in a large midwestern metropolitan area. CDS has built a reputation for high-quality customer service and job security for its employees. Quality service and customer satisfaction have been CDS's primary subgoals—retaining a skilled and motivated workforce has been an important factor in achieving those goals. In the past, temporary downturns in business did not mean layoffs of employees, though some employees were required to perform other than their usual tasks. In anticipation of growth in business, CDS leased new equipment that, beginning in August, added $10,000 per month in operating costs. Three months ago, however, a new competitor began offering the same services to CDS customers at prices averaging 19% lower than those of CDS. Rico Estrada, the company founder and president, believes that a significant price reduction is necessary to maintain the company's market share and avoid financial ruin, but he is puzzled about how to achieve it without compromising quality, service, and the goodwill of his workforce.

CDS has a productivity objective of 20 accounts per employee. Estrada does not think that he can increase this productivity and still maintain both quality and flexibility to customer needs. CDS also monitors average cost per account and the number of customer satisfaction adjustments (resolutions of complaints). The average billing markup rate is 25% of cost. Consider the following data from the past 6 months:

	June	**July**	**August**	**September**	**October**	**November**
Number of accounts	797	803	869	784	723	680
Number of employees	40	41	44	43	43	41
Average cost per account	$ 153	$ 153	$ 158	$ 173	$ 187	$ 191
Average salary per employee	$3,000	$3,000	$3,000	$3,000	$3,000	$3,000

1. Discuss the trade-offs facing Rico Estrada.
2. Can you suggest solutions to his trade-off dilemma?

9-51 Six Sigma

The chapter mentions four companies that use Six Sigma for measuring and controlling quality: Motorola, General Electric, 3M, and Dow Chemical. Go to the Web site for each of these companies and find what each says about its Six Sigma efforts.

9-52 Review of Chapters 1–9

William Whitebear, general manager of the Kamloops Division of Canada Enterprises, was preparing for a management meeting. His divisional controller gave him the following information:

1. The master budget for the fiscal year ended June 30, 20X4 follows:

Sales (50,000 units of A and 70,000 units of B)	$870,000
Manufacturing cost of goods sold	740,000
Manufacturing margin	$130,000
Selling and administrative expenses	120,000
Operating income	$ 10,000

2. The standard variable manufacturing cost per unit follows:

	Product A		Product B	
Direct materials	10 pieces at $.25	$2.50	5 pounds at $.30	$1.50
Direct labor	1 hour at $3.00	3.00	.3 hour at $2.50	.75
Variable overhead	1 hour at $2.00	2.00	.3 hour at $2.50	.75
Total		$7.50		$3.00

3. All budgeted selling and administrative expenses are common, fixed expenses; 60% are discretionary expenses.
4. The actual income statement for the fiscal year ended June 30, 20X4 follows:

Sales (53,000 units of A and 64,000 units of B)	$861,000
Manufacturing cost of goods sold	749,200
Manufacturing margin	$111,800
Selling and administrative expenses	116,000
Operating income	$ (4,200)

5. The budgeted sales prices for products A and B were $9 and $6, respectively. Actual sales prices equaled budgeted sales prices.
6. The schedule of the actual variable manufacturing cost of goods sold by product follows (actual quantities in parentheses):

Product A:	Materials	$134,500	(538,000 pieces)
	Labor	156,350	(53,000 hours)
	Overhead	108,650	(53,000 hours)
Product B:	Materials	102,400	(320,000 pounds)
	Labor	50,000	(20,000 hours)
	Overhead	50,000	(20,000 hours)
Total		$601,900	

7. Products A and B are manufactured in separate facilities. Of the budgeted fixed manufacturing cost, $130,000 is separable as follows: $45,000 to product A and $85,000 to product B. Ten percent of these separate costs are discretionary. All other budgeted fixed manufacturing expenses, separable and common, are committed.
8. There are no beginning or ending inventories.

During the upcoming management meeting, it is quite likely that some of the information from your controller will be discussed. In anticipation you set out to prepare answers to possible questions.

1. Determine the firm's budgeted break-even point in dollars, overall contribution-margin ratio, and contribution margins per unit by product.
2. Considering products A and B as segments of the firm, find the budgeted "contribution by segments" for each.
3. It is decided to allocate the budgeted selling and administrative expenses to the segments (in number 2) as follows: committed costs on the basis of budgeted unit sales mix and discretionary costs on the basis of actual unit sales mix. What are the final expense allocations? Briefly appraise the allocation method.
4. How would you respond to a proposal to base commissions to salespersons on the sales (revenue) value of orders received? Assume all salespersons have the opportunity to sell both products.
5. Determine the firm's actual "contribution margin" and "contribution controllable by segment managers" for the fiscal year ended June 30, 20X4. Assume no variances in committed fixed costs.
6. Determine the "sales-activity variance" for each product for the fiscal year ended June 30, 20X4.
7. Determine and identify all variances in variable manufacturing costs by product for the fiscal year ended June 30, 20X4.

NIKE 10-K PROBLEM

9-53 Strategy at Nike

Find "Item 7 Management's Discussion and Analysis of Financial Condition and Results of Operations" near the beginning of the **Nike** 10-K in Appendix C.

1. Outline Nike's strategy to convert revenue growth to shareholder value in five key areas.
2. What are four long-term financial goals?
3. How well have these financial goals been met?
4. List some nonfinancial goals that Nike might use in a BSC.

EXCEL APPLICATION EXERCISE

9-54 Wages for New Salary-Plus-Bonus Plan

Goal: Create an Excel spreadsheet to calculate the impact on employee wages of a new salary-plus-bonus plan established to motivate salesclerks to increase sales. Use the results to answer questions about your findings.

Scenario: As the department store manager, you must determine if the new plan is the best way to motivate salesclerks and meet the objective of increasing sales. The background data for the compensation plan appear in Exercise 9-34. Use only data for salesclerk A and salesclerk B to prepare your spreadsheet.

When you have completed your spreadsheet, answer the following questions:
1. Which salesclerk has the highest average total salary over the four-month period?
2. What part of the compensation plan had the most impact on the salesclerks' salaries? The least impact?
3. Do you see any problems with this compensation plan? Explain.

Step-by-Step:
1. Open a new Excel spreadsheet.
2. In column A, create a bold-faced heading that contains the following:
   Row 1: Chapter 9 Decision Guideline
   Row 2: Tokyo Department Store
   Row 3: Salary-Plus-Bonus Plan Analysis
   Row 4: Today's Date
3. Merge and center the four heading rows across columns A–H.
4. In column A, create the following row headings:
   Row 7: Salesclerk A
   Row 8: Month
   Row 9: January
   Row 10: February
   Row 11: March
   Row 12: April
   Skip three rows.

> Row 16: Salesclerk B
> Row 17: Month
> Row 18: January
> Row 19: February
> Row 20: March
> Row 21: April

5. Change the format of salesclerk names (rows 7, 16) to bold-faced, underlined headings.
6. Change the format of month (rows 8, 17) to bold-faced headings.
7. In rows 8 and 17, create the following bold-faced, right-justified column headings:
    Column B: Quota
    Column C: Sales
    Column D: Over Quota
    Column E: Base Salary
    Column F: Quota Bonus
    Column G: Commission
    Column H: Total Salary

    Note: Adjust column widths as necessary.

8. In column G, create the following right-justified cell headings:
    Row 14: Average:
    Row 23: Average:
9. Use the scenario data to fill in quota, sales, and base salary amounts from January–April for each salesclerk.
10. Use the appropriate IF statements to calculate over quota and quota bonus amounts when the salesclerks' sales met or exceeded their respective quotas (negative commissions should not be calculated).

$$= \text{IF (formula} > 0, \text{formula}, 0)$$
For Over Quota only.

$$= \text{IF (formula} < 0, 0, 68000) \text{ OR } = \text{IF (formula} > 0, 68000, 0)$$
For Quota Bonus only.

Hint: Go to the "Help" text and type "copy formulas" in the search area to obtain instructions for copying formulas from one cell to another. If done correctly, you should have to type in each of the formulas only once.

11. Use appropriate formulas to calculate commission and total salary amounts for each month, as well as an average amount for the January–April period for each salesclerk.
12. Format all amounts as follows:

Number tab:	Category:	Currency
	Decimal places:	0
	Symbol:	None
	Negative numbers:	Black with parentheses

13. To format specific amounts to display with a yen symbol, do the following:
    a. In an empty cell, hold down the Alt key and enter 0165 from the numeric keypad. When you stop holding the Alt key down, a yen sign will be displayed.
       Note: If your keyboard does not have a numeric keypad, use the shift and NumLk keys to activate the imbedded numeric keypad. Then, follow the instructions in part a. Use the shift and NumLk keys to turn the feature off.
    b. Highlight the yen character you have just created, select Edit, Cut. This will paste the yen sign to the clipboard. To see the clipboard, select View, Toolbars, Clipboard.
    c. Select the average amount for salesclerk A and open the Format, Cells .... dialog box.
    d. Select the custom category on the number tab. Scroll down toward the bottom of the type list and highlight the type shown next.

    Type: ($*#, ##0); ($*#, ##0); ($*"−"); (@)

    Change the data between the quotation marks in the third grouping from "−" to "0."
    Paste the yen sign over EACH occurrence of the dollar sign.
    Hint: Highlight the $ sign; press "Ctrl" and "V." This will paste the yen sign from the clipboard over the $ sign that has been highlighted in the Type field.

   e. Click the OK button.

   f. Utilize the custom format, which should now be at the bottom of the type list, to print the yen sign for all January amounts for both clerks and the average amount for salesclerk B.

14. Save your work to disk, and print a copy for your files.

> Note: Print your spreadsheet using landscape in order to ensure that all columns appear on one page.

COLLABORATIVE LEARNING EXERCISE

9-55 Goals, Objectives, and Performance Measures

There is increasing pressure on colleges and universities to develop measures of accountability. The objective is to specify goals and objectives and to develop performance measures to assess the achievement of those goals and objectives.

Form a group of four to six students to be a consulting team to the accounting department at your college or university. (If you are not using this book as part of a course in an accounting department, select any department at a local college or university.) Based on your collective knowledge of the department, its mission, and its activities, formulate a statement of goals for the department. From that statement, develop several specific objectives, each of which can be measured. Then, develop one or more measure of performance for each objective.

An optional second step in this exercise is to meet with a faculty member from the department, and ask him or her to critique your objectives and performance measures. To the department member, do the objectives make sense? Are the proposed measures feasible, and will they correctly measure attainment of the objectives? Will they provide proper incentives to the faculty? If the department has created objectives and performance measures, compare them to those your group developed.

INTERNET EXERCISE

9-56 Management Control System at Procter & Gamble

Setting up management control systems and determining measurement methods and who should be responsible for particular revenues, costs, and information can be a large task. The structure of the organization plays a part in how well a particular measure is likely to work. Ensuring that the goals of the organization are in concert with the management control system is also an important factor. It is not possible to evaluate a company's management control system from an Internet site. What we can do, however, is to use a site as an example and apply some of the concepts of the chapter to measures and tools that would be possibilities for a firm.

1. A well-known and well-established company with worldwide acceptance is **Procter & Gamble (P&G)**. Log on to the company's Web site at www.pg.com. Locate the most recent annual report by following the links under the "Investor Relations" tab to "Financial Reporting." Let's determine what P&G considers the most important factors in its success. P&G usually lists its "Core Strengths" in the "Letter to Shareholders" section of the annual report. What are the core strengths of the firm? How does P&G expect these to translate into success?

2. The company has numerous products, and the Web site divides them into different categories and brands to help customers find relevant product information. Click on "Brands." What are the major categories of brands listed on the Web site? Click on the "Household Care" category. What types of items are contained in this category? How could a system be set up to help measure the success of the firm's first goal to build established brands in the "Household Care" category? What would be three possible financial measures? What about three nonfinancial measures?

3. The "Letter to Shareholders" section of the annual report usually outlines growth strategies. What are these strategies? For each strategy, list at least one financial measure and one nonfinancial measure that could be used to track success of the strategy.

CHAPTER 10

Management Control in Decentralized Organizations

LEARNING OBJECTIVES

When you have finished studying this chapter, you should be able to:

1. Define *decentralization* and identify its expected benefits and costs.

2. Distinguish between responsibility centers and decentralization.

3. Explain how the linking of rewards to responsibility-center performance metrics affects incentives and risk.

4. Compute ROI, economic profit, and economic value added (EVA) and contrast them as criteria for judging the performance of organization segments.

5. Compare the advantages and disadvantages of various bases for measuring the invested capital used by organization segments.

6. Define *transfer prices* and identify their purpose.

7. State the general rule for transfer pricing and use it to assess transfer prices based on total costs, variable costs, and market prices.

8. Identify the factors affecting multinational transfer prices.

9. Explain how controllability and management by objectives (MBO) aid the implementation of management control systems.

▶ NIKE

In 30 years, Nike has become the largest sports and fitness company in the world. It has grown from a small Beaverton, Oregon, company into a global giant. Nike was the official sponsor and supplier for Chinese athletes for the 2008 Beijing Olympic Games. Ten years ago, Nike was only a minor factor in the world of soccer. Now Nike endorsement arrangements include the Italian and French national teams, as well as Arsenal, Manchester United, FC Barcelona, Inter Milan, Juventus, Aston Villa, Celtic, and PSV Eindhoven. Nike has placed itself at the center of attention for soccer fans worldwide.

From 1986 to 2008, Nike's revenues increased from $1 billion to more than $18 billion. During this same period, the percentage of revenues from outside the United States increased from 25% to 58%. Nike now has more stores outside the United States than inside. While footwear still accounts for more than half of Nike's sales, apparel sales now account for nearly one-third. A sampling of endorsements (promotional contracts with famous sports teams, individuals, and organizations) in addition to the soccer teams previously listed gives another perspective on the company's global presence: tennis stars Roger Federer, James Blake, Jim Courier, Andre Agassi, Rafael Nadal, Pete Sampras, Lindsay Davenport, Mary Pierce, Maria Sharapova, Serena Williams; seven-time Tour de France winner Lance Armstrong; basketball stars Kobe Bryant, Lebron James, Steve Nash, and Michael Jordan; and golf's Trevor Immelman and Paul Casey. Watch almost any sports event on television, and you are likely to see the Nike "swoosh" logo.

Nike made a conscious decision to go global—a process that has generated substantial financial rewards. What are some of the keys to success when a company like Nike decides to significantly expand its operations abroad? To manage effectively in this decentralized environment, Nike needs information to help coordinate and evaluate widely dispersed operations. A well-designed management control system is essential.

One critical element is understanding the relevance of the brand to local markets. Nike has gained this understanding by delegating management decision making to the local market level. For example, local Nike managers in Germany made the decision to sign an endorsement contract with world-champion racecar driver Michael Schumacher. According to CEO Philip Knight, "[Previously] it would have taken a move from within the company headquarters to strike such a deal.... But this time it was a decision made in country." The local German manager knew that Schumacher was extremely relevant to the German market and that this would be a "profit driven, culturally significant, and brand enhancing move." Knight credits this move toward decentralization for Nike's rapid increase in international sales: "It is a great example of what we are trying to do: Make decisions on the ground in faraway places."

As organizations like Nike grow and undertake more diverse and complex activities, many elect to delegate decision-making authority to managers throughout the organization. This delegation of the freedom to make decisions is called **decentralization**. Decentralization is a matter of degree. The lower in the organization that this freedom exists, the greater the decentralization. Increasing sophistication of communications—Internet, e-mail, and worldwide cellular phone coverage—aids decentralization. Geographical separation no longer implies lack of access to information. More companies are locating sales and production divisions far from headquarters without sacrificing knowledge of what is happening in the units. While communications technology can help Nike and others get information quickly, the management control system determines what information they receive.

Nike is a globally decentralized company. Customers throughout the world recognize its "swoosh" trademark. Achieving the appropriate balance between autonomy at the local level and efficiencies at the corporate level is a challenge when designing Nike's management control system.

Objective 1
Define *decentralization* and identify its expected benefits and costs.

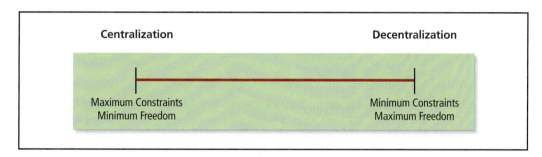

This chapter focuses on the role of management control systems in decentralized organizations. After providing an overview of decentralization, the chapter discusses how companies use performance metrics to motivate managers of decentralized units, including various ways of measuring unit profitability to encourage actions by managers that are in the company's best interests. Finally, we address the special problems created when one segment of an organization charges another for providing goods or services. ■

Centralization Versus Decentralization

Centralization is the process by which organizations concentrate decision making within a particular location or group. The best choice along the continuum between centralization and decentralization is seldom obvious. In fact, organizations and industries often seem to cycle from increasing decentralization to increasing centralization, and back again. For example, a decade or so ago most airlines, such as **South China Airlines**, **Iberia Airlines**, and **Air France**, decentralized. In contrast, at the same time, **Sabena**, Belgium's state-owned airline until its bankruptcy in 2001, undertook a centralization effort. In the insurance industry, **Aetna** decentralized at the same time **AXA Equitable** was centralizing. Let's take a look at some of the factors companies consider as they choose their position along the centralization/decentralization continuum.

Costs and Benefits

Most organizations realize benefits from some level of decentralization. Managers of lower-level units (which we will refer to as "local" managers), often have the best information concerning local conditions and, therefore, are able to make faster and better decisions on local issues than higher-level managers (which we will refer to as "central" managers). By delegating decision-making authority to local managers, central managers free up time to deal with larger issues and fundamental strategy. In addition, decentralization gives local managers an opportunity to develop their decision-making ability and other management skills that help them move upward in the organization, ensuring that the organization develops future leaders. Finally, local managers who are given more authority often have greater motivation and job satisfaction and enjoy higher status.

Decentralization also has its costs. Local managers may make decisions that are not in the organization's best interests. Why? Either because they act to improve their own segment's performance at the expense of the organization or because they do not fully understand the effects of their decisions on other segments and the organization as a whole. Innovative ideas to improve performance are less likely to be shared across units in a decentralized organization. Local managers in decentralized organizations also tend to duplicate services that might be less expensive if centralized (e.g., accounting, advertising, and personnel). Furthermore, costs of accumulating and processing information frequently rise under decentralization because top management needs additional accounting reports to learn about and evaluate decentralized units and their managers. Finally, managers in decentralized units may waste time negotiating with other units about goods or services that are being transferred between units. You can see some of the costs and benefits of decentralization in the Business First box on page 387.

Decentralization is more popular in profit-seeking organizations (where accountants can more easily measure outputs and inputs) than in nonprofit organizations (where it is more difficult to find reliable performance measures, so granting managers freedom is more risky). Central management can give local managers more freedom when it can more easily measure the results of their decisions and thereby hold the local managers accountable for the results. Poor decisions in a profit-seeking firm quickly become apparent from the inadequate profit generated.

Middle Ground

Organizations make many choices along the centralization/decentralization continuum and the optimal choice for one organization is likely to differ from the optimal choice for another. For every **Nike** that finds the benefits of increased decentralization exceeding the costs, another company finds the costs exceeding the benefits. In fact, the optimal choice for one part of the organization may differ from the optimal choice for another part. For example, many companies decentralize much of the controller's problem-solving and attention-directing functions and handle them at lower levels. In contrast, they generally centralize income tax planning and mass scorekeeping functions such as accounting for payroll.

Decentralization is most successful when an organization's segments are relatively independent of one another—that is, when the decisions of a manager in one segment will not affect other segments. When segments do much internal buying or selling, much buying from the same outside suppliers, or much selling to the same outside markets, they are candidates for more centralization.

In Chapter 9, we stressed that managers should consider cost-benefit tests, goal congruence, and managerial effort when designing a management control system. If management has decided in favor of heavy decentralization, then **segment autonomy**—the delegation of decision-making power to managers of segments of an organization—is also crucial. For decentralization to work, however, this autonomy must be real, not just lip service. In most circumstances, top managers must be willing to abide by decisions made by segment managers.

Responsibility Centers and Decentralization

Objective 2

Distinguish between responsibility centers and decentralization.

Design of a management control system should consider two separate dimensions of control: (1) the responsibilities of managers and (2) the amount of autonomy they have. Some managers confuse these two dimensions by assuming that profit-center managers always have more decentralized decision-making authority than cost-center managers. This does not need to be the case. Some profit center managers, such as those at **General Electric**, possess vast freedom to make decisions concerning labor contracts, supplier choices, equipment purchases, personnel decisions, and so on. In contrast, profit-center managers at other companies may need top-management

Business First

Benefits and Costs of Decentralization

Many companies believe that decentralization is important to their success, including **PepsiCo**, **DuPont**, and **Procter & Gamble**. But one company stands out from the others in its efforts to decentralize: **Johnson & Johnson**. Johnson & Johnson (with 2008 sales of $63.7 billion, more than 118,000 employees, and more than 250 companies operating in 57 countries) is the maker of products such as Tylenol, Listerine, Johnson's Baby Powder, Neutrogena, and Neosporin. The company has a long history of decentralization, beginning in the 1930s. Its 2008 annual report states "a decentralized management approach ... keeps our people close to their customers and their markets. It drove our business success in 2008, and it mobilizes us to capitalize on new health care opportunities while we meet the challenges ahead in an unprecedented, difficult global economic setting." Another recent annual report elaborated: "Our decentralized management system is also reflected in our strong performance, as it gives us focus and a sense of ownership in local markets through dedicated and empowered management groups. They can quickly pursue local avenues of opportunity."

Under the company's management structure, each of its operating companies functions autonomously. One benefit is that decisions are made by executives who are closer to the marketplace. One disadvantage is the additional expense because many of the operating companies duplicate many overhead costs. Although ultimately accountable to executives at Johnson & Johnson headquarters in New Brunswick, New Jersey, some segment presidents see their bosses as few as four times a year. Bill Weldon, Johnson & Johnson chairman of the board and CEO, extols the virtues of decentralization: "Johnson & Johnson has maintained a significant and well-established presence in these markets for decades, utilizing our decentralized operating model to stay close to patients, consumers and health care providers with local market insights, products, and strategies." He believes that the structure has been essential to its strategy of developing executives from within because young managers can be given responsibility for running whole companies. "This allows people to be entrepreneurial," he said, "and to grow."

BusinessWeek summarized Weldon's approach as follows: "[Johnson & Johnson's] success has hinged on its unique culture and structure.... Each of its far-flung units operates pretty much as an independent enterprise. Businesses set their own strategies; they have their own finance and human resources departments, for example. While this degree of decentralization makes for relatively high overhead costs, no chief executive, Weldon included, has thought that too high a price to pay."

As you can see, decentralization has benefits and costs. Some companies have vacillated between decentralization and centralization, sometimes believing that the benefits of centralizing common activities dominate the benefits of decentralization, while at other times seeking the decision-making advantages of decentralization. In contrast, Johnson & Johnson has continued its policy of decentralization in good times and bad, through a long succession of top management leadership. The company has a long-term credo that mandates decentralization. It would take a brave (or foolhardy) leader to change Johnson & Johnson's philosophy of decentralization.

Sources: Adapted from *Johnson & Johnson 2008 Annual Report*; M. Petersen, "From the Ranks, Unassumingly," *New York Times*, February 24, 2002, Section 3, page 2; and A. Barrett, "Staying on Top," *BusinessWeek*, May 5, 2003.

approval for almost all the decisions just mentioned. Similarly, cost centers may be more heavily decentralized than profit centers. The fundamental question in deciding between using a cost center or a profit center for a given segment is not whether heavy decentralization exists. Instead, the fundamental question is, for whatever level of decentralization that exists, "Will a profit center or a cost center better solve the problems of goal congruence and management effort?"

The management control system should be designed to achieve the best possible alignment between local manager decisions and the actions central management seeks. For example, a plant may seem to be a "natural" cost center because the plant manager has no influence over decisions concerning the marketing of its products. Nevertheless, some companies insist on evaluating a plant manager by the plant's profitability. Why? Because they believe this broader evaluation base will positively affect the plant manager's behavior. Instead of being concerned solely with running an efficient cost center, the system motivates the plant manager to consider quality control more carefully and react to customers' special requests more sympathetically. A profit center may thus provide more clear incentives for the desired plant-manager behavior than does a cost center. In designing accounting control systems, top managers must consider the system's impact on behavior desired by the organization.

Performance Metrics and Management Control

A major factor in designing decentralized management control systems is how the system's performance metrics affect managers' incentives. **Incentives** are the rewards, both implicit and explicit, for managerial effort and actions. A **performance metric** is a specific measure of

Objective 3

Explain how the linking of rewards to responsibility-center performance metrics affects incentives and risk.

management accomplishment. Organizations should choose performance metrics that improve the alignment of manager incentives with organizational objectives. The organization wants managers to use decision-making autonomy to meet the company's objectives, not to pursue other goals. For example, **Nike** executives wanted the company's manager of German operations to sign auto-racer Michael Schumacher to a contract only if it would create additional profits for Nike, not to provide an entree for the manager into the inner circles of auto racing.

Agency Theory, Performance, and Rewards

Agency theory provides a model to analyze relationships where one party (the principal) delegates decision-making authority to another party (the agent). Agency theory is useful to analyze situations where there is imperfect alignment between the principal's and agent's 1) information and 2) objectives. As discussed earlier, it is common for local managers to have better information about their units than do higher-level central managers. Because the local managers have different information than central managers, they make different decisions. Similarly, as discussed in Chapter 9, it is common for the objectives of local managers to differ in some ways from central manager and organizational objectives. Differences in objectives can again lead local managers to make different decisions. Agency theory provides a framework to analyze these differences in designing a management control system.

Exhibit 10-1 shows how the design of a management control system affects the actions of managers. Managers have beliefs about how alternative action choices will lead to outcomes for their unit, and the management control system specifies how outcomes translate into unit performance metrics and into both explicit and implicit rewards. Local managers choose the action that they believe will lead to the combination of outcomes, performance metrics, and rewards with the highest value to the local manager. Managers' preferences motivate them to select actions that generate outcomes measured and rewarded by a company's management control system. The manager's understanding of how the control system links outcomes, performance metrics, and rewards influences the manager's choice of actions. Thus, the right metrics and rewards motivate actions that are in the company's best interests. For example, if a company measures and explicitly rewards increases in divisional profit, managers have an incentive to expend effort to increase profits.

The links between outcomes and performance metrics and rewards are critical features of the management control system. While the importance of explicit links is clear, implicit links may be equally important. For example, the management control system might include an explicit link that specifies the amount of bonus that will be paid for different levels of profit, but there may be an important implicit link between performance and pay raises. Similarly, it is important to recognize that rewards may be monetary or nonmonetary. Examples of monetary rewards include pay raises and bonuses. Examples of nonmonetary rewards include promotions, praise, self-satisfaction, better offices, and other perquisites. Thus, while we often focus on explicit monetary rewards, remember that implicit and nonmonetary rewards associated with outcomes and metrics play important roles in the management control system.

One important rule for performance measurement is clear: *You get what you measure!* Managers focus their efforts in areas where an organization measures managerial performance, even when the management control system does not include explicit rewards tied to the measures. Therefore, it is important to choose accounting measures that provide objective and

Exhibit 10-1
Designing a Management
Control System

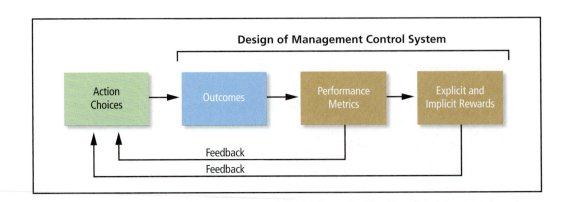

easy-to-understand evaluations of performance, where managers believe there is a clear connection between their action choices and the performance metric.

Agency Theory and Risk

Ideally, companies should reward managers based on their individual performance, but often an organization cannot directly measure a manager's performance. For example, a company may not be able to separate the manager's effect on responsibility-center results from the effect of other factors beyond a manager's control. The greater the influence of noncontrollable factors on responsibility-center results, the more problems there are in using the results to measure and reward a manager's performance.

Consider a particular Niketown store. Suppose its profits increased dramatically. The following factors all contributed to the increase in profits:

- A lengthy strike by employees of a competitor resulted in many customers switching to Nike.
- The store implemented a new cost management system resulting in a significant reduction in the costs of handling merchandise.
- Overall population growth in the store's region has been much higher than that in other Niketown locations.
- Labor costs in the region have not increased as much as in most Niketown locations.
- Employee turnover is lower than the system average. Employees cite their excellent relationship with fellow employees and management as the reason for their high level of job satisfaction.

How should Nike evaluate the performance of the store manager? Should it measure the manager's performance by profit results compared to those of other Niketown stores? What other measures could Nike use? From the factors listed, it is likely that a significant portion of the store's profit increase was due to factors the store manager could not control (the competitor's strike, population growth, and regional labor costs). However, it is also likely that the manager exerted a strong influence on other factors by improving the cost-management system and creating a productive working environment for all employees.

An ideal performance metric would measure and reward the manager for controllable factors and neither reward nor punish the manager for uncontrollable factors. Although this ideal is hard to achieve, agency theory can guide the design of a system to link performance metrics and rewards. When an organization hires a manager, the employment contract details performance metrics and how they will affect rewards. For example, the contract might specify that a manager will receive a bonus of 15% of his or her salary if his or her responsibility center achieves its budgeted profit. However, not all rewards are explicitly specified in the contract. For example, a company can reward a manager with a promotion, but seldom are the requirements for promotion spelled out in detail.

According to agency theory, employment contracts will balance three factors:

1. Incentive: The more a manager's reward depends on a performance metric, the more incentive the manager has to take actions that maximize that measure. Top management should define the performance metric to promote goal congruence and base enough reward on it to achieve managerial effort.
2. Risk: The more uncontrollable factors affect a manager's reward, the more risk the manager bears. People generally avoid risk, so a company must pay managers more if it expects them to bear more risk. Creating incentive by linking rewards to responsibility-center results, which is generally desirable, has the undesirable side effect of imposing risk on managers if noncontrollable factors affect some part of the center's results.
3. Cost of measuring performance: The incentive versus risk trade-off is not necessary if a manager's performance can be perfectly measured. Why? Because managers completely control their own performance, perfect measurement of controllable performance would eliminate risk to the manager. With perfect performance measurement, a manager could be paid a fixed amount if he or she performs as agreed, and nothing otherwise. But perfectly measuring controllable performance is usually inordinately expensive if not outright impossible. The cost-benefit criterion therefore leads companies to rely on imperfect but low-cost measures. Unfortunately, these more readily-available measures frequently confound the manager's controllable performance with uncontrollable factors.

Consider the example of a promoter hired by a group of investors to promote and administer an outdoor concert. Suppose the investors offer the promoter a contract with part guaranteed pay and part bonus based on total attendance. A larger bonus portion compared with the guaranteed portion creates more incentive, but it also creates more risk for the promoter. For example, what happens if it rains? The promoter could do an outstanding job promoting the concert but the weather might keep fans away. To compensate the promoter for added risk, the expected total payment to the promoter will have to be higher for a contract where a higher portion of the total payment is based on attendance. The investors must decide on the optimal tradeoff between the benefit from the added incentive created by a larger bonus and the extra total payment necessary to compensate for the added risk. Note that these contracting issues would not arise if the investors could directly measure the promoter's effort and judgment, rather than basing the bonus on attendance at the concert, a low-cost and readily-available measure that unfortunately is also influenced by factors outside the control of the promoter.

Regardless of how a company links rewards to performance metrics, one pervasive performance metric is profitability. While many organizations use performance measurement systems such as the balanced scorecard (discussed in Chapter 9) that incorporate goals and metrics beyond profitability, it is hard to imagine a company that does not include at least one measure of profitability among its performance metrics. We next look at how various measures of profitability affect managers' incentives.

Measures of Profitability

Objective 4

Compute ROI, economic profit, and economic value added (EVA) and contrast them as criteria for judging the performance of organization segments.

Companies often evaluate segment managers in decentralized units based on their segment's profitability. The trouble is that there are many ways to measure profitability, and it is not clear which is the best measure. Is it income? Is it income before or after interest and taxes? Is it an absolute amount? A percentage? If a percentage, is it a percentage of revenue or of investment? In this section, we consider the strengths and weaknesses of commonly used profitability measures.

Return on Investment

Too often, managers stress net operating income and ignore the investment associated with generating that income. Suppose **Nike** has two divisions, A and B. To say that division A, with an operating income of $200,000, has better performance than division B, with an operating income of $150,000, ignores an important aspect of profitability. A more comprehensive measure of profitability is the rate of **return on investment (ROI)**, which is income divided by the investment required to obtain that income. For any given amount of investment required, the investor wants the maximum income (holding risk constant). If division A requires an investment of $500,000 and division B requires only $250,000, division B has the higher ROI:

$$\text{ROI} = \frac{\text{income}}{\text{investment}}$$

$$\text{ROI division A} = \frac{\$200,000}{\$500,000} = 40\%$$

$$\text{ROI division B} = \frac{\$150,000}{\$250,000} = 60\%$$

Every dollar invested in division B is generating income of $.60, compared to the $.40 generated by every dollar invested in division A.

In ROI calculations, we should measure invested capital as an average for the period under review. Why? Because income is a flow of resources over a period of time, and we should measure the average investment that generates that flow. The most accurate measures of average investment take into account the amount invested month-by-month, or even day-by-day. However, a simple average of the beginning and ending balances often provides nearly the same result without going to the trouble required to produce greater accuracy. Suppose division A had $450,000 of investment at the beginning of the year and gradually increased it to $550,000 by the end of the year. The average of the beginning and ending investment amounts is ($450,000 + $550,000) ÷ 2 = $500,000.

ROI facilitates the comparison of a unit's performance with that of other segments within the company or with similar units outside the company. Why? Because, unlike income alone, ROI takes into account the investment required to generate the income. ROI is a return per unit of investment and does not depend on the size of the segments being compared.

As shown in the following equations, we can write ROI as the product of two items: **return on sales** (income divided by revenue) and **capital turnover** (revenue divided by invested capital).

$$\text{return on investment} = \frac{\text{income}}{\text{invested capital}}$$

$$= \frac{\text{income}}{\text{revenue}} \times \frac{\text{revenue}}{\text{invested capital}}$$

$$= \text{return on sales} \times \text{capital turnover}$$

ROI can be increased by increasing either return on sales or capital turnover without changing the other. Consider an example of these relationships (amounts are in thousands of dollars):

	Rate of Return on Invested Capital (%)	=	Income Revenue	×	Revenue Invested Capital
Present outlook	20	=	$\frac{16}{100}$	×	$\frac{100}{80}$
Alternatives:					
1. Increase return on sales by reducing expenses relative to sales	25	=	$\frac{20}{100}$	×	$\frac{100}{80}$
2. Increase capital turnover by decreasing investment	25	=	$\frac{16}{100}$	×	$\frac{100}{64}$

Alternative 1 improves return on sales by decreasing expenses relative to sales without increasing investment. Alternative 2 increases capital turnover by decreasing investment without reducing sales. Either alternative will increase ROI. Increasing capital turnover by decreasing investment means using fewer assets, such as cash, receivables, inventories, or equipment, for each dollar of revenue generated.

Increasing turnover is one of the advantages of implementing the just-in-time (JIT) philosophy (see Chapter 1). Many companies implementing JIT purchasing and production systems have realized dramatic improvements in ROI because capital turnover increased due to lower inventory levels while the return on sales stayed the same.

Although evaluation based on ROI causes managers to consider both income and investment in their decisions, it may provide inappropriate incentives for managers to reject profitable investment opportunities or accept unprofitable investment opportunities, as explained in the following section. Alternative performance measures—metrics that focus more on economic profit—address this issue.

Economic Profit or Economic Value Added (EVA)

Performance measurement systems should motivate managers to make decisions that increase the value of the company. ROI includes both profit and investment, focusing on income as a percentage of investment. However, there are advantages to a metric that emphasizes an absolute amount of income rather than a percentage. **Economic profit**, also called **residual income**, defined as net operating profit after-tax (NOPAT) less a capital charge, is such a metric. **Net operating profit after-tax (NOPAT)** is income before interest expense but after tax. The **capital charge** is the company's cost of capital multiplied by the amount of investment, where the **cost of capital** is the cost of long-term liabilities and stockholders' equity weighted by their relative size. In short, economic profit tells you how much a company's after-tax operating income exceeds what it is paying for capital. Consider division A in our earlier example. Suppose its after-tax operating income is $200,000, the average invested capital in the division for the year is $500,000, and the company's after-tax cost of capital is 10%:

Divisional after-tax operating income	$200,000
Minus charge for average invested capital (.10 × $500,000)	50,000
Equals economic profit (or residual income)	$150,000

There are different ways to calculate measures of economic profit, depending on exactly how a company chooses to define the terms used. One popular variant developed and marketed by the consulting firm **Stern Stewart & Co.** is **economic value added (EVA)**. In formula form, Stern Stewart defines EVA as

EVA = adjusted NOPAT − (after-tax cost of capital × adjusted average invested capital)

Stern Stewart makes specific adjustments to financial-reporting measures of after-tax operating profit and invested capital. These adjustments are designed to convert after-tax operating income into a closer approximation of cash income and invested capital into a closer approximation of the cash invested in the economic resources the company uses to create value. Examples of these adjustments include the following:

- Use taxes paid rather than tax expense.
- Capitalize (rather than expense) research and development expenses.
- Use FIFO for inventory valuation (thus companies using LIFO must add back the LIFO reserve to invested capital and add the increase or deduct the decrease in the LIFO reserve to after-tax operating income).
- If a company deducts interest expense in computing operating income, it must add back after-tax interest expense to find NOPAT.

To illustrate, suppose a division of Nike spent $4 million at the beginning of year 1 for research and development of a new shoe. The shoe proved to be a success with a product life cycle of 4 years. Assume that before accounting for R&D, the division's operating income each year was $12 million, the division's capital is $50 million each year, and Nike's cost of capital is 10%. For simplicity, we will ignore income taxes in our example, but remember that EVA uses after-tax numbers.

Normally, following U.S. financial reporting rules, the company would expense the entire $4 million of R&D as incurred with no asset reported on the balance sheet. In contrast, EVA companies look upon R&D as a capital investment. For purposes of calculating EVA, Nike's division capitalizes these expenditures and expenses them over the product's life cycle. In addition, the division deducts from operating income a capital charge of 10% of the average capital balance outstanding during the year, including the capitalized R&D.

Exhibit 10-2 shows a comparison of the income and capital effects between traditional economic profit and EVA. Total 4-year financial-reporting operating profit, the amount included on Nike's income statement, is $44 million. Traditional economic profit (without capitalizing R&D) is $44 million less a capital charge of $20 million, or $24 million. EVA also deducts a capital charge but capital is adjusted upward by $4 milion at the beginning of the year to reflect the capitalized investment in R&D and then declines by $1 milion per year as R&D is amortized. After incorporating the effect of these adjustments on both income and investment, EVA = $44 million − $20.8 million = $23.2 million. That is, EVA deducts an additional $.8 million capital charge for the capital used for the R&D. Stern Stewart has identified more than 160 different adjustments such as the adjustment illustrated for R&D but usually recommends only a few for a specific client. Many companies using economic profit for performance evaluation develop their own set of adjustments to income and capital, but all companies use the basic concept of net operating profit after-tax less a capital charge.

Economic profit and EVA have received much attention recently as scores of companies are adopting them as financial performance metrics. **AT&T, Coca-Cola, CSX, FMC,** and **Quaker Oats** claim that using EVA motivated managers to make decisions that increased shareholder value. All these companies are successful. Why? Because they do a better job than many of their competitors at allocating, managing, and redeploying scarce capital resources (fixed assets, such

Year	Accounting Operating Income	Adjusted Operating Income	Accounting Capital	Adjusted Average Capital†	Economic Profit Capital Charge at 10%‡	EVA Capital Charge at 10%§	Economic Profit	Economic Value Added
Year 1	$ 8	$8 + 4 - 1 = \$11^*$	$50	$53.5	$ 5	$ 5.35	$ 3	$ 5.65
Year 2	12	$12 - 1 = 11$	50	52.5	5	5.25	7	5.75
Year 3	12	$12 - 1 = 11$	50	51.5	5	5.15	7	5.85
Year 4	12	$12 - 1 = 11$	50	50.5	5	5.05	7	5.95
Total	$44	$44			$20	$20.80	$24	$23.20

†Adjusted average capital: Year 1, 1/2 × ($54 + $53); Year 2, 1/2 × ($53 + $52); Year 3, 1/2 × ($52 + $51); Year 4, 1/2 × ($51 + $50).
‡10% × accounting capital.
§10% × adjusted average capital.
*Accounting operating income + R&D expense – R&D amortization = $8 + $4 – $1 = $11.

Exhibit 10-2
Comparison of Economic Profit and EVA

as heavy equipment, computers, real estate, and working capital). Because EVA explicitly recognizes the cost of the capital deployed, it may help managers in these companies make better capital allocation decisions. Further, some investment companies, such as Manhattan-based broker-dealer **Matrix USA**, use economic profit to rate stocks for their investment clients.

Making Managerial Decisions

One company that improved its EVA performance dramatically during the 1990s is **IBM**. In 1993, its EVA was a negative $13 billion. By 2000, the company improved its EVA to $2.2 billion. Like most companies, the economic downturn in the early 2000s hurt its EVA, dropping it into the negative range by 2002. By 2005, IBM again had a positive EVA at just under $1 billion. Compute the EVA for IBM for 2008 using the following data (in billions of dollars) without any of the specific adjustments recommended by Stern Stewart. As a manager, how would you explain the past history of EVA and the current EVA to investors?

	2008
Net operating profit after tax	$ 12.8
Invested capital	67
Cost of capital (assumed)	10%

Answer

Amounts are in billions as follows:

$$EVA = \text{Net operating profit after tax} - \text{cost-of-capital percentage} \times \text{capital invested}$$
$$= \$12.8 - .10 \times \$67$$
$$= \$12.8 - \$6.7 = \$6.1 \text{ Billion}$$

The improvement from 1993 to 2000 was dramatic. The decline in EVA in 2002 was not unexpected since a majority of companies lost value in 2002. IBM had returned to positive EVA by 2005. Results for 2008 showed strong growth as EVA rose to $6.1 billion.

ROI or Economic Profit?

Why do some companies prefer economic profit (or EVA) to ROI? Because ROI can motivate divisional managers to make investment decisions that are not in the best interests of the company as a whole. Under ROI, the basic incentive is to maximize rate of return. This leads division managers to invest only in projects that will increase their division's ROI, that is, projects with an ROI greater than the division's current ROI. For example, if a company measures performance using only ROI, the manager of a division currently earning 20% may be reluctant to invest in projects that earn 18%, even if accepting such a project would be best for the company.

From the viewpoint of the company as a whole, division managers should accept projects that earn more than the cost of capital, rather than projects that earn more than the current ROI for the manager's division. Why? Suppose the company's cost of capital is 10%. Investing in projects earning more than 10% will increase the company's profitability. For every $100 of investment, the company gets more than $10 in operating income and pays only $10 for the capital, a net gain. When a company uses economic profit as a performance metric, managers have incentive to invest in any project earning more than the cost of capital because such an investment will increase the division's economic profit.

Consider two **Nike** divisions, division X with operating income of $200,000 and division Y with operating income of $40,000. Division X has average invested capital of $1 million and division Y has average invested capital of $800,000. Assume that Nike's cost of capital is 10%, and, for simplicity, ignore taxes. Suppose each division is considering a new proposed project. Division X is considering Project A that will earn 15% annually on a $500,000 investment, or $75,000 a year. Division Y is considering Project B that will earn 7% annually on an $800,000 investment, or $56,000 a year. Exhibit 10-3 shows ROI and economic profit with and without the project for each division.

Suppose Nike bases performance evaluation on ROI. Would the manager of division X invest in Project A? No. Even though Project A earns a return of 15% (which is above the 10% cost of capital), it would decrease ROI for division X from 20% to 18.3%. Now suppose you are the manager of division Y. Would you invest in Project B? Yes. Even though Project B earns a return of 7% (below the 10% cost of capital), it would increase ROI for division Y from 5% to 6%. In general, the ROI profitability metric provides an incentive for divisions to invest in new projects that earn a return in excess of their current return, rather than an incentive to invest in new projects with a return in excess of the cost of capital. Thus, performance evaluation based on ROI leads division X to reject a project with a 15% return and division Y to accept a project with a 7% return.

Now suppose top management evaluates performance using economic profit. For division X, investing in Project A would increase economic profit by $25,000, from $100,000 to $125,000. This $25,000 increase in economic profit is the $75,000 annual return from the new project less the $50,000 annual cost of capital for the new project. In contrast to the decision under ROI, the division X manager would accept Project A. For division Y, investing in Project B would decrease economic profit by $24,000, from $–40,000 to $–64,000. This $24,000 decrease is the $56,000 annual return from the new project less the $80,000 annual cost of capital for the new project. Thus, the division Y manager would reject Project B, where ROI evaluation led to its acceptance. Evaluation based on economic profit motivates both managers to invest in projects that earn a return in excess of the cost of capital, whereas evaluation based on ROI leads both managers to incorrect decisions—division A rejecting a desirable project and division B accepting an undesirable one. In general, use of economic profit or EVA will promote goal congruence and lead to better decisions than using ROI.

Many companies are convinced that EVA has played a large role in their success. James M. Cornelius, chairman of **Guidant Corporation**, a medical device company focused on cardiovascular disease, paid tribute to EVA on Stern Stewart's Web site:

From day one at Guidant, we linked management bonuses to EVA performance targets.... If a target acquisition isn't EVA positive here, we don't do it. We pay EVA performance bonuses to Guidant technologists who develop new products within specified time frames, and we are seeing product innovation here that we've never seen before. All of our employees ... are performing at levels we've never before experienced. I'm convinced

	Without Project		With Project	
	Division X	Division Y	Division X	Division Y
Net after-tax operating income	$ 200,000	$ 40,000	$ 275,000	$ 96,000
Invested capital	$1,000,000	$ 800,000	$1,500,000	$1,600,000
ROI (net operating income ÷ invested capital)	20%	5%	18.3%	6%
Capital charge (10% × invested capital)	$ 100,000	$ 80,000	$ 150,000	$ 160,000
Economic profit (net operating income − capital charge)	$ 100,000	$ (40,000)	$ 125,000	$ (64,000)

Exhibit 10-3
ROI and Economic Profit for Divisions X and Y

these results are largely because of EVA. [Employees] keep looking for ways to improve our business because at the end of the day a significant share of their annual cash bonuses are tied to EVA improvement.... All that they have accomplished couldn't have been done without EVA.

Siemens Corporation, Europe's largest electronics and electrical engineering firm and Stern Stewart's first EVA client in Europe, reported in its annual report that "Siemens focuses on EVA as the yardstick by which we measure the success of our efforts. The EVA performance standard encourages our people to be efficient, productive and proactive in thinking about our customers and their customers. These attributes translate into profitable growth and higher returns." Examples of actions taken by Siemens to improve EVA include the sale of **Siecor**, the fiberoptic cable business, to **Corning**, and the sale of its retail and banking business. As stated by Siemens, "Divesting selected businesses has generated funds for more strategic investments."

Salvatore Fazzolari, chairman and CEO, describes how **Harsco**, a company with $4 billion in sales of specialized industrial services and products, uses EVA to guide major business decisions:

We are equally committed to creating wealth and value for shareholders, and one way we do so is through our unwavering commitment to Economic Value Added. This enterprise-wide metric provides a consistent and transparent way to translate strategy into investment decisions and compensate all key managers in the Company based on performance. EVA discipline also drove our restructuring initiatives in the fourth quarter of 2008. As the economic climate deteriorated, we took necessary countermeasures that included rationalizing facilities, renegotiating contracts, amending benefit plans and trimming our global workforce. These initiatives should save more than $50 million per year.

Despite the success of economic profit and EVA, many companies still use ROI. Why? Probably because it is easier for managers to understand, and it facilitates comparison across divisions. Furthermore, combining ROI with appropriate growth and profit targets can minimize ROI's dysfunctional motivations.

Summary Problem for Your Review

PROBLEM

Suppose a division of **Google** has assets of $2,000,000, invested capital of $1,800,000, and net operating income of $600,000. Ignore taxes.

1. What is the division's ROI?
2. If the weighted-average cost of capital is 14%, what is the EVA?
3. Suppose management uses ROI as a performance metric. What effects on management behavior do you expect?
4. Suppose management uses economic profit as a performance metric. What effects on management behavior do you expect?

SOLUTION

1. ROI = $600,000 ÷ $1,800,000 = 33%.
2. EVA = $600,000 − .14 ($1,800,000) = $600,000 − $252,000 = $348,000.
3. If the company uses ROI, the division manager has an incentive to reject new projects that do not earn an ROI of at least 33%, the division's current ROI. From the viewpoint of the organization as a whole, this is undesirable if the cost of capital is only 14%. If a division is enjoying a high ROI, it is less likely to expand if top management evaluates performance using ROI than if it evaluates performance using EVA.
4. If the company uses EVA, the manager is inclined to accept all projects whose expected rate of return exceeds the weighted-average cost of capital. The manager is more likely to expand the division because his or her goal is to maximize a dollar amount rather than a rate.

A Closer Look at Invested Capital

To apply either ROI or economic profit, we must measure both income and invested capital. However, there are many different interpretations of these concepts. To understand what ROI or economic profit figures really mean for a particular company, you must first determine how the company defines and measures invested capital and income. We discussed various definitions of income in Chapter 9, pages 354–357, so we will not repeat them here. We will, however, explore various definitions of invested capital.

Definitions of Invested Capital

Consider the following balance sheet classifications:

Current assets	$ 400,000	Current liabilities	$ 200,000
Property, plant, and		Long-term liabilities	400,000
equipment, net	900,000	Stockholders' equity	700,000
Total assets	$1,300,000	Total liabilities and stockholders' equity	$1,300,000

Possible definitions of invested capital and their values on the preceding balance sheet include the following:

1. Total assets: All assets are included, $1,300,000.
2. Total assets less short-term liabilities: All assets except that portion financed by short-term creditors, $1,300,000 – $200,000 = $1,100,000, the definition commonly used for EVA. This is sometimes expressed as long-term invested capital. Note that because of the identity assets = short-term liabilities + long-term liabilities + stockholders' equity, this can also be computed by adding the long-term liabilities and the stockholders' equity, $400,000 + $700,000 = $1,100,000.
3. Stockholders' equity: Focuses on the investment of the owners of the business, $700,000.

For measuring the performance of division managers, we recommend one of the first two definitions rather than the third, stockholders' equity. If the division manager's mission is to put all assets to their best use without regard to their financing, then total assets is best. If the manager has direct control over obtaining short-term credit, then total assets less current liabilities is best. To increase return or economic profit measures, managers will focus attention on reducing the measure of invested capital that a company adopts. In practice, most companies using ROI or economic profit include all assets in invested capital, and about half (primarily companies using EVA) deduct some portion of current liabilities.

Valuation of Assets

Other issues in measuring invested capital are whether to value the assets contained in the investment base at **gross book value** (the original cost of an asset) or **net book value** (the original cost of an asset less any accumulated depreciation) and whether to base the values on historical cost or some version of current value. Practice is overwhelmingly in favor of using net book value based on historical cost. This means the numbers used for performance metrics are consistent with financial numbers reported to the public. However, the alternatives are attractive in certain circumstances. We first examine the historical cost versus current cost issue and then discuss gross versus net asset values.

HISTORICAL OR CURRENT COST? Most companies favor historical cost over any measure of current cost such as replacement cost or liquidation values. Yet, critics maintain that historical cost provides a faulty basis for decision making and performance evaluation. Historical costs may be far from what a company might pay to purchase the asset today or the amount it could get from selling it, the values relevant to decisions affecting the asset. Despite these criticisms, managers have been slow to depart from historical cost.

Why is historical cost so widely used? Some critics would say that sheer ignorance is the explanation. But a more persuasive answer comes from cost-benefit analysis. Accounting systems are costly. Companies must keep historical records for many legal purposes, so historical records are already in place. A company spends no additional money evaluating performance based on historical costs. Many top managers believe that a more sophisticated system would not improve collective operating decisions enough to warrant the added expense.

PLANT AND EQUIPMENT: GROSS OR NET?   In valuing assets, we need to distinguish between net and gross book values. Most companies use net book value in calculating their investment base. However, a significant minority uses gross book value. The proponents of gross book value maintain that it facilitates comparisons between years and between plants or divisions. Under gross values, performance evaluations depend only on what assets are in use, not on the depreciation assumptions or how old the assets are.

Consider an example of a $600,000 piece of equipment with a 3-year life and no residual value.

Year	Operating Income Before Depreciation	Depreciation	Operating Income	Average Net Book Value*	Net BV Rate of Return	Gross Book Value	Gross BV Rate of Return
1	$260,000	$200,000	$60,000	$500,000	12%	$600,000	10%
2	260,000	200,000	60,000	300,000	20	600,000	10
3	260,000	200,000	60,000	100,000	60	600,000	10

*($600,000 + $400,000) ÷ 2; ($400,000 + $200,000) ÷ 2; and so on.

Notice that the rate of return on net book value increases as the equipment ages. In contrast, the rate of return on gross book value is unchanged if operating income does not change. Proponents of using gross book value for performance evaluation maintain that a performance metric should not improve simply because assets are getting older. In contrast, advocates of using net book value maintain that it is less confusing because it is consistent with the assets shown on the conventional balance sheet and with net income computations.

Companies should focus on the effect on managers' incentives when choosing between net and gross book value. Managers evaluated using gross book value will tend to replace assets sooner than will managers in firms using net book value. Consider a division of **Nike** that has a 4-year-old machine with an original cost of $1,000 and net book value of $200. The division can replace the machine with a new one that also costs $1,000. The choice of net or gross book value does not affect net income. However, if Nike uses the net book value for measuring the investment base, replacement will increase the investment base from $200 to $1,000. In contrast, if Nike uses gross book value, the base is $1,000 both before and after the replacement. In summary, to maximize ROI or economic profit, managers in firms using net book value have incentives to keep old assets with their low book value. Those in firms using gross book value will have less incentive to keep old assets. Therefore, using gross book value will motivate managers to use more state-of-the-art production technology. Net asset value will motivate a more conservative approach to asset replacement.

There are no universally correct answers with respect to such controversial issues as historical values versus current values or gross versus net asset values. Instead, each organization must design its management control system to achieve the best possible decision making, taking into account the cost-benefit tradeoff. This approach is not concerned with "truth" or "perfection" by itself. Instead, the design should ask questions such as the following: Will improvements in the system be worth the added cost? Will a different system achieve better goal congruence and managerial effort? Or, will our existing imperfect system provide about the same set of decisions at lower cost?

Transfer Pricing

Now that you understand some of the issues in measuring profitability, we will look at something that can further complicate the use of profitability as a performance metric. When all the segments of a decentralized organization are independent of one another, managers' motivations that result from using profitability measures for performance evaluation are generally consistent with overall organizational goals. Segment managers can focus only on their own segments because what is best for their segment is generally best for the organization as a whole. In contrast, when segments interact, there is a possibility that what helps one segment hurts another segment badly enough to have a negative net effect on the entire organization. For example, two **Nike** sales divisions may compete for the same customer by cutting prices and thereby reducing the company's overall margin on the business.

A major source of potential conflicts between segment and organizational interests occurs when one segment sells products or services to another segment of the same organization for a price called the **transfer price**. For example, when one segment produces a subcomponent and sells it to another segment that then incorporates it in a final product, a transfer price is required. Transfer prices also apply to services, such as when a product manager buys advertising services from the marketing support segment. The transfer price for the subcomponent is revenue to the producing segment and a cost to the acquiring segment. Thus, a change in the transfer price increases the computed profit for one segment and decreases the profit for the other segment. However, it does not affect profit for the company as a whole.

Purposes of Transfer Pricing

Objective 6

Define *transfer prices* and identify their purpose.

What does a company want from its transfer pricing system? Ideally, it wants to ensure that managers who make decisions to improve their segment's performance also increase the performance of the organization as a whole. When a company evaluates a segment based on profitability, it wants profitability metrics that reward the segment manager for decisions that increase both a segment's profitability and the profitability of the entire company. For example, transfer prices should guide managers to make the best possible decisions regarding whether to buy or sell products and services inside or outside the total organization. Decisions by the buying and selling segment managers, acting without top management intervention, should be the best decisions for their segment and for the entire organization. In other words, decisions that increase a segment's profit should also increase the profits of the entire company.

Another common goal of transfer-pricing systems is to preserve segment autonomy. Top management could dictate how much of any product or service one segment transfers to another. However, if an organization has decided that decentralization, with its focus on autonomy of segment managers, is desirable, then segment managers should be free to make their own decisions.

Organizations use a variety of transfer prices, cost-based prices for some transfers, market-based prices for other transfers, and negotiated prices for others. Therefore, do not expect to obtain a single, universally applicable answer to the problem of transfer pricing. There is no perfect transfer-pricing system. Almost every manager in a decentralized organization has had experience with transfer-pricing systems that seem less than ideal. For example, a manager at **Weyerhaeuser**, a large wood-products firm, called transfer pricing his firm's most troublesome management control issue.

A General Rule for Transfer Pricing

Objective 7

State the general rule for transfer pricing and use it to assess transfer prices based on total costs, variable costs, and market prices.

Although no single rule always meets the goals of transfer pricing, a general rule can provide guidance:

$$\text{transfer price} = \text{outlay cost} + \text{opportunity cost}$$

As described on page 223, outlay costs require a cash disbursement. They are essentially the additional amount the selling segment must pay to produce and transfer a product or service to another segment. In many cases, outlay costs are the variable costs for producing the item transferred. Opportunity cost is the contribution to profit that the selling segment forgoes by transferring the item internally. For example, if capacity constraints force a segment to either transfer an item internally or sell it externally—that is, it cannot produce enough to do both—the opportunity cost for internal transfer is the contribution margin the segment could have received from the external sale.

Why does this rule generally work? Consider the following example of two hypothetical Nike divisions. The fabric division (the selling division) is considering transferring the fabric required for a golf shirt to the sportswear division (the buying division):

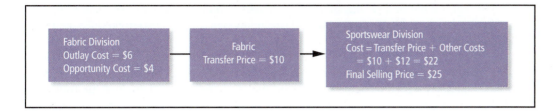

Suppose the fabric division's $4 opportunity cost arises because it can get $10 by selling the fabric to a buyer outside the company. Thus, the foregone contribution by not selling to the outside buyer is $10 – $6 = $4. At any transfer price less than $10, the selling division is better off selling the fabrics to the outside buyer rather than transferring it. Thus, the minimum transfer price it would accept is $6 + $4 = $10.

Now consider how much the item is worth to the sportswear division. For the fabric to be profitable to the sportswear division, it must be able to sell the final product for more than the transfer price plus the other costs it must incur to finish and sell the product. Because it can sell the golf shirt for $25 and its other costs are $12, the maximum price the sportswear division would be willing to pay is $25 – $12 = $13. At any higher price, the sportswear division would choose not to produce the shirt at all. But there is a second constraint: The sportswear division will not pay more to the fabric division than it would have to pay to an outside supplier for an equivalent fabric. Thus, the largest transfer price acceptable to the sportswear division is the lesser of (1) $13 or (2) the cost charged by an outside supplier.

Now, from the company's point of view, transfer is desirable whenever (1) the total cost to the company for producing the fabric internally ($10, including opportunity cost, as determined by the fabric division) is less than its value to the company ($13 as determined by the sportswear division), and (2) the fabric division's costs (again including opportunity costs) are less than the price the sportswear division would have to pay to an outside supplier. The first criterion guarantees that the company does not decide to produce a product where the total cost to produce exceeds the final selling price to the end user. The second guarantees that it does not pay more to produce the fabric internally than it would have to pay to buy it in the marketplace. The only transfer price that will always meet these criteria is $10, the fabric division's outlay cost plus opportunity cost. Why? Any price between $10 and $13 meets the first criterion. However, only $10 meets the second because the sportswear division should purchase the fabric for $10 from the outside supplier for any transfer price above $10.

Exhibit 10-4 summarizes the division's decision and the effect on Nike as a whole when an outside supplier offers the fabric at either greater than $10 or less than $10. At a $10 transfer price, regardless of what price outside suppliers offer, the division managers, acting independently, make the decision that is most profitable for the company as a whole. Any other transfer price creates a possibility of a manager making the decision that is best for his or her segment but not for the company as a whole. The fabric division would reject the transfer at less than $10

Outside Supplier Price	Decision by Division Managers	Decision Best for Company
Less than $10	Do not transfer—buying division rejects transfer because buying internally will reduce its profits	Buy from outside supplier because it is cheaper for the company as a whole
Greater than $10	If value to buying division is greater than $10: Transfer at $10—both divisions benefit	Transfer because internal price is less than external price
	If value to buying division is less than $10: Buying division rejects transfer	Do not transfer because the value of the fabric to the company is less than its cost

Exhibit 10-4

Summary Effects of a $10 Transfer Price

regardless of how much profit it creates for the sportswear division. The sportswear division would reject the transfer whenever the transfer price is greater than the price from alternative sources. Any transfer price greater than $10 runs the risk of the sportswear division purchasing outside the company even when the internal cost is lower. For example, with a transfer price of $12 and an outside bid of $11, the sportswear division would pay $11 to the outside supplier when the company could have spent only $10 (including opportunity cost) to produce the fabric in the fabric division.

This general rule doesn't always achieve all of the multiple goals of transfer-pricing systems; as we said earlier, there is no universally optimal transfer price. Nonetheless, it provides a good benchmark by which to judge transfer-pricing systems. We will analyze the following transfer-pricing systems, the most popular systems in practice, by examining how close the transfer price comes to the benchmark of outlay cost plus opportunity cost:

1. Market-based transfer prices
2. Cost-based transfer prices
   a. Variable cost
   b. Full cost (possibly plus profit)
3. Negotiated transfer prices

In addressing these transfer-pricing systems, we will assume that a company has multiple divisions that transfer items to one another, and that the company wants to preserve segment autonomy in a decentralized operation.

Market-Based Transfer Prices

When there is a ready market for an item or service transferred from one segment to another, transfer pricing policies are straightforward. The common maxim is "if a market price exists, use it." The more competitive the market, the better the maxim applies.

If there is a competitive market for the product or service being transferred internally, using the market price as a transfer price will generally lead to goal congruence. Why? Because the market price equals the variable cost plus opportunity cost.

$$\text{transfer price} = \text{variable cost} + \text{opportunity cost}$$
$$= \text{variable cost} + (\text{market price} - \text{variable cost})$$
$$= \text{market price} + \text{variable cost} - \text{variable cost}$$
$$= \text{market price}$$

If the selling division avoids some marketing and delivery costs when selling internally, many companies will deduct these costs from the market price when computing the transfer price. That is, the opportunity cost in the preceding expression is the net amount the selling division would receive selling the item on the market after deducting variable cost and marketing and delivery costs.

To illustrate market-based transfer prices, reconsider the two hypothetical divisions of Nike. The fabric division makes fabrics it sells directly to external customers as well as to other Nike divisions, such as the sportswear division. The fabric division makes a particular fabric for an outlay cost of $6 and can sell it to external customers for $10. The sportswear division can buy that same fabric on the market for $10 and use it to make a golf shirt, spending an extra $12 in production costs. The golf shirt sells for $25. Should the sportswear division obtain the fabric from the fabric division of Nike or purchase it from an external supplier?

Assume for the moment that the fabric division can sell its entire production to external customers without incurring any marketing or shipping costs. The manager of the fabric division will not sell the fabric for less than $10. Why? Because he or she can sell it on the market for $10, so any price less than $10 will reduce the manager's division's profit. Furthermore, the sportswear division manager will refuse to pay a transfer price greater than $10 for the fabric for each golf shirt. Why? Because if the transfer price is greater than $10, he or she will purchase the fabric from the external supplier for the lower price of $10 in order to maximize his or her division's profit. The only transfer price that allows both managers to maximize their division's profit is $10, the market price. If the managers had autonomy to make decisions, at any transfer price other than $10 one of the managers would decline the internal transfer of the fabric.

Now suppose the fabric division incurs a $.75 per square yard marketing and shipping cost that it can avoid by transferring the fabric to the sportswear division instead of marketing it to outside customers. Most companies would then use a transfer price of $9.25, often called a "market-price-minus" transfer price. The fabric division would get the same net amount from the transfer ($9.25 with no marketing or shipping costs) as from an external sale ($10 less $.75 marketing and shipping costs), whereas the sportswear division saves $.75 per shirt. Thus, Nike benefits overall.

This situation is similar to one where a noncompetitive market creates an external selling price for the fabric division of $9.25 and an external purchase price for the sportswear division of $10. A transfer price of $9.25 will motivate transfer of the fabric only when Nike as a whole will benefit from the transfer. The fabric division will produce and transfer the fabric only if the transfer price is at least $9.25, and the sportswear division will buy the fabric internally only if it costs less than $10 and is worth at least $9.25 to the division. These criteria drive a decision to transfer only if it is in Nike's overall best interests.

While market-based transfer prices generally provide the correct incentives, market prices are not always available. Therefore, we next discuss some other systems commonly used in the absence of market-based prices.

Transfers at Cost

When market prices don't exist, most companies resort to cost-based transfer prices. In fact, about half the major companies in the world use a cost-based transfer-pricing system. However, there are many possible definitions of cost. Some companies use only variable cost, others use full cost, and still others use full cost plus a profit markup. Some use standard costs, and some use actual costs. Cost-based transfer prices are easy to understand and use, but they can easily lead to **dysfunctional decisions**—decisions in conflict with the company's goals. The key to successful cost-based transfer prices is to minimize such dysfunctional decisions. Let's examine some of these cost-based transfer-pricing systems.

TRANSFERS AT VARIABLE COST   Companies that transfer items at variable cost implicitly assume that the selling division has no opportunity cost. Why? Because the outlay cost is generally about equal to variable cost: transfer price = outlay (variable) cost + $0. Therefore, a variable-cost transfer-pricing system is most appropriate when the selling division forgoes no opportunities when it transfers the item internally, for example when there is plenty of excess capacity in the selling division.

Variable-cost transfer prices cause dysfunctional decisions when the selling segment has significant opportunity costs. In our fabric division–sportswear division example, there are two ways this could happen. First, if there are positive opportunity costs, the fabric division manager would turn down any transfer, preferring to pursue the alternative opportunities, perhaps selling the fabric on the open market or using facilities to make a different, more profitable, fabric. This would be dysfunctional if the sportswear division could make more profit from its golf shirt than the fabric division makes from pursuing its alternative opportunities. Second, realizing the lack of incentive for the fabric division to transfer the fabric, top management might insist that it produce and transfer the fabric. This would be against the company's interests if the fabric division passes up opportunities that yield more profit than the sportswear division's golf shirt. In addition, this policy violates segment autonomy.

TRANSFERS AT FULL COST OR FULL COST PLUS PROFIT   Full-cost transfer prices include not only variable cost but also an allocation of fixed costs. In addition, some companies also add a markup for profit. This implicitly assumes that the allocation of fixed costs (and, if included, the profit markup) is a good approximation of the opportunity cost. In cases of constrained capacity, where the selling division cannot satisfy all internal and external demand for its products, the opportunity cost is positive. In such cases, variable-cost transfer prices are problematic. However, there is no guarantee that adding an allocation of fixed costs, with or without an additional profit component, is a good approximation of the opportunity cost. Yet, it may be a better approximation than assuming a zero opportunity cost. Some companies believe that using activity-based costing improves cost-based transfer prices, as described in the Business First box on page 402.

Business First

Activity-Based Costing and Transfer Pricing

Teva Pharmaceutical Industries Ltd. is a global health-care company specializing in pharmaceuticals. It is headquartered in Israel and had 2008 sales of $11.1 billion. Teva entered the lucrative generic drug market in the mid-1980s. Each of the marketing divisions purchases generic drugs from the manufacturing division. As part of its strategy, the company decentralized its pharmaceutical business into cost and profit centers. Prior to decentralization, each marketing division was a revenue center. With the new organizational structure, management had to decide how to measure marketing division costs because profits were now the key financial performance metric.

A key cost to the marketing divisions is the transfer price paid for drugs purchased from the manufacturing division. Management considered several alternative bases for the company's transfer prices. Market price was not a feasible basis for transfer pricing because there was not a ready market. Negotiated prices were rejected because management believed that the resulting debates over the proper price would be lengthy and disruptive. Teva adopted variable cost (raw material and packaging costs) transfer pricing for a short time but eventually rejected it because it did not lead to congruent decisions—managers did not differentiate products using many scarce resources from those using few. Further, when a local source for the drug did exist, the market price was always above the variable-cost transfer price. Thus, managers in Teva's manufacturing division had little incentive to keep costs low.

Management also rejected traditional full cost that did not capture the actual cost structure of the manufacturing division. Specifically, the traditional full-cost system undercosted the low-volume products and overcosted the large-volume products. The system traced only raw materials directly to products. It divided the remaining manufacturing costs into two cost pools and allocated them based on labor hours and machine hours. One problem with the traditional system was its inability to capture and correctly allocate the non-value-added cost of setup activity. Management did not know the size of the errors in product cost, but the lack of confidence in the traditional cost system led to rejection of full cost as the transfer-pricing base.

Then Teva's management adopted an activity-based-costing (ABC) system to improve the accuracy of its product costs. The ABC system has five activity centers and related cost pools: receiving, manufacturing, packaging, quality assurance, and shipping. Because of the dramatic increase in costing accuracy, management was able to adopt full activity-based cost as the transfer price.

Teva's managers are pleased with their transfer-pricing system. The benefits include increased confidence that the costs being transferred are closely aligned with the actual short- and long-run costs being incurred, increased communication between divisions, and an increased awareness of the costs of low-volume products and the costs of capacity required to support these products. They believe that their activity-based costs are the best approximation to outlay cost plus opportunity costs because the allocation of the fixed costs is a good measure of the value (opportunity cost) of the resources being consumed.

Sources: Adapted from Robert Kaplan, Dan Weiss, and Eyal Desheh, "Transfer Pricing with ABC," *Management Accounting*, May, 1997, pp. 20–28; and Teva Pharmaceutical Industries Ltd *2008 Annual Report*.

Dysfunctional decisions arise with full-cost transfer prices when the selling segment has opportunity costs that differ significantly from the allocation of fixed costs and profit. In our example, suppose the fabric division has excess capacity and thus nearly zero opportunity cost. Nevertheless, it has large fixed costs so that the full cost of the transferred fabric includes $8 of fixed cost in addition to the $6 variable cost. At a transfer price of $14, and assuming an external supplier either doesn't exist or would also charge at least $14, the sportswear division would refuse the transfer unless it could sell the golf shirt for at least $14 + $12 = $26. Therefore, because the shirt sells for $25, the sportswear division would decide not to produce it. But this decision costs Nike a contribution margin of $25 − ($6 + $12) = $7. The decision not to produce the shirt is dysfunctional—that is, it conflicts with Nike's goal of generating additional profit.

Cost-based transfer prices can create problems when a company uses actual cost rather than standard cost as a transfer price. Because the buying division will not know its actual cost in advance, it will not be able to accurately plan its costs. More importantly, a transfer price based on actual costs merely passes cost inefficiencies in the selling division along to the buying division. Therefore, the selling division lacks incentive to control its costs. Thus, we recommend using budgeted or standard costs instead of actual costs for cost-based transfer prices.

Finally, cost-based transfer prices can undercut segment autonomy and sometimes lead to conflicts between segment and organizational goals. Suppose managers believe that it's best for the company to transfer an item internally rather than purchasing it externally but also believe that the transfer price is unfair to their segment. They may either do what they think top management wants but resent its negative effect on their segment, or they may do what is best for their segment, ignoring its negative impact on the organization as a whole. Neither alternative is desirable.

Supporters of cost-based transfer prices point out that they are easy to understand and inexpensive to implement. However, any cost-based transfer price can lead to dysfunctional decisions. Companies transferring goods or services in the absence of market prices must decide whether the effects of dysfunctional decisions are great enough to abandon cost-based transfer prices. One alternative is to give up decentralized decision making—essentially have top management dictate whether to transfer items internally or purchase them from external suppliers. However, suppose the benefits of decentralization are large but so are the costs of dysfunctional decisions caused by cost-based transfer prices. In such a case, another alternative is negotiated transfer prices.

Making Managerial Decisions

Consider the following data concerning a subassembly that Willamette Manufacturing Company produces in its fabricating division and uses in products assembled in its assembly division.

Fabricating Division	
Variable cost of subassembly	$35
Excess capacity (in units)	1,000
Assembly Division	
Market price for buying the subassembly from external sources	$50
Number of units needed	900

If you were the manager of the fabricating division, what is the lowest transfer price you would accept for the subassembly? If you were the manager of the assembly division, what is the most you would be willing to pay for the subassembly? Is there a transfer price that would motivate production and transfer of the sub-assembly? If so, what is the price?

Answer

The fabricating division has excess capacity, so its manager would be willing to accept any price above the variable cost of $35. The assembly division can buy the subassembly for $50 on the external market, so its manager would be willing to pay no more than $50 to buy it from the fabricating division. The transfer would take place at some price between $35 and $50.

Negotiated Transfer Prices

Companies heavily committed to segment autonomy often allow managers to negotiate transfer prices. The managers may consider both costs and market prices in their negotiations, but no policy requires them to do so. Supporters of negotiated transfer prices maintain that the managers involved have the best knowledge of what the company will gain or lose by producing and transferring the product or service, so open negotiation allows the managers to make optimal decisions. Critics of negotiated prices focus on the time and effort spent negotiating, an activity that adds nothing directly to the profits of the company.

Let's look at how our fabric division and sportswear division managers might approach a negotiation of a transfer price. The sportswear division manager might look at the selling price of the golf shirt, $25, less the additional cost the division incurs in making it, $12, and decide to purchase fabric at any transfer price less than $25 – $12 = $13. The sportswear division will add to its profit by making and selling the shirt if the transfer price is below $13. At a transfer price above $13, the sportswear division will choose to not make and sell the shirt, assuming there is no other supplier of fabric at a price below $13.

Similarly, the fabric division manager will look at what it costs to produce and transfer the fabric. If there is excess capacity and thus no opportunity cost, any transfer price above $6 will increase the fabric division's profit. Negotiation will result in a transfer if the maximum transfer price the sportswear division is willing to pay is greater than the minimum transfer price the fabric division is willing to accept. The fabric division manager is willing to accept any price above $6 and the sportswear division manager will pay up to $13. The exact transfer price will depend on the negotiating ability and power of the two division managers.

Now suppose there is no excess capacity in the fabric division and an outside customer is willing to pay $10 for the fabric. Transferring the fabric internally causes the division to give up a contribution of $4 as well as paying variable costs of $6, so the minimum transfer price acceptable to the fabric division is now $10. A transfer will take place at a price between $10 and $13. If the opportunity cost had been more than $7, a transfer would not occur. Why?

Because the fabric division's minimum price of $6 variable costs plus opportunity cost would now be greater than $13 and the sportswear division's maximum price would be just $13. This decision is exactly what Nike would prefer. When the fabric division's opportunity cost is less than $7, the golf shirt is more profitable than the fabric division's other business, and the transfer should occur. When the fabric division's opportunity cost is greater than $7, the additional contribution from the fabric division's other business will be greater than the sportswear division's contribution on the shirt, and the transfer should not occur. Therefore, the manager's decisions are congruent with the company's best interests.

What should top management of a decentralized organization do if it sees segment managers making dysfunctional decisions through their negotiations? As usual, the answer is, "It depends." Top management can step in and force the "correct" decision, but doing so undermines segment managers' autonomy and the overall notion of decentralization. It also assumes that top management has the information necessary to determine the correct decision. Most important, frequent intervention results in recentralization. Indeed, if more centralization is desired, the organization might want to reorganize by combining segments.

Top managers who wish to encourage decentralization will often make sure that both producing and purchasing division managers understand all the facts and then allow the managers to negotiate a transfer price. Even when top managers suspect that the segments might make a dysfunctional decision, they may swallow hard and accept the segment manager's judgment as a cost of decentralization. (Repeated dysfunctional decision making may be a reason to change the organizational design or to change managers.)

Well-trained and informed segment managers who understand opportunity costs and the behavior of fixed and variable costs will often make better decisions than will top managers. The producing division manager knows best the various uses of its capacity, and the purchasing division manager knows best what profit can be made on the items to be transferred. In addition, negotiation allows segments to respond flexibly to changing market conditions when setting transfer prices. One transfer price may be appropriate in a time of idle capacity and another when demand increases and operations approach full capacity.

Multinational Transfer Pricing

Objective 8

Identify the factors affecting multinational transfer prices.

So far, we have focused on how transfer-pricing policies affect the motivation of managers. However, in multinational companies, other factors may dominate. For example, multinational companies use transfer prices to minimize worldwide income taxes, import duties, and tariffs. For example, Nike might prefer to make its profits in Singapore, where the marginal corporate tax rate is less than half the rate in the United States.

Suppose a division in a high-income-tax-rate country produces a subcomponent for another division in a low-income-tax-rate country. By setting a low transfer price, the company can recognize most of the profit from the production in the low-income-tax-rate country, thereby minimizing taxes. Likewise, items produced by divisions in a low-income-tax-rate country and transferred to a division in a high-income-tax-rate country should have a high transfer price to minimize taxes.

Sometimes import duties offset income tax effects. Most countries base import duties on the price paid for an item, whether bought from an outside company or transferred from another division. Therefore, low transfer prices generally lead to low import duties.

Tax authorities also recognize the incentive to set transfer prices to minimize taxes and import duties. Therefore, most countries have restrictions on allowable transfer prices. U.S. multinationals must follow an Internal Revenue Code rule specifying that transfers be priced at "arm's-length" market values, or at the price one division would pay another if they were independent companies. Even with this rule, companies have some latitude in deciding an appropriate "arm's-length" price.

Consider a high-end running shoe produced by an Irish Nike division with a 12% income tax rate and transferred to a division in Germany with a 40% rate. In addition, suppose Germany imposes an import duty equal to 20% of the price of the item and that Nike cannot deduct this import duty for tax purposes. Suppose the full unit cost of a pair of the shoes (translated to U.S. dollars) is $100, and the variable cost is $60. If tax authorities allow either variable- or full-cost transfer prices, which should Nike choose? By transferring at $100 rather than at $60, the company gains $3.20 per unit:

Effect of Transferring at $100 Instead of at $60	
Income of the Irish division is $40 higher; therefore, it pays 12% × $40 more income taxes	$(4.80)
Income of the German division is $40 lower; therefore, it pays 40% × $40 less income taxes	16.00
Import duty is paid by the German division on an additional $100 − $60 = $40; therefore, it pays 20% × $40 more duty	(8.00)
Net savings from transferring at $100 instead of $60	$ 3.20

Companies may also use transfer prices to avoid the financial restrictions imposed by some governments. For example, a country might restrict the amount of dividends paid to foreign owners. It may be easier for a company to get cash from a foreign division as payment for items transferred than as cash dividends.

In summary, transfer pricing is more complex in a multinational company than it is in a domestic company. Multinational companies try to achieve more objectives through transfer-pricing policies, and some of the objectives can conflict with one another.

Summary Problem for Your Review

PROBLEM

Reconsider Nike's fabric division and sportswear division described on page 399. In addition to the data there, suppose the fabric division has annual fixed manufacturing costs of $800,000 and expected annual production of enough fabric to make 100,000 golf shirts. The "fully-allocated cost" of the material for one golf shirt is as follows:

Variable costs	$ 6.00
Fixed costs, $800,000 ÷ 100,000 shirts	8.00
Fully allocated cost of the material for one golf shirt	$14.00

Assume that the fabric division has idle capacity. The sportswear division is considering whether to buy enough fabric for 10,000 golf shirts. It will sell each shirt for $25. The additional processing and selling costs in the sportswear division to produce and sell one shirt are $12. If Nike bases its transfer prices on fully-allocated cost, would the sportswear division manager buy? Explain. Would the company as a whole benefit if the sportswear division manager decided to buy? Explain.

SOLUTION

The sportswear division manager would not buy. The fully-allocated cost-based transfer price of $14 would make the acquisition of the fabric unattractive to the sportswear division:

Sportswear Division:		
Sales price of final product		$25
Deduct costs		
Transfer price paid to the fabric division (fully-allocated cost)	$14	
Additional processing and selling costs	12	
Total costs to the sportswear division		26
Contribution to profit of the sportswear division		$ (1)
Company as a whole:		
Sales price of final product		$25
Deduct variable costs and opportunity costs		
Fabric department	$ 6	
Sportswear department	12	
Total variable and opportunity costs		18
Contribution to company as a whole		$ 7

The company as a whole would benefit by $70,000 (10,000 shirts $\times$ $7) if the fabric division produces and transfers the fabric.

The major lesson here is that when there is idle capacity in the supplier division transfer prices based on fully-allocated costs may induce the wrong decisions. Working in his or her own best interests, the sportswear division manager has no incentive to buy from the fabric division.

Keys to Successful Management Control Systems

Like management in general, management control systems are more art than science. A company such as **Nike** will certainly include many subjective factors as well as more objective measures of profitability in its performance-evaluation system. Intelligent use of the available information is as important as generating the information itself. Next, we briefly explore three factors that help managers interpret and use management control information.

Focus on Controllability

Objective 9

Explain how controllability and management by objectives (MBO) aid the implementation of management control systems.

As Chapter 9 explained (see Exhibit 9-5, page 356), companies should distinguish between the performance of the division manager and the performance of the division as an investment by the corporation. Top management should evaluate segment managers on the basis of their controllable performance. However, management should base decisions such as increasing or decreasing investment in a division on the economic viability of the division, not on the performance of its managers.

This distinction helps to clarify some vexing difficulties. For example, top management may use an investment base to gauge the economic performance of a retail store, but judge the store's manager by focusing on income and ignoring any investment allocations. The aim is to evaluate the manager on controllable factors, but controllability depends on what decisions managers can make. In a highly decentralized company such as **Johnson & Johnson** or **General Electric**, for instance, managers can influence investments in assets and can exercise judgment regarding the appropriate amount of short-term credit and some long-term credit. Investment decisions that managers do not influence should not affect their performance evaluations.

Management by Objectives and Setting Expectations

Management by objectives (MBO) describes the joint formulation by managers and their superiors of a set of goals and plans for achieving the goals for a forthcoming period. For our purposes here, the terms *goals* and *objectives* are synonymous. The plans often take the form of a responsibility accounting budget (together with supplementary goals, such as levels of management training and safety that managers may not incorporate into the accounting budget). The company then evaluates a manager's performance in relation to these agreed-on budgeted objectives. It is important that managers' expectations be consistent with those of their superiors.

An MBO approach tends to reduce complaints about lack of controllability because managers first agree on a reasonable budget. That is, a particular manager and his or her superior negotiate a budget for a particular period and a particular set of expected outside and inside influences. For example, by evaluating results compared to expectations, a manager may more readily accept an assignment to a less successful segment. Why? Because a manager can reasonably expect to meet goals that recognize that the segment is economically struggling. Thus, an MBO system is preferable to a system that emphasizes absolute profitability for its own sake. Unless evaluation focuses on meeting reasonable expectations, able managers will be reluctant to accept responsibility for segments that are in economic trouble. Whether using MBO or not, skillful budgeting and intelligent performance evaluation will go a long way toward overcoming the common lament, "I'm being held responsible for items beyond my control."

MBO is also especially useful in nonprofit organizations where financial goals may be less important than nonfinancial goals. Managers can set objectives that fit well with overall organizational objectives. The Business First box on page 407 illustrates how an academic institution can use decentralization to further the university's financial and nonfinancial objectives.

Business First

Decentralization in Academia

Corporations are not the only types of organizations that decentralize. Many nonprofit organizations, such as universities, hospitals, and churches, also decentralize by delegating decision-making authority to segments of the organization. It is important for each segment to set objectives consistent with the overall organizational goals.

An example of such an organization is Harvard University. Using a philosophy of "every tub on its own bottom," Harvard is divided into ten academic units: (1) Faculty of Arts and Sciences, which includes Harvard College, Graduate School of Arts and Sciences, and Division of Continuing Education; (2) Business School; (3) Design School; (4) Divinity School; (5) Graduate School of Education; (6) John F. Kennedy School of Government; (7) Law School; (8) Faculty of Medicine, which includes the Medical School and School of Dental Medicine; (9) School of Public Health; and (10) Radcliffe Institute for Advanced Study. At the head of each unit is a dean appointed by the president. The dean is directly responsible for his or her unit's finances and organization. In essence, each unit functions like a division of a decentralized corporation. Although the units have a great deal of independence, they must still set financial and nonfinancial objectives that are consistent with Harvard's goals, and their accomplishments will be measured against their objectives.

Because each unit at Harvard is responsible for its own revenues and expenses, many of the issues are similar to those of a for-profit corporation. The governing board that is responsible for the day-to-day operations at Harvard—called the Harvard Corporation and known formally as the President and Fellows of Harvard College—is a seven-member board headed by the president. To effectively manage the university, the board needs information from the units, but it intentionally does not directly make decisions for the units—that is left to the deans. Only when reports indicate that something is awry does the board intervene.

To the extent that the units are independent of one another, decentralization works well. But, just as in a for-profit organization, difficulties can arise when there are real or potential interactions among units. For example, how is tuition divided among units when students admitted to one unit take classes in another? This is a classic transfer-pricing problem. Or what about two units (for example the Economics Department and the Business School) competing for a particular faculty member. How is the good of the entire university reflected in such hiring decisions? Or how does the university encourage cross-functional programs and research involving more than one unit? Or how does the university choose whether to invest scarce funds into the Law School or the Divinity School? These are all issues that arise from decentralization.

Like any organization, Harvard must balance overall organizational objectives versus the advantages of local decision making and superior motivation of divisional authority. While Harvard is an example of decentralization, other universities favor a more centralized approach.

Source: "Harvard's Ten Principal Academic Units" (http://www.news.harvard.edu/guide/underst/under2.html).

Budgets, Performance Targets, and Ethics

Organizations can minimize many of the troublesome motivational effects of performance evaluation systems by the astute use of budgets. We cannot overemphasize the desirability of tailoring budgets to a particular manager. For example, either an ROI or an economic profit system can promote goal congruence and managerial effort if top management gets everybody to focus on what is currently attainable in the forthcoming budget period.

Using budgets as performance targets also has its dangers. On pages 268-270 of Chapter 7 we pointed out how misuse of budgets for performance evaluation can lead to lying and cheating. Companies that make meeting a budget too important when evaluating managers may motivate unethical behavior. Top management at companies such as **WorldCom** gave "making the numbers" such a high priority that, when it became clear that a segment would not meet its goals, managers fabricated the accounting reports. At **Enron**, the consequences of poor performance evaluations were so great that managers played bookkeeping games and allegedly manipulated electricity prices to make their performance look better. The lesson is that "astute" use of budgets is good, but using budgets to put unreasonable pressure on managers can undermine the ethics of an organization.

As we said earlier in the chapter, "You get what you measure." It is important to use measures that are consistent with organizational goals. Yet, measurement is only part of the management control system. Accountants often focus too much on the measurements. Managers should also think hard about how they use the measures to achieve the organization's objectives. Even good measures can lead to dysfunctional decisions when managers misuse them. A management control system is only as good as the managers who use it.

Highlights to Remember

1. **Define *decentralization* and identify its expected benefits and costs.** As companies grow, the ability of managers to effectively plan and control becomes more difficult because top managers are further removed from day-to-day operations. One approach to effective planning and control in large companies is to decentralize decision making. This means that top management gives mid- and lower-level managers the freedom to make decisions that impact the subunit's performance. The more that decision making is delegated, the greater the decentralization. Often, the subunit manager is most knowledgeable of the factors that management should consider in the decision-making process.

2. **Distinguish between responsibility centers and decentralization.** Top management must design the management control system so that it motivates managers to act in the best interests of the company. This is done through the choice of responsibility centers and the appropriate performance metrics and rewards. The degree of decentralization does not depend upon the type of responsibility center chosen. For example, a cost-center manager in one company may have more decision-making authority than does a profit-center manager in a highly centralized company.

3. **Explain how the linking of rewards to responsibility-center performance metrics affects incentives and risk.** It is generally a good idea to link managers' rewards to responsibility-center results to promote goal congruence. However, linking rewards to results creates risk for the manager. The greater the influence of uncontrollable factors on a manager's reward, the more risk the manager bears.

4. **Compute ROI, economic profit, and economic value added (EVA) and contrast them as criteria for judging the performance of organization segments.** It is typical to measure the results of investment centers using a set of performance metrics that include financial measures, such as return on investment (ROI), economic profit, or economic value added (EVA). ROI is any income measure divided by the dollar amount invested and is expressed as a percentage. Economic profit, or economic value added, is operating income less a capital charge based on the capital invested (cost of capital). It is an absolute dollar amount.

5. **Compare the advantages and disadvantages of various bases for measuring the invested capital used by organization segments.** The way an organization measures invested capital determines the precise motivation provided by ROI, economic profit, or EVA. Managers will try to reduce assets or increase liabilities that a company includes in their division's investment base. They will adopt more conservative asset replacement policies if the company uses net book value rather than gross book value in measuring the assets.

6. **Define *transfer prices* and identify their purpose.** In large companies with many different segments, one segment often provides products or services to another segment. Deciding on the amount the selling division should charge the buying division for these transfers (the transfer price) is difficult. Companies use various types of transfer pricing policies. The overall purpose of transfer prices is to motivate managers to act in the best interests of the company, not just their segment.

7. **State the general rule for transfer pricing and use it to assess transfer prices based on total costs, variable costs, and market prices.** As a general rule, transfer prices should approximate the outlay cost plus opportunity cost of the producing segment. Each type of transfer price has its own advantages and disadvantages. Each has a situation where it works best, and each can lead to dysfunctional decisions in some instances. When a competitive market exists for the product or service, using market-based transfer prices usually leads to goal congruence and optimal decisions. When idle capacity exists in the segment providing the product or service, the use of variable cost as the transfer price usually leads to goal congruence. Cost-based prices are readily available but should usually be based on planned, rather than actual, costs. If a company uses actual costs, there is little incentive for the selling segment manager to minimize costs and the receiving segment manager does not know the cost in advance, which makes cost planning difficult.

8. **Identify the factors affecting multinational transfer prices.** Multinational organizations often use transfer prices as a means of minimizing worldwide income taxes, import duties, and tariffs.

9. **Explain how controllability and management by objectives (MBO) aid the implementation of management control systems.** Regardless of what measures a management control system uses, measures used to evaluate managers should focus on only the controllable aspects of performance. MBO can focus attention on performance compared to expectations, which is better than evaluations based on absolute profitability. Misuse of budgets and performance metrics can motivate managers to violate ethical standards. ■

Accounting Vocabulary

agency theory, p. 388
capital charge, p. 391
capital turnover, p. 391
centralization, p. 385
cost of capital, p. 391
decentralization, p. 385
dysfunctional decisions, p. 401
economic profit, p. 391

economic value added
   (EVA), p. 392
gross book value, p. 396
incentives, p. 387
management by objectives
   (MBO), p. 406
net book value, p. 396
net operating profit after-tax
   (NOPAT), p. 391

performance metric, p. 387
residual income, p. 391
return on investment
   (ROI), p. 390
return on sales, p. 391
segment autonomy, p. 386
transfer price, p. 398

Fundamental Assignment Material

10-A1 ROI and Economic Profit Calculations

Consider the following data (in thousands):

	Division		
	Tinker	**Evers**	**Chance**
Average invested capital	$2,000	$ 600	$1,800
Revenue	3,600	1,200	9,000
Income	180	126	360

1. For each division, compute the return on sales, the capital turnover, and the return on investment (ROI).
2. Which division is the best performer if evaluation is based on ROI? Explain.
3. Suppose each division is assessed a cost of capital of 10% on invested capital. Compute the economic profit for each division. Which division is the best performer based on economic profit? Explain.

10-A2 Transfer-Pricing Dispute

Bern Équipement, SA, a Swiss transportation equipment manufacturer, is heavily decentralized. Each division head has full authority on all decisions regarding sales to internal or external customers. The Graubunden division has always acquired a certain equipment component from the Ticino division. The Ticino division recently acquired specialized equipment that is used primarily to make this component. Because of the new depreciation charges on the equipment, the Ticino division has informed the Graubunden division that the unit price will be increased to CHF 325. However, the Graubunden division's management has now decided to purchase the component from outside suppliers at a price of CHF 300.

    The Ticino division has supplied the following production cost data for this component:

Annual production of component (all for sale to Graubunden division)	3,000 units
Ticino's variable costs per unit	CHF 280
Ticino's fixed costs per unit	CHF 30

1. Suppose there are no alternative uses of the Ticino facilities and that fixed costs will continue if Ticino no longer produces the component for Graubunden. Will the company as a whole benefit if the Graubunden division buys from the outside suppliers for CHF 300 per unit? Show computations to support your answer.
2. Suppose there is an alternative use for the Ticino facilities. If the Ticino facilities are used to produce the component for the Graubunden division, the Ticino division will give up a contribution of CHF 75,000 from this alternative use. Should the Graubunden division purchase from outsiders at CHF 300 per unit?
3. Suppose that there are no alternative uses for Ticino's internal facilities and that the outsiders' selling price drops by CHF 30 to CHF 270. Should the Graubunden division purchase from outsiders?

4. As the president, how would you respond if the Ticino division manager's requests that you require the Graubunden division to purchase the component from Ticino? Would your response differ depending on the specific situations described in numbers 1–3 above? Why?

10-A3 Transfer Pricing

Refer to problem 10-A2, number 1 only. Suppose the Ticino division could modify the component at an additional variable cost of CHF 17 per unit and sell the 3,000 units to other customers for CHF 325. Then, would the entire company benefit if the Graubunden division purchased the 3,000 components from outsiders at CHF 300 per unit?

10-A4 Rate of Return and Transfer Pricing

Consider the following data regarding budgeted operations for 20X7 of the Portland division of Machine Products:

Average total assets	
Receivables	$ 220,000
Inventories	290,000
Plant and equipment, net	450,000
Total	$ 960,000
Fixed overhead	$ 300,000
Variable costs	$1 per unit
Desired rate of return on average total assets	25%
Expected volume	150,000 units

1. a. What average unit sales price does the Portland division need to obtain its desired rate of return on average total assets?
   b. What would be the expected capital turnover?
   c. What would be the return on sales?
2. a. If the selling price is as previously computed, what rate of return will the division earn on total assets if sales volume is 170,000 units?
   b. If sales volume is 130,000 units?
3. Assume that the Portland division plans to sell 45,000 units to the Calgary division of Machine Products and that it can sell only 105,000 units to outside customers at the price computed in requirement 1a. The Calgary division manager has balked at a tentative transfer price of $4. She has offered $2.25, claiming that she can manufacture the units herself for that price. The Portland division manager has examined his own data. He had decided that he could eliminate $60,000 of inventories, $90,000 of plant and equipment, and $22,500 of fixed overhead if he did not sell to the Calgary division and sold only 105,000 units to outside customers. Should he sell for $2.25? Show computations to support your answer.

10-B1 ROI or Economic Profit

Melbourne Co. is a large integrated Australian conglomerate with shipping, metals, and mining operations throughout Asia. Melbourne is just starting a new manufacturing division and the newly-appointed general manager plans to submit a proposed capital budget for 20X8 for inclusion in the companywide budget.

The division manager has for consideration the following projects, all of which require an outlay of capital. All projects have equal risk.

Project	Investment Required	Return
1	$4,800,000	$1,200,000
2	1,900,000	627,000
3	1,400,000	182,000
4	950,000	152,000
5	650,000	136,500
6	300,000	90,000

The division manager must decide which of the projects to take. The company has a cost of capital of 20%. An amount of $12 million is available to the division for investment purposes.

1. What will be the total investment, total return, return on capital invested, and economic profit of the rational division manager if
   a. the company has a rule that managers should accept all projects promising a return on investment of at least 15%?
   b. the company evaluates division managers on their ability to maximize the return on capital invested (assume this is a new division so that invested capital will consist only of capital invested in new projects adopted by the manager)?
   c. the division manager is expected to maximize economic profit computed using the 20% cost of capital?
2. Which of the three approaches will induce the most effective investment policy for the company as a whole? Explain.

10-B2 Computing EVA

A company that uses EVA reported the following results for 20X4 and 20X5 (in millions):

	20X4	20X5
Pretax operating income	$5,698	5,700
Cash taxes	1,676	1,600

Average adjusted invested capital was $20,308 million in 20X4 and $18,091 million in 20X5, and the cost of capital was 9% in both 20X4 and 20X5.

1. Compute the company's EVA for 20X4 and 20X5.
2. Compare the company's performance in creating value for its shareholders in 20X5 with that in 20X4.

10-B3 Transfer Pricing

Hawkeye Enterprises runs a chain of drive-in ice cream stands in Iowa City during the summer season. Managers of all stands are told to act as if they owned the stand and are judged on their profit performance. Hawkeye Enterprises has rented an ice cream machine for the summer for $3,600 to supply its stands with ice cream. Hawkeye is not allowed to sell ice cream to other dealers because it cannot obtain a dairy license. The manager of the ice cream machine charges the stands $4 per gallon. Operating figures for the machine for the summer are as follows:

Sales to the stands (16,000 gallons at $4)		$64,000
Variable costs, at $2.10 per gallon	$33,600	
Fixed costs		
Rental of machine	3,600	
Other fixed costs	10,000	47,200
Operating margin		$16,800

The manager of the Coralville Drive-In, one of the Hawkeye drive-ins, is seeking permission to sign a contract to buy ice cream from an outside supplier at $3.35 a gallon. The Coralville Drive-In uses 4,000 gallons of ice cream during the summer. Elizabeth Chuk, controller of Hawkeye, refers this request to you. You determine that the other fixed costs of operating the machine will decrease by $900 if the Coralville Drive-In purchases from an outside supplier. Chuk wants an analysis of the request in terms of overall company objectives and an explanation of your conclusion. What is the appropriate transfer price?

10-B4 Rate of Return and Transfer Pricing

The Tokyo division of Kaycee Toy Company manufactures units of the game Shogi and sells them in the Japanese market for ¥7,200 each. The following data are from the Tokyo division's 20X8 budget:

Variable cost	¥ 5,000 per unit
Fixed overhead	¥ 6,080,000
Total assets	¥12,500,000

Kaycee has instructed the Tokyo division to budget a rate of return on total assets (before taxes) of 20%.

1. Suppose the Tokyo division expects to sell 3,400 games during 20X8.
   a. What rate of return will be earned on total assets?
   b. What would be the expected capital turnover?
   c. What would be the return on sales?
2. The Tokyo division is considering adjustments in the budget to reach the desired 20% rate of return on total assets.
   a. How many units must be sold to obtain the desired return if no other part of the budget is changed?
   b. Suppose sales cannot be increased beyond 3,400 units. How much must total assets be reduced to obtain the desired return? Assume that for every ¥1,000 decrease in total assets, fixed costs decrease by ¥100.
3. Assume that only 2,400 units can be sold in the Japanese market. However, another 1,400 units can be sold to the European marketing division of Kaycee. The Tokyo manager has offered to sell the 1,400 units for ¥6,700 each. The European marketing division manager has countered with an offer to pay ¥6,200 per unit, claiming that she can subcontract production to an Italian producer at a cost equivalent to ¥6,200. The Tokyo manager knows that if his production falls to 2,400 units, he could eliminate some assets, reducing total assets to ¥10 million and annual fixed overhead to ¥4.9 million. Should the Tokyo manager sell for ¥6,200 per unit? Support your answer with the relevant computations. Ignore the effects of income taxes and import duties.

Additional Assignment Material

QUESTIONS

10-1 "Decentralization has benefits and costs." Name three of each.

10-2 Sophisticated accounting and communications systems aid decentralization. Explain how they accomplish this.

10-3 Why is decentralization more popular in profit-seeking organizations than in nonprofit organizations?

10-4 "The essence of decentralization is the use of profit centers." Do you agree? Explain.

10-5 What kinds of organizations find decentralization to be preferable to centralization?

10-6 According to agency theory, employment contracts balance what three factors?

10-7 What is the major benefit of the ROI technique for measuring performance?

10-8 What two major items affect ROI?

10-9 How does economic profit differ from net income?

10-10 Define *economic value added* (*EVA*) and describe three ways a company can improve its EVA.

10-11 Division A's ROI is 20%, and B's is 10%. The company pays each division manager a bonus based on his or her division's ROI. Discuss whether each division manager would accept or reject a proposed project with a rate of return of 15%. Would either of them make a different decision if the company evaluated managers using economic profit with a capital charge of 11%? Explain.

10-12 Give three possible definitions of invested capital that we can use in measuring ROI or economic profit.

10-13 "Managers who use a historical-cost accounting system look backward at what something cost yesterday, instead of forward to what it will cost tomorrow." Do you agree? Why?

10-14 Ross Company uses net book value as a measure of invested capital when computing ROI. A division manager has suggested that the company change to using gross book value instead. What difference in motivation of division managers might result from such a change? Do you suppose most of the assets in the division of the manager proposing the change are relatively new or old? Why?

10-15 Why do companies need transfer-pricing systems?

10-16 Describe two problems that can arise when using actual full cost as a transfer price.

10-17 How does the presence or absence of idle capacity affect the optimal transfer-pricing policy?

10-18 "We use variable-cost transfer prices to ensure that we make no dysfunctional decisions." Discuss.

10-19 What is the major advantage of negotiated transfer prices? What is the major disadvantage?

10-20 Discuss two factors that affect multinational transfer prices but have little effect on purely domestic transfers.

10-21 Describe management by objectives (MBO).

10-22 How can performance measurement lead to unethical behavior by managers?

CRITICAL THINKING EXERCISES

10-23 Decentralization

Many companies implement organizational changes to centralize or decentralize operations only to follow with later changes in the opposite direction. Why might a company that at one time decentralizes decide later to centralize?

10-24 Comparing Financial Measures of Performance

"Both ROI and economic profit use profit and invested capital to measure performance. Therefore it really doesn't matter which we use." Do you agree? Explain.

10-25 Performance Metrics and Ethics

"Financial performance metrics cause managers to ignore ethics and focus just on meeting their profit targets. After all, look at what happened at Enron, Global Crossing, WorldCom, Tyco, HealthSouth, and several other companies." Evaluate this quote. Can financial performance metrics be compatible with ethical behavior?

10-26 Transfer Pricing and Organizational Behavior

The principle reason for transfer-pricing systems is to communicate data that will lead to goal-congruent decisions by managers of different business units. When managers take actions that conflict with organizational goals, dysfunctional behavior exists. Why does top management sometimes accept a division manager's judgments, even if the division manager appears to behave in a dysfunctional manner?

EXERCISES

10-27 Simple ROI Calculations

You are given the following data:

Sales	$120,000,000
Invested capital	$ 60,000,000
Net income	$ 6,000,000

Compute the following:

1. Turnover of capital
2. Return on sales
3. Return on investment (ROI)

10-28 Simple ROI Calculation

Fill in the blanks:

	Division		
	A	**B**	**C**
Return on sales	7%	3%	__%
Capital turnover	3	—	4
Rate of return on invested capital	__%	18%	20%

10-29 Simple ROI and Economic Profit Calculations

Consider the following data:

	Division		
	X	**Y**	**Z**
Invested capital	$1,000,000	$ _____	$1,250,000
Income	$ _____	$ 182,000	$ 162,500
Revenue	$2,500,000	$3,640,000	$ _____
Return on sales	4%	__%	__%
Capital turnover	_____	_____	3
Rate of return on invested capital	__%	14%	__%

1. Prepare a similar tabular presentation, filling in all blanks.
2. Suppose each division is assessed a capital charge based on a cost of capital of 12% of invested capital. Compute the economic profit for each division.
3. Which division is the best performer? Explain.

10-30 EVA at Briggs & Stratton

Briggs & Stratton Corporation is the world's largest maker of air-cooled gasoline engines for outdoor power equipment. The company's engines are used by the lawn and garden equipment industry. According to the company's annual report, "management subscribes to the premise that the value of Briggs & Stratton is enhanced if the capital invested in its operations yields a cash return that is greater than that expected by the providers of capital."

The following data are from Briggs & Stratton's 2008 annual report with operating profit and average invested capital adjusted to reflect the capitalization of R&D and the use of FIFO inventories (thousands of dollars):

	2008	2007
Adjusted before tax operating profit	$ 71,460	$ 52,190
Cash taxes	10,853	30,424
Adjusted average invested capital	1,687,082	1,652,321
Cost of capital	9.4%	9.9%

1. Compute the EVA for Briggs & Stratton for 2007 and 2008.
2. Did Briggs & Stratton's overall performance improve from 2007 to 2008? Explain.

10-31 Comparison of Asset and Equity Bases

Laurel Company has assets of $2 million and long-term, 10% debt of $1,200,000. Hardy Company has assets of $2 million and no long-term debt. The annual operating income (before interest) of both companies is $400,000. Ignore taxes.

1. Compute the rate of return on
   a. assets, and
   b. stockholders' equity.
2. Evaluate the relative merits of each base for appraising operating management.

10-32 Finding Unknowns

Consider the following data:

	Division		
	J	**K**	**L**
Income	$280,000	$_____	$_____
Revenue	$_____	$_____	$_____
Invested capital	$_____	$3,000,000	$16,000,000
Return on sales	7%	4%	_____%
Capital turnover	4	_____	3
Rate of return on invested capital	_____%	20%	15%
Cost of capital	16%	12%	_____%
Economic profit	$_____	$_____	$ 320,000

1. Prepare a similar tabular presentation, filling in all blanks.
2. Which division is the best performer? Explain.

10-33 Gross Versus Net Asset Value

The St. Cloud division of Upcraft Company just purchased an asset for $180,000. The asset has a 3-year life. Upcraft's top management evaluates Freida Ramirez, manager of the St. Cloud division, based on ROI for this asset. She can choose to measure the asset using either gross asset value or net asset value. Her operating income before depreciation each year is $80,000.

1. What is the St. Cloud division's ROI for each of the 3 years using the gross asset value?
2. What is the St. Cloud division's ROI for each of the 3 years using the net asset value?

3. If Ramirez expects Upcraft to transfer her to a different division in about a year, which asset valuation policy would she prefer?

10-34 Variable Cost as a Transfer Price

A chair's variable cost is $50 and its market value as a piece of unfinished furniture is $63 at a transfer point from the assembly division to the finishing division. The finishing division's variable cost of sanding and finishing the chair is $28, and the selling price of the finished chair is $85.

1. Prepare a tabulation of the contribution margin per unit for the finishing division's performance and overall company performance under the two alternatives of (a) selling to outsiders at the transfer point and (b) sanding and finishing the chair and then selling to outsiders.
2. As finishing division manager, which alternative would you choose? Explain.

10-35 Maximum and Minimum Transfer Price

Sherwin Company makes bicycles. Various divisions make components and transfer them to the Dayton division for assembly into final products. The Dayton division can also buy components from external suppliers. The Toledo division makes the wheels, and it also sells wheels to external customers. All divisions are profit centers, and managers are free to negotiate transfer prices. Prices and costs for the Toledo and Dayton divisions are as follows:

Toledo Division	
Sales price to external customers	$ 14
Internal transfer price	?
Costs	
Variable costs per wheel	$ 10
Total fixed costs	$320,000
Budgeted production	64,000 wheels*

*Includes production for transfer to Dayton

Dayton Division	
Sales price to external customers	$ 170
Costs	
Wheels, per bicycle	?
Other components, per bicycle	$ 85
Other variable costs, per bicycle	$ 45
Total fixed costs	$640,000
Budgeted production	16,000 bicycles

Fixed costs in both divisions will be unaffected by the transfer of wheels from Toledo to Dayton.

1. Compute the maximum transfer price per wheel the Dayton division would be willing to pay to buy wheels from the Toledo division.
2. Compute the minimum transfer price per wheel at which the Toledo division would be willing to produce and sell wheels to the Dayton division. Assume that Toledo has excess capacity.

10-36 Multinational Transfer Prices

Cambridge International has production and marketing divisions throughout the world. It produces one particular product in Ireland, where the income tax rate is 12%, and transfers it to a marketing division in Japan, where the income tax rate is 40%. Assume that Japan places an import tax of 10% on the product and that import duties are not deductible for income tax purposes.

The variable cost of the product is £200 and the full cost is £400. Suppose the company can legally select a transfer price anywhere between the variable and full cost.

1. What transfer price should Cambridge International use to minimize taxes? Explain why this is the tax-minimizing transfer price.
2. Compute the amount of taxes saved by using the transfer price in requirement 1 instead of the transfer price that would result in the highest taxes.

PROBLEMS

10-37 Agency Theory

The Tamura International Trading Company plans to hire a manager for its division in Mexico City. Tamura International's president and vice president of personnel are trying to decide on an appropriate incentive employment contract. The manager will operate far from the Tokyo corporate headquarters, so evaluation by personal observation will be limited. The president insists that a large incentive to produce profits is necessary; he favors a salary of ¥150,000 and a bonus of 10% of the profits above ¥1,200,000. If operations proceed as expected, profits will be ¥4,600,000, and the manager will receive ¥490,000. But both profits and compensation might be more or less than planned.

The vice president of personnel responds that ¥490,000 is more than most of Tamura International's division managers make. She is sure that the company can hire a competent manager for a guaranteed salary of ¥400,000. She argued, "Why pay ¥490,000 when we can probably hire the same person for ¥400,000?"

1. What factors would affect Tamura International's choice of employment contract? Include a discussion of the pros and cons of each proposed contract.
2. Why is the expected compensation more with the bonus plan than with the straight salary?

10-38 Margins and Turnover

Accountants often express ROI as the product of two components—capital turnover and return on sales. You are considering investing in one of three companies, all in the same industry, and are given the following information:

	Company		
	Abel	**Baker**	**Charlie**
Sales	$6,000,000	$ 2,500,000	$37,500,000
Income	$ 600,000	$ 375,000	$ 375,000
Capital	$3,000,000	$12,500,000	$12,500,000

1. Why would you desire the breakdown of return on investment into return on sales and turnover on capital?
2. Compute the return on sales, turnover on capital, and ROI for the three companies, and comment on the relative performance of the companies as thoroughly as the data permit.
3. Notice that Baker and Charlie have the same income and capital but vastly different levels of sales. Discuss the types of industries that Baker and Charlie might be in.

10-39 ROI by Business Segment

Multimedia Technology does business in three different business segments: (1) entertainment, (2) publishing/information, and (3) consumer/commercial finance. Results for a recent year were as follows (in millions):

	Revenues	**Operating Income**	**Total Assets**
Entertainment	$1,272	$223	$1,120
Publishing/Information	$ 705	$122	$1,308
Consumer/Commercial Finance	$1,235	$244	$ 924

1. Compute the following for each business segment:
   a. Return on sales
   b. Capital turnover
   c. ROI
2. Comment on the differences in ROI among the business segments. Include reasons for the differences.

10-40 EVA Versus Economic Profit, Briggs & Stratton

This is an expansion of Exercise 10-30. The primary difference between the EVA and economic profit measures is the increased focus on cash flow by EVA. EVA companies make several adjustments to both operating income from the income statement and invested capital from the balance sheet. Common examples of these adjustments include adjustments for LIFO and reporting warranty costs on a cash basis. Most EVA companies make only a few such adjustments (from 5 to 15).

The following data were taken from the 2008 annual report of **Briggs & Stratton** (thousands of dollars):

Income from operations	$ 66,227
Provision for income taxes	7,009
Net EVA adjustments added to income from operations	5,233
Additional capital employed from EVA adjustments	232,037
Ending total shareholders' equity	837,523
Cash taxes	10,853
Ending total current liabilities	333,602
Ending total assets	1,833,294
Beginning total shareholders' equity	838,454
Beginning total current liabilities	474,070
Beginning total assets	1,884,468
Management's estimate of the cost-of-capital	9.4%

Prepare a schedule that calculates and compares EVA to economic profit for Briggs & Stratton.

10-41 EVA at Hershey

The **Hershey Company** manufactures, distributes, and sells many items with the Hershey brand name. It also has many other brands including Almond Joy, Kit Kat, Milk Duds, and Twizzler. Its financial results for two recent fiscal years included the following (in millions):

	Year 2	Year 1
Revenues	$4,836	$4,429
Operating expenses	3,975	3,548
Cash Income taxes	280	237
Average invested capital (total assets less current liabilities)	$2,654	$2,764

1. Suppose that Hershey's cost of capital is 9.5%. Compute the company's EVA for years 1 and 2. Assume definitions of after-tax operating income and invested capital as reported in Hershey's annual reports without adjustments advocated by Stern Stewart or others.
2. Discuss the change in EVA between years 1 and 2.

10-42 EVA

The **Coca-Cola Company** uses EVA to evaluate top management performance. In 2008, Coca-Cola had net operating income of $8,446 million, income taxes of $1,632 million, and average noncurrent liabilities plus stockholders' equity of $27,531 million. The company's capital is about 15% long-term debt and 85% equity. Assume that the after-tax cost of debt is 5% and the cost of equity is 11%.

1. Compute Coca-Cola's EVA. Assume definitions of after-tax operating income and invested capital as reported in Coca-Cola's annual reports without adjustments advocated by Stern Stewart or others.
2. Explain what EVA tells you about the performance of the top management of Coca-Cola in 2008.

10-43 Evaluation of Divisional Performance

As the CEO of Friendly Hardware Company, you examined the following measures of the performance of three divisions (in thousands of dollars):

	Average Net Assets Based On		Operating Income Based On*	
Division	**Historical Cost**	**Replacement Cost**	**Historical Cost**	**Replacement Cost**
Tools	$15,000	$15,000	$2,600	$2,600
Appliances	44,000	55,000	6,750	6,150
Lighting	27,000	48,000	5,000	3,900

*The differences in operating income between historical and replacement cost are attributable to the differences in depreciation expenses.

1. Calculate for each division the rate of return on net assets and the economic profit based on historical cost and on replacement cost. For purposes of calculating economic profit, use 10% as the minimum desired rate of return.
2. Rank the performance of each division under each of the four different measures computed in number 1.
3. What do these measures indicate about the performance of the divisions? Of the division managers? Which measure do you prefer? Why?

10-44 Use of Gross or Net Book Value of Fixed Assets

Assume that a machine shop acquires $600,000 of fixed assets with a useful life of 4 years and no residual value. The shop uses straight-line depreciation. The company judges the shop manager based on income in relation to these fixed assets. Annual net income, after deducting depreciation, is $60,000.

Assume that sales, and all expenses except depreciation, are on a cash basis. Dividends equal net income. Thus, cash in the amount of the depreciation charge will accumulate each year. The plant manager's performance is judged in relation to fixed assets because all current assets, including cash, are considered under central-company control. Assume (unrealistically) that any cash accumulated remains idle. Ignore taxes.

1. Prepare a comparative tabulation of the plant's rate of return and the company's overall rate of return based on
   a. gross (i.e., original cost) assets.
   b. net book value of assets.
2. Evaluate the relative merits of gross assets and net book value of assets as investment bases.

10-45 Role of Economic Value and Replacement Value

(This problem requires understanding of the concept of present values. See Appendix B.)

"To me, economic value is the only justifiable basis for measuring plant assets for purposes of evaluating performance. By economic value, I mean the present value of expected future services. Still, we do not even do this on acquisition of new assets—that is, we may compute a positive net present value, using discounted cash flow; but we record the asset at no more than its cost. In this way, the excess present value is not shown in the initial balance sheet. Moreover, the use of replacement costs in subsequent years is also unlikely to result in showing economic values. The replacement cost will probably be less than the economic value at any given instant of an asset's life.

"Market values are totally unappealing to me because they represent a second-best alternative value—that is, they ordinarily represent the maximum amount obtainable from an alternative that has been rejected. Obviously, if the market value exceeds the economic value of the assets in use, they should be sold. However, in most instances, the opposite is true; market values of individual assets are far below their economic value in use.

"The obtaining and recording of total present values of individual assets based on discounted-cash-flow techniques is an infeasible alternative. I, therefore, conclude that replacement cost (less accumulated depreciation) of similar assets producing similar services is the best practical approximation of the economic value of the assets in use. Of course, it is more appropriate for the evaluation of the division's performance than the division manager's performance."

Critically evaluate these comments. Please do not wander; concentrate on the issues described by the quotation.

10-46 Profit Centers and Transfer Pricing in an Automobile Dealership

A large automobile dealership in Chicago is installing a responsibility accounting system and three profit centers: parts and service, new vehicles, and used vehicles. Top management has told the three department managers to run their shops as if they were in business for themselves. However, there are interdepartmental dealings. For example,

a. the parts and service department prepares new cars for final delivery and repairs used cars prior to resale.
b. the used-car department's major source of inventory has been cars traded in as partial payment for new cars.

The owner of the dealership has asked you to draft a company policy statement on transfer pricing, together with specific rules to be applied to the examples cited. He has told you that clarity is of paramount importance because he will rely on your statement for settling transfer-pricing disputes.

10-47 Transfer Pricing

The shocks and struts division of Transnational Motors Company produces strut assemblies for automobiles. It has been the sole supplier of strut assemblies to the automotive division and charges $45 per unit, the current market price for very large wholesale lots. The shocks and struts division also sells to outside retail outlets, at $57 per unit. Normally, outside sales amount to 25% of a total sales volume of 1 million strut assemblies per year. Typical combined annual data for the division follow:

Sales	$48,000,000	
Variable costs, at $37.50 per strut assembly		$37,500,000
Fixed costs		4,500,000
Total costs	$42,000,000	
Gross margin	$ 6,000,000	

Flint Auto Parts Company, an entirely separate entity, has offered the automotive division comparable strut assemblies at a firm price of $42 per unit. The shocks and struts division of Transnational Motors claims that it cannot possibly match this price because it could not earn any margin at $42.

1. Assume that you are the manager of the automotive division of Transnational Motors. Comment on the shocks and struts division's claim. Assume that normal outside volume cannot be increased.
2. Now assume the shocks and struts division believes that it can increase outside sales by 750,000 strut assemblies per year by increasing fixed costs by $3 million and variable costs by $4.50 per unit while reducing the selling price to $54. Assume that maximum capacity is 1 million strut assemblies per year. Should the division reject intracompany business and concentrate on outside sales?

10-48 Transfer-Pricing Concession

You are the divisional controller of the U.S. division of Samtech Electronics. Your division is operating at capacity. The Australian division has asked the U.S. division to supply a sound system (chip and speaker), which it will use in a new model Game Box that it is introducing. The U.S. division currently sells identical sound systems to outside customers at $11.00 each.

The Australian division has offered to pay $7.00 for each sound system. The total cost of the

Purchased parts from outside vendors	$28.10
Sound system from U.S. division	7.00
Other variable costs	17.50
Fixed overhead	10.00
Total	$62.60

Game Box is as follows:

The Australian division is operating at 50% of capacity, and this Game Box is an important new product introduction to increase its use of capacity. Based on a target-costing approach, the Australian division management has decided that paying more than $7.00 for the sound system would make production of the Game Box infeasible because the predicted selling price for the Game Box is only $62.00.

Samtech Electronics evaluates divisional managers on the basis of pretax ROI and dollar profits compared to the budget. Ignore taxes and tariffs.

1. As divisional controller of the U.S. division, would you recommend supplying the sound system to the Australian division for $7.00 each? Why or why not?
2. Would it be to the short-run economic advantage of Samtech Electronics for the U.S. division to supply the sound system to the Australian division? Explain your answer.
3. Discuss the organizational and behavioral difficulties, if any, inherent in this situation. As the U.S. division controller, what would you advise the Samtech Electronics president to do in this situation?

10-49 Transfer Prices and Idle Capacity

The Eugene division of Union Furniture purchases lumber, which it uses to fabricate tables, chairs, and other wood furniture. It purchases most of the lumber from Shasta Mill, also a division of Union Furniture. Both the Eugene division and Shasta Mill are profit centers.

The Eugene division proposes to produce a new Shaker-style chair that will sell for $95. The manager is exploring the possibility of purchasing the required lumber from Shasta Mill. Production of 800 chairs is planned, using capacity in the Eugene division that is currently idle.

The Eugene division can purchase the lumber needed for one chair from an outside supplier for $72. Union Furniture has a policy that internal transfers are priced at fully allocated cost.

Assume the following costs for the production of one chair and the lumber required for the chair:

Shasta Mill—Lumber Cost		Eugene Division—Chair Cost		
Variable cost	$48	Variable costs		
Allocated fixed cost	22	Lumber from Shasta Mill		$70
Fully allocated cost	$70	Eugene division variable costs		
		Manufacturing	$23	
		Selling	6	29
		Total variable cost		$99

1. Assume that the Shasta Mill has idle capacity and, therefore, would incur no additional fixed costs to produce the required lumber. Would the Eugene division manager buy the lumber for the chair from the Shasta Mill, given the existing transfer-pricing policy? Why or why not? Would the company as a whole benefit if the manager decides to buy from the Shasta Mill? Explain.
2. Assume that there is no idle capacity at the Shasta Mill and the lumber required for one chair can be sold to outside customers for $72. Would the company as a whole benefit if the Eugene manager buys from Shasta? Explain.

10-50 Transfer-Pricing Principles

A law firm, Cal Legal Services, is decentralized with 25 offices around the state of California. The headquarters is based in San Francisco. Another operating division is located in San Jose, 50 miles away. A subsidiary printing operation, CalPrint, is located in the headquarters building. Top management has indicated the desirability of the San Jose office using CalPrint for printing reports. All charges are eventually billed to the client, but Cal Legal Services was concerned about keeping such charges competitive.

CalPrint charges San Jose the following:

Photographing page for offset printing (a setup cost)	$.240
Printing cost per page	.014

At this rate, CalPrint sales have a 60% contribution margin to fixed overhead.

Outside bids for 100 copies of a 120-page report needed immediately have been as follows:

Print 4U	$203.50
Jiffy Press	179.25
Kustom Print	184.00

These three printers are located within a 5-mile radius of Cal Legal Services' San Jose office and can have the reports ready in 2 days. A messenger would have to be sent to drop off the original and pick up the copies. The messenger usually goes to headquarters, but in the past, special trips have been required to deliver the original or pick up the copies. It takes 3–4 days to get the copies from CalPrint (because of the extra scheduling difficulties in delivery and pickup).

Quality control at CalPrint is poor. Reports received in the past have contained wrinkled pages, have occasionally been mis-collated, or have had pages deleted altogether. (In one instance, an intra-company memorandum including the San Jose Office's financial performance statistics was inserted in a report prepared for an outside client. Fortunately, the San Jose office detected the error before the report was distributed to the client.) The degree of quality control in the three outside print shops is unknown.

(Although the differences in costs may seem immaterial in this case, regard the numbers as significant for purposes of focusing on the key issues.)

1. If you were the decision maker at the San Jose office of Cal Legal Services, to which print shop would you give the business? Is this an optimal economic decision from the entire organization's viewpoint?
2. What would be the ideal transfer price in this case, if based only on economic considerations?
3. Time is an important factor in maintaining client goodwill. There is potential return business from this client. Given this perspective, what might be the optimal decision for the company?
4. Comment on the wisdom of top management in indicating that CalPrint should be used.

10-51 Negotiated Transfer Prices

The Lighting division of Ibex Office Furniture needs 1,200 units of a leaded-glass lamp shade from the fabricating division. The company has a policy of negotiated transfer prices. The fabricating division has enough excess capacity to produce 2,000 units of the lamp shade. Its variable cost of production is $23. The market price of the lamp shade to external customers is $39.

What is the natural bargaining range for a transfer price between the two divisions? Explain why no price below your range would be acceptable. Also explain why no price above your range would be acceptable.

10-52 Transfer Prices and Minority Interests

This chapter discussed transferring profits between divisions of a multinational company. Another situation where transfer prices have a similar effect is when a parent company transfers items to or from a subsidiary when there are minority shareholders in the subsidiary. Consider the **Michelin Group** and its Polish subsidiary, **Stomil Olsztyn**, of which Michelin owns 70%. Michelin buys tires from Stomil Olsztyn at a transfer price. Since Michelin owns a majority of Stomil Olsztyn, it controls the transfer-pricing policy. The holders of the other 30% of Stomil Olsztyn claim that Michelin sets the transfer prices too low, thereby reducing the profits of Stomil Olsztyn. They maintain that Stomil Olsztyn would be more profitable if it were allowed to sell its tires on the market rather than transfer them to Michelin. In reply, Michelin managers maintain that Stomil Olsztyn is more profitable than other members of the Michelin Group, and, therefore, the transfer prices must be fair.

Discuss the incentives for Michelin to transfer tires at a low price from Stomil Olsztyn to its Michelin parent. What transfer price do the minority shareholders in Stomil Olsztyn favor? Use an example of a tire that Stomil Olsztyn produces at a variable cost of €20 that is transferred to Michelin for €25. How should Michelin and Stomil Olsztyn establish a fair transfer price?

10-53 Multinational Transfer Prices

American Medical Instruments produces a variety of medical products at its plant in Minneapolis. The company has sales divisions worldwide. One of these sales divisions is located in Uppsala, Sweden. Assume that the U.S. income tax rate is 34%, the Swedish rate is 60%, and a 12% import duty is imposed on medical supplies brought into Sweden.

One product produced in Minneapolis and shipped to Sweden is a heart defibrillator. The variable cost of production is $400 per unit, and the fully allocated cost is $650 per unit.

1. Suppose the Swedish and U.S. governments allow either the variable or fully allocated cost to be used as a transfer price. Which price should American Medical Instruments choose to minimize the total of income taxes and import duties? Compute the amount the company saves if it uses your suggested transfer price instead of the alternative. Assume import duties are not deductible for tax purposes.
2. Suppose the Swedish parliament passed a law decreasing the income tax rate to 50% and increasing the duty on heart monitors to 20%. Repeat number 1, using these new facts.

10-54 Review of Major Points in This Chapter

The Canadian Instruments Company uses the decentralized form of organizational structure and considers each of its divisions as an investment center. The Toronto division is currently selling 15,000 air filters annually, although it has sufficient productive capacity to produce 21,000 units per year. Variable manufacturing costs amount to $21 per unit, while the total fixed costs amount to $90,000. These 15,000 air filters are sold to outside customers at $40 per unit.

The Montreal division, also a part of Canadian Instruments, has indicated that it would like to buy 1,500 air filters from the Toronto division, but at a price of $37 per unit. This is the price the Montreal division is currently paying an outside supplier.

1. Compute the effect on the operating income of the company as a whole if the Montreal division purchases the 1,500 air filters from the Toronto division.
2. What is the minimum price that the Toronto division should be willing to accept for these 1,500 air filters?
3. What is the maximum price that the Montreal division should be willing to pay for these 1,500 air filters?
4. Suppose instead that the Toronto division is currently producing and selling 21,000 air filters annually to outside customers. What is the effect on the overall Canadian Instruments Company operating income if the Toronto division is required by top management to sell 1,500 air filters to the Montreal division at (a) $21 per unit and (b) $37 per unit?
5. For this question only, assume that the Toronto division is currently earning an annual operating income of $36,000, and the division's average invested capital is $300,000. The division manager has an opportunity to invest in a proposal that will require an additional investment of $20,000

and will increase annual operating income by $2,000. (a) Should the division manager accept this proposal if the Canadian Instruments Company uses ROI in evaluating the performance of its divisional managers? (b) If the company uses economic profit? (Assume a cost of capital of 7%.)

CASES

10-55 Profit Centers and Central Services

Star Manufacturing, manufacturer of Starlite brand small appliances, has a process engineering department (PED). The department's major task has been to help the production departments improve their operating methods and processes.

For several years, Star Manufacturing has charged the cost of consulting services to the production departments based on a signed agreement between the managers involved. The agreement specifies the scope of the project, the predicted savings, and the number of consulting hours required. The charge to the production departments is based on the costs to the Engineering Department of the services rendered. For example, senior engineer hours cost more per hour than junior engineer hours. An overhead cost is included. The agreement is really a "fixed-price" contract. That is, the production manager knows the total cost of the project in advance. A recent survey revealed that production managers have a high level of confidence in the engineers.

The PED department manager oversees the work of about 40 engineers and 10 technicians. She reports to the engineering manager, who reports to the vice president of manufacturing. The PED manager has the freedom to increase or decrease the number of engineers under her supervision. The PED manager's performance evaluation is based on many factors including the annual incremental savings to the company in excess of the costs of operating the PED department.

The production departments are profit centers. Their goods are transferred to subsequent departments, such as a sales department or sales division, at prices that approximate market prices for similar products.

Top management is seriously considering a "no-charge" plan. That is, production departments would receive engineering services at absolutely no cost. Proponents of the new plan maintain that it would motivate the production managers to take better advantage of engineering talent. In all other respects, the new system would be unchanged from the present system.

1. Compare the present and proposed plans. What are their strong and weak points? In particular, will the PED manager tend to hire the "optimal" amount of engineering talent?
2. Which plan do you favor? Why?

10-56 Management by Objectives

Roger Ravenhill is the CEO of Haida Company. Ravenhill has a financial management background and is known throughout the organization as a "no-nonsense" executive. When Ravenhill became CEO, he emphasized cost reduction and savings and introduced a comprehensive cost control and budget system. The company goals and budget plans were established by Ravenhill and given to his subordinates for implementation. Some of the company's key executives were dismissed or demoted for failing to meet projected budget plans. Under the leadership of Roger Ravenhill, Haida has once again become financially stable and profitable after several years of poor performance.

Recently, Ravenhill has become concerned with the human side of the organization and has become interested in the management technique referred to as "management by objectives" (MBO). If there are enough positive benefits of MBO, he plans to implement the system throughout the company. However, he realizes that he does not fully understand MBO because he does not understand how it differs from the current system of establishing firm objectives and budget plans.

1. Briefly explain what MBO entails and identify its advantages and disadvantages.
2. Does Roger Ravenhill's management style incorporate the human-value premises and goals of MBO? Explain your answer.

NIKE 10-K PROBLEM

10-57 ROI and Economic Profit

Examine Nike's segments as defined in Note 17 to its financial statements in the 10-K in Appendix C.

Determine the pretax ROI and economic profit for each segment in 2007 and 2008 using the pretax income information from the 10-K and the information on average total assets less current liabilities by segment in the table at the top of page 423. Assume that Nike's cost of capital is 10%. Use your results to evaluate the performance of each segment. Which segment management seems to be doing the best job? What subjective factors would you consider, in addition to ROI and economic profit, in assessing segment performance?

Segment	Average Total Assets Less Current Liabilities	
	2008	**2007**
United States	$2,591	$2,284
Europe, Middle East, and Africa	2,405	2,076
Asia Pacific	1,291	1,142
Americas	530	439
Other	1,247	1,127
Total	$8,064	$7,068

EXCEL APPLICATION EXERCISE

10-58 Return on Investment and Economic Profit

Goal: Create an Excel spreadsheet to calculate performance of divisional segments using the ROI and economic profit methods. Use the results to answer questions about your findings.

Scenario: The company has asked you to calculate ROI and economic profit for three divisions. The background data for your analysis appears in Fundamental Assignment Material 10-A1. Use an interest rate of 10% when calculating the capital charge.

When you have completed your spreadsheet, answer the following questions:
1. Which division has the best performance using the ROI method? Using the economic profit method?
2. Which division has the worst performance under both methods?
3. Based on your findings, what are your recommendations to management concerning which of these three divisions should receive an increase in invested capital?

Step-by-Step:
1. Open a new Excel spreadsheet.
2. In column A, create a bold-faced heading that contains the following:
   Row 1: Chapter 10 Decision Guideline
   Row 2: Divisions Tinker, Evers, and Chance
   Row 3: Measures of Profitability
   Row 4: Today's Date
3. Merge and center the four heading rows across columns A–I.
4. In row 7, create the following center-justified column headings:
   Column A: Division
   Column B: Invested Capital
   Column C: Revenue
   Column D: Income
   Column E: Capital Charge
   Column F: Economic Profit
   Column G: Return on Investment
   Column H: Return on Sales
   Column I: Capital Turnover
5. Change the format of Economic Profit and Return on Investment to bold-faced headings.
6. Change the format of the column headings in row 7 to permit the titles to be displayed on multiple lines within a single cell.

   Alignment tab: Wrap Text: Checked

   Note: Adjust column widths so the headings only use two lines.

   Adjust row height to insure that row is the same height as adjusted headings.
7. In column A, create the following center-justified row headings:
   Row 8: Tinker
   Skip a row.
   Row 10: Evers
   Skip a row.
   Row 12: Chance
8. Use the scenario data to fill in invested capital, revenue, and income amounts for each division.
9. Use the scenario data and appropriate formulas to calculate capital charge amounts for each division.

10. Use the appropriate formulas from this chapter to calculate economic profit, ROI, return on sales, and capital turnover amounts for each division.

11. Format amounts in columns B, C, D, E, and F for division A as follows:

Number tab:	Category:	Currency
	Decimal places:	0
	Symbol:	$
	Negative numbers:	Black with parentheses

12. Format amounts in columns B, C, D, E, and F for divisions B and C as follows:

Number tab:	Category:	Currency
	Decimal places:	0
	Symbol:	None
	Negative numbers:	Black with parentheses

13. Format amounts in columns G and H to display as percentages without decimal places.

Number tab:	Category:	Percentage
	Decimal places:	0

14. Format the capital turnover amounts to display two decimal places, followed by the word **times**.

Number tab:	Category:	Custom

From the Type list, highlight the type shown next:

	Type:	0.00

Change the data in the Type field from 0.00 to the following:

	Type:	0.00 "times"

Click the OK button.

15. Save your work to disk, and print a copy for your files.

Note: Print your spreadsheet using landscape in order to ensure that all columns appear on one page.

COLLABORATIVE LEARNING EXERCISE

10-59 ROI

Form groups of three to six students. Each student should select a company. Coordinate the selection of companies so that each group has companies from a wide variety of industries. For example, a good mix of industries for a group of five students would be a retail company, a basic manufacturing company, a computer software company, a bank, and an electric utility company.

1. Each student should find the latest annual report for his or her company. (If you cannot find the company's home page, try www.sec.gov, and search the Security and Exchange Commission's Edgar files for the company's 10-K report, which will contain its financial statements.) Compute the following:
   a. Return on sales
   b. Capital turnover
   c. ROI
2. As a group, compare these performance metrics for the chosen companies. Why do they differ across companies? What characteristic of the company and its industry might explain the differences in the measures?

INTERNET EXERCISE

10-60 Decentralization at Marriott International

Decentralization of an organization can occur for many reasons. It may be that the organization is involved in multiple activities that are not closely related to each other, such as construction and auto sales. In other cases, the decision may be due to the structure of the firm's ownership and how it chooses to manage its image. Let's look at a firm that falls under this category—**Marriott International**.

1. Go to Marriott International's Web site at www.marriott.com. What does the home page emphasize about Marriott's operations? What promotional information does Marriott include on its home page?

2. How has Marriott decentralized its businesses? Click on "Our Brands" near the bottom of the page to find a list of Marriott's divisions. Do you suppose the divisions are cost centers, profit centers, or investment centers?

3. Go to the most recent annual report by clicking on "About Marriott," "Investor Relations," "Financial Information," and finally click on "Financial Reports & Proxy" to find the most recent annual report. Locate the information on business segments in the Notes to Financial Statements. How many segments does Marriott identify? What are these segments? What information does the firm report with respect to each of the different segments?

4. Marriott provides both income from continuing operations and assets for each of the segments. Calculate the operating return on average total assets for the past 2 years for each of the segments.

5. What was the operating return on average total assets for the corporation as a whole for each of the past 2 years? Given the different kinds of business segments the company has, do you think that operating return on average total assets would be a good measure for evaluating the individual segments? What factors might influence your answer?

6. Is Marriott likely to have any transfer prices? If Marriott has transfers, how do you suppose the company determines its transfer prices?

Capital Budgeting

LEARNING OBJECTIVES

When you have finished studying this chapter, you should be able to:

1. Describe capital-budgeting decisions and use the net-present-value (NPV) method to make such decisions.

2. Evaluate projects using sensitivity analysis.

3. Calculate the NPV difference between two projects using both the total project and differential approaches.

4. Identify relevant cash flows for NPV analyses.

5. Compute the after-tax net present values of projects.

6. Explain the after-tax effect on cash received from the disposal of assets.

7. Use the payback model and the accounting rate-of-return model and compare them with the NPV model.

8. Reconcile the conflict between using an NPV model for making decisions and using accounting income for evaluating the related performance.

9. Compute the impact of inflation on a capital-budgeting project (Appendix 11).

▶ TOYOTA MOTOR CORPORATION

In 2008 Toyota Motor Corporation became the largest automobile company in the world, replacing General Motors. Toyota was founded in 1937 by Japanese entrepreneur, Kiichiro Toyoda, to produce and sell Toyoda autos. Almost immediately the name was changed to Toyota because (according to Wikipedia) "it took eight brush strokes (a fortuitous number) to write in Japanese, was visually simpler (leaving off two ticks at the end), and sounded better with two 't's." In 1957 Toyota entered the U.S. market with a car called the Toyopet Crown. Unfortunately, U.S. consumers associated these cars with toys and pets, so Toyota quickly dropped the Toyopet name. Nevertheless, the company continued selling Toyotas in the United States. In 1963 Toyota built its first car outside of Japan (in Australia) and in 1982 began producing cars in the United States. Now it has five major assembly plants in the United States, one under construction, and one on the drawing board. It has production or assembly plants in more than 25 countries.

Toyota was instrumental in developing lean manufacturing and just-in-time production. Its management philosophy focuses on four areas: 1) long-term thinking, 2) a process for problem-solving, 3) adding value by developing people, and 4) organizational learning. This has led to a variety of awards for quality, from the Deming Prize for Total Quality Management in 1965 to recent J.D. Power awards for automobile quality. This reputation for quality was instrumental in Toyota's worldwide growth.

Nearly a decade ago Toyota invested heavily in U.S. manufacturing facilities, especially those for full-size pickup trucks and sports-utility vehicles. With the downturn in the economy in 2008 and 2009, Toyota found itself with excess manufacturing capacity. The company moved quickly to shut down two factories for several months each and to switch production in another from the Highlander SUV to the Prius. The investment in production facilities for trucks and SUVs may not have turned out well, but it was based on the best information available at the time. Every forward-looking company must make long-term investment decisions based on uncertain predictions. All investment decisions will not be perfect, but making good investment decisions is critical to the long-term success of most organizations. This chapter focuses on the analyses that go into such decisions. ■

The Toyota Prius was the first mass-produced hybrid vehicle.

Capital Budgeting for Programs or Projects

Major corporations such as Toyota are not the only companies that face decisions about capital investment and expansion. At some time, every company needs to decide where and how to spend its money on major projects that will affect company financial results for years to come. This chapter concentrates on the planning and controlling decisions for programs or projects that affect financial results over a period longer than just the next year. Such decisions require investments of large amounts of resources—called capital outlays—in anticipation of future benefits that are often uncertain. The term **capital budgeting** describes the long-term planning for making and financing such outlays.

Capital budgeting has three phases: (1) identifying potential investments, (2) choosing which investments to make (which includes gathering data to aid the decision), and (3) follow-up monitoring, or "post-audit," of the investments. Accountants usually are not involved in the first phase, but they play important roles in phases 2 and 3.

Why are accountants involved in capital-budgeting decisions? They function primarily as information specialists. One of the purposes of a cost-management system is to provide cost measurements for strategic decisions, such as major capital-budgeting decisions.

Accountants gather and interpret information to help managers make capital-budgeting decisions. To help organize volumes of information, accountants rely on capital-budgeting models. Let's take a look at how some of these models work.

Discounted-Cash-Flow Models

The most widely used capital-budgeting models are **discounted-cash-flow (DCF) models**. These models focus on a project's cash inflows and outflows while taking into account the time value of money. They are based on the old adage that a bird in the hand is worth two in the bush—that a dollar in the hand today is worth more than a dollar to be received in several years. This adage applies because the receipt of money in the future has an opportunity cost—interest income forgone by not receiving the money now and earning interest on it in the interim period. Similarly, borrowing money now to use for a capital expenditure carries a cost for interest expense. More than 85% of the large industrial firms in the United States use a DCF model.

Major Aspects of DCF

As the name suggests, DCF models focus on expected cash inflows and outflows rather than on net income. They also compute **present values (PV)**, the value today of a future cash flow. Companies invest cash today in order to receive cash in future periods. DCF models compare the value of today's cash outflows with the present value of the future cash inflows.

DCF methods are based on the theory of compound interest. If your knowledge of compound interest and time value of money is a little rusty, be sure to read Appendix B, pages A5–A10. Do not try to learn about the DCF methods until you are able to use Tables 1 (p. A6) and 2 (p. A9) in Appendix B.

Net Present Value (NPV)

We will focus on the most popular version of DCF, the **net-present-value (NPV) method**. The NPV method computes the present value of all expected future cash flows using a minimum desired rate of return. The minimum desired rate of return depends on the risk of a proposed project—the higher the risk, the higher the rate. This minimum rate, called the **required rate of return**, **hurdle rate**, or **discount rate**, is based on the cost of capital—what the firm pays to acquire more capital. Using this required rate, managers sum the present values of all expected future cash flows (inflows and outflows, if any) from the project and subtract the initial investment. If this total, the **net present value**, is positive, the project is desirable. If the net present value is negative, the project is undesirable. Why? A positive NPV means that accepting the project benefits the firm because the present value of the project's cash inflows exceeds the present value of its cash outflows. Similarly, accepting a negative NPV project makes the firm worse off financially because its investment is more than the PV of the future benefits. (An NPV of zero means that the present value of the inflows equals the present value of the outflows so the project will make the firm neither better nor worse off.) When choosing among several investments, managers should pick the one with the greatest net present value.

Applying the NPV Method

Objective 1

Describe capital-budgeting decisions and use the net-present-value (NPV) method to make such decisions.

To illustrate how DCF models work, we will use the following example throughout the rest of this section: Managers at Toyota's Tupelo, Mississippi plant are contemplating the purchase of new, more efficient auto painting equipment that they expect will increase efficiency and produce operating savings of $2,000 cash per year. The useful life of the equipment is 4 years, after which it will have a net disposal value of zero. The equipment will cost $5,827 now, and the minimum desired rate of return is 10% per year.

To apply the NPV method, you can use the following three steps, which we illustrate in Exhibit 11-1.

1. *Identify the amount and timing of relevant expected cash inflows and outflows:* The right-hand side of Exhibit 11-1 shows how to sketch these cash flows. Outflows are in parentheses. Be sure to include the outflow at time zero, the date of acquisition. You do not have to use a sketch, but sketches can help you to see costs and cost relationships over time.

	Present Value of $1, Discounted at 10%	Total Present Value	0	1	2	3	4
				Sketch of Cash Flows at End of Year			
Approach 1: Discounting Each Year's Cash Flows Separately*							
Cash flows							
Annual savings	.9091	$1,818		$2,000			
	.8264	1,653			$2,000		
	.7513	1,503				$2,000	
	.6830	1,366					$2,000
Present value of future inflows		$6,340					
Initial outlay	1.0000	(5,827)	$(5,827)				
Net present value		$ 513					
Approach 2: Using Annuity Table†							
Annual savings	3.1699	$6,340		$2,000	$2,000	$2,000	$2,000
Initial outlay	1.0000	(5,827)	$(5,827)				
Net present value		$ 513					

*Present values from Table 1, Appendix B, page A6.

†Present value of annuity from Table 2, Appendix B, page A9. (Incidentally, calculators or computers may give slightly different answers than do the tables because of rounding differences.)

Exhibit 11-1

Net-Present-Value Method
Original investment, $5,827. Useful life, 4 years. Annual cash inflow from operations, $2,000. Minimum desired rate of return, 10%. Cash outflows are in parentheses; cash inflows are not. Total present values are rounded to the nearest dollar.

2. ***Find the present value of each expected cash inflow or outflow:*** Examine Table 1 in Appendix B on page A6. Find the PV factor for each year's cash flow from the correct row and column of the table. Multiply each expected cash inflow or outflow by the appropriate PV factor. For example, the $2,000 cash savings that will occur 2 years hence is worth $2,000 × .8264 = $1,653 today. Be sure to include the initial investment at time zero.

3. ***Sum the individual present values:*** The sum is the project's NPV. Accept a project whose NPV is positive, and reject a project whose NPV is negative.

The value today (at time zero) of the four $2,000 cash inflows is $6,340. The manager pays only $5,827 to obtain these cash inflows. Thus, the net present value is $6,340 − $5,827 = $513, so the investment is desirable.

Choice of the Correct Table

Exhibit 11-1 also shows another way to calculate the NPV, shown as approach 2. The basic steps are the same as for approach 1. The only difference is that approach 2 uses Table 2 in Appendix B (see page A9) instead of Table 1. Table 2 is an annuity table that provides a shortcut to reduce hand calculations. It gives discount factors for computing the PV of a series of equal cash flows at equal intervals. Because the four cash flows in our example are all equal, you can use Table 2 to make one PV computation instead of using Table 1 to make four individual computations. Table 2 merely sums up the pertinent PV factors of Table 1. Therefore, the annuity factor for 4 years at 10% is[1]

$$.9091 + .8264 + .7513 + .6830 = 3.1698$$

Beware of using the wrong table. You should use Table 1 for discounting individual amounts and Table 2 for a series of equal amounts. Table 1 is the basis for Table 2, and you can use it for all PV calculations if you wish.

You can avoid Tables 1 and 2 entirely by using the PV function on a handheld calculator or the PV function on a computer spreadsheet program. However, we encourage you to use the tables when learning the NPV method. Using the tables will help you better understand the process of PV computation. Once you are comfortable with the method, you can take advantage of the speed and convenience of calculators and computers.

Making Managerial Decisions

For major capital investments, managers usually prepare a detailed NPV analysis. For smaller items, sometimes they make a quick calculation or use intuition. Suppose you are in charge of a company's mail room. An employee has suggested the purchase of a $12,000 letter sorting machine. She says that it will save 1 hour per day for 250 working days a year for an employee making a total of $12 per hour. She indicates that the $12,000 expenditure will save $15,000 over the machine's 5-year life. Should you approve the purchase?

Answers

The employee is right about the $15,000 total savings:

1 hour × 250 days × $12/hour × 5 years = $15,000

However, her quick calculation ignores the time value of money. The $12,000 must be paid immediately, and the $15,000 of savings is spread over the next 5 years at $3,000 per year. You know that the present value of the savings is less than the $15,000 total, but the exact amount depends on the required rate of return. Therefore, you must know the required rate before you can answer the question.

Suppose the required rate is 10%. Then the NPV (using Table 1) is negative, $(627.90):

$.9091 × \$3,000 + .8264 × \$3,000 + .7513 × \$3,000 + .6830 × \$3,000 + .6209 × \$3,000 − \$12,000 = \$2,727.30 + \$2,479.20 + \$2,253.90 + \$2,049.00 + \$1,862.70 = \$11,372.10 − 12,000 = \$(627.90)$.

Using Table 2 it is 3.7908 × $3,000 − $12,000 = $11,372.40 − $12,000 = $(627.60), which differs from the Table 1 result by a rounding error. With a 10% required rate, the investment is not desirable.

Now, suppose the required rate is 5%. Using Table 2, the NPV is positive:

4.3295 × $3,000 − $12,000 = $12,988.50 − $12,000 = $988.50. In this case, the purchase is warranted. It is important to recognize the time value of money and to apply the right required rate of return.

---

[1]Rounding error causes a .0001 difference between the Table 2 factor and the summation of Table 1 factors.

Effect of Minimum Rate

The minimum desired rate of return can have a large effect on NPVs. The higher the minimum desired rate of return, the lower the PV of each future cash inflow. Why? Because the higher the rate of return, the more it costs you to wait for the cash rather than having it available to invest today. Thus, higher required rates lead to lower NPVs. For example, at a rate of 16%, the NPV of the project in Exhibit 11-1 would be −$231. That is, $2,000 × 2.7982 = $5,596, which is $231 less than the investment of $5,827, instead of the +$513 computed with a 10% rate. (PV factor 2.7982 is taken from Table 2 in Appendix B on page A9.) When the desired rate of return is 16% rather than 10%, the project should be rejected.

Assumptions of the NPV Model

We make two major assumptions when using the NPV model. First, we assume a world of certainty. That is, we act as if the predicted cash inflows and outflows are certain to occur at the times specified. Second, we assume perfect capital markets. That is, if we need to get extra cash or invest excess cash at any time, we can borrow or lend money at the same interest rate, which is our required rate of return. In a world that meets these assumptions, no model could possibly be better than the NPV model.

Unfortunately, the real world has neither certainty nor perfect capital markets. Nevertheless, the NPV model is usually preferred to other models because the assumptions of most other models are even less realistic. The NPV model is not perfect, but it generally meets our cost-benefit criterion. That is, the benefit of better decisions based on NPV is greater than the cost of applying it. More sophisticated models often do not improve decisions enough to be worth their cost.

Depreciation and NPV

NPV calculations do not include deductions for depreciation. Why not? Because NPV is based on inflows and outflows of cash and not on the accounting concepts of revenues and expenses.[2] Depreciation is not a cash flow. It is a way of allocating the cost of a long-lived asset (which a company usually pays for in cash upon purchase) to different periods. Because a capital budgeting analysis records and accounts for the cash outflow at the time of purchase, deducting depreciation from future cash flows would be like counting this cost twice—once at purchase and again over the asset's life.

Review of Decision Rules

Be sure that you understand why the NPV method works, not just how to apply it. The decision maker in our example cannot directly compare an immediate outflow of $5,827 with a series of future inflows of $2,000 each because of the time value of money. The NPV model aids comparison by expressing all amounts in today's monetary units (such as dollars, euros, or yen) at time zero. The required rate of return measures the cost of using money. At a rate of 14%, the comparison is as follows:

Outflow in today's dollars	$(5,827)
Inflow equivalent in today's dollars at 14%	5,827*
Net present value	$ 0

*$2,000 × 2.9137 from Table 2 = $5,827.

Therefore, at a required rate of return of 14%, the decision maker is indifferent between having $5,827 now or having a stream of four annual inflows of $2,000 each. If the interest rate were 16%, the decision maker would find the project unattractive because the net present value would be a negative $231. The following graph shows the relationship between the required rate of return and the project's NPV.

---

[2]Throughout this chapter, our examples often assume that cash inflows are equivalent to revenues and that cash outflows are equivalent to expenses (except for depreciation). If we account for the revenues and expenses on the accrual basis of accounting, there will be leads and lags of cash inflows and cash outflows that a precise DCF model must recognize. For example, we might record a $10,000 sale on credit as revenue in one period but not recognize the related cash inflow in a DCF model until collected, which may be in a second period. We do not make such refinements in this chapter.

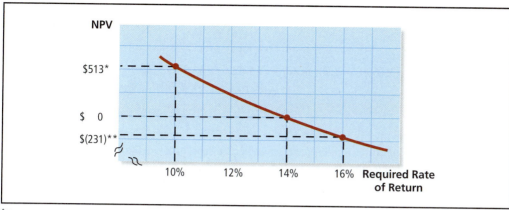

[*]($2,000 × 3.1699) − $5,827 = $513
^{**}($2,000 × 2.7982) − $5,827 = $(231)

At 10%, the NPV is a positive $513, so the project is desirable. At all rates below 14%, the NPV is positive. At all rates above 14%, the NPV is negative.

Internal Rate of Return (IRR) Model

Another popular DCF model is the **internal rate of return (IRR) model**. This model determines the interest rate at which the NPV equals zero. If this rate, called the IRR, is greater than the required rate of return, a project is desirable. If not, it is undesirable. Finance textbooks provide descriptions of the IRR method, and we will not go into details here. However, in most cases the IRR method gives equivalent decisions to the NPV method. In our example, the IRR is 14%; that is, the NPV of the equipment is zero using an interest rate of 14%. Thus, at our required rate of return of 10% (or any rate less than 14%) we accept the project. At any required rate above 14% we would reject it. In general, we find the following:

If IRR > required rate of return, then NPV > 0 and we should accept the project

If IRR < required rate of return, then NPV < 0 and we should reject the project

Because of the equivalence of NPV and IRR models for most investment proposals, we will use the NPV model for all the illustrations in this chapter.

Real Options

Whereas the IRR model is generally equivalent to the NPV model, the use of real options is an improvement on NPV. It is more sophisticated, and only a few companies are using it for routine capital-budgeting decisions. But it is an important innovation that is sure to grow in popularity. A **real options model** recognizes the value of contingent investments—that is, investments that a company can adjust as it learns more about their potential for success. For example, a project that a company can implement in stages, where investment in one stage occurs only if the previous stage was successful, has an advantage over an "all or nothing" project, one where the entire investment must take place up front. Suppose implementing a project in stages causes the expected NPV to fall because it is not as efficient as implementing it all at once. Staging the project might still be a preferred alternative if the company gains enough information in the early stages to make better decisions in the later stages. A real options model recognizes the value of such staging. Like the IRR model, we will leave the details of real options to the finance textbooks.

Sensitivity Analysis and Risk Assessment in DCF Models

Because the future is uncertain, actual cash inflows may differ from what was expected or predicted. To quantify this uncertainty, managers often use sensitivity analysis, which shows the financial consequences that would occur if actual cash inflows and outflows differ from those expected. It can answer what-if questions like *What will happen to the NPV if my predictions of useful life or cash flows change?* The best way to understand sensitivity analysis is to see it in action, so let's take a look at an example.

Suppose the Toyota managers know that the actual cash savings in Exhibit 11-1 could fall below the predicted level of $2,000. How far below $2,000 must the annual cash savings drop

Objective 2

Evaluate projects using sensitivity analysis.

before the NPV becomes negative? The cash inflow at the point where NPV = 0 is the "break-even" cash flow:

$$NPV = 0$$
$$(3.1699 \times \text{cash flow}) - \$5,827 = 0$$
$$\text{cash flow} = \$5,827 \div 3.1699$$
$$= \$1,838$$

If the annual cash savings is less than $1,838, the NPV is negative, and the managers should reject the project. Therefore, annual cash savings can drop only $2,000 − $1,838 = $162, or 8.1% below the predicted amount, before the managers would change their decision.

Managers like sensitivity analysis because it can give them immediate answers about possible future events. It also shows managers how risky a given project might be by showing how sensitive the decision is to changes in predictions. If a project has a positive NPV that would become negative with only a small change in cash flows, it can be a risky project. Sensitivity analysis can become complicated very quickly, and doing all the calculations by hand can be complex and tedious. Fortunately, there is a good deal of sensitivity analysis software available that lets computers do all the calculations, thus, permitting managers and accountants to focus on interpreting the results of the analysis.

The NPV Comparison of Two Projects

Objective 3

Calculate the NPV difference between two projects using both the total project and differential approaches.

So far we have seen how to use the NPV method to evaluate a single project. In practice, managers very rarely look at only one project or option at a time. Instead, managers compare several options to see which is the best or most profitable. We will now see how to use NPV to compare two or more alternatives.

Total Project Versus Differential Approach

Two common methods for comparing alternatives are (1) the total project approach and (2) the differential approach.

The **total project approach** computes the total impact on cash flows for each alternative and then converts these total cash flows to their present values. It is the most popular approach, and we can use it for any number of alternatives. The alternative with the largest NPV of total cash flows is best.

The **differential approach** computes the differences in cash flows between alternatives and then converts these differences to their present values. We cannot use this method to compare more than two alternatives. Often, the two alternatives being compared are (1) invest in a project and (2) do nothing.

Let's compare the differential and total project approaches. Consider a motor that drives one of the assembly lines at **Toyota**'s San Antonio plant. Assume that Toyota purchased the motor 3 years ago for $56,000. It has a remaining useful life of 5 years but will require a major overhaul at the end of two more years at a cost of $10,000. Its disposal value now is $20,000. Its predicted disposal value in 5 years is $8,000, assuming that the company does the $10,000 major overhaul on schedule. The predicted cash-operating costs of this motor are $40,000 annually. A sales representative has offered a substitute motor for $51,000. The new motor will reduce annual cash-operating costs by $10,000, will not require any overhauls, will have a useful life of 5 years, and will have a disposal value of $3,000. If the required rate of return is 14%, what should Toyota do to minimize long-run costs, keep the old machine or replace it with the new one? (Try to solve this problem yourself before examining the solution that follows.)

Regardless of the approach used, perhaps the hardest part of making capital-budgeting decisions is predicting accurately the relevant cash flows. Seeing which events will cause money to flow either in or out can be complex, especially when there are many sources of cash flows. However, you cannot compare alternatives if you do not know their cash flows, so the first step for either the total project or differential approach is to estimate the relevant cash flows. Exhibit 11-2 sketches these cash flows for each approach.

Total Project Approach: For the total project approach we list the cash flows for each project, replace or keep, separately. We then determine the NPV of the cash flows for each individual project and choose the project with the largest positive NPV or smallest negative NPV.

Exhibit 11-2

Total Project Versus Differential Approach to Net Present Value

	Present Value Discount Factor, at 14%	Total Present Value	Sketch of After-Tax Cash Flows at End of Year					
			0	1	2	3	4	5
I. Total Project Approach								
A. Replace								
Recurring cash operating costs, using an annuity table*	3.4331	$(102,993)		$(30,000)	$(30,000)	$(30,000)	$(30,000)	$(30,000)
Disposal value, end of year 5	.5194	1,558						$ 3,000
Initial required investment	1.0000	(31,000)	$(31,000)					
NPV of net cash flows		$(132,435)						
B. Keep								
Recurring cash operating costs, using an annuity table*	3.4331	$(137,324)		$(40,000)	$(40,000)	$(40,000)	$(40,000)	$(40,000)
Overhaul, end of year 2	.7695	(7,695)			$(10,000)			
Disposal value, end of year 5	.5194	4,155						$ 8,000
NPV of net cash flows		$(140,864)						
Difference in NPV between the alternatives		$ 8,429						
II. Differential Approach								
A–B. Analysis confined to differences								
Recurring cash operating savings, using an annuity table*	3.4331	$ 34,331		$ 10,000	$ 10,000	$ 10,000	$ 10,000	$ 10,000
Overhaul avoided, end of year 2	.7695	7,695			$ 10,000			
Difference in disposal values, end of year 5	.5194	(2,597)						$ (5,000)
Incremental initial investment	1.0000	(31,000)	$(31,000)					
Difference in NPV between alternatives		$ 8,429						

*Table 2, Appendix B.

Exhibit 11-2 shows that the NPV of replacing the motor, –132,435, is better than the – $140,864 NPV of keeping the old motor. The advantage is $140,864 − $132,435 = $8,429. Most cash flows are negative because these are the costs of operating the motor. The alternative with the lowest cost—the smallest negative NPV—is the most desirable.

Differential Approach: For the differential approach, we first list the difference in cash flow for each year. In other words, assume implementation of one of the projects as a baseline (for example, keeping the old machine) and perform a differential analysis as discussed in Chapter 6. Specifically, subtract the cash flows for keeping from the cash flows for replacement for each year. This isolates the advantages (cash inflows or cost savings) and disadvantages (cash outflows) of replacement compared to the baseline, keeping the machine. (Remember that cash inflows are positive numbers, while cash outflows are negative.) Next, calculate the NPV of the differential cash flows. If the NPV is positive, choose replacement; if it is negative, choose to keep the motor. Whereas the total project approach computed the difference in the NPVs of the two projects, the differential method computes the NPV of the difference in cash flows of the two projects. Both give the same total difference, an $8,429 advantage to replacement.

Exhibit 11-2 illustrates that both methods produce the same answer. As a result, you can use these methods interchangeably, as long as you are considering only two alternatives. If our example had more than two alternatives, our only choice would be to use the total project approach.

Relevant Cash Flows for NPV

Objective 4

Identify relevant cash flows for NPV analyses.

As we mentioned earlier, predicting cash flows is the hardest part of capital budgeting. When you array the relevant cash flows, be sure to consider three types of inflows and outflows: (1) initial cash inflows and outflows at time zero, (2) future disposal values, and (3) operating cash inflows and outflows.

INITIAL CASH INFLOWS AND OUTFLOWS AT TIME ZERO These cash flows include both outflows for the purchases and installation of equipment and other items required by the new project and either inflows or outflows from disposal of any items that are replaced. In Exhibit 11-2, we subtracted the $20,000 received from selling the old motor from the $51,000 purchase price of the new motor, resulting in a net cash outflow of $31,000. If the company could not sell the old motor, we would add any cost incurred to dismantle and discard it to the purchase price of the new motor.

FUTURE DISPOSAL VALUES Assets may have relevant disposal values. The disposal value at the end of a project's life is an increase in the cash inflow in the year of disposal. Errors in forecasting terminal disposal values are usually not crucial because the PV is usually small.

OPERATING CASH FLOWS The major purpose of most investments is to affect operating cash inflows and outflows. Many of these effects are difficult to measure, and three points deserve special mention:

1. The only relevant cash flows are those that will differ among alternatives. Often, fixed overhead will be the same under all the available alternatives. If so, you can safely ignore it. In practice, it is not easy to identify exactly which costs will differ among alternatives.
2. Remember that you are predicting cash inflows and outflows, not revenues and expenses. Therefore, you should ignore depreciation and book values. We recognize the cost of assets by the initial outlay, not by depreciation as computed under accrual accounting. Further, cash inflows may not occur in the same period as the related revenues, and cash outflows may not coincide with the related expense recognition.
3. We treat a reduction in a cash outflow the same as a cash inflow. Both signify increases in value.

Cash Flows for Investments in Technology

Many capital-budgeting decisions compare a potential investment with doing nothing. One such decision is investment in a highly automated production system to replace a traditional system. Cash flows predicted for the automated system should be compared with those predicted for continuation of the present system into the future. The latter predictions are not necessarily the

Business First

Does DCF Apply to Technology Investments?

Although DCF models are widely used, some have criticized them for leading to overly cautious investment decisions in information technology (IT). The critics maintain that the benefits of IT investments are difficult to quantify and such investments lead to unforeseen opportunities. By ignoring some of the potential benefits and opportunities, companies pass up desirable IT investments.

Such criticisms abated somewhat early this decade. The economic shakeout in 2001 and 2002 identified the winners and losers—and there were plenty of both. Winners (identified by *BusinessWeek*) included Expedia, Amazon, eBay, Yahoo!, and Dell. Losers, at least in the short run, included Hewlett-Packard, Barnes & Noble, AOL Time Warner, drkoop.com, and many startups. What differentiated winners from losers? Partly it was how they evaluated capital investment decisions. Some were overly cautious in employing technology. But others forgot the basic economics of investment analysis. Instead of focusing on cash flows and DCF analysis, companies touted their revenue per dollar of investment or, even worse, Web site hits per dollar of investment. They forgot that only net cash flows generate value. Increasing revenues are worthless if related expenses grow faster. No one became rich because of the number of visits to their Web site.

How did the winners approach capital-budgeting decisions? First, they identified ways to generate cash—either new inflows or savings of outflows—that technology solutions could produce. Their business plans showed at what point the company's technology investments would become profitable and how profitable they would be. Second, the companies did not try to protect current business while simultaneously pursuing new technology. If technology solutions better served customers, companies lagging in technology would lose them anyway. And finally, they used DCF analysis. They realized that dollars in the future are worth less than those today, so they needed large future profits to justify investments that would not pay off in the short term.

In the aftermath of the technology crash, many companies focused on how to correctly apply DCF to technology investments. Microsoft developed guides to its software that showed how to apply DCF to investments in technology and developed blogs to allow managers to share experiences applying DCF methods.

Companies also used new developments in finance and accounting to aid in the application of DCF analyses. For example, Scott Gamster of Grant Thornton's Performance Management Practice suggested using activity-based costing (ABC) to better estimate future cash flows. Analyses that focused primarily on how technology reduced direct costs ignored potentially large savings in indirect costs. Because an ABC system focuses on indirect costs, it can help identify other cost impacts of new technology systems. The attention to activities lets managers better assess the various impacts of new systems. For example, an ERP system will transform much of the work in many of a company's activities. Examining each activity in light of the potential implementation of an ERP system will help managers assess the full impact of the new system.

Options pricing theory is also useful for valuing technology investments. For example, the Yankee 24, a shared electronic banking network in New England that subsequently merged with NYCE Payments Network, applied real options theory to the decision on timing the deployment of point-of-sale debit services. The method explicitly recognized the future opportunities created by a current investment decision, and it used the complete range of possible outcomes to determine the investment's value.

Criticisms of using DCF for investment decisions were primarily criticisms of incorrect or incomplete applications of it. They have led to a better understanding of how to apply DCF to technology investments and to refinements in DCF analysis that are especially useful to investments in technology.

Sources: Adapted from S. Gamster, "Using Activity Based Management to Justify ERP Implementations," *Journal of Cost Management*, September/October 1999, pp. 24–33; M. Benaroch and R. J. Kauffman, "A Case for Using Real Options Pricing Analysis to Evaluate Information Technology Project Investments," *Information Systems Research*, March 1999, pp. 70–76; "The E-Business Surprise," *BusinessWeek*, May 12, 2003, pp. 60–68; Microsoft Dynamics, "Using ROI analysis to prioritize technology purchases," March 7, 2007, http://community.dynamics.com/blogs/articles/archive/2007/03/07/using-roi-analysis-to-prioritize-technology-purchases.aspx

current cash flows. Why? Because the competitive environment is changing. If others invest in automated systems, failure to invest may cause a decline in sales and an uncompetitive cost structure. The future without an automated system might be a continual decline in cash flows.

Suppose a company currently has a $10,000 net cash inflow annually using a traditional system. Investing in an automated system will increase the net cash inflow to $12,000. Failure to invest will cause net cash inflows to fall to $8,000. The benefit from the investment is a cash inflow of $12,000 − $8,000 = $4,000, not $12,000 − $10,000 = $2,000. This situation arises in many technology investments such as those described in the Business First box above.

Summary Problem for Your Review

PROBLEM

Review the example shown in Exhibit 11-2, page 433. Conduct three independent sensitivity analyses as indicated next.

1. Compute the difference in the NPV of the alternatives if the minimum desired rate of return were 20% instead of 14%.
2. Compute the difference in the NPV of the alternatives if predicted cash operating costs of the new motor were $35,000 annually instead of $30,000, using the 14% discount rate.
3. By how much may the annual cash operating savings fall short of the $10,000 predicted amount before the difference in NPV between the alternatives reaches zero? Use the original discount rate of 14%?

SOLUTION

1. You can use either the total project approach or the differential approach. The differential approach shows the following:

	Total Present Value
Recurring cash operating savings, using an annuity table (Table 2, p. 000): 2.9906 × $10,000 =	$29,906
Overhaul avoided: .6944 × $10,000 =	6,944
Difference in disposal values: .4019 × $5,000 =	(2,010)
Incremental initial investment	(31,000)
Difference in NPV between the alternatives	$ 3,840

2.

Difference in NPV value in Exhibit 11-2	$ 8,429
Present value of additional $5,000 annual operating costs 3.4331 × $5,000	(17,166)
Difference in NPV between the alternatives	$(8,737)

With $5,000 less in annual savings, the new motor yields a negative difference in the NPV between the alternatives, and therefore is not desirable.

3. Let X = annual cash operating savings and find the value of X so that the difference in NPV between the two alternatives = 0. Then,

$$0 = 3.4331(X) + \$7,695 - \$2,597 - \$31,000$$
$$3.4331(X) = \$25,902$$
$$X = \$7,545$$

(Note that the $7,695, $2,597, and $31,000 are at the bottom of Exhibit 11-2.)

If the annual savings fall from $10,000 to $7,545, a decrease of $2,455 or almost 25%, the NPV will hit zero.

An alternative way to obtain the same answer would be to divide the NPV of $8,429 (see bottom of Exhibit 11-2) by 3.4331, obtaining $2,455, the amount of the annual difference in savings that will eliminate the $8,429 of NPV.

Income Taxes and Capital Budgeting

Objective 5

Compute the after-tax net present values of projects.

We must consider another type of cash flow when making capital-budgeting decisions: income taxes. Income taxes paid by companies are cash outflows. Their basic role in capital budgeting does not differ from that of any other cash outflow. However, taxes tend to narrow the cash differences between projects. For example, if the cash savings from operations of one project over another were $1 million, a 40% tax rate would shrink the savings to $600,000. Why? Because the company would have to pay 40% × $1 million = $400,000 of the savings in taxes.

Corporations in the United States must pay both federal and state taxes on their income. Federal income tax rates rise as income rises. The current federal tax rate on ordinary corporate taxable income below $50,000 is 15%. Rates then increase until companies with taxable income over $335,000 pay between 34% and 38% on additional income. State tax rates vary widely from state to state. Therefore, the total tax rate a company has to pay, federal rates plus state rates, also varies widely.

In capital budgeting, the relevant tax rate is the **marginal income tax rate**, that is, the tax rate paid on additional amounts of pretax income. Suppose a corporation pays income taxes of 15% on the first $50,000 of pretax income and 30% on pretax income over $50,000. What is the company's marginal income tax rate when it has $75,000 of pretax income? The marginal rate is 30%, because the company will pay 30% of any additional income in taxes. In contrast, the company's average income tax rate is only 20% (that is, 15% × $50,000 + 30% × $25,000 = $15,000 of taxes on $75,000 of pretax income). When we assess tax effects of capital-budgeting decisions, we will always use the marginal tax rate because that is the rate applied to the additional cash flows generated by a proposed project.

Effects of Depreciation Deductions

Organizations that pay income taxes generally keep two sets of books—one for reporting to the public and one for reporting to the tax authorities. In the United States, this practice is not illegal or immoral—it is necessary. Tax reporting must follow detailed rules designed to achieve certain social goals. These rules do not usually lead to financial statements that best measure an organization's financial results and position, so it is more informative to financial statement users if companies use a separate set of rules for financial reporting. In this chapter, we are concerned with measuring cash payments for taxes. Therefore, we focus on the tax reporting rules, not those for public financial reporting.

One item that often differs between tax reporting and public reporting is depreciation. Recall that depreciation spreads the cost of an asset over its useful life. Income tax laws and regulations generally permit companies to spread the cost over depreciable lives that are shorter than the assets' useful lives. In addition, U.S. tax authorities allow **accelerated depreciation**, which charges a larger proportion of an asset's cost to the earlier years and less to later years. In contrast, an asset's depreciation for public reporting purposes is usually the same each year, called straight-line depreciation. For example, a $10,000 asset depreciated over a 5-year useful life results in straight-line depreciation of $10,000 ÷ 5 = $2,000 each year. In contrast, accelerated depreciation provides more than $2,000 of depreciation per year in the early years and less than $2,000 in the later years.

Exhibit 11-3 shows the interrelationship of income before taxes, income taxes, and depreciation for a hypothetical asset owned by Toyota. Assume that Toyota's U.S. operation purchases

Exhibit 11-3

Toyota Machine

Basic Analysis of Income Statement, Income Taxes, and Cash Flows

	Traditional Annual Income Statement	
(S)	Sales	$130,000
(E)	Less: Expenses, excluding depreciation	$ 70,000
(D)	Depreciation (straight-line)	25,000
	Total expenses	$ 95,000
	Income before taxes	$ 35,000
(T)	Income taxes at 40%	14,000
(I)	Net income	$ 21,000
	Total after-tax effect on cash is	
	either S − E − T = $130,000 − $70,000 − $14,000 = $46,000	
	or I + D = $21,000 + $25,000 = $46,000	

	Analysis of the Same Facts for Capital Budgeting	
	Cash effects of operations:	
(S − E)	Cash inflow from operations: $130,000 − $70,000	$ 60,000
	Income tax outflow at 40%	24,000
	After-tax inflow from operations (excluding depreciation)	$ 36,000
	Cash effects of depreciation:	
(D)	Straight-line depreciation: $125,000 ÷ 5 = $25,000	
	Income tax savings at 40%	10,000
	Total after-tax effect on cash	$ 46,000

for $125,000 cash a machine that produces replacement parts used in Lexus exhaust systems. The machine has a 5-year **recovery period**, which is the number of years over which a company can depreciate an asset for tax purposes, and also a 5-year useful life. Using the machine produces annual sales revenue of $130,000 and expenses (excluding depreciation) of $70,000. The purchase cost of the machine is tax deductible in the form of yearly depreciation.

Depreciating a fixed asset creates future tax deductions. In this case, these deductions will total the full purchase price of $125,000. The PV of this deduction depends directly on its specific yearly effects on future income tax payments. Therefore, the recovery period, the depreciation method selected, the tax rates, and the discount rate all affect the PV of the tax deduction.

Exhibit 11-4 analyzes Toyota's data for capital budgeting, assuming that the company uses straight-line depreciation for tax purposes. The NPV is $40,821 for the investment in this asset. The $125,000 investment really buys two streams of cash: (1) net inflows from operations over the useful life plus (2) savings of income tax outflows (which have the same effect in capital budgeting as do additions to cash inflows) from the depreciation deduction over the recovery period. The choice of depreciation method will not affect the cash inflows from operations. But different depreciation methods will affect the cash outflows for income taxes. That is, a straight-line method will produce one PV of total tax savings, and an accelerated method will produce a different (higher) PV.

Tax Deductions, Cash Effects, and Timing

Note that we computed the net cash effects of operations in Exhibit 11-4 by multiplying the pre-tax amounts by one minus the tax rate, or $1 - .40 = .60$. The total effect is the cash flow itself less the tax effect. Each additional $1 of sales also adds $.40 of taxes, leaving a net cash inflow of $.60. Each additional $1 of cash expense reduces taxes by $.40, leaving a net cash outflow of $.60. Thus, the after-tax effect of the $130,000 - $70,000 = $60,000 net cash inflow from operations is an after-tax inflow of $130,000 \times .6 - $70,000 \times .6 = ($130,000 - $70,000) \times .6 = $60,000 \times .6 = $36,000$.

In contrast, we compute the after-tax effects of depreciation by multiplying the tax deduction of $25,000 by the tax rate itself, or $25,000 \times .40 = $10,000$. Note that this is a cash inflow because it is a decrease in the tax payment. Without the depreciation deduction, taxes would be higher by $10,000 annually. The total cash effect of depreciation is only the tax-savings effect.

	12% Discount Factors, from Appropriate Tables	Total Present Value at 12%	Sketch of After-Tax Cash Flows at End of Year					
			0	1	2	3	4	5
Cash effects of operations, excluding depreciation, $60,000 × (1 −.4)	3.6048	$ 129,773		36,000	36,000	36,000	36,000	36,000
Cash effects of straight-line depreciation: savings of income taxes, $25,000 × .4	3.6048	36,048		10,000	10,000	10,000	10,000	10,000
Total after-tax effect on cash		165,821						
Investment	1.0000	(125,000)	(125,000)					
Net present value of the investment		$ 40,821						

Exhibit 11-4

Impact of Income Taxes on Capital-Budgeting Analysis

Assume: original cost of equipment, $100,000; 5-year recovery period; 5-year useful life; zero terminal disposal value; pretax annual net cash inflow from operations, $60,000; income tax rate, 40%; required after-tax rate of return, 12%. All items are in dollars except discount factors. The after-tax cash flows are from Exhibit 11-3.

Throughout the illustrations in this chapter, we assume that all income tax flows occur at the same time as the related pretax cash flows. For example, we assume that both the net $60,000 pretax cash inflow and the related $24,000 tax payment occurred at the end of year 1. We also assume that the companies in question are profitable. That is, the companies will have enough taxable income from all sources to use all income tax benefits in the situations described.

Summary Problem for Your Review

PROBLEM

Consider Toyota's purchase of the $125,000 machine analyzed in Exhibits 11-3 and 11-4. Suppose the machine had a useful life of 6 years, but the recovery period remains 5 years. What is the net present value of the investment?

SOLUTION

The present value of the tax savings will not change. Only the recovery period, not the useful life, affects the depreciation deductions. There will be one extra year of operating savings in year 6. Its present value is $36,000 × .5066 = $18,238. Therefore, the net present value is $59,059:

Original NPV (from Exhibit 11-4)	$40,821
Added PV of savings in year 6	18,238
NPV	$59,059

Note especially that the recovery period for tax purposes and the economic useful life of the asset need not be equal. The tax law specifies recovery periods for various types of depreciable assets. The economic useful life of the asset does not affect the recovery period. Thus, a longer useful life for an asset increases operating cash flows without decreasing the PV of the tax savings.

Accelerated Depreciation

Governments frequently allow accelerated depreciation to encourage investments in long-lived assets. To see why accelerated depreciation is attractive to investors, reconsider the facts in Exhibit 11-4. Suppose that, as is the case in some countries, companies could write off immediately the entire initial investment for income tax reporting. We see that NPV will rise from $40,821 to $54,773.

	Present Values	
	As in Exhibit 11-4	Complete Write-Off Immediately
Cash effects of operations	$129,773	$129,773
Cash effects of depreciation	36,048	50,000*
Total after-tax effect on cash	165,821	179,773
Investment	(125,000)	(125,000)
Net present value	$ 40,821	$ 54,773

*Assumes that the tax effect occurs simultaneously with the investment at time zero: $125,000 × .40 = $50,000.

In summary, the earlier you can take the depreciation, the greater the PV of the income tax savings. The total tax savings will be the same regardless of the depreciation method. In the example, the tax savings from the depreciation deduction is either .40 × $125,000 = $50,000 immediately or .40 × $25,000 = $10,000 per year for 5 years, a total of $50,000. However, the time value of money makes the immediate savings worth more than future savings. The mottoes in income tax planning are "When there is a legal choice, take the deduction sooner rather than later," and "Recognize taxable income later rather than sooner."

Managers have an obligation to stockholders to minimize and delay taxes to the extent permitted by law. For example, astute managers use accelerated depreciation instead of straight-line depreciation whenever the law permits its use. We call this tax avoidance. Careful tax planning can have large financial payoffs. In contrast, managers must not engage in tax evasion, which is illegally reducing taxes by recording fictitious deductions or failing to report income. Managers who avoid taxes get bonuses; those who evade taxes often land in jail. Among the charges that landed former Tyco CEO Dennis Kozlowski in jail was that he prepared false invoices and shipped empty boxes to the conglomerate's executive offices in New Hampshire to fool tax authorities. Because the line between tax evasion and tax avoidance is sometimes gray, it is important to act both legally and ethically when trying to minimize taxes.

Modified Accelerated Cost Recovery System (MACRS)

Under U.S. income tax laws, companies depreciate most assets using the **modified accelerated cost recovery system (MACRS)**. This system specifies a recovery period and an accelerated depreciation schedule for all types of assets. The MACRS system places each asset in one of the eight classes shown in Exhibit 11-5.

Exhibit 11-6 presents MACRS depreciation schedules for recovery periods of 3, 5, 7, and 10 years. Note that each schedule extends 1 year beyond the recovery period because MACRS assumes one half-year of depreciation in the first year and one half-year in the final year. Thus, a 3-year MACRS depreciation schedule has one half-year of depreciation in years 1 and 4 and a full year of depreciation in years 2 and 3. We can apply MACRS depreciation to the example in Exhibit 11-4 as follows, assuming that the machine that Toyota purchased is a 5-year MACRS asset:

Year	Tax Rate (1)	PV Factor at 12% (2)	Depreciation (3)	PV of Tax Savings (1) × (2) × (3)
1	.40	0.8929	$125,000 × .2000 = $25,000	$ 8,929
2	.40	0.7972	125,000 × .3200 = 40,000	12,755
3	.40	0.7118	125,000 × .1920 = 24,000	6,833
4	.40	0.6355	125,000 × .1152 = 14,400	3,660
5	.40	0.5674	125,000 × .1152 = 14,400	3,268
6	.40	0.5066	125,000 × .0576 = 7,200	1,459
				$36,904

How much did Toyota gain by using MACRS instead of straight-line depreciation? The $36,904 present value of tax savings is $856 higher with MACRS than the $36,048 achieved with straight-line depreciation (see Exhibit 11-4 on page 438).

Present Value of MACRS Depreciation

In capital-budgeting decisions, managers often want to know the PV of the tax savings from depreciation. Exhibit 11-7 provides present values for $1 to be depreciated over MACRS schedules for 3-, 5-, 7-, and 10-year recovery periods for a variety of interest rates. For example, consider a

3-year	Special tools for several specific industries, tractor units for over-the-road
5-year	Automobiles, trucks, research equipment, computers, machinery and equipment in selected industries
7-year	Office furniture, railroad tracks, machinery and equipment in a majority of industries
10-year	Water transportation equipment, machinery and equipment in selected industries
15-year	Most land improvements, machinery and equipment in selected industries
20-year	Farm buildings, electricity generation and distribution equipment
27.5-year	Residential rental property
31.5-year	Nonresidential real property

Exhibit 11-5

Examples of Assets in Modified Accelerated Cost Recovery System (MACRS) Classes

Tax Year	3-Year Property	5-Year Property	7-Year Property	10-Year Property
1	33.33%	20.00%	14.29%	10.00%
2	44.45	32.00	24.49	18.00
3	14.81	19.20	17.49	14.40
4	7.41	11.52	12.49	11.52
5		11.52	8.93	9.22
6		5.76	8.92	7.37
7			8.93	6.55
8			4.46	6.55
9				6.56
10				6.55
11				3.28

Exhibit 11-6

Selected MACRS Depreciation Schedules

company with a 3-year asset and 10% minimum desired rate of return. The PV of $1 of MACRS depreciation is as follows:

Year	Depreciation* (1)	PV Factor at 10% (2)	PV of Depreciation (1) × (2)
1	$0.3333	0.9091	$0.3030
2	0.4445	0.8264	0.3673
3	0.1481	0.7513	0.1113
4	0.0741	0.6830	0.0506
Total Depreciation	$1.0000		
Present Value of $1 depreciation, shown in Exhibit 11-7			$0.8322

*From the 3-Year Property column of Exhibit 11-6.

Discount Rate	3-year	5-year	7-year	10-year
3%	0.9439	0.9215	0.9002	0.8698
4%	0.9264	0.8975	0.8704	0.8324
5%	0.9095	0.8746	0.8422	0.7975
6%	0.8931	0.8526	0.8155	0.7649
7%	0.8772	0.8315	0.7902	0.7344
8%	0.8617	0.8113	0.7661	0.7059
9%	0.8468	0.7919	0.7432	0.6792
10%	0.8322	0.7733	0.7214	0.6541
12%	0.8044	0.7381	0.6810	0.6084
14%	0.7782	0.7055	0.6441	0.5678
15%	0.7657	0.6902	0.6270	0.5492
16%	0.7535	0.6753	0.6106	0.5317
18%	0.7300	0.6473	0.5798	0.4993
20%	0.7079	0.6211	0.5517	0.4702
22%	0.6868	0.5968	0.5257	0.4439
24%	0.6669	0.5740	0.5019	0.4201
25%	0.6573	0.5631	0.4906	0.4090
26%	0.6479	0.5526	0.4798	0.3985
28%	0.6299	0.5327	0.4594	0.3787
30%	0.6128	0.5139	0.4404	0.3606
40%	0.5381	0.4352	0.3632	0.2896

Exhibit 11-7

PV of $1 of MACRS Depreciation

You can find the PV of tax savings in three steps:

1. Find the PV factor from Exhibit 11-7 for the appropriate recovery period and required rate of return.
2. Multiply the factor by the tax rate to find the PV of the tax savings per dollar of investment.
3. Multiply the result by the amount of the investment to find the PV of the total tax savings.

Consider Toyota's investment of $125,000 in a machine with a 5-year MACRS recovery period. A 12% after-tax required rate of return and a 40% tax rate produce a tax savings with a present value of .7381 × .40 × $125,000 = $36,905. (This differs from the $36,904 calculated earlier by a $1 rounding error.)

Making Managerial Decisions

Why do managers like accelerated depreciation for tax purposes? Consider an investment of $100,000 in an asset with a 10-year economic life and a 10-year MACRS recovery period. The asset has no salvage value at the end of 10 years. The tax rate is 40%, and the required rate of return is 10%. What is the PV of the depreciation tax savings using straight-line (SL) depreciation? What is the PV of the depreciation tax savings using MACRS depreciation? Which depreciation method would you choose if you were managing the company?

Answers

Straight-line depreciation = $10,000 per year, so tax savings with SL is .40 × $10,000 = $4,000 per year. Thus, the present value of the SL tax savings is $4,000 × 6.1446 = $24,578.40.

The PV of MACRS depreciation tax savings is .6541 × .40 × $100,000 = $26,164.00. Although the total tax savings is $40,000 regardless of the depreciation method, the MACRS accelerated depreciation schedule creates a greater PV by $26,164.00 − $24,578.40 = $1,585.60. A good manager will choose MACRS and save $1,585.60 for the company.

Gains or Losses on Disposal

Objective 6

Explain the after-tax effect on cash received from the disposal of assets.

The disposal of equipment for cash can also affect income taxes. Suppose Toyota sells its $125,000 machine at the end of year 3 after taking 3 years of straight-line depreciation. If Toyota sells it for its net book value, $125,000 − (3 × $25,000) = $50,000, there is no tax effect. If Toyota receives more than $50,000, there is a gain and an additional tax payment. If the company receives less than $50,000, there is a loss and a tax savings. The following table shows the effects on cash flow for sales prices of $70,000 and $20,000:

(a)	Cash proceeds of sale	$70,000	$ 20,000
	Book value: [$125,000 − (3 × $25,000)]	50,000	50,000
	Gain (loss)	$20,000	$ (30,000)
	Effect on income taxes at 40%:		
(b)	Tax savings, an inflow effect: .40 × loss		$ 12,000
(c)	Tax paid, an outflow: .40 × gain	$ (8,000)	
	Net cash inflow from sale:		
	(a) plus (b)		$ 32,000
	(a) minus (c)	$62,000	

Summary Problem for Your Review

PROBLEM

Consider the investment opportunity in Exhibit 11-4, page 438: original cost of machine, $125,000; 5-year useful life; zero terminal salvage value; pretax annual cash inflow from operations, $60,000; income tax rate, 40%; required after-tax rate of return, 12%. Assume the equipment is a 5-year MACRS asset for tax purposes. The NPV is as follows:

	Present Values (PV)
Cash effects of operations,* $60,000 × (1 − .40) × 3.6048	$129,773
Cash effects of depreciation on income tax savings using MACRS, $125,000 × .40 × .7381[†]	36,905
Total after-tax effect on cash	$166,678
Investment	125,000
NPV	$ 41,678

*See Exhibit 11-4, page 438, for details.

†Factor .7381 is from Exhibit 11-7, page 441.

Consider each requirement independently. Compute the NPV of the investment for each. Assume the original depreciation schedule is not altered for either requirement.

1. Suppose Toyota ends up selling the equipment for $20,000 cash immediately after the end of year 5.
2. Ignore the assumption in number 1. Return to the original data. Suppose the economic life of the machine turns out to be 8 years, not 5 years. However, tax authorities still allow MACRS cost recovery over 5 years.

SOLUTION

1.

NPV as given		$41,678
Cash proceeds of sale	$20,000	
Book value	0	
Gain	$20,000	
Income taxes at 40%	8,000	
Total after-tax effect on cash	$12,000	
PV of $12,000 to be received in 5 years at 12%, $12,000 × .5674		6,809
NPV of investment		$48,487

2.

NPV as given		$41,678
Add the PV of $36,000 per year for 8 years		
Discount factor of 4.9676* × $36,000 =	$178,834	
Deduct the PV of $36,000 per year for 5 years	129,773	
Increase in PV		49,061
NPV		$90,739

*Factor 4.9676 is from Table 2.

The investment would be very attractive because there are additional operating savings but no change in the tax savings from depreciation.

Confusion About Depreciation

The meanings of depreciation and book value are widely misunderstood. Let's review their role in decisions. Suppose **Toyota** is considering the replacement of some old copying equipment with a book value of $30,000, an expected terminal disposal value of zero, a current disposal value of $12,000, and a remaining useful life of 3 years. For simplicity, assume that Toyota will take straight-line depreciation of $10,000 yearly. The tax rate is 40%.

You should be careful to examine these data in perspective, as Exhibit 11-8 indicates. In particular, note that the inputs to the decision model are the predicted income tax effects on cash.

Exhibit 11-8
Perspective on Book Value
and Depreciation

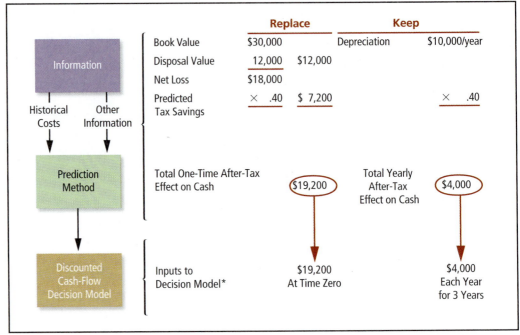

*There will be other related inputs to this decision model—for example, the cost of the new equipment and the differences in future annual cash flows from operations.

Book values and depreciation may be necessary for making predictions. By themselves, however, they are not inputs to the DCF decision model.

Other Models for Analyzing Long-Range Decisions

Although an increasing number of companies are using DCF models to make their capital-budgeting decisions, some companies still use simpler models, either in place of or in addition to the NPV model. We will examine two such models, the payback and accounting rate-of-return models.

Payback Model

Payback time or **payback period** is the time it will take to recoup, in the form of cash inflows from operations, the initial dollars invested in a project. Assume that **Toyota** spends $12,000 for a forklift that has an estimated useful life of 4 years. Toyota expects annual savings of $4,000 in cash outflows. The payback period is 3 years, calculated as follows:

$$\text{payback time} = \frac{\text{initial incremental amount invested}}{\text{equal annual incremental cash inflow from operations}}$$

$$P = \frac{I}{O} = \frac{\$12,000}{\$4,000} = 3 \text{ years}$$

We can use this formula for payback time only when there are equal annual cash inflows from operations. When annual cash inflows are not equal, we must add up each year's net cash inflows until they add up to the amount of the initial investment.

Assume the following cash flow pattern for the forklift:

End of Year	0	1	2	3	4
Investment	($12,000)				
Cash inflows		$4,000	$6,000	$5,000	$5,000

The calculation of the payback period is as follows:

Year	Initial Investment	Net Cash Inflows Each Year	Net Cash Inflows Accumulated
0	$12,000	—	—
1	—	$4,000	$ 4,000
2	—	6,000	10,000
2+	—	2,000	12,000

In this case, the payback time is slightly beyond the second year. Interpolation within the third year reveals that an additional 4/10 of a year is needed to recoup the final $2,000, making the payback period 2.4 years:

$$2 \text{ years} + \left(\frac{\$2,000}{\$5,000} \times 1 \text{ year} \right) = 2.4 \text{ years}$$

Three major weaknesses of the payback model are that (1) it does not measure profitability, which is a primary goal of businesses, (2) it ignores the time value of money, and (3) it ignores cash flows beyond the payback period. DCF models recognize all cash flows and allow for the force of interest and the timing of cash flows. The payback model merely measures how quickly a company will recoup its investment dollars. However, a project with a shorter payback time is not necessarily preferable to one with a longer payback time. After all, a company can recoup its entire investment immediately by not investing.

Sometimes managers use the payback period as a rough estimate of the riskiness of a project. Suppose a company faces rapid technological changes. Cash flows beyond the first few years may be extremely uncertain. In such a situation, projects that recoup their investment quickly may be less risky than those that require a longer wait until the cash starts flowing in.

Accounting Rate-of-Return Model

The **accounting rate-of-return (ARR) model** expresses a project's return as the increase in expected average annual operating income divided by the initial required investment.

$$\text{accounting rate-of-return (ARR)} = \frac{\text{increase in expected average annual operating income}}{\text{initial required investment}}$$

$$= \frac{O - D}{I} = \frac{\text{average annual incremental net cash in flow from operations} - \text{incremental average annual depreciation}}{\text{initial required investment}}$$

ARR computations dovetail most closely with conventional accounting models of calculating income and required investment, and they show the effect of an investment on an organization's financial statements.

To see how ARR works, assume the same facts as in Exhibit 11-1: Investment is $5,827, useful life is 4 years, estimated disposal value is zero, and expected annual cash inflow from operations is $2,000. Annual depreciation is $5,827 ÷ 4 = $1,456.75, rounded to $1,457. Substitute these values in the accounting rate-of-return equation:

$$\text{ARR} = \frac{(\$2,000 - \$1,457)}{\$5,827} = 9.3\%$$

Some companies use the "average" investment (often assumed to be the average book value over the useful life) instead of original investment in the denominator. Therefore, the denominator[3] becomes $5,827 ÷ 2 = $2,913.50:

$$\text{ARR} = \frac{(\$2,000 - \$1,457)}{\$2,913.50} = 18.6\%$$

The accounting rate-of-return model is based on the familiar financial statements prepared under accrual accounting. Unlike the payback model, the accounting model at least has profitability as an objective. Nevertheless, it has a major drawback—it ignores the time value of money. DCF models explicitly allow for the force of interest and the timing of cash flows. In contrast, the accounting model uses annual averages. It uses concepts of investment and income that accountants originally designed for a quite different purpose, accounting for periodic income and financial position.

The increasing use of DCF models as well as the continued use of payback and accounting rate of return models is described in the Business First box on page 447.

Performance Evaluation

Potential Conflict

Objective 8

Reconcile the conflict between using an NPV model for making decisions and using accounting income for evaluating the related performance.

Many managers who are evaluated on the basis of accounting income or an ARR model are reluctant to accept DCF models as the best way to make capital-budgeting decisions. To illustrate, consider the potential conflict that might arise in the example of Exhibit 11-1. Recall that the NPV was $513 based on a 10% required rate of return, an investment of $5,827, cash savings of $2,000 for each of 4 years, and no terminal disposal value. Using ARR with accounting income computed with straight-line depreciation, the evaluation of performance for years 1–4 would be as follows:

	Year 1	Year 2	Year 3	Year 4
Cash-operating savings	$2,000	$2,000	$2,000	$2,000
Straight-line depreciation, $5,827 ÷ 4	1,457	1,457	1,457	1,457[*]
Effect on operating income	543	543	543	543
Book value at beginning of year	5,827	4,370	2,913	1,456
ARR	9.3%	12.4%	18.6%	37.3%

*Total depreciation of 4 × $1,457 = $5,828 differs from $5,827 because of rounding error. Also, the ARR is based on the book value at the beginning of the year as a proxy for the investment.

Many managers would be reluctant to replace equipment, despite the positive NPV, if superiors evaluated their performance by accounting rate of return. They might be especially reluctant if they are likely to transfer to new positions (or retire) within a short time frame. Why? This accrual accounting system understates the return in early years, especially in year 1 when the return is below the required rate, and a manager might not be around to reap the benefits of the later overstatement of returns.

As Chapter 6 indicated, managers are especially reluctant to replace assets if a heavy book loss on old equipment would appear in year 1's income statement—even though such a loss is irrelevant in a properly constructed decision model. Thus, performance evaluation based on typical accounting measures can cause the rejection of major, long-term projects, such as investments in technologically advanced production systems. This pattern may help explain why many U.S. firms seem to be excessively short-term oriented.

Reconciliation of Conflict

The best way to reconcile any potential conflict between capital budgeting and performance evaluation is to use DCF for both capital-budgeting decisions and performance evaluation.

---

[3]The investment committed to the project would decline at a rate of $1,456 per year from $5,827 to zero; hence, the average investment would be the beginning balance plus the ending balance ($5,827 + 0) divided by 2, or $2,913.50.

Business First

Who Uses What Capital Budgeting Model?

Companies are increasingly using formal capital budgeting models and most use more than one model. Of the 1,000 largest U.S. companies, more than 95% use a DCF model for their large investment decisions, although about half of them use such methods only for investments over $500,000. The NPV model is the most popular DCF method, with many also using IRR. However, use of the payback model remains strong, with more than half of the companies using it for at least some decisions.

Many smaller companies also use DCF methods. However, there is a clear relationship between size and capital budgeting methods. The larger the company and the larger the investment, the more likely is the use of DCF methods. Smaller companies use the payback method more often. Companies that have high financial leverage and young, highly-educated CFOs are more likely to use DCF methods. Fast growing companies use the payback method more than similar-sized, low-growth companies.

DCF methods have also made inroads into nonprofit companies. For example, hospitals have huge capital investment decisions. A few years ago the payback model was the dominant capital budgeting model used, but recent studies show that DCF models are used as often as payback. Further, large, multi-hospital systems generally use DCF methods.

More companies in the United States use DCF methods than in other countries, but the usage is nearly as high in the United Kingdom, Australia, and the Netherlands. Even in China, nearly 90% of the large companies use DCF methods.

However, in China the dominant DCF method is IRR and a larger percentage of companies continue to use the payback method for some investments. As companies become more sophisticated and more dependent on capital markets, they tend to progress from payback to IRR and then to NPV.

Companies are also using more sophisticated techniques to analyze capital investment decisions. The most popular is sensitivity analysis. However, the use of real options is growing quickly. In 2002 a quarter of large U.S. companies already used real options, as did a third of Australian firms in 2008. Within the next few years it is likely that half of the large companies in the developed world will use capital budgeting models based on real options for at least some of their major investments.

Sources: G. Truong, G. Partington, and M. Peat, "Cost-of-Capital Estimation and Capital-Budgeting Practices in Australia," *Australian Journal of Management*, June 2008, pp. 95–121; C. Kocher, "Hospital Capital Budgeting Practices and Their Relation to Key Hospital Characteristics: A Survey of U.S. Manager Practices," *Journal of Global Business Issues*, July 1, 2007, pp. 21–30 ; J. Graham and C. Harvey, "How Do CFOs Make Capital Budgeting and Capital Structure Decisions?" *Journal of Applied Corporate Finance*, Spring 2002, pp. 8–23; P. Ryan and G. Ryan, "Capital Budgeting Practices of the Fortune 1000: How Have Things Changed?" *Journal of Business and Management*, Winter 2002, pp. 355–364; and N. Hermes, P. Smid, and L. Yao, "Capital Budgeting Practices: A Comparative Study of The Netherlands and China," November 2005, available at SSRN: http://ssrn.com/abstract=881754.

Companies that use EVA for performance evaluation, as described in Chapter 10, page 391, avoid some of the conflict. Although EVA has the weakness of using accrual accounting measures of profit and investment rather than cash flows, it has conceptual similarities to the NPV method of capital budgeting. Both EVA and NPV recognize that a firm creates value only after projects cover their cost of capital.

Another way to address this issue is to conduct a follow-up evaluation of capital-budgeting decisions, often called a **post-audit**. Most large companies (76% in a recent survey) post-audit at least some capital-budgeting decisions. The purposes of a post-audit include the following:

1. Seeing that investment expenditures are proceeding on time and within budget
2. Comparing actual cash flows with those originally predicted, in order to motivate careful and honest predictions
3. Providing information for improving future predictions of cash flows
4. Evaluating the continuation of the project

By focusing the post-audit on actual versus predicted cash flows, we can make the evaluation consistent with the decision process. However, post-auditing of all capital-budgeting decisions is costly. Most accounting systems are best at evaluating operating performances of products, departments, divisions, territories, and so on, year by year. In contrast, capital-budgeting decisions frequently deal with individual projects, not the collection of projects that are usually being managed at the same time by division or department managers. Therefore, most companies audit only selected capital-budgeting decisions.

The conflicts between the longstanding, pervasive accrual accounting model and various formal decision models create some of the most serious unsolved problems in the design of management control systems. Top management cannot expect goal congruence if it favors the use of one type of model for decisions and the use of another type for performance evaluation.

Highlights to Remember

1. **Describe capital-budgeting decisions and use the net-present-value (NPV) method to make such decisions.** Capital budgeting is long-term planning for proposed capital outlays and their financing. The net-present-value (NPV) model aids this process by computing the present value (PV) of all expected future cash flows using a minimum desired rate of return. A company should accept projects with an NPV greater than zero.

2. **Evaluate projects using sensitivity analysis.** Managers use sensitivity analysis to aid risk assessment by examining the effects if actual cash flows differ from those expected.

3. **Calculate the NPV difference between two projects using both the total project and differential approaches.** The total project approach compares the NPVs of the cash flows from each project, while the differential approach computes the NPV of the difference in cash flows between two projects. Both produce the same results if there are two alternatives. You have to use the total project approach if you have more than two alternatives.

4. **Identify relevant cash flows for NPV analyses.** Predicting cash flows is the hardest part of capital budgeting. Managers should consider four categories of cash flows: initial cash inflows and outflows at time zero, investments in working capital, future disposal values, and operating cash flows.

5. **Compute the after-tax NPV of projects.** Income taxes can have a significant effect on the desirability of an investment. Additional taxes are cash outflows, and tax savings are cash inflows. Accelerated depreciation speeds up a company's tax savings. Generally, companies should take depreciation deductions as early as legally permitted.

6. **Explain the after-tax effect on cash received from the disposal of assets.** When companies sell assets for more than their book value, the gain generates additional taxes. When they sell assets for less than their book value, the loss generates tax savings.

7. **Use the payback model and the accounting rate-of-return model and compare them with the NPV model.** The payback model is simple to apply, but it does not measure profitability. The accounting rate-of-return model uses accounting measures of income and investment, but it ignores the time value of money. Both models are inferior to the NPV model.

8. **Reconcile the conflict between using an NPV model for making decisions and using accounting income for evaluating the related performance.** NPV is a summary measure of all the cash flows from a project. Accounting income is a one-period measure. A positive NPV project can have low (or even negative) accounting income in the first year. Managers may be reluctant to invest in such a project, despite its positive value to the company, especially if they expect to be transferred to a new position before they can benefit from the positive returns that come later. ■

Appendix 11: Capital Budgeting and Inflation

Objective 9

Compute the impact of inflation on a capital-budgeting project (Appendix 11).

Capital-budgeting decision makers should also consider the effects of inflation on their cash-flow predictions. **Inflation** is the decline in the general purchasing power of the monetary unit. For example, a dollar today will buy only half as much as it did in the late-1980s. At a 5% annual inflation rate, average prices rise more than 60% over 10 years. The United States had double-digit inflation rates in the late 1970s, and some countries, such as Brazil and Argentina, have had triple-digit annual inflation rates (that is, average prices more than doubling each year). In the last decade, inflation rates in the United States have been low—generally around 3%—but it is possible that rates in the future might increase. If a company expects significant inflation over the life of a project, it should specifically and consistently recognize inflation in its capital-budgeting decisions.

Watch for Consistency

The key to appropriate consideration of inflation in capital budgeting is consistent treatment of the required rate of return and the predicted cash inflows and outflows. We can achieve such consistency by including an element for inflation in both the required rate and in the cash-flow predictions.

Many firms base their required rate of return on market interest rates, also called **nominal rates**, that include an inflation element. For example, consider three possible components of a 12% nominal rate:

(a)	Risk-free element—the "pure" rate of interest	3%
(b)	Business-risk element—the "risk" premium that is demanded for taking larger risks	5
(a) + (b)	Often called the "real rate"	8%
(b)	Inflation element—the premium demanded because of expected deterioration of the general purchasing power of the monetary unit	4
(a) + (b) + (c)	Often called the "nominal rate"	12%

Four percentage points out of the 12% return compensate an investor for receiving future payments in inflated dollars, that is, in dollars with less purchasing power than those invested. Therefore, basing the required rate of return on quoted market rates automatically includes an inflation element in the rate. Companies that base their required rate of return on market rates should also adjust their cash-flow predictions for anticipated inflation. For example, suppose a company expects to sell 1,000 units of a product in each of the next 2 years. Assume this year's price is $50, and inflation causes next year's price to be $52.50. This year's predicted cash inflow is 1,000 × $50 = $50,000, and next year's inflation-adjusted cash inflow is 1,000 × $52.50 = $52,500. Inflation-adjusted cash flows are the inflows and outflows expected after adjusting prices to reflect anticipated inflation.

Consider another illustration: purchase cost of equipment, $200,000; useful life, 5 years; zero terminal salvage value; pretax operating cash savings per year, $83,333 (in 20X0 dollars); income tax rate, 40%. For simplicity, we assume ordinary straight-line depreciation of $200,000 ÷ 5 = $40,000 per year. The after-tax minimum desired rate, based on quoted market rates, is 25%. It includes an inflation factor of 10%.

Exhibit 11-9 displays correct and incorrect ways to analyze the effects of inflation. The key words are *internal consistency*. The correct analysis (1) uses a minimum desired rate that includes an element attributable to inflation and (2) explicitly adjusts the predicted operating cash flows for the effects of inflation. Note that the correct analysis favors the purchase of the equipment, but the incorrect analysis does not.

The incorrect analysis in Exhibit 11-9 is inherently inconsistent. The predicted cash inflows exclude adjustments for inflation. Instead, they are stated in 20X0 dollars. However, the discount rate includes an element attributable to inflation. An analytical mistake like this might lead to an unwise refusal to purchase.

Role of Depreciation

The correct analysis in Exhibit 11-9 shows that we did not adjust the tax effects of depreciation for inflation. Why? Because U.S. income tax laws permit a depreciation deduction based on the original dollars invested, nothing more.

Critics of income tax laws emphasize that such laws discourage capital investment by not allowing companies to adjust depreciation deductions for inflationary effects. For instance, the NPV in Exhibit 11-9 would be larger if depreciation were not confined to the $40,000 amount per year. The latter generates a $16,000 savings in 20X1 dollars, then $16,000 in 20X2 dollars, and so forth. Defenders of existing U.S. tax laws assert that tax laws encourage capital investment in many other ways. The most prominent example is provision for accelerated depreciation over lives that are much shorter than the economic lives of the assets.

Exhibit 11-9
Inflation and Capital Budgeting

	At 25%		Sketch of Relevant Cash Flows (at End of Year)					
Description	PV Factor	Present Value	0	1	2	3	4	5
Correct analysis (Be sure the discount rate includes an element attributable to inflation and adjust the predicted cash flows for inflationary effects.)								
Cash operating inflows:								
Pretax inflow in 20X0 dollars $83,333								
Income tax effect at 40% 33,333								
After-tax effect on cash $50,000								
	.8000	$ 44,000		$55,000*				
	.6400	38,720			$60,500			
	.5120	34,074				$66,550		
	.4096	29,985					$73,205	
	.3277	26,388						$80,526
Subtotal		$ 173,167						
Annual depreciation								
$200,000 ÷ 5 = $40,000								
Cash effect of depreciation								
Savings in income taxes								
at 40% = $40,000 × .40 =	2.6893	43,029		$16,000†	$16,000	$16,000	$16,000	$16,000
$16,000								
Investment in equipment	1.0000	(200,000)	($200,000)					
Net present value		$ 16,196						
Incorrect analysis (A common error is to include an inflation element in the discount rate as above, but not adjust the predicted cash inflows.)								
Cash operating inflows after taxes	2.6893	$134,465		$50,000	$50,000	$50,000	$50,000	$50,000
Tax effect of depreciation	2.6893	43,029		16,000	16,000	16,000	16,000	16,000
Investment in equipment	1.0000	(200,000)	($200,000)					
Net present value		$ (22,506)						

*Each year is adjusted for anticipated inflation: $50,000 × 1.10, $50,000 × 1.10², $50,000 × 1.10³, and so on.

†Inflation will not affect the annual savings in income taxes from depreciation. Why? Because the income tax deduction must be based on original cost of the asset in 20X0 dollars.

Summary Problems for Your Review

PROBLEM

Examine the correct analysis in Exhibit 11-9. Suppose the cash-operating inflows persisted for an extra year. Compute the PV of the inflow for the sixth year. Ignore depreciation.

SOLUTION

The cash operating inflow would be $50,000 \times 1.10^6$, or $80,526 \times 1.10$, or $88,579. Its PV would be $88,579 \times .2621$, the factor from Table 1 of Appendix B (period 6 row, 25% column), or $23,217.

PROBLEM

Examine the MACRS depreciation schedule in Exhibit 11-7 on page 441. Assume an anticipated inflation rate of 7%. How would you change the PVs of depreciation to accommodate the inflation rate?

SOLUTION

The computations on page 441 would not change. Inflation does not affect the tax effects of depreciation. Income tax laws in the United States permit a deduction based on the original dollars invested, nothing more.

Accounting Vocabulary

accelerated depreciation, p. 437
accounting rate-of-return (ARR) model, p. 445
capital budgeting, p. 427
differential approach, p. 432
discount rate, p. 428
discounted-cash-flow (DCF) models, p. 427
hurdle rate, p. 428
inflation, p. 448

internal rate of return (IRR) model, p. 431
marginal income tax rate, p. 437
modified accelerated cost recovery system (MACRS), p. 440
net present value, p. 428
net-present-value (NPV) method, p. 428
nominal rate, p. 449

payback period, p. 444
payback time, p. 444
post-audit, p. 447
present value (PV), p. 427
real options model, p. 431
recovery period, p. 438
required rate of return, p. 428
total project approach, p. 432

Fundamental Assignment Material

Special note: In all assignment materials that include taxes, assume, unless directed otherwise, that (1) all income tax cash flows occur simultaneously with the pretax cash flows, and (2) the companies in question will have enough taxable income from other sources to use all income tax benefits from the situations described.

11-A1 Exercises in Compound Interest: Answers Supplied

Use the appropriate interest table from Appendix B (see page A6 or A9) to complete the following exercises. The answers appear at the end of the assignment material for this chapter, pages 470–471.

1. It is your sixtieth birthday. You plan to work 5 more years before retiring, at which point you and your spouse want to take $25,000 for a round-the-world tour. What lump sum do you have to invest now to accumulate the $25,000? Assume that your minimum desired rate of return is
   a. 5%, compounded annually.
   b. 10%, compounded annually.
   c. 20%, compounded annually.

2. You want to spend $2,000 on a vacation at the end of each of the next 5 years. What lump sum do you have to invest now to take the five vacations? Assume that your minimum desired rate of return is
   a. 5%, compounded annually.
   b. 10%, compounded annually.
   c. 20%, compounded annually.

3. At age 60, you find that your employer is moving to another location. You receive termination pay of $100,000. You have some savings and wonder whether to retire now.
   a. If you invest the $100,000 now at 5%, compounded annually, how much money can you withdraw from your account each year so that at the end of 5 years there will be a zero balance?
   b. Answer part a, assuming that you invest it at 10%.

4. Two NBA basketball players, LeBron and Kobe, signed 5-year, $60-million contracts. At 16%, compounded annually, which of the following contracts is more desirable in terms of present values? Show computations to support your answer.

Annual Cash Inflows (in thousands)

Year	LeBron	Kobe
1	$20,000	$ 4,000
2	16,000	8,000
3	12,000	12,000
4	8,000	16,000
5	4,000	20,000
	$60,000	$60,000

11-A2 NPV for Investment Decisions

A manager of the engineering department of Manchester University is contemplating acquiring 120 computers. The computers will cost £240,000 cash, have zero terminal salvage value, and a useful life of 3 years. Annual cash savings from operations will be £110,000. The required rate of return is 14%. There are no taxes.

1. Compute the NPV.
2. Should the engineering department acquire the computers? Explain.

11-A3 Taxes, Straight-Line Depreciation, and Present Values

A manager of Olympic Mutual Funds is contemplating acquiring servers to operate its Web site. The servers will cost $660,000 cash and will have zero terminal salvage value. The recovery period and useful life are both 3 years. Annual pretax cash savings from operations will be $300,000. The income tax rate is 40%, and the required after-tax rate of return is 12%.

1. Compute the NPV, assuming straight-line depreciation of $220,000 yearly for tax purposes. Should Olympic acquire the computers? Explain.
2. Suppose the computers will be fully depreciated at the end of year 3 but can be sold for $90,000 cash. Compute the NPV. Should Olympic acquire the computers? Explain.
3. Ignore number 2. Suppose the required after-tax rate of return is 8% instead of 12%. Should Olympic acquire the computers? Show computations.

11-A4 MACRS and Present Values

Managers of Midwest Gas & Electric are considering whether to buy some equipment for the company's Bismark plant. The equipment will cost $1.5 million cash and will have a 10-year useful life and zero terminal salvage value. Annual pretax cash savings from operations will be $380,000. The income tax rate is 40%, and the required after-tax rate of return is 16%.

1. Compute the NPV, using a 7-year recovery period and MACRS depreciation for tax purposes. Should the company acquire the equipment?
2. Suppose the economic life of the equipment is 15 years, which means that there will be $380,000 additional annual cash savings from operations in each of the years from 11 to 15. Assume that a 7-year recovery period is used. Should the company acquire the equipment? Show computations.

11-A5 Gains or Losses on Disposal

On January 1, 20X1, Brisbane Company sold an asset with a book value of $50,000 for cash.
   Assume two selling prices: $65,000 and $40,000. For each selling price, prepare a tabulation of the gain or loss, the effect on income taxes, and the total after-tax effect on cash. The applicable income tax rate is 40%.

11-B1 Exercises in Compound Interest

Use the appropriate table to compute the following:

1. You have always dreamed of taking a safari in Africa. What lump sum do you have to invest today to have the $16,000 needed for the trip in 3 years? Assume that you can invest the money at
   a. 4%, compounded annually.
   b. 10%, compounded annually.
   c. 16%, compounded annually.
2. You are considering partial retirement. To do so you need to use part of your savings to supplement your income for the next 5 years. Suppose you need an extra $20,000 per year. What lump sum do you have to invest now to supplement your income for 5 years? Assume that your minimum desired rate of return is
   a. 4%, compounded annually.
   b. 10%, compounded annually.
   c. 16%, compounded annually.
3. You just won a lump sum of $1,000,000 in a state lottery. You have decided to invest the winnings and withdraw an equal amount each year for 10 years. How much can you withdraw each year and have a zero balance left at the end of 10 years if you invest at
   a. 5%, compounded annually?
   b. 10%, compounded annually?
4. An NHL hockey player is offered the choice of two 4-year salary contracts, contract X for $1.4 million and contract Y for $1.3 million:

	Contract X	**Contract Y**
End of year 1	$ 200,000	$ 450,000
End of year 2	300,000	350,000
End of year 3	400,000	300,000
End of year 4	500,000	200,000
Total	$1,400,000	$1,300,000

Which contract has the higher PV at 14% compounded annually? Show computations to support your answer.

11-B2 NPV for Investment Decisions

The head of the oncology department of FH Research Center is considering the purchase of some new equipment. The cost is $420,000, the economic life is 5 years, and there is no terminal disposal value. Annual cash inflows from operations would increase by $140,000, and the required rate of return is 14%. There are no taxes.

1. Compute the NPV.
2. Should the research center acquire the equipment? Explain.

11-B3 Taxes, Straight-Line Depreciation, and NPV

The president of E-Games, an online gaming company, is considering the purchase of some equipment used for the development of new games. The cost is $400,000, the economic life and the recovery period are both 5 years, and there is no terminal disposal value. Annual pretax cash inflows from operations would increase by $130,000, giving a total 5-year pretax savings of $650,000. The income tax rate is 40%, and the required after-tax rate of return is 14%.

1. Compute the NPV, assuming straight-line depreciation of $80,000 yearly for tax purposes. Should E-Games acquire the equipment?
2. Suppose the asset will be fully depreciated at the end of year 5 but is sold for $25,000 cash. Should E-Games acquire the equipment? Show computations.
3. Ignore number 2. Suppose the required after-tax rate of return is 10% instead of 14%. Should E-Games acquire the equipment? Show computations.

11-B4 MACRS and Present Values

The general manager of a West Virginia mining company has a chance to purchase a new drill at a total cost of $250,000. The recovery period is 5 years. Additional annual pretax cash inflow from operations is $82,000, the economic life of the drill is 5 years, there is no salvage value, the income tax rate is 35%, and the after-tax required rate of return is 16%.

1. Compute the NPV, assuming MACRS depreciation for tax purposes. Should the company acquire the drill?
2. Suppose the economic life of the drill is 6 years, which means that there will be an $82,000 cash inflow from operations in the sixth year. The recovery period is still 5 years. Should the company acquire the drill? Show computations.

11-B5 Income Taxes and Disposal of Assets

Assume that the combined federal and state income tax rate for Quixote Company is 40%.

1. The book value of an old machine is $25,000. Quixote sold the machine for $10,000 cash. What is the effect of this decision on after-tax cash flows?
2. The book value of an old machine is $25,000. Quixote sold the machine for $35,000 cash. What is the effect of this decision on after-tax cash flows?

Additional Assignment Material

QUESTIONS

11-1 Capital budgeting has three phases: (a) identification of potential investments, (b) selection of investments, and (c) post-audit of investments. What is the accountant's role in each phase?

11-2 Why is discounted cash flow a superior method for capital budgeting?

11-3 "The higher the minimum desired rate of return, the higher the price that a company will be willing to pay for cost-saving equipment." Do you agree? Explain.

11-4 "The DCF model assumes certainty and perfect capital markets. Thus, it is impractical to use it in most real-world situations." Do you agree? Explain.

11-5 "Double-counting of costs occurs if depreciation is separately considered in DCF analysis." Do you agree? Explain.

11-6 Does the IRR model make significantly different decisions than does the NPV model? Why or why not?

11-7 What does the real options model recognize that the NPV and IRR models do not?

11-8 "We can't use sensitivity analysis because our cash-flow predictions are too inaccurate." Comment.

11-9 Why should the differential approach to alternatives always lead to the same decision as the total project approach?

11-10 "The NPV model should not be used for investment decisions about advanced technology, such as computer-integrated manufacturing systems." Do you agree? Explain.

11-11 Distinguish between average and marginal tax rates.

11-12 "Congress should pass a law forbidding corporations to keep two sets of books." Do you agree? Explain.

11-13 Distinguish between tax avoidance and tax evasion.

11-14 "Companies that try to avoid taxes are unethical." Do you agree? Discuss.

11-15 Explain why accelerated depreciation methods are superior to straight-line methods for income tax purposes.

11-16 "An investment in equipment really buys two streams of cash." Do you agree? Explain.

11-17 Why should companies take tax deductions sooner rather than later?

11-18 "The MACRS half-year convention causes assets to be depreciated beyond the lives specified in the MACRS recovery schedules." Do you agree? Explain.

11-19 "When there are income taxes, depreciation is a cash outlay." Do you agree? Explain.

11-20 "If DCF approaches are superior to the payback and the accounting rate-of-return methods, why should we bother to learn the others? All it does is confuse things." Answer this contention.

11-21 What is the basic flaw in the payback model?

11-22 Explain how a conflict can arise between capital-budgeting decision models and performance evaluation methods.

11-23 Study Appendix 11. What are the three components of market (nominal) interest rates?

11-24 Study Appendix 11. Describe how internal consistency is achieved when considering inflation in a capital-budgeting model.

CRITICAL THINKING EXERCISES

11-25 Investment in R&D

"It is impossible to use DCF methods for evaluating investments in R&D. There are no cost savings to measure, and we don't even know what products might come out of our R&D activities." This is a quote from an R&D manager who was asked to justify investment in a major research project based on its expected NPV. Do you agree with her statement? Explain.

11-26 Business Valuation and NPV

When a company elects to invest in a project with a positive NPV, what will generally happen to the value of the company? What will happen to this value when the company invests in a negative NPV project?

11-27 Replacement of Production Facilities

A manufacturing company recently considered replacing one of its forming machines with a newer, faster, more accurate model. What cash flows would this decision be likely to affect? List both cash flows that would be easy to quantify and those for which measurement would be difficult.

11-28 Capital Budgeting, Taxes, and Ethics

The U.S. tax law is complex. Sometimes the line between tax avoidance and tax evasion is not clear. Discuss the legal and ethical implications of the following two capital investment decisions:

a. A company invested in an asset that it expects to grow rather than decline in value. Nevertheless, the tax law allows the company to deduct depreciation on the asset. Therefore, the company depreciated the asset for tax purposes using an accelerated MACRS schedule.

b. There are often tax advantages to investments "offshore." For example, in Bermuda there are no taxes on profits, dividends, or income, and there is no capital gains tax, no withholding tax, and no sales tax. A U.S. company decided to invest in a manufacturing plant in Bermuda and use transfer prices to move as much of the company's profits as possible to the Bermuda plant.

EXERCISES

11-29 Exercise in Compound Interest

Chinn Wong wishes to purchase a $600,000 house. She has accumulated a $120,000 down payment, but she wishes to borrow $480,000 on a 30-year mortgage. For simplicity, assume annual mortgage payments occur at the end of each year and there are no loan fees.

1. What are Wong's annual payments if her interest rate is (a) 8%, (b) 10%, and (c) 12%, compounded annually?
2. Repeat number 1 for a 15-year mortgage.
3. Suppose Wong had to choose between a 30-year and a 15-year mortgage, either one at a 10% interest rate. Compute the total payments and total interest paid on (a) a 30-year mortgage and (b) a 15-year mortgage.

11-30 Exercise in Compound Interest

Suppose **Subaru of America, Inc.** wishes to borrow money from **UBS**. They agree on an annual rate of 10%.

1. Suppose Subaru agrees to repay $500 million at the end of 4 years. How much will UBS lend Subaru?
2. Suppose Subaru agrees to repay a total of $500 million at a rate of $125 million at the end of each of the next 4 years. How much will UBS lend Subaru?

11-31 Exercise in Compound Interest

Suppose you are a loan officer for a bank. A start-up company has qualified for a loan. You are pondering various proposals for repayment:

1. Lump sum of $500,000 four years hence. How much will you lend if your desired rate of return is (a) 12%, compounded annually, and (b) 16%, compounded annually?
2. Repeat number 1, but assume that the interest rates are compounded semiannually.
3. Suppose the loan is to be paid in full by equal payments of $125,000 at the end of each of the next 4 years. How much will you lend if your desired rate of return is (a) 12%, compounded annually, and (b) 16%, compounded annually?

11-32 Basic Relationships in Interest Tables

1. Suppose you borrow $100,000 now at 12% interest, compounded annually. You will repay the borrowed amount plus interest in a lump sum at the end of 8 years. How much must you repay? Use Table 1 (page A6) and the basic equation PV = future amount × conversion factor.
2. Assume the same facts as previously except that you will repay the loan in equal installments at the end of each of the 8 years. How much must you repay each year? Use Table 2 (page A9) and the basic equation: PV = future annual amounts × conversion factor.

11-33 PV and Sports Salaries

Because of a salary cap, National Basketball Association teams are not allowed to exceed a certain annual limit in total player salaries. Suppose the Portland Trailblazers had scheduled salaries exactly equal to their cap of $50 million for 2010. Roy Brandon, a star player, was scheduled to receive $14 million in 2010. To free up money to pay a prize rookie, Brandon agreed on July 1, 2010 to defer $6 million of his salary for 2 years, by which time the salary cap will have been increased. His contract called for salary payments of $14 million in 2010, $14 million in 2011, and $16 million in 2012, all on July 1 of the respective year. Now, he will receive $8 million in 2010, still $14 million in 2011, and $22 million in 2012. Brandon's minimum desired rate of return is 12%.

Did the deferral of salary cost Brandon anything? If so, how much? Compute the PV of the sacrifice as of July 1, 2010. Explain.

11-34 Simple NPV

Banerjee Company expects to receive $200 at the end of each of the next 5 years and an additional $1,000 at the end of the fifth year. Therefore, the total payments will be $2,000. What is the NPV of the payments at an interest rate of 8%?

11-35 NPV Relationships

Fill in the blanks.

	Number of Years			
	8	18	20	28
Amount of annual cash inflow*	$12,000	$	$ 9,000	$ 8,000
Required initial investment	$	$80,000	$65,000	$27,000
Minimum desired rate of return	14%	20%	$	25%
NPV	$ 5,613	($13,835)	$ 2,225	$

*To be received at the end of each year.

11-36 New Equipment

The Modesto Office Equipment Company has offered to sell some new packaging equipment to the Chavez Company. The list price is $36,000, but Modesto has agreed to allow a trade-in allowance of $15,000 on some old equipment. The old equipment was carried at a book value of $8,700 and could be sold outright for $10,000 cash. Cash-operating savings are expected to be $5,000 annually for the next 12 years. The minimum desired rate of return is 12%. The old equipment has a remaining useful life of 12 years. Both the old and the new equipment will have zero disposal values 12 years from now.

Should Chavez buy the new equipment? Show your computations, using the NPV method. Ignore income taxes.

11-37 Present Values of Cash Inflows

City View Restaurant is about to open at a new location. Operating plans indicate the following expected cash flows:

		Outflows	Inflows
Initial investment now		$235,000	$ —
End of year:	1	$150,000	200,000
	2	$200,000	250,000
	3	$250,000	300,000
	4	$300,000	450,000
	5	$350,000	500,000

1. Compute the NPV for all these cash flows. This should be a single amount. Use a discount rate of 14%.
2. Suppose the minimum desired rate was 12%. Without further calculations, determine whether the NPV is positive or negative. Explain.

11-38 Effect of Minimum Rate

Zielinsky Company has an opportunity to invest $5,000 in a new automated lathe that will reduce annual operating costs by $1,000 per year and will have an economic life of 7 years.

1. Suppose Zielinsky Company has a minimum desired rate of return of 5%. Compute the NPV of the investment and recommend to Zielinsky Company whether it should purchase the lathe.
2. Suppose Zielinsky Company has a minimum desired rate of return of 12%. Compute the NPV of the investment and recommend to Zielinsky Company whether it should purchase the lathe.
3. How does the desired rate of return affect the NPV of a potential investment?

11-39 NPV and IRR

Czick Company is considering an investment in a machine that costs $36,048 and would result in cash savings of $10,000 per year for 5 years. The company's cost of capital is 10%.

1. Compute the project's NPV at 10%, 12%, and 14%.
2. Compute the project's IRR.
3. Suppose the company uses the NPV model. Would it accept the project? Why or why not?
4. Suppose the company uses the IRR model. Would it accept the project? Why or why not?

11-40 Sensitivity Analysis

Bailey, Root, and Wylie, LLP, a law firm, is considering the replacement of its old accounting system with new software that should save $6,000 per year in net cash operating costs. The old system has zero disposal value, but it could be used for the next 12 years. The estimated useful life of the new software is 12 years, and it will cost $30,000. The minimum desired rate of return is 10%.

1. What is the payback period?
2. Compute the NPV.
3. Management is unsure about the useful life. What would be the NPV if the useful life were (a) 5 years instead of 12 or (b) 20 years instead of 12?
4. Suppose the life will be 12 years, but the savings will be $4,000 per year instead of $6,000. What would be the NPV?
5. Suppose the annual savings will be $5,000 for 8 years. What would be the NPV?

11-41 NPV and Sensitivity Analysis

Chippewa County Jail currently has its laundry done by a local cleaners at an annual cost of $46,000. It is considering a purchase of washers, dryers, and presses at a total installed cost of $52,000 so that inmates can do the laundry. The county expects savings of $15,000 per year, and it expects the machines to last 5 years. The desired rate of return is 10%.

Answer each part separately.

1. Compute the NPV of the investment in laundry facilities.
2. a. Suppose the machines last only 4 years. Compute the NPV.
   b. Suppose the machines last 7 years. Compute the NPV.
3. a. Suppose the annual savings are only $12,000. Compute the NPV.
   b. Suppose the annual savings are $18,000. Compute the NPV.
4. a. Compute the most optimistic estimate of NPV, combining the best outcomes in numbers 2 and 3.
   b. Compute the most pessimistic estimate of NPV, combining the worst outcomes in numbers 2 and 3.
5. Accept the expected life estimate of 5 years. What is the minimum annual savings that would justify the investment in the laundry facilities?

11-42 Depreciation, Income Taxes, Cash Flows

Fill in the unknowns (in thousands of dollars):

(S)	Sales	550
(E)	Expenses excluding depreciation	350
(D)	Depreciation	100
	Total expenses	450
	Income before income taxes	?
(T)	Income taxes at 30%	?
(I)	Net income	?
	Cash effects of operations	
	Cash inflow from operations	?
	Income tax outflow at 30%	?
	After-tax inflow from operations	?
	Effect of depreciation	
	Depreciation	?
	Income tax savings	?
	Total after-tax effect on cash	?

11-43 After-Tax Effect on Cash

The 20X9 income statement of United Cable Company included the following:

Sales	$1,100,000
Less: Expenses, excluding depreciation	$ 600,000
Depreciation	400,000
Total expenses	$1,000,000
Income before taxes	$ 100,000
Income taxes (40%)	40,000
Net income	$ 60,000

Compute the total after-tax effect on cash. Use the format of the second part of Exhibit 11-3, page 437, "Analysis of the Same Facts for Capital Budgeting."

11-44 MACRS Depreciation

In 2009, Victoria Athletic Shoe Company acquired the following assets and immediately placed them into service.

1. Special tools (a 3-year-MACRS asset) that cost $25,000 on February 1.
2. A desktop computer that cost $4,000 on December 15.
3. Special calibration equipment that was used in running-shoe research and cost $8,000 on July 7.
4. A set of file cabinets that cost $7,000, purchased on March 1.

Compute the depreciation for tax purposes, under the prescribed MACRS method, in 2009 and 2010.

11-45 Present Value of MACRS Depreciation

Compute the PV of the MACRS tax savings for each of the following five assets:

	Asset Cost	Recovery Period	Discount Rate	Tax Rate
(a)	$240,000	3-year	12%	35%
(b)	$650,000	5-year	10%	40%
(c)	$ 55,000	7-year	16%	50%
(d)	$900,000	10-year	8%	35%
(e)	$400,000	10-year	15%	28%

11-46 NPV, ARR, and Payback

TexaTaco is considering a proposal to invest in a speaker system that would allow its employees to service drive-through customers. The cost of the system (including installation of special windows and driveway modifications) is $36,000. Jessica Declan, manager of TexaTaco, expects the drive-through operations to increase annual sales by $25,000, with a 40% contribution margin ratio. Assume that the system has an economic life of 6 years, at which time it will have no disposal value. The required rate of return is 12%. Ignore taxes.

1. Compute the payback period. Is this a good measure of profitability?

2. Compute the NPV. Should Declan accept the proposal? Why or why not?
3. Using the ARR model, compute the rate of return on the initial investment.

11-47 Weaknesses of the Payback Model

De Luca Company is considering two possible investments, each of which requires an initial invest-ment of $12,000. Investment A will provide a cash flow of $3,000 at the end of each year for 4 years. Investment B will provide a cash flow of $2,000 at the end of each year for 10 years.

1. Determine the payback period for each investment. Which investment is most desirable using the payback method?
2. Compute the NPV of each investment using a desired rate of return of 5%. Which investment is most desirable using the NPV method?
3. Explain why the payback method does not lead to an optimal decision for the De Luca Company.

11-48 Comparison of Capital-Budgeting Techniques

The Jackson City parks department is considering the purchase of a new, more efficient pool heater for its Moorcroft Swimming Pool at a cost of $15,000. It should save $3,000 in cash operating costs per year. Its estimated useful life is 8 years, and it will have zero disposal value. Ignore taxes.

1. What is the payback time?
2. Compute the NPV if the minimum rate of return desired is 8%. Should the department buy the heater? Why?
3. Using the ARR model, compute the rate of return on the initial investment.

11-49 Inflation and Capital Budgeting

Study Appendix 11. The head of the corporate tax division of a major public relations firm has pro-posed investing $295,000 in personal computers for the staff. The useful life and recovery period for the computers are both 5 years. The firm uses MACRS depreciation. There is no terminal salvage value. Labor savings of $125,000 per year (in year-zero dollars) are expected from the purchase. The income tax rate is 45%, and the after-tax required rate of return is 20%, which includes a 4% element attributable to inflation.

1. Compute the NPV of the computers. Use the nominal required rate of return and adjust the cash flows for inflation. (For example, year 1 cash flow = 1.04 × year 0 cash flow.)
2. Compute the NPV of the computers using the nominal required rate of return without adjusting the cash flows for inflation.
3. Compare your answers in numbers 1 and 2. Which is correct? Would using the incorrect analysis generally lead to overinvestment or underinvestment? Explain.

11-50 Sensitivity of Capital Budgeting to Inflation

Study Appendix 11. Enrique Mendoza, the president of a Mexican wholesale company, is considering whether to invest 420,000 pesos in new semiautomatic loading equipment that will last 5 years, have zero scrap value, and generate cash operating savings in labor usage of 150,000 pesos annually, using 20X0 prices and wage rates. It is December 31, 20X0.

The minimum desired rate of return is 18% per year after taxes.

1. Compute the NPV of the project. Use 150,000 pesos as the savings for each of the 5 years. Assume a 40% tax rate and, for simplicity, assume ordinary straight-line depreciation of 420,000 pesos ÷ 5 = 84,000 pesos annually for tax purposes.
2. Mendoza is wondering if the model in number 1 provides a correct analysis of the effects of infla-tion. He maintains that the 18% rate embodies an element attributable to anticipated inflation. For purposes of this analysis, he assumes that the existing rate of inflation, 10% annually, will persist over the next 5 years. Repeat number 1, adjusting the cash operating savings upward by using the 10% inflation rate.
3. Which analysis, the one in number 1 or 2, is correct? Why?

PROBLEMS

11-51 Replacement of Office Equipment

Southeastern University is considering replacing some Xerox copiers with faster copiers purchased from Cannon. The administration is very concerned about the rising costs of operations during the last decade.

To convert to Cannon, two operators would have to be retrained. Required training and remodeling would cost $4,000. Southeastern's three Xerox machines were purchased for $10,000 each, 5 years ago. Their expected life was 10 years. Their resale value now is $1,000 each and will be zero in 5 more years. The total cost of the new Cannon equipment will be $50,000; it will have zero disposal value in 5 years.

The three Xerox operators are paid $8 an hour each. They usually work a 40-hour week. Machine breakdowns occur monthly on each machine, resulting in repair costs of $50 per month and overtime of 4 hours, at time-and-one-half, per machine per month, to complete the normal monthly workload. Toner, supplies, and so on, cost $100 a month for each Xerox copier.

The Cannon system will require only two regular operators, on a regular work week of 40 hours each, to do the same work. Rates are $10 an hour, and no overtime is expected. Toner, supplies, and so on, will cost a total of $3,300 annually. Maintenance and repairs are fully serviced by Cannon for $1,050 annually. (Assume a 52-week year.)

1. Using DCF techniques, compute the PV of all relevant cash flows, under both alternatives, for the 5-year period discounted at 12%. As a nonprofit university, Southeastern does not pay income taxes.
2. Should Southeastern keep the Xerox copiers or replace them if the decision is based solely on the given data?
3. What other considerations might affect the decision?

11-52 Replacement Decision for Railway Equipment

Suppose the **Norfolk Southern Railway** is considering replacement of a power jack tamper, used for maintenance of track, with a new automatic raising device that can be attached to a production tamper.

The present power jack tamper cost $24,000 five years ago and had an estimated life of 12 years. A year from now, the machine will require a major overhaul estimated to cost $5,000. It can be disposed of now via an outright cash sale for $4,000. There will be no value at the end of another 7 years.

The automatic raising attachment has a delivered selling price of $68,000 and an estimated life of 12 years. Because of anticipated future developments in combined maintenance machines, Norfolk Southern management predicts that the company will dispose of the machine at the end of the seventh year to take advantage of newly developed machines. Estimated sales value at the end of 7 years is $7,000.

Tests have shown that the automatic raising machine will produce a more uniform surface on the track than does the power jack tamper now in use. The new equipment will eliminate one laborer whose annual compensation, including fringe benefits, is $30,000.

Track maintenance work is seasonal, and the equipment normally works from May 1 to October 31 each year. Machine operators and laborers are transferred to other work after October 31, at the same rate of pay.

The salesman claims that the annual normal maintenance of the new machine will run about $1,000 per year. Because the automatic raising machine is more complicated than the manually operated machine, it will probably require a thorough overhaul at the end of the fourth year, at an estimated cost of $7,000.

Records show the annual normal maintenance of the power jack tamper to be $1,200. Fuel consumption of the two machines is equal. Should Norfolk Southern keep or replace the power jack tamper? The company requires a 10% rate of return. Compute PV. Ignore income taxes.

11-53 Discounted Cash Flow, Uneven Revenue Stream, Relevant Costs

Mildred Driver, the owner of a nine-hole golf course on the outskirts of a large city, is considering a proposal that the course be illuminated and operated at night. Ms. Driver purchased the course early last year for $480,000. Her receipts from operations during the 28-week season were $135,000. Total disbursements for the year, for all purposes, were $84,000.

The required investment in lighting this course is estimated at $90,000. The system will require 300 lamps of 1,000 watts each. Electricity costs $.08 per kilowatt-hour. The expected average hours of operation per night is 5. Because of occasional bad weather and the probable curtailment of night operation at the beginning and end of the season, it is estimated that there will be only 130 nights of operation per year. Labor for keeping the course open at night will cost $75 per night. Light bulb cost is estimated at $1,500 per year; other maintenance and repairs, per year, will amount to 4% of the initial cost of the lighting system. Annual property taxes on this equipment will be about 1.7% of its initial cost. It is estimated that the average revenue, per night of operation, will be $420 for the first 2 years.

Considering the probability of competition from the illumination of other golf courses, Ms. Driver decides that she will not make the investment unless she can make at least 10% per annum on her investment. Because of anticipated competition, revenue is expected to drop to $300 per night for years 3–5. It is estimated that the lighting equipment will have a salvage value of $35,000 at the end of the 5-year period.

Using DCF techniques, determine whether Ms. Driver should install the lighting system.

11-54 Investment in Machine

The Soho Ale Company has an old brewing machine with a net disposal value of £12,000 now and £4,000 five years from now. A new brewing machine is offered for £57,000 cash or £45,000 with a trade-in. The new machine will result in an annual operating cash outflow of £40,000 as compared with the old machine's annual outflow of £50,000. The disposal value of the new machine 5 years hence will be £2,000.

The minimum desired rate of return is 20%. The company uses DCF techniques to guide these decisions.

Should Soho Ale acquire the new brewing machine? Show your calculations. Company procedures require the computing of the PV of each alternative. The most desirable alternative is the one with the least cost. Assume that the PV of £1 at 20% for 5 years is £.40; the PV of an annuity of £1 at 20% for 5 years is £3.

11-55 Replacement Decision

The **Metropolitan Transit Authority (MTA)** has included a cafeteria car on the passenger train it operates. Yearly operations of the cafeteria car have shown a consistent loss, which is expected to persist, as follows:

Revenue (in cash)		$200,000
Expenses for food, supplies, etc. (in cash)	$100,000	
Salaries	110,000	210,000
Net loss (ignore depreciation on the dining car itself)		$ (10,000)

The Auto-Vend Company has offered to sell automatic vending machines to MTA for $22,000, less a $3,000 trade-in allowance on old equipment (which is carried at $3,000 book value, and which can be sold outright for $3,000 cash) now used in the cafeteria-car operation. The useful life of the vending equipment is estimated at 10 years, with zero scrap value. Experience elsewhere has led executives to predict that the equipment will serve 50% more food than the dining car, but prices will be 50% less, so the new revenue will probably be $150,000. The variety and mix of food sold are expected to be the same as for the cafeteria car. A catering company will completely service and supply food and beverages for the machines, paying 10% of revenue to MTA and bearing all costs of food, repairs, and so on. All dining-car employees will be discharged immediately. Their termination pay will total $35,000. However, an attendant who has some general knowledge of vending machines will be needed for one shift per day. The annual cost to MTA for the attendant will be $13,000.

For political and other reasons, the railroad will definitely not abandon its food service. The old equipment will have zero scrap value at the end of 10 years.

Using the preceding data, compute the following. Label computations. Ignore income taxes.

1. Use the NPV method to analyze the incremental investment. Assume a minimum desired rate of return of 10%. For this problem, assume that the PV of $1 at 10% to be received at the end of 10 years is $.400 and that the PV of an annuity of $1 at 10% for 10 years is $6.000.
2. What would be the minimum amount of annual revenue that MTA would have to receive from the catering company to justify making the investment? Show computations.

11-56 Minimization of Transportation Costs Without Income Taxes

J. Youle Company produces industrial and residential lighting fixtures at its manufacturing facility located in Scottsdale, Arizona. The company currently ships products to an eastern warehouse via common carriers at a rate of $.26 per pound of fixtures. The warehouse is located in Cleveland, 2,500 miles from Scottsdale.

Alexis Azra, the treasurer of Youle, is considering whether to purchase a truck for transporting products to the eastern warehouse. The following data on the truck are available:

Purchase price	$50,000
Useful life	5 years
Salvage value after 5 years	0
Capacity of truck	10,000 lb
Cash costs of operating truck	$.90 per mile

Azra feels that an investment in this truck is particularly attractive because of her successful negotiation with Retro to back-haul Retro's products from Cleveland to Scottsdale on every return trip from the warehouse. Retro has agreed to pay Youle $2,400 per load of Retro's products hauled from Cleveland to Scottsdale up to and including 100 loads per year.

Youle's marketing manager has estimated that the company will ship 500,000 pounds of fixtures to the eastern warehouse each year for the next 5 years. The truck will be fully loaded on each round trip.

Ignore income taxes.

1. Assume that Youle requires a minimum rate of return of 20%. Should it purchase the truck? Show computations to support your answer.
2. What is the minimum number of trips that Retro must guarantee to make the deal acceptable to Youle, based on the preceding numbers alone?
3. What qualitative factors might influence your decision? Be specific.

11-57 Straight-Line Depreciation, MACRS Depreciation, and Immediate Write-Off

Mr. Hiramatsu bought a new $50,000 freezer for his grocery store on January 2, 2010. The freezer has a 5-year economic life and recovery period, Mr. Hiramatsu's minimum desired rate of return is 12%, and his tax rate is 40%.

1. Suppose Mr. Hiramatsu uses straight-line depreciation for tax purposes. Compute the PV of the tax savings from depreciation. Assume that Mr. Hiramatsu takes a full year of depreciation at the end of 2010.
2. Suppose Mr. Hiramatsu uses MACRS depreciation for tax purposes. Compute the PV of the tax savings from depreciation.
3. Suppose Mr. Hiramatsu was allowed to immediately deduct the entire cost of the freezer for tax purposes. Compute the PV of the tax savings from depreciation.
4. Which of the three methods of deducting the cost of the freezer would Mr. Hiramatsu prefer if all three were allowable for tax purposes? Why?

11-58 MACRS, Residual Value

The Maddox Company estimates that it can save $10,000 per year in annual operating cash costs for the next 5 years if it buys a special-purpose machine at a cost of $33,000. Residual value is expected to be $4,000, although no residual value is being provided for in using MACRS depreciation (5-year recovery period) for tax purposes. The company will sell the equipment at the end of the fifth year. The minimum desired rate of return, after taxes, is 12%. Assume the income tax rate is 45%.

Using the NPV method, show whether the investment is desirable.

11-59 Purchase of Equipment

The Philadelphia Clinic, a for-profit medical facility, is planning to spend $45,000 for modernized X-ray equipment. It will replace equipment that has zero book value and no salvage value, although the old equipment would have lasted another 7 years.

The new equipment will save $16,000 in cash operating costs for each of the next 7 years, at which time the clinic will sell it for $8,000. A major overhaul costing $4,000 will occur at the end of the fourth year; the old equipment would require no such overhaul. The entire cost of the overhaul is deductible for tax purposes in the fourth year. The equipment has a 5-year recovery period. The clinic uses MACRS depreciation for tax purposes.

The minimum desired rate of return after taxes is 12%. The applicable income tax rate is 40%.

Compute the after-tax NPV. Is the new equipment a desirable investment?

11-60 MACRS and Low-Income Housing

Aaron Hersch is a real estate developer who specializes in residential apartments. A complex of 20 run-down apartments has recently come on the market for $332,500. Hersch predicts that after remodeling, the 12 one-bedroom units will rent for $380 per month and the 8 two-bedroom apartments for $440. He budgets 15% of the rental fees for repairs and maintenance. It should be 30 years before the apartments need remodeling again, if the work is done well. Remodeling costs are $15,000 per apartment. Both purchase price and remodeling costs qualify as 27.5-year MACRS property.

Assume that the MACRS schedule assigns an equal amount of depreciation to each of the first 27 years and one-half year to year 28. The PV at 10% of $1 of cost recovery spread over the 28 years in this way is $.3372.

Hersch does not believe he will keep the apartment complex for its entire 30-year life. Most likely he will sell it just after the end of the tenth year. His predicted sales price is $980,000.

Hersch's after-tax required rate of return is 10%, and his tax rate is 38%.

Should Hersch buy the apartment complex? What is the after-tax NPV? Ignore tax complications, such as capital gains.

11-61 PV of After-Tax Cash Flows, Payback, and ARR

Suppose that Mitsubishi Chemical Corporation is planning to buy new equipment to expand its production of a popular solvent. Estimated data are as follows (monetary amounts are in thousands of Japanese yen):

Cash cost of new equipment now	¥400,000
Estimated life in years	10
Terminal salvage value	¥ 50,000
Incremental revenues per year	¥330,000
Incremental expenses per year other than depreciation	¥165,000

Assume a 60% flat rate for income taxes. The company receives all revenues and pays all expenses other than depreciation in cash. Use a 14% discount rate. Assume that the company uses ordinary straight-line depreciation based on a 10-year recovery period for tax purposes. Also assume that the company depreciates the original cost less the terminal salvage value.

Compute the following:

1. Depreciation expense per year
2. Anticipated net income per year
3. Annual net cash flow
4. Payback period
5. ARR on initial investment
6. NPV

11-62 Investment Justification Analysis and Graphs

Consider a new video game developed by Dynamic Gaming, Inc. (DGI). DGI's development team was formed at the end of 2006 and has been working on the development of the game for several years. After spending $175,000 on the development, the team has reached the point in 2010 where it must make a decision on whether to proceed with production of the game. Production of the game will require an initial investment in facilities of $199,500 at the end of 2010. The project has an expected life cycle of 7 years (end of 2010 through 2017). Predicted cash flows for the game are as follows (assuming that all cash flows occur at the end of the year):

End of Year	Cash Inflow	Cash Outflow
2010	$ 0	$199,500
2011	100,000	100,000
2012	220,000	180,000
2013	340,000	260,000
2014	460,000	320,000
2015	470,000	280,000
2016	410,000	200,000
2017	150,000	120,000

DGI's applicable tax rate is 40%, and DGI uses straight-line depreciation over the asset's expected life for tax purposes. The salvage value of the facilities will be zero in 7 years. DGI uses two criteria to evaluate potential investments: payback time and NPV. It wants a payback period of 3 years or less and an NPV greater than zero. DGI has a cost of capital of 18%.

1. Prepare a table that shows the after-tax annual net cash flows, cumulative net cash flow, and cumulative discounted net cash flow each year.
2. Would DGI invest in production of the game if it uses the payback period?
3. Would DGI invest in production of the game if it uses the NPV model?
4. Use graph paper to prepare a well-labeled line chart that shows the cumulative after-tax net cash flow and the cumulative after-tax discounted net cash flow of this investment over its life cycle. On your chart, clearly identify the payback time and the NPV for the project.
5. Would you recommend that DGI invest in this project? Explain.

11-63 Fixed and Current Assets; Evaluation of Performance

Roxbury Clinic has been under pressure to keep costs down. The clinic administrator has been managing various revenue-producing centers to maximize contributions to the recovery of the operating costs of the clinic as a whole. The administrator has been considering whether to buy a special-purpose X-ray machine for $193,000. Its unique characteristics would generate additional cash operating income of $51,500 per year for the clinic as a whole.

The clinic expects the machine to have a useful life of 6 years and a terminal salvage value of $22,000. The machine is delicate. It requires a constant inventory of various supplies and spare parts.

When the clinic uses some of these items, it instantly replaces them so it maintains an investment of $15,000 at all times. However, the clinic fully recovers this investment at the end of the useful life of the machine.

1. Compute NPV if the required rate of return is 14%.
2. Compute the ARR on (a) the initial investment and (b) the "average" investment.
3. Why might the administrator be reluctant to base her decision on the DCF model?

11-64 Investment Before and After Taxes

Deer Valley Lodge, a ski area near Salt Lake City, has plans to eventually add five new chairlifts. Suppose that one of the lifts costs $2.2 million, and preparing the slope and installing the lift costs another $1.48 million. The lift will allow 300 additional skiers on the slopes, but there are only 40 days a year when the lodge needs the extra capacity. (Assume that Deer Valley will sell all 300 lift tickets on those 40 days.) Running the new lift will cost $500 a day for the entire 200 days the lodge is open. Assume that lift tickets at Deer Valley cost $65 a day and added cash expenses for each skier-day are $9. The new lift has an economic life of 20 years.

1. Assume that the before-tax required rate of return for Deer Valley is 14%. Compute the before-tax NPV of the new lift and advise the managers of Deer Valley about whether adding the lift will be a profitable investment.
2. Assume that the after-tax required rate of return for Deer Valley is 8%, the income tax rate is 40%, and the MACRS recovery period is 10 years. Compute the after-tax NPV of the new lift and advise the managers of Deer Valley about whether adding the lift will be a profitable investment.
3. What subjective factors would affect the investment decision?

11-65 After-Tax NPV

Berradi Corp. is considering the purchase of a new stamping machine to manufacture its product. The following information is available:

New Machine	
Purchase cost new	$85,000
Annual increase in cash revenues	60,000
Annual increase in cash operating costs	42,000
Salvage value—10 years from now	5,000

If Berradi purchases the new machine, it will use it for 10 years and then trade it in on another machine. The company computes depreciation on a straight-line basis, for both taxes and financial reporting purposes. Assume Berradi currently has an old stamping machine with a book value of $30,000 that it can currently dispose of for $8,000 if it buys the new machine. Assume Berradi's cost of capital is 14%, and its tax rate is 30%.

Should the new machine be purchased based on the NPV method?

11-66 Minimization of Transportation Costs After Taxes, Inflation

Study Appendix 11. (This problem is a version of Problem 11-56 that includes taxes and inflation elements.) The J. Youle Company produces industrial and residential lighting fixtures at its manufacturing facility in Scottsdale. The company currently ships products to an eastern warehouse via common carriers at a rate of $.26 per pound of fixtures (expressed in year-zero dollars). The warehouse is located in Cleveland, 2,500 miles from Scottsdale. The rate will increase with inflation.

Alexis Azra, the treasurer of Youle, is currently considering whether to purchase a truck for transporting products to the eastern warehouse. Refer to the table in Problem 11-56 for truck data.

Azra feels that an investment in this truck is particularly attractive because of her successful negotiation with Retro to back-haul Retro's products from Cleveland to Scottsdale on every return trip from the warehouse. Retro has agreed to pay Youle $2,400 per load of Retro's products hauled from Cleveland to Scottsdale for as many loads as Youle can accommodate, up to and including 100 loads per year over the next 5 years.

Youle's marketing manager has estimated that the company will ship 500,000 pounds of fixtures to the eastern warehouse each year for the next 5 years. The truck will be fully loaded on each round trip.

Make the following assumptions:
a. Youle requires a minimum 20% after-tax rate of return, which includes a 10% element attributable to inflation.
b. A 40% tax rate.
c. MACRS depreciation based on 5-year cost recovery period.
d. An inflation rate of 10%.

1. Should Youle purchase the truck? Show computations to support your answer.
2. What qualitative factors might influence your decision? Be specific.

11-67 Inflation and Nonprofit Institution

Study Appendix 11. MLK Elementary School is considering the purchase of a photocopying machine for $7,000 on December 31, 20X0. The machine will have a useful life of 5 years and no residual value. The cash operating savings are expected to be $2,000 annually, measured in 20X0 dollars.

The minimum desired rate is 14%, which includes an element attributable to anticipated inflation of 6%. (Remember that the school district pays no income taxes.)

Use the 14% minimum desired rate for numbers 1 and 2:

1. Compute the NPV of the project without adjusting the cash operating savings for inflation.
2. Repeat number 1, adjusting the cash operating savings upward in accordance with the 6% inflation rate.
3. Compare your results in numbers 1 and 2. What generalization seems applicable about the analysis of inflation in capital budgeting?

CASES

11-68 Investment in CAD/CAM

Aswega AS is an Estonian manufacturer of electromagnetic flowmeters, heatmeters, and calibration equipment located in Tallinn. Suppose that it is considering the installation of a computer-aided design/computer-aided manufacturing (CAD/CAM) system. The current proposal calls for implementation of only the CAD portion of the system. The manager in charge of production design and planning has estimated that the CAD portion of CAD/CAM could do the work of five designers, who are each paid EEK 500,000 per year (52 weeks × 40 hours × EEK 250 per hour), where EEK is the symbol for the Estonian kroon.

Aswega can purchase the CAD/CAM system for EEK 2.8 million. (It cannot purchase the CAD portion separately.) The annual out-of-pocket costs of running the CAD portion of the system are EEK 1.8 million. The company expects to use the system for 8 years. The company's minimum desired rate of return is 12%. Ignore income taxes.

1. Compute the NPV of the investment in the CAD/CAM system. Should Aswega purchase the system? Explain.
2. Suppose the manager was not certain about her predictions of savings and economic life. Possibly the company will replace only four designers, but if everything works out well, it may replace as many as six. If better systems become available, the company may use the CAD/CAM system for only 5 years, but it might last as long as 10 years. Prepare pessimistic, most likely, and optimistic predictions of NPV. Would this analysis make you more confident or less confident in your decision in number 1? Explain.
3. What subjective factors might influence your decision?

11-69 Investment in Technology

Nashville Tool Company is considering installation of a CIM system as part of its implementation of a JIT philosophy. Gretchen Torres, company president, is convinced that the new system is necessary, but she needs the numbers to convince the board of directors. This is a major move for the company, and approval at board level is required.

Maria, Gretchen's daughter, has been assigned the task of justifying the investment. She is a business school graduate and understands the use of NPV for capital-budgeting decisions. To identify relevant costs, she developed the following information.

Nashville Tool Company produces a variety of small automobile components and sells them to auto manufacturers. It has a 40% market share, with the following condensed results expected for 2011:

Sales		$12,000,000
Cost of goods sold		
Variable	$4,000,000	
Fixed	4,300,000	8,300,000
Selling and administrative expenses		
Variable	$2,000,000	
Fixed	400,000	2,400,000
Operating income		$ 1,300,000

Installation of the CIM system will cost $6 million, and the company expects the system to have a useful life of 6 years with no salvage value. Installation will occur at the beginning of 2012. In 2012, the training costs for personnel will exceed any cost savings by $400,000. In years 2013–2017, variable cost of goods sold will decrease by 35%, an annual savings of $1.4 million. There will be no savings in fixed cost of goods sold—it will increase by the amount of the straight-line depreciation on the new system. Selling and administrative expenses will not be affected. The required rate of return is 12%. Assume that all cash flows occur at the end of the year the revenue or expense is recognized, except the initial investment, which occurs at the beginning of 2012. Ignore income taxes.

1. Suppose that Maria assumes that production and sales would continue for the next 6 years as they are expected in 2011 in the absence of investment in the CIM. Compute the NPV of investing in the CIM.
2. Now suppose Maria predicts that it will be difficult to compete without installing the CIM. She has undertaken market research that estimates a drop in market share of three percentage points a year starting in 2012 in the absence of investment in the CIM (i.e., market share will be 37% in 2012, 34% in 2013, 31% in 2014, etc.). Her study also showed that the total market sales level will stay the same, and she does not expect market prices to change. Compute the NPV of investing in the CIM.
3. Prepare a memo from Maria to the board of directors of Nashville Tool Company. In the memo, explain why the analysis in number 2 is appropriate and why analyses such as that in number 1 cause companies to under-invest in high-technology projects. Include an explanation of qualitative factors that are not included in the NPV calculation.

11-70 Investment in Quality

The Sydney Manufacturing Company produces a single model of a high-quality DVD player that it sells to Australian manufacturers of sound systems. It sells each DVD player for $210, resulting in a contribution margin of $70 before considering any costs of inspection, correction of product defects, or refunds to customers.

On January 1, 2011, top management at Sydney is contemplating a change in its quality control system. Currently, the company spends $30,000 annually on quality control inspections for the 50,000 DVD players it produces and ships each year. In producing those DVD players, the company produces an average of 2,000 defective units. The inspection process identifies 1,500 of these, and the company spends an average of $85 on each to correct the defects. The company ships the other 500 defective players to customers. When a customer discovers a defective DVD player, Sydney Manufacturing refunds the $210 purchase price.

Many of Sydney's customers build the DVDs into home-entertainment units. As more of these customers change to JIT inventory systems and automated production processes, the receipt of defective goods poses greater and greater problems for them. Sometimes a defective DVD player causes them to delay their whole production line while they replace the DVD player. Companies competing with Sydney recognize this situation, and most have already begun extensive quality control programs. If Sydney does not improve quality, sales volume is expected to fall by 5,000 DVD players a year, beginning after 2011:

	Predicted Sales Volume in Units Without Quality Control Program	Predicted Sales Volume in Units with Quality Control Program
2011	50,000	50,000
2012	45,000	50,000
2013	40,000	50,000
2014	35,000	50,000

The proposed quality control program has two elements. First, Sydney would spend $950,000 immediately to train workers to recognize and correct defects at the time they occur. This is expected to cut the number of defective DVD players produced from 2,000 to 500 without incurring additional manufacturing costs. Second, an earlier inspection point would replace the current inspection. This would require purchase of an X-ray machine at a cost of $250,000 plus additional annual operating costs of $60,000 more than the current inspection costs. Early detection of defects would reduce the average amount spent to correct defects from $85 to $50, and only 50 defective DVD players would be shipped to customers. To compete, Sydney would refund one-and-one-half times the purchase price ($315) for defective DVD players delivered to customers.

Top management at Sydney has decided that a 4-year planning period is sufficient for analyzing this decision. The minimum required rate of return is 20%. For simplicity, assume that under the current quality control system, if the volume of production decreases, the number of defective DVD players produced remains at 2,000. Also assume that all annual cash flows occur at the end of the relevant year. Should Sydney undertake the new quality control program? Explain, using the NPV model. Ignore income taxes.

11-71 Make or Buy and Replacement of Equipment

International Hoists is one of the largest producers of hoists of all types. An especially complex part of a particular auto hoist needs special tools that are not useful for other products. The company purchased these tools on July 1, 2006, for $2,000,000.

It is now July 1, 2010. The manager of the auto hoists division, David Lee, is contemplating three alternatives. First, he could continue to produce the ship using the current tools; they will last another 5 years, at which time they would have zero terminal value. Second, he could sell the tools for $400,000 and purchase the parts from an outside supplier for $110 each. Third, he could replace the tools with new, more efficient tools costing $1,800,000.

Lee expects to produce 8,000 units of this particular hoist each of the next 5 years. Manufacturing costs for the hoist have been as follows, and no change in costs is expected:

Direct materials	$ 38
Direct labor	37
Variable overhead	17
Fixed overhead*	45
Total unit cost	$137

*Depreciation accounts for two-thirds of the fixed overhead. The balance is for other fixed overhead costs of the factory that require cash outlays, 60% of which would be saved if production of the parts were eliminated.

The outside supplier offered the $110 price as a once-only offer. It is unlikely it would make such a low price available later. International Hoists would also have to guarantee to purchase at least 7,000 parts for each of the next 5 years.

The new tools that are available would last for 5 years with a disposal value of $500,000 at the end of 5 years. The old tools are a 5-year MACRS property, the new tools are a 3-year MACRS property, and both use the current MACRS schedules. International Hoists uses straight-line depreciation for book purposes and MACRS for tax purposes. The sales representative selling the new tools stated, "The new tools will allow direct labor and variable overhead to be reduced by $21 per unit." Lee thinks this estimate is accurate. However, she also knows that a higher quality of materials would be necessary with the new tools. She predicts the following costs with the new tools:

Direct materials	$ 40
Direct labor	25
Variable overhead	8
Fixed overhead	60*
Total unit cost	$133

*The increase in fixed overhead is caused by depreciation on the new tools.

The company has a 40% marginal tax rate and requires a 12% after-tax rate of return.

1. Calculate the NPV of each of the three alternatives. Recognize the tax implications. Which alternative should Lee select?
2. What are some factors besides the NPV that should influence Lee's selection?

NIKE 10-K PROBLEM

11-72 Nike Capital Budgeting with NPV

Examine Nike's financial statements and notes 1 and 3 to those statements in Appendix C.

1. What method of depreciation does Nike use in reporting to shareholders? Do you think it uses the same method for tax purposes? If not, what method do you suppose they use for tax reporting? Why?
2. What is the original cost of the machinery and equipment currently used by Nike? If Nike generally invests $400 million per year in machinery and equipment, what is the average useful life of its machinery and equipment?

3. Nike's Statement of Cash Flows shows that the company invested $449.2 million in machinery and equipment during fiscal 2008. Assume that these assets have a useful life of 5 years and that Nike requires a 14% pretax rate of return. Compute the minimum average annual pretax net cash inflow that would justify this investment.

4. Using the $449.2 million of investment and the net cash flow you computed in requirement 3 (and assuming zero residual value), determine the investment's a) payback period and b) accounting rate of return on average investment.

EXCEL APPLICATION EXERCISE

11-73 Net Present Value and Payback Period for a Purchase Decision

Goal: Create a spreadsheet to compute the NPV and payback period to assist with a purchase decision. Use the results to answer questions about your findings.

Scenario: Amazon.com is planning to purchase a new bar-coding machine for one of its warehouses. You have been asked to prepare a simple analysis to determine whether Amazon should purchase the machine. The bar-coding machine costs $60,000. It has a 5-year economic life and an estimated residual value of $10,000. The estimated annual net cash flow from the machine is $16,000. Amazon.com's required rate of return is 16%.

When you have completed your spreadsheet, answer the following questions:

1. What is the machine's NPV?
2. What is the machine's payback period?
3. Should Amazon.com purchase the machine? Why or why not?

Step-by-Step:

1. Open a new Excel spreadsheet.
2. In column A, create a bold-faced heading that contains the following:
   Row 1: Chapter 11 Decision Guideline
   Row 2: Amazon.com
   Row 3: Analysis for Purchase of Bar-Coding Machine
   Row 4: Today's Date
3. Merge and center the four heading rows across columns A–H.
4. In row 7, create the following bold-faced headings:
   Column A: Cash Outflow
   Column B: Calculations
   Column D: Annualized Cash Flows
5. Center the heading in column A, row 7 and then shade the heading as follows:

   Patterns tab: Color: Lightest gray (above white)

   Note: Adjust column width as necessary.

6. Merge and center the heading in column B, row 7 across columns B–C.
7. Merge and center the heading in column D, row 7 across columns D–H and shade the heading as follows:

   Patterns tab: Color: Lightest gray (above white)

8. In row 8, create the following bold-faced, center-justified column headings:
   Column A: Investment
   Column B: Net Present Value
   Column C: Payback Period
   Column D: Year 1
   Column E: Year 2
   Column F: Year 3
   Column G: Year 4
   Column H: Year 5

   Note: Adjust the width of columns B and C as necessary.

9. Use the scenario data to fill in the investment and annualized cash flows for each of the 5 years.

   Note: The amount in the Investment column should be entered as a negative amount because it represents cash outflow. Be sure to include the machine's residual value in the appropriate column when entering the Annualized Cash Flows data.

10. Use the NPV function to calculate the NPV of the machine in column B, row 9.
    Click Insert on the tool bar and select Function. Then do the following:

Function category:	Financial
Function name:	NPV

Complete the fill-in form that appears with the appropriate data from the scenario.

Hint: Go to "Help" and search the topic "NPV." Review the help text that appears. Carefully read the examples given and their associated formulas. Use the formula that matches the Scenario data for the problem.

11. Enter a formula to calculate the payback period in column C, row 9. Ensure a positive result by using the absolute value function in your payback formula. (The formula can be found in the chapter.)

12. Modify the format of the payback period result by clicking in the cell containing the results. At the end of the formula that appears in the formula bar, type the following: & "years". Right justify the result.

13. Format row 9, columns A–B and columns D–H as follows:

Number tab:	Category:	Currency
	Decimal places:	2
	Symbol:	$
	Negative numbers:	Red with parentheses

14. Save your work to disk, and print a copy for your files.

Note: Print your spreadsheet using landscape to ensure that all columns appear on one page.

COLLABORATIVE LEARNING EXERCISE

11-74 Capital Budgeting, Sensitivity Analysis, and Ethics

Abrielle Rossi had recently been appointed controller of the soup division of a major food company. The division manager, Asim Sharma, was known as a hard-driving, intelligent, uncompromising manager. He had been very successful and was rumored to be on the fast track to corporate top management, maybe even in line for the company presidency. One of Abrielle's first assignments was to prepare the financial analysis for a new soup, Delhi Chicken. This product was especially important to Sharma because he was convinced that it would be a success and thereby a springboard for his ascent to top management.

Rossi discussed the product with the food lab that had designed it, with the market research department that had tested it, and with the finance people who would have to fund its introduction. After putting together all the information, she developed the following optimistic and pessimistic sales projections:

	Optimistic	Pessimistic
Year 1	$ 1,600,000	$ 800,000
Year 2	3,600,000	1,200,000
Year 3	5,000,000	1,000,000
Year 4	8,000,000	800,000
Year 5	10,000,000	400,000

The optimistic predictions assume a successful introduction of a popular product. The pessimistic predictions assume that the product is introduced but does not gain wide acceptance and is terminated after 5 years. Rossi thinks the most likely results are halfway between the optimistic and pessimistic predictions.

Rossi learned from finance that this type of product introduction requires a predicted pretax rate of return of 16% before top management will authorize funds for its introduction. She also determined that the contribution margin should be about 50% on the product but could be as low as 42% or as high as 58%. Initial investment would include $3.5 million for production facilities and $2.5 million for advertising and other product introduction expenses. The production facilities would have a value of $1.2 million after 5 years.

Based on her preliminary analysis, Rossi recommended to Sharma that the product not be launched. Sharma was not pleased with the recommendation. He claimed that Rossi was much too pessimistic and asked her to redo her numbers so that he could justify the product to top management.

Rossi carried out further analysis, but her predictions came out no different. She became even more convinced that her projections were accurate. Yet, she was certain that if she returned to Sharma with numbers that did not support introduction of the product, she would incur his wrath. And he could be right—that is, there is so much uncertainty in the forecasts that she could easily come up with believable numbers that would support going forward with the product. She would not believe them, but she believed she could convince top management that they were accurate.

The entire class could role-play this scenario or it could be done in teams of three to six persons. Here, it is acted out by a team.

Choose one member of the team to be Abrielle Rossi and one to be Asim Sharma.

1. With the help of the entire team except the person chosen to be Sharma, Rossi should prepare the capital-budgeting analysis used for her first meeting with Sharma.
2. Next, Rossi should meet again with Sharma. They should try to agree on the analysis to take forward to top management. As they discuss the issues and try to come to an agreement, the remaining team members should record all the ethical judgments each discussant makes.
3. After Rossi and Sharma have completed their role-playing assignment, the entire team should assess the ethical judgments made by each and recommend an appropriate position for Rossi to take in this situation.

INTERNET EXERCISE

11-75 Capital Budgeting at Carnival Corporation

Many companies strive to continue to grow and develop. Some companies grow through the expansion of existing operations and increased utilization of existing assets. Others grow through the acquisition of firms within their industry or by purchasing a firm that opens up new direction for them. No matter which method a company selects, capital budgeting is an important part of a systematic expansion plan. Consider the expansion activities of **Carnival Corporation**, the cruise ship company.

1. Go to Carnival Corporation's home page at www.carnivalcorp.com. What cruise lines does Carnival own or have an interest in? Now go to the page "Corporate Information." How many current ships does Carnival operate? What type of plans does the firm list for future expansion? What does this information indicate about the intent of the firm?
2. As we can see, the firm has looked ahead to buying new ships. To get additional information, click on the link to "Investor Relations" and then "Financial Reports." Select the most recent annual report and open it. Go to the section on Highlights near the beginning of the report. Looking at passengers carried and passenger capacity, examine how capacity available and capacity used have changed over the past 4 years.
3. Now examine the CEO's letter. What does the letter tell the investor about new investment during the current year? What form did the investment/expansion take? What are the investment plans for the future?
4. While acquiring contracts for new ships and increasing ownership of other lines is noteworthy, the firm must in some manner plan to pay for this expansion. Let's look at the Statement of Cash Flows to see if we can determine where the firm got the cash to pay for the new ships. Based on your review of the cash flow statement, how much money did the firm invest in new assets? Where did Carnival generate these funds?

Solutions to Exercises in Compound Interest, Problem 11-A1

The general approach to these exercises centers on one fundamental question: Which of the two basic tables am I dealing with? No calculations should be made until after this question is answered with assurance. If you made any errors, it is possible that you used the wrong table.

1. From Table 1, Appendix B, page A6:
   a. $19,587.50
   b. $15,522.50
   c. $10,047.50
   The $25,000 is an amount of future worth. You want the PV of that amount:

$$PV = \$20,000 \times \frac{1}{[(1 + i)^n]}$$

The conversion factor, $1/(1 + i)^n$, is on line 5 of Table 1. Substituting,

$$PV = \$25,000(.7835) = \$19,587.50$$
$$PV = \$25,000(.6209) = \$15,522.50$$
$$PV = \$25,000(.4019) = \$10,047.50$$

Note that the higher the interest rate, the lower the PV.

2. From Table 2, Appendix B, page A9:
   a. $8,659.00
   b. $7,581.60
   c. $5,981.20

   The $2,000 withdrawal is a uniform annual amount, an annuity. You need to find the PV of an annuity for 5 years:

   $$PV_A = \text{annual withdrawal} \times F, \text{ where F is the conversion factor.}$$

   Substituting:
   $$PV_A = \$2,000(4.3295) = \$8,659.00$$
   $$PV_A = \$2,000(3.7908) = \$7,581.60$$
   $$PV_A = \$2,000(2.9906) = \$5,981.20$$

3. From Table 2:
   a. $46,194.71
   b. $52,759.31

   You have $100,000, the PV of your contemplated annuity. You must find the annuity that will just exhaust the invested principal in 5 years:

   $$PV_A = \text{annual withdrawal} \times F$$
   $$\$100,000 = \text{annual withdrawal} \times 4.3295$$
   $$\text{annual withrawal} = \$100,000 \div 4.3295$$
   $$= \$23,097.36$$
   $$\$100,000 = \text{annual withdrawal} \times 3.7908$$
   $$\text{annual withdrawal} = \$100,000 \div 3.7908$$
   $$= \$26,379.66$$

4. Amounts are in thousands. From Table 1: LeBron's contract is preferable; its PV exceeds that of Kobe's contract by $43,143 − $35,441 = $7,702. Note that the nearer dollars are more valuable than the distant dollars.

Year	Present Value at 16% from Table 1	Present Value of LeBron's Contract	Present Value Of Kobe's Contract
1	.8621	$17,242	$ 3,448
2	.7432	11,891	5,946
3	.6407	7,688	7,688
4	.5523	4,418	8,837
5	.4761	1,904	9,522
		$43,143	$35,441

CHAPTER 12

Cost Allocation

LEARNING OBJECTIVES

When you have finished studying this chapter, you should be able to:

1. Describe the general framework for cost allocation.

2. Allocate the variable and fixed costs of service departments to other organizational units.

3. Use the direct and step-down methods to allocate service department costs to user departments.

4. Allocate costs from producing departments to products or services using the traditional approach.

5. Allocate costs associated with customer actions to customers.

6. Allocate the central corporate costs of an organization.

7. Allocate joint costs to products using the physical-units and relative-sales-value methods.

▶ L.A. DARLING

Recall the last time you shopped in one of the following stores—**Wal-Mart**, **Kmart**, **Dollar General**, **Best Buy**, **Walgreens**, or **Payless ShoeSource**. Do you remember anything about the store fixtures? Chances are, the answer is no. Store fixtures such as shelving, counters, garment racks, and displays are an important part of the merchandising programs of retail stores, but not many people are aware of them when shopping. An industry leader in store fixtures is **L.A. Darling Company**, which designs and manufactures metal, wood, and wire display systems for retail stores worldwide. Darling is one of 125 business units that operate independently within the **Marmon Group**. Member companies have collective revenues of approximately $7 billion. The Marmon Group derives its name from the Marmon Wasp—the racing car built by an engineer of the **Marmon Motor Car Company** that won the very first Indianapolis 500 race in 1911.

Recently, when a major retailer undertook an aggressive growth program, it selected Darling to meet its fixturing needs. According to Ray Watson, former controller, "One of the advantages Darling offers companies is its large production capacity." But while this gives the company a competitive advantage, accounting for capacity costs, most of which are fixed manufacturing overhead, is a real challenge.

Should Darling allocate these fixed overhead costs to individual products or services when assessing their profitability? When estimating a customer's profitability? When evaluating a manager's performance? These are important questions for managers as well as for accountants.

Many managerial decisions require information about product or customer profitability. For example, a sales manager at L.A. Darling knows that some customers such as Wal-Mart require different kinds and amounts of Darling's resources than small specialty stores. The mix of products that Wal-Mart orders from Darling is vastly different from products ordered by specialty stores, as are the costs of ordering, shipping, and customer service. Fortunately, improvements in computer technology and cost-allocation techniques enable better measurements of both product (or service) and customer profitability.

Fixed cost allocations also can affect the evaluation of managers. Darling evaluates managers based partly on the income of the organizational segment they manage. Therefore, both accountants and managers are concerned with how the allocations affect segment income.

Just as is the case for Darling, cost allocation is of strategic importance to most businesses. For example, many faculty use a university's computer systems for both teaching and performing government-funded research. How much of the computer systems' costs should we assign to the research projects? Or consider a special Los Angeles police unit set up to investigate a series of related assaults. What is the total cost of the effort, including various support costs? Finally, suppose a company uses a machine to make two different product lines. How much of the cost of the machine should we assign to each product line? These are all problems of cost allocation, the subject of this chapter. ■

You might not recognize the name L. A. Darling, but you have seen its displays in many stores like this Kmart store in Manhattan.

A General Framework for Cost Allocation

As described in Chapter 4, cost-allocation methods comprise an important part of a company's cost accounting system—the techniques it uses to determine the cost of a product, service, customer, or other cost objects. Why? Because, for most companies, accountants can directly trace less than 60% of operating costs to products and services. For the rest of a company's costs, accountants must either apply cost-allocation methods or leave costs unallocated. Most managers prefer to allocate these costs rather than leaving them unallocated.

Because of the importance to all organizations of products, services, or customers as final cost objectives, we focus on how companies assign direct costs and indirect (allocated) costs to these cost objects. A recent survey of over 400 organizations worldwide reported that companies trace or allocate a majority of costs in all value-chain functions to products or customers:[1]

Objective 1

Describe the general framework for cost allocation.

Value Chain Function	Percent of Costs Traced or Allocated to Products or Customers
Research and development	60%
Design	70%
Production	94%
Sales and marketing	68%
Distribution	79%
Customer service	67%
Corporate Support	70%

Of course, this also shows that, in all functions other than production, significant costs remain unassigned to products or customers.

Companies must assign all production costs and only production costs to products for external financial reporting purposes. They can elect to assign or not assign all other costs for internal management purposes. The significant percentages of unassigned costs reflect the difficulty and cost of developing useful allocation systems across the value chain. Still, most companies trace or allocate most value-chain costs to final cost objects. After developing a general framework for allocation, we will take a careful look at how allocation systems are developed and used.

We will use the framework in Exhibit 12-1 to show how cost allocation fits into the overall cost accounting system. Each of the arrows in Exhibit 12-1 represents an assignment of some costs to a cost objective. We show four types of cost objectives—service departments, producing departments, products/services, and customers. The cost accounting system first accumulates costs and assigns them to organizational units. We will call each unit a department. There are two

---

[1]W. Stratton, D. Desroches, R. Lawson, and T. Hatch "Activity-Based Costing—Is It Still Relevant?" *Management Accounting Quarterly*, Spring 2009, Vol. 10, No. 3, pp. 31–40.

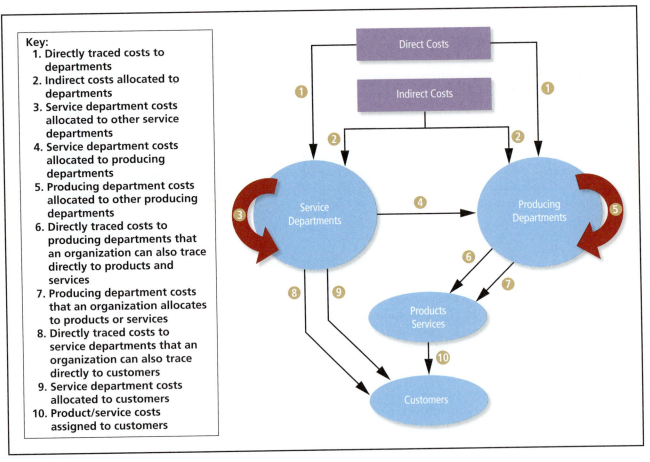

Key:
1. Directly traced costs to departments
2. Indirect costs allocated to departments
3. Service department costs allocated to other service departments
4. Service department costs allocated to producing departments
5. Producing department costs allocated to other producing departments
6. Directly traced costs to producing departments that an organization can also trace directly to products and services
7. Producing department costs that an organization allocates to products or services
8. Directly traced costs to service departments that an organization can also trace directly to customers
9. Service department costs allocated to customers
10. Product/service costs assigned to customers

Exhibit 12-1
Framework for Cost Accounting Systems

types of departments: (1) **producing departments**, where employees work on the organization's products or services, and (2) **service departments**, which exist only to support other departments or customers. Examples of service departments are personnel departments, laundry departments in hospitals, technical support centers, and facility management departments.[2] We can trace the *direct* costs to each department, shown by the arrows labeled 1. In contrast, we have to *allocate* the *indirect* costs, such as rent for facilities used by more than one department. We label these allocations as 2 in Exhibit 12-1.

Assume that a company has now assigned resource costs 1 and 2 to producing and service departments. Suppose some service departments provide services to other service departments. An example is personnel services provided to employees in the facilities maintenance department. Arrow 3 represents the allocation of these costs. After assignments 1, 2, and 3 have been made, managers can evaluate the performance of each service department.

To evaluate the costs of resources used in producing departments such as machine processing, installation, or assembly, many companies develop allocation methods to assign service department costs to the producing departments. Why? The reason is that managers want to know total costs, both producing-department costs and the costs of using resources from other departments. We show these assignments as 4 in Exhibit 12-1. Sometimes, producing departments transfer items to other producing departments as well as producing products or services. For example, a producing department may process a chemical resulting in several finished products and several products that need to be processed further. We transfer the costs of products that need further processing to other producing departments—labeled as 5 in Exhibit 12-1. Notice that direct service department costs—labeled as 1—become indirect costs to the producing department when they

---

[2]There are some costs associated with general (or central) support that we do not consider service department costs. Examples of these are public relations and corporate planning. We will discuss how these central costs are treated later in the chapter

are part of allocation 4. For example, the salaries of human resources personnel are a direct departmental cost for the human resources department. However, when we allocate these costs, along with all other human resource department costs, to producing departments, they become indirect to the producing department.

At this point, we have accumulated service department and producing department costs into the producing departments. The next step is to assign costs to products or services. There are significant producing department costs that are directly traceable to products and services. We indicate these costs as 6; examples are direct materials and direct labor. The other producing department costs are allocated to products and services, labeled as 7 in Exhibit 12-1. Again, because we have changed the cost objectives, some costs that were directly traceable to the producing departments will be indirect when the cost objective is the various products or services; examples include salaries of production supervisors, supplies, and most equipment costs.

All organizations accumulate product- or service-related costs for their products or services. They must do so for financial reporting purposes. Many organizations also accumulated and allocate other value-chain costs. So tracing and allocating costs as shown in arrows 1–7 are common to all organizations. However, an increasing number of organizations also choose to measure and manage the costs and profitability of their customers. Arrows 8–10 demonstrate how they do this.

Some service department activities support customers rather than the production process; examples include order processing and customer service activities. Therefore, we assign the costs of such services to customers rather than to the producing departments. We can trace some of these costs directly to customers—labeled 8 in Exhibit 12-1. Examples are sales commissions and dedicated customer support, such as presales negotiation. We then allocate the other customer-related services, such as order processing—arrow 9 in Exhibit 12-1. The last step shown in Exhibit 12-1 is to assign the cost of products or services to customers who purchase them. After this last assignment, a company can determine customer profitability by subtracting costs 8, 9, and 10 from customer revenue.

Why is it important to directly trace and allocate customer-related service department costs to customers (8 and 9 in Exhibit 12-1) rather than assigning them first to producing departments and then to customers? If we assigned these costs to producing departments and then to products, the allocation to products would be based on production-related output measures that may have little relationship to the cause of customer-service costs. This would cause cost distortions to both the product and customer cost objectives.

Each department will generally trace or allocate most of its direct and indirect costs to its outputs, although it might leave some costs unallocated if there is no logical basis for allocating them. Tracing or allocating these costs requires accountants to identify and measure a department's output (to which it will trace or allocate costs) and determine the cost-allocation base for the indirect costs. For example, the pediatrics department of a medical clinic might allocate its indirect costs to patients based on physician time per patient. Or the assembly activity of a manufacturing firm might allocate costs to units assembled based on machine hours used. Or the tax department of a CPA firm might allocate costs to clients based on professional hours spent.

As indicated in Chapter 4, we would like to use a cost driver as a cost-allocation base because of the driver's logical, cause-and-effect relationship to costs. For example, a logical cost-allocation base for allocating building rent costs to departments is the square feet that each department occupies. Other logical cost-allocation bases include cubic feet for allocating depreciation of heating and air conditioning equipment and total direct cost for allocating general administrative expense. Accountants use many different terms to describe cost allocation in practice. As indicated in Chapter 4, terms such as *allocate, apply, absorb, attribute, reallocate, trace, assign, distribute, redistribute, load, burden, apportion,* and *reapportion* are used interchangeably to describe the allocation of costs to cost objectives.

Some individual indirect costs are important enough that we allocate them using obvious cost-allocation bases. For example, we would allocate the cost of professional labor for a law firm to departments, jobs, and projects using labor hours used. We pool the other costs that are not important enough to justify being allocated individually and allocate them together. Recall that a cost pool is a group of individual costs that we allocate to cost objectives using a single cost-allocation base. For example, building rent, utilities cost, and janitorial services may be in the same cost pool because a company allocates all of them on the basis of square footage of space occupied; or a university could pool all the operating costs of its registrar's office and allocate them to its colleges on the basis of the number of students in each college.

The next section looks in detail at allocation of service department costs, and the following sections focus on allocation to products or services and to customers.

Allocation of Service Department Costs

In our general framework shown in Exhibit 12-1, service department allocations are labeled as 3, 4, and 9. Before discussing methods of allocation, we give some general guidelines that managers should consider when designing allocation systems.

General Guidelines

The preferred guidelines for allocating service department costs are as follows:

1. Establish part or all of the details regarding cost allocation in advance of rendering the service rather than after the fact. This approach establishes the "rules of the game" so that all departments can plan appropriately.
2. Allocate variable- and fixed-cost pools separately. Note that one service department (such as a computer department) can contain multiple cost pools if more than one cost driver causes the department's costs. At a minimum, there should be a variable-cost pool and a fixed-cost pool.
3. Evaluate performance using budgets for each service (staff) department, just as for each production or operating (line) department. Managers should evaluate the performance of a service department by comparing actual costs with a budget, regardless of how the company allocates costs. From the budget, variable-cost pools and fixed-cost pools can be identified for use in allocation.

Consider an example of a computer department of a university that serves two major users, the school of business and the school of engineering. Exhibit 12-2 shows the allocation system for this service department. Suppose there are two major reasons for the allocation: (1) predicting economic effects of the use of the computer, and (2) motivating the individuals in the two schools to use its capabilities more fully. How should the university allocate the costs of the computer department (salaries, depreciation, energy, materials, and so on) to the two schools?

We begin by analyzing the costs of the computer department in detail. The primary activity performed is computer processing. The university acquired the computer mainframe on a 5-year lease that is not cancelable unless it pays huge penalties. Resources consumed include processing time, operator time, energy, materials, and building space. Suppose the university performed cost-behavior analysis and determined the budget formula for the forthcoming year is $100,000 monthly fixed cost plus $200 variable cost per hour of computer time used. Refer to Exhibit 12-2 as we show how to apply guideline 2—the topic of the next two sections.

Variable-Cost Pool

Costs in the variable-cost pool include energy, operator labor costs, and materials. The cost-allocation base for the variable-cost pool is actual hours of computer time used. Therefore, the university should allocate variable costs as follows:

$$\text{budgeted unit rate} \times \text{actual hours of computer time used}$$

The cause-and-effect relationship is clear: The heavier the usage, the higher the total costs. In this example, the budgeted cost-allocation rate is $200 per hour, determined by dividing the total budgeted costs of energy, operators, and materials by the total budgeted hours of computer time.

The use of budgeted cost rates rather than actual cost rates for allocating variable costs of service departments protects the user departments from intervening price fluctuations and also often protects them from inefficiencies in the service departments. When an organization allocates *actual* total service department cost, it holds user department managers responsible for costs beyond their control and provides less incentive for service departments to be efficient. Both effects are undesirable.

Consider the allocation of variable costs to a department that uses 600 hours of computer time. Suppose inefficiencies in the computer department caused the variable costs to be $140,000 instead of the 600 hours × $200 = $120,000 budgeted. A good cost-allocation scheme

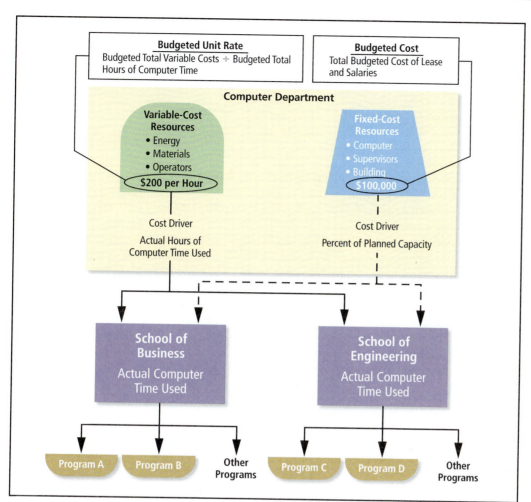

Exhibit 12-2
Allocation of Variable- and
Fixed-Cost Pools

would allocate only the $120,000 to the consuming departments and would let the $20,000 remain as an unallocated unfavorable budget variance of the computer department. This scheme holds computer department managers responsible for the $20,000 variance and reduces the resentment of user managers. User department managers sometimes complain more vigorously about uncertainty over allocations and the poor management of a service department than about the choice of a cost-allocation base (such as direct-labor dollars or number of employees). Such complaints are less likely if the service department managers have budget responsibility and the user departments are protected from short-run price fluctuations and inefficiencies.

Consider an automobile repair and maintenance department for a state government. Agencies that use the department's service should receive firm prices for various services. Imagine the feelings of an agency head who had an agency automobile repaired and was told, "Normally, your repair would have taken 5 hours. However, we had a new employee work on it, and the job took him 10 hours. Therefore, we must charge you for 10 hours of labor time."

Fixed-Cost Pool

Consider again our example of the university computer department. Costs in the fixed-cost pool include the lease payment on the computers, salaries of managers and supervisors, and building occupancy costs (depreciation, insurance, and so on). The cost-allocation base for the fixed-cost pool is the predicted amount of capacity needed by the two schools when the university acquired the computer facilities, measured in monthly hours of usage. Therefore, fixed costs are allocated as follows:

$$\text{predicted percent of capacity needed} \times \text{total budgeted fixed costs}$$

Suppose the deans had originally predicted the long-run average monthly usage by the school of business at 210 hours, and by the school of engineering at 490 hours, a total of 700 hours. These estimates resulted in a set of committed fixed costs that remain largely uncontrollable over many years. We should allocate the fixed-cost pool as follows:

	Business	Engineering
Fixed costs per month		
210/700, or 30% of $100,000	$30,000	
490/700, or 70% of $100,000		$70,000

This predetermined lump-sum approach is based on the long-run capacity available to the user, regardless of actual usage from month to month. The reasoning is that long-range planning regarding the expected required overall level of service affects the level of fixed costs, not short-run fluctuations in actual usage.

A major strength of using capacity available rather than capacity used when allocating budgeted fixed costs is that actual usage by user departments does not affect the short-run allocations to other user departments. Such a budgeted lump-sum approach is more likely to have the desired motivational effects with respect to the ordering of services in both the short run and the long run.

In practice, companies often inappropriately allocate fixed-cost pools on the basis of capacity used, not capacity available. Suppose for 2 successive months the computer department's actual fixed costs were exactly the $100,000 budgeted. The university allocated these costs based on actual hours used by the consuming departments. Compare the costs borne by the two schools in the first month when business uses 200 hours and engineering 400 hours.

Total fixed costs incurred, $100,000	
Business: 200/600 × $100,000 =	$ 33,333
Engineering: 400/600 × $100,000 =	66,667
Total cost allocated	$100,000

What happens if business uses only 100 hours during the following month, and engineering still uses 400 hours?

Total fixed costs incurred, $100,000	
Business: 100/500 × $100,000 =	$ 20,000
Engineering: 400/500 × $100,000 =	80,000
Total cost allocated	$100,000

Engineering's usage was unchanged, but it must bear an additional cost of $13,333, an increase of 20%. Its short-run costs depend on what other consumers have used, not solely on its own actions. This phenomenon is caused by a faulty allocation method for the fixed portion of total costs, a method whereby the allocations are highly sensitive to fluctuations in the actual volumes used by the various consuming departments. We can avoid this weakness by using a predetermined lump-sum allocation of fixed costs based on budgeted usage.

Consider the preceding automobile repair shop example. You would not be happy if you came to get your car and were told, "Our daily fixed overhead is $1,000. Yours was the only car in our shop today, so we are charging you the full $1,000. If we had processed 100 cars today, your charge would have been only $10."

Trouble with Using Lump Sums

Using lump-sum allocations is not without problems, however. If a company allocates fixed costs on the basis of long-range plans, there is a natural tendency on the part of managers to underestimate their planned usage and thus obtain a smaller fraction of the cost allocation. Top management can counteract these tendencies by monitoring predictions and by following up and using feedback to keep future predictions more honest.

In some organizations, there are even definite rewards in the form of salary increases for managers who make accurate predictions. Moreover, some cost-allocation methods provide for penalties for underpredictions. For example, suppose a manager predicts usage of 210 hours and then demands 300 hours. The manager either doesn't get the hours or pays a dear price for every hour beyond 210 in such systems.

Allocating Service Department Costs to Producing Departments

Recall from Exhibit 12-1 on page 474 that assignment type 4 is allocating service department costs to producing departments. We now explore methods commonly used for this type of allocation. Suppose one of **L.A. Darling**'s display facilities assembles parts into custom and standard displays that Darling sells to **Wal-Mart**, **Target**, and **Walgreens**. Exhibit 12-3 is a process map for the facility. There are two producing departments, processing and assembly. There are also two service departments, facilities management (rent, power, insurance, janitorial services, and some corporate resources such as administration and engineering) and human resources. In this section of the chapter, we focus on the processing and assembly departments as cost objectives. Let's assume that a single plausible and reliable cost driver serves as a cost-allocation base for each service department and that all resource costs vary in proportion to this cost driver—that is, these are variable-cost resources. Managers have determined that the cost driver for facilities management costs is the square footage occupied and the cost driver for human resources costs is the number of employees. Exhibit 12-3 shows the direct costs for a recent month when the company produced 200 custom and 1,200 standard displays. Exhibit 12-3 shows the square footage occupied and number of employees for each department. Note that facilities management provides services for the human resources department in addition to providing services for the producing departments, and that human resources aids employees in facilities management as well as those in production departments.

There are two popular methods for allocating service department costs to producing departments in such cases: the direct method and the step-down method.

DIRECT METHOD   The **direct method** ignores other service departments when allocating any given service department's costs to the producing departments. In other words, the direct method ignores the services that facilities management provides for human resources and the services

Objective 3

Use the direct and step-down methods to allocate service department costs to user departments.

Exhibit 12-3

L.A. Darling's Processing Facility: Service Department Allocation

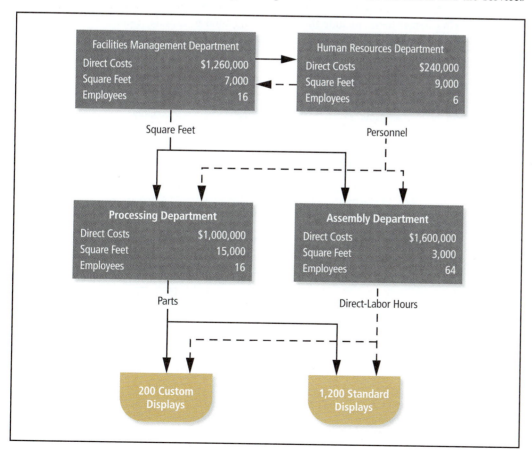

that human resources provides to facilities management. The direct method allocates facilities management costs based on the relative square footage occupied by the processing and assembly departments only.

- Total square footage in producing departments = 15,000 + 3,000 = 18,000
- Facilities management cost allocated to processing department = (15,000 ÷ 18,000) × $1,260,000 = $1,050,000
- Facilities management cost allocated to assembly department = (3,000 ÷ 18,000) × $1,260,000 = $210,000

Likewise, human resources department costs are allocated only to the producing departments on the basis of the relative number of employees in the producing departments.

- Total employees in producing departments = 16 + 64 = 80
- Human resources costs allocated to processing department = (16 ÷ 80) × $240,000 = $48,000
- Human resources costs allocated to assembly department = (64 ÷ 80) × $240,000 = $192,000

STEP-DOWN METHOD   The **step-down method** recognizes that some service departments support the activities in other service departments as well as those in producing departments. To apply the step-down method, we choose a sequence of service department allocations, starting with the service department that renders the greatest service (as measured by costs) to the greatest number of other service departments. The last service department in the sequence is the one that renders the least service to the least number of other service departments. We allocate the costs of one service department at a time, assigning the costs to the producing departments and to the remaining service departments. Once we allocate a department's costs to other departments, we never allocate other service department costs back to it.

In our example, we allocate facilities management department costs first. Why? Because facilities management renders more support to human resources than human resources provides to facilities management.[3] Examine Exhibit 12-4. After allocating facilities management costs, we do not allocate any costs back to facilities management, even though human resources does provide some services to facilities management. The $660,000 human resources costs allocated to the producing departments include the amount allocated to human resources from facilities management ($420,000) in addition to the direct human resources department costs of $240,000.

	Facilities Management	Human Resources	Processing	Assembly	Total
Direct department costs before allocation	$ 1,260,000	$ 240,000	$1,000,000	$1,600,000	$4,100,000
Step 1 Facilities Management	$(1,260,000)	(9 ÷ 27) × $1,260,000 = $ 420,000	(15 ÷ 27) × $1,260,000 = $ 700,000	(3 ÷ 27) × $1,260,000 = $ 140,000	
Step 2 Human Resources		$ (660,000)	(16 ÷ 80) × $ 660,000 = $ 132,000	(64 ÷ 80) × $ 660,000 = $ 528,000	
Total cost after allocation	$ 0	$ 0	$1,832,000	$2,268,000	$4,100,000

Exhibit 12-4
Step-Down Allocation

[3]How should we determine which of the two service departments provides more service to the other? One way is to carry out step 1 of the step-down method with facilities management allocated first, and then repeat it assuming personnel is allocated first. With facilities management allocated first, $420,000 is allocated to human resources, as shown in Exhibit 12-4. If human resources had been allocated first, (16 ÷ 96) × $240,000 = $40,000 would have been allocated to facilities management. Because $40,000 is smaller than $420,000, facilities management is allocated first.

Examine the last column of Exhibit 12-4. Before allocation, the four departments incurred costs of $4,100,000. In step 1, we deducted $1,260,000 from facilities management and added it to the other three departments. There was no net effect on the total cost. In step 2, we deducted $660,000 from human resources and added it to the remaining two departments. Again, total cost was unaffected. After allocation, all $4,100,000 remains, but it is all in the processing and assembly departments. None was left in facilities management or human resources.

COMPARISON OF THE METHODS   Compare the costs of the producing departments under direct and step-down methods, as shown in Exhibit 12-5. Note that the method of allocation can greatly affect the costs. Processing appears to be a more expensive operation to a manager using the direct method than it does to one using the step-down method. Conversely, assembly seems more expensive to a manager using the step-down method.

Which method is better? Generally, the step-down method.[4] Why? Because it recognizes the effects of the most significant support provided by service departments to other service departments. The greatest virtue of the direct method is its simplicity. If the two methods do not produce significantly different results, many companies elect to use the direct method because it is easier for managers to understand.

COSTS NOT RELATED TO COST DRIVERS   Our example illustrating direct and step-down allocation methods assumed that we could use a single cost driver as a cost-allocation base for all costs in a given service department. For example, we assumed that we could use square footage occupied to allocate all facilities management costs. But what if some of the costs in facilities management do not vary proportionately to the cost-driver square footage? For example, rent often consists of a single sum for the entire plant for a period of time. Another example occurs when the contract for an outside company to perform janitorial services specifies a fixed monthly charge plus an additional charge based on the square feet maintained.

We suggest two guidelines that are helpful in situations where costs are not related to cost drivers:

1. Identify additional cost drivers. Divide facilities management costs into two or more different cost pools and use a different cost-allocation base to allocate the costs in each pool. For example, rent and insurance costs often are fixed but we can allocate them using square footage occupied by the various service departments. Power costs are mostly variable and we can allocate them using a driver such as megawatt hours. The cost of janitorial services as described previously is a mixed cost. The allocation of the variable portion of janitorial services should be allocated based on the same measure used for billing—square feet maintained, for example. The fixed portion may not have a plausible or reliable cost driver and thus might remain unallocated.
2. Allocate all costs by the direct or step-down method using square footage as the cost-allocation base. In this alternative, we implicitly assume that, in the long run, square footage causes all facilities management costs—even if we cannot easily identify a short-term causal

	Processing		Assembly	
	Direct	**Step-Down***	**Direct**	**Step-Down***
Direct costs	$1,000,000	$1,000,000	$1,600,000	$1,600,000
Allocated from				
facilities management	1,050,000	700,000	210,000	140,000
Allocated from personnel	48,000	132,000	192,000	528,000
Total costs	$2,098,000	$1,832,000	$2,002,000	$2,268,000

*From Exhibit 12-4.

Exhibit 12-5
Direct Versus Step-Down Method

---

[4]The most defensible theoretical accuracy is generated by the reciprocal cost method, which is rarely used in practice because it is more difficult to understand. The method uses simultaneous equations and linear algebra to solve for the impact of mutually interacting services.

relationship. In other words, the need for more square footage may not cause an immediate increase in all facilities management costs, but eventually management will need to provide more space so the costs will increase.

Making Managerial Decisions

Suppose you are on a cross-functional team that is discussing how to allocate the costs of a purchasing department. One team member suggested that "number of purchase orders issued" is the best cost driver to use as a cost-allocation base. However, a scatter graph of total costs versus number of purchase orders issued shows the following:

discovered that a significant amount of work of the purchasing department was certifying new vendors in addition to issuing purchase orders. What alternative method of allocation would you recommend?

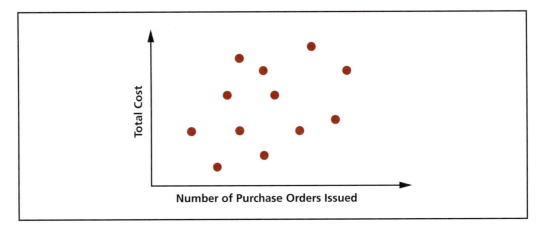

Because the data clearly indicate that the single cost driver "number of purchase orders issued" is not a reliable measure of the work done in the department (because there is too much scatter in the data), the team investigated further. It

Answer

Because a large percentage of the work of the purchasing department is not related to the single cost driver "number of purchase orders," the team should use a second cost pool with another cost-allocation base, such as "number of new vendors."

Allocation of Costs to Product or Service Cost Objects

After the allocation of service department costs, we have all production-related costs residing in the producing departments. All that remains is to allocate those costs to the product or service cost objects. Examples of such cost objects are products such as automobiles, furniture, and newspapers, and services such as bank accounts, patient visits, and student credit hours. Some accountants use the term **cost application** for the allocation of total departmental costs to the revenue-producing products or services.

A Traditional Approach

Objective 4

Allocate costs from producing departments to products or services using the traditional approach.

The traditional approach to cost allocation is as follows:

1. Divide the costs in each producing department, including both the direct department costs and all the costs allocated to it, into two categories: (1) the direct costs that you can physically trace to the product or service cost objectives and (2) the remainder, the indirect costs.
2. Trace the direct costs to the appropriate products or services. Note that some costs that are direct to the department will be indirect to the product or service cost objectives—for example, depreciation on the department's equipment.
3. Select cost pools and related cost-allocation bases in each production department, and assign all the indirect departmental costs to the appropriate cost pool. For example, you might assign a portion of the indirect departmental costs on the basis of direct-labor hours,

another portion on the basis of machine hours, and the remainder on the basis of number of parts. Be sure to use separate cost pools for fixed and variable costs.

4. Allocate (apply) the costs in each cost pool to the products or services in proportion to their usage of the related cost-allocation base. Apply variable costs on the basis of the actual amount of the cost-allocation base. Apply fixed costs on the basis of the budgeted amount of the cost-allocation base.

Consider our example of the **L.A. Darling** display facility. Exhibit 12-6 shows the process map for the facility assuming that the facility uses the step-down method for allocating service department costs. We now shift our focus from the two operating departments as cost objectives to the two types of displays—the products manufactured by the L.A. Darling display facility.

The first step is to determine the operating department costs that we can directly trace to displays. Of the $1,832,000 total costs in the processing department, we can trace the $800,000 cost of parts to custom and standard displays, as shown in Exhibit 12-6. Similarly, of the $2,268,000 total costs in the assembly department, we can directly trace the $200,000 of wages for direct labor to displays. The remaining resources and allocated costs from service departments are indirect costs with respect to the displays, and we will assume they are fixed-cost resources. Why is there no direct labor in the processing department? Because this is a machine intensive department with only indirect labor maintaining the machines.

In step 2, we trace the direct costs to the two display types as shown in Exhibit 12-6. Compare the processing department costs in Exhibits 12-3 and 12-6. How did $1,000,000 in direct processing department costs in Exhibit 12-3 decrease to only $800,000 direct costs in

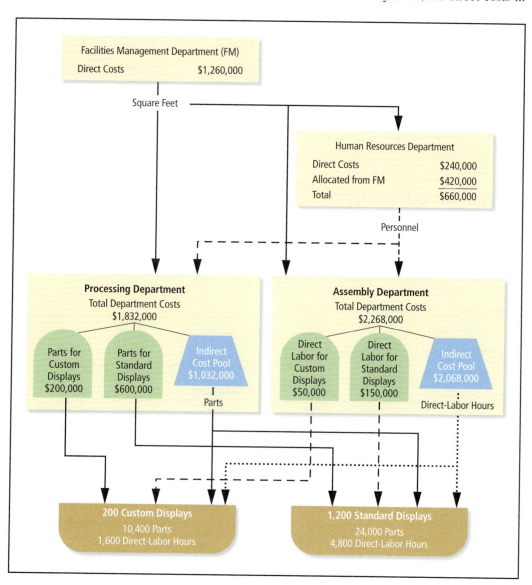

Exhibit 12-6

L.A. Darling's Display Facility: Allocation to Cost Objects Using Traditional Approach and Step-Down Allocation Method

Exhibit 12-6? The answer lies in our change in cost objectives. When we were interested only in determining the cost of the processing department, $200,000 of costs such as depreciation on department equipment and costs of supervisors were wholly in support of the department—a single cost object—and did not need to be allocated. When we changed the cost objective to the two displays, these resources became shared. Since we could find no economically feasible way to trace their use directly, we need to allocate their costs.

Next, in step 3, we select cost pools and related cost-allocation bases for the indirect costs of each department. We assign the remaining $1,032,000 of indirect costs in the processing department to one fixed-cost pool with budgeted number of parts as the cost-allocation base. Similarly, we assign all the remaining $2,068,000 indirect costs in the assembly department to one fixed-cost pool with budgeted direct-labor hours as the cost-allocation base.

Therefore, we allocate indirect departmental costs to the displays as follows:

$$\text{Processing: } \$1,032,000 \div (10,400 + 24,000) \text{ parts} = \$30.00 \text{ per part}$$
$$\text{Assembly: } \$2,068,000 \div (1,600 + 4,800) \text{ direct-labor hours}$$
$$= \$323.125 \text{ per direct-labor hour}$$

The total and unit costs of making 200 custom and 1,200 standard displays are as follows:

	200 Custom Displays		1,200 Standard Displays	
	Total	Unit	Total	Unit
Parts	$ 200,000	$1,000.00	$ 600,000	$ 500.00
Direct labor	50,000	250.00	150,000	125.00
Indirect costs—processing department	312,000*	1,560.00	720,000†	600.00
Indirect costs—assembly department	517,000‡	2,585.00	1,551,000§	1,292.50
	$1,079,000	$5,395.00	$3,021,000	$2,517.50

*$30.00 × 10,400 parts
†$30.00 × 24,000 parts
‡$323.125 × 1,600 direct-labor hours
§$323.125 × 4,800 direct-labor hours

Summary Problem for Your Review

PROBLEM

Nonmanufacturing organizations often find it useful to allocate costs to products or services. Consider a hospital. The output of a hospital is not as easy to define as the output of a factory. Assume the following measures of output in three revenue-producing departments:

Department	Measures of Output*
Radiology	X-ray films processed
Laboratory	Tests administered
Daily patient services†	Patient-days of care (i.e., the number of patients multiplied by the number of days of each patient's stay)

*These become the "product" cost objectives, the various revenue-producing activities of a hospital.

†There would be many of these departments, such as obstetrics, pediatrics, and orthopedics. Moreover, there may be both inpatient and outpatient care.

Budgeted output for 20X7 is 60,000 X-ray films processed in radiology, 50,000 tests administered in the laboratory, and 30,000 patient-days in daily patient services.

In addition to the revenue-producing departments, the hospital has three service departments: administrative and fiscal services, plant operations and maintenance, and laundry. (Real hospitals have more than three revenue-producing departments and more than three service departments. This problem is simplified to keep the data manageable.)

The hospital has decided that the cost-allocation base for administrative and fiscal services costs is the direct department costs of the other departments. The cost-allocation base for plant operations and maintenance is square feet occupied, and for laundry is pounds of laundry. The pertinent budget data for 20X7 are as follows:

	Direct Department Costs	Square Feet Occupied	Pounds of Laundry
Administrative and fiscal services	$1,000,000	1,000	—
Plant operations and maintenance	800,000	2,000	—
Laundry	200,000	5,000	—
Radiology	1,000,000	12,000	80,000
Laboratory	400,000	3,000	20,000
Daily patient services	1,600,000	80,000	300,000
Total	$5,000,000	103,000	400,000

1. Allocate service department costs using the direct method.
2. Allocate service department costs using the step-down method. Allocate administrative and fiscal services first, plant operations and maintenance second, and laundry third.
3. Compute the cost per unit of output in each of the revenue-producing departments using (a) the costs determined using the direct method for allocating service department costs (number 1) and (b) the costs determined using the step-down method for allocating service department costs (number 2).

SOLUTION

1. Exhibit 12-7 shows the solutions to all three problems. We present the direct method first. Note that we did not allocate service department costs to another service department. Therefore, we base allocations on the relative amounts of the cost-allocation base in the revenue-producing department only. For example, in allocating plant operations and maintenance, we ignore square footage occupied by the service departments. The cost-allocation base is the 95,000 square feet occupied by the revenue-producing departments.

   Note that the total cost of the revenue-producing departments after allocation, $1,474,386 + $568,596 + $2,957,018 = $5,000,000, is equal to the total of the direct department costs in all six departments before allocation.

2. The lower half of Exhibit 12-7 shows the step-down method. We allocate the costs of administrative and fiscal services to all five other departments. Because we do not allocate a department's own costs to itself, the cost-allocation base consists of the $4,000,000 direct department costs in the five departments excluding administrative and fiscal services. We allocate plant operations and maintenance second on the basis of square feet occupied. We allocate no cost to the department itself or back to administrative and fiscal services. Therefore, the square footage used for allocation is the 100,000 square feet occupied by the other four departments.

   We allocate laundry third. We do not allocate cost back to the first two departments, even if they had used laundry services.

   As in the direct method, note that the total costs of the revenue-producing departments after allocation, $1,430,000 + $545,000 + $3,025,000 = $5,000,000, equals the total of the direct department costs before allocation.

3. We label the solutions 3a and 3b in Exhibit 12-7. Compare the unit costs derived from the direct method with those of the step-down method. In many instances, the product costs may not differ enough to warrant investing in a cost-allocation method that is any fancier than the direct method. But sometimes even small differences may be significant to a government agency or anybody paying for a large volume of services based on costs. For example, in Exhibit 12-7 the "cost" of an "average" laboratory test is either $11.37 or $10.90. This may be significant for the fiscal committee of the hospital's board of trustees, who must decide on hospital prices. Thus, cost allocation often is a technique that helps answer the vital question, "Who should pay for what, and how much?"

Allocation Base	Administrative and Fiscal Services — Accumulated Costs	Plant Operations and Maintenance — Sq. Footage	Laundry — Pounds	Radiology	Laboratory	Daily Patient Services
1. Direct method:						
Direct departmental costs before allocation	$ 1,000,000	$ 800,000	$ 200,000	$1,000,000	$400,000	$1,600,000
Administrative and fiscal services	(1,000,000)	—	—	333,333*	133,333	533,334
Plant operations and maintenance		(800,000)		101,053†	25,263	673,684
Laundry			(200,000)	40,000‡	10,000	150,000
Total costs after allocation				$1,474,386	$568,596	$2,957,018
Product output in films, tests, and patient-days, respectively				60,000	50,000	30,000
3a. Cost per unit of output				$24.573	$11.372	$98.567
2. Step-down method:						
Direct departmental costs before allocation	$ 1,000,000	$ 800,000	$ 200,000	$1,000,000	$400,000	$1,600,000
Administrative and fiscal services	(1,000,000)	200,000§	50,000	250,000	100,000	400,000
Plant operations and maintenance		(1,000,000)	50,000‖	120,000	30,000	800,000
Laundry			(300,000)	60,000#	15,000	225,000
Total costs after allocation				$1,430,000	$545,000	$3,025,000
Product output in films, tests, and patient-days, respectively				60,000	50,000	30,000
3b. Cost per unit of output				$23.833	$10.900	$100.833

*$1,000,000 ÷ (1,000,000 + 400,000 + 1,600,000) = $.33, 1/3 × 1,000,000 = $333,333; and so on.

†$800,000 ÷ (12,000 + 3,000 + 80,000) = $8.4210526; $8.4210526 × 12,000 sq. ft. = $101,053; and so on.

‡$200,000 × (80,000 + 20,000 + 300,000) = $.50; $.50 × 80,000 = $40,000; and so on.

§$1,000,000 ÷ (800,000 + 200,000 + 1,000,000 + 400,000 +1,600,000) = $.25; .25 × 800,000 = $200,000; and so on.

‖$1,000,000 × (5,000 + 12,000 + 3,000 + 80,000) = $10.00; $10.00 × 5,000 sq. ft. = $50,000; and so on.

#$300,000 ÷ (80,000 + 20,000 + 300,000) = $.75; $.75 × 80,000 = $60,000; and so on.

Exhibit 12-7

Allocation of Service Department Costs: Direct and Step-Down Methods

An ABC Approach

The traditional approach to cost allocation focuses on accumulating and reporting costs by department. In the last couple of decades an alternative approach, activity-based costing, as described in Chapter 4, has become popular. It focuses on activities rather than departments. Let's examine how the same facility of **L.A. Darling** might apply ABC to determine the costs of custom and standard displays.

Assume that management decides to apply ABC only to the producing departments. The service departments will continue to use traditional costing. We will still use the step-down method to allocate the costs of the service departments to the producing departments. First, we allocate facilities management department costs to the human resources department and the specific activities identified in the producing departments. Then, we allocate the human resources department costs, both the direct department costs and the costs allocated from facilities management, to the various activities. Finally, we allocate the producing department activity-cost pools using a two-stage ABC system that uses a four-step procedure. Appendix 12 discusses a multistage ABC allocation system.

To apply ABC we use the following four steps:

STEP 1: DETERMINE THE KEY COMPONENTS OF THE SYSTEM   The costing objective is to determine the costs of custom and standard displays—the final cost objects for L.A. Darling. The structure of the service department component of the cost allocation system is unchanged—we still use the step-down method. The major differences are in the producing departments. The ABC accounting system traces the cost of parts and direct labor to each product—this is the same as the traditional approach. During the implementation of ABC, managers often discover ways to improve costing accuracy. In this case, management decided to combine the processing and assembly departments into one new production department with three major activities—design, processing, and assembly. The design activity's resources, engineers and CAD equipment, were previously part of the facilities management department. Managers believed that they could more accurately allocate these costs if they accumulate them separately as part of a production department design activity and allocate them using distinct parts as the cost-allocation base. In summary, the cost-allocation bases for design, processing, and assembly activities are distinct parts, machine hours, and direct-labor hours, respectively.

STEP 2: DEVELOP THE RELATIONSHIPS BETWEEN RESOURCES, ACTIVITIES, AND COST OBJECTS   Interviews with key personnel identified the interrelationships between the two service departments, three activities, resources, and final cost objects. Exhibit 12-8 is a process map that depicts these interrelationships. The newly formed production department is depicted by a dashed line in Exhibit 12-8. Why do we use a dashed line? The emphasis in the ABC approach is on allocations to activities without regard to departmental boundaries. Note that the exhibit also shows the cost behavior for each resource. Understanding the cost behavior of resources is vital during the planning process.

STEP 3: COLLECT RELEVANT DATA CONCERNING COSTS AND THE PHYSICAL FLOW OF COST-ALLOCATION BASE UNITS AMONG RESOURCES AND ACTIVITIES   Using the process map as a guide, accountants collected the required cost and operational data by further interviews with relevant personnel. Data collected are given in Exhibit 12-8. Note that the total costs of the facilities management department is only $1,000,000 instead of the $1,260,000 used under the traditional approach. The difference is the cost of engineers and CAD equipment that is now treated as part of the production department. Each of the three activities shows the total cost pool. For example, the processing activity cost pool is $1,476,000. We calculate this as follows:

Resource Supporting the Processing Activity	Allocation Calculation	Allocated Cost
Facilities management department resources	$1,000,000 \times [15,000 \div (9,000 + 3,000 + 15,000 + 3,000)]$	$ 500,000
Human resources department resources	$540,000 \times [16 \div (10 + 16 + 64)]$	96,000
Machines, tools, mechanics, and supplies	$1,200,000 \times 70\%$	840,000
Supervisors and equipment	$400,000 \times 10\%$	40,000
Total		$1,476,000

Exhibit 12-8

L.A. Darling Display Facility: Allocation to Final Cost Objectives Using the ABC Approach

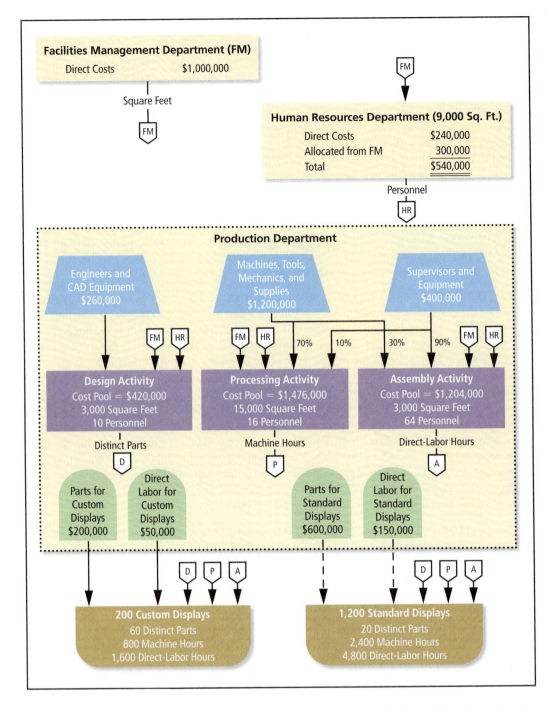

STEP 4: CALCULATE AND INTERPRET THE NEW ABC INFORMATION Exhibit 12-9 shows the last step of allocating the costs of activities to the custom and standard displays. For each activity, the exhibit shows the cost pool of indirect costs that results from allocations of service department costs and the first stage of resource allocations. Then, it shows how to allocate these costs to the displays via the appropriate cost-allocation bases.

Compare the cost per unit figures using the traditional and ABC approaches. There is a substantial difference in the reported cost as shown next:

	Allocated Cost	
	Custom Displays	Standard Displays
Traditional approach	$5,395.00	$2,517.50
ABC approach	$6,175.00	$2,387.50

Activity/Resource (Cost Driver)	Cost Pool	Physical Flow of Cost Driver	Cost per Driver Unit	Custom Displays		Standard Displays	
				Flow	Cost	Flow	Cost
Design (distinct parts)	$ 420,000	80	$5,250.000	60	$ 315,000	20	$ 105,000
Processing (machine hours)	1,476,000	3,200	461.250	800	369,000	2,400	1,107,000
Assembly (direct-labor hours)	1,204,000	6,400	188.125	1,600	301,000	4,800	903,000
Parts					200,000		600,000
Direct labor					50,000		150,000
Total direct and allocated cost					$1,235,000		$2,865,000
Units					÷ 200		÷ 1,200
Display cost per unit					$ 6,175.00		$ 2,387.50

Exhibit 12-9

L.A. Darling's Display Facility: Allocation to Final Cost Objects Using the ABC Approach

How important are these differences? Suppose that product costs are 40% of L.A. Darling's total costs. If the company desires an operating income of 20% of total costs, the required total revenue is [1.2 × product cost ÷ 0.4] = 300% × product cost or three times the product cost. This means that the price for custom displays would be 3 × $5,395 = $16,185 under the traditional approach compared to 3 × $6,175 = $18,525 under the ABC approach. Assuming the ABC cost is the more accurate estimate of actual costs, using the traditional approach would underprice custom displays by $2,340 or 12.6%. The bottom-line question for L.A. Darling's decision makers is as follows: Is it worth the cost of maintaining the more expensive ABC system to be able to avoid strategic pricing errors of this magnitude?

Another company that switched from traditional to ABC costing is **Dow Chemical**. The Business First box on page 490 explains how Dow used ABC to help implement a new business strategy.

So far, we have seen how to accumulate costs and trace or allocate them to products or services—numbers 1–7 in Exhibit 12-1. This enables the calculation of gross profit for products or services. Many managers recognize that to achieve overall profitability goals, it is necessary to have both profitable products or services and profitable customers. We now consider how organizations measure and manage customer profitability.

Allocation of Costs to Customer Cost Objects to Determine Customer Profitability

As shown in Exhibit 12-1, customer profitability depends on more than the gross margin of the products or services purchased. Customer profitability also depends on the costs incurred to fulfill customer orders and to provide other customer services such as order changes, returns, and expedited scheduling or delivery. Exhibit 12-10 shows how these two factors determine profitability.

Objective 5

Allocate costs associated with customer actions to customers.

Consider customer type 1. This customer buys a mix of products that have high gross margins yielding a high gross margin percentage, about 70%. Customer type 1 has a low cost-to-serve percentage (cost to serve ÷ sales revenue), about 30%. As a result, customer type 1 will have a high level of profitability, 70% – 30% = 40%. On the other hand, customer type 2 buys products with a lower gross margin and is very costly to serve resulting in a loss to the company of 50% – 70% = –20%. Most of this difference reflects the 40% higher cost to serve. The following list is a profile of low and high cost-to-serve customers.

Low Cost to Serve	High Cost to Serve
Large order quantity	Small order quantity
Few order changes	Many order changes
Little pre- and post-sales support	Large amounts of pre- and post-sales support
Regular scheduling	Expedited scheduling
Standard delivery	Special delivery requirements
Few returns	Frequent returns

Business First

Companies Use ABC to Improve the Allocation of Service Costs and Lower the Costs to Serve Customers

Dow Chemical believes that its ABC allocation system is the foundation of its cost-management system. Dow, with annual revenues of more than $54 billion, is the largest chemical company in the United States and number two worldwide. The company has three major business segments: plastics, chemicals, and agricultural products. Dow switched from a traditional allocation system to ABC as part of a major shift in its total strategy. It sold its pharmaceutical, energy, and consumer products businesses and set a goal to be the number one company in chemicals, plastics, and agroscience. Dow believed that, to accomplish its goal, it needed to improve the quality and accuracy of its costing system, including the costs of internal services such as those provided by the human resources and maintenance departments.

Service providers, such as human resources and maintenance, identified the major activities performed, determined the appropriate cost-allocation base for each activity, and computed costs for each activity and service provided to using departments. The focus on activities has led to a better understanding of costs by everyone and better cost control. Another advantage of the ABC system is improved resource planning and utilization. By focusing on activities and their related cost-allocation bases, Dow's maintenance department

managers can more effectively plan maintenance resource needs and availability. Overall, since the company integrated ABC into its cost management system, it has realized significant benefits.

Another company that used ABC to improve its allocation system is **Kemps LLC**, a manufacturer of dairy products such as milk, yogurt, and ice cream. Kemps' customers range from small convenience stores to large retailers such as **Target**. When Kemp changed its strategy to focus more on being a low-total-cost provider, it recognized the need to measure and manage the costs to serve its diverse customer base. Using an ABC system it was able to identify customers who had a high cost to serve and thus were unprofitable. Many of these customers ordered in low quantities or made frequent returns. By implementing a menu-based pricing strategy where Kemps charged higher prices for low-volume orders and offered discounts for lowering product returns, Kemps realized significant cost savings.

Sources: J. Damitio, G. Hayes, and P. Kintzele, "Integrating ABC and ABM at Dow Chemical," *Management Accounting Quarterly*, Winter 2000, pp. 22–26; R. Kaplan and S. Anderson, "Time-Driven Activity-Based Costing," *Harvard Business Review*, November 2004, pp. 131–138; and *Dow Chemical Company, 2007 Annual Report*.

Measuring and Managing Customer Profitability

In the general framework for cost allocation, we stated that it is important to directly trace or allocate costs associated with customer actions to customers rather than assigning them first to producing departments and then to customers. This is because if we assigned these costs to producing departments and then to products, the allocation to customers would be based on production-related output measures that may have little relationship to the cause of customer-service costs. Such allocations can lead to cost distortions and resulting erroneous customer-profitability measures. Let's consider an example that illustrates this important concept.

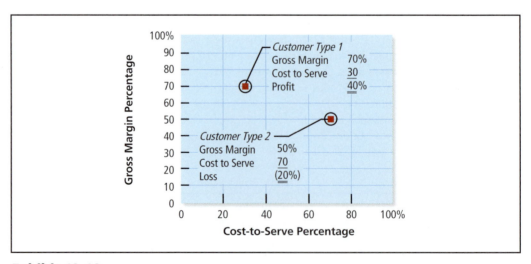

Exhibit 12-10
Customer Profitability as a Function of Customer Gross Margin and Cost to Serve

Cedar City Distributors (CCD) is a distributor of athletic apparel and sports gear. CCD distributes many products to retail outlets but classifies products into just two product groups—apparel and sports gear.

- Apparel items arrive at CCD in prepackaged cases and CCD ships them to customers in these cases. Examples include shirts, shorts, socks, and hats.
- CDD receives sports gear in bulk shipments. CCD must unpack these products and then repack them to meet small order quantities for specific gear. Examples include tennis rackets and balls, baseball bats and gloves, and golf clubs and bags.

CCD has two types of customers:

1. Small stores: stores that order low volumes (an average of 10 cases per order), the majority being apparel
2. Large stores: stores that order large volumes of both apparel and sports gear

CCD's management has set a strategic goal to improve both product and customer profitability. A related and necessary subgoal that supports this strategy is to identify profitable products and customers using an accurate cost-accounting system.

CCD currently uses a simple cost accounting system to calculate both product and customer profitability. The only direct costs are the purchase costs of apparel and sports gear products. CCD allocates indirect costs to the product groups using a single indirect cost pool for all indirect costs with "pounds of product" as the cost allocation base. Cost and operating data accumulated for the most recent year are shown in Exhibit 12-11.

To determine the profitability of a customer, we first calculate the profit margin per case for each product. Then, we use the product mix ordered by each customer to calculate profitability. Exhibit 12-12 shows how to calculate the profit margin per case and the profit margin percentage of both products. Based on the profit-margin percentage, apparel products are more profitable than sports gear. Since small stores' product mix is 75% apparel compared to only 50% for large stores, we expect small store customers have a larger profit margin percentage. We verify this in Exhibit 12-13, which shows customer profitability. Note that customer profitability is based solely on the product mix ordered by a particular customer.

Our analysis indicates that a strategy to increase CCD's overall profitability would involve an emphasis on apparel products and small stores. However, in setting this strategy, CCD's management relied on the accuracy of the cost. CCD's simple cost-accounting system may accurately allocate indirect costs if the single cost allocation base, pounds of product sold, is a plausible and reliable cost driver for all resources in the indirect cost pool. Let's see if that is the case.

Exhibit 12-11
Operating Data for Cedar City Distributors

Product Data

	Apparel	Sports Gear
Annual demand in cases	1,400	1,000
Average purchase cost per case	$80	$140
Average weight per purchased case	15 pounds	25 pounds
Average sales price per case	$570	$830

Customer Data

	Small Stores	Large Stores
Apparel demand in cases	600	800
Sports gear demand in cases	200	800
Total annual demand in cases	800	1,600
Orders	80	35

Indirect Cost Data

A single indirect cost pool consists of resources needed to perform receiving, storing, picking, packing, shipping, order processing, and customer service activities. The annual cost of these resources is $690,000. The cost-allocation base used to allocate this pool to the two product groups is pounds of product sold.

	Output Measure or Cost Allocation Base	Revenue or Cost per Unit	Apparel		Sports Gear	
			Amount of Output or Cost-Allocation Base	Total Revenue or Cost	Amount of Output or Cost-Allocation Base	Total Revenue or Cost
Apparel revenue	Cases	$570.00	1,400	$798,000		
Sports gear revenue	Cases	$830.00			1,000	$830,000
Apparel purchase cost	Cases	$ 80.00	1,400	112,000		
Sports gear purchase cost	Cases	$140.00			1,000	140,000
Indirect cost pool, $690,000	Pounds	$ 15.00*	21,000**	315,000	25,000	375,000
Total cost				427,000		515,000
Profit margin				$371,000		$315,000
Profit margin per case				$ 265.00		$ 315.00
Profit margin percentage				46.5%†		38.0%‡

*$690,000 ÷ (15 lb. per case × 1,400 cases) + (25 lb. per case × 1,000 cases)
**15 lb. per case × 1,400 cases
†$371,000 ÷ $798,000
‡$315,000 ÷ $830,000

Exhibit 12-12
Profit Margin Per Case of Apparel and Sports Gear

ALLOCATION OF THE COSTS TO SERVE We look again at Exhibit 12-11 and ask, "Is it plausible that all the activities and associated indirect resources included in the indirect cost pool are related solely to the weight of purchased product?" Might "number of customer orders" be a more plausible cost-allocation base for some items, like the order processing and customer service activities and related resources?

Let's assume that "number of orders" was indeed a better cost-allocation base for the order processing and customer service activities. The cost of the resources used by these two activities is $276,000 out of the total indirect cost pool of $690,000. CCD should exclude these costs from the computation of product profit margin. Instead, it should set up an additional cost pool and allocate these costs to customer types. (Note, this is shown as allocation type "9" in Exhibit 12-1 on page 474.)

The partial process map in Exhibit 12-14 shows how we can change CCD's old allocation system to reflect this refinement. Exhibit 12-14 does not contain revenue and direct product costs because they will not change. It shows only the $690,000 of indirect costs, separated into two cost pools. One cost pool is the $276,000 cost of resources used for processing customer orders and providing customer services. We will examine how to allocate this cost shortly. The other cost pool is the $690,000 – $276,000 = $414,000 associated with resources used for receiving, unpacking, storing, packing, and shipping that remains in the original indirect cost pool. The allocation of this $414,000 does not change and is still based on pounds of product.

In our refined system, we allocate the $276,000 to the customer cost objectives on the basis of number of orders, an allocation base that represents the cause of the costs much better than does

Exhibit 12-13
Customer Profitability at Cedar City Distributors

	Small Stores			Large Stores		
	Cases	Profit Margin Per Case	Total Profit Margin	Cases	Profit Margin Per Case	Total Profit Margin
Apparel	600	$265.00	$159,000	800	$265.00	$212,000
Sports Gear	200	315.00	63,000	800	315.00	252,000
			$222,000			$464,000
Total Profit Margin Percentage			43.7%*			41.4%†

*$222,000 ÷ (600 cases × $570 per case + 200 cases × $830 per case) = $222,000 ÷ ($342,000 + $166,000) = $222,000 ÷ $508,000 = .437
†$464,000 ÷ (800 cases × $570 per case + 800 cases × $830 per case) = $464,000 ÷ ($456,000 + $664,000) = $464,000 ÷ $1,120,000 = .414

pounds of product. An analysis of the allocation percentages in Exhibit 12-14 reveals how customer profitability will change under the refined allocation system. Consider the allocations of the $276,000 to large stores under both systems. In the old system, large stores receive (32,000 lbs. ÷ 46,000 lbs) × $276,000 = $192,000 because shipments to large stores weigh 32,000 pounds out of total shipments of 46,000 pounds. In the refined allocation system, the allocation of the $276,000 is based on the proportion of orders by large stores. Large stores make only 35 out of 115 orders, so the allocation is (35 ÷ 115) × $276,000 = $84,000. The refined cost-accounting system allocates

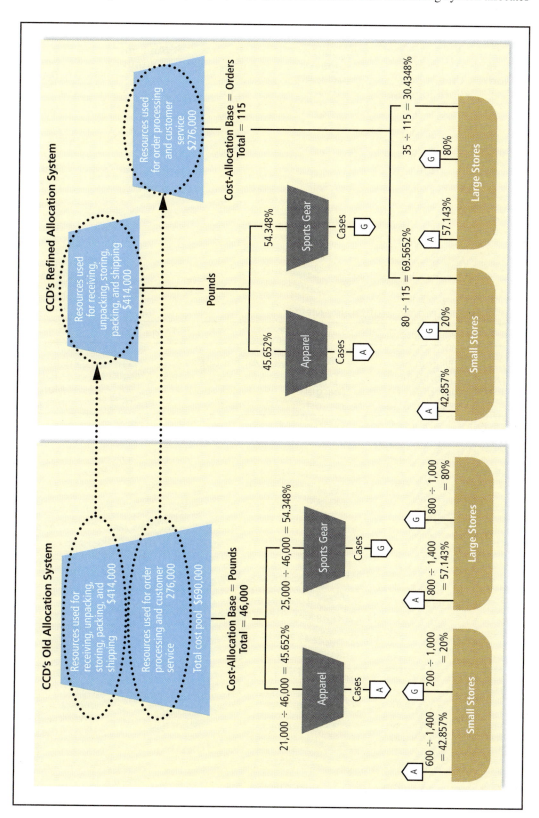

Exhibit 12-14
Cedar City Distributor's Refined Cost-Allocation System

$192,000 − $84,000 = $108,000 less indirect, customer-related costs to large stores and, correspondingly, $108,000 more cost to small stores.

The refined cost-allocation system significantly changes the profitability measures of small and large stores. Exhibit 12-15 shows the calculation of product gross margin, customer gross margin, customer cost to serve, and customer profitability.

Product Profitability Measures

	Output Measure or Cost-Allocation Base	Revenue or Cost per Unit of Cost-Allocation Base	Apparel		Sports Gear	
			Amount of Output or Cost-Allocation Base	Total Revenue or Cost	Amount of Output or Cost-Allocation Base	Total Revenue or Cost
Apparel revenue	Cases	$570.00	1,400	$798,000		
Sports gear revenue	Cases	830.00			1,000	$830,000
Apparel purchase cost	Cases	80.00	1,400	112,000		
Sports gear purchase cost	Cases	140.00			1,000	140,000
Indirect cost pool, $414,000	Pounds	9.00*	21,000	189,000	25,000	225,000
Total cost				301,000		365,000
Product gross margin				$497,000		$465,000
Product gross margin per case				$ 355.00		$ 465.00
Product gross margin percentage				62.3%		56.0%

Customer Profitability Measures

	Small Stores			Large Stores		
	Amount of Output or Cost-Allocation Base	Margin or Cost Per Unit of Cost-Allocation Base	Total Margin or Cost	Amount of Output or Cost-Allocation Base	Margin or Cost Per Unit	Total Margin or Cost
Apparel product gross margin	600 Cases	$355.00	$213,000	800 Cases	$355.00	284,000
Sports gear product gross margin	200 Cases	465.00	93,000	800 Cases	465.00	372,000
Gross margin for product mix			306,000			656,000
Cost to serve, $2,400 per order[§]	80 Orders	2,400	192,000	35 Orders	2,400	84,000
Customer profit margin			$114,000			$572,000
Customer gross margin percentage			60.2%[†]			58.6%[‡]
Cost to service percentage			37.8%			7.5%
Customer profit margin percentage			22.4%[¶]			51.1%[#]

*$414,000 ÷ (15 lb. per case × 1,400 cases + 25 lb. per case × 1,000 cases)
[†]$306,000 ÷ (600 cases × $570 per case + 200 cases × $830 per case)
[‡]$656,000 ÷ (800 cases × $570 per case + 800 cases × $830 per case)
[§]$276,000 ÷ (80 orders + 35 orders)
[¶]60.2% − 37.8% or $114,000 ÷ (600 cases × $570 per case + 200 cases × $830 per case)
[#]58.6% − 7.5% or $572,000 ÷ (800 cases × $570 per case + 800 cases × $830 per case)

Exhibit 12-15
Product and Customer Profitability Measures Based on CCD's Refined Cost-Allocation System

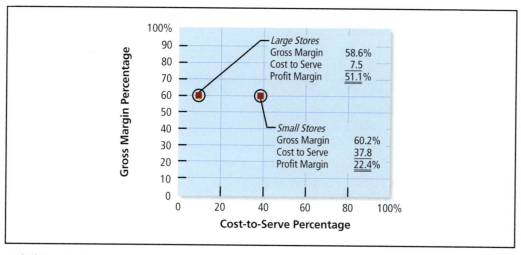

Exhibit 12-16
Customer Profitability at Cedar City Distributors

Contrary to the results based on the simple, existing cost-accounting system (Exhibit 12-13), the refined system shows that large stores are the most profitable customers. Exhibit 12-16 is based on Exhibit 12-15 and depicts both the customer product gross margin and cost to serve. It is easy to see why large stores are the major source of profit for CCD. The cost to serve is low and the product mix yields a substantial gross margin. This example demonstrates why it is important for accountants to carefully choose and measure cost-allocation bases. The refined system gives managers at CCD more insight into operations, and they have a tool to measure and manage customer profitability.

Summary Problem for Your Review

PROBLEM

Consider our example of **L.A. Darling**'s display facility. Exhibits 12-8 and 12-9 on pages 488 and 489 show how the company used the ABC approach to determine the cost of goods sold for custom and standard displays. Suppose that management wants to know the profitability of its major customers. Assume that two major customers are Southwest Hardware Stores (SHS) and **Target Corporation**. SHS orders a mix of custom and standard displays. It also has unique service requirements, orders relatively small order sizes, and requires substantial pre- and post-sales support from customer service and corporate staff. In contrast, Target orders only a few custom displays, has larger order quantities, and does not require much customer service or corporate staff support.

Accountants have performed an analysis of customer-related activities and concluded that two activities capture the main differences in cost to serve among the customers—sales activity and customer and corporate support. Both customers use these activities to some extent, and it is not economically feasible to directly trace these costs to customers. Therefore, L.A. Darling allocates these costs to customers. The cost-allocation bases chosen are number of orders for the sales activity cost pool and service and staff labor hours for the customer and corporate support cost pool.

To determine the profitability of the two customers, the company has collected the following data:

• Average price of a custom display	$12,000
• Average price of a standard display	$ 8,500
• Number of custom displays ordered by SHS	180
• Number of custom displays ordered by Target	20
• Number of standard displays ordered by SHS	220
• Number of standard displays ordered by Target	980
• Cost to serve activity analysis data:	
• Total sales and marketing cost pool	$3,000,000
• Total customer service and corporate support cost pool	$1,150,000
• Amount of each cost-allocation base used by each customer:	

Cost Allocation Base	SHS	Target
Orders	40	20
Hours	6,400	3,600

1. Calculate the gross margin percentage and cost-to-serve percentage for Southwest Hardware Stores and Target.
2. Construct a graph similar to Exhibit 12-16 that depicts customer profitability for Southwest Hardware Stores and Target.
3. Suggest a strategy for profit improvement for both customers.

SOLUTION

1. Exhibit 12-17 shows the calculation of customer gross margin and customer cost to serve.
2. Exhibit 12-18 depicts the profitability of SHS and Target.
3. You can use Exhibit 12-18 as a guide for setting strategy for profit improvement. Target is generating much more profit for the company than is SHS. L.A. Darling managers should protect customers such as Target from possible competitor actions, perhaps offering discounts to ensure continued business. In addition, the sales department manager should profile this type of customer to make it easier for salespersons to identify profitable new business. SHS is very expensive to serve because of its small order quantities and extensive pre- and post-sales support. Possible actions that would improve its profitability include charging for corporate support, reviewing internal processes within L.A. Darling's customer service and corporate support function to improve efficiencies, and increasing prices for custom displays.

	Cost-Allocation Base	Revenue/Cost per Unit of Cost-Allocation Base	SHS		Target	
			Amount of Cost-Allocation Base	Revenue/Cost	Amount of Cost Allocation Base	Revenue/Cost
Revenue—Custom	Displays	$12,000.00	180	$2,160,000	20	$ 240,000
Revenue—Standard	Displays	8,500.00	220	1,870,000	980	8,330,000
Total Revenue				4,030,000		8,570,000
Cost of goods sold—Custom	Displays	6,175.00*	180	1,111,500	20	123,500
Cost of goods sold—Standard	Displays	2,387.50*	220	525,250	980	2,339,750
Total cost of goods sold				1,636,750		2,463,250
Gross margin				2,393,250		6,106,750
Cost to serve:						
Sales	Orders	50,000.00†	40	2,000,000	20	1,000,000
Customer service and corporate support	Hours	115.00‡	6,400	736,000	3,600	414,000
Total cost to serve				2,736,000		1,414,000
Contribution to unallocated corporate overhead				$ (342,750)		$4,692,750
Gross margin percentage				59.4%		71.3%
Cost-to-serve percentage				67.9%		16.5%
Customer profit margin percentage				(8.5)%		54.8%

*From Exhibit 12-9
†$3,000,000 ÷ (40 orders + 20 orders)
‡$1,150,000 ÷ (6,400 hours + 3,600 hours)

Exhibit 12-17
Contribution to Unallocated Corporate Overhead at L.A. Darling Display Facility

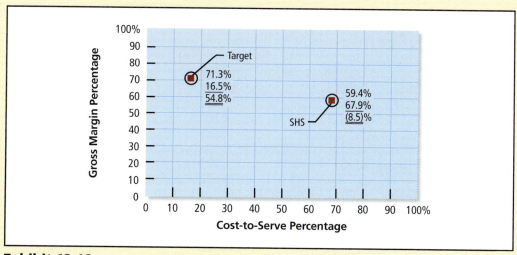

Exhibit 12-18
L.A. Darling's Display Facility: Customer Profitability Using the ABC Approach

Making Managerial Decisions

Louder Is Better Company makes two speaker models—standard (S) and deluxe (D). The following diagrams show how ABC and traditional allocation systems allocate overhead costs to the deluxe model. The production department has overhead costs of $36,000. Why does the cost allocated to the deluxe type speakers by the ABC system differ from that in the traditional system?

Answer

In the traditional system, the deluxe product receives only 25% of the overhead costs because it uses only 25% of the machine hours. But in the ABC system, it receives 72% of the overhead because it uses 63% of the parts and 83% of the setups.

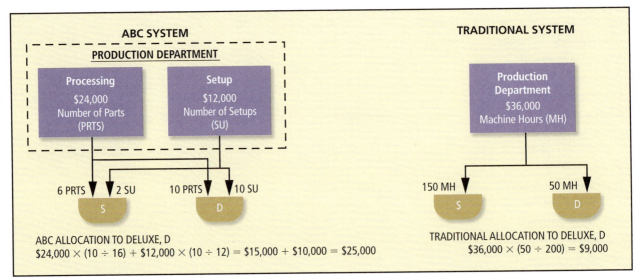

This concludes our discussion of service department allocation. We will next consider two specific types of cost allocations: (1) allocation of central corporate costs such as public relations and legal costs, and (2) allocation of joint and by-product costs.

Allocation of Central Corporate Support Costs

Objective 6
Allocate the central corporate costs of an organization.

Many managers believe it is desirable to fully allocate all of an organization's costs, including central corporate support costs, to the revenue-producing (operating) parts of the organization. Such allocations are not necessary from an accounting viewpoint and usually not useful as management information. For this reason, we do not consider central costs to be part of the value chain in this text. However, when a company allocates such costs, most managers accept them as a fact of life—as long as all managers seem to be treated alike and thus "fairly."

Whenever possible, the preferred cost-allocation base for central services is usage, either actual or estimated. But companies seldom allocate the costs of these central services on the basis of usage. They are more likely to choose usage as a cost-allocation base for data processing, advertising, and operations research.

Companies that allocate central costs by usage tend to generate less resentment over allocations. Consider the experience of **J. C. Penney Company** as reported in *BusinessWeek*:

> *The controller's office wanted subsidiaries such as* **Thrift Drug Co.** *and the insurance operations to base their share of corporate personnel, legal, and auditing costs on their revenues. The subsidiaries contended that they maintained their own personnel and legal departments, and should be assessed far less. . . . The subcommittee addressed the issue by asking the corporate departments to approximate the time (a measure of usage) and costs involved in servicing the subsidiaries. The final allocation plan, based on these studies, cost the divisions less than they were initially assessed but more than they had wanted to pay. Nonetheless, the plan was implemented easily.*

Usage is not always an economically viable way to allocate central costs, however. Also, it is difficult to allocate many central costs, such as the president's salary and related expenses, public relations, legal services, income tax planning, company-wide advertising, and basic research, on the basis of cause and effect. As a result, some companies use cost-allocation bases such as the revenue of each division, the cost of goods sold by each division, the total assets of each division, or the total costs of each division (before allocation of the central costs) to allocate central costs, even though these bases are not necessarily the cost drivers.

The use of the foregoing cost-allocation bases might provide a rough indication of a cause-and-effect relationship. Basically, however, they represent an "ability to bear" philosophy of cost allocation. For example, a company might allocate the costs of company-wide advertising, such as the sponsorship of a program on a PBS station, to all products and divisions on the basis of the revenues in each. But such costs precede sales. They are discretionary costs as determined by management policies, not by sales results. Although 60% of the companies in a large survey use sales revenue as a cost-allocation base for some cost-allocation purposes, it is seldom truly a cost driver in the sense of being an activity that causes the costs.

Use of Budgeted Sales for Allocation

If a company feels it must allocate the costs of central services based on sales, even though the costs do not vary in proportion to sales, it should use budgeted sales rather than actual sales as an allocation base. At least this method means that the fortunes of other departments will not affect the short-run costs of a given department.

For example, suppose **L.A. Darling Company** budgets central advertising as 10% of forecasted sales in two countries—Mexico and Canada. The forecasted sales are $500,000 in both Mexico and Canada so the total advertising budget, a fixed cost, is $100,000. Actual sales in Mexico and Canada are $300,000 and $600,000, respectively. How does the company allocate the $100,000 advertising budget if it uses forecasted sales compared to actual sales?

Allocation of $100,000 Central Advertising Budget

	Mexico	Canada
Forecast sales	$500,000	$500,000
Allocation based on forecast sales	50,000	50,000
Actual sales	300,000	600,000
Allocation based on actual sales	33,333	67,667

The preferred allocation is based on forecast sales. Why? Because it indicates a low ratio of sales to advertising in Mexico—it directs attention to a potential problem. In contrast, allocation based on actual sales soaks the Canadian operations with more advertising cost because of the achieved results and relieves Mexican operations despite its lower success. This is another example of the confusion that can arise when cost allocations to one company unit depend on the activity of other units.

Allocation of Joint Costs and By-Product Costs

Joint costs and by-product costs create especially difficult cost-allocation problems. By definition, such costs relate to more than one product, and we cannot separately identify them with an individual product. Let's examine these special cases, starting with joint costs.

Objective 7

Allocate joint costs to products using the physical-units and relative-sales-value methods.

Joint Costs

So far, we have assumed that we could identify cost-allocation bases with an individual product. For example, if we are allocating activity costs to products or services on the basis of machine hours, we have assumed that we can measure the amount of machine time consumed in making each product. However, sometimes we add inputs to the production process before we can separately identify individual products (i.e., before the split-off point). Recall from Chapter 6 (page 234) that we call such costs joint costs. Joint costs include all inputs of material, labor, and overhead costs that are incurred before the split-off point.

Suppose a department has more than one product and some costs are joint costs. How should we allocate such joint costs to the products? *Allocation of joint costs should not affect decisions about the individual products.* Nevertheless, companies routinely allocate joint product costs to products for purposes of inventory valuation and income determination.

Consider the example of joint product costs that we used in Chapter 6. A department in **Dow Chemical Company** produces two chemicals, X and Y. The joint cost is $100,000, and production is 1,000,000 liters of X and 500,000 liters of Y. X sells for $.09 per liter and Y for $.06 per liter. We want to find a method to allocate some part of the $100,000 joint cost to the inventory of X and the rest to the inventory of Y. Such allocations are useful for inventory purposes only. You should ignore joint cost allocations for decisions such as selling a joint product or processing it further.

There are two conventional ways of allocating joint costs to products: physical units and relative sales values. If a company uses physical units, it would allocate the joint costs as follows:

	Liters	Weighting	Allocation of Joint Costs	Sales Value at Split-Off Point
X	1,000,000	(10 ÷ 15) × $100,000	$ 66,667	$ 90,000
Y	500,000	(5 ÷ 15) × $100,000	33,333	30,000
	1,500,000		$100,000	$120,000

This approach shows that the $33,333 joint cost of producing Y exceeds its $30,000 sales value at the split-off point seemingly indicating that the company should not produce Y. However, such an allocation is not helpful in making production decisions. We can produce neither of the two products separately.

A decision to produce Y must be a decision to produce X and Y. Because total revenue of $120,000 exceeds the total joint cost of $100,000, we should produce both. The allocation was not useful for this decision.

The physical-units method requires a common physical unit for measuring the output of each product. For example, board feet is a common unit for a variety of products in the lumber industry. However, sometimes such a common denominator is lacking. Consider the production of meat and hides from butchering a steer. You might use pounds as a common denominator, but pounds is not a good measure of the output of hides. As an alternative, many companies use the relative-sales-value method for allocating joint costs. The following allocation results from applying the relative-sales-value method to the Dow Chemical department:

	Relative Sales Value at Split-Off Point	Weighting	Allocation of Joint Costs
X	$ 90,000	(90 ÷ 120) × $100,000	$ 75,000
Y	30,000	(30 ÷ 120) × $100,000	25,000
	$120,000		$100,000

The weighting is based on the sales values of the individual products. Because the sales value of X at the split-off point is $90,000 and total sales value at the split-off point is $120,000, we allocate 90 ÷ 120 of the joint cost to X.

This method might eliminate one problem, but it creates another. Note how the allocation of a cost to a particular product, such as Y, depends not only on the sales value of Y but also on the sales value of X. For example, suppose you were the product manager for Y. You planned to sell your 500,000 liters for $30,000, achieving a profit of $30,000 − $25,000 = $5,000. Everything went as expected except that the price of X fell to $.07 per liter for revenue of $70,000 rather than $90,000. Instead of 30 ÷ 120 of the joint cost, Y received 30 ÷ 100 × $100,000 = $30,000 and had a profit of $0. Despite the fact that Y operations were exactly as planned, the cost-allocation method caused the profit on Y to be $5,000 below plan.

We can also use the relative-sales-value method when we cannot sell one or more of the joint products at the split-off point. To apply the method, we approximate the sales value at split off as follows:

$$\text{sales value at split off} = \text{final sales value} - \text{separable costs}$$

For example, suppose the 500,000 liters of Y requires $20,000 of processing beyond the split-off point, after which we can sell it for $.10 per liter. The sales value at split off would be ($.10 × 500,000) − $20,000 = $50,000 − $20,000 = $30,000.

By-Product Costs

By-products are similar to joint products. A **by-product** is a product that, like a joint product, is not individually identifiable until manufacturing reaches a split-off point. By-products differ from joint products because they have relatively insignificant total sales values in comparison with the other products emerging at split off. In contrast, joint products have relatively significant total sales values at split off in comparison with the other jointly produced items. Examples of by-products are glycerine from soap making and mill ends of cloth and carpets.

If we account for an item as a by-product, we allocate only separable costs to it. We allocate all joint costs to the main products. We deduct any revenues from by-products, less their separable costs, from the cost of the main products.

Consider a lumber company that sells sawdust generated in the production of lumber to companies making particle board. Suppose the company regards the sawdust as a by-product. In 20X7, sales of sawdust totaled $30,000, and the cost of loading and shipping the sawdust (i.e., costs incurred beyond the split-off point) was $20,000. The inventory cost of the sawdust would consist of only the $20,000 separable cost. The company would allocate none of the joint cost of producing lumber and sawdust to the sawdust. It would deduct the difference between the revenue and separable cost, $30,000 – $20,000 = $10,000, from the cost of the lumber produced.

Highlights to Remember

1. **Describe the general framework for cost allocation.** Companies assign direct and indirect costs to various cost objects, including service departments, producing departments, products, and customers. All organizations allocate indirect costs to producing departments and to the products or services delivered to customers. These allocations often include the costs of service departments. Some organizations carry cost allocation one more step—to customers.

2. **Allocate the variable and fixed costs of service departments to other organizational units.** Companies should use separate cost pools for variable and fixed costs when allocating service department costs. They should allocate variable costs using budgeted cost rates times the actual cost-driver level. They should allocate fixed costs using budgeted percent of capacity available for use times the total budgeted fixed costs.

3. **Use the direct and step-down methods to allocate service department costs to user departments.** When service departments support other service departments in addition to producing departments, they can use either the direct or step-down method for allocation. The direct method ignores other service departments when allocating costs. The step-down method recognizes other service departments' use of services.

4. **Allocate costs from producing departments to products or services using the traditional approach.** When a company's products or services are the final cost object, it should integrate its service department allocation with the allocation system used to cost final cost objects. A traditional system traces the direct costs in each department to its products or services and allocates indirect costs using a cost-allocation base. The ABC approach uses four steps to assign costs to products or services: 1) Determine key components, 2) Identify resources, activities, and cost objects and their relationships, 3) Collect relevant data, and 4) Calculate and interpret ABC information. The ABC approach provides more accurate estimates of product or service costs than the traditional approach but is more costly to maintain.

5. **Allocate costs associated with customer actions to customers.** Customer profitability is a function of product mix and the cost to serve. Activities that can drive up the costs to serve customers include small order quantities, pre-sales work, order changes, returns, special delivery requirements, and post-sales work.

6. **Allocate the central corporate costs of an organization.** Central costs include public relations, top corporate management overhead, legal, data processing, controller's department, and company-wide planning. Often, it is best to allocate only those central costs of an organization for which measures of usage by departments are available.

7. **Allocate joint costs to products using the physical-units and relative-sales-value methods.** Companies often allocate joint costs to products for inventory valuation and income determination using the physical-units or relative-sales-value method. However, such allocations should not affect decisions. ∎

Appendix 12: Multistage ABC (MSABC) Systems

In Chapter 4 we introduced simple two-stage ABC systems. The first stage allocates costs to activities, and the second stage allocates the activity costs to products, customers, or other cost objectives. They have a financial accounting flavor because the general ledger is at the heart of all the cost data used. While two-stage ABC systems meet the decision-making needs of many organizations, some organizations (such as FedEx, Boeing, Allstate Insurance, and the United States Department of Labor) prefer to design **multistage ABC (MSABC) systems** with more than two stages of allocations and resource cost-allocation bases other than percentages.

There is a distinctive operational flavor to MSABC systems because much of the required data comes from operational data sources, not just the general ledger. Many companies, such as Pillsbury and AT&T, began their use of ABC by using the two-stage approach. However, they later converted to the multistage approach because of its focus on operations and its tendency to enhance operating managers' understanding of the business. According to one manager at Pillsbury,

> *Having already completed an ABC model within our organization using the two-stage ABC approach, my eyes were opened to the importance of the multistage ABC approach and how its scenario-playing capability and flexibility allows an organization to move past just ABC toward ABM.*

Managers at companies that use MSABC systems believe that their additional complexity yields more accurate costs and a deeper understanding of operations. A deeper understanding of the business leads to better ideas for process improvement. Process improvements, in turn, lead to more satisfied customers and a competitive edge. Three key attributes distinguish MSABC systems from two-stage ABC systems:

1. There are more than two stages of allocation.
2. Cost behavior of resources is considered.
3. There is a greater use of operational information such as cost-allocation bases and consumption rates.

Let's explore each of these attributes to see why MSABC systems offer so much value to managers.

Key Attributes of Multistage ABC Systems

Understanding the relationships between activities, resources, resource costs, and cost-allocation bases is the key to understanding MSABC systems and how they facilitate managers' understanding of operations. To gain more insight into how an ABC system actually works, we will look at one of the products produced by Woodland Park Company, a manufacturer of plastic components used in commercial trucks and buses.

One of the components Woodland Park makes, 102Z, is a plastic dashboard casing for the control panel of large trucks. Making 102Z requires resin material and several activities, such as receiving, production scheduling, material handling, setup, molding machine processing, assembly, inspection, packaging, and shipping. We will focus on the set-up and molding machine processing activities. The resources required by these activities include an injection-molding machine, operating labor, electrical energy, and the plant itself. Exhibit 12-19 shows the relationships between the setup and machine processing activities and the resources used.

The first key attribute of MSABC systems is the use of more than two stages of allocation. In Exhibit 12-19, notice that the plant resource costs are allocated to the final cost objective—truck dashboard casings—in three stages. In a two-stage ABC system, plant costs would be allocated to the truck casings in only two stages. In the MSABC system, we assume machine and labor resources consume plant costs as measured by the square feet that each occupies. In a two-stage ABC system, we would ignore the interrelationship between the plant and the machine and labor resources, and instead use a percentage to allocate plant costs directly to the setup and machine-processing activities. But this is difficult to interpret and does little to enhance our

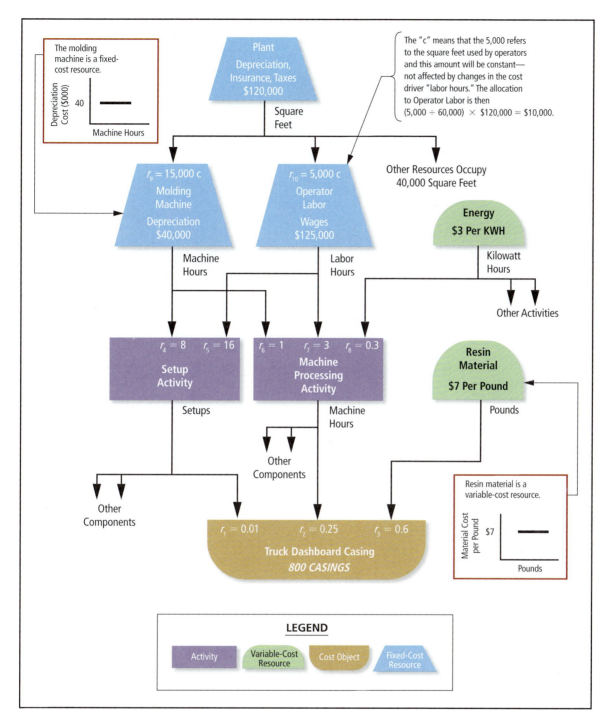

Exhibit 12-19
Relationship Between Cost Object, Activities, and Resources in an ABC System

understanding of operations. MSABC systems overcome this problem, allowing for any number of allocations necessary to accurately describe operations.

The second key attribute of MSABC systems is their extensive use of operational information. Look at the cost objective Truck Dashboard Casing in Exhibit 12-19. It takes 15 minutes of machine time to process each casing. This is shown by the activity-consumption rate, $r_2 = 0.25$ machine hours per casing. Similarly, r_1 gives the consumption rate for setup activity. Each production run produces 100 casings and requires one setup ($r_1 = 0.01$). Each casing requires 0.6 pounds of resin material. Therefore, the annual demand for 800 casings requires a total of 8 setups (800 × .01), 200 processing hours (800 × .25), and 480 pounds of resin (800 × 0.6).

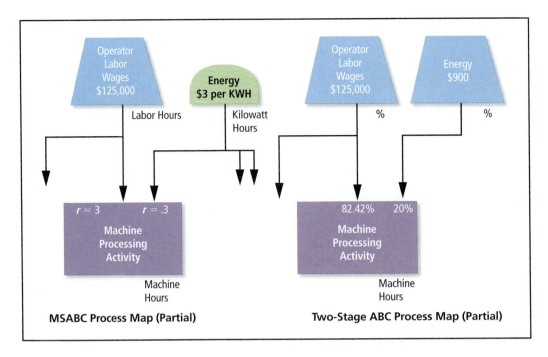

MSABC Process Map (Partial)

Two-Stage ABC Process Map (Partial)

A similar interpretation can be made for the activities. For example, each hour of machine-processing activity requires (consumes) one molding machine hour, three operator labor hours, and 0.3 kilowatt hours of energy. We can see that the cost-allocation bases are a measure of the activity level (setups and processing hours) and the amount of resources used (machine hours, labor hours, and kilowatt hours) to produce casings. The resource-consumption rates (the rs on each activity in Exhibit 12-19) give the rates at which the activity uses resources for each cost-driver unit of the activity.

Two-stage ABC systems differ in the treatment of the consumption of resources by activities. In two-stage ABC, percentages would be used to describe the relationships between resources and activities. Managers who use MSABC believe that resource-consumption rates provide more valuable operational information than percentages. In our example, the managers at Woodland Park Company now have cost and operational information that they can use to manage operations more effectively. For example, consider the portion of the process map shown at the top of this page. There is much more useful operational information in the MSABC map. Operational managers use information, such as the labor hours per machine hour or kilowatt hours per machine hour, to track operational improvements. Using the cost behavior feature of MSABC, managers can predict the effects on activity costs of such improvements. This is much more difficult—or impossible—using the two-stage approach.

Let's look at an example. Suppose that Woodland Park can increase its sales of truck casings to an annual total of 900 but does not have the machine time available for the extra 100 casings. It would require an additional 25 hours of processing time to meet this new demand. Management believes that by using special quick-change dies, it can reduce the setup time by 75%. Will this process improvement save enough time to produce the extra 100 casings? The new consumption rate for machine time, r_4, is 2 hours per setup. So, the total machine time consumed during setups will be 18 hours (900 casings $\times$ 0.01 setups per casing $\times$ 2 machine hours per setup) compared to the current 64 hours (800 $\times$ 0.01 $\times$ 8). Thus, the time savings of 46 hours is more than enough to produce the extra 100 casings. If a two-stage ABC system were being used, it would be much more difficult to analyze this improvement idea because we would not have the consumption rate for machine time. Instead, we would have a percentage based on historical relationships and general ledger data.

The third key attribute of MSABC systems is their recognition of cost behavior. In Exhibit 12-19, the variable-cost resources—energy and resin material—are modeled by using this symbol ⬤. Financial data for these resources are expressed as costs per cost-driver unit. For energy, this is $3 per kilowatt hour. Energy cost varies directly with changes in the processing activity because the power company charges Woodland Park based on the kilowatt hours used. One additional processing hour will require .3 additional kilowatt hours that will increase energy cost by $0.90 ($3.00 × .3). Thus, energy is a variable-cost resource, and it is easy to see that processing hours and kilowatt hours are factors that affect energy costs.

The fixed-cost resources—plant, machines, and labor—are modeled by using this symbol [blue symbol]. For financial data, we use total costs. The costs of the machine and labor resources are fixed with respect to changes (within the relevant range) in the cost-allocation bases. One additional processing hour requires one additional machine hour and three labor hours, but the costs of the machine (depreciation) and labor (wages) resources do not change as long as machine time and labor time are available. Have we violated our definition of cost driver? Not really. If the number of processing hours increases enough, the required machine hours or labor hours will exceed the capacities of the machine and labor. Management will then decide whether to purchase more machines or to hire additional operating laborers. Costs of fixed-cost resources do not change automatically when the level of a cost-allocation bases change—this involves a management decision.

In simple, two-stage ABC systems, the cost behavior of resources is usually ignored. This means that planning for future operations is difficult with two-stage ABC because the impact of changes in demand and related cost-driver levels cannot be predicted. For example, if we expect that the demand for casings will increase, a two-stage ABC system will not enable us to predict the increase in variable production costs such as materials and energy, but the MSABC system will correctly predict the variable resin and energy cost increases.

Summary Problem for Your Review

PROBLEM

Refer to the Chapter 4 discussion (Appendix 4, pages 143–152) of the billing department at one of **AT&T**'s customer care centers. Suppose the billing department has designed an MSABC system. Exhibit 12-20 shows the process map for the MSABC system. Consider the portion of the billing department's process map shown in Exhibit 12-21. Management wants to reduce activities that do not add value for the customer. One idea is to reduce the verification of commercial bills by verifying only 70% of commercial bills (at random) and, further, by verifying only certain parts of each bill. Verifying only part of each bill will reduce the verifying time from 6 minutes to only 3 minutes per bill (account). Management believes that this procedure would not result in any increase in the number of inquiries and that bill accuracy would be unchanged. Since only part of each bill will be verified, the number of computer transactions will also be reduced from 25 to 15 per account. AT&T's labor agreement specifies that whenever labor utilization for the combined billing and verification labor pool falls below 70% due to any process improvement, the company may lay off workers until the utilization level reaches 70%. Currently, billing labor (billing labor plus bill-verifying labor) utilization is at 85% (actual hours consisting of 1,804 labor hours for billing plus 440 labor hours for verification activity divided by capacity of 2,640 labor hours = 85%). Wages and benefits are $2,812.50 per month per laborer. Each laborer is available for 110 hours a month. Currently, there are 24 billing laborers, 4 of whom are dedicated to verifying bills—the verification team. Because of the negative impact that layoffs have on employee morale, management is hesitant to implement any layoffs unless the cost savings are significant.

1. Cost allocation in MSABC systems is complex and requires some form of computer software. To get a feel for this complexity, consider the various cost-allocations required to allocate occupancy cost to the residential accounts. Three of these paths are listed next and are also displayed in Exhibit 12-20.

   Allocation Path 1: Occupancy → Account Inquiry Labor → Correspondence Activity → Account Inquiry Activity → Residential Accounts

   Allocation Path 2: Occupancy → Supervision → Account Inquiry Labor → Account Inquiry Activity → Residential Accounts

   Allocation Path 3: Occupancy → Printers → Other Activities → Residential Accounts

A computer program, either a spreadsheet or commercial software, would compute the allocations for each step in these paths based on the percentage of cost-allocation bases used. For example,

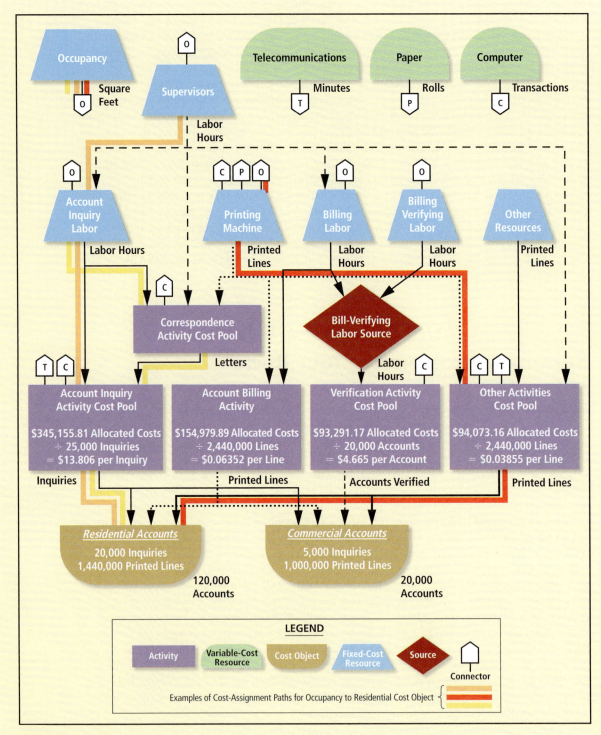

Exhibit 12-20
Multistage ABC System for Billing Department Operations

the first set of allocations of the $47,000 occupancy costs are based on the square feet occupied by account-inquiry labor, supervisors, printing machines, billing labor, and bill-verifying labor.

1. There are a total of eleven allocation paths to allocate occupancy costs to residential accounts. Give the other eight paths, using the same format shown previously.

2. In Exhibit 12-21, the relationship (indicated by arrows and consumption rates) between the computer resource and activities and resources such as account inquiry,

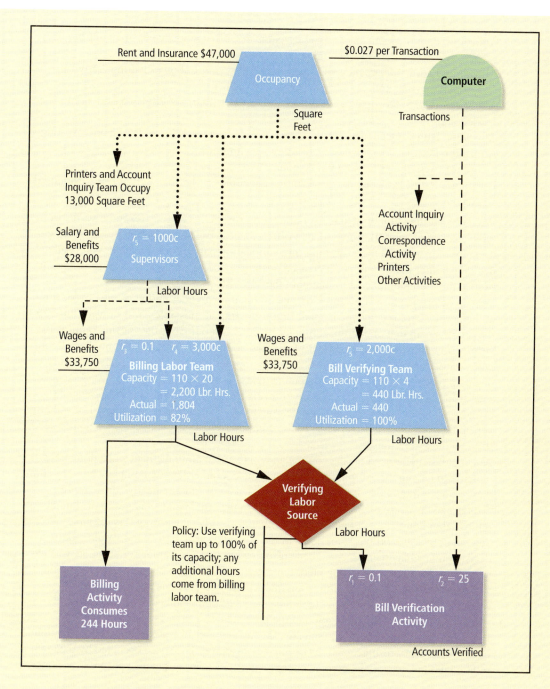

Exhibit 12-21
Billing Department Bill Verification Activity

correspondence, printing machines, and other activities is not shown. Explain why it is not necessary to know these relationships in order to determine the incremental billing labor cost savings from the process improvement.

3. Why is "transactions" a true cost driver for computer costs, whereas supervisor "labor hours" is not a true cost driver of billing labor costs?

4. Determine the billing labor and computer cost savings from this process improvement. What other potential cost savings may result? What action would you recommend?

SOLUTION

1. The remaining eight cost-allocation paths are as follows:

   Allocation Path 4: Occupancy → Account Inquiry Activity → Account Inquiry Labor → Residential Accounts

   Allocation Path 5: Occupancy → Supervision → Account Inquiry Labor → Correspondence → Account Inquiry Activity → Residential Accounts

Allocation Path 6: Occupancy → Supervision → Correspondence → Account Inquiry Activity → Residential Accounts

Allocation Path 7: Occupancy → Supervision → Billing Labor → Billing Activity → Residential Accounts

Allocation Path 8: Occupancy → Billing Labor → Billing Activity → Residential Accounts

Allocation Path 9: Occupancy → Supervision → Other Activities → Residential Accounts

Allocation Path 10: Occupancy → Printing Machines → Correspondence → Account Inquiry Activity → Residential Accounts

Allocation Path 11: Occupancy → Printing Machines → Billing Activity → Residential Accounts

We note that the number of stages of allocation for the occupancy resource varies from three (paths 4, 8, and 9) to five (path 5). Two-stage ABC has only two stages of allocations for all paths and there are only three allocation paths. As a manager, you need to decide whether the benefits of increased costing accuracy and operational information exceed the incremental cost to maintain the MSABC system.

2. We can determine how a resource will be affected by an operational change by starting at the point where the change is made and following all possible paths upward through the process map that end at the computer resource. In our case, the starting point is the verification activity. As the number of verified accounts is reduced, the number of computer transactions will also decline, as will computer costs. In this case, there is only one path linking verification to computers, and it is shown in Exhibit 12-20. As can be seen from Exhibit 12-20, the cost-driver levels for account inquiry, correspondence, printers, and other activities will not be affected by a decrease in the number of accounts verified. No other cost driver links to the computer resource changes so we do not need to show these relationships.

3. Any increase in demand for the computers will result in an immediate and automatic increase in the number of transactions. Since the computer leasing company bills the company on a per transaction basis, the computer costs will "automatically" decrease in response to the decrease in accounts verified. On the other hand, changes in the number of billing labor hours does not automatically change or drive the cost of this resource. We use the output measure billing labor hours as the cost-allocation basis but it would require a decision by management to change the resource cost. As the number of accounts verified decreases, the number of billing labor hours will also decrease but the total wages paid will stay the same—only the utilization rate will decrease. If this rate falls below 70%, management can decide whether to reduce the labor pool and hence the labor cost.

4. Exhibit 12-22 shows the calculation of the predicted cost savings from this process improvement—$41,580. Additional cost savings may result from the reduced utilization of the supervisory resource and the occupancy resource. The space occupied by the eight billing laborers who are let go may either be used for other productive purposes or rented.

Total Cost Analysis

Resource	Current Cost		Cost with Process Improvement	
Computer	20,000 acct × 25 trans/acct × $.027/trans =	$13,500	14,000 accts × 15 trans/acct × $.027/trans =	$ 5,670
Billing labor	$2,812.50/lbr × 24 lbrs =	$67,500	[(14,000 accts × .05 hr/acct) + 244 hr] ÷ .7 = desired capacity of 1,349 hr or 1,349 ÷ 110 ≈ 12 lbr.*	
			Cost is 12 lbr × $2,812.50 =	$33,750
	Total cost	$81,000	Total cost	$39,420
			Cost savings ($81,000 − $39,420)	$41,580

*Check for utilization: capacity = 12 × 110 = 1,320; actual = (14,000 acct × .05 hr/acct) + 244 hr = 944 hr. Utilization = 944 ÷ 1,320 = 71.5%. With 13 people, utilization would be 944 ÷ 1,430 = 66%, so one additional laborer can be laid off.

Exhibit 12-22
Total Cost Analysis of Process Improvement in Verification Activity

Accounting Vocabulary

by-product, p. 501
cost application, p. 482
direct method, p. 479

multistage ABC (MSABC)
   systems, p. 502
producing departments, p. 474

service departments, p. 474
step-down method, p. 480

Fundamental Assignment Material

12-A1 Direct and Step-Down Methods of Allocation; General Framework for Allocation

Manriquez Tool and Die has three service departments:

	Budgeted Department Costs
Cafeteria, revenue of $100,000 less expenses of $250,000	$ 150,000
Engineering	2,500,000
General factory administration	950,000

Cost-allocation bases are budgeted as follows:

Production Departments	Employees	Engineering Hours Worked for Production Departments	Total Labor Hours
Machining	120	50,000	300,000
Assembly	540	20,000	720,000
Finishing and painting	60	10,000	120,000

1. Manriquez allocates all service department costs directly to the production departments without allocation to other service departments. Show how much of the budgeted costs of each service department are allocated to each production department. To plan your work, examine number 2 before undertaking this question.

2. The company has decided to use the step-down method of cost allocation. General factory administration would be allocated first, then cafeteria, then engineering. Cafeteria employees work 36,000 labor hours per year. There were 60 engineering employees with 120,000 total labor hours. Recompute the results in number 1, using the step-down method. Show your computations. Compare the results in numbers 1 and 2. Which method of allocation do you favor? Why?

3. Refer to Exhibit 12-1 on page 474. For each type of cost assignment made in number 2 using the step-down method, indicate the assignment type from Exhibit 12-1.

12-A2 Customer Profitability

The following table gives sales, product cost, and cost-to-serve data for a company that makes three product lines: E, F, and G. The company has two customer types.

	Product E	Product F	Product G
Sales	$5,000	$6,000	$30,000
Cost of sales	4,500	4,800	15,000

	Customer Type 1	Customer Type 2	Total
Product E Sales	$ 500	$ 4,500	$ 5,000
Product F Sales	1,000	5,000	6,000
Product G Sales	16,000	14,000	30,000
Manager Visits	4	16	20

The cost to serve all customers is $12,000 and is allocated to customer types based on the number of manager visits to customer locations for pre- and post-sales support.

1. Determine the gross profit margin percentage of sales for each product. Which product is the most profitable?
2. Determine the gross profit margin and the gross profit margin percentage of sales for each customer type.
3. Determine the cost-to-serve percentage of sales for each customer type.
4. Determine the operating income and operating income percentage of sales for each customer type.
5. Which customer is the most profitable based the following profitability measures:
   a. Gross margin
   b. Gross margin percentage of sales
   c. Operating income
   d. Operating income percentage of sales

12-A3 Joint Products

Quebec Metals buys raw ore on the open market and processes it into two products, A and B. The ore costs $10 per pound, and the process separating it into A and B has a cost of $4 per pound. During 20X7, Quebec plans to produce 200,000 pounds of A and 600,000 pounds of B from 800,000 pounds of ore. A sells for $30 a pound and B for $15 a pound. The company allocated joint costs to the individual products for inventory valuation purposes.

1. Allocate all the joint costs to A and B using the physical-units method.
2. Allocate all the joint costs to A and B using the relative-sales-value method.
3. Suppose B cannot be sold in the form in which it emerges from the joint process. Instead, it must be processed further at a fixed cost of $300,000 plus a variable cost of $1 per pound. Then, it can be sold for $21.50 a pound. Allocate all the joint costs to A and B using the relative-sales-value method.

12-B1 Allocation of Service Department Costs; General Framework for Allocation

Dallas Cleaning provides cleaning services for a variety of clients. The company has two producing departments, residential and commercial, and two service departments, personnel and administrative. The company has decided to allocate all service department costs to the producing departments' personnel on the basis of number of employees and administrative on the basis of direct department costs. The budget for 20X7 shows the following:

	Personnel	Administrative	Residential	Commercial
Direct department costs	$70,000	$90,000	$240,000	$400,000
Number of employees	3	5	12	18
Direct-labor hours			24,000	36,000
Square feet cleaned			4,500,000	9,970,000

1. Allocate service department costs using the direct method.
2. Allocate service department costs using the step-down method. Personnel costs should be allocated first.
3. Suppose the company prices by the hour in the residential department and by the square foot cleaned in commercial. Using the results of the step-down allocations in number 2,
   a. compute the cost of providing 1 direct-labor hour of service in the residential department.
   b. compute the cost of cleaning one square foot of space in the commercial department.
4. refer to Exhibit 12-1 on page 474. For each type of cost assignment made in number 2 using the step-down method, indicate the assignment type from Exhibit 12-1.

12-B2 Customer Profitability

Hogenson Company makes three product lines and has two customer types. The following table gives sales, product cost, and cost-to-serve data for Hogenson:

	Product X	Product Y	Product Z
Sales	$2,000	$8,000	$20,000
Cost of goods sold	1,000	2,000	14,000

	Customer Type 1	Customer Type 2	Total
Product X Sales	$1,000	$ 1,000	$ 2,000
Product Y Sales	5,000	3,000	8,000
Product Z Sales	1,000	19,000	20,000
Manager Visits	6	4	10

The cost to serve all customers is $10,000 and is allocated to customer types based on the number of manager visits to customer locations for pre- and post-sales support.

1. Determine the gross profit margin percentage of sales for each product. Which product is the most profitable?
2. Determine the gross profit margin and the gross profit margin percentage of sales for each customer type.
3. Determine the cost-to-serve percentage of sales for each customer type.
4. Determine the operating income and operating income percentage of sales for each customer type.
5. Which customer is the most profitable based the following profitability measures:
   a. Gross margin
   b. Gross margin percentage of sales
   c. Operating income
   d. Operating income percentage of sales

12-B3 Joint Products

Des Moines Milling buys oats at $.60 per pound and produces CRM Oat Flour, CRM Oat Flakes, and CRM Oat Bran. The process of separating the oats into oat flour and oat bran costs $.30 per pound. The oat flour can be sold for $1.50 per pound, the oat bran for $2.00 per pound. Each pound of oats has .2 pounds of oat bran and .8 pounds of oat flour. A pound of oat flour can be made into oat flakes for a fixed cost of $240,000 plus a variable cost of $.60 per pound. Des Moines Milling plans to process 1 million pounds of oats in 20X7, at a purchase price of $600,000.

1. Allocate all the joint costs to oat flour and oat bran using the physical-units method.
2. Allocate all the joint costs to oat flour and oat bran using the relative-sales-value method.
3. Suppose there were no market for oat flour. Instead, it must be made into oat flakes to be sold. Oat flakes sell for $2.90 per pound. Allocate the joint cost to oat bran and oat flakes using the relative-sales-value method.

Additional Assignment Material

MyAccountingLab

QUESTIONS

12-1 Why is the cost-allocation method used by an organization an important part of its cost accounting system?

12-2 In a meeting among company executives and cost accountants, the CEO asked for the product costs for the company's newest product line. The cost accountant replied, "Product cost depends on the reason for knowing it." Do you agree? Explain briefly.

12-3 What are the 10 types of cost assignments?

12-4 When determining customer profitability, why is it important to directly trace and allocate customer-related service department costs to customers rather than assigning them first to producing departments and then to customers?

12-5 "The more the better!" was a comment made by the CEO of a major company when asked about allocation of sales, general, and administrative costs to products. Do you agree? Explain.

12-6 List three guidelines for the allocation of service department costs.

12-7 Explain how a direct department cost can become an indirect cost.

12-8 Why should budgeted cost rates, rather than actual cost rates, be used for allocating the variable costs of service departments?

12-9 "We used a lump-sum allocation method for fixed costs a few years ago, but we gave it up because managers always predicted usage below what they actually used." Is this a common problem? How might it be prevented?

12-10 Briefly describe the two popular methods for allocating service department costs.

12-11 "The step-down method allocates more costs to the producing departments than does the direct method." Do you agree? Explain.

12-12 What is a non-volume-related cost driver? Give two examples.

12-13 How are costs of various overhead resources allocated to products, services, or customers in an ABC system?

12-14 "A cost pool for a particular resource is either a variable cost pool or a fixed cost pool. There should be no mixed-cost pools." Do you agree? Explain.

12-15 Give four examples of activities and related cost-allocation bases that can be used in an ABC system to allocate costs to products, services, or customers.

12-16 Name the four steps used to allocate producing department activity cost pools using the ABC approach.

12-17 List several factors that determine whether a customer has a low or high cost to serve.

12-18 Chapter 6 explained that joint costs should not be allocated to individual products for decision purposes. For what purposes are such costs allocated to products?

12-19 Briefly explain each of the two conventional ways of allocating joint costs of products.

12-20 What are by-products and how do we account for them?

12-21 Suppose Winter Park Company has two plants—the Salem plant and the Youngstown plant. The Youngstown plant produces only three components that are very similar in material and production requirements. The Salem plant makes a wide variety of parts. Which type of costing system would you recommend for each plant (traditional or ABC)? Explain.

12-22 Study Appendix 12. Distinguish between two-stage and multistage ABC systems.

12-23 Study Appendix 12. In Exhibits 12-20 and 12-21, the *r*s represent resource- and activity-consumption rates. Why are these rates important to managers looking for ideas for process improvements?

12-24 Study Appendix 12. Explain the difference between resource-consumption rates and cost per driver unit.

12-25 Why is it necessary to know the profitability of customers? If all the products of a company are profitable, shouldn't its customers also be profitable? Explain.

CRITICAL THINKING EXERCISES

12-26 Allocation and Cost Behavior

There are three general guidelines to use when allocating service department (support) costs. One of these guidelines deals with the cost behavior of support costs. Why do many companies allocate fixed support costs separately from variable support costs?

12-27 Allocation and the Sales Function

Confusion can arise when cost allocations to one consuming department depend on the activity of another consuming department. "A commonly misused basis for allocation of central support costs is actual dollar sales." Explain.

12-28 Allocation and Marketing

Many companies are allocating more nonproduction costs because of the increasing magnitude of these value-chain costs. One value-chain function that is receiving more attention is marketing. How should national advertising costs be allocated to territories?

EXERCISES

12-29 Allocation of Computer Costs

Review the section Allocation of Service Department Costs, pages 476–482, especially the example of the use of the computer by the university. Recall that the budget formula was $100,000 fixed cost monthly plus $200 per hour of computer time used. Based on long-run predicted usage, the fixed costs were allocated on a lump-sum basis, 30% to business and 70% to engineering.

1. Show the total allocation if business used 210 hours and engineering used 390 hours in a given month. Assume that the actual costs coincided exactly with the budgeted amount for total usage of 600 hours.
2. Assume the same facts as in number 1 except that the fixed costs were allocated on the basis of actual hours of usage. Show the total allocation of costs to each school. As the dean of the school of business, would you prefer this method or the method in number 1? Explain.

12-30 Fixed- and Variable-Cost Pools

The city of Castle Rock signed a lease for a photocopy machine at $2,500 per month and $.02 per copy. Operating costs for toner, paper, operator salary, and so on are all variable at $.03 per copy. Departments had projected a need for 100,000 copies a month. The city planning department predicted its usage at 36,000 copies a month. It made 42,000 copies in August.

1. Suppose one predetermined rate per copy was used to allocate all photocopy costs. What rate would be used and how much cost would be allocated to the city planning department in August?
2. Suppose fixed- and variable-cost pools were allocated separately. Specify how each pool should be allocated. Compute the cost allocated to the city planning department in August.
3. Which method, the one in number 1 or the one in number 2, do you prefer? Explain.

12-31 Sales-Based Allocations

Johnny's Markets has three grocery stores in the metropolitan Philadelphia area. Central costs are allocated using sales as the cost-allocation base. The following are budgeted and actual sales during November:

	Sunnyville	Wedgewood	Capital
Budgeted sales	$600,000	$1,000,000	$400,000
Actual sales	600,000	700,000	500,000

Central costs of $200,000 are to be allocated in November.

1. Compute the central costs allocated to each store with budgeted sales as the cost-allocation base.
2. Compute the central costs allocated to each store with actual sales as the cost-allocation base.
3. What advantages are there to using budgeted rather than actual sales for allocating the central costs?

12-32 Direct and Step-Down Allocations, Activity-Based Allocation, and Process Map

Denver Building Maintenance provides cleaning services for a variety of clients. The company has two producing divisions, residential and commercial, and two service departments, personnel and administrative. The company uses an activity-based allocation system in each of its producing divisions. Previously, the costs of service support departments has been unallocated. However, the company has decided to allocate all service department costs to the producing departments' personnel on the basis of number of employees and administrative on the basis of the direct costs of the activities in each division. Denver uses a process map as part of its activity-based allocation system. The map based on the budget for 20X5 is shown in Exhibit 12-23 on page 514.

1. Determine the costs allocated to the residential and commercial divisions using the direct method.
2. Determine the costs allocated to the residential and commercial divisions using the step-down method. The personnel department costs should be allocated first.
3. Explain how costs would be allocated to each customer in both the residential and commercial divisions.

12-33 Direct and Step-Down Allocations

Butler Home Products has two producing departments, machining and assembly, and two service departments, personnel and custodial. The company's budget for April 20X7 is as follows:

	Service Departments		Production Departments	
	Personnel	Custodial	Machining	Assembly
Direct department costs	$32,000	$70,000	$600,000	$800,000
Square feet	2,000	1,000	10,000	25,000
Number of employees	15	30	200	250

Butler allocates personnel costs on the basis of number of employees. Butler allocates custodial costs on the basis of square feet.

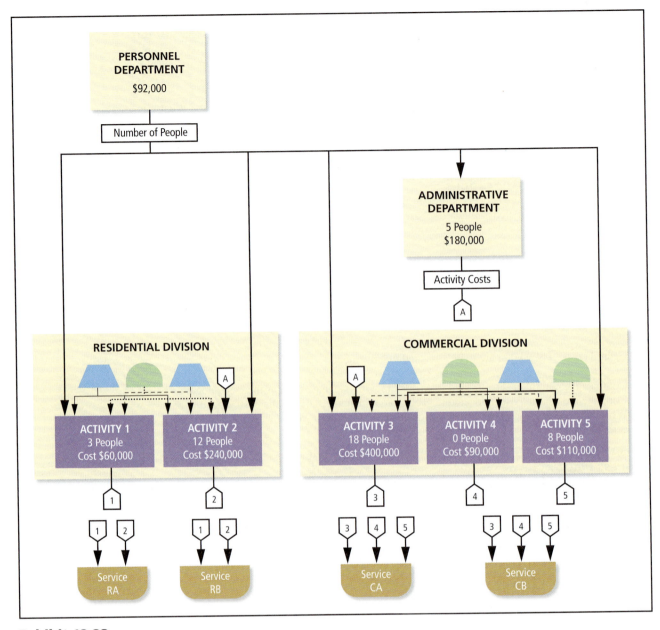

Exhibit 12-23
Denver Building Maintenance, Inc., Allocation System

1. Allocate personnel and custodial costs to the producing departments using the direct method.
2. Allocate personnel and custodial costs to the producing departments using the step-down method. Allocate personnel costs first.

12-34 Customer Profitability; Strategy

The table at the top of page 515 gives the sales, product cost, and cost-to-serve data for a merchandising store. The store has four types of merchandise and three types of customers.

The costs to serve all customers is $140,000 and is allocated to customer types based on the number of units sold.

1. Determine the gross profit margin percentage of sales for each product. Which product is the most profitable?
2. Determine the gross profit margin percentage of sales for each customer type.
3. Determine the cost-to-serve percentage of sales for each customer type.
4. Which customer is the most profitable?
5. Prepare a chart similar to Exhibit 12-18 that shows the customer gross margin percentage and cost-to-serve percentage for the three customers. Recommend a strategy for profit improvement for each customer.

	Product A		Product B		Product C		Product D
Sales	$32,000	Sales	$88,000	Sales	$280,000	Sales	$144,000
Cost of sales	20,000	Cost of sales	70,400	Cost of sales	224,000	Cost of sales	81,000

	Customer Type 1	Customer Type 2	Customer Type 3	Total Units Sold
Product A units	200	2,200	500	2,900
Product B units	100	1,200	3,000	4,300
Product C units	50	400	5,000	5,450
Product D units	400	800	400	1,600
Total units sold	750	4,600	8,900	14,250

12-35 Joint Costs

Robinson Chemical Company's production process for two of its solvents can be diagrammed as follows:

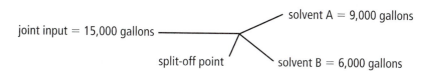

joint input = 15,000 gallons — split-off point — solvent A = 9,000 gallons / solvent B = 6,000 gallons

The cost of the joint input, including processing costs before the split-off point, is $300,000. Solvent A can be sold at split off for $30 per gallon and solvent B for $45 per gallon.

1. Allocate the $300,000 joint cost to solvents A and B by the physical-units method.
2. Allocate the $300,000 joint cost to solvents A and B by the relative-sales-value method.

12-36 Joint Costs and Process Map

Hernandez Chemical Company's production process for two of its solvents can be diagrammed using a process map as shown in Exhibit 12-24.

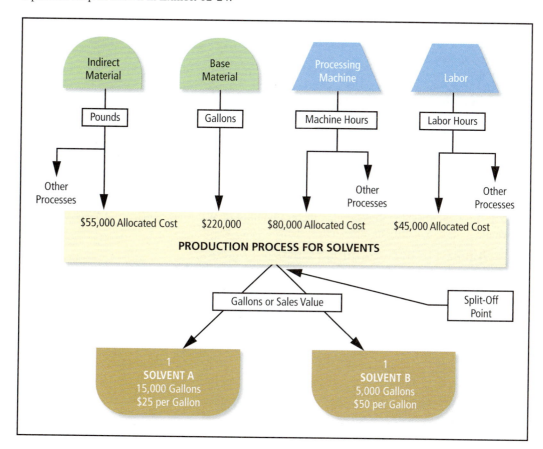

Exhibit 12-24
Hernandez Chemical Company's Joint Process

The cost of the joint input, including processing costs before the split-off point, is $400,000. Solvent A can be sold at the split-off point for $25 per gallon and solvent B for $50 per gallon.

1. Allocate the $400,000 joint cost to solvents A and B by the physical-units method.
2. Allocate the $400,000 joint cost to solvents A and B by the relative-sales-value method.

12-37 By-Product Costing

Wenatchee Apple Company buys apples from local orchards and presses them to produce apple juice. The pulp that remains after pressing is sold to farmers as livestock food. This livestock food is accounted for as a by-product.

During the 20X7 fiscal year, the company paid $1 million to purchase 8 million pounds of apples. After processing, 1 million pounds of pulp remained. Wenatchee spent $35,000 to package and ship the pulp, which was sold for $50,000.

1. How much of the joint cost of the apples is allocated to the pulp?
2. Compute the total inventory cost (and therefore the cost of goods sold) for the pulp.
3. Assume that $130,000 was spent to press the apples and $150,000 was spent to filter, pasteurize, and pack the apple juice. Compute the total inventory cost of the apple juice produced.

12-38 Cost Assignment Paths

Study Appendix 12, especially the Summary Problem for Your Review on pages 505. Exhibit 12-20 shows the MSABC system of the billing department. What costs would be included in the billing labor and bill-verifying labor resources? Compile a list of the cost-allocation paths from these two labor resources to the commercial accounts cost object.

PROBLEMS

12-39 General Framework for Allocation, Service Departments, ABC, Customer Profitability, and Process Maps

Consider one of **L.A. Darling**'s manufacturing facilities. Suppose this facility assembles parts for displays to be sold to **Wal-Mart**, **Kmart**, and **Walgreens**. There are three departments—assembly, power, and maintenance. The assembly department uses an ABC system. The general cost of occupancy is allocated to the maintenance department and the assembly department based on the space occupied. Power department costs are allocated based on megawatt hours used. The assembly process produces three different types of displays with diverse demands on various activities and resources. Display type A consists of simple parts that are produced in high volume. Display type B has parts that are of medium volume and complexity. Display type C consists of complex parts that are produced in small lots.

Management implemented ABC in this facility using the four-step procedure outlined on pages 487–489. The first steps have been completed, and the results are depicted in the process map shown in Exhibit 12-25.

1. Refer to Exhibit 12-1 on page 474. For each type of cost assignment listed in Exhibit 12-1, give an example from L.A. Darling. If no example exists, note as such.
2. What allocation method for service department costs does this facility use? Explain.
3. Calculate the allocations of service department and general costs to the assembly department activities.
4. Calculate the activity-based cost of each display type.
5. If L.A. Darling wanted to determine the profitability of Wal-Mart, Kmart, and Walgreens, how would it have to modify its allocation system?

12-40 Allocation of Automobile Costs

The motor pool of a major city provides automobiles for the use of various city departments. Currently, the motor pool has 50 autos. A recent study showed that it costs $2,400 of annual fixed cost per automobile plus $.10 per mile variable cost to own, operate, and maintain autos like those provided by the motor pool.

Each month, the costs of the motor pool are allocated to the user departments on the basis of miles driven. On average, each auto is driven 24,000 miles annually, although wide month-to-month variations occur. In April 20X7, the 50 autos were driven a total of 50,000 miles. The motor pool's total costs for April were $19,000.

The chief planner for the city always seemed concerned about her auto costs. She was especially upset in April when she was charged $5,700 for the 15,000 miles driven in the department's five autos. This is the normal monthly mileage in the department. Her memo to the head of the motor pool stated, "I can certainly get autos at less than the $.38 per mile you charged in April." The response was, "I am

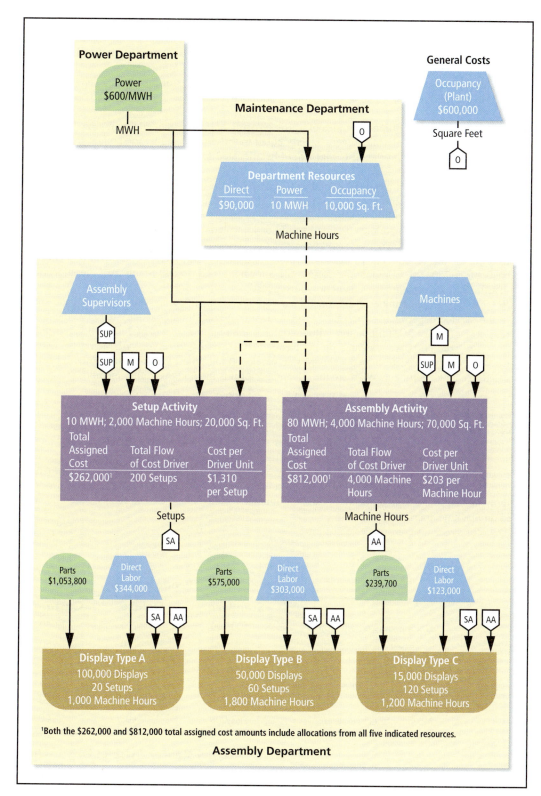

under instructions to allocate the motor pool costs to the user departments. Your department was responsible for 30% of the April usage (15,000 miles ÷ 50,000 miles) so I allocated 30% of the motor pool's April costs to you (.30 × $19,000). That just seems fair."

1. Calculate the city's average annual cost per mile for owning, maintaining, and operating an auto.
2. Explain why the allocated cost in April ($.38 per mile) exceeds the average in number 1.
3. Describe any undesirable behavioral effects of the cost-allocation method used.
4. How would you improve the cost-allocation method?

12-41 Allocation of Costs

The Vigil Trucking Company has one service department and two regional operating departments. The budgeted cost behavior pattern of the service department is $750,000 monthly in fixed costs plus $.75 per 1,000 ton-miles operated in the North and South regions. (Ton-miles are the number of tons carried times the number of miles traveled.) The actual monthly costs of the service department are allocated using ton-miles operated as the cost-allocation base.

1. Vigil processed 500 million ton-miles of traffic in April, half in each operating region. The actual costs of the service department were exactly equal to those predicted by the budget for 500 million ton-miles. Compute the costs that would be allocated to each operating region on an actual ton-miles basis.
2. Suppose the North region was plagued by strikes, so that the amount of freight handled was much lower than originally anticipated. North moved only 150 million ton-miles of traffic. The South region handled 250 million ton-miles. The actual costs were exactly as budgeted for this lower level of activity. Compute the costs that would be allocated to North and South on an actual ton-mile basis. Note that the total costs will be lower.
3. Refer to the facts in number 1. Various inefficiencies caused the service department to incur total costs of $1,250,000. Compute the costs to be allocated to North and South. Are the allocations justified? If not, what improvement do you suggest?
4. Refer to the facts in number 2. Assume that assorted investment outlays for equipment and space in the service department were made to provide a basic maximum capacity to serve the North region at a level of 360 million ton-miles and the South region at a level of 240 million ton-miles. Suppose fixed costs are allocated on the basis of this capacity to serve. Variable costs are allocated by using a predetermined standard rate per 1,000 ton-miles. Compute the costs to be allocated to each department. What are the advantages of this method over other methods?

12-42 Service Department Allocation and ABC, Product Costing

Fancy Fixtures makes displays for retail outlets. The company has three product lines—standard, deluxe, and custom. Fancy Fixtures integrates its service department allocation system with its ABC system. There are two service departments—power and facilities management. Fancy allocates its two service department costs to the processing department using the direct method based on megawatt hours and machine hours consumed. There are two activity centers in the processing department—setup/maintenance and assembly. Parts and assembly labor are traced directly to each product. Setup/maintenance costs are allocated based on number of setups, and assembly costs are allocated based on machine hours.

Data for a recent reporting period follow:

	Product Line		
	Standard	**Deluxe**	**Custom**
Units produced and sold	100,000	10,000	1,000
Sales price per unit	$ 20	$ 50	$ 250
Total parts costs	$1,003,800	$115,080	$15,980
Total direct-labor costs	$ 298,000	$ 72,000	$68,000
Setups	20	12	8
Machine hours in assembly	1,000	400	100

			Activity Centers' Use of Driver Unit	
Resource/Department	**Total Cost**	**Driver Unit**	**Setup/Maintenance**	**Assembly**
Assembly supervisors	$ 90,000	%	2%	98%
Assembly machines	$247,000	Machine hours	400	1,500
Facilities management department	$ 95,000	Machine hours	400	1,500
Power department	$ 54,000	Megawatt hours	10	80

Prepare a schedule that calculates the gross profit available to cover other value-chain costs for each product and Fancy Fixtures as a whole company.

12-43 Service Department Allocation and ABC; Product Profitability; Process Map

(This problem is the same as problem 12-42, but uses a process map to provide data.) Fancy Fixtures makes displays for retail outlets. The company has three product lines—standard, deluxe, and custom. Fancy Fixtures integrates its service department allocation system with its ABC system. There are two service departments—power and facilities management. Fancy allocates its two service department costs to the processing department using the direct method based on megawatt hours and machine hours consumed. There are two activity centers in the processing department—setup/maintenance and assembly. Parts and assembly labor are traced directly to each product. Setup/maintenance costs are allocated based on number of setups and assembly costs are allocated based on machine hours.

Exhibit 12-26 is a process map for operations at Fancy Fixtures.

Prepare a schedule that calculates the gross profit available to cover other value-chain costs for each product and Fancy Fixtures as a whole company.

12-44 Service Department Allocation and ABC; Customer Profitability

(This problem should not be assigned unless problem 12-42 or problem 12-43 is also assigned.) Refer to problem 12-42 or problem 12-43. Fancy Fixtures has two types of customers. Customer

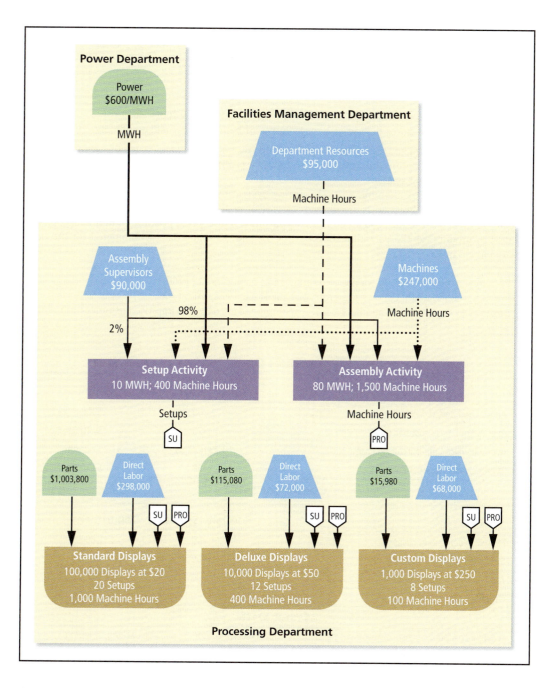

Exhibit 12-26
Allocation of Service Department Costs in Fancy Fixtures' ABC System

type 1 purchases mostly standard displays. Customer type 2 purchases all three product lines but is the only customer type that purchases custom displays. Data regarding the product mix for each customer follows:

| | **Units Sold by Product Line** | | | |
	Standard	Deluxe	Custom	Total
Customer type 1	75,000	5,000	0	80,000
Customer type 2	25,000	5,000	1,000	31,000
Total	100,000	10,000	1,000	111,000

Prepare a schedule that calculates the gross profit available to cover other value-chain costs for each customer type.

12-45 Customer Profitability at a Distributor

Mountain Cities Distributors (MCD) is a distributor of sports footwear and equipment. MCD distributes many products to retail accounts but classifies products into just two product groups—footwear and equipment.

- Footwear items arrive at MCD in cases and are shipped to customers in these cases.
- MCD receives equipment in bulk shipments. MCD must unpack these products and then repack them to meet small order quantities for specific equipment. Examples include weight-training equipment and golf clubs and bags.

MCD has two types of customers:

1. Specialty stores: stores that order low volumes, the majority being footwear
2. Department stores: stores that order large volumes of both footwear and equipment

MCD's management has set a strategic goal to improve both product and customer profitability. A related subgoal that supports this strategy is to identify profitable products and customers using an accurate cost-accounting system.

MCD currently uses a simple cost-accounting system to calculate both product and customer profitability. The only direct costs are the purchase costs of footwear and equipment products. MCD allocates indirect costs to the product groups using a single indirect cost pool for all indirect costs with "pounds of product" as the cost allocation base. Cost and operating data accumulated for the most recent year are in Exhibit 12-27.

1. Prepare a schedule that shows the gross margin of each product group.
2. Prepare a schedule that shows the gross margin of each customer type.
3. Based on your answers to numbers 1 and 2, recommend a strategy to improve customer profitability.

Exhibit 12-27
Operating Data for Mountain Cities Distributors

Product Data

	Footwear	Equipment
Annual demand in cases	2,800	2,000
Average purchase cost per case	$70	$120
Average weight per purchased case	18.75 pounds	31.25 pounds
Average sales price per case	$460	$790

Customer Data

Stores	Specialty Stores	Department
Footwear demand in cases	1,200	1,600
Equipment demand in cases	400	1,600
Total annual demand in cases	1,600	3,200
Orders	160	70

Other Data

A single cost pool consists of resources needed to perform receiving, storing, picking, packing, shipping, order processing, and customer service activities. The annual cost of these resources is $1,380,000. The cost-allocation base used to allocate this pool to the two product groups is pounds of product sold.

12-46 Customer Profitability and Allocation of Costs to Serve

(This problem is a continuation of problem 12-45 and should be assigned only if 12-45 is also assigned.)

Based on a study of operations at MCD, it was determined that "number of orders" was a better cost-allocation base for the order processing and customer service activities. The cost of the resources used by these two activities is $552,000 out of the total indirect cost pool of $1,380,000. MCD now wants to refine its costing system by allocating order processing and customer service activities to customers rather than to products.

1. Prepare a schedule that shows product gross margin for each of the products made by MCD.
2. Prepare a schedule that shows customer product gross margin, customer cost to serve, and customer profitability.
3. Prepare a chart that shows customer product gross margin percentage versus customer cost-to-serve percentage for each of the customer types. Based on this chart, recommend a strategy that can be used to improve customer profitability for each customer type.
4. Compare customer profitability results determined by this refined costing system to the results obtained in problem 12-45. Explain any significant differences.

12-47 Hospital Equipment

Many states have a hospital commission that must approve the acquisition of specified medical equipment before the hospitals in the state can qualify for cost-based reimbursement related to that equipment. That is, hospitals cannot bill government agencies for the use of the equipment unless the commission originally authorized the acquisition.

Two hospitals in one state proposed the acquisition and sharing of some expensive X-ray equipment to be used for unusual cases. The depreciation and related fixed costs of operating the equipment were predicted at $12,000 per month. The variable costs were predicted at $30 per patient procedure.

The commission asked each hospital to predict its usage of the equipment over its expected useful life of 5 years. University Hospital predicted an average usage of 75 X-rays per month, while Children's Hospital predicted 50 X-rays. The commission regarded this information as critical to the size and degree of sophistication that would be justified. That is, if the number of X-rays exceeded a certain quantity per month, a different configuration of space, equipment, and personnel would be required that would mean higher fixed costs per month.

1. Suppose fixed costs are allocated on the basis of the hospitals' predicted average use per month. Variable costs are allocated on the basis of $30 per X-ray, the budgeted variable-cost rate for the current fiscal year. In October, University Hospital had 50 X-rays and Children's Hospital had 50 X-rays. Compute the total costs allocated to University Hospital and to Children's Hospital.
2. Suppose the manager of the equipment had various operating inefficiencies so that the total October costs were $16,500. Would you change your answers in number 1? Why?
3. A traditional method of cost allocation does not use the method in number 1. Instead, an allocation rate depends on the actual costs and actual volume encountered. The actual costs are totaled for the month and divided by the actual number of X-rays during the month. Suppose the actual costs agreed exactly with the budget for a total of 100 actual X-rays. Compute the total costs allocated to University Hospital and to Children's Hospital. Compare the results with those in number 1. What is the major weakness in this traditional method? What are some of its possible behavioral effects?
4. Describe any undesirable behavioral effects of the method described in number 1. How would you counteract any tendencies toward deliberate false predictions of long-run usage?

12-48 Direct Method for Service Department Allocation

Wheelick Controls Company has two producing departments, mechanical instruments and electronic instruments. In addition, there are two service departments, building services and materials receiving and handling. The company purchases a variety of component parts from which the departments assemble instruments for sale in domestic and international markets.

The electronic instruments division is highly automated. The manufacturing costs depend primarily on the number of subcomponents in each instrument. In contrast, the mechanical instruments division relies primarily on a large labor force to hand-assemble instruments. Its costs depend on direct-labor hours.

The costs of building services depend primarily on the square footage occupied. The costs of materials receiving and handling depend primarily on the total number of components handled.

Instruments M1 and M2 are produced in the mechanical instruments department, and E1 and E2 are produced in the electronic instruments department. Data about these products follow:

	Direct-Materials Cost	Number of Components	Direct-Labor Hours
M1	$74	25	4.0
M2	86	21	8.0
E1	63	10	1.5
E2	91	15	1.0

Budget figures for 20X7 include the following:

	Building Service	Materials Receiving and Handling	Mechanical Instruments	Electronic Instruments
Direct department costs (excluding direct materials cost)	$150,000	$120,000	$680,000	$548,000
Square footage occupied		5,000	50,000	25,000
Number of final instruments produced			8,000	10,000
Average number of components per instrument			10	16
Direct-labor hours			30,000	8,000

1. Allocate the costs of the service departments using the direct method.
2. Using the results of number 1, compute the cost per direct-labor hour in the Mechanical Instruments department and the cost per component in the Electronic Instruments department.
3. Using the results of number 2, compute the cost per unit of product for instruments M1, M2, E1, and E2.

12-49 Step-Down Method for Service Department Allocation
Refer to the data in problem 12-48.

1. Allocate the costs of the service departments using the step-down method.
2. Using the results of number 1, compute the cost per direct-labor hour in the mechanical instruments department and the cost per component in the electronic instruments department.
3. Using the results of number 2, compute the cost per unit of product for instruments M1, M2, E1, and E2.

12-50 ABC Allocations; Process Map; What If Analysis
Yamaguchi Company makes printed circuit boards in a suburb of Kyoto. The production process is automated with computer-controlled robotic machines assembling each circuit board from a supply of parts and then soldering the parts to the board. Materials-handling and quality-assurance activities use a combination of labor and equipment. Although a few resources that are used are variable with respect to changes in the demand of boards, these costs are not material compared to the fixed-cost resources that are used.

Yamaguchi makes three types of circuit boards, models 1, 2, and 3. Steps 1–3 of the design process for an ABC system have been completed. Exhibit 12-28 shows the process-based map of Yamaguchi's operations.

1. Compute the cost of production for each of the three types of circuit boards and the cost per circuit board for each type.
2. What if the design of model 1 could be simplified so that it required only 10 distinct parts (instead of 20) and took only 3 minutes of testing time (instead of five). Compute the cost of model 1 circuit boards and the cost per circuit board. Will the costs per circuit board for models 2 and 3 change? You do not need to compute the costs per circuit board for models 2 and 3, only note whether the costs will increase, decrease, remain unchanged, or cannot be determined. Explain.

12-51 Activity-Based Allocations
St. Louis Wholesale Distributors uses an ABC system to determine the cost of handling its products. One important activity is receiving shipments in the warehouse. Three resources support that activity: (1) recording and record keeping, (2) labor, and (3) inspection.

Recording and record keeping is a variable cost driven by number of shipments received. The cost per shipment is $18.

Labor is driven by pounds of merchandise received. Because labor is hired in shifts, it is fixed for large ranges of volume. Currently, labor costs are running $32,200 per month for

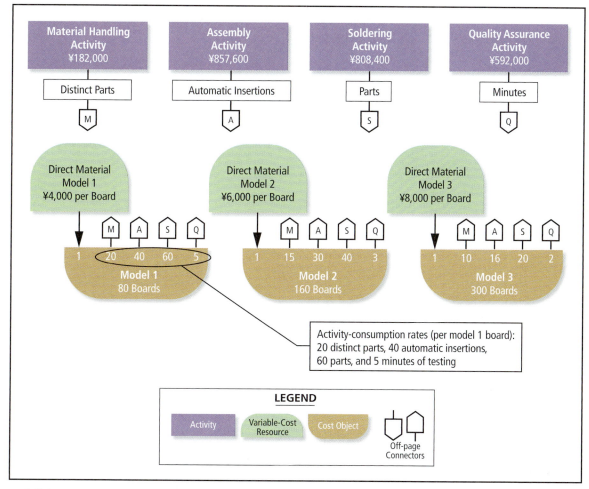

Activity-consumption rates (per model 1 board):
20 distinct parts, 40 automatic insertions,
60 parts, and 5 minutes of testing

LEGEND

| Activity | Variable-Cost Resource | Cost Object | Off-page Connectors |

Exhibit 12-28
Yamaguchi Company's Two-Stage ABC System

handling 460,000 pounds. This same cost would apply to all volumes between 300,000 pounds and 550,000 pounds.

Finally, inspection is a variable cost driven by the number of boxes received. Inspection costs are $3.75 per box.

One product distributed by St. Louis Wholesale Distributors is candy. There is a wide variety of candy so many different shipments are handled in the warehouse. In July, the warehouse received 500 shipments, consisting of 4,000 boxes weighing a total of 80,000 pounds.

1. Compute the cost of receiving candy shipments during July.
2. Management is considering elimination of brands of candy that have small sales levels. This would reduce the warehouse volume to 200 shipments, consisting of 3,000 boxes weighing a total of 60,000 pounds. Compute the amount of savings from eliminating the small-sales-level brands.
3. Suppose receiving costs were estimated on a per-pound basis. What was the total receiving cost per pound of candy received in July? If management had used this cost to estimate the effect of eliminating the 20,000 pounds of candy, what mistake might be made?

12-52 Allocation of Central Costs
The Union Atlantic Railroad allocates all central corporate overhead costs to its divisions. Some costs, such as specified internal auditing and legal costs, are identified on the basis of time spent. However, other costs are harder to allocate so the revenue achieved by each division is used as an allocation base. Examples of such costs are executive salaries, travel, secretarial, utilities, rent, depreciation, donations, corporate planning, and general marketing costs.

Allocations on the basis of revenue for 20X7 are shown at the top of page 524 (in millions). In 20X8, Northeast's revenue remained unchanged. However, Southeast's revenue soared to $280 million because of unusually large imports. The latter are troublesome to forecast because of variations in world markets. Mid-Atlantic had expected a sharp rise in revenue, but severe competitive conditions resulted in a decline to $200 million. The total cost allocated on the basis of revenue was again $30 million, despite rises in other costs. The president was pleased that central costs did not rise for the year.

Division	Revenue	Allocated Costs
Northeast	$120	$ 6
Mid-Atlantic	240	12
Southeast	240	12
Total	$600	$30

1. Compute the allocations of costs to each division for 20X8.
2. How would each division manager probably feel about the cost allocation in 20X8 as compared with 20X7? What are the weaknesses of using revenue as a basis for cost allocation?
3. Suppose the budgeted revenues for 20X8 were $120, $240, and $280, respectively, and the budgeted revenues were used as a cost-allocation base for allocation. Compute the allocations of costs to each division for 20X8. Do you prefer this method to the one used in number 1? Why?
4. Many accountants and managers oppose allocating any central costs. Why?

12-53 Joint Costs and Decisions

A chemical company has a batch process that takes 1,000 gallons of a raw material and transforms it into 80 pounds of X1 and 400 pounds of X2. Although the joint costs of their production are $1,200, both products are worthless at their split-off point. Additional separable costs of $350 are necessary to give X1 a sales value of $1,000 as product A. Similarly, additional separable costs of $200 are necessary to give X2 a sales value of $1,000 as product B.

You are in charge of the batch process and the marketing of both products. (Show your computations for each answer.)

1. a. Assuming that you believe in assigning joint costs on a physical basis, allocate the total profit of $250 per batch to products A and B.
   b. Would you stop processing one of the products? Why?
2. a. Assuming that you believe in assigning joint costs on a net-realizable-value (relative-sales-value) basis, allocate the total operating profit of $250 per batch to products A and B. If there is no market for X1 and X2 at their split-off point, a net realizable value is usually imputed by taking the ultimate sales values at the point of sale and working backward to obtain approximated "synthetic" relative sales values at the split-off point. These synthetic values are then used as weights for allocating the joint costs to the products.
   b. You have internal product-profitability reports in which joint costs are assigned on a net-realizable-value basis. Your chief engineer says that, after seeing these reports, he has developed a method of obtaining more of product B and correspondingly less of product A from each batch, without changing the per-pound cost factors. Would you approve this new method? Why? What would the overall operating profit be if 40 pounds more of B were produced and 40 pounds less of A?

12-54 Multistage Activity-Based Costing at AT&T

Study Appendix 12. Refer to the appendix discussion of the billing department at one of AT&T's customer care centers. Suppose the billing department has designed an MSABC system. Exhibit 12-20 on page 506 shows the process map for the MSABC system.

1. Calculate the cost per account for residential and commercial customers.
2. Based on this new MSABC information, what recommendation would you make to the billing department management concerning outsourcing to the local service bureau?
3. Prepare a table or chart that contrasts the residential cost per account to the commercial cost per account using the traditional, two-stage ABC, and MSABC systems. Comment on the results, indicating which system gives a greater level of accuracy and more information for management's strategic planning and operational control purposes.

CASES

12-55 Customer Profitability

Distribution Solutions, Inc., (DSI) is a regional distributor providing logistical support for merchandisers over a three-state area. Its distribution centers have been profitable until recently. DSI provides logistics solutions in industries such as fashion apparel, electronics, housewares, building materials, automotive tools, and beverage. Its locations are convenient to major ports and transportation hubs. DSI has an outstanding reputation for customer service.

Profit margins have declined over the past several years due mostly to a weak regional economy and competition from larger merchandisers such as **Home Depot**, **Lowe's**, and **Wal-Mart** who use logistic services of larger national distributors. Thus, the market share of merchandisers has declined along with their need for logistics support from DSI.

DSI orders supplies from a variety of manufacturers. All goods processed through the warehouse are stored on pallets and are handled by forklifts driven by forklift operators, who are assisted by warehouse labor. Processing of product consists of unloading at the receiving area (receiving activity), moving to the warehouse storage (put away activity), moving/shifting within the warehouse (warehousing activity), removal from racks (picking activity), and repacking (repacking activity). Customer-specific processing consists of order taking, customer service, order changes, returns, scheduling (regular or expedited), and shipping.

Prices at DSI are set using a cost-plus formula based on the average cost per case delivered during the previous year. Two markups are used. The first markup covers the cost of warehousing and distribution. The second markup covers the costs of general and selling expenses and an allowance for profit. Currently (20X7) this price is $7.25 per case. However, with the various discounts and promotions, this year's actual price averages $4.75 per case for all products.

DSI has six distinct product groups:

1. Regular products are prepackaged arriving and leaving in cases.
2. Fragile products are prepackaged but require care in handling.
3. Bulk products arrive in loose lots in crates or cases and are repackaged in smaller boxes, polybags, or small cartons before packing in cases.
4. High-security products must be locked in high-security area.
5. Short shelf-life products are dated products.
6. Singles are received in bundles and will be unbundled and hand-stacked for storage.

Traditionally, the regular prepackaged product has generated both high margins and high volume. Fragile pre-packaged product has high margin but low volume. Bulk products and singles have poor margins but have been part of DSI's offerings because of customer demands for a full-line distributor. As DSI focused on increasing sales, mega stores and local small stores have increased their purchases of bulk products and singles. Until now, no premium has been charged for these products.

DSI has for many years classified its customer base into various types. Prior to 20X2, almost all its customers were mega stores or large local stores. Since 20X2, local small store and specialty store business has been aggressively pursued. The customer types can be described as follows:

- Mega stores (CT1): a few very large stores that order large volumes of all product types (7,680,000 cases annually)
- Local small stores (CT2): many stores that order low volumes of all products for each store (6,000,000 cases annually)
- Local large stores (CT3): many stores that order large volumes of only regular, fragile, and bulk products (14,400,000 cases annually)
- Specialty stores (CT4): a few stores that order low volumes of only regular, high-security, and short shelf-life products (600,000 cases annually)

Over the past several months, Paul Doxey, controller, working closely with Jane Stratford, chief marketing officer, and a cross-functional implementation team have been developing the ABC system to include all costs as well as customer profitability. A study has been conducted to determine the key drivers of work associated with the various customer types. These drivers include order frequency, order size, pallets ordered, customer-specific service, and order changes.

Key activities associated with serving customers include the following:
- Shipping
- Parcel delivery
- Truck delivery
- Customer support
- Regular scheduling
- Expedited scheduling
- Order processing
- Order changes
- Corporate support

The implementation team headed by Paul Doxey has completed the activity analysis interviews, prepared a process map, collected data, and validated the new model both operationally and financially. The new process map is shown in Exhibit 12-29 on page 526. In order to link the product and customer models the product mix for each customer is specified giving the gross profit for each customer. Exhibit 12-30 on page 527 shows the product mix for each of the four customer types. Exhibit 12-31 on page 527 shows the cost-to-serve data for each driver.

1. Using Excel, construct an exhibit that calculates customer gross margin percentage and customer cost-to-serve percentage for the four customer types. Plot these points along with one for customer type 2 on a graph similar to Exhibit 12-18 on page 497.
2. For each customer type, recommend a strategy to improve profitability.

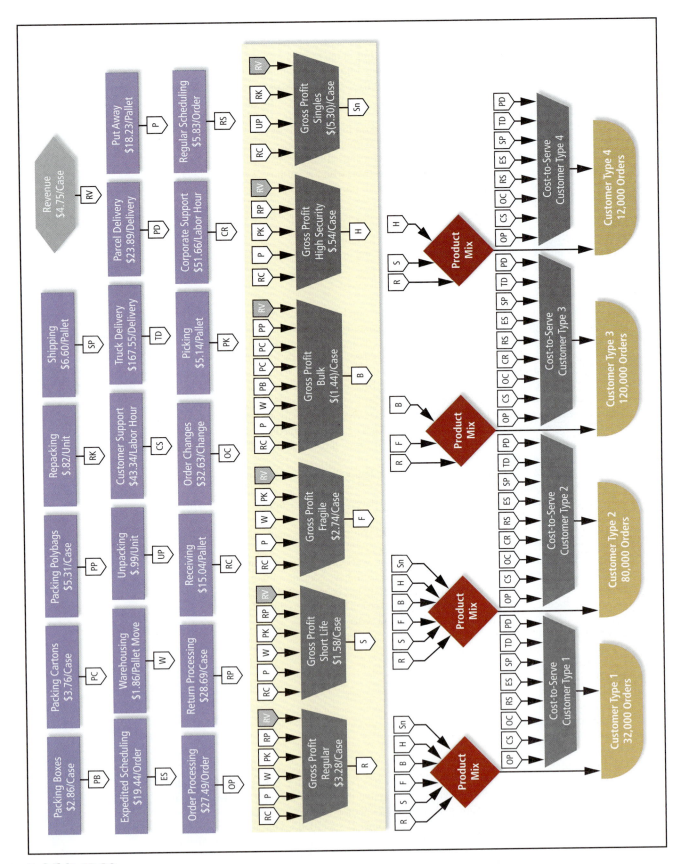

Exhibit 12-29
Process Map for Product/Customer Profitability

Product Mix (%)

Exhibit 12-30
Product Mix Data for
Product/Customer
Profitability Model

	Regular	Short Lived	Fragile	Bulk	High Security	Singles
Customer Type 1 Mega Stores	60%	5%	5%	20%	5%	5%
Customer Type 2 Local Small Stores	50	5	5	30	8	2
Customer Type 3 Local Large Stores	80	—	10	10	—	—
Customer Type 4 Specialty Stores	10	20	—	—	70	—

Cost-to-Serve Activities

	Order Processing	Customer Support	Order Changes	Corporate Support	Scheduling— Regular	Scheduling— Expedited	Shipping	Delivery— Truck	Delivery— Parcel
Cost Driver	Orders	Labor Hours	Number of Changes	Labor Hours	Orders	Orders	Pallets	Deliveries	Deliveries
Cost per Driver Unit	$27.49	$43.34	$32.63	$51.66	$5.83	$19.44	$6.60	$167.55	$23.89
				Number of Driver Units (Thousands)					
CT1	32	18.7	3.2	0	29	3	416	25.6*	1.6*
CT2	80	100.0	8.0	20	72	8	640	68.0	8.0
CT3	120	70.0	2.4	80	108	12	840	90.0	6.0
CT4	12	30.0	1.2	0	10	2	60	4.8	2.4

*The sum of deliveries (25.6 + 1.6 = 27.2 on average) is less than the number of orders (29 + 3) because a few customers picked up their order at the distribution center.

Exhibit 12-31
Cost Driver Data by Customer Type and Cost-to-Serve Activity

12-56 Allocation of Data Processing Costs

The Gibraltar Insurance Co. (GIC) established a systems department to implement and operate its own data processing systems. GIC believed that its own system would be more cost-effective than the service bureau it had been using.

GIC's three departments—claims, records, and finance—have different requirements with respect to hardware and other capacity-related resources and operating resources. The system was designed to recognize these differing needs. In addition, the system was designed to meet GIC's long-term capacity needs. The excess capacity designed into the system would be sold to outside users until needed by GIC. The estimated resource requirements used to design and implement the system are shown in the following schedule:

	Hardware and Other Capacity- Related Resources	Operating Resources
Records	25%	60%
Claims	50	15
Finance	20	20
Expansion (outside use)	5	5
Total	100%	100%

GIC currently sells the equivalent of its expansion capacity to a few outside clients.

At the time the system became operational, management decided to redistribute total expenses of the systems department to the user departments based on actual computer time used. The actual costs for the first quarter of the current fiscal year were distributed to the user departments as shown at the top of page 528.

The three user departments have complained about the cost-distribution method since the systems department was established. The records department's monthly costs have been as much as three times the costs experienced with the service bureau. The finance department is concerned about the costs distributed to the outside user category because these allocated costs form the basis for the fees billed to the outside clients.

Department	Percentage Utilization	Amount
Records	60%	$330,000
Claims	15	82,500
Finance	20	110,000
Outside	5	27,500
Total	100%	$550,000

Mostafa Al Rashed, GIC's controller, decided to review the cost-allocation method. The additional information he gathered for his review is reported in Tables 1, 2, and 3 below.

Al Rashed has concluded that the method of cost allocation should be changed. He believes that the hardware and capacity-related costs should be allocated to the user departments in proportion to the planned long-term needs. Any difference between actual and budgeted hardware costs would not be allocated to the departments, but would remain with the systems department.

The costs for software development and operations would be charged to the user departments based on actual hours used. A predetermined hourly rate based on the annual budget data would be used. The hourly rates that would be used for the current fiscal year are as shown at the top of page 529.

Al Rashed plans to use first-quarter activity and cost data to illustrate his recommendations. The recommendations will be presented to the systems department and the user departments for their comments and reactions. He then expects to present his recommendations to management for approval.

TABLE 1 Systems Department Costs and Activity Levels

| | Annual Budget | | First Quarter | | | |
| | | | Budget | | Actual | |
	Hours	Dollars	Hours	Dollars	Hours	Dollars
Hardware and other capacity-related costs	—	$ 600,000	—	$150,000	—	$155,000
Software development	18,750	562,500	4,725	141,750	4,250	130,000
Operations						
Computer related	3,750	750,000	945	189,000	920	187,000
Input/output related	30,000	300,000	7,560	75,600	7,900	78,000
Total		$2,212,500		$556,350		$550,000

TABLE 2 Historical Usage

| | Hardware and Other Capacity Needs | Software Development | | Operations | | | |
| | | | | Computer | | Input/Output | |
		Range	Average	Range	Average	Range	Average
Records	25%	0%–30%	15%	55%–65%	60%	10%–30%	15%
Claims	50	15–60	40	10–25	15	60–80	75
Finance	20	25–75	40	10–25	20	3–10	5
Outside	5	0–25	5	3–8	5	3–10	5
	100%		100%		100%		100%

TABLE 3 Usage of Systems Department s Services First Quarter (in hours)

| | Software Development | Operations | |
		Computer Related	Input/Output
Records	450	540	1,540
Claims	1,800	194	5,540
Finance	1,600	126	410
Outside	400	60	410
Total	4,250	920	7,900

Function	Hourly Rate
Software development Operations	$ 30
Computer related	200
Input/output related	10

1. Calculate the amount of data-processing costs that would be included in the claims department's first-quarter budget according to the method Al Rashed has recommended.
2. Prepare a schedule to show how the actual first-quarter costs of the systems department would be charged to the users if GIC adopts Al Rashed's recommended method.
3. Explain whether Al Rashed's recommended system for charging costs to the user departments will
   a. improve cost control in the systems department.
   b. improve planning and cost control in the user departments.

12-57 Library Research and AT&T Corporation

AT&T was highlighted on in Chapter 4 and on page 505. AT&T used multistage ABC as described in Appendix 12 of this chapter. AT&T first tried the two-stage ABC approach but was not happy with it. A detailed description of AT&T's experience with ABM is given in the article "Activity-Based Management at AT&T," by T. Hobdy, J. Thomson, and P. Sharman, *Management Accounting* (April 1994).

Compare the approach to designing and implementing an ABC system described in the text to that described in the article by answering the following questions:

1. In the article, how were "some billing costs" allocated to different customer classes (invoice types) prior to implementing the process modeling approach to ABC?
2. In the article, what business unit was selected for the pilot ABC project, and what were the overall goals of the pilot study from the managers' perspective?
3. From the article, give examples of cost objects, activities, resources, and cost drivers.
4. For AT&T, "the cost of service support to these individual customers was determined by identifying activity and driver consumption characteristics." For the bill verification activity described in Exhibit 12-21, what is meant by the cost consumption characteristics for the labor resource?
5. Exhibit 12-20 on page 506 shows the operations of the billing department at AT&T. A similar flowchart is described in the article. What function did it perform?
6. In the article, "each cost object was costed by multiplying the quantity of driver units of each activity consumed by the cost per driver unit." Using the data from Exhibit 12-20, explain how this method applies for the residential customer class.
7. In the article, the ABC study revealed that "25% of total center costs were assignable to message investigation (account inquiry and correspondence)." For the text illustration, what is the percent of total billing department costs assigned to account inquiry investigation?
8. What process improvements were implemented at AT&T for the message investigation activity?

NIKE 10-K PROBLEM

12-58 Customer Profitability

Part of the supply chain for **Nike**'s athletic footwear, apparel, and equipment can be depicted as follows:

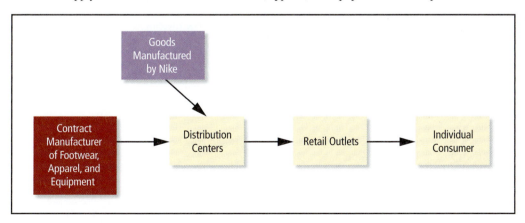

Based on information from Nike's 10-K, describe where most of Nike's customers are in the supply chain. Who is Nike's largest customer? If you wanted to calculate the profitability of this customer, describe the information you would need that is not contained in Nike's 10-K.

EXCEL APPLICATION EXERCISE

12-59 Allocating Costs Using Direct and Step-Down Methods

Goal: Create an Excel spreadsheet to allocate costs using the direct method and the step-down method. Use the results to answer questions about your findings.

Scenario: Dallas Cleaning has asked you to help them determine the best method for allocating costs from its service departments to its producing departments. Additional background information for your spreadsheet appears in Fundamental Assignment Material 12-B1. Exhibit 12-4 on page 480 illustrates the types of calculations that are used for allocating costs using the direct method and the step-down method.

When you have completed your spreadsheet, answer the following questions:
1. What are the total costs for the residential department using the direct method?
   What are the total costs for the commercial department using the direct method?
2. What are the total costs for the residential department using the step-down method?
3. What are the total costs for the commercial department using the step-down method?
4. Which method would you recommend that Dallas Cleaning use to allocate its service departments' costs to its producing departments? Why?

Step-by-Step:
1. Open a new Excel spreadsheet.
2. In column A, create a bold-faced heading that contains the following:
   Row 1: Chapter 12 Decision Guideline
   Row 2: Dallas Cleaning
   Row 3: Cost Allocations from Service Departments to Producing Departments
   Row 4: Today's Date
3. Merge and center the four heading rows across columns A–H.
4. In row 7, create the following bold-faced, center-justified column headings:
   Column B: Personnel
   Column C: Administrative
   Column D: Residential
   Column E: Commercial
   Column F: Total Res/Comm
   Column G: Total Admin/Res/Comm
   Column H: Grand Total
5. Change the format of the column headings in row 7 to permit the titles to be displayed on multiple lines within a single cell.

   Alignment tab: Wrap Text: Checked

   Note: Adjust column widths so that headings use only two lines.

   Adjust row height to ensure that row is same height as adjusted headings.
6. In column A, create the following row headings:
   Row 8: Direct Department Costs
   Row 9: Number of Employees
   Skip two rows.
   Note: Adjust the width of column A to 27.14.

7. In column A, create the following bold-faced, underlined row heading:
   Row 12: Direct Method:
8. In column A, create the following row headings:
   Row 13: Direct Department Costs
   Row 14: Personnel Allocation
   Row 15: Administrative Allocation
   Row 16: Total Costs
   Skip two rows.
9. In column A, create the following bold-faced, underlined row heading:
   Row 19: Step-Down Method:
10. In column A, create the following row headings:
   Row 20: Direct Department Costs
   Row 21: Step 1—Personnel Allocation
   Row 22: Step 2—Administrative Allocation
   Row 23: Total Costs
11. Use data from Fundamental Assignment 12-B1 to enter the amounts in columns B–E for rows 8, 9, 13, and 20.
12. Use the appropriate calculations to do the totals in row 8 for columns F and H.
   Use the appropriate calculations to do the totals in row 9 for columns F and G.

13. Use the appropriate formulas to allocate the costs from the service departments to the producing departments using each of the methods.
14. Use the appropriate calculations to do the totals in columns B–E and in column H, rows 16 and 23.
15. Format amounts in columns B–H, rows 8, 13, 16, 20, and 23 as follows:

Number tab:	Category:	Accounting
	Decimal:	0
	Symbol:	$

16. Format the amount in columns B–E, rows 14, 15, 21, and 22 as follows:

Number tab:	Category:	Accounting
	Decimal:	0
	Symbol:	None

17. Change the format of the total costs amounts in columns B–E, rows 16 and 23, to display a top border, using the default line style.

Border tab:	Icon:	Top Border

18. Change the format of the amounts in row 9, columns B–G to center justified.
19. Save your work to disk, and print a copy for your files.
    Note: Print your spreadsheet using landscape in order to ensure that all columns appear on one page.

COLLABORATIVE LEARNING EXERCISE

12-60 Library Research on ABC and Customer Profitability

Form groups of three to five people each. Each member of the group should pick one of the following industries:

- Manufacturing
- Insurance
- Health care
- Government
- Service

Each person should explore the Internet for an example of a company that implemented ABC and ABM with a focus on determining customer profitability. One way to do this is to go to the Web site www.sas.com and choose one company from the industry chosen. Prepare and give a briefing for your group. Do this by completing the following:

1. Describe the company and its business.
2. What was the scope of the ABC/ABM project?
3. What were the goals for the ABC/ABM project?
4. Summarize the results of the project.

   After each person has briefed the group on his or her company, discuss within your group the commonalities between the ABC/ABM applications.

INTERNET EXERCISE

12-61 Cost Allocation at Sears Holdings Corporation

Allocating indirect costs can be a challenging task. Almost all firms have some type of cost centers (departments), whether it is the administration overseeing the corporation as a whole or the accounting department processing billing and invoicing customers. What to do with the costs generated by these cost centers can be a tricky task. Let's take a look at Sears Holdings Corporation, a firm that has three major operating segments.

1. Go to the home page for Sears Holdings at www.searsholdings.com. How many companies are listed under the umbrella of Sears Holdings Corporation? What are these companies? How many of them are located in the area where you are located? If one or more is not located in your area, have you heard of it before?
2. Locate Sears Holdings' most recent annual report by clicking on "Investors" at Sears Holdings' home page. Click on "Financial Information" and then on the most recent annual report. Look at the "Notes to Consolidated Financial Statements." Did the firm provide any information on segment revenues? Sum the operating income of the segments for the current year. What is this figure? Now, look at the income statement for the current year. What is the operating income for the year? Why is it different from the sum of the segment pretax profit? What portion of company-wide operating costs are allocated to segments? What percent of the total selling and administrative costs are allocated to each segment?
3. If Sears Holdings wants to allocate the selling and administrative costs to the major segments based on total segment revenue, what percent of selling and administrative expenses is allocated to each segment? What would be the allocation if the corporation used the total assets as the allocation basis?

Accounting for Overhead Costs

▶ **DELL**

Dell is the world's leading direct-sale marketer of made-to-order computer systems. Dell does not manufacture computer components (e.g., circuit boards, hard drives), but instead assembles them into computers on a made-to-order basis.

Dell pioneered the "direct business model"—selling directly to end users instead of using a network of dealers, which avoids the dealer markup and gives Dell a competitive price advantage. Customers can design their own computer systems to specifications they desire, choosing from among a full complement of options. Before ordering, customers can receive advice and price quotes for a wide variety of computer configurations.

Once an order is taken, Dell assembles it in a manufacturing work cell called a "mod." There is a separate mod for each of Dell's lines of business (Dimension Desktop PCs, OptiPlex Desktops for networked environments, Latitude and Inspiron Notebooks, PowerEdge and PowerApp network servers, and Precision workstation products). Management considers rapid response to customer orders a key to gaining and maintaining a competitive edge.

Dell takes orders over the phone or over the Internet. Dell derives about 50% of its revenues from the company's Web site, www.dell.com, with daily revenues in excess of $40 million and weekly "hits" of over 3,000,000. Customers may review, configure, and price systems within Dell's entire product line. Dell's Web site also offers personalized system-support pages and technical services. Customers of all kinds prefer Dell's direct business model, and the Internet affords Dell a perfect way to implement this model. They like the immediacy, convenience, savings, and personal touches the Internet-direct customer experience provides.

Why are managers at a highly profitable company like Dell interested in knowing as much as possible about the cost of their individual product lines? With strong profits being reported over the years, is there a clear need for costs for other management purposes? The answer is yes—most of the reason why Dell's profitability has been strong is the strategic and operational decisions its managers make. These decisions are based on detailed cost information. For example, Dell's cost accounting systems supply product costs to managers for evaluating pricing policy and product lines. Dell managers need to know the cost of each kind of computer being produced to set prices, to determine marketing and production strategies for various models, and to evaluate production operations. At the same time, product costs appear as cost of goods sold in income statements and as finished-goods inventory values in balance sheets. Although it would be possible to have two product-costing systems, one for management decision making and one for financial reporting, seldom do the benefits of using two completely separate systems exceed the costs. Therefore, both decision-making and financial-reporting needs influence the design of a company's product-costing system.

In Chapter 4, you learned about three types of costs in a manufacturing company, direct materials, direct labor, and factory overhead (or indirect manufacturing) costs. You also learned that for many organizations, indirect costs account for as much as 40% of total operating costs. Thus, this is an important area of concern for managers. In this chapter, we focus on overhead. ■

Dell sells computers directly to customers around the world.

Accounting for Factory Overhead

Years ago, direct materials and direct labor were the largest costs for most companies. Today, automated companies such as **Dell** have less direct labor but much larger overhead costs. Thus, methods for assigning overhead costs to the products is an important part of accurately measuring product costs.

How to Apply Factory Overhead to Products

Managers need to know product costs in order to make ongoing decisions, such as which products or services to emphasize or deemphasize and how to price each product or service. Ideally, managers would know all costs precisely, including overhead, when they make these decisions. Because accountants directly trace direct materials and direct labor costs to products and services, these costs are available immediately on completion of production and they are known precisely. In contrast, because it is not economically feasible to know all of the indirect manufacturing costs immediately, accountants must estimate them. For this reason, accountants use budgeted (predetermined) overhead rates to apply overhead to jobs. This makes an estimate of total product cost available for managerial decisions as soon as products or services are completed, if not sooner. When the relative size of the overhead costs is large, we can understand how important it is for companies to have an accurate system for factory overhead accounting.

The size of overhead costs in many manufacturing companies is large enough to motivate companies to search for ways to convert them into direct costs. Dell has increased the accuracy of its product cost information by converting some of its factory-overhead costs from indirect to direct costs. How did the company do this? By dedicating assembly labor and factory equipment to specific product lines. Work cells (mods) do the assembly and software loading for specific product lines. This makes it easier to trace some of the equipment costs to products. Nevertheless, significant overhead costs remain to be allocated. So let's look at how companies such as Dell allocate these overhead costs to products and services.

Budgeted Overhead Application Rates

The following steps summarize how to account for factory overhead:

1. Select one or more cost-allocation bases for applying overhead costs to products or services. In this chapter, we often use the term *apply* instead of *allocate* when assigning overhead costs to a product or service. However, the concept is essentially the same—determining the amount of each cost pool to assign to each cost object. Examples of cost-allocation bases include direct-labor hours, direct-labor costs, machine hours, and production setups. The

Objective 1

Compute budgeted factory-overhead rates and apply factory overhead to production.

cost-allocation base should be a measure of the amount of overhead resources—a cost or a group of costs such as machinery cost, set-up costs, or energy cost—used by each product. The cost-allocation base(s) should be the most plausible and reliable measure(s) available of the cause-and-effect relationships between overhead costs and production volume.

2. Prepare a factory-overhead budget for the planning period, ordinarily a year. The two key items are (a) budgeted overhead and (b) budgeted volume of the cost-allocation base. There will be a set of budgeted overhead costs and an associated budgeted cost-allocation base level for each overhead cost pool.[1] In businesses with simple production systems, there may be just one set.

3. Compute the **budgeted factory-overhead rate(s)** by dividing the budgeted total overhead for each cost pool by the budgeted cost-allocation base level.

4. Obtain actual cost-allocation base data (such as direct-labor hours or machine hours) used for each product.

5. Apply the budgeted overhead to the products or services by multiplying the budgeted rate(s) in step 3 times the actual cost-allocation base data from step 4.

6. At the end of the year, account for any differences between the amount of overhead actually incurred and overhead applied to products.

Illustration of Overhead Application

Now that you know the steps in accounting for factory overhead, let's examine how they work in a realistic example. Consider the Enriquez Machine Parts Company.[2] Its manufacturing-overhead budget for 20X0 follows:

	Machining	Assembly
Indirect labor	$ 75,600	$ 36,800
Supplies	8,400	2,400
Utilities	20,000	7,000
Repairs	10,000	3,000
Factory rent	10,000	6,800
Supervision	42,600	35,400
Depreciation on equipment	104,000	9,400
Insurance, property taxes, etc.	7,200	2,400
Total	$277,800	$103,200

Enriquez selected a single cost-allocation base in each department, machine hours in machining and direct-labor cost in assembly, for applying overhead. As Enriquez works on a product, it applies the factory overhead to the product using a budgeted overhead rate, computed as follows:

$$\text{budgeted overhead application rate} = \frac{\text{total budgeted factory overhead}}{\text{total budgeted amount of cost driver}}$$

The overhead rates for the two departments are as follows:

	Year 20X0	
	Machining	Assembly
Budgeted manufacturing overhead	$ 277,800	$103,200
Budgeted machine hours	69,450	
Budgeted direct-labor cost		$206,400
Budgeted overhead rate, per machine hour: $277,800 ÷ 69,450 =	$ 4	
Budgeted overhead rate, per direct labor dollar: $103,200 ÷ $206,400 =		50%

---

[1]Cost pools were defined in Chapter 4, page 126, as a group of individual costs that a company allocates to activities or cost objectives using a single cost driver.

[2]If Chapter 14 and job-order costing have been assigned prior to this chapter, you will notice that the chapter illustration of Enriquez Machine Parts Company in both Chapters 13 and 14 are the same, with all data completely compatible.

Note that the overhead rates are budgeted; they are estimates. Accountants at Enriquez then use these budgeted rates to apply overhead based on actual events. That is, the total overhead applied to a particular product is the result of multiplying the budgeted overhead rates by the actual machine hours or labor cost used by that product. Thus, we would apply $44 of overhead to a product that uses 6 machine hours in machining and incurs direct-labor cost of $40 in assembly:

Machining: 6 actual machine hours × $4 per machine hour	$24
Assembly: $40 of direct-labor cost × 50%	20
Total overhead	$44

Suppose that at the end of the year Enriquez had used 70,000 machine hours in machining and incurred $190,000 of direct-labor cost in assembly. It would have applied a total of $375,000 of overhead to the products produced:

Machining: 70,000 actual machine hours × $4	$280,000
Assembly: $190,000 actual direct-labor cost × 50%	95,000
Total factory overhead applied	$375,000

This $375,000 is an estimate of Enriquez's overhead for the year, and it will become part of the cost of goods sold expense on Enriquez's income statement when the units produced are subsequently sold. If the actual overhead costs differ from $375,000, the company will usually charge the difference to expense in the period of production. For example, if Enriquez's actual overhead in 20X0 were $392,000, it would add $392,000 − $375,000 = $17,000 additional expense in 20X0.

This completes our six steps. Next let's go back to step 1 and explore how a company might choose appropriate cost-allocation bases.

Choice of Cost-Allocation Bases

As you have seen several times in this text, no one cost-allocation base is appropriate in all situations. The accountant's goal is to find the cost-allocation base that best links cause and effect. In the Enriquez machining department, use of machines causes most overhead cost, such as depreciation and repairs. Therefore, machine hours is the most appropriate cost-allocation base for applying overhead costs. Thus, Enriquez must keep track of the machine hours used for each product, creating an added data collection cost. That is, it must accumulate machine hours in addition to direct-materials costs and direct-labor costs for each product.

In contrast, direct labor is the principal cost-allocation base in the Enriquez assembly department because employees assemble parts by hand. Suppose the company records the time each worker spends on each product (or batch of products). Then, all that is needed is to apply the 50% overhead rate to the cost of direct labor already recorded. No additional data are needed.

If the hourly labor rates for workers differ greatly for individuals performing identical tasks, Enriquez might use the hours of labor, rather than the dollars spent for labor, as a base. Otherwise, Enriquez would apply more overhead to a product when a $10-per-hour worker works an hour than when an $8-per-hour worker works an hour, even though each employee uses the same facilities and generally consumes the same overhead support. However, sometimes direct-labor cost is the best overhead cost-allocation base even if wage rates vary within a department. For example, higher-skilled labor may use more costly equipment and have more indirect labor support than low-skilled workers. Moreover, many factory-overhead costs include expensive labor fringe benefits such as pensions and payroll taxes. Direct-labor cost rather than direct-labor hours often drive such fringe-benefit costs.

If a department identifies more than one cost-allocation base for overhead costs, it should accumulate a separate cost pool for each cost-allocation base and put each overhead cost into the appropriate cost pool. In practice, such a system is too costly for many organizations. Instead, these organizations select a few cost-allocation bases (often only one) to serve as a basis for allocating overhead costs. We often use the 80–20 rule in these situations—20% of the cost-allocation bases drive 80% of the overhead costs. For example, suppose a company identifies 10 separate overhead pools with 10 different cost-allocation bases. Often, it can accurately apply approximately 80% of the total overhead cost with only two allocation bases. It may be too costly to devise separate cost pools for the other 20%, so it arbitrarily assigns those costs to the two main cost pools.

Objective 2

Determine and use appropriate cost-allocation bases for overhead application to products and services.

Consider **Dell**. As we mentioned earlier, Dell has converted many of its overhead costs into direct costs. However, two important costs that it cannot directly trace (that is, that remain indirect costs) are facilities and engineering. Facilities costs include occupancy costs such as depreciation, insurance, and taxes on the factory. Dell applies these costs using the cost-allocation base "square footage used by each line of business (assembly line)." Dell incurs large product and process engineering costs as part of the design phase of the company's value chain. It applies these costs to lines of business using a "complexity" cost-allocation base such as number of distinct parts in the motherboard. Server computer products, for example, require much more engineering time and effort due to the number of distinct parts in the motherboard (complexity of the product) compared to laptops or PCs. Thus, server products receive a much greater allocation of engineering costs than laptops or PCs.

Another example is **Harley-Davidson**, which changed from using direct labor as a cost-allocation base to using process hours, as we describe in the Business First box on page 537.

Problems of Overhead Application

Normalized Overhead Rates

Objective 3
Identify the meaning and purpose of normalized overhead rates.

The Enriquez illustration demonstrated what we call the normal costing approach. Why the term *normal*? Because we use an annual average overhead rate consistently throughout the year for product costing, without altering it from day to day and from month to month. The resultant "normal" product costs include an average or normalized chunk of overhead. Hence, in a **normal costing system** the cost of the manufactured product is composed of actual direct material, actual direct labor, and normal applied overhead.

A department's applied overhead will rarely equal the actual overhead incurred. Managers can analyze this variance between applied and incurred cost. The most common—and important—contributor to these variances is operating at a different level of volume than the level used as a denominator in calculating the budgeted overhead rate (for instance, using 100,000 budgeted direct-labor hours as the denominator and then actually working only 80,000 hours). Other frequent causes include poor forecasting, inefficient use of overhead items, price changes in individual overhead items, erratic behavior of individual overhead items (e.g., repairs made only during slack time), and calendar variations (e.g., 20 workdays in one month, 22 in the next).

Companies generally prefer to use an annual budgeted factory-overhead rate regardless of the month-to-month peculiarities of specific overhead costs. Such an approach is more defensible than, for example, applying the actual overhead for each month. Why? Because a normal product cost is more useful for decisions, and more representative for inventory-costing purposes, than an "actual" product cost that is distorted by month-to-month fluctuations in production volume and by the erratic behavior of many overhead costs. For example, the employees of a gypsum plant using an "actual" product cost system had the privilege of buying company-made items "at cost." Employees joked about the benefits of buying "at cost" during high-volume months, when unit costs were lower because volume was higher, as the following table illustrates:

	Actual Overhead			Direct-Labor	Actual Overhead Application
	Variable	Fixed	Total	Hours	Rate per Direct-Labor Hour
Peak-volume month	$60,000	$40,000	$100,000	100,000	$1.00
Low-volume month	30,000	40,000	70,000	50,000	1.40

*Divide total overhead by direct-labor hours. Note that the presence of fixed overhead causes the fluctuation in unit overhead costs from $1.00 to $1.40. The variable component is $.60 an hour in both months, but the fixed component is $.40 in the peak-volume month ($40,000 ÷ 100,000) and $.80 in the low-volume month ($40,000 ÷ 50,000).

Disposition of Underapplied or Overapplied Overhead

The last step on page 534 dealt with differences between actual and applied overhead. Let's look in more detail at options for accounting for such differences. Recall that in 20X0 Enriquez applied $375,000 of overhead to its products but actually incurred $392,000 of overhead costs. The difference is a $17,000 variance, which we call **underapplied overhead** because the amount applied is less than the amount incurred. The opposite, **overapplied overhead**, occurs when the amount applied exceeds the amount incurred. At year-end, the company needs to produce its financial

Business First

Overhead Allocation at Harley-Davidson

Milwaukee-based Harley-Davidson, the motorcycle manufacturer, recently celebrated its one hundredth birthday. As happy as everyone at Harley-Davidson is today, it is a bit surprising to some how far the company has come over the past several decades. From near collapse, Harley-Davidson turned its business around during the 1980s and 1990s, and in 1999 captured the number one market position from Honda for the first time in three decades. Harley-Davidson (2008 sales of $5.6 billion) is the only major U.S.-based motorcycle producer. One of the keys to the company's return to competitiveness was the adoption of a JIT philosophy. It is not unusual for a company to discover that a change in an important component of operations requires a corresponding change in the company's accounting system. The main focus of the old accounting system was direct labor, which not only made up a part of product cost itself, but also functioned as an all-purpose base for allocating overhead. However, direct labor was only 10% of total product cost. It certainly did not generate a majority of overhead costs. Although Harley-Davidson's production process had changed, the accounting system remained static.

The JIT system served to emphasize that detailed information on direct-labor costs was not useful to managers. It was costly to have each direct laborer record the time spent on each product or part and then enter the information from these time cards into the accounting system. For example, if each of 500 direct laborers works on 20 products per day, the system must record 10,000 entries per day, which is 200,000 entries per month. The time spent by direct laborers to record the time, by clerks to enter the data into the system, and by accountants to check the data's accuracy, is enormous—and all to produce product cost information that was used for financial reporting but was useless to managers.

The JIT system forced manufacturing managers to focus on satisfying customers and minimizing non-value-added activities. Gradually, accountants began to focus on the same objectives. Accounting's customers were the managers who used the accounting information, and effort put into activities that did not help managers was deemed counterproductive (non-value-added). Therefore, eliminating the costly, time-consuming recording of detailed labor costs became a priority. Harley-Davidson eliminated direct labor as a direct cost, and consequently could not use it for overhead application. After considering process hours, flow-through time, materials value, and individual cost per unit as possible cost-allocation bases for applying overhead, the company selected process hours. Direct labor and overhead were combined to form conversion costs, which accountants applied to products on the basis of total process hours. This did not result in costs significantly different from the old system, but the new system was much simpler and less costly. The company traced only direct material directly to the product. It applied conversion costs at completion of production based on a simple measure of process time.

Accounting systems should generate benefits greater than their costs. More sophisticated systems are not necessarily better systems. Harley-Davidson's main objective in changing its accounting system was simplification—elimination of unnecessary tasks and streamlining others. These changes resulted in a revitalized accounting system.

Sources: Adapted from W. T. Turk, "Management Accounting Revitalized: The Harley-Davidson Experience," in B. J. Brinker, Ed., *Emerging Practices in Cost Management* (Boston: Warren, Gorham & Lamont, 1990), pp. 155–166; K. Barron, "Hog Wild," *Forbes*, May 15, 2000; and *Harley-Davidson 2008 Annual Report*.

statements, which require production costs based on the actual costs incurred. To yield this result, it must dispose of any under- or overapplied overhead, either by an immediate write-off to the income statement or through proration between the balance sheet and income statement.

Recall that Enriquez applied $375,000 to the products produced during the period. This amount is part of the cost of goods sold expense for those units that were sold and is included in ending inventory for those units that remain unsold at the end of 20X0. Enriquez still needs to account for the $17,000 variance (which is the amount of actual cost not yet applied to product). Accountants use one of two methods to account for the overhead variance: 1) a simple but imprecise approach is to dispose of the whole amount as a write-off to cost of goods sold, and 2) a better but more complex approach is **proration**, which means applying over- or underapplied overhead to cost of goods sold, work-in-process inventory, and finished-goods inventory in proportion to the ending balances of each account.

IMMEDIATE WRITE-OFF   The immediate write-off method regards the $17,000 underapplied overhead as a reduction in current income by adding it to the cost of goods sold. By the same logic, we would deduct any overapplied overhead from the cost of goods sold.

The reasoning behind this method is that the company has probably sold most of the goods produced during the period, so that prorating part of the variance to inventory accounts would not produce a materially different result. Another justification is that, if the extra overhead costs result from inefficiencies in the current period, they do not qualify as part of ending inventory costs because they do not represent assets. Because of its simplicity, the immediate write-off method is most commonly used.

the only variable selling and administrative cost is a sales commission of 5% of dollar sales. Actual product quantities are as follows:

	20X0	20X1
In units (computers)		
Opening inventory	—	3,000
Production	17,000	14,000
Sales	14,000	16,000
Ending inventory	3,000	1,000

There are no variances from the standard variable manufacturing or selling and administrative costs, the actual fixed manufacturing overhead incurred is exactly $1,500,000 each year, and the actual fixed selling and administrative cost is $650,000 each year.

Based on this information, we can

1. prepare income statements for 20X0 and 20X1 under variable costing.
2. prepare income statements for 20X0 and 20X1 under absorption costing.
3. show a reconciliation of the difference in operating income for 20X0, 20X1, and the two years as a whole.

Variable-Costing Method

Objective 4

Construct an income statement using the variable-costing approach.

We begin by preparing income statements under variable costing. The variable-costing statement shown in Exhibit 13-3 has a familiar contribution-approach format, the same format introduced in Chapter 5. The only new characteristic of Exhibit 13-3 is the presence of a detailed calculation of cost of goods sold, which is affected by changes in the beginning and ending inventories. In contrast, the income statements in earlier chapters assumed that there were no changes in the beginning and ending inventories.

We account for the costs of the product by applying all variable manufacturing costs to the goods produced at a rate of $300 per computer. This values inventories at standard variable costs. We do not apply any fixed manufacturing costs to products; instead we regard them as expenses in the period they are incurred.

		20X0	20X1
Sales, 14,000 and 16,000 computers, respectively	(1)	$7,000	$8,000
Variable expenses:			
Variable manufacturing cost of goods sold			
Opening inventory, at standard variable costs of $300		$ —	$ 900
Add: variable cost of goods manufactured at standard, 17,000 and 14,000 computers, respectively		5,100	4,200
Available for sale, 17,000 computers in each year		$5,100	$5,100
Deduct: ending inventory, at standard variable cost of $300		900*	300†
Variable manufacturing cost of goods sold		$4,200	$4,800
Variable selling expenses, at 5% of dollar sales		350	400
Total variable expenses	(2)	4,550	5,200
Contribution margin	(3) = (1) – (2)	$2,450	$2,800
Fixed expenses:			
Fixed factory overhead		$1,500	$1,500
Fixed selling and administrative expenses		650	650
Total fixed expenses	(4)	2,150	2,150
Operating income, variable costing	(3) – (4)	$ 300	$ 650

*3,000 computers at $300 = $900,000.
†1,000 computers at $300 = $300,000.

Exhibit 13-3

Desk PC Division: Comparative Income Statements Using Variable Costing
Years 20X0 and 20X1 (thousands of dollars)

Before reading on, be sure to trace the facts from our Desktop PC division example to the presentation in Exhibit 13-3, step-by-step. Note that we deduct both variable cost of goods sold and variable selling and administrative expenses in computing the contribution margin. However, variable selling and administrative expenses are not inventoriable. Why? They are not incurred in production and so are not considered to be product costs. Only the level of sales, not changes in inventory, affect them.

Absorption-Costing Method

Exhibit 13-4 shows the standard absorption-costing framework. As you can see, it differs from the variable-costing format in three ways.

First, the unit product cost used for computing cost of goods sold is $400, not $300. Why? Because we add fixed manufacturing overhead of $100 to the $300 variable manufacturing cost. The $100 of fixed manufacturing overhead applied to each unit is the **fixed-overhead rate**. We determine this rate by dividing the budgeted fixed overhead by the expected cost-allocation base activity, in this case expected volume of production, for the budget period:

Objective 5

Construct an income statement using the absorption-costing approach.

$$\text{fixed-overhead rate} = \frac{\text{budgeted fixed manufacturing overhead}}{\text{expected volume of production}}$$

$$= \frac{\$1,500,000}{15,000 \text{ units}}$$

$$= \$100$$

Second, fixed factory overhead does not appear as a separate line in an absorption-costing income statement. Instead, the fixed factory overhead appears in two places: as part of the cost of goods sold and as a production-volume variance.[4] A **production-volume variance** (which we explain further in the next section) appears whenever actual production deviates from the expected volume of production used in computing the fixed overhead rate:

$$\text{production-volume variance} = (\text{actual volume} - \text{expected volume}) \times \text{fixed-overhead rate}$$

		20X0		20X1
Sales			$7,000		$8,000
Cost of goods sold:					
Opening inventory, at standard absorption cost of $400*	$ —		$1,200	
Cost of goods manufactured at standard of $400	6,800		5,600	
Available for sale	6,800		6,800	
Deduct: ending inventory at standard absorption cost of $400	1,200		400	
Cost of goods sold, at standard		5,600		6,400
Gross profit at standard		1,400		1,600
Production-volume variance†		200 F		100 U
Gross margin or gross profit, at "actual"		1,600		1,500
Selling and administrative expenses		1,000		1,050
Operating income		$ 600		$ 450

Exhibit 13-4

Desk PC Division: Comparative Income Statements Using Absorption Costing
Years 20X0 and 20X1 (thousands of dollars)

*Variable cost $300
Fixed cost ($1,500,000 ÷ 15,000)   100
Standard absorption cost $400
†Computation of production-volume variance based on expected volume of production of 15,000 computers:

20X0	$200,000 F	(17,000 − 15,000) × $100
20X1	100,000 U	(14,000 − 15,000) × $100
Two years together	$100,000 F	(31,000 − 30,000) × $100

U = Unfavorable, F = Favorable

---

[4]In general, this will be a cost-driver activity variance. In our example, production volume is the only cost driver, so it can be called a production-volume variance.

For example, the production-volume variance for 20X1 is $(14{,}000 - 15{,}000) \times \$100 = -\$100{,}000$, an under-applied overhead. At $100 per computer, Dell applies only $1,400,000 of fixed overhead to production while actual overhead is exactly equal to its budget of $1,500,000. Assuming it uses the immediate write-off approach, Dell must add the $100,000 to the 20X1 cost of goods sold.

Finally, the format for an absorption-costing income statement separates costs into the major categories of manufacturing and nonmanufacturing. In contrast, a variable-costing income statement separates costs into the major categories of fixed and variable. In an absorption-costing statement, revenue less manufacturing cost (both fixed and variable) is gross profit or gross margin. In a variable-costing statement, revenue less all variable costs (both manufacturing and nonmanufacturing) is the contribution margin. We illustrate this difference by a condensed comparison of 20X1 income statements (in thousands of dollars):

Variable Costing		Absorption Costing	
Revenue	$8,000	Revenue	$8,000
All variable costs	5,200	All manufacturing costs*	6,500
Contribution margin	2,800	Gross margin	1,500
All fixed costs	2,150	All nonmanufacturing costs	1,050
Operating income	$ 650	Operating income	$ 450

*Standard absorption cost of goods sold (16 × $400) plus the production-volume variance ($100).

Making Managerial Decisions

When making decisions, it is important for managers to distinguish between gross margin and contribution margin. List the ways in which these two margins differ.

Answer

Among the differences are the following:
- Gross margin appears in an absorption-costing income statement; contribution margin is in a variable-costing income statement.
- Gross margin is revenue less manufacturing cost; contribution margin is revenue less all variable costs.

- Gross margin is based on a categorization of costs by function (manufacturing versus non-manufacturing); contribution margin separates costs by cost behavior pattern (variable versus fixed).
- Gross margin is required for external financial reporting; contribution margin is most useful for short-term management decisions and other settings where the variable versus fixed cost distinction is relevant.

Fixed Overhead and Absorption Costs of Product

The differences between variable- and absorption-costing formats arise because the two formats treat fixed manufacturing overhead differently. In this and subsequent sections, we explore how to account for factory overhead in an absorption-costing system. We do not further examine this issue under variable costing because its treatment of fixed manufacturing overhead is straightforward—we simply deduct the total amount of actual fixed factory overhead on the current-period income statement.

Variable and Fixed Unit Costs

Continuing our example of the Desktop PC division, we begin by comparing (1) the manufacturing overhead costs in the flexible budget used for departmental budgeting and control purposes with (2) the manufacturing overhead costs applied to products under an absorption-costing system. To stress the basic assumptions behind absorption costing, we will also split manufacturing overhead into variable and fixed components.

Consider the following graphs of variable-overhead costs:

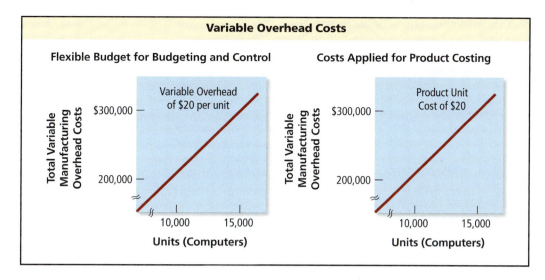

Note that the two graphs are identical. The expected variable-overhead costs from the flexible budget are the same as the variable-overhead costs applied to the products. Both budgeted and applied variable overhead are $20 per computer. Each time we produce 1,000 additional computers, we expect to incur an additional $20,000 of variable overhead, and we add $20,000 of variable-overhead cost to the inventory account for computers. The variable costs used for budgeting and control are the same as those used for product costing.

In contrast, the graph for applied fixed-overhead costs differs from that for the flexible budget:

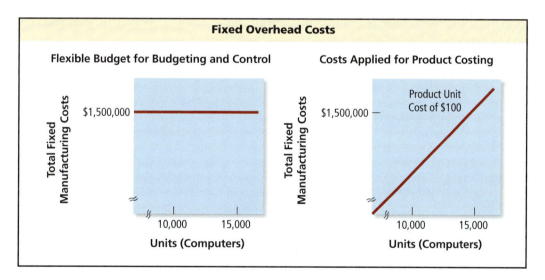

The flexible budget for fixed overhead is a lump-sum budgeted amount of $1,500,000. Volume does not affect it. In contrast, the applied fixed cost depends on actual volume and the predicted volume (denominator level) used to set the budgeted rate for fixed factory overhead.

$$\text{Fixed cost applied} = \text{actual volume} \times \text{fixed-overhead rate}$$

$$= \text{units produced} \times \$100$$

Suppose actual volume equals the expected volume of 15,000 computers. Applied fixed overhead would be 15,000 computers $\times$ $100 per computer = $1,500,000, the same as the flexible-budget amount. However, whenever actual volume differs from expected volume, the costs used for budgeting and control differ from those used for product costing. For budgeting and control purposes, managers use the true cost behavior pattern for fixed costs. In contrast, as the graphs indicate, the absorption product-costing approach treats and applies these fixed costs as though they had a variable-cost behavior pattern. The difference between applied and budgeted fixed overhead is the production-volume variance.

Objective 6

Compute the production-volume variance and show how it should appear in the income statement.

Nature of Production-Volume Variance

We calculate the production-volume variance as follows:

$$\text{production-volume variance} = \text{applied fixed overhead} - \text{budgeted fixed overhead}$$

$$= (\text{actual volume} \times \text{fixed-overhead rate})$$

$$- (\text{expected volume} \times \text{fixed-overhead rate})$$

or

$$\text{production-volume variance} = (\text{actual volume} - \text{expected volume}) \times \text{fixed-overhead rate}$$

In practice, accountants often call the production-volume variance simply the **volume variance**. We use the term *production-volume variance* because it is a more precise description of the fundamental nature of the variance. Using production-volume variance also distinguishes it from the sales-volume variance described in Chapter 8. Despite similar nomenclature, they are completely different concepts.

A production-volume variance arises when the actual production volume achieved does not coincide with the expected volume of production used as a denominator for computing the fixed-overhead rate for product-costing purposes:

1. When expected production volume and actual production volume are identical, there is no production-volume variance.
2. When actual volume is less than expected volume, the production-volume variance is unfavorable because usage of facilities is less than expected and fixed overhead is underapplied. It is measured in Exhibit 13-4 for 20X1 as follows:

$$\text{production-volume variance} = (\text{actual volume-expected volume}) \times \text{budgeted fixed-overhead rate}$$

$$= (14,000 \text{ units} - 15,000 \text{ units}) \times \$100$$

$$= -\$100,000 \text{ or } \$100,000 \text{ U}$$

or

$$\text{production-volume variance} = \text{budget minus applied}$$

$$= \$1,500,000 - \$1,400,000 = \$100,000 \text{ U}$$

The $100,000 unfavorable production-volume variance increases the manufacturing costs shown on the income statement. Why? Recall that the department incurred $1,500,000 of fixed manufacturing cost, but applied only $1,400,000 to inventory. Therefore, the department will charge only $1,400,000 as expense when it sells the inventory. But eventually it must charge the actual cost of $1,500,000 to the income statement as expense. Recall for simplicity that we assumed any variance is not prorated, so **Dell** writes off the extra $100,000 to Cost of Goods Sold in the current income statement.

3. When actual volume exceeds expected volume, as was the case in 20X0, the production-volume variance is favorable because use of facilities is better than expected, and fixed overhead is overapplied.

$$\text{production-volume variance} = (17,000 \text{ units} - 15,000 \text{ units}) \times \$100 = \$200,000 \text{ F}$$

In this case, the department will charge $1,700,000 through inventory. Because the department incurs actual costs of only $1,500,000, future expenses will be overstated by $200,000. Therefore, we reduce current period expenses by the $200,000 favorable variance.

The production-volume variance is the conventional measure of the cost of departing from the level of activity originally used to set the fixed-overhead rate. Most companies consider production-volume variances to be beyond immediate control, although sometimes a manager responsible for volume has to do some explaining or investigating. Sometimes, idle facilities caused by disappointing total sales, poor production scheduling, unusual machine breakdowns, shortages of skilled workers, strikes, storms, and the like are responsible for the failure to reach the expected volume.

There is no production-volume variance for variable overhead. Why? The concept of production-volume variance arises for fixed overhead because of the conflict between accounting for control (by flexible budgets) and accounting for product costing (by application rates), and there is no such conflict for variable overhead costs. Above all, remember that fixed costs are simply not divisible as variable costs are. Rather, they come in large lump sums and are related to the provision of large amounts of production or sales capability, not to the production or sale of a single unit of product.

Making Managerial Decisions

Some accountants claim that the production-volume variance is a good measure of how well a company uses its capacity: Favorable (unfavorable) variances imply effective (ineffective) use of capacity. As a manager, be careful not to fall into that trap. Why?

Answer

The production volume variance tells you one thing and only one thing—whether actual production was above or below the predicted volume used in setting the fixed overhead rate.

Suppose a manager can avoid an unfavorable production-volume variance by lowering the product's selling price to increase sales volume enough to use up the idle capacity. However, if the result is a decline in total contribution margin, this would not be an effective use of the capacity. Similarly, a favorable production-volume variance is not desirable if it occurs because management forces excess production through the facility, despite quality declines or other inefficiencies caused by overburdened production facilities.

Reconciliation of Variable Costing and Absorption Costing

We can easily reconcile the operating incomes shown in Exhibits 13-3 and 13-4. The difference in income equals the difference in the total amount of fixed manufacturing overhead charged as an expense during a given year. Examine Exhibit 13-5. The total fixed manufacturing overhead incurred ($1,500,000 in 20X1) is always recognized as an expense on a variable-costing income

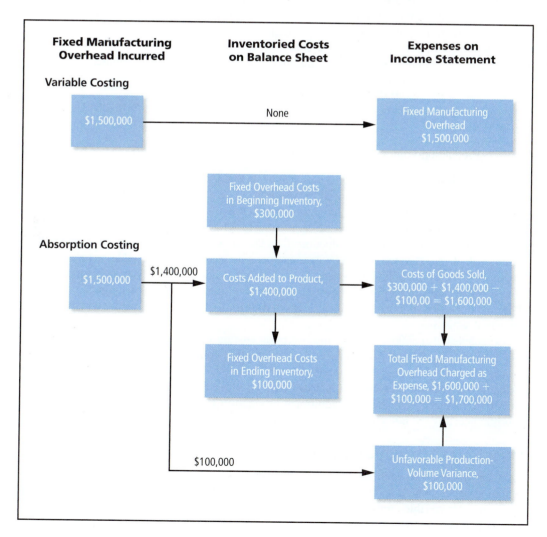

Exhibit 13-5
Flow of Fixed Manufacturing Overhead Costs During 20X1

statement. Under absorption costing, fixed manufacturing overhead appears in two places on the income statement: cost of goods sold and production-volume variance.

Under absorption costing, the beginning inventory includes $300,000 of fixed costs incurred before 20X1. During 20X1, accountants added $1,400,000 of fixed manufacturing overhead to inventory, and $100,000 remained in the ending inventory of 20X1 (1,000 units in ending inventory times the $100 fixed factory overhead rate applied to them). Thus, the fixed manufacturing overhead included in cost of goods sold for 20X1 was $300,000 + $1,400,000 − $100,000 = $1,600,000. In addition, the production-volume variance is $100,000, unfavorable. The total fixed manufacturing overhead charged as 20X1 expenses under absorption costing is $1,700,000, or $200,000 more than the $1,500,000 charged under variable costing. Therefore, 20X1 variable-costing income is higher by $200,000.

We can quickly explain the difference in variable-costing and absorption-costing operating income by multiplying the fixed-overhead product-costing rate by the change in the total units in the beginning and ending inventories. Consider 20X1: The change in inventory was 2,000 units, so the difference in net income would be 2,000 units × $100 = $200,000.

Remember that it is the relationship between sales and production that determines the difference between variable-costing and absorption-costing income. Whenever units sold are greater than [less than] units produced, variable-costing income is greater than [less than] absorption-costing income. This means that when inventories decrease [increase], variable-costing income is greater than [less than] absorption-costing income.

Why Use Variable Costing?

Objective 7

Explain why a company might prefer to use a variable-costing approach.

Why do many companies use variable costing for internal statements? One reason is that production volume affects absorption-costing income but has no effect on variable-costing income. Consider the 20X1 absorption-costing statement in Exhibit 13-4, which shows operating income of $450,000. Suppose a manager decides to produce 1,000 additional units in December 20X1 even though they will remain unsold. Will this affect operating income? First, note that the gross profit will not change because both revenue and goods sold are based on units sold, not on production volume. However, the production-volume variance will change:

$$\text{If production} = 14,000 \text{ units}$$
$$\text{Production-volume variance} = (15,000 - 14,000) \times \$100 = \$100,000 \text{ U}$$
$$\text{If production} = 15,000 \text{ U}$$
$$\text{Production-volume variance} = (15,000 - 15,000) \times \$100 = 0$$

Because there is no production-volume variance when the department produces 15,000 units, the new operating income equals gross profit less selling and administrative expenses, $1,600,000 − $1,050,000 = $550,000. Therefore, increasing production by 1,000 units without any increase in sales increases absorption-costing operating income by $100,000, from $450,000 to $550,000.

How will such an increase in production affect the variable-costing statement in Exhibit 13-3? Nothing will change. Production does not affect operating income under variable costing.

Suppose the evaluation of a manager's performance is based primarily on operating income. If the company uses the absorption-costing approach, a manager might be tempted to produce additional unneeded units just to increase reported operating income. No such temptation exists with variable costing.

Companies also choose variable or absorption costing based on which system they believe gives a better signal about performance. A sales-oriented company may prefer variable costing because the level of sales is the primary effect on its income. In contrast, a production-oriented company, for example, a company that can easily sell all the units it produces, might prefer absorption costing. Why? Because additional production increases the operating income with absorption costing but not with variable costing.

Effect of Other Variances

So far, our example has deliberately ignored the possibility of any variance except the production-volume variance, which appears only on an absorption-costing statement. All other variances appear on both variable- and absorption-costing income statements. In this section, we will consider these other variances that you encountered in Chapter 8.

Flexible-Budget Variances

Returning again to the Desktop PC division, we will assume some additional facts for 20X1 (the second of the 2 years covered by our example):

Flexible-budget variances		
Direct materials		None
Direct labor	$	170,000 U
Variable factory overhead	$	30,000 U
Fixed factory overhead	$	70,000 U
Supporting data (used to compute the preceding variances as shown in Appendix 13):		
Standard direct-labor hours allowed for 14,000 units of output produced		87,500
Standard direct-labor rate per hour	$	12.00
Actual direct-labor hours of inputs		100,000
Actual direct-labor rate per hour	$	12.20
Variable manufacturing overhead actually incurred		$ 310,000
Fixed manufacturing overhead actually incurred		$1,570,000

As Chapter 8 explained, flexible-budget variances may arise for both variable overhead and fixed overhead. Consider the following:

	Actual Amounts	Flexible Budget Amounts at 14,000 Units	Flexible Budget Variances
Variable factory overhead	$ 310,000	$ 280,000	$30,000 U
Fixed factory overhead	1,570,000	1,500,000	70,000 U

Exhibit 13-6 shows the relationship between the fixed-overhead flexible-budget variance and the production-volume variance. The difference between the actual fixed overhead and that applied to products is the underapplied (or overapplied) overhead. Because the actual fixed overhead of $1,570,000 exceeds the $1,400,000 applied, fixed overhead is underapplied by $170,000, which means that the variance is unfavorable. The $170,000 underapplied fixed overhead has two components: (1) a production-volume variance of $100,000 U and (2) a fixed-overhead flexible-budget variance (also called the fixed-overhead spending variance) of $70,000 U.

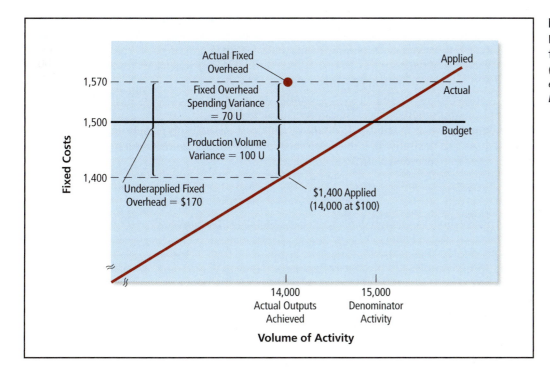

Exhibit 13-6
Fixed-Overhead Variances for 20X1
(dollar amounts in thousands except per unit amounts)
Data are from Exhibit 13-4

Exhibit 13-7 contains the income statement under absorption costing that incorporates these new facts. These new variances decrease income by 270,000 because, like the production-volume variance, they are all unfavorable variances that are charged against income in 20X1. When cost variances are favorable, they increase operating income.

		(in thousands)
Sales, 16,000 at $500		$8,000
Opening inventory at standard, 3,000 at $400	$1,200	
Cost of goods manufactured at standard, 14,000 at $400	5,600	
Available for sale, 17,000 at $400	$6,800	
Deduct ending inventory at standard, 1,000 at $400	400	
Cost of goods sold at standard, 16,000 at $400		6,400
Gross profit at standard		$1,600
Flexible-budget variances, both unfavorable		
Variable manufacturing costs ($170,000 + $30,000)	$ 200	
Fixed factory overhead	70	
Production-volume variance (arises only because of		
fixed overhead), unfavorable	100	
Total variances		370
Gross profit at "actual"		$1,230
Selling and administrative expenses		1,050
Operating income		$ 180

Exhibit 13-7

Absorption Costing Modification of Exhibit 13-4 for 20X1

(additional facts are in text)

Summary Problem for Your Review

PROBLEM

1. Reconsider Exhibits 13-3 and 13-4 on pages 542 and 543. Suppose production in 20X1 was 14,500 units instead of 14,000 units, but sales remained at 16,000 units. Assume that the net variances for all variable manufacturing costs were $200,000, unfavorable. Regard these variances as adjustments to the standard cost of goods sold. Also assume that actual fixed costs were $1,570,000. Prepare income statements for 20X1 under variable costing and under absorption costing.

2. Explain why operating income was different under variable costing from what it was under absorption costing. Show your calculations.

3. Without regard to number 1, would variable costing or absorption costing give a manager more flexibility in influencing short-run operating income through production-scheduling decisions? Why?

SOLUTION

1. See Exhibit 13-8 and Exhibit 13-9. Note that the ending inventory will be 1,500 units instead of 1,000 units.

Sales		$8,000
Opening inventory, at variable		
standard cost of $300	$ 900	
Add: Variable cost of goods manufactured	4,350	
Available for sale	$5,250	
Deduct: Ending inventory, at variable		
standard cost of $300	450	
Variable cost of goods sold, at standard	$4,800	
Net flexible-budget variances for		
all variable costs, unfavorable	200	
Variable cost of goods sold, at actual	$5,000	
Variable selling expenses, at 5% of dollar sales	400	
Total variable costs charged against sales		5,400
Contribution margin		$2,600
Fixed factory overhead	$1,570*	
Fixed selling and administrative expenses	650	
Total fixed expenses		2,220
Operating income		$ 380†

Exhibit 13-8
Desk PC Division
Income Statement (variable costing), Year 20X1 (thousands of dollars)

*This could be shown in two lines, $1,500,000 budget plus $70,000 variance.
†The difference between this and the $650,000 operating income in Exhibit 13-3 occurs because of the $200,000 unfavorable variable-cost variances and the $70,000 unfavorable fixed-cost flexible-budget variance.

Sales		$8,000
Opening inventory, at standard cost of $4	$1,200	
Cost of goods manufactured, at standard	5,800	
Available for sale	$7,000	
Deduct: Ending inventory, at standard	600	
Cost of goods sold, at standard	$6,400	
Net flexible-budget variances for all variable		
manufacturing costs, unfavorable	$200	
Fixed factory overhead flexible-budget		
variance, unfavorable	70	
Production-volume variance, unfavorable	50*	
Total variances	320	
Cost of goods sold, at actual "		6,720†
Gross profit, at "actual"		$1,280
Selling and administrative expenses		
Variable	400	
Fixed	650	1,050
Operating income		$ 230‡

Exhibit 13-9
Desk PC Division
Income Statement (absorption costing), Year 20X1 (thousands of dollars)

*Production-volume variance is $100 × (15,000 expected volume − 14,500 actual production).
†This format differs slightly from Exhibit 13-7. The difference is deliberate; it illustrates that the formats of income statements are not rigid.
‡Compare this result with the $180,000 operating income in Exhibit 13-7. The only difference is traceable to the production of 14,500 units instead of 14,000 units, resulting in an unfavorable production-volume variance of $50,000 instead of $100,000.

2. Decline in inventory levels is 3,000 − 1,500, or 1,500 units. The fixed-overhead rate per unit in absorption costing is $100. Therefore, $150,000 more fixed overhead was charged against operations under absorption costing than under variable costing. The variable-costing statement shows fixed factory overhead of $1,570,000, whereas the absorption-costing statement includes fixed factory overhead in three places: $1,600,000 in cost of goods sold, $70,000 U in fixed factory-overhead flexible-budget variance, and $50,000 U as a production-volume variance, for a total of $1,720,000. Generally, when inventories decline, absorption costing will show less income than will variable costing; when inventories rise, absorption costing will show more income than variable costing.

3. Absorption costing will give a manager more discretion in influencing operating income via production scheduling. Operating income will fluctuate in harmony with changes in net sales under variable costing, but both production and sales influence it under absorption costing. For example, compare the variable costing operating income in Exhibits 13-3 and 13-8. As

the second note to Exhibit 13-8 indicates, assorted variances (but not the production-volume variance) may affect operating income under variable costing, but production scheduling per se will have no effect on operating income.

On the other hand, compare the operating income of Exhibits 13-7 and 13-9. As the third note to Exhibit 13-9 explains, production scheduling as well as sales influence operating income. Production was 14,500 rather than 14,000 units. So $50,000 of fixed overhead became a part of ending inventory (an asset) instead of part of the production-volume variance (an expense)—that is, the production-volume variance is $50,000 lower, and the ending inventory contains $50,000 more fixed overhead in Exhibit 13-9 than in Exhibit 13-7. The manager adds $100 to 20X1 operating income with each unit of production under absorption costing, even if the department does not sell the unit.

Highlights to Remember

1. **Compute budgeted factory-overhead rates and apply factory overhead to production.** Accountants usually apply indirect manufacturing costs (factory overhead) to products using budgeted overhead rates. They compute the rates by dividing total budgeted overhead by a measure of cost-allocation base activity such as expected machine hours.

2. **Determine and use appropriate cost-allocation bases for overhead application to products and services.** There should be a strong cause-and-effect relationship between cost-allocation bases and the overhead costs that are applied using these bases.

3. **Identify the meaning and purpose of normalized overhead rates.** Budgeted overhead rates are usually annual averages. The resulting product costs are normal costs, consisting of actual direct materials, actual direct labor, and applied overhead using the budgeted rates. Normal product costs are often more useful than true actual costs for decision-making and inventory-costing purposes.

4. **Construct an income statement using the variable-costing approach.** Two major methods of product costing are variable (contribution approach) and absorption costing. The variable-costing method emphasizes the effects of cost behavior on income. This method excludes fixed manufacturing overhead from the cost of products and expenses it immediately.

5. **Construct an income statement using the absorption-costing approach.** The absorption or traditional approach ignores cost behavior distinctions. As a result, all costs incurred in the production of goods become part of the inventory cost. Thus, we add fixed manufacturing overhead to inventory and it appears on the income statement only when the company sells the goods.

6. **Compute the production-volume variance and show how it should appear in the income statement.** Whenever a company employs the absorption method and the actual production volume does not equal the expected (budgeted) volume that it used for computing the fixed-overhead rate, a production-volume variance arises. When the actual production volume is less than budgeted, the variance is unfavorable; when actual volume exceeds budgeted volume, the variance is favorable. The amount of the variance is equal to the fixed-overhead rate times the difference between the budgeted and actual volume. Companies usually dispose of this variance by adjusting the current-period income. Favorable variances increase current-period income and unfavorable variances reduce current-period income.

7. **Explain why a company might prefer to use a variable-costing approach.** Companies that use operating income to measure results may prefer variable costing. This is because changes in production volume affect absorption-costing income but not variable-costing income. A company that wants to focus managers' energies on sales would prefer to use variable costing, since the level of sales is the primary driver of variable-costing income. ■

Appendix 13: Comparisons of Production-Volume Variance with Other Variances

The only new variance introduced in this chapter is the production-volume variance, which arises because companies use fixed-overhead accounting for both control and product-costing purposes. Let's examine this variance in perspective by using the approach originally demonstrated in Exhibit 8-9 of Chapter 8 (p. 322). The results of the approach appear in Exhibit 13-10,

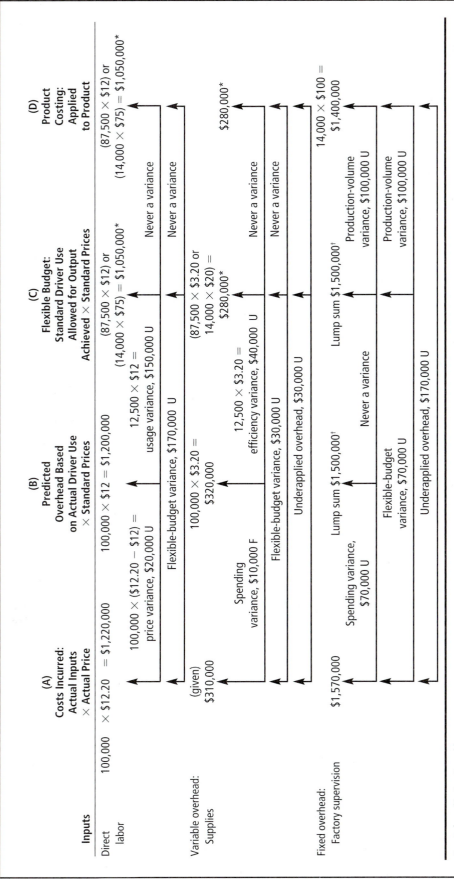

	(A) Costs Incurred: Actual Inputs × Actual Price	(B) Predicted Overhead Based on Actual Driver Use × Standard Prices	(C) Flexible Budget: Standard Driver Use Allowed for Output Achieved × Standard Prices	(D) Product Costing: Applied to Product
Inputs				
Direct labor	100,000 × $12.20 = $1,220,000	100,000 × $12 = $1,200,000	(87,500 × $12) or (14,000 × $75) = $1,050,000*	(87,500 × $12) or (14,000 × $75) = $1,050,000*

100,000 × ($12.20 − $12) = price variance, $20,000 U

12,500 × $12 = usage variance, $150,000 U

Never a variance

Never a variance

Flexible-budget variance, $170,000 U

Variable overhead: Supplies	(given) $310,000	100,000 × $3.20 = $320,000	(87,500 × $3.20 or 14,000 × $20) = $280,000*	$280,000*

Spending variance, $10,000 F

12,500 × $3.20 = efficiency variance, $40,000 U

Never a variance

Never a variance

Flexible-budget variance, $30,000 U

Underapplied overhead, $30,000 U

Fixed overhead: Factory supervision	$1,570,000	Lump sum $1,500,000†	Lump sum $1,500,000	14,000 × $100 = $1,400,000

Spending variance, $70,000 U

Never a variance

Production-volume variance, $100,000 U

Flexible-budget variance, $70,000 U

Production-volume variance, $100,000 U

Underapplied overhead, $170,000 U

U = Unfavorable, F = Favorable.

*Note especially that the flexible budget for variable costs rises and falls in direct proportion to production. Note also that the control-budget purpose and the product-costing purpose harmonize completely. The total costs in the flexible budget will always agree with the standard-variable costs applied to the product because they are based on standard costs per unit multiplied by units produced.

†In contrast with variable costs, the flexible-budget total for fixed costs will always be the same regardless of the units produced. However, the control-budget purpose and the product-costing purpose conflict; whenever actual production differs from expected production, the standard costs applied to the product will differ from the flexible budget. This difference is the production-volume variance. In this case, the production-volume variance may be computed by multiplying the $100 rate times the difference between the 15,000 expected volume and the 14,000 units of output achieved.

Exhibit 13-10
Analysis of Variances
(data are from text for 20X1)

which deserves your careful study, particularly the two footnotes. Please ponder the exhibit before reading on.

Exhibit 13-11 graphically compares the variable- and fixed-overhead costs analyzed in Exhibit 13-10. Note how the control-budget line and the product-costing line (the applied line) are superimposed in the graph for variable overhead but differ in the graph for fixed overhead.

Underapplied or overapplied overhead is always the difference between the actual overhead incurred and the overhead applied. An analysis may then be made:

$$\text{underapplied overhead} = \left(\begin{array}{c}\text{flexible-budget}\\\text{variance}\end{array}\right) + \left(\begin{array}{c}\text{production-volume}\\\text{variance}\end{array}\right)$$

$$\text{for variable overhead} = \$30,000 + 0 = \$30,000$$
$$\text{for fixed overhead} = \$70,000 + \$100,000 = \$170,000$$

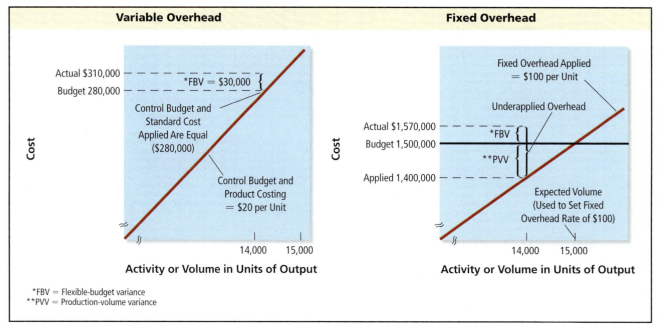

*FBV = Flexible-budget variance
**PVV = Production-volume variance

Exhibit 13-11
Comparison of Control and Product-Costing Purposes, Variable Overhead, and Fixed Overhead (not to scale)

Accounting Vocabulary

budgeted factory-overhead rate, p. 534
fixed-overhead rate, p. 543
normal costing system, p. 536

overapplied overhead, p. 536
production-volume variance, p. 543
proration, p. 537

underapplied overhead, p. 536
volume variance, p. 546

 **Fundamental Assignment Material**

13-A1 Accounting for Overhead; Budgeted Rates

Donald Aeronautics Company uses a budgeted overhead rate in applying overhead to products on a machine-hour basis for department A and on a direct-labor hour basis for department B. At the beginning of 20X0, the company's management made the following budget predictions:

	Department A	Department B
Direct-labor cost	$1,500,000	$1,200,000
Factory overhead	$1,820,000	$1,000,000
Direct-labor hours	90,000	125,000
Machine hours	350,000	20,000

Cost records of recent months show the following accumulations for product M89:

	Department A	Department B
Material placed in production	$12,000	$32,000
Direct-labor cost	$10,800	$10,000
Direct-labor hours	900	1,250
Machine hours	3,500	150

1. What is the budgeted overhead rate that should be applied in department A? In department B?
2. What is the total overhead cost of product M89?
3. If 120 units of product M89 are produced, what is their unit cost?
4. At the end of 20X0, actual results for the year's operations were as follows:

	Department A	Department B
Actual overhead costs incurred	$1,300,000	$1,200,000
Actual direct-labor hours	80,000	120,000
Actual machine hours	300,000	25,000

Find the underapplied or overapplied overhead for each department and for the factory as a whole.

13-A2 Disposition of Overhead

Penski Precision Tooling applies factory overhead using machine hours and number of component parts as cost-allocation bases. In 20X0, actual factory overhead incurred was $125,000 and applied factory overhead was $135,000. Before disposition of underapplied or overapplied factory overhead, the cost of goods sold was $525,000, gross profit was $60,000, and ending inventories were as follows:

Direct materials	$ 25,000
WIP	75,000
Finished goods	100,000
Total inventories	$200,000

1. Was factory overhead overapplied or underapplied? By how much?
2. Assume that Penski writes off overapplied or underapplied factory overhead as an adjustment to cost of goods sold. Compute adjusted gross profit.
3. Assume that Penski prorates overapplied or underapplied factory overhead based on end-of-the-year unadjusted balances. Compute adjusted gross profit.
4. Assume that actual factory overhead was $140,000 instead of $125,000, and that Penski writes off overapplied or underapplied factory overhead as an adjustment to cost of goods sold. Compute adjusted gross profit.

13-A3 Comparison of Variable Costing and Absorption Costing

Consider the following information pertaining to a year's operation of Blair Company:

Units produced	2,500
Units sold	2,100
Direct labor	$4,000
Direct materials used	$3,000
Selling and administrative expenses (all fixed)	$ 900
Fixed manufacturing overhead	$5,000
Variable manufacturing overhead	$2,500
All beginning inventories	$ 0
Gross margin (gross profit)	$2,200
Direct-materials inventory, end	$ 400
Work-in-process inventory, end	$ 0

1. What is the ending finished-goods inventory cost under variable costing?
2. What is the ending finished-goods inventory cost under absorption costing?
3. Would operating income be higher or lower under variable costing? By how much? Why?
   (Answer: $800 lower, but explain why.)

13-A4 Comparison of Absorption and Variable Costing

Examine the Trahn Company's simplified income statement based on variable costing. Assume that the budgeted volume for absorption costing in 20X0 and 20X1 was 1,400 units and that total fixed costs were identical in 20X0 and 20X1. There is no beginning or ending work in process.

Income Statement
Year Ended December 31, 20X1

Sales, 1,260 units at $13		$16,380
Deduct variable costs		
Beginning inventory, 100 units at $7	$ 700	
Variable manufacturing cost of goods manufactured, 1,200 units at $7	8,400	
Variable manufacturing cost of goods available for sale	$9,100	
Ending inventory, 40 units at $7	280	
Variable manufacturing cost of goods sold	$8,820	
Variable selling and administrative expenses	600	
Total variable costs		9,420
Contribution margin		$ 6,960
Deduct fixed costs		
Fixed factory overhead at budget	$4,900	
Fixed selling and administrative expenses	350	
Total fixed costs		5,250
Operating income		$ 1,710

1. Prepare an income statement based on absorption costing. Assume that actual fixed costs were equal to budgeted fixed costs.
2. Explain the difference in operating income between absorption costing and variable costing. Be specific.

13-B1 Disposition of Overhead

MacLachlan Manufacturing had underapplied overhead of $40,000 in 20X0. Before adjusting for over-applied or underapplied overhead, the ending inventories for direct materials, WIP, and finished goods were $75,000, $150,000, and $100,000, respectively. Unadjusted cost of goods sold was $250,000.

1. Assume that the $40,000 was written off solely as an adjustment to cost of goods sold. Compute the adjusted cost of goods sold.
2. Management has decided to prorate the $40,000 to the appropriate accounts (using the unadjusted ending balances) instead of writing it off solely as an adjustment of cost of goods sold. Would gross profit be higher or lower than in requirement 1? By how much?

13-B2 Application of Overhead Using Budgeted Rates

The Bellevue Clinic computes a cost of treating each patient. It allocates costs to departments and then applies departmental overhead costs to individual patients using a different budgeted overhead rate in each department. Consider the following predicted 20X0 data for two of Bellevue's departments:

	Pharmacy	Medical Records
Department overhead cost	$225,000	$300,000
Number of prescriptions filled	75,000	
Number of patient visits		50,000

The cost-allocation base for overhead in the pharmacy is number of prescriptions filled; in medical records it is number of patient visits.

In June 20X0, David Li paid two visits to the clinic and had four prescriptions filled at the pharmacy.

1. Compute departmental overhead rates for the two departments.
2. Compute the overhead costs applied to the patient David Li in June 20X0.
3. At the end of 20X0, actual overhead costs were as follows:

Pharmacy	$218,000
Medical records	$321,000

The pharmacy filled 85,000 prescriptions, and the clinic had 63,000 patient visits during 20X0. Compute the overapplied or underapplied overhead in each department.

13-B3 Comparison of Variable Costing and Absorption Costing

Consider the following information pertaining to a year's operations of Youngstown Manufacturing:

Units sold	1,400
Units produced	1,900
Direct labor	$4,500
Direct materials used	3,500
Fixed manufacturing overhead	2,850
Variable manufacturing overhead	300
Selling and administrative expenses (all fixed)	700
Beginning inventories	0
Contribution margin	5,600
Direct-material inventory, end	800

There are no work-in-process inventories.

1. What is the ending finished-goods inventory cost under absorption costing?
2. What is the ending finished-goods inventory cost under variable costing?

13-B4 Extension of Chapter Illustration

Reconsider Exhibits 13-3 and 13-4, pages 542 and 543. Suppose that in 20X1 production was 15,500 computers instead of 14,000 computers, and sales were 15,000 computers. Also assume that the net variances for all variable manufacturing costs were $18,000, unfavorable. Also assume that actual fixed manufacturing costs were $1,560,000.

1. Prepare income statements for 20X1 under variable costing and under absorption costing. Use a format similar to Exhibits 13-8 and 13-9, page 551.
2. Explain why operating income was different under variable costing and absorption costing. Show your calculations.

Additional Assignment Material

MyAccountingLab

QUESTIONS

13-1 Suppose a company uses machine hours as a cost-allocation base for factory overhead. How does the company compute a budgeted overhead application rate? How does it compute the amounts of factory overhead applied to a particular job?

13-2 "Each department must choose one cost-allocation base to be used for cost application." Do you agree? Explain.

13-3 "Sometimes direct-labor cost is the best cost-allocation base for overhead application even if wage rates vary within a department." Do you agree? Explain.

13-4 Identify four cost-allocation bases that a manufacturing company might use to apply factory overhead costs to jobs.

13-5 Is the comparison of actual overhead costs to budgeted overhead costs part of the product-costing process or part of the control process? Explain.

13-6 What are some reasons for differences between the amounts of incurred and applied overhead?

13-7 "Under actual overhead application, unit costs soar as volume increases, and vice versa." Do you agree? Explain.

13-8 Define *normal costing*.

13-9 What is the best theoretical method of allocating underapplied or overapplied overhead, assuming that the objective is to obtain as accurate a cost application as possible?

13-10 "As data processing becomes more economical, more costs than just direct materials and direct labor will be classified as direct costs wherever feasible." Give three examples of such costs.

13-11 Compare variable and absorption costing regarding the treatment of fixed manufacturing costs.

13-12 Compare variable and absorption costing regarding the treatment of production-volume variance.

13-13 In the United States, about one in every four companies uses variable costing for internal-reporting purposes. These companies must make adjustments to these reports for external-reporting purposes. Explain.

13-14 "With variable costing, only direct materials and direct labor are inventoried." Do you agree? Why?

13-15 "Absorption costing regards more categories of costs as product costs." Explain. Be specific.

13-16 "An increasing number of companies are using variable costing in their corporate annual reports." Do you agree? Explain.

13-17 Why is variable costing used only for internal reporting and not for external financial reporting or tax purposes?

13-18 Compare the contribution margin with the gross margin.

13-19 How is fixed overhead applied to products?

13-20 Name the three ways that an absorption-costing format differs from a variable-costing format.

13-21 "The flexible budget for budgeting and control differs from the costs applied for product costing." What type of cost is being described? Explain.

13-22 "Variable costing is consistent with cost-volume-profit analysis." Explain.

13-23 "In a standard absorption-costing system, the amount of fixed manufacturing overhead applied to the products rarely equals the budgeted fixed manufacturing overhead." Do you agree? Explain.

13-24 "The dollar amount of the production-volume variance depends on what expected volume of production was chosen to determine the fixed-overhead rate." Explain.

13-25 Why is there no production-volume variance for direct labor?

13-26 "An unfavorable production-volume variance means that fixed manufacturing costs have not been well controlled." Do you agree? Explain.

13-27 "The fixed cost per unit is directly affected by the expected volume selected as the denominator." Do you agree? Explain.

13-28 "Absorption-costing income exceeds variable-costing income when the number of units sold exceeds the number of units produced." Do you agree? Explain.

13-29 Suppose a manager is paid a bonus only if standard absorption-costing operating income exceeds the budget. If operating income through November is slightly below budget, what might the manager do in December to increase his or her chance of getting the bonus?

13-30 Why are companies with small levels of inventory generally unconcerned with the choice of variable or absorption costing?

13-31 "Overhead variances arise only with absorption-costing systems." Do you agree? Explain.

CRITICAL THINKING EXERCISES

13-32 Relationship Between Cost-Allocation Bases and Factory Overhead
"There should be a strong relationship between the factory overhead incurred and the cost-allocation base chosen for its application." Why?

13-33 Cost Application in Service Firms
"Service firms trace only direct-labor costs to jobs. All other costs are applied as a percentage of direct-labor cost." Do you agree? Explain.

13-34 Accounting for Fixed Costs
Applying fixed costs to products seems to cause all kinds of problems. Why do companies continue to use accounting systems that assign fixed costs to products on a per unit basis?

13-35 Marketing Decisions and Absorption Costing
Product pricing and promotion decisions should usually be based on their effect on contribution margin, not on gross margin. Explain how using an absorption costing format for the income statement can provide misleading information on the effect of pricing and promotion decisions.

13-36 Evaluating Production Using the Production-Volume Variance
The sales-volume variance (see Chapter 8) highlights the effect on income of sales exceeding or falling short of sales targets. Does the production-volume variance provide parallel information for evaluating the effect of exceeding or falling short of production targets? Explain.

13-37 Absorption Costing and the Value Chain
Many costs on a product's value chain, such as R&D and product design costs, are considered period costs and are not assigned to units of product. An absorption-costing system could be expanded to apply such costs to the products. What would be the advantages and disadvantages of doing so? Would this help managers make better decisions?

EXERCISES

13-38 Discovery of Unknowns

The Hatch Manufacturing Company has the following budgeted overhead cost and other data for its machining department for the month of December:

Budgeted Data:	
Indirect labor and supplies	$ 70,000
Factory rent	$ 19,000
Supervision	$ 84,000
Depreciation on equipment	$139,000
Cost-allocation base for overhead application	Machine hours
Budgeted overhead application rate	$6 per machine hour
Other Data:	
Actual machine hours during December	68,000
Actual overhead cost incurred during December	$439,000

Compute the total budgeted machine hours, total applied overhead cost, and indicate how any difference between the actual overhead cost incurred and applied overhead would be treated on Hatch's income statement for the month of December.

13-39 Discovery of Unknowns

The Lawson Manufacturing Company has the following budgeted overhead cost and other data for its assembly department for the month of April:

Budgeted Data:	
Indirect labor and supplies	$170,000
Factory rent	$ 52,000
Supervision	$ 67,000
Depreciation on equipment	$216,000
Cost-allocation base for overhead application	Direct-labor hours
Total budgeted direct-labor hours	50,000
Other Data:	
Total applied overhead costs for April	$616,100
Actual overhead cost incurred during April	$577,000

Compute the budgeted factory overhead rate, actual direct-labor hours, and indicate how the difference between the actual overhead cost incurred and applied overhead would be treated on Lawson's income statement for the month of April.

13-40 Relationship Among Overhead Items

Fill in the unknowns:

	Case 1	Case 2
a. Budgeted factory overhead	$600,000	$420,000
b. Cost-allocation base, budgeted direct-labor cost	400,000	?
c. Budgeted factory-overhead rate	?	120%
d. Direct-labor cost incurred	570,000	?
e. Factory overhead incurred	830,000	425,000
f. Factory overhead applied	?	?
g. Underapplied (overapplied) factory overhead	?	35,000

13-41 Underapplied and Overapplied Overhead

Wosepka Welding Company applies factory overhead at a rate of $8.50 per direct-labor hour. Selected data for 20X0 operations are as follows (in thousands):

	Case 1	Case 2
Direct-labor hours	30	36
Direct-labor cost	$220	$245
Indirect-labor cost	32	40
Sales commissions	20	15
Depreciation, manufacturing equipment	22	32
Direct-materials cost	230	250
Factory fuel costs	35	47
Depreciation, finished-goods warehouse	5	17
Cost of goods sold	420	510
All other factory costs	138	204

Compute for both cases

1. factory overhead applied.
2. total factory overhead incurred.
3. amount of underapplied or overapplied factory overhead.

13-42 Disposition of Year-End Underapplied Overhead

Liz's Cosmetics uses a normal cost system and has the following balances at the end of its first year's operations.

WIP inventory	$200,000
Finished-goods inventory	200,000
Cost of goods sold	400,000
Actual factory overhead	413,000
Factory overhead applied	453,000

Compute cost of goods sold for two different ways to dispose of the year-end overhead balances. By how much would gross profit differ?

13-43 Simple Comparison of Variable and Absorption Costing

Khalid Company began business on January 1, 20X1, with assets of $150,000 cash and equities of $150,000 capital stock. In 20X1, it manufactured some inventory at a cost of $60,000 cash, including $16,000 for factory rent and other fixed factory overhead. In 20X2, it manufactured nothing and sold half of its inventory for $43,000 cash. In 20X3 it manufactured nothing and sold the remaining half for another $43,000 cash. It had no fixed expenses in 20X2 or 20X3.

There are no other transactions of any kind. Ignore income taxes.

Prepare an ending balance sheet plus an income statement for 20X1, 20X2, and 20X3 under (1) absorption costing and (2) variable costing (direct costing). Explain the differences in net income between absorption and variable costing.

13-44 Comparisons over Four Years

The Balakrishnan Corporation began business on January 1, 20X0, to produce and sell a single product. Reported operating income figures under both absorption and variable costing for the first 4 years of operation are as follows:

Year	Absorption Costing	Variable Costing
20X0	$80,000	$60,000
20X1	70,000	60,000
20X2	50,000	50,000
20X3	40,000	70,000

Standard production costs per unit, sales prices, application (absorption) rates, and expected volume levels were the same in each year. There were no flexible-budget variances for any type of cost. All non-manufacturing expenses were fixed, and there were no nonmanufacturing cost variances in any year.

1. In what year(s) did "units produced" equal "units sold"?
2. In what year(s) did "units produced" exceed "units sold"?

3. What is the dollar amount of the December 31, 20X3, finished-goods inventory? (Give absorption-costing value.)
4. What is the difference between "units produced" and "units sold" in 20X3, if you know that the absorption-costing fixed-manufacturing overhead application rate is $3 per unit? (Give answer in units.)

13-45 Variable and Absorption Costing

Chan Manufacturing Company data for 20X0 follow:

Sales: 12,000 units at $18 each	
Actual production	15,000 units
Expected volume of production	18,000 units
Manufacturing costs incurred	
Variable	$120,000
Fixed	60,000
Nonmanufacturing costs incurred	
Variable	$ 24,000
Fixed	18,000

1. Determine operating income for 20X0, assuming the firm uses the variable-costing approach to product costing. (Do not prepare a statement.)
2. Assume that there is no January 1, 20X0, inventory; no variances are allocated to inventory; and the firm uses a "full absorption" approach to product costing. Compute (a) the cost assigned to December 31, 20X0, inventory; and (b) operating income for the year ended December 31, 20X0. (Do not prepare a statement.)

13-46 Computation of Production-Volume Variance

Osaka Manufacturing Company budgeted its 20X0 variable overhead at ¥14,100,000 and its fixed overhead at ¥26,230,000. Expected 20X0 volume was 6,100 units. Actual costs for production of 5,800 units during 20X0 were as follows:

Variable overhead	¥14,160,000
Fixed overhead	26,340,000
Total overhead	¥40,500,000

Compute the production-volume variance. Be sure to label it favorable or unfavorable.

13-47 Reconciliation of Variable-Costing and Absorption-Costing Operating Income

Blackstone Tools produced 12,000 electric drills during 20X0. Expected production was only 10,500 drills. The company's fixed-overhead rate is $7 per drill. Absorption-costing operating income for the year is $18,000, based on sales of 11,000 drills.

1. Compute the following:
   a. Budgeted fixed overhead
   b. Production-volume variance
   c. Variable-costing operating income
2. Reconcile absorption-costing operating income and variable-costing operating income. Include the amount of the difference between the two and an explanation for the difference.

13-48 Overhead Variances

Study Appendix 13. Consider the following data for the Rivera Company:

	Factory Overhead	
	Fixed	**Variable**
Actual incurred	$14,400	$13,600
Budget for standard hours allowed for output achieved	12,500	11,000
Applied	11,600	11,000
Budget for actual hours of input	12,500	11,400

From the preceding information, fill in the following blanks. Be sure to mark your variances F for favorable and U for unfavorable.

a. Flexible-budget variance $_____   Fixed $_____
                                       Variable $_____

b. Production-volume variance $_____   Fixed $_____
                                       Variable $_____

c. Spending variance $_____   Fixed $_____
                                       Variable $_____

d. Efficiency variance $_____   Fixed $_____
                                       Variable $_____

13-49 Variances

Study Appendix 13. Consider the following data regarding factory overhead:

	Variable	Fixed
Budget for actual hours of input	$45,000	$70,000
Applied	41,000	64,800
Budget for standard hours allowed for actual output achieved	?	?
Actual incurred	48,100	66,500

Using the preceding data, fill in the following blanks with the variance amounts. Use F for favorable or U for unfavorable for each variance.

	Total Overhead	Variable	Fixed
1. Spending variance	_____	_____	_____
2. Efficiency variance	_____	_____	_____
3. Production-volume variance	_____	_____	_____
4. Flexible-budget variance	_____	_____	_____
5. Underapplied overhead	_____	_____	_____

PROBLEMS

13-50 Choice of Cost-Allocation Base at Enriquez Machine Parts Company

Refer to the chapter discussion of Enriquez Machine Parts Company beginning on page 534. Suppose Enriquez decided to use only one overhead cost pool for both departments with machine hours as the single cost-allocation base.

1. Compute the budgeted overhead application rate for the factory using the budgeted data on page 534.
2. If Enriquez used 70,000 machine hours during 20X0, what was the total factory overhead applied to products?
3. The applied factory overhead based on separate application rates for the machining and assembly departments was $375,000. Explain why this amount is different than the applied amount from requirement 2.

13-51 Choice of Cost-Allocation Base at Enriquez Machine Parts Company

Refer to the chapter discussion of Enriquez Machine Parts Company beginning on page 534. Suppose Enriquez decided to use only one overhead cost pool for both departments with direct labor cost as the single cost-allocation base.

1. Compute the budgeted overhead application rate for the factory using the budgeted data on page 534.
2. If Enriquez incurred $190,000 of direct labor cost during 20X0, what was the total factory overhead applied to products?
3. The applied factory overhead based on separate application rates for the machining and assembly departments was $375,000. Explain why this amount is different than the applied amount from requirement 2.

13-52 Choice of Cost-Allocation Bases in Accounting Firm

Brenda McCoy, the managing partner of McCoy, Brennan, and Cable, a public accounting firm, is considering the desirability of tracing more costs to jobs than just direct labor. In this way, the firm will be able to justify billings to clients.

Last year's costs were as follows:

Direct-professional labor	$ 5,000,000
Overhead	10,000,000
Total costs	$15,000,000

The following costs were included in overhead:

Computer time	$ 750,000
Secretarial cost	700,000
Photocopying	250,000
Fringe benefits to direct labor	800,000
Phone call time with clients (estimated but not tabulated)	500,000
Total	$3,000,000

The firm's data processing techniques now make it feasible to document and trace these costs to individual jobs.

As an experiment, in December Brenda McCoy arranged to trace these costs to six audit engagements. Two job records showed the following:

	Engagement	
	Eagledale Company	**First Valley Bank**
Direct-professional labor	$15,000	$15,000
Fringe benefits to direct labor	3,000	3,000
Phone call time with clients	1,500	500
Computer time	3,000	700
Secretarial costs	2,000	1,500
Photocopying	500	300
Total direct costs	$25,000	$21,000

1. Compute the overhead application rate based on last year's costs.
2. Suppose last year's costs were reclassified so that $3 million would be regarded as direct costs instead of overhead. Compute the overhead application rate as a percentage of direct labor and as a percentage of total direct costs.
3. Using the three rates computed in numbers 1 and 2, compute the total costs of engagements for Eagledale Company and First Valley Bank.
4. Suppose that client billing was based on a 30% markup of total job costs. Compute the billings that would be forthcoming in number 3.
5. Which method of costing and overhead application do you favor? Explain.

13-53 Allocated Costs and Public Services

The Napa County (California) grand jury charged the city of St. Helena with overbilling customers for water and sewer services. The city allocated "administrative overhead" to the water and sewer department's budget. These costs were then added to the "jobs," that is, to the accounts of the customers of the water and sewer department. The grand jury called the $76,581.20 allocated to the department in 1996–1997 "merely a ruse" to generate funds to cover city expenses that are unrelated to water and sewer services, resulting in "bloated water bills" for local customers.

The city finance director explained that the overhead allocation was the way in which the city bills the water and sewer department for time that other departments spend on water and sewer issues. Mayor John Brown concluded that "it was very clear to me that they [the grand jury] didn't know what they were talking about."

1. Was the overhead charge to the water and sewer department a legitimate cost to be covered by water and sewer bills? Explain your reasoning to the citizens of St. Helena.

2. Assume that at least part of the overhead charge is a legitimate cost of the water and sewer department. Suggest possible changes in the accounting system that would provide a more accurate measure of the cost of services provided to the water and sewer department by other departments.

13-54 Overhead Accounting for Control and for Product Costing

The pickle department of a major food manufacturer has an overhead rate of $5 per direct-labor hour, based on expected variable overhead of $150,000 per year, expected fixed overhead of $350,000 per year, and expected direct-labor hours of 100,000 per year.

Data for the year's operations follow:

	Direct-Labor Hours Used	Overhead Costs Incurred*
First 6 months	52,000	$264,000
Last 6 months	42,000	239,000

*Fixed costs incurred were exactly equal to budgeted amounts throughout the year.

1. What is the underapplied or overapplied overhead for each 6-month period? Label your answer as underapplied or overapplied.
2. Explain briefly (no more than 50 words for each part) the probable causes for the underapplied or overapplied overhead. Focus on variable and fixed costs separately. Give the exact figures attributable to the causes you cite.

13-55 Comparison of Variable Costing and Absorption Costing

Simple numbers are used in this problem to highlight the concepts covered in the chapter.

Assume that the Perth Woolen Company produces a rug that sells for $20. Perth uses a standard cost system. Total standard variable costs of production are $8 per rug, fixed manufacturing costs are $150,000 per year, and selling and administrative expenses are $30,000 per year, all fixed. Expected production volume is 25,000 rugs per year.

1. For each of the following nine combinations of actual sales and production (in thousands of units) for 20X0, prepare condensed income statements under variable costing and under absorption costing.

	(1)	(2)	(3)	(4)	(5)	(6)	(7)	(8)	(9)
Sales units	15	20	25	20	25	30	25	30	35
Production units	20	20	20	25	25	25	30	30	30

Use the following formats:

Variable Costing		Absorption Costing	
Revenue	$ aa	Revenue	$ aa
Cost of goods sold	(bb)	Cost of goods sold	(uu)
Contribution margin	$ cc	Gross profit at standard	$ vv
Fixed manufacturing costs	(dd)	Favorable (unfavorable)	
Fixed selling and administrative expenses	(ee)	production-volume variance	ww
		Gross profit at "actual"	$ xx
		Selling and administrative expenses	(yy)
Operating income	$ ff	Operating income	$ zz

2. a. In which of the nine combinations is variable-costing income greater than absorption-costing income? In which is it lower? The same?
   b. In which of the nine combinations is the production-volume variance unfavorable? Favorable?
   c. How much profit is added by selling one more unit under variable costing? Under absorption costing?
   d. How much profit is added by producing one more unit under variable costing? Under absorption costing?
   e. Suppose sales, rather than production, is the critical factor in determining the success of Perth Woolen Company. Which format, variable costing or absorption costing, provides the better measure of performance?

13-56 All-Fixed Costs

The Gibraltar Company has built a massive water-desalting factory next to an ocean. The factory is completely automated. It has its own source of power, light, heat, and so on. The salt water costs nothing. All producing and other operating costs are fixed; they do not vary with output because the volume is governed by adjusting a few dials on a control panel. The employees have flat annual salaries.

The desalted water is not sold to household consumers. It has a special taste that appeals to local breweries, distilleries, and soft-drink manufacturers. The price, $.60 per gallon, is expected to remain unchanged for quite some time.

The following are data regarding the first 2 years of operations:

	In Gallons		Costs (All Fixed)	
	Sales	Production	Manufacturing	Other
20X0	1,500,000	3,000,000	$600,000	$200,000
20X1	1,500,000	0	600,000	200,000

Orders can be processed in 4 hours so management decided, in early 20X1, to gear production strictly to sales.

1. Prepare three-column income statements for 20X0, for 20X1, and for the 2 years together using (a) variable costing and (b) absorption costing.
2. What is the break-even point under (a) variable costing and (b) absorption costing?
3. What inventory costs would be carried on the balance sheets on December 31, 20X0 and 20X1, under each method?
4. Comment on your answers in numbers 1 and 2. Which costing method appears more useful?

13-57 Semifixed Costs

The Plymouth Company differs from the Gibraltar Company (described in problem 13-56) in only one respect: It has both variable and fixed manufacturing costs. Its variable costs are $.14 per gallon, and its fixed manufacturing costs are $390,000 per year.

1. Using the same data as in the preceding problem, except for the change in production-cost behavior, prepare three-column income statements for 20X0, for 20X1, and for the 2 years together using (a) variable costing and (b) absorption costing.
2. What inventory costs would be carried on the balance sheets on December 31, 20X0 and 20X1, under each method?

13-58 Absorption and Variable Costing

The Trapani Company had the following actual data for 20X0 and 20X1:

	20X0	20X1
Units of finished goods		
Opening inventory	—	2,000
Production	15,000	13,000
Sales	13,000	14,000
Ending inventory	2,000	1,000

The basic production data at standard unit costs for the 2 years were as follows:

Direct materials	$22
Direct labor	18
Variable factory overhead	4
Standard variable costs per unit	$44

Fixed factory overhead was budgeted at $98,000 per year. The expected volume of production was 14,000 units so the fixed overhead rate was $98,000 ÷ 14,000 = $7 per unit.

Budgeted sales price was $75 per unit. Selling and administrative expenses were budgeted at variable, $9 per unit sold, and fixed, $80,000 per year.

Assume that there were absolutely no variances from any standard variable costs or budgeted selling prices or budgeted fixed costs in 20X0.

There were no beginning or ending inventories of work in process.

1. For 20X0, prepare income statements based on standard variable (direct) costing and standard absorption costing. (The next problem deals with 20X1.)
2. Explain why operating income differs between variable costing and absorption costing. Be specific.

13-59 Absorption and Variable Costing

Assume the same facts as in the preceding problem. In addition, consider the following actual data for 20X1:

Direct materials	$ 285,000
Direct labor	174,200
Variable factory overhead	36,000
Fixed factory overhead	95,000
Selling and administrative costs	
Variable	118,400
Fixed	80,000
Sales	1,068,000

1. For 20X1, prepare income statements based on standard variable (direct) costing and standard absorption costing.
2. Explain why operating income differs between variable costing and absorption costing. Be specific.

13-60 Fundamentals of Overhead Variances

The Durant Company is installing an absorption standard-cost system and a flexible-overhead budget. Standard costs have recently been developed for its only product and are as follows:

Direct materials, 3 pounds at $20	$60
Direct labor, 2 hours at $14	28
Variable overhead, 2 hours at $5	10
Fixed overhead	?
Standard cost per unit of finished product	$?

Expected production activity is expressed as 7,500 standard direct-labor hours per month. Fixed overhead is expected to be $60,000 per month. The predetermined fixed-overhead rate for product costing is not changed from month to month.

1. Calculate the proper fixed-overhead rate per standard direct-labor hour and per unit.
2. Graph the following for activity from 0 to 10,000 hours:
   a. Budgeted variable overhead
   b. Variable overhead applied to product
3. Graph the following for activity from 0 to 10,000 hours:
   a. Budgeted fixed overhead
   b. Fixed overhead applied to product
4. Assume that 6,000 standard direct-labor hours are allowed for the output achieved during a given month. Actual variable overhead of $31,000 was incurred; actual fixed overhead amounted to $62,000. Calculate the following:
   a. Fixed-overhead flexible-budget variance
   b. Fixed-overhead production-volume variance
   c. Variable-overhead flexible-budget variance
5. Assume that 7,800 standard direct-labor hours are allowed for the output achieved during a given month. Actual overhead incurred amounted to $99,700, $62,000 of which was fixed. Calculate the following:
   a. Fixed-overhead flexible-budget variance
   b. Fixed-overhead production-volume variance
   c. Variable-overhead flexible-budget variance

13-61 Production-Volume Variance at L.A. Darling Company

Review the Chapter 12 opening vignette on **L.A. Darling Company** (pages 472–473). L.A. Darling receives about $6 billion of revenue each year from designing, manufacturing, and installing store fixtures in retail stores. Accounting for fixed manufacturing overhead is a challenge for the company. Suppose a manufacturing division of the company has the following budgeted costs for production of 800,000 shelving units in 2009:

Direct materials	$160,000,000
Direct labor	24,000,000
Other variable manufacturing costs	20,000,000
Fixed manufacturing costs	100,000,000
Total manufacturing cost	$304,000,000

During 2009, this division of L.A. Darling produced 850,000 of the shelving units and sold 820,000 of them for $450 million. Assume that L.A. Darling does not allocate selling or administrative costs to the individual products.

1. Compute the following budgeted unit costs for 2009:

Variable manufacturing costs per unit	?
Fixed manufacturing costs per unit	?
Total manufacturing costs per unit	?

2. Compute the production-volume variance for 2009. Be sure to label it favorable or unfavorable.
3. Compute the 2009 profit from the production and sales of the shelving using absorption costing. Ignore selling and administrative costs.
4. Compute the 2009 profit from the production and sales of the shelving using variable costing. Ignore selling and administrative costs.
5. Which measure of profit, absorption-costing profit or variable-costing profit, is a better measure of performance during 2009? Explain.

13-62 Fixed Overhead and Practical Capacity

The expected activity of the paper-making plant of Goldberg Paper Company was 45,000 machine hours per month. Practical capacity was 60,000 machine hours per month. The standard machine hours allowed for the actual output achieved in January were 54,000. The budgeted fixed-factory-overhead items were as follows:

Depreciation, equipment	$340,000
Depreciation, factory building	64,000
Supervision	47,000
Indirect labor	234,000
Insurance	18,000
Property taxes	17,000
Total	$720,000

Because of unanticipated scheduling difficulties and the need for more indirect labor, the actual fixed factory overhead was $747,000.

1. Using practical capacity as the base for applying fixed factory overhead, prepare a summary analysis of fixed-overhead variances for January.
2. Using expected activity as the base for applying fixed factory overhead, prepare a summary analysis of fixed-overhead variances for January.
3. Explain why some of your variances in numbers 1 and 2 are the same and why some differ.

13-63 Selection of Expected Volume

Rosanne McIntire is a consultant to Georgia Paper Products Company. She is helping one of the company's divisions to install a standard cost system for 20X0. For product-costing purposes, the system must apply fixed factory costs to products manufactured. She has decided that the fixed-overhead rate should be based on machine hours, but she is uncertain about the appropriate volume to use in the denominator. Georgia Paper has grown rapidly; the division has added production capacity approximately every

4 years. The last addition was completed in early 20X0, and the total capacity is now 2,800,000 machine hours per year. McIntire predicts the following operating levels (in machine hours) through 20X4:

Year	Capacity Used
20X0	2,250,000 hours
20X1	2,450,000 hours
20X2	2,700,000 hours
20X3	2,800,000 hours
20X4	2,900,000 hours

The current plan is to add another 500,000 machine hours of capacity in 20X4. McIntire has identified three alternatives for the application base:
a. Predicted volume for the year in question
b. Average volume over the 4 years of the current production setup
c. Practical (or full) capacity

1. Suppose annual fixed factory overhead is expected to be $36,400,000 through 20X3. For simplicity, assume no inflation. Calculate the fixed-overhead rates (to the nearest cent) for 20X1, 20X2, and 20X3, using each of the three alternative application bases.
2. Provide a brief description of the effect of using each method of computing the application base.
3. Which method do you prefer? Why?

13-64 Analysis of Operating Results

Leeds Tool Company produces and sells a variety of machine-tooled products. The company employs a standard cost accounting system for record-keeping purposes.

At the beginning of 20X0, the president of Leeds Tool presented the budget to the company's board of directors. The board accepted a target 20X0 profit of £16,800 and agreed to pay the president a bonus if profits exceeded the target. The president has been confident that the year's profit would exceed the budget target, since the monthly sales reports that he has been receiving have shown that sales for the year will exceed budget by 10%. The president is both disturbed and confused when the controller presents an adjusted forecast as of November 30, 20X0, indicating that profit will be 14% under budget:

Leeds Tool Company		
Forecasts of Operating Results		
	Forecasts as of	
	1/1/X0	**11/30/X0**
Sales	£156,000	£171,600
Cost of sales at standard	108,000*	118,800
Gross margin at standard	£ 48,000	£ 52,800
Over- (under-) absorbed fixed manufacturing overhead	0	(6,000)
Actual gross margin	£ 48,000	£ 46,800
Selling expenses	£ 11,200	£ 12,320
Administrative expenses	20,000	20,000
Total operating expenses	£ 31,200	£ 32,320
Earnings before tax	£ 16,800	£ 14,480

*Includes fixed manufacturing overhead of £30,000.

There have been no sales price changes or product-mix shifts since the January 1, 20X0, forecast. The only cost variance on the income statement is the underapplied manufacturing overhead. This arose because the company produced only 16,000 standard machine hours (budgeted machine hours were 20,000) during 20X0, as a result of a shortage of raw materials while its principal supplier was closed by a strike. Fortunately, Leeds Tool's finished-goods inventory was large enough to fill all sales orders received.

1. Analyze and explain why the profit has declined despite increased sales and good control over costs. Show computations.
2. What plan, if any, could Leeds Tool adopt during December to improve its reported profit at year-end? Explain your answer.

3. Illustrate and explain how Leeds Tool could adopt an alternative internal cost-reporting procedure that would avoid the confusing effect of the present procedure. Show the revised forecasts under your alternative.

4. Would the alternative procedure described in number 3 be acceptable to the board of directors for financial-reporting purposes? Explain.

13-65 Standard Absorption and Standard Variable Costing

Schlosser Company has the following results for a certain year. All variances are written off as additions to (or deductions from) the standard cost of goods sold. Find the unknowns, designated by letters.

Sales: 150,000 units, at $20	$3,000,000
Net variance for standard variable manufacturing costs	$ 33,000 unfavorable
Variable standard cost of goods manufactured	$ 11 per unit
Variable selling and administrative expenses	$ 3 per unit
Fixed selling and administrative expenses	$ 650,000
Fixed manufacturing overhead	$ 165,000
Maximum capacity per year	190,000 units
Expected production volume for year	150,000 units
Beginning inventory of finished goods	15,000 units
Ending inventory of finished goods	10,000 units
Beginning inventory: Variable-costing basis	a
Contribution margin	b
Operating income: Variable-costing basis	c
Beginning inventory: Absorption-costing basis	d
Gross margin	e
Operating income: Absorption-costing basis	f

13-66 Disposition of Variances

In January 20X0, Louisiana Garden Equipment Company started a division for making grass clippers. Management hoped that these grass clippers were significantly better than most competitors in the market. During 20X0, it produced 100,000 grass clippers. Financial results were as follows:

- Sales: 75,000 units at $18
- Direct labor at standard: 100,000 × $8 = $800,000
- Direct-labor variances: $34,000 U
- Direct materials at standard: 100,000 × $5 = $500,000
- Direct-material variances: $9,500 U
- Overhead incurred at standard: 100,000 × $4 = $400,000
- Overhead variances: $3,500 F

Louisiana uses an absorption-costing system and allows divisions to choose one of two methods of accounting for variances:

a. Direct charge to income

b. Proration to the production of the period; method b requires variances to be spread equally over the units produced during the period

1. Calculate the division's operating income (a) using method a and (b) using method b. Assume no selling and administrative expenses.

2. Calculate ending inventory value (a) using method a and (b) using method b. Note that there was no beginning inventory.

3. What is the major argument in support of each method?

13-67 Straightforward Problem on Standard Cost System

Study Appendix 13. The Winnipeg Chemical Company uses flexible budgets and a standard cost system.

- Direct-labor costs incurred, 12,000 hours, $150,000
- Variable-overhead costs incurred, $37,000
- Fixed-overhead flexible-budget variance, $1,600, favorable
- Finished units produced, 1,800
- Fixed-overhead costs incurred, $38,000
- Variable overhead applied at $3 per hour
- Standard direct-labor cost, $13 per hour
- Denominator production per month, 2,000 units
- Standard direct-labor hours per finished unit, 6

Prepare an analysis of all variances (similar to Exhibit 13-10, p. 553).

13-68 Straightforward Problem on Standard Cost System

Study Appendix 13. The München Company uses a standard cost system. The month's data regarding its single product follow (where € is the symbol for the euro, the currency of most countries of the European Union):

- Fixed-overhead costs incurred, €6,300
- Variable overhead applied at €11 per hour
- Standard direct-labor cost, €44 per hour
- Denominator production per month, 220 units
- Standard direct-labor hours per finished unit, 5
- Direct-labor costs incurred, 1,000 hours, €42,500
- Variable-overhead costs incurred, €10,400
- Fixed-overhead flexible-budget variance, €300, favorable
- Finished units produced, 180

Prepare an analysis of all variances (similar to Exhibit 13-10, p. 553).

CASES

13-69 Multiple Overhead Rates and Activity-Based Costing

A division of **Hewlett-Packard** assembles and tests printed circuit (PC) boards. The division has many different products. Some are high volume; others are low volume. For years, manufacturing overhead was applied to products using a single overhead rate based on direct-labor dollars. However, direct-labor has shrunk to 6% of total manufacturing costs.

Managers decided to refine the division's product-costing system. Abolishing the direct-labor category, they included all manufacturing labor as a part of factory overhead. They also identified several activities and the appropriate cost-allocation base for each. The cost-allocation base for the first activity, the start station, was the number of raw PC boards. The application rate was computed as follows:

$$\text{application rate for start station activity} = \frac{\text{budgeted total factory overhead at the activity}}{\text{budgeted raw PC boards for the year}}$$

$$= \frac{\$150,000}{125,000}$$

$$= \$1.20$$

Each time a raw PC board passes through the start station activity, $1.20 is added to the cost of the board. The product cost is the sum of costs directly traced to the board plus the indirect costs (factory overhead) accumulated at each of the manufacturing activities undergone.

Using assumed numbers, consider the following data regarding PC board 37:

Direct materials	$55.00
Factory overhead applied	?
Total manufacturing product cost	?

The activities involved in the production of PC board 37 and the related cost-allocation bases were as follows:

Activity	Cost-Allocation Base	Factory-Overhead Costs Applied for Each Activity
1. Start station	Number of raw PC boards	1 × $1.20 = $1.20
2. Axial insertion	Number of axial insertions	39 × .07 = ?
3. Dip insertion	Number of dip insertions	? × .20 = 5.60
4. Manual insertion	Number of manual insertions	15 × ? = 6.00
5. Wave solder	Number of boards soldered	1 × 3.20 = 3.20
6. Backload	Number of backload insertions	8 × .60 = 4.80
7. Test	Standard time board is in test activity	.15 × 80.00 = ?
8. Defect analysis	Standard time for defect analysis and repair	.05 × ? = 4.50
Total		$?

1. Fill in the numbers where there are question marks.
2. How is direct labor identified with products under this product-costing system?
3. Why would managers favor this multiple-overhead rate, ABC system instead of the older system?

13-70 Inventory Measures, Production Scheduling, and Evaluating Divisional Performance

The Calais Company stresses competition between the heads of its various divisions, and it rewards stellar performance with year-end bonuses that vary between 5% and 10% of division net operating income (before considering the bonus or income taxes). The divisional managers have great discretion in setting production schedules.

The Brittany division produces and sells a product for which there is a long-standing demand but which can have marked seasonal and year-to-year fluctuations. On November 30, 20X0, Veronique Giraud, the Brittany division manager, is preparing a production schedule for December. The following data are available for January 1 through November 30 (€ is the symbol for euro, the currency for most countries of the European Union):

Beginning inventory, January 1, in units	10,000
Sales price, per unit	€ 400
Total fixed costs incurred for manufacturing	€ 9,350,000
Total fixed costs: Other (not inventoriable)	€10,200,000
Total variable costs for manufacturing	€18,150,000
Total other variable costs (fluctuate with units sold)	€ 4,000,000
Units produced	110,000
Units sold	100,000
Variances	None

Production in October and November was 10,000 units each month. Practical capacity is 12,000 units per month. Maximum available storage space for inventory is 25,000 units. The sales outlook for December–February is 6,000 units monthly. To retain a core of key employees, monthly production cannot be scheduled at less than 4,000 units without special permission from the president. Inventory is never to be less than 10,000 units.

The denominator used for applying fixed factory overhead is regarded as 120,000 units annually. The company uses a standard absorption-costing system. All variances are disposed of at year-end as an adjustment to standard cost of goods sold.

1. Given the restrictions as stated, and assuming that Giraud wants to maximize the company's net income for 20X0, answer the following:
   a. How many units should be scheduled for production in December?
   b. What net operating income will be reported in 20X0 as a whole, assuming that the implied cost-behavior patterns will continue in December as they did throughout the year to date? Show your computations.
   c. If December production is scheduled at 4,000 units, what would reported net income be?
2. Assume that standard variable costing is used rather than standard absorption costing.
   a. What would net income for 20X0 be, assuming that the December production schedule is the one in part a of number 1?
   b. What would net income for 20X0 be, assuming that December production was 4,000 units?
   c. Reconcile the net incomes in this requirement with those in number 1.
3. From the viewpoint of the long-run interests of the company as a whole, what production schedule should the division manager set? Explain fully. Include in your explanation a comparison of the motivating influence of absorption and variable costing in this situation.
4. Assume standard absorption costing. Giraud wants to maximize her after-income tax performance over the long run. Given the data at the beginning of the problem, assume that income tax rates will be halved in 20X1. Assume also that year-end write-offs of variances are acceptable for income tax purposes. How many units should be scheduled for production in December? Why?

13-71 Performance Evaluation

A division of Iowa/Illinois Corn Company produces seed corn for farmers throughout the Midwest. Jens Jensen became president in 20X0. He is concerned with the ability of his division manager to control costs. To aid his evaluation, Jensen set up a standard cost system.

Standard costs were based on 20X0 costs in several categories. Each 20X0 cost was divided by 1,520,000 cwt, the volume of 20X0 production, to determine a standard for 20X1 (cwt means hundredweight, or 100 pounds):

	20X0 Cost (thousands)	20X1 Standard (per hundredweight)
Direct materials	$1,824	$1.20
Direct labor	836	.55
Variable overhead	1,596	1.05
Fixed overhead	2,432	1.60
Total	$6,688	$4.40

At the end of 20X1, Jensen compared actual results with the standards he established. Production was 1,360,000 cwt, and variances were as follows:

	Actual	Standard	Variance
Direct materials	$1,802	$1,632	$170 U
Direct labor	735	748	13 F
Variable overhead	1,422	1,428	6 F
Fixed overhead	2,412	2,176	236 U
Total	$6,371	$5,984	$387 U

Jensen was not surprised by the unfavorable variance in direct materials. After all, corn prices in 20X1 averaged 10% above those in 20X0. But he was disturbed by the lack of control of fixed overhead. He called in the production manager and demanded an explanation.

1. Prepare an explanation for the large unfavorable fixed-overhead variance.
2. Discuss the appropriateness of using one year's costs as the next year's standards.

13-72 Converting an Income Statement from Absorption Costing to Variable Costing

Holden Corp. has the following income statement under standard absorption costing:

Sales		$1,000,000
Cost of goods sold:		
Beginning inventory	$ 0	
Production	$ 975,000	
Ending inventory	$ 225,000	
Cost of goods sold:	$ 750,000	
Less adjustment for variances	$ 95,000	
Adjusted cost of goods sold		$ 655,000
Gross profit		$ 345,000
Selling and administrative expenses		
Variable selling and administrative	$ 30,000	
Fixed selling and administrative	$ 170,000	
Net income		$ 145,000

During the period Holden produced 130,000 units and sold 100,000 units. There was no beginning or ending WIP inventory. Budgeted fixed factory overhead was $150,000, actual fixed factory overhead was $90,000, and denominator level was 100,000 units. Holden does not prorate variances.

Present a variable costing income statement. Be sure to list the amount of any variance in an adjustment for variances.

13-73 Converting an Income Statement from Variable Costing to Absorption Costing

Moseley Corp. currently uses variable costing in its accounting system, with the following selected results (assume there were no variances):

Contribution margin	$300,000
Variable selling and administrative	$100,000
Fixed selling and administrative	$ 60,000
Net income	$150,000

During the period Moseley produced 160,000 units and sold 80,000 units. Selling price is $10/unit. There was no beginning or ending WIP inventory, and no beginning FG inventory. Moseley is considering a standard absorption costing system. It estimates that if it had used such a system this year, it would have budgeted fixed factory overhead at $100,000, and would have selected a denominator level of 200,000 units. The company also estimates that there would have still been no variances related to direct materials, direct labor, and variable factory overhead.

Present a standard absorption costing income statement with proration. Be sure to present the adjustment for variances amount on the income statement.

NIKE 10-K PROBLEM

13-74 Overhead Costs at Umbro

Read **Nike**'s 10-K Item 1 description of its business. Although Nike does not manufacture the products it sells, its subsidiaries do some manufacturing. For example, Nike's subsidiary, **Umbro**, headquartered in Cheadle, England, manufactures and distributes soccer equipment and clothing.

1. What kinds of sports gear does Umbro make? Consider the Umbro plant that makes soccer clothing. List five variable-cost resources and five fixed-cost resources that are part of the plant's overhead.
2. Suppose that Umbro uses a dedicated production line to make only soccer shoes. What are some resources that are normally part of overhead that would be directly traceable to the soccer-shoe cost object?

EXCEL APPLICATION EXERCISE

13-75 Computing Budgeted Factory Overhead

Goal: Create an Excel spreadsheet to compute budgeted factory overhead rates and apply factory overhead to production. Use the results to answer questions about your findings.

Scenario: Donald Aeronautics Company has asked you to determine its budgeted factory overhead rates. It would also like you to apply the appropriate factory overhead amounts to actual production and determine any variances. Additional background information for your spreadsheet appears in Fundamental Assignment Material 13-A1. (Ignore data in the Fundamental Assignment Material for product M89.)

When you have completed your spreadsheet, answer the following questions:

1. What was the budgeted factory overhead rate for department A? Department B?
2. What overhead amount was distributed to department A? Was the overhead over- or underapplied? By what amount?
3. What overhead amount was distributed to department B? Was the overhead over- or underapplied? By what amount?

Step-by-Step:
1. Open a new Excel spreadsheet.
2. In column A, create a bold-faced heading that contains the following:
   Row 1: Chapter 13 Decision Guideline
   Row 2: Donald Aeronautics Company
   Row 3: Overhead Applications Using Budgeted Rates
   Row 4: Today's Date
3. Merge and center the four heading rows across columns A–G.
4. In row 7, create the following column headings:
   Column B: 20X0 Budget
   Column D: 20X0 Actual
   Column F: Variances
5. Merge and center the 20X0 Budget heading across columns B–C.
6. Merge and center the 20X0 Actual heading across columns D–E.
7. Merge and center the Variances heading across columns F–G.
8. In row 8, create the following center-justified column headings:
   Columns B, D, and F: Dept. A
   Columns C, E, and G: Dept. B
9. In column A, create the following row headings:
   Row 9: Factory Overhead
   Row 10: Direct-Labor Hours
   Row 11: Machine Hours
   Skip a row.
   Row 13: Overhead Rate

Row 14: Distributed Overhead

Row 15: Over/(Under) Applied

Note: Recommended column widths: column A = 18, columns B–G = 12.

10. Use data from Fundamental Assignment Material 13-A1 to enter the amounts for the department A and B 20X0 budget predictions and 20X0 actual results.

11. Use the appropriate formulas to calculate the following amounts:

20X0 budgeted overhead rates for depts. A and B	Row 13, columns B and C
20X0 distributed overhead for depts. A and B	Row 14, columns D and E
20X0 over/under applied overhead	Row 15, columns D and E
Flexible budget variances for depts. A and B	Row 9, columns F and G
Activity budget variance for dept. B	Row 10, column G
Activity budget variance for dept. A	Row 11, column F
Total variances for depts. A and B	Row 15, columns F and G

12. Format amounts in rows 10 and 11 as follows:

Number tab:	Category:	Accounting
	Decimal:	0
	Symbol:	None

13. Format amounts in rows 9, 14, and 15 as follows:

Number tab:	Category:	Accounting
	Decimal:	0
	Symbol:	$

14. Format amounts in row 13 as follows:

Number tab:	Category:	Accounting
	Decimal:	2
	Symbol:	$

15. Modify the format of the total variances in row 15, columns F and G to display a top border using the default Line Style.

Border tab:	Icon:	Top Border

16. Save your work to disk, and print a copy for your files.

Note: Print your spreadsheet using landscape in order to ensure that all columns appear on one page.

COLLABORATIVE LEARNING EXERCISE

13-76 Accounting for Overhead

Form groups of four to six persons. Each group should identify a cost accountant at a local company to interview. The interviewee could be the top financial officer of a small company, but a division controller or cost analyst might be more appropriate for a large company. The essential factor is that the person chosen understands how overhead costs are allocated to products or services in the company.

Set up an interview with the cost accountant, and explore the following issues. Be prepared with follow-up questions if your question receives a superficial answer. Your goal should be to get as much operational detail as possible about the procedures used for allocating overhead costs at the company. If the company is large, you may want to focus on one department, one product line, or some other subdivision of the company.

The issues to explore are as follows:

1. What types of costs are included in overhead? How large is overhead compared with direct materials and labor costs?
2. What types of overhead cost pools exist? Are there different pools by department? By activity? By cost-allocation base? By fixed or variable cost? Be prepared to explain what you mean by these terms because terminology varies widely.
3. How is overhead applied to final products or services? What cost-allocation bases are used?

After the interview, draw a diagram of the cost application system in as much detail as possible. Be prepared to share this with the entire class, using it to explain the overhead cost application system at the company your group studied.

INTERNET EXERCISE

13-77 Dell

Published income statements use the absorption-costing basis—after all, that is the method that is acceptable for use under GAAP. But the absorption-costing statement might not really provide the information that management needs to make future decisions because it does not separate fixed from variable costs. This exercise focuses on extracting contribution information from published absorption-costing financial statements of Dell Computer. As a manufacturer of computers, Dell has become a well-known, household name.

1. Go to the home page for Dell at www.dell.com. Take a look at one of the computers for home being offered. Once you've arrived at the product page, what type of information do you find about the computer? What information is available about prices? Is it possible that the model could have more than one price? Why or why not?

2. Look at the most recent 10-K report for Dell by following links to Investor Relations, Financials, and 10-K filings. Go to the section, "Management's Discussion and Analysis of Financial Condition and Results of Operations." What was the total revenue for Dell? What is the average selling price per unit shipped? What is the change in the average selling price for the firm? Why do you think this change occurred?

3. Look at the most recent Consolidated Statement of Operations. What were the cost of goods sold and the selling, administrative, and engineering expenses for the current year? Refer to the cash flow statement for the current year. How much was the depreciation and amortization for the current year? Assume that $3 billion of operating expense in addition to all depreciation and amortization are fixed expenses. Compute the average variable cost of goods sold per unit. Compute the average contribution margin per unit. What would be the break-even number of units to produce and sell under this scenario? Does this seem reasonable, given the current operating income reported by the firm?

Job-Order Costing and Process-Costing Systems

LEARNING OBJECTIVES

When you have finished studying this chapter, you should be able to:

1. Distinguish between job-order costing and process costing.

2. Prepare summary journal entries for the typical transactions of a job-order costing system.

3. Use an ABC system in a job-order environment.

4. Show how service organizations use job-order costing.

5. Explain the basic ideas underlying process costing and how they differ from job-order costing.

6. Compute output in terms of equivalent units.

7. Compute costs and prepare journal entries for the principal transactions in a process-costing system.

8. Demonstrate how the presence of beginning inventories affects the computation of unit costs under the weighted-average method.

9. Use backflush costing with a JIT production system.

▶ JELLY BELLY

Here is a trivia question: Name the favorite candy of former President Ronald Reagan, the candy featured in the hit movie Harry Potter (with flavors like dirt, grass, and vomit), and the first candy to travel into outer space. The answer is jelly beans. And one of the most famous brands is **Jelly Belly Candy**. As noted by the authors of this text, this candy often shows up on the desks of students taking long, difficult management-accounting exams.

Jelly Belly is the world's number one gourmet jelly bean. The Jelly Belly Candy Company makes candy corn and more than 100 mouthwatering candies, including such delights as chocolates, gummies, sour candies, and confections for all the major seasons. To make a Jelly Belly jelly bean in either of its two factories, several processes are required. A hot kettle of gooey mix is flavored and colored with ingredients such as real peanut butter, peach puree, or milk chocolate. Then, 1,260 tiny beans are placed in a tray, cooled, and coated with corn starch and sugar before a shell is added. The final processes include polishing, printing the Jelly Belly name on each piece, and packaging.

How do Jelly Belly's accountants, affectionately called bean counters, determine the cost of each of these processing steps? How is the cost of flavoring transferred to the sugar-coating process and then to the process that adds a shell? Finally, how are all these processing costs combined to determine the cost of the hundreds of products that are sold worldwide? The answers to these questions enable management to determine the profit of each of the products sold and to set prices. To answer such questions, the accountants at Jelly Belly have developed a process-costing system with capabilities that are carefully tailored to meet the decision-making needs of management. ■

Distinction Between Job-Order Costing and Process Costing

The two most common systems of product costing are job-order costing and process costing. **Job-order costing** (or simply **job costing**) allocates costs to products that are readily identified by individual units or batches, each of which requires varying degrees of attention and skill. Industries that commonly use job-order methods include construction, printing, aircraft, furniture, special-purpose machinery, and any manufacturer of tailor-made or unique goods.

Process costing averages costs over large numbers of nearly identical products. It is most often found in such industries as chemicals, oil, plastics, rubber, lumber, food processing, glass, mining, cement, and meatpacking. These industries mass produce homogeneous units that usually pass in continuous fashion through a series of uniform production steps called operations or processes.

The distinction between the job-cost and the process-cost methods centers largely on how they measure product costs. Job costing applies costs to specific jobs, which may consist of either a single physical unit (such as a custom sofa) or a few like units (such as a dozen tables) in a distinct batch or job lot. In contrast, process costing deals with great masses of identical units and computes broad averages of unit costs.

The most important point is that product costing is an averaging process. The unit cost used for inventory purposes is the result of taking some accumulated cost of production (e.g., the sum of production-related activity costs) and dividing it by some measure of production. The basic distinction between job-order costing and process costing is the breadth of the denominator: In job-order costing, the denominator is small (e.g., 1 painting, 100 advertising circulars, 1 special packaging machine, or 1 highway bridge); however, in process costing, the denominator is large (e.g., thousands of pounds, gallons, or board feet).

Job costing and process costing are extremes along a continuum of potential costing systems. Each company designs its own accounting system to fit its underlying production activities. Some companies use **hybrid costing systems**, which are blends of ideas from both job costing and process costing.

Jelly Belly produces fun as well as candy, as is evident from the smiles of these two tour conductors at the company's Kenosha Jelly Belly Candy Store.

Objective 1
Distinguish between job-order costing and process costing.

Illustration of Job Costing

Job costing is best learned by example. But first we examine the basic records used in a job-cost system. The centerpiece of a job-costing system is the **job-cost record** (also called a **job-cost sheet** or **job order**), shown in Exhibit 14-1. The job-cost record contains all costs for a particular product, service, or batch of products. A file of job-cost records for partially completed jobs provides supporting details for the Work-in-Process Inventory account, often simply called Work in Process (WIP). A file of completed job-cost records comprises the Finished-Goods Inventory account.

As Exhibit 14-1 shows, the job-cost record summarizes information contained on source documents, such as materials requisitions and labor time tickets. **Materials requisitions** are records of materials used in particular jobs. **Labor time tickets** (or **time cards**) record the time a particular direct laborer spends on each job.

Today, job-cost records and other source documents are likely to be computer files, not paper records. With online data entry, bar coding, and optical scanning, much of the information needed for such records enters the computer without ever being written on paper. Nevertheless, whether records are on paper or in computer files, the accounting system must collect and maintain the same basic information.

As each job begins, we create its own job-cost record. As units are worked on, we make entries on the job-cost record. We accumulate three classes of costs on the job-cost record as units pass through the departments: Materials requisitions are the source of direct-materials costs, time tickets provide direct-labor costs, and budgeted overhead rates (a separate rate for each overhead cost pool) are used to apply factory overhead to products. (The computation of these budgeted rates will be described later in this chapter.)

Exhibit 14-1
Completed Job-Cost Record
and Sample Source
Documents*
*Note that 7 of the 8 hours and
$105 of the $120 in time ticket
7Z4 belong to job no. 963.

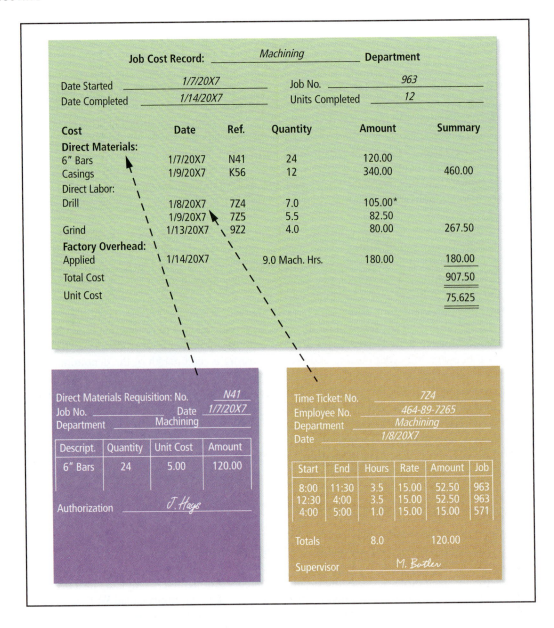

Basic Records of Enriquez Machine Parts Company

To illustrate the functioning of a job-order costing system, we will use the records and journal entries of the Enriquez Machine Parts Company. The following is a summary of pertinent transactions for the year 20X1:

		Machining	Assembly	Total
1.	Direct materials purchased on account	—	—	$1,900,000
2.	Direct materials requisitioned for manufacturing	$1,000,000	$890,000	1,890,000
3.	Direct-labor costs incurred	200,000	190,000	390,000
4a	Factory overhead incurred	290,000	102,000	392,000
4b.	Factory overhead applied*	280,000	95,000	375,000
5.	Cost of goods completed and transferred to finished-goods inventory	—	—	2,500,000
6a.	Sales on account	—	—	4,000,000
6b.	Cost of goods sold	—	—	2,480,000

*We explain the nature of factory overhead applied in Chapter 13, pages 534–535.

On December 31, 20X0, the firm had the following inventories:

Direct materials (12 types)	$110,000
Work in process	—
Finished goods (unsold units from two jobs)	12,000

Exhibit 14-2 is an overview of the general flow of costs through the Enriquez Machine Parts Company's job-order costing system.[1] The exhibit summarizes the effects of transactions on the key manufacturing accounts in the firm's books. As you proceed through the following transaction-by-transaction summary analysis, keep checking each explanation against the overview in Exhibit 14-2 (companies usually make entries as transactions occur but to obtain a sweeping overview, our illustration uses summary entries for the entire 20X1 year). Essentially, we bring into WIP the costs of direct material used, direct labor, and factory overhead applied. In turn, we transfer the costs of completed goods from WIP to Finished Goods. As the company sells goods, its costs become expense in the form of Cost of Goods Sold.

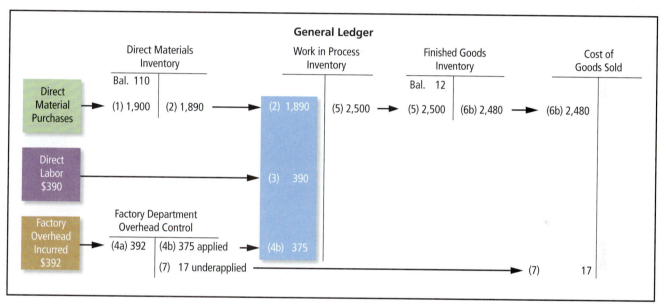

Exhibit 14-2
Job-Order Costing, General Flow of Costs (thousands)

---

[1]Exhibit 14-2 and the following explanation of transactions assume knowledge of basic accounting procedures. We will use the T-account format for a company's accounts. Entries on the left of the T are debits and those on the right are credits. Asset T-accounts, such as the inventory accounts, show increases on the left (debit) side and decreases on the right (credit) side of the T:

Inventory	
Beginning Balance	Decreases
Increases	
Ending Balance	

We record transactions affecting the accounts as journal entries. We show debit (left-side) entries flush with the left margin, we indent credit (right-side) entries, and often we include an explanation. For example, we would show a $10,000 transfer from Direct-Materials Inventory to WIP Inventory as follows:

WIP Inventory... 10,000

    Direct-Materials Inventory 10,000

To increase WIP Inventory and decrease

    Direct-Materials Inventory by $10,000.

Objective 2

Prepare summary journal entries for the typical transactions of a job-costing system.

Applying Direct Materials and Direct Labor Costs

The first three transactions in Exhibit 14-2 trace direct materials and direct labor costs to WIP. The entries are straightforward.

1. Transaction: Direct materials purchased, $1,900,000 on account
       Analysis: The asset Direct-Materials Inventory is increased. The liability
                   Accounts Payable is increased.
    Journal Entry: Direct-Materials Inventory 1,900,000
                           Accounts Payable 1,900,000

2. Transaction: Direct materials requisitioned, $1,890,000
       Analysis: The asset WIP Inventory is increased. The asset
                   Direct-Materials Inventory is decreased.
    Journal Entry: WIP Inventory 1,890,000
                           Direct-Materials Inventory 1,890,000

3. Transaction: Direct-labor cost incurred, $390,000
       Analysis: The asset WIP Inventory is increased. The liability Accrued Payroll is increased.
    Journal Entry: WIP Inventory 390,000
                           Accrued Payroll 390,000

Applying Factory Overhead Costs

Transactions 4a and 4b deal with factory overhead costs. In transaction 4a we charge the actual factory overhead costs as a debit to a summary account called Factory Department Overhead Control, which we temporarily regard as an asset. Each department will have a variety of detailed overhead accounts to help control overhead, but for our purposes we summarize them all into the Factory Department Overhead Control account.

4a. Transaction: Actual factory overhead incurred, $392,000
        Analysis: The temporary account Factory Department Overhead Control is increased.
                    Assorted asset accounts are decreased and/or liability accounts increased.
     Journal Entry: Factory Department Overhead Control 392,000
                    Cash, Accounts Payable, and various other balance
                    sheet accounts... 392,000

In transaction 4b we apply factory overhead costs to WIP.[2] While accountants directly trace direct materials and direct labor costs to products (as in transactions 2 and 3), they apply factory overhead costs to WIP via budgeted (predetermined) overhead rates. As described in Chapter 13 (pp. 533–535), to compute the budgeted overhead rates we need the following for each department: 1) cost-allocation base, 2) budgeted overhead costs, and 3) budgeted amount of each cost-allocation base. Enriquez allocates overhead based on machine hours in machining and direct-labor cost in assembly, resulting in the following overhead rates:

	Machining	Assembly
Budgeted manufacturing overhead	$277,800	$103,200
Budgeted machine hours	69,450	
Budgeted direct-labor cost		$206,400
Budgeted overhead rate per machine hour: $277,800 ÷ 69,450	$ 4	
Budgeted overhead rate per direct-labor dollar: $103,200 ÷ $206,400		50%

---

[2]Refer to pages 533–535 in Chapter 13 for an expanded discussion of the application of overhead. For our example here, we use the same overhead cost scenario and values for Enriquez Machine Parts Company found on pages 534–535 in Chapter 13.

Using these rates, the applied overhead for 20X1 is $375,000:

Machining: Actual machine hours of 70,000 × $4	$280,000
Assembly: Actual direct-labor cost of $190,000 × 50%	95,000
Total factory overhead applied	$375,000

The summary journal entry for this application follows:

4b.   Transaction: Factory overhead applied, $95,000 + $280,000 = $375,000

          Analysis: The asset WIP Inventory is increased. The asset Factory Department Overhead Control is decreased.

      Journal Entry: WIP Inventory 375,000

                         Factory Department Overhead Control 375,000

Finished Goods, Sales, and Cost of Goods Sold

Transactions 5 and 6 recognize the completion of production and the eventual sale of the goods. When Enriquez completes a particular job, it transfers the costs assigned to that job to Finished-Goods Inventory, and when it sells the job those same costs become expenses on the income statement in the form of Cost of Goods Sold.

5.   Transaction: Cost of goods manufactured, $2,500,000

          Analysis: The asset Finished-Goods Inventory is increased. The asset WIP Inventory is decreased.

      Journal Entry: Finished-Goods Inventory 2,500,000

                         WIP Inventory 2,500,000

6a.   Transaction: Sales on account, $4,000,000

          Analysis: The asset Accounts Receivable is increased. The revenue account Sales is increased.

      Journal Entry: Accounts Receivable 4,000,000

                         Sales 4,000,000

6b.   Transaction: Cost of goods sold, $2,480,000

          Analysis: The expense Cost of Goods Sold is increased. The asset Finished-Goods Inventory is decreased.

      Journal Entry: Cost of Goods Sold 2,480,000

                         Finished-Goods Inventory 2,480,000

Finally, transaction 7 in Exhibit 14-2 deals with differences between actual and applied overhead. In 20X1, Enriquez applied $375,000 of overhead to its products but actually incurred $392,000 of overhead costs. We call this difference underapplied overhead because the amount applied is less than the amount incurred. The opposite, overapplied overhead, occurs when the amount applied exceeds the amount incurred. As discussed more fully on pages 536–538 of Chapter 13, the Enriquez Company disposes of under- or overapplied overhead by some method at year-end. We will assume it uses the immediate write-off method, so it adds the $17,000 of underapplied overhead to cost of goods sold:

7.   Transaction: Underapplied overhead, $17,000

          Analysis: Cost of Goods Sold is increased and Factory Department Overhead Control is decreased.

      Journal Entry: Cost of Goods Sold 17,000

                         Factory Department Overhead Control 17,000

These seven transactions have accounted for all direct materials, direct labor, and factory overhead costs incurred during 20X1. As shown in Exhibit 14-2, all these costs ended up in either Direct-Materials Inventory, WIP Inventory, Finished-Goods Inventory, or Cost of Goods Sold.

Making Managerial Decisions

Suppose you are a manager of a manufacturing department. Confirm your understanding of product costing in a job-order environment by indicating the transactions that occurred for each of the following journal entries. Which of these transactions records actual costs versus cost estimates?

1. WIP Inventory XXX

    Accrued Payroll XXX

2. WIP Inventory XXX

    Factory Department
    Overhead Control................................XXX

3. Cost of Goods Sold........................XXX

    Finished Goods XXX

Answer

The first entry records the actual cost of direct labor that the accounting system traces to the specific job being costed. We make the second entry to record the application of factory overhead. This is an estimate of the costs of indirect resources used in producing the job. The last entry records the cost of goods sold when the company sells the product from the job. The cost in this transfer from finished-goods inventory to cost of goods sold is a mix of actual costs (direct material and direct labor) and estimated costs (applied factory overhead).

Activity-Based Costing/Management in a Job-Costing Environment

Regardless of the nature of its production system, firms will inevitably have resources they share among different products. The costs of these resources are part of the overhead the company must account for. In many cases, the magnitude of overhead is large enough to justify a significant investment in a costing system that provides accurate cost information. Whether companies use this cost information for planning and control or product costing, often the benefits of more accurate costs exceed the costs of installing and maintaining the cost system. As we have seen, ABC usually increases costing accuracy because it focuses on the cause-and-effect relationships between work performed (activities) and the consumption of resources (costs).

Illustration of ABC in a Job-Order Environment

Objective 3

Use an ABC system in a job-order environment.

We illustrate an ABC system in a job-order environment by considering **Dell**. Recall that Dell was the subject of the introduction to Chapter 13, page 532. A few years ago, Dell adopted an ABC job-order costing system. What motivated Dell to adopt ABC? Company managers cite two reasons: (1) the aggressive cost-reduction targets set by top management and (2) the need to understand product-line profitability. As is the case with any business, understanding profitability means understanding the cost structure of the entire business. One of the key advantages of an ABC system is its focus on understanding how work (activity) is related to the consumption of resources (costs). So, an ABC system was a logical choice for Dell. And, once Dell's managers improved their understanding of the company's cost structure, cost reduction through ABM (activity-based management) was much easier.

Like most companies that implement ABC, Dell began developing its ABC system by focusing on the most critical (core) processes across the value chain. These were the design and production processes. After it put the initial system in place, Dell added the remaining phases of the value chain. Exhibit 14-3 shows the functions (or core processes) that add value to the company's products and how Dell assigns the costs of these functions to an individual job under the current ABC system.

To understand product-line profitability, Dell managers identified key activities for the R&D, product design, production, marketing, distribution, and customer service phases. Then, they used appropriate cost drivers to allocate activity costs to the produced product lines. While each of the phases shown in Exhibit 14-3 is important, we will focus on the product design and production phases. Product design is one of Dell's most important value-adding functions, providing a defect-free computer product that is easy to manufacture and reliable to use. Engineering costs (primarily salaries and CAD equipment depreciation) account for most of the design costs. These costs are indirect and, thus, Dell must allocate them to product lines using a cost-allocation base.

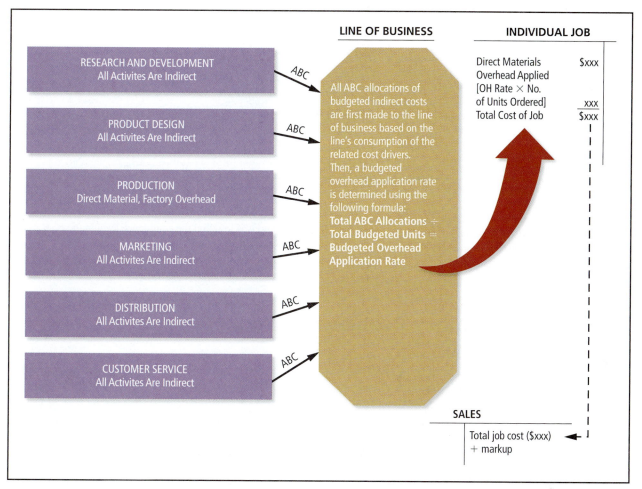

LINE OF BUSINESS

INDIVIDUAL JOB

RESEARCH AND DEVELOPMENT
All Activites Are Indirect

PRODUCT DESIGN
All Activites Are Indirect

PRODUCTION
Direct Material, Factory Overhead

MARKETING
All Activites Are Indirect

DISTRIBUTION
All Activites Are Indirect

CUSTOMER SERVICE
All Activites Are Indirect

ABC

All ABC allocations of budgeted indirect costs are first made to the line of business based on the line's consumption of the related cost drivers. Then, a budgeted overhead application rate is determined using the following formula: **Total ABC Allocations ÷ Total Budgeted Units = Budgeted Overhead Application Rate**

Direct Materials $xxx
Overhead Applied
[OH Rate × No.
of Units Ordered]   xxx
Total Cost of Job $xxx

SALES

Total job cost ($xxx)
+ markup

Exhibit 14-3
Dell Computer Corporation's Value Chain and ABC System

The production costs include direct materials and factory overhead. Factory overhead consists of six activity centers and related cost pools: receiving, preparation, assembly, testing, packaging, and shipping. Facility costs (plant depreciation, insurance, taxes) are considered part of the production function and are allocated to each activity center based on the square feet occupied by the center.

Dell divided the total annual budgeted indirect cost allocated to a product line by the total budgeted units produced to find a budgeted overhead rate. It then used this rate, which is adjusted periodically to reflect changes in the budget, to cost individual jobs.

Dell now breaks down the costs in each activity center into value added and non-value added and targets non-value-added costs for cost reduction programs. An example of a non-value-added activity is the preparation activity in the production function.

Making Managerial Decisions

Refer to Exhibit 14-3. One of the primary purposes of an ABC system is to increase the accuracy of product costs so that managers can make better cost-based decisions. Assume that you are a manager at **Dell** and that you have to determine prices for computers by adding a markup to the cost accumulated by the costing system. For example, if the accumulated total job cost is $800, a markup sufficient to "cover" all unallocated costs and provide a reasonable profit is added. Using the table at the top of page 584, determine whether the percentage markup under the ABC system is higher or lower than under the previous system. Which system gives you a higher degree of confidence that the price for a computer is adequate to cover all costs and provide a reasonable profit? Why?

	ABC or Unallocated	
Value-Chain Function	Previous Costing System	ABC Costing System
Research and development	Unallocated	ABC Allocations
Design	Unallocated	ABC Allocations
Production	Traditional Allocation	ABC Allocations
Marketing	Unallocated	ABC Allocations
Distribution	Unallocated	ABC Allocations
Customer service	Unallocated	ABC Allocations

Answer

Under the previous costing system, Dell determined prices by marking up only the cost of production. Thus, the markup was relatively high so that the company would cover all the unallocated costs and also achieve a reasonable profit, and managers had a low level of confidence in this cost system. The ABC system provided estimates of all value-chain costs, so the size of the markup was low, and the confidence level in the costs provided was high.

Summary Problem for Your Review

PROBLEM

Review the Enriquez illustration, especially Exhibit 14-2 on page 579. Prepare an income statement for 20X1 through the gross profit line. Use the immediate write-off method for overapplied or underapplied overhead.

SOLUTION

Exhibit 14-4 recapitulates the final impact of the Enriquez illustration on the financial statements. Note how the immediate write-off means that we add the $17,000 to the cost of goods sold. As you study Exhibit 14-4, trace the three major elements of cost (direct materials, direct labor, and factory overhead) through the accounts.

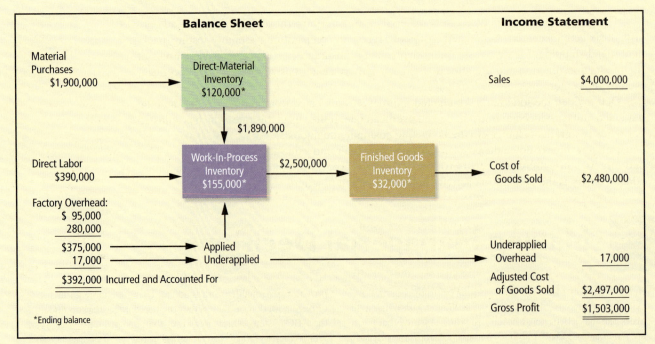

Exhibit 14-4
Relation of Costs to Financial Statements

Job Costing in Service and Nonprofit Organizations

So far, this chapter has concentrated on applying costs to manufactured products. However, the job-costing approach is used in nonmanufacturing situations, too. For example, universities have research "projects," airlines have repair and overhaul "jobs," and public accountants have audit "engagements." In such situations, the focus shifts from the costs of products to the costs of services, projects, or programs.

Objective 4

Show how service organizations use job costing.

Service and nonprofit organizations do not usually call their "product" a "job order." Instead, they may call it a program or a class of service. A "program" is an identifiable group of activities that frequently produces outputs in the form of services rather than goods. Examples include a safety program, an education program, or a family counseling program. Accountants can trace costs or revenues to individual hospital patients, individual social welfare cases, and individual university research projects. However, internal departments in service organizations often work simultaneously on many programs, so the "job-order" costing challenge is to "apply" the various department costs to the various programs. Only then can managers best allocate limited resources among competing programs.

In service industries—such as repairing, consulting, legal, and accounting services—each customer order is a different job with a special account or order number. Accountants can trace just costs, just revenues, or both to jobs. For example, automobile repair shops typically have a repair order for each car worked on, with space for allocating materials and labor costs. Customers see only a copy showing the retail prices of the materials, parts, and labor billed to their orders. Meanwhile, accountants trace the actual parts and labor costs of each order to a duplicate copy of the repair order, providing a measure of profit for each job. To get these actual costs, auto mechanics must enter their starting and stopping times on time tickets for each new order. This is why you might see them stamping a time card each time they start or end a job.

Budgets and Control of Engagements

In many service organizations and some manufacturing operations, job orders serve not only for product/service costing, but also for planning and control purposes. For example, a public accounting firm might have a condensed budget for 20X1 as follows:

Revenue	$10,000,000	100%
Direct labor (for professional hours charged to engagements)	2,500,000	25%
Contribution to overhead and operating income	$ 7,500,000	75%
Overhead (all other costs)	6,500,000	65%
Operating income	$ 1,000,000	10%

In this illustration,

$$\text{budgeted overhead rate} = \frac{\text{budgeted overhead}}{\text{budgeted direct labor}}$$

$$= \frac{\$6,500,000}{\$2,500,000}$$

$$= 260\%$$

To prepare a budget for each engagement, the partner in charge of the audit predicts the expected number of necessary direct-professional hours. Direct-professional hours are those that partners, managers, and staff auditors work to complete the engagement. The budgeted direct-labor cost is the pertinent hourly labor costs multiplied by the budgeted hours. Accounting firms charge partners' time to the engagement at much higher rates than subordinates' time.

How do such firms apply overhead? Accounting firms usually use either direct-labor cost or direct-labor hours as the cost driver for overhead application. In our example, the firm uses direct-labor cost. The budgeted total cost of an engagement is the direct-labor cost plus applied overhead, 260% of direct-labor cost in this illustration, plus any other direct costs.

This practice implies that partners require proportionately more overhead support for each of their hours charged. For example, 1 hour of partner work that has a direct-labor cost of $200 would result in a projected overhead support cost of $520. If this work can be done by a staff person whose charge rate is only $50, the projected overhead is only $130.

The engagement partner uses a budget for a specific audit job that includes detailed scope and steps. For instance, the budget for auditing cash or receivables on the engagement would specify the exact work to be done; the number of hours; and the necessary hours of partner time, manager time, and staff time. The partner monitors progress by comparing the hours logged to date with the original budget, and with the estimated hours remaining on the engagement. If the firm quoted a fixed audit fee, the profitability of an engagement depends on whether it can accomplish the audit within the budgeted time limits.

Accuracy of Costs of Engagements

Managers of service firms, such as auditing and consulting firms, frequently use budgeted costs of engagements as guides to pricing and to allocating effort among particular services or customers. Hence, the accuracy of projected costs of various engagements may affect pricing and operational decisions.

Suppose the accounting firm's policy for price quotes for engagements is 200% of total projected professional costs plus travel costs. The firm projects costs and sets the price on an auditing engagement as follows:

	Projected Cost	Price
Direct-professional labor	$ 50,000	$100,000
Applied overhead, 260% of direct-professional labor	130,000	260,000
Total professional costs excluding travel costs	$180,000	360,000
Travel costs	14,000	14,000
Total projected costs of engagement	$194,000	$374,000

Note that costs reimbursed by the client—such as travel costs—do not add to overhead costs and so are not subject to any markups in the setting of fees. Once the client accepts the offer, the firm needs to monitor the assignment of work as well as the overhead incurred to insure control of costs.

Process Costing Basics

In this mine, owned and operated by **Nally & Gibson Georgetown**, limestone rock is mined from a quarry, and transported by a conveyor system to plant areas. Nally & Gibson uses a process-costing system to determine the costs of mining, crushing, transporting, processing, and storing limestone.

As indicated on page 577, an alternative to job costing is process costing. Before we examine the procedures of process costing, let's examine a real application. **Nally & Gibson Georgetown** is a leading producer of limestone products used for industrial and commercial purposes. Limestone is used in highways, high school track beds, concrete sidewalks, buildings, soil enhancement products, residential homes, and about a million other places (yes, even in some toothpastes).

The making of limestone products is an excellent example of a process production system. A single raw material—limestone rock—is subjected to several processes that result in finished limestone products. The basic production processes that convert limestone rock into usable limestone are easy to understand and are reasonably simple. Basically, the limestone rock is mined from Nally & Gibson's quarry and mine in Georgetown, Kentucky, and transported to the processing facility. There it passes through several stages of crushing and grinding, depending on how fine the finished product needs to be. The ease and homogeneous nature of these processes might make you think that the cost accounting system used to track product costs should also be fairly simple and perhaps even unimportant to the success of the company. However, accurate and timely cost information is critical for both product costing and decision-making purposes at Nally & Gibson.

For example, the accurate allocation of the costs of mining and transporting limestone and then crushing the limestone to form the various products is essential to the success of the company. The company's cost accounting system accumulates the costs of these processes and then calculates an average cost per ton of product using a process-costing system. According to company president Frank Hamilton Jr., "If Nally & Gibson did not keep a handle on costs, we would not be here."

One of Nally & Gibson's costs is transporting quarried rock from the mine to plants. Using trucks that have to travel up to a mile into the mine and then up a steep grade is expensive and hazardous. The solution to this transportation problem was provided by **Process Machinery, Inc**, a full-service equipment dealer servicing Kentucky, Indiana, and Ohio. Process Machinery designed, constructed, and installed a 3,000-foot conveyor system used by Nally & Gibson. The accounting system used by Process Machinery to account for this job is an excellent example of a job-order system. There is a customer-specific product that requires a unique combination of resources.

The result—Nally & Gibson increased its production by up to 50% with increased safety and at a reduced cost. We can see from this example that the cost accounting system a company uses depends on the nature of its products and services. The cost information needed by managers dictates the type of cost accounting system. Process Machinery's managers need costs for specific products that have unique features. Nally & Gibson's managers, whose product is crushed limestone, have much different cost-information needs.

Companies like **Jelly Belly** and Nally & Gibson that produce in a continuous process large quantities of a generic or homogeneous product, such as staples or sliced potato strips for cooking french fries, do not use the job-costing techniques that you just learned. Why? Because a method called process costing fits their production process better and so is a more efficient costing system for such companies.

Why doesn't Nally & Gibson use a job-cost system to assign costs to its products? First, because there are no discrete jobs. The company does not wait for a specific customer order before producing the product. The company makes a forecast of the demand for the product and produces to meet this expected demand. Second, it is amazingly difficult (and costly) to trace costs to a specific truckload of limestone. And there would be no benefit in doing so in terms of increased accuracy. So the cost-benefit criterion clearly dictates that the company determines unit costs using much larger quantities—for example, a whole month's production.

As we noted early in this chapter, all product costing uses averaging to determine costs per unit of production. Sometimes those averages apply to a relatively small number of units, such as a particular printing job produced in a job-order production system. Other times, the averages might have to be extremely broad, based on generic products from a continual-process production system, such as limestone road fill. Process-costing systems apply costs to homogeneous products that a company mass produces in continuous fashion through a series of production processes. These processes usually occur in separate departments, although a single department sometimes contains more than one process.

Process Costing Compared with Job Costing

It is easiest to understand process costing if you compare it with something you already know: job costing. Companies use job costing and process costing for different types of products. As mentioned previously, firms in which each unit or batch (job) of product is unique and easily identifiable use job-order costing. However, when there is mass production through a sequence of several processes, such as mixing and cooking, we use process costing. Examples include chemicals, flour, glass, toothpaste, and limestone.

Objective 5

Explain the basic ideas underlying process costing and how they differ from job costing.

Exhibit 14-5 shows the major differences between job-order costing and process costing. Job-order costing has one WIP for each job. In contrast, process costing requires one WIP account for each process. As goods move from process to process, accountants transfer their costs accordingly.

Consider Nally & Gibson's process-costing system. The company's production system has four core processes as shown in Exhibit 14-6. The company first obtains limestone rock from surface quarries or from mines. It then transports the rock to the plant by rail or truck. At the plant, machines crush the rock and screen it to various sizes demanded by customers. The crushed limestone is then stocked in large piles of inventory for shipment. Each process requires resources. The direct-materials resource is the limestone rock itself. All four processes use direct-labor and overhead resources.

The process-costing approach does not distinguish between individual units of product. Instead, it accumulates costs for a period and divides them by quantities produced during that period to get broad, average unit costs. We can apply process costing to nonmanufacturing activities as well as to manufacturing activities. For example, we can divide the costs of giving state automobile driver's license tests by the number of tests given, and we can divide the cost of a post office sorting department by the number of items sorted.

To get a rough feel for process costing, consider Magenta Midget Frozen Vegetables. This company quick-cooks tiny carrots, beans, and other vegetables before freezing them. It has only two processes, cooking and freezing. As the following T-accounts show, the costs of cooked vegetables (in millions of dollars) are transferred from the cooking department to the freezing department:

Work in Process—Cooking

Direct materials	14	Transfer cost of goods completed to next department	23
Direct labor	4		
Factory overhead	8		
	26		
Ending inventory	3		

Work in Process—Freezing

Cost transferred in from cooking	23	Transfer cost of goods complete do finished goods	21
Direct labor	1		
Factory overhead	2		
	26		
Ending inventory	5		

We determine the amount of cost to be transferred by dividing the accumulated costs in the cooking department by the pounds of vegetables processed. We then multiply the resulting cost per pound by the pounds of vegetables physically transferred to the freezing department.

The journal entries for process-costing systems are similar to those for the job-order costing system. That is, we account for direct materials, direct labor, and factory overhead as before. However, now there is more than a single WIP account for all units being manufactured. There is one WIP account for each processing department, WIP—Cooking and WIP—Freezing, in our example. The Magenta Midget data are recorded as follows:

1. Work in Process—Cooking 14
        Direct-Materials Inventory 14
    To record direct materials used.

2. Work in Process—Cooking 4
        Accrued Payroll 4
    To record direct labor incurred.

3. Work in Process—Cooking 8
        Factory Overhead 8
    To record factory overhead applied to product.

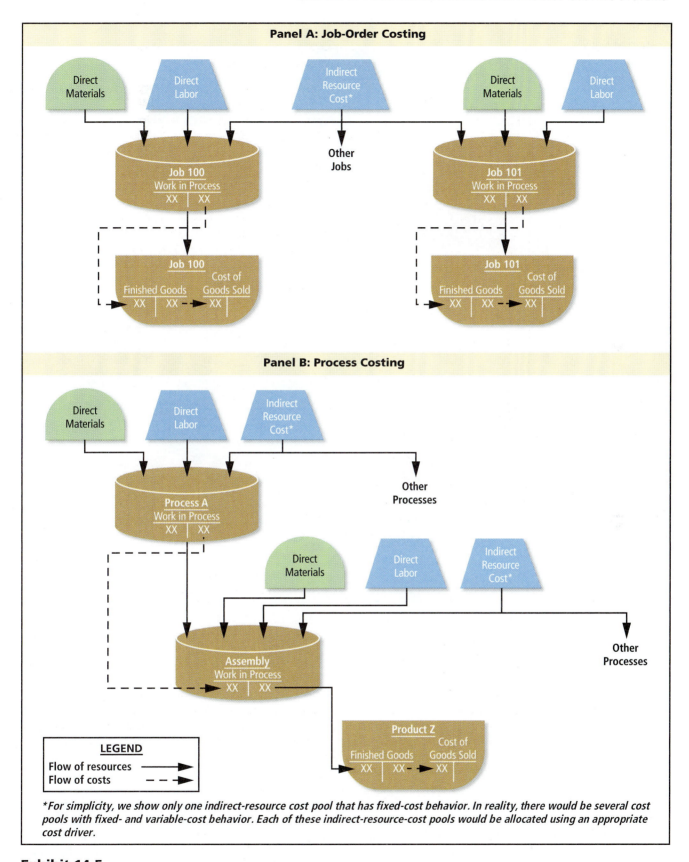

Exhibit 14-5
Comparison of Job-Order and Process Costing

Exhibit 14-6
Process Costing at Nally & Gibson

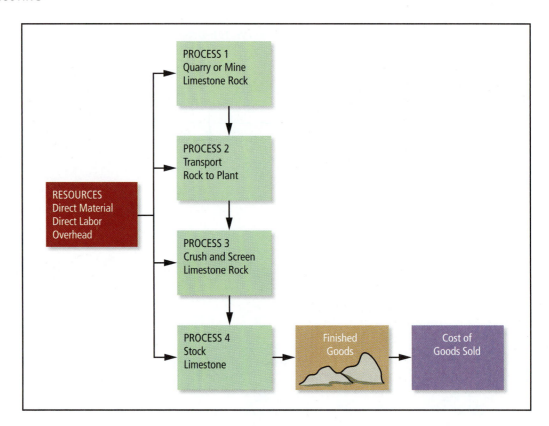

4. Work in Process—Freezing 23

      Work in Process—Cooking 23

    To transfer goods from the cooking process; 3 million remains in cooking.

5. Work in Process—Freezing 1

      Accrued Payroll 1

    To record direct labor incurred.

6. Work in Process—Freezing 2

      Factory Overhead 2

    To record factory overhead applied to product.

7. Finished Goods 21

      Work in Process—Freezing...21

    To transfer goods from the freezing process; 5 million remains in freezing.

Process manufacturing systems vary in design. The design shown in panel B of Exhibit 14-5 (as well as Exhibit 14-6) is sequential—units pass from process A to process B and so on until the product is finished. You will find many other designs in practice—each tailored to meet specific production requirements. For example, the firm can operate processes in parallel until final assembly. In this case, process A and process B might occur at the same time to produce different parts of the finished product. Whatever the specific layout, the basic principles of process costing are the same.

The central product-costing problem is how each department should compute the cost of goods transferred out and the cost of goods remaining in the department. If the same amount of work were done on each unit transferred out and on each unit in ending inventory, the solution would be easy. We could simply divide total costs by total units. Then, we would use this unit cost to calculate the total cost of units transferred out and the remaining cost of unfinished units. However, this is not possible because units in ending inventory cannot be complete, which makes them different from the completed units transferred out. Thus, the product-costing system must distinguish between the costs of fully completed units that a department transfers out and the costs of partially completed units that still remain in ending inventory. Let's now see how process costing systems accomplish this.

Application of Process Costing

To help you better understand our discussion of process costing, we will use the example of Oakville Wooden Toys. The company buys wood as a direct material for its forming department, which processes only one type of toy, marionettes. It inserts all the wood into this department at the beginning of the process. After forming, the company transfers the marionettes to the finishing department where workers hand shape them and add strings, paint, and clothing.

The forming department had no beginning inventory and completely manufactured 25,000 identical units during April, leaving no ending inventory. Its costs that month were as follows:

Direct materials		$ 75,000
Conversion costs		
Direct labor	$15,000	
Factory overhead	40,000	55,000
Costs to account for		$130,000

Since there is no ending inventory, the unit cost of goods completed is simply $130,000 ÷ 25,000 = $5.20. An itemization would show the following:

Direct materials, $75,000 ÷ 25,000	$3.00
Conversion costs, $55,000 ÷ 25,000	2.20
Unit cost of a whole completed marionette	$5.20

But what if not all 25,000 marionettes were completed during April? For example, assume that 5,000 were still in process at the end of April—only 20,000 were started and fully completed. All units—both those transferred out and those still in inventory—have obviously received all the necessary direct materials. However, only the transferred units have received the full amount of conversion resources. Oakville determined that the 5,000 marionettes that remain in process have received, on average, only 40% of conversion resources. How should the forming department calculate the cost of goods transferred and the cost of goods remaining in the ending WIP inventory? The answer lies in the following five key steps:

- Step 1: Summarize the flow of physical units.
- Step 2: Calculate output in terms of equivalent units.
- Step 3: Summarize the total costs to account for, which are the costs applied to WIP.
- Step 4: Calculate cost per equivalent unit.
- Step 5: Apply costs to units completed and to units in the ending WIP.

We now work through each of these five steps. Keep in mind that each step provides managers with data that are useful for product costing and operational control purposes.

Physical Units and Equivalent Units (Steps 1 and 2)

Step 1, as the first column in Exhibit 14-7 shows, tracks the physical units of production. How should we measure the output—the results of the department's work? This tracking tells us we have a total of 25,000 physical units to account for, but not all these units count the same in the forming department's output. Why not? Because only 20,000 units were fully completed and transferred out. The remaining 5,000 units are only partially complete, and we cannot assign partially completed units the same cost as the completed output. As a result, we have to state output not in terms of physical units but in terms of a different unit measure called an "equivalent unit."

Equivalent units are the number of completed (whole) units that the department could have produced from the inputs applied. For example, four units that are each one-half completed represent two equivalent units. Similarly, if each unit had been one-fourth completed, the four together would represent one equivalent unit. So, we determine equivalent units by multiplying physical units by the percent of completion. This equivalent unit measure correctly equates the

Objective 6
Compute output in terms of equivalent units.

Exhibit 14-7
Forming Department Output
in Equivalent Units
Month Ended April 30, 20X0

| | (Step 1) | (Step 2) Equivalent Units | |
| | Physical | Direct | |
Flow of Production	Units	Materials	Conversion
Started and completed	20,000	20,000	20,000
Work in process, ending inventory	5,000	5,000	2,000*
Units accounted for	25,000		
Work done to date		25,000	22,000*

*5,000 physical units × .40 degree of completion of conversion costs.

completed physical units that are transferred out with the partially completed physical units in ending inventory.

In our example, as step 2 in Exhibit 14-7 shows, we measure the output as 25,000 equivalent units of direct-materials cost but only 22,000 equivalent units of conversion costs. Why? Because direct materials had been fully added to all 25,000 units. In contrast, only 40% of the conversion costs were applied to the 5,000 partially completed units, which would have been sufficient to complete only 2,000 equivalent units in addition to the 20,000 units that were actually completed.

To compute equivalent units, you need to estimate how much of a given resource was applied to units in process, which is not always an easy task. Some estimates are easier to make than others. For example, estimating the amount of direct materials used is fairly easy. However, how do you measure how much energy, maintenance labor, or supervision was incurred for a given unit? Conversion costs can involve a number of these hard-to-measure resources, which leaves you estimating both how much total effort it takes to complete a unit and how much of that effort has already been put into the units in process. Coming up with accurate estimates is further complicated in industries such as textiles, where there is a great deal of work in process at all times. To simplify estimation, some companies may decide that all unfinished work in process must be deemed either one-third, one-half, or two-thirds complete. In other cases where continuous processing leaves roughly the same amount in process at the end of every month, accountants ignore work in process altogether and assign all monthly production costs to units completed and transferred out.

Measures in equivalent units are not confined to manufacturing situations. Such measures are a popular way of expressing workloads in terms of a common denominator. For example, radiology departments measure their output in terms of weighted units. Various X-ray procedures are ranked in terms of the time, supplies, and related costs devoted to each. A simple chest X-ray may receive a weight of one. But a skull X-ray may receive a weight of three because it uses three times more resources (for example, technicians' time) than a procedure with a weight of one.

Calculation of Product Costs (Steps 3 to 5)

Objective 7

Compute costs and prepare journal entries for the principal transactions in a process-costing system.

Exhibit 14-8 is a production-cost report. It shows steps 3–5 of process costing. Step 3 summarizes the total costs to account for (that is, the total costs incurred and applied to WIP—Forming). Step 4 obtains unit costs by dividing the two categories of total costs by the appropriate measures of equivalent units. The unit cost of a completed unit—materials cost plus conversion costs per equivalent unit—is $3.00 + $2.50 = $5.50. Why is the unit cost $5.50 instead of the $5.20 calculated on page 591? Because the $55,000 conversion cost is spread over 22,000 units instead of 25,000 units. Step 5 then uses these unit costs to apply costs to products. The 20,000 finished units are complete in terms of both direct materials and conversion costs. Thus, we can multiply the full unit cost times the number of completed units to determine their costs, which is 20,000 units times $5.50, or $110,000. The 5,000 physical units in ending work-in-process inventory are fully completed in terms of direct materials. Therefore, the direct materials applied to ending work in process are 5,000 equivalent units times $3.00, or $15,000. In contrast, the 5,000 physical units are 40% completed in terms of conversion costs. Therefore, the conversion costs applied to work in process are 2,000 equivalent units (40% of 5,000 physical units) times $2.50, or $5,000. Thus, the total cost of the ending inventory is $20,000.

		Total Costs	Details Direct Materials	Details Conversion Costs
(Step 3)	Costs to account for	$130,000	$75,000	$55,000
(Step 4)	Divide by equivalent units		÷ 25,000	÷ 22,000
	Unit costs	$ 5.50	$ 3.00	$ 2.50
(Step 5)	Application of costs			
	To units completed and transferred to the finishing department, 20,000 units at $5.50	$110,000		
	To units not completed and still in process, April 30, 5,000 units			
	Direct materials	$ 15,000	5,000 ($3.00)	
	Conversion costs	5,000		2,000 ($2.50)
	Work in process, April 30	$ 20,000		
	Total costs accounted for	$130,000		

Exhibit 14-8

Forming Department Production Cost Report
Month Ended April 30, 20X0

Journal entries for the data in our illustration would appear as follows:

1. Work in Process—Forming.................................75,000
        Direct-Materials Inventory...75,000
    Materials added to production in April.

2. Work in Process—Forming.................................15,000
        Accrued Payroll 15,000
    Direct labor incurred in April.

3. Work in Process—Forming.................................40,000
        Factory Overhead 40,000
    Factory overhead applied in April.

4. Work in Process—Finishing 110,000
        Work in Process—Forming...110,000
    Cost of goods completed and transferred in April from forming to assembly.

The $130,000 added to the Work in Process—Forming account less the $110,000 transferred out leaves an ending balance of $20,000:

Work in Process—Forming			
1. Direct materials	$ 75,000	4. Transferred out to finishing	
2. Direct labor	15,000		
3. Factory overhead	40,000		$110,000
Costs to account for	130,000		
Bal. April 30	$ 20,000		

Summary Problem for Your Review

PROBLEM

Consider **Nally & Gibson**'s plant operations in Georgetown. The plant processes limestone rock that is quarried in a nearby mine. Exhibit 14-6 (page 590) shows the various processing steps. Process 3 is crushing and screening the rock. To produce the crushed limestone, the company starts with limestone rocks from its quarry in Georgetown, Kentucky, and puts the rocks through a crushing process. Suppose that during May, the company quarried and shipped to its processing plant 288 tons of rock from its quarry, and at the end of the month 15 tons remained in process, on average 20% complete. The cost of rocks from the quarry for the last 5 months has been $120 per ton, so the cost of the limestone rock put into Process 3 is $120/ton times 288 tons, or $34,560. Labor and overhead cost during May in the rock crushing process were $35,880. Assume there was no work in process at the beginning of May.

1. Compute the cost of crushed rock processed and transferred out in May.
2. Compute the cost of the work in process inventory at the end of May.

SOLUTION

	(Step 1)	(Step 2) Equivalent Units in Tons	
Flow of Production	Physical Units (Tons)	Direct Materials	Conversion
Started and completed	273	273	273
Ending work in process	15	15*	3*
Units accounted for	288		
Work done to date		288	276

*15 × 100% = 15; 15 × 20% = 3.

		Details	
	Total Costs	Limestone Rock	Conversion Costs
(Step 3) Costs to account for	$70,440	$34,560	$35,880
(Step 4) Divide by equivalent units		÷ 288	÷ 276
Unit costs	$250.00*	$120.00	$130.00
(Step 5) Application of costs			
To units completed and transferred, 273 tons at $250.00	$68,250		
To ending work in process, 15 tons			
Direct materials	$ 1,800	15 × $120.00	
Conversion costs	390		3 × $130.00
Work in process, ending inventory	$ 2,190		
Total costs accounted for	$70,440		

*Cost per ton ($250) = limestone rock costs ($120) + conversion costs ($130).

Effects of Beginning Inventories

Objective 8

Demonstrate how the presence of beginning inventories affects the computation of unit costs under the weighted-average method.

So far, our example has been very straightforward because all units were started during the period. In other words, there were no units in beginning inventory. The presence of units in beginning inventory actually complicates matters a great deal.

There are several ways to deal with beginning inventories, but we will describe only the most popular alternative, the weighted-average method. In the next two sections, we will explore this method using the following data from our Oakville example for the month of May. Recall that the ending WIP inventory for April in the forming department was 5,000 units. These units become the beginning inventory for May.

Units

    Work in process, April 30: 5,000 units; 100% completed for materials,
        but only 40% completed for conversion costs

    Units started in May: 26,000

    Units completed in May: 24,000

    Work in process, May 31: 7,000 units; 100% completed for materials,
        but only 60% completed for conversion costs

Costs

    Work in process, April 30

Direct materials	$15,000	
Conversion costs	5,000	$ 20,000
Direct materials added during May		84,200
Conversion costs added during May		62,680
Total costs to account for		$166,880*

*Note that the $166,880 total costs to account for include the $20,000 of beginning inventory in addition to the $146,880 added during May.

Weighted-Average Method

The **weighted-average (WA) process-costing method** determines total costs by adding together the cost of (1) all work done in the current period and (2) the work done in the preceding period on the current period's beginning inventory of work in process. Then, you divide this total cost by the total equivalent units of work done to date, whether that work was done in the current or previous period.

Why do we use the term *weighted-average* to describe this method? Primarily because the unit costs used for applying costs to products are based on the total cost incurred to date, regardless of whether the department incurred those costs in the current period or in the prior period. If costs of materials, labor, or overhead changed across periods, essentially the weighted-average method reweights these comingled costs to determine revised unit cost.

Exhibit 14-9 shows the first two steps in this process-costing method, computation of physical units and equivalent units. The computation of equivalent units ignores where the 31,000 units to account for came from, either beginning work in process or those started in May. Exhibit 14-10 presents a production-cost report, summarizing steps 3–5 regarding computations of unit product costs and the resulting cost allocations to inventory accounts.

Transferred-In Costs

Many companies that use process costing have sequential production processes. For example, Oakville Wooden Toys transfers the items completed in its forming department to the finishing department. The finishing department would label the costs of the items it receives from the forming department **transferred-in costs**—costs incurred in a previous department for items that have been received by a subsequent department. They are similar to, but not identical to, additional

	(Step 1)	(Step 2) Equivalent Units	
Flow of Production	**Physical Units**	**Direct Materials**	**Conversion**
Work in process, April 30	5,000 (40%)*		
Started in May	26,000		
To account for	31,000		
Completed and transferred out			
during current period	24,000	24,000	24,000
Work in process, May 31	7,000 (60%)*	7,000	4,200†
Units accounted for	31,000		
Work done to date		31,000	28,200

*Degrees of completion for conversion costs at the dates of inventories.
†.60 × 7,000 = 4,200.

Exhibit 14-9
Forming Department Output in Equivalent Units, Weighted-Average Method
Month Ended May 31, 20X0

Business First

Process Costing at a Snack Peanut Company

Americans consume more than 300 million pounds of snack peanuts each year. The leading producer of snack peanuts is **Planters Specialty Products Company**, an operating unit of **Kraft Foods**. Planters markets regular-roast, dry-roast, salted, and unsalted peanuts in the United States. Processing a peanut snack food involves several activities. Most snack peanuts are blanched (removing the skins) before roasting. Peanuts can be oil-roasted or dry-roasted before being packaged and shipped.

The major activities in the processing of peanuts are shown next. This system not only tracks transferred-in costs between operating departments, such as the "blanching and frying department" and the "packing and shipping department," it also tracks these costs for support (services) departments, such as receiving, moving, and storing activities within the overall process costing sequence. This is because Planters incorporates ABC concepts within its process costing environment, designing a system that focuses on tracking and reporting costs by key activities within the system, regardless of traditional operating versus support department boundaries.

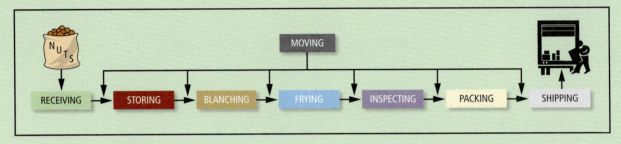

direct-materials costs incurred in the finishing department. Because transferred-in costs are a combination of all types of costs (direct-materials and conversion costs) incurred in previous departments, they should not be called a direct-materials cost in the finishing department.

We account for transferred-in costs just as we account for direct materials that the finishing department adds at the beginning of its process, with one exception: We keep transferred-in costs separate from the direct materials added in the department. Therefore, Exhibit 14-10 includes three columns of costs instead of two: transferred-in costs, direct-materials costs, and conversion costs. The total unit cost will be the sum of all three types of unit costs. For an interesting look at how one major snack food company designed its costing system with numerous transferred-in costs, see the Business First box above.

Exhibit 14-10
Forming Department
Production-Cost Report,
Weighted-Average Method
Month Ended May 31, 20X0

		Totals	Direct Materials	Conversion Costs
			Details	
(Step 3)	Work in process, April 30	$ 20,000	$15,000	$ 5,000
	Costs added currently	146,880	84,200	62,680
	Total costs to account for	$166,880	$99,200	$67,680
(Step 4)	Divisor, equivalent units for work done to date*		÷31,000	÷28,200
	Unit costs (weighted averages)	$ 5.60	$ 3.20	$ 2.40
(Step 5)	Application of costs			
	Completed and transferred, 24,000 units ($5.60)	$134,400		
	Work in process, May 31, 7,000 units			
	Direct materials	$ 22,400	7,000 ($3.20)	
	Conversion costs	10,080		4,200* ($2.40)
	Total work in process	$ 32,480		
	Total costs accounted for	$166,880		

*Equivalent units of work done. For more details, see Exhibit 14-9.

Summary Problem for Your Review

PROBLEM

Consider the cooking department of **Middleton Foods**, a British food-processing company. Compute the cost of work completed and the cost of the ending inventory of work in process using the weighted-average method.

Units		
Beginning work in process: 5,000 units; 100% completed for materials, 40% completed for conversion costs		
Started during month: 28,000 units		
Completed during month: 31,000 units		
Ending work in process: 2,000 units; 100% completed for materials, 50% for conversion costs		
Costs		
Beginning work in process		
Direct materials	£8,060	
Conversion costs	1,300	£ 9,360
Direct materials added in current month		41,440
Conversion costs added in current month		14,700
Total costs to account for		£65,500

SOLUTION

Flow of Production	(Step 1) Physical Units	(Step 2) Equivalent Units Material	Conversion
Completed and transferred out	31,000	31,000	31,000
Ending work in process	2,000	2,000*	1,000*
Equivalent units	33,000	33,000	32,000

*2,000 × 100% = 2,000; 2,000 × 50% = 1,000.

Weighted-Average Method	Total Cost	Direct Materials	Conversion Costs
Beginning work in process	£ 9,360	£ 8,060	£ 1,300
Costs added currently	56,140	41,440	14,700
Total costs to account for	£65,500	£49,500	£16,000
Equivalent units, weighted-average		÷33,000	÷32,000
Unit costs, weighted-average	£ 2.00	£ 1.50	£ 0.50
Transferred out, 31,000 × £2.00	£62,000		
Ending work in process			
Direct materials	£ 3,000	2,000 (£1.50)	
Conversion cost	500		1,000 (£.50)
Total work in process	£ 3,500		
Total costs accounted for	£65,500		

Process Costing in a JIT System: Backflush Costing

Objective 9

Use backflush costing with a JIT production system.

Tracking costs through various stages of inventory—raw material, work in process inventory for each process (or department), and finished-goods inventory—makes accounting systems complex. If there were no inventories, we could charge all costs directly to cost of goods sold, and accounting systems would be much simpler. Organizations using JIT production systems usually have very small inventories or no inventories at all. For them, a traditional accounting system that traces costs through several different types of inventories may be inappropriate or of limited value. One such company is **American Gypsum Company**. The company manufactures gypsum wallboard for commercial and residential use. Like many companies that use the JIT production system, American Gypsum has very low inventory levels and uses **backflush costing**, an accounting system that applies costs to products only when the production is complete. How does backflush costing work? As we shall see, it is a fairly simple costing system.

Principles of Backflush Costing

Backflush costing has only two categories of costs: materials and conversion costs. Its unique feature is an absence of a WIP account. Accountants enter actual material costs into a materials inventory account, and they enter actual labor and overhead costs into a conversion costs account. They then transfer costs from these two temporary accounts directly into finished-goods inventories. Some backflush systems even eliminate the finished-goods inventory accounts and transfer costs directly to cost of goods sold, especially if the company does not have a finished-goods inventory but rather sells products before producing them so that it can ship them immediately upon completion. Backflush systems assume that the company completes production so soon after the application of conversion activities that balances in the conversion costs accounts remain near zero as it transfers costs out almost immediately after initially recording them.

Example of Backflush Costing

Speaker Technology, Inc., (STI) produces speakers for automobile stereo systems. STI recently introduced a JIT production system and backflush costing. Consider the July production for speaker model AX27. The standard material cost per unit of AX27 is $14, and the standard unit conversion cost is $21. During July, STI purchased materials for $5,600, incurred conversion costs of $8,400 (which included all labor costs and manufacturing overhead), and produced and sold 400 units of AX27.

Backflush costing is accomplished in three steps:

1. Record actual materials and conversion costs. For simplicity, we initially assume that actual materials and conversion costs were identical to the standard costs. As a company purchases materials, backflush systems add their cost to the Materials Inventory account:

   Materials Inventory 5,600

       Accounts Payable (or Cash) 5,600

   To record material purchases.

   Similarly, we add direct labor and manufacturing overhead costs to the Conversion Costs account when the company incurs them:

   Conversion Costs...8,400

       Accrued Wages and Other Accounts...8,400

   To record conversion costs incurred.

2. Apply costs to completed units. When production is complete, we transfer the costs from Materials Inventory and Conversion Costs accounts to Finished-Goods Inventory, based on the number of units completed and the standard cost of each unit:

   Finished-Goods Inventory (400 × $35)...14,000

       Materials Inventory 5,600

       Conversion Costs..8,400

   To record costs of completed production.

Because of short production cycle times, there is little lag between additions to the Conversion Costs account and transfers to Finished-Goods Inventory. The Conversion Costs account, therefore, remains near zero.

3. Record cost of goods sold during the period. We transfer the standard cost of the items sold from Finished-Goods Inventory to Cost of Goods Sold:

Cost of Goods Sold 14,000
    Finished-Goods Inventory 14,000

To record cost of 400 units sold at $35 per unit.

Suppose the company immediately delivers completed units to customers so that finished goods inventories are negligible. We can combine steps 2 and 3 to eliminate the Finished-Goods Inventory account:

Cost of Goods Sold 14,000
    Material Inventory 5,600
    Conversion Costs 8,400

What if actual costs added to the Conversion Costs account do not equal the standard amounts that are transferred to Finished-Goods Inventory? We treat the variances like overapplied or underapplied overhead. Backflush systems assume that account balances for conversion costs are approximately zero at all times. Thus, we charge any remaining balance in the account at the end of an accounting period to Cost of Goods Sold. Suppose actual conversion costs for July had been $8,600 and the amount transferred to finished goods (that is, applied to the product) was $8,400. We would write off the $200 balance in the Conversion Costs account to Cost of Goods Sold at the end of the month:

Cost of Goods Sold 200
    Conversion Costs 200

To recognize underapplied conversion costs.

Summary Problem for Your Review

PROBLEM

The most extreme (and simplest) version of backflush costing makes product costing entries at only one point. Suppose STI had no Materials Inventory account (in addition to no WIP Inventory account). It purchases materials only when it needs them for production. Therefore, STI enters both materials and conversion costs directly into its Finished-Goods Inventory account.

Prepare journal entries (without explanations) and T-accounts for July's production of 400 units. As given earlier, materials purchases totaled $5,600, and conversion costs were $8,400. Why might a company use this extreme type of backflush costing?

SOLUTION

In one step, material and conversion costs are applied to finished goods inventories:

Finished-Goods Inventories 14,000
    Accounts Payable 5,600
    Wages Payable and Other Accounts 8,400

Finished Goods Inventories		Accounts Payable, Wages Payable, and Other Accounts	
Materials	5,600		5600
Conversion costs	8,400		8400

This example shows that backflush costing is simple and inexpensive. Backflush costing provides reasonably accurate product costs if (1) materials inventories are low (most likely because of JIT delivery schedules), and (2) production cycle times are short, so that at any time a company has incurred only inconsequential amounts of materials costs and conversion costs for products that have yet to be completed.

Highlights to Remember

1. **Distinguish between job-order costing and process costing.** Product costing is an averaging process. Process costing deals with broad averages and large volumes of homogeneous units. Job-order costing deals with narrow averages and unique units or a small batch of similar units.

2. **Prepare summary journal entries for the typical transactions of a job-costing system.** The focus of journal entries in a job-order costing system is on inventory accounts. The WIP Inventory account receives central attention. Direct materials used, direct labor, and factory overhead applied are accumulated in WIP. In turn, the cost of completed goods is transferred from WIP to Finished Goods.

3. **Use an ABC system in a job-order environment.** ABC can be used for any type of business that has significant levels of shared resources. In a job-order system, ABC helps managers understand the cost structure of the business on a job-by-job basis. Overhead costs are assigned to activity centers and then to jobs based on appropriate cost drivers. ABM uses ABC information and the increased understanding of the organization's cost structure to control and reduce overhead costs.

4. **Show how service organizations use job costing.** The job-costing approach is used in non-manufacturing as well as in manufacturing. Examples include costs of services such as auto repair, consulting, and auditing. For example, the job order is a key device for planning and controlling an audit engagement by a public accounting firm.

5. **Explain the basic ideas underlying process costing and how they differ from job costing.** Process costing is used for inventory costing when there is continuous mass production of homogeneous units. Process-cost systems accumulate costs by department (or process); each department has its own WIP account. Job-order cost systems differ because costs are accumulated and tracked by the individual job order.

6. **Compute output in terms of equivalent units.** The key concept in process costing is that of equivalent units, the number of fully completed units that could have been produced from the inputs applied.

7. **Compute costs and prepare journal entries for the principal transactions in a process-costing system.** There are five basic steps to process costing:

   1. Summarize the flow of physical units.
   2. Calculate output in terms of equivalent units.
   3. Summarize the total costs to account for.
   4. Calculate unit costs (step 3 ÷ step 2).
   5. Apply costs to units completed and to units in the ending work in process.

   Steps 3 and 5 provide the data for journal entries. These entries all involve the WIP accounts for the various departments (processes) producing products.

8. **Demonstrate how the presence of beginning inventories affects the computation of unit costs under the weighted-average method.** Process costing is complicated by the presence of beginning inventories. The weighted-average method calculates a unit cost that includes the work done in previous periods on the current period's beginning inventory with work done in the current period.

9. **Use backflush costing with a JIT production system.** Many companies with JIT production systems use backflush costing. Such systems have no WIP Inventory account and apply costs to products only after the production process is complete. ■

Accounting Vocabulary

backflush costing, p. 598
equivalent units, p. 591
hybrid costing systems, p. 577
job costing, p. 577
job-cost record, p. 577

job-cost sheet, p. 577
job order, p. 577
job-order costing, p. 577
labor time tickets, p. 577
materials requisitions, p. 577

process costing, p. 577
time cards, p. 577
transferred-in costs, p. 595
weighted-average (WA) process-
    costing method, p. 595

Fundamental Assignment Material

14-A1 Job-Order Costing, Basic Journal Entries

The following data (in thousands) summarize the factory operations of the Smothers Manufacturing Company for the year 20X1, its first year in business:

a.	Direct materials purchased for cash	$360
b.	Direct materials issued and used	325
c.	Labor used directly on production	130
d1.	Indirect labor	90
d2.	Depreciation of plant and equipment	50
d3.	Miscellaneous factory overhead (ordinarily would be detailed)	40
e.	Overhead applied: 180% of direct labor	?
f.	Cost of production completed	625
g.	Cost of goods sold	425

1. Prepare summary journal entries. Omit explanations. For purposes of this problem, combine the items in part d as "overhead incurred."
2. Show the T-accounts for all inventories, Cost of Goods Sold, and Factory Department Overhead Control. Compute the ending balances of the inventories. Do not adjust for underapplied or overapplied factory overhead.

14-A2 Basic Process Costing

CellTel produces cellular phones in large quantities. For simplicity, assume that the company has two departments, assembly and testing. The manufacturing costs in the assembly department during February were as follows:

Direct materials added		$ 66,000
Conversion costs		
Direct labor	$62,000	
Factory overhead	33,000	95,000
Assembly costs to account for		$161,000

There was no beginning inventory of work in process. Suppose work on 20,000 phones was begun in the assembly department during February, but only 18,000 phones were fully completed. All the parts had been made or placed in process, but only half the conversion costs had been completed for each of the phones still in process.

1. Compute the equivalent units and unit costs for February.
2. Compute the costs of units completed and transferred to the testing department. Also compute the cost of the ending work in process. (For journal entries, see problem 14-34.)

14-A3 Weighted-Average Process-Costing Method

The Magnatto Company manufactures electric drills. Material is introduced at the beginning of the process in the assembly department. Conversion costs are applied uniformly throughout the process. As the process is completed, goods are immediately transferred to the finishing department.

Data for the assembly department for the month of July 20X1 follow:

Work in process, June 30: $175,500 (consisting of $138,000 materials and $37,500 conversion costs); 100% completed for direct materials, but only 25% completed for conversion costs	10,000 units
Units started during July	80,000 units
Units completed during July	70,000 units
Work in process, July 31: 100% completed for direct materials, but only 50% completed for conversion costs	20,000 units
Direct materials added during July	$852,000
Conversion costs added during July	$634,500

1. Compute the total cost of goods transferred out of the assembly department during July.
2. Compute the total costs of the ending work in process. Prepare a production-cost report or a similar orderly tabulation of your work. Assume weighted-average product costing. (For journal entries, see Exercise 14-38.)

14-A4 Backflush Costing

Digital Controls makes electronic thermostats for homes and offices. The Kansas City Division makes one product, Autotherm, which has a standard cost of $36, consisting of $20 of materials and $16 of conversion costs. In January, actual purchases of materials totaled $45,000, labor payroll costs were $10,000, and manufacturing overhead was $20,000. Completed output was 2,000 units.

The Kansas City Division uses a backflush-costing system that records costs in materials inventory and conversion costs accounts and applies costs to products at the time production is completed. There were no finished goods inventories on January 1 and 20 units on January 31.

1. Prepare journal entries (without explanations) to record January's costs for the Kansas City Division. Include the purchase of materials, incurrence of labor and manufacturing overhead costs, application of product costs, and recognition of cost of goods sold.
2. Suppose January's actual manufacturing overhead costs had been $24,000 instead of $20,000. Prepare the journal entry to recognize underapplied conversion costs at the end of January.

14-B1 Job-Order Costing, Basic Journal Entries

Consider the following data for Cambridge Printing Company (in thousands):

Inventories, December 31, 2009	
Direct materials	£ 22
Work in process	27
Finished goods	102

Summarized transactions for 2010 are as follows:

a.	Purchases of direct materials	£109
b.	Direct materials used	90
c.	Direct labor	140
d.	Factory overhead incurred	92
e.	Factory overhead applied, 80% of direct labor	?
f.	Cost of goods completed and transferred to finished goods	275
g.	Cost of goods sold	350
h.	Sales on account	620

1. Prepare summary journal entries for 2010 transactions. Omit explanations.
2. Show the T-accounts for all inventories, Cost of Goods Sold, and Factory Department Overhead Control. Compute the ending balances of the inventories. Do not adjust for underapplied or overapplied factory overhead.

14-B2 Basic Process Costing

Hassan Company produces digital watches in large quantities. The manufacturing costs of the assembly department were as follows:

Direct materials added		$1,750,000
Conversion costs		
Direct labor	$550,000	
Factory overhead	137,500	687,500
Assembly costs to account for		$2,437,500

For simplicity, assume that this is a two-department company, assembly and finishing. There was no beginning work in process.

Suppose 700,000 units were started in the assembly department. There were 400,000 units completed and transferred to the finishing department. The 300,000 units in ending work in process were fully completed regarding direct materials but half-completed regarding conversion costs.

1. Compute the equivalent units and unit costs in the assembly department.
2. Compute the costs of units completed and transferred to the finishing department. Also compute the cost of the ending work in process in the assembly department. (For journal entries, see Exercise 14-35.)

14-B3 Weighted-Average Process-Costing Method

The Rainbow Paint Company uses a process-costing system. Materials are added at the beginning of a particular process, and conversion costs are incurred uniformly. Work in process at the beginning of the month is 40% complete, while at the end it is 20% complete. One gallon of material makes one gallon of product. Data follow:

Beginning inventory	600 gal
Direct materials added	8,200 gal
Ending inventory	1,000 gal
Conversion costs incurred	$25,800
Cost of direct materials added	$55,700
Conversion costs, beginning inventory	$ 2,200
Cost of direct materials, beginning inventory	$ 3,700

Use the weighted-average method. Prepare a schedule of output in equivalent units and a schedule of application of costs to products. Show the cost of goods completed and cost of ending work in process. (For journal entries, see Exercise 14-37.)

14-B4 Backflush Costing

Audio Components recently installed a backflush-costing system. One department makes 4-inch speakers with a standard cost as follows:

Materials	$ 9.60
Conversion costs	5.40
Total	$15.00

Speakers are scheduled for production only after orders are received, and products are shipped to customers immediately on completion. Therefore, no finished goods inventories are kept, and product costs are applied directly to cost of goods sold.

In October, 1,600 speakers were produced and shipped to customers. Materials were purchased at a cost of $16,200, and actual conversion costs (labor plus manufacturing overhead) of $6,800 were recorded.

1. Prepare journal entries to record October's costs for the production of 4-inch speakers.
2. Suppose October's actual conversion costs had been $6,000 instead of $6,800. Prepare a journal entry to recognize overapplied conversion costs.

Additional Assignment Material

QUESTIONS

14-1 "There are different product costs for different purposes." Name at least two purposes.

14-2 Distinguish between job costing and process costing.

14-3 Describe the supporting details for work in process in a job-cost system.

14-4 What types of source documents provide information for job-cost records?

14-5 State three examples of service industries that use the job-costing approach.

14-6 "Law firms use job-costing to cost engagements. Thus, the markup required to cover overhead costs is not as great as in companies that use a process-costing system." Do you agree? Explain.

14-7 Give three examples of industries where process-costing systems are probably used.

14-8 Give three examples of nonprofit organizations where process-costing systems are probably used.

14-9 "There are five key steps in process-cost accounting." What are they?

14-10 Identify the major distinction between the first two and the final three steps of the five major steps in accounting for process costs.

14-11 Suppose a university has 10,000 full-time students and 5,000 half-time students. Using the concept of equivalent units, compute the number of "full-time equivalent" students.

14-12 Present an equation that describes the physical flow in process costing when there are beginning inventories in work in process.

14-13 How are transferred-in costs similar to direct materials costs? How are they different?

14-14 Explain what happens in a backflush-costing system when the amount of actual conversion cost in a period exceeds the amount applied to the products completed during that period.

CRITICAL THINKING EXERCISES

14-15 Purposes of Accumulating Job Costs
"Job costs are accumulated for purposes of inventory valuation and income determination." State two other purposes.

14-16 Job-Order Compared to Process Costing
"The basic distinction between job-order costing and process costing is the breadth of the denominator." Explain.

14-17 Cost Allocation in Service Firms
"Service firms trace only direct-labor costs to jobs. All other costs are applied as a percentage of direct-labor cost." Do you agree? Explain.

14-18 Purpose of Product Costing in a Process Production Environment
All product costing uses averages to determine costs per unit of product produced. In job-order production systems, the averages are based on a relatively small number of units. In a process production environment, the number of units is much larger. Once the average unit cost is determined, what is the central product-costing problem in process costing?

14-19 Process Costing in a JIT Environment
Companies using JIT production systems usually have very small inventories or no inventories at all. As a result, a traditional accounting system may be inappropriate. Many of these companies have adopted backflush-costing systems. Do backflush-costing systems work only for companies using a JIT production system? Explain.

EXERCISES

14-20 Job Costing in Business Sectors
Job costing systems are used in all business sectors. For each example listed, indicate whether the company is in the manufacturing, merchandising, or service sector:
  a. Audit engagements by **Ernst & Young**
  b. Advertising new products by **Target**
  c. Assembly of desktop computers by **Dell**
  d. Consulting engagement by **McKensey & Co.**

14-21 Direct Materials

For each of the following independent cases, fill in the blanks (in millions of dollars):

	1	2	3	4
Direct-materials inventory, December 31, 20X0	8	8	5	—
Purchased	5	9	—	8
Used	7	—	7	3
Direct-materials inventory, December 31, 20X1	—	6	8	7

14-22 Use of WIP Inventory Account

April production resulted in the following activity in a key account of Cheung Casting Company (in thousands):

WIP Inventory	
April 1 balance	12
Direct materials used	50
Direct labor charged to jobs	25
Factory overhead applied to jobs	55

Job Orders A13 and A37, with total costs of $72,000 and $56,000, respectively, were completed in April.

1. Journalize the completed production for April.
2. Compute the balance in WIP Inventory, April 30, after recording the completed production.
3. Journalize the credit sale of Job A13 for $101,000.

14-23 Job-Cost Record

Western State University uses job-cost records for various research projects. A major reason for such records is to justify requests for reimbursement of costs on projects sponsored by the federal government.

Consider the following summarized data regarding a cancer research project in the Medical School:
- January 5   Direct materials, various medical supplies, $925
- January 7   Direct materials, various chemicals, $780
- January 5–12   Direct labor, research associates, 120 hours
- January 7–12   Direct labor, research assistants, 180 hours

Research associates receive $32 per hour, while assistants receive $19. The overhead rate is 70% of direct-labor cost.

Sketch a job-cost record. Post all the data to the project-cost record. Compute the total cost of the project through January 12.

14-24 Analysis of Job-Cost Data

Job-cost records for Ganz Construction contained the following data:

Job No.	Dates Started	Finished	Sold	Total Cost of Job at May 31
1	April 19	May 14	May 15	$4,200
2	April 26	May 22	May 25	7,600
3	May 2	June 6	June 8	6,300
4	May 9	May 29	June 5	8,300
5	May 14	June 14	June 16	4,700

Compute Ganz's (1) WIP Inventory at May 31, (2) Finished-Goods Inventory at May 31, and (3) Cost of Goods Sold for May.

14-25 Analysis of Job-Cost Data

The Cabrillo Construction Company constructs houses on speculation. That is, the houses are started before any buyer is known. Even if the buyer agrees to purchase a house under construction, no sales are recorded until the house is completed and accepted for delivery. The job-cost records contained the following (in thousands):

Job No.	Dates Started	Dates Finished	Sold	Total Cost of Job at September 30	Total Construction Cost Added in October
43	4/26	9/7	9/8	$180	
51	5/17	9/14	9/17	170	
52	5/20	9/30	10/4	150	
53	5/28	10/14	10/18	200	$50
61	6/3	10/20	11/24	115	20
62	6/9	10/21	10/27	180	25
71	7/7	11/6	11/22	118	36
81	8/7	11/24	12/24	106	48

1. Compute Cabrillo's cost of (a) construction-in-process inventory at September 30 and October 31, (b) finished-houses inventory at September 30 and October 31, and (c) cost of houses sold for September and October.
2. Prepare summary journal entries for the transfer of completed houses from construction in process to finished houses for September and October.
3. Record the cash sale (price = $345,000) and the cost of the house sold for Job 53.

14-26 Discovery of Unknowns

DeMond Chemicals has the following balances (in millions) on December 31, 20X1:

Factory overhead applied	$450
Cost of goods sold	900
Factory overhead incurred	415
Direct-materials inventory	30
Finished-goods inventory	180
WIP inventory	140

The cost of goods completed was $880. The cost of direct materials requisitioned for production during 20X1 was $210. The cost of direct materials purchased was $225. Factory overhead was applied to production at a rate of 150% of direct-labor cost.

Compute the beginning inventory balances of direct materials, WIP, and finished goods. Make these computations before considering any possible adjustments for overapplied or underapplied overhead.

14-27 Discovery of Unknowns

The Ramakrishnan Manufacturing Company has the following balances (in millions) as of December 31, 20X1:

WIP inventory	$ 14
Finished-goods inventory	175
Direct-materials inventory	65
Factory overhead incurred	180
Factory overhead applied at 150% of direct-labor cost	150
Cost of goods sold	350

The cost of direct materials purchased during 20X1 was $275. The cost of direct materials requisitioned for production during 20X1 was $235. The cost of goods completed was $493, all in millions.

Before considering any year-end adjustments for overapplied or underapplied overhead, compute the beginning inventory balances of direct materials, WIP, and finished goods.

14-28 Relationships Among Overhead Items

Fill in the unknowns:

	Case A	Case B	Case C
Budgeted factory overhead	$3,600,000	$?	$1,500,000
Budgeted cost drivers			
Direct-labor cost	$2,000,000		
Direct-labor hours		450,000	
Machine hours			250,000
Overhead application rate	?	$ 5	?

14-29 Process Costing in Business Sectors

Process-costing systems are used in all business sectors. For each example listed, indicate whether the company is in the manufacturing or service sector.
a. Beverage bottling at **Coca-Cola**
b. Postal delivery of mail by the U.S. Post Office
c. Limestone production at **Nally & Gibson**
d. Processing a life insurance application by **State Farm**

14-30 Process Map and Process Costing

Refer to Exhibit 14-5, panel B, on page 589. Identify an example of (1) a transferred-in cost, (2) a variable-cost resource, (3) a direct fixed-cost resource, and (4) an indirect resource cost for the process-costing system.

14-31 Equivalent Units

Confirm your understanding of the equivalent units concept by computing the equivalent units for material, direct labor, and overhead for the following hypothetical case at Nally & Gibson (refer to Exhibit 14-6, page 590).

In Process 3—crush and screen limestone rock—400 tons of limestone rock were transported to the plant during March. There was no beginning inventory of rock. During March, 320 tons were crushed, screened, and stocked. At the end of March, 80 tons of rock were 40% crushed and screened. Direct labor and overhead are incurred evenly during the crushing and screening process.

14-32 Basic Process Costing

A department of Jamestown Textiles produces cotton fabric. All direct materials are introduced at the start of the process. Conversion costs are incurred uniformly throughout the process.

In April, there was no beginning inventory. Units started, completed, and transferred were 650,000. Units in process on April 30 were 220,000. Each unit in ending work in process was 60% converted. Costs incurred during April were direct materials at $3,654,000 and conversion costs at $860,200.

1. Compute the total work done in equivalent units and the unit cost for April.
2. Compute the cost of units completed and transferred. Also, compute the cost of units in ending work in process.

14-33 Uneven Flow

One department of Dallas Instruments Company manufactures basic handheld calculators. Several materials are added at various stages of the process. The outer front shell and the carrying case, which represent 10% of the total materials cost, are added at the final step of the assembly process. All other materials are considered to be "in process" by the time the calculator reaches a 50% stage of completion.

During 20X0, 74,000 calculators were started in production. At year-end, 6,000 calculators were in various stages of completion, but all of them were beyond the 50% stage and, on the average, they were regarded as being 70% completed.

The following costs were incurred during the year: direct materials, $205,520; conversion costs, $397,100. There was no beginning WIP inventory.

1. Prepare a schedule of physical units and equivalent units.
2. Tabulate the unit costs, cost of goods completed, and cost of ending work in process.

14-34 Journal Entries

Refer to the data in problem 14-A2. Prepare summary journal entries for the use of direct materials, direct labor, and factory overhead applied. Also prepare a journal entry for the transfer of goods completed and transferred. Show the postings to the WIP account.

14-35 Journal Entries

Refer to the data in problem 14-B2. Prepare summary journal entries for the use of direct materials, direct labor, and factory overhead applied. Also prepare a journal entry for the transfer of goods completed and transferred. Show the posting to the WIP—Assembly Department account.

14-36 Compute Equivalent Units

Consider the following data for 20X1:

	Physical Units
Started in 20X1	90,000
Completed in 20X1	80,000
Ending inventory, work in process	40,000
Beginning inventory, work in process	30,000

The beginning inventory was 80% complete regarding direct materials and 40% complete regarding conversion costs. The ending inventory was 20% complete regarding direct materials and 10% complete regarding conversion costs.

Prepare a schedule of equivalent units for the work done to date.

14-37 Journal Entries

Refer to the data in problem 14-B3. Prepare summary journal entries for the use of direct materials and conversion costs. Also, prepare a journal entry for the transfer of goods completed, assuming that the goods are transferred to another department.

14-38 Journal Entries

Refer to the data in problem 14-A3. Prepare summary journal entries for the use of direct materials and conversion costs. Also, prepare a journal entry for the transfer of the goods completed and transferred from the assembly department to the finishing department.

PROBLEMS

14-39 Job Costing at Dell Computer

Dell's manufacturing process at its Austin, Texas, facility consists of assembly, functional testing, and quality control of the company's computer systems. The company's build-to-order manufacturing process is designed to allow the company to quickly produce customized computer systems. For example, the company contracts with various suppliers to manufacture unconfigured base Latitude notebook computers and then Dell customizes these systems for shipment to customers. Quality control is maintained through the testing of components, parts, and subassemblies at various stages in the manufacturing process.

Describe how Dell might set up a job-costing system to determine the costs of its computers. What is a "job" to Dell? How might the costs of components, assembly, testing, and quality control be allocated to each "job"?

14-40 Relationships of Manufacturing Costs

Selected data concerning the past fiscal year's operations of the Woodson Manufacturing Company are as follows (in thousands):

	Inventories	
	Beginning	Ending
Raw materials	$ 70	$ 90
WIP	75	35
Finished goods	100	120
Other data:		
Raw materials used		$ 468
Total manufacturing costs charged to production during the year (includes raw materials, direct labor, and factory overhead applied at a rate of 80% of direct-labor cost)		864
Selling and general expenses		50

Answer each of the following items:

1. Compute the cost of raw materials purchased during the year.
2. Compute the direct-labor costs charged to production during the year.
3. Compute the cost of goods available for sale during the year.
4. Compute the cost of goods sold during the year.

14-41 Relationship of Subsidiary and General Ledgers, Journal Entries

The following summarized data are available on three job-cost records of Red Lake Manufacturing Company, a producer of packaging equipment:

	Job 412		Job 413		Job 414
	April	**May**	**April**	**May**	**May**
Direct materials	$9,000	$2,500	$12,000	—	$13,000
Direct labor	4,000	1,500	5,000	2,500	2,000
Factory overhead applied	8,000	?	10,000	?	?

The company's fiscal year ends on May 31. Factory overhead is applied as a percentage of direct-labor costs. The balances in selected accounts on April 30 were as follows: direct-materials inventory, $19,000; finished-goods inventory, $18,000.

Job 412 was completed during May and transferred to finished goods. Job 413 was still in process at the end of May, as was Job 414, which had started May 24. These were the only jobs worked on during April and May.

Job 412 was sold, along with other finished goods, by May 30. The total cost of goods sold during May was $33,000. The balance in Cost of Goods Sold for sales through April 30 was $450,000.

1. Prepare a schedule showing the balance of the WIP Inventory for April 30. This schedule should show the total costs of each job record. Taken together, the job-cost records are the subsidiary ledger supporting the general ledger balance of work in process.
2. What is the overhead application rate?
3. Prepare summary general journal entries for all costs added to WIP during May. Also prepare entries for all costs transferred from WIP to Finished Goods and from Finished Goods to Cost of Goods Sold. Post to the appropriate T-accounts.
4. Prepare a schedule showing the balance of the WIP Inventory, May 31.

14-42 Job Costing in a Consulting Firm

Lubbock Engineering Consultants is a firm of professional civil engineers. It mostly does surveying jobs for the heavy construction industry throughout Texas. The firm obtains its jobs by giving fixed-price quotations, so profitability depends on the ability to predict the time required for the various subtasks on the job. (This situation is similar to that in the auditing profession, where times are budgeted for such audit steps as reconciling cash and confirming accounts receivable.)

A client may be served by various professional staff members who hold positions in the hierarchy from partners to managers to senior engineers to assistants. In addition, there are secretaries and other employees.

Lubbock Engineering has the following budget for 20X1:

Compensation of professional staff	$3,600,000
Other costs	1,449,000
Total budgeted costs	$5,049,000

Each professional staff member must submit a weekly time report, which is used for charging hours to a client job-order record. The time report has seven columns, one for each day of the week. Its rows are as follows:

- Chargeable hours
    Client 156
    Client 183
    etc.
- Nonchargeable hours
    Attending seminar on new equipment
    Unassigned time
    etc.

In turn, these time reports are used for charging hours and costs to the client job-order records. The managing partner regards these job records as absolutely essential for measuring the profitability of various jobs and for providing an "experience base for improving predictions on future jobs."

1. This firm applies overhead to jobs at a budgeted percentage of the professional compensation charged directly to the job ("direct labor"). For all categories of professional personnel, chargeable hours average 85% of available hours. Nonchargeable hours are regarded as additional overhead. What is the overhead rate as a percentage of "direct labor," the chargeable professional compensation cost?

2. A senior engineer works 48 weeks per year, 40 hours per week. His compensation is $60,000. He has worked on two jobs during the past week, devoting 10 hours to Job 156 and 30 hours to Job 183. How much cost should be charged to Job 156 because of his work there?

14-43 Weighted-Average Process Costing at Nally & Gibson

Nally & Gibson produces crushed limestone, among other products, used in highway construction. To produce the crushed limestone, the company starts with limestone rocks from its quarry in Georgetown, Kentucky, and puts the rocks through a crushing process. Suppose that on May 1, Nally & Gibson has 24 tons of rock (75% complete) in the crushing process. The cost of that beginning WIP inventory was $6,000. During May, the company added 288 tons of rock from its quarry, and at the end of the month 15 tons remained in process, on average one-third complete. The cost of rocks from the quarry for the last 5 months has been $120 per ton. Labor and overhead cost during May in the rock-crushing process were $40,670. Nally & Gibson uses weighted-average process costing.

1. Compute the cost per ton of crushed rock for production in May.
2. Compute the cost of the WIP inventory at the end of May.
3. Suppose the flexible budget for labor and overhead was $16,000 plus $80 per ton. Evaluate the control of overhead and labor costs during May.

14-44 Process and ABC

Consider the potato chip production process at a company such as **Frito-Lay**. Frito-Lay uses a continuous flow technology that is suited for high volumes of product. At the Plano, Texas, facility, between 6,000 and 7,000 pounds of potato chips are produced each hour. The plant operates 24 hours a day. It takes 30 minutes to completely produce a bag of potato chips from the raw potato to the packed end product.

1. What product and process characteristics of potato chips dictate the cost accounting system used? Describe the costing system best suited to Frito-Lay.
2. What product and process characteristics dictate the use of an ABC system? What implications does this have for Frito-Lay?
3. When beginning inventories are present, product costing becomes more complicated. Estimate the relative magnitude of beginning inventories at Frito-Lay compared to total production. What implication does this have for the costing system?

14-45 Nonprofit Basic Process Costing

The IRS must process millions of income tax returns yearly. When the taxpayer sends in a return, documents such as withholding statements and checks are matched against the data submitted. Then, various other inspections of the data are conducted. Some returns are more complicated than others so the expected time allowed to process a return is geared to an "average" return.

Some work-measurement experts have been closely monitoring the processing at a particular branch. They are seeking ways to improve productivity.

Suppose 3 million returns were received on April 15. On April 22, the work-measurement teams discovered that all supplies (punched cards, inspection check-sheets, and so on) had been affixed to the returns, but 40% of the returns still had to undergo a final inspection. The other returns were fully completed.

1. Suppose the final inspection represents 20% of the overall processing time in this process. Compute the total work done in terms of equivalent units.
2. The materials and supplies consumed were $600,000. For these calculations, materials and supplies are regarded just like direct materials. The conversion costs were $4,830,000. Compute the unit costs of materials and supplies and of conversion.
3. Compute the cost of the tax returns not yet completely processed.

14-46 Two Materials, Basic Process Costing

The following data pertain to the blending department at Pennsylvania Chemicals for April:

Units		
	Work in process, March 31	0
	Units started	50,000
	Completed and transferred to finishing department	40,000
Costs		
	Materials	
	Plastic compound	$450,000
	Softening compound	$ 60,000
	Conversion costs	$220,000

The plastic compound is introduced at the start of the process, while the softening compound is added when the product reaches an 80% stage of completion. Conversion costs are incurred uniformly throughout the process.

The ending work in process is 40% completed for conversion costs. None of the units in process reached the 80% stage of completion.

1. Compute the equivalent units and unit costs for April.
2. Compute the total cost of units completed and transferred to finished goods. Also compute the cost of the ending work in process.

14-47 Materials and Cartons in Basic Process Costing

A Manchester, England, company manufactures and sells small portable digital voice recorders. Business is booming. Several materials are added at various stages in the assembly department. Costs are accounted for on a process-cost basis. The end of the process involves conducting a final inspection and adding a cardboard carton.

The final inspection requires 5% of the total processing time. All units inspected during the period successfully passed inspection. All materials, besides the carton, are added by the time the recorders reach an 80% stage of completion of conversion.

There were no beginning inventories. During 20X1, 150,000 recorders were started in production. At the end of the year, which was not a busy time, 5,000 recorders were in various stages of completion. All the ending units in work in process were at the 95% stage. They awaited final inspection before being placed in cartons.

Total direct materials consumed in production, except for cartons, cost £2,250,000. Cartons used cost £319,000. Total conversion costs were £1,198,000.

1. Present a schedule of physical units, equivalent units, and unit costs of direct materials, cartons, and conversion costs.
2. Present a summary of the cost of goods completed and the cost of ending work in process.

14-48 Backflush Costing

Adirondak Meter manufactures a variety of measuring instruments. One product is an altimeter used by hikers and mountain climbers. Adirondak adopted a JIT viewpoint with an automated, computer-controlled, robotic production system. The company schedules production only after an order is received, materials and parts arrive just as they are needed, the production cycle time for altimeters is less than one day, and completed units are packaged and shipped as part of the production cycle.

Adirondak's backflush-costing system has only three accounts related to production of altimeters: materials and parts inventory, conversion costs, and finished-goods inventory. At the beginning of April (as at the beginning of every month), each of the three accounts had a balance of zero. Following are the April transactions related to the production of altimeters:

Materials and parts purchased	$287,000
Conversion costs incurred	$ 92,000
Altimeters produced	11,500 units

The budgeted (or standard) cost for one altimeter is $24 for materials and parts and $8 for conversion costs.

1. Prepare summary journal entries for the production of altimeters in April.
2. Compute the cost of goods sold for April. Explain any assumptions you make.
3. Suppose the actual conversion costs incurred during April were $95,000 instead of $92,000, and all other facts were as given. Prepare the additional journal entry that would be required at the end of April. Explain why the entry was necessary.

14-49 Review of Chapters 13 and 14

Tucson Co. uses normal absorption costing. Factory overhead is applied to production at a budgeted rate based on direct labor cost. At the end of the period, there are two unfinished jobs. Additional information is available as follows:

Direct materials used = $50,000

Direct labor = $100,000

Beginning balance of work in process = $100,000

Cost of goods manufactured = $150,000

Finished goods beginning inventory = $140,000

Finished goods ending inventory = $110,000

Factory overhead is overapplied by $60,000

Actual factory overhead = $90,000

Determine the following:

1. The cost of goods sold before disposition of overapplied overhead
2. Ending balance in WIP
3. Budgeted rate for applying factory overhead
4. Assuming the overapplied factory overhead is not prorated, what is adjusted cost of goods sold?

14-50 Review of Chapters 13 and 14

Clark Co. uses normal absorption job order costing. Factory overhead is applied to production at a budgeted rate of 300% of prime costs (direct materials plus direct labor). Clark Co.'s policy is to not prorate any over- or underapplied overhead amounts. All inventory amounts listed next are after disposition of any over- or under- applied overhead:

Direct labor = $100,000

Beginning balance of stores (direct materials) = $20,000

Ending balance of stores = $20,000

Purchased $50,000 of direct materials during period

Beginning balance of work in process = $300,000

Ending balance of work in process = $300,000

Cost of goods sold = $350,000

Finished goods beg. inventory = $100,000

Finished goods ending inventory = $200,000

Determine the following:

1. Direct materials used
2. Factory overhead applied
3. Cost of goods manufactured
4. Actual factory overhead for the period

NIKE 10-K PROBLEM

14-51 ABC and Distribution Centers

Read **Nike**'s 10-K in Appendix C. Item 1 describes of its business, especially in the United States. A simplified description of Nike's supply chain follows.

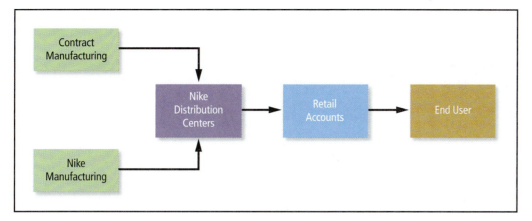

What kind of production system and associated costing system would you expect at the contract manufacturers? Nike distribution centers? How many distribution centers does Nike operate in the United States? Where are they located? How many retail accounts are in the United States? Suppose Nike is implementing an ABC system to improve its accounting for overhead costs at its Memphis facility. Some of the activities performed at a Nike distribution center are listed along with a resource used by the activities. Because each of the resources is also used by more than one activity, its cost must be allocated. For each of the activities-resource pairs, suggest a plausible cost-allocation base that could be used to allocate the resource cost to the activities.

Activities	Resource Used
Receiving, put away apparel, picking products to fill an order, loading pallets onto trucks for shipment	Forklift
Receiving, put away apparel, repacking in boxes, repacking in cartons, shipping	Occupancy costs
Supplies ordering, customer order processing, invoicing and payment for parcel deliveries	Variable computer costs

EXCEL APPLICATION EXERCISE

14-52 Value of Units Produced

Goal: Create an Excel spreadsheet to compute the value of units produced using the weighted-average process-costing method. Use the results to answer questions about your findings.

Scenario: The Magnatto Company has asked you to compute costs for the electric drills produced in its assembly department during the month of July. You will need to use the weighted-average process-costing method to determine costs for beginning work in process, completed units, and ending work in process. Additional background information for your spreadsheet appears in Fundamental Assignment Material 14-A3.

When you have completed your spreadsheet, answer the following questions:
1. At the end of July, what is the value of the 20,000 units remaining in the WIP ending inventory?
2. What were the materials, conversion, and total cost of goods amounts for the units transferred to the finishing department during the month of July?
3. What are the materials and conversion cost per unit amounts for the accumulated units and costs in July?

Step-by-Step:
1. Open a new Excel spreadsheet.
2. In column A, create a bold-faced heading that contains the following:
   Row 1: Chapter 14 Decision Guideline
   Row 2: Magnatto Company
   Row 3: Weighted-Average Process Costing for July, 20X1
   Row 4: Today's Date
3. Merge and center the four heading rows across columns A–K.
4. In row 7, create the following column headings justified as indicated:

Column B: Number	Center-justify
Column C: Percent Complete	Merge and center across columns C and D
Column E: Equivalent Units	Merge and center across columns E and F
Column G: Cost of Goods	Merge and center across columns G–I
Column J: Cost per Unit	Merge and center across columns J and K

5. In row 8, create the following center-justified column headings:
   Column B: of Units
   Columns C, E, G, and J: Materials
   Columns D, F, H, and K: Conversion
   Column I: Total

6. In column A, create the following row headings:
   Row 9: Beginning WIP
   Skip a row.
   Row 11: Units started
   Row 12: Less: Ending units
   Row 13: Units started and completed in July
   Row 14: Beginning units completed
   Skip a row.
   Row 16: Accumulated units and costs in July
   Skip a row.
   Row 18: Value of transferred units

   Note: Recommended column widths:

   Column A = 28
   Column B = 7
   Columns C, E, and J = 8
   Columns D, F, G, H, and K = 9
   Column I = 11

7. Format columns C and D as follows:

Number tab:	Category:	Percentage
	Decimal places:	0

8. Use data from Fundamental Assignment Material 14-A3 to enter the following amounts:

Beginning WIP:	units, percent complete, cost of goods
Units started:	units
Less: Ending units:	units, percent complete
Accumulated units and costs in July:	cost of goods for materials and conversion
Value of transferred units:	units

9. Calculate the following amounts:

Units started and completed in July:	units, percent complete
Beginning units completed:	units, percent complete

10. In the sequence listed, use formulas to calculate the following amounts:

Equivalent units for:	Beginning WIP
	Less: Ending units
	Units started and completed in July
	Beginning units completed
	Accumulated units and costs in July
Cost per unit for:	Beginning WIP
	Accumulated units and costs in July
Materials cost of goods for:	Less: Ending units
	Units started and completed in July
	Beginning units completed
	Value of transferred units
Conversion cost of goods for:	Less: Ending units
	Units started and completed in July
	Beginning units completed
	Value of transferred units
Total cost of goods for:	Less: Ending units
	Units started and completed in July
	Beginning units completed
	Accumulated units and costs in July
	Value of transferred units
Cost per unit for:	Value of transferred units

11. Format columns B, E, F, G, H, and I as follows:

Number tab:	Category:	Number
	Decimal places:	0
	Use 1000 Separator (,):	Checked
	Negative numbers:	Red with parentheses

12. Format columns J and K as follows:

Number tab:	Category:	Currency
	Decimal places:	2
	Symbol:	$
	Negative numbers:	Red with parentheses

13. Format the cost of goods rows 9, 12, 16, and 18 as follows:

Number tab:	Category:	Accounting
	Decimal places:	0
	Symbol:	$

14. Modify the format of column B, rows 13 and 18; and row 16, columns E–I to display a top border using the default Line Style.

Border tab:	Icon:	Top Border

15. Modify the format of row 7, columns C, D, G, H, and I; and row 8, columns E, F, J, and K to display with a light gray fill.

Patterns tab:	Color:	Lightest Grey (above white)

16. Save your work to disk, and print a copy for your files.

Note: Print your spreadsheet using landscape in order to ensure that all columns appear on one page.

COLLABORATIVE LEARNING EXERCISE

14-53 Job and Process Costing

Form into groups of three to six students. For each of the following production processes, assess whether a job-cost or process-cost system is most likely to be used to determine the cost of the product or service. Also, explain why you think that system is most logical. (This can be done by individuals, but it is a much richer experience when done as a group, because the knowledge and judgment of several students interact to produce a much better analysis than a single student can produce.)

a. Producing Cheerios by **General Mills**
b. Processing an application for life insurance by **Prudential**
c. Producing a couch by **Ethan Allen**
d. Building a bridge by **Kiewit Construction Co.**
e. Producing gasoline by **Chevron**
f. Producing 200 copies of a 140-page course packet by **FedEx Office**
g. Producing a superferry by **Todd Shipyards**

INTERNET EXERCISE

14-54 Process Costing at a Variety of Companies

Process costing assigns costs by measuring overall production costs and averaging them based on total production in units over a period of time, usually a month. The resulting average unit costs are then used to determine inventory cost and the cost of goods sold. Let's look at some companies and see if any of them might be candidates for using a process-costing system.

1. Log on to **Lands' End**'s Web site at www.landsend.com. Click on "About Us" on the bottom of the page. What type of firm is Lands' End? What is its main activity? Do you think that the firm would be a good candidate for using a process-costing system? Why or why not?
2. Log on to **La-Z-Boy**'s Web site at www.lazboy.com. Click on "About La-Z-Boy." What type of firm is La-Z-Boy? What is its main activity? Do you think that the firm would be a good candidate for using a process-costing system? Why or why not?
3. Log on to **Tasty Baking Company**'s Web site at www.tastykake.com. What type of firm is Tasty Baking Company? What is its main activity? Do you think that the firm would be a good candidate for using a process-costing system? Why or why not?
4. Refer to Tasty Baking Company's most recent annual report. What type of inventory accounts do you find? Where did you locate the information on inventory? Can you tell from the information provided what type of costing system that Tasty Baking Company uses?

Appendix A   Recommended Readings

The following readings will aid readers who want to pursue some topics in more depth than is possible in this book. There is a hazard in compiling a group of recommended readings. Inevitably, we will omit some worthwhile books or periodicals. Moreover, such a list cannot include books published subsequently to the compilation date. Although this list is not comprehensive, it includes many excellent readings.

Periodicals

Professional Journals

The following professional journals are typically available in university libraries and include articles on the application of management accounting:

- *Accounting Horizons.* Published by the American Accounting Association; stresses current practice-oriented articles in all areas of accounting
- *CMA Management.* Published by CMA Canada; includes much practice-oriented research in management accounting
- *Cost Management.* Published by Thompson Reuters; stresses cost management tools
- *Financial Executive.* Published by Financial Executives International; emphasizes general policy issues for accounting and finance executives
- *The Journal of Corporate Accounting & Finance.* Published by Wiley; dirercted to corporate accounting and finance executives and outside auditors and accountants working for the corporation
- *Harvard Business Review.* Published by Harvard Business School; directed to general managers but contains excellent articles on applications of management accounting
- *Journal of Accountancy.* Published by the American Institute of CPAs; emphasizes financial accounting and is directed at the practicing CPA
- *Management Accounting Quarterly.* An online journal published by the Institute of Management Accountants; practical articles with an academic focus
- *Strategic Finance.* Published by the Institute of Management Accountants; many articles on actual applications by individual organizations
- *BusinessWeek, Forbes, Fortune,* the *Economist,* and the *Wall Street Journal.* Popular publications that cover a variety of business and economics topics; often their articles relate to management accounting

Academic Journals

The academic journal that focuses most directly on current management and cost accounting research is the *Journal of Management Accounting Research*, published by the Management Accounting section of the American Accounting Association. *The Accounting Review*, the general research publication of the American Accounting Association; *Journal of Accounting Research*, published at the University of Chicago; and *Contemporary Accounting Research*, published by the Canadian Academic Association, cover all accounting topics at a more theoretical level. *Accounting, Organizations and Society*, a British journal, publishes research on behavioral aspects of management accounting. The *Journal of Accounting and Economics* covers economics-based accounting research. *Research on Professional Responsibility and Ethics in Accounting*, published by Emerald Group Publishing, is an annual journal devoted to ethical issues.

Books in Management Accounting

Most of the topics in this text are covered in more detail in the many books on cost accounting, including *Cost Accounting: A Managerial Emphasis*, 13th edition, by C. T. Horngren, G. Foster, S. Datar, and Madhav Rajan (Prentice Hall, 2008). You can find more advanced coverage in *Advanced Management Accounting*, 3rd edition, by R. S. Kaplan and A. A. Atkinson (Prentice Hall, 1998). Current management accounting issues are discussed in *Issues in Management Accounting* by Trevor Hopper, Robert W. Scapens, and Deryl Northcott (Prentice Hall, 2007).

The Financial Executives Institute, 200 Campus Drive, P.O. Box 674, Florham Park, NJ 07960, and the Institute of Management Accounting, 10 Paragon Drive, P.O. Box 433, Montvale, NJ 07932, have long lists of accounting research publications.

Handbooks, General Texts, and Case Books

The books in this list have wide application to management accounting issues. The handbooks are basic references. The textbooks are designed for classroom use but may be useful for self-study. The case books present applications from real companies.

- Adkins, T. C., *Case Studies in Performance Management: A Guide from the Experts*, Hoboken, NJ: John Wiley & Sons, 2006.
- Allen, B. R., E. R. Brownlee, M. E. Haskins, L. J. Lynch, and J. W. Rotch, *Cases in Management Accounting and Control Systems*, 4th ed. Upper Saddle River, NJ: Prentice Hall, 2004.
- Bierman, H., Jr., and S. Smidt, *The Capital Budgeting Decision: Economic Analysis of Investment Projects*, 9th ed. Routledge, 2006. This text expands the capital budgeting discussion from Chapter 11.
- Bierman, H., Jr., and S. Smidt, *Advanced Capital Budgeting: Refinements in the Economic Analysis of Investment Projects*, Routledge, 2007.
- Render, B., R. Stair, and M. Hanna, *Quantitative Analysis for Management*, 10th ed. Prentice Hall, 2008.
- Groot, T., and K. Lukka (eds.), *Cases in Management Accounting: Current Practices in European Companies*, Harlow: Prentice Hall/Pearson, 2000.
- Innes, J., *Handbook of Management Accounting*, 3rd ed. London: CIMA, 2005.
- Manning, G. A., *Financial Investigation and Forensic Accounting*, 3rd ed. Boca Raton, FL: CRC Press, 2005.
- Pryor, T., et al., *Activity Dictionary: A Comprehensive Reference Tool for ABM and ABC: 2000 Edition*, Arlington, TX: ICMS, Inc., 2000.
- Seitz, N., and M. Ellison, *Capital Budgeting and Long-Term Financing Decisions*, Cincinnati, OH: South-Western, 2004.
- Shank, J., *Strategic Cost Management: The New Tool for Competitive Advantage*, Free Press, 2008.
- Young, S. M., *Readings in Management Accounting*, 5th ed. Upper Saddle River, NJ: Prentice Hall, 2007.

Accounting Ethics

Integrity is essential for accountants. An increasing emphasis on ethics has led to a number of books devoted to the subject.

- Brooks, L. J., and P. Dunn, *Business and Professional Ethics for Directors, Executives, & Accountants*, Mason, OH: South-Western, 2009.
- Cheffers, M. L., and M. Pakaluk, *Understanding Accounting Ethics*, 2nd ed. Manchaug, MA: Allen David Press, 2007.
- Duska, R. F., and B. S. Duska, *Accounting Ethics*, Malden, MA: Blackwell Publishing, 2003.
- Mintz, S. M., and R. E. Morris, *Ethical Obligations and Decision Making in Accounting: Text and Cases*, New York: McGraw-Hill/Irwin, 2008.

The Strategic Nature of Management Accounting

Management accountants realize that cost and performance information is most useful to organizations when it helps define strategic alternatives and helps in the management of resources to achieve strategic objectives. The books in this list, though not necessarily accounting books, provide a valuable foundation to the interaction of strategy and accounting information.

- Ansari, S., and J. Bell, *Target Costing: The Next Frontier in Strategic Cost Management*, Mountain Valley Publishing, 2009.
- L. Carr and A. Nanni Jr., *Delivering Results: Managing What Matters*, Springer, 2009.

- Grant, J. L., *Foundations of Economic Value Added*, 2nd ed. New York: Wiley, 2002.
- Porter, M., *The Michael Porter Trilogy: Competitive Strategy, Competitive Advantage, the Competitive Advantage of Nations*, New York: The Free Press, 1998.
- Small, P., *The Ultimate Game of Strategy: Establish Your Personal Niche in the World of e-Business*, Upper Saddle River, NJ: Prentice Hall, 2001.
- Stern, J., J. Shiely, and I. Ross, *The EVA Challenge: Implementing Value-Added Change in an Organization*, New York: Wiley, 2003.

Modern Manufacturing

The following books provide background on the role of accounting in modern manufacturing environments.

- Atkinson, A. A., R. S. Kaplan, S. M. Young, and E. M. Matsumura, *Management Accounting*, 5th ed. Upper Saddle River, NJ: Prentice Hall, 2006.
- Carriera, B., *Lean Manufacturing That Works: Powerful Tools for Dramatically Reducing Waste and Maximizing Profits*, New York: AMACOM, 2004.
- Carreira, B, and B. Trudell, *Lean Six Sigma That Works: A Powerful Action Plan for Dramatically Improving Quality, Increasing Speed, and Reducing Waste*, New York: AMACOM, 2006.
- Chase, R., N. Aquilano, and F. R. Jacobs, *Operations Management for Competitive Advantage*, Homewood, IL: McGraw-Hill/Irwin, 2005.
- Cooper, R., and R. Kaplan, *Design of Cost Management Systems*, 2nd ed. Upper Saddle River, NJ: Prentice Hall, 1999.
- Goldratt, E. M., *Theory of Constraints*, Croton-on-Hudson, NY: North River Press, Inc., 2000.
- Goldratt, E. M., and J. Cox, *The Goal*, 3rd ed. Croton-on-Hudson, NY: North River Press, 2004. This is a novel illustrating the new manufacturing environment.
- Kaplan, R. S., and R. Cooper, *Cost & Effect*, Boston: Harvard Business School Press, 1998.
- Morgan, J., *Lean Six Sigma for Dummies*, Indianapolis: Wiley-Blackwell Publishing, 2009.
- Pyzdek, T., *The Six Sigma Handbook*, 2nd ed. New York: McGraw-Hill, 2003.
- Rubrich, L., and M. Watson, *Implementing World Class Manufacturing*, 2nd ed. Fort Wayne, IN: WCM Associates, 2004.

Management Control Systems

The topics of Chapters 7–10 can be explored further in several books, including the following:

- Anthony, R. N., and V. Govindarajan, *Management Control Systems*, 12th ed. McGraw-Hill/Irwin, 2006.
- Arrow, K. J., *The Limits of Organization*, New York: Norton, 1974. [This is a readable classic by a Nobel laureate.]
- Gupta, P., and A. W. Wiggenhorn, *Six Sigma Business Scorecard: Creating a Comprehensive Corporate Performance Measurement System*, 2nd ed. New York: McGraw-Hill, 2006.
- Kaplan, R. S., and D. P. Norton, *Alignment: Using the Balanced Scorecard to Create Corporate Synergies*, Boston: Harvard Business School Press, 2006.
- Kaplan, R. S., and D. P. Norton, *The Balanced Scorecard: Measures That Drive Performance*, Boston: Harvard Business School Press, 1996.
- Merchant K., and W. Van der Stede, *Management Control Systems*, 2nd ed. Upper Saddle River, NJ: Prentice Hall, 2007.
- Niven, P. R., *Balanced Scorecard Step-by-Step: Maximizing Performance and Maintaining Results*, Hoboken, NJ: John Wiley & Sons, 2006.
- Simons, R., *Performance Measurement and Control Systems for Implementing Strategy*, Upper Saddle River, NJ: Prentice Hall, 2000.
- Solomons, D., *Divisional Performance: Measurement and Control*, New York: Markus Wiener, 1983. [This is a reprint of a 1965 classic that is still relevant.]

Management Accounting in Nonprofit Organizations

Many books discuss management accounting in nonprofit organizations, especially in health care. Five examples are as follows:

- Anthony, R. N., and D. W. Young, *Management Control in Nonprofit Organizations*, 7th ed. Homewood, IL: Irwin, 2003.
- Baker, J. J., and R. W. Baker, *Health Care Finance: Basic Tools for Nonfinancial Managers*, 2nd ed. Sudbury, MA: Jones and Bartlett, 2006.
- Brimson, J., and J. Antos, *Activity Based Management for Service Industries, Government Entities, and Non-Profit Organizations*, New York: John Wiley & Sons, 1998.
- Finkler, S. A., D. M. Ward, and J. J. Baker, *Essentials of Cost Accounting for Health Care Organizations*, 3rd ed. Sudbury, MA: Jones and Bartlett, 2007.
- Gapenski, L. C., *Healthcare Finance: An Introduction to Accounting and Financial Management*, 4th ed. Washington DC: Health Administration Press, 2008.
- Neumann, B., and K. Boles, *Management Accounting for Healthcare Organizations*, 5th ed. Chicago: Precept Press, 1998.
- Niven, P., *Balanced Scorecard: Step-by-Step for Government and Nonprofit Agencies*, New York: John Wiley & Sons, 2003.
- Young, D., *Management Accounting in Health Care Organizations*, 2nd ed., Jossey-Bass, 2009.

Online Resources

The online resources related to management accounting are too extensive to create a comprehensive list. The best way to access them may be to use a good search engine. However, we list a few URLs that can help you get started.

- AICPA's Financial Management Center: Information for CPAs in business and industry, at http://fmcenter.aicpa.org/
- Balanced Scorecard Institute: Includes a variety of resources related to the balanced scorecard, at http://www.balancedscorecard.org
- BetterManagement.com: Includes materials on both activity-based management and balanced scorecard, at http://www.bettermanagement.com
- CMA Canada: Many services, including strategic management accounting practices and management accounting standards, at http://www.cma-canada.org
- Consortium for Advanced Manufacturing International (CAM-I): Online library, at http://www.cam-i.org
- Financial Executives International: Information for corporate financial officers, at http://www.fei.org
- Hyperion Solutions: Software for both activity-based management and the balanced scorecard, now owned by Oracle, at http://www.oracle.com/hyperion/index.html
- Institute of Management Accountants: A variety of services, including an index of research publications, at http://www.imanet.org/
- Metrus Group: A variation of the balance scorecard, at http://www.metrus.com/products/balanced-scorecards.html
- Stern Stewart & Co.: Information about economic value added by the firm that developed the technique, at http://www.sternstewart.com/

Appendix B   Fundamentals of Compound Interest and the Use of Present-Value Tables

The Nature of Interest

Interest is the cost of using money. It is the rental fee for money, similar to the rental fees charged for the use of automobiles or machinery.

Suppose you invest $10,000 in a savings account in a financial institution. This $10,000 is the *principal*. Interest is the amount you earn on the investment each period. In this appendix, we focus on compound interest, where we add each period's interest to the beginning-of-the-period principal to come up with the principal for the next period. For example, suppose the financial institution promised to pay 10% interest per year on your $10,000 investment. The 10% × $10,000 = $1,000 interest the first year would create a principal of $10,000 + $1,000 = $11,000 at the start of the second year. If you let the amount accumulate for 3 years before withdrawing the full balance of the deposit, the deposit would accumulate to $13,310:

	Principal	Compound Interest	Balance, End of Year
Year 1	$10,000	$10,000 × 0.10 = $1,000	$11,000
Year 2	11,000	11,000 × 0.10 = 1,100	12,100
Year 3	12,100	12,100 × 0.10 = 1,210	13,310

Because compound interest accumulates on both the original principal and the previously accumulated interest that has been added to principal each period, the "force" of compound interest can be staggering. For example, the $10,000 deposit would accumulate as follows:

At End of			
3 Years	10 Years	20 Years	40 Years
$13,310	$25,937	$67,275	$452,593

Step-by-step calculations of compound interest quickly become burdensome. Therefore, experts have constructed compound interest tables to ease computations. In addition, the computations in these tables are built into many handheld calculators and computer software programs. This appendix explains how to use the two compound interest tables most commonly used in capital budgeting. Both provide measures of *present value*, the value today of a future amount.

Table B-1: Present Value of $1

How do you express a future cash inflow or outflow in terms of its equivalent today (at time zero)? Table B-1 provides factors that give the present value of a single, lump-sum cash flow that you will receive or pay at the end of a future period.

Suppose you invest $1.00 today at 6% interest. It will grow to $1.06 in one year.; that is, $1 × 1.06 = $1.06. At the end of the second year, its value is ($1 × 1.06) × 1.06 = $1 × (1.06)^2 = $1.124; and at the end of the third year it is $1 × (1.06)^3 = 1.191. In general, $1.00 grows to (1 + i)^n in n years at i percent interest.

To determine the present value, you reverse this accumulation process. If you will receive $1.00 in one year, it is worth $1 ÷ 1.06 = $0.9434 today at an interest rate of 6%. Stated differently, if you invest $0.9434 today, in one year you will have $0.9434 × 1.06 = $1.00. Thus, $0.9434 is the present value of $1.00 a year hence at 6%.

Suppose you will receive the $1 in 2 years instead of in 1 year. Its present value is then $1.00 ÷ (1.06)^2 = $0.8900. The general formula for the present value (PV) of an amount S that you will receive or pay in n periods at an interest rate of i% per period is as follows:

$$PV = \frac{S}{(1 + i)^n}$$

TABLE B-1 Present Value of $1

Period	3%	4%	5%	6%	7%	8%	10%	12%	14%	16%	18%	20%	22%	24%	25%	26%	28%	30%	40%
1	.9709	.9615	.9524	.9434	.9346	.9259	.9091	.8929	.8772	.8621	.8475	.8333	.8197	.8065	.8000	.7937	.7813	.7692	.7143
2	.9426	.9246	.9070	.8900	.8734	.8573	.8264	.7972	.7695	.7432	.7182	.6944	.6719	.6504	.6400	.6299	.6104	.5917	.5102
3	.9151	.8890	.8638	.8396	.8163	.7938	.7513	.7118	.6750	.6407	.6086	.5787	.5507	.5245	.5120	.4999	.4768	.4552	.3644
4	.8885	.8548	.8227	.7921	.7629	.7350	.6830	.6355	.5921	.5523	.5158	.4823	.4514	.4230	.4096	.3968	.3725	.3501	.2603
5	.8626	.8219	.7835	.7473	.7130	.6806	.6209	.5674	.5194	.4761	.4371	.4019	.3700	.3411	.3277	.3149	.2910	.2693	.1859
6	.8375	.7903	.7462	.7050	.6663	.6302	.5645	.5066	.4556	.4104	.3704	.3349	.3033	.2751	.2621	.2499	.2274	.2072	.1328
7	.8131	.7599	.7107	.6651	.6227	.5835	.5132	.4523	.3996	.3538	.3139	.2791	.2486	.2218	.2097	.1983	.1776	.1594	.0949
8	.7894	.7307	.6768	.6274	.5820	.5403	.4665	.4039	.3506	.3050	.2660	.2326	.2038	.1789	.1678	.1574	.1388	.1226	.0678
9	.7664	.7026	.6446	.5919	.5439	.5002	.4241	.3606	.3075	.2630	.2255	.1938	.1670	.1443	.1342	.1249	.1084	.0943	.0484
10	.7441	.6756	.6139	.5584	.5083	.4632	.3855	.3220	.2697	.2267	.1911	.1615	.1369	.1164	.1074	.0992	.0847	.0725	.0346
11	.7224	.6496	.5847	.5268	.4751	.4289	.3505	.2875	.2366	.1954	.1619	.1346	.1122	.0938	.0859	.0787	.0662	.0558	.0247
12	.7014	.6246	.5568	.4970	.4440	.3971	.3186	.2567	.2076	.1685	.1372	.1122	.0920	.0757	.0687	.0625	.0517	.0429	.0176
13	.6810	.6006	.5303	.4688	.4150	.3677	.2897	.2292	.1821	.1452	.1163	.0935	.0754	.0610	.0550	.0496	.0404	.0330	.0126
14	.6611	.5775	.5051	.4423	.3878	.3405	.2633	.2046	.1597	.1252	.0985	.0779	.0618	.0492	.0440	.0393	.0316	.0254	.0090
15	.6419	.5553	.4810	.4173	.3624	.3152	.2394	.1827	.1401	.1079	.0835	.0649	.0507	.0397	.0352	.0312	.0247	.0195	.0064
16	.6232	.5339	.4581	.3936	.3387	.2919	.2176	.1631	.1229	.0930	.0708	.0541	.0415	.0320	.0281	.0248	.0193	.0150	.0046
17	.6050	.5134	.4363	.3714	.3166	.2703	.1978	.1456	.1078	.0802	.0600	.0451	.0340	.0258	.0225	.0197	.0150	.0116	.0033
18	.5874	.4936	.4155	.3503	.2959	.2502	.1799	.1300	.0946	.0691	.0508	.0376	.0279	.0208	.0180	.0156	.0118	.0089	.0023
19	.5703	.4746	.3957	.3305	.2765	.2317	.1635	.1161	.0829	.0596	.0431	.0313	.0229	.0168	.0144	.0124	.0092	.0068	.0017
20	.5537	.4564	.3769	.3118	.2584	.2145	.1486	.1037	.0728	.0514	.0365	.0261	.0187	.0135	.0115	.0098	.0072	.0053	.0012
21	.5375	.4388	.3589	.2942	.2415	.1987	.1351	.0926	.0638	.0443	.0309	.0217	.0154	.0109	.0092	.0078	.0056	.0040	.0009
22	.5219	.4220	.3418	.2775	.2257	.1839	.1228	.0826	.0560	.0382	.0262	.0181	.0126	.0088	.0074	.0062	.0044	.0031	.0006
23	.5067	.4057	.3256	.2618	.2109	.1703	.1117	.0738	.0491	.0329	.0222	.0151	.0103	.0071	.0059	.0049	.0034	.0024	.0004
24	.4919	.3901	.3101	.2470	.1971	.1577	.1015	.0659	.0431	.0284	.0188	.0126	.0085	.0057	.0047	.0039	.0027	.0018	.0003
25	.4776	.3751	.2953	.2330	.1842	.1460	.0923	.0588	.0378	.0245	.0160	.0105	.0069	.0046	.0038	.0031	.0021	.0014	.0002
26	.4637	.3607	.2812	.2198	.1722	.1352	.0839	.0525	.0331	.0211	.0135	.0087	.0057	.0037	.0030	.0025	.0016	.0011	.0002
27	.4502	.3468	.2678	.2074	.1609	.1252	.0763	.0469	.0291	.0182	.0115	.0073	.0047	.0030	.0024	.0019	.0013	.0008	.0001
28	.4371	.3335	.2551	.1956	.1504	.1159	.0693	.0419	.0255	.0157	.0097	.0061	.0038	.0024	.0019	.0015	.0010	.0006	.0001
29	.4243	.3207	.2429	.1846	.1406	.1073	.0630	.0374	.0224	.0135	.0082	.0051	.0031	.0020	.0015	.0012	.0008	.0005	.0001
30	.4120	.3083	.2314	.1741	.1314	.0994	.0573	.0334	.0196	.0116	.0070	.0042	.0026	.0016	.0012	.0010	.0006	.0004	.0000
40	.3066	.2083	.1420	.0972	.0668	.0460	.0221	.0107	.0053	.0026	.0013	.0007	.0004	.0002	.0001	.0001	.0001	.0000	.0000

Table B-1 on page A6 provides factors computed using this formula. It shows the present value of a single, lump-sum cash flow at the end of a future period at a particular interest rate.

Present values are also called *discounted values*, and the process of finding the present value is called *discounting*. You can think of this as discounting (decreasing) the value of a future cash inflow or outflow. Why is the value discounted? Because you will receive or pay the cash in the future, its value today is reduced or discounted from the future amount to be received.

Assume that a municipality issues a 3-year non-interest-bearing note payable that promises to pay you a lump sum of $1,000 exactly 3 years from the issue date. You desire a rate of return of 6%, compounded annually. How much would you be willing to pay now for the 3-year note? The situation is sketched as follows:

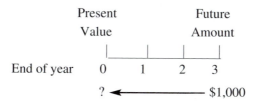

The factor in the period 3 row and 6% column of Table B-1 is 0.8396. The present value of the $1,000 payment is $1,000 × 0.8396 = $839.60. You would therefore be willing to pay $839.60 today for the $1,000 that you will receive in 3 years; $839.60 is the discounted value of the $1,000 future amount.

Compounding can occur more frequently than once per year. Suppose interest is compounded semiannually rather than annually. In our previous example, the 3 years become six semiannual interest compounding periods. How much would you be willing to pay, assuming the rate of return you demand per semiannual period is half the annual rate, or 6% ÷ 2 = 3%? The factor in the period 6 row and 3% column of Table B-1 is 0.8375. You would be willing to pay $1,000 × 0.8375, or only $837.50 rather than $839.60.

As a further check on your understanding, review the earlier example of your $10,000 investment. Suppose the financial institution promised to pay $13,310 at the end of 3 years. How much would you be willing to deposit at time zero if you desired a 10% rate of return compounded annually? Using Table B-1, the period 3 row and the 10% column show a factor of 0.7513. You multiply this factor by the future amount:

$$PV = 0.7513 \times \$13,310 = \$10,000$$

A diagram of this computation follows:

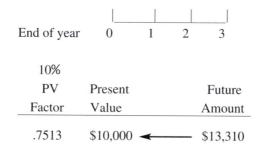

Pause for a moment. Use Table B-1 to obtain the present values of

1. $1,700 at 20% at the end of 20 years.
2. $8,300 at 10% at the end of 12 years.
3. $8,000 at 4% at the end of 4 years.

Answers:

1. $1,700 × 0.0261 = $44.37
2. $8,300 × 0.3186 = $2,644.38
3. $8,000 × 0.8548 = $6,838.40

Table B-2: Present Value of an Ordinary Annuity of $1

An annuity is a series of equal cash flows spaced equally in time. An ordinary annuity has the equally spaced payments occurring at the end of each period. (We will not discuss the other type of annuity, an annuity due, which has payments at the beginning of each year.) Assume that you buy a note from a municipality that promises to pay $1,000 at the end of each of the next 3 years. How much should you be willing to pay if you desire a rate of return of 6%, compounded annually? This series of payments is a 3-year ordinary annuity. You denote the present value of an ordinary annuity as PV_A.

Before we introduce a computational method to deal with an annuity, note that you can simply treat this as a series of individual amounts and solve the problem using Table B-1. First, you find the present value of each payment, and then you add the present values. As shown next, you would be willing to pay $943.40 for the first payment, $890.00 for the second, and $839.60 for the third, for a total of $2,673.00:

Payment	Table 1 Factor	Present Value	0	1	2	3
End of Year						
1	$\dfrac{1}{1.06} = .9434$	$ 943.40	$1,000			
2	$\dfrac{1}{(1.06)^2} = .8900$	890.00		1,000		
3	$\dfrac{1}{(1.06)^3} = .8396$	$\underline{839.60}$				$1,000
Total		$\underline{\underline{\$2,673.00}}$				

Although you can always treat an annuity as a series of individual amounts, this approach is computationally inconvenient for a long annuity. Instead, the factors in Table B-2 on page A9 provide a computational shortcut. Let's examine the conceptual basis for Table B-2 using our 3-year annuity. The three present value factors corresponding to the three annuity payments are the first three numbers from the 6% column of Table B-1. Because you multiply each of these factors by the $1,000 annuity payment, you can sum the factors and then multiply by $1,000 instead of multiplying each factor by $1,000 and then summing. For this example, the sum of the factors is .9434 + .8900 + .8396 = 2.6730, and this is the value that you find in Table B-2 for a three-period annuity with an interest rate of 6%. The present value of the annuity is simply the value from Table B-2, 2.6730, multiplied by $1,000: 2.6730 × $1,000 = $2,673.00. This shortcut is especially valuable if the cash payments or receipts extend over many periods. Consider an annual cash payment of $1,000 for 20 years at 6%. The present value, calculated from Table B-2, is $1,000 × 11.4699 = $11,469.90. To use Table B-1 for this calculation, you would have to perform 20 multiplications and then add the 20 products.

The factors in Table B-2 could be calculated by summing the factors in Table B-1, but they could also be calculated using the following general formula:

$$PV_A = \frac{1}{i}\left[1 - \frac{1}{(1 + i)^n}\right]$$

Applied to our illustration,

$$PV_A = \frac{1}{.06}\left[1 - \frac{1}{(1.06)^3}\right] = \frac{1}{.06}(1 - .8396) = \frac{.1604}{.06} = 2.6730$$

TABLE B-2 Present Value of Ordinary Annuity of $1

Period	3%	4%	5%	6%	7%	8%	10%	12%	14%	16%	18%	20%	22%	24%	25%	26%	28%	30%	40%
1	.9709	.9615	.9524	.9434	.9346	.9259	.9091	.8929	.8772	.8621	.8475	.8333	.8197	.8065	.8000	.7937	.7813	.7692	.7143
2	1.9135	1.8861	1.8594	1.8334	1.8080	1.7833	1.7355	1.6901	1.6467	1.6052	1.5656	1.5278	1.4915	1.4568	1.4400	1.4235	1.3916	1.3609	1.2245
3	2.8286	2.7751	2.7232	2.6730	2.6243	2.5771	2.4869	2.4018	2.3216	2.2459	2.1743	2.1065	2.0422	1.9813	1.9520	1.9234	1.8684	1.8161	1.5889
4	3.7171	3.6299	3.5460	3.4651	3.3872	3.3121	3.1699	3.0373	2.9137	2.7982	2.6901	2.5887	2.4936	2.4043	2.3616	2.3202	2.2410	2.1662	1.8492
5	4.5797	4.4518	4.3295	4.2124	4.1002	3.9927	3.7908	3.6048	3.4331	3.2743	3.1272	2.9906	2.8636	2.7454	2.6893	2.6351	2.5320	2.4356	2.0352
6	5.4172	5.2421	5.0757	4.9173	4.7665	4.6229	4.3553	4.1114	3.8887	3.6847	3.4976	3.3255	3.1669	3.0205	2.9514	2.8850	2.7594	2.6427	2.1680
7	6.2303	6.0021	5.7864	5.5824	5.3893	5.2064	4.8684	4.5638	4.2883	4.0386	3.8115	3.6046	3.4155	3.2423	3.1611	3.0833	2.9370	2.8021	2.2628
8	7.0197	6.7327	6.4632	6.2098	5.9713	5.7466	5.3349	4.9676	4.6389	4.3436	4.0776	3.8372	3.6193	3.4212	3.3289	3.2407	3.0758	2.9247	2.3306
9	7.7861	7.4353	7.1078	6.8017	6.5152	6.2469	5.7590	5.3282	4.9464	4.6065	4.3030	4.0310	3.7863	3.5655	3.4631	3.3657	3.1842	3.0190	2.3790
10	8.5302	8.1109	7.7217	7.3601	7.0236	6.7101	6.1446	5.6502	5.2161	4.8332	4.4941	4.1925	3.9232	3.6819	3.5705	3.4648	3.2689	3.0915	2.4136
11	9.2526	8.7605	8.3064	7.8869	7.4987	7.1390	6.4951	5.9377	5.4527	5.0286	4.6560	4.3271	4.0354	3.7757	3.6564	3.5435	3.3351	3.1473	2.4383
12	9.9540	9.3851	8.8633	8.3838	7.9427	7.5361	6.8137	6.1944	5.6603	5.1971	4.7932	4.4392	4.1274	3.8514	3.7251	3.6059	3.3868	3.1903	2.4559
13	10.6350	9.9856	9.3936	8.8527	8.3577	7.9038	7.1034	6.4235	5.8424	5.3423	4.9095	4.5327	4.2028	3.9124	3.7801	3.6555	3.4272	3.2233	2.4685
14	11.2961	10.5631	9.8986	9.2950	8.7455	8.2442	7.3667	6.6282	6.0021	5.4675	5.0081	4.6106	4.2646	3.9616	3.8241	3.6949	3.4587	3.2487	2.4775
15	11.9379	11.1184	10.3797	9.7122	9.1079	8.5595	7.6061	6.8109	6.1422	5.5755	5.0916	4.6755	4.3152	4.0013	3.8593	3.7261	3.4834	3.2682	2.4839
16	12.5611	11.6523	10.8378	10.1059	9.4466	8.8514	7.8237	6.9740	6.2651	5.6685	5.1624	4.7296	4.3567	4.0333	3.8874	3.7509	3.5026	3.2832	2.4885
17	13.1661	12.1657	11.2741	10.4773	9.7632	9.1216	8.0216	7.1196	6.3729	5.7487	5.2223	4.7746	4.3908	4.0591	3.9099	3.7705	3.5177	3.2948	2.4918
18	13.7535	12.6593	11.6896	10.8276	10.0591	9.3719	8.2014	7.2497	6.4674	5.8178	5.2732	4.8122	4.4187	4.0799	3.9279	3.7861	3.5294	3.3037	2.4941
19	14.3238	13.1339	12.0853	11.1581	10.3356	9.6036	8.3649	7.3658	6.5504	5.8775	5.3162	4.8435	4.4415	4.0967	3.9424	3.7985	3.5386	3.3105	2.4958
20	14.8775	13.5903	12.4622	11.4699	10.5940	9.8181	8.5136	7.4694	6.6231	5.9288	5.3527	4.8696	4.4603	4.1103	3.9539	3.8083	3.5458	3.3158	2.4970
21	15.4150	14.0292	12.8212	11.7641	10.8355	10.0168	8.6487	7.5620	6.6870	5.9731	5.3837	4.8913	4.4756	4.1212	3.9631	3.8161	3.5514	3.3198	2.4979
22	15.9369	14.4511	13.1630	12.0416	11.0612	10.2007	8.7715	7.6446	6.7429	6.0113	5.4099	4.9094	4.4882	4.1300	3.9705	3.8223	3.5558	3.3230	2.4985
23	16.4436	14.8568	13.4886	12.3034	11.2722	10.3711	8.8832	7.7184	6.7921	6.0442	5.4321	4.9245	4.4985	4.1371	3.9764	3.8273	3.5592	3.3254	2.4989
24	16.9355	15.2470	13.7986	12.5504	11.4693	10.5288	8.9847	7.7843	6.8351	6.0726	5.4509	4.9371	4.5070	4.1428	3.9811	3.8312	3.5619	3.3272	2.4992
25	17.4131	15.6221	14.0939	12.7834	11.6536	10.6748	9.0770	7.8431	6.8729	6.0971	5.4669	4.9476	4.5139	4.1474	3.9849	3.8342	3.5640	3.3286	2.4994
26	17.8768	15.9828	14.3752	13.0032	11.8258	10.8100	9.1609	7.8957	6.9061	6.1182	5.4804	4.9563	4.5196	4.1511	3.9879	3.8367	3.5656	3.3297	2.4996
27	18.3270	16.3296	14.6430	13.2105	11.9867	10.9352	9.2372	7.9426	6.9352	6.1364	5.4919	4.9636	4.5243	4.1542	3.9903	3.8387	3.5669	3.3305	2.4997
28	18.7641	16.6631	14.8981	13.4062	12.1371	11.0511	9.3066	7.9844	6.9607	6.1520	5.5016	4.9697	4.5281	4.1566	3.9923	3.8402	3.5679	3.3312	2.4998
29	19.1885	16.9837	15.1411	13.5907	12.2777	11.1584	9.3696	8.0218	6.9830	6.1656	5.5098	4.9747	4.5312	4.1585	3.9938	3.8414	3.5687	3.3317	2.4999
30	19.6004	17.2920	15.3725	13.7648	12.4090	11.2578	9.4269	8.0552	7.0027	6.1772	5.5168	4.9789	4.5338	4.1601	3.9950	3.8424	3.5693	3.3321	2.4999
40	23.1148	19.7928	17.1591	15.0463	13.3317	11.9246	9.7791	8.2438	7.1050	6.2335	5.5482	4.9966	4.5439	4.1659	3.9995	3.8458	3.5712	3.3332	2.5000

Now, use Table B-2 to obtain the present values of the following ordinary annuities:

1. $1,600 at 20% for 20 years
2. $8,300 at 10% for 12 years
3. $8,000 at 4% for 4 years

Answers:

1. $1,600 × 4.8696 = $7,791.36
2. $8,300 × 6.8137 = $56,553.71
3. $8,000 × 3.6299 = $29,039.20

In particular, note that the higher the interest rate, the lower the present value.

Appendix C   Excerpts from Form 10-K of NIKE, Inc.

SECURITIES AND EXCHANGE COMMISSION
Washington, D.C. 20549

Form 10-K

(Mark One)

☑ **ANNUAL REPORT PURSUANT TO SECTION 13 OR 15(d) OF THE SECURITIES EXCHANGE ACT OF 1934**

For the fiscal year ended May 31, 2008

or

☐ **TRANSITION REPORT PURSUANT TO SECTION 13 OR 15(d) OF THE SECURITIES EXCHANGE ACT OF 1934**

For the transition period from   to   .

Commission File No. 1-10635

NIKE, Inc.
(Exact name of Registrant as specified in its charter)

Oregon	**93-0584541**
(State or other jurisdiction of incorporation)	*(IRS Employer Identification No.)*
One Bowerman Drive	**(503) 671-6453**
Beaverton, Oregon 97005-6453	*(Registrant's Telephone Number, Including Area Code)*
(Address of principal executive offices) (Zip Code)	

Securities registered pursuant to Section 12(b) of the Act:

Class B Common Stock	New York Stock Exchange
(Title of Each Class)	*(Name of Each Exchange on Which Registered)*

Part I

Item 1. *Business*

GENERAL   NIKE, Inc. was incorporated in 1968 under the laws of the state of Oregon. As used in this report, the terms "we", "us", "NIKE" and the "Company" refer to NIKE, Inc. and its predecessors, subsidiaries and affiliates, unless the context indicates otherwise. Our Internet address is *www.nike.com.* On our NIKE Corporate web site, located at *www.nikebiz.com,* we post the following filings as soon as reasonably practicable after they are electronically filed with or furnished to the Securities and Exchange Commission: our annual report on Form 10-K, our quarterly reports on Form 10-Q, our current reports on Form 8-K and any amendments to those reports filed or furnished pursuant to Section 13(a) or 15(d) of the Securities and Exchange Act of 1934, as amended. All such filings on our NIKE Corporate web site are available free of charge. Also available on the NIKE Corporate web site are the charters of the committees of our board of directors, as well as our corporate governance guidelines and code of ethics; copies of any of these documents will be provided in print to any shareholder who submits a request in writing to NIKE Investor Relations, One Bowerman Drive, Beaverton, Oregon 97005-6453.

Our principal business activity is the design, development and worldwide marketing of high quality footwear, apparel, equipment, and accessory products. NIKE is the largest seller of athletic footwear and athletic apparel in the world. We sell our products to retail accounts, through NIKE-owned retail including stores and internet sales, and through a mix of independent distributors and licensees, in over 180 countries around the world. Virtually all of our products are manufactured by independent contractors. Virtually all footwear and apparel products are produced outside the United States, while equipment products are produced both in the United States and abroad.

PRODUCTS   NIKE's athletic footwear products are designed primarily for specific athletic use, although a large percentage of the products are worn for casual or leisure purposes. We place considerable emphasis on high quality construction and innovation in products designed for men, women and children. Running, training, basketball, soccer, sport-inspired urban shoes, and children's shoes are currently our top-selling footwear categories and we expect them to continue to lead in product sales in the near future. We also market shoes designed for aquatic activities, baseball, bicycling, cheerleading, football, golf, lacrosse, outdoor activities, skateboarding, tennis, volleyball, walking, wrestling, and other athletic and recreational uses.

We sell sports apparel and accessories covering most of the above categories, sports-inspired lifestyle apparel, as well as athletic bags and accessory items. NIKE apparel and accessories are designed to complement our athletic footwear products, feature the same trademarks and are sold through the same marketing and distribution channels. We often market footwear, apparel and accessories in "collections" of similar design or for specific purposes. We also market apparel with licensed college and professional team and league logos.

We sell a line of performance equipment under the NIKE brand name, including bags, socks, sport balls, eyewear, timepieces, electronic devices, bats, gloves, protective equipment, golf clubs, and other equipment designed for sports activities. We also have agreements for licensees to produce and sell NIKE brand swimwear, team sports apparel, training equipment, children's clothing, electronic devices, eyewear, golf accessories, and belts. We also sell small amounts of various plastic products to other manufacturers through our wholly-owned subsidiary, NIKE IHM, Inc.

UNITED STATES MARKET   In fiscal 2008, sales in the United States including U.S. sales of Cole Haan, Converse, Exeter Brands Group (which we sold in December, 2007), Hurley, Umbro, NIKE Bauer Hockey (which we sold in April, 2008) and NIKE Golf accounted for approximately 43 percent of total revenues, compared to 47 percent in fiscal 2007 and 47 percent in fiscal 2006. We estimate that we sell to more than 25,000 retail accounts in the United States. The NIKE brand domestic retail account base includes a mix of footwear stores, sporting goods stores, athletic specialty stores, department stores, skate, tennis and golf shops, and other retail accounts. During fiscal year 2008, our three largest customers accounted for approximately 24 percent of NIKE brand sales in the United States.

We utilize 18 NIKE sales offices to solicit sales in the United States. We also utilize 4 independent sales representatives to sell specialty products for golf, and 2 for skating and outdoor products. In addition, we sell NIKE brand products through our internet website, *www.nikestore.com*, and we operate the following retail outlets in the United States:

U.S. Retail Stores	Number
NIKE factory stores (which carry primarily overstock and close-out merchandise)	121
NIKE stores (including one NIKE Women store)	14
NIKETOWNs (designed to showcase NIKE products)	12
NIKE employee-only stores	3
Cole Haan stores (including factory and employee stores)	102
Converse stores (including factory and employee stores)	35
Hurley stores	9
Total	296

NIKE's United States distribution centers for footwear are located in Wilsonville, Oregon, and Memphis, Tennessee. Apparel and equipment products are shipped from our Memphis,

Tennessee, Tigard, Oregon, and Foothill Ranch, California distribution centers. Cole Haan products are distributed primarily from Greenland, New Hampshire, Converse products are shipped from Ontario, California, and Hurley products are distributed from Irvine, California.

INTERNATIONAL MARKETS   In fiscal 2008, non-U.S. sales (including non-U.S. sales of Cole Haan, Converse, Exeter Brands Group, Hurley, NIKE Bauer Hockey, Umbro, and NIKE Golf) accounted for 57 percent of total revenues, compared to 53 percent in fiscal 2007 and 53 percent in fiscal 2006. We sell our products to retail accounts, through NIKE-owned retail stores, and through a mix of independent distributors and licensees around the world. We estimate that we sell to more than 27,000 retail accounts outside the United States, excluding sales by independent distributors and licensees. We operate 11 distribution centers outside of the United States. In many countries and regions, including Canada, Asia, some Latin American countries, and Europe, we have a futures ordering program for retailers similar to the United States futures program described above. NIKE's three largest customers outside of the U.S. accounted for approximately 9 percent of total non-U.S. sales.

We operate the following retail outlets outside the United States:

Non-U.S. Retail Stores	Number
NIKE factory stores	141
NIKE stores	46
NIKETOWNs	3
NIKE employee-only stores	12
Cole Haan stores	57
Hurley stores	1
Total	260

International branch offices and subsidiaries of NIKE are located in Argentina, Australia, Austria, Belgium, Brazil, Bulgaria, Canada, Chile, Croatia, Cyprus, Czech Republic, Denmark, Finland, France, Germany, Greece, Hong Kong, Hungary, Indonesia, India, Ireland, Israel, Italy, Japan, Korea, Lebanon, Macau, Malaysia, Mexico, New Zealand, the Netherlands, Norway, People's Republic of China, the Philippines, Poland, Portugal, Russia, Singapore, Slovakia, Slovenia, South Africa, Spain, Sri Lanka, Sweden, Switzerland, Taiwan, Thailand, Turkey, the United Arab Emirates, the United Kingdom, Uruguay and Vietnam.

MANUFACTURING   Virtually all of our footwear is produced outside of the United States. In fiscal 2008, contract suppliers in China, Vietnam, Indonesia and Thailand manufactured 36 percent, 33 percent, 21 percent and 9 percent of total NIKE brand footwear, respectively. We also have manufacturing agreements with independent factories in Argentina, Brazil, India, Italy, and South Africa to manufacture footwear for sale primarily within those countries. Our largest single footwear factory accounted for approximately 6 percent of total fiscal 2008 footwear production.

Almost all of NIKE brand apparel production was manufactured outside of the United States by independent contract manufacturers located in 34 countries. Most of this apparel production occurred in China, Thailand, Indonesia, Malaysia, Vietnam, Turkey, Sri Lanka, Honduras, Mexico, Taiwan, Israel, Cambodia, India and Bangladesh. Our largest single apparel factory accounted for approximately 8 percent of total fiscal 2008 apparel production.

COMPETITION   The athletic footwear, apparel and equipment industry is keenly competitive in the United States and on a worldwide basis. We compete internationally with an increasing number of athletic and leisure shoe companies, athletic and leisure apparel companies, sports equipment companies, and large companies having diversified lines of athletic and leisure shoes, apparel and equipment, including Adidas, Puma, and others. The intense competition and the rapid changes in technology and consumer preferences in the markets for athletic and leisure footwear and apparel, and athletic equipment, constitute significant risk factors in our operations.

NIKE is the largest seller of athletic footwear and athletic apparel in the world. Performance and reliability of shoes, apparel, and equipment, new product development, price, product identity through marketing and promotion, and customer support and service are important aspects of competition in the athletic footwear, apparel and equipment industry. To help market our products, we contract with prominent and influential athletes, coaches, teams, colleges and sports leagues to endorse our brands and use our products, and we actively sponsor sporting events and clinics. We believe that we are competitive in all of these areas.

EMPLOYEES   We had approximately 32,500 employees at May 31, 2008. Management considers its relationship with employees to be excellent. None of our employees is represented by a union, with the exception of 23 employees in Mexico, the collective bargaining agreement for which expires in 2009. Also, in some countries outside of the United States, local laws require representation for employees by works councils (such as in the EU, in which they are entitled to information and consultation on certain Company decisions) or other representation by an organization similar to a union, although collective bargaining agreements are not involved. There has never been a material interruption of operations due to labor disagreements.

EXECUTIVE OFFICERS OF THE REGISTRANT   The executive officers of NIKE as of July 25, 2008 are as follows:

Philip H. Knight, Chairman of the Board—Mr. Knight, 70, a director since 1968, is a co-founder of NIKE and, except for the period from June 1983 through September 1984, served as its President from 1968 to 1990, and from June 2000 to December 2004. Prior to 1968, Mr. Knight was a certified public accountant with Price Waterhouse and Coopers & Lybrand and was an Assistant Professor of Business Administration at Portland State University.

Mark G. Parker, Chief Executive Officer and President—Mr. Parker, 52, was appointed CEO and President in January 2006. He has been employed by NIKE since 1979 with primary responsibilities in product research, design and development, marketing, and brand management. Mr. Parker was appointed divisional Vice President in charge of development in 1987, corporate Vice President in 1989, General Manager in 1993, Vice President of Global Footwear in 1998, and President of the NIKE Brand in 2001.

David J. Ayre, Vice President, Global Human Resources—Mr. Ayre, 48, joined NIKE as Vice President, Global Human Resources in July 2007. Prior to joining NIKE, he held a number of senior human resource positions with Pepsico, Inc. since 1990, most recently as head of Talent and Performance Rewards.

Lewis L. Bird III, President, Affiliates—Mr. Bird, 44, joined NIKE in July 2006 as President, Affiliates, which currently includes the businesses of Cole Haan, Converse, Hurley, and Umbro. Prior to joining NIKE, he held a number of management positions within multinational companies with diverse brand portfolios. He was Executive Vice President of New Business Development for Gap Inc. from September 2005 to March 2006. Prior to that, Mr. Bird served as Chief Operating Officer of Gap Inc.'s North American division from March 2003 to September 2005, Chief Financial Officer of Gap Inc.'s Old Navy division from 2001 to 2003, Vice President Finance & Operations of Gateway, Inc. from 1999 to 2001, Director of Business Analysis & Planning at AlliedSignal Inc. from 1998 to 1999, and prior to that held financial management positions with AlliedSignal, Ford Motor Company and BayBanks, Inc.

Donald W. Blair, Vice President and Chief Financial Officer—Mr. Blair, 50, joined NIKE in November 1999. Prior to joining NIKE, he held a number of financial management positions with Pepsico, Inc., including Vice President, Finance of Pepsi-Cola Asia, Vice President, Planning of PepsiCo's Pizza Hut Division, and Senior Vice President, Finance of The Pepsi Bottling Group, Inc. Prior to joining Pepsico, Mr. Blair was a certified public accountant with Deloitte, Haskins, and Sells.

Bernard F. Pliska, Vice President, Corporate Controller—Mr. Pliska, 46, joined NIKE as Corporate Controller in 1995. He was appointed Vice President, Corporate Controller in 2003. Prior to NIKE, Mr. Pliska was with Price Waterhouse from 1984 to 1995. Mr. Pliska is a certified public accountant.

Item 2. *Properties*

The following is a summary of principal properties owned or leased by NIKE.

The NIKE World Campus, owned by NIKE and located in Beaverton, Oregon, USA, is a 176 acre facility of 17 buildings which functions as our world headquarters and is occupied by almost 6,000 employees engaged in management, research, design, development, marketing, finance, and other administrative functions from nearly all of our divisions of the Company. We also lease various office facilities in the surrounding metropolitan area. We lease a similar, but smaller, administrative facility in Hilversum, The Netherlands, which serves as the headquarters for the Europe, Middle East and Africa ("EMEA") Region.

There are three significant distribution and customer service facilities for NIKE brand products in the United States. Two of them are located in Memphis, Tennessee, one of which is leased, and one is located in Wilsonville, Oregon, which is also leased. Cole Haan also operates a distribution facility in Greenland, New Hampshire, which is owned by us. Smaller leased distribution facilities for other brands and non-NIKE brand businesses are located in various parts of the United States. We also own or lease distribution and customer service facilities in many parts of the world, the most significant of which are the distribution facilities located in Tomisatomachi, Japan, and in Laakdal, Belgium, both of which we own.

We manufacture NIKE AIR-SOLE cushioning materials and components at NIKE IHM, Inc. manufacturing facilities located in Beaverton, Oregon and St. Charles, Missouri, which are owned by us, and at NIKE (Suzhou) Sports Company, Ltd., facilities in the People's Republic of China, which are owned by us.

Aside from the principal properties described above, we lease 6 production offices outside the United States, over 100 sales offices and showrooms worldwide, and over 70 administrative offices worldwide. We lease approximately 556 retail stores worldwide, which consist primarily of factory outlet stores. *See "United States Market" and "International Markets" on page 4 of this Report.* Our leases expire at various dates through the year 2034.

Item 7. *Management's Discussion and Analysis of Financial Condition and Results of Operations*

OVERVIEW   NIKE designs, develops and markets high quality footwear, apparel, equipment and accessory products worldwide. We are the largest seller of athletic footwear and apparel in the world and sell our products primarily through a combination of retail accounts, NIKE-owned retail, including stores and e-commerce, and independent distributors, franchisees and licensees in the United States and worldwide. Our goal is to deliver value to our shareholders by building a profitable global portfolio of branded footwear, apparel, equipment and accessories businesses. Our strategy is to create long-term revenue growth by creating compelling consumer experiences by creating and delivering innovative, "must have" products; deep personal connections with our brands; and compelling retail presentation.

We strive to convert revenue growth to shareholder value by driving operating excellence in several key areas:

- Making our supply chain a competitive advantage, through operational discipline
- Reducing product costs through a continued focus on lean manufacturing and product design that strives to eliminate waste
- Improving selling and administrative expense productivity by focusing on investments that drive economic returns in the form of incremental revenue and gross margin, and leveraging existing infrastructure across our portfolio of brands to eliminate duplicative costs
- Improving working capital efficiency
- Deploying capital effectively to create value for our shareholders

By executing this strategy, we aim to deliver the following long-term financial goals:

- High single-digit revenue growth;
- Mid-teens earnings per share growth;
- Increased return on invested capital and accelerated cash flows; and
- Consistent results through effective management of our diversified portfolio of businesses.

In fiscal 2008 we met or exceeded these financial goals. Our revenues grew 14% to $18.6 billion, net income grew 26% to $1.9 billion, and we delivered diluted earnings per share of $3.74, a 28% increase versus fiscal 2007. These reported results included combined gains from the sale of our Starter Brand and NIKE Bauer Hockey businesses of $35.4 million, net of tax, in fiscal 2008 and the gain recognized on the sale-leaseback of the Oregon Footwear Distribution Center of $10.0 million, net of tax, in fiscal 2007, one-time tax benefits of $105.4 million and $25.5 million recognized in fiscal 2008 and 2007, respectively, operational losses of $13.3 million, net of tax, from Umbro, which we acquired in the fourth quarter of fiscal 2008, and a $9.6 million gain, net of tax, from the Converse arbitration ruling settlement in fiscal 2007. We estimate that the combination of favorable translation of foreign currency-denominated profits from international businesses and the foreign currency losses included in other (expense) income, net resulted in a year-over-year increase in consolidated income before income taxes of approximately 6%.

For the year, the increase in net income was higher than our rate of revenue growth due to a reduction in our effective tax rate and improved gross margins, partially offset by higher selling and administrative expenses as a percentage of revenue. Fiscal 2008 results were positively affected by a reduction in our effective tax rate of 7.4 percentage points as compared to fiscal 2007, primarily as a result of the $105.4 million one-time tax benefit received in the first quarter of fiscal 2008. Also reflected in the year-over-year effective tax rate improvement was a reduction in our ongoing effective tax rate resulting from our profits earned outside of the United States; our effective tax rates for these operations are generally lower than the U.S. statutory rate. Gross margins for the year grew 110 basis points versus the prior year as inventory management and strategic price increases were partially offset by higher product costs and increased close-out sales. The increase in selling and administrative expenses was attributable to higher investments in growth drivers such as athlete and sport team endorsers of our products, spending around major sporting events, key product initiatives, investments in company owned retail and non-NIKE brand businesses as well as normal wage increases. Our earnings per share for the year grew at a higher rate than net income given lower outstanding shares due to repurchases made under our share repurchase program. In addition, we increased cash flow from operations and continued to return larger amounts of cash to shareholders through higher dividends and increased cash paid for share repurchases. Our return on invested capital increased as compared to fiscal 2007. Although we may not meet all of the financial goals outlined above in any particular fiscal quarter or fiscal year, we continue to believe these are appropriate long-term goals.

RESULTS OF OPERATIONS

	Fiscal 2008	Fiscal 2007	FY08 vs. FY07 % Change	Fiscal 2006	FY07 vs. FY06 % Change
	(In millions, except per share data)[1]				
Revenues	$ 18,627.0	$ 16,325.9	14%	$ 14,954.9	9%
Cost of sales	10,239.6	9,165.4	12%	8,367.9	10%
Gross margin	8,387.4	7,160.5	17%	6,587.0	9%
Gross margin %	45.0%	43.9%		44.0%	
Selling and administrative expense	5,953.7	5,028.7	18%	4,477.8	12%
% of Revenues	32.0%	30.8%		9.9%	
Income before income taxes	2,502.9	2,199.9	14%	2,141.6	3%
Net income	1,883.4	1,491.5	26%	1,392.0	7%
Diluted earnings per share	3.74	2.93	28%	2.64	11%

[1]All per share information has been restated to reflect the two-for-one stock split affected in the form of a 100% common stock dividend distributed on April 2, 2007.

CONSOLIDATED OPERATING RESULTS

Revenues

	Fiscal 2008	Fiscal 2007	FY08 vs. FY07 % Change	Fiscal 2006	FY07 vs. FY06 % Change
	(In millions)				
Revenues	$ 18,627.0	$ 16,325.9	14%	$ 14,954.9	9%

Fiscal 2008 Compared to Fiscal 2007 During fiscal 2008, changes in foreign currency exchange rates contributed 5 percentage points of consolidated revenue growth. Strong demand for NIKE brand products continued to drive revenue growth, as all four of our geographic regions and, on a consolidated basis, all three of our product business units delivered revenue growth. The U.S. Region contributed nearly 2 percentage points of the consolidated revenue growth for fiscal 2008. Excluding the effects of changes in currency exchange rates, our international regions contributed nearly 7 percentage points of the consolidated revenue growth for fiscal 2008, as all of our international regions posted higher revenues. Our Other businesses, comprised of results from Cole Haan, Converse, Exeter Brands Group (whose primary business was the Starter brand business which was sold on December 17, 2007), Hurley International, NIKE Bauer Hockey (which was sold on April 17, 2008), NIKE Golf, and Umbro (which was acquired on March 3, 2008) contributed the remaining consolidated constant-currency revenue growth, as Cole Haan, Converse, Hurley and NIKE Golf posted higher year-over-year revenues.

By product group, our worldwide NIKE brand footwear revenue grew 14% and contributed more than $1.2 billion of incremental revenue for fiscal 2008. Our worldwide NIKE branded apparel and equipment businesses reported revenue growth of 14% and 10% for the year, respectively, and combined added approximately $750 million of incremental revenue. Our Other Businesses reported revenue growth of 15% and combined added more than $330 million of incremental revenue.

Gross Margin

	Fiscal 2008	Fiscal 2007	FY08 vs. FY07 Change	Fiscal 2006	FY07 vs. FY06 Change
			(In millions)		
Gross Margin	$ 8,387.4	$ 7,160.5	17%	$ 6,587.0	9%
Gross Margin %	45.0%	43.9%	110 bps	44.0%	(10)bps

Fiscal 2008 Compared to Fiscal 2007 During fiscal 2008, the primary factors contributing to the 110 basis point increase in the consolidated gross margin percentage versus the prior year were as follows:

1. Higher footwear in-line gross pricing margins, most notably in the U.S. Region, primarily due to strategic price increases;
2. Improved hedge rates relative to the prior year, primarily in the Europe, Middle East and Africa ("EMEA") Region;
3. Higher footwear close-out net pricing margins, most notably in the EMEA Region, primarily due to better inventory management.

The factors driving an increased gross margin percentage were partially offset by lower apparel in-line gross pricing margins primarily driven by higher product costs, most notably in the U.S. and EMEA Regions, and increased apparel close-out sales, primarily in the U.S. Region.

Selling and Administrative Expense

	Fiscal 2008	Fiscal 2007	FY08 vs. FY07 Change	Fiscal 2006	FY07 vs. FY06 Change
			(In millions)		
Operating overhead expense[1]	3,645.4	3,116.3	17%	2,737.6	14%
Demand creation expense[2]	2,308.3	1,912.4	21%	1,740.2	10%
Selling and administrative expense	5,953.7	5,028.7	18%	4,477.8	12%
% of Revenues	32%	30.8%	120 bps	29.9%	90 bps

[1]Fiscal 2008 and fiscal 2007 operating overhead expense includes charges related to stock-based compensation associated with stock options and ESPP shares issued to employees and expensed in accordance with Statement of Financial Accounting Standards ("SFAS") No. 123R "Share Based Payment" ("FAS 123R"). We adopted FAS 123R during the first quarter of fiscal 2007 using the modified prospective transition method. This expense was not reflected in our results of operations for fiscal 2006. *(See Note 1—Summary of Significant Accounting Policies in the Notes to the Consolidated Financial Statements)*

[2]Demand creation consists of advertising and promotion expenses, including costs of endorsement contracts.

Fiscal 2008 Compared to Fiscal 2007 In fiscal 2008, selling and administrative expenses increased as a percentage of revenues by 120 basis points, driven primarily by strategic investments in both demand creation and operating overhead. Changes in currency exchange rates increased selling and administrative expense growth by four percentage points.

On a constant-currency basis, demand creation expense increased 15% versus the prior year. The year-over-year increase was primarily attributable to investments in athlete and sport team endorsers of our products, spending around major sporting events including the 2008 Olympics in Beijing and the European Football Championships, key product initiatives such as Men's Training in the U.S. and retail presentation.

Excluding the effects of changes in exchange rates, operating overhead increased 14% versus the prior year. The increase in operating overhead was attributable to investments in growth drivers such as NIKE-owned retail, non-NIKE brand businesses, emerging markets and normal wage inflation and performance compensation.

We believe total selling and administrative expenses will grow faster than our rate of revenue growth in fiscal 2009 driven primarily by strategic investments in demand creation, including spending around the 2008 Olympics in Beijing and the European Football Championships and increased investments in athlete and team endorsers of our products.

Other (Expense) Income, net

	Fiscal 2008	Fiscal 2007	FY08 vs. FY07 % Change	Fiscal 2006	FY07 vs. FY06 % Change
			(In millions)		
Other (expense) income, net	$ (7.9)	$ 0.9	978%	$ (4.4)	120%

Fiscal 2008 Compared to Fiscal 2007 Other (expense) income, net is comprised substantially of gains and losses from hedging and re-measurement of non-functional currency balances, disposals of fixed assets, as well as other unusual or non-recurring transactions that are outside the normal course of business. Foreign currency hedge gains and losses reported in other (expense) income, net are reflected in the Corporate line in our segment presentation of pre-tax income in the *Notes to Consolidated Financial Statements (Note 17—Operating Segments and Related Information).*

In fiscal 2008, other (expense) income, net included foreign currency hedge losses that were partially offset by the $32.0 million gain on the sale of NIKE Bauer Hockey and the $28.6 million gain on the sale of the Starter brand business. Other (expense) income, net in fiscal 2007 is primarily comprised of the $14.7 million gain on the sale-leaseback of our Oregon footwear distribution center and the $14.2 million benefit from the settlement of the Converse arbitration, partially offset by foreign currency hedge losses.

In fiscal 2008, we estimate that the combination of favorable translation of foreign currency-denominated profits from international businesses and the foreign currency losses included in other (expense) income, net resulted in a year-over-year increase in consolidated income before income taxes of approximately $122 million.

Income Taxes

	Fiscal 2008	Fiscal 2007	FY08 vs. FY07 Change	Fiscal 2006	FY07 vs. FY06 Change
Effective tax rate	24.8%	32.2%	(740) bps	35.0%	(280) bps

Fiscal 2008 Compared to Fiscal 2007 Our effective tax rate for fiscal 2008 was 24.8%, 7.4 percentage points lower than the prior year. Over the last few years, several of our international entities generated losses for which we did not recognize the corresponding tax benefits, as the realization of those benefits was uncertain. In the first quarter of fiscal 2008, we took steps necessary to realize these benefits, resulting in a one-time tax benefit of $105.4 million. Also reflected in the year-over-year effective tax rate improvement was a reduction in our on-going effective tax rate resulting from our profits earned outside the United States; our effective tax rates for these operations are generally lower than the U.S. statutory rate.

OPERATING SEGMENTS   The breakdown of revenues follows:

	Fiscal 2008	Fiscal 2007	FY08 vs. FY07 % Change	Fiscal 2006	FY07 vs. FY06 % Change
			(In millions)		
U.S. Region					
Footwear	$ 4,326.8	$ 4,067.2	6%	$ 3,832.2	6%
Apparel	1,745.1	1,716.1	2%	1,591.6	8%
Equipment	306.1	323.8	(5)%	298.7	8%
Total U.S	6,378.0	6,107.1	4%	5,722.5	7%
EMEA Region					
Footwear	3,112.6	2,608.0	19%	2,454.3	6%
Apparel	2,083.5	1,757.2	19%	1,559.0	13%
Equipment	424.3	358.1	18%	13.3	14%
Total EMEA	5,620.4	4,723.3	19%	4,326.6	9%
Asia Pacific Region					
Footwear	1,499.5	1,159.2	29%	1,044.1	11%
Apparel	1,140.0	909.3	25%	815.6	11%
Equipment	242.2	214.9	13%	194.1	11%
Total Asia Pacific	2,881.7	2,283.4	26%	2,053.8	11%
Americas Region					
Footwear	792.7	679.6	17%	635.3	7%
Apparel	265.4	193.9	37%	201.8	(4)%
Equipment	96.0	79.0	22%	67.8	17%
Total Americas	1,154.1	952.5	21%	904.9	5%
	16,034.2	14,066.3	14%	13,007.8	8%
Other	2,592.8	2,259.6	15%	1,947.1	16%
Total Revenues	$ 18,627.0	$ 16,325.9	14%	$ 14,954.9	9%

The breakdown of income before income taxes ("pre-tax income") follows:

	Fiscal 2008	Fiscal 2007[1]	FY08 vs. FY07 % Change	Fiscal 2006[1]	FY07 vs. FY06 % Change
			(In millions)		
U.S. Region	$ 1,391.9	$ 1,367.3	2%	$ 1,315.2	4%
EMEA Region	1,266.2	1,036.2	22%	992.6	4%
Asia Pacific Region	692.6	508.3	36%	436.4	16%
Americas Region	239.3	192.7	24%	177.6	9%
Other	336.4	299.7	12%	153.6	95%
Corporate	(1,423.5)	(1,204.3)	(18)%	(933.8)	(29)%
Total Pre-tax Income	$ 2,502.9	$ 2,199.9	14%	$ 2,141.6	3%

[1]Certain prior year amounts have been reclassified to conform to fiscal year 2008 presentation. These changes had no impact on previously reported results of operations or shareholders' equity.

The following discussion includes disclosure of pre-tax income for our operating segments. We have reported pre-tax income for each of our operating segments in accordance with SFAS No. 131, "Disclosures about Segments of an Enterprise and Related Information." As discussed in *Note 17—Operating Segments and Related Information* in the accompanying *Notes to Consolidated Financial Statements,* certain corporate costs are not included in pre-tax income of our operating segments.

U.S. Region

	Fiscal 2008	Fiscal 2007	FY08 vs. FY07 % Change	Fiscal 2006	FY07 vs. FY06 % Change
			(In millions)		
Revenues					
Footwear	$ 4,326.8	$ 4,067.2	6%	$ 3,832.2	6%
Apparel	1,745.1	1,716.1	2%	1,591.6	8%
Equipment	306.1	323.8	(5)%	298.7	8%
Total Revenues	$ 6,378.0	$ 6,107.1	4%	$ 5,722.5	7%
Pre-tax Income	$ 1,391.9	$ 1,367.3	2%	$ 1,315.2	4%

Fiscal 2008 Compared to Fiscal 2007 During fiscal 2008, the increase in U.S. footwear revenue was the result of low-single digit growth in unit sales and a slight increase in the average selling price per pair. The growth in unit sales and average selling price per pair was driven by higher demand for our NIKE brand sportswear products and Brand Jordan products, partially offset by a decrease in demand for our NIKE brand basketball products. The increase in average selling price per pair was also attributable to strategic price increases and an increased sales mix of higher priced NIKE brand sportswear and Brand Jordan products.

The year-over-year increase in U.S. apparel revenues during fiscal 2008 reflected an increase in unit sales, mostly offset by lower average selling prices. The increase in unit sales was primarily driven by higher close-out sales and increased demand for NIKE brand sports performance products, partially offset by lower unit sales of sportswear and Brand Jordan products. Average selling prices decreased primarily as a result of a higher mix of close-out sales.

The year-over-year decrease in U.S. equipment revenues during fiscal 2008 was primarily the result of lower unit sales of accessory products and fewer close-out sales.

Pre-tax income for the U.S. Region grew at a slower rate than revenue in fiscal 2008 as a result of higher demand creation and operating overhead expenses, partially offset by higher gross margins, driven by footwear. The increase in demand creation was driven by higher sports marketing expenses and investments in the retail presentation of our key wholesale customers. The increase in operating overhead was attributable to investments in NIKE-owned retail and normal wage inflation.

EMEA Region

	Fiscal 2008	Fiscal 2007	FY08 vs. FY07 % Change	Fiscal 2006	FY07 vs. FY06 % Change
			(In millions)		
Revenues					
Footwear	$ 3,112.6	$ 2,608.0	19%	$ 2,454.3	6%
Apparel	2,083.5	1,757.2	19%	1,559.0	13%
Equipment	424.3	358.1	18%	313.3	14%
Total Revenues	$ 5,620.4	$ 4,723.3	19%	$ 4,326.6	9%
Pre-tax Income	$ 1,266.2	$ 1,036.2	22%	$ 992.6	4%

Fiscal 2008 Compared to Fiscal 2007 For the EMEA Region, changes in currency exchange rates contributed 11 percentage points of the revenue growth during fiscal 2008. Nearly all markets within the region increased revenues during the year. The emerging markets in the region grew nearly 25%, driven by strong results in Russia, Turkey and South Africa. Increases in Northern Europe and the U.K. also contributed significantly to the revenue growth.

Excluding changes in exchange rates, footwear revenues increased 8 percentage points during fiscal 2008 compared to the prior year. The increase in footwear revenue was attributable to double-digit growth in unit sales, partially offset by a low single-digit decrease in the average selling price per pair. The growth in unit sales was driven primarily by higher demand for our NIKE brand soccer and sportswear products. The decrease in average selling price per pair resulted from a shift in product mix from higher priced to lower priced product models, most notably within our NIKE brand sportswear product lines.

On a currency neutral basis, EMEA apparel revenue increased 8 percentage points during fiscal 2008 compared to the prior year, primarily as a result of increased unit sales and a slight increase in average selling prices. The increase in unit sales was driven primarily by increased demand for sports performance products, most notably soccer.

The increase in pre-tax income for the EMEA Region during fiscal 2008 compared to the prior year was primarily driven by the increase in revenues, favorable foreign currency translation and a higher gross margin percentage, partially offset by higher selling and administrative expenses as a percentage of revenues. The gross margin improvement in fiscal 2008 was primarily attributable to improved year-over-year hedge rates and improved margins on close-out product. The increase in selling and administrative expenses was driven by an increase in demand creation spending, primarily attributable to spending around the European Football Championships. As a result of retail expansion and overall business growth across the region, operating overhead expenses increased for the year, but at a slower rate than revenue growth.

Asia Pacific Region

	Fiscal 2008	Fiscal 2007	FY08 vs. FY07 % Change	Fiscal 2006	FY07 vs. FY06 % Change
			(In millions)		
Revenues					
Footwear	$ 1,499.5	$ 1,159.2	29%	$ 1,044.1	11%
Apparel	1,140.0	909.3	25%	815.6	11%
Equipment	242.2	214.9	13%	194.1	11%
Total Revenues	$ 2,881.7	$ 2,283.4	26%	$ 2,053.8	11%
Pre-tax Income	$ 692.6	$ 508.3	36%	$ 436.4	16%

Fiscal 2008 Compared to Fiscal 2007 In the Asia Pacific Region, changes in currency exchange rates contributed 6 percentage points of revenue growth for fiscal 2008. Nearly all countries across the region delivered revenue growth on a currency neutral basis. China continues to be the primary driver of growth within the region as fiscal 2008 revenues increased 50% on a currency-neutral basis, driven by the expansion in both the number of stores selling NIKE product and sales through existing stores. Constant-currency revenues in Japan increased at a low single digit rate during fiscal 2008.

Footwear revenue growth for fiscal 2008 reflected increased unit sales, most notably in China, partially offset by lower average selling prices driven primarily by a shift in mix from higher priced to lower priced models. The year-over-year increase in apparel revenue was driven by increased demand in China.

The increase in pre-tax income for the Asia Pacific Region for fiscal 2008 was driven by higher revenues, improved gross margins and favorable foreign currency translation, which more than offset slightly higher selling and administrative expenses as a percentage of revenue. The gross margin improvement versus the prior year was primarily driven by reduced warehousing costs, improved year-over-year currency hedge rates and improved margins on close-out product. The increase in selling and administrative expenses during fiscal 2008 was primarily attributable to spending around the 2008 Olympics in Beijing. Overall business growth across the region combined with retail expansion, primarily in China, also contributed to an increase in operating overhead expenses, which grew slightly slower than revenues.

Americas Region

	Fiscal 2008	Fiscal 2007	FY08 vs. FY07 % Change	Fiscal 2006	FY07 vs. FY06 % Change
			(In millions)		
Revenues					
Footwear	$ 792.7	$ 679.6	17%	$ 635.3	7%
Apparel	265.4	193.9	37%	201.8	(4)%
Equipment	96.0	79.0	22%	67.8	17%
Total Revenues	$ 1,154.1	$ 952.5	21%	$ 904.9	5%
Pre-tax Income	$ 239.3	$ 192.7	24%	$ 177.6	9%

Fiscal 2008 Compared to Fiscal 2007 In the Americas Region, changes in currency exchange rates contributed 7 percentage points of revenue growth for fiscal 2008. Excluding changes in foreign currency exchange rates, the Americas Region reported growth in all markets, led by Argentina, Mexico and Brazil.

The increase in pre-tax income for fiscal 2008 versus the prior year was primarily attributable to higher revenues, improved gross margins and operating overhead leverage, combined with favorable foreign currency translation. These factors were partially offset by higher demand creation spending as a percentage of revenue. The gross margin improvement was driven primarily by higher in-line net pricing margins resulting from a better mix of products sold and fewer discounts offered in fiscal 2008 compared to fiscal 2007. The increase in demand creation spending during fiscal 2008 was primarily attributable to investments in sports marketing, most notably in soccer, brand events including spending around Run Americas III and investments in the retail presentation of NIKE + and NIKE Pro products.

Other Businesses

	Fiscal 2008	Fiscal 2007	FY08 vs. FY07 % Change	Fiscal 2006	FY07 vs. FY06 % Change
			(In millions)		
Revenues	$2,592.8	$2,259.6	15%	$1,947.1	16%
Pre-tax Income	$ 336.4	$ 299.7	12%	$ 153.6	95%

Fiscal 2008 Compared to Fiscal 2007 The increase in Other business revenues was driven by higher revenues across all businesses, most notably Converse and NIKE Golf. In fiscal 2008, revenues at Converse increased more than 29% versus the prior year to approximately $729 million, driven by strong consumer demand in the United States and internationally, while NIKE Golf grew 12% to nearly $725 million. Revenues at Cole Haan increased 6% to $496 million, driven by strong results at company-owned retail stores. Revenues at Hurley increased 14% to $171 million.

During fiscal 2008, growth at Converse and NIKE Golf, combined with margin improvements across most businesses drove the year-over-year increase in pre-tax income. Fiscal 2007 pre-tax income included a $14.2 million benefit relating to the settlement of an arbitration ruling involving Converse and a former South American licensee. Fiscal 2008 pre-tax income for our Other businesses would have increased approximately 18% versus fiscal 2007 excluding this favorable settlement.

As part of our long term growth strategy, we continually evaluate our existing portfolio of businesses as well as new business opportunities to ensure the Company is investing in those businesses with the largest growth potential and highest returns. On March 3, 2008 we completed the acquisition of 100% of the outstanding shares of Umbro Plc ("Umbro"), a leading United Kingdom-based global soccer brand, for a purchase price of £290.5 million in cash (approximately $576.4 million), inclusive of direct transaction costs. This acquisition is intended to significantly strengthen our market position in the United Kingdom and expand NIKE's global leadership in soccer, a key area of growth for the Company. This acquisition also provides scaled positions in emerging soccer markets such as China, Russia and Brazil. The results of Umbro's operations have been included in the Company's consolidated financial statements and in the Other operating segment since the date of acquisition. Umbro, which was listed on the London Stock Exchange prior to our acquisition, reported in their 2006 annual report that revenues for calendar year 2006 were approximately $276 million (£149.5 million), and estimated that the combination of Umbro's calendar year 2006 wholesale revenue and estimated sales revenue earned by Umbro's licensees from the sale of Umbro products totaled approximately $755 million (£409.4 million).

Following a strategic review of the Company's existing business portfolio, we concluded that the Starter and Bauer Hockey businesses did not align with our long-term growth priorities. On December 17, 2007 we completed the sale of the Starter brand business for $60 million in cash. On April 17, 2008 we completed the sale of the Bauer Hockey business for net proceeds of $189.2 million after working capital adjustments. These transactions resulted in gains of approximately $28.6 million and $32.0 million, respectively, which are reflected in the Corporate line in our segment presentation of pre-tax income in the *Notes to Consolidated Financial Statements (Note 17—Operating Segments).*

LIQUIDITY AND CAPITAL RESOURCES

Fiscal 2008 Cash Flow Activity Cash provided by operations was approximately $1.9 billion in both fiscal 2008 and fiscal 2007. Our primary source of operating cash flow in fiscal 2008 was net income of $1.9 billion. Adjustments for non-cash depreciation and stock-based compensation were offset by increases in deferred income taxes as well as investments in working capital and other assets and liabilities to support growth in the business. The increase in working capital during fiscal 2008 was primarily attributable to an increase in inventories and accounts receivable, partially offset by increases in accounts payable and accrued liabilities. The increase in accounts receivable is attributable to higher sales in the last quarter of 2008. The increase in inventories reflects year-over-year growth in reported futures and higher inventories to support the expansion of NIKE-owned retail stores, slightly offset by better inventory management. The increase in accounts payable and accrued liabilities was primarily due to the timing of payments and inventory receipts compared to the prior year.

Cash used by investing activities was $0.4 billion during fiscal 2008, compared to $0.1 billion provided by investing activities during fiscal 2007. The year-over-year increase in cash used by investing activities was primarily due to our acquisition of Umbro for approximately $0.6 billion offset by proceeds from the divestitures of our NIKE Bauer Hockey and Starter brand businesses of $0.2 billion.

Cash used in financing activities was $1.2 billion during fiscal 2008, compared to $1.1 billion used in fiscal 2007. The increase versus fiscal 2007 was primarily due to an increase in share repurchases and dividends paid, discussed below, partially offset by a decrease in payments of long term debt as we made a $250 million repayment of corporate bonds in fiscal 2007.

In fiscal 2008, we purchased approximately 20.6 million shares of NIKE's Class B Common Stock for $1.2 billion. As of the end of fiscal 2008, we have repurchased 38.6 million shares for $2.1 billion under the $3 billion program approved by our Board of Directors in June 2006. We expect to fund share repurchases from operating cash flow, excess cash and/or debt. The timing and the ultimate amount of shares purchased under the programs will be dictated by our capital needs and stock market conditions.

Dividends declared per share of common stock for fiscal 2008 were $0.875, compared to $0.71 in fiscal 2007. We have paid a dividend every quarter since February 1984. Our current dividend policy is to provide an annual dividend equal to 20% to 30% of the trailing twelve-months' earnings per share, paid out on a quarterly basis. We review our dividend policy from time to time, and based upon current projected earnings and cash flow requirements, we anticipate continuing to pay a quarterly dividend in the foreseeable future.

Off-Balance Sheet Arrangements In connection with various contracts and agreements, we provide routine indemnifications relating to the enforceability of intellectual property rights, coverage for legal issues that arise and other items that fall under the scope of Financial Accounting Standards Board ("FASB") Interpretation No. 45, "Guarantor's Accounting and Disclosure

Requirements for Guarantees, Including Indirect Guarantees of Indebtedness of Others." Currently, we have several such agreements in place. However, based on our historical experience and the estimated probability of future loss, we have determined that the fair value of such indemnifications is not material to our financial position or results of operations.

Contractual Obligations Our significant long-term contractual obligations as of May 31, 2008, and significant endorsement contracts entered into through the date of this report are as follows:

	Cash Payments Due During the Year Ending May 31,						
Description of Commitment	2009	2010	2011	2012	2013	Thereafter	Total
	(In millions)						
Operating Leases	$ 312.4	$ 264.4	$ 228.9	$ 192.1	$ 163.9	$ 692.3	$ 1,854.0
Long-term Debt	6.3	31.3	6.3	153.4	46.3	197.5	441.1
Endorsement Contracts[1]	700.4	599.3	518.3	480.3	407.2	1,122.0	3,827.5
Product Purchase Obligations[2]	2,272.0	1.9	—	—	—	—	2,273.9
Other[3]	250.7	76.4	62.6	55.1	50.7	1.2	496.7
Total	$ 3,541.8	$ 973.3	$ 816.1	$ 880.9	$ 668.1	$ 2,013.0	$ 8,893.2

[1]The amounts listed for endorsement contracts represent approximate amounts of base compensation and minimum guaranteed royalty fees we are obligated to pay athlete and sport team endorsers of our products. Actual payments under some contracts may be higher than the amounts listed as these contracts provide for bonuses to be paid to the endorsers based upon athletic achievements and/or royalties on product sales in future periods. Actual payments under some contracts may also be lower as these contracts include provisions for reduced payments if athletic performance declines in future periods.

In addition to the cash payments, we are obligated to furnish our endorsers with NIKE products for their use. It is not possible to determine how much we will spend on this product on an annual basis as the contracts do not stipulate a specific amount of cash to be spent on the product. The amount of product provided to the endorsers will depend on many factors including general playing conditions, the number of sporting events in which they participate, and our own decisions regarding product and marketing initiatives. In addition, the costs to design, develop, source, and purchase the products furnished to the endorsers are incurred over a period of time and are not necessarily tracked separately from similar costs incurred for products sold to customers.

[2]We generally order product at least four to five months in advance of sale based primarily on advanced futures orders received from customers. The amounts listed for product purchase obligations represent agreements (including open purchase orders) to purchase products in the ordinary course of business, that are enforceable and legally binding and that specify all significant terms. In some cases, prices are subject to change throughout the production process. The reported amounts exclude product purchase liabilities included in accounts payable on the Consolidated Balance Sheet as of May 31, 2008.

[3]Other amounts primarily include service and marketing commitments made in the ordinary course of business. The amounts represent the minimum payments required by legally binding contracts and agreements that specify all significant terms, including open purchase orders for non-product purchases. The reported amounts exclude those liabilities included in accounts payable or accrued liabilities on the Consolidated Balance Sheet as of May 31, 2008.

The total long-term liability for uncertain tax positions was $251.1 million, excluding related interest and penalties, at May 31, 2008. We are not able to reasonably estimate when or if cash payments of the long-term liability for uncertain tax positions will occur.

We also have the following outstanding short-term debt obligations as of May 31, 2008. Please refer to the accompanying *Notes to Consolidated Financial Statements (Note 6—Short-Term Borrowings and Credit Lines)* for further description and interest rates related to the short-term debt obligations listed below.

	Outstanding as of May 31, 2008
	(In millions)
Notes payable, due at mutually agreed-upon dates within one year of issuance or on demand	$ 177.7
Payable to Sojitz America for the purchase of inventories, generally due 60 days after shipment of goods from a foreign port	$ 65.9

As of May 31, 2008, letters of credit of $193.4 million were outstanding, generally for the purchase of inventory.

Capital Resources In October 2001, we filed a shelf registration statement with the SEC under which $1 billion in debt securities may be issued. In May 2002, we commenced a medium-term note program under the shelf registration that allows us to issue up to $500.0 million in medium-term notes as our capital needs dictate. We entered into this program to provide additional liquidity to meet our working capital and general corporate cash requirements and since commencement of the program have issued $240.0 million in medium-term notes. As of May 31, 2008, $215.0 million in medium-term notes remained outstanding. We may issue additional notes under the shelf registration in fiscal 2009 depending on general corporate needs.

During fiscal 2008, one of our Japanese subsidiaries entered into a total of ¥5.0 billion (approximately $47.4 million as of May 31, 2008) in short-term loans to meet general operating needs. The interest rates on the loans are based on the prevailing Tokyo Interbank Offer Rate of our election plus a spread, resulting in a weighted average all-in rate of 1.06% at May 31, 2008.

During fiscal 2007, another of our Japanese subsidiaries entered into a ¥3.0 billion (approximately $28.5 million as of May 31, 2008) loan facility that replaced certain intercompany borrowings. The interest rate on the facility is based on the six-month Japanese Yen London Interbank Offer Rate ("JPY LIBOR") plus a spread resulting in an all in rate of approximately 1.12% at May 31, 2008. This loan facility was renewed during fiscal 2008. Subsequent to May 31, 2008, this loan facility expired and was replaced with intercompany borrowings.

During fiscal 2007, the same Japanese subsidiary entered into a ¥5.0 billion (approximately $47.4 million as of May 31, 2008) term loan that replaced certain intercompany borrowings and matures on February 14, 2012. The interest rate on the loan is approximately 1.5% and interest is paid semi-annually.

As of May 31, 2008, we had no amounts outstanding under our multi-year, $1 billion revolving credit facility in place with a group of banks. The facility matures in December 2012 and can be extended for one additional year on its next anniversary date. Based on our current long-term senior unsecured debt ratings of A+ and A1 from Standard and Poor's Corporation and Moody's Investor Services, respectively, the interest rate charged on any outstanding borrowings would be the prevailing London Interbank Offer Rate ("LIBOR") plus 0.15%. The facility fee is 0.05% of the total commitment.

If our long-term debt rating were to decline, the facility fee and interest rate under our committed credit facility would increase. Conversely, if our long-term debt rating were to improve, the facility fee and interest rate would decrease. Changes in our long-term debt rating would not trigger acceleration of maturity of any then outstanding borrowings or any future borrowings under the committed credit facility. Under this committed credit facility, we have agreed to various covenants. These covenants include limits on our disposal of fixed assets and the amount of debt secured by liens we may incur as well as a minimum capitalization ratio. In the event we were to have any borrowings outstanding under this facility, failed to meet any covenant, and were unable to obtain a waiver from a majority of the banks, any borrowings would become immediately due and payable. As of May 31, 2008, we were in full compliance with each of these covenants and believe it is unlikely we will fail to meet any of these covenants in the foreseeable future.

Liquidity is also provided by our commercial paper program, under which there was no amount outstanding at May 31, 2008 or May 31, 2007. We currently have short-term debt ratings of A1 and P1 from Standard and Poor's Corporation and Moody's Investor Services, respectively.

We currently believe that cash generated by operations, together with access to external sources of funds as described above, will be sufficient to meet our operating and capital needs in the foreseeable future.

Item 8. *Financial Statements and Supplemental Data*

Management of NIKE, Inc. is responsible for the information and representations contained in this report. The financial statements have been prepared in conformity with the generally accepted accounting principles we considered appropriate in the circumstances and include some amounts based on our best estimates and judgments. Other financial information in this report is consistent with these financial statements.

Our accounting systems include controls designed to reasonably assure that assets are safeguarded from unauthorized use or disposition and which provide for the preparation of financial statements in conformity with generally accepted accounting principles. These systems are supplemented by the selection and training of qualified financial personnel and an organizational structure providing for appropriate segregation of duties.

An Internal Audit department reviews the results of its work with the Audit Committee of the Board of Directors, presently consisting of three outside directors. The Audit Committee is responsible for the appointment of the independent registered public accounting firm and reviews with the independent registered public accounting firm, management and the internal audit staff, the scope and the results of the annual examination, the effectiveness of the accounting control system and other matters relating to the financial affairs of NIKE as they deem appropriate. The independent registered public accounting firm and the internal auditors have full access to the Committee, with and without the presence of management, to discuss any appropriate matters.

Management's Annual Report on Internal Control Over Financial Reporting

Management is responsible for establishing and maintaining adequate internal control over financial reporting, as such term is defined in Exchange Act rule 13a-15(f). Under the supervision and with the participation of our Chief Executive Officer and Chief Financial Officer, our management conducted an evaluation of the effectiveness of our internal control over financial reporting based upon the framework in *Internal Control — Integrated Framework* issued by the Committee of Sponsoring Organizations of the Treadway Commission. We have excluded from our evaluation the internal controls over financial reporting of Umbro Ltd., which we acquired on March 3, 2008. As of May 31, 2008 and for the period from March 3, 2008 through May 31, 2008, total assets and total revenues subject to Umbro Ltd.'s internal control over financial reporting represented 7.3% and 0.3% of the Company's consolidated total assets and total revenues, respectively. Based on the results of our evaluation, our management concluded that our internal control over financial reporting was effective as of May 31, 2008.

Internal control over financial reporting cannot provide absolute assurance of achieving financial reporting objectives because of its inherent limitations. Internal control over financial reporting is a process that involves human diligence and compliance and is subject to lapses in judgment and breakdowns resulting from human failures. Internal control over financial reporting also can be circumvented by collusion or improper management override. Because of such limitations, there is a risk that material misstatements may not be prevented or detected on a timely basis by internal control over financial reporting. However, these inherent limitations are known features of the financial reporting process. Therefore, it is possible to design into the process safeguards to reduce, though not eliminate, this risk.

PricewaterhouseCoopers LLP, an independent registered public accounting firm, has audited (1) the consolidated financial statements and (2) the effectiveness of our internal control over financial reporting as of May 31, 2008, as stated in their report herein.

Mark G. Parker
Chief Executive Officer and President

Donald W. Blair
Chief Financial Officer

Report of Independent Registered Public Accounting Firm

To the Board of Directors and Shareholders of NIKE, Inc.:

In our opinion, the consolidated financial statements listed in the index appearing under Item 15(a)(1) present fairly, in all material respects, the financial position of NIKE, Inc. and its subsidiaries at May 31, 2008 and 2007, and the results of their operations and their cash flows for each of the three years in the period ended May 31, 2008 in conformity with accounting principles generally accepted in the United States of America. In addition, in our opinion, the financial statement schedule listed in the appendix appearing under Item 15(a)(2) presents fairly in all material respects, the information set forth therein when read in conjunction with the related consolidated financial statements. Also in our opinion, the Company maintained, in all material respects, effective internal control over financial reporting as of May 31, 2008, based on criteria established in *Internal Control—Integrated Framework* issued by the Committee of Sponsoring Organizations of the Treadway Commission (COSO). The Company's management is responsible for these financial statements and financial statement schedule, for maintaining effective internal control over financial reporting and for its assessment of the effectiveness of internal control over financial reporting, included in Management's Annual Report on Internal Control Over Financial Reporting appearing under Item 8. Our responsibility is to express opinions on these financial statements, on the financial statement schedule, and on the Company's internal control over financial reporting based on our integrated audits. We conducted our audits in accordance with the standards of the Public Company Accounting Oversight Board (United States). Those standards require that we plan and perform the audits to obtain reasonable assurance about whether the financial statements are free of material misstatement and whether effective internal control over financial reporting was maintained in all material respects. Our audits of the financial statements included examining, on a test basis, evidence supporting the amounts and disclosures in the financial statements, assessing the accounting principles used and significant estimates made by management, and evaluating the overall financial statement presentation. Our audit of internal control over financial reporting included obtaining an understanding of internal control over financial reporting, assessing the risk that a material weakness exists, and testing and evaluating the design and operating effectiveness of internal control based on the assessed risk. Our audits also included performing such other procedures as we considered necessary in the circumstances. We believe that our audits provide a reasonable basis for our opinions.

As discussed in Note 1 to the consolidated financial statements, effective June 1, 2006, the Company changed the manner in which it accounts for stock-based compensation in accordance with the Statement of Financial Accounting Standards No. 123R "Share-Based Payment."

A company's internal control over financial reporting is a process designed to provide reasonable assurance regarding the reliability of financial reporting and the preparation of financial statements for external purposes in accordance with generally accepted accounting principles. A company's internal control over financial reporting includes those policies and procedures that (i) pertain to the maintenance of records that, in reasonable detail, accurately and fairly reflect the transactions and dispositions of the assets of the company; (ii) provide reasonable assurance that transactions are recorded as necessary to permit preparation of financial statements in accordance with generally accepted accounting principles, and that receipts and expenditures of the company are being made only in accordance with authorizations of management and directors of the company; and (iii) provide reasonable assurance regarding prevention or timely detection of unauthorized acquisition, use, or disposition of the company's assets that could have a material effect on the financial statements.

Because of its inherent limitations, internal control over financial reporting may not prevent or detect misstatements. Also, projections of any evaluation of effectiveness to future periods are subject to the risk that controls may become inadequate because of changes in conditions, or that the degree of compliance with the policies or procedures may deteriorate.

As described in Management's Annual Report on Internal Control Over Financial Reporting, management has excluded Umbro Ltd. from its assessment of internal control over financial reporting as of May 31, 2008 because it was acquired by the Company in a purchase business combination during fiscal 2008. We have also excluded Umbro Ltd. from our audit of internal control over financial reporting. Umbro Ltd. is a wholly-owned subsidiary whose total assets and total revenues represent 7.3% and 0.3%, respectively, of the related consolidated financial statement amounts as of and for the year ended May 31, 2008.

/s/ PRICEWATERHOUSECOOPERS LLP

Portland, Oregon
July 24, 2008

NIKE, INC.

CONSOLIDATED STATEMENTS OF INCOME

	Year Ended May 31,		
	2008	2007	2006
	(In millions, except per share data)		
Revenues	$ 18,627.0	$ 16,325.9	$ 14,954.9
Cost of sales	10,239.6	9,165.4	8,367.9
Gross margin	8,387.4	7,160.5	6,587.0
Selling and administrative expense	5,953.7	5,028.7	4,477.8
Interest income, net (Notes 1, 6 and 7)	77.1	67.2	36.8
Other (expense) income, net (Notes 15 and 16)	(7.9)	0.9	(4.4)
Income before income taxes	2,502.9	2,199.9	2,141.6
Income taxes (Note 8)	619.5	708.4	749.6
Net income	$ 1,883.4	$ 1,491.5	$ 1,392.0
Basic earnings per common share (Notes 1 and 11)	$ 3.80	$ 2.96	$ 2.69
Diluted earnings per common share (Notes 1 and 11)	$ 3.74	$ 2.93	$ 2.64
Dividends declared per common share	$ 0.875	$ 0.71	$ 0.59

The accompanying notes to consolidated financial statements are an integral part of this statement.

NIKE, INC.

CONSOLIDATED BALANCE SHEETS

	May 31,	
	2008	2007
	(In millions)	
ASSETS		
Current assets:		
Cash and equivalents	$ 2,133.9	$ 1,856.7
Short-term investments	642.2	990.3
Accounts receivable, net	2,795.3	2,494.7
Inventories (Note 2)	2,438.4	2,121.9
Deferred income taxes (Note 8)	227.2	219.7
Prepaid expenses and other current assets	602.3	393.2
Total current assets	8,839.3	8,076.5
Property, plant and equipment, net (Note 3)	1,891.1	1,678.3
Identifiable intangible assets, net (Note 4)	743.1	409.9
Goodwill (Note 4)	448.8	130.8
Deferred income taxes and other assets (Note 8)	520.4	392.8
Total assets	$ 12,442.7	$ 10,688.3
LIABILITIES AND SHAREHOLDERS' EQUITY		
Current liabilities:		
Current portion of long-term debt (Note 7)	$ 6.3	$ 30.5
Notes payable (Note 6)	177.7	100.8
Accounts payable (Note 6)	1,287.6	1,040.3

	May 31,	
	2008	2007
	(In millions)	
Accrued liabilities (Notes 5 and 16)	1,761.9	1,303.4
Income taxes payable	88.0	109.0
Total current liabilities	3,321.5	2,584.0
Long-term debt (Note 7)	441.1	409.9
Deferred income taxes and other liabilities (Note 8)	854.5	668.7
Commitments and contingencies (Notes 14 and 16)	—	—
Redeemable Preferred Stock (Note 9)	0.3	0.3
Shareholders' equity:		
Common stock at stated value (Note 10):		
Class A convertible — 96.8 and 117.6 shares outstanding	0.1	0.1
Class B — 394.3 and 384.1 shares outstanding	2.7	2.7
Capital in excess of stated value	2,497.8	1,960.0
Accumulated other comprehensive income (Note 13)	251.4	177.4
Retained earnings	5,073.3	4,885.2
Total shareholders' equity	7,825.3	7,025.4
Total liabilities and shareholders' equity	$12,442.7	$10,688.3

The accompanying notes to consolidated financial statements are an integral part of this statement.

NIKE, INC.

CONSOLIDATED STATEMENTS OF CASH FLOWS

	Year Ended May 31,		
	2008	2007	2006
	(In millions)		
Cash provided (used) by operations:			
Net income	$ 1,883.4	$ 1,491.5	$ 1,392.0
Income charges not affecting cash:			
Depreciation	303.6	269.7	282.0
Deferred income taxes	(300.6)	34.1	(26.0)
Stock-based compensation (Notes 1 and 10)	141.0	147.7	11.8
Gain on divestitures (Note 15)	(60.6)	—	—
Amortization and other	17.9	0.5	(2.9)
Income tax benefit from exercise of stock options	—	—	54.2
Changes in certain working capital components and other assets and liabilities excluding the impact of acquisition and divestitures:			
Increase in accounts receivable	(118.3)	(39.6)	(85.1)
Increase in inventories	(249.8)	(49.5)	(200.3)
Increase in prepaid expenses and other current assets	(11.2)	(60.8)	(37.2)
Increase in accounts payable, accrued liabilities and income taxes payable	330.9	85.1	279.4
Cash provided by operations	1,936.3	1,878.7	1,667.9

	May 31,		
	2008	2007	2006
	(In millions)		
Cash provided (used) by investing activities:			
Purchases of short-term investments	(1,865.6)	(2,133.8)	(2,619.7)
Maturities of short-term investments	2,246.0	2,516.2	1,709.8
Additions to property, plant and equipment	(449.2)	(313.5)	(333.7)
Disposals of property, plant and equipment	1.9	28.3	1.6
Increase in other assets, net of other liabilities	(21.8)	(4.3)	(34.6)
Acquisition of subsidiary, net of cash acquired (Note 15)	(571.1)	—	—
Proceeds from divestitures (Note 15)	246.0	—	—
Cash (used) provided by investing activities	(413.8)	92.9	(1,276.6)
Cash provided (used) by financing activities:			
Proceeds from issuance of long-term debt	—	41.8	—
Reductions in long-term debt, including current portion	(35.2)	(255.7)	(6.0)
Increase (decrease) in notes payable	63.7	52.6	(18.2)
Proceeds from exercise of stock options and other stock issuances	343.3	322.9	225.3
Excess tax benefits from share-based payment arrangements	63.0	55.8	—
Repurchase of common stock	(1,248.0)	(985.2)	(761.1)
Dividends — common and preferred	(412.9)	(343.7)	(290.9)
Cash used by financing activities	(1,226.1)	(1,111.5)	(850.9)
Effect of exchange rate changes	(19.2)	42.4	25.7
Net increase (decrease) in cash and equivalents	277.2	902.5	(433.9)
Cash and equivalents, beginning of year	1,856.7	954.2	1,388.1
Cash and equivalents, end of year	$ 2,133.9	$ 1,856.7	$ 954.2
Supplemental disclosure of cash flow information:			
Cash paid during the year for:			
Interest, net of capitalized interest	$ 44.1	$ 60.0	$ 54.2
Income taxes	717.5	601.1	752.6
Dividends declared and not paid	112.9	92.9	79.4

The accompanying notes to consolidated financial statements are an integral part of this statement.

NIKE, INC.

CONSOLIDATED STATEMENTS OF SHAREHOLDERS' EQUITY

	Common Stock				Capital in Excess of Stated Value	Accumulated Other Comprehensive Income (Loss)	Retained Earnings	Total
	Class A		Class B					
	Shares	Amount	Shares	Amount				
	(In millions, except per share data)							
Balance at May 31, 2005	143.8	$ 0.1	378.4	$ 2.7	$ 1,171.5	$ 73.4	$ 4,396.5	$ 5,644.2
Stock options exercised			8.0		253.7			253.7
Conversion to Class B Common Stock	(16.0)		16.0					—

NIKE, INC.

CONSOLIDATED STATEMENTS OF SHAREHOLDERS' EQUITY

| | Common Stock | | | | Capital in Excess of Stated Value | Accumulated Other Comprehensive Income (Loss) | Retained Earnings | Total |
| | Class A | | Class B | | | | | |
	Shares	Amount	Shares	Amount				
	(In millions, except per share data)							
Repurchase of Class B Common Stock			(19.0)		(11.3)		(769.9)	(781.2)
Dividends on Common stock ($0.59 per share)							(304.9)	(304.9)
Issuance of shares to employees			1.0		26.9			26.9
Stock-based compensation (Note 10):					11.8			11.8
Forfeiture of shares from employees			(0.2)		(5.3)		(0.3)	(5.6)
Comprehensive income (Note 13):								
Net income							1,392.0	1,392.0
Other comprehensive income:								
Foreign currency translation and other (net of tax benefit of $19.7)						87.1		87.1
Net loss on cash flow hedges (net of tax benefit of $2.8)						(5.6)		(5.6)
Reclassification to net income of previously deferred gains related to hedge derivatives (net of tax expense of $15.3)						(33.2)		(33.2)
Comprehensive income						48.3	1,392.0	1,440.3
Balance at May 31, 2006	127.8	$ 0.1	384.2	$ 2.7	$ 1,447.3	$ 121.7	$ 4,713.4	$ 6,285.2
Stock options exercised			10.7		349.7			349.7
Conversion to Class B Common Stock	(10.2)		10.2					—
Repurchase of Class B Common Stock			(22.1)		(13.2)		(962.0)	(975.2)
Dividends on Common stock ($0.71 per share)							(357.2)	(357.2)
Issuance of shares to employees			1.2		30.1			30.1
Stock-based compensation (Note 10):					147.7			147.7

NIKE, INC.

CONSOLIDATED STATEMENTS OF SHAREHOLDERS' EQUITY

	Common Stock				Capital in Excess of Stated Value	Accumulated Other Comprehensive Income (Loss)	Retained Earnings	Total
	Class A		Class B					
	Shares	Amount	Shares	Amount				
	(In millions, except per share data)							
Forfeiture of shares from employees			(0.1)		(1.6)		(0.5)	(2.1)
Comprehensive income (Note 13):								
Net income							1,491.5	1,491.5
Other comprehensive income:								
Foreign currency translation and other (net of tax expense of $5.4)						84.6		84.6
Net loss on cash flow hedges (net of tax benefit of $9.5)						(38.1)		(38.1)
Reclassification to net income of previously deferred losses related to hedge derivatives (net of tax benefit of $3.6)	—	—	—	—	—	21.4	—	21.4
Comprehensive income						67.9	1,491.5	1,559.4
Adoption of FAS 158 (net of tax benefit of $5.4) (Note 12):						(12.2)		(12.2)
Balance at May 31, 2007	117.6	$ 0.1	384.1	$ 2.7	$ 1,960.0	$ 177.4	$ 4,885.2	$ 7,025.4
Stock options exercised			9.1		372.2			372.2
Conversion to Class B Common Stock	(20.8)		20.8					—
Repurchase of Class B Common Stock			(20.6)		(12.3)		(1,235.7)	(1,248.0)
Dividends on Common stock ($0.875 per share)							(432.8)	(432.8)
Issuance of shares to employees			1.0		39.2			39.2
Stock-based compensation (Notes 1 and 10):					141.0			141.0
Forfeiture of shares from employees			(0.1)		(2.3)		(1.1)	(3.4)
Comprehensive income (Note 13):								
Net income							1,883.4	1,883.4
Other comprehensive income:								
Foreign currency translation and other (net of tax expense of $101.6)						211.9		211.9

NIKE, INC.

CONSOLIDATED STATEMENTS OF SHAREHOLDERS' EQUITY

	Common Stock				Capital in Excess of Stated Value	Accumulated Other Comprehensive Income (Loss)	Retained Earnings	Total
	Class A		Class B					
	Shares	Amount	Shares	Amount				
				(In millions, except per share data)				
Realized foreign currency translation gain due to divestiture (Note 15)						(46.3)		(46.3)
Net loss on cash flow hedges (net of tax benefit of $67.7)						(175.8)		(175.8)
Net loss on net investment hedges (net of tax benefit of $25.1)						(43.5)		(43.5)
Reclassification to net income of previously deferred losses related to hedge derivatives (net of tax benefit of $49.6)						127.7		127.7
Comprehensive income						74.0	1,883.4	1,957.4
Adoption of FIN 48 (Notes 1 and 8)							(15.6)	(15.6)
Adoption of EITF 06-2 Sabbaticals (net of tax benefit of $6.2) (Note 1)							(10.1)	(10.1)
Balance at May 31, 2008	96.8	$ 0.1	394.3	$ 2.7	$ 2,497.8	$ 251.4	$ 5,073.3	$ 7,825.3

The accompanying notes to consolidated financial statements are an integral part of this statement.

NIKE, INC.
NOTES TO CONSOLIDATED FINANCIAL STATEMENTS

Note 1—Summary of Significant Accounting Policies

Basis of Consolidation

The consolidated financial statements include the accounts of NIKE, Inc. and its subsidiaries (the "Company"). All significant intercompany transactions and balances have been eliminated.

Stock Split

On February 15, 2007 the Board of Directors declared a two-for-one stock split of the Company's Class A and Class B common shares, which was effected in the form of a 100% common stock dividend distributed on April 2, 2007. All references to share and per share amounts in the consolidated financial statements and accompanying notes to the consolidated financial statements have been retroactively restated to reflect the two-for-one stock split.

Recognition of Revenues

Wholesale revenues are recognized when the risks and rewards of ownership have passed to the customer, based on the terms of sale. This occurs upon shipment or upon receipt by the customer depending on the country of the sale and the agreement with the customer. Retail store revenues are recorded at the time of sale. Provisions for sales discounts, returns and miscellaneous claims from customers are made at the time of sale.

Shipping and Handling Costs

Shipping and handling costs are expensed as incurred and included in cost of sales.

Advertising and Promotion

Advertising production costs are expensed the first time the advertisement is run. Media (TV and print) placement costs are expensed in the month the advertising appears.

A significant amount of the Company's promotional expenses result from payments under endorsement contracts. Accounting for endorsement payments is based upon specific contract provisions. Generally, endorsement payments are expensed on a straight-line basis over the term of the contract after giving recognition to periodic performance compliance provisions of the contracts. Prepayments made under contracts are included in prepaid expenses or other assets depending on the period to which the prepayment applies.

Through cooperative advertising programs, the Company reimburses its retail customers for certain of their costs of advertising the Company's products. The Company records these costs in selling and administrative expense at the point in time when it is obligated to its customers for the costs, which is when the related revenues are recognized. This obligation may arise prior to the related advertisement being run.

Total advertising and promotion expenses were $2,308.3 million, $1,912.4 million, and $1,740.2 million for the years ended May 31, 2008, 2007 and 2006, respectively. Prepaid advertising and promotion expenses recorded in prepaid expenses and other assets totaled $266.7 million and $253.0 million at May 31, 2008 and 2007, respectively.

Cash and Equivalents

Cash and equivalents represent cash and short-term, highly liquid investments with maturities of three months or less at date of purchase. The carrying amounts reflected in the consolidated balance sheet for cash and equivalents approximate fair value.

Short-Term Investments

Short-term investments consist of highly liquid investments, primarily commercial paper, U.S. Treasury, U.S. agency, and corporate debt securities, with maturities over three months from the date of purchase. Debt securities which the Company has the ability and positive intent to hold to maturity are carried at amortized cost, which approximates fair value. Short-term investments of

$124.9 million and $975.4 million at May 31, 2008 and 2007, respectively, were classified as held-to-maturity and primarily comprised of U.S. Treasury and U.S. agency securities. All held-to-maturity securities at May 31, 2008 have maturity dates within one year.

Available-for-sale debt securities are recorded at fair value with net unrealized gains and losses reported, net of tax, in other comprehensive income, unless unrealized losses are determined to be other than temporary. The Company considers all available-for-sale securities, including those with maturity dates beyond 12 months, as available to support current operational liquidity needs and therefore classifies these securities as current assets within Short-term investments on the consolidated balance sheet. As of May 31, 2008, the Company held $432.3 million of available-for-sale securities with maturity dates within one year and $85.0 million with maturity dates over one year and less than five years.

Investments classified as available-for-sale consist of the following at fair value:

	As of May 31,	
	2008	2007
	(In millions)	
Available-for-sale investments:		
U.S. treasury and agencies	$ 194.1	$ 6.6
Corporate commercial paper and bonds	323.2	8.3
Total available-for-sale investments	$ 517.3	$ 14.9

Included in interest income, net for the years ended May 31, 2008, 2007, and 2006, was interest income of $115.8 million, $116.9 million and $87.3 million, respectively, related to short-term investments and cash and equivalents.

Allowance for Uncollectible Accounts Receivable

Accounts receivable consists principally of amounts receivable from customers. We make ongoing estimates relating to the collectibility of our accounts receivable and maintain an allowance for estimated losses resulting from the inability of our customers to make required payments. In determining the amount of the allowance, we consider our historical level of credit losses and make judgments about the creditworthiness of significant customers based on ongoing credit evaluations. Accounts receivable with anticipated collection dates greater than twelve months from the balance sheet date and related allowances are considered non-current and recorded in other assets. The allowance for uncollectible accounts receivable was $78.4 million and $71.5 million at May 31, 2008 and 2007, respectively, of which $36.7 million and $33.3 million was recorded in other assets.

Inventory Valuation

Inventories related to our wholesale operations are stated at lower of cost or market and valued on a first-in, first-out ("FIFO") or moving average cost basis. Inventories related to our retail operations are stated at the lower of average cost or market using the retail inventory method. Under the retail inventory method, the valuation of inventories at cost is calculated by applying a cost-to-retail ratio to the retail value inventories. Permanent and point of sale markdowns, when recorded, reduce both the retail and cost components of inventory on hand so as to maintain the already established cost-to-retail relationship.

Property, Plant and Equipment and Depreciation

Property, plant and equipment are recorded at cost. Depreciation for financial reporting purposes is determined on a straight-line basis for buildings and leasehold improvements over 2 to 40 years and for machinery and equipment over 2 to 15 years. Computer software (including, in some cases, the cost of internal labor) is depreciated on a straight-line basis over 3 to 10 years.

Impairment of Long-Lived Assets

The Company estimates the future undiscounted cash flows to be derived from an asset to assess whether or not a potential impairment exists when events or circumstances indicate the carrying value of a long-lived asset may be impaired. If the carrying value exceeds the Company's estimate of future undiscounted cash flows, the Company then calculates the impairment as the excess of the carrying value of the asset over the Company's estimate of its fair market value.

Identifiable Intangible Assets and Goodwill

Goodwill and intangible assets with indefinite lives are not amortized but instead are measured for impairment at least annually in the fourth quarter, or when events indicate that an impairment exists. As required by Statement of Financial Accounting Standards ("SFAS") No. 142, "Goodwill and other Intangible Assets" ("FAS 142"), in the Company's impairment test of goodwill, the Company compares the fair value of the applicable reporting unit to its carrying value. The Company estimates the fair value of its reporting units by using a combination of discounted cash flow analysis and comparisons with the market values of similar publicly traded companies. If the carrying value of the reporting unit exceeds the estimate of fair value, the Company calculates the impairment as the excess of the carrying value of goodwill over its implied fair value. In the impairment tests for indefinite-lived intangible assets, the Company compares the estimated fair value of the indefinite-lived intangible assets to the carrying value. The Company estimates the fair value of indefinite-lived intangible assets and trademarks using the relief from royalty approach, which is a standard form of discounted cash flow analysis used for the valuation of trademarks. If the carrying value exceeds the estimate of fair value, the Company calculates impairment as the excess of the carrying value over the estimate of fair value.

Intangible assets that are determined to have definite lives are amortized over their useful lives and are measured for impairment only when events or circumstances indicate the carrying value may be impaired.

Foreign Currency Translation and Foreign Currency Transactions

Adjustments resulting from translating foreign functional currency financial statements into U.S. dollars are included in the foreign currency translation adjustment, a component of accumulated other comprehensive income in shareholders' equity.

Transaction gains and losses generated by the effect of foreign exchange rates on recorded assets and liabilities denominated in a currency different from the functional currency of the applicable Company entity are recorded in other (expense) income, net, in the period in which they occur.

Accounting for Derivatives and Hedging Activities

The Company uses derivative financial instruments to limit exposure to changes in foreign currency exchange rates and interest rates. The Company accounts for derivatives pursuant to SFAS No. 133, "Accounting for Derivative Instruments and Hedging Activities," as amended and interpreted ("FAS 133"). FAS 133 establishes accounting and reporting standards for derivative instruments and requires that all derivatives be recorded at fair value on the balance sheet. Changes in the fair value of derivative financial instruments are either recognized in other comprehensive income (a component of shareholders' equity) or net income depending on whether the derivative is being used to hedge changes in cash flows or fair value.

See Note 16 for more information on the Company's Risk Management program and derivatives.

Stock-Based Compensation

On June 1, 2006, the Company adopted SFAS No. 123R "Share-Based Payment" ("FAS 123R") which requires the Company to record expense for stock-based compensation to employees using a fair value method. Under FAS 123R, the Company estimates the fair value of options granted under the NIKE, Inc. 1990 Stock Incentive Plan (the "1990 Plan") (see Note 10) and employees' purchase rights under the Employee Stock Purchase Plans ("ESPPs") using the Black-Scholes option pricing model. The Company recognizes this fair value, net of estimated forfeitures, as selling and administrative expense in the Consolidated Statements of Income over the vesting period using the straight-line method.

The Company has adopted the modified prospective transition method prescribed by FAS 123R, which does not require the restatement of financial results for previous periods. In accordance with this transition method, the Company's Consolidated Statement of Income for the year ended May 31, 2008 and 2007 includes (1) amortization of outstanding stock-based compensation granted prior to, but not vested, as of June 1, 2006, based on the fair value estimated in accordance with the original provisions of SFAS No. 123, "Accounting for Stock-Based Compensation" ("FAS 123") and (2) amortization of all stock-based awards granted subsequent to June 1, 2006, based on the fair value estimated in accordance with the provisions of FAS 123R.

The following table summarizes the Company's total stock-based compensation expense recognized in selling and administrative expense:

	Year Ended May 31,		
	2008	2007	2006
	(in millions)		
Stock options[1]	$127.0	$134.9	$ 0.3
ESPPs	7.2	7.0	—
Restricted stock	6.8	5.8	11.5
Total stock-based compensation expense	$141.0	$147.7	$11.8

[1]In accordance with FAS 123R, stock-based compensation expense reported during the years ended May 31, 2008 and 2007 includes $40.7 million and $36.3 million, respectively, of accelerated stock-based compensation expense recorded for employees eligible for stock option vesting upon retirement.

Prior to the adoption of FAS 123R, the Company used the intrinsic value method to account for stock options and ESPP shares in accordance with Accounting Principles Board Opinion No. 25, "Accounting for Stock Issued to Employees" as permitted by FAS 123. If the Company had instead accounted for stock options and ESPP shares issued to employees using the fair value method prescribed by FAS 123 during the year ended May 31, 2006 the Company's pro forma net income and pro forma earnings per share would have been reported as follows:

	Year Ended May 31, 2006
	(In millions, except per share data)
Net income as reported	$1,392.0
Add: Stock option expense included in reported net income, net of tax	0.2
Deduct: Total stock option and ESPP expense under fair value based method for all awards, net of tax[1]	(76.8)
Pro forma net income	$1,315.4
Earnings per share:	
Basic — as reported	$ 2.69
Basic — pro forma	2.54
Diluted — as reported	2.64
Diluted — pro forma	2.50

[1]Accelerated stock-based compensation expense for options subject to accelerated vesting due to employee retirement is not included in the pro forma figures shown above for the year ended May 31, 2006. This disclosure reflects the expense of such options ratably over the stated vesting period or upon actual employee retirement. Had the Company recognized the fair value for such stock options on an accelerated basis in this pro forma disclosure, the Company would have recognized additional stock-based compensation expense of $17.5 million, net of tax, or $0.03 per diluted share for the year ended May 31, 2006.

To calculate the excess tax benefits available for use in offsetting future tax shortfalls as of the date of implementation, the Company is following the alternative transition method discussed in FASB Staff Position No. 123R-3, "Transition Election Relating to Accounting for the Tax Effects of Share-Based Payment Awards."

See Note 10 for more information on the Company's stock programs.

Income Taxes

The Company accounts for income taxes using the asset and liability method. This approach requires the recognition of deferred tax assets and liabilities for the expected future tax consequences of temporary differences between the carrying amounts and the tax basis of assets and liabilities. United States income taxes are provided currently on financial statement earnings of non-U.S. subsidiaries that are expected to be repatriated. The Company determines annually the amount of undistributed non-U.S. earnings to invest indefinitely in its non-U.S. operations. The Company recognizes interest and penalties related to income tax matters in income tax expense. See Note 8 for further discussion.

Earnings Per Share

Basic earnings per common share is calculated by dividing net income by the weighted average number of common shares outstanding during the year. Diluted earnings per common share is calculated by adjusting weighted average outstanding shares, assuming conversion of all potentially dilutive stock options and awards. See Note 11 for further discussion.

Management Estimates

The preparation of financial statements in conformity with generally accepted accounting principles requires management to make estimates, including estimates relating to assumptions that affect the reported amounts of assets and liabilities and disclosure of contingent assets and liabilities at the date of financial statements and the reported amounts of revenues and expenses during the reporting period. Actual results could differ from these estimates.

Reclassifications

Certain prior year amounts have been reclassified to conform to fiscal year 2008 presentation. These changes had no impact on previously reported results of operations or shareholders' equity.

Note 2—Inventories

Inventory balances of $2,438.4 million and $2,121.9 million at May 31, 2008 and 2007, respectively, were substantially all finished goods.

Note 3—Property, Plant and Equipment

Property, plant and equipment includes the following:

	May 31,	
	2008	2007
	(In millions)	
Land	$ 209.4	$ 193.8
Buildings	934.6	840.9
Machinery and equipment	2,005.0	1,817.2
Leasehold improvements	757.3	672.8
Construction in process	196.7	94.4
	4,103.0	3,619.1
Less accumulated depreciation	2,211.9	1,940.8
	$ 1,891.1	$ 1,678.3

Capitalized interest was not material for the years ended May 31, 2008, 2007 and 2006.

Note 4—Identifiable Intangible Assets and Goodwill:

The following table summarizes the Company's identifiable intangible assets balances as of May 31, 2008 and May 31, 2007:

	May 31, 2008			May 31, 2007		
	Gross Carrying Amount	Accumulated Amortization	Net Carrying Amount	Gross Carrying Amount	Accumulated Amortization	Net Carrying Amount
	(In millions)					
Amortized intangible assets:						
Patents	$ 47.5	$ (14.4)	$ 33.1	$ 44.1	$ (12.3)	$ 31.8
Trademarks	13.2	(7.8)	5.4	49.8	(17.5)	32.3
Other	65.2	(19.7)	45.5	21.6	(17.3)	4.3
Total	$ 125.9	$ (41.9)	$ 84.0	$ 115.5	$ (47.1)	$ 68.4
Unamortized intangible assets—Trademarks	———		$ 659.1			$ 341.5
Total	══		$ 743.1			$ 409.9

Amortization expense of identifiable assets with definite lives, which is included in selling and administrative expense, was $9.2 million, $9.9 million and $9.8 million for the years ended May 31, 2008, 2007, and 2006, respectively. The estimated amortization expense for intangible assets subject to amortization for each of the years ending May 31, 2009 through May 31, 2013 is as follows: 2009: $9.0 million; 2010: $8.6 million; 2011: $8.2 million; 2012: $7.5 million; 2013: $5.7 million.

During the fourth quarter ended May 31, 2008 the Company completed the acquisition of Umbro Plc ("Umbro"). As a result, $378.4 million was allocated to unamortized trademarks, $319.2 million was allocated to goodwill and $41.1 million was allocated to other amortized intangible assets consisting of Umbro's sourcing network, established customer relationships and the United Soccer League Franchise. The gross carrying amount of unamortized and amortized trademarks were reduced by $59.6 million and $37.5 million, respectively, as a result of our divestitures of the Starter brand business and NIKE Bauer Hockey Corp. during the year ended May 31, 2008. See Note 15 for more information on the Company's acquisition and divestitures.

The following table summarizes the Company's goodwill balances as of May 31, 2008 and May 31, 2007 (in millions):

Goodwill, May 31, 2007	$ 130.8
Acquisition of Umbro Plc (Note 15)	319.2
Other[1]	(1.2)
Goodwill, May 31, 2008	$ 448.8

[1]Other consists of foreign currency translation adjustments on Umbro goodwill.

Note 5—Accrued Liabilities

Accrued liabilities include the following:

	May 31,	
	2008	2007
	(In millions)	
Compensation and benefits, excluding taxes	$ 538.0	$ 451.6
Endorser compensation	203.5	139.9
Fair value of derivatives	173.3	90.5
Taxes other than income taxes	147.6	133.4
Advertising and marketing	121.4	70.6
Dividends payable	112.9	92.9
Import and logistics costs	78.8	81.4
Other[1]	386.4	243.1
	$ 1,761.9	$ 1,303.4

[1]Other consists of various accrued expenses and no individual item accounted for more than $65 million of the balance at May 31, 2008 or 2007.

Note 6—Short-Term Borrowings and Credit Lines

Notes payable to banks and interest-bearing accounts payable to Sojitz Corporation of America ("Sojitz America") as of May 31, 2008 and 2007, are summarized below:

	May 31,			
	2008		2007	
	Borrowings	Interest Rate	Borrowings	Interest Rate
	(In millions)			
Notes payable:				
U.S. operations	$ 18.6	0.00%[1]	$ 14.6	0.00%[1]
Non-U.S. operations	159.1	6.80%	86.2	9.85%
	$ 177.7		$ 100.8	
Sojitz America	$ 65.9	3.51%	$ 44.6	6.09%

[1]Weighted average interest rate includes non-interest bearing overdrafts.

The carrying amounts reflected in the consolidated balance sheet for notes payable approximate fair value.

The Company purchases through Sojitz America certain athletic footwear, apparel and equipment it acquires from non-U.S. suppliers. These purchases are for the Company's operations outside of the United States, the Europe, Middle East, and Africa Region and Japan. Accounts payable to Sojitz America are generally due up to 60 days after shipment of goods from the foreign port. The interest rate on such accounts payable is the 60-day London Interbank Offered Rate ("LIBOR") as of the beginning of the month of the invoice date, plus 0.75%.

The Company had no borrowings outstanding under its commercial paper program at May 31, 2008 and 2007.

In December 2006, the Company entered into a $1 billion revolving credit facility with a group of banks. The facility matures in December 2012 and can be extended for one additional year on its next anniversary date. Based on the Company's current long-term senior unsecured debt ratings of A+ and A2 from Standard and Poor's Corporation and Moody's Investor Services, respectively, the interest rate charged on any outstanding borrowings would be the prevailing London Interbank Offer Rate ("LIBOR") plus 0.15%. The facility fee is 0.05% of the total commitment. Under this agreement, the Company must maintain, among other things, certain minimum specified financial ratios with which the Company was in compliance at May 31, 2008. No amounts were outstanding under these facilities as of May 31, 2008 or 2007.

During the year ended May 31, 2008, one of the Company's Japanese subsidiaries entered into a total of ¥5.0 billion (approximately $47.4 million as of May 31, 2008) in short-term loans to meet general operating needs. The interest rates on the loans are based on the prevailing Tokyo Interbank Offer Rate of our election plus a spread, resulting in a weighted average all-in rate of 1.06% at May 31, 2008.

In January 2007, another one of the Company's Japanese subsidiaries entered into a ¥3.0 billion (approximately $28.5 million as of May 31, 2008) loan facility that replaced certain intercompany borrowings. The interest rate on the facility is based on the six-month Japanese Yen London Interbank Offer Rate plus a spread resulting in an all-in-rate of approximately 1.12% at May 31, 2008. The loan facility was replaced with intercompany borrowings subsequent to May 31, 2008.

Note 7—Long-Term Debt

Long-term debt includes the following:

	May 31,	
	2008	2007
	(In millions)	
4.8% Corporate Bond, payable July 9, 2007	—	$ 25.0
5.375% Corporate Bond, payable July 8, 2009	25.5	24.8
5.66% Corporate Bond, payable July 23, 2012	26.1	24.8
5.4% Corporate Bond, payable August 7, 2012	15.4	14.6
4.7% Corporate Bond, payable October 1, 2013	50.0	50.0
5.15% Corporate Bonds, payable October 15, 2015	104.5	99.6
4.3% Japanese yen note, payable June 26, 2011	99.6	86.4
1.5% Japanese yen note, payable February 14, 2012	47.4	41.1
2.6% Japanese yen note, maturing August 20, 2001 through November 20, 2020	54.5	51.2
2.0% Japanese yen note, maturing August 20, 2001 through November 20, 2020	24.4	22.9
Total	447.4	440.4
Less current maturities	6.3	30.5
	$ 441.1	$ 409.9

The fair value of long-term debt is estimated using discounted cash flow analyses, based on the Company's incremental borrowing rates for similar types of borrowing arrangements. The fair value of the Company's long-term debt, including current portion, is approximately $450.8 million at May 31, 2008 and $443.2 million at May 31, 2007.

Since 2001, the Company has had an effective shelf registration statement with the Securities and Exchange Commission for $1 billion of debt securities. The Company has a medium-term note program under the shelf registration ("medium-term note program") that allows the Company to issue up to $500 million in medium-term notes. Since commencement of this program, the Company has issued $240 million in medium-term notes of which $215 million and $240 million were outstanding as of May 31, 2008 and 2007, respectively. The issued notes have coupon rates that range from 4.70% to 5.66%. The remaining maturities range from July 8, 2009 to October 15, 2015. For each of these notes, except for the swap for the $50 million note maturing October 1, 2013, the Company has entered into interest rate swap agreements whereby the Company receives fixed interest payments at the same rate as the notes and pays variable interest payments based on the three-month or six-month LIBOR plus a spread. Each swap has the same notional amount and maturity date as the corresponding note. The swap for the $50 million note maturing October 1, 2013, expired October 2, 2006. At May 31, 2008, the interest rates payable on these swap agreements range from approximately 2.6% to 3.5%.

In June 1996, one of the Company's Japanese subsidiaries, NIKE Logistics YK, borrowed ¥10.5 billion (approximately $99.6 million as of May 31, 2008) in a private placement with a maturity of June 26, 2011. Interest is paid semi-annually. The agreement provides for early retirement after year ten.

In July 1999, NIKE Logistics YK assumed ¥13.0 billion in loans as part of its agreement to purchase a distribution center in Japan, which serves as collateral for the loans. These loans mature in equal quarterly installments during the period August 20, 2001 through November 20, 2020. Interest is also paid quarterly. As of May 31, 2008, ¥8.3 billion in loans were outstanding (approximately $78.9 million).

In February 2007, NIKE Logistics YK entered into a ¥5.0 billion (approximately $47.4 million as of May 31, 2008) term loan that replaced certain intercompany borrowings and matures on February 14, 2012. The interest rate on the loan is approximately 1.5% and interest is paid semi-annually.

Amounts of long-term debt maturities in each of the years ending May 31, 2009 through 2013 are $6.3 million, $31.3 million, $6.3 million, $153.4 million and $46.3 million, respectively.

Note 8—Income Taxes

Income before income taxes is as follows:

	Year Ended May 31,		
	2008	2007	2006
	(In millions)		
Income before income taxes:			
United States	$ 713.0	$ 805.1	$ 838.6
Foreign	1,789.9	1,394.8	1,303.0
	$ 2,502.9	$ 2,199.9	$ 2,141.6

The provision for income taxes is as follows:

	Year Ended May 31,		
	2008	2007	2006
	(In millions)		
Current:			
United States			
Federal	$ 469.9	$ 352.6	$ 359.0
State	58.4	59.6	60.6
Foreign	391.8	261.9	356.0
	920.1	674.1	775.6

	Year Ended May 31,		
	2008	2007	2006
	(In millions)		
Deferred:			
United States			
Federal	(273.0)	38.7	(4.2)
State	(5.0)	(4.8)	(6.8)
Foreign	(22.6)	0.4	(15.0)
	(300.6)	34.3	(26.0)
	$ 619.5	$ 708.4	$ 749.6

Deferred tax assets and (liabilities) are comprised of the following:

	May 31,	
	2008	2007
	(In millions)	
Deferred tax assets:		
Allowance for doubtful accounts	$ 13.1	$ 12.4
Inventories	49.2	45.8
Sales return reserves	49.2	42.1
Deferred compensation	158.4	132.5
Stock-based compensation	55.2	30.3
Reserves and accrued liabilities	57.0	46.2
Property, plant, and equipment	7.9	16.3
Foreign loss carry-forwards	40.1	37.5
Foreign tax credit carry-forwards	91.9	3.4
Hedges	42.9	26.2
Other	40.5	33.0
Total deferred tax assets	605.4	425.7
Valuation allowance	(40.7)	(42.3)
Total deferred tax assets after valuation allowance	564.7	383.4
Deferred tax liabilities:		
Undistributed earnings of foreign subsidiaries	(113.2)	(232.6)
Property, plant and equipment	(67.4)	(66.1)
Intangibles	(214.2)	(97.2)
Hedges	(1.3)	(2.5)
Other	(0.7)	(17.8)
Total deferred tax liability	(396.8)	(416.2)
Net deferred tax asset (liability)	$ 167.9	$ (32.8)

A reconciliation from the U.S. statutory federal income tax rate to the effective income tax rate follows:

	Year Ended May 31,		
	2008	2007	2006
Federal income tax rate	35.0 %	35.0 %	35.0 %
State taxes, net of federal benefit	1.4	1.6	1.5
Foreign earnings	(12.9)	(4.1)	(1.5)
Other, net	1.3	(0.3)	—
Effective income tax rate	24.8%	32.2%	35.0%

The effective tax rate for the year ended May 31, 2008 of 24.8% decreased from the fiscal 2007 effective tax rate of 32.2%. Over the last few years, a number of international entities generated losses for which the Company did not recognize offsetting tax benefits because the realization of those benefits was uncertain. The necessary steps to realize these benefits have now been taken resulting in a one-time reduction of the effective tax rate for the year ended May 31, 2008 of 4.2 percentage points. Also reflected in the effective tax rate for the year ended May 31, 2008 is a reduction in our on-going effective tax rate resulting from our operations outside of the United States; our tax rates on these operations are generally lower than the U.S. statutory rate. The effective tax rate for the year ended May 31, 2007 of 32.2% decreased from the fiscal 2006 effective tax rate of 35.0%. The decrease is primarily due to a European tax agreement entered into during the three months ended November 30, 2006. The Company recorded a retroactive benefit for the European tax agreement during the year ended May 31, 2007.

The Company adopted FIN 48 effective June 1, 2007. Upon adoption, the Company recognized an additional long-term liability of $89.4 million for unrecognized tax benefits, $15.6 million of which was recorded as a reduction to the Company's beginning retained earnings, and the remaining $73.8 million was recorded as a reduction to the Company's noncurrent deferred tax liability. In addition, the Company reclassified $12.2 million of unrecognized tax benefits from income taxes payable to other long term liabilities in conjunction with the adoption of FIN 48.

At the adoption date of June 1, 2007, the Company had $122.5 million of gross unrecognized tax benefits, excluding related interest and penalties, $30.7 million of which would affect the Company's effective tax rate if recognized in future periods. Including related interest and penalties and net of federal benefit of interest and unrecognized state tax benefits, at June 1, 2007, the Company had $135.0 million of total unrecognized tax benefits, $52.0 million of which would affect the Company's effective tax rate if recognized in future periods. As of May 31, 2008, the total gross unrecognized tax benefits, excluding related interest and penalties, were $251.1 million, $60.6 million of which would affect the Company's effective tax rate if recognized in future periods. The Company does not anticipate that total unrecognized tax benefits will change significantly within the next 12 months.

The following is a reconciliation of the changes in the gross balance of unrecognized tax benefits for the year (in millions):

Unrecognized tax benefits — June 1, 2007	$ 122.5
Gross increases related to prior period tax positions	71.6
Gross decreases related to prior period tax positions	(23.1)
Gross increases related to current period tax positions	87.7
Settlements	(13.4)
Lapse of statute of limitations	(0.7)
Changes due to currency translation	6.5
Unrecognized tax benefits — May 31, 2008	$ 251.1

The Company is subject to taxation primarily in the United States, China and the Netherlands as well as various state and other foreign jurisdictions. The Company has concluded substantially all U.S. federal income tax matters through fiscal year 2004. The Company is currently under audit by the Internal Revenue Service for the 2005 and 2006 tax years. The Company's major foreign jurisdictions, China and the Netherlands, have concluded substantially all income tax matters through calendar year 1997 and fiscal year 2002, respectively.

The Company recognizes interest and penalties related to income tax matters in income tax expense. Upon adoption at June 1, 2007, the Company had $32.0 million (excluding federal benefit) accrued for interest and penalties related to uncertain tax positions. The liability for payment of interest and penalties increased $41.2 million during the year ended May 31, 2008. As of May 31, 2008, accrued interest and penalties related to uncertain tax positions was $73.2 million (excluding federal benefit).

During the quarter ended November 30, 2005, the Company's CEO and Board of Directors approved a domestic reinvestment plan as required by the American Jobs Creation Act of 2004 (the "Act") to repatriate $500 million of foreign earnings in fiscal 2006. The Act created a temporary incentive for U.S. multinational corporations to repatriate accumulated income earned outside the U.S. by providing an 85% dividend received deduction for certain dividends from controlled foreign corporations. A $500 million repatriation was made during the quarter ended May 31, 2006 comprised of both foreign earnings for which U.S. taxes have previously been provided and foreign earnings that had been designated as permanently reinvested. Accordingly, the provisions made did not have a material impact on the Company's income tax expense or effective tax rate for the years ended May 31, 2008, 2007 and 2006.

The Company has indefinitely reinvested approximately $1,808.6 million of the cumulative undistributed earnings of certain foreign subsidiaries. Such earnings would be subject to U.S. taxation if repatriated to the U.S. Determination of the amount of unrecognized deferred tax liability associated with the permanently reinvested cumulative undistributed earnings is not practicable.

Deferred tax assets at May 31, 2008, 2007 and 2006 were reduced by a valuation allowance relating to tax benefits of certain foreign subsidiaries with operating losses where it is more likely than not that the deferred tax assets will not be realized.

During the years ended May 31, 2008, 2007, and 2006, income tax benefits attributable to employee stock-based compensation transactions of $68.9 million, $56.6 million, and $54.2 million, respectively, were allocated to shareholders' equity.

Note 9—Redeemable Preferred Stock

Sojitz America is the sole owner of the Company's authorized Redeemable Preferred Stock, $1 par value, which is redeemable at the option of Sojitz America or the Company at par value aggregating $0.3 million. A cumulative dividend of $0.10 per share is payable annually on May 31 and no dividends may be declared or paid on the common stock of the Company unless dividends on the Redeemable Preferred Stock have been declared and paid in full. There have been no changes in the Redeemable Preferred Stock in the three years ended May 31, 2008, 2007 and 2006. As the holder of the Redeemable Preferred Stock, Sojitz America does not have general voting rights but does have the right to vote as a separate class on the sale of all or substantially all of the assets of the Company and its subsidiaries, on merger, consolidation, liquidation or dissolution of the Company or on the sale or assignment of the NIKE trademark for athletic footwear sold in the United States.

Note 10—Common Stock

The authorized number of shares of Class A Common Stock, no par value, and Class B Common Stock, no par value, are 175 million and 750 million, respectively. Each share of Class A Common Stock is convertible into one share of Class B Common Stock. Voting rights of Class B Common Stock are limited in certain circumstances with respect to the election of directors.

In 1990, the Board of Directors adopted, and the shareholders approved, the NIKE, Inc. 1990 Stock Incentive Plan (the "1990 Plan"). The 1990 Plan provides for the issuance of up to 132 million previously unissued shares of Class B Common Stock in connection with stock options and other awards granted under the plan. The 1990 Plan authorizes the grant of non-statutory stock options, incentive stock options, stock appreciation rights, stock bonuses and the issuance and sale of restricted stock. The exercise price for non-statutory stock options, stock appreciation rights and the grant price of restricted stock may not be less than 75% of the fair market value of the underlying shares on the date of grant. The exercise price for incentive stock options may not be less than the fair market value of the underlying shares on the date of grant. A committee of the Board of Directors administers the 1990 Plan. The committee has the authority to determine the employees to whom awards will be made, the amount of the awards, and the other terms and conditions of the awards. The committee has granted substantially all stock options at 100% of the market price on the date of grant. Substantially all stock option grants outstanding under the 1990 plan were granted in the first quarter of each fiscal year, vest ratably over four years, and expire 10 years from the date of grant.

The weighted average fair value per share of the options granted during the years ended May 31, 2008, 2007 and 2006, as computed using the Black-Scholes pricing model, was $13.87, $8.80 and $9.68, respectively. The weighted average assumptions used to estimate these fair values are as follows:

	Year Ended May 31,		
	2008	2007	2006
Dividend yield	1.4%	1.6%	1%
Expected volatility	20%	19%	21%
Weighted average expected life (in years)	5.0	5.0	4.5
Risk-free interest rate	4.8%	5.0%	4.0%

The Company estimates the expected volatility based on the implied volatility in market traded options on the Company's common stock with a term greater than one year, along with other factors. The weighted average expected life of options is based on an analysis of historical and expected future exercise patterns. The interest rate is based on the U.S. Treasury (constant maturity) risk-free rate in effect at the date of grant for periods corresponding with the expected term of the options.

The following summarizes the stock option transactions under the plan discussed above:

	Shares	Weighted Average Option Price
	(In millions)	
Options outstanding May 31, 2005	38.7	$ 27.49
Exercised	(8.0)	24.68
Forfeited	(1.8)	35.75
Granted	11.5	43.68
Options outstanding May 31, 2006	40.4	32.31
Exercised	(10.7)	27.55
Forfeited	(1.6)	37.17
Granted	11.6	39.54
Options outstanding May 31, 2007	39.7	$ 35.50
Exercised	(9.1)	33.45
Forfeited	(0.9)	44.44
Granted	6.9	58.50
Options outstanding May 31, 2008	36.6	$ 40.14
Options exercisable at May 31,		
2006	16.6	$ 25.68
2007	15.3	29.52
2008	16.2	32.35

The weighted average contractual life remaining for options outstanding and options exercisable at May 31, 2008 was 6.9 years and 5.4 years, respectively. The aggregate intrinsic value for options outstanding and exercisable at May 31, 2008 was $1,034.1 million and $582.3 million, respectively. The aggregate intrinsic value was the amount by which the market value of the underlying stock exceeded the exercise price of the options. The total intrinsic value of the options exercised during the years ended May 31, 2008, 2007 and 2006 was $259.4 million, $204.9 million and $144.0 million, respectively.

As of May 31, 2008, the Company had $90.9 million of unrecognized compensation costs from stock options, net of estimated forfeitures, to be recognized as selling and administrative expense over a weighted average period of 1.9 years.

In addition to the 1990 Plan, the Company gives employees the right to purchase shares at a discount to the market price under employee stock purchase plans ("ESPPs"). Employees are eligible to participate through payroll deductions up to 10% of their compensation. At the end of each six-month offering period, shares are purchased by the participants at 85% of the lower of the fair market value at the beginning or the ending of the offering period. Employees purchased 0.8 million shares in each of the years ended May 31, 2008, 2007 and 2006.

From time to time, the Company grants restricted stock and unrestricted stock to key employees under the 1990 Plan. The number of shares granted to employees during the years ended May 31, 2008, 2007 and 2006 were 110,000, 345,000 and 141,000 with weighted average values per share of $59.50, $39.38 and $43.38, respectively. Recipients of restricted shares are entitled to cash dividends and to vote their respective shares throughout the period of restriction. The value of all of the granted shares was established by the market price on the date of grant. During the years ended May 31, 2008, 2007 and 2006, the fair value of restricted shares vested was $9.0 million, $5.5 million and $13.4 million, respectively, determined as of the date of vesting.

During the years ended May 31, 2007 and 2006, the Company also granted shares of stock under the Long-Term Incentive Plan ("LTIP"), adopted by the Board of Directors and approved by shareholders in September 1997. During the year ended May 31, 2007, LTIP participants agreed to amend their grant agreements to eliminate the ability to receive payments in shares of stock; shares of stock are no longer awarded. Prior to the amendment, the LTIP provided for the issuance of cash or up to 2.0 million shares of Class B Common Stock to certain executives based on performance targets established over three-year time periods. Once performance targets are achieved, cash or shares of stock are issued. The shares are immediately vested upon grant. The value of the shares is established by the market price on the date of issuance. Under the LTIP, 3,000 and 6,000 shares with a price of $38.84 and $40.79, respectively, were issued during the years ended May 31, 2007 and 2006 for the plan years ended May 31, 2006 and 2005, respectively. Compensation expense recognized relating to shares issued during the years ended May 31, 2007 and 2006 was not material. The Company recognized $35.9 million, $30.0 million and $21.7 million of selling and administrative expense related to the cash awards during the years ended May 31, 2008, 2007 and 2006, respectively.

Note 11—Earnings Per Share

The following represents a reconciliation from basic earnings per common share to diluted earnings per common share. Options to purchase an additional 6.6 million, 9.5 million and 11.3 million shares of common stock were outstanding at May 31, 2008, 2007 and 2006, respectively, but were not included in the computation of diluted earnings per share because the options were antidilutive.

	Year Ended May 31,		
	2008	2007	2006
	(In millions, except per share data)		
Determination of shares:			
Weighted average common shares outstanding	495.6	503.8	518.0
Assumed conversion of dilutive stock options and awards	8.5	6.1	9.6
Diluted weighted average common shares outstanding	504.1	509.9	527.6
Basic earnings per common share	$ 3.80	$ 2.96	$ 2.69
Diluted earnings per common share	$ 3.74	$ 2.93	$ 2.64

Revenues by Major Product Lines.

Revenues to external customers for NIKE brand products are attributable to sales of footwear, apparel and equipment. Other revenues to external customers primarily include external sales by Cole Haan Holdings Incorporated, Converse Inc., Exeter Brands Group LLC (whose primary business was the Starter brand business which was sold December 17, 2007), Hurley International LLC, NIKE Bauer Hockey Corp. (through April 16, 2008), NIKE Golf, and Umbro Ltd. (beginning March 3, 2008).

| | Year Ended May 31, | | |
	2008	2007	2006
	(In millions)		
Footwear	$ 9,731.6	$ 8,514.0	$ 7,965.9
Apparel	5,234.0	4,576.5	4,168.0
Equipment	1,068.6	975.8	873.9
Other	2,592.8	2,259.6	1,947.1
	$18,627.0	$16,325.9	$14,954.9

Revenues and Long-Lived Assets by Geographic Area.

Geographical area information is similar to that shown previously under operating segments with the exception of the Other activity, which has been allocated to the geographical areas based on the location where the sales originated. Revenues derived in the United States were $7,938.5 million, $7,593.7 million, and $7,019.0 million, for the years ended May 31, 2008, 2007, and 2006, respectively. The Company's largest concentrations of long-lived assets primarily consist of the Company's world headquarters and distribution facilities in the United States and distribution facilities in Japan and Belgium. Long-lived assets attributable to operations in the United States, which are comprised of net property, plant & equipment were $1,109.9 million, $991.3 million, and $998.2 million at May 31, 2008, 2007, and 2006, respectively. Long-lived assets attributable to operations in Japan were $303.8 million, $260.6 million, and $296.3 million at May 31, 2008, 2007, and 2006, respectively. Long-lived assets attributable to operations in Belgium were $219.1 million, $198.3 million and $145.4 million at May 31, 2008, 2007, and 2006, respectively.

Major Customers.

During the years ended May 31, 2008, 2007 and 2006, revenues derived from Foot Locker, Inc. represented 9 percent, 10 percent and 10 percent of the Company's consolidated revenues, respectively. Sales to this customer are included in all segments of the Company.

Glindex A combined Glossary/Subject Index

contribution approach A method of internal (management accounting) reporting that emphasizes the distinction between variable and fixed costs for the purpose of better decision making., 182

    absorption approach versus, 183, 195

    in cost-plus pricing, 194–195

    in management control systems, 354–357

contribution margin A term used for either unit contribution margin or total contribution margin., 44. *See also* Product-mix decisions

    in break-even point calculation, 44–45

    equation method versus, 46

    gross margin and, 54–55

    in management control systems, 355–356

    in product-mix decisions, 232

contribution-margin percentage Total contribution margin divided by sales or 100% minus the variable cost percentage., 45, 52–53

contribution-margin ratio Contribution margin percentage expressed as a ratio., 45

control Implementing plans and using feedback to evaluate the attainment of objectives., 7

    cost allocation supporting, 125

    in performance evaluation, 406

    planning versus, 7, 347 (*see also* Management control systems)

    for product life cycles, 9–11

    in service organizations, 585–586

    for value chain, 9–11

controllable cost Any cost that a manager's decisions and actions can influence., 354

controller (comptroller) The top accounting officer of an organization who deals mainly with operating matters, such as aiding management decision making., 13

    versus treasurers, 13–14

Cooper, Cynthia, 18

Coordination, budgets as tool for, 267

Cornelius, James M., 394

Corporate Responsibility Officer, 30

Corporate support cost allocation, 498–499

cost A sacrifice or giving up of resources for a particular purpose., 122. *See also* Unit cost; Variable costs

    ABC system in controlling, 149–150

    avoidable, 231

    capacity, 83

    controllable, 354

    differential, 223–225

    direct, 124

    expenses versus, 132

    indirect, 124, 126–127

    irrelevant or misspecified, 238–240 (*see also* Relevant information)

    labor and materials, 129, 580

    unallocated, 357

    uncontrollable, 354

    value-added, 140

cost accounting That part of the cost management system that measures costs for the purposes of management decision making and financial reporting., 122

cost accounting systems The techniques used to determine the cost of a product, service, customer, or other cost object., 122–123. *See also* Activity-based costing (ABC) systems; Cost management system (CMS)

    business type affecting, 130–132

    cost allocation in, 473 (*see also* Cost allocation)

    for external reporting, 129–132

    processes in, 123

    role of, 122–123

    terminology, 122–123, 127, 129–130

    traditional, 133–140, 143–145

cost accumulation Collecting costs by some natural classification, such as activities performed, labor, or materials., 123

cost allocation Assigning indirect costs to cost objects in proportion to the cost object's use of a particular cost-allocation base., 124. *See also* Activity-based costing (ABC) systems; Overhead cost allocation

    case study, 472–473

    central corporate support, 498–499

    in customer profitability measurement, 489–497

    framework for, 473–476

    joint and by-product, 499–501

    methods of, 126–127

    in MSABC systems, 502–505

    production-related, 482–486

    purposes of, 125–126

    service department, 476–482

    unallocated costs and, 127–129

cost-allocation base A measure of input or output that determines the amount of cost to be allocated to a particular cost object. An ideal cost-allocation base would measure how much of the particular cost is caused by the cost object., 124, 475. *See also* Overhead cost allocation

cost application The allocation of total departmental costs to the revenue-producing products or services., 482

cost assignment Attaching costs to one or more cost objects, such as activities, departments, customers, or products., 123

Cost-based transfer price, 401–403

cost behavior How the activities of an organization affect its costs., 35. *See also* Cost-volume-profit (CVP) analysis; Measurement of cost behavior

    break-even point in, 43–49

    case studies, 34–35, 80

    cost drivers affecting, 35–36, 81–83

    income tax impacts in, 58–59

    management influence on, 83–85

    variable and fixed, 37–38 (*see also* Fixed costs; Variable costs)

cost-benefit balance Weighing estimated costs against probable benefits, the primary consideration in choosing among accounting systems and methods., 6, 389

cost center A responsibility center in which managers are responsible for costs only., 354, 386–387

Cost-control incentives, 85

cost driver A measure of activities that requires the use of resources and thereby cause costs., 35. *See also* Cost allocation; Cost behavior; Cost-volume-profit (CVP) analysis; Measurement of cost behavior

    allocation bases as, 124

    cost behavior and, 81–83

    costs not related to, 481–482

    identifying, 35–36, 87–88

internal auditors Accountants who review and evaluate accounting systems, including their internal controls., 6

internal controls Policies to protect and make the most efficient use of an organization's assets., 5

internal rate of return (IRR) model A capital-budgeting model that determines the interest rate at which the NPV equals zero., 431

International Accounting Education Standards Board (IAESB) The body that sets educational standards for auditors throughout the world., 14

International Financial Reporting Standards (IFRS) Generally accepted accounting principles set by the IASB and applied in the European Union and in more than 100 countries worldwide., 5

Inventory
    affecting process costing, 594–596
    cost allocation for, 125, 130

inventory turnover The number of times the average inventory is sold per year., 233

Invested capital, 396–397

investment center A responsibility center where managers are responsible for investment as well as profits., 355

Irrelevant information, 179–180, 238–240. *See also* Relevant information

J

James, Lebron, 384

Jensen, Michael, 268

job costing *See* job-order costing.

job-cost record (job-cost sheet, job order) A document that shows all costs for a particular product, service, or batch of products., 577

job-cost sheet *See* job-cost record.

job order *See* job-cost record.

job-order costing (job costing) The method of allocating costs to products that are readily identified by individual units or batches, each of which requires varying degrees of attention and skill., 577
    activity-based costing and, 582–583
    case study, 576–577
    illustration, 577–581
    process costing versus, 577, 587–590 (*see also* Process costing)
    service and nonprofit organizations, 585–586

Joint cost allocation, 499–501

joint costs The costs of manufacturing joint products prior to the split-off point., 234

joint products Two or more manufactured products that (1) have relatively significant sales values and (2) are not separately identifiable as individual products until their split-off point., 234–235

Jordan, Michael, 384

just-in-time (JIT) philosophy A philosophy to eliminate waste by reducing the time products spend in the production process and eliminating the time products spend on activities that do not add value, 16, 391, 537, 598–599

K

kaizen costing The Japanese term for continuous improvement during manufacturing, 200

Kaplan, Robert, 365

Kaufman, Stephen, 350

Kertley, Todd, 226

key performance indicators Measures that drive the organization to achieve its goals, 365–366

key success factor Characteristics or attributes that managers must achieve in order to drive the organization toward its goals, 349

Knight, Philip, 385

Kozlowski, Dennis, 440

L

Labor standards variance, 316, 319–320

labor time tickets (time cards) The record of the time a particular direct laborer spends on each job, 577

Lay, Kenneth, 18

lean manufacturing Applying continuous process improvements to eliminate waste from the entire enterprise., 16

Learning culture, 351–353

least-squares regression (regression analysis) Measuring a cost function objectively by using statistics to fit a cost function to all the data., 96

Least-squares regression, 96–99

Leverage, 53–54

limiting factor (scarce resource) The item that restricts or constrains the production or sale of a product or service., 232

linear-cost behavior Activity that can be graphed with a straight line because costs are assumed to be either fixed or variable., 81

line managers Managers who are directly involved with making and selling the organization's products or services., 12

London Suite (Simon), 257–258

long-range plan Forecasted financial statements for 5- to 10-year periods., 271

Losses, 442

Lump-sum approach, 478–479

M

Make-or-buy decisions, 225–228

Management accountants, opportunities for, 14

management accounting The branch of accounting that produces information for managers within an organization. It is the process of identifying, measuring, accumulating, analyzing, preparing, interpreting, and communicating information that helps managers fulfill organizational objectives., 3
    career opportunities in, 14
    case study, 2–3
    controllers versus treasurers in, 13–14
    current trends in, 11, 14–17
    financial accounting versus, 3
    role of, 11–14

management audit A review to determine whether managers are implementing the policies and procedures specified by top management., 6

management by exception Concentrating on areas that deviate from the plan and ignoring areas that are presumed to be running smoothly., 8

management by objectives (MBO) The joint formulation by managers and their superiors of a set of goals and plans for achieving the goals for a forthcoming period., 406

management control system A logical integration of techniques for gathering and using information to make planning and control decisions, for motivating employee behavior, and for evaluating performance., 347

managerial effort   Exertion toward a goal or objective, including all conscious actions (such as supervising, planning, and thinking) that result in more efficiency and effectiveness., 349

manufacturing overhead   *See* indirect production costs., 129

marginal cost   The additional cost resulting from producing and selling one additional unit., 190

marginal income   The unit sales price minus the variable cost per unit., 44, 48–49

marginal income tax rate   The tax rate paid on additional amounts of pretax income., 437

marginal revenue   The additional revenue resulting from the sale of an additional unit., 190

Marginal revenue curve, 190–191

margin of safety   The planned unit sales less the break-even unit sales; it shows how far sales can fall below the planned level before losses occur., 54

Market-based transfer price, 400–401

markup   The amount by which price exceeds cost., 193

master budget   An extensive analysis of the first year of the long-range plan. It summarizes the planned activities of all subunits of an organization., 271. *See also* Budget

materials requisitions   Records of materials used in particular jobs., 577

Material standards variance, 316, 319–320

measurement of cost behavior   Understanding and quantifying how activities of an organization affect its levels of costs., 80. *See also* Cost behavior

mixed costs   Costs that contain elements of both fixed- and variable-cost behavior., 82, 86

modified accelerated cost recovery system (MACRS)   The method companies use to depreciate most assets under U.S. income tax laws., 440–442. *See also* Accelerated depreciation

motivation   The drive toward some selected goal that creates effort and action toward that goal., 349–350, 386–387. *See also* Incentive systems; Performance evaluation; Reward systems

Mulally, Alan, 35

Multinational transfer pricing, 404–405

multistage ABC (MSABC) systems   Costing systems with more than two stages of allocations and cost drivers other than percentages., 502–505

N

Nadal, Rafael, 384

Nardelli, Bob, 353

Nash, Steve, 384

Negotiated transfer price, 403–404

net book value   The original cost of an asset less any accumulated depreciation., 236, 396

net operating profit after-tax (NOPAT)   Income before interest expense but after tax., 391

net present value   The sum of the present values of all expected cash flows., 428

net-present-value (NPV) method   A discounted-cash-flow approach to capital budgeting that computes the present value of all expected future cash flows using a minimum desired rate of return., 428. *See also* Capital budgeting; Discounted-cash-flow (DCF) models

New York Times, 257

nominal rate   Quoted market interest rate that includes an inflation element., 449

Nonfinancial performance measures

Nonproduction costs, 129–130

Nonprofit organizations. *See also* Service organizations

non-value-added costs   Costs that a company can eliminate without affecting a product's value to the customer., 140

normal costing system   The cost system in which the cost of the manufactured product is composed of actual direct material, actual direct labor, and normal applied overhead., 536

Norton, David, 365

NYCE Payments Network, 435

O

Office of Federal Housing Oversight (OFHEO), 266

operating budget (profit plan)   A major part of a master budget that focuses on the income statement and its supporting schedules., 272, 274–276, 280

in JIT system, 598–599

job-order costing versus, 577, 587–590 (*see also* Job-order costing)

reasons for using, 586–587

process map A schematic diagram capturing interrelationships between cost objects, activities, and resources., 133–134. *See also* Activity-based costing (ABC) systems

producing departments Departments where employees work on the organization's products or services., 474, 482–486. *See also* Cost allocation

product costs (inventoriable costs) Costs identified with goods produced or purchased for resale., 130

production-volume variance A variance that appears whenever actual production deviates from the expected volume of production used in computing the fixed overhead rate. It is calculated as (actual volume – expected volume) × fixed-overhead rate., 543, 546–548, 552–554

productivity A measure of outputs divided by inputs., 362–363

product life cycle The various stages through which a product passes, from conception and development to introduction into the market to maturation and, finally, withdrawal from the market., 9

planning and control, 9–11

Product-mix decisions, 232–234

Products

adding or deleting, 230–232

joint, 234–235

Profitability measurement, 390–395, 489–497

Profit and loss statement. *See* Income statement

profit center A responsibility center in which managers are responsible for revenues as well as costs—that is, profitability., 354, 386–387

profit plan *See* operating budget.

proration To assign underapplied overhead or overapplied overhead to cost of goods sold, work-in-process inventory, and finished-good inventory in proportion to the ending balances of each account., 537–538

Purchases budget, 275–276

Q

quality control The effort to ensure that products and services perform to customer requirements., 360–362

quality-control chart The statistical plot of measures of various product quality dimensions or attributes., 360–362

quantity variance The difference between the actual quantity of inputs used and the standard quantity allowed for the good output achieved multiplied by the standard price of the input., 317–319, 319–321

R

rate variance A price variance applied to labor., 319

Ratio analysis, 45

real options model A capital-budgeting model that recognizes the value of contingent investments—that is, investments that a company can adjust as it learns more about their potential for success., 431

Reciprocal cost method, 481n

Reciprocal services, 479–482

recovery period The number of years over which a company can depreciate an asset for tax purposes., 438

regression analysis *See* least-squares regression.

relevant information The predicted future costs and revenues that will differ among alternative courses of action., 179. *See also* Operational decisions; Pricing decisions

on alternative income statements, 181–184

in decision process, 180–181

irrelevant information versus, 179–180, 238–240

in net-present-value method, 434

relevant range The limit of cost-driver level within which a specific relationship between costs and the cost driver is valid., 41, 81–83

Reliability, of cost functions, 87

required rate of return (hurdle rate, discount rate) The minimum desired rate of return, based on the firm's cost of capital., 428

residual income *See* economic profit.

responsibility accounting Identifying what parts of the organization have primary responsibility for each action, developing performance measures and targets, and designing reports of these measures by responsibility center., 354

responsibility center A set of activities and resources assigned to a manager, a group of managers, or other employees., 354, 386–387

return on investment (ROI) A measure of income divided by the investment required to obtain that income., 390–391, 393–395

return on sales Income divided by revenue., 391

Revenue

curves, 190–191

differential, 223

variances, 305–306

Reward systems, 314, 388–389. *See also* Incentive systems; Motivation; Performance evaluation

Risk, 389, 431–432

rolling budget *See* continuous budget.

Rowan, Jim, 279

S

sales-activity variances The activity-level variances when sales is used as the cost driver., 310

sales budget The result of decisions to create conditions that will generate a desired level of sales., 270, 275, 499

sales forecast A prediction of sales under a given set of conditions., 270–271

sales mix The relative proportions or combinations of quantities of products that constitute total sales., 48, 57–58

Sampras, Pete, 384

Sarbanes-Oxley Act A 2002 law that requires more top-management oversight of a company's accounting policies and procedures., 5, 20

scarce resource *See* limiting factor.

Schumacher, Michael, 385, 388

scorekeeping The accumulation and classification of data., 4

managerial decisions, 5

Scott, Tom, 222

segment autonomy The delegation of decision-making power to managers of segments in an organization., 386, 398, 402, 403

segments Responsibility centers for which a company develops separate measures of revenues and costs., 355

contribution by, 357

Index of Companies

Photo Credits